*The
Right Word
at the
Right Time*

The Right Word at the Right Time

A GUIDE TO THE ENGLISH LANGUAGE AND HOW TO USE IT

PUBLISHED BY
THE READER'S DIGEST ASSOCIATION LIMITED
London   New York   Montreal   Sydney   Cape Town

THE RIGHT WORD AT THE RIGHT TIME
was edited and designed by
The Reader's Digest Association Limited, London

First Edition Copyright © 1985
The Reader's Digest Association Limited
25 Berkeley Square, London W1X 6AB
Reprinted with amendments 1987

Copyright © 1985
Reader's Digest Association Far East Limited
Philippines Copyright
1985 Reader's Digest Association Far East Limited

The original idea for this book derives from
SUCCESS WITH WORDS, Copyright © 1983
The Reader's Digest Association Inc., Pleasantville, USA.
Some of the entries in THE RIGHT WORD AT THE RIGHT TIME
have been adapted from that publication.

Printed in Hong Kong

Acknowledgments

Principal contributors

EDITOR
John Ellison Kahn, MA, DPhil

CONSULTANT EDITOR
Robert Ilson, MA, PhD
Associate Director of The Survey of English Usage,
and Honorary Research Fellow, University College London

The publishers also thank the following people
for their valuable contributions to this book:

Nicolette Jones, MA

Loreto Todd, MA, PhD
Senior Lecturer, School of English, University of Leeds

Faye Carney, MA

Sylvia Chalker, MA

Jenny Cheshire, BA, PhD
Lecturer in Linguistics, Birkbeck College, University of London

Derek Davy
Professor of English, University of Canterbury, Christchurch, New Zealand

John Dodgson, MA, FSA
Reader in English, University College London

Stanley Ellis, MA, FIL
Honorary Fellow, School of English, University of Leeds

Peter Hawkins, MA, MPhil, PhD
Lecturer in Linguistics, Queen Margaret College, Edinburgh

Frederick Jones, MA, PhD
Lecturer in English, Fourah Bay College, University of Sierra Leone

Bernard Lott, OBE, MA, PhD
formerly Controller, English Language Teaching, the British Council

Geoffrey Lucy

Mary Penrith, MA, MLitt

Alan R. Thomas
Reader in Linguistics, University College of North Wales, Bangor

J.C. Wells, MA, PhD
Reader in Phonetics, University College London

Janet Whitcut, MA

The publishers are indebted to:

André Deutsch Ltd,
for permission to quote 'The Lama' by Ogden Nash
(copyright 1931, 1983) from *I Wouldn't Have Missed It*;
Canadian rights by kind permission
of Little, Brown and Company

Using the right word

WHY BOTHER WITH THE RIGHT WORD? 'People understand me well enough' is the typical response of the uncaring speaker to any criticism of his usage — that is, of the way he talks or writes. But do people understand such a speaker well enough? And even if they do, what is their impression of him or of anyone who speaks and writes in a sloppy, careless way? Much the same, probably, as their impression of someone who is sloppily dressed. Using the right word at the right time is rather like wearing appropriate clothing for the occasion: it is a courtesy to others, and a favour to yourself — a matter of presenting yourself well in the eyes of the world.

The comparison goes further than that: just as dressing appropriately can help you to feel more confident and to act more effectively, so speaking and writing appropriately can help you to reach clearer decisions and persuade others to agree with you. Sloppy language makes for muddled thinking:

> The English language ... becomes ugly and inaccurate because our thoughts are foolish, but the slovenliness of our language makes it easier for us to have foolish thoughts.
> – George Orwell,
> 'Politics and the English Language'

Respecting words

IF YOU HAVE THIS BOOK, you care about English. Not everybody does: standards are distressingly low in many schools, in much of broadcasting and the press, and in much of public life — so much so that many educationalists are even urging a return to traditional grammar lessons in the school curriculum.

Certainly correct grammar is important, and many common grammatical errors or disputes are discussed in this book — ✕ *between you and I*; ? *She ran faster than me*, ? *to boldly go*, and so on. But good English is more than a matter of grammar, or the combination of words. It involves too a respect for individual words — the use of the right word at the right time ... the correct meaning, for instance, of *enormity* (which does not mean the same as *enormousness*) and *fortuitously* (which does not mean the same as *fortunately*).

This book discusses hundreds of such snares in our vocabulary and problems of English usage. How should you deal with the different senses that attach to *decimate* or *billion*? What is the difference between *alternately* and *alternatively*? Should a proposal be described as *practical* or as *practicable*? How acceptable is it to use *hopefully* to mean 'I hope'? Can *to aggravate* be legitimately used in the same way as *to irritate*?

Disrespect for words is all too easy to find — in the use of clichés and vogue words, such as *meaningful dialogue* instead of *serious discussions*, and in the misuse or confusion of other terms: *flaunt* for *flout*, *disinterested* for *uninterested*, *Frankenstein* for *Frankenstein's monster*, *infer* for *imply*, *mitigate against* for *militate against*.

Passing judgment

NOT ALL USAGE PROBLEMS are as clear-cut as these, of course. Sometimes the dispute is finely balanced — the pronunciation of *controversy*, for instance, or the need for *whom*, or the difference between *further* and *farther*. But you will always find here a clear discussion of the dispute, airing the arguments on both sides, referring to the history of the language, quoting modern examples, and suggesting a solution.

Sometimes the judgment is a decisive one: no matter how weighty the tradition of disapproval might be, an expression will be given the seal of approval if it deserves one; and no matter how popular an expression may be, it will be condemned if it deserves to be. But it is not enough just to condemn a usage: you will always find an acceptable alternative proposed here — even if it takes the form of a recommendation to avoid the impasse altogether, and to approach your intended meaning by another route.

Many changes in meaning and usage cannot be resisted, no matter how undesirable they may appear to be. Dr Johnson struck the right note in the introduction to his famous *Dictionary of the English Language* (1755): 'It remains that we retard what we cannot repel, that we palliate what we cannot cure.'

Not all changes are undesirable, however; yet the welcome given to them is still sometimes qualified by caution. Consider again the modern use of *hopefully*. The case against it is weak, and there are in fact good linguistic reasons for tolerating it. And yet ... people of the old school do object to it and might well be distracted from what you are saying, or be prejudiced against your line of reasoning, if you use such an 'objectionable' formation. The same holds true for some long-established usages, such as the 'split infinitive', that are traditionally considered 'wrong'.

Unless you are spoiling for a fight over usage, you should consider submitting to the sensitivities of your audience or readers. There is no point in stubbornly acting on your belief that *hopefully* is a legitimate aid to communication if, through parading it, you simply provoke an interruption and thereby impede communication.

A lively approach

AS A BACKGROUND and supplement to these debates on good English usage, this book features articles defining and discussing the various parts of speech and the various punctuation marks; long articles on spelling and pronunciation; descriptions of the national varieties of English — American English, Australian English, South African English, Canadian English, and so on; articles on pidgins and creoles, on English dialects and the history of the language, on metaphors, slang, and jargon, on euphemisms, misquotations, and ambiguity.

The discussions of controversial usages are illustrated with a wealth of quotations — good and bad — drawn from current newspapers, magazines, books, and radio programmes. Where a quotation or example shows a misuse, it is clearly marked as wrong by means of a cross printed in red: ×. And if it is a doubtful or ill-advised usage, it is marked with a red question mark, ?, or double question mark: ??. Bear in mind that a mistake attributed to an author or journalist may not really be of his or her own making: in newspapers in particular, a writer's words might have been hurriedly recast by a sub-editor, or mis-set by the typesetter. And note too that the extracts quoted are usually printed in the standard spelling and pronunciation used in this book, even if the original text used different conventions.

English today is closer to being a World Language than any other language has been in history. It is the international language of science, of pilots and sea-captains, and frequently of diplomatic, sporting, and trade contacts. It is used, and even cherished, by untold millions whose mother tongue is quite different. This should be at once a source of pride to those whose mother tongue is English, and an inducement — perhaps even an obligation — to use the language well.

KEY TO RED SYMBOLS

? **doubtful or informal usage** — think twice before using this word or construction

?? **inappropriate or nonstandard usage** — avoid if possible in formal contexts

× **incorrect usage** — avoid

GUIDE TO PRONUNCIATION

Pronunciations are printed between slash marks or diagonal lines: the pronunciation of *genuine*, for instance, is represented as /**jen**new-in/.

Note how stress is marked in words of more than one syllable: the stressed syllable is printed in **bold type** to distinguish it from unstressed syllables.

Where alternative pronunciations are given, these are sometimes represented simply by the syllables that vary: the pronunciation of *adversary*, for instance, is printed /**ad**vər-səri, -sri/.

Where a foreign sound cannot be perfectly expressed by any of the symbols listed below, an approximation to it is given wherever this is possible.

a, **a**	as in *trap* /trap/, *backhand* /**bak**-hand/
aa, **aa**	as in *calm* /kaam/, *father* /**faa**thər/
air, **air**	as in *scarce* /skairss/, *parent* /**pair**-ənt/
ar, **ar**, **aar**	as in *cart* /kart/, *party* /**par**ti/, *carnation* /kaar-**naysh**'n/, *sari* /**saa**ri/
aw, **aw**	as in *thought* /thawt/, *daughter* /**daw**tər/
awr, **awr**	SEE or, **or**
ay, **ay**	as in *face* /fayss/, *native* /**nay**tiv/
b, bb	as in *stab* /stab/, *rubber* /**rub**bər/
ch	as in *church* /church/, *nature* /**nay**chər/
ck	SEE k
d, dd	as in *dead* /ded/, *ladder* /**lad**dər/
e, **e**	as in *ten* /ten/, *ready* /**red**di/
ee, **ee**	as in *meat* /meet/, *machine* /mə-**sheen**/
eer, **eer**	as in *fierce* /feerss/, *serious* /**seer**-i-əss/
er, **er**	as in *term* /term/, *defer* /di-**fer**/
ew, **ew**	as in *few* /few/, *music* /**mew**zik/
ewr, **ewr**	as in *pure* /pewr/, *curious* /**kewr**-i-əss/
ə	as in *about* /ə-**bowt**/, *cannon* /**kan**nən/
ər	as in *persist* /pər-**sist**/, *celery* /**sel**ləri/
f, ff	as in *sofa* /**sō**fə/, *suffer* /**suf**fər/
g, gg	as in *stag* /stag/, *giggle* /**gig**g'l/
h	as in *hat* /hat/, *ahead* /ə-**hed**/
i, **i**	as in *grid* /grid/, *ticket* /**tick**it/
ī, **ī**	as in *price* /prīss/, *mighty* /**mī**ti/
īr, **īr**	as in *fire* /fīr/, *tyrant* /**tīr**-ənt/
j	as in *judge* /juj/, *age* /ayj/
k, ck	as in *kick* /kik/, *pocket* /**pock**it/, *six* /siks/, *quite* /kwīt/
l, ll	as in *fill* /fil/, *colour* /**kul**lər/
'l	as in *needle* /**need**'l/, *channel* /**chann**'l/
m, mm	as in *man* /man/, *summer* /**sum**mər/
'm	as in *rhythm* /**rith**'m/, *blossom* /**bloss**'m/
n, nn	as in *fan* /fan/, *honour* /**onn**ər/
'n	as in *sudden* /**sudd**'n/, *cotton* /**kott**'n/
ng	as in *tank* /tangk/, *finger* /**fing**-gər/
o, **o**	as in *rod* /rod/, *stockpot* /**stok**-pot/
ō, **ō**	as in *goat* /gōt/, *dodo* /**dō**-dō/
o͞o, **o͞o**	as in *would* /wo͞od/, *pusher* /**po͞o**shər/
o͞o, **o͞o**	as in *shoe* /sho͞o/, *prudent* /**pro͞o**d'nt/
oor, **oor**	as in *poor* /poor/, *surely* /**shoor**li/
or, **or**, **awr**, **awr**	as in *north* /north/, *portion* /**por**-sh'n/, *swarm* /swawrm/, *warden* /**wawrd**'n/
ow, **ow**	as in *stout* /stowt/, *powder* /**pow**dər/
owr, **owr**	as in *sour* /sowr/, *dowry* /**dowr**-i/
oy, **oy**	as in *boy* /boy/, *poison* /**poyz**'n/
p, pp	as in *crop* /krop/, *pepper* /**pep**pər/
r, rr	as in *red* /red/, *terror* /**terr**ər/
s, ss	as in *list* /list/, *box* /boks/, *sauce* /sawss/, *fussy* /**fuss**i/
sh	as in *ship* /ship/, *pressure* /**presh**ər/
t, tt	as in *state* /stayt/, *totter* /**tott**ər/
th	as in *thick* /thik/, *author* /**aw**thər/
th	as in *this* /this͟s/, *mother* /**muth͟**ər/
u, **u**	as in *cut* /kut/, *money* /**mun**ni/
v, vv	as in *valve* /valv/, *cover* /**kuv**vər/
w	as in *wet* /wet/, *away* /ə-**way**/
y	as in *yes* /yess/, *beyond* /bi-**yond**/
z, zz	as in *zoo* /zo͞o/, *scissors* /**sizz**ərz/
zh	as in *vision* /**vizh**'n/, *pleasure* /**plezh**ər/

FOREIGN PRONUNCIATIONS

kh	as in Scottish *loch* /lokh/, Arabic *Khalid* /**khaa**-lid/, or German *Achtung* /**akh**-to͞ong/
aN, oN	as in French *Saint-Saëns* /saN-**soN**ss/ — the N indicates that the preceding vowel is nasalised.

A

a, an 1. Is it wrong to say *an hotel*? Not really wrong — but not recommended any longer, particularly in writing.

The general rule is this: it is pronunciation, not spelling, that governs the choice between *a* and *an*. Words beginning with a consonant-sound take *a*; words beginning with a vowel-sound take *an*; words beginning with the 'glides' or 'weak' consonants — /h/, /w/, and /y/ — take *a*. So: *an umbrella* but *a unit* and *a eucalyptus tree*; *a £1 note* but *an only child*, *a young child*, and *a weak child*; *a haircut* but *an honour*. And since the standard pronunciation of *hotel* today requires an audible *h*-sound (though it is often dropped in the speech of the lower and upper classes), the preferred form is *a hotel*.

The fact remains that it is not easy to say *a hotel* out loud. In rapid speech, the *h* is so weak that it seems quite natural to say *an hotel*, *an habitual liar*, and so on. And this is often transferred to writing:

> Two entertaining talks by John Pemble, an historian, on Radio 3 'reflected' . . . on the tuberculous British abroad in the nineteenth century.
> – Paul Ferris, *The Observer*

> Harrison agreed to publish the book and was then let into the secret — which she, like Gottlieb, has kept for an heroic 2½ years.
> – Claire Tomalin, *The Sunday Times*

Note how different things are, however, when it comes to ✗ *an hostel,* ✗ *an horrible liar,* and so on. Clearly these sound impossibly awkward today, though, as old texts show, they used to be standard:

> It was a curious little green box on four wheels, . . . drawn by an immense brown horse, displaying great symmetry of bone. An hostler stood near, holding by the bridle another immense horse.
> – Charles Dickens,
> *The Pickwick Papers* (1837)

The *h* of *hostler* was probably pronounced very faintly by Dickens, if at all. Today, however, this use of *an* is unacceptable: the *h*-sound is now too prominent, even in rapid speech, since *hostel* and *horrible* are stressed in the first syllable. In *hotel* and *habitual* the first syllable is unaccented and the *h*-sound much softer accordingly, so *an* is less awkward here.

The rule applies to abbreviations too: pronunciation, not spelling, determines the use of *a* or *an*. So a standard written sentence might be: *I saw an MP reading a MS* — **an** *MP* because *MP* is intended to be pronounced /**em-pee**/; and **a** *MS* because *MS* is intended to be read as *manuscript*. But if you intended *MP* to be read as *Member of Parliament* (or *Military Policeman* or *Mounted Policeman*), then you would write *a MP*. In the following quotation, the writer must have intended *SF* to be read as *Science Fiction*, rather than as /**ess eff**/:

> I remember a SF story, too, that set up another speculation: a bunch of people equipped with a time machine . . .
> – Katharine Whitehorn, *The Observer*

Interestingly enough, the original form of the indefinite article, in Old English, was *an*, meaning 'one'. (Compare *un* and *ein* in modern French and German.) It was only later, in Middle English, that *an* began to be reduced to *a* before consonants.

2. One common way of dealing with the difficulty of saying *a hotel* is to pronounce *a* as /ay/ rather than /ə/ — the way you might pronounce the *the* of *the hotel* as /t͟hee/ rather than /t͟hə/. This is a fair compromise in this particular case, but the pronunciation /ay/, like /t͟hee/, when used before full consonants, attracts a great deal of criticism. With one exception, the pronunciation of *a lamp* as ✗/ay lamp/ is nonstandard. In British English it is considered overdeliberate and prissy, or else vulgar — just one step away from pronouncing it /hay lamp/.

. The exception is when *a* is being used emphatically, as a contrast to some other word:

> You said *a* lamp, not *the* lamp.
> I asked for *a* lamp, not for *150* lamps!

Here the strong pronunciation /ay/ is acceptable.

American English is rather more tolerant of the pronunciation /ay/ — it is in fairly common use there to indicate deliberation, hesitation, or emphasis, as in Bob Dylan's line 'Like /ay/ rolling stone'.

3. A single *a* or *an* can sometimes be used to refer to several linked singular nouns:

> Whether it takes a minute, hour, or day, I'll do it gladly.
> In his time, he's been an explorer, bricklayer, dustman, and schoolteacher.

Strictly speaking, of course, *a* cannot be correctly applied to *hour* in the first example — *hour* takes *an*. Similarly, *an* in the second example is inappropriate for *bricklayer, dustman,* and *schoolteacher*. Pedants would therefore urge the insertion of the 'correct' article: *a minute, an hour, or a day*. This is quite unnecessary, however: convention allows the 'correct' form to be understood, rather as **a** *timely entrance* is understood as **an** *entrance that is timely*.

Where it might be appropriate, however, to insert the article before each noun is where the various items are considered independently rather than together:

> A policeman and a criminal will obviously interpret things differently.

> a stone, a leaf, an unfound door (a motif in Thomas Wolfe's novel *Look Homeward, Angel*)

> A spaniel, a woman, and a walnut tree — the more they're beaten, the better they be.

> A random scattering of objects surrounded the corpse — a brick, a broken radio set, an umbrella, a pressure cooker ... perhaps one of them had been used to bludgeon the unfortunate man to death.

> A book of verses underneath the bough,
> A jug of wine, a loaf of bread — and thou
> Beside me ...
> — Edward Fitzgerald,
> *The Rubaiyat of Omar Khayyam* (1879)

And the *a* or *an* must be reinserted if the list of items is interrupted by any item (a plural noun or a mass noun) that does not take either *a* or *an*. In fact, it is best to use *a* or *an* wherever possible if any of the items marks an exception by not taking an indefinite article:

> For this recipe you need a carrot, an onion, a tomato, beef-stock, a large potato, three leeks, a cooking apple, a patient soul, and a lot of luck.

4. The positioning of *a* or *an* in a sentence, and

even its presence there, are not always straightforward matters. The indefinite article usually comes before both the adjective and the noun: *a sweet smile, an inviting smile* ... but: *such a smile, so sweet a smile, what an inviting smile, many an inviting smile, how sweet a smile, too sweet a smile*.

(Note that some of these constructions are now rather old-fashioned: *many a sweet smile* would today usually be expressed instead by *many sweet smiles* or *a lot of sweet smiles*.)

There is a temptation to follow this inverted pattern in similar constructions where it is not in fact appropriate to do so:

> ✗ Have you ever seen more inviting a smile?
> ✗ That's not sufficiently sweet a smile.

These should read:

> Have you ever seen a more inviting smile?
> That's not a sufficiently sweet smile.

Sometimes *a* or *an* is not simply wrongly positioned but wrongly included in the first place — notably when the adjective *no* is used in the sentence to qualify the noun: *no* then means 'not a', so the inclusion of an explicit *a* is redundant:

> ✗ No more inviting a smile had he ever seen than the one the mermaid now directed towards him.

The *a* should be omitted. If the sentence is restructured, you can see more easily that the *a* is unnecessary: *No smile more inviting had he ever seen* ...

Sometimes the *a* or *an* is optional — before idiomatic pairs or lists of nouns, for a start:

> All you need is (a) needle and thread.
> We shall provide (a) table and chairs, but you must bring your own cutlery.

> He's not one of those priests who arrive with (a) bell, book, and candle whenever summoned.

The *a* or *an* is also optional after *as*:

> He is more famous as (a) poet than as (a) novelist.

And *a* or *an* is also optional when the noun is in apposition to a person's name (that is, when it simply stands after the name, to expand or explain it, and has the same grammatical role in the sentence):

> ? Mrs Sylvia Wilkins, (an) avid amateur astronomer from Glasgow, reports a sighting of an unidentified comet.

? (A) Nicaraguan diplomat Nico Yepes has won the pools in three different countries.

In these last examples, the omission of *a* or *an* would be slightly dubious perhaps — common enough in journalism, but probably considered informal elsewhere.

5. When the first word of a book, play, film, or the like is *A*, it is — with the full sanction of convention — often dropped to make the sentence flow more smoothly:

> There's an excellent *Midsummer Night's Dream* on at the Alhambra.
> Robert Bolt's *Man for All Seasons* converted easily to the screen.

abbreviations In private and informal writings, people abbreviate words and names in any way they find useful and understandable.

In print and formal writing, rules are needed for the thousands of possible abbreviated forms, to avoid confusion and prevent overuse. The first rule is: When in doubt, spell it out. This applies to all general writing such as fiction, history, news, and formal letters. Only a handful of extremely well-known abbreviations tend to be used in such texts — *a.m.*, *M.P.*, *Mrs.*, *St.* (= Saint, as in *St. John*), or *U.S.A.*, but probably not *e.g.*, *lb.*, *Mt.*, *St.* (= street), *SW*, or *U.K.* In technical and business writing, however, abbreviations are heavily used, and provide an invaluable space-saving service.

1. Abbreviations are often identified by full stops:

> M.A. (*M*aster of *A*rts)
> a.m. (*a*nte *m*eridiem)
> T.S. Eliot (*T*homas *S*tearns *E*liot)

There is wide variation in practice, however. For example, the 1984 London telephone directory includes both *B & E Contractors* and *B. & E. Hardware.*

The tendency to leave out full stops is particularly strong in abbreviations that consist entirely of capital letters: *BBC*, *MA*, *TLS*, *NNW*. This tendency is less strong with the abbreviations of people's names: *T S Eliot* is less likely than *T.S. Eliot.*

Only if the capital letter stands for a complete word can it take a full stop: *TB* (tuberculosis), *TV* (television), and *MS* (manuscript) therefore cannot take a full stop. And full stops tend to be omitted in acronyms (see **6. c.** below) such as *UNICEF* or *NATO.*

2. When an abbreviation ends with the last letter of the word abbreviated, British English often

considers it a 'contraction' (see below) rather than a true abbreviation, and writes it without a full stop (*Dr*, *Mr*, *Jr*). American English is far more likely to use a full stop (*Dr.*, *Mr.*, *Jr.*) — this is still quite acceptable in British English, of course, though less and less common.

The distinction is a controversial one, however. It seems rather odd to find *Dr* ('contraction' — no stop) and *Prof.* (abbreviation — hence full stop) in a single text or even sentence; similarly *Lat.* (abbreviation of *Latin*) and *Gk* (contraction of *Greek*), or *Pvt.* (abbreviation of *private*) and *Sgt* (contraction of *Sergeant*). And what of *Col/Col.* (Colonel) and *Lieut/Lieut.* or *Lt/Lt.* — are they contractions or abbreviations; do they omit the stop or take it? Finally, the occasional glaring exception: *ms*, for *manuscript*, is almost never seen with a full stop after it, though according to the 'rule' it ought to have one.

3. For consistency's sake then (or perhaps more often through ignorance), the recommended distinction is more and more being disregarded, in British English at least, in favour of the blanket omission of the full stop after abbreviations. The effect is certainly streamlined, as the following extracts make clear:

> See now, for instance, the approach adopted in *SA Wire Co (Pty) Ltd* v *Durban Wire & Plastics (Pty) Ltd* 1968 (2) SA 777 (D) at 781, cited by Hosten and others (n 25 above) 241.
> ... R W M Dias *Jurisprudence* 4 ed (1976) ch 7 pp 218 – 45 ...
> Gramsci op cit 321 – 43. Cf Maureen Cain 'Optimism, Law and the State: A Plea for the Possibility of Politics' in C M Campbell and C J Schuyt (eds) *European Yearbook in Law and Sociology* (1974) 26.
> — footnotes,
> *The South African Law Journal*

4. *plurals and possessives.* A few single-letter abbreviations indicate their plural form by simply doubling the letter: the full stop, if it is used at all, is placed after the second of these letters. So, the word *page* can be abbreviated as *p.* or *p*, and *pages* accordingly becomes *pp.* (with a stop after the second *p*) or *pp* (without any stop at all).

A few abbreviations undergo fairly drastic changes when cast in the plural, notably *Mr*, which becomes *Messrs*, from French *Messieurs* (obviously it could not be spelt as *Mrs*).

For the most part, a simple *s* is added to the abbreviation: *five backbench MPs/M.P.s*; do not be tempted to insert a needless apostrophe here — *M.P.'s* is the possessive, not the plural. Note that if the abbreviation contains more than one full stop, the full stops are unaffected by the addition of the *s* — *five M.P.s*; *three successive l.b.w.s* — but if the abbreviation has only a single, final full stop, this shifts its position and follows the *s*: *a message for Capts. Kane and Hilson*. (For more details, see PLURALS.)

Scientific terms tend to retain the singular form when the plural sense is intended: *one kg*; *four kg*, and so on. (See section **6.d.i** below.)

The possessive is formed by the simple addition of *-'s* or *-s'*: *the PM's latest proposal* (or *P.M.'s*); *the J.P.s' conference*, and so on.

See also A, AN **1**.

5. Note that if an assertion ends with an abbreviation, and that abbreviation ends with a full stop, no more full stops are needed:

She works for the B.B.C.
She works for the BBC.

In other words, an assertion should end with only one full stop, even if it is the full stop of an abbreviation.

6. Several types of construction resemble abbreviations but have rather different punctuation rules:

a. *contractions* — *can't, mustn't, shan't*, and so on: these take an apostrophe to represent the missing letter/s. Note, however, that *shan't* has only one apostrophe, whereas it should really have two. Take care to place the apostrophe in the correct position — it corresponds to the missing letter, not to the syllable break: *shouldn't*, not × *should'nt*.

See also AIN'T; CONTRACTIONS OF VERBS.

b. *clipped forms of words* — *flu, phone, Tom, fo'c's'le*, and so on: few of these are spelt with an apostrophe nowadays — *fo'c's'le* (for *forecastle*) and *bo's'n* (for *boatswain*) are extreme examples. *Cello* used to be spelt with an apostrophe in front of it, the full form being *violoncello*, but this would seem pedantic today. And to spell *flu* as *'flu* is not only pedantic but inconsistent, since there are missing letters after as well as before the contracted form, and an apostrophe might be expected at the end too.

Cello is today quite at home in even the most formal contexts — so too are *bus, chips, cinema, cox, curio, perm, pram, taxi*, and *zoo,* so much so that many people are scarcely aware of the fuller forms (*omnibus, chipped potatoes, cinematograph, coxswain, curiosity, permanent wave, perambulator, taximeter cabriolet*, and *zoological gardens*).

Flu is slightly less formal, but still perfectly suited to most ordinary contexts: similarly *bike,*

disco, exam, fan (in the sense of 'enthusiastic supporter' — from *fanatic*), *fridge, gym, phone, photo, pop music* (from *popular music*), *pub, quad, recap* (from *recapitulate*), *vet* (from *veterinary surgeon*), and so on.

Some clipped forms are fairly informal still — *telly* and *ref,* for example; also *ad* (for *advertisement*), *bookie* (*bookmaker*), *deli* (*delicatessen*), *gent, info* (*information*), *mike* (*microphone*), *prelims* (*preliminaries*), *prof* (*professor*), *wellies* (*Wellington boots*), and so on.

All varieties — from the most formal and assimilated to the most slangy — tend to be spelt without any apostrophe.

See also APOSTROPHE **3, 4.**

c. *acronyms* — these are strings of letters or syllables that are pronounced as if they spelt a complete word. *U.N.* or *UN* is an abbreviation, whereas *UNESCO* (/yoō-neskō/) and *Comintern* (/kommin-tern/) are acronyms — the former from initial letters, the latter from the initial syllables of *Com*munist *Intern*ational. Syllable acronyms such as *Comintern* (or *Benelux*) are never written with full stops, and letter acronyms such as *UNESCO* (*Fiat, NAAFI, NATO, OPEC, Wrens*, and so on) almost never have full stops either nowadays. Acronyms denoting common objects — such as *radar* (*ra*dio *d*etection *a*nd *r*anging) and *scuba* (*s*elf-*c*ontained *u*nderwater *b*reathing *a*pparatus) — are by now fully accepted as common nouns, and of course take no full stops.

d. *scientific terms.* **i.** *weights and measures.* The full stop is seldom used here — *kg*, without the stop, stands for *kilogram/s*; *cwt* for *hundredweight*; *ft* for *foot* or *feet*; *amp* for *ampere/s*; *yd* for *yard*. The standard abbreviation of *yards* should be *yds*, though in fact *? yds.* with the full stop seems to be just as common. The abbreviation of *miles per hour* seems equally acceptable without and with full stops — *mph* and *m.p.h.*

Note that *lb* stands for *pound* or *pounds*: the form *? lbs* represents an undesirable mix of the English plural-ending *-s* and the Latin *libra* (singular) or *librae* (plural).

ii. *chemical symbols* — such as *Ca* (calcium) and *Fe* (iron). These never have full stops, whether of the *Ca* type, reflecting the current English term *calcium,* or of the *Fe* type reflecting the Latin word for 'iron', *ferrum.*

abjure, adjure, conjure These three fairly uncommon verbs may cause problems, *abjure* and *adjure* being so similar in sound and spelling, and *adjure* and *conjure* being confusingly close in meaning.

Abjure comes via Middle English and Old French from Latin *abjurare,* 'to deny on oath', from *ab-,* 'away' + *jurare,* 'to swear'. *To abjure* means 'to renounce or repudiate or abstain from, as if under oath': *He has a history of alcoholism, but is reformed and now abjures drink.* As the prefix *ab-* suggests, the word refers to staying *away* from something.

Adjure comes via Middle English from the Latin *adjurare,* 'to swear to', from *ad-,* 'to' + *jurare,* 'to swear'. Like *abjure* the word contains the sense of 'as if by an oath', but this time the solemnity of the act is directed towards something or someone else rather than away from oneself. *To adjure* means 'to command or entreat earnestly, as if under an oath'. The *ad-* element in the word suggests the meaning 'to appeal *to*':

> He need not have adjured me to keep up my spirits, which were as high as possible . . .
> I was, as it were, really new-born.
> – William Morris,
> *News from Nowhere* (1890)

Abjure and *adjure* are both stressed on the second syllable. *Conjure* is usually stressed on the first, though in the first sense given below it should be pronounced /kən-**joor**/ — but rarely is, except in American English.

The word comes through Old and Middle English from Medieval Latin *conjurare,* 'to invoke with oaths or incantations' — in Latin, it meant 'to swear together, conspire', from *com-,* 'together' + *jurare,* 'to swear'. *To conjure* can mean 'to call upon or entreat solemnly, especially by an oath', which brings it very near to the meaning of *adjure.* The difference is perhaps that *conjuration* of someone carries the implication of 'conspiracy', of urging him to follow one's own example: *He conjured his friend to join him in voting with the reformers.*

A related meaning of the verb *to conjure* is 'to summon (especially a devil or spirit) by incantation or by magic'.

There are extended meanings of the verb: 'to perform magic tricks' (hence *conjurer),* and 'to cause or effect as if by magic': *The argument seemed endless until Mary arrived and conjured away all the problems.* Similarly, the phrase *to conjure up* means, 'to bring into existence, as if by magic' — *He conjured up a feast at an hour's notice* — or 'to bring to the mind's eye, evoke': *Her speech conjured up a utopia of freedom, equality, and justice.*

The verbs *abjure* and *adjure* are fairly rare now, as is *conjure* in the senses of 'to entreat' or 'to summon'. It would be just as well, then, to con-

sider other words instead, and at the same time avoid the risk of confusion: for *abjure,* the alternatives *renounce, give up, reject,* and *repudiate* are possible; for *adjure — implore*, *beg*, and *entreat*; and for conjure — *entreat*, or *summon*, *enlist*, and *call upon.*

about   **1.** In the sense of 'approximately', *about* is often used redundantly:

> ? The victim is a man of about 60 to 65.
> ? Damage was caused that is estimated to be about £60,000.
> ? I'll arrive at about 9 or 10.

About should ideally apply to only one figure: since a margin of error is implied by the word, an alternative figure is unnecessary. The first specimen sentence above seems, therefore, to be saying the same thing twice. In the second example, the word *estimated* indicates that the figure cited is only approximate: the *about* is redundant and should be omitted. In the third sentence, the phrase *at 9 or 10* is an idiomatic way of admitting uncertainty about the time of arrival: no additional indication is needed, and the *about* should accordingly be deleted. There is also some objection to the use of *about* with precise figures rather than round figures: it is odder to hear ? *about 1528* than *about 1525.*

2. In the sense of 'approximately', *around* and *about* are equally acceptable, but *around* is more common in North American than in British English. The expression *round about* is chiefly British English: *I'll arrive round about 10 o'clock.* (See AROUND.)

3. Three constructions, all involving the word *about*, are fairly common in American English and are becoming more noticeable in British English. In their different ways, and to different degrees, they are undesirable additions to the language.

a. First, *about* in the sense of 'aiming at, intending to achieve':

> ? Historically, the Populist Party was about the redistribution of economic power.
> – Arthur M. Schlesinger, Jr. (U.S.),
> *The New York Times*

The problem is that this is different from the older sense of *about,* 'dealing with, treating'. The Schlesinger example is unambiguous because only the newer sense is possible in it. But there can be ambiguity in a sentence such as ? *Politics is about power.* Does this mean that politics is concerned with power as a subject of study — in the abstract, as it were — or that politics is concerned with how to *achieve* power?

b. The extended form *what it's all about* has become a fashionable tag:

? Broadcasting? Broadcasting isn't a 'public service'. It's a business, like any other. It's there to make money. Money — that's what it's all about.

? Disappointed, the lovers fall out of love. Love has failed to give meaning to their lives and that, in a way, is what all the various concepts which are covered by the single word 'love' are about: a drive towards meaning.
   – Eleanor Bron, 'Words', BBC Radio 3

This usage was no sooner established than it became a cliché, rather like *the name of the game,* which could replace *what it's all about* in the example above.

Although the current popularity of *what it's all about* seems to be due to American influence, the phrase itself was perhaps of British origin: it is found in the old nursery jingle 'Looby Loo', and is, more or less, the refrain of the song 'The Cokey-Cokey' (1942).

c. The phrase *not about to,* in the sense of 'unwilling to' or 'unlikely to', is not yet — fortunately — so widespread in British English:

? If I'd followed that suggestion, I would have had to mortgage my house a second time, and I was not about to do that.

The expression is not particularly elegant, and it duplicates quite unnecessarily the work of *unwilling to* or *unlikely to.* But the chief objection to it is its ambiguity. The established sense of *not about to do that* is 'not on the verge of doing that'. If the new sense gains a secure foothold in British English, then a sentence such as *She is not about to organise another conference* will become intolerably ambiguous, as it already is in American English. Resist this new usage, or we are in danger of losing the old one.

In fairness, it should be noted that the expression *not going to* probably underwent a similar development, and can indicate unwillingness as well as futurity: *I'm not going to say it.* In fact, the positive form *going to* can be used to indicate willingness or insistence — *I am going to resign* (though the positive form *about to* cannot really be used in this way).

The forms *will not* and *will* can similarly be used to express both futurity and (un)willingness — *I will not agree to it* — though here (as in many languages) the development was in the opposite

direction: *will* began as a verb expressing willingness or determination, and only later came to be used to indicate the future.

● *Recommendation* Of these three new uses of *about* — listed above in ascending order of respectability — **b.** is a cliché, and, like all clichés, is best reserved for special effects, such as deliberate informality or irony. Use **a.** can lead to ambiguity, and should be allowed only with appropriate caution. Use **c.** can also lead to ambiguity, though this ambiguity is associated with a general, perhaps universal, development within certain verbs — combining a sense of willingness with a sense of futurity.

above The use of *above* as a noun — *as the above makes clear* — is common in legal, official, technical, or business writing, but is considered stilted in ordinary writing, and is best avoided there:

? The percipient reader will have observed the hand of Toomey in the above. The stress of invention is less arduous than the strain of word for word copying.
   – Anthony Burgess, *Earthly Powers*

? The problem with writing your autobiography is that you feel a reluctance to include puffs like the above.
   – Veronica Lake (U.S.), *Veronica*

It might have been more appropriate to say simply *puffs of this kind* or *puffs like those just mentioned.*

Note that there is no equivalent noun use of *below.*

Both *above* and *below* are used in corresponding ways as adjectives and adverbs, and this use is quite acceptable. There is nothing wrong with saying, for instance, *puffs like those mentioned above.* Both *above* and *below* are freely used in this way throughout this book: *as all the above examples make clear*; *as all the examples above make clear*; *as all the examples listed above make clear.*

The use is slightly metaphorical: the example referred to as *the above example* may in fact occur at the foot of the previous column or page, and thus literally be *below.* (Similarly, a list referred to as *the list below* may appear at the top of the following column, and thus literally be *above.*) Nevertheless, the adjectives *above* and *below* cannot easily be replaced: *foregoing, aforementioned, previous, preceding, following,* and so on are all slightly stilted or misleading in their own way.

absolute adjectives See ADJECTIVES; UNIQUE; VERY.

abstemious, abstinent The adjective *abstemious* means 'sparing in the consumption of food and drink, not self-indulgent'. The word comes from the Latin *abstemius* from *ab-, abs-,* 'away from' + *temetum,* 'alcoholic drink'. *Abstinent* comes from a different Latin word, *abstinere,* 'to abstain', from *ab-, abs-,* 'away from', + *tenere,* 'to hold'. It means 'denying one's appetites completely; doing without'.

Abstinent differs from *abstemious* in two respects: first, it refers to all appetites and desires, whereas *abstemious* tends to refer only to food and drink, or even more specifically to alcoholic drink alone; secondly, *abstinent* suggests total self-denial, *abstemious* simply suggests moderation.

The noun derived from *abstemious* is *abstemiousness; abstinent* has two related nouns — *abstinence* and *abstention. Abstention,* unlike *abstinence,* has no suggestion of denying the appetites: it refers simply to refraining from something — a single act of abstaining (commonly, abstaining from voting). *Abstinence* suggests continuous abstaining (as from drink). In the Roman Catholic Church, *abstinence* has (or had) the special sense of 'going without certain specific foods on days of penitence'. So a Catholic might practise *abstinence* by occasional *abstention* from meat.

abstract nouns *Abstract nouns* refer to qualities, emotions, concepts, and relationships that cannot usually be perceived with our senses: *hopelessness, vacancy, rejection,* and *parenthood* (and the words *quality, emotion, concept,* and *relationship* themselves), as contrasted with *concrete nouns* such as *tortoise, bicycle, leather, parent* and *airport.* You need abstract nouns every now and again to communicate your ideas, but if you use too many of them, and particularly if you use too many long ones ending in *-ity, -ence, -ment, -ness,* and *-tion,* your language will become heavy and unreadable. It is usually neater and clearer to reformulate the sentence with a verb or adjective or concrete noun rather than rely on the abstract noun. If possible use *opaque* in preference to *opacity, sleepy* to *somnolence, achieve* to *achievement, distribute* to *distribution, the members* to *the membership, the leaders* to *the leadership.*

Such nouns as *basis, situation, conditions,* and *nature* can often be removed, to the advantage of the text. You could rephrase *work on a part-time basis* as *part-time work; They negotiated in a face-to-face situation* as *They negotiated face to face; the weather conditions* as *the weather; acts of a ceremonial nature* as *ceremonies;* and *have an alcohol problem* as *drink too much.*

Sociologists and academic writers tend to make extremely heavy use of abstract nouns. These might sound impressive, but often at the expense of elegance and clarity:

If there really is a pattern of incompatibility and an incapacity for resolution of differences, then reconciliation is simply not an option.

How much clearer had the wording been:

If you really are incompatible and cannot resolve your differences, you simply cannot live together again.

The following extract would have benefited from rephrasing:

Some people, I know, will see that as an argument for bringing the IRA into the negotiating process.
— Conor Cruise O'Brien,
The Observer

This could simply have read *for bringing the IRA into the negotiations* or *for negotiating with the IRA.*

See also JARGON.

acceptation This noun used to deputise for *acceptance* in many of its uses, but is now quite distinct from it. Its only common current sense is 'the usual or accepted meaning of a word or phrase (or the interpretation of an idea)': *I use the word 'code' in its usual acceptation; His acceptation of a warm welcome is a sullen 'Very well, come in then'.*

accessory, accessary Both these words are spelt with double *c* and double *s.* In American English, *accessory* is the only current form, and covers all the meanings; but in British English the different spellings are usually reserved for different meanings, though here too *accessary* is losing ground.

An *accessary* is a helper, willingly aiding or consenting in an activity, especially a criminal act. *Accessary before the fact* is a former legal term referring to a person who aids or encourages a crime but is not present when it is committed. *Accessary after the fact* is the former term referring to a person who is once again not present at the crime, but who helps the criminal after it has been committed. The phrase *accessary to* is used when mentioning the crime (not the criminal): *being accessary to the train-robbery.* In general, *accessary* can be used either as a noun or as an adjective: *the safebreaker's accessary; his accessary concealment of the escaped convict.* (Note that the actual perpetrator of the crime, to whom the accessary is secondary, is the *principal.*)

Accessory, with an *o,* can also be used either as a noun or as an adjective. As an adjective, it means 'additional, supplementary'; as a noun, 'an additional feature, often subordinate and inessential'. It has two common specialised meanings. An *accessory* in a person's wardrobe is a supplementary item of clothing that accompanies and harmonises with an outfit — for example, a handbag, belt, scarf, hat, gloves, or even shoes. The *accessories* of a car, machine, or kit are inessential extras: of a car, the cigarette lighter or the radio, perhaps; of a tape recorder, a hand-held microphone or earphones or extra tapes, and so on.

The spelling *accessory* is now encroaching on the meaning of *accessary;* to write *accessory after the fact* is almost common practice today:

? Michael Chamberlain was found guilty of being an accessory after the fact of murder.
— Michael Davie, *The Observer*

None the less, this change of spelling has still not secured complete acceptance, and it is best to retain the old distinction. Do not be surprised, however, to find uninformed people 'correcting' your *-ary* spelling to *-ory.*

acquirement, acquisition Both of these nouns can refer either to the faculty (or power or act) of acquiring, or to the thing acquired. The difference is in the nature of the thing acquired — *acquirement* is used when referring to skills, qualities, and abilities; *acquisition* is used when referring to physical objects or people.

So: *impressive acquirements in musicianship; the acquisition of a small fortune* (note the prepositions — an acquirement *in,* the acquisition *of*); and *Ballroom dancing may not be as generally useful an acquirement today as it once was; Have you seen my latest acquisition — a 64K microcomputer?*

Nowadays, however, *acquirement* is not much used, the noun *accomplishment* being preferred. See also REQUIREMENT.

acronyms See ABBREVIATIONS **6.c.**

act The verb *to act* is sometimes followed by an adjective. This is generally felt to be nonstandard in British English, though it is more acceptable in North America: *?? He's acting crazy; ?? Don't act stupid.* Standard usage favours an adverb: *Don't act stupidly.*

activate, actuate *Activate* is an increasingly fashionable word, and in the view of many people an increasingly misused one as well, appearing all too often in contexts where *actuate* would be strictly correct. *To activate* first appeared in about 1626, and meant simply 'to make active', as in *to activate the heart.* The word's resurgence is perhaps the result of its recently taking on a number of specialist scientific uses. In chemistry, for example, *to activate* means 'to accelerate (a reaction), as by heat'; *to activate sewage* is to blow compressed air through it to speed up its decomposition. In physics, *to activate* means 'to make radioactive'. In American military usage, it means 'to call to active duty; organise': *to activate the commando unit.*

To actuate, from medieval Latin *actuare,* 'to execute', appeared in about 1596. It means 'to set in motion or put into mechanical action', and also 'to inspire or motivate': *The project was actuated, but they had to wait for results; By flipping the switch, I inadvertently actuated the alarm system; She was actuated by good intentions.*

Activate is now often encountered in such sentences in the place of *actuate.* And in some cases — notably in reference to machinery or electrical circuits, as in *to activate the alarm* — the usage is well established and quite permissible today. But when used in reference to people and their motives, *to activate* still jars unacceptably: *a man actuated by malice* remains the only correct form; *activated* is not an acceptable alternative in such constructions.

active and passive **1.** These are two forms of what is technically called 'voice', a grammatical category that makes it possible to view the events described in a sentence in two ways, without making any difference to the facts reported: *The cameraman photographed the President* is in the *active* voice. *The President was photographed by the cameraman* is in the *passive* voice.

Passive verbs are formed with the verb *to be,* or informally sometimes with *to get,* and the *-en* or *-ed* form (past participle) of another verb. They are most often used when the focus is on the person or thing that undergoes the action. There is no need even to mention the person or thing that performs the action (the element corresponding to *by the cameraman* is often simply omitted): *The President was photographed; The boy got* *hurt*; *Postal rates are to be increased*.

Curiously, however, if the *by* part of the sentence is retained, the effect is often to focus attention on the performer of the action more emphatically than if the sentence had remained in the active: *These Christmas cards were painted by sufferers from cerebral palsy* is more effective than *Sufferers from cerebral palsy painted these Christmas cards*.

2. The passive is also often used to conceal the identity of the person who is actually responsible for something unpleasant. An inspector might write *It is felt that you have no grounds for complaint* when he is reluctant to admit plainly that it is he who feels that way himself. Such a construction may be frowned on by some critics as cowardly, but it is a typical part of the weaponry of the language. Still, it is best to keep the passive to a minimum. Use active sentences unless there is some good reason against them. Such formulas as *Your cooperation is greatly appreciated* or *The inconvenience caused is much regretted* would be better rephrased as *We greatly appreciate your cooperation* and *I much regret the inconvenience caused*.

3. The *double passive* is a fairly common stylistic or grammatical fault: it consists of putting into the passive both verbs of an active sentence rather than just one. Consider the sentence *We endeavour to create a cheerful atmosphere*: the passive version all too often emerges as × *A cheerful atmosphere is endeavoured to be created*. If you really must avoid the active form here, rephrase as *An attempt is made to create a cheerful atmosphere*. The faulty double passive is common with the verbs *attempt, begin, desire, hope, intend, propose, threaten*, and *omit*:

× The mountain was attempted to be climbed.
× The contract is proposed to be cancelled.
× The grant is threatened to be withdrawn.

There is no objection to the double passive if it is generated from a sentence already containing one passive. The sentences *They believed him to have been drowned* and *She ordered the family to be rehoused* can quite correctly become *He was believed to have been drowned* and *The family were ordered to be rehoused*.
Compare the following two sentences:

We hope to resume the service shortly.
We expect to resume the service shortly.

They seem similar enough, but *expect* has a versatility that *hope* lacks. The second sentence can be rephrased as *We expect the service to be resumed*, and hence as an acceptable double passive: *The service is expected to be resumed shortly*.

Perhaps on the analogy of this past sentence, *hope* is often used in the double passive too — unacceptably: × *The service is hoped to be resumed shortly*. This is not legitimate, since the intermediate stage is impossible: × *We hope the service to be resumed*.

Note, however, that the *hope*-sentence can be rephrased with two passives (not really a double passive), if the verbs are kept apart and treated separately: *It is hoped that the service is to be resumed*.

actuate See ACTIVATE.

AD, BC **1.** The simplest and best forms of these terms are: AD and BC — full capital letters, no full stops, no italics, no space between the letters. The most common variants have full stops — A.D. and B.C. Small capital letters are sometimes used (with or without full stops) in place of full capital letters: AD/A.D. and BC/B.C.

These variants are fully acceptable; less acceptable are the use of italics and the placing of a space between the letters: *?* 276 *BC*; *?* A D 30.

2. AD stands for *Anno Domini* (/**an**no **dom**minī/; usually /-nee/ in American speech), 'in the year of the Lord', meaning 'in the (specified) year after the birth of Jesus Christ'. Scholars have disputed the date of Jesus' birth — some favouring 7 BC, some AD 4, for instance — but that does not affect the calendar in the least. Traditionally, AD comes before the number of the year — as in the previous sentence. This is in keeping with the full reading 'in the year-of-the-Lord 4'.

BC, on the other hand, traditionally follows the number of the year — *died in 327 BC*. This is in keeping with the full reading 'in the year 327 before Christ'. So:

Augustus was born in 63 BC and died in AD 14.

Another traditional distinction is that BC can be applied to centuries and millennia — *archaeological finds dating back to the 13th century BC* — but that AD should be omitted when referring to centuries: *the development of the English language during the 13th century*. This traditional 'rule' has little basis, however, and can be safely ignored where appropriate — especially when both epochs are mentioned together: *the Roman Empire from the second century BC to the third century AD*.

Note too that AD here follows rather than precedes the number of the century. Increasingly, AD is being used after rather than before the year as well: *? died in 1430 AD*. But the traditional rule governing this question is rather more vigorous, and objections persist to such constructions as *? 1430 AD*. The plaque left on the moon by the Apollo astronauts reads:

? Here men from the planet Earth first set foot upon the Moon, July 1969, A.D.

A letter to the *Los Angeles Times* drew attention to an alleged grammatical error, suggesting that the correct form should be *July, A.D. 1969*. Users of British English might add a further objection — that the word *in* has been omitted before *July*. It is advisable, in formal contexts, to continue to place AD before the number of the year.

3. Note, finally, that people of persuasions other than Christianity sometimes avoid using BC and AD altogether (just as they avoid referring to *Christian names*). The standard alternative formulations are BCE and CE, standing for 'before the common era' and 'in the common era'. In both cases, the year comes first. So: *63 BCE* and *14 CE*.

See also CENTURIES.

adequate   In the sense of 'sufficient for a particular purpose or need', *adequate* can be followed by *for* (before a noun) or *to* (before a verb): *The amount was adequate for our needs*; *There was adequate food for our needs*; *The amount was adequate to feed four people*.

In the sense of 'having the right qualities to meet the requirements of a situation', *adequate* is usually followed by *to*: *He proved adequate to the task*.

adherence, adhesion   The verb *to adhere* comes from the Latin *adhaerere*, meaning 'to stick or cling to', and is used both literally — *a stamp adhering to the envelope*; *a tyre that adheres well to the road* — and figuratively: *adhering closely to the plan*; *disciples who adhere to a charismatic leader*.

There are two pairs of words related to *adhere* — *adhesive* and *adherent*; and *adhesion* and *adherence*: in each case, the first of the pair emphasises the literal sense of the verb, and the second the figurative sense.

Adhesive, both as noun and as adjective, covers the literal sense: *the adhesive properties of adhesive plaster*; *wallpaper needing a strong adhesive*. And *adherent*, as a noun (and as a rare adjective), covers the figurative sense: *one of Hitler's earliest adherents*.

Adherence corresponds to *adherent*, and covers such abstract senses as 'abiding by' and 'loyal devotion to': *strict adherence to the rules*; *adherence to the President and his policies*. *Adhesion*, however, is not quite so clear-cut: it does have the literal sense, corresponding to *adhesive*, of 'the act or state of sticking together': *preventing the adhesion of mud to their shoes*. But it also has a more figurative sense — 'agreeing or assenting to join or associate oneself with some cause or group': *an act of adhesion to the new revivalist movement*. And in medical parlance it can refer to the pathological results of organic fusion: *painful adhesions due to inflammation*.

See also COHERENT.

adjacent, adjoining   These two adjectives are often interchangeable, but in their primary meanings are distinct and should not be confused. If two things are *adjoining*, they are literally joined: *adjoining rooms* have some wall or door or passage in common.

There was a scuffling, followed by a heavy thud, as if the young man had been flung violently against the door. The thud roused Mr Norris to action. With a single, surprisingly agile movement, he dragged me after him into the adjoining room.
— Christopher Isherwood, *Mr Norris Changes Trains*

If two things are *adjacent*, they are simply near each other or next to each other, as in *adjacent angles, adjacent epochs*, or *a garden adjacent to the towpath*. (The Latin roots of the word have the literal meaning 'to be thrown down close to'.) They may or may not be in physical contact with each other.

The traveller will pass the main police barracks on his left and then, on his right, the Court house and the adjacent cluster of buildings, well shaded by trees.
— Paul Scott, *The Jewel in the Crown*

The word *contiguous* can be used in both ways. However, in its primary sense it is virtually synonymous with *adjoining*, as its Latin roots suggest (literally, 'touching on all sides').

adjectives   **1.** Adjectives are words that give some information about a noun or noun equivalent, by limiting, qualifying, or specifying it. *Nice* is an adjective, as in *nice house*, and *French*, as in *French house*; less obviously, so is *this* in *this house* and *first* in *first house*.

Most adjectives can be used in more than one position in a sentence. They can come before the noun they describe, as with *green* in *green door*. Here, *green* is in the 'attributive' position. Or they can follow a verb, as with *green* in *The door is green*. Here, *green* is in the 'predicative' position. A rarer position for an English adjective is directly after the noun, as with *old* in *three years old*, *thick* in *two metres thick*, *errant* in *knights errant*, and *elect* in *president elect*. These adjectives are in the 'postpositive' position.

Some adjectives can be only attributive. We can say *the main problem* but not × *The problem is main*. Others can be only predicative. We can say *The pilot is alive* but not × *the alive pilot*. Only a few adjectives are regularly used post-positively, but many others can be so used for certain effects of style — *A man alone has got no chance* — and must be so used in certain constructions: *a child eager to learn*.

Note that certain words other than adjectives can be used attributively to describe nouns. This is particularly true of names of materials, as in *glass bottles, silk ties, iron railways*; and of participles of verbs, as in *the coming months, a deserved rebuke*.

Many *compound adjectives* are formed from longer phrases and clauses: a *soft-spoken negotiator* is one who speaks softly. So too *time-honoured, tax-free, tongue-tied, straight-from-the-shoulder*. Such combinations are usually hyphenated.

For nouns ('attributive nouns') used like adjectives, as with *railway* in *railway station* and *sports* as in *sports car*, see NOUNS; NEWSPAPER ENGLISH. For adjectives used like nouns, as in *the rich, the deaf, the good*, see NOUNS. For adjectival clauses and phrases, as in *the man (that) you met* and *the house at the corner*, see CLAUSES; PHRASES.

The possessive forms of the personal pronouns *I, he,* and so on are *my, his*, and so on, and these are often classified as *possessive adjectives* when they come before a noun: *my/your/our/his/her/its/their house*. (For the problem of whether to say *He doesn't like me whistling* or *He doesn't like my whistling*, see -ING FORMS OF VERBS.)

Some ambiguity can arise when *my, his, Joe's, the dogs',* and so on are used with certain abstract nouns (typically those based on verbs), though the context will usually clear things up: the phrase *the students' evaluation* or *their evaluation* can have either an active or a passive sense. So: *the students' evaluation of the problem* means that they evaluate the problem, while *the students' evaluation by the examiner* means that they are evaluated by the examiner.

Where more than one adjective, or adjective equivalent, is used before a noun, some ambiguity may creep in. There is no problem over expressions such as *a large black leather briefcase*, since *large, black,* and *leather* all describe the briefcase; but *small children's toys* may be either *toys for small children* or *small toys for children*, and it would be clearer to express the idea in one of those ways.

2. *comparison.* Most adjectives and adverbs can be used not only in the 'positive' form (*bright, good, fast*) but in the 'comparative' (*brighter, better, faster*) and the 'superlative' (*brightest, best, fastest*). The comparative is the intermediate degree: *Anna is fatter than her sisters.* It must be used where only two items are compared: *the fatter* (not *the fattest*) *of the two girls.* The superlative is the extreme degree: *Anna is the fattest in the family.* It is used for more than two: *the fattest of the three girls.*

Comparatives and superlatives are formed in one of three ways: first, by adding the endings *-er, -est*, which is the usual way for words of one syllable and some words of two — *taller, tallest; sooner, soonest; stupider, stupidest.*

The second way of indicating degrees of comparison is by using *more* and *most*; this is done with some words of two syllables and almost all words of more than two — *more complex, most serious/ly*. (Conversely, *less* and *least* are used, and these usually suit one-syllabled words as well as those of two or more syllables: *less quick/ly, least desirable*.) Some adjectives, including many compound adjectives, can form their comparatives and superlatives in both ways: *more kind-hearted, most kind-hearted* or *kinder-hearted, kindest-hearted.*

The third way of indicating the comparative and superlative is by using quite different words. The two main 'irregular' comparisons in English are these: *good/well, better, best; bad/badly, worse, worst.*

Advertisers often use comparative adjectives without providing any basis for comparison, as when they speak of the *better* class of hotel, or say that a detergent washes *whiter*. Whiter than what? Avoid this dubious linguistic trick.

See also MORE; MOST.

3. *absolute adjectives.* Some adjectives cannot be used in the comparative or superlative. Obviously you cannot say × *a more nuclear missile* or × *the most medical student*. You cannot even say that the missile is × *very nuclear* or the student × *nearly medical*. They are nuclear and medical, and that is that.

Some adjectives should not normally be used in the comparative or superlative, since they already imply a complete or final degree. If something is *perfect*, for instance, it cannot be improved on, so × *more perfect* and × *most perfect* are not usually possible. Neither are × *less perfect* and × *least perfect*, since once something is less than perfect, it is imperfect.

Strictly speaking, such *absolute adjectives* should also not be modified by words such as *absolutely, totally, utterly*, and *very*: ? *an absolutely perfect somersault*. Yet idiom seems to have given its blessing to such constructions, though they are really tautologous.

Absolute adjectives can be modified by *nearly, not quite*, and so on: *an almost perfect somersault*.

There are dozens of other absolute adjectives. Here is a sampling: *absolute, complete, contemporary, entire, essential, everlasting, extreme, supreme, total, unique*. (See PERFECT; UNIQUE; VERY, MUCH.)

Many apparently absolute adjectives are usually exempted from the restrictions, however. Few people would object to the use of *the purest water*; *a fuller description*; *an even more cloudless day*; *a very thorough search*.

In the following examples, however, the absolute adjectives are surely being misused:

× This [*Roget's Thesaurus*] must surely be the most indispensable publication ever compiled. In its revised form it is even more invaluable.
    – review, in *John O'London's*

Indispensable and *invaluable* do not really allow modification. The reviewer should have written *most useful* and *most valuable* instead. Here is another example:

× It seems that the last few hours of the average person's sleep are not so essential, and probably have little restorative value for the brain.
    – Dr Jim Horne, *The Guardian*

There are no degrees of *essentialness*. The author should have written *not so necessary*. A last example:

× Mr James, a keen canoeist for the past six years, has travelled to Spain and Austria in search of 'wild water' to test his skills. Yesterday he found the most ideal conditions in his home city, as 13ft of floodwater turned the river into a torrent.
    – caption, *The Times*

Here *the most nearly ideal conditions* would have

been correct though rather pedantic. Perhaps the *most favourable* or simply *the best* would be most appropriate.

4. *adjective or adverb*? When a word is to follow a verb, there may be a problem over whether to use a predicative adjective or an adverb. Use the adjective if the word describes the subject — *He looked hungry* — and use the adverb if the word describes how the activity was done: *He looked hungrily at the steak*. Similarly *The market closed steady* and *The market rose steadily*.

The test is whether or not the verb can be replaced by the verb *to be*. It is correct to say *He looked hungry* because it could be that *He was hungry*. Similarly, *The market closed steady* means in effect *The market was steady* when it closed. If the verb *to be* does fit the construction, then use the adjective.

Note that some words can function as both adjective and adverb — *late* and *fast*, for instance: *The train was fast, The train is late* (adjectives); *The train went fast, The train is running late* (adverbs).

In some such cases, there is an alternative regular adverb ending in *-ly*: *the direct train* (adjective), *The train goes direct to York* (adverb), *The train is leaving directly* (adverb). Similarly: *They were educated free; They moved about freely*. Here, the two adverbs have different meanings in each case. Where the two adverbs have the same meaning, the *-ly* form is usually better for formal contexts: it is chiefly in informal speech that one says *Come here quick*; *You're working too slow*; *They're selling apples very cheap*, and so on. In the following piece of serious writing, *quicker* seems rather out of place — *more quickly* would have been more suitable:

Throughout its history, English has had scribes, printers and conscious reformers who have tried to make spelling adequately represent pronunciation. But always the pronunciation has changed quicker than the spelling.
    – Professor C.L. Wrenn,
    The English Language

The adjectives *sure* and *real* are used like adverbs before other adjectives in informal language, particularly in American English. Expressions such as ? *real nice* and ? *I sure don't* should be rephrased in formal writing as *really nice* and *I certainly do not*.

Some apparent adjectives are conventionally used in certain phrases and situations where you might expect an adverb: *He arrived late, doubtless* (not *doubtlessly*) *because of the heavy traffic. He acted contrary* (not *contrarily*) *to my wishes*. Similar phrases are *preparatory to, previous to, prior to, irrespective of*, and *regardless of*, all of which really function as complex prepositions. *Prior to* is a formal substitute for *before*.

5. *too many adjectives.* It is a common fault of weak stylists to use too many adjectives and hackneyed adjectives. Public officials and business executives write of *an integral part, real danger, prime responsibility, active consideration, sudden emergency*, and *true facts*, where the nouns in question could be sufficiently effective on their own. Literary aspirants are equally guilty, with *silvery moon, briny ocean, arid desert*, and *fond farewell*.

The best policy here is to be as exact and specific as possible, using adjectives of kind rather than those of degree. To say that a *crisis* is an *economic crisis* tells us much more than to say that it is an *acute crisis*. To call an action *virtuous, efficient,* or *generous* tells us more than to praise it as merely *good*.

Much can be done too by using more exact nouns and verbs, rather than leaving all the work to the adjectives and adverbs: *He slouched into the dive* is more vivid than *He walked limply into the seedy bar*. In appropriate contexts, *a rattletrap* would be more effective than *a noisy worn-out car*, and *a greybeard* than *an old man*.

adjure   See ABJURE.

admission, admittance   The verb *to admit* has two main meanings: 'to acknowledge or confess' and 'to allow to enter'. When the noun relates to the first of these senses, and means 'a confession or acknowledgment', the word used is always *admission*: *by his own admission*; *an admission of guilt*; *his admission that they were right*.

> Despite Boy George's frocks and scarlet lips, most men are trying hard not to have a public image that might confuse them with women, and they know that the key thing to avoid is anything smacking of the emotional, the admission of personal problems and any accompanying confusions — the very stuff that females are supposed to be made of.
> – Helen Franks, *The Observer*

> Arthur didn't say much about his business affairs; he was more guarded than of old. 'Times are bad, but, but, on the whole, I can't complain,' was his only admission.
> – Christopher Isherwood,
> *Mr Norris Changes Trains*

Sometimes, *admittance* is used in this sense too — mistakenly:

> ✕ The strategy which England chose was to put the ball behind the Springboks by persistent kicking and then to chase and harry over the advantage line. It was an admittance of their lack of confidence in their capacity to achieve anything in constructive attack. And so it proved.
> – Clem Thomas, *The Observer*

For the sense 'entrance, right of entrance, or permission to enter', *admission* and *admittance* are both possible. *Admission* is far more common in general use, and is the recommended form: *There is an admission charge*. The form *admittance* has an official, formal feel to it, and most often appears on signs or notices, in the forbidding phrase *No admittance*. In the following examples it is used in the contexts of enrolment at an exclusive school and entrance to a religious sanctuary:

> As to the matter of Mrs Humbert's daughter, she wished to report that it was too late to enrol her this year; but that she ... was practically certain that if Mr and Mrs Humbert brought Dolores over in January, her admittance might be arranged.
> – Vladimir Nabokov, *Lolita*

> A bell is rung in the main sanctuary: by a devotee of Lord Venkataswara warning the god that he seeks admittance.
> – Paul Scott, *The Jewel in the Crown*

admit   **1.** The phrase *to admit of* now means only 'to allow the possibility of; to leave room for', and can no longer replace *to admit* in its various other senses: ✕ *I admit of the justice of your claim.* Leave out the first *of* here. (It is no improvement to replace it with *to*: see below.)

A simple pointer to alert you to a faulty *of* is the use of a human subject. Typically, *to admit of* takes an abstract subject. You can say, for instance:

> The proposals admit of a certain margin of error.
> Such a decisive refusal admits of no further discussion.

But you should not say:

> ✕ I admit of a certain margin of error in my proposals.
> ✕ The managers admit of no further discussion of the subject.

2. The phrase *to admit to* should be restricted to the sense 'to lead in to; to afford access to': *This door admits to the main hall.*

To admit to is widely used, however, where *to admit* alone is appropriate:

?? I admit to the justice of your claim.
?? Do you admit to the error of your ways?
?? They admitted to juggling the figures.

It is advisable to leave out the *to* in each case. It was probably adopted originally on the model of *to confess to,* which is usually an acceptable variant of *to confess.*

See also ADMISSION, ADMITTANCE.

adoptive Take care not to use *adoptive* as a supposedly impressive synonym of *adopted.* The two adjectives regard the relationship of adoption from opposite directions. Children are *adopted*; parents are *adoptive.* So: *My adopted son is six years old*; *My adoptive father was very good to me, but I always harboured the wish to find my real father.*

advance, advancement The verb *to advance* means either 'to go forward' or 'to bring forward'. *Advance* is the noun relating to the first sense, and means 'going forward or ahead'. *Advancement* is the noun from the second sense, and means 'bringing or putting forward or upwards; promotion'. The two nouns are never interchangeable; to use *advancement* as a long variant of *advance* is an error. So: *His advance through the enemy ranks was devastating*; *His advancement through the ranks smacked of favouritism. The advance of learning* refers to the increase or refinement of knowledge; *the advancement of learning* refers to its promotion by encouragement, subsidies, and so on.

Advance can also, of course, be used like an adjective, meaning 'going before': *They sent an advance party.* Remember that the word is superfluous in such phrases as × *advance warning*, × *advance preparations*, or × *advance planning*, since *warning, preparations,* and *planning* already refer to the future.

You can, however, speak of *advanced planning* or *advanced preparations.* The participle *advanced*, used as an adjective, has a quite different sense from *advance. Advanced* means 'far on in development or years or sophistication': *advanced technology, an advanced age.*

adventitious *Adventitious* sounds as though it might be close in meaning to *adventurous* or *advent* — and it does have a shared origin with them in the Latin verb *advenire,* 'to arrive'. But its sense is quite distinct from theirs. *Adventitious* means 'added by chance, extraneous, accidental, not inherent': *adventitious decorations with no relation to the overall design of the building.*

In legal terminology *an adventitious inheritance* is one that falls to someone who would not normally receive it (for example, a person unknown or unrelated to the deceased). In botany, *adventitious* means 'random, appearing irregularly or in unusual positions': *adventitious roots.* (Note also the botanical term *adventive,* meaning 'not native and not fully established in a new habitat; newly arrived'. *Adventive* in the sense of 'immigrant' was formerly in more general use, but today is confined to botanical contexts).

adverbs **1.** 'Adverb' is a somewhat unsatisfactory name for this part of speech. Adverbs modify verbs: *to continue steadily*; or adjectives: *amazingly steady*; or other adverbs: *surprisingly steadily*, or prepositional phrases: *right into my eyes*; or whole clauses or sentences: *Frankly, I don't care.* They can also link a sentence with what precedes it: *Yes, she is; Therefore, it's false.* In fact, it would be tempting to say that grammarians call a word an 'adverb' if they cannot confidently describe it as anything else.

The commonest kind of adverb is formed by adding *-ly* to an adjective: *steadily, carefully, resourcefully, instantaneously.* But note that many adverbs do not end in *-ly*: *soon, therefore*; and that some have forms both with and without *-ly*: *free/freely*; *direct/directly* (see ADJECTIVES **4**). Note too that many *-ly* words, such as *friendly* and *lonely*, are not adverbs but adjectives (see -LY).

Adverbs that in effect answer the question How? are sometimes called adverbs of 'manner'; the answer may be *gratefully, slowly*, or *eagerly.* Those that answer the question When? are adverbs of 'time': *now, yesterday*; and those that answer the question Where? are adverbs of 'place': *here, upstairs.* This system of classification is convenient in some ways, but it does not really belong to grammar.

2. *the placement of adverbs.* It is perfectly legitimate to insert an adverb between the parts of a verb: *I should probably have gone; They may sometimes refuse; They couldn't possibly remember.* (But see SPLIT INFINITIVE.) An adverb should not normally intervene between a verb and its object, but this depends upon the length of the object. ?? *We explained carefully the matter* should be corrected to *We carefully explained the matter* or *We explained the matter carefully.*

However, *We explained carefully that we wanted all the doors painted purple* sounds idiomatically acceptable: *carefully* could still be placed before *explained*, but it could not be postponed until the end. Sometimes the dubious positioning of the adverb can cause ambiguity: *? The review criticised unnecessarily modernist novels.* Here, *unnecessarily* could be taken to apply to *modernist*. If it is intended to apply to *criticised*, place it before rather than after the verb, or else at the end of the sentence.

Certain adverbs, particularly *only, even, quite, just, hardly,* and *scarcely,* are usually best placed as close as possible to the part of the sentence to which they apply, at least in formal writing. Although the natural place for *only* may be quite early in the sentence, as in *He's only lost one election,* the order *He's lost only one election* is usually considered more precise. (See ONLY.)

Usually and *generally* are more correctly placed after a negative than before it: *He doesn't usually wear a tie* rather than *? He usually doesn't wear a tie.*

For comparison of adverbs (*sooner, most pleasantly*) see ADJECTIVES 2, and for overuse of adverbs, see ADJECTIVES 5. For adverbial clauses and phrases, as in *He left before we arrived* and *We meet every other day,* see CLAUSES; PHRASES.

adverse See AVERSE.

advice, advise Take care to spell these two words correctly. In both British and American English, the noun is *advice* ('counsel, guidance'); and the verb is *to advise* ('to give helpful suggestions, give counsel').

A spelling error here is all the less excusable, since the two forms are pronounced differently — ending with an *s* sound and a *z* sound respectively — unlike (in British English) the pairs *practice/practise* and *licence/license.*

advise Commercial jargon has long favoured the verb *to advise* as an impressive-sounding substitute for *to tell,* or *to mention. ? Further to your inquiry, we would advise you that the cheque is in the post.* Sometimes the *you* might be left out here, further irritating the purists in the process. To them, *advise* means 'to counsel; to offer advice or recommendations to (someone), or to suggest or recommend (something)'.

If you wish to tell someone something, then it is best to *notify* him, *inform* him, or simply *tell* him. There is no need to *advise* him unless you are actually giving him advice.

? When the crew abandoned the manoeuvre the braking was so severe that the brake overheat light came on. The control tower was advised of the situation and emergency services were called.
> – Peter Durisch, *The Observer*

Another extended sense, chiefly in American English, is equally unwelcome to careful speakers. This is the sense 'to consult, or take counsel': *?? The president is advising with his aides.*

aerie, eyrie Both mean 'an eagle's nest'. *Eyrie* is the more usual spelling in British English. The variant *aerie* is common in America; the further variant *aery* slightly less so.

All these pronunciations are possible: /**eer**-i/, /**air**-i/, and /**ī**r-i/; /**eer**-i/ is safest.

aesthetic The branch of philosophy called *aesthetics* is concerned with beauty — what counts as beautiful and how it is perceived. (Note that it usually takes a singular verb: *Aesthetics appeals more to female than to male students.*) There is also the noun *aesthetic,* meaning 'a principle or theory of beauty'. And *an aesthete* is a person who cultivates the appreciation of beauty and art — the word is now sometimes used disparagingly, the way *arty* is.

The adjective *aesthetic* refers to the study of aesthetics or to the general appreciation of beauty and the criticism of taste: *Much modern architecture has abandoned aesthetic considerations in favour of functional efficiency.*

By a slight extension, *aesthetic* has come to be used of people. *An aesthetic young man* is one who has good taste and is interested in art, music, and so on (perhaps in contrast to *an athletic young man*).

The meaning of *aesthetic* is often extended further still, across the borderline of acceptability this time. Careful users of English flinch at the appearance of *aesthetic* in the senses of 'guided by good taste' or 'beautiful': *?? a most aesthetic flower arrangement; ?? an aesthetic little country cottage.* Such uses perhaps developed from a phrase such as *aesthetically pleasing.* If so, the wrong element has been singled out in the shorter form. It would be better to speak of *a very pleasing flower arrangement.* And it is much less pretentious (and less provoking) to speak simply of *a beautiful little country cottage.*

The word *aesthetic* goes back through French, German, and New Latin to the Greek *aisthetikos,* which meant 'pertaining to sense perception' (the question of beauty was not originally involved), from *aistheta,* 'perceptible things', from *ais-thenasthai,* 'to perceive'. The same Greek root is the ultimate source of *anaesthetic,* which relates to the *loss* of sensation or sense perception.

The commonest pronunciation in British English is probably /eess-**thet**tik/, though /iss-/ and /ess-/ are acceptable too. The noun *aesthete* has only one standard pronunciation in British English: /**eess**-theet/.

In American English the first syllable of *aesthete* is pronounced /**ess**-/ and the first syllable of *aesthetics* is pronounced /**ess**-/ or /**iss**-/. In both words the pronunciation /eess-/ is regarded as British. In accordance with its preference for /ess-/ in pronunciation, American English allows *esthete* and *esthetic* as variant spellings of *aesthete* and *aesthetic.*

affect, effect The most common use of *effect* is as a noun meaning 'a result':

> The whole theory of modern education is radically unsound. Fortunately, in England, at any rate, education produces no effect whatsoever. If it did, it would prove a serious danger to the upper classes.
> – Lady Bracknell, in Oscar Wilde's *The Importance of Being Earnest*

The noun also commonly means 'an influence': *His speech had a profound effect on my thinking.*

The commonest use of *affect* is as a verb related to this second sense of *effect,* meaning principally 'to have an effect upon, to influence': *Alcohol affects different people in different ways.*

Effect can also be used as a verb, meaning 'to bring into existence, bring about or cause'. Thus, *to effect a reform* is to bring it into existence; *to affect a reform* is to have an influence — to have an effect — on a reform already in existence. In the following passage, *effect* is used as a formal equivalent of *make:*

> It wasn't [him], but 'he looked incredibly like him', recalled the pensioner, Professor Jim Gower. 'I nearly effected a citizen's arrest.'
> – Lindsay Vincent, *The Observer*

Effect is frequently misspelt as *affect,* especially since the two words are often pronounced the same: /ə-**fekt**/. (Strictly speaking, however, the correct pronunciation of *effect* is /i-**fekt**/.)

To return to *affect* — three other common senses are 'to move emotionally, to touch': *I am deeply affected by all your kind messages of support*; 'to have a harmful effect on, influence adversely': *The moist climate is affecting my health*; and 'to assume, pretend, feign': *to affect indifference, affected an Oxford accent.*

> It would be equitable to see a major increase in the child benefit allowance in this Budget; alas, this is a forlorn hope. Mr Lawson affects little sympathy with the poor and downtrodden.
> – leading article, *The Observer*

It is from this last sense that the adjective *affected* takes its sense of 'insincere and conceited': *a nasty, snobbish, affected little man.*

Affect does have a use as a noun, but in a rare and specialist psychological sense, to mean 'emotion'. This is unlikely to be confused with *effect* because the stress now falls on the first syllable: /**af**fekt/. The adjective from this is *affective* — 'relating to emotion rather than to thought'. Here the stress is back on the second syllable, and there is the danger of confusion in spelling with *effective,* 'having a substantial, or desired, effect'.

The following quotation illustrates helpfully the commonest senses of *effect* and *affective*:

> This failure has damaging effects on Josipovici's whole critical manner and mode of address. For all his professed modernism he is really an old-fashioned affective critic who likes books which are 'moving', 'profoundly moving', even 'splendid'. A trim and nimble literary impresario, he tends to project his own face into the critical mirror.
> – Tom Paulin, *The Observer*

See also EFFECTIVE.

affixes See PREFIXES AND SUFFIXES.

affluent *Affluent* originally meant 'flowing freely', the Latin roots being *ad-,* 'towards' + *fluere,* 'to flow'. (As a noun, *affluent* still refers to a tributary river.) By a natural extension, it came to mean 'copious or abundant' — *an affluent harvest* — and by a further extension, 'well-stocked, amply provided': *a writer affluent in comic ideas; a valley affluent in good farming land.* Such uses are now rare, however.

Today the word has been further extended — distorted, in the view of many careful speakers — to serve as a synonym of *rich* or *wealthy* or *well-to-do*: *?an extremely affluent barrister.* It is perhaps the euphemistic rather than pompous element of the word that irritates the purists. If you mean 'rich or wealthy', they would urge, then say *rich* or *wealthy.* The noun *affluence* is similarly considered a needless synonym of *riches* or *wealth.* It might not always be appropriate, however, to speak so forthrightly, and *affluence* seems to have become fully established now in this sense. But do use it sparingly.

African English English is the most extensively used language in West and East Africa, even though it is the mother tongue of only a tiny minority of the population. As a second language, and as an official language, it is spread across Nigeria, Ghana, Sierra Leone, the Gambia, Cameroon, and Liberia in West Africa; Kenya, Tanzania, and Uganda in East Africa; and Malawi, Botswana, Zambia, Zimbabwe, and other southerly Black African states. (The English of South Africa is usually treated as a different variety, and discussed separately. See SOUTH AFRICAN ENGLISH.)

Most of these countries were once part of the British Empire and are now part of the Commonwealth. Perhaps the Empire's greatest legacy to the Commonwealth has been the strong bond of the English language.

The History of English in Africa The first Europeans to visit Black Africa in modern times were the Portuguese. In the early 16th century, British seamen began to challenge Portuguese domination, establishing settlements in West Africa and engaging in regular trade with the native inhabitants. Within a century, a pidginised variety of English was spoken all along the West African coast.

The slave trade then conveyed much of this pidgin English across the Atlantic (see WEST INDIAN ENGLISH), but the movement was again reversed during the late 18th and early 19th centuries. Freetown in Sierra Leone was established as a haven for former slaves. A small number of these, the 'Black Poor' returning from London, brought British varieties of English back with them; the majority — mainly freed Jamaican slaves, or 'Maroons', and escaped American slaves temporarily resettled in Nova Scotia by the British after the American War of Independence — spoke American varieties of English or creole.

Sierra Leone became a British Crown Colony in 1808: throughout the 19th century, thousands of West Africans being shipped to America as slaves were recaptured and settled in Freetown. These disparate groups eventually forged a common English-based creole, Krio, a mother tongue now widespread in Sierra Leone and parts of Gambia.

The American influence is more specific in Liberia, established — as its name implies — as a refuge for freed American slaves in 1821. In 1867, when the country became an independent republic, about one per cent of its population were 'Americo-Liberians' who spoke (and whose descendants still speak) a variety of Black American English, often called *Merico*, as their mother tongue.

But elsewhere it is British rather than American English that is the norm; many other West African countries, and many East and Southern African countries, came under British rule between the mid-19th and early 20th centuries. (Of the European powers, only France and possibly Portugal can be said to have acquired anything like a comparable administrative, and hence linguistic, stake in the continent.) English secured its currency and high prestige in Africa mainly through the efforts of missionaries and traders during the 19th century. Today standard English is the medium of instruction in most secondary and tertiary education. It is also the language of administration and legislation, of the higher law courts, of broadcasting and the press, of large business, and of science and technology. And it serves, of course, as a vital link with the rest of the world.

In day-to-day matters, English serves as the lingua franca — the common language between people of different mother tongues — in one of the world's most complex linguistic conglomerations. In West Africa, for instance, in a population of about 140 million, there are perhaps as many as 2000 indigenous languages. Not surprisingly, English (in a range of varieties, including pidgins that are not always mutually intelligible) is to all intents and purposes the national language of at least three-quarters of the inhabitants of the region. Even in the French-speaking countries of West Africa, English is widely studied and highly regarded for its regional value, not just its overseas value.

The picture is slightly different in East Africa: with its more agreeable climate the region attracted British settlers in greater numbers during the colonial period, and standard English thus gained a more natural foothold there. (There are no English-based pidgins in East Africa.) True enough, East Africa does have a widely spoken indigenous language, Swahili, that rivals English as a lingua franca, and even as an administrative medium. But Swahili has more than one variety: the standardised variety in Tanzania (used now as an official language and the language of early education) is not easily understood in Kenya. The position of English seems secure: its value in higher education and in international communications, at least outside the immediate region, remains unchallenged.

The nature of African English 'African English' differs from country to country, even from region to region, so the features discussed here are generalisations at best. There is a range of varieties — a linguistic 'continuum' from pidgins to standard English. Any one speaker may be quite versatile, changing his position along the continuum according to the social context he finds himself in at the time.

Many identifiable features of African English reflect the influence of the speakers' mother tongues. This 'mother-tongue interference' declines according to educational attainment. At its most 'proficient', African English does not differ strikingly from mother-tongue World English, except perhaps in aspects of pronunciation. Such deviations as there are in vocabulary and grammar are much debated: they are often widespread, stable, and locally acceptable enough to be 'West Africanisms', or even 'Nigerianisms' and 'Ghanaianisms' as the case may be. But are they to be welcomed as permanent features of the language, incorporated into official usage, and countenanced in schools, newspapers, and broadcasting; or are they to be treated as aberrations, and scorned and shunned? Many educated speakers take this latter view, and attach considerable social prestige to 'correct' grammar and 'standard' vocabulary. In its extreme form, this attitude (coupled with another factor — that in many places English is still taught as a written rather than spoken language) can give rise to a florid, even archaic, style of English — sometimes to the point of an incongruous stiltedness or a quite inappropriate formality.

Pronunciation The pronunciation of African English is orientated towards RP — (the 'received pronunciation' of educated people in southeast England). Even Liberia is moving away from its form of American accent towards a more British form. It is generally considered socially undesirable, however, to affect a pronunciation that draws attention to itself as imitating RP too closely.

Neither East Africa nor West Africa has a stable homogeneous accent within itself; but some generalisations are possible, and 'typical' West African pronunciation can be differentiated from 'typical' East African pronunciation. In each case, the deviations from RP are largely the result of interference from the mother-tongue sound-system. Here are some of the more striking features that are often found in spoken African English.

African English gives considerable prominence to every syllable, resulting in a smoother 'syllable-timed' rhythm more like that of French than the typical undulating 'stress-timed' rhythm of RP.

When a stress-timed pattern is attempted, the stress is sometimes shifted: *edu***cate**, *suc***cess**, *exer***cise**, *doctor***ate**. In phrases or sentences the stress is sometimes placed on the less important words or syllables:

I like *it* very much.

'Spelling pronunciations' abound, perhaps because so much English-teaching is, or was, based on the written rather than spoken word: *chalk* is sometimes pronounced /chawlk/, with the *l* clearly heard; *Christmas* is often /krīst-mas/, *Anthony* /**an**thōnee/, *apostle* /a**pos**tel/, *camera* /**kam**eera/, and *country* /**kown**-tree/.

Similarly, the *g* of the -*ng* sequence is often sounded — *singing* might be pronounced /**sing**-ging-g/ — as is the *b* in words ending in -*mb*: *climbing* might be pronounced /**klīm**-bing-g/. These consonant-patterns often occur in the local languages, and so are transferred to English pronunciation.

Other consonant-clusters, however, are typically absent from African mother tongues, and are either broken up or reduced when they occur in English: the final consonants of *against* might be broken up by an intrusive vowel sound — /a-**gay**-nist/; the final consonant-combination of words like *lend* and *learned* tend to be reduced — to produce /len/ in both cases.

The consonants /th/ and /t̲h̲/, being typically absent in African mother tongues, are usually rendered as /t/ and /d/ in West Africa, and as /s/ and /z/ in East Africa. So the phrase *those three* might sound like /dōz tri/ in Nigeria, and /zōz sri/ in Kenya.

Similarly, 'voiced' consonants are often pronounced as 'voiceless' at the end of a word; *bag* might sound the same as *back*, and *cub* as *cup*.

The contrast between 'short' and 'long' vowels tends to disappear in African English, and there are fewer diphthongs; accordingly, many pairs or groups of words that sound quite distinct in RP are homophonous (identically pronounced) in African English: *head* and *heard* — /hed/; *pick* and *peak* — /peek/; *pull* and *pool* — /pōol/; *bird, bud, bod,* and *board* — /bod/ (in West Africa); *bird, bud, bad,* and *bard* — /bed/ (in East Africa).

The neutral vowel /ə/ is little used — *colour* and *collar*, for instance, take a more distinct final vowel than they would in RP: both words sound something like /**kul**lo/ in West Africa. (Note the absence of a final *r* sound; like RP, African English tends not to pronounce the *r* except before vowels.) And the 'syllabic consonant' on the end of such words as *hospital* or *happen* is expanded to a full syllable with a distinct vowel: /**hos**-pi-tal/; /**hap**-pin/.

Grammar Some common modifications of standard British English are:

● different uses of adverbs and prepositions in some constructions:

> You can pick me at home (= pick me up)
> She has a child for him (= by him) (West African)
> I'm going to stay with this pen (= keep this pen) (East African)

● the widespread use of the unvarying tags *isn't it?* and *not so?*

> You like the idea, isn't it?
> Everything's fine, not so?

(This feature is common in several other varieties of English.)

● in West Africa, the use of *o* to end a sentence or greeting:

> I am sorry o.
> Morning o!

● the pluralisation of nouns that are normally singular or 'uncountable': *slangs, funs, furnitures, advices.*

● the different distribution of *the, a, one,* and the frequent omission of them (this is a common feature in pidgins and creoles and other varieties of English as a second language).

> I am going to bank this morning (= to the bank)
> I saw the very one (= that very one)
> I bought one fine dress (= a nice outfit — whether for men or women)
> I stayed with one very nice somebody (= with somebody very nice) (West African)

● the tendency to use the *-ing* form of a verb, or the base form, in a way that goes against the idiom of standard English:

> He is not usually feeling very well (= does not usually feel)
> She has learn the whole book (= has learned/learnt)
> We have post 16 cards (= have posted)

● a tendency to use *he/him/his* and *she/her/hers* indiscriminately of a man or a woman:

> Give it to my mother, and tell him I am well.

Vocabulary African English has borrowed words from indigenous languages where needed.

These may be widespread or localised, reflecting the general African culture or local cultural differences: *kente* refers to a Ghanaian-made cloth, for instance; *oga* means 'a boss' or 'a superior person'; *fon* means 'a chief'.

Other African words are at least well-known in other parts of the world — *bwana* and *uhuru* (both from Swahili, but adapted from Arabic roots). And many words of African origin have been fully absorbed into World English: *safari* (adopted from Swahili, again from an Arabic source), *banana, banjo, chimpanzee, cola, voodoo, yam, zombie* (all adopted from various West African languages).

There are a number of 'calques' or 'loan translations' in African English — literal English translations of African idioms or metaphors: *to enstool* (in Ghana, 'to select and install as chief'); *to have long legs* ('to have influence'); *outdooring* (referring to a traditional naming ceremony); *to be a native of rice* (in East Africa, 'to eat rice habitually'); *palm wine; head tie* ('a head scarf'). English is now in such extensive use that local slang and colloquial idioms are constantly being created: *go-slow* for 'a traffic jam'; *senior brother* for 'elder brother'; *been-to*, referring to a person who has been overseas, typically to study, and since returned.

Finally, some standard English terms, while retaining their original senses, have acquired extended senses too: the word *carpet*, for instance, can also refer to a linoleum surface; *to hear a language* can mean 'to understand' it; *to try* can also mean 'to do well'; and *to bluff* can also mean 'to show off' or 'to dress in a flashy way'; *soup* can refer to a stew; *wedding bells* can mean 'an invitation to a wedding'; *to germinate*, used of a girl, means 'to mature into an adolescent'; *to take in* can mean 'to become pregnant', and *to be in a state*, 'to be pregnant'.

The future of African English It is impossible to be certain how the English language will develop in Africa. No one could have predicted, for instance, the recent impact of Indian English in Nigeria, where thousands of Indians are employed in village schools, urban colleges, and universities.

Some guesses, however, can be made. It seems likely, for a start, that English will continue to thrive in Africa, and that more and more Africans will extend their spoken repertoires, especially through exposure to British and American radio and television programmes. It seems probable too that American English will come to exercise a greater influence than it does now, especially among the young. Finally, it is likely that the similarities among the various African varieties of English — in the east, west, or south of the continent — will be reinforced by increased economic contact and cultural exchange.

See also PIDGINS AND CREOLES; SOUTH AFRICAN ENGLISH.

aggravate The purists' objection to *aggravate* in the sense of 'to irritate or exasperate' persists in the face of widespread use of the extended meaning — a meaning that dates back to Shakespeare's time! It seems that the extended sense occurs most often in the present participle, *aggravating*: *? What an aggravating thing to happen!* The noun *aggravation* is also used quite widely in the sense of 'an annoyance, irritation':

? It is then, of course, that the roller-coaster ride of anxiety really gets under way, when no worry, no matter how trivial, is given less than the most massive scrutiny. What might start off as a vague aggravation at 11.30 at night has developed into a major crisis of conscience by dawn.
– Ray Connolly, *The London Standard*

To aggravate means primarily 'to make worse or more serious', from Latin *aggravare,* 'to make heavier', from *ad-*, 'in addition to' + *gravare,* 'to burden', from *gravis,* 'heavy'. So: *Infection aggravated the wound*; *Her attempts at mediation only aggravated the dispute.*

The seriousness of any deterioration of relations between Moslems and Hindus was aggravated by the 40 million or more who were numbered among the scheduled castes.
– Lord Butler, *The Art of the Possible*

But in many cases it is hard to avoid a further charge. ... Their offence, in fact, is aggravated by cowardice and hypocrisy.
– Robert Conquest, *Daily Telegraph*

The modern sense must have developed cut of contexts such as *Her jibes aggravated my anger*; *His well-meant enquiries only aggravated her temper.* This is typical of the way in which words extend their meaning; indeed, the Latin sense of 'to make heavier' in *aggravare* was extended in a similar way into the English sense of 'to make more serious' in *aggravate.* Similarly, *to irritate* originally meant 'to stimulate, excite, or arouse' (which it still can mean) before acquiring its present sense of 'to annoy' — unobjectionable even to a purist.

Nevertheless, the force of the purists' objection has kept *to aggravate* from securing full accept-

ability in the sense of 'to vex or exasperate'. It is best to restrict this use to informal speech. There are, after all, several quite suitable synonyms: *irritate, exasperate, annoy, anger, bother, provoke, vex,* and so on.

ago, since 1. Compare the following two sentences:

It was only 10 days ago that the accident happened.
It is only 10 days since the accident happened.

When the sentence has two clauses like this, and is viewed from the present time, *ago* is preceded by the simple past tense (*was*), and *since* by the present or present perfect tense (*is, has been*). In addition *ago* is followed by *that,* whereas *since* is not (*ago* is an adverb, and the conjunction *that* is needed here to link the clauses; *since* is a conjunction in the example above, and needs no further conjunction to link the clauses).

A common error is to use *ago* and *since* side by side:

× It was only 10 days ago since the accident happened.

This is a fusion of the two standard structures illustrated in the earlier examples.

Another combination of *since* and *ago* is possible in such a sentence as:

?? I've been here since 10 days ago.

This sentence appears to violate no rule of English, but it sounds very awkward, and the following equivalent is preferred:

I've been here for 10 days.

Here is another example of the dubious combination:

?? It was 'Roy Hobbs Day', that had been in the making since two weeks ago, when Max Mercy printed in his column: 'Roy Hobbs, El Swatto, has been ixnayed on a pay raise.'
– Bernard Malamud (U.S.), *The Natural*

2. *Since* serves not just as a conjunction but as a preposition too (*awake since 5.30*), and as an adverb (*long since forgotten, stayed here ever since*). As an adverb, it was formerly an equivalent of *ago* in single-clause constructions. But no longer. Compare:

The accident happened 10 days ago.
? The accident happened 10 days since.

The use of *since* here is archaic. It would have

been idiomatic 200 years ago perhaps, but is now even more old-fashioned than its temporal opposite, *hence*: *? The meeting will take place 10 days hence.*

agree   The verb *to agree* is followed by a variety of prepositions, according to the sense intended.

To agree with means 'to regard favourably': *I agree with his views*; 'to share the opinion of': *Do you agree with me?*; 'to accord with': *The copy agrees with the original*; *The verb must agree with the noun*; and 'to have a beneficial or neutral effect on the health of': *Oysters don't agree with me.*

To agree to means 'to accept, endorse, or consent to': *He agrees to all your proposals except the last*; *I can't agree to your demands.* So you might agree *to* a policy and yet not agree *with* it.

To agree on (or *upon* or *about*) means 'to reach an understanding of; to have the same opinion of': *Let's try to agree on an approach to the problem.*

British (but not American) usage allows — just — the preposition to be dropped in this last case: *Let's try to agree an approach*; *They agreed terms.*

> Mr Foot is probably right: for while Mr Healey was talking about the precise method of phasing out Polaris, Mr Callaghan seemed to be advocating a nuclear Britain in perpetuity. Still, Mr Healey and Mr Foot should have agreed their story and stuck to it.
> – Alan Watkins, *The Observer*

Informal usage goes further, and often omits the preposition from *agree to*: *?? He agreed all our demands*; *?? The suggested procedure has not yet been agreed by the arbitrator.* To careful users of English, these constructions are quite unacceptable. Use instead *to approve, to accept, to ratify, to permit,* or — *to agree to.*

agreement   Any one part of a sentence has to correspond to the other parts: the form of a verb has to be in harmony with its subject, the pronoun or possessive adjective has to be of the appropriate gender, number, and person, and so on. This harmony is known as 'agreement' or 'concord'.

To native English speakers, agreement in a sentence is intuitive: when writing or speaking the sentence *Mr Graham sends his apologies*, for instance, no deliberate thinking is needed in choosing *sends* rather than *send*, and *his* rather than *her*. Yet errors in agreement are still very common — sometimes simply because of carelessness, sometimes because a sentence is distractingly complex, sometimes because the decision is very difficult to make.

Here, in ascending order of difficulty, are some examples of mistakes in agreement:

× Each soldier solemnly saluted, stepped forward, and pledged their allegiance to the Republic.

This should read *pledged his allegiance*. The middle section of the sentence delayed the implementation of agreement between *each member* and *his allegiance*; the writer had by this time lost sight of the grammatically singular subject, and in keeping with the plural feel of the sentence, chose *their* by mistake.

× Each of the recruits solemnly saluted, stepped forward, and pledged their allegiance to the Republic.

The same factors are at work here too, with the added complication of a plural noun, *recruits*, to reinforce the plural feel of the sentence. But the subject is not *recruits*: it is *each* — and *his*, not *their*, is the possessive adjective that corresponds to it. (See EACH.)

× The result of all these delays and cancellations, even though they were due to factors beyond our control, were several claims for damages and even two threats of legal action.

This should read *was several claims*: the subject is singular — *the result* — and the plural verb *were* is not in agreement with it. The writer was, understandably enough, distracted by all the plural nouns intervening — *delays, cancellations, factors,* even *claims* — and was therefore tempted into using the plural verb *were*. (See PLURALS Part II.)

× Simon together with Margaret are now going to perform an encore.

The subject is simply *Simon* and requires the singular verb *is*. If the sentence had begun *Simon and Margaret*, the subject would have been plural and *are* would have been correct. But *together with*, unlike *and*, does not link two singular nouns into a plural subject. Similarly:

?? Either the birds or the postman wake me in the morning.
?? Neither you nor she ever wake before 11.

In both examples here, *wakes* would be preferable to *wake*. When there is a 'compound' subject like this, the verb takes its form from the noun that is nearer to it: *the postman wakes, she wakes.* Had the elements in each subject been reversed, then *wake* would have been correct — *Either the postman or the birds wake me* . . . ; *Neither she nor you ever wake* . . . (See EITHER; NEITHER.)

Many people feel that this is still not a satisfactory solution. The impasse remains. The best course then is this: since it is the structure of the sentence that produces the impasse, simply change the structure of the sentence:

> Either the birds wake me or the postman wakes me.
> Either the birds wake me or the postman does.

Similarly, instead of puzzling over the correct verb to use in the sentence *One or both of them is/are lying,* unravel the syntax and say instead *One of them is lying, or both (of them) are.*

Keep trying new constructions until you are happy with the wording. English is a remarkably versatile language. One version after another might be unsatisfactory, but persistence will turn up a suitable construction in the end. Consider this sequence:

> ?Everybody in favour is to raise their right hand. (Unsatisfactory: *Everybody* is singular, whereas *their* is plural.)
> ?Everybody in favour is to raise his right hand. (But there are women present: perhaps *his* is not appropriate.)
> ?Everybody in favour is to raise his or her right hand. (A bit awkward.)

The next version is commonly considered correct, but it might create a new problem:

> All those in favour are to raise their right hands.

Now *their* is in agreement, since the subject is plural — *All those.* But is it correct to say *raise their right hands*? — that might imply that a person has more than one right hand. Is it correct then to say *raise their right hand*? — but that sounds odd. Finally:

> If you are in favour, raise your right hand.

At last — this version sounds just right in this particular setting. Persistence has paid. After trial and error, the solution has emerged.

See also EVERYBODY; NONE; ONE 5; PARALLEL CONSTRUCTIONS.

aid, aide As a noun, *aid* usually means 'help'. But it can also sometimes mean 'a helper', and this leads to confusion with *aide,* 'an assistant,

a right-hand man'. *Aide* has a much more official ring to it than *aid* does. *Aide* was originally a military term, the slightly less formal form of *aide-de-camp.* It is now widely used in government, diplomatic, and even business contexts: *The managing director's aide scuttled about trying to look useful.*

> Christian Heritage was launched at Westminster Abbey on May 9 with an ecumenical service, a sermon preached by the Archbishop of Canterbury — and an empty space where the Queen should have been. The Queen withdrew from the occasion on the advice of one of her close aides.
> – Mary Kenny, *Sunday Telegraph*

ain't *Ain't* is in fairly wide use in colloquial speech, both in British English and, especially, in American English. But it is nowadays also widely considered nonstandard, and should be avoided in writing (except in dialogue) and in formal speech — except when you are deliberately aiming at a humorous effect or using a fixed phrase such as *Einstein he ain't; It ain't necessarily so; You ain't heard nothing yet,* or *Things ain't what they used to be.*

Ain't, formerly *an't,* is strictly a contraction of *am not,* the way *don't* is a contraction of *do not,* and should be no more objectionable when used in that way than *don't* is — informal but not nonstandard. Yet generations of schoolroom disapproval have tainted *ain't* forever: ✗ *Ain't I getting a share?* is 'wrong'; *Don't I get a share?* is simply 'informal'.

The reason for this condemnation of *ain't* is probably that it came to be used in other, less acceptable, ways — to mean *is not, are not, has not,* and *have not:*

> ✗ 'Ain't he getting a share?'
> ✗ 'No, and you ain't getting any either.'
> ✗ 'He ain't got any, and I ain't got any either.'

These are clearly unsatisfactory: after all, the appropriate contractions *isn't, aren't, hasn't,* and *haven't* are available. But it is a pity that *ain't* as a form of *am not* is subject to this general condemnation too: there is no satisfactory alternative contraction this time. Certainly *I'm not* is suitable in statements or exclamations — *I'm not getting a share!* — but what about questions? Since *Am I not getting a share?* sounds extremely formal in ordinary conversation, some contraction clearly is needed — and the form *aren't* has been adopted for this purpose: ?*Aren't I getting a share?*; ?*I'm getting a share, aren't I?* Some purists object to it, since it suggests the combination ✗ *I are*; but it is now widely accepted in informal usage. There is another contraction — *amn't I?* — but this is restricted to certain regional varieties of English, especially in Scotland and Ireland, and even there is considered dubious.

albumen, albumin *Albumen* is the scientific word for the white of an egg. (It was originally a Latin word, derived from the adjective *albus,* 'white'.) It is also used to refer to the endosperm, the nutritive tissue surrounding the embryo in plant seeds.

Albumin is a more specific chemical term. It refers to any of several simple protein substances. They can be dissolved in water and coagulated by heat, and are found not only in egg whites, but also in blood serum, milk, and many animal and plant tissues. So *albumen* contains *albumins*.

Albumin is sometimes found spelt as *albumen,* but *albumen* should never be spelt as *albumin*. The two words are usually pronounced identically, /**al**-bew-min/, though you can distinguish the final syllables if you want to make it clear which word you intend. The stress is usually on the first syllable, though a second-syllable stress is an acceptable variant.

alibi *Alibi* has a specific legal sense: 'a form of legal defence, by which the accused tries to prove that he was somewhere else when the crime was committed; also, the evidence supporting this claim'. (In Latin, *alibi* meant 'elsewhere', from *alius,* 'other' + *ubi,* 'where'.)

> The culprit's alibi was hopeless: he claimed to have been at home watching TV, but he knew nothing about the programmes he had apparently watched.

In a slightly extended sense, common in American English but still slightly dubious in British English, *alibi* means 'the person vouching for the claim; the person who was allegedly in the suspect's company at the time':

? If she cites me as her alibi, she's in trouble — I'm not going to perjure myself to save her skin.

The word has extended its range in another way, and is often used loosely — unacceptably loosely — as a synonym of *excuse*.

?? Late for work again, Jones — what's your alibi this time?

?? You're always using your insomnia as an alibi for unsatisfactory work.

?? All were agreed, however, that at 35 Holmes is only a shadow of the fighter he once was. ... Holmes even offered an alibi for his poor performance — a fractured right thumb in training in July.
> – W.J. Weatherby, *The Guardian*

This usage is nonstandard, and should be avoided except in the most informal contexts. The concept in these examples is already served by the words *excuse, justification, pretext,* and *defence,* whereas the true sense of *alibi* can be served by no other word: *alibi* is needless in the one case, and too precious in the other to risk corrupting.

Another informal use of *alibi,* though less objectionable, is its use as a verb — 'to provide an alibi for':

? The barman agreed to alibi the thief in return for a share of the loot.

The pronunciation of *alibi* is /**al**-i-bī/ — it has remained quite unaffected by the vogue for a more Latinised pronunciation of Latin words in English. The plural is *alibis.*

all 1. *All,* whether as adjective or pronoun, can occur in conjunction with either a singular or plural verb. If a plural noun is present or understood, then obviously the verb will be in the plural too: *All (councillors) are attending the meeting.* But if a mass noun, or an 'uncountable' noun, is present or understood, then the singular verb is correct: *All human life is here*; *All is stolen or lost.*

The use of *of* after *all* is necessary before pronouns: *all of them, all of which* — though not if the pronoun is in apposition (that is, if it is followed directly by a noun). It is then optional: *All (of) you thieves are in trouble; warned all (of) us thieves.* The *of* cannot be used directly before plural nouns — *All councillors are attending the meeting* — or before most mass nouns: *All paper has a high carbon content.* Finally, the *of* is optional before some uncountable nouns — *All (of) human life is here* — and before *the, these, those* or *our, your, my,* and so on introducing plural nouns: *all (of) our knives and forks; all (of) the councillors.*

Where the *of* is optional, American English slightly favours the use of it, and British English prefers to leave it out: it is usually included, however, when contrasted with *some of, a few of, much of, none of,* and the like. So: *some of our knives and all of our forks.*

Abraham Lincoln's celebrated apophthegm is often quoted in the form:

You can fool all of the people some of the time, and some of the people all of the time, but you can't fool all of the people all of the time.

In this form it strikes many British people as relentlessly American in its use of *all of the* instead of *all the*. However, the most reliable account of Lincoln's words is strikingly different on this point:

You can fool all the people some of the time, and some of the people all the time, but you can not fool all the people all of the time.

2. All is often used redundantly: *All visitors must report to reception*; *All OAPs are entitled to a discount*. Omit the *all* here: it is unnecessary.

3. The expressions *All is not lost* and *All that glisters is not gold* are established idioms, and unlikely to be misunderstood. But their grammar is distinctly odd. (Strictly, the correct forms would be *Not all is lost*; *Not all that glisters is gold*.) Take care not to imitate the structure of these idioms when creating new sentences:

?? They seem happy together, but in fact all is not well between them.

?? You cannot say that all should be forgiven — some things should be forgiven, but all should not be forgiven.

These should read *not all is well between them* and *not all should be forgiven*.

Of course, *all* as a non-personal pronoun is now very old-fashioned. Current idiom favours *everything*. But the same grammatical requirements apply: *not everything should be forgiven*. *All* has survived better in reference to people, as before *who*: *All who know her love her*. However, *everyone/everybody* is again more in keeping with current idiom: *Everyone who knows her loves her*.

See NOT 1.

4. *All* should of course be used of three or more elements. If there are only two, then *both* is the usual form, with *each* applicable to two or more. There is one common context in which *all* applies to only two elements, however — sports matches:

With five minutes to go, the score is still two all.
At 30 all, McEnroe served two successive aces to take the match.

Purists might urge the substitution of *each* for *all* here, but the weight of idiom is overwhelmingly in favour of *all*.

See also BOTH; EACH; EVERYBODY.

all right   In the words of an old rule, *It is not all right to write 'alright'*. The correct form, for both adverb and adjective, remains two separate words — *all right*.

The temptation to use the spelling *?? alright* is threefold: first, it is usually pronounced as a single word, the *all* being only weakly sounded; secondly, there is the analogy of *almost, already,* and *altogether*; thirdly, there is the urge to distinguish the usual uses of the phrase — 'satisfactory, correct, permitted', and so on (for which the spelling *alright* is common) from the use in which the two words are quite independent, as in *He did 20 sums and got them all right*. Nevertheless, the spelling *?? alright* has not been accepted into standard English, and should be used, if at all, only in very informal writing.

It is striking that purists who claim to want English to make more distinctions rather than fewer have nevertheless here set their faces against one distinction (that between *all right* and *alright*) that is firmly based on analogy with other similar pairs. But *all right* remains the only standard form, even when an independent *all* precedes it: *I visited the five patients today, and can report that they're all all right*.

If *all right* is wanted as an informal adjective directly before a noun, it is best hyphenated: *an all-right guy*.

allegory, fable, parable   All three words refer to a story (or in the case of *allegory*, a painting as well) in which there are two levels of meaning: the simple surface meaning that meets the eye and a hidden, deeper meaning.

An *allegory* is usually a long narrative full of symbols conveying a moral message. Thus, John Bunyan's *Pilgrim's Progress* is on the surface an account of the journey of its hero, Christian; but it is also an allegory of the course of a Christian life. In art, an *allegory* is a picture that appears to tell a story, and features images that carry a symbolic meaning. This reflects the source of the word — the Greek verb *allegorein*, 'to speak in other terms'.

A *parable* is a special kind of allegory — a short narrative, again invested with a moral message. It is now most commonly used to refer to the stories told by Jesus in the Gospels, illustrating the right way to live. The word goes back to the Greek *parabalein*, 'to set beside'.

A *fable*, too, has a moral message. But while a parable uses events in common experience to make its moral clear and immediate (*The Good Samaritan* or *The Prodigal Son*), a fable uses impossible events to teach its lessons. In Aesop's

Fables, for example, animals speak and have human emotions. The tortoise races against the hare, so that Aesop can make the point that slow, steady plodding can often be more effective than flashy but sporadic brilliance. This idea of unreality or impossible events is contained in the adjective *fabulous*, now debased in informal usage to mean simply 'extremely good'.

Fable can also be used to mean 'a mythical or legendary story' and 'a lie'. The word comes via Old French and Middle English from the Latin *fabula*, 'narration, or a story', from *fari*, 'to speak'.

See also METAPHOR.

alligator, crocodile, cayman, gavial The order *Crocodilia* consists of three families: *Crocodylidae* (crocodiles), *Alligatoridae* (alligators and caymans), and *Gavialidae* (gavials). Strictly, these various amphibious reptiles are quite distinct creatures, but in some parts of the world (such as Australia) *alligator* is used to refer to crocodiles, and in Madagascar, crocodiles are called *caymans*. Many people, uncertain which creature is which, use the names *alligator* and *crocodile* interchangeably.

There are several varieties of crocodile, alligator, and cayman, so exact details of size and shape do not help very much in distinguishing the species. In general, alligators have a somewhat broader, shorter snout than crocodiles, but the only foolproof test for telling a crocodile from an alligator or cayman is this: crocodiles have the teeth of their upper jaw more or less exactly above the teeth of the lower jaw and all their teeth can be seen when their jaws are closed — which is what gives crocodiles a reputation for having a permanent grin. Furthermore, the lower jaw's fourth tooth on either side is longer than the others and sticks up outside the mouth. So a crocodile looks as though it has a pair of short tusks on the side of its nose. In alligators and caymans the long teeth fit into a space in the upper jaw inside the mouth, and the teeth of the bottom jaw are set further back than the top ones; so none of the teeth is visible when the jaws are shut (though sometimes an aged alligator's long tooth is so long that it protrudes through the upper jaw).

Caymans and alligators belong to the same family and strongly resemble each other; accordingly, they are difficult to tell apart at a glance. Both are found in the Americas; but only the alligator is found in parts of Asia. The caymans are quicker and more agile than the alligators, and some kinds have larger eyes — or a ridge across the nose that looks like the bridge of a pair of glasses and gives rise to the name 'spectacled cayman'. The term *alligator* can be understood in two different ways — as excluding caymans, or as referring to both the cayman and the alligator proper.

The *gavial* has much the longest and thinnest jaw of all this order, with more pointed teeth than the others. One crocodile, the African Long-nosed or Slender-nosed crocodile, might be mistaken for a gavial, but the 'real' African gavial is distinguished by a high, convex forehead. The term *gavial* is usually restricted to a single Asian species, found mainly in India, that has in the male a distinctive bulbous protuberance rising from the snout.

The distribution of the various families is as follows: crocodiles are found in Africa, southeast Asia, New Guinea, Australia, and parts of America; alligators are restricted to America and small parts of Asia; caymans are restricted to America, and gavials occur mainly in India.

The word *crocodile* comes from Greek (via Latin, Old French and Middle English) and was originally the name of a Greek lizard: *krokodilos* meaning 'worm of the pebbles', from *kroke,* 'pebbles' + *drilos* 'worm' (so called because the lizard liked basking on pebbles: the Egyptian crocodile shares this habit, and the Greeks gave it the same name accordingly).

The name *alligator* comes from a fusion of name and article in Spanish: *el,* 'the' + *lagarto,* 'lizard'.

Cayman is often spelt *caiman*. The plural is *caymans*. The name comes through Spanish or Portuguese from the Carib *acayuman*.

A *gavial* is also known as a *gharial* — a less distorted form of its Hindi name *ghariyal,* which is the origin, through French, of the English name.

allude, allusion Properly, *allude to* means 'to mention or convey (something) in an indirect way'. It derives from Latin *alludere*, 'to play with', which in turn is made up of *ad-*, 'to' + *ludere*, 'to play': *allude* is thus a distant relative of the word *ludicrous*. To refer to 'the victor of Austerlitz' or 'the exile of Saint Helena' is to *allude to* Napoleon. To refer to 'Napoleon' is to mention him, but not to allude to him. The useful distinction between alluding to something and mentioning it is worth preserving. If a speaker braces his audience for hard times ahead by referring to 'the Dunkirk spirit', do not, in reporting the speech, say that he *alluded* to the Dunkirk spirit. What he did was *mention* it.

In the first of the following quotations, *allude to* is used correctly; in the second, *alluded to* is clearly a mistake — the actual words are quoted, so it is hardly an *indirect* reference — and should be replaced by *mentioned* or *spoken of*:

> Porter was the son of a wealthy family, a Yale man. His stage songs allude to the smart set but also to Sappho, Freud, Engels, Eugene O'Neill.
> – Anthony Burgess, *The Observer*

× 'Theo's parties in the old days', occasionally alluded to by Pimlico Price in tones of mock-nostalgia, had presumably been attended by some of this crowd.
> – A.N. Wilson,
> *The Sweets of Pimlico*

You can allude not only to a person or an event, but to a word or a phrase as well:

> ... those trips abroad, for instance, each more grotesque and perhaps damaging than the last. Most recently it was *Carry On Up Castro*: and what a sinister farce.
> – Colin Welch, *The Spectator*

Here there is an allusion to the titles of a series of popular British screen farces, each of which begins with the words *Carry On*, and one of which is called *Carry On Up The Khyber*; the allusion is reinforced by the subsequent use of the word *farce*. Such allusions can create powerful and sometimes hilarious effects, but they must be used with care, since a reader who does not know the source of the allusion will be completely mystified by it.

Take care not to confuse *allude*, *allusion*, and the adjective *allusive* with the similar-sounding words *elude*, *illusion*, *elusive*, and so on. To *elude* is to avoid capture or understanding: *The fugitive eluded the search patrol*; *The meaning of her glance eluded me*. So whereas an *allusive* literary style is full of *allusions*, an *elusive* style is one whose effects are hard to define. An *illusion* is, chiefly, a mistaken perception, and a *delusion* a mistaken belief. (See DELUSION.)

already, all ready 1. In the sense of 'before, previously', *already* requires a verb in the perfect — that is, a *have*-form or *had*-form of the verb: *I've already discussed it with her*. In much informal American English, and increasingly in British English, the simple past tense is used: × *I already discussed it with her*. This usage remains non-standard. In a different sense of *already* — 'by a specified or implied time' — the simple past can

be used: *He was already dead when the ambulance arrived*; *By midnight I already knew the answer*.

In this sense, *already* seems to have established itself in scholarly prose, especially before the prepositions *in* and *at*:

> ? Already in the 18th century, the idea of the intellectual's alienation from society was common coin.
> ? Already at the end of the 19th century, the music of Wagner was a force that could not be ignored.

This use of *already in* or *already at* has not attracted much criticism, yet it seems an unnecessary alternative to *as early as, even in* or *even at,* or simply *by,* or the like:

> As long ago as the 18th century ...
> Even in the 18th century ...
> By the end of the 19th century ...

The *already*-constructions may be based on the German form — *Schon im achtzehnten Jahrhundert* — and German has no handy equivalent of the simple English *by*.

2. Be careful not to spell *all ready* as *already*:

> Breakfast was all ready and waiting for us, and by dawn we were all ready to go.
> Breakfast was already waiting for us, and by first light we had already progressed two miles from the camp.

The rule of thumb is: if the *all* can be dropped without much damage to the sentence, then it is a separate word.

3. *Already* has a slang use in American English — especially in New York, and in those media circles influenced by New York idiom — that is now sometimes heard in British English as well. It is used to express impatience, and can be understood as the equivalent of *for goodness' sake*: *That's enough complaining already!* It is presumably an adoption from the comparable use of the Yiddish or German word for 'already', *schon*. Obviously this use of *already* should be restricted to extremely informal contexts. Compare the slang use of *yet* (see YET 6).

also 1. *Also* is increasingly being used as a substitute for *and, but,* or *as well as*:

> ? She studies politics and economics, also a little sociology.
> ? He is fluent in French and German, also he can read Spanish and Italian.

Strictly speaking, *also* is an adverb, not a conjunction, and purists object to the extended use. In the examples above, *also* should really be replaced, or at least preceded, by *and*. Yet if a semicolon or a dash were used in place of the comma in each case, the objection to *also* would weaken: the punctuation mark could be said to serve instead of a conjunction, and *also* could then be classified as the adverb it is meant to be.

2. As with *only*, *also* needs careful placing within a sentence. According to its position, it affects the meaning of the sentence in different ways. Compare the likely interpretations, out of context, of the following sentences:

The colonel has also climbed Mont Blanc (as well as sailed up the Amazon).
The colonel has climbed Mont Blanc also (as well as the Matterhorn).
The colonel also has climbed Mont Blanc (so the major is not alone in having done this).

(In this last example, *too* rather than *also* would normally be used.)
See ONLY 1. for a further discussion.

altar, alter There is no danger of confusing the meaning of these two words, but take care not to spell the sacramental table as though it were the verb 'to change, adjust'. The table has an *a,* and goes back to the Late Latin *altare,* 'a high place', from Latin *altus,* 'high'. *Alter* goes back to the Medieval Latin *alterare,* from Latin *alter,* 'other'.

alternate, alternative Both these adjectives come from the Latin *alternus,* 'by turns, interchangeable', from *alter,* 'other'. Formerly both meant what *alternate* now means: 'by turns, one after the other'. But now *alternative* has the quite distinct meaning of 'offering or necessitating a choice between two or more possibilities'. So: *An alternative exercise, if you don't like jogging, is alternate running and walking.* Again: *The two of you could use the two-handed saw together — alternatively, use the hacksaw alternately.*

The breadline can scarcely be such a terrifying place as its name suggests. What, in fact, does it mean? It might be a bread queue along the lines of the old soup kitchens ... Alternatively, it might imply that 15 million live so close to starvation that only a diet of bread saves them from death by malnutrition.
– Auberon Waugh, *The Spectator*

He read through the note again, frowning. Then he went over to the window and gazed down into Hand and Ball Court for several minutes, frowning and pushing up his lower lip alternately.
– Michael Frayn,
Towards the End of the Morning

There is a tendency, particularly in the United States, to use *alternate* and *alternately* instead of *alternative* and *alternatively:*

× In cases where the two forms of the word are not equally used ... the alternate spelling appears at the end of the entry.
– Introduction to
The World Book Dictionary (U.S.)

× *Boche* is thought to derive from *caboche,* medieval slang for head and, as an alternate possibility, from a dialectal pronunciation of *bois* (wood) as *boche.*
– Charles Berlitz (U.S.),
Native Tongues

But in British English, *alternate* is no longer an alternative to *alternative*. Here, however, is an example by a British writer of the opposite mistake, the use of *alternative* in the place of *alternate:*

× The wind had dropped now and the cloud was breaking up, we walked to the quay in alternative light and shade. The tide was coming in fast.
– Ian McEwan,
First Love, Last Rites

Alternate can be a verb as well as an adjective, of course, but this involves a change in pronunciation and (in British English) a shift of stress. The verb is /**awl**-tər-nayt/; the adjective is in British English /awl-**ter**-nət/, and in American English /**awl**-tər-nət/.

In American English, though rarely in British English, *alternate* is used as a noun as well, meaning 'a person acting in the place of another, a substitute': *1450 full delegates and 650 alternates.* The pronunciation this time is /**awl**-tər-nət/.

Alternative (with the stress always on the second syllable) is either an adjective or a noun, in both British and American English.

As a noun, it raises a few questions of usage. Some pedants argue that because the Latin word *alter* referred to one or other of two, *alternative* should be used only where there is a choice of two items. This view is now largely discredited, however, and a statement such as *We must consider all the alternatives* is regarded as acceptable.

However, etymology casts its shadow still: we would be more likely to say *few alternatives* than

? many alternatives; in the second case, *many options/choices* would be preferred.

There is a slight danger too in specifying a number before *alternatives*. To say *There are three alternatives* is probably to imply that a total of three possibilities exists, but it could suggest a total of four possibilities — one chief possibility, and three alternatives. It is best, when specifying a number, to use some less ambiguous word: *There are three choices/options/possible courses of action.*

When *alternative* is used in the sense of 'a range of choice, a pair or set of possibilities', it may be represented in the pattern *A or B*: *The alternative is economising or bankruptcy.* However, if it is used in the sense of 'one of the options from that set of possibilities', it can be used in the plural, and the choice then takes the pattern *A and B*: *The alternatives are economising and bankruptcy* (not *or*).

× Paralysis or catastrophe seem the grim alternatives during this terminal phase of British influence in India. Codes formerly followed have become meaningless.
— Peter Kemp,
The Times Literary Supplement

Alternative is frequently accompanied by the word *other* when *other* is redundant: × *We must pursue this policy — there is no other alternative.* The *other* here should be omitted, since *alternative* already means 'other policy or course of action'.

× It so happened that the car was spending the night in a repair shop downtown. I had no other alternative than to pursue on foot the winged fugitive.
— Vladimir Nabokov, *Lolita*

The correct wording here would be either *no alternative but to pursue* or *no other course of action than to pursue.* (*Other alternative* can occur, however, when the purpose is a contrast: *Having tried one alternative without success, we switched to the other alternative*).

As an adjective, *alternative* is often used pretentiously or wrongly in contexts where a simpler word such as *other, new,* or *revised* would be preferable or necessary — *? an alternative date, ? an alternative venue,* and so on: *? The alternative plan has replaced the one which was scrapped* (*new* or *revised* would be better here than *alternative*); *? While this project is held up, there is alternative work for you to do* (*other* would be quite adequate).

Recently, the adjective has taken on a new meaning: 'opposed to convention or the establishment'. So, *alternative theatre* is nontraditional, and often politically opposed to the status quo, and *alternative medicine* is different from what most doctors do at the moment. The word is now in danger of being overused, ousting *unconventional, unusual, untraditional,* and so on at the least excuse. Furthermore, this new sense creates the risk of ambiguity, yet more reason for limiting its use: *He left his teaching job and went to work in an alternative school* — this could mean simply 'He found a job in another school', or it could mean 'He found an unconventional school to work in'.

although, though 1. The contracted forms *altho'* and *tho'* (sometimes without the apostrophe) should be avoided today except in informal writing. They are pronounced the same as the full forms.

2. *Though* can always be used in place of *although* — they share the role of conjunction meaning 'regardless of the fact that, notwithstanding that'. But the reverse does not hold good: *though* has certain senses and functions that *although* lacks.

First, *though* appears frequently in the compound conjunctions *as though* and *even though* — *although* cannot be used here.

Secondly, *though* is mobile in certain constructions: *I kept silent, though/although I was angry* but *I kept silent, angry though I was* — *although* cannot be used in this position.

Thirdly, *though* alone can serve as an adverb meaning 'however': *? I liked the play — the acting wasn't much good, though.* (For the acceptability of this usage, see section 4. below.)

Even where *though* and *although* are interchangeable, certain factors may favour one or the other. *Although* used to be considered more emphatic (though not as strong as *even though*) and slightly more formal, and is still preferred at the beginning of a sentence — provided that it introduces a full factual clause: *Although I was angry, I kept silent.* If the clause is hypothetical, however (see section 5. below), or if the verb is omitted from the clause (as in the previous sentence), then *though* is preferable: *Though angry, I kept silent.* Finally, *though* is far more frequent than *although* as a synonym of *but*:

? I suspect you're right, though I'd have to check in my manual.

? She's in her forties, though you'd never think so to look at her.

Although in such sentences, though not incorrect, produces a rather odd impression of formality combined with informality.

3. The use of *though* (and *although*) in place of *but*, as in the examples just used, is discouraged by purists, and should be avoided in more formal usage.

4. Also opposed by the purists is the use of *though* as an adverb meaning 'however' or 'nevertheless'. It is in common use in informal contexts, where *however* and *nevertheless* would sound far too stiff:

?It's overcast — not at all cold, though.

?Sorry I can't help ... I'll tell you what, though — why don't you try *Bickley's* down the road?

?What's whipped up by the video nasties is hardly a constructive force. There's one serious reason, though, that we've been slow to do something about the nasties, which is less easy to resolve.
– Katharine Whitehorn, *The Observer*

Increasingly, however, it is found in formal writing too:

?The work chronicles a jolting process from colonialism to chaos. It is the individuals caught in the turmoil who receive most attention, though. Profusion and detail of character are Scott's fictional forte.
– Peter Kemp,
The Times Literary Supplement

?While Seepersad Naipaul suffered the nullity of the writer *manqué,* his son has resplendently fulfilled that lost ambition. Paradoxically, though, Naipaul is happiest with misery, most deeply stirred by failure.
– Martin Amis, *The Observer*

Clearly this use of *though* is well on the way to acceptance as standard English. It has still not fully secured that acceptance, however, and in strictly formal writing should give way to *however,* as in this sentence.

Note that *though* is virtually never used, in this sense, at the beginning of a sentence. Note too the punctuation surrounding *though* in such constructions: a comma before it, and either a comma or a full stop after it. In streamlined American writing, the first comma is often omitted. Such an omission in British English would provoke further objections from the purists.

5. The verb after *though* or *although* is often cast in the subjunctive form when theoretical rather than real conditions are under discussion:

Though your sins be as scarlet, they shall be as white as snow; though they be red like crimson, they shall be as wool.
– Isaiah 1:18

This construction is now rather archaic: the first clause would today tend to be worded as *Though your sins may be like scarlet*, or *Even if your sins were/are like scarlet,* or *Even supposing ...* ; it could not, however, be rewritten as *Though your sins are like scarlet* without seriously distorting the sense. Compare:

Though the road be long, your heart beats strong

and

Though the road is long, your heart beats strong

(The hypothetical nature of the first sentence would tend today to be expressed by *Even if ...* again, or by the addition of *may: Though the road may be long ...*)
See also AS IF; BUT **3**; SUBJUNCTIVE.

altogether, all together   As with *anyone* and *any one,* the two-word phrase is sometimes misspelt as one word. *All together* is used when referring to several people, things, or ideas that have been brought together, physically or metaphorically: *dozens of prisoners herded all together*; *singing the chorus all together*; *the Third World nations standing all together in their support of the resolution.* Be careful not to fuse the separate words into *altogether* in such contexts. The rule of thumb is: if you can leave out the *all* without making the sentence sound odd, then *all* has to be a separate word when it is included.

Altogether means 'entirely': *not altogether pleased with the result*; 'in all': *100 guests altogether*; and 'on the whole': *Altogether, I'm not sorry it happened.* It does not mean 'gathered in one place' or 'united'.

The informal expression *in the altogether,* meaning 'in the nude, naked', is derived from the phrase *altogether naked,* and came into use in about 1894.

ambiance, ambience   The atmosphere or character of a place (usually congenial) can be referred to as either the *ambiance* or the *ambience.* Both spellings are acceptable, *-iance* via the French and *-ience* closer to the Latin.

Technically, the Frenchified pronunciation /**amb**i-ɒɴss/ should be restricted, therefore, to the French spelling *ambiance.* This can also be pronounced /**am**bi-ənss/, as *ambience* is. If in doubt, use the English pronunciation.

The word, in either of its forms, has become something of a vogue word, a fashionable variant of *atmosphere*. Use it sparingly.

Note that the related adjective can be spelt only as *ambient*; it means 'surrounding, in the immediate environment', and is used especially in the phrase *the ambient temperature*.

ambiguity Ambiguity — being open to more than one interpretation — is eagerly exploited by poets and comedians alike. In ordinary speech and writing, however, ambiguity is obviously an obstacle to clear communication, and care needs to be taken to avoid it.

1. The sounds of English are sometimes the source of ambiguity. Two quite different words might sound the same, whether spelt alike (*maroon,* 'to cast away', and *maroon,* 'purplish brown') or differently (*sail* and *sale*), and the occasional misunderstanding might arise as a result.

Equally, two distinct phrases might sound very similar, as all children know — *I scream* and *ice cream,* for instance. Such similarity of sound is one of the chief sources of puns. One famous example will bear this out: three brothers inherited a cattle ranch from their father, and promptly renamed it 'Focus' — because that was where *the sons raise meat* (= *the sun's rays meet*). In French, such oral ambiguities abound. The 'famous last words' of a French king were reputedly as follows: /sharlə-toɴ/. This can be understood as *Charlatans!* ('Charlatans!' — addressed to the king's family or courtiers) or *Charles attend* ('Charles is waiting' — to invade, or to succeed to the throne). And another royal French utterance was apparently /massakray-tōo/, which could be understood as *Massacrez tout* ('Massacre the lot of them!' — referring to rioters and revolutionaries presumably) or as *Ma sacrée toux!* ('My blasted cough!').

In practice, most apparent ambiguities in English speech are avoided, because intonation and word-breaks distinguish one sense from another: *I scream* and *ice cream* do not in fact sound identical when spoken, any more than *blackboard* and *black board* do. Thus, many phrases which are ambiguous in written English would not be in danger of being misunderstood if spoken. In speech, the words *Do you understand?* can be spoken as a question or as a threat. No such distinction is possible on the page.

Similarly, the phrases *an American history teacher* or *a large man's suit,* both ambiguous when written, can both be stressed and timed in two different ways when spoken, according to the meaning intended. Compare the two ways of saying *a large man's suit*: you can phrase it either as 'a (large) (man's suit)', in which case it means 'a man's suit that is large', or as 'a (large man's) suit', in which case it means 'a suit for, or belonging to, a large man'.

2. There are many other sources of ambiguity apart from confusion of sound. The traps for the unwary speaker or writer seem endless. Unless you are aiming deliberately at a comic or poetic effect (or deliberately hoping to mislead your listener without actually telling a lie!), ambiguity stands out as a serious blemish on what you say or write.

Perhaps the commonest cause of ambiguity is careless word-order. It is important to structure sentences in such a way that the intended relationship between words or phrases is clear, and that no unintended relationship is inadvertently set up. The rule-of-thumb is to place related words as near to each other as possible. Two traditional examples show the comic results of failing to do this, one from the small ads column in a newspaper, the other from the inscription on a tombstone in Edinburgh:

✗ A piano is being sold by a lady with carved legs.

✗   Erected to the Memory
      of John McFarlane
   Drown'd in the Water of Leith
   By a few affectionate friends.

In each case, the final phrase should have come earlier, in order to relate to the correct noun or verb (*piano, erected*). By being left until the end, each phrase relates grammatically to the wrong noun or verb (*lady, drown'd*) — and suffers the consequences.

Here are some further examples:

✗ On government orders, a volley of gunshot was used to disperse the riot by the police.

✗ Please send us your ideas about water-skiing on a postcard.

✗ She told me to slow down with great impatience.

✗ The car stalled in the dark tunnel, but I calmed the children by telling them the story of the bear who wouldn't speak until the engine started.

✗ I sat contentedly in the park, watching the dogs playing and smoking my pipe.

✗ Now that you've watched me at target practice, why don't you try shooting yourself?

✗ An estate agent's first duty is to secure the highest price for his client.

Once again, the final word or phrase in each case has been left too late, and a false grammatical relationship has been created in consequence.

More generally, the reason for ambiguous sentences such as these is a reluctance to exploit the full resources of English word-order. It is true that the normal English word-order after the subject is verb + object + adverbial phrase, represented in our last example by the order of elements *secure* + *the highest price* + *for his client*. However, that is not the only order possible in English. It is perfectly correct to say *secure* + *for his client* + *the highest price* (verb + adverbial phrase + object). Unusual or 'marked' word-order of this kind should be used sparingly, of course — as a rule, only when striving for emphasis or contrast — but it is an essential resource for preventing ambiguity.

All the examples so far listed are ambiguous only in theory. In each case, the writer's intention is clear, even if his grammar is not.

In some cases, however, the two rival meanings seem equally likely:

? The committee made recommendations for educational reforms in 1981.

What does *in 1981* relate to? The committee's discussions, or the educational reforms? It is possible that the context would make this clear — if the sentence appeared in a newspaper in 1975, for example, then the phrase *in 1981* would obviously be referring to *educational reforms*. If the context does not make it clear, then the preferable reading is again that *in 1981* relates to *educational reforms,* since it is placed closer to it than it is to *committee* or *made*. Yet the cautious reader would still hesitate, sensing that the alternative meaning was possibly the one intended. Ideally, the sentence should be reworded. The two meanings would be distinguished by these two versions:

In 1981, the committee made recommendations for educational reforms.

The committee recommended educational reforms due to come into effect in 1981.

Here are some further examples of genuinely puzzling ambiguity. In each case, the dubiously placed word or phrase should be repositioned or the sentence thoroughly reworded:

? You won't catch butterflies resting on your bed.

(Does *resting on your bed* relate to *you* or to *butterflies*? See MISRELATED CONSTRUCTIONS **2**.)

? We have decided to cancel tonight's performance in honour of Sir William.

Is Sir William being honoured by the cancellation or by the performance? If by the cancellation, it would be better to say:

We have decided, in honour of Sir William, to cancel tonight's performance.

If the performance itself was planned in honour of Sir William, it would be better to say:

We have decided that tonight's performance in honour of Sir William is to be cancelled.

? They are trying to get the project started again.

(Was the project once under way in the past; or is it just that previous attempts have been made to start it?)

? The courts were not able to convict for technical reasons.

? The attack was not launched because of intelligence reports.

? I did not protest because I lost the election.

(Did the courts convict or not? Was the attack launched at all? Did I in fact protest or not? See NOT **1**.)

? The machine only seems to go wrong when Jessie is operating it.

(Does the machine in fact go wrong when Jessie operates it? Or does it only *seem* to go wrong? See ONLY **1**.)

3. Another common source of ambiguity in a sentence is the ambiguity of a word or phrase within it. There are many traditional examples of this. Consider the pessimistic interpretation that could be put on the optimistic proverb:

? No news is good news.

Lord Palmerston's 'famous last words' were reported as being:

? Die, my dear doctor? — That's the last thing I shall do.

Or consider such old jokes as:

? The peasants are revolting.
? The captain bowled a maiden over.

A celebrated example from a linguist is:

? Visiting aunts can be a bore.

(The phrase *visiting aunts* can be understood here to mean either 'to go and visit aunts' or 'aunts who come to visit'.)

Two notorious boasts, next, that were less than flattering. A pharmacist is said to have paraded in his window the dubious slogan:

? We dispense with accuracy.

And a firm of furniture-removers advertised itself as:

? Removers of distinction.

Here are some amusingly ambiguous newspaper headlines — ambiguous in theory at least:

? Health Minister appeals to nurses.
? Icelandic fish talks.
? PM lashes backbenchers.
? Spotted man wanted for questioning.
? Bigamy more common than thought in U.S.

The following newspaper headline is really ambiguous:

? Envoy critical after shooting.
　　　　　　　　　　　　　　– The Guardian

Does *critical* mean 'disapproving' here — the envoy was critical of the lax security arrangements, perhaps — or does it have the modern sense of 'critically ill'? (The article revealed that the second of these meanings was the intended one.)

Here are some further examples from the British press:

? The Oxford United coach was held up in a traffic jam and arrived with only three minutes to spare.
　　　　　　　　　　　　　　– The Times

It became clear later in the article that *coach* referred not to the man in charge of training the team, but to the bus carrying the team to its match.

? I came to know Pulo while he was at Oxford in 1977 – 79. He has just spent his third birthday in jail without trial, and I again urge President Kaunda to free him.
　　　　　– Professor Kenneth Kirkwood,
　　　　　　　　　　　quoted in *The Observer*

Of course, the professor's statement is ambiguous only in theory. The prisoner is presumably much older than three. But the words *third birthday* are almost always used to mean 'the birthday on which one becomes three years old'. What the professor meant was 'the third in a row of his many birthdays', and he would have expressed himself better had he said *a third birthday* or else

He has just spent another birthday — the third in a row — in jail without trial ...

Many common misunderstandings are caused by the different senses that people attach to a particular word or phrase. Where most English speakers would say *Shall I open the door?*, a Scot or Irishman might say *Will I open the door?* — which sounds a very foolish question to those who are unaware of this regional difference. And the phrase *just now* is notoriously variable in meaning: literally, it means 'at this very moment'; it is also widely used to mean 'in the recent past, a short while ago'; and in South African English it tends to mean 'in the near future, very soon'. So both of the following sentences are ambiguous: ? *I'm leaving just now* and ? *They cost £5 just now.*

Similarly, the phrase *next Wednesday* can be understood in two different ways, as the Welsh poet Dannie Abse learnt to his cost:

'I'll expect you next Wednesday,' I had said. She never arrived. When I phoned her later, she said, 'Oh dear, a verbal misunderstanding. You should have said *this Wednesday*. By *next Wednesday* I assumed you meant the Wednesday of the following week.'
　　　– Dannie Abse,'Words', BBC Radio 3

In the following exchange, there is some momentary confusion over the meaning of the phrase *take on*, which can mean both 'to adopt' and 'to oppose':

'Is it difficult to take on the government's attitudes?'
　'You mean, to *challenge* them? ...'
　　　– Frank Delaney and Nadine Gordimer,
　　　　　　　　　'Bookshelf', BBC Radio 4

Here is a final selection of sentences whose ambiguity is due to the uncertain meaning of a word or a phrase within them:

? He played Caesar as well as Romeo.
? The chicken is off.
? Tell me if you want an answer.
? It's too hot to eat.
? The country had no capital at the time.
? How would you like to die?
? I saw the repairman about the house.
? I must replace that ashtray.
? The doctor prescribed a certain remedy.
? You must meet my old friend.
? He was driven from his home by his wife.
? The two of them seemed to enjoy rowing.
? There are three outstanding results.
? Mountaineering, which is the subject of my

last chapter ...
? I don't discuss my wife's affairs with my friends.
? I came by and found you out.
? The police are trying to stop drinking at football matches.
? She couldn't allow herself to take advantage of them.
? The editor wants more humorous stories.
? Avoid such ambiguous sentences.

The context will often indicate the preferred meaning. Even then, however, it is usually worth making the meaning of a sentence clear, in its own terms.

4. A word can be quite unambiguous in itself, and yet create ambiguity in a sentence by failing to make clear what part of the sentence it refers to. This is especially true of pronouns. Once again, there is a famous traditional example:

? If the baby does not thrive on fresh milk, boil it.

The pronoun *it* is obviously intended to refer to *milk,* but it could grammatically refer to *the baby* — hence the comic effect.

George Bernard Shaw is supposed to have made a mischievously ambiguous remark to the effect that:

? Men chase after women until they catch up with them.

The natural interpretation of the sentence here is undercut by the possibility of a different and ironic interpretation.

And consider the following quotations — who does *he* refer to in each case, or rather, who is suggested by the grammar as being the referent?

? Solicitors for Mr Duncan Campbell, an investigative journalist, yesterday gave the Metropolitan Police Commissioner, Sir Kenneth Newman, 48 hours to hand over belongings confiscated by the police after he had an accident on his bicycle in London last Thursday.
  – The Times

? Mr Dyke joined the breakfast television station when it was close to collapse and bankruptcy — it couldn't even pay its newspaper bill and a man once called round to turn the electricity off. He built up the dwindling audience from a mere handful of insomniacs to a level that has overtaken its BBC 'Breakfast Time' rival.
  – Peter Hillmore, The Observer

Here are a few similar examples:

? The President told Mr Jones that his own hometown would not get special treatment.
? Tom phoned his brother before he left for work.
? He dragged the box from the car's bonnet, and jumped on to it.

A rather more complicated example is this:

? Where were you wounded?

The 18th-century author Lawrence Sterne exploited very cleverly the ambiguity in such phrasing. In *Tristram Shandy,* the Widow Wadman keeps putting this question, in one form or another, to Uncle Toby, a retired soldier. She is eager to marry him but worried that his war wounds might incapacitate him as a husband. Eventually Uncle Toby overcomes his shyness, and agrees to show the Widow the very spot where he received his wound ... only to spread a map of Europe out in front of her, and point to the town where he was stationed at the time he was wounded.

Finally, this quotation — how much blood makes one unit?

? In 1982, more than 32,000 units (about two-thirds of a pint) of blood were supplied to private hospitals.
  – The Times

5. A closely related cause of ambiguity is uncertainty over the *range* of a word's reference.

? The moths have attacked all my fine imported hats.

This could mean that moths have attacked all my hats, which are always fine imported hats; or it could mean that moths have attacked some of my hats — all the fine imported ones, as luck would have it — but left my other hats untouched. Similarly:

? She went travelling with her two scholarly friends.
? He had only one rotting tooth.

And if the crucial word *and* had been dropped from a sentence in the previous section, it would have read, very ambiguously, as follows:

? The natural interpretation of the sentence here is undercut by the possibility of a different ironic interpretation.

The addition of *and* between the two adjectives *different* and *ironic* restores the sentence to its single correct meaning. Other devices, such as commas or brackets, can also clarify the meaning in this way: *my fine, imported hats*; *one (rotting) tooth.*

As it happens, however, the word *and* is responsible for causing ambiguity far more often than it is for relieving it. The *and* in the middle of a sentence tends to generate doubts about the range of a word's reference: does the adjective in the first noun phrase, for instance, apply to a second noun phrase as well?

? We offer iced lemonade and tea to drink, and chocolate eclairs and biscuits to eat.

Are the biscuits all chocolate biscuits? And is the tea iced tea? If so, the adjectives *iced* and *chocolate* should perhaps have been repeated, to make the meaning quite clear. If not, each pair of nouns should have been reversed, to make the unambiguous sentence:

We offer tea and iced lemonade to drink, and biscuits and chocolate eclairs to eat.

Similarly:

? He had a bizarre collection of hunting trophies — elephants' tusks, skulls, and hides.

(Are the skulls and hides all from elephants, or are they from other animals too?)

? She is inclined to refuse to cooperate and to report on her colleagues' behaviour.

(Does she tend to report on her colleagues' behaviour, or does she usually refuse to report on her colleagues' behaviour?)

The word *to,* as the above example shows, is a fertile source of confusion.

? It is easy to imagine the chaos that would ensue if a member of these forces refused to obey the orders of his commanding officer if his union told him not to.
— G.C. Hampson,
letter to *The Times*

(If his union told him not to — what? Not to obey? Or not to refuse to obey?)

Relative pronouns are often of uncertain scope. What does the *that* relate to in the following example? Is it the hills or the flowers that tourists find so attractive?

? Further south are the hills covered in wild flowers that tourists find so attractive.

Finally, the scope of negative words — *not, never, hardly,* and so on — is notoriously difficult to control.

? He was hardly happy and eager to get rid of me.

(A comma after *happy* would resolve the ambiguity in one way. To resolve it the other way, you could change the *and* to an *or*; or you could insert an extra *hardly* before *eager*.)

? You were not paying attention the whole time.

(Does this mean that you paid attention only some of the time, or that you did not pay attention at all? The context might indicate which. If not, a major rephrasing of the sentence would be needed.)

6. Another common source of ambiguity is thoughtless brevity. The lazy omission of words on the one hand, and the overzealous attempt to pack too much meaning into too little space on the other — these are responsible for many an awkward construction or outright blunder. As the Roman poet Horace put it, 'I toil to be brief, and become obscure'.

One traditional example is:

? He likes me more than you.

The context might indicate which of the two possible meanings is intended here. If not, the ambiguity must be eliminated by the addition of a word or phrase. On the one hand,

He likes me more than he likes you.

On the other,

He likes me more than you do.

Here is a similar example:

? I've just read in *Options* magazine that a young woman called Luella from Plymouth has won a tycoon-of-the-year award for her meteoric success in the window business. I wish Luella had come to me instead of Sid.
— Sue Arnold, *The Observer*

(Does this mean 'I wish Luella rather than Sid had come to me' or does it mean 'I wish Luella had come to me instead of going to Sid'?)

Another traditional example, cited earlier, is *? a large man's suit* or *? an American history teacher.* If the context is unhelpful, this latter phrase would have to be reworded either as *a teacher of American history* or as *an American teacher of history.* Similar constructions, while unlikely to be misunderstood, do theoretically offer an amusing alternative reading: *? a pickled onion seller, ? second-hand ladies' clothing,* and so on. (As the next section shows, the occasional hyphen can 'disentangle' the meanings: *An American-history teacher*; *a pickled-onion seller.*)

Here is a selection of rather more complicated examples of ambiguity that result from the omission of a word or phrase:

? The border guards were accused of bombarding the sentry posts opposite for half an hour without causing any injuries.

(After *half an hour,* add a comma and the words *though admittedly.*)

? The little boy walked amiably towards the man intending to kidnap him.

(Add *who was* after *the man.*)

?? Very few inmates bothered to protest at this abuse, and just took the new indignity with silent submissiveness.

This reads *Very few inmates ... took the new indignity with silent submissiveness,* which is clearly not the intended meaning. Add *most of them* after *and,* and the correct meaning now comes across unambiguously. Similarly:

?? The total vocabulary of English is immense and runs to about half a million items. None of us as individuals, of course, knows more than a fairly limited number of these, and uses even less.

> – Sir Randolph Quirk,
> *The Use of English*

This reads *none of us ... uses even less.* What the writer meant was *each of us uses even less* (or more correctly, *even fewer*) or *we use even less,* and that is what he should have written.

7. Careless punctuation, finally, is a major cause of ambiguity. Telegrams are a traditional source of such ambiguities. One joke has it that Stalin received a telegram from Trotsky, which he read as an apology:

You were right. I should apologise.

What Trotsky had in fact meant was:

You were right? I should *apologise?!*

Another joke, from a time before the age of telegrams, concerns a message (reported in English, though perhaps originally in French or German) that was supposedly passed to the French sage Voltaire by a lackey of Frederick the Great. The message read:

Frederick says Voltaire is an ass.

Voltaire turned the tables by adding a pair of commas:

Frederick, says Voltaire, is an ass.

A true historical example is the telegram sent to Dr Jameson at the time of the notorious 'Jameson Raid' in 1895 in southern Africa. The text, without punctuation, was as follows:

It is under these circumstances that we feel constrained to call upon you to come to our aid should a disturbance arise here the circumstances are so extreme that we cannot but believe that you and the men under you will not fail to come to the rescue of people who are so situated.

Now, where was the first full stop intended to go? Those who sent the telegram probably meant it to come after *should a disturbance arise here* — thereby simply putting Jameson on the alert, in case his help should be needed. But when the text was wired to *The Times* in London, the full stop was placed after *come to our aid* instead — thus creating the impression of a firm and urgent invitation, and 'justifying' Dr Jameson's unauthorised invasion of the Transvaal.

A famous literary example of confused meaning through punctuation occurs in *A Midsummer Night's Dream,* when Quince the carpenter reads the prologue to the 'Pyramus and Thisby' play:

Consider then we come but in despite.
We do not come as minding to content you,
Our true intent is. All for your delight
We are not here. That you should here
  repent you,
The actors are at hand ...

> – Quince, in
> *A Midsummer Night's Dream* V i

A more correct reading would be:

Consider then: we come (but in despite
We do not come) as minding to content you.
Our true intent is all for your delight.
We are not here that you should here repent
  you.
The actors are at hand ...

Here are some further examples of confusion caused by faulty punctuation. First, a misplaced comma produces nonsense:

× The victim, rather then phoning the police foolishly, failed to report her suspicion and paid the price.

In these next examples, it is the insertion of a needless comma that produces the nonsense:

× Few of the children behaved themselves, as we hoped.

× I refuse to admire the play, simply because the acting is excellent.

× The new regulation applies to all restaurants, where kitchen conditions are considered a hazard to health.

In this last example, the comma has the effect of turning the subordinate clause into a nonrestrictive clause, where clearly it is intended to be a restrictive clause (see RESTRICTIVE AND NONRESTRICTIVE CLAUSES). The implication now is that *all* restaurants have dangerously unhygienic kitchens; without the comma, the sentence would imply, as intended, that only *some* restaurants represent a health hazard.

The examples cited so far in this section are not true ambiguities. What the faulty punctuation has generated is an unintended meaning in each case, rather than a pair of rival meanings. The following examples, however, are all truly ambiguous:

? For all the members know the chairman will resign.

(To distinguish the two meanings, insert either a comma or the word *that* after *know*.)

? Once I learnt that I could no longer rely on him.

(Insert a comma either after *once* or after *that*.)

? She published a book of stories and then a novel following encouraging reviews.

(A comma should be placed either after *stories* or after *novel,* in order to clarify which of the two possible meanings is intended.)

? The shell killed Private Hutchinson and Corporal Edwards and the two lieutenants are seriously injured.

(Place a comma either after *Private Hutchinson,* or after *Corporal Edwards.*)

? Very little was known when Miss Hill was writing about the life of Flora Mayor, and her three novels for some reason ... failed to interest those who have written critical histories of the novel.
 – David Holloway, *Daily Telegraph*

Does the *about* here relate to *known* or to *writing*? If to *known,* then commas should be inserted either side of the clause *when Miss Hill was writing*; if to *writing,* then a single comma could be placed before the clause, or else a small rephrasing could be made, such as *Very little was known when Miss Hill was studying the life of Flora Mayor* ...

? Dr Magpie is the author of *Islands, Archipelagoes, Peninsulas, The Greek Isles, Sicily, Sardinia, Corsica,* and so on.

How many books are being cited here? On the face of it, seven. But the number intended was perhaps only three, and the sentence should then have read:

Dr Magpie is the author of *Islands, Archipelagoes, Peninsulas; The Greek Isles; Sicily, Sardinia, Corsica,* and so on.

Where an individual item in a list contains commas within itself, it has to be separated from neighbouring items by a semi-colon rather than a comma. Even if the writer had intended to list seven books, the possibility of confusion remained, and he or she would have done better to reword the sentence along the following lines:

Dr Magpie is the author of many works, among them these seven — *Islands, Archipelagoes, Peninsulas, The Greek Isles, Sicily, Sardinia,* and *Corsica.*

To finish, a few light-hearted uncertainties involving missing hyphens. Consider these newspaper phrases, and think how a well-placed hyphen (and sometimes comma) might resolve the ambiguity or else restore the intended meaning. First, two headlines:

× Man eating wolf.
× Scarlet coated woman in nightclub scandal.

Next, an item from the small-ads column:

× For sale: little used car.

Finally, two captions under photographs:

× The long sought after dachshund safely back home.

× Mr and Mrs Staple, celebrating their ruby wedding, surrounded by their eight children and twenty odd grandchildren.

The way to avoid ambiguity in speech and writing is very simple — and very difficult. The trick is merely to think carefully before you speak, and to check carefully after you write. Sensitivity to language is something that everybody has in some measure or other — but not everybody is patient or concerned enough to use it, let alone develop it. The more you monitor your own writing (and that of others), the more instances of carelessness and ambiguity you are at first likely to discover. And the more your powers of observation sharpen in this way, the fewer careless errors and ambiguities you will in due course find yourself perpetrating.

See also AMBIGUOUS; MISRELATED CONSTRUCTIONS; NOT; ONLY; PUNCTUATION.

ambiguous, ambivalent *Ambiguous* comes from the Latin word *ambiguus,* meaning 'wandering about, uncertain'. *Ambiguous* means 'open to more than one interpretation, uncertain in meaning': *This line of poetry is ambiguous*; *His behaviour towards her was ambiguous.*

> An agent's relationship with an author is undoubtedly an ambiguous and subtle affair.
> – Pamela Todd,
> *The Fiction Magazine*

The word *ambivalence* (hence *ambivalent*) was coined in its German form by Sigmund Freud, the founder of psychoanalysis, from Latin words meaning roughly 'double values'. It refers to the simultaneous presence in a person's mind of conflicting feelings towards someone or something. The adjective *ambivalent* (pronounced /am-**biv**və-lənt/; sometimes /**am**bi-**vay**lənt/) has become a vogue word, used very loosely to mean something like 'wanting two different and incompatible things':

> ? The Russians are ambivalent — they want disarmament and they want a strong defence system.

This is probably an unacceptably loose usage. The furthest that the word should be allowed to stray from its original technical sense is to a meaning something like 'with mixed feelings, or involving contradictory emotions':

> She was ambivalent about her ex-husband — full of fond memories but angry and hurt at the same time.

> Cowboys have always been selfish drivers, and the attitude of the civilised world to them has always been ambivalent (a word I am in two minds about), partly admiring their freedom, partly fearing their lawlessness.
> – Philip Howard, *Words Fail Me*

> Shepard is ambivalent about the movie industry. He talks disparagingly of Hollywood and the studio system, but admits that his plays could not have been created without the lessons of cinema. His dialogue is filled with allusions to old movies.
> – William Scobie,
> *The Observer*

Instead of wittily writing *a word I am in two minds about,* Mr Howard might have written *a word I am ambivalent about,* and just got away with it.

What would be quite unacceptable is the use of *ambivalent* to refer to meanings rather than to feelings or attitudes — the use of *ambivalent* as a substitute for *ambiguous.*

> × Only one outsider remains, Alex's 20-year-old mistress Chloe (Meg Tilly), who lives without hope or illusion and is the ambivalent clue to Alex's state of mind.
> – Philip French, *The Observer*

> ?? Scott made his fateful return visit to India in 1964. The obsession suddenly took shape; he saw a way of making India intelligible even though his understanding of it was built on a new perception of how many-sided the country was and of how ambivalent the British role had been.
> – Sebastian Faulks, *Sunday Telegraph*

The two adjectives can sometimes be used in the same context, where either feelings or meaning might be uncertain. *An ambiguous piece of writing* would be one which could be understood in more than one way. *An ambivalent piece of writing* might express an emotional contradiction. *Ambivalent* has the related noun *ambivalence*; *ambiguous* has two related nouns — *ambiguousness* and *ambiguity*. Both refer to the state of being *ambiguous* — the *ambiguity/ ambiguousness of her reply* — but *ambiguity* has the further sense of 'something ambiguous': *There's an ambiguity in the first sentence*; *poetry full of subtle ambiguities.*

> These concentrated, enigmatic stories address their subjects with such intelligent conviction and clarity that their ambiguities are not left to be stumbled on by the reader, but are challengingly displayed.
> – Alan Hollinghurst,
> *The Times Literary Supplement*

Note, finally, the word *bivalent* (/**bī-vay**lənt/). This is a technical term used in chemistry, genetics, and logic, and refers to a chemical valency of 2, or to a pair of chromosomes, or to a true-false logical system.

See also AMBIGUITY.

amend See EMEND.

America, American Take care, when using these words, that your meaning is quite clear to your listener or reader. The words are sometimes used in reference to the United States, and sometimes in reference to 'the Americas' — that is, North America, Central America, and South America (possibly including the Caribbean islands as well).

The name *America* was coined by a German map-maker in 1507, in honour of Americus Vespucius (the Latinised form of Amerigo Vespucci), the Italian navigator who explored the New World coastline in about 1500, shortly after Columbus. The name was originally applied to the entire landmass, north and south.

In general usage, however, it remains a fair assumption that *American*, without qualifications, refers to the USA. or to a U.S. citizen. If the reference were to a Canadian or Brazilian person or thing, then obviously the words *Canadian* and *Brazilian* would be used instead:

> Canadians would like to claim Vinland as theirs because of the saga references to maple trees ... Americans, on the other hand, would also like to claim Vinland as theirs.
> – Magnus Magnusson, *Vikings!*

The Americas can be divided up in several different ways, so the terms *North*, *South*, and *Central America* are not always clear. *South America* technically refers to the area south of the Panama Canal, or south of the Panama-Colombia border.

Central America refers to those states lying between Mexico in the north and Colombia in the south (excluding Mexico and Colombia themselves).

North America strictly refers to Canada, the United States, and Mexico, though it is often loosely used to refer to Canada and the United States alone. If the whole landmass is divided simply into *North* and *South* America, then North America would probably be understood to include all lands above the Panama Canal, or all countries north of the Panama-Colombia border.

A cultural rather than geographical division is sometimes made: the common term *Latin America* and the rare term *Anglo-America*. *Latin America* usually refers to Mexico and Central and South America. (The term would usually include the Spanish-speaking Caribbean islands of Cuba and Puerto Rico as well as the Dominican Republic.) Not all these areas are Spanish- or Portuguese-speaking, however. Belize and Guyana, for instance, being former British colonies, should strictly speaking not be considered part of Latin America, nor should those areas where Dutch is spoken. (However, French-influenced areas, such as French Guiana and Haiti, may well qualify for inclusion.) The term *Spanish America* is of course limited to Spanish-

speaking areas, and should not include Brazil.

Spanish-speakers have conventions of their own. In Spanish, the word *Americano*, though often used of people from the USA, attracts criticism from those who feel it should be used of anyone from North, South, or Central America. There is another problem in referring to the USA, since some Latin American countries are also 'United States': the United States of Mexico, the United States of Brazil, and the United States of Venezuela. Spanish-speakers often therefore refer to the USA as *Los Estados Unidos del Norte* ('the United States of the North'), and to a U.S. citizen as an *estadounidense* or *estadinense*, or as a *norteamericano* (though this could apply to a Canadian as well).

See also BRITAIN; UNITED STATES.

American English   American English originated in the British English of the 17th and 18th centuries, with various features of the old regional dialects all recombined and reshaped in America. Today's American English has lost some features that British English has kept, and kept some that British English has lost.

Gotten for instance, retained by Americans (though some American purists have criticised it), has been eliminated from standard British English except in *ill-gotten gains*, though it still survives tenuously in some British dialects. (On the other hand, the adjectival *?boughten,* 'bought in a shop rather than homemade', is nonstandard in both British and American English but survives in dialects on both sides of the Atlantic.)

Other 'Americanisms' that are in fact old British usages include: *cute* and *invite* (an invitation) — both of these were British slang terms in the 18th century or earlier; *fall* (autumn), *to loan* (to lend), *mad* (angry), *I guess* (I suppose), *-wise* (as in *sympathywise*), *moonshine* (whisky), *handy* (near), *to meet with*, and *mugging*.

Oscar Wilde's description of Britain and America as 'two great countries divided by a common language' contains truth as well as wit. British and American speakers have never had much serious trouble in understanding each other, but they have had a long history of being irritated by each other. British purists have felt that uncouth Americanisms were corrupting their language; some seem to think that everything they dislike about English must be of American origin. (Such attitudes are rather similar to those of speakers of other languages towards English if they feel threatened by its influence.) And American language patriots have claimed that British English is effete, and American university handbooks of composition and usage have warned users against pretentiously larding their writing with Briticisms (*lift* rather than *elevator*), or 'foreignisms' generally (*garçon* rather than *waiter*).

A forceful though idiosyncratic view of how the British and the Americans felt about each other's writers was expressed in these words by a famous British writer in 1950:

> To the American, English writers are like prim spinsters fidgeting with the china, punctilious about good taste, and inwardly full of thwarted, tepid and perverse passions. We see the Americans as gushing adolescents, repetitive and slangy, rather nasty sometimes in their zest for violence and bad language.
> – Evelyn Waugh,
> 'Literary Style in England and America'

However, kinder views have also been expressed. Some people in Britain regard American English as vigorous, imaginative, and above all classless. (The British poet Vernon Scannell once noted that British politicians merely 'stand' for office, while American politicians 'run' for office.) And some people in America admire the ability of British writers to achieve a wide range of effects without having to veer in their prose from one stylistic level to another: their American counterparts, treating the same theme, might be tempted to lurch between stilted formality and inappropriate slanginess without being able to establish a basic 'tone' to give coherence to the text as a whole.

British and American English have continued to borrow from each other. Up to about 1900, American English was probably more influenced by British English than British English was by American, with such expressions as *central heating* and *weekend* crossing the Atlantic from east to west. But throughout the 20th century the tendency has been powerfully reversed. In recent years, modern British English has borrowed far more from American English than American English has borrowed from British. In both directions the borrowings are more extensive than either side realises. Some words or expressions are well known to be Americanisms or Briticisms and are resisted or welcomed accordingly; but others are never noticed until they have become so fully established that they are felt to have been native all along. And a further complication is that people in Britain tend to know far more about American English than people in America know about British English. Modern British dictionaries include many Americanisms; modern American dictionaries include relatively few Briticisms. Furthermore, modern British dictionaries tend to label not only Americanisms but also Briticisms: not only is *elevator* labelled American but *lift* is labelled British. Most American dictionaries would label *lift* British but would not label *elevator* at all.

The trade in terms, then, tends to appear more one-sided than it really is. America does continue to import Briticisms. Here is a brief selection of words and expressions of 20th-century British origin that have made themselves at home in America: *miniskirt, the Establishment, mandarin* (a high-ranking civil servant), *iron curtain* (popularised by Winston Churchill), *Big Brother* (coined in its sinister sense by George Orwell), *the corridors of power* (coined by C.P. Snow), *opposite number* (one's counterpart), *gentrification, brain drain, breathalyser, gamesmanship* (coined by Stephen Potter), *hovercraft, kiss of life, Parkinson's Law, smog,* and *tabloid.*

More surprising, perhaps, is that even some British slang and informal terms have established themselves in America. These include *bonkers, gay* (homosexual, now especially male homosexual), *mod, posh, spoof,* and *swanky,* with *perks* and *trendy* as recent additions. *Brunch* is a good example of the thoroughly Americanised British import: British by origin, the word came into American English in the 1920s, died out until recently in Britain, and is now widely — but mistakenly — felt on both sides of the Atlantic to be an Americanism.

American exports to Britain are more numerous, though not overwhelmingly so: *to categorise* and *to hospitalise, stunt, baby sitter, teenager, gimmick, know-how, commuter, snarl-up, tailback,* and the vogue meanings of *blueprint* and *authentic.* Furthermore, new Americanisms seem to find their way to Britain very soon after surfacing in America: the neologisms *laid-back, palimony, rip-off,* and *no way,* and the new general sense of *lifestyle.* More slowly, though just as surely, the disputed senses of *hopefully* and *alibi* appeared fairly promptly in Britain.

It is borrowings of this last sort, of course, that especially outrage British purists. However, American purists denounce these usages with equal fury and equal lack of success. It is remarkable that most of the major usage issues, such as the use of *whom,* the split infinitive, the placement of *only,* and the meaning of *disinterested,* are in fact treated in much the same way in America and Britain. The same deviations occur; conservatives condemn them; progressive linguists justify them, and a large number of British and American speakers pay no attention to either type of advice.

Despite the continuing interaction of British and American English, there remain important differences between them in virtually every aspect of language use: pronunciation and intonation, spelling, grammar, vocabulary, and even style. It is impossible in one article to survey these differences comprehensively. Besides, many individual differences are discussed in individual articles throughout this book. The aim of the following sections is therefore simply to give a general idea of the types of difference that exist, illustrated by some typical examples. A few preliminary points to note:

First, American English, like British English, includes many regional, urban, and even class dialects. But there are enough features common to the speech and writing of most educated Americans to make possible a comparison of their language with that of most educated people in Britain.

Secondly, many features of British English are shared by the English of other countries, both Commonwealth and non-Commonwealth, including those where English is a second language. And many features of American English are shared by Canadian English and by the English of the Philippines, where English is an important second language.

Finally, the research done for this book suggests that there are also some features of standard British English that are *not* shared by any other variety of English. One such feature, discussed below, is the '*do*-reinforcement' of such phrases as *They must have done* — it occurs very occasionally in Australian English, but is otherwise peculiar to Britain.

Pronunciation A few of the more glaring differences between American and British pronunciation are extremely well-known: *tomato* is pronounced /tə-**maat**ō/ by most British speakers, and /tə-**mayt**ō/ by most, though not all, Americans. Similarly, for *privacy*, the pronunciation /**priv**və-si/ is favoured in Britain, and /**prīv**ə-si/ in the U.S. And *schedule,* pronounced /**shed**dewl/ in Britain, is /**skej**-əl, -ōōl/ in the U.S., and typically /**shej**-əl, -ōōl/ in Canada.

But these are all isolated cases. The important differences between American and British pronunciation are the systemic differences — that is, differences affecting whole sets of words.

1. The most conspicuous single British-American difference is that most Americans pronounce *r* whenever it is found in the spelling of a word, whereas in standard British pronunciation — the 'received pronunciation' (RP) of educated people in southeastern England — it is not pronounced after a vowel unless another vowel follows it. Thus most Americans pronounce the *r* in such words as *far, hard,* and *mother*. The standard American treatment of *r* is actually older than its treatment in RP. Of course, many dialects of British English also retain 'post-vocalic *r*', and in America the eastern New England dialect, the dialect of New York City, and some Southern dialects often lose it.

The result is that in London there is more prestige attached to dropping post-vocalic *r* than to pronouncing it, whereas in New York there is more prestige in pronouncing it than in dropping it. The American sociolinguist William Labov found that in New York City, the posher the department store, the more likely its employees were to pronounce post-vocalic *r*.

Furthermore, the majority of Americans who pronounce *r* wherever it is written do not use the so-called 'intrusive *r*': for them, *law and order* could never be mistaken for *lore and order*.

The American vowels preceding written *r* are often 'higher' than their RP counterparts: American *mirror*, for instance, may sound rather like *merer*. This can create some strange 'sound effects' for British people listening to Americans, but is unlikely to produce real misunderstanding.

2. The second most conspicuous British-American difference concerns the treatment of the vowel in such words as *path, pass, dance, ask,* and *laugh*. In Shakespeare's time this vowel was something like /a/. Southern British English changed it to /aa/ in the 18th century, and this pronunciation became part of RP. Most Americans use /a/. But note that northern and some western British English retains a vowel even closer to Shakespeare's /a/; and in America, eastern New England and coastal Southeastern speech often have /aa/, perhaps because they stayed under the influence of London speech longer than other parts of the United States. Even today, Americans who do not use /aa/ in such words as *pass* tend to regard its use there as either British or affected — perhaps both.

3. Most Americans have no distinctive vowel corresponding to the RP /o/ of such words as *cod, dog, bomb,* or *orange*. They use instead one of their other vowels in these words — usually /aa/ or /aw/. This means that the American pronunciation of *cod*, /kaad/, can sound somewhat like the RP pronunciation of *card*, and that the American pronunciation of *impossible* can sound like the RP pronunciation of *impassable*. Real confusion can result when Americans talk to British people. However, Americans understand each other perfectly, because those who pronounce *cod* as /kaad/ pronounce *card* as /kaard/, and those who pronounce *impossible* with /aa/ pronounce *impassable* with /a/.

4. In such words as *tune, duke,* and *student,* most Americans say /o͞o/ whereas RP keeps a *y*-sound as well: /ew/. This is a feature of American pronunciation often mimicked by British speakers — and by Canadians, who also tend to use /ew/. However, there is some evidence that it is on the increase in British English, too.

5. Many Americans, though not most, pronounce such words as *pin* and *bin* so that they sound like *pen* and *Ben.* This can cause real confusion, not only for British people and for the majority of Americans who distinguish /i/ from /e/, but even among speakers of those American dialects that merge the two vowels in certain positions. This regional feature of American pronunciation is the inverse of a feature of New Zealand pronunciation, in which *pen* sounds like *pin.*

6. When faced with a word containing *t* or *tt* between a stressed and an unstressed vowel, many Americans will pronounce the *t* so that it sounds almost like /d/. British people will find it hard to tell the difference between such Americans' pronunciations of *latter* and of *ladder.* The distinction is not always clear to Americans themselves, but real confusion is unlikely to arise. On the other hand, American English does not usually replace /t/ with a virtually soundless 'glottal stop' — a tendency apparently becoming more widespread in British English, where *latter* is sometimes pronounced something like /la-ə/.

7. When *nt* comes between a stressed and an unstressed vowel, the *t* is often pronounced weakly or even lost altogether, with the result that *winter* can sound like *winner* in many American pronunciations.

8. Many Americans do not distinguish between the 'clear' *l*, before a vowel, and the 'dark' *l* (approaching a *w*-sound), after a vowel: they 'darken' the first *l*'s of *Lil* and *lull* into sounding like the final *l*'s. This feature of American pronunciation is the inverse of certain West Indian pronunciations of English, in which the *l*'s are generally 'clear'. The American tendency to use 'dark' *l* before vowels does not cause misunderstanding, but is one of the features of American English that British actors tend to seize on when trying to imitate an American accent. However, most Americans are unaware of the American tendency to merge 'clear' and 'dark' *l*'s, and regard British attempts to imitate this feature as exaggerated to the point of caricature. Besides, many Americans do distinguish between the two types of /l/.

9. Another set of more or less consistent British-American differences is the placement of stress in various types of word.

In words borrowed from French and still perceived as French, American English tends to leave the stress on the last syllable, but British English tends to bring it forward. *Ballet* and *croquet* are /**bal**-ay, **bal**-i/ and /**krō**-kay, **krō**-ki/ in British English, but usually /ba-**lay**/ and /krō-**kay**/ in American English. In British English, *garage* is /**garr**aa<u>zh</u>, **garr**ij/, but in American English /gə-**raazh**, gə-**raaj**/.

The reverse applies to two-syllable verbs that end in *-ate.* Here British English accentuates the last syllable and American English the first. So British speakers say *to dic**tate*** and *to frus**trate*** but Americans usually say *to **dic**tate* and almost always *to **frus**trate.*

10. There is a British-American difference too in the pronunciation of certain suffixes. Americans generally pronounce the suffix *-ary/-ory* with some stress on its first syllable, but British RP gives this syllable no special stress, or eliminates it entirely. Furthermore, the last syllable of the suffix *-ary/-ory* (like unstressed final *-y* generally) is pronounced /ee/ by most Americans but is generally /i/ in RP (though many speakers of standard British English now use /ee/ here, too). Thus the RP pronunciation of *dictionary* is /**dik**-sh'n-əri/ or, more often, /**dik**-sh'n-ri/, but the most common American pronunciation is /**dik**-sh'n-erree/. Likewise, the prevailing American pronunciation of *library* is /**lī**-brerree/; of *military,* /**mil**i-terree/; and of *preliminary,* /pri-**lim**min-erree/.

With the ending *-ile,* on the other hand, things are again usually reversed. British English gives this syllable a full 'spelling'-pronunciation, with some stress — as does standard Canadian English — whereas American English generally uses a reduced or virtually silent vowel: *docile, fragile,* and *futile* are in RP /**dō**-sīl/, /**fraj**-īl/, and /**few**-tīl/, but in American English usually /**daa**ss'l/, /**fraj**əl/, and /**few**-t'l/, the result is that for many Americans *hostile* sounds the same as *hostel,* and *missile* as *missal.* However, the longer or more technical a word in *-ile,* the more likely Americans are to pronounce its ending as /-īl/. So for Americans *juvenile* and *prehensile* can end in either /-əl/ or /-īl/, *motile* is rather more likely to end in /-īl/ than *mobile* is, and *percentile* almost always ends in /-īl/, just as it does for the British.

11. There is far less diversity of pronunciation in America than there is in Britain (though some regional or social dialects — Black American English, for instance — are very different from the mainstream). In the words of the British language expert Simeon Potter, 'dialectal differences are more marked in England between Trent and Tweed than in the whole of North America'. For one thing, there is, and always has been, much greater mobility in America, so accents there have tended to meet, mingle, and — not merge perhaps, but certainly modify one another. The main regional divisions are simply the Western, Northern, Southern, and Midland dialects, the last of these commonly divided into North Midland and South Midland. There are of course important sub-divisions within each group, New England dialect and New York City dialect being two of the most notable.

Furthermore, Americans are far less concerned about accents than the British are. Certainly they were aware of President Carter's Georgia accent, and they are taking an increasing interest and pride in their regional and ethnic roots. Yet authenticity of accent is less important to them: an American play set in Texas might well have New England actors in it speaking with their natural New England accents, and causing little critical comment in doing so. Imagine, by contrast, the protests that would be generated in Britain by an actor's Cockney or Yorkshire or Scottish accent in a play set in Wales, for example. (In the case of American Westerns, however, this linguistic nonchalance may be justified historically: the American West was indeed settled by people from all over the country, though it has since developed speech patterns of its own.)

But just as British audiences can usually tell when an American actor is putting on a British accent, so Americans can usually tell when a British actor is trying to speak American. The giveaway is not so much the residue of British English in his voice as his general inability to imitate one regional dialect alone. Americans do not mind New Yorkers playing hillbillies, but they do find it strange when someone playing a hillbilly sounds like a hillbilly some of the time, like a New Yorker some of the time, and like a Mid-Westerner the rest of the time.

Pronunciation can, it is true, be a marker of social position in America, especially in big cities such as New York. But it is far less intensely discussed and scrutinised there than it is in Britain. In America, someone *well-spoken* speaks fluently and effectively. In Britain, someone *well-spoken* speaks fluently and effectively, too — but above all he uses the right accent. Moreover, Americans — white Americans at least — seldom indulge in the British habit of switching accents in relaxed conversation as a way of associating the ideas they are expressing with the posh, the pretentious, or the boorish. (Many black Americans, however, do use this code-switching in humorous conversation.) In fact, it is not quite certain that social dialects in America are sufficiently distinct to make this kind of switching possible on a large scale.

Spelling The differences between British and American spelling are more important for sociological reasons than for linguistic ones. They serve to identify a written text as of British or American origin when otherwise it might not be possible to. Many of the spelling differences were promoted by the great American lexicographer Noah Webster (with his spelling manual in 1783 and his dictionary in 1828), and they were adopted as badges of linguistic nationalism by the young American republic.

Not all the spellings that are today regarded as distinctively American are of American origin. In Shakespeare's day *color* and *colour* coexisted, and so did *center* and *centre*. But the fact that Americans plumped enthusiastically for *color* and *center* helped to ensure that people in Britain would eventually decide that *they* preferred *colour* and *centre* (whereas Canadians tend to mix typically 'British' and typically 'American' spellings in variable proportions).

Americans would argue, as Noah Webster did, that their spellings are simpler, more logical, and etymologically sounder than those that have come to prevail in Britain. However, they do not usually regard British spellings as wrong in the way that many British people would regard American spellings as wrong. Besides, some British spellings linger on in odd ways in America as a reminder of times past: New York City boasts a mammoth World Trade Center not far from an old Manhattan road called Centre Street.

Some of the major British-American spelling differences are as follows:

1. Many words that in British English end in *-our*, in American English end in *-or*: *arbor*, *armor*, *behavior*, *candor*, *clamor*, *color*, *favor*, *flavor*, *harbor*, *labor*, *neighbor*, *rigor*, *splendor*, *vigor*, and so on; but both British and American English have *error*, *horror*, *pallor*, *stupor*, *torpor*, and others, and American English still prefers *glamour* to *glamor*. The American preference for *-or* makes it easy for Americans to form inflections and derivatives of the words in this group: compare British *colour*, *colourful*, *coloration* and the more regular American *color, colorful, coloration*.

Both British and American English have *-or* for agent nouns such as *author, doctor, collaborator, tractor*; but American English often has *saviour*, especially as an appellation of Jesus: *the Saviour*. (The witty charge levelled at Noah Webster — that he wanted to take *u* from *the Saviour* — turned out to be a not quite accurate prediction.)

2. There is a tendency in American English to prefer *e* where British English has *ae* or *oe*: Americans can write *eon, anemia, esophagus*, and *homeopathic* where British English has *aeon, anaemia, oesophagus*, and *homoeopathic*. However, this is a tendency rather than a rule: the British spellings are also acceptable in America.

3. American English has *-er* where British has *-re* in *center, goiter, miter, specter*, and so on, but allows both *theater* and *theatre*. Both British and American English have *acre, lucre*, and *mediocre*. American English has *meter* both for 'a measuring instrument' (as in British English) and for 'a measurement of length, just over three feet' (which in British English is spelt *metre*). British *manoeuvre* differs in two respects from American *maneuver*.

4. American English prefers *defense, offense, pretense*, and *license* (noun and verb), where British has *defence, offence, pretence*, and *licence* (noun), reserving *license* for the verb. The British distinction between *practice* (noun) and *practise* (verb) is not usually maintained in American spelling, where *practice* is common for both. But in all these cases the 'British' spelling is acceptable in America.

5. When a verb ends in *-l* preceded by a single written vowel, British English doubles the *l* when adding a suffix that begins with a vowel: *rebel, rebelling; travel, travelling*. American English is obliged to double the *l* only when it ends a stressed syllable: *rebel, rebelling* but *travel, traveling*. However, American English sometimes doubles the *l* in the same way as British English does: *travelling* is sometimes found in American writing. By contrast, certain verbs that in British English end in *-l* have *-ll* in American English. These include *appall, distill, enroll, fulfill*, and *instill*. Such verbs keep *-ll* in American English in all inflections and derivatives, producing a contrast between American *enrollment* and *fulfillment* and British *enrolment* and *fulfilment*.

Furthermore, some verbs that end in *-all* in both varieties — *enthrall, install* — keep their *-ll* in American English even when they lose their final *l* in British English: Americans write *enthrallment*

and *installment* where British people write *enthralment* and *instalment*. Likewise, *skill* loses one *l* in the British spelling of *skilful* but retains it in American *skillful*.

6. American English uses *-ize* where possible: it has *civilize* rather than *civilise, organize* rather than *organise*. British English is evenly divided in its preferences. However, American English does encourage *-ise* where *-ise* is obligatory in British English; that is, in such verbs as *advise* and *surprise*. (See -ISE, -IZE.)

The American preference for *z* is carried over into inflections and derivatives of words ending in *-ize*: *civilization, organizer*.

American English also has *-lyze* where British English has *-lyse*: *analyze, paralyze*. However, it does *not* extend this to derivatives (where there is a pronunciation change anyway), having *analysis* and *paralysis* as in British English.

7. Several words having the sequence *-moul-* in British English are spelt *-mol-* in American English: so British *mould, moulder, moult*, and *smoulder* are usually *mold, molder, molt*, and *smolder* in American spelling.

8. Finally, a handful of miscellaneous spelling differences: the British *cheque, kerb*, and *tyre* (usually nouns) are in American spelling *check, curb*, and *tire*. The British might claim to have a more sensible policy here, differentiating these words, in the spelling, from the quite different words *check, curb*, and *tire* (usually verbs).

Some other examples: British *dyke, grey*, and *sulphur*; American usually *dike, gray*, and *sulfur*; British *mollusc, pyjamas*, and *sceptic*; American usually *mollusk, pajamas*, and *skeptic*. The British *moustache* differs in both spelling and pronunciation from the American *mustache*.

See also SPELLING.

Punctuation The differences between British and American punctuation are discussed in detail in the articles devoted to the individual punctuation marks. Here are two of the most important general differences:

1. For quotation marks, American English prefers double quotation marks (" ") to single ones, and generally insists that commas and full stops should go to the left of the quotation marks, producing *He said "nice."* ... where British English would tend to have *He said 'nice'*. — the full stop here usually (though not always) being placed outside the quotation marks. The rules for the use of quotation marks and the placement relative to them of commas and full stops are enforced quite strictly in printed American English, where there is much less variation in style than in printed British English.

2. American English has a marked preference for so-called 'serial commas' before *and* and *or*, strongly preferring *x, y, and z* to *x, y and z*. The form *x, y and z* is much more common in Britain than in America.

Other specific but important differences include:

3. The American distinction between *Dear Mr Smith:* ... as the salutation of a business letter, and *Dear John,* ... as the salutation of a friendly letter. British English would use a comma in both cases — *Dear Mr Smith,* ...; *Dear John,* ... .

4. The complex symbol :— is now almost unknown in American English, being replaced by a simple colon.

5. The symbol # is frequently used in American English as the equivalent of *no.*, meaning 'Number': *# 1534*. It is not used in this way in British English.

6. The date 10/5/53 means '5 October 1953' in American English, but '10 May 1953' in British English.

Grammar There are many grammatical differences between British and American English. Fortunately they do not usually lead to misunderstanding, and in some cases usage in the two varieties seems actually to be converging. The following discussion presents only some of the more important points of difference.

1. Many British speakers might say *Yes, I have done* or *Yes, they will do* as well as *Yes, I have* or *Yes, they will*. The possibility of using reinforcing forms of *to do* in this way is largely limited to British English (it occurs very occasionally in Australian English too). Americans and most other English speakers say only *Yes, I have*; *Yes, they will*; *Yes, I suppose they can*, and so on. This suggests that the development of the so-called '*do*-reinforcement' in British English is relatively recent.

2. British English uses a wide variety of 'tags', and uses them often — *He's here, isn't he? He isn't here, is he? So he's here, is he? So he didn't do it, didn't he?* — and regional forms such as: *He's really quick, is John.* American English feels comfortable only with the first two types, though it can cope with the third. The last two types are virtually unknown in American speech. In other words, American English tends to prefer constructions in which a positive statement is followed by a negative tag or a negative statement is followed by a positive tag. Furthermore, there is evidence (as from modern British and American plays) that tags occur *several times* more frequently in British speech than in American speech.

It is possible that other varieties of English in the world are closer to American English than to British English in this respect. Some varieties of English, as a second language, tend to have only the one all-purpose tag, *isn't it? — It's cold, isn't it? They read the book, isn't it?* American English, and to some extent British English, can use *right?* in that way, and other languages tend also to prefer a single all-purpose formula to the multiplicity of English tags: French *n'est-ce pas?*; Spanish *¿verdad?* or *¿vale?*; German *nicht (wahr)?* or *oder—?*

As with *do*-reinforcement, the greater variety of tags in British English than in other varieties of English suggests that their current frequency may be a relatively recent development. And of course some uses of tags in British English are nonstandard: *? I was walking down the street, wasn't I? ? And I saw the door open, didn't I? ? And I helped myself to a few things on the counter, didn't I?* Such tic-like uses of tags are often exploited by British writers to represent the speech of the lower classes and sometimes of criminals. This sort of thing is unknown in American English.

3. In the use of *have* (to indicate possession) in questions and negative sentences, there used to be different tendencies in American and British English. Americans would say, and still do say, *Do you have any children?* and *I don't have any children*, which the British used to consider Americanisms. British usage tended to favour *Have you any children?* and *I haven't any children*, which Americans used to consider, and still consider, Briticisms.

British usage has now changed: it now considers its former preference slightly old-fashioned, and has come to accept the 'American' forms as more or less natural; its own preference is now for the forms *Have you got any children?* and *I haven't got any children*, which are also acceptable to Americans, though used only occasionally by them. (The past forms *had got* and *hadn't got* are very rare in American English, and may be considered Briticisms.) Both British and American English make frequent use, in informal speech, of the form *Got any money?* (For more details, see HAVE **2**.)

Note the likely answers to the questions just discussed. To the question *Do you have any children?*, both British and American parents would reply *Yes, I do*. To the question *Have you (got) any children?*, a British parent would reply *Yes, I have*. So too might an American parent, but he or she might also reply *? Yes, I do*. This 'Americanism' can now be heard increasingly in British English too. It is criticised by purists on both sides of the Atlantic.

4. *Gotten* has fallen out of use in standard British English except in the phrase *ill-gotten gains.* It continues to flourish in American English, however (despite criticisms at one time by American purists). Thus American English can make a useful distinction:

a. I've got to go to that boring party (= I have to go).

b. I've gotten to go to that swell party (= I've managed to wangle an invitation).

In British English, sentence *a.* would be ambiguous, and to make clear that sense *b.* was intended, a British speaker would have to use a form such as *managed to go* or *managed to get myself invited* — which Americans could say, too.

Some British writers believe that Americans do not use *got* at all as a past participle, and would represent sentence *a.* in American speech with *gotten.* That is quite wrong.

5. With such words as *yet*, *already*, and *just*, British English prefers the present perfect forms of verbs in such expressions as:

a. Have you eaten yet?
b. I've already said so.
c. He's just left.

These forms are also recommended in American English. But American English frequently uses the simple past:

a. ? Did you eat yet?
b. ? I already said so.
c. ? He just left.

This use of the past is informal or nonstandard in American English. And there are signs — particularly with *just* — that it is starting to appear in British English. But its much greater frequency in American than in British English marks a notable difference between the two varieties.

6. With verbs allowing a choice of past forms — *learned*, *learnt*; *spilled*, *spilt* — and so on, British and American usage have different tendencies. British English favours the *-t* forms slightly. American English has a slight preference for *-ed* forms, especially *leaned, learned,* and *spelled* — the alternative *-t* forms here are considered distinctly British by Americans. On the other hand, Americans seem to use *dwelt, knelt*, and *leapt* as often as, or even more often than, *dwelled, kneeled*, and *leaped.* (For a fuller discussion, see -ED, -T.)

7. After certain expressions of recommendation or request, British English can use several constructions:

It is desirable/I demand that he should go there/that he go there
It was desirable/I demanded that he should go there/that he go there/ ? that he went there.

Should go is favoured; *go* alone seems slightly formal; *went*, used principally after past expressions (*was desirable*, *demanded*) is often considered nonstandard.

In American English, *go* is favoured; *should go* is less common and may actually strike some people as strange to the point of being foreign (rather than being British); *went* seems to be extremely unusual.

The use of *go* on its own seems to be increasing in British English, so that the two varieties are converging here (much as in the treatment of *have*). Nevertheless, British speakers are still often amazed at the way this 'subjunctive' *go* is negated in American English:

It is desirable/I demand that he not go there.

British speakers would almost always use a *should* before the *not* here.

8. There are a number of British-American differences in the use of auxiliary and modal verbs:

a. *shall.* Though some American writers have occasionally tried to follow the traditional rules about *shall* and *will*, ordinary American English, like Scottish and Irish English, uses *I will* and *we will* on a par with *you will*, *they will*, and the like. Unlike most Scottish and Irish English, however, American English retains *shall* in questions:

i. Shall I clean the windows?
ii. Shall we clean the windows, Miss Jones?
iii. Shall we dance, Miss Jones?

In *i.* and *ii.*, *should* is an American alternative to *shall.* But in *iii.*, *shall* is unchallenged. The difference between *ii.* and *iii.* is that in *ii.*, *we* is 'exclusive' (it does not include Miss Jones), whereas in *iii.*, *we* is 'inclusive' (it includes Miss Jones and means 'you and I'). The contraction *shan't* is much rarer in American English than in British English. (For a more detailed discussion, see SHALL, WILL.)

b. *should.* Americans do not ordinarily use *I should* to mean, in effect, *I would.* They are amazed when British speakers say:

i. I should dress warmly (if I were you) (= You should dress warmly).

ii. I should behave yourself (= You should behave yourself).

Admittedly, not all British speakers would use *ii.*

either. (For a further discussion, see SHOULD, WOULD.)

c. *let's.* Three ways of negating *let's* are found in British and American English:

i. Let's not.
ii. Don't let's.
iii. ? Let's don't.

The first is common in both varieties, and standard. The second is perhaps even more common in British English than the first, but is usually considered somewhat informal. In American English it is relatively rare. The third is widespread in American English, and very rare in British English. In both varieties, it is considered informal or nonstandard. The principal difference between standard British and standard American English is the greater currency of *ii.* in British English.

d. *used to.* The forms *Used you to?* and *You used not to* are British rather than American (though they are becoming rare in British English too). The forms *Did you use(d) to?* and *You didn't use(d) to* are common in both British and American English. In spelling, the forms without the last *d* are to be preferred on the ground that auxiliary *do* is supposed to be followed by the infinitive, but there is no difference in pronunciation between *used to* and *use to* here.

e. *dare* and *need.* The treatment of these verbs as auxiliaries, as in *You needn't leave* and *Dare he stay?* is probably less common in America than in Britain. The forms *You don't need to leave* and *Does he dare (to) stay?* are possible in both varieties.

The phrase *I dare say* is more British than American.

f. *ought to.* Research suggests that *ought to* is somewhat less common in American English than in British English. But American English can drop the *to* in negative sentences, especially when referring to past time: *He oughtn't have done that.* This is far less acceptable in British usage.

g. *may* and *might.* The use of *may* instead of *might*, as in *?? She may have lived if the doctors had heeded the warning signs*, receives far less attention from Americans than from the British, suggesting that it is more of a problem in British English than in American English.

The contraction *mayn't* is rare in Britain, and even rarer in America. Some authorities have even claimed that it is unknown in America, but that is probably an exaggeration. (See MAY, MIGHT; and also CAN, MAY.)

h. *must* and *have to.* When *must* indicates assumption, it can be negated in these ways:

i. It must not be very cold out.
ii. It can't be very cold out.
iii. It must not have been very cold out.
iv. It can't have been very cold out.

The form *i.* is found in standard American English and in some British dialects; *ii.* is found in standard British English and also in standard American English; *iii.* in standard American English and in some British dialects; *iv.* is found in standard British English but is relatively rare in American English.

Furthermore, in affirmative sentences the *must* of assumption (*You must be joking*) can be replaced by *have to* or *have got to* in American English (*You have to be joking/You've got to be joking*). This replacement is clearly catching on in British English, but is still felt by many to be an Americanism.

j. *meant to.* In British English, *supposed to* can sometimes be replaced by *meant to*: *Brighton is supposed to be/? is meant to be very pleasant.* This does not happen in American English. Note that it is considered nonstandard by some British speakers.

k. *wasn't to, weren't to.* In British English *couldn't have* can be replaced by *wasn't to* or *weren't to*:

i. He couldn't have known that the door would be locked.

ii. He wasn't to know that the door would be locked.

In American English, only *i.* is possible. Of course, *wasn't to* and *weren't to* are available to both British and American English in their other functions:

iii. The plan wasn't to be put into operation until 1924.

9. The negative recommendation with *not to* (*Not to worry*; *Not to panic*) is British. However, it has achieved considerable popularity among fashion-conscious Americans in recent years.

10. The words *directly* and *immediately* can be used as conjunctions in British English (though purists disapprove of such use):

? Immediately/Directly I saw her, I knew she was right for the job.

Americans do not use this construction. They would have to say:

As soon as I saw her, I knew she was right for the job.

Of course, this is also standard in British English.

11. Another conjunction peculiar to British English is *whilst*. In American English it has been entirely replaced by *while*, and is on its way to being ousted in British English too.

12. Consider the following constructions with adjectives (or adverbs):

a. Honest though he is, I still don't like him.
b. Honest as he is, I still don't like him.
c. As honest as he is, I still don't like him.
d. Honest that he is, he returned the cheque to me.

The forms *a.* and *b.* are used in both British and American English, *c.* is American only; and *d.*, with its very different effect, is British only.

13. British English allows both *The government has decided* ... and *The government have decided* ... . Americans strongly resist giving plural verbs to group nouns (*government, committee, jury,* and the like), and much prefer *The government has decided* ... . Americans will use plural verbs with such nouns only if compelled to, as in: *The government are fighting among themselves.* But even here, Americans would rather say *The members of the government are fighting among themselves.*

Some speakers of British English do not like this use of plural verbs either, and many who would accept it in the examples above would bridle at the following notice seen in the Senate House of the University of London:

? The Institute of Education have moved to Bedford Square.

This would be unthinkable to an American.

The ability of British English to use plural verbs with group nouns makes certain useful distinctions possible, as between:

a. England has defeated Argentina in the Falklands (= two countries).
b. England have defeated Argentina in the World Cup (= two teams).

Of course, speakers of British English could also say what speakers of American English must say:

c. England has defeated Argentina in the World Cup.

See also COLLECTIVE NOUNS; PLURALS Part II.
Vocabulary Everybody knows that there are substantial differences between British and American vocabulary. A list of some of these differences follows. But first, a few general considerations to bear in mind.

1. *words and things.* British *lift* corresponds to American *elevator.* They are two names for the same thing: just the sort of lexical difference that is worth including here. But *President* is not the American word for *Prime Minister.* The President of the United States is chosen in a quite different way from the British Prime Minister, has many different functions, and, above all, is part of a different political system. An American would never think of calling Margaret Thatcher × *the British President* any more than a British person would think of calling Ronald Reagan × *the American Prime Minister.* The difference between *President* and *Prime Minister* is not really a difference between two *words,* but a difference between two *things.* Such pairs have no place in a list of vocabulary differences between British and American English.

Even so, the distinction between 'word differences' and 'thing differences' sometimes blurs. What about *underground* and *subway*? It could be argued that they are like *lift* and *elevator.* But many American speakers would distinguish between the New York *subway* and the London *underground,* and many British speakers would do the same. (Such speakers, whether British or American, would tend, in talking about Paris, to use neither *underground* nor *subway,* but *metro* — or perhaps even *métro*.) Do British *underground* and American *subway* both mean 'an underground railway within a city', or does *underground* mean 'an underground railway within a British city, especially London', and *subway* 'an underground railway within an American city'? In the first case we would be dealing with two words for the same thing; in the second case, with two words for different things, rather like *Prime Minister* and *President.* The decision to list or not to list such pairs as *underground* and *subway* is difficult and to some extent arbitrary.

2. *words and senses.* The example of *subway* raises another problem. The word has another sense in British English: what Americans call a *pedestrian underpass* or simply an *underpass.* Many an American tourist in search of public transport has rushed down a stairway labelled 'Subway' only to find himself eventually on the other side of the street rather than at the other end of London. Lists of British-American vocabulary differences traditionally look like lists of words, but they are in fact lists of *senses.* To say that *elevator* equals *lift* is to say that there is one sense of *elevator* that in American English is equivalent to one sense of *lift* in British English. The difference between words and senses is of no immediate importance when words are compared that have only one sense each, but it is important when you are comparing words with more than one sense. In the list below, a gloss, or short definition, has been appended to each word when necessary to show which sense is being dealt with.

Some words are particularly interesting in having a unique sense in both varieties: *rubber* is a famous example — both varieties refer to the latex substance, a person or thing that rubs, and so on; British English, unlike American English, uses *rubber* very commonly to refer to an eraser; American English, unlike British English, uses *rubber* to refer informally to a contraceptive sheath, and *rubbers* to refer to rubber waterproof overshoes or galoshes.

In America, a play might *bomb* (be a hopeless failure) while in Britain it might *go like a bomb* (be a great success). A different play might in America be *slated* (= scheduled, or destined) for a long run, but in Britain it might be *slated* (harshly reviewed) by the critics.

A British *slot machine* is called a *vending machine* in America; to an American a *slot machine*, or informally a *one-armed bandit*, is what the British call a *fruit machine*.

A *vest* in British English is an *undershirt* in American English; a *vest* in American English is a *waistcoat* in British English.

Suspenders occurs only in British English, not in American English, when referring to the fasteners (and sometimes the strap supporting them) used to keep women's stockings, or men's socks, in place — for stockings, at least, Americans refer instead to *garters* or *a garter-belt* (as the British can do too). And *suspenders* occurs only in American English, not in British English, when referring to the elasticated shoulder-straps used to hold men's trousers up — *braces* in British English (and sometimes in American English too).

The phrases *to knock up* and *to wash up* have senses peculiar to each variety: *to knock up*, in British English, is an informal term having as one of its meanings, 'to wake (someone) by knocking on the bedroom door'; in American English, (and now in British English too sometimes), it is a slang term meaning 'to make (a woman) pregnant'. *To wash up* means 'to wash the dishes, pots, and cutlery' in Britain; and 'to wash one's dirty hands (and sometimes face)' in America.

3. *equivalents and definitions. Lift* and *elevator* are equivalents. But not all expressions in one variety of English have equivalents in the other. This is particularly clear in the case of idioms. In American English *to shoot the breeze* means 'to pass the time in an informal conversation'. It does not correspond to any well-known fixed expression in British English, and so cannot be provided with a British English equivalent

in the way that *elevator* can be. Instead, it must be given an explanation or definition.

Once again, the boundary between an equivalent and a definition is by no means always clear. But in the list that follows, definitions will be enclosed in quotation marks, whereas equivalents will not.

4. *American English and British English as labels.* American and British English are two standard varieties of one language that are in continuous and ever-growing contact. Furthermore they are of supranational importance: they provide reference norms for other varieties of English — national and local, standard and nonstandard, first-language and second-language. British English, as already pointed out, is often the model for the English of most Commonwealth and former Commonwealth countries; and American English influences Canadian and Philippine English. Yet some features considered American are to be found also in other varieties of 'Commonwealth English' and local varieties of British English, and some features considered British are to be found in local varieties of American English or as minority forms in standard American English.

More important still, British and American English influence each other, so that the boundary between them is constantly shifting. The best-known current example of this interaction is the way in which the American sense of *billion* is rapidly ousting the British sense of *billion* in Britain itself. (See BILLION.)

A remarkable picture emerges if you take a historical view. Consider the terminology of the following fields of interest: sailing, railways, motor cars, aircraft, and computers. The picture that emerges very clearly is this: British-American differences are small in sailing, great in railways and motor cars, very small again in aircraft, and virtually nonexistent in computers (where even American spelling is widespread in Britain: witness *disk* and *program*). This suggests that in areas of interest developed before America was colonised, differences were small; in the 19th century they were at their greatest; and in the 20th century, as international communication became easier, they shrank again. Not that British and American English will ever become identical (nor that local varieties of either will disappear). The needs of international communication will bring them together; the desire to preserve national and local identity will keep them apart. British and American English will probably become as similar as is necessary for easy mutual understanding, but not more similar than that unless Americans and Britons feel no further need to regard themselves as culturally distinct. As the late Professor J.R. Firth is said to have observed of pronunciation: 'It is part of the meaning of an American to sound like one.'

5. *representing British and American differences*. Word-lists of British-American differences must be read with caution. The difference is sometimes a gulf, sometimes a mere tendency. Remember that there is constant interaction of British and American English, and a richness within each variety allowing more than one way to express any given idea. To say, for example, that *fall* is an American equivalent of *autumn* does not imply that *autumn* is a British word: Americans use it, too, and generally speak of *autumn leaves* rather than of *? fall leaves*. Perhaps the clearest way to display British-American differences is in three columns, with the British preference on one side, the American preference on the other side, and in the middle, either a definition (where no equivalent term exists in the other variety) or an equivalent that is used in both varieties — and thus often labelled 'World English'. Bear in mind that the list that follows is no more than a selection. (A comprehensive list would take up a whole book.) In particular, it excludes many British-American differences discussed elsewhere in this book, and also colloquial and slang expressions (where the differences are greatest), and neologisms (most American neologisms, such as *palimony*, cross the Atlantic with amazing speed nowadays).

6. First of all, here is a selection of terms in which the British and the American forms differ only very slightly, through an element within the word or phrase. The two forms in each pair are sometimes called 'morphological variants':

British English	World English	American English
accommodation	—	accommodations
aeroplane	aircraft	airplane
aluminium	—	aluminum
—	burgle	burglarize
candidature	—	candidacy
—	centenary	centennial
cookery book	—	cookbook
—	doll's house	dollhouse
to double-declutch	—	to double-clutch
haulier	—	hauler
jewellery	—	jewelry
maths	—	math
mum(my)	—	mom(my)
parting (in one's hair)	—	part
—	pernickety	persnickety

British English	World English	American English
racialism	racism	—
rowing boat	—	rowboat
—	sailing boat	sailboat
—	sanatorium	sanatarium, sanitarium
—	titbit	tidbit
zip	—	zipper

7. Now for a list of fuller differences in vocabulary or meaning. Remember that it is no more than a selection.

British English	World English	American English
—	aerial	antenna (of a radio)
anticlockwise	—	counterclockwise
aubergine	eggplant	—
—	autumn	fall
bank holiday	legal or public holiday	—
—	bath	bathtub
beetroot	—	beet
bird (slang for 'a girl')	chick (slang)	—
biscuit (sweet-tasting)	—	cookie
—	blind (over a window)	window shade
bonnet (of a car)	—	hood
boot (of a car)	—	trunk
bottom drawer	—	hope chest
—	bowler (hat)	derby
call box	telephone booth	—
camp bed	—	cot
candy floss	—	cotton candy
caravan	—	trailer, mobile home
catapult (toy)	—	slingshot
chemist	pharmacist	druggist
—	chest of drawers	bureau
chips	French fries	—
—	chiropodist	podiatrist
—	Christian name, first name	given name
crisps	—	potato chips
cooker	stove	—
cor anglais	English horn	—
cornflour	—	cornstarch
cot	—	crib
courgettes	—	zucchini
crotchet	—	quarter note
—	cutlery	silverware
current account	—	checking account
cutting (from a newspaper)	—	clipping
cut-price	—	cut-rate

British English	World English	American English	British English	World English	American English
dialling code	—	area code	—	'a lavatory in a public building'	restroom
Directory Enquiries	—	Information			
drawing pin	—	thumbtack	to lay a table	to set a table	—
dummy (baby's)	—	pacifier	lead (of a dog)	leash	—
dustbin	—	garbage can, trashcan	leader (in a newspaper)	editorial	—
engaged (telephone)	busy	—	leader (of an orchestra)	—	concertmaster
engine driver	—	engineer	lift	—	elevator
estate agent	—	real-estate agent, realtor	liver sausage	—	liverwurst
			—	lodger	roomer
ex-directory	—	unlisted	lorry	truck	—
ex-serviceman	—	veteran	market garden	—	truck farm
fanlight	—	transom	mileometer	—	odometer
Father Christmas	Santa Claus	—	mince	—	ground meat, chopped meat, hamburger
fire brigade	—	fire department			
flat (housing unit)	apartment	—	minim	—	half note
			motorway	—	expressway, freeway
flex	—	(electric) cord			
follow-my-leader	—	follow-the-leader	nail varnish	nail polish	—
fortnight	'two weeks'	—	nappy	—	diaper
founder member	—	charter member	No Entry (sign)	—	Do Not Enter
—	frying pan	skillet	notice board	—	bulletin board
—	garden party	lawn party	noughts and crosses	—	tick-tack-toe
gents	—	men's room	number plate	—	license plate
Girl Guide	—	Girl Scout	oven glove	—	pot holder
Give Way (road sign)	—	Yield (also in other national varieties)	paraffin	—	kerosene
			—	patience (the card-game)	solitaire
—	glasses	eyeglasses	pavement	—	sidewalk
goods train	—	freight train	pelmet	—	valance
to grill	—	to broil	petrol	—	gas, gasoline
hair grip	—	bobby pin	pillar box, postbox	—	mailbox
—	handbag	purse			
hardwearing	—	longwearing	plimsolls	—	sneakers
the high street	—	(the) main street	points (electric)	socket	outlet
hire-purchase	—	the installment plan	—	'a policeman on the beat'	patrolman
hoarding	—	billboard	post code	—	zip code
holidaymaker	—	vacationer	pram	—	baby carriage
houseman	—	intern	quaver	—	eighth note
house-trained	—	housebroken	queue	—	line
Inland Revenue	—	Internal Revenue Service	—	railway	railroad
			removal man	—	moving man
interval (in a cinema or theatre)	—	intermission	return (ticket)	—	round trip
			reverse-charge (call)	—	collect (call)
—	jeans	blue jeans	right-angled triangle	—	right triangle
jug	—	pitcher	—	ring binder	loose-leaf notebook
jumble sale	—	rummage sale			
launderette	—	laundromat	to ring (up)	to (tele)phone, to call (up)	—
lavatory	toilet	washroom			

British English	World English	American English
rise (in salary)	—	raise
Roadworks (sign)	—	Men Working
roundabout	—	traffic circle (also in other national varieties)
rowlock	—	oarlock
saloon (car)	—	sedan
sandpit	—	sandpile
secateurs	pruning shears	—
serviette	napkin	—
shop assistant	—	salesclerk
shopwalker	—	floor walker
—	'shorthand writer'	stenographer
silencer (of a car)	—	muffler
single (ticket)	—	one-way
skirting board	—	baseboard
sledge	—	sled
spring onion	scallion	—
stalls (in a theatre)	—	orchestra
standard lamp	—	floor lamp
swede (vegetable)	—	rutabaga
sweets	—	(hard) candy
—	tap	faucet
terrace(d) house	—	row house
telly (informal)	TV	—
—	tie	necktie
—	timber	lumber
tin (of food)	can	—
torch (battery-operated)	—	flashlight
tower block	high-rise (building)	—
—	traffic light	stoplight
tram	—	streetcar, trolley (car)
treacle	molasses	—
—	undertaker	mortician
unit trust	—	mutual fund
—	veranda	porch
washbasin, wash-handbasin	—	sink, bathroom sink
—	wastepaper basket	wastebasket
white coffee	'coffee with milk'	—
wholemeal	—	wholewheat
windscreen	—	windshield
wing (of a car)	—	fender
witness box	—	(witness) stand
zed	—	zee

8. Here are some equivalent British and American idioms that are quite similar in their phrasing:

British English	American English
at a loose end	at loose ends
to blow one's own trumpet	to blow one's own horn
to bowl someone a googly	to throw someone a curve
cash on the nail	cash on the barrelhead
green fingers	green thumb
home from home	home away from home
to lead someone a merry dance	to lead someone a merry chase
to let well alone	to let well enough alone
like a cat on hot bricks	like a cat on a hot tin roof
to lock the stable door after the horse has bolted	to lock the barn door after the horse is stolen
not by a long chalk	not by a long shot
on second thoughts	on second thought
a storm in a teacup	a tempest in a teacup/teapot

And here, finally, are a few idioms with quite different equivalents:

British English	World English	American English
as sure as eggs is eggs	—	dollars to doughnuts
—	between the devil and the deep blue sea	between a rock and a hard place
Gordon Bennet!	Goodness Gracious!	Heavens to Betsy!
—	when the chips are down	when push comes to shove

amiable, amicable These two adjectives both derive, by slightly different routes, from the Latin *amicus,* 'a friend'. They have developed slightly different uses, as careful users of English recognise.

Amiable tends to be applied to people, and means 'friendly, good-natured, likable': *a most amiable fellow*; *an amiable grin*; *a strong, but amiable personality.*

It was an amiable crowd and nobody seemed to mind how much you pushed, and eventually, sweating and exhausted, we forced our way to the front.

– Lynn Reid Banks,
The L-Shaped Room

It can also refer to a social environment, conversation, piece of writing, or the like, and mean 'congenial, cordial': *the amiable atmosphere of the social club.*

61

At his most characteristic he introduces the reader to some harmlessly amiable, even comic scene or episode, and then reverses the feeling to the limit.

– Kingsley Amis, *The Observer*

Amicable tends to refer to relationships, or joint enterprises, or decisions. It means 'characterised by good will, showing a friendly attitude, harmonious': *They arrived at an amicable settlement of their dispute.*

The paper was threatened a few weeks ago by a row between Mr Rowland and the editor, Mr Donald Trelford, over a story by Mr Trelford alleging army atrocities in Zimbabwe, where Lonrho has important assets. That dispute was eventually settled amicably.

– John Ardill, *The Guardian*

In the following quotation, *amicable* was a dubious choice for the adjective — *amiable* would have been better.

? And, in truth, he had to concede also that Dalmire had always been amicable and subservient; there was no evident cause for the poisonous hate he now nurtured in his breast.

– William Boyd,
A Good Man in Africa

amid, amidst   These words sound rather literary or old-fashioned today, and their shortened forms *'mid* and *'midst* even more so. The modern preference is for *in the midst of* or *in the middle of*, or above all for *among*.

Among is not always a suitable replacement, however. It can be used before plural nouns — *among the spectators* — and before some collective nouns: *among the crowd, among the aristocracy.* But it is not really suited to other singular nouns ? *among the traffic*, ? *among the alien corn*, ? *among the rubbish*, ?? *among the tumult*. In such phrases, *amid* or *amidst* is far more appropriate:

Perhaps the self-same song that found a path
Through the sad heart of Ruth, when, sick for home
She stood in tears amid the alien corn . . .
– John Keats, 'Ode to a Nightingale'

E. Box, the painter, is a favourite correspondent and she has painted the Lady Torte de Shell's portrait on the lid of a box, setting her amidst foliage and beneath a mysterious moon.

– Sir Roy Strong, *The Times*

In this second example, the old-fashioned feel of *amidst* is effective in the context. In most modern writing, however, *in the midst of* would probably seem more natural.

See also AMONG.

amoeba   See GERM.

amok, amuck   Most often encountered in the phrase *to run amok/amuck*, meaning 'to go berserk, to be in an uncontrollable frenzy', this word can be spelt quite acceptably in either way.

Figurative uses of the phrase are also possible, as in *Inflation must not be allowed to run amok/amuck.*

The word is Malay in origin, and it used to be maintained by some purists that only a Malay could run amok. This was, perhaps, taking pedantry too far, but their concern at least served to make people think twice before applying the word to any sort of angry or uncontrolled behaviour short of frenzy.

? If you're planning a holiday party Angela Hollest and Penelope Gaine have just written a useful book, *Children's Parties* . . . Their practical advice will take a great deal of panic out of the prospect of energetic youngsters running amok on your territory.

– Julia Watson, *The Observer*

among, amongst   There seems to be little agreement about these words. Some people regard *amongst* as obsolete, serving no use that is not better served by *among*. Others regard *amongst* as an acceptable variation that is not even old-fashioned, and that is in fact preferable to *among* before vowels. However, *amongst* is clearly less common today, and is probably becoming even rarer.

Nevertheless, *amongst* may still have some currency in figurative uses (especially at the beginning of a sentence): *Amongst all the great leaders of the ancient world, Julius Caesar stood out for his political sagacity.*

A favourite pastime amongst the hard-working journalists who covered last winter's cricket tour (one of the few relaxations indeed for which they could find any time) was to lay wagers about England's pair of opening batsmen for the Fifth Test this summer.

– Scyld Berry, *The Observer*

Among would still be quite suitable here, of course. And in literal uses, especially *within a* sentence, *among* is plainly preferable: *Caesar stood among a crowd of senators. Amongst* would be far less suitable here.

Note that there is a poetic form *'mongst* corresponding to *amongst,* but no form × *'mong* corresponding to *among.*

See AMID; BETWEEN.

among other things The phrase *among other things,* and similar phrases such as *among other excuses* and *among other reasons,* are so much the common idiom of today that we tend not to notice how silly and self-contradictory they are. If things are *other,* then this thing cannot be *among* them; if this thing is *among* various things, then they cannot be *other.*

The phrases seem to be a confused blend of two different phrases in each case: *among several excuses* and *in addition to other excuses.*

Curiously, no such objection seems to have been raised to the Latin phrase corresponding to *among other things: inter alia.* This Latin precedent probably accounts for the existence, and general acceptance, of the English phrases.

amoral See IMMORAL.

an See A, AN.

analyse, analysis 1. These words are extremely common today in general use — too common in fact. They have become vogue words, far removed from their proper technical contexts — chemistry, mathematics, philosophy, psychology, and so on. Today the most trivial of matters are *analysed* or subjected to an *analysis*:

> Let's analyse the possibilities — we can stay at home and eat, we can go to a restaurant, or we can accept your parents' invitation to dine with them...

The old words such as *consider, examine, look at, discuss,* and so on are perhaps thought to indicate an insufficiently serious attitude. An earnest or 'committed' weighing up of things involves an *analysis.*

The words are losing their old sharp outlines — the sense of the breaking down of complex wholes into parts in order to study and understand them more easily. Think twice before using the words outside a technical context, and try in that way to slow down their descent into banality.

2. The phrases *in the last analysis, in the final analysis, in the ultimate analysis,* and so on are seldom anything more than impressive-sounding ways of saying *in the end, finally,* or *at last.* Once

again, avoid using *analysis* unless there is in fact some analysis involved.

3. Note the spelling: *analyse,* with an *s.* In American English, *analyze* is also acceptable, but in Britain — despite its increasing frequency — this is still regarded as an Americanism. The same applies to *catalyse* and *paralyse.*

With *-ise* verbs, the choice of spelling holds good for the noun form as well. If you choose to spell *civilise* as *civilize,* then you will also spell *civilisation* as *civilization.* But with *-lyse* verbs, the pronunciation shift — from /z/ in the verb to /s/ in the noun — means that even those Americans who write *analyze* spell the derived noun *analysis*; similarly *paralysis* and *catalysis.*

Note finally that the plural of *analysis* is *analyses.*

and 1. *And* has been commonly used as the first word of a sentence for ten centuries now — throughout the history of written English. The schoolroom prohibition on using *and* to begin a sentence has not been going on quite that long, but it has become a well-entrenched traditional 'rule' of English grammar. And pedantic schoolteachers and stylists continue to abide by it and impose it on others.

But there seems no basis for the traditional rule — in grammar or logic — other than tradition itself, just as there is no good basis for the rule prohibiting *but* at the start of a sentence. By all means begin a sentence with *and,* so long as doing so remains in keeping with good style (and so long as you do not care if pedantic readers are perhaps going to be alienated from the rest of your writing).

Where good style might discourage the use of *and* to begin a sentence is where both that sentence and the preceding one are very short. A single sentence is then preferable:

> John looked guilty, and Mary looked innocent.

Only if you are aiming at some special staccato effect should you break such a sentence up into two. And when such sentences are streamlined, by omitting a word or words from the second clause —

> John looked guilty, and Mary innocent

— the comma should not be replaced by a full stop. To break the sentence up in this way, and use *and* to begin the second sentence, might perhaps be effective in thrillers, advertising, certain kinds of journalism, and so on, but it would not be acceptable in ordinary formal writing:

? John looked guilty. And Mary innocent.

See also SENTENCES.

2. When *and* joins two nouns, even two singular nouns, the resulting compound is usually plural, and should take a plural verb:

Mary and Jane are driving me insane.

Sometimes a pair of nouns fuses into a single concept, however, and is often treated as a singular subject and allocated a singular verb:

Your son and heir looks very fit.
The long and the short of it is that you're fired.
Sausage and mash is available only on Friday nights.
Bread and butter is all you're getting for tea.
? The wind and rain is driving me insane.
? Love and marriage remains even today the deepest ambition of the average adolescent boy.

In the first two examples, the singular verb is not just acceptable; it is obligatory. *Son and heir,* for instance, clearly refers to a single person and is accordingly a singular subject.

The third and fourth examples are acceptable though optional: *sausage and mash* can be understood as *the dish of sausage and mash*; and *bread and butter* can be understood as *bread with butter* — in each case, the subject can be regarded as singular. But the last two examples are more controversial. Opinion is divided on the acceptability of the singular verb here.

Those who allow it argue that the subject in each case is one concept and virtually one word, as though it were spelt with hyphens: *the wind-and-rain, love-and-marriage.* The modern trend seems to favour this view.

What is clearly a mistake is the use of a singular verb when the subject remains indisputably plural:

× The love of a good woman and marriage to her remains even today the deepest ambition of the average adolescent boy.

Use *remain,* not *remains.*

The mistake is particularly common when the verb comes before the subject:

× Never before has Britain in particular, and Europe in general, been so severely affected by American interest rates.
× Does Judas College in *Zuleika Dobson* and Lazarus College in *Barchester Towers* represent any actual Oxford College, and if so, which in particular?

The verbs *has* and *does* should be replaced by *have* and *do.*

The converse mistake is also common — the use of a plural verb when the subject, despite the presence of *and*, is clearly singular:

× The use of the double exclamation mark and the double question mark at the end of a sentence, though common enough in popular novels and tabloid newspapers, are frowned on by careful stylists.

The subject is in fact singular — *the use ...* — and *are* should accordingly be changed to *is.* Had the words *The use of* been left out, then the subject would indeed have been in the plural — *the double exclamation mark and the double question mark* — and *are* would then have been appropriate.

See also AGREEMENT; PLURALS Part II.

3. A related error is the misuse of the subject-form of a pronoun after *and,* especially the pronoun *I.* It is quite correct to say *John and I betrayed Maria* but not at all correct to say *×* *Maria betrayed John and I,* or *×* *I betrayed John and she.* For a more detailed discussion of this common mistake, see BETWEEN YOU AND I.

4. Another stylistic peculiarity favoured by journalists, advertisers, and modern novelists is the complete omission of *and* from lists of items. Traditionally, a list of three or more items will have commas between any pair of items, reserving *and* for a single appearance between the last pair of items:

Hector has worked as a telephone-connector, a mine inspector, a debt-collector, and a company director.

The trend, in certain kinds of writing, is to leave out the *and.* This omission can be an effective device: in the specimen sentence above, it might suggest the bustle and variety of Hector's working life, and also perhaps that the list is open-ended — that the four jobs specified are only examples of Hector's diverse career, and that the roll-call could continue for some time. It is as if the sentence ends not with a full stop but with the dot-dot-dot of an ellipsis:

Hector has worked as a telephone-connector, a mine inspector, a debt collector, a company director (. . .)

The more often this trick of style is used, the less effective it becomes, of course — and the more irritating. If you do leave out the *and,* do so only very occasionally.

5. The converse also occurs — using *and*

repeatedly, instead of or in addition to commas, between each pair of items on a list:

> Hector has worked as a telephone-connector, and a mine inspector, and a debt-collector, and a company director.

With or without the commas, the effect of the repeated *and* is to emphasise each item in the series and slow down the reader's or hearer's pace. The device can be useful for suggesting a boring routine:

> She had to deal with the washing, and the shopping, and the children, and the dinner.

But the danger is that the device will not just suggest boredom in the subject of the sentence, but also induce boredom in the reader!

6. The pattern *A, B, C, and D* when listing items is not always applicable, unfortunately: it applies only if all the items have the same status in grammar. Suppose items *A, B, and C* are of one kind, and item *D* of another: the pattern then has to be *A, B, and C, and D*. The omission of that first *and* would result in a faulty construction:

> ✗ Hector has worked as a mine-inspector, a debt-collector, a company director, and has had several other jobs besides.

Another *and* is needed before *a company director* in order to link the three grammatically equivalent elements *a mine-inspector, a debt-collector,* and *a company director* with one another, before all of them as a group are linked by the second *and* with the grammatically different element *has had several jobs besides.* (It could be argued that the omission of *and* before *a company director* is justifiable as a stylistic device along the lines discussed in section **4.** above. Perhaps so, but this particular specimen sentence would not really be a good place to use such a stylistic device.) The omission of this first *and* is an extremely common fault of style, and reveals a weak grasp of grammar on the part of the perpetrator.

7. In lists of items, the comma before the final *and* is optional. The policy in this book is to include the 'serial' comma — it helps to make things that slight bit clearer — but the modern tendency in British English is towards leaving it out:

> Hector has worked as a telephone-connector, a mine inspector, a debt-collector and a company-director.

In printed American English, however, the use of the 'serial' comma is strongly favoured: a comma would be inserted after *debt-collector.* (See COMMA.)

Elsewhere, the punctuation before *and* is fairly straightforward. Those who dislike the use of *and* as the first word of a sentence also tend to dislike the use of a semi-colon or colon before *and.* Again, this objection can usually be ignored. In fairly complex sentences, a comma is usually placed before *and*:

> John was sentenced to three years' hard labour, and Maria was fined £2000.

The comma should always be inserted where momentary ambiguity might otherwise result:

> Hector betrayed John, and Maria betrayed Casey.

Without the comma to guide him, the reader might at first assume that Hector had betrayed John and Maria. And a streamlined version of that sentence —

> Hector betrayed John, and Maria Casey

— would be quite ambiguous without the comma. It could be taken to mean that Hector betrayed two people, one called John (or John Casey) and the other called Maria Casey.

In simpler and unambiguous sentences, especially where the subject is omitted in the *and*-clause, the comma is optional:

> Hector came from a poor home (,) and left school at 13 to begin work.

And in short sentences where both the subject and the verb are omitted in the *and*-clause, the comma is usually omitted as well:

> Hector worked as a mine inspector during the day and as a debt-collector in the evenings.

8. A few dubious uses of *and,* finally: first, the use of *and* rather than *to* after *try, be sure,* and a few other verbs or verb phrases:

> ? Try and behave now, there's a good boy.

> ?? 'You must be sure and get enough rest in the next days,' said a kindly middle-aged woman whose husband stood solemnly beside her.
> – Patricia Highsmith (U.S.), *Slowly, Slowly, in the Wind*

(See TRY AND for further details.)

A more clear-cut misuse of *and,* but rather more difficult to detect, is the insertion of *and* between two quite distinct parts of a sentence. The speaker or writer unthinkingly tries, by a linking *and,* to yoke two successive ideas together into a single idea, when in fact they stubbornly remain two separate ideas:

The investigation is being hampered by the fact that only small quantities of wreckage have been found, and a naval vessel with sensitive sonar equipment is still trying to locate the remains of the aircraft in the sea off Cromer.

– Rodney Cowton, *The Times*

The *and* serves no proper purpose here. At most, a colon might be allowed after *found* perhaps, though a full stop is really what is needed, to give appropriate prominence to the two distinct ideas. Either way, the word *and* should be omitted.

And is also disliked in front of *moreover* and *nor*. However, *and* can precede *neither* — *I can't help, and neither can my wife* — and idiom usually allows the combinations *and yet* and *and also*, even though they seem redundant: *I liked her, and yet I couldn't help distrusting her*; *I distrusted her, and also I suspected her husband.* See also AND WHICH.

and all, and that 1. In British English, this is an increasingly common tag added to the end of a spoken statement:

? The barman poured the beer over my head and all, and then picked me up and shoved me out the door and all.

It seems to be a kind of spoken punctuation mark, rather like *you know*, and just as irritating when inserted every ten seconds into the conversation.
    2. The informal expression *and all that*, meaning 'and so on, et cetera', seems to have acquired an even more informal variant in British English — *and that*:

? My mother kept complaining how I was slacking and going to seed and that, and how I never tidied my room or helped with the washing-up and that.

When used in informal settings, it cannot very well be criticised for its informality. But it can, once again, be criticised for overuse — it tends to become a distracting tic. If you use it at all, use it sparingly.

and/or This complex conjunction is used in legal, business, and technical contexts, and in informal messages, to set forth in a concise way three distinct and exclusive possibilities: of the two elements linked by *and/or,* the first may be applicable, or the second, or both.

Its usefulness is clear in an expression such as *a crime punishable by a fine and/or imprisonment*: it is so much more succinct than *a crime punishable by a fine, or by imprisonment, or by both (a fine and imprisonment)*.

Outside these official or scientific or informal contexts, however, *and/or* attracts criticism as an ugly or lazy short-cut. It is best avoided in other texts, and in speech it is best avoided altogether: it is safer and more elegant to spell out all three options clearly.

?? This, and other irrelevant cuteness concerning Garp's relationship to Jenny, made Garp very angry that his book couldn't be read and discussed for its own faults and/or merits, but John Wolf explained to him the hard fact that most readers were probably more interested in who he was than in what he'd actually written.

– John Irving (U.S.),
The World According to Garp

Worst of all is to use *and/or* unthinkingly when *and* alone or *or* alone would be enough: ✗ *This paint is resilient indoors and/or outdoors.*

and which, but which An old rule of grammar outlaws such phrases as *and which*, *but which*, *and who*, *but where*, and so on, unless certain conditions are met.

The conditions, of varying importance, are these:
    a. The relative pronouns (*which, where, who,* and so on) should already have appeared in a previous clause:

? The several stars he discovered, of enormous size but which emitted no light, have since been classified as black holes.

Although not strictly illogical, a sentence such as this is awkward to the point of unacceptability. The two descriptive elements joined by *but* should be similar in structure — either both phrases or both clauses:

The several stars he discovered, of enormous size but emitting no light ...

or:

The several stars he discovered, which were of enormous size but (which) emitted no light ...

Note that the second *which* is optional here: the first is compulsory.
    The following description is also in breach of the rule:

? ... a distant cousin called Thomas Knight,
a landowner with property both in Kent and
Hampshire and who lives in a big mansion,
Godmersham Park near Canterbury.
  – Lord David Cecil,
  A Portrait of Jane Austen

To bring the two elements into line, the writer
might have inserted a *who was* before the words
a landowner, or else changed *and who lived* to
and living.

In the absence of a prior relative pronoun, then,
it is not strictly permissible to use *that* relative pronoun after the conjunction: *? The man she
cheated, and whom she has been avoiding all
week, has tracked her down at last.* It is far better to include the *whom* in the first clause as well:
*The man whom she cheated, and whom she has
been avoiding* ...

The same holds true for *that* as conjunction:
*? She said she owed him money, and that she was
avoiding him.* The *that* should preferably be used
to introduce the first clause as well: *She said that
she owed him money, and (that she) was avoiding
him.* Note that the second *that* can be omitted (or
both *that*'s can be omitted), but if the second *that*
is used, the first *that* should be retained. Other
words can be omitted too, of course. There are
often several acceptable variations of a single
sentence:

> She said that she liked him and that she
> admired him.
> She said that she liked (him) and admired
> him.
> She said she liked and admired him.

But preferably not:

> ? She said she liked him and that she admired
> him.

And certainly not:

> × She said she liked and that she admired him.

b. Ideally, the two relative pronouns should be
identical, as in the first of the examples below.
The examples following it are increasingly
awkward and dubious, in proportion to the
increasing dissimilarity of the relative pronouns:

> The man whom she cheated, and whom she
> has been avoiding ...
> The man to whom she owes the money, and
> whom she has been avoiding ...
> The man who cheated her, and whom she has
> been avoiding ...
> ? The town where I grew up, and that we are
> going to visit tomorrow ...

The way of avoiding the slight imbalance in the
late examples here is simply to leave out the
and: *The man who cheated her, whom she has
been avoiding* ...

c. The two relative pronouns must relate to the
same antecedent noun or noun phrase. If two different antecedents are involved, the conjunction
is not permissible: × *These are the people that
brought the gifts and that we wanted to unwrap
at once.* The *and* should be omitted here.

d. The two clauses should either both be restrictive clauses or both be nonrestrictive clauses (for
details of the difference, see RESTRICTIVE AND
NONRESTRICTIVE CLAUSES).

> The coypu that you've just seen and that you
> thought was dead is now racing around in
> its cage. (Both defining clauses.)

> The coypu, which is a large rodent and which
> is valued for its fur, was introduced into Bri-
> tain from South America. (Both nonrestric-
> tive clauses.)

However, if one clause is restrictive and the
other nonrestrictive, they should not be linked by
a conjunction:

> ? The views which I hold, and which I arrived
> at only after much study, are obviously in
> conflict with yours.

Here the *and* should be omitted. (The first *which*
could be omitted too, or changed to *that*.)

> The views (which/that) I hold, which I
> arrived at only after much study, are obvi-
> ously in conflict with yours.

e. Finally, if the second of two relative pronouns
is omitted but the first is retained, the retained
pronoun should have the same grammatical case
and function in both relative clauses. It is all right
to say *the gifts that arrived and pleased everybody*
(where *that* is the subject of the verbs *arrived* and
pleased), but it would be very awkward to say
?? the gifts that arrived and we wanted to unwrap
(where *that* is the subject of *arrived* but the object
of *unwrap*). In the second example both relative
pronouns should be kept: *the gifts that arrived
and that we wanted to unwrap.*

ante-, anti- *Ante-* means 'in front of': *anteroom*;
or 'earlier than': *antenatal*. It is a Latin prefix.
Anti-, a Greek prefix and a much commoner form
in English, means 'against': *antiabortion, anti-
freeze*; or 'opposite to': *anticlockwise, antihero*.
Anti is also used as a freestanding word meaning
'opposed to', as in this example:

I'm not anti-American; I'm not anti the present state of affairs.

– Professor Christopher Ricks,
'The Frank Delaney Programme',
BBC 2

Words formed with *ante-* are virtually never hyphenated. Words with *anti-* tend to be hyphenated only if the second element begins with a capital (*anti-British*), or if it begins with *i* (*anti-intellectual*), or where lack of a hyphen would bring too many vowels together (*anti-aesthetic*).

Note that American English prefers *prenatal clinic* to *antenatal clinic*, and uses *counterclockwise* rather than *anticlockwise*.

American pronunciation often distinguishes the two prefixes: *anti-*, /**an**tī/, and *ante-*, /**an**ti/. In British English, they are both usually pronounced /**an**ti/.

anticipate The verb *to anticipate* still attracts criticism from purists when used as a (rather pompous) synonym of *to expect*: *?Everyone is anticipating a change of government before July.*

In its various older senses, *to anticipate* would convey the idea not just of expecting or foreseeing, but also of preventive — or premature — action:

We anticipated that the enemy would attack at dawn, and made preparations to rebuff them.
For once, Korchnoi anticipated Karpov's every move, and had forced his resignation within an hour.
She was about to protest, but I anticipated her, and explained my reasons.
In the identity-crises and occasional moral anarchy of his later works, Dickens anticipated the modernist movement.
They were foolish enough to anticipate the outcome of the election, and printed headlines announcing that Dewey had won.

The first and second of these examples are still quite current; the third is rather formal perhaps; the fourth is slightly old-fashioned, and the last is perhaps so old-fashioned that it could be misunderstood.

To the dismay of the purists, this rich variety of established uses has been overshadowed by the newer and weaker sense of simple forecast or expectation. Most dictionaries now accept this modern sense as fully standard, with only a few purists fighting a rearguard action. The language has been slightly impoverished, but there is nothing that can be done about it: the old clear distinction between *to expect* and *to anticipate* has been eroded, and a new ambiguity has arisen.

As it happens, popular idiom may still, without realising it, use *to anticipate* and *to expect* in different ways — ways that do reflect the purists' distinction between the two words. Consider these two sentences:

I expect that there will be problems within the next ten minutes.
I expect that he will be here within the next ten minutes.

If you were to replace *expect* with *anticipate* in the first example, the result would sound all right:

I anticipate that there will be problems within the next ten minutes.

But if you replace *expect* with *anticipate* in the second of the examples, the result sounds inflated and pompous, if not downright odd:

?I anticipate that he will be here within the next ten minutes.

Perhaps the reason for this difference is that *anticipate* is, even now, more at home introducing something that requires action (such as *a problem*) than something that seems not to (such as *his arrival*).

Note further, that in some constructions, *to expect* cannot be replaced by *to anticipate* at all: *She expects me to pay for the damage*; *He expects to see us soon*; *The peace talks are expected to take place in Oman,* and so on.

In principle, whatever distinction is made between the verbs *to anticipate* and *to expect* should apply similarly to the nouns *anticipation* and *expectation*. So there should be an objection to such phrases as:

?We arrived in anticipation of a pleasant evening.

In fact, purists seem not to discuss these noun forms, but we may *expect* that their judgment of the example above would be negative, and *anticipate* that judgment by appropriate evasive action — using the noun *expectation* instead.

See also EXPECT.

anxious *Anxious* primarily means 'worried': *I am anxious about the results of my exam.* Many careful speakers dislike the modern use of it to mean 'eager or desirous': *I am anxious to hear the results of my exam*; *The critics seem anxious to praise this new Australian film.* The first of these examples seems fair enough: *anxious* here adds overtones of nervousness that are absent from *eager*. In the second example, however, *eager* seems more appropriate.

Either way the usage is now fully established. So too is the revived sense of 'worrying': *This is an anxious time for her.* In very formal contexts, however, where purists might take you to task, it is perhaps best to avoid these contentious uses. The words *eager* and *worrying* are more than adequate substitutes.

any *Any* can be used with either a singular or a plural verb: *Is any of these books suitable?* (implying 'any one') or *Are any of these books available?* (implying 'some').

There are several uses of *any* that are very dubious. It occurs, for example, in place of *every* or *all* in such phrases as ? *the finest man of any*; ? *the best master of colour of any painter ever*.

> ? We boast that we belong to the nineteenth century and are making the most rapid strides of any nation.
> – Henry David Thoreau (U.S.),
> *Walden* (1854)

Although a fairly well-established idiom, this remains an illogical usage. The clash can be averted by changing the superlative to a comparative, or by changing the *any* to *all*: *making more rapid strides than any other nation; making the most rapid strides of all nations.*

Any sometimes mistakenly appears in place of *any other* in such phrases as × *a finer painting than any he had attempted.*

Any also appears, especially in American English, as an informal form of *in any way* or *at all* in questions or negative statements: ? *Your suggestion does not advance the debate any*; ? *Would it help any if I gave you a lift?*

Some is the positive counterpart of *any* here and elsewhere, and is equally inappropriate in formal usage: ? *Your suggestion helps some*; ? *It would help some if you gave me a lift.*

See also EVERYBODY.

anyone, any one As one word, *anyone* is the pronoun meaning 'anybody': it can be used only of people. As two words, *any one* can be used of either people or things, in such sentences as *They come in several different colours — we can supply any one you like*; *He's not much good, but he's better than any one of you* (or more probably, *better than any of you*).

Similarly *everyone* ('everybody' considered as a group) and *every one* (considered individually): *I'll fight and beat every one of you*; *But there were nine apples here — you can't have eaten every one.* With

minor adjustments, the same is true of *someone* and *some one* as well.

However, *no one* is the preferred form both in the sense of 'nobody' and in such sentences as *There is no one computer that I can recommend above all others.* Some publishers prefer the spelling *no-one* for the word in the sense of 'nobody', and even *noone* appears occasionally. But the most favoured form is still the two separate words *no one.*

See also EVERYBODY.

apostrophe 1. The apostrophe is used to indicate possession and other kinds of relationship: *Mary's book, the court's decision, the drivers' canteen, for pity's sake.* For the rules governing the use of the apostrophe here, see -'S, -S'. See also -ING FORMS OF VERBS 1.

2. The apostrophe is used to form contractions involving certain verbs: *isn't, I'm, where's.* Such contractions tend to fuse the words (*I'm = I am*) into one. They are very common in speech, and much informal writing. For very formal writing they are usually not considered appropriate. See CONTRACTIONS OF VERBS for a fuller discussion.

3. The apostrophe is also found in the contracted ('clipped') forms of some single words.

a. Some of these survive chiefly in older poetry: they are useful for the purposes of metre, having one syllable less than the corresponding full forms. The commonest of these literary contractions are *e'en* ('even'), *e'er* ('ever'), and *o'er* ('over'). Note that the letter omitted in all three cases is *v*. Note too that these contractions are literary, and so rather formal, whereas the contractions involving verbs, mentioned in 2. above, are somewhat informal.

b. Similarly, the word *of* is sometimes contracted to *o'*, especially in certain set phrases: *Jack-o'-lantern, will-o'-the-wisp.* The most common of these is *o'clock.*

c. English has a number of contracted words that are in current use, and are marked as contractions by the presence of the apostrophe: *ass'n* (used in writing to represent 'association'), *'cos* ('because'), *ma'am, fo'c's'le,* and so on. The modern tendency is to drop the apostrophes today if possible: *phone, plane, flu,* and even *assn* and *cos* are commonly spelt without an apostrophe nowadays. Many contractions never had one in the first place: *pub,* for example ('public house'). (See ABBREVIATIONS 6.b.)

Note that the contraction of a single word is sometimes called *elision.* The loss of a letter, if at the end of a word, is called *apocope* (*goin'* for *going*); if at the beginning, *aphesis* ('*ware* for *beware*); and if in the middle, *syncope* (*e'en* for *even*).

4. The apostrophe can be used to indicate the omission of part of a number: *songs from the '20s; the '14-'18 war*. The modern tendency would again be to omit the apostrophes here.

5. The form *O'* is found in many surnames typically of Celtic origin: *O'Connor, O'Reilly, O'Herlihy*. The *O* is derived from the Irish *ō*, 'a grandson or descendant'; the apostrophe is inserted to link this element to the rest of the name. It is not always present, however. The two elements might occasionally be fused — *Oherlihy* — or left quite open: *O Herlihy*.

The form *M'* is occasionally found in Celtic surnames too: *M'Quillan*. Here the apostrophe marks a contraction, of *Mac-* or *Mc-*. The Gaelic *Mac-* means 'son of'.

6. The apostrophe is used to indicate certain plural forms.

a. An apostrophe is often used to indicate the plural of a word referred to as a word, without regard to its meaning:

There are three *but*'s in the sentence.

Note that the word itself is in italics, but the *'s* is in roman in the example above. This change of typeface is itself an indication of the sense intended, so the apostrophe is sometimes omitted even here. Note also that the regularly formed plural is used if a meaning is attached to the word:

The ayes have it.
There are eight threes in twenty-four.

b. The apostrophe is often used to form the plurals of letters, numerals, and symbols:

Mind your p's and q's.
There are three 5's in 555.
He had £'s painted on his cheeks.

The apostrophe is particularly useful when it helps to avoid confusion between pluralised letters and words of similar appearance: *a*'s, *as*.

c. The apostrophe is also sometimes used to form the plurals of abbreviations and of expressions that use numerals: *three OK's*; *several MP's*; *the 1920's*. However, the apostrophe is often omitted in these cases, and with reason: a plural can so easily be confused with a possessive. Consider, as an extreme case, the headline *1980's Hit*. Does this refer to an attack on the decade 1980-1990, or to a successful pop record, say, of the year 1980? Furthermore, if you use an apostrophe to form the plural, you will end up with two apostrophes when forming the

possessive plural — *? the MP's' votes* — a very ungainly formation. It is best, then, to pluralise without an apostrophe where possible: *three OKs*; *several MPs*; *the 1920s*.

See PLURALS; -'S, -S'.

d. Note the common tendency, as in greengrocers' displays, to use the apostrophe when pluralising an ordinary noun: × *Potato's 11p* or × *Potatoe's 11p*. This is quite wrong.

7. Another frequent misuse of the apostrophe is its needless insertion in the possessive adjectives or possessive pronouns *hers, theirs, ours*, and *its*: × *Is this report their's or our's?*

× Mr Sainsbury, who was a close friend of her's some years before, was deeply moved by her death.

    — Pearce Wright, *The Times*

There is a formation *it's*, but this is a contraction of *it is* or *it has*: *It's two o'clock; It's been fun*. But the possessive of *it* is simply *its*: *The dog wants its dinner*. The two forms (and three functions) are illustrated together in this example: *Poor dog — it's yelping because it's lost its bone*. See ITS, IT'S.

8. Finally, the apostrophe is used in forming other inflections or abbreviations, as when an abbreviation functions as a verb:

She OK'd the proposal.
He KO'd his opponent.
They OD'd on heroin.

The most typical case seems to be with the *'d* ending of the past tense and past participle.

appendix The plural of *appendix* is usually *appendices*, /ə-**pen**di-seez/, when referring to books or documents, *appendixes* when referring to the anatomical part.

appraise, apprise Take care not to confuse these two verbs. *To appraise* means 'to evaluate, estimate the worth of': *The surveyor appraised the property*; *She appraised our contribution with a sceptical eye*.

In the corridor she had passed compartments full of young men playing cards, who looked up and appraised her face and figure with impersonal interest.

    — Michael Frayn,
    Towards The End of the Morning

The word goes back to the Late Latin *appretiare*, 'to set a value on', from the Latin noun *pretium,* 'a price' (the source too of *praise*).

The usual noun from *appraise* used to be

appraisement, meaning 'putting a value on'. *Appraisal* used to be a rather formal or literary usage in British English, but American influence has now made it the general form.

> Vague references to Western norms and liberal values are no substitute for concrete appraisal of the structural changes now under way and a just assessment of what Unesco's programmes have achieved in many different spheres.
> – Professor Malcolm Skilbeck, letter to *The Times*

> It was the response to the urgency of these pressures, and not any appraisal of commercial viability, that triggered the vast increase in lending after 1974.
> – Lord Lever, *Time and Tide*

Appraisal appears especially in political, military, and business uses. In fact, *appraisal*, and the flourishing word *reappraisal*, have become overused and clichéd. A *reappraisal* is often simply 'a second look'.

To apprise means 'to inform, make aware, cause to know'. It is usually used in the passive and almost always followed by *of* — *They were apprised of the history of the case* — but it can just be used without the *of*: *They were apprised that the case was now closed*. *Apprise* comes from the French *apprendre*, now meaning 'to learn' but formerly 'to teach', in turn derived from the Latin *appre(he)ndere*, 'to seize'. Never write or say × *appraised of* for *apprised of*. Remember the distinction: *The directors were apprised of the plan to appraise the company's assets.*

× He told the engineer that he had removed the reports from the mailbag because he thought that Herr Direktor should, as a matter of courtesy, be appraised of their contents before they were posted.
– Thomas Keneally, *Schindler's Ark*

appreciate This word has a strong connection with the idea of value. It derives from the Late Latin verb *appretiare*, 'to put a value on', from *ad-*, 'to' + *pretiare*, 'to value', from *pretium*, 'a price'. *To appreciate* a wine is to recognise its value and enjoy it in a discerning way. An *appreciation* of a writer is an assessment or evaluation of his works. If a house *appreciates*, it rises in value or price. And so on.

A well-established extended sense of *to appreciate* is 'to be grateful for': *I should appreciate a prompt reply*. Some careful users of English dislike the word in this role, regarding it as a bit pompous, and preferring the unpretentious *to be grateful for* as in *I should be grateful for a very prompt reply*.

A sense of *appreciate* still further removed from the idea of value is 'to realise or understand'. Many purists object more strongly to this sense. Typically it occurs when conveying a warning:

? You will appreciate the need for speed.
? He had better appreciate that the deadline is final.

It is a favourite term in business jargon:

? It is appreciated that the original delay was unavoidable, and we shall not activate the penalty clause.

It is also often used as a kind of preface to bad news — a linguistic bomb-alert, as it were:

? We appreciate that you have worked hard for us — nevertheless we cannot renew your contract.

The simple verbs *to realise* and *to understand* are usually available in such contexts, should you wish to heed the purists' protests. Curiously, the criticism of *appreciate* in these senses is perhaps slightly less telling when the word is used in negative sentences, questions, or subordinate clauses:

> You fail to appreciate the need for speed.
> Does he appreciate that the deadline is final?
> If you appreciated the need for speed, you would work faster.

And even in positive statements, *to appreciate* in the sense of 'to realise' can now be considered acceptable if it clearly suggests a subtle or sensitive perception. The following extract, for instance, seems unobjectionable:

> He appreciated that new forces were bursting the crust of the old social and political order.
> – Philip Magnus, *Edward VII*

The danger lies not so much in its use as in its overuse. And if there is nothing fine or sensitive about the judgment, then *to appreciate* is best left alone: use a straightforward verb such as *to understand*, *to recognise*, or *to conclude* instead.

apprise See APPRAISE.

apt See LIKELY, APT, LIABLE, PRONE.

Arab, Arabian, Arabic *Arab,* as both adjective and noun, applies to the Semitic people originally from the Arabian Peninsula in southwest Asia, who now inhabit large areas of the Middle East and North Africa: *Arab nations*; *the history of the Arabs*.

Arabian means primarily 'of or relating to Arabia'. It is mostly used in reference to geography or culture: *Arabian customs*; *Arabian settlements*. In its broader sense — 'of or relating to the Arabs' — it is now poetic or old-fashioned: *Arabian hospitality*; *Arabian mystique*.

The word *Araby* is an even more archaic term: it was formerly used as a poetic and romantic variant of *Arabia*.

Arabic as a noun refers to the language spoken by the Arabs, and as an adjective is used to describe this language, whether written or spoken: for instance, *Arabic script* (which contrasts with the Roman alphabet we use) or *Arabic numerals* (the figures *0* to *9,* as distinct from the Roman numerals we only rarely use). These numerals were in fact invented in India, and are known to the Arabs as 'Indian numerals'. (Moreover, they are written rather differently in Arab countries from the way that they are written in the West.) And *gum arabic,* by the way, is actually a gum exuded by the acacia trees of Africa.

As an adjective, *Arab* is increasingly being used to cover many of the meanings of *Arabian* and *Arabic*. This is quite understandable, since the language and all things Arabian are also 'of the Arabs'.

Two extended senses, finally: an *Arab* horse, or simply an *Arab* (sometimes, though rarely, an *Arabian* horse), is a horse of a swift, graceful breed originating in Arabia. All thoroughbred racehorses are descended from Arab stallions. And a *street Arab* or *city Arab* or simply *Arab* or *arab* used to refer to a homeless urchin or other vagrant. The terms were in wide use in 19th-century England (Sherlock Holmes used *street arabs* as his 'irregulars' — spies and informers, in effect) but are no longer current. The terms no doubt arose from the image of the Arab as a nomad.

archaeology, archeology The study of the material remains of past ages can be spelt either *archaeology* or *archeology*. *Archaeology* is the commoner spelling, though in American English *archeology* now rivals it. What is rarely found nowadays is the æ fused as a digraph.

The word is originally Greek; *arkhaiologia*, 'the study of antiquity'. The æ appeared in the Late Latin form, *archæologia*.

archaisms *Archaisms* in a language are words or expressions that sound to a greater or lesser degree old-fashioned. Some, such as *lest, hence, mirth,*

weep, whilst, or *amid*(*st*) are merely a little formal or bookish; others, such as *peradventure, trow,* or *varlet* are quite outside the scope of an everyday working vocabulary.

People naturally differ in their views on what is or is not archaic. The two lists here therefore do not pretend to be definitive — and they do not pretend to be exhaustive either. The first list is of words that almost always sound silly. Even when used for humorous effect, they tend to produce an irritatingly pompous 'Merrie England' atmosphere, as the quoted examples should demonstrate.

The words in the second list, by contrast, are quite often used by good writers, sometimes with a slightly ironic effect.

unusable archaisms

alas	peradventure
amain	perchance
anon	quaff
aright	quoth
belike	right glad
betwixt	sans
bosky	suffer (= to allow)
bounden duty	surcease
chide	thou (except in prayers)
choler	'tis
drear	trow
ere	'twas
goodly	varlet
methinks	ween
nay	wench
ne'er	whilom
o'er	yon
oft	yonder
ope	of yore

Here are examples of *nay* and *whilom* in actual use:

The New World Information Order exists, nay it flourishes, even if its worst aspects, such as compulsory identity cards for foreign journalists, have been forestalled for the time being.
— leading article, *Daily Telegraph*

Esther's whilom graduates Paul Heiney and Chris Searle have meanwhile returned with a fresh series of the always engaging *In at the Deep End*, now furnished with a David Hockney-ish titles sequence.
— Philip Purser, *Sunday Telegraph*

For some at least, it is difficult to read such passages with a straight face.

The following archaisms, by contrast, are not

really outrageous, and can reasonably be used now and then:

usable archaisms

afar	howbeit
albeit	lest
amid(st)	nary
bar (= except)	parlous
be he ...	save (= except)
behest	thence
behove	unbeknownst
beset	well-nigh
to boot	whence
brethren	whilst
erstwhile	whit
hence	whither
hither and thither	wonted

Here are examples, from five competent journalists, of current uses of *lest*, *albeit*, *to boot*, *whilst*, and *nary*:

This will inevitably increase the already strong pressures from Liberal activists to break up the Alliance lest the SDP end by swallowing them.
　　　　　　　　– Ian Waller, *Sunday Telegraph*

To their astonishment, in 11 weeks they have done 'incredibly well'. Albeit accidentally, they think they have discovered a basic truth about people who go into second-hand bookshops.
　　　　　　　　– Michael Davie, *The Observer*

In a way, of course, their Englishness makes the meeting even more distressing. For not only are they the foreign enemy but also, in our eyes, not far off traitors to boot.
　　　　　　　　– Peregrine Worsthorne, *Sunday Telegraph*

It concerned William Barnes, about whom — until last week — I knew only two facts. The first is that his statue stands in Dorchester High Street, whilst Thomas Hardy is up the hill and round the corner. The second is that an essay about him appears in Two Cheers for Democracy.
　　　　　　　　– Roy Hattersley, *The Listener*

Make Abu Dhabi your souk visit, for if you go on to Sharjah you will find a modern shopping mall calling itself a souk, with nary a craftsman, only a salesman in view.
　　　　　　　　– Serena Sinclair, *Daily Telegraph*

aren't I?　See AIN'T.

arise　See RISE.

around, round　**1.** In most cases, American usage favours *around,* whereas British usage now favours *round.* It seems to be the more usual idiom, in British English, to say *looked round in vain*; *spinning round and round*; *the Earth's motion round the Sun*; *just round the corner.*

Striding to the door, she flung it open and waved imperiously for Mesterbein to return. She swung round, hands on hips, and stared at Charlie, and her big pale eyes were a dangerous and alarming void.
　　　　　　　　– John le Carré,
　　　　　　　　The Little Drummer Girl

But professional soccer depends on spectators. Spectators don't flock round losing teams. So teams must win.
　　　　　　　　– Katharine Whitehorn, *The Observer*

Americans would tend to use *around* in each case. In most such phrases, the word *about* can also be used, though it is less favoured in both British and American English. But *about* cannot be used when *round* is repeated for emphasis: *The wheel spun round and round.*

In certain contexts, British usage might opt for *around* as well: *famous for miles around*; *He does get around*; *seated around the table.* Sometimes the rhythm seems to demand *around* in preference to *round*: *a ring around the moon*; *Around the world I've searched for you.* In general, it is safe to use the form which best suits your ear.

2. In the sense of 'roughly, approximately', *around* is standard American usage as well as *about*: *around 20 guests. Around* is used increasingly in this way in British English too, but the traditional *about* is still preferred: *about 20 guests.* This preference remains strongest in expressions referring to points of time: *at about half-past five.*

In certain other expressions too, British usage favours *about* slightly, where American English has *around*; *wandering about/around aimlessly*; *sitting about/around doing nothing*; *left his toys lying about/around.*

3. *Around* has recently begun encroaching on the territory of other prepositions, especially in political discussions. People *?argue around* issues, *?hold debates around* problems, *?base policies around* theories, and so on. Perhaps the vagueness of *around* (as contrasted with *on* or *over*) is what appeals to speakers and writers: using *around* is conveniently non-committal. But careful users of English will still opt for the more precise preposition.

See also CENTRE AROUND.

arouse See RISE.

artist, artiste It is a mistake to regard *artiste* as the feminine form of *artist*. *Artiste* was borrowed separately from French, and is used in a quite distinct way — of professional entertainers, especially singers and dancers, of either sex. And even then, the word now seems to be out of fashion, perhaps because considered rather affected.

Artist is the term to use of someone whose work (whether in the traditional arts, or entertainment, or trades, or the like) reaches the level of fine art: *That plumber is an artist — his work is so beautifully done.* A singing or dancing *artiste* could claim to be an *artist* only if the standard of his or her work is especially high.

Obversely, if a serious *artist* — a sculptor, a violinist, or a ballet dancer, say — were referred to as an *artiste*, he or she would be entitled to feel insulted.

as **1.** What form should pronouns take after *as* — subject or object? Do we say *as I* or *as me,* for example? It depends on the context. Since there is almost always a missing verb (such that *as* may be considered a conjunction), the rule is this: just add the missing verb (and any other missing words) mentally to the sentence, and that will decide the case of the pronoun for you. So:

The teacher scolded her as severely as me =
The teacher scolded her as severely as (he scolded) me.
The teacher scolded her as severely as I =
The teacher scolded her as severely as I (scolded her).

The two sentences clearly mean different things, and highlight the importance of using the correct form of the pronoun. If only this rule were consistently followed, there would be no ambiguity in such sentences. Unfortunately, careless users of English are likely to say *The teacher scolded her as severely as me* when what they really mean is *The teacher scolded her as severely as I (did).* To make quite sure of being correctly understood, it is perhaps advisable to add the missing verb not just mentally but explicitly. If your listener is going to be in any doubt about the meaning of *The teacher scolded her as severely as me,* then you are doing a favour to both him and yourself by filling your sentence out to *The teacher scolded her as severely as he scolded me.*

The danger of ambiguity is even greater when the final pronoun is *you* (which remains unchanged in form whether it is the subject or the object) or when the final word is a noun rather than a pronoun. The following two sentences are hopelessly ambiguous as they stand:

?I dislike her as much as you.
?I dislike her as much as Mary.

Of course, a fuller context might distinguish the correct sense from the incorrect one. And in speech, tone of voice would probably indicate the required sense. But to be on the safe side, you could add the missing word or words explicitly to the sentence, and in that way leave no doubt which sense you intend: *I dislike her as much as you do/I dislike her as much as I dislike you.*

Note these examples:

She is just as strong a chess player as he.
I could never beat as strong a chess player as he.
No portrait could do justice to so pretty a child as he.

It has to be said, however, that many millions of people in this country who are not archbishops are in exactly the same position as he.

— Bernard Levin, *The Times*

The temptation here is to use *as him* rather than *as he* at the end of each sentence, and in informal usage it almost always would be *as him.* But the *as* here is a conjunction in each case, not a preposition: a missing verb can be supplied in each sentence — namely the verb *is.* It would go at the end of each sentence. So strictly speaking, *as he* is the correct form, and should be retained in formal speech and writing.

Not that *as him* is always wrong. *As* can be a preposition — when its meaning is 'in the capacity of, or in the role of' — and is then followed by a pronoun or pronouns in the object form: *I identified the suspect as him; Why are you disguised as him?* (See also SUCH 2.)

2. *As* is often slipped into a sentence in a thoughtless way, and has come to be used in many quite unnecessary combinations. In the two fashionable prepositional phrases *as from* and *as of,* for example, the *as* is usually quite superfluous:

?As from today, there will be no morning tea-breaks.

?The new regulations are effective as of tomorrow.

In both sentences, the simple preposition *from* is all that you need.

The one case where *as from* is justifiable is when

the phrase concerns rules, agreements, or the like that are implemented retrospectively: *The new bonus awards will be calculated as from last November.* This can be understood to mean *as (if they had dated) from last November.*

See also AS TO; AS YET; and EQUALLY AS.

And after such verbs as *to name, to elect, to pronounce,* and *to nominate, as* is often superfluously inserted: ✗ *She was elected as president at last.* The correct wording is simply *was elected president.* Similarly, the verb *to consider:* ✗ *Andrew was considered as unsuitable for the position.* The correct form is *was considered unsuitable:* perhaps the intrusive *as* is due to the model of *was regarded as unsuitable.*

3. A traditional rule states that the negative form of *A is as good as B* is *A is not so good as B* — the first *as* changing to a *so* when prefaced by *not.* Although still perfectly acceptable, and often more elegant, this use of *so* is by no means compulsory today. It is just as acceptable to say *A is not as good as B.*

In positive clauses, *so* cannot usually be used in the pattern ✗ *A is so good as B.* But where *B* is an infinitive phrase beginning with *to,* then *so* is often used: *Please be so good as to give this to the editor.* And where the adjective in question is used figuratively in idioms such as *as far as* or *as long as,* then *so* is usually an acceptable substitute for the first *as: It's all in order as/so far as I can tell.*

So long as men can breathe or eyes can see,
So long lives this, and this gives life to thee.
— Shakespeare, Sonnet 18

In the following three quotations, one writer uses *so,* one uses *as,* and one uses both. All are fully acceptable:

I am suggesting that international law is immature and defective in this important area of relations between nations. Perhaps that is inevitable so long as Russia and a few countries which follow her instructions are ready to deal in subversion and takeover.
— Lord Home, *The Times*

The resuscitated programme was pretty routinely awful, and no surprise. Long-running shows are always mired in the time when they began; though as long as they sustain uninterrupted life their old-fashionedness is barely visible.
— Julian Barnes, *The Observer*

Does language really exist in the singular, like music, or are there only languages which must remain permanently foreign to each other, as long as they survive at all? Modern linguists are much concerned with this problem, but so far as I know, they are still a long way from solving it.
— Professor John Weightman, 'Words', BBC Radio 3

4. Among its various uses, *as* can be a conjunction meaning 'because'. It is not very elegant perhaps, and it is often considered nonstandard in American English, but it is acceptable and fairly widespread in British usage. Take care to avoid ambiguity, however. If *as* (or *since*) could be understood in a different sense, it is best to drop it in favour of *because:* ? *I pulled the alarm switch, as I was told to;* ? *Mother took the call, as Father was getting into the bath.* In each case the comma probably just saves the sentence from being misinterpreted as *in the way that I was told to* and *just when Father was getting into the bath* — but it would be safer to use *because* or *since* instead of *as* (see BECAUSE).

5. *As,* not *that,* is the appropriate relative pronoun after *such* and *same: the same donkey as you rode last week; noted such incidents as deserved to be reported.* The substitution of *that* for *as* here is a common error, both in American English and increasingly in British English.

Conversely, *as* is sometimes mistakenly used as the relative pronoun in place of *that* (or *who* or *which*), especially among children, or in dialect: ✗ *I'm going to kill the man as stole my horse.* Similarly, *as* (or *as how*) should not replace *that* as a conjunction: ✗ *She forgot as I was following her;* ✗ *But you've just told me as how paper was originally made from cloth.*

6. *As,* like *though,* can be used in such constructions as:

Nice as/though it was, I don't want to go there again. (= Though it was nice, I don't want to go there again.)

In American English, *as ... as* is also possible here:

? As nice as it was, I don't want to go there again.

But this *as ... as* is seldom used in such constructions in British English, and would be considered an Americanism.

See also AS GOOD OR BETTER THAN; LIKE 1; MISRELATED CONSTRUCTIONS 2.

as far as ... is concerned The construction *as far as X is concerned* or *so far as X is concerned* (or *are concerned*) is cumbersome, especially when there is a long noun phrase in the middle. It should be used sparingly, and avoided where a single preposition, such as *for*, would serve just as well: *? The budget contains some unwelcome surprises as far as the self-employed are concerned*. It would be far better to say, quite simply, *The budget contains some unwelcome surprises for the self-employed*.

None the less, the construction is very useful in its proper place:

> The second oil shock had a still more devastating effect upon both Western and Third World economies. ... As a result we have been back, so far as wasted output and wasted lives are concerned, ... in the conditions of the Thirties.
> — Roy Jenkins, *The Observer*

Since the phrase is awkward and inelegant sometimes, there is an increasing tendency just to leave out the second half altogether. This is not acceptable:

> ✕ As far as any investigation of members of Congress, however, I am not familiar with that at all.
> — Jimmy Carter (U.S.), quoted in *The New York Times*

> ? The Supreme Court ... has the final say on a range of things at issue, as far as human behaviour itself. It has ruled on capital punishment, religious authority, racial discrimination.
> — Alistair Cooke, 'Letter from America', BBC Radio 4

(The second example here is ambiguous. Perhaps *as far as* was intended to mean 'extending as far as' rather than 'as far as ... is concerned'.)

It might be argued that *as far as* should be regarded as a complex preposition in its own right now, equivalent to *as for* or *with regard to*. But if a short prepositional phrase is wanted, why not use an established complex preposition such as *as for* or *with regard to* in the first place?

One ingenious way of reducing the ungainliness of the larger construction is demonstrated in the following quotation:

> Miss World herself comes down to marry Peisthetairos, bringing with her ... good counsels, happy laws, sound common sense, and all the other blessings that were fast disappearing from fifth-century Greece, to say nothing of vegetarianism, at least as far as concerns the flesh of birds.
> — Philip Howard, *New Words for Old*

The advantage of the form *as far as concerns X* is that the phrase remains unseparated, with no intrusive noun or noun phrase splitting it down the middle; the disadvantage, of course, is that it goes against the natural idiom.

If you do decide to use *as far as concerns ...*, remember that it must be singular. Do not say ✕ *as far as concern X, Y, and Z*; say *as far as concerns X, Y, and Z*.

Another variant is the simpler *as/so far as X goes*:

> Those who deny this would argue, if they produced an argument at all, that language merely reflects existing social conditions, and that we cannot influence its development by any direct tinkering with words and constructions. So far as the general tone or spirit of a language goes, this may be true, but it is not true in detail.
> — George Orwell, 'Politics and the English Language'

as follows   This phrase remains unchanged even when there are several items that follow. Do not, out of a mistaken sense of grammatical correctness, say ✕ *The winners are as follow: X, Y, and Z*. The construction *as follows* is impersonal — the phrase should be understood as meaning *as (it) follows* — and the verb is not dependent for its form on the item or items mentioned afterwards (or before).

as for   See AS TO.

as good or better than   Two common forms of comparison are *A is as good as B* (or *as quick as* or *as talented as*) and *A is better than B* (or *quicker than* or *more talented than*). When these two forms are joined, the correct combination is *A is as good as, or better than, B*; or *A is as good as, if not better than, B*. The second *as* cannot be omitted; if it were, the sentence would read, in effect, ✕ *A is as good ... than B*. (See PARALLEL CONSTRUCTIONS.)

Yet this *as* is left out extraordinarily often. Certainly the sentence sounds smoother without it, but that is no justification. (French is lucky in having a single word, *que*, that serves as both *as* and *than*.) Another possible reason for its omission is the analogy of the related construction: *It is as good if not better*. (The comparison is left unstated here, so neither *as* nor *than* is needed.)

Here are a few examples of this common error:

> ✕ Nothing seems to matter more to him than that he should pass these assets on in as good

or better shape than he received them.
– Robert Lacey, *The Listener*

✗ I went to Oxford and talked to young Dr Fulder who ... told me as much if not more than I ever wanted to know about ginseng.
– Sue Arnold, *The Observer*

✗ On 4 December 1877 Dr Price conveyed their views on the specimens to him. It was as bad, or worse, than he had anticipated.
– K.M. Elizabeth Murray,
Caught in the Web of Words

✗ She believes, unlike so many research psychologists, that a person's own observations about him or herself are at least as important, or more important, than what researchers think they detect in their own controlled studies of human behaviour.
– Polly Toynbee, *The Guardian*

✗ A knight in his full armour in those days was generally carrying as much or more than his own weight in metal.
– T.H. White, *The Sword in the Stone*

Here, reassuringly, is an example of the correct construction:

The miners know as well as, or better than, the rest of us that a generation hence there will be a no-less important British coal industry.
– Enoch Powell, *The Times*

An acceptable compromise between the correct form and the smoother but incorrect form is this: *A is as good as B, or better*.

Note that the same careless omission affects other combinations: *similar (to) if not the same as*; *within reach (of) or even level with*, and so on:

✗ He can help Mary to produce Olympic performances which are equal or better than her world championships performances which resulted in two gold medals.
– Christopher Brasher, *The Observer*

as if, as though These two expressions mean much the same, and are both fully acceptable. There is a slight difference in emphasis, however, and one is sometimes more appropriate than the other in a given context.

For example, *as if* is preferable in exclamations, as where an allegation is being dismissed: *Kill his wife! As if he could even raise his voice in anger!* In negative sentences too, *as if* is probably the more idiomatic: *Let him complain — it's not as if he'd been invited here*. When a very far-fetched

comparison is put forward, *as though* is perhaps preferable: *His mouth opened wider, as though he were a python about to swallow a rabbit*.

My heart aches, and a drowsy numbness pains
My sense, as though of hemlock I had drunk.
– John Keats,
'Ode to a Nightingale' (1819)

Note that the verb following may be either in the indicative or in the subjunctive mood, according to the sense intended. (See SUBJUNCTIVE.)

The verb is in the indicative if the assumption is possibly true: *It looks as if she is in love again*. On the other hand, if the assumption is clearly false or purely imaginary, then the verb is in the subjunctive: *She always goes about grinning stupidly, as though she were in love*.

In the following examples, the writers seem to have got things back to front. In the first example, the writer clearly believes that marriage is *not* 'a unified and coherent construct'. He should then have written *as if it were* rather than *as if it was*:

?? Such an idea deserves to be resuscitated. It would, for one thing, prevent us talking about 'marriage' as if it was a unified and coherent construct instead of being a multidimensional phenomenon.
– Professor Anthony Clare,
The Listener

And in the next quotation the opposite mistake is made. Quite possibly snow was coming on, so *as if snow was coming on* would be better than *as if snow were coming on*:

? The light, though late now, was sharp, as if snow were coming on ... behind that freezing iron leaf he watched the slice of cold evening, and pulled his coat across his chest.
– Thomas Keneally, *Schindler's Ark*

as such This is a useful phrase, in its proper place. It can mean 'accordingly' — *a modest man, and as such difficult to draw out* — or 'in the nature of the case' — *A diplomat as such must be diplomatic* — or 'in itself, on its own': *Money as such won't bring happiness*.

But *as such* has also come to be used very widely, especially in British English, in contexts where it is not really suitable. It is often, for example, used to qualify or moderate a blunt expression (thereby applying to a verb, not just to a noun): ? *I didn't fail as such*; ? *I wasn't rejected as such — more told to wait and see*. The more traditional

— and more acceptable — form would be *I didn't exactly fail* or *I wasn't really rejected.* The person who says *I have no objection to the plan as such* probably does object to the plan, in practice if not in theory, and it would be more straightforward to say so: *I have no objection to the plan in theory/in principle, but ...*

Even worse, *as such* sometimes seems quite meaningless in a sentence, its purpose being nothing more, apparently, than to make the sentence sound more impressive: *? I don't believe that history as such is relevant to our discussion.*

as to   *As to* is correctly used in such contexts as *No one would be so silly as to fall into that trap.* Here, the *as* forms part of the pair *so ... as.*

As to is also a complex preposition. As such it can be a useful variant of *as for* or *with regard to,* especially in British English: *As to the supposed health hazards of the drug, opinions are divided.*

> One remained faced by the fact of a man blown to bits for nothing even most remotely resembling an idea, anarchistic or other. As to the outer wall of the Observatory it did not show as much as the faintest crack.
> – Joseph Conrad, Author's Note to
> *The Secret Agent*

When there is a strong contrast with what has gone before, however, *as for* is better: *Many succeeded — (but) as for Max, he failed.*

As a complex preposition *as to* is unfortunately very much overused. It is, for example, redundant when placed in front of relative pronouns such as *whether, who, what,* and *why*: *? The question as to whether the Minister is obliged to declare his financial interests is being hotly debated by constitutional lawyers.* The *as to* serves no purpose here, and should be omitted (or possibly replaced by *of*). Similarly, *as to* could be deleted in these examples:

> ? The programme was also in two minds as to whether to present the verse in costume and *in situ* or simply in modern dress.
> – Geoffrey Nicholson, *The Observer*

> ? In addition, there was the growing doubt as to whether competition, in fact, existed.
> – J.K. Galbraith (Canadian),
> *The Affluent Society*

And it is particularly slipshod to use *as to* directly after a full clause or main verb, as happens fairly often in British English: × *The committee discussed with him as to whether he*

intended to continue in the post. The *as to* must be deleted here.

As to is also used needlessly in place of established single prepositions: *? odd ideas as to his own role*; *? doubts as to that claim*; *? Is there any news as to the whereabouts of the superintendent?* Use *of* or *about* instead. It would be better, for example, to say *Is there any news of/about the whereabouts of the superintendent?*

In the following examples, *as to* should perhaps have been replaced by *about, on,* and *over* (or *at*) respectively:

> ? Fryn herself had no illusions as to the strength or durability of her small but genuine talent as a writer.
> – Hilary Spurling, *The Observer*

> ? The brochures tend ... towards exaggeration. ... You can do a rough check as to how closely the descriptive prose matches reality by comparing the age and appearance of the couples in the photographs with your own.
> – Edward Mace, *The Observer*

> ?? If Shadbold felt resentment as to Winterwade's transient pre-eminence — in the light of subsequent events it is unlikely he did not — he showed no outward sign.
> – Anthony Powell,
> *O, How the Wheel Becomes It!*

Not that *as to* should automatically be shunned after a noun. In the following example, *about* would probably be unidiomatic, and would convey a different sense; *as to* was the correct form to use:

> Despite the mystery surrounding the presence and status of the fallow deer from Khirokitia, it has at least provided a hint as to the origin of early humans on Cyprus.
> – Dr Simon Davis, *New Scientist*

as well as   1. Be careful of your grammar when using this phrase: it is not the equivalent of *and*: × *The pilot, as well as three of the five passengers, have survived the crash.* The correct form of the verb is *has survived,* since the phrase introduced by *as well as* is regarded as additional information rather than as an essential part of the subject. (For just the same reason, it is correct to say: *The pilot, together with three of the five passengers, has survived.*)

2. Purists and old-fashioned grammarians consider *as well as* to be a conjunction rather than a preposition. It should be understood as *and not*

only, rather than as *besides.* Strictly speaking, therefore, the pronouns and verbs following *as well as* should be in the same form — subject or object, *-ed* or *-ing* — as the corresponding noun (or pronoun) or verb preceding it. So:

The pilot, as well as I, survived the crash

— not:

✗ The pilot, as well as me, survived the crash.

And:

The pilot suffered internal injuries, as well as broke a leg (this is rather old-fashioned: a good way out is *as well as a broken leg*)

— rather than:

The pilot suffered internal injuries, as well as breaking a leg.

The final example, however, sounds quite natural today; and it is probably acceptable now to regard *as well as* as a preposition too, not just as a conjunction. Clearly when *as well as* comes at the beginning of a sentence, it almost always takes the *-ing* form of the verb, regardless of the form of the verb in the later clause:

As well as breaking a leg, the pilot suffered internal injuries.

(The purists, however, would argue that *as well as* should not be used at the start of a sentence — nor should its equivalent *and not only.*)

3. Note that *as well as* distinguishes two items of information in a sentence — one the important or new information, the other unimportant background information. This obvious or 'given' information is what follows *as well as* directly; it is the other element in the sentence that contains the important or new information. So:

Michelangelo was a poet as well as a sculptor.
As well as serving fine food, this restaurant will look after your dog while you're eating.

But look at what happens when the elements are reversed. The sentence would then sound quite odd:

?? Michelangelo was a sculptor as well as a poet.

Surely everyone knows that Michelangelo was a sculptor: the important or new information is that he was a poet as well, and this information should *not* appear directly after *as well as.*

4. Since *as well as* can be understood also in a literal sense ('as ably as; in as competent a man-

ner as'), it is worth making sure when using the phrase that no possible ambiguity is lurking in the construction. Note, for example, the two possible senses of the sentence: *? The pilot recovered, as well as the three passengers.* (The comma after *recovered* would usually, it is true, be omitted if *as well as* was really intended to mean *as completely as.*)

as yet This phrase has its uses: *Only a little progress has been made as yet.* (The implication is that things will, or should, change.) However, when the sentence is a question or in the negative, *as yet* should be avoided. A simple *yet* is quite enough:

? Have you made any progress as yet?
? We have not as yet made any progress.
? Hardly any progress has been made as yet.

In each case, *as yet* is an affected and unnecessary substitute for *yet.*

The phrase *as of yet* is even more affected, and should be avoided in affirmative statements as well as in negative statements and questions.

Asian, Asiatic *Asiatic* (attested since 1602), as both noun and adjective, is today considered discourteous or disparaging, and has now been supplanted by the slightly older term *Asian* (attested since 1599): *the Asian nations; Asian flu; the Asians of South Africa; the Asian community of South London.*

Asiatic can still be used however, in *Asiatic cholera* and *Asiatic elephant* (a rare name for the Indian elephant), and is official in the name of the *Royal Asiatic Society.*

In British English, but not American English, the word *Asian* has come to be used frequently to refer to people from the Indian subcontinent or Sri Lanka living elsewhere, or to their descendants. This usage is illustrated in two of the examples listed above: *the Asians of South Africa; the Asian community of South London.* Similarly, *Britain's largest-selling Asian weekly.* In British English such phrases would not normally be taken to refer to people from elsewhere in Asia.

A convention has also developed whereby the Indian subcontinent and Sri Lanka are collectively called *South Asia,* with *South-East Asia* referring to Indo-China, including Thailand, Malaysia, Singapore, and usually Burma. The term *East Asia* is uncommon but might be used for China and Japan.

The pronunciation of *Asian* is /aysh'n/ or /ay<u>zh</u>'n/, the first being slightly preferable in

British English, the second being much the more common in American English. The three-syllable pronunciations ?/**ay**si-ən/ or ?/**ay**zi-ən/ are not really standard, though the corresponding four-syllable pronunciation of *Asiatic* is acceptable.

See also BLACK; INDIAN.

aside, a side   1. Among its various senses as noun and adverb, *aside* means 'on one side, to the side': *She pushed me aside.* It does not mean 'on both sides' — for that sense, use the phrase *a side*: *After all those injuries, the teams are now down to 13 a side.*

If used before a noun, *a side* is likely to be hyphenated in combination with a specified number: *We played five-a-side football today.*

2. The phrase *aside from* is originally American: it is now fairly widespread in British English, but purists still prefer *apart from, except,* or *excluding,* all of which are also used in America.

assignation   *Assignation* — a rather formal word — does not mean exactly the same as *assignment.* It can be a rare and formal alternative to *assignment* in the sense of 'the act of assigning': *the assignation/assignment of the task to his deputy.* However, *assignation* cannot be an alternative to *assignment* in the sense of 'a task assigned' (or 'the post or duty to which one is assigned'): *The assignment was easy to complete,* not × *The assignation was easy to complete.*

The usual sense of *assignation* is 'a rendezvous or meeting', especially one for a romantic or shady purpose:

> It belongs to one war-scarred elderly American who makes the journey almost daily, knows his favourite seat and the first name of the air hostess. For two pins, you think, he will slip her a packet of Lucky Strikes and make an assignation with her behind the commissary.
>
> – John le Carré,
> *The Little Drummer Girl*

Note the pronunciation of *assignation*; unlike in other derivatives of *assign*, the *g* is sounded here: /assig-**nay**sh'n/.

Assignation can also, in Scotland, have the legal sense of *assignment,* referring to the transfer of a claim or property or right, or to the document or deed certifying this transfer, or to the thing transferred.

assume, presume   Each of these verbs has a number of different senses, and few of them cause any trouble. The problem arises with the sense

'to suppose or take for granted', which is common to the two verbs.

The truth is that *to assume* and *to presume,* in the sense of 'to suppose', are almost always used as exact synonyms today. Nevertheless, there are traditionally a few points of difference between them, and it is worth knowing these.

First of all, *to assume* is 'assumed' to be more timid, weaker, more tentative; *to presume* is thought to be more positive, bolder, more confident.

Then, *to assume* tends to refer to completed actions or agreements or conditions, and *to presume* tends to refer to present or future actions or conditions. (There is some slight backing for this in the respective origins of the two words: *presume* goes back to the Latin roots *prae-* + *sumere,* 'to take before, take in advance'; *assume* goes back to *ad* + *sumere,* 'to take to oneself'.) So you are perhaps more likely to say *I assume you were at the meeting* than *I presume you were at the meeting.* However, you are equally likely to say *I presume you agree with me* and *I assume you agree with me,* and also *I presume you will be at the meeting* and *I assume you will be at the meeting.* In these cases, the difference is supposed to be that *assume* implies a past agreement or understanding, whereas *presume* implies a present guess and future surprise if it turns out differently.

This may at first sight appear to contradict the earlier suggestion that *to assume* is more timid and *to presume* more forthright. But if anything it strengthens that notion: if there is a prior understanding, then it is in effect a timid act to ask for confirmation by *assuming*; if on the other hand you are just speculating about the present or future, then it is bold to air that speculation. (This is not to suggest that Stanley was being in the least discourteous when uttering the famous words *Doctor Livingstone, I presume.* As will become clear in a moment, there are other, very polite, overtones in his greeting.)

The third traditional difference is this: when you *assume,* you are putting forward a (previously formulated) theory; when you *presume,* you are stating your opinion or belief. The related adverbs bear this out. The rare adverb *assumedly* means 'as has been already proposed in a hypothesis': *Jack the Ripper assumedly had some medical training: we should then ask 'Where did he receive it?'* The common adverb *presumably,* by contrast, means 'as might reasonably be concluded from the currently available evidence': *If she has a cold, then presumably she won't be singing in the choir tonight.*

While not always quite so delightful as James believed that literary correspondence could be, they are invariably poignant and altogether more revealing than he presumably intended.

— Stephen Koss, *The Observer*

Assume and *presume* have many other senses, which should be apparent from the following common combinations. *To assume* is used in such phrases as *assume a pose/attitude/human form*; *assume the crown/the presidency*; *assume responsibility/new duties*; *assume jurisdiction* ('claim'); *assume the proportions of a crisis*; *assume a garment* and *assume a wife* (both rather old-fashioned); *assume surprise* ('feign') — in its past-participle form, it is used as an adjective to mean 'pretended, fictitious': *an assumed name*; finally, *assume that A is correct* ('grant for the sake of argument') — in its present-participle form, it works as a conjunction, much like *if*: *Assuming the scheme falls through, how do you propose to pay me back?*

To presume is used in such phrases as: *missing, presumed dead* (a legal phrase); *to presume upon my good nature* ('take advantage'); *don't presume* ('take liberties; be presumptuous'); *presumed to criticise me* ('undertake without proper authority; dare'). The last example is equivalent to *had the presumption/presumptuousness to criticise me.*

It is this last sense that makes Stanley's celebrated greeting, *Doctor Livingstone, I presume,* so appropriate — and so polite. Had he said *Doctor Livingstone, I assume,* he would have been implying that he was already in possession of sufficient information to reach a conclusion. In using *presume* he was in effect saying: 'Regardless of my previous knowledge, it is still slightly improper and *presumptuous* of me to be *assuming* anything about you' or 'I know I am being *presumptuous* in saying your name without your confirming it'.

Of the nouns *assumption* and *presumption*, *presumption* implies a greater degree of acceptance or conviction: *The presumption is she is lying.* (A legal term, *presumption of guilt,* suggests a very high probability or a near-certainty that the suspect or accused is guilty.) It should be used only of an established theory or common belief:

From this, of course, absolutely nothing can be deduced — not even the strictly limited presumption that Chernenko is the kind of man who plays things safe.

— David Watt, *The Times*

But *presumption* is probably most often used today in the sense of 'presumptuousness, arrogance, effrontery':

However, I shall not bore my learned readers with a detailed account of Lolita's presumption. Suffice it to say that not a trace of modesty did I perceive in this beautiful hardly formed young girl.

— Vladimir Nabokov, *Lolita*

Assumption is much more tentative than *presumption,* and implies a lesser degree of belief:

On the charitable assumption that Perry has actually read '1984' I invite him to read it again and see how many references he can find in it to specific evils of capitalist America and Western democracy, as compared with how many to specific evils of Stalin's Russia.

— Conor Cruise O'Brien, *The Observer*

In theology, the *Assumption* refers to the bodily taking up of the Virgin Mary into heaven. It also refers to the church feast on August 15 celebrating this miracle.

assure, ensure, insure These three verbs all have the core sense of attaining certainty or security, and in several contexts they can be interchanged. But as a rule, one or other is clearly preferable. The commonest meaning of *to assure* is 'to attempt to convince': *I shall assure her of my loyalty.* The past participle *assured* has come to function as an independent adjective: it can mean 'self-confident' — *a very assured young salesman* — and 'undoubted, guaranteed, certain': *an assured success.* The two meanings are illustrated by the following examples:

As they took their seats in the salon, she sat near them, as if to gain some bravery, some confidence, from their utterly assured presence.

— Anita Brookner, *Hotel du Lac*

Ingrid worked at the Cs' hardware outlet in Stradom Street. ... The rumour was that Schindler himself had got the girl appointed so that he would have an assured outlet for his kitchenware.

— Thomas Keneally, *Schindler's Ark*

In British English, in the world of personal finance, *to assure* yourself is to acquire financial protection for yourself or your dependants in anticipation of those personal misfortunes that are certain to happen — notably death.

In this context, *to insure* yourself, strictly speaking, is to acquire financial protection in anticipation of various misfortunes that may *possibly* happen — loss of property through fire or theft, medical expenses, loss of earnings through illness, and so on. However, *to insure* can be used as the all-embracing term, and is applied to *assured* policies as well. (So that a *life insurance policy* and a *life assurance policy* can amount to the same thing.) *To insure* is used in this general way very often in British English, and virtually always in American English. Finally, *to insure* has a still wider sense of protecting against harm: *measures to insure the village against famine.*

> The repercussions of this would be calamitous not only to the debtors and their creditors but to the world economy and to world politics. Clearly the first requirement of any sound policy must be to insure against this grave danger.
> – Lord Lever, *Time and Tide*

Note the terms *the insured* and (in British English) *the assured*: they function as nouns in legal language, referring to the holder or holders of an insurance policy. (They remain unchanged in form, whether singular or plural in reference.)

To ensure, finally, means 'to make certain, guarantee': *Please ensure that you leave the building by 5.30.*

> His economic policies were intended to ensure, he said, that Australia takes advantage of the rapidly growing economy of the region. It must be helped to do so through changes in education, job training, and in the labour force.
> – Michael Davie, *The Observer*

In American English, the spelling *insure* would often be used in preference.

astronomy, astrology *Astronomy* is the scientific study of the stars and planets, especially their size, position, and movement. It comes from Greek roots meaning roughly 'the arrangement of the stars'. *Astrology*, although its Greek roots suggest the meaning 'the study of the stars', is not a science; it is the art of revealing the supposed influence of the stars on human affairs, and particularly of outlining future events and speculating on personal characteristics by reference to the position of the stars and planets on a person's day of birth.

A person who studies *astronomy* is an *astronomer*; a person who practises *astrology* is an *astrologer* or *astrologist*.

The common adjectives from these two nouns are *astronomical* and *astrological*. (The main stress is shifted here from the second syllable to the third.) *Astronomical* has recently taken on a figurative sense that is different from its simple meaning of 'relating to astronomy'. It has come to be used, or rather over-used, to refer to very large numbers or amounts, and means 'very high or immense'. This sense probably developed through reference to the very large measurements or numbers that astronomers use in describing galaxies. It has the added suggestion of the sense 'so high that it reaches the stars'. This use has found its way into dictionaries, but it is at best likely to be somewhat exaggerated and at worst inappropriate, as in *an astronomical rise in interest in astrology*.

> ? These days figures, however astronomical they might be, are comparatively meaningless. VW say that £500 millions have been spent on development.
> – Roy Harry, *The Guardian*

> ? So it was with the Nazis and their disgusting adventure. It went on for so long, the casualties were so astronomic, that although the element of horror still lingers round every individual case, the wholesale figures fall numbly on the ear.
> – Peter Ustinov, *We Were Only Human*

Try to use a more straightforward word or phrase, such as *huge*, *extreme*, or *enormous*.

attend See TEND.

attribute You can attribute something *to* a person or thing, as in: *She attributed her success to her father and his encouragement.* You cannot, correctly, *attribute* a person or thing *with* something, as in ✗ *She attributed her father with a major role in her success.* Use *credited* for the second construction (it can be used in the first pattern too).

Here are two quotations containing *attribute*, one illustrating the correct use, and the other the incorrect use:

> He would not, for the love of Barbara or anyone else, attribute a date which he believed to be false to a manuscript or object of antiquity.
> – Muriel Spark,
> *The Mandelbaum Gate*

> ✗ The man whose friends all attribute him with lack of promptness can turn up on time to

every engagement in the year, but on the one occasion when he fails to do so, he will provoke the delighted response that his lapse is 'just like him'.

– A.N. Wilson,
The Sweets of Pimlico

It is true that many verbs have expanded from one pattern to the other. You can not only *spray water on the lawn* or *spread jam on the toast*, but also *spray the lawn with water* or *spread the toast with jam*. This seems a fairly common development in English. But efforts to force *attribute* into this versatility — and also other one-pattern verbs such as *imbue*, *instil*, and *inculcate* — are ill-advised. In due course, such verbs may become acceptable in both patterns, but at the moment only one pattern is considered correct.

Note that *attribute*, as a verb, should be stressed on the second syllable, and as a noun on the first syllable. Increasingly, however, the verb too is being stressed on its first syllable. Careful speakers consider this incorrect.

attributive See ADJECTIVES 1.

auger, augur Both of these words are pronounced /**aw**gər/, but they are quite distinct in origin and meaning. Be careful not to confuse the spellings.

An *auger* is a tool for boring holes — either a hand-held device, rather like a gimlet, used for piercing wood, or a larger mechanical device used in road-repairs or in drilling narrow wells. The word is of Old English origin.

Augur is most often used as a verb, meaning 'to prophesy or predict (as from signs or omens)', or 'to presage, foreshadow, herald, bode': *It augurs well for the company that our half-year profits have beaten last year's level*. As a noun, *augur* refers to the Roman official who made predictions from omens, or by extension to any prophet or soothsayer. A related noun, *augury* (pronounced /**aw**gewri/), refers both to the practice of such predictions or a rite involving them, and to an omen or prophetic sign.

In Latin the word *augur* was perhaps partly derived from *avis*, 'a bird': soothsayers would observe the flight of birds or examine their viscera for clues to the future.

aural, oral These two words are both pronounced /**aw**rəl/, and misspelling is all too easy in consequence. Some speakers now try to avoid confusion by pronouncing *aural* ?/**ow**-rəl/, and *oral* is often pronounced ?/**orr**əl/ or ō-rəl/.

None of these pronunciations is acceptable in formal speech, however.

Aural means 'having to do with the ear, or with hearing'. A test of musical perception, then, is *an aural examination*. And so is an inspection of the ear by a doctor. The word can also be used as a noun: *an aural* is again either a musical test or a medical examination of the ear. *Aural* comes from the Latin *auris*, 'an ear'. (There is, by the way, another word *aural*, meaning 'relating to an aura'.) And the adjective *auditory* refers specifically to hearing rather than to the ear — it goes back to the Latin verb *audire*, 'to hear'.

The principal senses of *oral* are 'having to do with the mouth or speech' and 'spoken rather than written'. *An oral examination* is therefore either an examination of the mouth (as by a dentist) or an examination in which the questions and answers are spoken, not written. It comes from Latin *oralis*, 'of the mouth', from *os*, 'a mouth'. As a noun *oral*, like *aural*, can mean 'an examination' — in this case, of course, an examination conducted in speech rather than writing. The plural form *orals* is often used in this sense, too.

Note that the adjective *verbal* is sometimes used when what is really meant is *oral*: the phrase ? *a verbal agreement* is particularly notorious in this regard. People use it to mean 'a spoken agreement' when all it really means is 'an agreement in words': *a verbal agreement* could, accordingly, just as well be written as spoken.

Verbal has in fact been used to mean 'spoken' for about 400 years. The objection to this use is not, then, that it is unestablished and modern, but rather that it can be misleading.

If you want to refer to an agreement based on speech rather than confirmed in writing, then use *an oral agreement* or simply *a spoken agreement*.

Australian English The first English settlement in Australia dates back to January 1788, with the establishment of a penal colony of about 1000 settlers at Botany Bay, today bordered by the suburbs of Sydney. About two-thirds of these settlers were convicts, 'transported' in order to relieve the pressure on Britain's overcrowded jails. The rest were soldiers, officials, and wives and children. Until about 1840, convicts remained the majority of the English-speaking population in Australia. But free settlers had begun to arrive, attracted by the country's potential for raising sheep and cattle.

The varieties of English spoken by these early settlers would have been very diverse. Records show that the convicts were drawn from all over

Britain, though more heavily from London and the south of England, and chiefly from towns rather than country areas. For a brief spell around 1800, Irish political prisoners constituted one-third of the population. A distinctive Australian accent appears to have developed within the first few decades of settlement — no doubt helped by the desire of 'old hands' to signal their status to new arrivals, and for the 'new chums' to conform quickly so as not to be mocked.

The term *Australian English* today covers a number of different varieties that are not easily separable. Unlike English in North America and Britain, Australian English has almost no regional accents or dialects, so that the English spoken in one state is much the same as the English spoken in another. There is social variation within Australian English, however, with differences in pronunciation and grammar reflecting mainly the various socioeconomic levels in the large towns, where the majority of the population lives today. There are also creole and pidgin varieties of English spoken by some descendants of the Aborigines who originally inhabited the conti-nent. It is not always recognised that these nonstandard varieties of Australian English are just as well-formed as the standard variety — con-flict therefore develops between standard and nonstandard English, and creates educational and other social problems in Australia, much as it does in other English-speaking countries.

Written forms of Australian English hardly dif-fer from British standard English, unless some specifically Australian vocabulary is used. The main differences in grammar and vocabulary occur in colloquial speech.

Pronunciation The pronunciation of Australian English has a number of distinctive char-acteristics.

The popular use in Britain of the term *Strine* for *Australian* points to one of the vowel dif-ferences between Australian English and Receiv-ed British Pronunciation (RP) — the change of the diphthong /ay/ to /ī/. (Hence the well-known joke about the Australian visitor to London who was understood as saying that he had 'come here to die' when he meant that he had only just arrived.) The diphthong /ī/ in turn approaches /oy/, so that *tie* can sound rather like *toy*. Other typical differences between RP and a broad Australian accent are the shifts of the RP vowels /a/ towards /e/, and /e/ towards /i/, and sometimes of the /aa/ sound to a long /a/. So the phrase *hard bad bed* might sound like *had bed bid* to an English ear.

Australians (like South Africans and many Americans) also tend to change /i/ to the neutral /ə/ in some unstressed syllables (*boxes* and *box-ers* are usually indistinguishable in Australia, as /**bok**-səz/, whereas British RP would pronounce *boxes* as /**bok**-siz/). The same /i/ sound can become /ee/ in other syllables. So, *stud-ded* and *studied*, which are usually indis-tinguishable in British RP as /**stud**did/, diverge in Australian pronunciation as /**stud**dəd/ and /**stud**-eed/).

Note how the *r* is not pronounced when it occurs before another consonant, as in *hard* and *boxers*. This is common to British RP, and South African and New Zealand English, but differs from many North American varieties, and Scot-tish and Irish English.

There are differences in intonation too. For example, when a question expecting the answer *yes* or *no* is asked, Australian speakers tend to use a continuous rise pattern, whereas in British RP the pitch of the voice tends to drop before a final rise:

Australian: Do you want some tea?

British RP: Do you want some tea?

These differences can cause problems for the uninitiated. British RP-speakers are often mistakenly assumed, in Australia, to be anxious, irritated, or even condescending when simply ask-ing a question in their natural way.

The characteristics discussed so far occur in their purest form in 'Broad' Australian. There are 'milder' accents that are closer to British RP (and that are, incidentally, seen by many Australians as 'affected') and a range of intermediate accents that fall between these two extremes. Milder ac-cents seem to be found more often among older speakers and among the better-off.

Vocabulary All 'transplanted' varieties of a language have to develop new words or new meanings to reflect the different conditions of the new country — both natural and social condi-tions. There tends to be a regular pattern to the way the transplanted language develops. First, words are borrowed from indigenous languages — especially to refer to animals, artefacts, features of the landscape, and so on, that simply did not exist in the home country. In Australia, English naturally turned to native Aboriginal languages for such terms as *kangaroo, kookaburra, koala, boomerang* and *billabong* (a waterhole).

Secondly, words and phrases are often coined from English roots to meet new conditions of life.

Hence the Australian English terms: *outback* (the inland bush country), *back country* (remote areas), *bushranger* (a fugitive), *stockman* (a livestock farmer), *swagman* (an itinerant worker).

Thirdly and conversely, some old terms are used with altered or extended meanings to refer to features of the new country. The words *oak, broom*, and *cedar*, for example, can refer in Australia not just to the British varieties, but to quite different indigenous trees and shrubs as well. Similarly, the word *station* can mean 'a ranch', as in *sheep station* and *cattle station*, as well as being used in *railway station* and *police station*; *squatter* refers to a prosperous farmer, usually a sheep-farmer, and *paddock* refers to fenced-in land of any size and function (with *field* now used in a more restricted sense, usually in contexts such as *playing field*).

Colloquial and slang terms traditionally differ far more than standard vocabulary does from country to country. Many Australian slang terms derive either from the English dialects or the prison jargon of the early settlers — terms that have died out, or simply never caught on widely, in British English: hence *bodger* (useless), *cobber* (a friend), *dinkum* (genuine), and *to fossick* (to search).

Some colourful examples of more recent slang are *to chunder* (to vomit), *to nick off* (to depart) and *to rubbish* (to criticise contemptuously — this term has now entered British English too). The best-known of all colloquial Australian terms, perhaps, is the word *pommy*, or *pom*, which is used to refer deprecatingly to a British person. There are various theories about its source. It might come from the abbreviation POME (Prisoner of Mother England) or POHM (Prisoner of His/Her Majesty) by which an early convict would perhaps have been known. Or it might come from *pomegranate*: perhaps by a play on words, a recent *immigrant*, long known as a *Jimmy Grant*, came finally to be called a *pomegranate*; or perhaps the red, sunburnt face of a new arrival from Britain was thought by weathered native Australians to resemble a pomegranate. Or perhaps early migrant ships supplied their passengers with pomegranates as a supplement to their vitamin-deficient diet on board (in much the same way as British sailors once drank lime juice to ward off scurvy: hence the disparaging American slang term for a British person — a *limey*).

One particularly interesting tendency in colloquial Australian speech (though common too in South African English and other varieties) is to abbreviate words and add the suffix *-ie* or *-o*,

resulting in forms such as *wharfie* (a wharf labourer), *arvo* (afternoon), *gladdie* (a gladiolus), *galvo* (a sheet of galvanised iron), *garbo* (a garbage collector), and *nasho* (national service).

Many familiar English words have extended senses in Australian English that might well confuse an outsider: *station* and *paddock*, as already mentioned, have a wider range of meanings in Australian English than elsewhere; similarly, *theatre* can refer readily to a cinema as well as to a theatre proper, and *footpath* can refer to the pavement or sidewalk as well as to a narrow pathway. This divergence is all the greater in colloquial usage: *good day* is an informal rather than very formal way of saying 'hello', and *hooray* can mean 'goodbye'. The adjective *crook* means 'unwell' or 'out of order'; *never-never* refers to distant sparsely inhabited regions; and *maggoty* means 'angry or irritated'.

Grammar There are very few grammatical differences between standard Australian English and standard British English. There might sometimes be a distinct preference in Australia for one form where British English allows greater variation between two alternative forms. Of the southern British variants *The government has/have blundered*; *Perhaps I could/could do*; *Give it to her/Give it her*; and *I've got/I have a new house*, Australian English usually favours the first option in each case (in the first three cases) as does American English.

The divergence is slightly more noticeable in colloquial usage. One example is the use of *she* rather than *it* or *that* in impersonal constructions and in referring to inanimate nouns. *She's a stinker* means 'The weather — or day — is very hot'. The British equivalent might be *It's a scorcher*. And the informal Australian *She'll do*, meaning 'Enough — let's stop', would be expressed by British speakers as *That'll do*.

The nonstandard English spoken by less educated Australians has much in common with the nonstandard English varieties spoken in other parts of the world. For example, older negative constructions containing two or more negatives are used, as in *She didn't do nothing*.

Trends Australians have tended in the past to look to Britain for their standard language. The term *Far East*, for instance, is widely used in Australia, even though the countries referred to are in fact relatively near.

Recently, however, there have been signs that Australian English is becoming increasingly influenced by American English. Many young Australians now use a sound like a /d/ instead of the standard *t*-sound between two vowels, so that *butter* sounds like /**bud**də/.

There are indications too that Australian English is developing a sense of independence. Younger people seem to be adopting 'broader' accents than their parents, and dictionaries compiled in Australia are increasingly used in place of British or American dictionaries. Now that Australia is acquiring such an impressive international reputation for its achievements in literature, in films, and even in pop music, its cultural self-confidence is increasing rapidly, and it is likely to look to its own linguistic resources, rather than to Britain or America, for its future development.

authoritarian, authoritative The adjectives *authoritarian* and *authoritative* should not be confused. *Authoritarian* has negative associations and means 'based on the principle of authority rather than on individual freedom'.

> And if on set she was humble, quiet, not obviously authoritarian, power was nonetheless being exercised. 'I was frightened of so much power,' she admitted, 'so I tried to appear unpowerful.'
> – Jeannette Kupfermann,
> *The Sunday Times*

An *authoritarian* system is one that dictates much of the course of citizens' lives, and that demands unquestioning obedience. *Authoritarian* is also a noun, referring to a person who favours an *authoritarian* system or *authoritarianism*.

It is possible to speak of *an authoritarian person*, but it would be unusual to speak of *? an authoritative person*. True enough, *authoritative* used to have the meaning 'authoritarian, dictatorial', but it no longer has. It now almost always has more positive associations. It means, in a favourable way, 'possessing authority, and therefore deserving respect or obedience': *To find out what a word means, consult an authoritative dictionary*. It also means 'proceeding from a competent authority; based on expertise and therefore reliable': *Her work was authoritative — she had a perfect command of the subject*.

> During the 1960s and 1970s heavy scholarly editions, weighty with apparatus, were encouraged by the Center of Editions of American Authors of the Modern Language Association of America. They were attacked by Edmund Wilson, who called for something closer to an American Pléiade, unfussy authoritative editions of classic authors accessible to the general public.
> – Malcolm Bradbury, *The Observer*

Authoritative may also mean 'commanding' — *His voice was authoritative* — or 'official': *The information came from authoritative sources*. The noun related to *authoritative*, is usually *authority*, but *authoritativeness* is also possible.

Take care to avoid the common mistake, in spelling or pronouncing *authoritative*, of leaving out the *-it-* or *-at-* in the middle of the word.

auxiliary verbs See VERBS 3.

averse, adverse These two words are sometimes confused. Their Latin roots help to clarify the difference between them. Both come from the verb *vertere*, 'to turn', but the prefix of *averse* comes from *ab-*, 'away', and the prefix of *adverse* from *ad-*, 'towards'.

Averse, then, comes from the same roots as *averted*, and similarly suggests 'turned away', though it is used only in a figurative sense. It means 'disinclined, reluctant' — mildly rather than vehemently opposed: *The villagers were hostile to the idea of a car park, and even averse to the new bus stop*. It is perhaps most often encountered in the phrase *not averse to,* which is an understated way of saying 'in favour of', or even 'eager for':

> Such a study, ideally, would have to encompass a whole range of approaches, from sociology to academic gossip (to which the Leavises themselves were by no means averse).
> – John Gross, *The Observer*

> His book is the work of someone who, while liking to crack the jokes, might not be averse to cracking the odd whip either. Perhaps that is why he has been seen signing copies with the motto: 'Quick to give, and quick to take, offence'.
> – John Naughton, *The Observer*

Averse, as these examples illustrate, usually applies to people.

Adverse is not used of people. The Latin word *adversus* meant 'turned towards (with hostility)', so *adverse* means 'opposed, hostile, antagonistic', as in *adverse criticism*; or 'unfavourable, unpropitious', as in *adverse conditions*; or sometimes simply 'in an opposing direction': *adverse winds*.

> I was not muddling the two issues. I was commenting adversely on an approach which magnified one of them, and ignored the other.
> – Conor Cruise O'Brien, *The Observer*

In the following extract, *adverse* is used mistakenly for *averse*:

✗ It's all very well for Tam Dalyell to explain nobly that he missed the Belgrano show at the Commons on Wednesday because it would have meant cancelling previous engagements. But, strangely, he wasn't that adverse to cancelling previous engagements last week, when something more interesting came up.

> – Peter Hillmore, *The Observer*

Both words are used with the preposition *to*: *He was averse to my suggestion*; *restrictions adverse to my interests*. *Adverse* can probably also be used with *for*: *conditions adverse for sailing*. And it has been argued that *averse* should be used with *from*, as in the example below, because of the prefix *ab-*, 'away'. This is a fallacy, however, since even Latin authors used *aversus* with the dative case, which expresses the idea of 'to'. The correct preposition is *to*; *from* is just pedantic:

? Sir Edward Grey was strongly averse from making any formal protest.

> – Philip Magnus, *Edward VII*

? In principle Shadbold was not averse from tasks of that kind, if made worth while. He was, however, sufficiently experienced to guess ... that a good deal of effort would be needed even to read the MS.

> – Anthony Powell,
> *O, How the Wheel Becomes It!*

Note, however, that the formal verb *to avert* does take *from*: *He averted his gaze from the carnage*.

Averse is always stressed on the second syllable: /ə-**verss**/; *adverse* may be stressed on either the first or the second: /**ad**-verss/ or /ad-**verss**/.

The noun related to *averse* is *aversion*, 'an intense dislike'. The preposition *to* is again the appropriate one: *a strong aversion to garlic*.

Adverse, in its usual sense, has the corresponding noun *adverseness*: the adverseness of the conditions. The noun *adversity* has a rather different sense, referring to misfortune — a state of hardship or a calamitous event: *showed great heroism in the face of adversity*; *beset by a series of adversities*.

await See WAIT.

awake, awaken See WAKE.

awfully Poor word! Its early meanings were associated with the word *awe,* and suggested fear or reverence or sublimity: 'awesomely', 'majestically', 'fearfully' — *awfully* would, in the past, have been used with senses such as these: *The king swept awfully into the chamber and the courtiers fell awfully to their knees*, and so on.

> The awful shadow of some unseen Power
> Floats though unseen among us.
>
> > – P.B. Shelley,
> > 'Hymn to Intellectual Beauty' (1816)

This impressive term then went into a decline, in two directions: first, in step with *awful*, it came to suggest great ugliness or sloppiness or the like: *He sings awfully*; secondly, it became a mere intensifier, a synonym of *very* and *extremely*: *You're awfully late*.

> He has tried awfully hard in the past few years to stretch his liberal conscience.
>
> > – Alistair Cooke, *The Americans*

Much the same development has affected *dreadfully*, *fearfully*, *frightfully*, *terribly*, and *terrifically*. It is impossible for anyone to restore such words to a full and useful life. What we can do, however, is to keep them, in their present feeble senses, out of formal English. Restrict these adverbs and their corresponding adjectives to informal contexts and try to use them sparingly even there.

The use of *awful* for *awfully*, as in ? *awful hard*, is found sometimes in nonstandard American English.

B

back-formation See VERBS 7.

bacteria See GERM.

bail, bale There are several words covered by these two spellings. *Bail* refers to the system of exchanging a cash security for the release of a prisoner. The word can be used of the security, the person providing it, or the release itself: hence *to go* (or *stand*) *bail for* someone, and *to jump bail*. The word goes back to the Latin noun *bajulus*, 'a porter or carrier'. As a verb, usually in the form *to bail (someone) out*, it means 'to provide bail for (a prisoner)', or, informally, 'to help (someone) get out of a tricky situation'.

That person might *bale out* of the tricky situation on his own, however — that is, he might abandon it. This is an extension of *to bale out* in the sense 'to parachute from an aircraft, especially in an emergency' — probably from the idea of dropping a bundle or *bale* through a trap-door. (This is sometimes spelt *bail out*, mainly in American English.) The noun here, *bale*, refers to a large packaged bundle, as of wool. The word comes from Old French, but is probably of Germanic origin.

Another word *bale*, from Old English, is an archaic term for 'evil influence' or 'mental anguish': it survives in the word *baleful*. (See BALEFUL.)

Bale is also a variant, especially in American spelling, of a different word *bail*, noun or verb, referring to the removal of water from a boat. The immediate source is the Middle English word *baille*, 'a bucket', again probably going back, via Middle French, to the Latin *bajulus*, 'a porter or carrier'.

Bale is also a variant of yet another word *bail*, referring either to the hooplike handle of a bucket or kettle, or to the hoops supporting the top of a covered wagon. This probably goes back to the Old Norse word *beygja*, 'to bend'.

Finally, there is the word *bail* referring to the small crosspieces of a wicket in cricket, and also to other forms of bar, as in a stable or on a typewriter. This word is of Old French origin, from *bailler*, 'to enclose' (presumably by means of wooden bars).

baleful, baneful These two adjectives share a great deal of their meaning. *Baneful* today means approximately 'harmful, destructive', though it formerly had a stronger sense of 'poisonous, deadly'. *Baleful* means 'having an evil influence or result', and sometimes also 'foreboding evil, ominous'. In many contexts, either word might be used with equal appropriateness: *the baneful/baleful effect of television on children's reading ability*.

Baleful is the commoner word, at least in British English, and usually seems the more natural choice:

> The Munich agreement had its baleful consequences throughout Europe.
> – Anthony Eden, *The Reckoning*

Baleful is perhaps most often used of facial expressions, and in such contexts *baneful* is unlikely to be used. *Baleful* here means 'threatening, vindictive': *He gave me a baleful stare and I retreated to my desk*.

Baleful was once used to mean 'sad, doleful' as well: *the dog's baleful brown eyes*. However, this meaning is no longer current.

Baleful and *baneful* have quite different sources. *Bale*, an archaic word for 'misery, trouble, evil', comes from the Old English *bealu*, 'anguish'. *Bane*, from Old English *bana*, 'a slayer', has the archaic sense of 'death, or cause of death, or poison' (as in the name of *henbane*), and the milder current sense of 'a major annoyance, or the cause of serious trouble', as in *a child who is the bane of my life*.

balk See BAULK.

balmy, barmy These two adjectives are pronounced identically by many speakers: /**baa**mi/. To confuse the spellings of them, however, at least in British English, is likely to produce laughable results: the one is such a poetic word, the other such an informal word, and this incongruity constitutes the extra threat to the careless writer.

Balmy literally means 'fragrant, sweet-smelling'. It is the adjective from *balm*, 'an aromatic, oily resin exuded by various tropical trees and shrubs'.

Balm is often used in medicines; by extension, the word came to refer to medicinal ointments, especially soothing creams. This sense of soothing is all the stronger in that *balmy* has extended its meaning from 'fragrant' to 'mild and pleasant' — probably because it usually appears in such phrases as *balmy air* and *balmy breezes*, and was understood to mean 'warm' as much as 'sweet-smelling'.

> Bright and pleasant was the sky, balmy the air, and beautiful the appearance of every object around, as Mr Pickwick leant over the balustrades of Rochester Ridge, contemplating nature, and waiting for breakfast.
> – Charles Dickens, *The Pickwick Papers*

Balm comes from the same root as the word *balsam,* going back via Middle English and Old French to the Latin *balsamum,* 'balsam'. This word goes further back through Greek to the Hebrew word for spice. *Balsam* is, however, not the same thing as *balm*: it is an oily resin as well, but from a different tree. (*Balsa* wood comes from a different tree again: the word has a quite different source — the Spanish *balsa,* 'a raft'). *Balsam* is the gummier substance, *balm* the more aromatic.

Barmy is an informal or even slang term meaning 'eccentric, insane, or simple-minded'. Its original meaning was 'frothy, foamy' — *barm* is an old-fashioned word for yeast. In the 17th century, there was a Yorkshire saying, *His brains will work without barm*, which perhaps gave rise to the current sense of *barmy*. The word *barmish* was used by Robert Burns in the 18th century; the dialectal expression *barmy in the crumpet* is recorded from 1909. The words *barmy* and *barmish* probably meant 'fermenting like barm, frothy, flighty, empty-headed'.

To remember the distinction in spelling, try to associate the *l* in *balmy* with the *l* in *calm*.

The spelling difference is obviously an important one in British English. In American English, however, *balmy* is the principal spelling for both meanings; *barmy* (= crazy) is no more than a secondary variant, and has distinctly British overtones.

British English is regrettably beginning to follow the American example, and although *barmy* remains the preferred spelling of the word meaning 'crazy', many British dictionaries now list *balmy* as a minor but acceptable variant. The distinction is worth preserving, however, and the spelling of *barmy* as *balmy* is to be discouraged.

baneful See BALEFUL.

baroque, rococo These two words — and the two styles of art that they refer to — are not easy to distinguish. But there is a distinction, and it should be observed.

Baroque art and architecture developed in Europe, chiefly in Italy, in the late 16th century, and lasted until the mid-18th century. It is typically ornate in style, characterised by bold ornamentation such as elaborate scrolls and flamboyant curves. Many outstanding examples of baroque architecture survive in the churches of Bavaria and Austria, for example. Painters such as Rubens and Caravaggio display baroque qualities in their formal flourish and use of bright colours. Bernini is the most famous of the baroque sculptors. And much of the music of that period too, such as Bach's and Vivaldi's, is called *baroque,* being equally rich in detailed ornamentation; in an extended sense, *baroque* might be used of any music reminiscent of true baroque music in its ornateness.

In French, *baroque* originally meant 'irregular in shape', and was applied to pearls. The use of the word in architecture was probably borrowed from Italian *barroco* rather than from French. The term goes back beyond both French and Italian, however, to Portuguese or Spanish.

In general, *rococo* is even more highly detailed and embellished than *baroque,* but through its use of lighter colours (or lighter musical texture) and looser composition achieves a more delicate, less ponderous effect, though at the expense of grandeur.

Rococo design developed in France in the early 18th century, towards the end of the baroque period, and it can be argued that a rococo work is a kind of baroque work, rather than something different from a baroque work. (In music, however, the two periods are usually considered quite distinct, the dividing-date lying somewhere between 1710 and 1730: rococo composers include Telemann and the early Haydn and Mozart.) Rococo painters include Watteau, Boucher, and Tiepolo. *Rococo* is very much a decorative style, being characterised by even more intricate ornamentation and the use of contrasting materials such as tapestry, stucco, and shellwork. (The French word *rococo* is a fanciful alteration of *rocaille,* 'rockwork, shellwork'.)

Applied to literature, *baroque* means 'extravagant, strange, and ingenious' — especially in the use of unlikely or ambiguous imagery. The Metaphysical Poets, including John Donne, may be described as *baroque*. So too might various modern novelists. (*Rococo* does not have a specialist literary sense.)

Garp was an excessive man. He made everything baroque, he believed in exaggeration; his fiction was also extremist.

> – John Irving (U.S.),
> *The World According To Garp*

Both words are sometimes used as disparaging adjectives in nontechnical contexts: *baroque* is used to mean either 'heavily ornate' or 'bizarre, grotesque', and *rococo* to mean 'excessively florid, overdone'. The following quotation attempts, dubiously, to rank the two adjectives in order of weirdness:

> As the scientific mastermind behind the whole affair, Freddie Jones seems to be challenging Donald Pleasance for the title of the international cinema's number one loony. But if Jones's mad scientist is baroque, George C. Scott's half-Indian CIA hitman is positively rococo. Combining the most extreme features of his General Turgidson from 'Dr Strangelove' and his Fagin in a recent cut-price 'Oliver Twist', Scott's bizarre behaviour would cause eyebrows to be raised in the corridors of Broadmoor or Charenton.
>
> – Philip French, *The Observer*

Note the pronunciations: *baroque*, /bə-**rok**/, /bə-**rōk**/ (in American English the latter is always used); *rococo*, /rə-**kōkō**/ or /rō-**kōkō**/ (in American English, sometimes /**rōkə-kō**/).

basically In recent years, this term has come to be used — overused — as the opening word of a reply to a question:

> 'How do you, as team-manager, feel about today's match?'
> 'Basically, the midfield-players let too many opportunities go by . . .'

It is the modern equivalent, perhaps, of clearing your throat — it gives you a moment to collect your thoughts, and secures the attention of the listener. But a brief silence could serve these two purposes just as effectively — and far less irritatingly. *Basically* has become a cliché: the automatic and mindless way it tends to be trotted out casts doubt on the rest of the reply — is it equally thoughtless? you wonder; can it be trusted?

Even more irritating than its frequency, perhaps, is the misleading way in which it is used. The information that follows *basically* is all too often extremely abstruse and detailed — anything but basic.

Try to restrict *basically* to its literal sense — typically just in front of an adjective: *The engine is basically sound, but it does need careful tuning.* Think twice before using *basically* as the first word of a sentence.

See also HOPEFULLY.

bath British and sometimes American English use *to bathe* when referring to swimming in the sea or applying liquid in a soothing way; in American usage *to bathe* can occasionally also mean 'to take a bath'.

In British English, you say *I am going to bath the baby*; in American English you have to say *I am going to give the baby a bath*.

Spelling is often no guide to the verb being used. The forms *bathing* or *bathed* can be derived from *to bath* or *to bathe*. In speech, a distinction is made: *bath* produces /**baa**thing/ and /baatht/, *bathe* produces /**bay**thing/ and /baythd/.

baulk, balk *Baulk* is the usual spelling of this word in all senses. *Balk* is standard in American English, and is sometimes favoured in British English too.

As a noun, *baulk* is little used today except in its various specialised senses — in farming, building, fishing, and snooker. It is still in wide use as a verb, however, in such senses as 'to refuse', 'to be reluctant', and 'to thwart': *At the last jump, the horse baulked*; *We were baulked of victory*; *The judge baulked at imposing the death penalty*.

> I resented the interference but didn't see it as a serious obstacle until they baulked at the presentation of the spastic child.
>
> – Peter Nichols, *The Observer*

> I gave her the number and hung up feeling baulked of my escape, almost as if I'd expected that the thing could be done now, tonight.
>
> – Lynne Reid Banks, *The L-Shaped Room*

The standard pronunciation, surprisingly perhaps, is /bawk/, but /bawlk/ is an alternative.

BC See AD, BC.

be In dialects, *be* is still used in contexts where *am, is,* and so on are now standard: *My boy Ethan be 16 next January*. The commonest uses today are in imperatives: *Be good!*; after *to*: *Try to be good*; and after an auxiliary verb: *He will be 16 soon*. Its use as a subjunctive form sounds rather old-fashioned now, though it is still heard:

No matter how old he be, he's still a fool. The modern tendency would be to insert a *may* before the *be* here, or to use *is* instead: *No matter how old he is/may be . . .*

In British English, the colloquial construction *been and* is used to express surprise: *? He's been and got married!* This should be restricted to informal contexts.

The double use of *be*, in *be being* or *been being*, sounds very inelegant, but it sometimes seems unavoidable: *Jane's the one who ought to be being questioned like this.* Here, *be being* emphasises the duration of the action. A slight rewording may be possible, however, without any loss of effectiveness: *Jane's the one who ought to be undergoing questioning like this.*

The use of *being* followed by *as* or *that* instead of *because* or *since* is strictly for informal use: *?? Being as you're tired, you might as well stay home.*

because, as, since, for All these words introduce clauses giving a reason for the action or state of affairs mentioned in the main clause. But the words are not always equally appropriate.

At the beginning of a sentence, *as* and *since* are often favoured. They are preferred where the main statement is more important than the reason for it:

> As/Since the luggage weighed over two tons, the back axle broke.

> Other patients came and went but we four great-bellied matrons formed the hardcore of the ward. Since she'd been there longest — apparently within minutes of conception — in deference to rank we invariably discussed Mrs Baker's clots first.
> – Sue Arnold, *The Observer*

Here, Mrs Baker's clots are the focus of interest. *As* could have replaced *since* here, but *because* would have been slightly awkward. Take care not to use *as* or *since* if there is any chance of ambiguity, however. In *As the car swerved, he slammed on the brakes*, the *as* is more likely to mean 'at the moment that' than 'for the reason that'. And in *Since he won the prize, he's been very pleased with himself*, the *since* is more likely to mean 'from the time that' than 'for the reason that'.

Because emphasises the cause rather than the main statement: *You're tired because you went to bed late.* Here, 'you' are already aware of your own tiredness, but I am telling you the cause of it. *As* and *since* would be unsuitable here.

Because (like *for*) may also introduce the reason for asserting a fact, as opposed to the cause of the fact asserted. It is often used in this way in speech and informal writing:

> I blame you for the broken axle, because/for it was you who overloaded the boot.

> Helen's head was flung forward, narrowly missing the steering column, which caught her at the back of her neck. Many wrestlers' children have hardy necks, because Helen's did not break — though she wore a brace for almost six weeks and her back would bother her for the rest of her life.
> – John Irving (U.S.),
> *The World According to Garp*

Here, *because* means 'which is why'. The part of the sentence after *because* is too important to be introduced by *as* or *since*, although *for* would be preferred in more formal prose. Best of all perhaps would be to use no introductory word at all, but simply a colon.

For is rather different from the other three words. It does not introduce the cause of a fact asserted; it introduces the reason for asserting the fact — the (subjective) explanation rather than the (objective) cause. *For* always comes between the two elements it joins, not at the beginning. It needs a comma, or even a semi-colon, before it, and can even stand at the head of a whole sentence, explaining the statement in the previous sentence:

> But he never lived to see the project through. For shortly before its completion, he collapsed from overwork, and was found by the office cleaner on a Monday morning, slumped over his desk, lifeless.

For emphasises about equally the main statement and the reason for making it. It is a rather formal word. It might have been a better choice than *because* in the following:

> It was too late, because there was a certain surge forward.
> – D.M. Thomas, *The White Hotel*

Here, *because* means something like 'as is shown by the fact that'.

See also REASON.

been and See BE.

begrudge, grudge These two verbs are often used interchangeably, but their primary meanings are distinct, and the distinction is worth observing.

To begrudge suggests envy; *to grudge* suggests reluctance: *Stephanie begrudged Sam his invitation, and therefore grudged him the loan of two pounds for his taxi-fare.* This means that Stephanie felt an envious resentment towards Sam over his possession of an invitation, and that she therefore was unwilling to lend him the money, or that she lent it only very reluctantly (that is, *grudgingly*). The slight ambiguity of *grudge* here (did she lend him the money, or not?) serves as a warning that the verb should be used only with great caution. *Grudge* is also a noun, of course.

Here are some examples of the two words in actual use:

If she met other men, he would become jealous, Mr Justice Sheldon said in the High Court Family Division. He 'begrudged her any independent life'.
— *The Times*

Spira's Political Section would go beyond the demands of grudging cooperation and would be full of ... men with complexes, with puerile grudges about the social and intellectual slights they'd received.
— Thomas Keneally, *Schindler's Ark*

behalf British and American English both use *on behalf of* in two senses:
1. 'as a representative of' (*spoke on behalf of her client*);
2. 'in the interest of' (*spoke on behalf of justice*).
American English can use *in behalf of* as a variant of *on behalf of* in both senses.

Some usage writers have argued that *on behalf of* should be limited to sense *1.* and that *in behalf of* should be used in sense *2.* This distinction is no longer possible in British English, where *in behalf of* is hardly used at all. The distinction can still be made in American English, but it appears that many Americans are unaware of it.

Note that *on behalf of* is often wrongly used in place of *on the part of*: × *The accident was caused by negligence on behalf of the driver.*

behove, behoove, behoof The British spelling of the formal verb, which means 'to be proper for', is *behove*, rhyming with 'wove'. The American spelling is *behoove*, rhyming with 'move'. It is used only impersonally: *It behoves us to consider the question carefully.* The example below, although the *it* is not present, is still correct, since the verb remains impersonal, with *as* (= which) as the subject:

He is certainly one of the most 'bookish' of Prime Ministers as behoves the only one who has been — and very successfully, too — a publisher by trade.
— Lord Blake, *The Times*

The noun *behoof*, which means 'benefit, advantage', is decidedly archaic. Even in the following passage, written almost 100 years ago, the modern *behalf* would have been more idiomatic — *behoof* was chosen to create a medieval effect:

A word or two from Robert the weaver, and they bustled about on our behoof, and presently came and took us by the hands and led us to a table in the pleasantest corner of the hall, where our breakfast was spread for us.
— William Morris, *News from Nowhere* (1890)

being as See BE.

below See ABOVE.

benevolent, beneficial, benign, beneficent These adjectives all suggest good intentions and results. A source word common to them all is the Latin *bene*, 'well'. Essentially, *benign* means 'kindly, well-disposed'; *benevolent* means 'wanting to do good' (the other Latin source word here is *velle*, 'to wish'); *beneficent* and *beneficial* both mean 'doing good' (the other Latin source word here is *facere*, 'to do or make'). The chief difference between *beneficent* and *beneficial* is that *beneficent* tends to be used of people, and *beneficial* of things or abstractions. So, a *benevolent* philanthropist of *benign* temperament may become a *beneficent* patron of the arts by making donations that will have *beneficial* effects.

The noun forms of these adjectives are *benignity* (the *g* is now pronounced), *benevolence*, *beneficence*, and *benefit* or the rare *beneficialness*. Here are some examples of these words in actual use:

In certain cases, REM sleep deprivation can be positively beneficial to us, and can be used successfully to treat certain forms of depression.
— Dr Jim Horne, *The Guardian*

Aeneas wants to rouse the pity of Dido for the cruel betrayal of the Trojans by Sinon's abuse of their benevolence, so that he can gain returns from that pity in good will to the remnant of the Trojans.
— Owen Dudley Edwards, *The Listener*

Perhaps it reflects people's willingness to give credence to the reassuring notion that a benignly disposed God or Nature has compensated the deaf for their deafness by not visiting upon them the calamitous consequences of the great confusion of tongues.
– Professor Roy Harris,
The Times Literary Supplement

In addition, we need a new theory of beneficence to cope with the problem of how to deal with future generations that are created by our present policies.
– Stephen Lukes, *The Observer*

These adjectives have, typically, developed transferred or extended uses: a *benign* or *benevolent* person can have a *benign* or *benevolent* smile; a climate as well as people can be *benign*; and the Sun, if personified, can be as *beneficent* as any philanthropist.

The opposite of *benign* is *malign* or *malignant* (*benignant*, with the *g* pronounced, is much less likely than *malignant*). The opposite of *benevolent* is *malevolent*. As opposites of *beneficent* and *beneficial* (rarely *benefic*), *maleficent* and *malefic* are possible, though hardly common.

The opposition of *benign* and *malignant* extends into the field of medicine. A *malignant* tumour is cancerous, a *benign* tumour is not.

Some years ago the curious compound *benign neglect* was used to describe a U.S. government policy that avoided actively promoting racial equality on the controversial ground that progress towards racial equality would meet less resistance in the absence of such intervention.

Compare MALICIOUS.

bereaved, bereft These words were originally variant past-tense or past-participle forms of the verb *to bereave*, from Old English roots. *Bereaved* is the usual word for 'deprived by death': *a bereaved father*. It can be used as a noun, either singular or, more commonly, plural: *The bereaved stood round the coffin*. *Bereft* means 'deprived' in a more general way, so it is often necessary to specify what the person is *bereft of*: *a man bereft of his sense of purpose*. But *bereft of* now sounds rather old-fashioned.

Note that *bereft* usually stands after the noun to which it applies, or after a verb:

Although he loved reviewing, and would have felt bereft without this work, he regarded it principally as a means of earning his daily bread.
– Jessica Mitford, *The Observer*

Bereft should not really be used to mean merely 'without' or 'devoid of', as in the following:

? But Argentina's students seem as bereft of any sense of history as everybody else's.
– Peregrine Worsthorne, *Sunday Telegraph*

Where the deprivation is an actual 'bereavement', a writer may still choose to use *bereft* rather than *bereaved*, to emphasise the sense of desolate loneliness rather than the mere loss of a loved one:

A year after Charles's death his ashes were incorporated in the base of a memorial urn in the Fellows' Garden at Christ's ... As I write, it is nearly two years since Charles's death and I am bereft.
– Philip Snow, *Stranger and Brother*

beside, besides *Beside* is only a preposition, meaning 'next to' — *Sit beside me* — or 'in comparison with': *Our problems are insignificant beside theirs*. It is not now usually used, as in the following example, to mean 'as well as':

? 'Leave poor Helen alone', Jenny advised him. 'I thought you were going to write something beside letters.'
– John Irving (U.S.),
The World According to Garp

Most writers would have chosen *besides* here. *Besides* can be either a preposition or an adverb. It means 'as well as' — *Besides his books, there were lots of maps* — or 'moreover': *I can't swim ... besides, I'm tired*. *Besides* can also mean 'except for, other than', as in *There's nothing we can do besides wait*. But note that it is inclusive in meaning, like *in addition to*, rather than exclusive like *except for*. So, *We all want to go, besides Mary* implies that she wants to go too.

best Strictly speaking, *best* should be used only when three or more people or things are being compared. Thus, correct usage contrasts *He's the best of all the players* with *He's the better of the two players*. In casual speech, however, this distinction is frequently lost, and sentences such as ? *He's the best of the two players* can be heard. In particular, ? *May the best man win* is commonly heard at a contest between two men — far more commonly, in fact, than the theoretically correct *May the better man win*.

bettor, better Someone who lays a bet is either a *bettor* or a *better*. Some people prefer *bettor*, in order to distinguish the word from the comparative of *good* or *well*. But it is not necessarily a better spelling.

between, among 1. The traditional rule is this: *between* is used when relating two elements; *among* when relating three or more:

> We sensed an uncomfortable tension between the president and the interviewer.
> There was unconcealed hostility among the various candidates for the job.

The second part of the rule — the part dealing with *among* — is easy and accurate enough; the first part of the rule, however — the part dealing with *between* — is not quite true to the facts. The use of *between* is rather complicated. First, *between* is used where there is a single two-way relationship involved, regardless of the number of participants.

> We sensed an uncomfortable tension between the president's advisers and the interviewers.
> The American Civil War is often called the War Between the States (that is, the Northern States and the Southern States).

Then, *between* is still preferable when more than one relationship is involved, provided that every relationship is a well-defined two-way relationship — typically when every element is named.

> Switzerland lies between France, Germany, Austria, Liechtenstein, and Italy.
> Constructive talks took place between Britain, Denmark, and Iceland over fishing-rights.

> With almost every expense spared, it falls between three stools, lacking the kind of extended treatment a TV-serial might provide, the ebullience of Lionel Bart's stage musical, and the visual intensity of David Lean's 1948 film that merged Cruikshank caricature with cinematic expressionism.
> – Philip French, *The Observer*

When the exact number of elements is specified, *between* can still be used, even though the elements are not named:

> The prize was divided equally between the seven winners.

Here, *among* would be equally appropriate; and if the participants are neither named nor numbered, then *among* should be used:

> The prize was divided equally among the winners (if there are more than two winners).

If a cooperative group activity is being discussed, then *between* is always the appropriate pronoun: *between ourselves.*

> The workers secured over £20,000 compensation between them.
> Between them the apprentices at last managed to get the engine assembled.

2. The word that follows *between* as its 'correlative' partner is *and,* not *or, to, in contrast to, whereas,* or the like:

✗ the choice between spending all your income or trying to save a certain proportion of it
✗ salaries ranging between £5000 to £20,000

✗ It looks as if we have to make a choice between submitting the video trade to control, with the risk of censorship spreading, or having the youngsters corrupted.
> – Katharine Whitehorn, *The Observer*

✗ There was no intermediate zone of study. Either the enormity of the desert space, or the sight of a tiny flower. You had to choose between the tiny or the vast.
> – Paul Theroux (U.S.), *The Old Patagonian Express*

These common mistakes seem to be based on a confusion between two different constructions in each case. The correct wording is:

> the choice between spending all your income and trying to save/the choice of spending all your income or trying to save
> salaries ranging between £5000 and £20,000/salaries ranging from £5000 to £20,000
> a choice of submitting ... or having the youngsters corrupted/a choice between submitting ... and having ...
> to choose the tiny or the vast/to choose between the tiny and the vast

One other reason for the use of *or* in place of *and* may sometimes be that the first element itself includes an *and,* so a subsequent *and* might seem repetitive and misleading:

✗ The menu offers a choice between soup and entrée or entrée and dessert.

Certainly it would be confusing simply to change the *or* to *and* in this sentence. But that is no excuse for retaining the ungrammatical *or.* One solution is just to change *between* to *of.* But if you want to retain *between,* the best course of action is to mark off the two separate choices by adding the phrases *on the one hand* and *on the other.* So:

The menu offers a choice between soup and entrée on the one hand, and entrée and dessert on the other.

The constant interplay between the academic lecture and the 'elite' essay on the one hand, and the presentation of the same or closely related material and signatures by the media — the quality papers, the weeklies, the radio-talk — on the other, have produced hybrid forms.

> – Professor George Steiner,
> *The Times Literary Supplement*

(But notice the wrong use of the plural verb *have* here: it should be *has*, in keeping with the singular subject of the sentence, *interplay*.)

3. *Between* cannot be repeated before each element in the way that other prepositions can. You can say:

To the winner and to the runner-up, our warmest congratulations.

But you cannot of course say:

× Between the winner and between the runner-up was a distance of over thirty yards.

The second *between* must be deleted. When the two elements are widely separated in a sentence, however, by subordinate clauses or parentheses, it is easy to lose track of the construction, and to repeat the *between* in a desperate effort to pick up the threads again:

× The distance between the winner, who has just crossed the finishing line to a volley of flash-bulbs from the assembled photographers and a barrage of questions from the reporters, and between the runner-up, who is just approaching the finishing line now, must be well over 150 metres.

4. The phrase *between each* or *between every* is a very common lapse of logic:

× The interval between each buzz is ten seconds.

× The distance between each marker varies from 1.5 kilometres to 3.75 kilometres.

A moment's thought will show that the correct phrasing would take any of the following forms:

The interval between buzzes is ten seconds

The interval between one buzz and the next is ten seconds

The interval from one buzz to the next is ten seconds.

It is also best to avoid such constructions as *the interval between each/every/any two buzzes is ten seconds.* After all, the interval between the first buzz and the last, say, is surely longer than ten seconds.

See also AMONG; BETWEEN YOU AND I.

between you and I This phrase is so widely used nowadays (and is found in writing as far back as Shakespeare) that some experts now accept it as standard usage. It is clearly wrong grammatically — this becomes obvious when you reverse the order of the pronouns: × *between I and you.* The preposition *between* requires the object-form of pronouns that follow it. The correct wording is *between you and me.*

The reason for the popularity of *between you and I* is probably, paradoxically, the early coaching that middle-class children receive in good grammar. Children have a tendency to use the phrase *you and me* where *you and I* is appropriate — × *You and me* (or, *Me and you*) *are going to get our hair cut today* — which concerned parents and schoolteachers are at pains to correct, perhaps too insistently: 'No, not *you and me:* you must say *you and I* . . .'

The responsive child therefore develops a suspicion of the phrase *you and me,* and uses *you and I* instead — even when grammar requires the object-form *you and me.* This 'hypercorrection' as it is known — 'correcting' a construction that is already correct into a form that is incorrect — occurs in many other contexts: × *Let you and I pray*; ? *Let's you and I talk this over*; × *Let Sally and I give you a lift home*; × *The news came as a great shock to my husband and I*; × *They must be cursing you and I back at company headquarters.*

> Surely the champions of the Queen's English must acknowledge defeat after hearing the Governor-General of Canada, twice over in a three-minute speech in front of our City Hall use the expression: 'For my wife and I'!
> – Dr A.C. Henderson (Canadian),
> letter to *The Toronto Star*

There are two ways in which the phrase ? *between you and I* might be defended: first, you might argue that it is now so widespread that, whatever the rights and wrongs of its *grammar,* it is established *idiom* and therefore acceptable. Most careful users of English, however, do not acknowledge this claim of idiomatic immunity — it is not yet a natural idiom, they counter, and must not be allowed to become one: it should be corrected whenever it is encountered, and its encroachment resisted in that way.

Secondly, you could perhaps argue that *? between you and I* is in a way grammatical after all: *you and I,* you might suggest, is a kind of composite pronoun, as though it were spelt *you-and-I,* and this pronoun does not change its form, in the way that *I* does, when it shifts from being a grammatical subject to being a grammatical object: so *You-and-I saw Henry*; but also *Henry saw you-and-I*; *Henry walked past you-and-I*; *Between you-and-I*; *Henry envies you-and-I, and is trying to give you-and-I a bad name.* Again, however, most careful users of English are quite unconvinced: it seems an overingenious attempt at defending the indefensible.

● *Recommendation* Avoid the phrase × *between you and I,* no matter how widely you might hear it used. It is often a giveaway sign that the user is trying (and failing) to show a superior grasp of grammar or a superior education. The correct form is *between you and me.*

See also IT'S ME.

biennial, biannual The Latin prefix *bi-,* from *bis,* 'twice', creates confusion. The reference to 'two' is obvious in such words as *bicycle, binoculars, bilingual,* but it is not always clear whether the reference is to two wholes or two halves. *To bisect,* for instance, might be defined as 'to divide into two' or 'to cut in half'.

In other words, *bi-* can suggest either 'double' or 'half'. *Biannual* and *biennial* (both from the Latin *bi-* + *annus,* 'a year') divide these two functions between them.

Biannual is the word meaning 'every half-year, twice a year, semiannual'. *Biennial* means either 'lasting two years' or 'happening every second year'. So *a biannual event* might take place in January and June each year; *a biennial event* might take place in 1984, 1986, 1988, and so on. One way of remembering the difference is this: *biennial* has the related (though rare) noun *biennium,* which refers to a two-year period in the way that *millennium* refers to a thousand-year period.

Note that *biennial* is both adjective and noun. As a noun, it refers most often to plants with a two-year life-cycle, which sprout leaves in the first year, flower and fruit in the second year, and then die. Compare *annuals* which have a one-year life-cycle, and *perennials* which continue to flower and fruit year after year.

In view of the danger of confusion between *biennial* and *biannual,* it might sometimes be advisable to use an alternative adjective, such as *two-yearly* for *biennial,* and *twice-yearly, half-yearly,* or *semiannual* for *biannual.* This applies all the more to other formations with *bi-* that are genuinely ambiguous, such as *biweekly* and *bimonthly.* These can mean either 'once in two weeks/months' or 'twice a week/month'. If a doctor intended a patient to take a certain medicine once a fortnight, and advised him to take it *biweekly,* the results might be fatal if the patient understood this to mean twice a week. Specify *twice-weekly, fortnightly, every two months, half-yearly,* and so on, to make your meaning clear.

Exemption may, however, be granted to *bicentennial* (or *bicentenary*), a legitimate formation for which there is no succinct alternative. The word is clearly understood to refer to intervals of two hundred years, not to half-centuries.

See also YEAR.

billion 1. The traditional British *billion* is a million million — 1,000,000,000,000. To Americans, this is *a trillion*; for them *a billion* has long been a thousand million — 1,000,000,000. Traditionally, this was supposed to be referred to, in British English, as a *milliard,* though the term *milliard* now seems to have passed out of use completely.

The 'small' *billion* is in fact a much more useful figure — having some role in the language of economics, population control, and so on. The 'large' *billion* is of use only to those interested in astronomy and one or two other specialised sciences.

British usage, in tacit recognition of this, has now begun to follow American usage. A few years ago, *The Times,* for instance, announced that it was henceforth going to use *billion* to mean a thousand million. But such declarations are not enough, of course: when usage is divided, as it now is in British English, things have to be spelt out in case the reader or listener misunderstands. So the word *billion* is now perhaps best avoided in favour of *a thousand million* or *a million million.*

Similarly, if you ever encounter or use the terms *trillion, quadrillion,* and so on, make sure that you understand or convey the meaning clearly.

2. Like *million, billion* retains its singular form when used in specific plurals. It is not followed by *of.*

There is a trade deficit of three billion dollars.
Several billion molecules would be needed to fill a thimble.

When the relevant noun is omitted, however,

British English probably allows *billions*, as it does *millions*:

The war must have cost many billions.

And when an indefinite quantity is suggested, then *billions* is correct. It is often followed by *of*.

Billions of molecules would be needed to fill a thimble.
There were billions of people at the party.

(This last usage, with its outrageous exaggeration, should be restricted to informal contexts.)
See also NUMBER STYLE.

bison See BUFFALO.

black Both as noun and as adjective, *black* is now the preferred term to use when referring to a person from the dark-skinned ethnic groups, especially those of African origin. It is also the term used by the black community itself, as in the slogan *Black is beautiful*, to express its pride in its African heritage.

However, the use of *black* in Britain may cause offence when applied to immigrants (and their descendants) from India, Pakistan, Bangladesh, and Sri Lanka. Members of these groups are now in British English normally referred to as *Asian* to reflect their ethnic origins. (See ASIAN.)

The term *coloured* (plural *coloureds*) is also considered offensive, especially when used as a noun, as it lumps together all non-Caucasians indiscriminately; in South Africa, it is a technical term denoting people of mixed race.

The terms *Negro* and *Negress* are now often considered offensive, and should be avoided except in specialised anthropological contexts, or when generalised in constructions such as *the growing economic power of the Negro*. If used at all, *Negro* and *Negress* should begin with a capital letter as *Asian* and *Asians* do, though *white* and *whites*, *black* and *blacks*, and *coloured* and *coloureds* generally do not.

Black English See WEST INDIAN ENGLISH.

blame The traditional pattern is *to blame someone for something*. The pattern *to blame something on someone* is more recent, and some purists still object to it. It is so well entrenched in everyday idiom now, however, that it can be safely used except in extremely formal contexts. Hardly anyone sees anything odd in saying *I blame inflation on the government*; *Don't blame it on me*; *The investigators blamed the accident on low visibility*, and so on.

As it happens, English is remarkably versatile when it comes to using a single verb in different patterns: *to shower her with compliments* and *to shower compliments on her*; *to divide 21 by 3* and *to divide 3 into 21*, and so on.

blanch, blench, bleach All these verbs are used, both transitively and intransitively, to mean 'to turn white or pale'. But the contexts in which they can appear are restricted by idiomatic usage. The commonest uses are exemplified by *to blench with fear*; *to blanch almonds* or *celery*, or *to blanch at the sight*; and *to bleach linen*.

The pink lilies folded up and disappeared. The plains were swallowed up by the yellow dust again. The sun frizzled the grasses and blazed on the rocks of Kasauli. All was either bleached or blackened by heat and glare.
– Anita Desai, *Fire on the Mountain*

To bleach is never used of people except metaphorically: *He was a man bleached of all fellow-feeling*. *To blanch* is sometimes used of people:

Restaurants charging prices that would make a Londoner blanch are packed. Ulster cuisine leaves you pale, too.
– Patrick Bishop, *The Observer*

But it is perhaps preferable to use *to blench* in such contexts, and in that way maintain a distinction:

Drage knelt down, and there was a tearing noise like old canvas. A large polished expanse of dome was presented to the bishop. He said afterwards that he blenched rather because Drage looked so extraordinary. Bits of dry glue were sticking to his scalp here and there.
– Antrobus, in Lawrence Durrell's *Esprit de Corps*

Blench and *blanch* are variants of a single word deriving from the Old French word for 'white'. *To bleach* is the modern form of an Old English verb. There is another distinct word, *to blench*, also from an Old English verb this time, meaning 'to shy away, flinch, cower'. (All these words probably derive from a single remote Germanic ancestor.) *To blench with fear* can therefore mean 'to recoil' as well as 'to turn white' — an ambiguity worth bearing in mind.

blatant, flagrant These two words carry suggestions both of offensive behaviour and of the conspicuousness of such behaviour. But *blatant* stresses the conspicuousness, and *flagrant* stresses the offensiveness.

Blatant can simply suggest a conspicuous or obtrusive presence:

> I looked out across the river. It was such a familiar view, the green towpath on one side, the old houses and angular blatant factories on the other.
> – Lynne Reid Banks, *The L-Shaped Room*

But *blatant* is used of people as well as things. A *blatant cheat* is a person whose cheating is glaringly obvious, and who apparently makes no attempt to conceal it or to show shame:

> He was terrified of blatant liars like Joe and always felt a ruinous urge to conspire with them, as he did with his mother, to the effect that they were honest people.
> – Muriel Spark,
> *The Mandelbaum Gate*

Equally, in a phrase such as *blatantly cheating* or *a blatant error*, the adverb or adjective indicates how easily perceptible the offence is to the onlooker:

> He also persuaded six people to join his 'team', but they were 'blatantly and cruelly deceived', the judge said.
> – *The Times*

The word has a secondary sense of 'unpleasantly loud or noisy, blaring': this reinforces the suggestion of conspicuousness and obtrusiveness. (The ultimate source of *blatant* is possibly the Latin verb *blatire*, 'to blab or gossip'.)

Flagrant is today used only of abstract things, no longer of people. It derives originally from a Latin verb meaning 'to burn or blaze' (hence the word *conflagration*): the word implies a shocking wrongness that is as undeniable and conspicuous as a blazing fire. It carries a stronger sense of wrongdoing than *blatant* does, suggesting notoriety or even evil. *A flagrant miscarriage of justice* is not only an open, unashamed, and even delighted defiance, but a particularly wicked one as well. (It also points to an intense feeling of outrage on the part of the speaker.)

> Finally, his egg-shell personality shattered under his wife's cruel taunts about his sexual inadequacies, his long-standing mental disorders, and her flagrant promiscuity.
> – *The Times*

The UN High Commission for Refugees, in a confidential memorandum to the two Governments, calls the exchange a 'flagrant violation of international obligations'.
> – Richard Hall, *The Observer*

The different emphases of the two words can be summed up perhaps in the following pair of short definitions: *blatant*, 'offensively conspicuous'; *flagrant*, 'conspicuously offensive'.

Each of the following quotations, the second in particular, might have been the better for using the other word:

> In a series of blatant frauds, gangs of London-based confidence tricksters have stolen as much as £200 million from German and other European investors.
> – Lorana Sullivan (U.S.), *The Observer*

> ? There is much rubbish (usually judicial) talked about women saying No when they mean Yes; but this was an 'I want to be alone' which flagrantly meant 'Don't you dare leave me alone'.
> – Julian Barnes, *The Observer*

Note, finally, the legal phrase *in flagrante delicto*, meaning 'red-handed, in the actual act of committing an offence'. In Latin, the literal meaning of the words is roughly 'with the crime still blazing'. In general use, the phrase is often shortened to *in flagrante*, and tends to be used of sexual misdemeanours, especially adultery.

bleach, blench   See BLANCH.

bona fide, bona fides   These terms are pronounced /**bō**nə **fī**di, **fī**deez/ rhyming with *tidy*, *tidies*. In American English *bona fide* is often /**bō**nə **fīd**/ rhyming with *tide*. The terms are a source of some confusion. *Bona fides* in Latin, means 'good faith'; *bona fide* is the ablative form of it, and means 'with good faith'. Strictly speaking, therefore, *bona fide* is an adverb — though little used nowadays: *The truce was settled bona fide.*

Bona fide is also used, more commonly today, as the adjective (the hyphenated form *bona-fide* is also used). It means not just 'in good faith, sincere, without intent to deceive' — *hardly a bona-fide agreement* — but also, loosely, 'authentic, genuine': *a certified, bona fide Rembrandt.*

Bona fide should not be used as a noun. The noun, in the singular, is *bona fides*; it means 'honest intention, good faith':

> The prisoner's bona fides was not enough for the magistrate, and bail was set at £5,000 (note the use of *was,* not *were*).

It was only much later, with the arrival of some genuine Italian prisoners from North Africa, that doubts were cast on his nationality, but by that time Blott had established his bona fides by displaying no interest in the course of the war and by resolutely demonstrating a reluctance to escape that was authentically Italian.

    – Tom Sharpe, *Blott on the Landscape*

There is no plural form. *Bona fides* is really a 'mass noun', just as *good faith* is. When referring to the *bona fides* of more than one person, you can just perhaps continue to use the term with a singular verb, but it is best to adopt some other strategy and restructure the sentence slightly, along the following lines:

? The bona fides of all the prisoners was rejected by the magistrate.
All the prisoners' declarations of bona fides were rejected by the magistrate.
All the prisoners' credentials were rejected by the magistrate.
The bona fides of each prisoner was rejected by the magistrate.

Note that the terms are now regarded as fully established in English and are therefore usually not printed in italics.

bonus   *A bonus*, from the Latin word for 'good', refers principally to an additional payment, such as shareholders might get supplementary to their expected dividend, or employees might get at Christmas or in acknowledgment of higher productivity.

    An extended sense has attracted criticism from purists — 'an incidental benefit; a plus': *It was a lovely drive, and the bonus was that the sun came out for half an hour.* The objections seem slightly unfair: the word is no more objectionable than *plus*, and there seems no other single-word equivalent. But do use *bonus* with restraint. If everything is a *bonus*, then bonuses soon lose their value.

    One criticism that is well-founded, however, is that directed against the common phrase *?? an added bonus*. This is tautologous: a bonus is by definition something added to the main payment or advantage.

both   **1.** *Both* applies to two and only two elements — *damaged both the bark and the foliage of the tree* — though either or both of these elements (ideally, only the second of them) may itself be in the plural: *damaged both the bark*

and the branches of the tree. If more than two elements are listed, then *both* cannot be used:

  ✕ The beetles cause damage to both the bark, foliage, and branches of the tree.

Omit the *both* here.

    2. With nouns, such as *children*, the following three constructions are all acceptable: *Both children are crying*; *Both the children are crying*; *Both of the children are crying*. American English uses the *of* freely; British English, until fairly recently, tended to avoid it, but today probably includes it as often as not.

    3. *Both* is used not simply when speaking of two elements, but when considering them together. If they are being considered separately, then *each* is preferable to *both*:

  ?? Both boys pointed at the other in silent accusation.

It would be more in keeping with idiom here to say: *Each boy pointed at the other* or *The boys pointed at each other*. If the word *other* appears in a sentence, the chances are that *both* is less appropriate than *each*.

    And note a possible difference between the following two sentences:

    Anna and I each received a letter this morning.
    Anna and I both received a letter this morning.

The first example indicates that two letters arrived — one for Ann and one for me. The second example should be used to indicate that a single letter arrived — addressed jointly to Ann and me. However, it is perhaps more commonly and certainly more dubiously used to mean the same as the first example.

    Again:

  ? There is a filling station on both sides of the road.

This suggests that the filling station straddles the road. It is far better to say:

    There is a filling station on each/either side of the road.

Another possible construction, *? There are filling stations on both sides of the road*, is again slightly ambiguous unfortunately: it is unclear whether there is one filling station, or more than one, on each side of the road.

    See EACH; EITHER.

    4. *Both* is often used together in a sentence with some other intensifying word or phrase — such as *also*, *as well as*, *same*, *agree*, *jointly*, *alike*, and *equally* — resulting in redundancy:

× This line seems to have been misunderstood both by the critics as well as by the poet himself.

Either omit *both* or change *as well as* to *and*. Again:

? Judge Teller, having both a jurisprudence degree and also a sound medical training, is chosen to hear the tricky ethical cases.

The *also* is best omitted; alternatively change the *both . . . and* construction to a *not only . . . but also* construction: *. . . having not only a jurisprudence degree but also a sound medical training*. Again:

× They both belong to the same club.

Omit the *both* or the *same*. Similarly:

?? The environment regulations are aimed at conserving the habitat of both tribesman and animal alike.

Omit either *both* or *alike*.

5. a. The phrase *the both* is used in regional varieties of English, but should be avoided elsewhere: ? *I'll thrash the both of you*. Use either *the two of you* or simply *both of you*.
b. Some constructions with *both* at the end, such as ? *She is a doctor and a lawyer both* or ? *He loves Anne and Mary both,* are characteristic of northern British English and American English, but seem strange to speakers of southern British English.
6. When *both* and *and* are used as correlative conjunctions, the words, phrases, or clauses that follow them have to be of similar structure:

The storm stripped the tree of both its foliage and its branches.
The storm stripped the tree both of its foliage and of its branches.
The storm both stripped the tree of its foliage and tore down its branches.

Note how, in the second example, the *of* is repeated after *and* to correspond with the *of* that follows *both*; and how, in the third example, an entire clause is used after *both* and *and*. To neglect this correlation between the two structures in each case is to fall into grammatical error:

× The storm stripped the tree of both its foliage and of its branches.
× The storm stripped the tree both of its foliage and its branches.

× The storm both stripped the tree of its foliage and of its branches.

× Most Grenadian politicians now appear to favour at least an 18-month delay before elections to choose a Government for their tiny, traumatised island, and some even suggest that two years will be needed both to prepare the electorate and avoid the return to power of former Premier Sir Eric Gairy.
    – Robert Chesshyre, *The Observer*

An extra *to* is needed before *avoid* in order to restore the balance.

For a more detailed discussion, see PARALLEL CONSTRUCTIONS.

7. Since *both* can be used like an adjective as well (technically, it is a 'determiner' or 'predeterminer'), the danger of ambiguity arises. Suppose the elements had been reversed in one of the examples listed above:

? The storm stripped the tree of both its branches and its foliage.

Two interpretations are possible here: first, that conveyed by the original sentence —

The storm stripped the tree of both its foliage and its branches

— and secondly, that conveyed by either of the following sentences:

The storm stripped the tree of its two branches and its foliage.
The storm stripped the tree of its foliage and both its branches.

For the sake of clarity, these three unambiguous sentences are preferable.

Another slight ambiguity occurs in such constructions as:

Professor Roberts and Dr Crick have both joined the protest group and signed the petition.

The *both* could be understood as referring either backwards (to the two men) or forwards (to the two actions), though the two versions at least remain similar in meaning. Be on the alert for ambiguous uses of *both*, and take evasive action if you find any.

8. Ambiguity can also arise in a purely adjectival use of *both*. Consider the following confusing sentence:

? Both (of) your cars are due for a service.

Is the speaker addressing two people, each having one car, or is he addressing one person who owns two cars? Without a context as a clue, the sentence is ambiguous.

Perhaps out of fear of such ambiguity, some purists discourage the construction *both our Xs, both their Xs,* and so on, recommending instead the construction *the Xs of both of us/them,* and so on. The example above would accordingly be reworded as:

The cars of both of you are due for a service.

Similarly:

The eldest sons of both of them go to Eton.

Better still, however, is to cast everything in the singular:

The eldest son of each of them goes to Eton.

Of course, when a single subject belongs to two people jointly, the construction × *both our X* is impossible:

× We're twins — today is both our birthday/s.
× They should share the credit — it was both of their idea/it was both of them's idea.

These should read *the birthday of both of us* and *the idea of both of them.*

A further preference of the purists, in the case of *both* with pronouns, is for just such phrases as *both of us* and *both of them* over *us both* and *them both.* It is perhaps slightly less formal, though no less acceptable, to say:

We both work at the British Museum

than to say:

Both of us work at the British Museum.

● *Recommendation* For most purposes there is little to choose between the constructions *both (of) their fathers* and *the fathers of both of them* (provided, of course, that they are equally unambiguous), and similarly between *we both are* and *both of us are.* Purists favour the second item in each pair; in very formal contexts, that is perhaps the one to choose. But the former item in each pair is quite standard too, and often feels more natural and less stiff.

bottleneck This is a useful image, referring to a traffic holdup or other restricted flow, or to something that causes it: *a bottleneck in the processing of visa applications, owing to a go-slow by consulate clerks.*

The original sense, dating back to 1896, was of a narrow road or intersection where a traffic jam was likely to build up. Today it is so widely used that it has been criticised as a vogue word. Use it sparingly; there are often more precise terms available (sometimes also metaphors in origin): *backlog, holdup, congestion,* and so on.

One limitation on the use of *bottleneck* is the intensifying of it. People speak of *? a big bottleneck,* which, if you think about it, suggests an easy flow rather than a difficult one. On the other hand, *a narrow bottleneck* does not sound very impressive. Perhaps an adjective like *troublesome* is the best that one can do.

Bottleneck also refers to a style of guitar-playing. There is a verb too, *to bottleneck,* meaning 'to impede or slow down by creating a bottleneck'.

brackets 1. These crescent-shaped marks of punctuation, ( ), are to be distinguished from the square marks, [ ]. The coexistence of ( ) and [ ] has led to confusion over the names of each type of symbol:

British English	*American English*
( ) brackets, round brackets	parentheses
[ ] square brackets	brackets, square brackets

(Note that the curly mark linking items on two or more separate lines — {tea coffee} — is called a *brace,* not a *bracket*; the brackets < > are called *angle brackets.*)

Material enclosed in brackets is often (especially in Britain), called a 'parenthesis', or said to be 'in parenthesis'. The Welsh writer David Jones called his poetic novel about the First World War *In Parenthesis,* suggesting, perhaps, that the war experience was 'cut off' or separated from the peace-time world that preceded and followed it.

2. The notion that bracketed material is fundamentally separated from what surrounds it points to the principal use of brackets. They enclose material that supplements or explains — material that could be omitted without changing the truth of the sentence. In the previous paragraph, for example, the phrase (*especially in Britain*) is important but not absolutely essential to the sentence in which it appears.

Typical examples of short bracketed material include dates and references:

William Shakespeare (1564-1616)
in chapter 3 (pp 48-51)

But the use of brackets is often more sophisticated than this. The examples that follow in this section — and in the whole article — are all taken from a single issue of *The Times Literary Supplement* (*TLS*), unless otherwise noted.

The principal Catholic service, the Mass, was never broadcast by the BBC (except occasionally in Northern Ireland) until the Second World War.
— John Whale, *TLS*

However, the family connection with the trade (as he acknowledges) made it easier for him to gain the cooperation of the sixty or so practitioners he interviewed.
— Donald Gould, *TLS*

It sets out to expose the grimness that exists beneath the beauty and grace in a dancer's life: in her case, ... the illnesses that invariably coincided with first nights; the collapse of marriages (two), and her difficult double role as a mother.
— Julie Kavanagh, *TLS*

...reproduced from the British Journal of Photography Annual 1984 *(203pp. Henry Greenwood, 28 Great James Street, London WC1. £9.95. 0 90041 429 4).*
— caption, in *TLS*

In *Homo Hierarchicus* he analysed the capacity of a caste-system to ascribe rigid roles to each individual, and in *From Mandeville to Marx* (the French edition is called *Homo Equalis*) he turned to the origins of contemporary economic individualism.
— Adrian Wooldridge, *TLS*

3. In general, material set off by brackets is less closely integrated with its surroundings than material set off by commas. This can be seen clearly in the first example above. Both *the Mass* and *(except occasionally in Northern Ireland)* can in theory be omitted from the sentence. But the omission of the former would seriously impair the sense of the sentence, whereas omission of the latter would not.

Furthermore, bracketed material can connect or contrast with its surroundings more than material set off by commas usually does. That difference too is illustrated by the first example. If, however, the contrast is particularly abrupt, dashes may be used instead of brackets. And only brackets or dashes, not commas, can enclose a complete sentence, as in the last example. Another example from the same edition of *The Times Literary Supplement*:

Her free, unorthodox way of moving (Seymour has never been considered a true classical dancer), and her directness as an actress, could make an audience forget the

artificiality of the genre and allow them to concentrate on the character.
— Julie Kavanagh, *TLS*

4. All the examples so far have been of bracketed material within a sentence. But there are also bracketed sentences within paragraphs:

It was Frederick Ashton who confirmed Seymour's stylistic affinity with Isadora Duncan in a wonderful solo which he devised for her, to five Brahms waltzes, as an evocation of the dances he remembered seeing Duncan perform. (Seymour recently surfaced from 'retirement' once more to take Royal Ballet classes — albeit in sneakers — to prepare for her performance of the Isadora solo at the Met's celebratory gala in New York.) Ashton was also to provide ... the perfect role for a mature ballerina — Natalya Petrovna, in *A Month in the Country*.
— Julie Kavanagh, *TLS*

This example also shows the use of dashes to set off material *within* material already bracketed: it is usually clearer to use dashes or commas for this purpose than to have brackets within brackets.

Even entire paragraphs can sometimes be found bracketed off from the surrounding text, though they are not very common.

5. The last example also shows that a complete and independent sentence within brackets is treated as a proper sentence: it can end with a full stop and would begin with a capital letter even if its first word were not a name: *(She recently surfaced ...).* But bracketed material within a sentence does not end with a full stop (even when it comes at the end of a sentence: the full stop should then fall outside the bracket, as here). And it does not usually begin with a capital letter: even if it has the form of a *complete* sentence, it is not an independent one:

This is one reason so many things slipped by him. And the imagination (he himself said it, echoing Shelley) is 'a fading coal'.
— Professor Hugh Kenner (U.S.), *TLS*

The only important exception is adages, mottoes, quotations, and the like — and even here there is no full stop:

She embroidered her favourite saying (Well begun is half done) on a pillow.

In other respects, punctuation within brackets is straightforward; in particular, full stops after abbreviations are permitted, as are question marks and exclamation marks, as in the following hypothetical example:

She became (who would have thought it?) the Chairman of the Board.

As for punctuation surrounding bracketed material, it too is straightforward. But in general no mark of punctuation should come immediately before an opening bracket in the middle of a sentence. Thus the following example is incorrect:

✕ The monarch of Etna and Vesuvius ... was not Ferdinand I of Austria, 'der Gütige', roughly Ferdinand the Harmless, (even though he was married to a daughter of the King of Sardinia), the one who ... whinged 'Kaiser bin i', und Knödel müss i' haben'.
— Eric Korn, *TLS*

The comma before the first bracket should have been omitted; but the comma after the closing bracket is quite in order.

6. Some writers put brackets round certain adjectives or phrases that come before nouns, as in the following hypothetical example:

a number of (unconfirmed) sightings of the Loch Ness monster.

The effect is to 'demote' the bracketed material from an essential, restrictive part of the noun phrase to a nonessential, nonrestrictive part, as if one had written:

a number of sightings, unconfirmed, of the Loch Ness monster.

Yet, paradoxically, the bracketed material is also given greater prominence than if the author had written:

a number of unconfirmed sightings of the Loch Ness monster.

7. Brackets are used to enclose alternative material: *The person(s) who did this will be apprehended.* This is roughly equivalent to *The person or persons who did this will be apprehended.* Similarly:

This is a clangorous irony, of a kind the play is full of. Simon Gray makes a lot, in particular, of juxtapositions between literary and biological (in)fertility. Stuart's wife has an abortion at just the time when, with his magazine failing, he most wants a child.
— Jeremy Treglown, *TLS*

This might be glossed as 'literary and biological fertility or infertility, as the case may be'.

8. In line with their use to present supplementary or explanatory material, brackets also enclose figured numerals that confirm written numbers or that 'translate' one system of reckoning into another, as in these hypothetical examples:

at forty-five (45) revolutions per minute
at 2/6 (12½p)
the year 1985 (5745 in the Jewish calendar)

They also enclose abbreviations when these are introduced:

Acquired Immunodeficiency Syndrome (AIDS)

Subsequently the abbreviation may be used instead of the expression it stands for: this is a common space-saving convention in technical and semi-technical writing. Obversely, brackets can enclose the expansion of an abbreviation:

the degree of B.Mus. (Bachelor of Music)

9. Brackets can also enclose letters or numbers used to order items in a list:

... an author who hadn't actually finished the book when its typescripts went to the printers, and was simultaneously (a) composing two whole episodes while (b) trying to cope with proofs on the margins of which he (c) added some 30 per cent of the final text while (d) intermittently rolling on the floor with pain ...
But it evidently corresponds not only with a *Ulysses* cross-reference but with a scenario whereby (1) the typist didn't correct an error of fact but simply made a mistake; (2) Joyce didn't see the error in the list but caught the resulting fault in the arithmetic, having (3) ... had all his wits about him, whereas when he saw to the errata the coal had faded.
Professor Hugh Kenner (U.S.), *TLS*

Normally, here as elsewhere, the brackets are used in pairs. But sometimes it is possible to use the final bracket only, especially when the listed items appear on separate lines:

There are three points to consider here:
1) ...
2) ...
3) ...

10. In mathematics an important use of brackets is to indicate the order in which operations are performed:

$(2 \times 3) + 1 = 7$ but $2 \times (3 + 1) = 8$
$xy^2(z + [x^3y^2]^4)^2$

11. Note the brackets-within-brackets in the example above. The change from round brackets to square brackets is designed to help the reader isolate the subdivision — but, unlike the change from single to double quotation marks, this change is not essential. The formula could just as well have been written:

$$xy^2(z + (x^3y^2)^4)^2$$

Similarly in prose: some publishers favour using square brackets for sub-divisions; others favour repeating the round brackets; but most would probably agree that it is best to avoid brackets-within-brackets wherever possible. Here are the three options — the last, though not quite self-consistent, certainly looks the best:

Read the last part of chapter 3 (pp 48-51) and the whole of chapter 4 (and also, if you can, the first part of chapter 5 [pp 89-97]).
Read the last part of chapter 3 (pp 48-51) and the whole of chapter 4 (and also, if you can, the first part of chapter 5 (pp 89-97)).
Read the last part of chapter 3 (pp 48-51) and the whole of chapter 4 (and also, if you can, the first part of chapter 5, pp 89-97).

12. In books about language, such as this one, brackets have a number of special functions. They can enclose optional material:

There are other problems (,) too.

The brackets round the comma mean that the sentence illustrated is correct with or without the comma.

In dictionaries, brackets are especially important. They can enclose the word typically modified by an adjective:

addled *adj.* (of an egg) spoilt: *an addled egg*

They can enclose the typical subject of a verb:

capsize *verb intransitive* (of a boat or ship) to turn over: *The boat capsized*

They can enclose the typical object of a transitive verb:

capsize *verb transitive* to cause (a boat or ship) to turn over: *The waves capsized the boat.*

They can also make it possible to use a single definition for more than one part of speech:

white *adj., n.* (of) the colour of snow

With the *of,* the definition is of an adjective: *The sheets are white = The sheets are of the colour of snow.* Without the *of,* the definition is that of a noun: *White is my favourite colour =*

The colour of snow is my favourite colour.

Dictionaries and other language books often also use brackets to enclose the pronunciation of words:

kite (kīt) *n.*

There is considerable variation in the use of these conventions by dictionaries, though English-language dictionaries are generally agreed on the use of brackets to enclose the objects of verbs. See also SQUARE BRACKETS.

bravura, bravado *Bravura* is a brilliant showy style of performance. The word was originally applied to the performance of music — *a bravura violin passage* — but is now used more widely:

The bravura cameos in *The Hypnotist*, with which the Sigmund saga continued on BBC2 last night, were numerous, fulfilling for the cast but ... leaving one quite enervated at the end.
  As the Baroness, Miriam Margolyes proved that when bravura is called for, she can make the most of it.
  — Dennis Hackett, *The Times*

Bravado is a defiant swaggering show of courage: *He had bravado all right, but I doubted his competence, and even his courage, on the actual field of battle.*

The words are related in origin, *bravado* coming through Spanish, and *bravura* through Italian, and both (like *brave*) going back to the Latin *barbarus* and Greek *barbaros*, 'foreign, barbarous'. With their similarity of form and the slight overlap of meaning, the two words are sometimes confused. Specifically, *bravura* is used mistakenly in place of *bravado*:

✗ With amazing bravura, Ned rang GK's New York number on a pretext.
  — John le Carré,
  The Little Drummer Girl

✗ In spite of this known danger, Japanese men continue to eat the dangerous fish in a spirit of bravura, and every year a number of people die as a result of these banquets.
  — Charles Berlitz (U.S.), *Native Tongues*

breach, breech *Breach* and *breech* present an old spelling problem. The words have quite different meanings, and their frequent misspelling can produce some very strange results.
  The noun *breach*, with an *a*, is 'an opening, a fissure, a gap broken through something' — whether literal or metaphorical:

And as he talked she had that unsettling feeling which she had had about him from the start: that his outward nature, like his presence here, was a pretext — his task was to force a breach through which he could spirit his other and totally larcenous nature.
— John le Carré,
The Little Drummer Girl

A more common metaphorical sense is 'a rift in or rupturing of relations': *The argument over the loot only widened the breach between us.*

But Dennis Robertson, the most gifted economist among those who fought in the First World War, never fully recovered from the breach with the man whom he had worked with and so much admired.
— Piers Brendon, *The Observer*

Bear in mind that *breach* is related to the word *break*, or think of it as meaning '*a*perture', and the spelling should be easier to remember.

Breach also refers to the breaking of any moral or legal or emotional bond, as in *breach of contract* or *a breach of promise* — the breaking of a verbal commitment, usually to marry. It is frequently used in the idiom *in breach of*:

Adams is seeking a declaration that in charging him with industrial espionage for leaking papers to the commission, the Swiss Government was in breach of the free trade agreement it enjoys with the Community.
— Nigel Hawkes, *The Observer*

As a verb, *to breach* means 'to make or cause a breach in':

In the eighth round he had the champion in big trouble, but his failure to follow up and breach Holmes's skilful defences lost him his chance of winning.
— W.J. Weatherby, *The Guardian*

Take care not to confuse *to breach* with *to broach,* which literally means 'to pierce' but is often used to mean 'to open, embark upon', as in *to broach a subject.*

The word *breach* is a fusion of two source words: Old High German *brehhan* (via Old French) and Old English *brecan*, both of which mean 'to break'.

Breech, with the double *e*, refers to the back or lower part of something. It applies especially to the rear of the barrel of a gun, or the lower part of the human trunk, or the buttocks. As a memory aid, think of the spelling as having the extra *e* for 'end'. There is sometimes confusion

over the spelling of *breech* in *breech birth* (or *delivery*). The phrase refers to a birth in which the baby is born feet or buttocks (*breech*) first.

The word *breeches,* meaning 'trousers, especially knee-length trousers', functions as a plural, although it has no singular. Note that it should properly be pronounced /**brich**iz/.

Breech and *breeches* come from the Old English *brec*, the plural of *broc*, 'a leg-covering'.

Britain, Great Britain, the British Isles, the United Kingdom, England

Britain is a name without any official status. It is used loosely as a substitute for various other names, listed in the title of this item, especially *Great Britain*.

Great Britain refers mainly to the large island shared by England, Scotland, and Wales, and has been used since 1707 to refer to the political union of these three regions. The various small islands considered to be English, Scottish, or Welsh are also usually understood to be covered by the designation *Great Britain,* but that does not include the Isle of Man, the Channel Islands (Jersey, Guernsey, and so on), and the province of Northern Ireland.

The *United Kingdom,* or to give it its full official title, the *United Kingdom of Great Britain and Northern Ireland*, refers to a political rather than a geographical unit — the state, the constitutional monarchy. It does include Northern Ireland, of course, but strictly speaking, not the Isle of Man and the Channel Islands — these are, in different degrees, self-governing, though 'possessions' of the British Crown.

The United Kingdom was built up in this way: Wales became an English principality in 1284. Scotland and England were officially united in 1707 to form Great Britain. And in 1801, the political union of Ireland with Great Britain produced the United Kingdom. When the south of Ireland gained its independence in 1921, the present state — and full official title — emerged.

The British Isles is an unofficial name again, referring to the United Kingdom and the Republic of Ireland together, as well as the Isle of Man and the Channel Islands (sometimes including those governed by France).

England refers, strictly, to just one of the political divisions of the United Kingdom, but it is loosely used, especially by foreigners, to refer to Great Britain and sometimes the United Kingdom as a whole. Some set-phrases encourage this careless usage, especially *the Queen* (or *King*) *of England* and, of course, *the English language.* A Scot or Welshman is happy to admit to speaking *English*, but would not take kindly to being called *an Englishman*. It is a pity that no natural, elegant and simple term exists for 'a citizen of the United Kingdom' — *Briton* is rather haughty, *Brit* is slangy and possibly offensive, *Britisher* is an ugly and outdated Americanism, and all three are probably inappropriate anyway for someone from Northern Ireland.

Note, finally, that there are six counties of Northern Ireland included in the United Kingdom — Antrim, Armagh, Down, Fermanagh, Derry or Londonderry, and Tyrone. Northern Ireland is sometimes referred to as *Ulster*, but strictly speaking Ulster consists of these six counties plus three others — Cavan, Donegal, and Monaghan — that are now part of the Republic of Ireland.

See also AMERICA; UNITED STATES.

broach   See BREACH.

brutalise   *To brutalise* is a powerful word: it means 'to make brutal' — *His nature was brutalised by an impoverished childhood* — or, more loosely 'to treat brutally': *The murderer had whipped, burnt, and otherwise brutalised his victim before finally slitting her throat.*

This second sense, dubious enough as it is in the eyes of some purists, has given rise to a still weaker sense — 'to mistreat or maltreat': ? *Stop that child brutalising its doll like that.* Surely there is little feeling here of the beast in human nature — the notion that *brutalise* ought to be conveying.

Limit *brutalise* to truly brutal contexts, or you will in a small way be contributing to the decline in its effectiveness.

buffalo, bison   There are four main types of animal covered by the names *buffalo* and *bison*. All are heavy, ox-like, horned creatures of the family *Bovidae*. Only one of the four — the famous North American animal — can be referred to by either name.

Two of the animals may be called *buffalo* but not *bison*. One is the 'water buffalo' or 'carabao' (*Bubalis bubalis*), a draught animal originally from India and now more widespread in Asia. It has long spreading horns that curve backwards, and heavy, coarse black hair. The other is the African buffalo, the 'Cape buffalo', which is more lightly built, and has horns spreading sideways from the crown of its head in the shape of a handlebar moustache.

The animal that can be called either *buffalo* or *bison* (or *wild ox*) is the *Bison bison*. Of its two names, *buffalo* is by far the more usual in American English. This is the animal that the American Indians once hunted for meat, and that

the white settlers and hunters almost wiped out. 'Buffalo' Bill Cody earned his name by shooting a huge number of buffalo: in one single year, he shot over 3000. The buffalo/bison has a humped body, a shaggy mane, and small horns.

The word *bison* (but not *buffalo*) is also used to refer to a somewhat smaller European animal, the *Bison bonasus*. This creature is also known by the German name of *wisent*, pronounced /**weez**n't/ or /**veez**n't/ and possibly related in origin to *bison*.

The word *buffalo* comes from the Portuguese *bufalo*. This goes back to Latin *bubalus* and Greek *boubalos,* 'African antelope, buffalo', probably in turn from *bous,* 'ox, cow'.

Bison comes from the Latin *bison,* and seems to be of Germanic origin.

The plural of *bison* is again *bison*. The plural of buffalo is *buffaloes* or *buffalos,* or collectively *buffalo*.

burn   The past tense and past participle of *to burn* can be either *burnt* or *burned*. In British English, *burnt* tends to be used when the idea is of a fully completed action, and *burned* when the idea is of a continuing or repeated process. So: *The house burnt down; They burnt some incense*, but *Her cheeks burned*; *They burned logs all night to keep warm*.

North Americans tend to favour *burned* in all contexts, though they seem happy to use *burnt* directly before a noun: *burnt toast*.

Note that *burned* can be pronounced /burnt/ as well as /burnd/.

See -ED, -T.

but   1. Generations of schoolteachers have solemnly warned generations of schoolchildren against beginning a sentence with *But*. But there is no good reason, grammatical or logical, for this prohibition. Historically *but*, like *and*, has been used at the start of sentences through every period of the language's development. It is true that other words are available, and sometimes preferable — *yet, still*, or *nevertheless* — but often *but* is the only appropriate word.

The schoolroom-rule can be ignored then — with the following provisos or risks.

First, two very short clauses should be linked into a single sentence if the second clause starts with *but*, unless you are aiming for some special staccato effect by writing short, sharp, separate sentences.

Secondly, a useful streamlining results from linking the two clauses into a single sentence. Compare:

George was quite prepared to join us, but not to pay his share

and:

George was quite prepared to join us. But he was not prepared to pay his share.

Note how the single-sentence version requires fewer words than the two-sentence version. (The two versions can be combined, and produce quite effective results for a journalist or advertiser:

? George was quite prepared to join us. But not to pay his share.

In ordinary formal usage, however, this would be unadvisable.)

Thirdly, pedants will continue to criticise you if you start a sentence with *but,* and it might in certain circumstances be worth yielding in order to avoid a distracting debate on the subject.

The most common alternative to *but* is *however.* However, objections are also sometimes raised to the use of *however,* in this sense, as the first word of a sentence (see HOWEVER 3.).

However is at least versatile enough to shift its position: *That was, however, not the true story*; *That was not the true story, however.* In standard English, *but* cannot of course appear in the middle or at the end of its clause in this way. But it is worth noting that in colloquial Australian and New Zealand English, and in some regional dialects elsewhere, *but* can appear at the end of a sentence: ? *It's nice and sunny — cold, but.*

2. The punctuation used with *but* is fairly straightforward. Those who criticise the use of *but* as the first word of a sentence will again criticise the use of a semicolon or colon just before *but.* Again, this criticism can — with similar provisos — be ignored. The punctuation mark usually preceding *but* is a comma.

He lay motionless in a pool of blood on the floor, but I was taking no chances — I shot him once more from close range.

The comma is particularly necessary in sentences where *but* might otherwise be understood momentarily to have a different meaning:

The man at the door was not Casey, but Stevenson bade him enter just the same.

Without that comma to guide him, the reader might at first take the construction to mean that the man at the door was Stevenson.

In shorter and unambiguous sentences, especially where the subject is omitted in the *but*-clause, the comma is optional:

She is not a strong player(,) but is so enthusiastic that the team cannot do without her.

And in short sentences where both the subject and verb are omitted from the *but*-clause, the comma is better left out than kept in:

He was defeated but not disgraced.

So much for the comma before *but.* Is it ever permissible to use a comma directly after *but,* as it is used after *however?*

Merchants were good to the firefighters then, because they expected firefighters to be good in return as they made their annual, semi-annual, or monthly fire inspections. But, the system has changed now.
— Dennis Smith (U.S.),
Report From Engine Company 82.

The comma after *but* here reflects the dramatic and emphatic pause in speech. Many careful users disapprove of the comma, however, preferring to use a dash or ellipsis (three dots) to represent a spoken pause.

3. *But* is often used unnecessarily or incorrectly.

a. It should not be used if *however* occurs in the same clause and conveys the same meaning:
× *But this offer of help, however, arrived too late.* (Of course, *however* in its other senses can be combined with *but*: *He wanted very much to win, but however hard he fought, his opponent always got the better of him.*)

Other ways of reinforcing or expanding the meaning of *but* are less objectionable, however. *But nevertheless, but despite that, but even so* grate less than *but, however*:

? Peter Levi's election to Professor of Poetry at Oxford is gratifying ... his poems, browsed through or taken en masse, informally or intravenously, are often lovely things ... But what *kind* of poetry professor will he be, though? Will he do as Auden admirably did, will he sit in the cafés and bars of Oxford and talk of poems with anyone who cares to listen?
— Frank Delaney, *The Listener*

And *but still* has become almost fully accepted as an idiomatic turn of phrase.

b. In its usual sense, *but* links two ideas that are in opposition: *He was rich but he was very unhappy.* (The assumption here is that wealth and unhappiness are opposing ideas.) Take care not to use *but* when the two ideas are in harmony with each other:

✗ He made futile attempts to scare away the locusts, but was unable to save his crops.

The word *futile* already suggests that the crop might be lost, and the two clauses in the sentence are therefore in harmony. The word *but* is accordingly inappropriate. If *futile* were changed to *desperate* or *heroic,* the *but* would then be correct.

A subtler but similar case is

✗ He fled from the approaching figure, but it was she who stood her ground and confronted the irate gamekeeper.

The second half of this sentence expresses contrast in two ways: one, by *but,* two, by the use of *it was she who* instead of the normal *she.* These two devices achieve much the same effect, so one of them is redundant. Say *He fled, but she stood her ground* or *He fled: it was she who stood her ground* or else *He fled, and it was she who stood her ground.*

At its simplest, the contrast between a correct and an incorrect use of *but* is demonstrated in the following pair of sentences.

She is not cross but pleased.
✗ She is not cross but she is pleased.

4. *But* in the sense of 'except' raises a problem. Should we say *No one but I can tell* or *No one can tell but me*? The experts differ: the majority probably consider *but* to be a conjunction here, and would therefore recommend *No one but I can tell.* But *but* was originally a preposition (meaning 'outside'), and can still be regarded as one — in which case, the correct form is *No one can tell but me.*

Since there is no clear answer in grammar, the answer must be sought in idiom. And idiom endorses both of the forms so far suggested. What idiom finds less acceptable are the forms *? No one can tell but I* and *? No one but me can tell.* In other words, if the *but*-phrase follows the verb, treat *but* as a preposition, and use *me, him, her,* or *them*; if the *but*-phrase comes before the verb, treat *but* as a conjunction, and use *I, he, she,* or *they.* So the two best forms would be:

The boy stood on the burning deck whence all but he had fled.

The boy stood on the burning deck whence all had fled but him.

Of course in some sentences, the pronoun has to be in the objective case: *You have no supporters but me.* Whether *me* is taken as the object of the preposition *but* or the object of the verb *have* is immaterial.

When *but* in the sense of 'except' is followed directly by the infinitive form of a verb, it usually takes *to*:

We had no alternative but to confess our guilt.

But in similar phrases with *anything, nothing,* and the like, the *to* is omitted:

We'll do anything/everything but confess our guilt.
We did nothing but protest our innocence.

● *Recommendation* But, in the sense of 'except', has to be followed by *me, him,* or the like if the *but*-phrase relates to the object of the sentence. But where the *but*-phrase relates to a subject, there is a choice between *me, him,* or the like, and *I, he,* or the like. There is a slight idiomatic preference for one form over the other according to the position of *but* in the clause. The rule of thumb is this: use *but I, but he,* and so on in the middle of a clause (as before the verb), and *but me, but him,* and so on at the end of a clause.

5. *But* in the sense of 'only': this rather old-fashioned adverb occurs in such constructions as *There is but one man for the job.*

In markets such as these — 14-point falls in the Financial Times 30-share index come expensive — one should not invest; one should but gamble.
– Melvyn Marckus, *The Observer*

If you intend the sentence to be positive, take care not to slip a negative adverb into it as many speakers of dialect or nonstandard English do: *? He doesn't earn but £50 a week*; *? She never had but two happy days in her life.*

Take care too, as with *only,* to position *but* correctly within the sentence: *There is time for but one further question,* not ✗ *There is time but for one further question.* See ONLY.

6. *but that*: this old-fashioned idiom is still useful in negative and interrogative constructions after such words as *to know* and *to be sure.* The double conjunction *but that* indicates both hesitation and optimism:

Who knows but that the war is almost over?
I am not sure but that spring has arrived.

The modern tendency would be to replace *but that* with *that . . . not,* where possible:

I am not sure that spring has not arrived.

The hesitant optimism of *but that* is now rather weakened, however.

Where *but that* is no longer quite acceptable is in sentences where *that* by itself can replace it, especially in negative or interrogative sentences after the verbs *to doubt* and *to wonder:*

? I don't doubt but that he's telling the truth.
I don't doubt that he's telling the truth.

Strictly speaking, the first of these sentences contains a kind of double negative (in *don't* and *but*), and is therefore misleadingly constructed (see DOUBLE NEGATIVE). And the effect is in any case one of pompousness rather than mere formality. The use of the shorter *but* rather than *but that* is usually no improvement. In the following quotation, however, the construction lends itself to the slightly archaic *but*. To replace it by *that ... not*, or the equivalent, would produce an inelegant jar with the *not*'s already present in the sentence:

True, it is not dull — indeed there is not a paragraph in it but sparkles with lucidity and grace — and the final essay, an account of the achievements and fates of the members of the Vienna Circle, is an eloquent and even moving tribute to 'those heroes of my youth'.
— Bernard Levin, *The Observer*
See also NO QUESTION.

7. *but what*: This combination has a strange appeal for writers and speakers of English. Presumably it is felt to add something stylish to a sentence: in fact, it sounds affected or just silly today, and probably did even in the days when it was widely used. Nowadays, all its functions have been taken over by more idiomatic and less archaic forms.

? I don't doubt but what she will be re-elected. (= I don't doubt that she will be re-elected.)
? And I don't know but what I shan't tell her so. (= And I don't know that I shan't tell her so.)
? I never hear Gigli records but what I think of my childhood singing-teacher. (= I never hear Gigli records without thinking of my childhood singing-teacher.)

This last example could be altered less drastically by the simple omission of the *what*:

I never hear Gigli records but I think of my childhood singing-teacher.

The *but* here is an old-fashioned conjunction introducing an adverbial clause, as in *It never*

rains but it pours. The meaning is roughly 'without its also happening that'.

One place where *but what* has survived, however, is in the informal idiom *not but what ... not*, roughly equivalent to 'although, to be sure':

It's getting late — not but what I couldn't do with a pint before we go.

See also AND WHICH; CAN BUT; NOT ONLY ... BUT ALSO; NOT SO MUCH ... AS.

but which See AND WHICH.

buzz words See JARGON; VOGUE WORDS.

by, bye Confusion sometimes arises between these two spellings; remember that *by* is a preposition or adverb, meaning 'near' or 'next to', whereas *bye* is a noun, meaning 'a side issue or secondary matter'. Here are a few common phrases illustrating the difference:

by the bye. (*By* is used here as a preposition meaning 'beside', and *bye* is a noun, meaning 'side issue or wayside'. Nevertheless, the phrase is often spelt *by the by*, and most dictionaries now accept this as a variant.)

by and by. (Both *by*'s are adverbs.)

a leg bye. (*Bye* is a noun, referring to a run scored in cricket without the batsman's actually hitting the ball with his bat.)

In compound words, it is safest to spell the prefix *by* (with or without a hyphen). Sometimes *bye* is allowable too — *by-election/bye-election*; *bylaw/bye-law* — but even here it is not recommended. In most such words, *by* is the only permitted form: *by-blow, bygone, by-line, by-product, bypass/by-pass, byroad, bystander, bypath/by-path, byplay, byway/by-way, byword*.

Take care not to confuse the *by-* prefix with the combining form *bi-*, which means 'twice' or 'doubly', as in *bifocal spectacles* or *bicentennial*. (See PREFIXES AND SUFFIXES.) *Bi-* is of Latin origin, whereas *by* (which gave rise to *bye*) is from Old English.

Note that the *by-* in *bylaw* is not related to the common adverb or preposition *by*. It seems instead to go back to the Old Norse *byr*, 'a village'.

Goodbye is an old contraction for 'God be with you'. Its informal version is accordingly spelt *bye-bye*. The baby-talk word *bye-byes*, meaning 'sleep', may be related to *bye-bye*, but perhaps developed simply as a soothing sound used in lullabies.

C

cabal, cabala *Cabal* and *cabala* both come originally from a Hebrew word *qabbalah*, 'received doctrine, tradition'. The *cabala* is an occult philosophy of Medieval rabbinic origin, and is based on mystical interpretations of the Old Testament. Its meaning has now been extended to cover any secret doctrine.

Cabal came from *cabala* via the French *cabale*, 'an intrigue'. It means primarily 'a group of political conspirators' — a sense reinforced by the coincidence that Charles II had Ministers whose initials spelt *cabal*: Clifford, Arlington, Buckingham, Ashley, Lauderdale. Although these men belonged to rival groupings, the word often applies now to political allies with sinister motives.

Cabal also refers to the intrigue or scheme in which the members of a *cabal* are involved. The word is pronounced /kəbal/ or /kəbaal/.

Cabala can also be spelt *cabbala*, *kabala*, or *kabbala*, and often has a capital *C*. The stress is usually on the second syllable, /kə-baalə/, but is now sometimes heard on the first: /kabbələ/. The derived adjective *cabalistic* is quite common. It is mostly used figuratively to mean 'occult, mysterious, having a secret or apparently magical significance': *the impenetrable and cabalistic texts of modern literary criticism.*

cacao, cocoa The *cacao* (pronounced /kə-kaa-ō/ or /kə-kay-ō/) is a tropical tree, a South American evergreen (*Theobroma cacao*) with yellowish flowers and reddish seed pods. The seed pods contain *cocoa beans* — also known as *cacao beans*. They are ground to make *cocoa powder* and squeezed to make *cocoa butter* (also called *cacao* butter). *Cocoa powder* is also known as *cocoa*, as is the drink made from it. (The powder known as *drinking chocolate*, which is made into the drink *chocolate* or *chocolate milk,* is technically distinct from *cocoa,* being made by a different process.) Both *cocoa* and *chocolate* are also used to refer to various shades of brown.

The words *cacao* and *chocolate* both come through Spanish from Nahuatl, the language of the Aztecs — *cacao* from *cacahuatl*, 'the cacao tree', and *chocolate* from *xocolatl*, literally 'bitter water'.

The word *cocoa* arose from a confusion between *cacao* and the *coco* palm tree on which the *coconut* grows.

As for the word *coco* itself, it comes through Spanish from Portuguese *coco*, 'a goblin, or grimace', referring to the marks on the base of a coconut shell which resemble a monkey's grinning face. A subsequent confusion with *cocoa* led to the spelling *cocoanut*: most dictionaries now accept this as a secondary variant, but it is best avoided. In either form, the word is pronounced /kokə-nut/ — not ×/kōkō-/ as in *cocoa*.

A third tropical plant contributes to the possible confusion: the South American shrub the *coca*, whose leaves are chewed as a stimulant. The word comes through Spanish from the Quechua name of the plant.

Cocoa, then, comes from the *cacao* tree, *coconuts* come from the *coco* palm, and *cocaine* comes from the *coca* shrub.

caddie, caddy The person who carries a golfer's clubs around the course is usually referred to as a *caddie. To caddie* is the intransitive verb, meaning 'to act as caddie'. But *caddy* is a possible variant spelling for both noun and verb.

A tea *caddy*, on the other hand, 'a small container for tea', is always spelt with a *y*.

Caddie is a Scottish borrowing from the French *cadet*, 'a young soldier, cadet'.

Caddy comes from Malay *kati*, a unit of weight (about 600 grams, or 1⅓ lb) that was used as a measure on colonial tea plantations.

café The spelling of this word without the accent is now widespread in informal written English, and is increasingly to be found in shop signs and advertisements. In speech, the most common British pronunciation is nowadays /kaffi/, with /kaffay/ restricted to careful use. The British mispronunciations /kaf/ and /kayf/, which are based on the informal, accentless spelling of the word, are never heard in educated usage except when intended as a joke. The spelling *caff* is a humorous attempt to represent the first of these nonstandard pronunciations.

American English stresses *café* on the last syllable, in line with its general treatment of French borrowings.

callous, callus *Callous*, 'hard-hearted', is related to *callus*, 'hard skin': both come from Latin *callosus*, 'having hard skin'.

The adjective *callous* means principally 'emotionally hardened, insensitive, unfeeling'. The noun *callus* refers to a hardened patch of skin, as on the hands or feet, caused by pressure and friction. A second sense of *callous* is 'having calluses', though the adjective *callused*, sometimes *calloused*, is commonly preferred.

camel, dromedary The dromedary is in fact a kind of camel — a one-humped Arabian camel, bred especially for racing and riding. (The Greek source word means 'running' or 'a race' or 'a road', as in *hippodrome*.) Camels can have one hump (Arabian camels, including dromedaries) or two (Bactrian camels).

Geographical distribution helps to distinguish the camel from the dromedary, but only up to a point. The Bactrian camel is found in central Asia and the Arabian camel or dromedary in North Africa (and now in Australia, where they were imported), but both are found in southwest Asia (*Bactria* is in fact the name of an ancient country in southwest Asia).

can, may Generations of teachers have tried to drum the rule into their pupils' heads: *can* expresses capability, but if you want to express permission you have to use *may*.

Yet children, and adults, continue to use *can* in requesting permission: *? Can I leave the room, please? ? Can I have some more?* In speech at any rate, there is seldom any ambiguity. The typical sarcastic correction on the part of the schoolteacher — *I dare say you can leave the room, but may you?* or *Not until you ask properly* — is in keeping with formal usage, but is flying in the face of current idiom. Furthermore, if ambiguity is the problem, *can* is less likely to be guilty of it than *may*:

The agency may not release the news until the government issues its own report.

In this example we do not know without a larger context whether *may not* refers to permission ('is not allowed to') or to possibility ('perhaps will not'). But suppose *may* is replaced by *can*:

The agency cannot release the news until the government issues its own report.

The sentence is again ambiguous, as between ability ('is not able to') and permission ('is not allowed to'). But the ambiguity is trivial: in either case, the agency is unlikely to release the news. Similarly:

The agency may release the news once the government issues its own report.
The agency can release the news once the government issues its own report.

Once again, the ambiguity is more serious with *may* than with *can*. So the purists' preference for *may* over *can* to indicate permission actually seems to make things less clear rather than more.

Besides, in negative sentences in particular, the 'rule' tends to produce a stiff, overformal effect: *Mayn't we help? You mayn't have more than two* — these sound far less natural than *Can't we help? You can't have more than two.* (Curiously, *may not* sounds rather less stiff than the contracted form *mayn't*.)

With affirmative sentences, however, *may* is perhaps best retained in formal writing (provided that there is no serious ambiguity) — until purists finally stop demanding compliance with the rule.

The rule extends to the past tense as well: *? She asked if she could help with the cooking.* Strictly speaking, *might* rather than *could* is the correct verb here. Similarly: *? You and your big mouth — you could have got arrested!* But it is sometimes impossible or at least excessively formal to use *might* as the past tense of *may*; *could* is then unavoidable — specifically in the sense 'was/were allowed to':

Department stores these days may open for trade on Sundays, but until the autumn of 1984 they could trade only on weekdays.

If *could* were 'corrected' to *might* here, the sentence would be both stiff and ambiguous.

One last point: the negative of *can* has three distinct written forms: *can not, cannot*, and *can't*. The negative of *may* is *may not* or *mayn't*: *mayn't* is not very common in British English, and extremely rare in American English.

See also MAY, MIGHT.

can but, cannot but, cannot help but These expressions are almost archaic, and tend to sound very old-fashioned or pretentious when used today:

One can but hope that nobody ever finds out about it.
I cannot but suspect her of treachery.
? I cannot help but suspect her of treachery.

In this extract, a diplomat recognises the pomposity of the phrase:

> He introduced himself in rather a mincing fashion. His eyes were certainly glassy. I put him down as a rather introverted type. I must say, however, that his opening remark 'could not but' (as we say in despatches) fill me with misgiving.
> – Lawrence Durrell, *Esprit de Corps*

A further objection is the apparent inconsistency: *can but* and *cannot but,* instead of being opposite in sense, appear to have a very similar meaning.

> You can but succeed.
> You cannot but succeed.

In each case, success is forecast, though the emphasis may vary from one form to the other. The inconsistency here, as it happens, is only apparent: in the one case, *but* means 'only'; in the other, it means roughly 'except': *cannot but,* in other words, involves a double negative, and hence has a positive meaning (see DOUBLE NEGATIVE). With *cannot help but,* however, there is a real inconsistency: the expression involves a triple negative! Grammatically, it should be negative in meaning, therefore, but the intended meaning is always positive.

? Yet five weeks later Carter accepted it as a fait accompli. That couldn't help but be perceived by the Soviets as a sign of weakness.
> – Gerald R. Ford (U.S.),
> *A Time to Heal*

The combination *cannot help but* is the most objectionable of the three constructions, and is best avoided at all times.

Not that the other two combinations, *can but* and *cannot but,* should be used very readily either. The old-fashioned or pompous tone cannot be wished away. Far preferable to the modern ear are the following idiomatic versions of the first two specimen sentences cited above:

> One can only hope that nobody ever finds out about it.
> I can't help suspecting her of treachery.

Canadian English Canadian English has a history of just 200 years or so, as against the 300-year history of Canadian French. A popular myth, still fairly widespread, is that Canadian English was originally just a variety of British English brought over by the early settlers, and is still basically 'British' though much 'corrupted' by the influx of Americanisms from its powerful neighbour to the south. This view is also reflected in a long-standing joke, that a Canadian is someone who is taken for an American by the British, but for an English person by the Americans. There is some truth in the joke: Canadian English is in so many respects similar to American that an outsider could well confuse them, and yet sufficiently different for an American to realise that it is a foreign variety of English — possibly British English.

The 'British origin' theory for Canadian English is almost certainly false: the first major settlement of English-speakers comprised not British newcomers but American 'Loyalists' (later known as the 'United Empire Loyalists') — Americans who had remained loyal to the British crown, and who moved northwards into Canada to escape retribution at the time of the American Revolution. Coming mainly from the Eastern seaboard of the United States, these settlers would have brought with them the speech of 18th-century New England and Pennsylvania, a group of dialects that already differed substantially from 18th-century British English. The big influx of British settlers into Canada took place later — throughout the 19th century. But the character of a dialect tends to be established by the first substantial group of settlers — later settlers assimilate to the existing dialect as quickly as possible, to avoid being taken for 'novices'. Canadian English is thus almost certainly American in origin, with a British component (especially Scottish) added to it. Canadians themselves are not committed to either model. For historical reasons, they like to distance themselves from Americans, in language as in other respects. Equally, however, they do not want the image of a British colony, and standard British English is not urged as a model except perhaps in a few private schools.

To determine what Canadian English is, then, you have to ask how it differs from American English; whether these differences are attributable to British influence; and whether there is anything distinctively and originally Canadian.

Pronunciation Canadian pronunciation is on the whole very similar to neighbouring accents in the United States — hardly surprising in view of the history of the region and the easy and regular communications across the border (sometimes easier than East-West communications within Canada).

● Canadian English is 'rhotic' — the *r* is pronounced in words like *star, four, earth.*

● The flat /a/ of *cat* is found also in words like *bath*, *laugh*, *ask*, and *aunt*, where British RP, the 'received pronunciation' of educated people in southeastern England, has the 'broad' /aa/.

● A /t/ and /d/ in the middle of a word are often given the same sound, so that *latter* sounds like *ladder* and *kitty* like *kiddy*, and the capital 'ciddy' is called (and sometimes even spelt!) 'Oddawa'.

● Sometimes the /t/ is dropped after *n*, so that *winter* sounds like *winner* and *Toronto* is 'Toronno' (or 'Traano').

In these and many other ways, Canadian pronunciation resembles much American pronunciation and differs from RP.

When Canadians are asked what distinguishes their speech from Americans, they usually mention the pronunciation of particular words, such as *schedule* with /sh-/ rather than /sk-/, *leisure* with /e/ instead of /ee/, and *new* with /ny-/ in preference to simple /n-/. (And yet the *Survey of Canadian English*, published in 1972, reported that a majority of Canadians, and particularly the young, favour the American pronunciations of *schedule* and *leisure*.) Many Canadians also follow British usage rather than American in pronouncing words such as *progress* (/**prō**-/ not /**praa**-/), *been* (/been/ not /bin/), *suggest* (/sə-**jest**/ not /sug-**jest**/), *docile* (/**dō**sīl/ not /**doss**'l/), and *lever* (/**lee**vər/ not /**lev**vər/).

These examples, though conspicuous, are limited. But there are two general features of pronunciation (possibly both influenced by the accents of Scottish immigrants) that distinguish most Canadians from most Americans. First, Canadians tend to use a single vowel sound /aa/ to represent three RP sounds: /aa, o, aw/. So, many Canadians would pronounce *collar* and *caller* identically, as /**kaa**lər/. (Similarly *don* and *dawn*, *cot* and *caught*, *stock* and *stalk*, and *knotty* and *naughty*.) In the United States (apart from some regions, notably the Upper Midwest), *collar* and *caller* are kept distinct, as /**kaa**lər/ and /**kaw**lər/.

Secondly, Canadians — or at least those in eastern Canada — sometimes 'raise' the vowels /ī/ and /ow/, as in *price* and *house*, to something nearer /ay/ and /ō/. (This occurs only when the vowel precedes a 'voiceless' consonant such as /p, t, k, f, th, s/.) So *rice* sounds fairly close to *race*, and *bout* to *boat*. This peculiarity is again not unknown in the United States, but it occurs in different regions from the *collar-caller* peculiarity. The combination of these two general pronunciation-features in a person's speech would identify that person unmistakably as a Canadian.

There are small regional differences across Canada, though Canadian pronunciation is, in view of the size of the country, surprisingly uniform. The glaring exception is Newfoundland: it was settled early and remained long in isolation. It retains many features of 17th-century English from Ireland and southwest England — the use of /v/ instead of /f/, for example, as though *finger* and *farmer* were *vinger* and *varmer*; and the use of /t/ and /d/ instead of /th/ and /<u>th</u>/, so that *the thin brother* sounds like *de tin brudder*.

Spelling Spelling is perhaps a more sensitive indicator of people's attitudes to their language than anything else. Canadians, torn between the influence of the United States and the prestige of Britain, use a variety of spelling systems in which distinctively U.S. elements and distinctively British ones are mixed in varying proportions depending on the writer, the intended audience, and, of course, the publisher's 'house style'.

In general, the more 'up-market' the readership, the more British the spelling; the more popular the readership, the more American the spelling. Writing intended for the middle range of readers sometimes exhibits a mixture of spellings that people in either Britain or the United States find both charming and disconcerting. A recent study of Canadian English by a linguist in Canada uses both *defense* (the prevailing U.S. spelling of *defence*) and *skilful* (the British spelling of a word spelt *skillful* in the United States). Whether this mixed style is what the author wrote or what his publisher wanted is immaterial. This blend of British and U.S. spellings is coming to be a distinctive and interesting feature of Canadian English.

Grammar There seem to be few grammatical constructions that are peculiarly Canadian. For the most part, Canadians seem to follow U.S. usage (sometimes even more keenly than U.S. speakers themselves do), though now and then they shy away from U.S. practice.

So, Canadians tend to say *He dove*, *They just left*, and *to have drank* even more freely than speakers in the United States do, though the forms favoured in British English — *He dived*, *They have just left*, and *to have drunk* — are also available throughout North America. Conversely, Canadians tend to avoid the U.S. constructions *a quarter of ten*, *to visit with relatives*, and *in back of*: like the British (and many U.S. speakers), Canadians consistently use *a quarter to ten*, *to visit relatives*, and *behind* instead. And Canadian English, like British English, still prefers *Have you (got) the time?* to the U.S. form *Do you have the time?*

Vocabulary Of all the features of language, it is vocabulary that travels farthest and fastest. Today, when contacts between Canada and the United States, or across the Atlantic to Britain, are so frequent, and when films, television programmes, books, and magazines are circulated internationally, it soon becomes hard to tell where a word first came from. None the less, long-established differences may persist: American *cookie, elevator, freeway, gas,* and *thumbtack* are the British *biscuit, lift, motorway, petrol,* and *drawing pin.* (See AMERICAN ENGLISH.)

In vocabulary, as in much else, Canadians tend to use the American terms — all of those just listed, for instance, and also the variant forms *airplane, aluminum,* and *specialty* in preference to the British *aeroplane, aluminium,* and *speciality.*

On the other hand, some British forms are preferred in Canada: *blinds, porridge, tap,* and the letter *zed,* for instance, rather than the American *shades, oatmeal, faucet,* and the letter *zee.* Similarly, Canadians tend to wear *ties* rather than *neckties,* and to wash in a *basin* rather than a *sink* or *bowl.*

Sometimes usage is strangely mixed: Canadians tend to take *luggage* (British), though they might store it in the *baggage-car* of a train, and label it with a *baggage-check* (both American).

And usage is sometimes divided within Canada: some Canadians take *holidays,* others a *vacation*; some have the letters delivered by a *postman,* some by a *mailman*; some do *odd jobs* around the house and some do *chores.* This divided usage is sometimes identifiably regional: a language survey revealed that most people in Ontario (81 per cent) use the British term *braces* to refer to the over-the-shoulder straps that hold trousers up, whereas most English speakers in Montreal (58 per cent) use the American term *suspenders.*

Strangely enough, regions near the United States border are often more likely to use the non-U.S. term: *asphalt road,* for instance, in preference to the U.S. *blacktop, verandah* rather than *porch,* and *chesterfield* rather than *sofa* or *couch.* Canadian use of *eh?* for *pardon?* was so typical, according to the survey, that immigration officers used it as a means of identifying travellers as Canadians.

In some areas of meaning, American terminology is very strong: Canadian terms for road, rail, and air transport, for example, are almost always American — though the British *shunting* (U.S. *switching*) and *level crossing* (U.S. *grade crossing*) do survive. But in one area at least, a British component remains strong — the field of politics. Partly, this is because Canada follows the British model of parliamentary democracy. Canada has a *Prime Minister* (in addition to the Governor-General) instead of a *President*; a *House of Commons, Members of Parliament,* and a *Leader of the Opposition*; *backbenchers, constituencies,* and *by-elections.*

There are, of course, many words, or word meanings, of a distinctively Canadian character: *the Mounties,* for example, or *Acadians* (the inhabitants of the French-influenced areas of the Maritime provinces). Historically, *factory* and *concession* were used to refer to a fur-trading post and a grant of land respectively. A *separate school* is a denominational or church school. The *hydro* is the electricity service, and *to jack* can mean 'to hunt illegally at night'.

Many of these Canadian terms refer to fauna and flora: a *black cat* (a marten), the *Land of the Little Sticks* (a region of stunted trees adjacent to the *Barren Lands*), *saskatoon* (a species of juneberry, with edible purple fruit).

Some words are Canadian Indian in origin: *muskeg* (a grassy bog or swamp, from Algonquian) and *whiskey jack* (a blue jay, from Cree *wisketjan*). Some of the Canadian Indian words came in via French, and retain a French spelling: *babiche* (leather thong), and *caribou.* A few Indian words have now passed into general English: *toboggan, hooch,* and *totem,* as have a number of Innuit (Eskimo) words, such as *igloo* and *kayak.*

Canadian French has contributed a few loan words, such as *bateau* (a type of flat-bottomed boat), *lacrosse* (the game) and, more recently, *Anglophone, Francophone,* and *tuque* (a woolly cap).

The uniqueness of Canadian vocabulary, as of its other aspects of language, lies in the combination of British and American elements, sometimes side by side. It is the particular flavour of the mixture that distinguishes Canadian from other varieties of English. Whether this flavour can persist in the face of the strong influence of American English remains to be seen.

canon, cannon These two nouns provide a common source of spelling confusion.

The big gun is the *cannon,* with two *n*'s in the middle. The word also refers to the loop at the top of a bell, by which it is suspended; to a round bit for a horse, and also to a particular bone in a horse's leg; and, in British English, to a shot in billiards in which the cue ball strikes two other balls in succession (in American English the word for this last sense is *carom,* both noun and verb).

As a verb, *cannon* means 'to bombard', 'to fire cannon', 'to collide', or 'to make a cannon shot in billiards'. The word goes back to the Italian *cannone,* 'a large tube or barrel', from the Latin *canna* and Greek *kanna,* 'a reed or tube' (from which the word *cane* comes as well).

Note that the plural of *cannon* is *cannons* if they are thought of individually — *16 cannons and 44 muskets* — but simply *cannon* if thought of collectively: *reinforcements of horse and cannon*; *Cannon to right of them/Cannon to left of them* (Tennyson).

There are two words written as *canon,* with one *n* in the middle. They are related, both going back to the Latin *canon,* 'a measuring line, a rule, or a model', from the Greek *kanon,* 'a rod or rule'. It is not too difficult to see how the various modern senses developed from these ancient meanings: the first *canon* refers to a church law or set of laws, and hence to various other religious items — the official list of books of the Bible, a part of the Mass, and the calendar of Saints. It also refers to an ordinary law or set of laws; hence a basis or standard for judgment — a criterion, as in *canons of taste*; and also an authoritative list, as of a writer's works or a cultural tradition:

> The British are long used to having an established 'history' of English Literature, a well-recognised, classic canon of major authors: Chaucer and Shakespeare, Milton and Wordsworth, Dickens and George Eliot.
> – Malcolm Bradbury, *The Observer*

Canon is a technical term in music and printing as well.

The second *canon* is a priest in a cathedral chapter or collegiate church, or else a member of a close-knit religious community.

Priests and guns should be kept apart: take care with your spelling, and avoid referring inadvertently to one when you mean the other.

canvas, canvass The noun *canvas* refers to the coarse cloth that artists paint on, sails are made of, and Boy Scouts sleep under. The verb *to canvass*, enlisting another *s*, means 'to enlist support or solicit votes', 'to survey people's opinions', or 'to examine and discuss; scrutinise':

> Over the next few weeks Lady Maud was intensely active. She took legal advice from Mr Turnbull daily. She canvassed opposition to the proposed motorway and sat almost continuously on committees.
> – Tom Sharpe, *Blott on the Landscape*

> A colleague and I went down a street of council houses which Benn had canvassed a few days before. Roughly one-in-five said that they wouldn't vote for the party this time, because of Benn.
> – Simon Hoggart, *The Observer*

The two words are related in a curious way. In the 16th century *canvassing* meant tossing someone in a canvas sheet as a practical joke or part of an initiation ceremony. From this came the sense of 'beating or buffeting, or shaking out a subject under discussion'. The political sense of 'soliciting votes' seems to have arisen from this, perhaps through the sifting of people for potential supporters, or the thrashing out of arguments in order to muster support.

capital, capitol In all but a few senses, the correct spelling is *capital* — whether a noun referring to wealth or the chief city, or an adjective meaning 'principal', 'excellent', 'upper-case', and so on.

Capitol, with an *o*, is reserved for the following uses. With a capital *C, the Capitol* can refer to the Ancient Temple of Jupiter in Rome (on the Capitoline Hill), to the seat of the United States Congress in Washington, D.C., or to the building in which the legislature of any U.S. State assembles. Only this last can be spelt with a small *c*.

Capital and *capitol* both derive ultimately from the Latin root, *caput* 'a head'.

capital letters It can be amusing — and puzzling — to consult various style manuals on the rules of capitalisation. One authority approves of *the Mayor of Camden*; another endorses *the mayor of Camden*. One urges you to write *Board of Directors*; another says the correct form is *board of directors*. At first glance this kind of disagreement among 'the authorities' is utterly confusing and even depressing. At second glance, however, it provides the key to understanding the function of capitalisation.

Capitalisation gives importance, distinction, and emphasis to whatever it touches. This explains why every sentence begins with a capital letter — to emphasise that a new thought has begun; why the simple phrase *white house* becomes the *White House* when it signifies the seat of presidential (sometimes Presidential) power in the United States; and why certain photocopying equipment is trademarked Xerox — to stop it from becoming a generic, undistinguished (and thus uncapitalised) term for any kind of photocopy.

Once capitalisation is viewed as a process of assigning special significance to words, it becomes obvious why the authorities are bound to disagree. They tend to assign significance to those things that loom largest in their lives and to play down things that seem more remote. Thus, government insiders are more likely to write *the Government* and *the Mayor* than those outside; people outside a company are less likely to care about its *board of directors* than those who work for the company or own shares in it.

In short, your use of capital letters is likely to vary with your perspective. Instead of trying to choose the 'correct' form, astute writers will recognise that each possibility may have its appropriate uses, depending on the circumstances and the context. Instead of approaching capitalisation as a number of flat rules to be applied mechanically, effective writers will view it as a flexible instrument of style that can give special force and vigour to their writing.

The only blanket rule is: be consistent. If you decide to capitalise a word in one place, make sure that you capitalise it throughout. Inconsistency in these small matters arouses in the reader, rightly or wrongly, a suspicion of inconsistency in larger matters such as your opinions and the expression of them in the text.

Capital letters are often referred to as 'upper-case letters' or as 'in the upper case', and small letters are often called 'lower-case' letters. Both terms come from printing. In the days when type was set by hand, all the letters for each typeface were kept in a large tray that was divided into dozens of compartments — one for each letter or punctuation mark. In use, the tray, known as a 'case', was propped on a sloping rack so that the printer could reach all the compartments easily and slide out the letters more quickly. Capital letters were invariably stored at the top end of the rack, the 'upper case', farther from the printer's darting fingers, because they were used less often. Ordinary letters, which were needed more often, were stored close to hand for speed, in the 'lower case'.

The guidelines to capitalisation that are given in this entry have been divided into 17 topics:

1. Proper nouns
2. Common nouns
3. First words
4. Personal names
5. Titles with personal names
6. Organisations
7. Governmental organisations
8. Place names
9. Names of academic subjects or disciplines
10. Compass points
11. Calendar references, seasons, and events
12. Ethnic terms
13. Religious terms
14. Scientific terms
15. Words with numbers or letters
16. Titles of artistic and literary works
17. Avoiding ambiguity

1. *Proper nouns* The formal or official names of particular persons, places, or things — in short, proper nouns — are always capitalised because of the distinction these names deserve: *William Shakespeare, Mount Everest, British Leyland, the Red Cross, Oxford University*. For the same reason, capitalise nicknames and imaginative names that refer to particular people, places, or things: *Capability Brown, the King of Rock, the New World, the Golden Horn*.

Capitalise proper adjectives too (forms derived from proper nouns): *Danish* (from *Denmark*), *Shakespearean* (from *Shakespeare*), *Dantesque* (from *Dante*). In a few cases it is customary to use lower-case letters for the adjective derived from a proper noun: *constitutional, parliamentary, senatorial* (referring, respectively, to a specific *Constitution, Parliament*, and *Senate*).

Some proper names give rise to ordinary expressions (and are then called 'eponyms'). Of these, many retain their capitals: *an Arcadia, an Adonis, a Casanova*. Others are now considered to have lost their connection with the original name, so they take the lower case:

ampere	jersey
to anglicise	morocco leather
boycott	to pasteurise
brussels sprouts	platonic love
cardigan	quisling
chinaware	silhouette
diesel engine	watt

The following expressions, however (and others like them), do not command the same measure of general agreement. They are in a state of transition. Some authorities still recommend capitalising; others do not. In such cases you can choose the form you prefer or select one authority and follow that style consistently:

bohemian existence	herculean
danish pastry	pullman car
dutch oven	scotch whisky
french windows	turkish bath

Note that when a lower-case prefix is attached to a proper noun or adjective, the main part of the word usually keeps its capital letter (and is usually preceded by a hyphen): *un-American, anti-British, pro-Nazi, non-Jewish, mid-Atlantic* (but *transatlantic*).

2. *Common nouns* Broadly, the rule is this: capitalise a common noun when it forms part of a proper name but not when it is used alone or in place of the proper name. For example: *Uncle David, my uncle; the National Westminster Bank, the bank; the Savoy Hotel, this hotel; Buckingham Palace, a fairy-tale palace.*

The common-noun element of a proper name, when used in place of the full name, is often referred to as a 'short form': *the company* may, in a legal document for example, stand for *the Ford Motor Company.* In a few special cases, which will be noted in due course, these short forms are capitalised because they carry the full force of complete proper names. However, these cases are clear exceptions to the rule given above. Writers who capitalise all types of short forms, beyond the well-established exceptions, run the risk of exhausting the special emphasis that capitalisation is intended to convey. When everything stands out, nothing stands out. In general then, if you choose to capitalise a common noun when it stands alone, make sure that you have a good reason for it.

3. *First words* The initial letter of the 'first word' should usually be capitalised.

a. Capitalise the first word of a *sentence* and of any phrase that is used as a sentence:

Do you believe her story? Not me. Incredible!

Capitalise the first word of a sentence that is *quoted*:

I myself heard Jennings say: 'There's no chance that I will resign. If they want me out of this office, they'll have to dig me out.'

The words *yes* and *no* sometimes take a capital letter in the middle of a sentence even when not enclosed in quotation marks:

If your answer is Yes, place a tick in the box.

See QUOTATION MARKS.

b. Capitalise the first word of an *independent question* within a sentence:

The question now is, Will funds be available to implement the defence policy?

When several independent questions follow a common introduction, capitalise the first word of each question:

Here's what I'd like to know: Who authorised the repaving of the car park? When? Was the project put out to tender? If not, why not?

c. Capitalise the first word *following a colon* under any of these conditions:
i. If the material preceding the colon is a short introductory word like *Remember* or *Note*;
ii. If the material following the colon starts on a new line;
iii. If the material following the colon is a quoted sentence or starts with a proper noun, a proper adjective, or the pronoun *I*;
iv. If the material following the colon consists of two or more sentences.

However, if the material following the colon cannot stand alone as a separate sentence and none of the first three conditions applies, then do not capitalise the first word.

The only difficult decision about capitalising after a colon occurs when two independent clauses (in effect, two complete sentences) are brought together within the same sentence with only a colon between them. The decision whether or not to capitalise depends on the importance assigned to the second clause. If the second clause simply explains or illustrates the idea presented in the first clause, do not capitalise the start of it.

If they accept your terms, it's for only one reason: they need the business.

However, if the second clause is presented as a formal rule or if it expresses the main thought (and the first clause simply serves to introduce it), then the beginning of the second clause may safely be capitalised:

Our new policy on gift matching is as follows: For every pound that an employee contributes to a recognised charity, the company will contribute two pounds.

d. Capitalise the first word of each item displayed in an *outline* or a *list*:

This book will tell architects of public buildings —
● How to achieve designs that are economically responsible, yet responsive to community needs.
● How to incorporate open space into designs intended for high population density.
● How to modernise existing structures.

e. The first word of each line of *poetry* is customarily capitalised:

St George he was for England,
And before he killed the dragon
He drank a pint of English ale
Out of an English flagon.
    – G.K. Chesterton, 'The Englishman'

Some poets deviate from this rule — and other rules of punctuation — for special effect:

as freedom is a breakfastfood
or truth can live with right and wrong
or molehills are from mountains made
— long enough and just so long
will being pay the rent of seem
and genius please the talentgang
and water most encourage flame ...
    – e. e. cummings (U.S.), *Fifty Poems*

f. Note that some dictionaries begin their definitions with a capital letter, but others do not.

4. *Personal names* As a rule, capitalise the first letter of each word in a person's name, as well as any initials used in the name. However, respect individual preferences on this point. The poet quoted above, e. e. cummings, wanted his name treated without capitals at all. And British surnames beginning with *ff* are often written without capitals. The London telephone directory has both Ffoulkes and ffoulkes, both Ffytche and ffytche. As it happens the *ff* used in such surnames originated not as a double *f* at all, but as an old-fashioned form of the capital, *F*.

Names with prefixes sometimes pose special problems. In surnames beginning with *O'*, capitalise both the *O* and the first letter following the apostrophe: *O'Malley, O'Rourke*. In surnames beginning with *d', da, de, del, della, di, du, l', la, le, van*, and *von*, individual preferences on capitalisation (as well as spacing and spelling) can vary quite widely: the London telephone directory includes Van Den Berg, van den Berg, Van den Berg, and Van Denbergh. There is similar variation in *Mc –* or *Mac –* surnames: the London telephone directory lists McNair, Mac-Nair, Macnair, and even Mcnair.

When a surname begins with an uncapitalised particle and is used on its own in running text, without a title, a first name, or even initials preceding it, it is common practice to capitalise the particle in order to prevent a misreading: *General de Gaulle, Charles de Gaulle, C. A. de Gaulle*, but *De Gaulle*.

When a name like *La Salle* (with a space after the particle) has to be written all in capital letters, write *LA SALLE*. However, if the name is *LaSalle* (with no space after the prefix), write *LaSALLE*; similarly, *McGREGOR*.

5. *Titles with personal names* Capitalise all titles that precede personal names — titles of a personal nature (*Mr, Mrs, Ms, Miss*) as well as titles that indicate rank in an organisation or status in a profession (*President, Chairman, Mayor, General, Corporal, Dr, Professor*).

When these titles follow a personal name or take the place of a personal name, they are not capitalised as a rule: *Mr Bullen, the chairman of the housing committee*. Exceptions are often made, however, for:

a. High-ranking government or opposition officials: *the Prime Minister, the Leader of the Opposition, the President, the Foreign Secretary* (and other members of the cabinet).

b. Heads of state and other international figures: *the Queen, the Pope, the Dalai Lama, the Polish Ambassador*.

However, when such titles are used with a general rather than specific reference, they are often lower-cased: *a Polish ambassador, various foreign secretaries, a 19th-century prime minister, one of the more liberal popes*.

6. *Organisations* Capitalise the formal names of all types of organisation — business, political, educational, religious, and social: *Smith Box Company, Fabian Society, McGill University, Church of St Aloysius, Upper Canada Country Club*. Follow the organisation's style when you know it. If you do not, capitalise all words except articles (*the, a, an*), short prepositions (*of, for*), and short conjunctions (*and, or*). Do not capitalise short forms (such as *company* or *association*) except in legal documents or other formal material where the short form is intended to convey the full force of the complete name.

So, in ordinary material you might write:

The managers I talked with at the Fox Umbrella Company said that the company would not raise its prices during the next 12 months.

In a contract or a letter of agreement, however, a Fox official would probably write:

For a period of 12 months from the date of this agreement, the Company agrees not to increase the prices shown in the attached catalogue.

Note, however, that when two or more organisations are referred to that share the same short form, that short form is often not capitalised: *the Conservative Party, the Labour Party, the Liberal Party*, but *the Conservative, Labour, and Liberal parties*; *the Roman Catholic*

Church, the Eastern Orthodox Church, but *the Roman Catholic and Eastern Orthodox churches.*

7. *Governmental organisations* Capitalise the formal names of all governmental organisations at national, county, provincial, and local level: *Ministry of Agriculture, Dorset County Council, the Camden Council of Social Services.* The word *administration* is sometimes capitalised: *the Reagan Administration, the Administration.* And capitalise the names of all international organisations: *the United Nations Security Council*; *the World Bank*; *the Council of Europe*; *the Organisation of African Unity.*

It is customary to capitalise short forms of key national-government organisations: *the House* (of Commons); *the Ministry* (of Agriculture, Defence, and the like). However, short forms of local bodies are not usually capitalised except by insiders. Thus, you might write to urge friends to join you in a protest *at the next meeting of the council.* But the local council itself might be issuing this announcement: *At its next meeting the Council will discuss its plan to close its day-care centre.*

The term *government* alone (referring to the national government) commonly takes lower case except when used by people in government. However, in a context where it has the full force of an official name, it can safely be capitalised: *The Government is against the scheme.*

In the United States, the word *federal* is capitalised when it is part of the official name of an agency or a piece of legislation: *the Federal Trade Commission, the Federal Insurance Contributions Act.* It is often lower-cased in other contexts: *the federal tax laws, federal regulators, federal government.*

Political parties take capital letters: *the Liberal Party, the Republican Party.* So do the members of political parties: *the Liberals, the Conservatives.* But if political views, rather than political parties, are being referred to, then a small letter is used: *outraged liberal opinion*; *a more conservative policy.* Note too: *the Right, the hard Left, the Centre*, but *right-wing* and *left-wing.*

8. *Place names* Capitalise names of places, both natural and man-made: *Sydney Harbour, the North Circular Road, Table Mountain, Ayers Rock, the Mississippi River, Lake Windermere, the Tower of London, the Chrysler Building, Gatwick Airport, the Golden Gate Bridge.* As a rule, however, do not capitalise a short form used in place of the full name: *the mountain, the river, the bay.* In a few special cases, because of longstanding identification of a short form with

a specific place, the short form is capitalised. Thus, you might fly out to *the Coast* (referring to the West Coast of the United States) or cross *the Channel* (English, of course) on your way over to *the Continent* (of Europe). By the same token, imaginative or poetic-sounding names clearly identified with a specific place are capitalised: *the Vale of Health* (Hampstead); *the Bay Area* (San Francisco); *the Big Apple* (New York City).

Capitalise *city* only when it is part of the official name or part of a well-established imaginative name: *Oklahoma City, the Eternal City* (Rome), but *the city of Detroit.*

New York can be simply *the city of New York*, but also both *New York City* and *the City of New York.* Note the difference in meaning between *the City of New York*, which embraces all five boroughs, and *the City of London* (usually shortened to *the City*), which is just one part of the Greater London conurbation.

Similarly, capitalise *state* only when it follows the state name or is part of an imaginative name: *the state of Washington*, but *Washington State*; *the Tarheel State* (North Carolina); *the States* (referring to the United States).

9. *Names of academic subjects or disciplines* The names of recognised subject fields are often not capitalised, but tend to be capitalised when the reference is to a course, degree, or examination in the subject: *She studied chemistry* (= the subject chemistry), *She won the Nobel Prize for chemistry* (= the subject chemistry), but *She got a distinction in Chemistry* (= a chemistry exam or course).

10. *Compass points* Capitalise *north, south, east*, and *west* (and related words like *northern, northeast*, and *southwest*) when they are part of a proper name — *North Island* (New Zealand), *South America, East Riding* (formerly part of Yorkshire), *Northwest Territories* (Canada), *Northern Territory* (Australia), *Southeast Asia.* Similarly, when they refer to a specific region that is distinctive because of certain social, cultural, or political characteristics: *out West* (in the United States), *out East* (in or to Asia as seen from Britain), *up North, down South.* However, put these words in lower case when they simply indicate location or direction: *northern Australia* (as distinct from *Northern Territory*), *somewhere east of Suez, travelled west of the Rockies.* Thus, you would visit the shops in *the West End* (if that is what that part of town is actually called, as it is in London); otherwise, you would simply visit the shops on *the west side of town.*

Similarly, capitalise *northern, southern, eastern,*

and *western* (and related words) when they refer to social, cultural, or political aspects of a region: *Eastern religions, Western governments* (but a film about cowboys is a *western*). And lower-case these terms when they refer simply to the climate, the geography, or the general location of a region: *southerly breezes, the northern slopes of the Matterhorn, the southwestern region of the country.*

11. *Calendar references, seasons, and events* Capitalise the names of days and months, but use lower case for the names of seasons except in the rare instances when they are personified: *Thursday, January, all through the spring and summer,* but *harsh Winter with her bitter winds.*

Capitalise the names of all holidays and religious days: *New Year's Eve, April Fool's Day, May Day, Ash Wednesday, Holy Week, Passover, Rosh Hashanah, Ramadan, Tet.*

Do not capitalise the names of decades and centuries except in imaginative references: *before the sixties, during the nineteen-thirties, in the twenty-first century, the early nineteen hundreds,* but *the Roaring Twenties, the Gay Nineties.* (Usually, numerals rather than words would be used here. See NUMBER STYLE.)

Capitalise the names of events and the imaginative names given to historical or cultural periods: *the Renaissance, the Enlightenment, the Civil War, the French Revolution, the Second World War, Prohibition, International Year of the Disabled.*

References to cultural and geological periods are usually capitalised: *the Stone Age, the Dark Ages, the Middle Ages, the Elizabethan Age, the Age of Reason, the Neolithic Period, the Jurassic.* However, more recent references, such as *the space age* and *the nuclear age,* are usually lower case, unless they appear in the same context with a capitalised reference to an age; then, for the sake of consistency, they are capitalised also.

12. *Ethnic terms* Capitalise the names of races, nationalities, tribes, languages, and similar terms referring to ethnic groups: *Caucasians, Basques, Saudi Arabians, the Sioux, Slavonic.* Designations based on colour are customarily in lower case: *a black girl of about 13; a white man.*

13. *Religious terms* Capitalise all references to a supreme being: *God, the Father, the Son, the Holy Spirit, the Lord, the Messiah, Allah, the Almighty, the Word, the Supreme Being.* The pronouns *he, his,* and *him* used to be capitalised under all circumstances when referring to a supreme being. Today these pronouns are often put in the lower case when there is a specific

reference to God nearby: *Trust in the Lord and honour him* (or *Him) always;* but *Pray with your heart and He will hear you.*

Capitalise all references to people revered as especially holy: *Blessed Virgin, Mother of God, the Apostles, John the Baptist, Saint Jude, the Prophet, Buddha.*

Capitalise all references to the Bible and other sacred writings; however, do not underline or italicise these references:

> the Apostles' Creed
> the Authorised Version
> the Bhagavad Gita
> the Book of Mormon
> the Dead Sea Scrolls
> Genesis
> the Gospels
> the King James Bible
> the Koran
> the Lord's Prayer
> the Old Testament
> Psalm 23
> the Revised Standard Version
> Scripture
> the Sermon on the Mount
> the Talmud
> the Ten Commandments

The adjective derived from the word *Bible* is also often capitalised still, but the current trend favours lower case: *a fine biblical scholar; in biblical times.*

Capitalise the names of religions, their members, and their buildings: *Anglican, Orthodox Judaism, Jehovah's Witnesses, Buddhism, Roman Catholicism, the Dome of the Rock, St Paul's Cathedral* (the official name of a specific building), but *the only cathedral in the county* (merely a reference to a specific building). The word *church,* when it refers to the total institution, can be capitalised or lower-cased: *the Church of England; the Baptist church.* But note once again the form when two or more are referred to together: *the Roman Catholic and Eastern Orthodox churches.*

Capitalise references to important religious events: *the Creation, the Fall, the Flood, the Exodus, the Last Supper, the Crucifixion, the Resurrection, the Second Coming.* However, as a general rule lower-case references to religious rites and services: *attend a mass* (but *celebrate the Mass), a vesper service, a baptism, a christening* (and *a christian name), a bar mitzvah; a seder.* The names of certain Christian sacraments are capitalised: *Eucharist, Holy Communion, Anointing of the Sick.*

14. *Scientific terms* For names of plants and animals, the scientific convention is to capitalise the name of the genus but not the name of the species (even if derived from a proper name): *Arum maculatum* (lords-and-ladies), *Sorbus acuparia* (European mountain ash), *Sus scrofa* (pig), *Monodon monoceros* (narwhal), *Equus caballus* (horse). When writing the popular names of plants and animals, capitalise only proper nouns and adjectives: *London pride, Virginia creeper, Labrador retriever, Shetland pony*.

Names of chemical elements and compounds go in lower case, but the corresponding symbols are capitalised: *calcium chloride ($CaCl_2$), boric acid (H_3BO_3)*.

15. *Words with numbers or letters* Capitalise words followed by a number or a letter to indicate sequence: *in Room 303, proceed to Gate 12A for Flight 617, in Form 2B*. In literary references, the terms *page, paragraph, line, verse*, and *note* are lower-cased; other such terms are often capitalised: *Volume III, Chapter 4, Section Two, Figure 6-4, Table 8, Appendix B*.

16. *Titles of artistic and literary works* Capitalise the first and last words in titles, and all other words except articles (*the, a, an*), short conjunctions (such as *and, but, or*), and short prepositions (such as *by, for, to*). Authorities disagree on how short is 'short'. In general, capitalise any conjunction or preposition of five or more letters:

The Taming of the Shrew
Gone with the Wind
A Tale of Two Cities
The House at Pooh Corner
The Man Without a Country

Authorities disagree on the treatment of hyphenated words in titles. Many capitalise only the first element, but on the whole it is better to treat each element according to the guidelines given above, for the sake of both consistency and appearance:

The Looking-Glass War
Nineteen Eighty-Four
The L-Shaped Room

17. *Avoiding ambiguity* Although the trend is to avoid capitals if there is a choice, it is best to use the capital if that would prevent ambiguity. In *The cabinet is collapsing*, it is unclear whether *cabinet* refers to a piece of furniture or the council of government Ministers. In *The Cabinet is collapsing*, this ambiguity has been resolved: so *Cabinet*, referring to the council of Ministers, is still given a capital *C* by many publishers, and

Minister a capital *M* (to distinguish the government official from a clergyman). So, too, the *Opposition*, an *Act* (of Parliament), *Bill* (before Parliament), the *Bench*, the *Bar*, the *Continent*, a *Scout* (a Boy Scout), a *Mason* (a Freemason), and so on.

Two final points. If you remain uncertain about any particular word, consult a good dictionary. Apply its recommendations consistently if possible, in order to keep your own usage consistent. And note that other languages have other rules: German, for example, capitalises all common nouns as well as proper nouns. English, too, tended to do this in the past, but the practice died out in the 18th and 19th centuries. In French, the title of a book or film or organisation has all initial letters in lower case except those of one or two important words near the beginning. In Spanish, the first word of a line of poetry is often, traditionally, in lower case.

See also ABBREVIATIONS.

capitol See CAPITAL.

carat, karat *Carat* has two meanings. It refers either to a unit of weight (200 milligrams) used for measuring precious stones, or to a unit of fineness for measuring gold.

This second meaning is usually spelt *karat* in American English. Pure gold is 24 carats, so each carat is ¹⁄₂₄ part of pure gold. *Twelve-carat gold*, then, is an alloy, part of gold, half of other metal.

The word *carat* or *karat* comes through French from Arabic *qirat*, referring to a small weight (actually about four grams); this in turn comes from Greek *keration*, 'a little horn' (also referring to a small weight, or to a carob fruit).

case **1.** In such senses as 'a state of affairs or set of circumstances', *case* is a sadly overworked word, pressed into service by insensitive writers and readers whenever they are too lazy to phrase a thought carefully or too vain to phrase it simply.

It is quite acceptable to use it — sparingly — in sentences such as these:

I shall make an exception in your case.
In that case, I resign.
Certainly it applies in some cases, but that does not mean it applies universally.
Your whole argument rests on the assumption that the disease is air-borne — which is simply not the case.

But all too often, *case* is used thoughtlessly where a more precise word is available or where no word is needed at all. The previous paragraph, for instance, might easily have begun:

? It is quite acceptable to use it — sparingly — in cases such as these.

But it would have been less sharp and efficient as a result.

The following sentences all use the phrase *in the case of,* and would all benefit from the removal of this verbal padding:

? A cooker is expensive enough to run as it is, but in the case of an electric cooker, it will cost you half as much again (= ... but an electric cooker will cost you half as much again).

? In the case of the *Pastoral Symphony,* Beethoven turned his back on 'absolute' music and opted unashamedly for 'programme' music (= In the *Pastoral Symphony* ...).

? And in the case of crabs, their shells do not expand, but have to be shed by moulting and then re-formed in a larger size (= As for crabs ... or simply: Crabs' shells do not expand ...).

The following sentences use *case,* or a phrase with *case,* as a supposedly more elegant word or phrase than the obvious one, or as a way of avoiding repetition — when there is nothing wrong with repetition:

? The chief superintendent has denied all responsibility in the case of the signals failure (= denied all responsibility for the signals failure).

? Despite antibiotics, the disease is even more widespread today than was the case 100 years ago (= than it was 100 years ago).

? The safety officer is to check all fire-doors and certify that they are in every case capable of being opened from the inside (= and certify that every one of them is capable ...).

? Is it or is it not the case that you have exceeded the budget? (= Is it or is it not true ... or: Have you or have you not ...).

? Such behaviour may be acceptable in your part of the world, but this is not the case here (= but it is not acceptable here).

2. In British English, the phrase *in case* means 'to provide for the possibility that':

In case you get home before I do, I'll leave the key under the mat.

Note that the clause is often left unfinished in informal speech and writing:

I'll leave the key under the mat, just in case.

In more formal contexts, the verb should be inserted to complete the clause.

The use of *in case* in the sense simply of 'if' or 'in the event that' is fairly common in American English, but is not considered standard British English:

In case you get home before I do, could you start preparing dinner?

caster, castor In some of their meanings, *caster* and *castor* are acceptable variants; in others they are not. The finely ground white sugar is always *caster sugar* (more common in British than in American usage), but the perforated jar from which it is shaken can be either a *sugar caster* or a *sugar castor.*

The foul-tasting medication inflicted on reluctant children to purge their bowels is *castor oil,* extracted from the bean of an Indian plant.

Fortunately, this is not the same *castor* that is used as a fixative in perfumes, and that consists of a brown, odorous secretion from glands in a beaver's groin. (Nevertheless, *castor oil* is probably so called because it was thought to resemble perfume *castor*: this word comes originally from the Greek *kastor,* 'a beaver'.)

The small swivelling wheel, fitted under a piece of furniture to make it easy to move, is usually a *castor* but can be a *caster.* The opposite applies in the case of 'someone who casts' — *caster* is more commonly used, but *castor* is also acceptable.

Catholic, catholic The word *catholic* or *Catholic* comes from Greek roots meaning 'universal' (literally, 'according to the whole'). With a small *c, catholic* still means this, or more broadly, 'general, all-inclusive, liberal, comprehensive in interests and sympathies': *She is a person of catholic tastes.*

The reviewer's own preferences in children's literature are perforce pretty catholic. A combination of drollery and didacticism is most likely to draw an instant paternal purr of approval, but parental canons can never be sovereign in these things for groundlings are not a passive audience.
— Philip Waller, *The Literary Review*

The phrase *the Catholic Church* (or *the Church Catholic*) originally meant 'the universal Christian Church'. The title *Catholic* is now most often associated with the Roman Catholic Church, but strictly speaking it also covers any of the churches that have claimed to be part of or in the tradition of the ancient undivided Christian church. (One tendency in the Church of England, for example, is referred to as *Anglo-Catholic*.) If there is any danger of confusion, it is best to use *Roman Catholic,* but often enough, especially when used in contrast with *Protestant,* the term *Catholic* alone is sufficient.

Note that *Catholic* (like *Protestant*) can be a noun or an adjective, whereas *catholic* can be used only as an adjective. The noun from *catholic* is *catholicity* (/**kathə-liss**əti/), meaning 'universality, or broad-mindedness'. From *Catholic* the more usual noun is *Catholicism* (/kə-**tholli**-siz'm/).

ceiling In the sense of 'an upper limit', *ceiling* is now widely used in economic and other official contexts: *a ceiling of five per cent for pay increases in the public sector.* The trouble is that the older sense of *ceiling* still lurks within the modern sense, and can produce some very odd effects: *? reduce the ceiling, ? abolish the ceiling*, and so on. Use the word with care: it is not yet a completely dead metaphor.

The opposite, *floor*, is rarer but no less risky: *? to increase the floor of the wage scale*; *a flexible floor to entrance qualifications.*

Celtic, Gaelic Typically, *Celtic* refers to a whole set of languages, *Gaelic* to a specific language, either of the Scottish or of the Irish variety. Both *Celtic* and *Gaelic* can serve as noun or adjective. The Celtic languages are so called after the original speakers, the Celts, a people of Europe and Asia Minor that included the Gauls and the ancient Britons.

The Celtic languages constitute a branch of the Indo-European language family, and are divided in turn into the Brythonic group — comprising Cornish, Welsh, and Breton — and the Goidelic group, comprising Scottish Gaelic, Irish, and Manx.

Note that Scottish Gaelic is sometimes known as *Gaelic*, Irish as *Irish Gaelic* or *Gaelic*, and Manx as *Manx Gaelic. Gaelic* can in fact refer to any of the three Goidelic languages, or to the Goidelic group as a whole (*Gaelic* and *Goidelic* are really just different forms of the same word). Note too that *Erse,* which usually refers specifically to Irish Gaelic, can also be used to refer to the Goidelic group as a whole.

Gaelic is pronounced /**gay**lik/ or /**gal**-lik/, and sometimes /**gaa**lik/. *Celtic* is pronounced with a hard *c* as /**kel**tik/; only rarely is a soft *c* used — /**sel**tik/ — though the Scottish football team is always pronounced this way. The spelling *Keltic* (and *Kelt*), once favoured by scholars, is now very little used.

censor, censure These two verbs should not be confused. *To censure* is to disapprove of or to criticise strongly, sometimes by an official decision. Its object can be human or nonhuman: *voted to censure the treasurer*; *censured the withdrawal agreement.*

> The *Mail on Sunday* newspaper failed to give proper prominence to an adjudication which censured it, the Press Council says today.
> The paper was censured earlier for failing to correct a front-page lead story which alleged, wrongly, that two Soviet generals had been entertained at Edinburgh University at the taxpayers' expense.
> – Adam Raphael, *The Observer*

To censor something is to impose censorship upon it — this involves checking mail and other communications, or inspecting material (written, performed, or graphic) that is intended for publication, with a view to bringing it into line with official policy by changing or deleting parts of it:

> The Mrs Grundys on the town council wanted to censor the Christmas pantomime by cutting out all the rude jokes and covering the actresses' legs with long skirts.

To censor tends to have nonhuman objects, though when used in a transferred sense it can sometimes have a human object: *once again threatening to censor dissident writers.*

Note the pronunciations of the two verbs: *censor* is pronounced /**sen**-sər/, and *censure* is pronounced /**sen**-shər/. The words are closely related in origin, both going back to the Latin verb *censere*, 'to judge'.

There is also a danger of confusing the related adjectives: *censorial* (/sen-**saw**ri-əl/) is the adjective counterpart of *to censor,* and *censorious* (/sen-**saw**ri-əss/) of *to censure.*

> Sometimes I longed to have someone to talk to ... Dottie was the obvious choice, but when I imagined her probable reaction it didn't entice me. It wasn't that I was afraid she'd be shocked or censorious, but that I felt she would regard the whole thing in the light of her own situation.
> – Lynne Reid Banks, *The L-Shaped Room*

Note too the various nouns related to the two verbs: *a censor* and *censorship* for *to censor*; and *a censurer* and *censure* for *to censure*.

Take care not to confuse the spelling of *censor* with that of *censer*, 'a vessel in which incense is burned'. *Censer* and *incense* are related in origin, both going back to the Latin verb *incendere*, 'to set on fire'.

centre around The phrases *? to centre around*, *? to centre round*, and *? to centre about* are often condemned by usage experts. Logically, a *centre*, of all things, cannot be *around* anything. Yet the expression is widely used, and does not seem to cause any trouble or misunderstanding. Respected writers of the past have been quite happy with it:

? The life of the widow ... was like one long service to the departed soul; its many annual observances centring about the funeral urn.
– Walter Pater,
Marius the Epicurean (1885)

? *This* book is *that* story, reduced to manageable proportions, its whole course suggested and centred round the absurd cruelty of the Greenwich Park explosion.
– Joseph Conrad,
Author's Note to *The Secret Agent*

Strictly speaking, something centres *on* or *upon* something else (or *at* or *in* a place: *an organisation centred at Chichester*).

During the hectic preparations in Jerusalem for the Summit, talk centred on how far the two governments would agree to a new programme of strategic cooperation, and whether such cooperation would really strengthen Israel's hand.
– Christopher Walker, *The Times*

William Boyd's screenwriting debut centred on a group of such well-schooled rotters, and on one of their forgotten victims who 10 years later turns avenger.
– Julian Barnes, *The Observer*

Despite the disapproval by purists of *? to centre around*, writers continue to use it unabashed:

? In an exclusive interview, the company's founder chairman, Sir Clive Sinclair, revealed that he is investing 'millions of pounds' on the project, centred around a research team based at his MetaLab think tank in Cambridge.
– Steven Vines, *The Observer*

? In 'Lunette', which centres round the barely disguised figure of a famous art historian at

the beginning of the century, we find the same awareness of the physical impact of the Italian countryside.
– Joan Haslip, *The Literary Review*

? *To focus around* has recently been criticised for the same reason. The more accurate phrase would be *to focus on*. Yet idiom seems to have welcomed *? to focus around*, just as it now accepts *? to centre around*. In the long run, logic will have to yield to idiom here, but in the meantime the criticism remains strong, and it is best to use *to focus on* and *to centre on*.

centuries The 20th century began on 1 January 1901 — not 1900. The last day of our century will be 31 December 2000 — not 1999. There was no such year as the year 0: the 1st century AD is considered as running from year AD 1 up to and including year AD 100. Similarly, the centuries BC — the 1st century BC ran, as it were, from the beginning of 100 BC, through the end·of that year and on to the beginning of 99 BC and so on through to the end of the year 1 BC; to be followed immediately by the beginning of the year AD 1.

Human age is sometimes reckoned in a similar way: a newborn child is in his 'first year'; a person of 21 is in his '22nd year'.

If you are worried about being misunderstood when referring to various earlier ages, you can use a less confusing system: *the 1600s* is roughly the same as *the 17th century,* and more immediately graspable. It is a rather vaguer term too, of course, but if precise limits have to be set, they would probably be the years 1600 to 1699 inclusive, whereas the 17th century refers to the years 1601 to 1700 inclusive.

In other words, a century includes the year that in effect bears its name: the 19th century includes the year 1900, the 18th century 1800, and so on. The 20th century AD will include the year AD 2000, though the name of that year will almost certainly be pronounced *two thousand* (as with 2000 BC) rather than *twenty hundred*. The 21st century will therefore not begin until AD 2001 (in spoken English, as in the name of the film and book, *two thousand and one*).

See also AD, BC.

ceremonial, ceremonious *Ceremonial* can be a noun, meaning 'a set of ritual ceremonies' (or 'the observance of these ceremonies'):

What's going on, apart, that is, from an author's zealous tribute to the literary tradition that keeps on celebrating this sad ceremonial within the old American dreams, no one finds out, not even young Xavier, fledgling detective and devotee of the writings of Poe and Conan Doyle.

– Valentine Cunningham, *The Observer*

It is often used in the plural:

The Druid priests observed all the due ceremonials in welcoming the spring.

More commonly it is used as an adjective. It relates to the noun *ceremony* in the sense of a traditional, formal procedure or ritual custom: *ceremonial dress*; *the ceremonial opening of Parliament*; *a job that is largely ceremonial and involves no real responsibility.*

The dropsical man sat on his stool as an old god carried out among them, the grotesque ceremonial presence without which carnival forgets its origin is in fear of death.

– Nadine Gordimer, *July's People*

The adjective *ceremonious,* on the other hand, relates to the noun *ceremony* in the sense of pomp or formality in general. It means 'full of formality or ceremony', and usually has a distinct flavour of self-importance: *She dismissed the servant with a ceremonious wave of the hand.* Similarly, the adverb *ceremoniously*:

Sometimes Lola would slouch in while we pondered the board — and it was every time a treat to see Gaston ceremoniously rise to shake hands with her, and forthwith release her limp fingers and descend again into his chair.

– Vladimir Nabokov, *Lolita*

Unceremonious can mean 'informal, not standing on ceremony'. But is is now very likely to have the related meaning 'brusque, rude, without the ceremonies or conventions of politeness'. The adverb *unceremoniously* has taken on this meaning, too: *We were unceremoniously shown the door by the irate manager.*

When Father came to fetch us home, I rode in front beside him holding David in my arms. On the way from the car I said 'Hold him a second while I get the things out of the back', and dumped him unceremoniously into Father's arms before he could protest.

– Lynne Reid Banks, *The L-Shaped Room*

cession   Take care not to confuse *cession* with *secession*, *cessation*, or *session*. *Cession*, pronounced /**sesh**'n/, means 'the act or an instance

of giving up something to which one has a claim'. It particularly applies to a surrendering of territory to another country by treaty: *the cession of Alsace-Lorraine by Germany to France.* The related verb is *to cede* (/seed/), which comes from the Latin verb *cedere*, 'to yield or go away'.

Secession comes from the verb *to secede*, 'to withdraw formally from membership in an organisation or alliance'. *Secession* is the act or an instance of such withdrawal: *The American War of Independence was a war of secession.* With a capital *S*, *the Secession* refers to the withdrawal of 11 Southern States from the Federal Union in 1860-61, precipitating the American Civil War. *Secession* is pronounced /si-**sesh**'n/, and *secede* /si-**seed**/. Their origin is the Latin *secedere*, 'to go away': *se-*, 'apart' + *cedere* again 'to go away'.

Cessation is the noun related to the verb *to cease*. It means 'a stopping or discontinuance': *a cessation of all human activity.* Interestingly enough, the Latin root verb *cessare*, 'to stop', is related to the verb *cedere* once again, which is the origin of *cession* and *secession*.

Session literally means 'a sitting', and goes back to the Latin verb *sedere*, 'to sit'. It refers particularly to a meeting of a legislative or judicial body, or to the term during which such meetings are held. It also now applies, more broadly, to any period of time devoted to a specific activity, including recording music in a studio: hence the adjectival use of *session*, as in *a session guitarist* — one who plays for recording sessions. (In other senses, the adjective from *session* is *sessional*, as in *a sessional system of parliament.*)

The pronunciation of *session* is of course the same as the pronunciation of *cession*, and *cession* is therefore often misspelt.

chairman, chairwoman, chairperson, chair
The word *chairman* has been the centre of attention in feminist debates about the English language. Since so many of the people who today preside over committees or companies are women, the term *chairman* was criticised as misleadingly masculine in form. The forms *lady chairman* and *woman chairman,* and the form of address *Madam Chairman,* were felt to be no answer: the *-man* element had to go — hence *chairwoman.*

But the problem remained of how to refer to the presiding officer when his or her sex was unknown or irrelevant. If an organisation's constitution read *The chairman shall have the casting vote,* should this be changed, and if so, how? Here and there, the neutral term *chairperson* was adopted, and the simple *chair* (dating back to the 17th century) reinvigorated. Neither is entirely satisfactory. *Chair* can sound ludicrous: *? What does the chair think? ? Madam Chair, I object. Chairperson* can sound prissy or strident or overearnest, and is not very versatile: you can say *Madam Chairman* and even perhaps *Madam Chairwoman,* but you cannot very well say *?? Madam Chairperson.*

It is virtually impossible to use either term unselfconsciously, and without drawing the listener's or reader's attention to it. To use either term is, willy-nilly, to make a statement about one's views on the question of women's rights.

This often applies too, no doubt, to the use of *chairman* in a neutral sense — to a slightly lesser extent, however, so *chairman* probably remains the most commonly used neutral term. A renowned report recently compiled carries the following title:

Report of the Committee of Inquiry into Human Fertilization and Embryology. Chairman:—Dame Mary Warnock DBE.

Conversely, an American law journal describes one of its (male) contributors in the following rather awkward way:

Abner J. Mikva, judge of the U.S. Court of Appeals for the District of Columbia Circuit, and vice-chairperson of the ABA Section of Individual Rights and Responsibilities.
— *The American Bar Association Journal* (U.S.)

There are no easy answers, unfortunately. A traditionalist might object to *chairperson;* a feminist might object to *chairman.* You can, if you want to keep the peace, adjust your terminology to one or the other — but what if there are both traditionalists and feminists among your listeners or readers? In that case, *chairman* would probably be the safer bet, as being slightly less conspicuous a term.

Much the same considerations apply to such coinages as *layperson, salesperson,* and *spokesperson.* But there has been no real need for *airperson* or *newsperson,* since the neutral terms *pilot* and *reporter* are available. And no -*person* compounds have yet been adopted for *alderman/ alderwoman,* for instance, or *businessman/ businesswoman, congressman/congresswoman, countryman/countrywoman, horseman/horsewoman, policeman/policewoman,* or *sportsman/ sportswoman.*

The words *chairman, chairwoman,* and *chairperson* are recorded as dating from 1654,

1685, and 1971 respectively. As for *layperson* and *spokesperson,* they are attested from 1972 — but *salesperson* is attested from 1901.

Another problem presented by words ending in -*person* is that of their plural form: is it -*persons* or -*people? Salespeople,* one of the oldest of these plurals, dates from 1876 — some 25 years before the singular *salesperson* was first recorded! But today the plural -*persons* seems to predominate: *salespersons* seems as common as *salespeople,* and *chairpersons* and *spokespersons* seem far more common than *chairpeople* and *spokespeople* (*lay persons* and *lay people* both seem common, but would probably be written as two separate words). The tendency to prefer -*persons* to -*people* smacks a little of formality or prissiness: in general, *Many people came to the party* sounds more vigorous and straightforward than *Many persons came to the party.* So perhaps those who advocate -*person* in the interests of greater forthrightness of language might consider trying -*people* instead of -*persons* as its plural.

Note, finally, that the use of *to chair* as a verb, meaning 'to preside over (a meeting)', aroused a chorus of objections when it emerged about 60 years ago. This opposition still continues today, though far less intensely. Most dictionaries now accept the word fully, and there no longer seems any need to avoid it.

See also -ESS; MAN; SEXISM IN THE ENGLISH LANGUAGE.

character   There is a strange tendency to invest anything with a *character* — *? paintings of a puzzling character; ? contributions of a praiseworthy character; ? the bland character of the food; ? It is heartening to know that adventures of this character are still undertaken today.* Why speakers and writers should want to make their meaning more abstract and their sentences more woolly is one of the mysteries of modern language use. It is more efficient and just as precise to speak of undertaking *such adventures,* or of *praiseworthy contributions, puzzling paintings,* and the *blandness of the food.*

If an abstract noun is needed, the traditional *quality, type, sort,* and *kind* are preferable to *character.* To be on the safe side, limit *character* as far as possible to people, and try to avoid using it of things. Of course, if *character* is used in a more precise way, to mean 'charm and interest', it can suit things as well as people: *a market town with a lot of character.*

charisma   *Charisma,* pronounced /kə-**riz**mə/, is one of those vogue words that tend, through overuse, to lose their force. Adopted from Greek, it was originally used in theological contexts to refer to a special power, divinely given, such as the power of healing. (The ultimate source is the Greek *kharis*, 'grace, favour'.) Used in this sense, *charisma* has the plural *charismata*, and the variant form *charism*.

In the 1950s, *charisma* and its adjective *charismatic*, pronounced /**karr**iz-**mat**tik/, were drawn into general use by being applied to the U.S. President John F. Kennedy and some of his entourage, who allegedly displayed a special appeal and personal magnetism. This was fair enough: there was a lexical gap in English and no better word — then or since — has been suggested to fill it.

Since then, however, *charisma* has become further diluted, and is now frequently used as no more than a synonym for *charm*. (The two words are not related in origin: *charm* goes back to the Latin *carmen*, 'a song or incantation'.) The debasement of the word seems inevitable, but until it has been drained of all its old potency, it is worth keeping it in reserve for special occasions.

chauvinist, chauvinism The model chauvinist, though not the first (for the condition existed long before it had a name), was a French soldier, Nicolas Chauvin, an ardent follower of Napoleon, noted for his patriotic fervour. He was popularised as a character in a French play in 1831, and his name gave rise — first in French and then in English — to the words referring to fanatical patriotism.

> ... the most ferocious of the new American films cropped up in the atmosphere of the second cold war. This is a film which should very reliably generate real terror and chauvinist hatred among the millions of naive and impressionable American teenagers likely to see it.
> – David Robinson, *The Times*

In our own day, the feminist movement has given currency to the phrase *male chauvinist* (sometimes shortened to the simple form *chauvinist*), which denotes a man with an unreasonable bias against women:

> Intent on securing a place in a merchant bank themselves, male undergraduates view women's job-hunting endeavours with something of an amused indulgence. Nor are such chauvinistic attitudes confined to the Junior Common Room. Legion are the

stories of male tutors who reduce their female students to tears.
> – Alison Payne, *The Guardian*

Chauvinist and *chauvinism* have now extended their range further, to any prejudiced belief in the superiority of one's own group.

> Who is the best living British cartoonist of the topical political variety? Our Deputy Editor, Anthony Howard, showing exemplary resistance to in-house chauvinism, nominates Nicholas Garland of the *Telegraph* newspapers.
> – Russell Davies, *The Observer*

As so often happens with a new sense, especially when it becomes fashionable, the original sense tends to be overshadowed. The danger is that if you speak of a *chauvinist* today without clarifying the context, people may assume that you are referring to a sexist man rather than to a zealous patriot. Take care not to lay yourself open to misunderstanding: the terms *jingoist* on the one hand, and *sexist* or *male chauvinist* on the other, can be enlisted if there is any danger of ambiguity.

check, cheque What in British English is a *cheque,* as in *traveller's cheque* or *cheque book,* is spelt *check* in American English. The Americans also use the word *check* in restaurants, to mean 'an invoice' — what in British English is called a *bill*. To continue the domino effect, in American English a *bill,* as in *a ten-dollar bill,* is what the English mean by a *note,* as in *a ten-pound note*. In restaurants, the British can pay a *bill* with a *cheque*; Americans might pay a *check* (in cash) with a *bill*.

Other senses of *check* that are exclusive to American English are 'a tick' (a mark of approval) or 'to tick', and 'a ticket or guarantee slip' — such a check may, for example, be handed in at a cloakroom (also called a *checkroom* in America) to reclaim property. *To take a rain check* in colloquial American English (and increasingly in British English too) is not to check if it is raining, but to postpone something until later. When a baseball game ('match') is rained out ('off'), a spectator can use his ticket-stub, or get a special ticket, to gain free admission to a later game: hence the idiom. Americans also use *check* as a verb, meaning 'to deposit (something) at a checkroom' or 'to take (something) for deposit'. Thus an American cloakroom attendant who asks *Can I check your bag?* probably does not want to examine its contents: he is merely reminding you that you can leave the bag in his safekeeping until you are ready to leave.

Another American usage, increasingly adopted in British English though widely criticised, is the phrase *? to check out.* Traditional usage has allowed *to check up* and *to check up on* something, so the objection to the 'unnecessary' word *out* in *to check out* seems rather unfair. None the less, the phrase is still best avoided in formal usage:

> *?* First, check out the school or playgroup yourself; never rely on other parents' opinions, however much you respect them.
> – Judy Froshang, *The Times*

The spelling *check* is standard, in both British and American English, for all other senses of the word (to restrain, to verify, an inspection, a small square, a chess position, and so on).

The game of draughts, played with discs on a squared board, is sometimes called *checkers* or *chequers*: in American English it is known and spelt only as *checkers*. A small piece in a game of draughts is sometimes a *draught* or *draughtsman,* and often a *chequer* or *checker* (always a *checker* in American English). The game is played on a *draughtboard* or *chequerboard* in British English; on a *checkerboard* in American English.

Chequers, finally, with a capital *C,* is the country residence of the British Prime Minister.

childish, childlike These adjectives tend nowadays to be applied not to young children at all, but to adults or older children. *Childish* is a disparaging term, *childlike* is usually a complimentary one. Both can be applied to people, works of art, attitudes, and so on. *Childish* means 'displaying qualities of a child that are irritating in an older person; foolishly immature':

> Stop being so childish! All I want is to borrow the car.
> I thought it a rather childish play, with a very simple-minded view of nuclear disarmament.

> Near his parent's apartment at Number 48, repeating a childish trick, he jumped from the moving vehicle before the air brakes went on, letting the momentum of the jump, combined with that of the tram, bring him up with a soft thud against the door jamb of his parents' building.
> – Thomas Keneally, *Schindler's Ark*

Childlike means 'displaying qualities of a child that remain endearing in an older person' — such as innocence and guilelessness:

The delightfully childlike paintings of Douanier Rousseau are in fact the product of a deliberate and very astute artistic consciousness.
The maestro tossed off the Liszt scherzo with a fresh, childlike charm.

> To suggest as some have that any woman would be pleased with partial possession of Oskar is to demean the women involved. The problem was, perhaps, that if you wanted to talk to Oskar about fidelity, a look of childlike and authentic bewilderment entered his eyes, as if you were proposing some concept like relativity which could be understood only if the listener had five hours to sit still and concentrate.
> – Thomas Keneally, *Schindler's Ark*

In the following extract, the distinction between *childish* and *childlike* is drawn explicitly:

> It's always been a policy on the programme not to talk down to children, to treat them as adults. .... I suppose, as a result, I tend to look at life in a childlike way — as opposed to childish. I'd like to think I have a childlike enthusiasm for things.
> – Simon Groom, *The Sunday Times*

Childish used to serve too as the neutral adjective applicable to young children: *The toddler sighed in her childish sleep; intent on their childish games in the playground.* But its more modern meaning, with its disapproving tone, has made such neutral usage virtually impossible today. A likelier and safer word is *child's* or *children's* or *childhood: in her child's sleep; children's games in the playground.*

Chinese *Chinese,* as in *a group of Chinese,* is the preferred term for a person or people of Chinese origin, other words being considered derogatory or nonstandard. *??* *Chinaman,* in particular, is regarded as old-fashioned and as offensive to Chinese people.

Singular uses such as *a Chinese* strike many people as awkward, however, and an adjectival construction is often used to get round this: *There was a Chinese man sitting at the table.* The singular form *×* *a Chinee* is both nonstandard and offensive, and can no longer be considered even humorous.

Christian name, first name, forename, given name 1. A *Christian name* (sometimes with a small c) was originally the baptismal name of a Christian; and in past centuries, when the vast majority of English-speakers were Christians, it was appropriate to refer to first names as *Christian names.*

Today the term is sometimes criticised, though still widely used in spoken British English. Jews, Hindus, and Muslims (and even atheist descendants of Christians) might reasonably object to being asked for their *Christian names.* In American English, the term is not much used, and may even be frowned on as insensitive. The usual term in American English is *first name/s* — which is now increasingly common in British English too.

In official forms and documents, *forename/s* and *given name/s* are the terms commonly used. These are both rather formal, and *given name/s* has the further disadvantage of being slightly misleading — in a sense, your surname is 'given' to you just as much as your first names are.

However, *given name* has one advantage over *first name*: it can be used without qualms about people whose mother tongues put the *surname* first, as Chinese and Hungarian do, for example: the Hungarian composer known to us as *Béla Bartók* is known to his compatriots as *Bartók Béla,* and *Mao Ze-dong* (Mao Tse-Tung) began life as a member of the *Mao* family.

● *Recommendation* Unless specifically addressing or referring to Christians, avoid the term *Christian name.* In speech and in most writing, *first name* is the most appropriate term. In formal and official writing, *forename* or *given name* is perhaps slightly more suitable, and *given name* is technically more appropriate when dealing with languages that put surnames first.

2. First names are in far commoner use today than in past times. In keeping with the old British tradition, schoolteachers may still address schoolboys by their surnames — even schoolboys may sometimes address fellow schoolboys in this way — but it is no longer the norm, and no longer sounds quite natural in the way it once did. About 200 years ago, it would even have been natural for wives to address their husbands as *Mr Stevens, Mr Lumley,* and so on. Today, by contrast, it is not unusual for children to address their parents and even grandparents by their first names.

The use of first name and surname together in addressing a person has respectable antecedents in the usage of certain religious groups:

Josiah Hawley, picture yourself cast
Into a brick-kiln where the blast
Fans your quick vitals to a coal.
         – Robert Lowell (U.S.),
         'Mr Edwards and the Spider'

The adoption of this style in general discourse seems a fairly recent habit, and one that has attracted some criticism. The two contexts in which this practice chiefly occurs are radio broadcasts and letters to strangers.

In interviews and discussions on the radio (and occasionally on television too), the interviewer or chairman might typically say *If I can turn to you, Joseph Carling, what is your view? ... David Burns, how do you respond to that? ... Mary Shawcross, you've been quoted as saying ... .* The practice probably developed as an aid to the listener — an intermittent reminder of the full name of the invisible interviewee or panel member — though why plain, old-fashioned *Mr Burns* or *Dr Shawcross* should be thought insufficient is not quite clear.

In the salutations in personal letters to strangers, the form *Dear Philip Howarth, Dear Beverley Trew,* or the like is probably prompted by an attempt to strike a balance between overfamiliarity and cold formality. Suppose you want to send a note to a film critic, pointing out an error he made in a review in a magazine: it might seem presumptuous to address him or her as *Dear Philip* or *Dear Beverley*, and yet reproachful or even hostile to write *Dear Sir* or *Dear Madam* or even *Dear Mr Howarth* or *Dear Miss Trew.* And is it not perhaps *Dr* Howarth or *Mrs* Trew — or perhaps she would prefer to be called *Ms* Trew, or might she be insulted to be called that ... or is *Beverley Trew* perhaps *Mr* Trew?

To write *Dear Philip Howarth* or *Dear Beverley Trew* seems a good compromise — hitting an appropriate tone and playing safe. Yet many people complain of being addressed in this way: Evelyn Waugh called it a 'deplorable ... form of address'. If in doubt, revert to the old-fashioned form *Dear Miss* (or *Mrs* or *Mr*) *Trew*, and so on. If you are uncertain about the correct title, try checking in a reference book such as *Who's Who,* or phoning his or her place of work and asking a colleague or assistant.

See also CAPITAL LETTERS **4.**

chronic A *chronic disease* is one that lasts for a long time or develops slowly, as distinct from an acute disease, which has a rapid onset. *Chronic unemployment* is the kind that lasts for years. Both usages take account of the word's origin — through French and Latin back to the Greek *khronikos,* from *khronos,* 'time'.

It is probably because of the word's frequent association with unpleasant medical conditions that it has developed the slang sense in British English of 'dreadful, very bad'. So people will talk of someone as having *a chronic sense of humour*, or put forward the opinion that *Last night's television was chronic*.

Restrict such uses to informal contexts, and use them sparingly even then.

circumstances *Under the circumstances* vs *in the circumstances*. The Latin roots of *circumstance* — *circum*, 'around' + *stare*, 'to stand or be' — have led pedants to argue that the correct phrase must be *in the circumstances*: if something is *around* us, we are surely *in* it rather than *under* it.

Such a severely logical approach is simply not appropriate to the English language. Idiom allows both *in the circumstances* and *under the circumstances*, and has done so for centuries.

Not that the two phrases are absolute equivalents. There is a theoretical distinction between them, and it is perhaps worth trying to observe it. *In the circumstances* is the more general term, meaning roughly 'in such a situation; this being the case'.

> There was nothing I could do in the circumstances other than sit and wait.
> In the circumstances, I'm inclined to overlook the offence and release you with a warning.

> Mr Gormann had not appeared to be disconcerted by the emergence of Jeremy on to that already confused scene. He took the boy's presence, if his bearing was anything to judge by, as unsurprising in the circumstances, one more or less member of the Tradescant family being unable to disrupt the tranquillity of his afternoon more than the tactlessness of their mother.
> — A.N. Wilson, *The Sweets of Pimlico*

Under the circumstances traditionally suggests a greater degree of connection between the circumstances mentioned and the action taken. It means roughly 'all things considered; taking these influences into account':

> Duran was brought up in the roughest neighbourhood in town, and under the circumstances, it's no surprise that he knows how to throw a punch.

> Night was falling, and the enemy was closing in on the left flank — under the circumstances, Marshall Strol was wise to withdraw hastily to the north.

> Unless I'm dreaming I have never written a word about Claire Brétecher in the *New Statesman*, or anywhere else. Under the cir-

cumstances I would very much like to disagree with the words mysteriously attributed to me.
> — Richard Boston, *The Observer*

Perhaps in conflict with this distinction, *under* is far more common before *no circumstances*, or *any circumstances*: *Under no circumstances am I prepared to overlook this offence*; *He won't budge under any circumstances*.

Various other forms of the phrases are common too: *in/under these circumstances, in such circumstances, in straitened circumstances*, and so on.

claim 1. Purists object to the loose way that the verb *claim* has come to be used. Strictly, it has a sense of forceful demand about it — as when laying claim to something or urging some unlikely belief or defiant boast or desperate contention:

> The composer claimed to be under the direct guidance of Chopin's spirit.

> The reason, baldly stated, is that the prosecution evidence may well have been faked from the very beginning, just as the five convicted men have always claimed.
> — Robin Lustig, *The Observer*

> Once Sedlacek had the question out, Schindler hesitated ... It should not be a surprise if he sat back in his padded chair and claimed ignorance.
> — Thomas Keneally, *Schindler's Ark*

> Each of the accused solemnly claimed that he had remained fast asleep throughout the shoot-out.

Some purists even go to the extent of objecting to the last of these examples, arguing that *claim* should never be followed by the conjunction *that*. This blanket ban is too harsh, but certainly *claim that* should not be used in very tame sentences, where the 'claim' is simply an allegation or a statement rather than some very assertive or implausible protestation. Among the milder or more appropriate verbs to choose from are *state, assert, contend, explain, argue, insist, maintain, charge, allege*, and — often best of all — *say*.

> ? Jackson claims that the table is mahogany, and I claim that it is teak. (Preferably *maintains, insists*, or *says*.)

> ? The plaintiff claimed that the landlord had clearly failed to give her the required four weeks' notice. (Preferably *argued, contended*, or *alleged*.)

?The Original Michael Frayn (Salamander Press, £4.95) does not wear so well. This assortment of old *Guardian* and *Observer* essays originally published between 1959 and 1968 is prefaced by a laboured introduction from the editor, James Fenton, who claims that we will hoot our heads off despite their 'period flavour'.

— Peter Jones, *The Times*

(Preferably *assures us, suggests,* or *contends.*)

2. A second dubious use of *claim* is in the recently popular phrase *to claim responsibility for.* This phrase has often been used in reports of terrorist outrages:

The Liberation Front yesterday claimed responsibility for the bombing.

The objection is this: that when *claim* is followed by a noun, it typically marks a good or desirable achievement — *to claim credit, to claim victory.* (Even *to claim ignorance*, as in an earlier example, is not to boast of ignorance, but to *disclaim* a responsibility one wants to evade.) To speak, then, of *claiming responsibility* for a bombing or a kidnapping is to make the act seem like a celebration rather than a confession. Terrorists might well see things in this light, but there is no need for reporters to go along with such a view. Writers and broadcasters have accordingly been urged to use other formulations, such as:

The Liberation Front yesterday admitted responsibility for the bombing.

The Liberation Front yesterday declared that it was responsible for the bombing.

classic, classical These two adjectives overlap in meaning. It is difficult, for instance, to detect any difference between *a practical joke of classic simplicity* and *a practical joke of classical simplicity.* Both words in this context seem to mean 'pure, unalloyed, undiluted'.

However, the two words are not, as a rule, interchangeable: in most contexts, either they would have quite different meanings, or else only one of them would be suitable in the first place.

Essentially, *classic* means 'typical of, or outstanding in, its class'. So it can mean 'of highest quality', as in *a classic performance of the blues* (which suggests a superb, standard-setting performance). Or it may simply mean 'perfectly characteristic', as in *a classic case of gangrene.* In both instances, the criterion is perfect accordance with the rules or expectations for a type or class. Here are two citations illustrating the two senses:

It was the usual freelancing pot-pourri: pieces on stockings, fashion, Truman Capote, John Lennon, Vidal Sassoon. As early as 1963 she wrote the classic exposé, 'I Was a Playboy Bunny'.

— Martin Amis, *The Observer*

Sentimentalising other cultures is to over-emphasise aspects which appeal, while not considering the whole picture; rose coloured spectacles obscure the vision. This is a classic tradition among discontented westerners: both Russia and China have been glamorised in this way — by Arthur Scargill, Beatrice Webb and Shirley Maclaine for instance.

— Minette Marrin, *The Observer*

If *classic* corresponds to *class,* then *classical* corresponds to *classics,* 'the study of Latin and ancient Greek' (and sometimes other *classical languages,* such as Biblical Hebrew and ancient Chinese): *a classical education; classical allusions.* The *classical age* is usually that of the ancient Greek and Roman civilisations; however, the phrase can refer too to other ancient civilisations and also to more recent eras in which a comparable peak of culture was achieved, especially when viewed as the culmination of what preceded rather than as the beginning of what followed.

There is a danger of confusion in contexts where either *classic* or *classical* might be used in their respective senses. *A classic play* and *a classical play* are not necessarily the same: Arthur Miller's *Death of a Salesman* and Harold Pinter's *The Caretaker* are *classic plays* — and modern plays. Pierre Corneille and his brother Thomas were both French *classical* dramatists of the 17th century — but only Pierre is considered a *classic* dramatist today. A *classical garment* might be a toga; a *classic garment* could be a Chanel suit — that is, one of simple and elegant style that survives the whims of passing fashion. It is theoretically possible to combine *classic* and *classical* in such a phrase as *a classic example of classical tragedy.*

The most common confusion — if it is one — is the use of *classical* where idiom favours *classic,* as in *a classic case* or *a classic example:*

? It is natural to the literary mind to be unduly observant of the choice of words. Logan Pearsall Smith was the classical case. I met him once only. He did not speak to me until we stood on the doorstep leaving.

— Evelyn Waugh, *.Encounter*

? Professor Bernard Crick's new critical edition — out this week — of George Orwell's

'1984' is a most ingenious contrivance. I propose to argue that it is a classical example of misplaced and excessive ingenuity, obfuscating the text it is intended to illuminate.
– Conor Cruise O'Brien, *The Observer*

Both *classic* and *classical* have several other shades of meaning. In informal contexts, for example, *classic* can mean 'traditional, well-known', as in *a classic mistake, a classic practical joke. Classical* can refer to achievements that were pinnacles in their time, even if now outmoded — *classical physics* is the physics of Newton, now in large part superseded by Einstein's theories of relativity.

Classical can also suggest a formal elegance or purity within any quality or ability — appearance, movement, thoughts, and so on:

> We all admire the spangled acrobat with classical grace meticulously walking his tightrope in the talcum light; but how much rarer art there is in the sagging rope expert wearing scarecrow clothes and impersonating a grotesque drunk!
> – Vladimir Nabokov, *Lolita*

The following quotation probably uses the word *classical* in more than one sense:

> This for me was a great problem as I felt that I needed some sort of classical frame upon which to expose the tapestry which I wanted to weave. I did not know whether I could use some of the by-products of this crisis and use them as if they were classical unities. The disintegration of the stable ego, the subject-object relationship ... Could I make myself a classical backcloth out of the by-products of relativity?
> – Lawrence Durrell, *The Fiction Magazine*

In the history of visual art, *classical* refers, strictly speaking, to Greek art of the 5th century BC, taken as the peak of the artistic achievement of the ancient world. (More generally, it is used to refer to all Greek and Roman art, or to any specified ancient culture or its traditions.) It is characterised by a formal idealisation of Nature that dispenses with all transitory and human irregularities, and relies on such principles as mathematical symmetry and harmony, unity and simplicity, and ideal beauty. The *neo-Classical* artists and critics of 18th-century Europe revered this tradition, and sought to restore it.

Classicism in art came to be defined as the opposite of a new rival movement, *Romanticism*, and eventually acquired more negative senses,

such as 'coldly formal' or even 'sterile'. And in 20th-century art, the adjective *classic* (now divorced from *classical,* but adopting much of its meaning) suggests clarity, proportion, and deliberate, rule-governed craftsmanship, and implies a contrast with expressionist and emotional works:

> As a painter he is both classic and modern; classic in composition and texture (he is great on walls, streets and interiors) and modern in his audacious foreshortenings, in his choice of subject matter.
> – Richard Roud, *The Guardian*

Classical music (also referred to as *the classics*), is used in at least three different senses. In its most general sense, it refers to any music of the serious educated European tradition, as distinct from folk music and pop music. In this sense, we can speak of classical music as still being written today. (The term *classical music* can be used in an equivalent sense of any culture, in contrast to its folk music: *a concert of Indian classical music.*) Rather more narrowly, it refers to all such music composed between about 1600 and 1800 and characterised by formal design and the search for beauty, as distinct from Romantic music, which developed instead the less abstract aims of expressing emotion and even representing ideas. More narrowly still, *classical music* refers to the serious music composed between about 1750 and 1800, notably that of Haydn and Mozart, as opposed to both Baroque music that came before and Romantic music that followed.

A similar threefold interpretation is possible of *classical ballet*, finally; but now the order of *classical* and *romantic* is reversed — *romantic ballet* referring usually to French ballet of the early 19th century, and *classical* to Russian ballet in the late 19th century.

Finally, remember that although *classical* is only an adjective, *classic* can be used, in various senses, as a noun:

> His book is none the less as rich a meal as a nineteenth-century feast, and his aggressively psychoanalytic approach will undoubtedly make this a classic of its kind.
> – Phyllis Grosskurth, *The Observer*

clauses A clause is a group of words containing a 'subject' and a 'predicate' (see SENTENCES) — typically a noun or noun equivalent followed by a full verb.

1. A *main clause* is one that can stand alone as a sentence: *The door was open*. A sentence may

contain more than one main clause: *The door was open and I went in.* Or it may contain one or more *subordinate* or *dependent clauses* in addition to the main clause. A subordinate clause is one that cannot stand alone. The words *when I arrived* constitute a subordinate clause in the sentence *The door was open when I arrived.*

2. a. Subordinate clauses function within the sentence in the same way as single adjectives, adverbs, or nouns do. A clause that does the work of an adjective is usually called a *relative clause*. Instead of saying *the open door* or *the kitchen door*, you could speak of *the door that leads to the kitchen*: the clause *that leads to the kitchen* identifies the door, just as the adjective *open* does in *the open door.* Similarly, *where we camped* is a relative clause in the sentence *The place where we camped is now flooded.*

Relative clauses can be of two types — *restrictive* (or *defining*) *clauses,* which define or specify the noun and are essential to the meaning of the sentence, and *nonrestrictive* (or *nondefining*) *clauses,* which simply present some extra information about the noun. For details, see RESTRICTIVE AND NONRESTRICTIVE CLAUSES.

b. An *adverbial clause* does the work of an adverb, usually in connection with a verb in some other clause. As with single adverbs, adverbial clauses can make a comment on the time or place of a verb:

When the cat's away, the mice will play. (time)
Put it where you can reach it. (place)

Adverbial clauses can also say something about the cause, effect, condition, or purpose of a verb. Grammarians have perhaps gone to unnecessary detail in the past in classifying the types. Here are some more examples:

You're tired because you went to bed so late. (cause)
You went to bed so late that you're tired. (effect)
He stayed till Thursday so that he could avoid the traffic. (purpose)
She will sing only if she's paid. (condition)

c. A *noun clause* does the work of a noun in the sentence. Instead of saying *They believed his story,* you could say *They believed what he told them,* using the noun clause *what he told them* as the object of the verb. In *What he told them will never be known,* the same noun clause is the subject of the verb. Instead of saying *We sold it for £10,* you could say *We sold it for what it would fetch,* using a noun clause as the object of

the preposition *for.*

3. A common characteristic of immature or oversophisticated style is the overuse of subordinate clauses — especially relative clauses dependent on other relative clauses:

? I shouldn't trust any agreement that contains a provision that offers the possibility, which either of the signatories can exploit, of cancellation at short notice.

Such a sentence may be grammatically correct, but it is hardly elegant. It should be broken down into two or three separate sentences. Alternatively, the relative clauses could be blended unobtrusively into the mainstream of the sentence:

I shouldn't trust any agreement that contains a provision offering either of the signatories the possibility of cancellation at short notice.

See also MISRELATED CONSTRUCTIONS.

claustrophobic See NOSTALGIA.

clichés 'Avoid clichés like the plague' is, as a joke, something of a cliché itself, and as a piece of advice, slightly overstated. But the principle is sound (perhaps even tautologous — a cliché might almost be defined as an overused idiom that you should avoid). Language reflects thought: it even, to a large extent, controls thought. So tired, unimaginative wording suggests tired, unimaginative thinking. Listeners and readers tend to suspect the opinions of a cliché-user as secondhand. If he cannot take the trouble to *express* his thoughts in a fresh or careful way, people feel, then he has probably been too lazy to *consider* his thoughts in a fresh and careful way. (True enough, all clichés must once have been freshly coined, and their persistence is a tribute to the vigour of the original thought in each case. Even so, their use is not to be recommended. Express the thought by all means, but express it in your own way.)

Clichés are not always the product of laziness or heedlessness. Sometimes they are chosen all too deliberately, out of facetiousness or the wish to show off. Clichéd allusions and quotations are usually prompted by the conscious urge to impress in this way: a bore who criticises a book or film as being *a curate's egg,* or who on hearing a bell tolling is moved to say *For whom the bell tolls,* is thinking too much about his words rather than too little. Foreigners too, wishing to parade their competence in English, often defeat this object by trotting out a rigmarole of extremely *unim-*

pressive idioms: *That film was not my cup of tea*; *It's raining cats and dogs*. No native speaker of English could say such things without sounding slightly silly, insensitive, or banal. To use thumping clichés like those would be something of an insult to the intelligence of the listener — rather like telling him a very stale joke.

The word *cliché* comes from the French. Its literal meaning there is 'stereotype(d)' — a *stereotype* being, originally, a metal printing plate cast from a mould. (The French verb referring to this process, *clicher*, developed in imitation of the sound made when the matrix, or mould of type, was dropped into the molten metal to make a stereotype plate.) From this image of a printing-plate that turns out the same page again and again came the sense of 'a phrase, idea, or situation that has been used too often — a trite, hackneyed expression', a *cliché*.

Clichés come in many shapes and sizes (to use a cliché). An inventory of types of cliché follows, with examples of each. But before that, a few notes of qualification. First, the word *cliché* can be applied to personal relationships, plot-devices, and so on, not just to verbal expressions: a playwright's use of disguised characters or lucky coincidences, for instance, might be criticised as a dramatic cliché.

Secondly, there is no clear dividing line between a verbal cliché and a useful phrase. Not every widely used idiom is a cliché. It would be unnecessary to expunge the following selection of expressions, for example, from your everyday vocabulary: *a bone of contention, tongue in cheek, to take someone down a peg or two, the old school tie, a man of straw, bored to tears, in the limelight, a wild-goose chase, to wash your hands of something, in the heat of the moment, a house of cards, to have the edge*.

Thirdly, even an indisputable cliché may sometimes be appropriate. Its very familiarity and forthrightness might be just what is needed. If a discussion has been too vague or petty, for instance, you might want to focus it by suggesting: *Let's get down to brass tacks*. There is no arguing over the meaning of that.

At least one celebrated Fleet Street editor has openly declared considerable tolerance of clichés:

> It is impossible to ban them because they serve a natural inclination. At best they are a form of literary shorthand, with the attraction of economy ... What deskmen can do with clichés in copy is to ration them, and tolerate only the best.
> – Harold Evans, *Newsman's English*

Finally, even the best of writers are prone to the occasional cliché — Lord Butler, for instance, in his famous volume of memoirs:

> With Birkenhead his relations were superficially easy, but in temperament and philosophy the two men stood poles apart. ...
> Thus our people had to put their best foot forward. I held many a meeting of the U.B.I. in my flat. ...
> The lecture would be printed for distribution throughout the Empire. All this encouraged me to put first things first. ...
> Within a few days of my going to the Foreign Office, Hitler had given us one more indication of the shape of things to come by his forcible incorporation of Austria in Germany.
> – Lord Butler, *The Art of the Possible*

Note the clichés *stood poles apart*, *put their best foot forward*, *put first things first*, and *the shape of things to come*.

Here now is a suggested list of the varieties of cliché. There is naturally some overlap among the examples.

● *homilies, platitudes, and stale proverbial sentiments*. Well-intentioned though these no doubt are, as advice or consolation, they often succeed only in irritating the hearer:

All good things must come to an end.
Seeing is believing.
He who pays the piper calls the tune.
You can't have your cake and eat it (too).
It's no good crying over spilt milk.
Slow and steady wins the race.
Fools rush in where angels fear to tread.
It takes all kinds to make a world.

> 'For the Pen,' said the Vicar; and in the sententious pause which followed I felt I would offer all the gold of Peru to avert the solemn, inevitable ... 'is mightier than the Sword.'
> – Logan Pearsall Smith (U.S.), *All Trivia*

● *the overused idiom*.
to heave a sigh of relief
conspicuous by his absence
to add insult to injury
to praise to the skies
Take it or leave it.
much of a muchness
a tower of strength
to make a mountain out of a molehill
few and far between

It warms the cockles of my heart.
to hit the nail on the head
On your own head be it.
six of one and half-a-dozen of the other
to give him a taste of his own medicine
none the worse for wear
to wend one's way
a blessing in disguise
to put all your eggs in one basket
from time immemorial
to nip something in the bud
just the ticket (chiefly British)
to pop the question
to snatch victory from the jaws of defeat
an uphill battle
the object of the exercise
to throw the book at someone
on a hiding to nothing (chiefly British)
to bite the bullet
to live the life of Riley
a climate of opinion
to make mincemeat of
to ride roughshod over
to pull your punches
at the drop of a hat

For *put your money where your mouth is*:

But there is all the difference in the world between making the right noises on this delicate subject and actually putting your money where your mouth is.
— Auberon Waugh, *Sunday Telegraph*

A particularly common kind of clichéd idiom is the 'duet' — a pair of words that seems to be an inseparable combination, to go together like '. . . a horse and carriage':

to pick and choose
goods and chattels
fine and dandy
part and parcel
trials and tribulations
without let or hindrance
to chop and change (chiefly British)
by leaps and bounds
slow but sure
home and dry
kith and kin
short and sweet
cut and thrust
sadder but wiser
neither rhyme nor reason
a hue and cry
to toss and turn
fast and furious
neither hide nor hair

There are 'trios' too:

cool, calm, and collected
hook, line, and sinker
every Tom, Dick, and Harry
lock, stock, and barrel

● *tarnished images and faded similes* Various metaphors, which might have been sparkling when they first appeared, have been dulled by overuse ('to coin a phrase'), and the original metaphorical point of them is hardly noticed any longer:

to take the lid off
in winter's icy grip
Silence reigned supreme.
to dice with death
a shot in the arm
to give the green light to
balanced on a knife edge
teething troubles
to keep your nose to the grindstone
the calm before the storm
to leave no stone unturned
a bolt from the blue
to stick to your last
clutching at straws
to burn the midnight oil
the parting of the ways
to take the bull by the horns
to beat about the bush
to turn over a new leaf
the march of time
to upset the apple-cart
a storm of protest
to snowball
at the end of my tether
to take the wind out of someone's sails

For *spike someone's guns*, *top dog*, and *reach the end of the road*:

By refusing to lend TUC support to the NGA in its lawless picketing, he has in effect spiked the Labour Left's guns ... As top dogs, organised labour in Britain has reached the end of the road.
— Peregrine Worsthorne,
Sunday Telegraph

A close relative of the dead metaphor is the faded simile:

as bright as a button
as bold as brass
to sell like hot cakes
as cunning as a fox
bleeding like a stuck pig

as cool as a cucumber
as tough as old boots (chiefly British)
as thick as two short planks (chiefly
    British)
to drink like a fish
a memory like a sieve
dead as a doornail
drunk as a lord
to fight like a lion
free as a bird
to come down like a ton of bricks
as large as life and twice as natural
like a bat out of hell
to turn up like a bad penny
flat as a pancake
to grin like a Cheshire cat
to get on like a house on fire
pure as the driven snow
to stick out like a sore thumb

● *the dead quotation or pointless allusion.* This type of cliché is particularly appealing to the showing-off personality. As always, Shakespeare and the Bible are most vulnerable, though Aesop runs a close third.

more sinned against than sinning
the writing on the wall
sour grapes
to turn the other cheek
an eye for an eye
all things to all men
no respecter of persons
There's method in his madness.
a rose by any other name
to out-herod Herod
hoist with his own petard
But who will bell the cat?
a dog in the manger
to cry wolf
Achilles' heel
warts and all
an ugly duckling
things fall apart
not with a bang but a whimper
the gentle art of ...
Yes sir, no sir, three bags full.
Down and out in ...

● *the inevitable adjective.* Many writers and speakers seem unable to use a noun without using its traditional accompanying adjective as well.

Questions may be raised — *burning* questions — that challenge traditional beliefs — *cherished* beliefs. A *grave* crisis might result, though *undue* alarm will be discouraged. After *active* consideration and a *concerted* effort, those involved will

decide matters by an *acid* test, producing *hard* facts that necessitate an *agonising* reappraisal. Even so, *flat* denials are likely to be issued as a *bounden* duty by those with *vested* interests. There will be *blunt* allegations of *gaping* holes in the research, and the so-called *full* inquiry will be branded a *grotesque* parody. So you are likely to remain in *blissful* ignorance of the results, and you will not be alone — in *splendid* isolation — in your ignorance. You will have a *bewildering* variety of *boon* companions, in fact — preferable at least to being left to the *tender* mercies of the *serried* ranks of *total* strangers.

Similarly, needs tend to be *crying,* brides *blushing,* thuds *dull,* accounts *graphic,* victims *hapless,* gentlemen *perfect*, and deterrents *credible*. In journalism, binoculars always seem to be *powerful* binoculars; similarly, *categorical* denials, *derisory* prison sentences, *pitched* battles, and *card-carrying* communists.

Adverbs too are sometimes tightly linked to a particular verb or adjective: *inextricably* linked, you might say. So: *hermetically* sealed, *deadly* serious, *desperately* poor, *wickedly* funny, *hopelessly* lost, *stony* broke.

This type of cliché provoked an amusing correspondence in a national British newspaper:

SIR — Why is daylight always referred to as 'broad'? Is this a special width discernible only by policemen and crime reporters?
TOM H. HOBBS

SIR — Mr T.H. Hobbs should be grateful that daylight is still broad since every dimension is currently qualified by the one adjective, massive; I trust no reporter will take this as a broad hint.

L.S. BOYS
– letters to the *Daily Telegraph*

The cliché irritates *me* because it is a cliché: an almost unvarying formula which suggests (surely wrongly?) that the news editor has not the time, wit or verbal armoury to ring a few changes. Why must all battles be 'pitched', all shots 'ring out', all struggles 'ensue'? Does *everything* that could be big, large, great, enormous, giant or vast *have* to be 'massive'? With synonyms like 'new', 'renewed' and 'more', etc. available, do we *have* to have everything 'fresh'? Fresh talks, fresh initiatives, fresh fighting and — in one memorable report, 'Three weeks after the earthquake, fresh bodies have been discovered.'

– Fritz Spiegl, *The Listener*

● *nicknames, titles, or sobriquets.* Again, the showing-off side of people prompts them to avoid calling a person, place, or thing by its ordinary name and to choose instead some 'different' title — facetious or solemn — that is in fact no different from the title used by millions of others:

the Emerald Isle
your better half
your good lady/lady wife (chiefly British)
she who must be obeyed
the Antipodes
our four-legged friends
crowned heads
a nation of shopkeepers
the supreme sacrifice
the city fathers
Reynard
the fair sex
the Mother of Parliaments
yours truly
the clerk of the weather (chiefly British)
Knacker of the Yard
Muggins
the Hammer of the Scots
the happy couple
the Bard of Avon
Father Time
twelve good men and true
the city of dreaming spires

For the *Groves of Academe*, referring to universities or scholarship:

He must also be the only Professor of Modern History anywhere in the world who has been charged by the police as an accessory to murder (I expect readers are reaching for their pens even now to tell me of the 23 other history professors who have been similarly accused — the Groves of Academe are probably stuffed with them. I'm sorry).

– Peter Hillmore, *The Observer*

● *rhetorical flourishes and professional slogans.* Toastmasters, politicians, lawyers, journalists, sociologists, 'celebrities', and any other set of culprits you choose to single out — in fact, all those given to making public or official pronouncements — have a repertoire of formulas 'suitable for all occasions'. Here is a very small sampling:

if I may venture an opinion
No comment.

our children and our children's children
a man who needs no introduction
be that as it may
in point of fact
when all is said and done
first and foremost
No names, no packdrill. (chiefly British)
without fear or favour
in no uncertain terms
by any standards
a dramatic new move
circumstances over which I have no control
if I may make so bold (as to say . . .)
it would ill become me to suggest
my lips are sealed
last but not least
agree to differ
negotiations are in train (chiefly British)
going about his lawful business
a tissue of lies
the burden of proof
benefit of the doubt
unconfirmed reports
a last-ditch attempt

● *needless foreign phrases.* Foreign languages are favourite hunting-grounds of show-off clichémongers:

noblesse oblige
persona non grata
la dolce vita
de rigueur
o tempora o mores
plus ça change
terra firma
c'est la vie
deo volente
in medias res
comme il faut

Finally, some cliché phrases of recent coining — from various walks of life, and various countries of origin — as evidence that the clichéindustry is 'alive and well and living in our midst'.

Three types can be identified here: first, those irritating counters used unthinkingly in daily conversation:

Know what I mean?
over the moon (chiefly British)
sick as a parrot (chiefly British)
This is it. (*That's it* is still quite all right.)
It makes you think.
No way.
to scare the pants off someone
clear as mud

to do your thing

I kid you not.

Surely you jest.

Do me a favour! (disagreeing, or rejecting a proposal)

Pull the other one. (expressing disbelief)

I like it. (after a joke)

Don't call us, we'll call you. (after a poor joke or suggestion)

What are the damages? (paying a bill)

many moons ago

You name it.

at a rate of knots (chiefly British)

I tell a lie.

I need it like a hole in the head.

Take a pew. (chiefly British)

a whole new ballgame (chiefly American English)

the name of the game (chiefly American English)

I must love you and leave you.

Look who's come crawling out of the woodwork.

the old U.S. of A.

Am I right or am I right?

29 going on 40

even Stevens

I don't mean maybe.

Secondly, some modern journalistic clichés:

political wilderness
a legal minefield
strife-torn
a peace initiative
a fact-finding mission
to drop a bombshell
a rising tide of violence
swingeing cuts (chiefly British)
political dynamite
reliable/informed/authoritative/unimpeachable sources

Thirdly, those clichés used in business and bureaucratic language — a combination of cliché and jargon:

at the end of the day
in the pipeline
to keep a low profile
to get down to the nitty-gritty
in this day and age
a proven track record
to spell it out loud and clear
on the table
to tell it like it is
to lay it on the line
to read someone the riot act

at this point/moment in time

the bottom line (chiefly American English: it means 'the result, or the really important element'.)

lowest common denominator

Let's run it up the flagpole. (American English: it means 'Let's try it out'.)

The opera isn't over till the fat lady sings. (American English: it is the equivalent of 'Don't count your chickens before they've hatched'.)

Note the modern clichés in the following quotations.

For *in the pipeline*:

As a result of timely interventions earlier this year and a lengthy period of debate, the British Government is well placed to follow up its criticism and proposals by a strong declaration of support for changes now in the pipeline.

– Professor Malcolm Skilbeck,
letter to *The Times*

For *on the table*:

We have placed on the table all the money we have. There is nothing further.

– Ian MacGregor,
quoted in the *Daily Telegraph*

For *Brownie points*:

I long ago learned that to expose an idol's feet of clay is no way to earn Brownie points, but I remain bemused by the violence of much of the Indian reaction to *Springing Tiger*.

– David Boulton, *New Statesman*

For *across the board*:

Mr Heseltine will look to increased efficiency across the board to meet this challenge: and the margins of the defence industries will have to make their proper contribution.

– Julian Critchley, *Daily Telegraph*

For *on the ground*:

From now on we would be well advised to take rather more account of the realities of the situation on the ground and, as Mr F. Noel Baker points out (November 21), to avoid 'megaphone diplomacy'.

– Julian Amery, letter to *The Times*

For *at the end of the day*:

I would not want them to be too cautious, but I would expect them to be sensible. At

the end of the day the safeguard would lie in their having no executive powers.
— Sir Douglas Wass,
quoted in the *Daily Telegraph*

For other modern clichés, see NEWSPAPER ENGLISH; SLANG; VOGUE WORDS.

climacteric This word is distinct in meaning from *climax* and its adjective *climactic* (though it does have the same Greek source as these words) — not to mention *climate* and *climatic*.

? It was the evening of little Belle's recital, the climacteric of her musical year.
— William Faulkner (U.S.), *Sartoris*

The word *climax* seems to be what Faulkner really had in mind here.

Climacteric as a noun refers primarily to the menopause, in both men and women — the physical and psychological changes that set in during middle age.

'How old is he?' 'About sixty.' The doctor nodded. 'After the climacteric, many manic-depressive patients spontaneously recover.'
— Mary McCarthy (U.S.), *The Group*

In a more general sense the noun *climacteric* refers to any critical period or turning point.

Adrian Noble's interesting production, strikingly designed by Bob Crowley in black silks and rotting fabric walls, with a towering tenement of bawds to observe the action, sets the play somewhere in the climacteric of the European Enlightenment — if programme-references are taken literally, between Hume's 'Philosophical Essays Concerning Human Understanding' in 1748 and Gluck's opera 'Orpheus and Eurydice' in 1762.
— Victoria Radin, *The Observer*

As an adjective, *climacteric* (or *climacterical*) means 'to do with a critical stage': *that climacteric year of his life.* The word is a rare one, of course. People are far more likely to speak of *a critical year* or *a climactic year,* depending on their meaning.

Climacteric goes back through Latin to the Greek *klimakter,* 'a crisis', originally 'the rung of a ladder', from *klimax,* 'a ladder' (also the source of *climax*).

Climacteric is pronounced /klī-**mak**tərik/ or /**klī**mak-**ter**rik/.

climatic, climactic Take care when you say or write these words that you have distinguished them properly. *Climatic* is the adjective meaning 'having to do with climate, weather, or atmosphere': *Climatic changes herald the next Ice Age.* It goes back to the Late Latin *clima,* 'a climate, or zone of latitude', from Greek *klima,* 'the sloping surface of the earth'.

Climactic is the adjective from *climax,* 'a culmination, or point of greatest intensity': *the climactic words of his speech. Climax* goes back, via Latin, to the Greek word *klimax,* which means 'a ladder'. The two Greek source words are distantly related, but the English derivatives could hardly be further apart in meaning.

See also CLIMACTERIC.

cocoa, coconut See CACAO.

coherent, cohesive, cogent *Coherent* is sometimes confused with *cohesive* on the one hand, and with *cogent* on the other.

Both *cohesive* and *coherent* (and their respective nouns *cohesion* and *coherence*) stem from the verb *to cohere,* which derives from the Latin base words *co-,* 'together' + *haerere,* 'to cling'. But they have different meanings. *Cohesive* means 'showing or producing fusion or attachment, especially between the parts of a whole': *tar and similar cohesive substances; the enhanced cohesive properties of the new cement. Cohesive* can also be used metaphorically of humans: *Cohesive family life gives a child a greater sense of security.*

Football has, in almost every sense, lost its innocence since the great days when Di Stefano and Puskas were inspiring Real. They went out to bury the opposition under an avalanche of cohesive virtuosity.
— Hugh McIlvanney, *The Observer*

They had been polite, they had drunk no alcohol, they had patiently spread their nets and preserved among themselves the dark-eyed Oriental cohesion of a fighting unit.
— John le Carré,
The Little Drummer Girl

Coherent means 'marked by an orderly or logical relationship of parts, in such a way as to aid comprehension or recognition': *incapable of coherent speech; few coherent arguments in favour of the proposal.*

He was peacefully asleep . . . it took some time to waken him.
'Are you part of a dream?' he asked. They were his first coherent words.
— C.P. Snow, *The Masters*

The seven Fraser years, he went on, had been years of 'ad hoc-ery': no vision of Australia's future, no coherent notion of what sort of country Australia was trying to be, no picture of Australia's place in its region.
— Michael Davie, *The Observer*

At first one hatches books, stories, poems, as they arrive, with pleasure and surprise, and quite without guarantees, as one produces babies. It is only after five or ten years that one ... begins to trace an inner coherence which relates all these separate parts into a system of ideas or a philosophy of life of a distinctive kind. ... India was just as important to me as England was. I reacted creatively to both styles of vision, and I often criticised both tartly, perhaps unjustly even, for it was difficult to match such opposing attributes and to make something coherent of the lessons they taught me. ...

And man? His coherence and self-possession had become dispersed and tarnished by doubts about his identity.
— Lawrence Durrell,
The Fiction Magazine

In the following example, *cohesive* would have been slightly more appropriate than *coherent*:

Under Gower, assisted by Mike Gatting, England became a coherent unit in the field. Their ability was translated into effect, unlike in the first Test in Wellington when everything started to go wrong.
— Scyld Berry, *The Observer*

The adjective *cogent* (noun *cogency*) comes from the Latin roots *co-* + *agere,* 'to force or drive together', and means 'convincing in a very forceful way; compelling'. It too is used to refer to arguments or reasoning — hence the danger of confusion. *Cogent arguments* are likely to be coherent, but *coherent arguments* are not necessarily cogent, since an argument may make sense without being persuasive.

A huge burden will fall on the network of district and borough councils which are to replace the six metropolitan councils and the GLC. The Government's paper says 'there are cogent reasons for voluntary co-operation between councils concerned to share funding and administration'.
— Joan Bakewell, *The Observer*

Whenever he goes into the child's bedroom to remonstrate, still bleary with port, the boy is ready with a cogent defence for the motion that it is not in fact two in the morning but four in the afternoon and time for *Playschool*.
— Alan Franks, *The Times*

See also ADHERENCE.

collective nouns Nouns such as *government, audience, crew, committee,* and *majority,* and others such as *flock* (*of sheep* or *geese*), *gang* (*of slaves*), *bunch* (*of grapes*) are called *group nouns* or *collective nouns*, though sometimes the term *collective noun* refers specifically to the second type.

A noun of either type (but especially the first type), particularly in British rather than American English, may be treated as plural, with plural verbs and pronouns. This happens when their members are thought of as a number of individuals: *The audience* (= its members) *were all waving their programmes. Chrysler* (= the car people) *have announced a price increase.* We use singular verbs and pronouns when we think of such a group as a single entity: *Chrysler is a public corporation*; *The audience was large.*

Where there is any doubt, it is best to use singular verbs and pronouns in referring to a group. Whichever course you do decide on, do not change your policy in midstream, by writing something like *The jury has retired to consider their verdict.* (For further details, see PLURALS Part II.)

Here is a selection from the colourful list of collective nouns that English sports:

a bevy of larks or quails (or girls)
a brood of chicks
a cete of badgers
a clowder of cats (U.S.)
a covey of partridges
a drove of oxen
an exaltation of larks
a fleet of cars
a flock of sheep or birds
a gaggle of geese
a gang of slaves or (in the U.S.) elks
a herd of cattle or elephants
a kindle of kittens
a litter of pups or cubs
a muster of peacocks
a nest of hornets, rabbits, tables, and missiles
a nye of pheasants (dialectal)
a pack of hounds
a plump of waterfowl, mallards, and so on, or (archaic) spears
a pride of lions
a rout of wolves or knights

a school of whales or porpoises
a shoal of fish
a skein of flying geese
a skulk of foxes, friars, or thieves (perhaps archaic)
a sounder of wild pigs
a stud of horses
a swarm of insects
a team of oxen or (in regional dialects) ducks
a troop of monkeys
a wisp of snipe

There are many other dialectal or jocular collective nouns that modern dictionaries tend to question or dismiss: *a chattering of choughs, a doylt of pigs, a labour of moles, a lepe of leopards,* and *a shrewdness of apes,* for example.

Note how many collective nouns are based on metaphors: *a pride of lions, a skulk of foxes, an exaltation of larks.* Note too that some collective nouns apply only to animals in certain circumstances: *a skein of geese* refers only to flying geese, probably wild geese; *a gaggle of geese* is typically a group of geese on the ground, and almost certainly domesticated geese.

colon 1. **a.** The colon (:) is a tricky and insufficiently understood form of punctuation. Use it to introduce material that explains, amplifies, or interprets what precedes it:

They haven't eaten all day: they must be hungry.
They are hungry: they haven't eaten all day.
They are hungry: give them something to eat.

A sentence or phrase that follows the colon is sometimes found with a capital letter, but this should be avoided except in special cases (mentioned below) or when special emphasis is required.

b. What precedes the colon need not be a complete sentence:

Another fine day: the sun was shining.

c. What follows the colon need not be a sentence either:

In this regard, there is another poet worth ʹ discussing: Hölderlin.

Here the colon functions rather like such expressions as *namely* or *that is.* In fact, a colon is sometimes used before or after these expressions too, and also after *to sum up, as I was saying,* and so on.

d. Similarly, the colon can come between a title and a subtitle:

The Astonished Heart: A Study in Romantic Poetry.

(The subtitle generally begins with a capital letter.)

e. Note that what precedes the colon should typically be able to stand on its own. So it would be incorrect to write:

⨉ Another poet worth discussing is: Hölderlin.
⨉ There are other poets worth discussing, including: Hölderlin and Rilke.

The colon should be omitted in each case here. However, the colon is acceptable if the examples it introduces are listed or numbered separately:

There are other poets worth discussing, including:
(a) Hölderlin
(b) Rilke.

2. a. As in the last example, a colon is often used to introduce a list, even one without separate numbering:

Dyson at once rushed after him, pelting him with the old beer cans and whatever else came to hand, which included: Tetley's tea-bags, ex-U.S. Air Force sparking plugs, overdue library books, rubber reducing garments, and genuine reproductions of Old Masters.
— Michael Frayn,
Towards The End Of The Morning

b. When the listed items are indented, the colon may be supplemented by a dash or hyphen:

The debris allegedly included:—
(a) Tetley's tea-bags
(b) sparking plugs
(c) overdue library books
(d) reducing garments.

This double punctuation mark is now quite rare in British English, and almost extinct in American English.

3. A colon may be used between expressions of parallel (or contrasting) structure or meaning:

Man proposes: God disposes.
To the left, a whirlpool: to the right, a desert.

It is possible to have more than two such parallel constructions:

Man proposes: God disposes: posterity benefits.

Nowadays, a semicolon would be likely to replace the colon in these examples:

Man proposes; God disposes; posterity benefits.

Nevertheless, the parallel or balancing colon is graceful and elegant, and perhaps deserves a revival.

4. a. The colon is used, after the identification of the speaker or writer, to introduce a quotation.

i. In the text of a play:

Apemantus: Beast!
Timon: Slave!
Apemantus: Toad!

– Shakespeare,
Timon of Athens IV iii

Note that quotation marks are not used here.

ii. In the published accounts of official proceedings, speeches, and so on, to introduce a fairly long passage in direct speech:

Opening the meeting, the Mayor said: ... (Then comes a word-for-word report of the speech, either in inverted commas, or indented within the surrounding text.)

A shorter passage would be introduced with a comma.

iii. Similarly, when introducing any long quotation, especially when it is not heralded directly by *said, remarked,* or the like:

It was a trying time for Surrey, as his diary makes clear: 'The generals were reluctant to put my plan into effect; morale was low among the men; even the weather seemed to discourage the implementation of Operation Ajax. In the event, however, its postponement was just as well.'

Again, the long quotation need not have quotation marks: it can be indented (as throughout this book). Note that the first word after the colon is usually capitalised now, though purists would permit this only if the original quotation had a capital letter at that point. Otherwise, they would use a small letter, possibly introduced by the dot-dot-dot of an ellipsis.

b. When a motto, adage, or slogan follows a colon, the first word is again capitalised:

My father had a favourite saying: Why shouldn't it be perfect?

c. i. The colon may also be used after a formal salutation preceding a message:

Ladies and gentlemen: It gives me great pleasure ...
My fellow Americans: Let me say at the outset ...
To whom it may concern: Regarding the ruling ...

Instead of the colon, a comma may be used after salutations like the first two, particularly if the following message is short. If the colon is preferred, a capital letter tends to follow it.

ii. In American English, a colon is used in the salutation of a business letter, whereas a comma is used in the salutation of a friendly letter:

Dear Sirs:　　　Dear Tom and Bill,

But in British English a comma is used everywhere:

Dear Sirs,　　　Dear Tom and Bill,

5. a. The colon is used after various headings in business correspondence:

To:　　Subject:　　Reference:

b. In bibliographical references it may be used after the place of publication:

London: 1961
London: Athenaeum Press

c. The colon may also be used after the volume number of a serial publication to introduce issue numbers or page numbers:

The London Review IV:3
The London Review 29:368-72

The volume number will often be in Roman numerals.

d. The colon may also be used between the act number and the scene number of a play:

Timon of Athens IV:iii

Here, too, the act number and scene number will usually be in Roman numerals.

e. In Biblical references, the colon comes between chapter and verse:

Isaiah 16:23-27

f. In American English, the colon is used in expressions of clock time between the hour and the minutes:

9:30 a.m.

In British English, this would be:

9·30 a.m. or 9.30 a.m.

g. In both British and American English the colon may be used in abbreviated dates:

1 : 3 : 61

However, this is much rarer than *1/3/61* or the British forms *1.3.61* or *1·3·61*. Remember, too, that in America these formulas would be the equivalent of *January 3rd, 1961* whereas in Britain they would be understood as *1 March 1961*.

h. In mathematics and in general contexts, a colon indicates a proportion or ratio:

The ratio of successes to failures was 1:2.
Mix the ingredients in the proportions 3:7:8.

Note that a double colon is used between analogous proportions:

1:2 :: 2:4 :: 3:6

This means that one is to two as two is to four as three is to six.

j. In many dictionaries and books about language, such as this one, a colon is used to introduce examples of usage (which are often in italics):

rec·ord ... **5.** The best performance known officially, as in a sport: *broke the world record.*

– Reader's Digest Great Illustrated Dictionary

See also CAPITAL LETTERS **3.c.**

coloured See BLACK.

combining forms See PREFIXES AND SUFFIXES.

comic, comical There is a traditional distinction between these two adjectives: *comic* implies an intention to be funny (whether or not the result is in fact funny); *comical* implies a funny effect or result (whether amusement was intended or not).

The two words tend therefore to combine with different sets of nouns — *a comic story, a comic mask, a comic actor* (these all aim at being funny, but might turn out to be not in the least funny); *a comical appearance, a comical expression, a comical situation* (all of these do cause amusement, though they might well be perfectly earnest in spirit or outlook).

Since the laughter-provoking effect of *comical* things is so often unintended or even at odds with a very serious background, *comical* frequently has a strong sense of 'odd, incongruous, ludicrous' about it: *a comical attempt, a comical excuse.*

Comic is often found in literary contexts, as the adjective for *comedy* (another adjective, *comedic*, is rather technical and is rarely used). *Comic* acquires much of its meaning through its contrast with *tragic*: once again, laughter is not necessarily implied by the word. A *comedy* is opposed to a *tragedy* in being fairly light and perhaps whimsical, and in having a relatively happy ending. (The original Greek roots of *comedy* mean 'sing-

ing at a celebration'.)

Comic is also used as a noun, in various senses. It can mean 'a comedian', though there is now a slightly disparaging or disapproving tone to the word. It can mean 'a comical person', as in *That baby of yours is such a comic!* And it can mean 'a magazine of cartoon stories': the stories may be adventure stories or science fiction or funny stories, but the magazine is still likely to be called a *comic* (or, in the United States, a *comic book*).

comma **1. a.** The comma separates main clauses that are linked by coordinating conjunctions such as *and, but, or, for,* and *nor*:

The house was almost in ruins, but the garden was entrancing.

The comma is most likely to be used when the clauses are long, contrasted, and complete. The following compound sentences may, but need not, have commas:

The house was old(,) but the garden was new. (short clauses)
The house was almost in ruins(,) and the garden was a mess. (clauses with similar meaning, linked by *and* rather than *but*)

And the following compound sentence will probably *not* have a comma:

Martha washed the clothes and mended the boiler.

Here, the subject of the second clause, *Martha*, has been omitted, being identical to the subject of the first clause.

When such clauses as those above are *not* linked by a coordinating conjunction, a semicolon is generally recommended instead of a comma:

The house was almost in ruins; the garden looked entrancing.

When the clauses are parallel in structure or have a logical relationship, a colon is also possible:

The house was old: the garden was ancient.

Note the difference in the treatment of *nor* and *neither*:

The house was not old, nor was the garden.
The house was not old; neither was the garden.

Nor is considered a conjunction, but *neither* is considered a linking adverb. A semicolon may also be used instead of a comma before a coordinating conjunction such as *but* if greater contrast is wanted or needed:

> The house was in ruins; but the garden was a sheer delight.

b. In several cases, clauses may be separated by commas even though they are, or resemble, main clauses and have no coordinating conjunctions:

> The higher the price (is), the worse the quality (is).

Such 'proportional' expressions with *the ... the ...* take commas, unless the expressions are very short: *The more the merrier.* A quite different example, now:

> It's a nice day, isn't it?

This is a 'tag question', and with it the comma is almost obligatory. Similarly:

> He's right, you know.

Before short 'comment clauses' such as *you know*, the comma is almost always used. Then:

> I came, I saw, I conquered.

Here we have very short main clauses — and more than two of them. In such cases a comma can be used, though a semicolon or colon would also be possible. Similarly:

> Cricket is his wife, rugby is his religion.
> I don't make the rules, I enforce them.

These are just acceptable: although unrelated grammatically, the two main clauses in each case are related structurally. When a balanced contrast is being made, and the two ideas are constructed symmetrically, a comma is permissible, though a semicolon or colon would usually be appropriate too.

c. Despite the possibility of such sentences as those just listed, the use of commas between main clauses not linked by coordinating conjunctions can give rise to the sort of error called a 'comma splice' or 'run-on sentence'. The error is particularly common in British English, and particularly among inexperienced or young writers, as the following mimicking example recognises:

✗ I wanted to impress Pandora with my multi talents, I think she is getting a bit bored with my conversation about great literature and the Norwegian leather industry.
> – Sue Townsend, *The Secret Diary of Adrian Mole Aged 13¾*

The author's hero would be marked down in an examination for writing this sentence with a comma rather than a colon or semicolon.

As these next examples show, however, it is not only young writers (or impersonators of them) who are guilty of the comma splice. The author of the following sentences was for many years literary editor of *The Listener*:

✗ I suggested to my father, nervously through my mother, that this waiter might be given the job. He was a most attractive boy, we had all been affected by his charm and friendliness ...

✗ ... His scanty grey hair had been doctored, obviously by himself, no barber could have made such a mess of it.

✗ ... My friend criticised this and I agreed with him; the book is *not* an autobiography, its intention is narrower and is stated in the title and the text, it is no more than an investigation of the relationship between my father and myself and should be confined as strictly as possible to that theme.
> – J.R. Ackerley, *My Father and Myself*

2. The comma can also be used to indicate an ellipsis — that is, the omission of certain words in a clause — in this case, the omission of an element given in an earlier clause:

> Antony loved Cleopatra; Romeo, Juliet.

The comma between *Romeo* and *Juliet* stands for the absent *loved*. The comma could perhaps be omitted here, because Romeo and Juliet are so well known; but in the next example the comma is strongly recommended: without it, people might think there is someone called 'Héloise Abélard'.

> Cleopatra loved Antony; Héloise, Abélard.

Here is another, more complex example: the comma after *wet* is in effect shorthand for the words *she wore*:

> Miss Crane had become used to ignoring the weather. In the dry she wore wide-brimmed hats, cotton or woollen dresses and sensible shoes; in the wet, blouses and gaberdine skirts, gumboots when necessary, with a lightweight burberry cape and an oilskin-covered sola topee.
> – Paul Scott, *The Jewel in the Crown*

3. a. The comma is used to separate nonessential (or 'parenthetical') elements from the rest of a simple sentence — that is, elements that are not an essential part of the sentence or its main clauses:

Tell her, if you see her, that I still love her.
Tell her, however, that I still love her.
Tell her, Patrick, that I still love her.
Tell her, above all, that I still love her.
Tell her, please, that I still love her.
Tell her, that proud and cruel beauty, that I still love her.

Among the elements that can be separated in this way are the following:

i. elements in contrast with the core of the sentence:

Tell her, not her sister.

ii. elements that supplement the core of the sentence:

She reported that many, if not most, of the victims were under the age of ten.

In keeping with the modern tendency to streamline the text by reducing punctuation, you could omit the commas in a construction of this kind. If not, make sure to retain both commas, not just one or the other. And make sure that the commas are correctly positioned: all too often the second comma is wrongly placed:

⨉ She reported that many, if not most of the victims were under the age of ten.

⨉ Symes was an important influence in, perhaps the major contributor, to the development of the system.

iii. nonrestrictive relative clauses — that is, those that describe rather than identify or define:

This book, which is about horses, is more interesting than that one.

(See RESTRICTIVE AND NONRESTRICTIVE CLAUSES.)
iv. elements 'presenting' or giving the source of direct quotations:

'I know,' she replied, 'that he still loves me.'

(For the positioning of the comma here, see QUOTATION MARKS.)
v. 'appositional' material — that is, a noun or noun phrase that follows another directly and explains or describes it, and serves the same function in the sentence:

Sue Townsend, the author of the book, impersonates a teenager.

Commas are not always wanted in appositional material, however:

James Caan the actor views things differently.

In this second example, the words *the actor* is a 'defining' or 'restrictive' phrase; in the first example, *the author of the book* describes rather than defines: it is a 'nonrestrictive' phrase, and demands commas before and after. (See again RESTRICTIVE AND NONRESTRICTIVE CLAUSES.)
b. This principle of using commas to set off nonessential material from the main clause is applied in a very varied way. Commas are most likely to set off single words:

Ah, I still love her, Patrick.

If the expression is more than one word long, commas are, paradoxically, more likely with longer ones than with shorter ones:

On Thursday the 26th of September, rumours began circulating in Fleet Street.
In 1964(,) rumours began circulating in Fleet Street.

When I'm tired after a hard day's work, I sit down.
When I'm tired(,) I sit down.

And commas are more likely if the subordinate expression is at the beginning or in the middle of a sentence than if it is at the end:

If you see her, don't hesitate to tell her.
Don't hesitate, if you see her, to tell her.
Don't hesitate to tell her(,) if you see her.

This difference in likelihood corresponds to differences in the intonation of these elements when spoken.
c. Remember, however, that a comma is *not* used between two elements that are essential to the sentence (as between subject and verb, or between verb and object). It is quite correct to write:

Tell her, if you see her, that I love her.

But it is incorrect to write:

⨉ Tell her, that I love her.

The phrase *that I love her* functions here as object of the verb *tell*, and should not be separated from it by a comma.
d. Note that there is considerable leeway in deciding what is essential information and what is additional or parenthetical information, especially in respect of adverbial expressions. It would be correct to write:

Davy Gam died gloriously at Agincourt.

But it would also be correct to write:

Davy Gam died gloriously, at Agincourt

if you meant 'Davy Gam died gloriously, and it happened at Agincourt'. Similarly, you could write:

Davy Gam died, gloriously, at Agincourt

if you meant 'Davy Gam died at Agincourt, and his death was glorious'.

4. a. Commas are used between items in lists of more than two, but are optional before *and* and *or*:

I came, saw(,) and conquered.
shoes, ships(,) and sealing-wax
an interesting, intelligent(,) and beautiful woman
in, on(,) or under the home

... strong in will
To strive, to seek, to find, and not to yield.
— Tennyson, 'Ulysses' (1842)

In British usage, the tendency nowadays is to omit the final comma. But where fine distinctions are essential — as in this book throughout — the final comma is retained to ensure that the last two items on the list are clearly distinguished.

The final comma is sometimes necessary to avoid ambiguity:

For breakfast they like juice, bacon and eggs, and bread and butter.

Here the final comma not only splits up a sub-series of three *and*'s, but helps to make it clear that *bacon and eggs* is one unit and that *bread and butter* is another.

b. When the series consists of only two items, and those items are connected by a conjunction, commas are not usual:

Hard work and good luck are essential to success.

Sometimes, in fact, commas are impossible, as when the linked items interact:

Hard work and good luck are sometimes interdependent.

But sometimes commas are useful in giving greater emphasis to an item, or in drawing attention to its unlikely presence in the sentence:

Hard work, and good luck, are essential to success.

Here, the meaning is perhaps 'Hard work is essential to success — but don't forget good luck'. You could use brackets or dashes instead:

Hard work — and good luck — are essential to success.

c. Adjective sequences present a number of special problems when they do not include *and*, *or*, or *but*. First, some types of adjective have relatively fixed positions in relation to one another. Sequences of such adjectives need not have commas:

a round red ball.

This sequence exhibits the typical order, in English, of adjectives of shape before adjectives of colour. When such adjectives occur out of sequence, however, commas are more likely:

a red, round ball.

With sequences of other adjectives, commas are possible but no longer obligatory:

an interesting(,) intelligent(,) beautiful woman
a beautiful(,) intelligent(,) interesting woman.

However, non-gradable adjectives (those that do not take *more*, *most*, *-er*, or *-est*) are rarely preceded by commas:

a red, round rubber ball
a beautiful(,) intelligent(,) interesting Italian woman.

Note the absence of commas before *rubber* and *Italian*.

The 'head' (usually a simple noun) of the adjective sequence is not normally preceded by a comma. Obviously it would be wrong to write × *a red, ball*; and similarly, the second comma in ? *a large, red, ball* should be omitted, unless some special emphasis is wanted.

When the head is a compound noun, there may be problems. Compare *important white papers* (= white papers that are important) and *stiff, white paper* (= paper that is white and stiff). In the first example, the head is not simply *papers* — it is *white papers*; there is therefore no comma after *important*. In the second example, the head is the single word *paper*, and *white* is simply an adjective in the same way as *stiff* is; a comma may therefore be placed before *white* this time.

5. The comma can change the meaning of a sentence. Sometimes its presence or absence affects the sense crucially:

a jolly fat man and a pretty haughty lady
a jolly, fat man and a pretty, haughty lady

We oppose tax increases which would slow down investment.
We oppose tax increases, which would slow down investment.

(See RESTRICTIVE AND NONRESTRICTIVE CLAUSES.)
Sometimes the positioning of the comma is crucial:

> To the pure by nature, all things are pure.
> To the pure, by nature all things are pure.

> For numbers of four figures only, commas are optional.
> For numbers of four figures, only commas are optional.

Sometimes the presence of a comma, although not strictly required by the syntax or the sense of the sentence, can save the reader from a false start. Think how confusing the following sentence might seem initially if the first comma had been omitted:

> In writing, the battered simile and the forgotten metaphor may well be ludicrous or inept or repellent.
>   – Eric Partridge, *A Charm of Words*

And think how much less confusing (and amusing) this next example would have been had a comma been inserted before the *and*:

> Juliane Koepcke, a 17-year-old German girl, survived a 10,000 foot fall when her aeroplane broke up and then walked for ten days through the Peruvian jungle.
>   – *The Times*

(See AMBIGUITY.)
6. In the punctuation of numbers, commas are used to separate large whole numbers into units of three, as for thousands and millions:

> 153,601   3,561,245

For numbers of four figures only, commas are optional:

> 4635 or 4,635

But commas are not used in four-figure years, page numbers, house numbers, or room numbers:

> AD 2001   page 1525   2647 Durham Drive
> Suite 1016

In certain contexts, there is an increasing tendency to use a half-space instead of a comma. This is not very widespread in English, but is officially recommended in calculations made in the metric system. The *Reader's Digest Great Illustrated Dictionary* says of the African volcano Kilimanjaro that it

> has two peaks, Mount Kibo (5 895 metres; 19,340 feet), Africa's highest peak, and Mount Mawenzi (5 354 metres; 17,564 feet).

The reason for using a space rather than a comma in metric numeration is this: in European countries and South Africa, a comma is used (instead of a full-stop 'decimal point') to separate whole numbers from decimal fractions — so that 2.8 is written as 2,8. To retain the commas in large whole numbers would cause dangerous confusion, so those commas have now been replaced by small spaces. Where British usage might still favour *33,426.525 litres*, continental and South African conventions require *33 426,525 litres*. Imagine the confusion if that half-space were still a comma.

7. In lists of names arranged by surname, the comma comes after the surname. The *Reader's Digest Great Illustrated Dictionary*, for instance, lists:

> **Cooper, Gary** ...
> **Cooper, James Fenimore** ...

This procedure is also followed with certain titles and the official names of some countries. The same dictionary lists:

> **Domingo, Placido** ...
> **Dominic, Saint** ...
> **Dominica, Commonwealth of** ...

Note, however, that a different convention is followed in the listing of fictional or legendary characters: **Hood, Thomas** will be found under the letter *H*, but **Robin Hood** will be found at *R*.

8. The comma is used between a name and a following title or honour:

> Arabella Smith, BA, MA, PhD
> Steven Strut, MP
> T.S. Eliot, OM
> Ronald Reagan, President of the United States.

9. The comma is used between the name of a street and the name of a town:

> 35 Blenheim Road, Manchester.

Similarly between the name of a town and the name of a county:

> Stoke Poges, Bucks

— and between the name of a town and the name of a country:

> Salzburg, Austria.

(This last is the usual American practice, even in ordinary text. In British usage, however, people usually limit this form to the address on an envelope or at the head of a letter. In ordinary text, it is usual to write *Salzburg in Austria*.)

Note that when an address is reproduced on separate lines, as on an envelope, the commas are nowadays often left out.

Finally, it used to be common in British usage to find a comma between a house number and a street name:

35, Blenheim Road

This practice is no longer recommended, though it is still fairly widespread.

10. In dates, a comma is frequently used to separate day, month, and year:

Tuesday, July 31st, 1984

In the following pattern, however, the comma is optional nowadays:

31 July(,) 1984

If only the month and year are specified, the comma is even more likely to be omitted:

July(,) 1984

Note that short dates do not have to be followed by a comma when used in a continuous text:

In July 1984 something important happened.

However, if a comma is used before the year, you have to use one after the year as well.

In July, 1984, something important happened.

(See also NUMBER STYLE.)

11. In letters, commas are used after the 'salutation' and the 'complimentary close':

Dear Sam,   Dear Mr Perkins,
Yours sincerely,

American English, however, would follow the salutation of a business letter with a colon:

Dear Mr Perkins:

12. In some dictionaries, the comma is used between definitions or translations that are nearly synonymous, whereas those further apart in meaning are separated by semicolons. Other dictionaries use commas only *within* definitions, and separate definitions or translations by semicolons, colons, or numbers and letters.

See also PARALLEL CONSTRUCTIONS.

committee In standard British English, the word *committee* can take a singular or a plural construction, depending on the emphasis or effect intended. It takes a singular construction when the members are acting as a single, unanimous body: *The committee has completed its report.*

When the members are acting individually, or are not unanimous, a plural construction follows: *The committee have signed their report*; *The committee are split over the issue.*

Do not mix singular and plural: × *The committee have signed its report.*

See COLLECTIVE NOUNS; PLURALS Part II.

common See MUTUAL.

common nouns See CAPITAL LETTERS 2; NOUNS.

comparative See ADJECTIVES 2.

comparatively See RELATIVELY.

compare with, compare to These two forms are often used interchangeably today, but there is a valuable traditional distinction that is worth preserving.

To compare to means 'to liken to' — to note similarities. Paradoxically it is the construction to choose when comparing two *dissimilar* things: there is then no need to discuss their obvious points of difference, but there is the need to discuss their surprising points of similarity. So Shakespeare chose well when he wrote *Shall I compare thee to a summer's day?* A lover is in most respects different from a summer's day, but, surprisingly, some points of comparison may be found — beauty, constancy, and the like. (In the event, Shakespeare shows that his beloved is *superior* to, more 'summery' than, the summer's day.)

In a famous essay, 'The Gangster as Tragic Hero', Robert Warshow compared the protagonists of the early 1930s crime films to Shakespeare's alluring villains.
– Philip French, *The Observer*

To compare with is a combination of *to compare to* and *to contrast with*. That is, it means to examine and discuss both points of similarity and points of dissimilarity, as in *Shall I compare my first husband with my second?* Husbands may reasonably be expected to be both alike and different.

When we compare Britain with other countries, we angrily point out that we're almost the only country in the EEC with such a silly voting system, or where they won't let you prod the fruit on market stalls.
– Katharine Whitehorn, *The Observer*

In their extreme forms, the two procedures might be distinguished in this way: *to compare to* is a convergent procedure, showing that two unlike things are alike; *to compare with* is a divergent procedure, showing that two like things are unalike. In the following extracts, the wrong preposition has been chosen:

?? And, in one notorious passage, he compared the novelist with the shoemaker.
> – James Pope Hennessy,
> *Anthony Trollope*

Here, a surprising similarity is being pointed out, and the preposition ought really to be *to*. And in the following example the preposition *with* would have been preferable:

?? He ponders on Great Commuters of the Past: Eliot, of course, and Trollope. ... He asks why British railways are so dull compared to those of Europe and America.
> – Simon Hoggart, *The Observer*

The intransitive sense of *to compare,* 'to compete; to bear comparison', is always followed by *with*: *This ice-cream compares favourably with Domenico's*; *Her latest novel can't compare with her previous one.* Similarly, the phrases *in/by comparison* and *(as) compared* should almost always be followed by *with*: *My son is pretty dim, but in comparison with my daughter he's a genius!* — or *compared with my daughter* or *as compared with my daughter*. (American English seems to ignore the 'rule', and tends to favour *compared to*; British English is, to the dismay of purists, tending in this direction as well. In particular, the adjectival form *comparable to* seems far more widely used now than *comparable with* is.)

It is possible in certain contexts to use either *with* or *to,* with a slight change of meaning:

> Today's editorial compares Mrs Thatcher's conduct during the Falklands campaign to/with Mr Churchill's during the Second World War.

If *to* is used, the editorial was probably flattering to Mrs Thatcher. Like Churchill, Mrs Thatcher was well informed, determined, and so on; if *with* is used, the editorial could perhaps also have intended a favourable assessment — examining Mrs Thatcher's record point for point against Churchill's, and finding it much the same — but more probably it intended an unfavourable assessment, suggesting that Mrs Thatcher was less far-sighted, less level-headed, and so on than Churchill was.

compass points See CAPITAL LETTERS 10.

complacent, complaisant, compliant The word *complaisant* is sometimes confused with *complacent* because of their similarity of sound and origin, and sometimes confused with *compliant* because of their similarity of sense.

Complacent and *complaisant* (and their related nouns *complacency/complacence* and *complaisance*) both derive from a Latin word meaning 'pleasing'. They have developed quite distinct meanings, however. *Complacent* can mean simply 'easy to please, contented, satisfied', but it usually has a rather more negative tone to it — either 'unduly contented with oneself, smug, self-satisfied', or 'unjustifiably contented, ignoring potential dangers, unperturbed by problems': *a complacent government that heeded too late the evidence of enemy rearmament.*

> Both in academia and in *belles-lettres,* be they 'deconstructively post-modern' or rancorously traditional, a note of complacent solipsism, of isolation from self-questioning, is unmistakable.
> – Professor George Steiner,
> *The Times Literary Supplement*

> The Law Society is also the ideal organisation to advise on the profitability of being a solicitor, as it was recently censured for its inaction and complacency when a solicitor overcharged a client by a mere £100,000.
> – Peter Hillmore, *The Observer*

Complaisant is rather an old-fashioned word now, and no longer in very wide use. It means 'eager to please, cheerfully obliging': *a complaisant hotel manager.* In some contexts, the word has a sense almost the opposite of *complacent*: *a complaisant employer* would do a great deal in response to the complaints and requests in his suggestions-box; a *complacent employer* would do nothing. Not that *complaisant* always has favourable associations; it can suggest a refusal to stand up for your own rights, an excessive wish to please others. For example, *a complaisant husband* overlooks or even encourages his wife's infidelities.

> Instead he agreed, almost without argument, to marry a girl she had picked out for him in her own village, the daughter of a childhood friend, a plump and uneducated girl, it was true, but so old-fashioned, so placid, so complaisant that she slipped into the household and settled in like a charm, seemingly too lazy and too good-natured to even try and make Rakesh leave home and

set up independently, as any other girl might have done.

— Anita Desai, *Games at Twilight*

Dooley, a large dark man with an oily complexion and appearance of not having shaved too well that morning, accepted with complaisance this reputation as a retailer of hair-raising anecdote.

— Anthony Powell, *The Valley of Bones*

Compliant (with its related noun *compliance,* sometimes *compliancy*) derives from a Latin verb meaning 'to fill up'. It also involves acting upon another's wishes, but there is an implication of docile submissiveness now, rather than of a genuine desire to please. A *compliant* person is usually one who has a natural tendency to yield unprotestingly to authority.

Mabel also entered into a 10-year liaison with Austin, the brother of Emily Dickinson ... Because they were both pillars of the community, society tolerated the relationship. More remarkable still was David Todd's compliance in, even encouragement of, the affair.

— Phyllis Grosskurth, *The Observer*

It was rather the result of decades of paternalistic authoritarianism under Walpole and the Pelhams, which had put a premium on dumb compliance and the maintenance of a low profile, so that after them a generation of politicians emerged which was simply not trained in policy-making.

— Professor John Kenyon, *The Observer*

Note the preferred pronunciations of the three words: *complacent* is pronounced /kəm-**play**ss'nt/; *complaisant* usually /kəm-**play**z'nt/, though in North America it is sometimes pronounced just like *complacent. Compliant* is pronounced /kəm-**pli**-ənt/.

complement, supplement There is an important difference in meaning between these two words. *To supplement* something is to add a part to it when it is already whole and complete; *to complement* something is to add a part to it and thereby make it a complete whole. (As a helpful reminder, note the resemblance in form between *to complement* and *to complete*; also between *to supplement* and *to supply*: in each pairing, the two words are closely related by origin.) So, you might say that a waistcoat would *supplement* a man's two-piece suit, whereas it would *complement* the jacket and trousers of a three-piece suit.

Mrs Wheaton wears her knowledge lightly, leading us with skill and humour through this rich banquet of a book. Its lucidity is complemented by a scholarly approach which provides excellent notes, a massive bibliography and two indices.

— Wendy Rowland, *The Literary Review*

It would be pointless for a biographer to try competing with 'Father and Son' on its own ground, and Ann Thwaite is too wise to make the attempt. She has, in fact, unearthed a good deal of new material about Gosse's childhood which usefully supplements and in a few minor cases corrects his self-portrait, but the main interest of her excellent biography inevitably lies in showing what happened next.

— John Gross, *The Observer*

Used as a noun, *a complement* is accordingly a crucial part, secondary perhaps to the main part but a necessary addition to it in making up the whole; *a supplement* by contrast is an extra part, additional to the whole, not essential to it. The more concrete senses of the two nouns confirm this abstract distinction: *complement* in its specialised senses in music and grammar, and referring to the full crew of officers and men on a ship; *supplement* as an addition to your diet, or as an extra section of a newspaper. In geometry *a complement* is either of two adjacent angles that together measure 90°; *a supplement* is either of two adjacent angles that together measure 180°, or else either of two arcs that make up a semicircle.

Both *complement* and *supplement* go back to the Latin verb *plere,* 'to fill', but with a different Latin prefix in each case.

The adjectives *complementary* and *supplementary* have to be distinguished in a corresponding way:

At ground level, the spectrum contracted into ranges of exhausted greys and yellows. Even the scarlet flower in a woman's braided hair, lacking its temperate complementary green, was scorched to an insipid brown.

— Paul Scott, *The Jewel in the Crown*

That illusion — as such a point of view was, in due course, to appear — was closely related to another belief: that existence fans out indefinitely into new areas of experience, and that almost every additional acquaintance offers some supplementary world with its own hazards and enchantments.

— Anthony Powell, *A Buyer's Market*

Note, finally, the difference in pronunciation between the noun forms and the verb forms of *supplement* and *complement*. As nouns, they have their stress on the first syllable, and the final syllable has a weak vowel sound — /-mənt/. As verbs they can have a second stress (a complementary or supplementary stress) on the last syllable, and whether or not they do, that last syllable is always pronounced with a full short *e* sound — /-ment/.

See also COMPLIMENT, COMPLEMENT.

complete   Purists point out that anything that is *complete* is absolutely so, and that it is therefore incorrect to use such qualifying words as *more*, *most*, *very*, *quite*, and so on. But where *complete* is used to refer to comprehensive scope or thorough treatment, the use of *more* and *most* is quite acceptable: *Her report gives a more complete account of the situation than mine.*

See ADJECTIVES 3; UNIQUE; VERY, MUCH.

compliant   See COMPLACENT.

complicated, complex   These two adjectives are often interchangeable, but there are slight differences that are worth remembering. The words' origins give a clue to one of these differences: *complicated* comes from the Latin verb *complicare* meaning 'to fold together'; *complex* comes from the past participle of the Latin verb *complectere*, meaning 'to plait or entwine, to twist or weave together'.

Something that is *complicated* has a bewildering number of aspects and is accordingly difficult to understand or solve or develop: *a complicated debate, a complicated puzzle, a complicated strategy.* But the sense of a *single* entity remains: there are many facets or folds, as it were, but all of a single, central, difficult theme.

> It is popularly supposed to have been suffering a 'profits crisis' for at least 20 years. The truth is more complicated.
> – Tim Congdon, *The Times*

Something that is *complex* has many parts or strands or stages that are inextricably bound up together — they combine into a composite whole that cannot be dismantled or disentangled: *a complex lifestyle; a complex relationship; a complex mechanism.* Less emphasis is put on the notion of difficulty here, and more on the notion of intricate interweaving:

> In other words, nearly all the inhabitants of these outwardly disconnected empires turn

out at last to be tenaciously interrelated; love and hate, friendship and enmity, too, becoming themselves much less clearly defined, more often than not showing signs of possessing characteristics that could claim, to say the least, not a little in common; while work and play merge indistinguishably into a complex tissue of pleasure and tedium.
> – Anthony Powell, *A Buyer's Market*

The distinction is a very fine one, it is true. Most cases are far from clear-cut: *a complicated problem* and *a complex problem* could be used alternatively in almost every context.

A second slight difference between the two words lies in their tone. *Complicated* sometimes has a negative nuance: *complicated language* suggests needless and almost deliberate difficulty; *complex language* sounds more favourable, or at least neutral, as though the intricacy were unavoidable or even praiseworthy. (When language teachers speak of someone's increasing mastery of a language, they call the process *complexification* rather than *complication*.) And when you refer to someone as *a complicated woman*, for example, you are probably feeling less sympathetic towards her than when you refer to her as *a complex woman*. Similarly:

> But the effect for which one has aimed is a difficult one — to make public the private side of a complicated man without distorting him into a 'character' or unacceptably invading his privacy.
> – Robert Kee, *The Observer*

In the following sentence, the two words appear in typical roles, and the difference is easily discernible: *The theory is complex enough as it is — don't make it more complicated by using unnecessary jargon.* Similarly:

> The mixture of state-of-the-art high-tech and run-of-the-mill low cunning is familiar. The ideas and dramatic structure are confused and complicated rather than complex.
> – Philip French, *The Observer*

There is an interesting complication when it comes to the noun forms from these adjectives. You would think that *complication* is the noun from *complicated*, and *complexity* the noun from *complex*. In fact, however, a *complication* tends to be a problematic *addition*. The state of being *complicated* (or of being *complex*) is usually best referred to as *complexity*. So, a dangerous development in an illness is commonly referred to as a *complication*; and a complicated puzzle is difficult because of its *complexity*.

To Barbara, one of the first attractions of her religion's moral philosophy had been its recognition of the helpless complexity of motives that prompted an action, and its consequent emphasis on actual words, thoughts and deeds.
– Muriel Spark, *The Mandelbaum Gate*

In traditional psychology, a *complex* is a strongly associated group of ideas in the memory, which are established as a group when a child first learns them. The term was first used in about 1906, by the Zurich school of the psychologist Carl Jung, and given wide currency by Sigmund Freud: it refers to a group of repressed emotional ideas responsible for an abnormal mental condition. *Complex* quickly caught on, and has been misused by non specialists ever since. It is often used today to mean 'an obsession' (or 'a thing', as it is often called nowadays), as in: *? He has a complex about replacing the top on the toothpaste tube.*

? The proposed beatification of Princess Grace is a piece of embarrassing nonsense dreamed up by one Monsignor Piero Pintus, 60, an insignificant Monégasque in Rome who has a Grace complex.
– Edward Steen, *Sunday Telegraph*

Complex is also used to refer to an excessive fear: *? She has a complex about men and will never go out on a date.*

In its proper sense, a *complex* is an unconscious state of mind that affects behaviour, and should not be used as if it meant merely a 'problem' or 'preoccupation', both of which are very much present in the consciousness.

The term *inferiority complex*, associated with the psychologist Alfred Adler, is not only over-used but also wrongly used. It refers to unconscious fears caused by past hurtful frustrations of the impulse to seek recognition. It manifests itself in defensive behaviour and aggression. People too often use it to mean a feeling of inferiority, which is common to almost everyone and which usually manifests itself in shyness and lack of confidence: × *She has such an inferiority complex that she won't even take part in the school play.*

Complex also of course has the simple meaning of 'a whole composed of interrelated parts', including a group of related buildings:

It is a title which totally resists translation, connoting as it does a complex of very British

attitudes, the chief of which are guarded affection and cautious derision.
– Anthony Burgess, *The Observer*

July's knowledge or instinct that in country dorps the black petrol attendants often live in sheds behind the garage-and-general-store complex — on that they had kept going, on and on, although they had left with only enough fuel to take them less than half-way.
– Nadine Gordimer, *July's People*

Note that in British English, *complex* is always pronounced with the stress on the first syllable, whether the word is being used as noun or adjective; in spoken American English, however, a useful distinction is usually observed: the noun has its stress on the first syllable, but the adjective shifts the stress to the second syllable — /kəm-**pleks**/. In both British and American English, the noun *complexity* has its stress on the second syllable.

compliment, complement A common source of misspelling here, especially as the words are pronounced identically. (They also have the same origin, in the Latin verb *complere*, 'to fill up'.) *Compliment*, as noun and verb, and the adjective *complimentary* relate to praise or flattery (*complimented me on my promotion*), and also to something acquired for free (*a complimentary ticket*).

His proposal wasn't any sort of a compliment, when you came right down to it; it was simply an attempt at expiation. I was fond of him, but I didn't respect him, any more than he did me.
– Lynne Reid Banks, *The L-Shaped Room*

Complement, as noun and verb, and the adjective *complementary* relate to the completion of a whole by adding a part. As a reminder, think of *complementing* as *completing*.

It is the unknown land which all of us have known and have longed to find in youth. It is the undiscovered complement of all that we have seen and known, the lost half of our dark heart.
– Thomas Wolfe (U.S.), *The Web and the Rock*

Edited with graceful intelligence, this magnificent collection deserves to have been more comprehensively indexed ... Equally complementary to Professor Edel's multi-volume biography and to James's *oeuvre*, these letters may be savoured for their own sake.

— Stephen Koss, *The Observer*

See also COMPLEMENT, SUPPLEMENT.

compose, comprise, constitute All three of these verbs can be used when relating a whole to its parts. But they are used in different ways.

To compose and *to constitute* can mean 'to make up, to be the elements of, to come together to produce (a whole)'. But *compose* is usually used in the passive: *The league is composed of fourteen teams all told.*

The Quartet's form tells us, in effect, that the history of the end of the Raj was largely composed of the doings of the officer class and its wife. Indians get walk-ons, but remain, for the most part, bit-players in their own history.

— Salman Rushdie, *The Observer*

Constitute in this sense is almost always in the active voice, and tends to take the plural form: *Fourteen teams all told constitute the league.*

A series of collisions, trifling in themselves, now began to take place. The Chief Economic Adviser to the Treasury, Comrade Cicic, was dancing with a wife whose massive proportions and enormous buffer constituted a dance floor hazard at the best of times. In a waltz it was hair-raising to image what might happen.

— Antrobus, in Lawrence Durrell's *Esprit de Corps*

(In a related sense, however, 'to be equivalent to, to be a sufficient condition of', *constitute* can just as easily be used in the singular: *As far as I'm concerned, pacifism constitutes treason.*)

Comprise is sometimes used in the same sense as *compose* and *constitute*, but it should be restricted to the converse sense — 'to be made up of, to consist of, to contain as constituent parts': *The league comprises fourteen teams all told.* It is not really acceptable to say ✕ *Fourteen teams comprise the league.*

✕ When she had done that, she chose a dozen postcards ... with facetious messages intended to embarrass him in front of the prim ladies who comprised his office staff.

— John le Carré, *The Little Drummer Girl*

✕ Given the link between the PSBR and the money supply, the Treasury thought the City

would get the message that there would be some 'awkward' money supply figures in the early months too.

But the stockbroking analysts who comprise the 'City' for this purpose, did not get the message.

— William Keegan, *The Observer*

✕ The three American divisions comprised General Truscott's VIth Corps.

— Winston Churchill, *Triumph and Tragedy*

Churchill would have pleased the stylistic purists better had he used *constituted*. Remember the rule — a whole comprises its parts (not the other way around):

Here is the second volume, seven years later; at the same rate, the book will be finished in 1998. Or rather, at that rate it *would* be finished then, were it not for the fact that we now learn that it will ultimately comprise five volumes, not four, which means that unless he gets a move on, it will not be finished before 2005.

— Bernard Levin, *The Observer*

A common mistake is to say ✕ *comprised of.* It is, for instance, quite wrong to say ✕ *The league is comprised of fourteen teams.*

✕ While etiquette is surely a factor, acceptable behaviour is comprised of a great deal more.

— Fran Lebowitz (U.S.), *Metropolitan Life*

This common error is clearly based on a confusion with the form *is composed of* or *consists of*. See also CONSIST OF.

concern, concerned When used as a noun, meaning 'anxiety' or 'uncertainty', *concern* is followed by *over* or *at* or *about*: *There is widespread concern over/at/about the growing number of unemployed.* However when *concern* means 'interest arising from personal involvement', it is followed by *for*: *Our concern for him/his well-being was genuine.* The verb *to concern oneself*, meaning 'to get involved in', is followed by *with*: *You've no need to concern yourself with such problems.* The adjectival form *concerned* is followed by *with* when it means 'interested, involved' — *I'm not concerned with the wider issues here* —and by *about* (or, less commonly, *for*), when it means 'anxious, worried': *We have been extremely concerned about him/his safety.*

See also AS FAR AS ... IS CONCERNED.

concur To concur, meaning 'to agree, share an opinion', is commonly used in this pattern: to concur with someone in something (a plan, opinion, course of action): I concur with my colleagues in deploring the use of violence; I concur with him in his dislike of the scheme.

conjunctions A conjunction is a word, such as and, but, because, when, if, that connects other words, phrases, clauses, and sentences.

A coordinating conjunction connects parallel sentence elements of equal rank. The English coordinating conjunctions are and, but, and or: cold and hungry; tired but happy; Peter or Edward; They shouted and laughed; He's old but I'm young. It is, incidentally, perfectly legitimate and often very effective to begin a sentence with and, but, or or.

A subordinating conjunction connects a subordinate clause to the main clause of the sentence. In He laughed when I told him, the conjunction when subordinates I told him to the main clause, He laughed. Other examples are because, where, who, and if: You're tired because you went to bed late; There's no canteen where I work; The man who came to dinner was French; She'll sing only if she's paid.

Correlative conjunctions are pairs of words such as either . . . or and neither . . . nor that are reciprocally related and regularly used together: Either you leave quietly now or I throw you out bodily.

And is sometimes called a copulative conjunction, since it couples the elements and expresses the sum of their meanings, rather like the + sign in arithmetic. Compound subjects joined by and become plural, and take a plural verb: Two and two are four; John and I have taken up yoga. (But if the compound is thought of as one unit, a singular verb is used: My son and heir is still at school.)

The word plus is now often used as a conjunction meaning 'and': ? I'm late already, plus I don't know what to wear. This usage is not fully acceptable, however. In formal use, plus should be used only as a preposition, meaning roughly 'with'; the verb following is therefore singular or plural according to the number of the noun before plus:

Their determination plus their resources makes them very strong.
Their resources plus their determination make them very strong.

The same is true of together with, as well as, in addition to, and alongside:

John, as well as his parents, has died.
The teacher, in addition to the students, enjoys the course.
The prisoners, alongside their guard, are entering the courtroom.

Some words (such as since) can function as adverbs, prepositions, and conjunctions: I haven't seen him since (adverb); I haven't seen him since then (preposition); I haven't seen him since he arrived (conjunction). A number of disputed words are approved when they function as prepositions but condemned when they function as conjunctions:

He won't succeed without working hard.
× He won't succeed without he works hard. (Use unless here.)
He won't succeed like her.
× He won't succeed like she will. (Use as or (in) the way (that) here.)

See AND; AS; BUT; LIKE; THAN.

conjure See ABJURE.

connote, denote To denote is to reveal or indicate directly; what a word denotes is what it means literally, or the actual thing or idea it refers to. The word home, for instance, might denote a house or flat, or a special hospital, and so on.

To connote is to suggest something beyond the literal meaning — to convey various secondary associations and emotions. The word home probably connotes security, happiness, and welcome to most people, though to others it might connote fear or discomfort.

The Latin roots of the two words are a guide to the difference in their meanings. The Latin notare, 'to note', from nota, 'a mark or sign', was combined with the prefixes de-, 'completely', and com-, 'together with'. To denote is to give a complete or literal meaning; to connote is to convey those secondary meanings that come together with the literal sense.

The noun forms connotation, 'an association, implication, or nuance', and denotation, 'an indication, sign, or meaning', are widely used more than the verbs — too widely in the view of some people. To ask ? What are the connotations of this decision? is a needlessly grand way of saying What does this decision mean/imply?

consensus The phrases consensus of opinion and general consensus attract criticism; they contain a redundant element: consensus itself means 'unanimity of opinion' or 'generally received view', as in *The consensus of critics is that.* ...

Nevertheless these tautological expressions still occur frequently, and have become part of the stock-in-trade of journalistic writing:

?? It seems, however, that anti-Semitism, in the second half of the twentieth century, has been in continuous decline ... That was the general consensus — though not without some reservations — of a conference on anti-Semitism which I attended last month.
 — Conor Cruise O'Brien, *The Observer*

?? What psychologists are good at is getting a consensus of opinion by psychologists who've been trained in the same way.
 — *The Listener*

The phrase *consensus politics* has become part of the political jargon of our day, used to refer to the views of an allegedly moderate majority.

Finally, beware of the common misspelling × *concensus*, probably modelled on *census, concentric,* or *concerted.* Remember that *consensus* is closely related, in its Latin origins, to *consent,* and the correct spelling should then stay in your mind. Both of these words go back to the Latin verb *consentire,* 'to feel together', from *com-,* 'together' + *sentire,* 'to feel'.

consequent, consequential, subsequent The word *consequent* is sometimes confused with *consequential* on the one hand, and with *subsequent* on the other.

Subsequent means simply 'following in time, occurring afterwards'; *consequent* means 'following as a natural result or logical conclusion': *The assault was far more serious than the subsequent robbery: it was the consequent hospital bills that nearly ruined me.*

When detached from their nouns, the two adjectives take different prepositions: *subsequent to,* but *consequent on* or *upon* (*to* is sometimes used, but it increases the danger of confusion and is best avoided): *The scandal consequent on the prisoner's death occurred only subsequent to the prison governor's resignation.*

Consequential has lost most of the senses it once had, including the sense of 'consequent'. In the following quotation, the word seems almost archaic when used in this way:

? Ministers are now more concerned about a collapse of the American banking system, and its consequential effects here, than they are about the miners' strike.
 — Alan Watkins, *The Observer*

Not that *consequent* would be much better here: ? *consequent effects* is quite redundant.

Consequential retains one or two technical senses in legal and parliamentary contexts, but the only general sense still current is 'self-important, pompous'. It can no longer be used to mean 'important' as such. However, its opposite, the word *inconsequential,* can mean 'unimportant, trivial': *an inconsequential delay that hardly affected us.* And a *man of consequence* does still mean 'an important man'.

conservative *A conservative estimate* is a restrained estimate, moderate, prudent, and cautious in the way that you would expect from a person of conservative temperament. It is usually a low estimate, but that is really incidental.

By a natural shift of emphasis, however, *a conservative estimate* has come to be understood as 'a low estimate', and the word *conservative* is now often used to refer to low or modest quantities:
? *These figures that I forecast are conservative*;
? *Do put in a conservative tender, or else they will assign the project elsewhere.*

This is a reasonable and fairly typical extension of the meaning of a word, but it has not yet become fully established, and is best avoided in careful speech and writing.

consider 1. *To consider,* in the sense of 'to regard as, to think of as being', usually occurs in the following pattern:

I consider the boy a fool.
I consider him foolish.

There is no preposition or verb between the first element (noun or pronoun) after *consider* and the second (noun or adjective). It is possible to insert the infinitive phrase *to be* or *to have been* between the two elements, especially when referring to the past:

I consider the boy to be/to have been a fool.
I consider him to be/to have been foolish.

What is unacceptable is to insert the preposition *as* between the two elements, on the mistaken model of *to regard as*:

× I consider the boy as no better than a fool.

Either omit the *as* here, or change *consider* to *regard.* (See REGARD 6.) Of course, in different constructions, *as* can follow *consider* — there is nothing wrong, for example, in saying:

I consider him second-rate as a writer.
Considered as a writer, he is second-rate.

2. *To consider* also attracts the criticism of purists when used in the sense of 'to believe or conclude':

? The tribunal considers that the complaint is groundless, and awards costs to the defendant.

The objection seems rather dated now: *to consider* is widely used before a *that*-clause in this way nowadays. But if you want to avoid the risk, then use any of the available synonyms instead: *believe, judge, decide, conclude*, or the like.

3. The word *considering* should be used carefully, since it gives rise to potential ambiguity. On the one hand, it is a preposition meaning 'in view of, taking into account', or a conjunction (slightly informal still, perhaps) meaning 'in view of the fact that, because'. (See MISRELATED CONSTRUCTIONS 3.) On the other hand, it is the present participle of the verb *to consider* in any of its senses: 'to ponder', 'to believe', and so on. So:

? Considering John's advanced age, I wonder why he doesn't slow down a bit (= either 'In view of his advanced age' or 'When I think about his advanced age').
? Considering he's innocent, John is behaving in a most uncooperative way (= either 'In view of the fact that he's innocent' or 'Judging himself to be innocent').

4. These uses of *considering* as preposition and conjunction are slightly informal still. The conjunction in particular is best avoided in very formal contexts. Even more informal is the use of *considering* as an adverb:

? John's so old and such a heavy drinker — mind you, he's very fit, considering.
? She still dances very well, considering.

A more formal wording would be *considering these handicaps* or *all things considered*.

considerable   The adjective *considerable*, in the sense of 'much; a good deal of', has traditionally in British English been limited to abstract nouns: *spoke with considerable feeling; in considerable pain; a musician of considerable experience*.

In American English, it has long been used to qualify concrete nouns as well: ? *discovered considerable sawdust in the flour*; ? *lost considerable blood*. Such constructions are now entering British English too, though they are not recommended. The preferred idiom remains *a considerable quantity/amount/measure of*, as in *lost a considerable amount of blood*.

In its closely related senses of 'large', 'severe',

and so on, *considerable* can probably be used acceptably to qualify concrete nouns: *a considerable barrel of beer*; *suffered considerable injuries*. The same is true of the sense 'important; reputable': *a considerable poet*.

There is a broader question about *considerable*, and that is the desirability of using such a vague word in the first place: ? *The strike-leaders claimed considerable support for their views among the rank and file*. The word is a favourite in political debate because it blurs the outlines of a statement and absolves the speaker from having to make specific claims.

consist of, consist in   Be careful to keep these two phrasal verbs distinct. *To consist of* means 'to be made up of, have as ingredients, comprise': *The survival pack consists of six water-purifying capsules, two aspirins, and a bar of chocolate*.

To consist in means 'to have as the essential or principal element': *True love consists in accepting each other's nature totally, not in submission or subordination or absorption*.

Note that *consist in* tends to occur in definitions and to introduce verbal or abstract nouns, whereas *consist of* introduces a constituent or list of constituents usually concrete nouns:

The police who were out in force, patrolling the main street, consisted of six men and the assistant sub-inspector.
   – Paul Scott, *The Jewel in the Crown*

These two extracts from a single essay neatly illustrate the difference:

As I have tried to show, modern writing at its worst does not consist in picking out words for the sake of their meaning and inventing images in order to make the meaning clearer. It consists in gumming together long strips of words which have already been set in order by someone else, and making the results presentable by sheer humbug. The attraction of this way of writing is that it is easy . . .

Thus political language has to consist largely of euphemism, question-begging and sheer cloudy vagueness. Defenceless villages are bombarded from the air, the inhabitants driven out into the countryside, the cattle machine-gunned, the huts set on fire with incendiary bullets: this is called *pacification*.
   – George Orwell,
'Politics and the English Language'

See also COMPOSE.

constitute See COMPOSE.

contact 1. Some old-fashioned purists still object to the use of *to contact* in the sense of 'to communicate with or convey news to', regarding it as an intrusive Americanism: *Please contact me as soon as the plans are ready.*

> Frau Hoffmann ... was writing about the women in Hitler's life when I contacted her.
> – David Pryce-Jones, *Unity Mitford*

It is very well established in British English now, however, and there is surely nothing more objectionable to it on linguistic grounds than there is in the phrase *to get in touch with*: the Latin roots of *contact* are just the same: *com-*, 'together with' + *tangere*, 'to touch'.

It might be fair to object on other grounds to the verb *to contact* — that it is overused, for example, or that it is imprecise. If you want someone specifically to write to you, or telephone you, or inform you, then why not say what you mean — namely, *Please write to/phone/inform me* — instead of the easy, glib *Please contact me*? But if you are not sure what form the communication will take, then the vagueness implied in *to contact* is very useful.

2. The noun *contact* is also very useful in its modern sense of 'being in communication, a link, a relationship': *sporting and business contacts between our two countries.* One modern noun sense of *contact* has attracted criticism, however — 'an acquaintance who might be of use; a connection': *I made a number of useful contacts at the conference*; *Who's your contact at the BBC?* But the word does fill a lexical gap, and should be welcomed rather than rebuffed: the older term *connection* does not have quite the same range, and might itself, in any case, be criticised as an intrusive metaphorical extension of an abstract noun.

However, there is one area in which the older term *connection* has received a new lease of life: the world of illicit drugs. Here, since at least 1934, a person who supplies narcotics to another has been called, in slang, a *connection*. The use of *connection* to mean 'the practice of supplying drugs' seems to be more recent — the earliest example cited in the Supplement to the Oxford English Dictionary is dated 1967. So, Jack Gelber's famous American play *The Connection* (1960) referred first and foremost to a drug dealer, while the American films *The French Connection* (1971) and *French Connection II* (1975) seemed to refer to the dealing as well as to the dealers.

contemporary, contemporaneous 1. Until fairly recently, *contemporary* was used primarily in the sense of 'occurring at the same time; belonging to the same era; coinciding or overlapping in time'. The Latin roots point to this traditional sense: *con-*, 'together' + *tempus*, 'time'. So: *Among the contemporary playwrights of Shakespeare's London years were Marlowe and Fletcher*. The word is used as a noun too in this sense: *Christopher Marlowe was a contemporary of Shakespeare's.*

The more recent senses are 'belonging to the present time, current' — *contemporary ballet* — and hence, 'very modern, up-to-date': *? the most contemporary attitudes towards the arms race.* The first of these recent senses is now firmly established (though some old-fashioned purists still object to it), and so too is the corresponding noun sense: *I think of Shakespeare as a contemporary.* The second sense is still on the borderline of acceptability, however, and is best avoided. One danger signal is the use of *very, extremely, more, most,* or the like in front of it. Instead of *contemporary* use *present-day, modern, latest, up-to-date,* or even *avant-garde.*

2. The various senses of *contemporary* can give rise to ambiguity: *an Elizabethan play performed in contemporary dress* could mean either that the costumes are those of today, or that the costumes are those of Elizabethan times. This is not to argue against the more recent sense of *contemporary* — only to warn against the confusing use or misunderstanding of the word. After all, even the original sense of *contemporary* could be ambiguous: *Richard II, performed in contemporary dress* could, even in the earlier sense, mean either that the costumes are those of the late 16th century (when the play was written), or that the costumes are those of the late 14th century (when the action of the play took place).

3. Note the various ways of expressing the idea that two people lived at the same time, or went to school together, or the like:

> Christopher Marlowe was contemporary with Shakespeare
> Christopher Marlowe was a contemporary of Shakespeare's
> Christopher Marlowe and Shakespeare were contemporaries
> ? Christopher Marlowe and Shakespeare were contemporary with each other
> × Christopher Marlowe and Shakespeare were contemporaries of each other.

This last wording is redundant: *of each other* should be omitted.

4. *Contemporaneous* means 'originating, existing, or occurring during the same period of time'. It is often interchangeable with *contemporary,* therefore:

> Marlowe's life was contemporary/ contemporaneous with Shakespeare's — though much shorter.

Unlike *contemporary, contemporaneous* cannot be used in the sense of 'current' or 'modern', and it cannot be used as a noun. But it does have two advantages over *contemporary*. First, it is far likelier to provide the adverb — *contemporaneously* occurs much more frequently than *contemporarily*:

> Marlowe's plays were written contemporaneously with the early works of Shakespeare.

Secondly, *contemporaneous/ly* is far likelier to be used of nonhuman subjects:

> The extinction of the dinosaurs seems to have been contemporaneous with the disappearance of many fern-species, and a connection has been proposed.

> Leibniz's calculus and Newton's were almost exactly contemporaneous, yet were devised quite independently.

contemptible, contemptuous These two adjectives are not interchangeable. *Contemptible* means 'deserving contempt, despicable, worthy of scorn':

> 'Well,' I began, 'first of all, you see ...' It was a long, silly story, which seemed to take hours to tell. I hadn't realised how foolish, how contemptible some of it would sound. I felt horribly ashamed of myself ... The story seemed to involve a confession of all my weaknesses to that silent, attentive man. I have never felt so humiliated in my life.
> – Christopher Isherwood,
> *Mr Norris Changes Trains*

Contemptuous means 'showing contempt, disdainful, scornful':

> Poldek Pfefferberg, runner for Oskar Schindler, had earlier in the year been ordered to begin tutoring the children of Symche Spira, exalted glazier, chief of the OD.
> It was a contemptuous summons, as if Spira were saying, 'Yes, we know you're not fit for man's work, but at least you can pass

on to my kids some of the benefits of your education.'
> – Thomas Keneally, *Schindler's Ark*

> A dish of coffee and milk was respectfully submitted to the cat, who drank it contemptuously and then retired to her box of shavings with an air of having sustained an insult.
> – Lynne Reid Banks,
> *The L-Shaped Room*

In some contexts both *contemptible* and *contemptuous* could be used, though with quite different meanings: *She was repelled by his contemptuous manner* (his haughty, scornful manner); *She was repelled by his contemptible manner* (his loathsome, despicable manner).

contiguous See ADJACENT.

continual, continuous *Continual* and *continuous* are often used interchangeably, but careful writers tend to distinguish them.
Of the two, only *continuous* can be used to refer to continuity through space: *a continuous line* but not × *a continual line.*
Both *continuous* and *continual* can refer to continuity through time, but in different ways: *continuous* means 'unbroken, going on without a pause'; *continual* means 'repeated, going on at regular intervals'. (The same distinction applies to the adverbs *continuously* and *continually*.)

> He looked at her with love, and his restlessness, his striving, his strenuous ambition, all died away; his nerves were steadied, he was content to the marrow of his bones. And she was happy through and through, with a happiness more continuous than a man could know.
> – C.P. Snow, *The Masters*

The author is emphasising the unbrokenness of the woman's happiness. Similarly:

> The clink and wrench of tools on metal was taken up against the single continuous note of the cicadas.
> – Nadine Gordimer, *July's People*

In the following passage, *continuous* is probably again the intended sense. The author perhaps avoided it because in context the sound of it would jar with *monotonous*. But that is not sufficient excuse for using the dubious *continual* instead:

> ? The cicadas sang their grating song with a frenzied energy; it was as continual and

monotonous as the rustling of a brook over the stones.

> – W. Somerset Maugham,
> 'The Force of Circumstances'

In the following passage, conversely, *continual* would probably have been preferable to *continuous*: surely the 'acts of definition' are repeated regularly rather than going on incessantly without a break?

? He was demanding a definition. By the long habit of her life, and by temperament, she held as a vital principle that the human mind was bound in duty to continuous acts of definition.
> – Muriel Spark, *The Mandelbaum Gate*

Continual should be used of events that are repeated rather than uninterrupted:

She had been almost relieved at their departure, for their continual anxious popping in and out of her room with warnings about this and that had exhausted her.
> – Muriel Spark, *The Mandelbaum Gate*

The haze had lifted in this cooler altitude, and I could see for fifty miles or more across a blue-green plain. Because the train kept switching back and forth on the hillside, the view continually altered, from this plain to a range of hills and to fertile valleys ...
> – Paul Theroux (U.S.),
> *The Old Patagonian Express*

The intrusions and the changes of scenery described here occur repeatedly but intermittently, rather than uninterruptedly.

In some contexts, a choice is possible: the event might be a repeated rather than an uninterrupted one (thus favouring the adjective *continual*), yet the author might want to convey metaphorically its ceaselessness (and so tend to use *continuous*). In the following two quotations, the alternative term could have been used instead:

There is nothing to suggest it will be anything other than a continuous process of killing and reprisal. What will change is the status of the Protestants.
> – Patrick Bishop, *The Observer*

Galbraith argues that whereas much of history is taught in terms of personalities and battles, it can be seen as one continual power struggle, with a natural tendency for existing power structures to lead to the setting up of opposing forces.
> – William Keegan, *The Observer*

continuance, continuation, continuity These three nouns are sometimes interchangeable, though each has special uses of its own.

Continuance and *continuation* can both mean 'the act or fact of continuing', but *continuance* suggests 'a continuing without having stopped; duration', whereas *continuation* tends to mean 'a continuing after a break; a resumption, prolongation, supplement, or sequel'. So *continuance* is appropriately used in these examples:

But Mrs Thatcher, who last December surprised Treasury officials by supporting the continuance of the £1 note, said: 'I do not think I can offer you very much hope.'
> – Robin Young, *The Times*

I drove through the slumbering town at a fifty-mile-per-hour pace in continuance of my smooth highway swoosh, and a twosome of patrolmen put their spotlight on the car, and told me to pull over.
> – Vladimir Nabokov, *Lolita*

And *continuation* is appropriate in such contexts as: *This episode is a continuation of last week's story; the continuation of play after the tea interval.*

Continuity relates more to the adjective *continuous* than to the verb *to continue*. *Continuity* is often interchangeable with the noun *continuousness*, but with certain special uses. *Continuity* is similar in meaning to *uninterruptedness, consistency, smoothness of progression*. Hence the use of the word in filmmaking to refer to the flow of sequences without discrepancies, and in broadcasting to refer to the announcer's conversation linking one programme to the next.

contractions of verbs The contracted forms in commonest use in standard speech are:

1. those of the present tense of *be* (*I'm, you're, he's, she's, it's, we're, they're*).

2. those of the auxiliary verb *have* (*I've, you've, he's, she's, it's, we've, they've*).

3. those of the auxiliary verb *had* (*I'd, you'd, he'd, she'd, it'd, we'd, they'd*).

4. those of the auxiliary verb *will* (*I'll, you'll, he'll, she'll, it'll, we'll, they'll*; it is possible that *I'll* and *we'll* also mark contractions of *shall*).

5. those of the auxiliary verb *would* (*I'd, you'd, he'd, she'd, it'd, we'd, they'd*).

6. the negative auxiliaries (*isn't, aren't, wasn't, weren't, won't, can't, couldn't, wouldn't, shouldn't, oughtn't, doesn't, didn't, haven't, hasn't, hadn't, mustn't*).

7. *let's.*

Note that *'s* can mean 'is' or 'has'; *'d*, 'had', or 'would'. In British English *has* and *had* are seldom represented by *'s* or *'d* when functioning as full verbs, though *She'd a new dress on* is possible. In American English such a sentence would virtually never be used.

The contractions *shan't*, *needn't*, and *daren't* are chiefly British; the contraction *mayn't* is almost exclusively British; and the contraction *usedn't to* is British and old-fashioned, though still common in Australia and New Zealand. It is also old-fashioned British English to write *they'ld* for *they'd* (= they would). *'Tis* and *'twas* are archaic or dialectal for *it is* and *it was*.

Take care in spelling all these contractions to place the apostrophe where it belongs. The temptation is sometimes to shift it to an earlier position: × *was'nt*, × *did'nt*.

The conservative policy is never to use contractions of these kinds in writing (except when representing speech). Most people use them in informal writing such as personal letters, and many now also use them in business letters, news reporting, and creative literature. Judicious use of the contracted forms can give a relaxed and mildly informal tone in all but the most ceremonial contexts. Occasionally, contracted and possessive forms are confused. (See APOSTROPHE; ITS, IT'S; -'S, -S'.)

George Bernard Shaw's efforts to do away with the apostrophe in contractions — *youre*, *theyd*, *oughtnt* — were doomed to founder on such 'contractions' as *Ill*, *shell*, *hell*, *shed*, and *well*, which tend instead to be read as quite different words.

See also ABBREVIATIONS 6; AIN'T.

controversy This word has been the subject of considerable ... controversy, and is perhaps the best-known of all pronunciation-problems in British English: is it **con***troversy* or *con***trov***ersy*? In fact, both are now generally considered standard in British English, but purists still prefer the first-syllable stress, /**kon**trə-versi/, as being longer established and truer to the word's Latin roots: *contro-* or *contra-*, 'against' + *versus,* 'turned', from *vertere,* 'to turn'. In American English, it remains the only acceptable pronunciation.

In British English, but not in American English, *labor**atory* and *met**allurgy* have undergone a similar shift of stress; *for**midable* is approaching acceptability; the incorrect stressing *cap**italist*, *lam**entably*, and *ir**revocably* are increasingly heard, and so on. It seems that British English finds it unnatural to string three or more unaccented syllables together. Despite the pattern of such words as *ad**miralty*, *dif**ficulty*, *ex**cellency*,

and *pres**idency*, such unaccented strings are rare: the more common patterns involve either an extra stress on the third syllable — *micro**scop***ic*, *cele**bra***tion* — or a second-syllable stress: *a***pol***ogy*, *hy***poc***risy*, *rhi***noc***eros*. The traditional pronunciation **con***troversy* follows the first, minority pattern; the second pattern is represented by the adjective **con***trov***ersial**; and the increasingly common *con***trov***ersy* follows the third pattern.

● *Recommendation* Purists, Americans, and older speakers of British English are likely to say **con***troversy*, and to think ill of *con***trov***ersy* — this more recent, and easier, pronunciation is today probably used by a majority of speakers of British English under 50, however, and many of them are likely to regard **con***troversy* as old-fashioned or pretentious.

So the chances are that someone or other is going to dislike your pronunciation, no matter which pronunciation you adopt. The choice is yours, then — including the choice of changing your pronunciation, chameleon-like, to suit the taste of your audience, and the safest (but also the silliest) choice of all ... to avoid using the word altogether in conversation. If you do want to use it, and to use it consistently, it is probably advisable to throw in your lot with the big guns rather than the big brigades, and to side with the purists and **con***troversy*.

corporal, corporeal In the past, these two adjectives were interchangeable, but today there is a clear distinction between them.

They both derive from the Latin *corpus*, 'a body', but the ways in which they refer to a body are slightly different.

Corporal means simply 'of or relating to the human body', and is seldom used outside the phrase *corporal punishment*, referring to caning or flogging. (It is often explicitly contrasted to *capital punishment,* from the Latin *caput*, 'a head' — that is, punishment of the head, rather than punishment of the body, which is what *corporal punishment* is. *Capital punishment* originally suggested beheading, but now refers to the death penalty carried out by any means.)

Other combinations with *corporal* are possible — *corporal beauty, corporal needs, corporal disfigurements*, and so on — but an adjective such as *physical* or *personal* or *bodily* is more likely to be used nowadays.

Corporeal is even less common, being restricted usually to religious or philosophical contexts. It refers to the body specifically as opposed to the spirit, and means 'material, tangible': *the corporeal presence of Christ; our corporeal existence.*

It is to warn Creed never to cross that barrier that the dreamed of, but all too corporeal, dead student returns.
– Bill Greenwell, *The Fiction Magazine*

The opposite, *incorporeal* — 'disembodied, spiritual, intangible' — is probably used more widely.

Corporal as a noun, referring to the military non-commissioned officer, really derives from the Latin word for the head rather than the body. Strictly speaking the word should be *caporal*, as it is in French (*caporale* in Italian), from the Latin *caput*, 'a head' (hence *capo*, Italian for 'a chief'). But *corporal* became the French form for a time, probably by association with the idea of 'a leader of a body (or *corps*) of troops', and it was at that time that English borrowed the word from French.

Note that the adjectives *corporal* and *corporeal* both refer to a body in the sense of a human body. They cannot be used to refer to a body in the sense of a group of people. The appropriate adjective here is *corporate*, as in *corporate strength*, meaning 'collective strength, the strength produced by a number of people uniting into a single group'. *Corporate* is also, of course, the adjective referring to *corporations* — that is, legally constituted business enterprises.

Note that *corporal* and *corporate* are stressed on the first syllable, whereas *corporeal* is stressed on the second.

See also CORPS.

corps, corpse, corpus A wide range of English words derives from the Latin word *corpus*, 'a body'. In English, *corpus* now means primarily 'a collection or body of texts or literary works': *A corpus of 350 spoken and written texts was analysed for information about contemporary English usage.*

The Zuckerman novels look like life looks, before art has properly finished with it. And Roth's corpus still gives the impression of a turbulent talent searching for a decorous way to explode.
– Martin Amis, *The Observer*

There are specialised senses of *corpus* in finance and anatomy as well.

The derivative *corps*, originally French, refers generally to a group ('a body') of people associated in some common endeavour, and more specifically, to a unit of the army. It also refers to the group of dancers in a ballet troupe who have no solo parts: the official term is *corps de ballet*.

Both *corps* and *corpus* give rise to problems with the plural. *Corps* is written the same way in the singular and the plural, but in the singular is pronounced /kor/ and in the plural /korz/ in English. The plural of *corpus* is technically *corpora*; *corpuses* is also used, but has not gained wide acceptance.

Corpse (pronounced /korps/) as a noun is used to refer to a dead body, usually a human body. The dead body of an animal is usually a *carcass* (also spelt *carcase*). Curiously, there is no English word for the dead body of a plant. As a verb, *to corpse* is an informal theatre term in British English; when one actor confuses another or spoils his performance, he is said to *corpse* (that is, 'to kill') him or it: *She corpsed my soliloquy by mistiming her exit.* Similarly, when an actor forgets his lines, he is said to *corpse* (that is, 'to die').

See also CORPORAL.

correspond If Abélard and Héloïse send each other letters, then Abélard and Héloïse *correspond with* each other, or simply *correspond*. If the left foreleg of a horse is related in function, position, and evolution to the left arm of a human being, then foreleg *corresponds to* arm, or simply, foreleg and arm *correspond*.

But *correspond with* is now widely used as a variant of *correspond to* (though not vice versa). A foreleg might *correspond with* an arm; a theory might fail to *correspond with* the facts. (There is in fact some ground for preferring *with* to *to* here: the Latin source *correspondere* contains the element *cor-*, a form of *com-*, whose basic sense is something like 'together' or 'with'. So it may be better in keeping with the word's history to say *correspond with* than *correspond to*.)

But the loss of the distinction is a pity, and purists continue to recommend *correspond to* in comparisons.

For another *to-with* distinction, of a different kind, see COMPARE WITH.

could See CAN, MAY.

council, counsel A *council* is a committee, or an assembly, or a meeting. The noun *counsel* means 'advice or consultation'; the verb *to counsel* means 'to advise': *He counselled the council, and his counsel was acted upon.*

After a few days of this, Kurtz got sick of the sight of him — 'haunting me like my own bad conscience' — and threatened openly to forbid him the house, until wiser counsels got the better of him.

– John le Carré,
The Little Drummer Girl

Council and *counsel* go back to two different Latin words: *council* comes from the noun *concilium*, 'a meeting or assembly'; *counsel* comes from the noun *consilium*, 'deliberation, consultation', which is akin to the verb *consulere*, 'to consult or take counsel'.

In Britain, *council* has a particular significance: it refers to the basic representative unit of local government, the administrative body of a town or county; hence also *a council house,* one which belongs to the local council. Town and city *councils* also exist in America, but the term *council house* is not used.

Generally, one who gives *counsel* is a *counsellor*, not to be confused with a *councillor,* who is a member of a council. Thus: *a marriage-guidance counsellor* but *a Yorkshire County Councillor.* In North America, members of town or city councils are called *council(l)ors*, *councilmen*, or *councilwomen*.

A *counsellor* in North America (sometimes spelt *counselor* there), can also be a guardian of children at a summer camp, or an adviser to students at a college or university. The word can also be used in addressing a lawyer, sometimes humorously.

Counsel can also mean 'an adviser' and is used without *a* or *the*. In legal terminology, usually with a capital *C*, *Counsel* is the lawyer who represents clients in litigation. The plural is also *counsel/Counsel*: *Several prominent Counsel were present.* But the abbreviation *QC* for *Queen's Counsel* is *QCs* in the plural.

Counsel are not allowed to lead their own witnesses to the answers they want from them by putting leading questions.
– Philip Howard, *Weasel Words*

The idiom *to keep your (own) counsel* means 'to keep your opinion to yourself, or to keep a secret'.

couple In informal usage, the meaning of *couple* has extended, so that it is no longer restricted to two, but has the less specific sense of 'a few'. As the strict meaning of 'two' is still very much alive, however, the word is often ambiguous. *There are a couple of points I'd like to make* does not necessarily mean only two (though it might). On the other hand, *I met a couple of young lads* is likely to be understood in the precise meaning of

the word, and all the more so such phrases as *the happy couple.* (See also PLURALS Part II.)

cowardly The adjective *cowardly* is a favourite standby of journalists and official spokesmen when describing a terrorist attack, mugging, or the like. Careful users of English object to such an application of the word: *cowardly* should suggest a lack of courage, whereas a terrorist outrage or mugging — however nasty, brutal, or stupid — is not, strictly speaking, the act of a coward. Traditionally it is a retreat, not an attack, that is regarded as cowardly.

Terrorists or muggers do, true enough, have this much in common with cowards — that they tend to be evasive and act in secret rather than declare themselves publicly; and this is presumably the reason for the development of the new sense of *cowardly*. But it is not really a sufficient reason, and *cowardly* should be restricted to its older and more precise meaning.

credible, creditable, credulous These three adjectives all derive ultimately from the Latin verb *credere*, meaning 'to believe or entrust'. *Credible* and *credulous* both retain the notion of believing, but in very different ways. *Credible* means 'believable' or 'reliable': *a credible alibi, a credible liar,* or *a credible account of the incident*.

The narrative is lightened at several points with some untypical Gordimer satire. She puts the knife into a smugly suburban Afrikaner couple, who remain credible nevertheless.
– Paul Bailey, *The Observer*

There is also an extended sense, 'authentic, convincing, sound': *hardly a credible candidate for the by-election; She makes a credible wife.*

It was the failure of the Opposition parties to convince the electorate that they had a credible alternative to the growing dole queues.
– Adam Raphael, *The Observer*

Credible in this sense has been criticised as a vogue word. Use it sparingly. The opposite, *incredible,* cannot apply to these extended senses: it means only 'unbelievable' and, informally, 'wonderful, marvellous': *an incredible holiday*.
Credulous is used exclusively of humans and human behaviour, never of things. It is applied to people who are, as it were, on the receiving end of a 'credible' story, and means 'believing too readily, gullible': *a credulous simpleton, a*

credulous electorate. Note the pronunciation: /**kred**dewləss/.

There are also signs of stupendous naivety. Feigenbaum and McCorduck, for example, are limitlessly credulous about the ability of the Japanese to achieve their immoderate objective.

– John Naughton, *The Observer*

The opposite *incredulous* means 'disbelieving, sceptical' or 'expressing disbelief': *an incredulous stare.*

The feeling persisted until teatime, when in front of his incredulous eyes the starboard outer propeller came spinning to a halt, and they landed in some haste, with fire-engines and ambulances standing by, at Ljubljana.

– Michael Frayn,
Towards the End of the Morning

Creditable, finally, has lost all connection with the notion of believing, and means primarily 'worthy of credit, deserving praise or commendation': *a creditable attempt, a creditable collaboration, a creditable result.* It is rarely if ever applied directly to people.

Polk-Mowbray threw himself into the arrangements with great abandon ... It promised to be the most original party of the year ... All in all it was most creditable to those concerned.

– Antrobus, in Lawrence Durrell's
Esprit de Corps

The noun *credit* has senses relating to both aspects: it can mean 'belief or trust, confidence in the truth of something', and it can also mean 'a good reputation' or 'a source of honour' or 'praise'.

'I want to thank all you gentlemen, and particularly Mr Brown, for what you've done for the boy ...' ...
'I'm sure that we all regard him as doing you the greatest credit,' said Brown.

– C.P. Snow, *The Masters*

The verb *to credit* means 'to believe or trust', and also 'to award, attribute', and so on:

You don't see why? Really, dear boy, I must own I credited you with more finesse. No, that's entirely out of the question.

– Arthur Norris, in Christopher Isherwood's
Mr Norris Changes Trains

Then he released himself with a small sound, inconclusive, disbelieving. Perhaps he didn't

credit death could be so clean; thought he had looked it back in the eye; perhaps he was too young to believe it existed.

– Nadine Gordimer, *July's People*

Discredit is both a noun and, more commonly, a verb — meaning chiefly 'to dishonour' or 'to cast doubt on':

She at once felt guilty for even thinking such a ridiculous thought, which somehow seemed to discredit her feelings about John's absence, and about separation in general.

– Michael Frayn,
Towards the End of the Morning

Among the many other related nouns are *credence,* 'acceptance, belief', pronounced /**kreed**'nss/; *credibility* (from *credible*); and *credulity* (from *credulous*), pronounced /kri-**dew**ləti/.

No one in the telecommunications industry gives much credence to Baker's other assertion that 'British Telecom needs time to adjust'. Armed with the initial advantage of a near monopoly, BT is felt well able to take care of itself.

– Colin Clifford, *The Observer*

If this hypothesis is correct — and all the available evidence points that way — it clearly casts the most serious doubt on the credibility of the police's case against the five men. This is not the same as saying the men are innocent — although that is their claim.

– Robin Lustig, *The Observer*

Nobody could claim that this prospect grew to match the ever growing mountain of debt: this was bound to bring into question the credibility of most of the debtors and of the lending system itself.

– Lord Lever, *Time and Tide*

He shares the tastes of the great medieval historian of chivalry, Jean Froissart, although without the latter's verbosity and without his wide-eyed credulity. Mr Keen knows how to colour his palette, but never loses his judgment.

– Jonathan Sumption,
Sunday Telegraph

At the trial, and during the court reviews of the case, one central question was whether any dingo could really have carried off a baby clad in a jump-suit. The jurors'

incredulity on this point was said to have had a strong influence on their decision.
— Michael Davie, *The Observer*

Take care to observe all the distinctions in this confusing group of related words.

creole See PIDGINS AND CREOLES; WEST INDIAN ENGLISH.

crescendo *Crescendo* is primarily a musical term. As a noun, it refers to a gradual increase in the volume of sound, or to a passage played in this way, or to the symbol indicating the increase in sound: <. It has related senses as an adjective, adverb, and intransitive verb.

A *crescendo* can apply to noises in general — *While I was waiting, the wind rose in a crescendo from a whisper to a roar* — and even, metaphorically, to developments other than sounds: *The election campaign has built up in an almost imperceptible crescendo over the autumn.*

This is hardly straining the sense at all: *crescendo* means literally 'growing' in Italian, from *crescere*, 'to increase or grow', from the Latin *crescere*, 'to grow'.

The idea of a growing or developing, a *process*, seems to be essential to the word. There is a tendency, however, to use the word to refer to the result of the development — to the *product* rather than the process. Purists rightly protest at this abuse: × *The roar of the wind rose to a crescendo*; × *Exams! — the crescendo of the academic year.*

× The rhythm of the seasons affects this branch of agriculture as much as others; it reaches a crescendo at this time of year in harmony with the annual price-fixing operation at Brussels.
— leading article, *The Times*

Use the established terms *climax, culmination, milestone, high point,* or the like instead. Note that as a rule, a sound or development rises *in* a crescendo, not *to* a crescendo. And it cannot usually *reach* a crescendo.

Take care too not to use a superfluous adjective before *crescendo*. It is acceptable to speak of *a slow crescendo,* but not of × *a growing crescendo* — there is a redundancy in that phrase. Just passable, perhaps, though best avoided, is *? a gradual crescendo.*

The pronunciation is /kri-**shen**-dō/. The plural is either *crescendos* or *crescendi.* The verb forms are spelt *crescendoed, crescendoing, crescendoes.*

The reverse of a *crescendo* is a *decrescendo* or a *diminuendo.* The inflexions and derivatives of these words are analogous to those of *crescendo.*

crisis *Crisis* entered English from Latin, which borrowed it from the Greek *krisis,* 'a turning point', from *krinein,* 'to separate or decide'. Deep within the word, then, is the notion of a decisive switch — specifically, a switch that is on the verge of happening or that threatens to happen. Whether the word is used of a disease, a drama, or a political state of affairs, it should suggest that some sudden change, for the better or worse, is about to take place. Careful users avoid the word in the loose sense it has recently acquired — 'any serious, urgent, worrying, or dangerous state of affairs':

? It looks like England has a crisis on its hands — the first three wickets have tumbled within the space of two hours.

It is interesting to note that the currently popular phrase *mid-life crisis* does actually use *crisis* close to its etymological sense of 'turning-point'.

Note, finally, that the plural of *crisis* is *crises.* Compare CRUCIAL.

criterion, criteria *Criterion* is the singular form; *criteria* is the plural. *Criterions* is found fairly often as well now, but purists still object to it. *Criterion* is Greek in origin, going back to the verb *krinein,* 'to separate or choose'; it retains the Greek neuter endings, *-on* for the singular, *-a* for the plural.

Criteria is often mistakenly used as the singular noun, with × *criterias* as its plural — presumably by analogy with certain Latin-based words such as *arena* and *formula.* Unlike *agenda, insignia,* and so on — also originally plurals — *criteria* is most unlikely to be accepted as a standard singular form.

See also DATA; MEDIA; PHENOMENON; PLURALS.

crocodile See ALLIGATOR.

crucial *Crucial* has a stronger sense than merely 'important', and careful speakers and writers avoid using it in this loose way as a synonym of *important:* ?? *The opening match of the season is always crucial for Rangers.* Surely not: the closing match of the season may be crucial, since that might determine whether Rangers are promoted or relegated, become league champions, or the like. The opening game, on the other hand, however *important* it may be, is most unlikely to be *crucial,* 'decisive, critical; of vital importance in deciding an outcome'.

Similarly *crucially*: call something *crucially important* only if it is so — that is, if its result is of decisive importance.

Crucial goes back, through French, to the Latin *crux*, 'a cross'. The idea is, presumably, of a clear change of direction. The related English word *crux*, 'the essential feature', is a reminder of the full strength of *crucial*. The following quotation illustrates the correct use of *crucial*, suggesting as it does a decisive point or crux:

Ordination of women will be discussed again in the Church's 44 dioceses but the next crucial test will come in the election of the General Synod which assembles in November 1985; a year before the actual legislative process over the issue is expected to begin.
— Martyn Halsall, *The Guardian*

Compare CRISIS.

crumpet See MUFFIN.

curate's egg This phrase has become something of a cliché in British English, and a misused one in addition. It is widely understood to refer to something that has both good and bad aspects — *That play was something of a curate's egg* — and so is sometimes taken for moderate praise.

The origin of the phrase suggests a different interpretation. A cartoon in *Punch* in 1895 showed a shy curate sitting at table with his bishop. The boiled egg placed in front of him is all too clearly a bad egg. When this is remarked on, he replies, not wanting to give offence, that 'parts of it are excellent'.

Now, a bad egg is bad through and through. The phrase *curate's egg* should therefore refer to something that is bad throughout, or at least something that cannot be redeemed even if there are a few good aspects. Use the phrase with caution: it is really a damning criticism, not a half-hearted compliment.

curb, kerb For the noun referring to the border round the edge of a pavement, *kerb* is the British spelling and *curb* the American.

Two sailors, their caps thrust back on their heads, came out of a shooting-alley and sat down on the kerb to share their last cigarette.
— Bruce Chatwin,
in *Great Rivers of the World*

As a verb, *to kerb* means 'to provide with a kerb': *to kerb the footpath*.

For all other senses, as both noun and verb, *curb* is the standard form in both British and American English. A *curb* is a chain for restraining a horse, or an enclosing frame or fender. *To curb* something is to restrain or control it:

It was then that we came closer to detection than ever before, and no wonder the experience curbed forever my yearning for rural amours.
— Vladimir Nabokov, *Lolita*

The words are related to *curve*, going back through Old French to the Latin *curvus*, 'a curve'.

current, currant A possible spelling problem here. The rule is simple: use *currant* only when referring to the small dried grapes or the small wild fruits resembling them, notably the *redcurrant* and *blackcurrant,* and the plants that bear them. *Current* is used in all other senses — such as the adjective meaning 'present, now in progress' — *current business* — and the noun meaning 'a flow, a movement in one direction': *electric current, the current of the river*.

Currant comes via Middle English from Anglo-French *raisins de corauntz,* 'grapes of Corinth' — Corinth being the place from which they were originally exported. *Current* goes back to the Latin *currere,* 'to run'.

cyclone, hurricane, typhoon, whirlwind, tornado All these words refer to high winds, usually destructive, which whirl or spiral around an axis or 'eye' of low pressure. There are small technical differences of size, shape, speed, and duration; the most important difference is their distribution — the part of the world where each occurs.

A *hurricane* can be any wind travelling at above 120 km/h (75 mph) — or Force 12 on the Beaufort wind-scale. More specifically, it refers to a tropical storm with winds of over 160 km/h (100 mph), torrential rain, and thunder and lightning. Hurricanes form in the late summer, typically in the West Indies or the gulf of Mexico, and drift across the sea until they exhaust themselves inland. Such storms occurring off the North of Australia are also called *hurricanes*, though there is an Australian name as well — a *willy-nilly* (more commonly referring to a cyclonic dust storm).

In the Northern Hemisphere hurricanes whirl anti-clockwise; in the Southern Hemisphere they whirl clockwise (they always arise in bands north and south of the Equator and drift away from it — so they do not cross the Equator).

The cylindrical body of swirling air can be up

to 960 km (600 miles) in diameter; the winds are fastest, up to 320 km/h (200 mph), nearest to the eye — although the eye itself, about 32 km (20 miles) across, is calm.

A *cyclone* is a small hurricane from 80-400 km across (50-250 miles), with an eye about 20 km across (12 miles). The winds can be just as fast as those of a hurricane, however — 200-300 km/h (120-180 mph). *Cyclones* occur in the Arabian Sea and the Bay of Bengal. Confusingly, a hurricane is sometimes referred to as a *tropical cyclone*.

There is also another sense of the word *cyclone*: it can mean the opposite of an *anticyclone*; that is, *cyclone* can refer to any area of low pressure. However, to avoid confusion between these two meteorological terms, this kind of cyclone is usually referred to as a *depression*.

A *typhoon* is also a small hurricane, occurring this time in the China Sea and along the margins of the Western Pacific.

Whirlwind is sometimes used as a general term for a whirling column of air, to cover cyclones and hurricanes alike; but it is usually more specific, referring to a small, tight, extremely destructive windstorm, of as little as 90 metres or so (100 yards) across, and visible as a moving funnel of cloud, spray, or dust.

In the southern United States, these wind-columns are known as *tornados*; they usually occur in early summer, and last only an hour or two. They are also sometimes informally called *twisters*; the present U.S. lookout centre which issues tornado-warnings is in Kansas — the very place from which Dorothy was transported by a twister to the Land of Oz.

There is a technical difference between a *whirl-wind* and a *tornado*. A tornado usually spirals downwards, from the clouds to the ground; a whirlwind does the reverse.

A tornado that occurs over desert is sometimes known informally as a *dust devil,* and one that forms over the sea causes (and is sometimes therefore called) a *waterspout.*

The word *hurricane* comes through Spanish from Carib *furacan, huracan,* 'a hurricane'.

Tornado comes from Spanish *tronada,* 'a thunderstorm', but was distorted into its present form by the influence of the word *tornado,* Spanish for 'turned'.

Typhoon is Chinese in origin, its elements meaning 'great wind'. The English form is partly due to the influence of the name of a Greek monster, *Typhon.* He had a hundred heads, each with a terrible voice, and made war on Zeus, the King of the Gods — an appropriate personification of a violent, noisy, terrifying windstorm.

czar   See TSAR.

D

dangling participles See MISRELATED CONSTRUCTIONS.

dare *Dare* as a verb is used in two different ways in standard English. It can be a full verb, taking an *-s* ending in the third person, followed by *to*, and having a past tense: *She dares to answer; She dared to answer; Does she dare to answer?; She didn't dare to answer.*

Dare can also be an auxiliary verb, with no endings and no *to*, though with a past tense — *dared* (archaic *durst*): *She dare not/daren't/dared not answer; Dare she answer?*

The full verb construction is more frequent, since the auxiliary can be used only in negatives and questions, or in sentences with at least some negative implication: *How dare you say that? I wonder how he dared mention it; That's as much as I dare spend; a statement that none of us dare question.*

Where there is a choice, Americans often prefer the full verb — *She doesn't dare to answer* — where the British would say *She daren't answer.*

It is important not to mix the constructions. Say either *if she dares to answer* or *if she dare answer*, but not × *if she dares answer*.

dash 1. The dash (—) is used, like the comma and the bracket, to surround any material that is included in a sentence without being structurally essential to it:

> The author, a good friend of mine, denied the charge.
> The author (a good friend of mine) denied the charge.
> The author — a good friend of mine — denied the charge.

The common comma is the least striking of these three marks of punctuation, the bracket is more striking, the dash most of all. It is the visibility of the dash that makes it so appropriate when setting off the parenthetical material from its surroundings. This separation of part of the sentence is either for the sake of emphasising it or because it is very long or markedly different in tone or structure. The following series illustrates the likely choice of punctuation:

> The author, a good friend of mine, denied the charge.
> The author (a good friend of mine, incidentally) denied the charge.
> The author — and he claims to be a good friend of mine! — denied the charge.

2. As the last example shows, material set off by dashes can be followed by an exclamation mark (or a question mark), though not by a full stop. Even when such material has the form of a full sentence, however, it does not usually begin with a capital letter. Bracketed material usually behaves in the same way, though it is possible to enclose a complete sentence in brackets. But material set off by commas cannot have any other final punctuation and cannot have the form of a complete sentence.

3. a. As a rule nowadays, neither of the dashes enclosing a piece of text is preceded by a comma, and the second dash is no longer followed by one (in the way that the second bracket can be), even when the grammar seems to demand such a comma. So it is not only wrong now to write:

> × The author, — he claims to be a friend of mine, — denied the charge.

It is probably also wrong, however logical, to write:

> ?? Although he is a friend of mine — or so he claims —, I have to admit he looks guilty.

b. Dashes (like commas) are not usually adjacent to full stops or semicolons or colons either. So if the parenthetical material comes at the end of a sentence (or before a colon or semicolon), it would have only the one dash (or comma) — in front of it, as here. (But if brackets are used, as here, the closing bracket cannot be left out.)

> Many of the subtleties reveal themselves only on second reading — a backhanded compliment, probably, in a fiction-crammed, hurried world.
>
> – Joy Grant,
> *The Times Literary Supplement*

4. The parenthetical material that the single dash

167

introduces in this last example might be called an afterthought. Here is another example:

And so it was the vicar himself who ended up paying for the party that was held in his honour — an interesting sidelight on the generosity and neighbourliness of the parishioners.

Another item typically introduced by the single dash is the change of direction in a train of thought:

The incident took place in 1963, the year of my marriage as it happens — but I digress.

The single dash also introduces an explanation or elaboration of a word, which is first repeated:

You could call it a compliment — a compliment of a very backhanded kind, of course, but a compliment nevertheless.

The single dash also introduces a punchline or surprise announcement (sometimes an anti-climax), after a careful build-up:

The footsteps came nearer and nearer, up the gravel pathway, step by step onto the porch, and along the groaning boards to the front door . . . the handle turned, the door slowly creaked open — and in walked my wife.

5. The single dash may also be used before or after a clause that summarises a series of words or phrases. There is a relatively sharp transition between the two halves of such sentences as:

a. Talent, hard work, good luck — these are the ingredients of success.
b. Success has three ingredients — talent, hard work, good luck.

A colon may appear instead of the dash, and is more common than the dash in examples such as *b.* above; that is, after the summarising clause:

c. Success has three ingredients: talent, hard work, good luck.

Related to this use of the dash is its use to 'explain' preceding material:

+ — plus
× — times
= — equals

Here the dash may be read out as 'means'.

6. The single dash may come at the end of a sentence — if the sentence is incomplete or interrupted:

Josephine and Constantia got up too.

'I should like it to be quite simple,' said Josephine firmly, 'and not too expensive. At the same time I should like —'
'A good one that will last,' thought dreamy Constantia, as if Josephine were buying a nightgown.

> – Katherine Mansfield,
> 'The Daughters of the Late Colonel'

Instead of the dash here, the writer could have used the dot-dot-dot convention of the ellipsis (*I should like . . .*) but this would suggest a gradual trailing off rather than a sudden interruption.

7. The single dash is also used to indicate the omission of all or part of a taboo word:

The —y door's stuck!
B— off!

(The expression *Dash it!*, as a softened version of *Damn it!*, derives from this practice. In former times, when the exclamation *Damn it!* was considered unfit for print, the printed form used instead was — *it!*, which was read out as *Dash it!*)

The dash also indicates the omission of all or part of a name that the author must not or will not reveal:

I first met the Count von O— in the picturesque Alpine village of H—.

This use of the dash is now rather rare: as regards obscenities, readers seem today to want them in full if they are prepared to tolerate them at all.

8. Dashes are also used to indicate hesitant speech. Usually at least two are used, but there may be more:

Going – going – gone!
I – um – er – well – that is – I love you.

Here, the 'en-dash' may be used — shorter than an ordinary dash (an 'em-dash') but longer than a hyphen. (The dot-dot-dot or ellipsis may also be used here — with a slightly different effect.)

Note, however, that for the stammering of sounds or syllables, hyphens are used rather than dashes:

I l-l-love you.

9. The single dash is also used between the first and last points in space or time:

Dover – Calais;   Monday – Friday;
1795 – 1822

This dash can be read out as 'to'. Once again, it is often printed as the shorter 'en-dash'.

Furthermore, several such dashes may be used, especially when listing the points on an itinerary:

London – Dover – Calais – Brussels

10. The single dash is also the traditional way of indicating the source of a quotation:

> – *TLS*, 22 June 1984
> – George Eliot, *Middlemarch*

11. The single dash is also used by many dictionaries for a variety of purposes, as can be seen in the following extracts from the *Reader's Digest Great Illustrated Dictionary*:

bondage ... — See Synonyms at **servitude**.
bone ... —**feel in (one's) bones** ...
bone·head ... —**bone·head·ed** ... *adj.*
— **bone·head·ed·ness** *n.*
eat ... *v.* ... — *tr.* ... — *intr.* ...

The single dash introduces cross-references, idioms, and simple derivatives of the word being defined. Some dictionaries use it in other ways, too: for example, to introduce explanatory notes that replace or supplement definitions.

12. In mathematics, the dash is used as the minus sign to indicate subtraction $(6-2=4)$, and together with a colon as the division sign $(6\div2=3)$.

The dash combines with the colon to form another symbol (:—), rather old-fashioned now, and almost unknown in American English. It is used to introduce a detailed list, usually one in which each item appears on a separate line.

13. Ordinary typewriters do not feature the dash. It can be represented either by two successive hyphens, or by a single hyphen with a space either side. The difference between an en-dash and an em-dash cannot really be represented.

data *Data* is pronounced /**day**-tə/ though /**daa**-tə/ and /**dat**tə/ can be heard, especially in American English. It is a plural noun, the Latin plural of *datum,* 'a given (fact)' — the way *bacteria* is the plural of *bacterium, strata* of *stratum,* and so on. (See PLURALS.)

The singular *datum* is rarely used nowadays, its commonest appearance probably being in an adjectival role, as in *the poverty datum-line.* If the singular is needed, a likelier term is *one of the data.* But *data* itself should not be used as a singular noun. Unlike *agenda* or *insignia,* for example, it has not yet graduated from plural form to singular function, though it is a very common mistake to treat it as singular:

× The available data on acid rain in Northern Europe suggests that Britain is the chief culprit.

× All that anthropological data on Samoan teenagers, collected by the late Margaret Mead, has recently been challenged as unreliable.

× But there are major issues that have not been addressed. For one thing, although it is assumed that all 'legalese' is incomprehensible, there is no real data, aside from anecdotes, to support this assumption or to elucidate the exact nature of the problem.
> – Robert P. Charrow (U.S.) and
> Veda R. Charrow (U.S.),
> *The Columbia Law Review*

In the first example, *suggests* should be changed to *suggest* — alternatively, *data* should be replaced by *information* or *evidence*; the second example should read *All those ... data ... have recently been challenged.* In the third example, × *there is no real data* should be changed to *there are no real data.*

The difficulty is less easily resolved when it comes to talking about the quantity of data. You cannot really count data as you can count the referents of ordinary plural nouns: it sounds odd to speak of *?? three data.* People tend to use a bridging, or 'partitive', expression in such cases: *three items of data*; *? three pieces of data*; *three of the data.* It is also slightly odd to say *? There aren't many data in support of the claim*; it sounds better to say *? There isn't much/a lot of data in support of the claim,* but this is unfortunately still considered unacceptable by purists. The only alternative seems to be to avoid using *data* altogether in such constructions, replacing it with *facts, evidence,* or the like: *There aren't many facts in support of the claim; There isn't much evidence in support of the claim.*

Compare CRITERION; MEDIA; PHENOMENON.

dates See NUMBER STYLE.

day See YEAR.

deceptive, deceitful Both these adjectives convey the idea of cheating or false appearance. But *deceitful* implies an intention to deceive (whether or not the result is in fact a successful deception); and *deceptive* implies a misleading effect or result (whether it was intended or not). *Deceitful* means primarily 'motivated by deceit or dishonesty'; *deceptive* means primarily 'resulting in deception or misapprehension'.

Deceitful therefore has a negative or morally disapproving tone, whereas *deceptive* is often quite neutral.

The words tend to combine with different ranges of nouns, in keeping with these different nuances: *his deceitful words of love, a deceitful little minx; deceptive appearances, an impression of being well-informed that proved quite deceptive.*

The corresponding nouns *deceit* and *deception* share several senses, but their emphases are rather different. Once again, *deceit* clearly implies an intention to mislead, and would be used most often in reference to deliberate human dishonesty; *deception* often implies deliberate trickery too, but it can refer to an accidental misrepresentation or natural illusion, and it can deal with non human subjects: *the deceptions to which the human eye is so often subjected by ordinary sunlight.*

The above example points to another slight difference in usage between the two nouns: *deception,* although it can mean general dishonesty, tends more often to refer to a particular act of trickery, and can easily be used in the plural therefore. *Deceit,* on the other hand, is less often used in such a concrete way, and is rarely found in the plural form; it more commonly has the abstract sense of *deceitfulness,* 'a tendency to deceive or the habit of deceiving'.

See also DECEPTIVELY.

deceptively   This is a deceptively easy adverb to use. It is usually placed directly in front of an adjective (as in the previous sentence) and implies that the outward appearances are misleading.

But what kind of adjective should be used? Suppose a contract seems very straightforward, but in fact has a lot of technical small print — is it *a deceptively simple contract* or *a deceptively complicated contract*? And if a woman turns out to be shorter than she looks, is she *deceptively short* or *deceptively tall*?

The correct answers are *a deceptively simple contract* and *deceptively tall.* The word *deceptively* in effect negates the adjective (*simple, tall*) and thus affirms the reality (complexity and shortness). The words *seemingly* and *apparently* can function in a similar though slightly milder way: *an apparently simple contract, seemingly tall.*

Deceptively is much better suited to some adjectives than to others. It sounds quite natural to talk about *a deceptively straightforward proposal*, but the phrase *? a deceptively devious proposal* sounds distinctly odd. Idiom seems to want a favourable rather than unfavourable adjective to combine with *deceptively.* (If the proposal really were straightforward but looked devious, the idiomatic way of describing it would be as *an apparently devious proposal.*)

The question raised by this appeal is one which, to the tyro, appears deceptively simple ... it is discouraging to one whose unfamiliarity with this field is unrivalled to find what appears to be a simple construction point overlaid by a great weight of authority.

– Lord Justice Oliver, quoted in
The All England Law Reports

'Nothing but the best here', as King George is said to have boomed when congratulated by Kenneth Clark on the Leonardos at Windsor. It is his subtlety, lack of ostentation and deceptively conservative approach that have made it easy to overlook the extent of Pritchett's originality.

– Hilary Spurling,
The Observer

It is difficult to see what drew Powell to this lemony subject. *O, How The Wheel Becomes It!* has none of his usual flair for catching real voices in real rooms. It is a dyspeptic footnote in a deceptively pretty wrapper.

– Jonathan Raban,
The Sunday Times

Perhaps because of this idiomatic preference for a favourable adjective, *deceptively* is often used in quite the wrong sense, as though it meant 'surprisingly' or 'despite appearances' or 'deceptive and'. Remember that *deceptively easy* means 'difficult', not 'easy despite appearances' or 'surprisingly easy' or 'deceptive and easy'. Here are two examples of the incorrect use:

✗ The problems that she faces, and which come to concern us, are simple, like trying to explain to her dying husband how much she has loved him. Of course simple is used here in the sense of infinitely complex, which is precisely the strength of Mr Edwards' book. It is short, cool and deceptively strong.

– Howard Davies,
The Literary Review

✗ **CHELSEA**   A small recently built cottage that is located in a deceptively quiet location and has its own private patio garden. It has a double and single bedroom, reception room, kitchen and bathroom.

– advertisement in *The Times*

The more appropriate wording would have been *surprisingly strong* (or *strong in spite of its mild presentation*, or the like) and *a surprisingly quiet location* (or *a location that is very quiet, considering the area*).

One last warning: the phrase *deceptively simple* has been criticised as a cliché: use it sparingly, and at all times use *deceptively* with great caution.

decided, decisive These adjectives overlap considerably in meaning, but there are subtle differences in the way they are used. *Decisive* still has a strong sense of decision-making about it: *a decisive chairman* suggests either a persuasive person who has his decisions ratified and executed, or a person who is able to make firm decisions without much hesitation or agonising. *A decided chairman* is one who is confident of his opinions, and expresses them without any doubts or qualifications.

The adverb *decidedly* means 'unquestionably, definitely': *a decidedly unwelcome development*. *Decisively* cannot be used in its place here.

When they are used in the same construction, notably *a decided/decisive advantage*, the two adjectives have different emphases. In a tennis match, for instance, *a decided advantage* is a clear and unquestionable advantage, but the contest is still in doubt; the player with *a decisive advantage*, however, virtually cannot lose: he is in the strongest possible position.

decimate *To decimate* originally meant — and still means, according to some — 'to kill a tenth of'. In classical times, a Roman military unit guilty of mutiny or cowardice might be punished by having one soldier in ten put to death: the Latin verb *decimare* developed from the adjective *decimus,* 'tenth' (from *decem,* 'ten').

The sound of the word, however, suggests a more serious disaster — perhaps through its similarity to *devastate* — and an extended sense duly developed, virtually reversing the proportions of the original practice:

? It was during this conference that Kapuściński got to know Teferra Gebrewold, an official who later served as the vital intermediary between the reporter and the survivors of the imperial court, their ranks decimated by firing squads, imprisonment and flight.

— David Caute, *The Observer*

? We participated in the famous 'Turkey Shoot' in the Marianas, during which we decimated the enemy's forces.

— Gerald R. Ford (U.S.),
A Time to Heal

Purists object to this new sense, though it seems to be firmly rooted now, and even more to looser senses such as 'to destroy', 'to get rid of', 'to defeat thoroughly', or the like:

?? Morinaga's sales so far this month are down 30 per cent (some £5 million) on the same period last year, and could halve by the end of the month. October sales for the entire Japanese confectionery industry could be decimated.

— Peter McGill, *The Observer*

× Regarding the discharge of suicidal patients from a mental hospital, the fault lies in decimating beds in asylums without having ensured the community services and hostels to accommodate these patients.

— Dr N.M. Tweedie-Stodart,
letter to the *Daily Telegraph*

× In last night's junior national title he easily defeated Andrew Salvidge ... Between them, they decimated the field of promising youngsters to meet each other.

— David Hunn, *The Observer*

decisive See DECIDED.

decry, descry *To decry* and *to descry* derive from the same source, but their uses are now quite separate. They should not be confused.

The common source is the old French *descrier,* meaning 'to cry down'. *To decry,* adopted from modern French, retains something of this sense; it means 'to belittle or disparage openly, to censure or denounce': *He decries the use of nuclear power as dangerous and uneconomical*. It can also, in rare technical contexts, mean 'to depreciate or devalue (a currency, for instance) by official proclamation or by rumour'.

To descry comes from a Middle English form of the Old French, and has moved far from the original sense. It means 'to discern something difficult to perceive, to catch sight of' or 'to discover by careful observation and investigation': *They descried a ship through the mists*. The word now has a poetic or very formal tone to it.

Note the pronunciations: decry, /di-**kri**/; descry, /di-**skri**/.

deduction, induction *Deduction* is the noun for two distinct verbs — *to deduct* and *to deduce*. *Induction* similarly is the noun for *to induct* and *to induce*.

To induct, first of all, means 'to install formally in office' — *She was inducted as mayor* — or 'to initiate, introduce to knowledge': *They inducted him into the mysteries of freemasonry.*

To deduct means 'to subtract': *The company deducts a small percentage of your salary for its pension scheme.*

To induce can mean 'to persuade, prevail upon' — *We finally induced her to give up smoking* — or 'to stimulate the occurrence of', especially to hasten childbirth artificially by the use of drugs. In physics, one can *induct* (and *induce*) an electric current or magnetic effect. *To induce* also means 'to reach a conclusion by generalising, to infer by means of induction' — though in this meaning, *to infer* is far more common than *to induce*.

To deduce, analogously, means 'to reach a conclusion by reasoning from general principles, to conclude by means of deduction'.

The difference between these two processes of reasoning, *induction* and *deduction*, is this: *induction* is reasoning from the particular to the general, drawing conclusions about all the members of a class of things by examining only a few of those members. *Deduction* moves in the other direction — it is reasoning from the general to the specific, drawing specific conclusions from more general premises.

For example, suppose that you studied a certain number of rosebushes and noticed that they all had thorns; you might then conclude, by *induction*, that 'All rosebushes have thorns'. This is the way that scientific laws are arrived at. From a number of observations, a generalisation or 'law' is drawn: the greater the number of observations, the more reliable the conclusion is likely to be.

Suppose on the other hand, that you believed, as a general statement or premise, that 'All rosebushes have thorns'. You might then conclude, by *deduction*, that the rosebush in the Prime Minister's garden has thorns — even though you have never inspected that rosebush. This would be a correct use of logic. But it would not necessarily be a true statement: if the premise itself is false, as in 'All apples are green', then a conclusion drawn from it, even if in keeping with the laws of logic, might also be false, as in 'The apple in Tom's lunch-box is green'. After all, the apple in Tom's lunch-box might in fact be red.

Note that *induction* and *deduction* can both refer to the process of reasoning and to the conclusions yielded. So 'The apple in Tom's lunch-box is green' might be, at one and the same time, a correct deduction (that is, a correct application of logic) and a false deduction (that is, an incorrect statement).

Note too that *deduction* is by far the more com-

mon term, and is often used in more general contexts to refer to any sort of inference or conclusion (including one arrived at by induction). Sherlock Holmes's *deductions* are sometimes really just *inductions* (or *inferences*).

Of course, *deduction* and *induction* have other senses corresponding to the meanings of their respective verbs: *a generous tax deduction, the induction of electricity, the induction of the mayor*, and so on.

Note the various other derivatives: *deducible, deductible, deductive; inducible, inductive, inducter, inductance, inducement.*

Take care, in working backwards from the nouns *induction* and *deduction*, to use the correct form of the verb: it is all too easy to say *deduct* when you mean *deduce* or *infer*:

✗ In this story, Poe's famous amateur French detective, the reclusive Auguste Dupin, solves a bizarre and brutal murder by deducting that the criminal is an escaped orangutan.

> – Hermione Lee,
> 'Book Four', Channel 4 TV

defective, deficient   These two words appear in similar contexts and are sometimes interchangeable, but they do mean different things. *Defective* means 'having a defect or defects'; *deficient* means 'having a deficiency or deficencies'. A *defect* is a fault; a *deficiency* is a lack. A new car may be *defective* if it has a faulty engine; and this defect may make it *deficient* in power or speed.

Deficient and *defective* thus overlap when a defect is felt to be a lack, or when a lack constitutes a fault. It would be quite legitimate to say both *Your technique is defective* (because it produces bad results) and *Your technique is deficient* (because it lacks something important).

Nevertheless, the words *defective* and *deficient* can rarely be contrasted so clearly. There are two reasons for this. First, *defective* is far more likely than *deficient* to be used of concrete, man-made objects: *My car is defective* is acceptable, but not ordinarily *? My car is deficient.*

Filmed on one set in a series of 10-minute takes (a seamless effect somewhat marred in a defective print) 'Rope' is a companion piece to that other virtuoso exercise in filmed theatre, the 3-D 'Dial M for Murder'.

> – Philip French, *The Observer*

Secondly, *deficient* is typically not used by itself — you usually have to specify where the deficiency lies: *technically deficient*; *deficient in technique*.

Note that *mental deficiency* is the term commonly used to refer to a condition of abnormally low intelligence, whereas *mental defective* is used to refer to a person suffering from this condition. (The term *mental defective* is now regarded as objectionable, however, and though still widely used, is to be discouraged.) When it comes to the adjective form, both *mentally defective* and *mentally deficient* are acceptable, *mentally deficient* rather more so.

Deficient is not the same as *insufficient*, which means 'not sufficient'. If the food supply is *deficient*, something is missing from it — say, an essential nutrient. If it is *insufficient*, there is not enough of it. So *insufficient* emphasises inadequate quantity; *deficient*, inadequate quality.

> At a time when the nation's manhood has proved uniquely deficient, and when even the lion on England's sweater (representing of course Ian Botham) looks tired, there is one solution to be found before our eyes.
> – Scyld Berry, *The Observer*

Note that *deficient* serves as the adjective for two distinct nouns — *deficit* (which means primarily 'a financial lack') and *deficiency*. However, *deficit* itself is sometimes used before a noun, and functions in much the same way as an adjective: *a deficit budget*; *deficit spending*.

Deficient and *defective* both go back to the same Latin verb *deficere*, 'to remove from, fail, desert, be wanting', from *de-*, 'away from' + *facere*, 'to do, set, make'.

defining and nondefining clauses See RESTRICTIVE AND NONRESTRICTIVE CLAUSES.

definite, definitive These adjectives both apply to what is explicitly set forth, and suggest in some way setting or having limits of completeness. (The Latin roots in each case are *de*, 'off' + *finis*, 'an end or boundary'.) But there is not much more overlap in meaning than this.

What is *definite* is precise, not ambiguous: *I want a definite decision one way or the other*. By contrast, *a definitive decision* is unalterably final, not provisional. *Definitive* suggests that complex and important issues have received authoritative attention. *A definitive literary work*, such as a biography, is one that is unlikely to be superseded:

> And I learnt how that master of lexicography James Murray, the first editor, organised the vast, infinitely daunting mass of material into the definitive history of the English language.
> – John Silverlight, *The Observer*

Definitive can also mean 'serving to define precisely'. It is correctly used in that sense in the following quotations:

> It was the wife of the Deputy Commissioner who was responsible for creating an image of Miss Crane which the ladies of Mayapore had now come to regard as definitive of her.
> – Paul Scott, *The Jewel in the Crown*

> For the re-opening, the museum has put together an international survey of recent paintings and sculpture, which is intended to be a definitive statement of where art is now at.
> – Michael Davie, *The Observer*

Definitive seems often to be misused: many speakers and writers tend to regard it merely as a grander word for *definite*:

> ✗ In the first of his new series (BBC-2), he asked Sir Clive Sinclair, the electronics warlock, if he felt that because a thing could be made, it should be made. The answer was a definitive no, and I sat forward for the follow-up.
> – Hugh Herbert, *The Guardian*

Definite and *definitely* are frequently used for almost meaningless emphasis: *? definitely harmful*; *? a definite mistake*. They may often be better omitted.

degrees of comparison See ADJECTIVES 2.

delusion, illusion These nouns are sometimes interchangeable, but there is an underlying difference between them. A *delusion* is a false belief; an *illusion* is a false appearance, or the false impression or idea produced by it.

Illusions are more easily eradicated: once the appearance is rectified, the false idea or impression tends to disappear. A delusion is more clinging: it is held despite appearances. A delusion is stronger in another way too: it tends to influence behaviour.

In the two quotations below, *delusion* is used correctly in the first, but dubiously in the second:

> This 'banana-skin' interpretation of current events is a dangerous delusion, detracting attention from the real weaknesses in Britain's economy, weaknesses that have

been sniffed out by the financial blood-hounds.
— John Eatwell, *The Listener*

? Ned stared from one to the other of them, and for a moment he had the delusion that their four eyes were controlled by one optic muscle.
— John le Carré,
The Little Drummer Girl

In the second extract here, *illusion* would have been more appropriate than *delusion*.

One other distinction, a difficult one: the vision or appearance is a delusion, the thing (which does not really exist) is the illusion: so, a mirage is a delusion, and the (non-existent) oasis is the illusion.

Certain idioms favour one term or the other: *suffering from delusions*; *labouring under an illusion*; *without illusion*; *delusions of grandeur*; *optical illusions*; *conjurors' illusions*.

Delusion has the corresponding verb *to delude* and the corresponding adjective *delusive* or sometimes *delusory*. Corresponding to *illusion*, the verb *to illude* is no longer current, and the adjective *illusive* is rarer than *illusory*.

Both sets of words go back to the Latin *ludere*, 'to play', from *ludus*, 'a game': *deludere* meant 'to play false, deceive'; *illudere*, 'to mock, jeer at'.

Take care to keep these terms quite distinct from *allusion, allusive*, and *elusive*. (See ALLUDE.)

denote See CONNOTE.

depend 1. The verb *to depend* is almost always followed by the preposition *on* or *upon* (understandably enough, considering its Latin roots, *de*, 'down' + *pendere*, 'to hang'):

Carey still depends on my advice.
That depends upon the weather.

After the phrase *it depends* (and sometimes *that depends*), the preposition tends to be left out when an indirect question follows:

? As for getting her approval, it all depends what kind of mood she's in at the time.

This omission of the *on* or *upon* is now very widespread, but many purists still object to the omission, and it is safest to retain or reinstate the preposition. In the following example, however, the omission of *on* seems unavoidable, unless the sentence were to be slightly restructured so as to read, for example, *It depends, dear, on which law you refer to*:

'Have you no respect at all for the law?'
'It depends, dear, to which law you refer. Like the ten commandments. I can't take very seriously the one about the ox and the ass.'
— Graham Greene, *Travels With My Aunt*

When used as a full sentence in itself, ? *It (all) depends* is still unsuited to formal contexts. In everyday conversation, however, it is very useful as a noncommittal reply to a question.

2. The related adjective and noun — *dependent* and *dependant* — are almost always strictly distinguished in British English by their spelling. The adjective is *dependent*: *still a very dependent child*; *Is he still dependent on his aunt for living expenses?*

The noun is *dependant*: *No, his aunt is now a dependant of his — she'd starve without his support*.

American English, while still able to make this distinction, favours *dependent* for the noun as well as the adjective (with *dependant* a secondary variant of both noun and adjective).

The Libyans also sent 137 dependents out of the country that day. In Tripoli, meanwhile, 30 British Embassy employees and dependents waited at the airport for permission to leave for home.
— *Newsweek* (U.S.)

The abstract noun from *dependent* is *dependence* in both British and American English (*dependance* is a secondary variant in American English): *reducing his dependence on his aunt*; *a dependence on painkillers*. And the noun referring to a subject territory is *dependency*, with *dependancy* as a secondary American variant.

deprecate, depreciate The distinction between these words is not widely observed today, but it is worth knowing. *To deprecate* something is to express disapproval of it, to protest or plead against it: *He deprecated the use of force*.

Knollys and Fisher deprecated all talk in the royal circle about compulsory military training, which they regarded as ridiculous.
— Philip Magnus, *Edward VII*

The Latin source *deprecari* meant 'to ward off by prayer', from *de-*, 'away' + *precari*, 'to pray'.

To depreciate something is to belittle it, to reduce its value: *He always depreciates my achievements*.

The Antiquarian Bookseller's Association did not at first admit the charges, later

depreciated Blackwell's one-man crusade, but finally yielded to these pressures, and by stiffening their rules made it much more difficult for the members to break the law.
– obituary notice, *The Times*

The idea of value is contained in the Latin roots, *de-*, 'down from, away' + *pretium*, 'a price'.

To depreciate is also used in financial contexts, when referring to a decrease in value. When used in this way, it tends now to be an intransitive verb (lacking a direct object): *This car has depreciated by 40 per cent in a single year.*

There is a slight overlap in meaning between the two words, and this has inevitably been reinforced by the similarity in their form. The shift has been mainly in one direction: *to deprecate* is increasingly used in place of *to depreciate* (rarely the other way round), and this development is widely, though not universally, accepted. It is not uncommon to hear *?* *He always deprecates my achievements*, though some careful speakers still avoid such uses. Similarly:

? Depending on his mood and the nature of the audience, Johnson told the story different ways. On some occasions he tended to deprecate his own role in the mission, insisting that he was not really the one who should have received the Silver Star.
– Doris Kearns (U.S.), *Lyndon Johnson and the American Dream*

The adjective *deprecatory* has approached *depreciatory*, and now commonly means 'discouraging compliments, dismissive':

'It must be quite a source of income.' Arthur made a deprecatory gesture. 'I should hardly go so far as to say that.'
– Christopher Isherwood, *Mr Norris Changes Trains*

Similarly, the adjective *self-deprecating* or *self-deprecatory*, meaning 'inclined to undervalue oneself and one's achievements; unduly modest', is now fully established as standard usage, even though it should strictly speaking be *self-depreciating* or *self-depreciatory*:

Yet Henry told others that story about himself, in a self-deprecating way, and you had to like him for it.
– William Safire (U.S.), *Before the Fall*

The noun *deprecation* has long had the extended sense of 'the disclaiming of credit or praise; modest and courteous behaviour':

'After you.'
'No, please.'
'I couldn't think of it.'
There was a good deal more polite deprecation and bowing before the two of them finally got through the doorway.
– Christopher Isherwood, *Mr Norris Changes Trains*

The noun *self-deprecation* is now widely accepted in the sense of 'humble estimation of one's own worth; modest self-disparagement':

So they went on confessing to faults and failings which — needless to say — they did not regard as faults and failings at all. All this self-deprecation meant only: how wonderful we must be if we can afford to admit so much against ourselves.
– George Mikes, *English Humour for Beginners*

In the following quotation, however, the writer has carefully opted for *self-depreciation*, more strictly correct, rather than *self-deprecation*, which is probably in wider use nowadays:

To her nephew Edward she described her work, with humorous self-depreciation, as 'that little bit (two inches wide) of ivory, in which I work with so fine a brush as produces little effect after much labour'.
– Lord David Cecil, *A Portrait of Jane Austen*

deprivation, privation *To deprive* is to deny someone something, either by keeping it from him or by taking it from him. So *deprivation* (sometimes *deprival*) contains the idea of loss, of lacking something you once had or which you would have had in normal circumstances: *the deprivation of his rights because of his crime.*

I bought a Mars Bar on the way to my first health farm. I don't even like Mars Bars very much, but I was convinced that three days of yogurt and yoga would be the end of me. I am not into deprivation.
– Beryl Downing, *The Times*

Deprivation comes from the verb *to deprive*. There is of course no verb ✗ *to prive*, but there is the noun *privation*. This means 'the lack of life's necessities or comforts, or the resulting condition', and so refers to serious basic need. It is more extreme than *poverty*. *Privation* can be used in a similar way to *deprivation* — *the privation of basic rights* — where the deprivation brings about a serious fundamental need.

The miners, despite the privations suffered by their families, have refused to comply with the Government's attempt to increase labour-market flexibility by closing their pits.
— John Eatwell, *The Listener*

Deprivation is now often used in a sense that has nothing to do with the removal of past or even automatic advantages. It is used loosely to refer to the lack of anything that a person thinks he ought to have. It has become a politically loaded vogue word, and as such should be used with caution. Consider, when using it, whether there is a genuine loss, or at least a lack of something otherwise expected. Similarly, do not use *privation* lightly; it should not be applied to anything less than serious necessity. The writer of the following passage might have picked up the earlier word *trimmed* and changed the poorly chosen *privations* to *trimmings*:

? Package prices can always be trimmed, of course, and travelling by coach has recently become a popular way of saving money. As a method of transport it suggests other privations, however, and may only help cut bills very slightly.
— Robin McKie, *The Observer*

The stress in *deprivation* falls on the first and third syllables and the word is pronounced /**dep**pri-**vaysh**'n/. *Privation* is pronounced /prī-**vaysh**'n/.

Both words go back to the Latin verb *privare*, 'to deprive', from *privus*, 'individual, private'.

derisive, derisory These two adjectives have long been interchangeable. But nowadays a clear distinction seems to be developing between the two words.

Derisive is becoming limited to the meaning 'expressing derision, laughing scornfully, mocking, contemptuous':

After the first rush of derisive publicity women's liberation has adopted a suspicious and uncooperative attitude to the press.
— Germaine Greer, *The Female Eunuch*

Derisory is retreating to the sense of 'deserving derision', especially by being 'laughably inadequate, ridiculously small': *considered the new pay offer derisory*.

Lewis, of course, came to the end of the line last year, when he was forced to fight the general election as an Independent Labour candidate, after being ousted by his constituency activists despite 33 years' service at

Westminster: he came fourth with a derisory 3000 votes.
— Dr Julian Lewis,
letter in *The Sunday Times*

Note the preferred pronunciations: *derisive*, /di-**rī**-siv/; *derisory*, /di-**rī**-sə-ri/ or /di-**rī**-zə-ri/; *derision*, /di-**rizh**'n/.

descriptive, prescriptive   See PRESCRIBE.

descry   See DECRY.

despite, in spite of   There used to be — perhaps still is — a preference among journalists for *in spite of* over *despite*. Both are shortened forms of the earlier *in despite of*.

Despite was apparently felt to be a slightly affected form of *in spite of*, rather in the way that *prior to* or *preparatory to* is sometimes used as an affected substitute for *before*, or *subsequent to* for *after*, or *in the vicinity of* for *near*.

This all seems rather unfair on *despite*, which might often, through its brevity, actually be preferable to *in spite of*.

There is an affected, cumbersome form worth mentioning, however — *in spite of the fact that* or *despite the fact that*, an attempt to convert a preposition into a conjunction:

People still complain in spite of the fact that improvements have been made.

There is nothing grammatically wrong with this sentence, but it would read more elegantly and simply if *even though* or *although* were used in place of *in spite of the fact that*.

Note that *in spite of* is three words: a common misspelling is × *inspite of*, probably through the analogy of *despite* or *instead of*.

despoil   To despoil does not mean 'to damage', in the way that *to spoil* does. You cannot say, for instance, × *Her suitcase was despoiled by being stored in a damp cellar*. To despoil means 'to deprive of possessions or contents by force, to plunder': *The village was despoiled by the invading soldiers*.

However, *despoil* is related to *spoil*. There is an archaic sense of *to spoil*, meaning 'to despoil'. And the noun *spoils*, as in *the spoils of war*, still refers to booty — the goods seized from a defeated opponent.

The nouns *despoliation* and *spoliation* refer to the act of plundering or pillaging. But the usual noun from *to spoil* in the sense 'to damage' is *spoilage*.

All these forms go back through Old French to the Latin noun *spolium*, 'the hide torn from an animal; booty'.

devil's advocate A *devil's advocate* is not a tempter (that is the devil himself) and not, strictly speaking, a person who tries to make bad things seem better than they are. He is the person who tries to make good things seem worse than they are — but purely for the sake of argument, not in a genuinely cynical way. In an attempt to liven up a dull conversation, for instance, you might play devil's advocate and pretend, in a contrary and provocative way, to dislike a person or film that everyone else admires. But the term is used loosely today, and more or less acceptably, to refer to someone who argues in the other direction, pretending to admire what other people dislike.

These uses are an extension of the technical sense, still current in the Roman Catholic Church. The devil's advocate here is a church official appointed to argue the case against the proposed canonisation or beatification of a candidate for sainthood. His formal title is *Promoter of the Faith*, a rather more complimentary title than *devil's advocate*.

diagonal See SOLIDUS.

dialectal, dialectical *Dialectal* is the adjective from the noun *dialect*; *dialectical* (occasionally *dialectic*) is the adjective from *dialectic* or *dialectics*. Both sets of words go back to the Greek verb *dialegesthai*, 'to converse or discuss' (from *dia-*, 'with one another' + *legein*, 'to tell'). *Dialectal* relates more to the sense 'to converse'; *dialectical* to the sense 'to discuss'.

A *dialect* is any variety of a language that differs from other varieties in accent, and to a lesser extent in vocabulary and grammar, according to the region, social group, or setting in which it is used. *Dialectal*, then, means 'characteristic of such a variety of language'.

Dialectic is a philosophical term referring to the art of discovering truth by reconciling opposites. The dialectic of the ancient Greek philosopher Socrates was a process of question and answer that exposed the contradictions in his opponent's position, and found the truth by overcoming these contradictions. The German philosopher G.W. F. Hegel (1770–1831) proposed that the flaws in any proposition (or *thesis*) implied an opposite (or *antithesis*), and that the interaction between these two (their *synthesis*) was the way to approach reality (which to Hegel was Mind or

Thought). Marxist dialectic, known as *dialectical materialism*, adapts Hegel's views: it regards the changing oppositions of the dialectic as material, not mental; history and fact, not just mind and thought, are the realities it claims to discover.

Sometimes *dialectic* is used more loosely to refer to the contradiction itself between the conflicting forces — this contradiction being the factor that determines their continued interaction. *Dialectic* might be used still more loosely to mean the relationship between any two opposing things. The Marxist dialectic is sometimes loosely understood simply as the opposition between classes.

Dialectics, with an -*s*, is the method of argument that weighs and tries to resolve contradictions. Here it is used with a singular verb (see -ICS). It can be used with a singular or plural verb when it refers to the Marxist doctrine of change through the conflict of opposing forces, and also when it refers to logic, especially logic as used to expose invalid reasoning.

Both *dialectics* and *dialectic* are in danger of becoming vogue words, used in an apparently grandiose but really slovenly way as synonyms of *reasons*, *basis*, *arguments*, *discussions*, and so on: ?? *I don't want to get into a dialectic about it*; ?? *What are the dialectics of your objection?*

Dialectical is the adjective from both *dialectic* and *dialectics*. Its meaning is clearly very different from that of *dialectal*. Take care not to confuse the two words by adding or omitting a syllable incorrectly.

dialects Anyone who has lived in Britain for any length of time will be able to distinguish two main pronunciations of the word *last*. The short *a* sound, /last/, is used by people from the northern half of Britain, in contrast to the long *a* of southern England: /laast/. A speaker's choice of pronunciation here is an initial pointer to his dialect — the kind of English he uses.

The dialects of a language are the distinct varieties of that language, marked off from each other by many differences in pronunciation, vocabulary, or grammar. Everybody is familiar with the different English accents, and to some extent the different grammar and vocabulary, of people from another country, or another part of the country, or another sphere of society.

Dialects are usually divided into regional and social dialects. Social dialects are based chiefly on status (class, occupation, and income), age, sex, ethnic origin, and social setting. A London lawyer will speak an identifiably different form of English from a London market trader, or perhaps even from his own children. The market trader will perhaps speak differently from his wife, and also from a fellow market trader of African or Indian birth, and will address his neighbours differently from the way he addresses his bank manager. He will also speak quite differently from a market trader in Edinburgh, or New York, or Canberra — but this marks a difference of regional rather than social dialect.

Regional dialects are based on geography. Linguistic atlases are compiled to show the range of various regional features. The boundary between any two features — say the pronunciation of *either* as /ee-thər/ or as /ī-thər/ — is called an 'isogloss'. Naturally, these regional features vary in their distribution, and it is not always easy to draw a line between two dialects: they might share many peculiarities, even though differing considerably in other respects. Nevertheless, the isoglosses do reveal some patterns, and in this way dialects are identified and defined.

The basis for geographical dialects is usually 'linguistic drift' — the tendency for speech habits to change with time. If two groups, speaking the same language, are cut off from each other (for geographical or political reasons, usually), their forms of the language will tend to drift apart. The less the contact between the two groups, and the longer the separation, the greater the divergence.

Note that geographical dialects are not always of the same rank. A 'Geordie dialect' might be identified within a wider-ranging northeast England dialect, within a northern England dialect, within a northern British dialect: it all depends on where you draw the line.

Dialects imply some 'norm', and are examined in relation to a 'standard' form of the language — the dominant form, used in educated speech, official and literary texts, and dictionaries. But a standard variety is in a sense just another dialect, and has no absolute claim to being more 'correct' than a regional variation.

Just as it is not always easy to draw a line between any two neighbouring dialects, so it is not always easy to decide when a dialect becomes a distinct language. The usual criterion is mutual intelligibility: if speakers of two varieties can no longer understand each other properly, they might be regarded as speaking different languages. But this test is not always accurate: a New Yorker might find it far more difficult to communicate with a Glaswegian, both reputedly speaking a single language, than a Spaniard would with a Portuguese, speaking different languages. A better test, in advanced societies, is the existence of a standard, written variety, often based on nationalism.

With political and cultural changes, a dialect might become a language, or vice versa. Afrikaans, for instance, was once considered a dialect of Dutch, achieving recognition as a language in its own right only in 1875 (and becoming an official language of South Africa only in 1925). Conversely, in 1973 the Belgian government renamed its Ministry of Flemish Culture the Ministry of Dutch Culture, effectively reclassifying the Flemish 'language' as a variety or dialect of Dutch.

Dialects tend to erode when people move from one area to another, and when communications are increased between various areas, as by a railway line or a national broadcasting network. And yet the surprising thing is how little they do erode. Regional speakers might be more proficient in standard English now than in times past, but they are not necessarily less proficient in their local or regional dialect. Within the family and among close friends, particularly away from big towns, regional dialects still flourish. Perhaps regional pride has something to do with it.

The dialects of Britain have a long history. Even in Anglo-Saxon times, northern English was markedly different from that of the Midlands or the southwest. This differentiation was due to the differing speech habits of the original Anglo-Saxon settlers, later reinforced by the settlement patterns of the Danish and Viking conquerors, and by their differing dialects in turn.

In Middle English too, regional dialects were strongly marked — Chaucer's use of English is strikingly different from that of his great provincial contemporary Langland, for instance. It was only in the 16th and 17th centuries, well after Chaucer's time, that the idea of a 'standard' English really began to develop: the growing social importance of the London court, and the scholarly influence of the universities of Oxford and Cambridge, exerted a combined pressure, and the dialect of London and the southeast Midlands became the 'prestige' variety — the standard language.

Not that this variety remained uninfluenced by regionalisms. Provincial pronunciations were accepted from time to time. Even after standard spelling had been established, a regional pronunciation might be adopted that went against the drift of the word's spelling: hence, in part, our legacy today of such discrepancies as *laughter* and *daughter*, which did once rhyme as their spelling suggests, but today have very different pronunciations in standard English.

The maps here provide guides to a few of the thousands of dialectal differences in Britain. The

BOUNDARIES OF DIALECT TERMS

CHILDREN

bairns
children

weans
bairns

weans

bairns

childer

bairns
childer

children

In Middle English, the plural of *child* was *childer,* still heard in parts of northwest England. (The standard form *children,* from *childer + -en,* is in fact a double plural.) Further north, *bairns* and *weans* (from *wee anes,* 'small ones') persist.

HAND

hond

hond

'ond

hand

For 700 years, the West Midland dialect has used /o/ for /a/ before *n, m,* or *ng.* There is a similar, though more erratic, tendency in Scotland: whereas *hond* for *hand* is common, *mon* for *man* is comparatively rare.

I AM

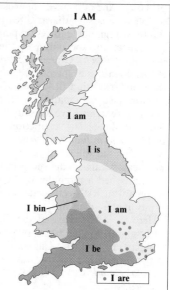

I am

I is

I bin

I am

I be

I are

The standard forms of the verb *to be* — *I am, we are,* and so on — are still sometimes disregarded in both British and American speech, and both in social dialects (*We is ready*) and in regional dialects (*I be ready*).

TO BREW (TEA)

mask

brew

mash
also
brew

brew
exclusively

wet

soak

To *brew* is used in all regions, but there is often another form available. In addition to those shown on the map, there are many that have no clear pattern of regional distribution: *to damp, to draw, to scald,* and *to steep.*

INITIAL H

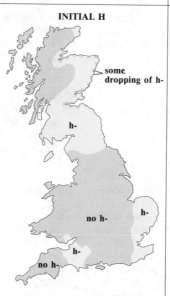

some
dropping of h-

h-

no h-

h-

h-

no h-

In social dialects, 'dropping your *h*'s' is considered nonstandard or undesirable. In regional dialects, speakers are not inhibited by any sense of stigma. The map is based on the use or non-use of *h* in the words *hammer, hair,* and *head.*

SHE

In Shetlands:
sher *and* **shur**

she

shay

oo

shoo

her

she

her

her

her

she

Many regional dialects still resist the standard use of *she* and *her.* In some, a variant form of *she* survives — *shay* or *shoo,* for example. In others, *her* is used as both subject and object: *Her got lost, but I found her.*

isoglosses are somewhat simplified, for the sake of clarity. And of course, not everyone within any dialect area uses the dialectal feature all the time. But these regional features do persist — regional pronunciation especially (see the maps headed *hand* and *initial h*). Grammatical peculiarities too, at least in informal speech, seem to have survived the standardisation processes of education and fashion (see the maps *I am* and *she*), and vocabulary items have as well, though these are most in danger of extinction (see the maps *children* and *to brew tea*). When the British Prime Minister used the word *frit* in parliament — a northeast Midlands dialect term for 'frightened' — she issued a reminder of how effective and colourful such dialect words can be. It would be a pity if they died out.

Here are a few more of the dialectal features of England, to give some idea of their flavour.

In parts of northeast England, the local people pronounce *among* as though it were *amang*, *walk* as *waak*, *spade* as *speed*, *take* as *teck*, and *cold* as *card*.

In the West Country of England they 'burr' their *r*'s, and pronounce *week* as *wick* and *deaf* as *diff*; *daughter* and *a loaf* are widely pronounced as *darter* and *aloof*, and *farmer* and *cider* as *varmer* and *zoider*.

As for grammar, people in some parts of the country say *we'm* instead of *we are*, *they han* for *they have*, *she do* for *she does*, *housen* for *houses*, *we* for *us*, *t'* for *the*, *hisn* and *theirn* for *his* and *theirs*, and so on.

And in vocabulary, there are many colourful regional terms: according to which part of the country you are in, you might hear a *newt* referred to as an *ask*, *asker*, *askert*, *askel*, *esk*, *esp*, *eff*, *eft*, *evet*, *ebbet*, or *swift*.

A *cowshed* or *stable* might be a *cow house*, a *cow hovel*, a *cow lodge*, a *cow stall*, a *beast house*, a *byre*, a *mistal*, a *shippon*, or a *skeeling*.

Children's truce words — the words children shout to gain a respite during games or fights — come in an extraordinary variety of forms. *Pax* is in wide use in private schools, but is not really a regional form. The true dialectal forms include *barley*, *bars*, *blobs*, *boosey*, *bruises*, *creams*, *crease*, *cree*, *crogs*, *croggies*, *crosses*, *cruce*, *exes*, *fainites*, *keppies*, *keys*, *kings*, *nicks*, *peril*, *scores*, *scrames*, *scrases*, *screams*, *screase*, *screens*, *scribs*, *scrogs*, *scruces*, *skinch*, *snakes*, and *trucie*.

And there is a wide range of dialectal terms, usually derisive, applied to left-handers: *corrie-flug*, *cuddy-wifted*, *kervag*, *kittaghy*, *left-couch*, *marlborough*. Most of these words are combinations of two elements: the second element might be *-handed*, *-fisted*, *-pawed*, or in Scotland, *-klookit*. The first element might be the simple *left-*, or any of the following: in Scotland, *corrie-*, *kerrie-*, *kippie-*, *pallie-*, *skerrie-*; in England, *back-*, *bang-*, *bollock-*, *carr-*, *click-*, *clicky-*, *cork-*, *corky-*, *cowie-*, *cuddy-*, *cue-*, *cutchy-*, *dollock-*, *galley-*, *gallock-*, *gammy-*, *gawky-*, *kack-*, *keck-*, *kecky-*, *keg-*, *keggy-*, *kaggy-*, *scrammy-*, *scrummy-*, *scutchy-*, *skiffy-*, *squiver-*, *watty-*.

These tell-tale variations in pronunciation, grammar, or vocabulary used to carry a social stigma. Some regions, transformed by the Industrial Revolution, were thought of as factory cultures and their dialects were branded as proletarian; other dialects, from traditionally rural areas, were branded as peasantlike. Even as late as the 1930s, children in remote grammar schools were pressed by parents and teachers to assume an artificial, educated standard English alien to their background.

Nowadays regional dialects, or at least accents, are widely accepted and even welcomed. This is partly due to the non-exclusive tolerance of the modern age, and partly too to greater exposure — through the increased movement of people, notably university students, from one part of the country to another, and through broadcasting. Phone-in programmes, chat-shows, quizzes, and so on present to a large audience, day after day, the language of successful, influential, and articulate men and women who still retain their dialectal characteristics, and who are no less intelligible and intelligent for having withstood the levelling influences of education or ambition.

dichotomy This noun has escaped from its special philosophical, botanical, and astronomical contexts into general usage, and become a vogue word there. The underlying idea in each case is a division into two parts: the Greek roots are *dikha*, 'in two' + *temnein*, 'to cut'.

In general contexts, the word is now widely used in the place of the traditional terms *schism*, *difference of opinion*, *split*, *division*: *A new dichotomy is emerging between the left and right within the Conservative Party*. And it is also used as a synonym for *discrepancy*, in the sense of 'a lack of agreement or correspondence': *a dichotomy between their election promises and their performance*.

Both of these uses are fair enough on occasion, though you might reasonably suspect the user of trying too hard to impress his listener or reader. The fault lies more in overuse. If you find you are drawn to the word, do at least try to use it sparingly.

different 1. Three linking words are commonly used after *different*: *from*, *to*, and *than*. *Different from* is the commonest and best form:

My outline is different from his in two crucial respects.

Different from is the only form accepted by the purists. Since we have to say *My outline differs from his* (not ×*differs to* or ×*differs than*), they argue, we should say *is different from*, not *is different to* or *is different than*. However, there is no rule requiring the same preposition for different parts of speech: we say *accords with* but *according to,* for example.

A more cogent argument in favour of *different from* is this: that the preposition *from* suggests divergence or separation, and therefore seems more appropriate than *to,* which suggests convergence or similarity. This is not to disqualify *different to,* however, which is in wide use in British English (though not in American English). The following extract from a children's book wittily illustrates the two opposing attitudes:

'We hope you won't find it too much of a comedown, being here,' Joanne said. 'We're probably rather different to what you're used to'.
'Different *from,*' Helen said automatically. There was a startled silence.
'Well, listen to that!' Joanne said at last. 'We'll have to remember to talk properly, girls, won't we? Different *from,*' she trilled in imitation. 'You must excuse me if I forget and drop an 'h' now and then. ... I was very badly brought up, wasn't I, Lorraine? ...'
– Tim Kennemore,
The Middle of the Sandwich

It is in fact very convenient to have the variant form *different to* available. If there is already a *from* or two in the sentence, the choice of *different to* instead of *different from* would avoid a monotonous surplus of *from*'s:

? The hotel that the family from Exeter was ejected from is different from the hotel that we were ejected from.

The substitution of *different to* here would surely improve a very awkward sentence. (On the question of the preposition at the end of the sentence, see PREPOSITION ENDING A SENTENCE.)
Note also, for what it is worth, that *indifferent* and *similar* are followed by *to*; and that *different to* at least fits their pattern.
Here is another example of the use of *different to*. It seems reasonably natural and idiomatic:

Women have emerged as the major new force of the '80s in American politics. In 1980, for the first time, they were the majority of voters and they cast their ballots in a significantly different way to that of their male counterparts, creating what has been termed the gender gap.
– Carol Thatcher, *Daily Telegraph*

? *Different than* is another matter: it is in wide use in American English, though not always regarded as acceptable there. In British English it is considered nonstandard, especially in simple constructions where a straightforward pronoun, noun, or noun phrase follows, rather than a clause:

× My outline is different than his.

Nevertheless, a case can be made for *different than*. *Than* is properly used after the comparative form of an adjective or adverb: *longer than*. The one exception is *other,* which is not a comparative yet which can legitimately be followed by *than*: *any day other than Sunday*. If *other* is allowed *than,* perhaps its near-synonym *different* should also be allowed to take *than*. Furthermore, *different* has one feature in common with comparative forms such as *longer*: it can be negated by a preceding *no,* as well as a preceding *not*: *not longer than 10 minutes*; *no longer than 10 minutes* — similarly *not different from his*; *no different from his*. Virtually no adjectives other than *different* can be negated by *no* in the way that comparatives can: *not long to go* but not ×*no long to go*. Since *different* shares this one property with comparative adjectives, perhaps it should be allowed to share another — the right to be followed by *than*.
Different than is particularly useful when it introduces a clause rather than a phrase or word: since *than* can be a conjunction as well as a preposition, it can be followed by a clause (full or 'verbless'), and this often makes the construction lighter and less awkward. Compare the following two sentences, the first with *different than,* the second with *different from*:

Her personality is very different than (it used to be) before she became addicted to tranquillisers.
Her personality is very different from the way it used to be before she became addicted to tranquillisers.

The lighter touch of *than* before clauses is even more apparent when *different* is separated from *than* or *from* either by a noun (*a different hotel from yours*) or by the *-ly* suffix of the adverb form (*works differently from mine*):

> We're staying in a different hotel than (we did) on our last visit.
> We're staying in a different hotel from the one we stayed in on our last visit.
> She sang that aria differently than before.
> She sang that aria differently from the way in which she sang it before.

Here are two quotations, by extremely careful writers, in which *than* is perhaps far enough away from *different* to be considered appropriate:

> ? You will say I am being unfair; Scott is a writer of a different calibre than M.M. Kaye. What's more, very few of the British characters come at all well out of the Quartet.
>   – Salman Rushdie, *The Observer*

Careful users of it pick their words judiciously to suit the occasion and register in which they are performing. You use a different sort of English in a *Times* leader than in a conversation in a pub.
>   – Philip Howard, *Vogue*

● *Recommendation Different from* is always correct, but not always very elegant.

Different to is a useful British variant to keep in reserve; there is no need to avoid it unless purist objections threaten to divert the flow of what you are saying or writing.

Different than should be avoided in simple comparisons when a mere noun, pronoun, or short noun phrase follows. When followed by a full or disguised clause, however, *different than* allows a far more streamlined and less wordy text than *different from* does. Even then, however, it remains widely discouraged in British English, and is still not regarded as acceptable formal usage.

2. *Different* is often inserted quite unnecessarily into a sentence:

> ? During their tour of New Zealand, they stayed in no fewer than 26 different hotels.
> ? A three-dial combination-lock allows a total of 1000 different combinations.
> ? There are well over 50 different brands of tinned tomato soup marketed in the States.

In each of these, the word *different* is strictly speaking redundant, and could be left out altogether without damaging the literal sense of the sentence. It does, however, have a useful intensifying effect, suggesting that the number or amount is unexpectedly large. It would be a pity to lose this function, at least in informal English. In very formal usage, however, the redundant *different* is best avoided. Try *separate* or *distinct* instead: critics have not yet started complaining about them.

3. Also to be avoided, in formal English, is the use of *different* in place of *various* or *unusual*, as in:

> ? Different experts have attempted to decipher it — all have failed. (Use *various*.)
> ? This is a new and different detergent! (Use *unusual*.)

4. The use of *different* as an adverb is unacceptable in standard English:

> × We do things different here.

Formal usage requires *differently*.

differential *Differential* has several senses, both technical and nontechnical, as both noun and adjective. Its commonest use is in reference to wages or salaries: *differential rates of pay*; *The typesetters want the differential restored*. The *differential* here is not simply a difference: it is a gap based on related differences — differences in skill, working-hours, or the like.

A *differential* is, strictly speaking, a factor that makes or constitutes or depends on a difference, not the difference itself. You should not speak of ?? *a differential of £2 per hour in the rate of pay*. What you mean is simply *a difference of £2 per hour*. And *differential* should not be used as a grandiose variant of *difference* in other contexts: × *The differential is that he has played the part before and I have not*.

difficulty In informal English, *difficulty* is often followed directly by the *-ing* form of a verb:

> ? There won't be any difficulty buying tickets, will there?

Formal usage requires the insertion of the preposition *in*:

> There will be no difficulty in buying tickets, will there?

dilemma A *dilemma* is more than a mere 'difficulty' or 'problem': strictly, it is a predicament or situation offering two equally balanced, and usually equally unattractive, solutions or courses of action. The idiom that comes to mind is *caught between the devil and the deep blue sea* — neither option is satisfactory:

Shreeve was in the same old dilemma — if he refused to go on holiday with his in-laws, his wife would make his life a misery; if he agreed to go on holiday with his in-laws, they would make his life a misery.

He was faced with a difficult dilemma: feed them less and save coins, or continue to feed them so that they would look better at the auction in Cuba.
– James A. Michener (U.S.), *Chesapeake*

The term comes from logic, where it refers to an argument that forces an opponent to make one or other of two responses, both of which weaken his own case. He is then 'impaled on the horns of a dilemma'. Indeed, the roots of the word *dilemma* reinforce this idea of two choices: the word goes back through Latin and Greek to the Greek roots *di-*, 'two, twice' + *lemma,* 'a proposition, argument, or proof' (from *lambanein,* 'to grasp or take').

Sometimes there are more than two choices: *dilemma* remains acceptable in this extended use, so long as all the choices are still undesirable ones.

Avoid the term if you are referring to a choice between attractive or neutral alternatives:

?? She's in such a dilemma — she's been offered two jobs, and can't decide between them.

?? Food is not optional. It is central, not just to creatures (obviously), but to cultures; and whether the reasonable man should or should not bother if they've put Marmite in his *boeuf bourguignon* is a far harder dilemma to resolve than whether he should wince if the singer doesn't hit her high C.
– Katharine Whitehorn,
The Observer

Above all, avoid the term if simply referring to a problem, without any indication of a choice:

× Here's my dilemma — how to get to the airport for the six a.m. flight when the first bus gets there at 20 past six.

Both common pronunciations are acceptable: /di-**lemm**ə, dī-**lemm**ə/. But purists prefer the first: /di-**lemm**ə/.

The standard plural is *dilemmas*; the Greek form *dilemmata* would be very unlikely even in works of logic.

direct, directly **1.** *Direct* is an adverb as well as an adjective. So you can say *This train goes direct to Swansea* as well as *This is the direct train to Swansea.*

It is incorrect to substitute *directly* for *direct* to mean 'uninterruptedly, straight' or 'without intermediary': × *This train goes directly to Swansea*; × *dial directly*. The adverb *directly* means 'immediately', 'exactly', and so on: *This train leaves directly for Swansea*; *directly in front of the station*.

2. The use of *directly* as a conjunction, chiefly in British English, is strictly colloquial, and the word should not be used in this way in formal contexts: ? *I rushed round directly I heard the news*. Either insert a *when* after the *directly* or use the standard conjunction *as soon as*. Alternatively, the construction can be changed to allow *directly* to function as part of an adverbial phrase: *I rushed round directly on hearing the news.*

direct speech See INVERTED WORD ORDER **8**; QUOTATION MARKS.

disc, disk *Disc* is the usual British spelling: *disc brakes*, *slipped disc*. *Disk* is the usual American spelling, but is also used in British English in connection with computers: *disk pack*, *floppy disk*. Compare PROGRAMME.

discomfit Although *discomfit* has a similar pronunciation to *discomfort*, and overlaps with it in meaning to a certain extent, it should not be regarded as a synonym of the more common verb. *To discomfit* comes from an old French word meaning 'to defeat, rout', and formerly had this sense in English:

Kings with their armies did flee and were discomfited: and they of the household divided the spoils.
– Psalm 68, *Book of Common Prayer*

In modern usage, it means either 'to thwart the plans of, foil' or 'to perplex, disconcert, or embarrass':

Otto, in his narrative, dwelt on the kick with special pride and pleasure ... And Otto began to laugh now, as he said it. He laughed heartily, without the least malice or savagery. He bore the discomfited Schmidt no grudge.
– Christopher Isherwood,
Mr Norris Changes Trains

Note that *discomfit*, unlike *discomfort*, cannot serve as a noun. The related noun is *discomfiture*.

Ted came down from the dais blushing furiously, and once back in his place he turned a frowning sulky face to the congratulatory and sly witticisms of his friends. I minded his discomfiture and yet I enjoyed it too.

– L.P. Hartley, *The Go-Between*

The British, to a lesser but still significant degree, have for some time dictated what a good ice-dance consists of, to the equal and opposite discomfiture of the Russians.

– Russell Davies, *The Observer*

discreet, discrete Take care not to confuse the spelling of these two adjectives.

Discreet means 'showing prudence, judiciously reserved', especially in the matter of keeping secrets — *a discreet silence* — and also 'modest, unobtrusive': *discreet lettering on his nameplate*; *kept at a discreet distance.*

Hoxha, however, ruthless enough to make Stalin look soft, is fading fast. The French, whose medical establishment possesses a doctor well acquainted with Hoxha's health, are typically most discreet about their medical intelligence. Few people, however, give him more than two years.

– Charles Meynell, *The Times*

Discrete means 'separate, distinct', and was a learned term from logic, the opposite of *concrete* when *concrete* means 'taken together, indivisible'. So: *several discrete sounds*; *developing in discrete stages.*

Of course long ago the Indians had told us that the notion of the discrete and separate ego was also an illusion — perhaps a dangerous one. Under the probings of Freud and Co. it had all but disintegrated already!

– Lawrence Durrell, *The Fiction Magazine*

Both words come from Latin *discernere,* 'to discern'. The word *discerning* still encapsulates a connection between 'showing good judgment' and 'picking out, telling apart'. So does the word *discriminating*. But *discreet* and *discrete* cannot stand in for each other; they are *discrete* words with distinct meanings, and should not be confused.

The writer of the following extract — admittedly not a native English speaker — has made the common mistake of spelling the *-eet* form as *-ete*. Or perhaps it was the typesetter.

So, I don't fit very well into the identikit picture of an exiled East European 'dissident'. I can't be used for the cold war crusade of the present British government, nor can I be popular among overtly or discretely pro-

Soviet left-wingers. Neutral institutions, like the BBC Czech Service, won't employ me: I am too political, too outspoken.

– Zdena Tomin, *The Listener*

The words used to be distinguished in pronunciation as well as in spelling: *discrete,* like *concrete,* used to be stressed on the first syllable, and it is still acceptable to stress it in this way. But it is more commonly stressed on the second syllable today, and is thus indistinguishable, when spoken, from *discreet.*

discriminating, discriminatory, indiscriminate, undiscriminating The verb *to discriminate* comes from the Latin *discriminare,* 'to divide or distinguish' from *discrimen,* 'a distinction'. Its primary meaning is now 'to distinguish, differentiate', but it has also taken on the sense 'to be unfairly selective, to act on the basis of prejudice'. This double sense can obviously lead to confusion when it comes to using the various adjectival forms.

The adjective that refers to prejudice is *discriminatory,* not *discriminating. Discriminatory* is unfavourable in tone; it means 'unjust, especially in a racist or sexist way'. *Discriminating* (or simply *discriminate*) has a quite different, positive meaning; it means 'discerning, tasteful, wisely selective'.

Accordingly, the adjectives meaning 'acting without prejudice' are *nondiscriminatory* or *undiscriminatory. Undiscriminating* means 'lacking in taste and discernment': *an undiscriminating drinker of wine.*

Indiscriminate approaches *undiscriminating* in sense, but usually has the more specific meaning of 'random, general, unrestrained, unselective': *the indiscriminate denunciation of government policies; the indiscriminate bombing of civilian targets.*

Note that in the verb *to discriminate,* as in the participle *discriminating,* the stress is on the second syllable and the *a* is pronounced /ay/: /dis-**krim**mi-nayt/. *Discriminate* as an adjective loses that /ay/ sound; it is pronounced /dis-**krim**mi-nət/. *Discriminatory* is pronounced either /dis-**krim**mi-**nay**təri/, with a stress on both the second and fourth syllables, or /dis-**krim**mi-nətri/, with the stress only on the second.

Finally, the rare adjective *discriminative,* /dis-**krim**mi-nətiv/: this covers several of the meanings of *discriminating* and even *discriminatory.* It is unlikely to be used of people, however. It tends to mean 'drawing distinctions' or 'distinguishing': *Providence is discriminative; the* *extraordinary discriminative powers of this new ultraviolet camera.*

disingenuous See INGENIOUS.

disinterested The adjective *disinterested* is traditionally distinguished from *uninterested*, and means primarily 'impartial, not swayed by or concerned with personal considerations'. Whereas *uninterested* suggests a lack of all interest, *disinterested* suggests a lack only of self-interest. The distinction is encapsulated in an old joke: the *disinterested* judge listens in an unbiased way to the evidence of both sides; the *uninterested* judge falls asleep while the trial is in progress.

Disinterested can be used with reference both to people and to actions or states of mind.

Disinterested intellectual curiosity is the lifeblood of real civilisation.
– G.M. Trevelyan, *English Social History*

They would get some competent and disinterested person to hear him play, and if that person said he showed promise of becoming a first-rate pianist no further obstacle would be placed in his way.
– W. Somerset Maugham, 'The Alien Corn'

He keeps a soul's watch upon the world, as passionate as ever and yet disinterested now, with no stake in the outcome.
– Martin Amis, *The Observer*

Uninterested can occasionally be used to refer to states of mind — *schoolboys slumped in an uninterested stupor* — but is usually applied to people or groups.

For a long time now our society has been thoroughly uninterested in the message of the artist.
– Henry Miller (U.S.), *The Time of the Assassins*

She became worried about the appearance of the place, about her cooking, and about her anomalous position in the household. But Morris turned out to be completely uninterested in all three.
– Michael Frayn, *Towards the End of the Morning*

Increasingly since the 1920s, however, the useful distinction between *disinterested* and *uninterested* has been under threat; *disinterested* has more and more been used in the sense of 'uninterested, indifferent, bored':

?? Maston was waiting for him to speak, but he was tired and suddenly utterly disinterested. Without a glance at Maston he got up and walked out.
– John le Carré, *Call for the Dead*

?? Mrs Reilly stared at her huffing son. She was disgusted and tired, disinterested in anything that Ignatius might have to say.
– John Kennedy Toole (U.S.), *A Confederacy of Dunces*

Many careful speakers and writers regard this modern 'misuse' of *disinterested* as a sure sign of philistinism in the user, and insist — out of concern for the sharpness and variety of the English vocabulary — on preserving the distinction between *disinterested* and *uninterested*.

Ironically, *disinterested* originally meant 'uninterested'. It is in fact the older form, dating back to Shakespeare's lifetime. And *uninterested,* to make matters worse, was once used to mean 'impartial or disinterested'. This is hardly an argument in favour of abandoning the current distinction between the two words, of course. The return of *disinterested* in its original sense was not a deliberate revival; it was originally just an ignorant reinterpretation.

The reasons for this modern misuse of *disinterested* are interesting to speculate on. For a start, *uninterested* is not a very common word, particularly when it follows the noun in question. *He was not interested in my theories* is a far more likely way of expressing this idea than *He was uninterested in my theories.* The nouns *uninterest* and *uninterestedness* are even rarer than *uninterested* (though *uninteresting* is very common). *Disinterested* is probably a much more familiar word, therefore, and when speakers or writers are reaching for the adjective that means the opposite of *interested,* they are likely to grab unthinkingly at *disinterested.*

The noun *disinterest* might well reinforce this tendency, since it is probably used far more often to mean 'uninterest, lack of interest, indifference' than to mean 'impartiality, lack of self-interest'. Compare the following two quotations:

? For Miss Crane she seemed to have no feelings whatsoever; a disinterest that might have been due to her discovery by direct questioning at the first dinner they attended together that Miss Crane had no degree, in fact no qualifications to teach other than the rough and ready training she had received years ago in Lahore.
– Paul Scott, *The Jewel in the Crown*

All he got from the organised Left at the time was either uninterest — Europe was not seen as 'an issue' — or scorn.
— 'Islander', *The New Statesman*

The purist objection to the 'misuse' of *disinterest* is, for some reason, nothing like as strong as the objection to the misuse of *disinterested*. Perhaps *disinterest* is rather easier to say than *uninterest,* and has for that reason virtually come to replace it. In view of the ambiguity of *disinterest,* the noun that should be used to convey the proper sense of *disinterested* is *disinterestedness.*

disk See DISC.

disorient, disorientate See ORIENT.

dispassionate, impassive, impassioned *Dispassionate* means 'without passion; calm': *dispassionate judgment*. (*Impassionate* is an archaic synonym of *dispassionate*.) *Impassive* means 'apathetic' or, particularly, 'revealing no emotion': *his impassive countenance.*

Impassive is quite different from *impassioned*, which like *passionate* means 'full of passion; ardent':

> Wolf had fetched Elke on Sunday afternoon in his open Volkswagen car ... while his wife, an impassioned grower of green vegetables, continued her work in the rear garden.
>
> — John le Carré,
> *The Little Drummer Girl*

dispersal, dispersion Both these nouns refer to the act of dispersing or spreading, or the state of being dispersed, but there is a slight difference of emphasis. In ordinary use, *dispersal* is chiefly the process of scattering: *the dispersal of a crowd by the troops*; *dispersion* is chiefly the resulting situation: *the widespread dispersion of the rioters throughout the town.*

Dispersion, not *dispersal*, is also used in various technical senses in optics, statistics, and chemistry. There it may mean either the process or the result.

dissatisfied, unsatisfied *Dissatisfied* means 'discontented; particularly, disappointed at the lack of something'. *Unsatisfied* is simply the opposite of *satisfied*, and thus has a wider range of meaning: we might speak, for instance, of an *unsatisfied demand for studio flats*, or *an unsatisfied obligation*, or *an unsatisfied creditor* or *an unsatisfied* (unconvinced) *investigating officer*. An *unsatisfied* person has generally not had enough of something, but may not feel actively *dissatisfied* about it.

dissemble Take care not to use *to dissemble* to mean 'to dis-assemble', on the model of *to dissociate*, which means 'to dis-associate'. *To dissemble* means either 'to feign' or 'to disguise', in each case by adopting a false appearance: *He dissembled laughter in order to hide his fear* (feigned); *He dissembled his fears with laughter* (disguised); *She gave every sign of loving me, but she was just dissembling* (feigning).

To dissemble is related in its origins to *resemble*, not to *assemble* or *disassemble*. The chief source word of *to dissemble* and *to resemble* is the Old French *sembler*, 'to be like, appear, seem', going back to the Latin *similis*, 'similar'. The main Latin source word of *assemble* and *disassemble* is *simul*, 'together, at the same time'.

distinct, distinctive These two adjectives are very often used in place of each other, though they are not in fact interchangeable. Do use them with care.

Distinct has several closely related senses, such as 'clearly noticeable, unmistakable, positive, marked': *a distinct chill in relations between the neighbouring states*; or 'separate, individual, definite': *a thought that has not yet become distinct in her mind*; or 'different': *a distinct species.*

Distinctive means 'characteristic; serving to identify and distinguish; expected': *One could hardly avoid noticing his distinctive tone of haughty condescension.*

> It went to prove what they had feared in their marrow when the Volkdeutsch official first spoke to them — that these days it didn't do to stand out, to acquire a distinctive face.
> — Thomas Keneally, *Schindler's Ark*

Both words imply some kind of comparison or distinction. They are related to the verb *to distinguish,* but suggest different aspects of it; *distinct* can be roughly defined as 'distinguishable', *distinctive* as 'distinguishing'. So: *This cake has a distinct taste of soap* (the soapy taste is distinguishable above the various other tastes), but: *Soap has a distinctive taste* (its taste is peculiar to itself, distinguishing it from the taste of any other product).

Do not confuse the two words; they have their own distinctive meanings, and should always be kept quite distinct.

distrust, mistrust   As verbs, these two words are often both suitable in any given context, though *distrust* is much more common. There are three small differences to bear in mind.

First, *to distrust* is rather more emphatic than *to mistrust*. *To mistrust* suggests vague doubts and a slight anxiety. *To distrust* suggests positive suspicions, even a complete lack of trust:

> One way and another he had a bright time of it, distrusted on all sides, yet frequently confided in on the mere hypnotic strength of his attractive personality.
> – Muriel Spark, *The Mandelbaum Gate*

Secondly, *to mistrust* is the preferred form when one's doubts are directed against oneself: *I mistrusted my own motives*; *He mistrusted himself in such matters*; *Elizabeth didn't for a moment mistrust her first impressions of Mr Darcy*.

Thirdly, *to mistrust* can perhaps still be used intransitively, in the sense of 'to be cautious or wary': *Have no fear — there is no need to mistrust: I know the road well.* Such usage is virtually archaic today, however, and is more likely to be found in old-fashioned romances than in modern speech and writing.

The difference in emphasis between the two words applies also when they are used as nouns, though it is perhaps less marked here. Once again, *distrust* is used far more frequently than *mistrust*.

dived, dove   The verb *to dive* has a regular past tense, *dived*, in British and American English. However, an alternative past, *dove*, occurs in some British dialects and is the standard form in some areas of the United States: *The demonstrators dove for cover.* Its use, especially in spoken American English, appears to be growing, and in American English it is now regarded as an acceptable alternative in all but the most formal written contexts.

> Dean Bodger, on the run, dove for the bird, which struck his chest with an impact even Bodger was not wholly prepared for. The pigeon sent the dean reeling.
> – John Irving (U.S.),
> *The World According to Garp*

However, the past participle of *dive* remains *dived* even in American English: *The demonstrators had already dived for cover.*

diverse, divers   *Diverse* can mean 'different, unlike' — *with two such diverse proposals to consider* — or it can mean 'of various or different kinds': *The committee came up with diverse proposals, yet the stubborn president found something to object to in each one of them.*

> From diverse sources — from the policeman Toffel as well as drunken Bosch of Ostfaser (the SS textile company) — Oskar Schindler heard rumours that 'procedures in the ghetto' were growing more intense.
> – Thomas Keneally, *Schindler's Ark*

Divers was once used in similar ways to these, but has long been obsolete in such senses. Today it survives as a poetic or very formal word meaning 'numerous, several': *She received divers proposals, but preferred to remain unmarried.*

Note the difference in pronunciation: *diverse*, /dī-**verss**/, sometimes /**dī**-verss/ or /di-**verss**/; *divers*, /**dī**vərz/.

do   1. One of the important functions of *to do* and *to do so* is to stand in for a verb phrase that has already been used in a sentence, and thereby save the sentence from an ugly repetition of that verb phrase — in much the same way as *it* stands in for a noun phrase:

> The perfect gyroscope spins at a regular speed and continues to do so until friction of some kind is applied.

Or simply: *... and does so until ...* or even *... and does until ...* or *... and continues to until....* In each case, there is a saving on the full form *... and (it) spins at a regular speed until ...* or *... and it continues to spin at a regular speed until ....* Similarly:

> She spun the gyroscope as I wanted her to do (or simply: *...as I wanted her to*).

Here *to do* replaces the full form *to spin the gyroscope*.

In Britain (and perhaps Australia), *do* can be inserted after an auxiliary verb (*can, should, used to,* and the like), and *done* can be inserted after the *have* of a perfect-form construction:

> 'Do you pass the library on the way home?' — 'I could do.'
> 'Do you go swimming before breakfast?' — 'I used to do, but not any longer.'
> 'Has she finished it?' — 'She might have done, but I'm not sure.'

In most other varieties of English — North American, South African, and so on — the *do* would almost never be used in the reply in each case here. Instead, people would simply say *I could, I used to,* and *She might have,* or more formally, *I could do so, I used to do so,* and *She might have done so.* (And in fact, many British speakers too — perhaps the majority — would claim not to use *do* or *done* by itself here.)

The substitution of *do* or *do so* for an earlier verb phrase is not always a straightforward matter, unfortunately. A *do* or *does* all too often appears quite inappropriately in a construction — relating to a noun rather than a verb, for example, or replacing the verb *to be* or a verb in the passive voice, and so on. Here are some examples of these various errors:

× Such callous neglect of a child is something that only a madman could do.

You cannot × *do neglect*; you might *be guilty of neglect, allow neglect,* or the like. So the sentence might be reworded as:

Such callous neglect of a child is something that only a madman could allow.

The use of *do* would be appropriate in British English if *neglect* were used as a verb rather than noun:

He neglected the child as only a madman could do.

Next:

× You are always agreeable to a 'compromise' when you think that doing so is in your interest.

The first verb here is a form of the verb *to be* — *are* — and the rule is that only the verb *to be* (not *do*) can 'replace' the verb *to be* later in a construction. The sentence should read:

You are always agreeable to a 'compromise' when you think that being so is in your interest.

The use of *doing* would have been appropriate if the earlier verb had been *agree* (or *compromise*) rather than *are*:

You always compromise/agree to a 'compromise' when you think that doing so is in your interest.

Some purists apply a similar rule to *have*:

? Your mother has no right, any more than I do, to tell you how to run your life.
? 'Have you got a car?' — 'No, I don't.'

? I avoid discussing this with the Prime Minister; she has a science degree and I don't.
— Peter Walker, quoted in *The Times*

The rule would require the verb *have* (not *do*) to 'replace' *have* in these constructions — *Your mother has no right, any more than I have...*; *I haven't.* But the prohibition on *do* here is less rigorously enforced, especially in American English, than it is with the verb *to be.*

Next:

× If you exclude overheads from the balance sheet, as can be done under the new bookkeeping-system, the company actually shows a slight profit.
× If overheads are excluded from the balance sheet, as the new bookkeeping-system allows you to do, the company actually shows a slight profit.

When *to do* replaces an earlier verb phrase, it should be in the same voice — active or passive — as that verb phrase. Changing from one voice to the other, as in the two examples above, is unacceptable.

2. The principal parts of the verb *to do* are *do, did, done.* The past-tense form is *did: Who did it?* The present perfect equivalent is *Who has done it?* But the form × *Who done it?* — despite the humorous noun *a whodunit* — is nonstandard; similarly × *He done it,* × *They done it,* and so on.

Interestingly enough, however, those speakers who do say × *He done it* tend to add a correct 'tag' to it: × *He done it, didn't he?* Similarly: *'Did he tell them?'* — *'Yes, he did'.* In both of these examples, *did(n't)* is the auxiliary verb rather than the main verb, and is almost never mistakenly replaced by *done.*

3. Another very common nonstandard usage is × *He don't* instead of *He doesn't.* This use of × *He/She/It don't* is prevalent in popular music: × *It don't mean a thing,* × *She don't love me no more,* and so on. The single-syllabled *don't* often suits the rhythm better than the grammatically correct two-syllabled *doesn't.* It is perhaps the influence of popular music that is behind the widespread occurrence of this nonstandard construction in ordinary speech.

4. *To do* has long been something of a jack-of-all-trades verb: *She did a landscape rather than a still life* (painted); *Shall I do the dinner?* (prepare); *The Thespians are doing Cinderella as this year's pantomime* (performing).

Some of these uses are too recent or too loose to qualify as fully standard: ? *Let's do the Tate Gallery this morning* (visit); ? *I'm off to Parliament to do a demonstration* (take part in). And other such usages are clearly informal or slang: ? *That conman has just done me for £500*; ? *She did a Houdini and escaped from the cell*; *? They did the pickpocket for six months.*

dolphin, porpoise, dorado Those two gregarious mammals of the ocean, the *dolphin* and the *porpoise,* have much in common, so much so that the name *porpoise* is often applied to both of them. But they are quite distinct creatures.

The dolphin, unlike the porpoise proper, has a long beak-like snout, and of the two the dolphin is the larger and more streamlined. Dolphins, in their various species, are members of the family *Delphinidae*, related to whales but smaller; the most common species is *Delphinus delphis*. The word *dolphin* goes back through Latin to the Greek *delphis*, apparently unrelated to the place-name *Delphi*.

Porpoises, in their various species, belong to the genus *Phocaena*. Their distinguishing characteristic is suggested by their name — literally, 'pig-fish'. The porpoise has a blunt nose and slightly resembles a pig in the appearance of its head. The word goes back through Old French and Vulgar Latin to the Latin words *porcus,* 'a pig', and *piscis,* 'a fish'.

Both the porpoise and the dolphin are considered highly intelligent animals: the dolphin has the largest brain relative to its size of any animal after man, and has prompted many scientific experiments designed to assess the extent of its understanding.

To add to the confusion over *dolphin* and *porpoise,* sailors have for centuries applied the name *dolphin* to two fish quite unrelated to the mammalian dolphin. They are large sea fish of the genus *Coryphaena*; they grow to about six feet long, and are renowned for their iridescent colouring, which changes dramatically when they have been caught and are dying. They are also known as *dorados*, but to refer to them by this name is not to put an end to the confusion, since *dorado* is also used of another, unrelated, salmon-like fish, of the genus *Salminus*, from the River Plate in South America. *Dorado* is a Spanish word, and means literally 'golden'.

If you are concerned not to be misunderstood, you can always identify the animal precisely by specifying its genus or family. Above all, be sure to establish whether the creature you are talking about is a true fish or a sea-mammal.

The word *dauphin* (/**daw**fin, dō-faN/), French for 'dolphin', was the title of the French crown prince in former times. The title was taken from the name of a French province, which in turn took its name from the dolphins on the coat of arms of the lords of the province.

dominate, domineer Be careful to distinguish these two verbs. *To dominate* has the primary sense of 'to exercise power or influence over, or to control something or somebody'. The authority is often, though not invariably, appropriate and justified: *She dominated the entire department, and with her flair and wit had soon transformed her colleagues into willing disciples.*

To domineer is usually followed by the preposition *over* before taking an object. It means 'to tyrannise, bully, exercise power in an overbearing way'. It is often used in domestic contexts: *Her husband domineered over her to the point where she lost confidence in herself entirely.*

To domineer is commonly found in its present participle form, functioning as an adjective: *a domineering manner, a domineering guardian.*

Mr Hulford said afterwards: 'I don't see myself as having the attitudes of a Victorian husband. I do not accept that I was domineering or chauvinist. I just consider myself to be an ordinary English husband ... '
– *The Times*

To dominate can also mean 'to overlook from a high or prominent position': *The castle dominates the village.*

Both verbs go back to the Latin *dominari*, from *dominus*, 'a lord or master' — *dominate* directly from the Latin, *domineer* via Dutch and French.

To predominate can mean 'to dominate', though it is very rarely used in this way nowadays. Usually it is used intransitively (without a direct object) in the sense 'to be more or most important, numerous, or the like': *Red squirrels are returning to the woods, but the grey squirrels still predominate.*

done See DO 2.

don't See DO 3.

dot-dot-dot See ELLIPSIS.

double negative The following exchange is typical of both British and American speech:

'... I don't owe you nothing.'
'Don't owe me anything,' I said. 'When are you going to learn two negatives cancel each other? If you don't owe me nothing that means you do owe me something.'
'O.K.,' Sammy said agreeably, 'so I don't owe you anything.'
– Budd Schulberg (U.S.),
What Makes Sammy Run?

In standard modern English, as in arithmetic, the rule is that two negatives make a positive: *I don't consider it impossible* means more or less the same as *I do consider it possible* (though the double negative *not ... impossible* adds an effect of cautious qualification). 'Negative' is here understood to refer not just to *no, not,* and related words (*never, nowhere, nobody,* and the like), but also to such prefixes as *un-* and *im-*; to negative-sounding words and phrases such as *deny, miss, doubt, neglect, prevent, without, unless, too much to,* and *except*; and to such semi-negative adverbs as *hardly* and *scarcely*.

One of the first experiences of English grammar that children encounter is the warning to avoid such double-negative constructions as × *I don't want nothing*; and × *I'm not listening to no more lies*.

In nonstandard English, such constructions remain fairly common. In various English dialects (as in many other languages, and indeed in Elizabethan English), a second negative element is used to reinforce, rather than to cancel, the first. The way in which the double negative has survived generations of repression in English shows at least that the construction has a robustness about it. One such construction is so widespread that even careful speakers of standard English often slip into it:

? I shouldn't be surprised if it doesn't snow tonight

— which is spoken with an intonation that makes it clear that the meaning intended is the same as:

I shouldn't be surprised if it snows tonight.

If the original sentence were written rather than spoken, however, it would be in danger of being understood in the opposite way, as a prediction that it will not snow.

The real danger lies not in short, simple sentences, of course, but in more complicated constructions. In a very long sentence, the original negative might be forgotten and a second one inadvertently inserted. Or a clumsily worded sentence might contain three or four negative or negative-sounding words or phrases, and it would be all too easy to lose count of them:

× No judge but the most stony-hearted could deny the ice-dancers anything but full marks.
× Even a train-strike could not stop Henry's thousands of fans from missing his fight against Crossley.
× I can't deny that I might not change my mind in the future.

? Doubtless one could also argue (as implied by the extension of the image) that the wheel often symbolises the manner in which nobody can tell where things are going to lead, nor to what purpose they may not be twisted.

> – Anthony Powell,
> *O, How the Wheel Becomes It!*

Even if such sentences had correctly reflected the intended meaning, rather than contradicting it, they would still have been less than fully acceptable. The accumulation of negatives is a discourtesy to the reader or listener, and should be avoided. No reader or listener should have to disentangle such knotty constructions as:

You surely don't doubt that your troops might not fail to disobey you in a crisis.

Shakespeare, in keeping with Elizabethan custom, used the double negative freely:

I am not valiant neither,
But every puny whipster gets my sword.
> – Othello, in *Othello* V ii

By innocence I swear, and by my youth,
I have one heart, one bosom, and one truth,
And that no woman has; nor never none
Shall mistress be of it, save I alone.
> – Viola, in *Twelfth Night* III i

But he was aware of the possible ambiguities in a double negative, and could use these ambiguities to good effect. In *Coriolanus,* the hero, at the gates of Corioli, asks if his enemy Tullus Aufidius is in the city. From the walls, the First Senator shouts a defiant reply:

No, nor a man that fears you less than he —

and then, realising that this might suggest that Aufidius fears Coriolanus *more* than anyone else in the town, he adds a 'clarification':

That's lesser than a little.
> – *Coriolanus* I iv

doubt, doubtful Several prepositions and conjunctions are commonly used after *doubt* (both noun and verb) and *doubtful*.

The most common preposition after *doubt* (noun) and *doubtful* is *about*:

I have my doubts about that doctor.
I'm very doubtful about all these medical tests.

A tone of scepticism is usually apparent in such cases. When a sense of alarm or fearful uncertainty is intended, then *of* is the preposition to choose:

I am doubtful of the outcome.

Of tends to be limited to future events or situations, whereas *about* can be used for the past, present, or future.

The two most suitable conjunctions are *that* and *whether*. Formerly, they conveyed a slightly different meaning: *doubt that* or *doubtful that* tended to imply a high degree of certainty — very little doubt, in other words:

I doubt that he'll try overcharging us again!

Doubt whether and *doubtful whether*, on the other hand, suggested uncertainty — a fair degree of doubt, that is:

It is doubtful whether she'll be well enough to travel on Monday, but if she is, I'll bring her along.

Today, this distinction is no longer widely observed. Instead, what determines the choice of *whether* or *that* is the sentence-structure: *that* tends to be used in questions and negative statements; *whether* is preferred in ordinary positive statements.

Can you doubt that she will recover?
There's no doubt that she's seriously ill.
I have no doubt that she'll be up and about soon.

I have my doubts whether she will be up and about as early as next week.
It is doubtful whether she'll be able to leave next week.
The doctor doubts whether she will ever regain the full use of her right leg.

Other conjunctions often used after *doubt* or *doubtful* are as follows:

● *if*: an acceptable substitute for *whether* as a rule, though perhaps best avoided in very formal contexts.
● *as to whether*: useful at times, though in most cases just a flabby variant of *whether* (see AS TO).
● *but* or *but that*: often found in questions and negative constructions — an affected variant of *that*, and a misleading one, since it produces a kind of double negative. (See BUT 6.)
● *but what*: an even more pretentious substitute for *that* in questions and negative sentences. (See BUT 7.)

Sometimes the conjunction is left out altogether, especially after *doubtful*. Such omission sometimes attracts considerable criticism:

? I'm doubtful she will be able to leave next week.
? It's scarcely doubtful she will recover completely.

Restore the *whether* to the first of these, and the *that* to the second (*scarcely* here functions much like *not* or *never*, and is regarded as making a sentence negative).

● *Recommendation* The ear is a good guide here, discouraging the affected *as to whether*, *but that*, and *but what*, allowing the slightly informal *if* in most contexts, favouring the use of *that* in questions and negative statements, and slightly preferring *whether* to convey uncertainty in positive statements.

See also DOUBTFUL; UNDOUBTEDLY.

doubtful, dubious These two adjectives share most of their senses, and can be used interchangeably in most contexts. You can regard something as *a doubtful prospect* or as *a dubious prospect*: in either case you are sceptical or uncertain, and have doubts or suspicions about the outcome.

Nevertheless, there are slight differences in emphasis between the two words. *Doubtful* is more subjective perhaps: the doubt seems to be in the mind of the beholder. *Dubious* suggests a more objective assessment: the fault, it implies, lies in the object of the doubt as much as in the mind of the doubter. *Dubious* is more definite, in other words, *doubtful* more tentative: when you are *dubious* about an outcome or a claim, you have greater misgivings than when you are just *doubtful* about it. And *a remark in doubtful taste* or *a book of doubtful literary merit* is a more vague, less confident criticism than *a remark in dubious taste* or *a book of dubious literary merit*.

A rough but helpful guide to the difference in tone is to think of *doubtful* as meaning 'uncertain', and *dubious* as meaning 'suspicious'. To refer to someone as *a man of doubtful origins* is to express your own sense of uncertainty about him; to refer to him as *a man of dubious origins* is to impute something suspicious to him, and in effect to make a veiled accusation.

Though they all insisted that what they were recalling did happen, I was doubtful. Like children described by Freud, they seemed to be groping in a twilight of half-truths and wished-for fulfilments.

— Peter Conrad, *The Observer*

Schmidt had picked himself up, slowly and

painfully, sobbed out some inarticulate threat, and limped away downstairs. And Arthur, who had been present in the background, had shaken his head doubtfully and protested. 'You shouldn't have done that, you know.'

> – Christopher Isherwood,
> *Mr Norris Changes Trains*

The air is full of confident *no questions* being used to hustle dubious statements and arguments past audiences too slow or too polite to object.

> – Philip Howard, *Weasel Words*

This inanity was uttered a few days after Bush's fellow citizens had enjoyed the dubious benefit of seeing their leader flounder about the television screen unedited.

> – Robert Chesshyre, *The Observer*

One construction where *doubtful* is clearly preferable to *dubious* is the *It is . . .* construction:

> It is highly doubtful whether Barbie came up with anything useful about communists, the Russians, or even the French, but it is certain that he accumulated knowledge which could have been extremely embarrassing to the Americans.
> – Chaim Bermant, *Daily Telegraph*

The use of *dubious* in such constructions is dubious if not incorrect:

> ? It is dubious whether there should be a collective organisation of senior civil servants at all, except perhaps for such purposes as organising an annual picnic or a darts competition.
> – John O'Sullivan, *Daily Telegraph*

See also DOUBT.

doubtless See UNDOUBTEDLY.

douse, dowse Both these verbs are fairly rare and both are concerned with water. Their spellings are all too easily confused.

To dowse is, primarily, to seek or find underground water or minerals using a divining rod or pendulum — hence *a dowsing rod*. By extension, the word can also mean 'to use apparently paranormal powers to make discoveries'. *Dowse* in these senses is usually pronounced /dowz/, but sometimes /dowss/ — which increases the likelihood of confusion with *douse,* also pronounced /dowss/.

Dowse is a 17th-century word of obscure origin.

There are really three words spelt *douse*. The first means, as a verb, 'to plunge into liquid or drench' — *doused in the pool by his classmates* — or 'to become thoroughly wet; soak'. As a noun, it means 'a drenching'. Confusingly, this word can be spelt *dowse* as well, though it rarely is.

The second *douse* is a verb meaning 'to put out or extinguish (a light or fire)': *They doused the candles and went to bed.* These two versions of *douse* are probably related in origin. The original 16th-century word, of obscure origin, meant 'to strike or smite', and the modern senses seem to have developed from this. The two modern senses are unfortunately liable to be confused. In the following quotation, the sense of *doused* is presumably 'drenched, damped down'. But a hasty reading of the metaphor *fire . . . being . . . doused* might well be of fires being extinguished — a reading quite at odds with the writer's intention:

> And yet Kentridge, the latest in that great line of lawyers, from Cicero to Clarence Darrow, who have served truth against its enemies, comes to full life upon the stage indicting wickedness in words of fire that burn the more savagely for being so carefully doused.
> – Bernard Levin, *The Times*

The third word *douse* is a nautical term, and means 'to lower (a sail)' or 'to close (a porthole)'. It is thought to derive from a Low German word, again perhaps having the sense of 'to strike or beat'.

dove See DIVED.

down As a general rule, *down* is used for travel in a southerly direction, *up* for travel to the north. Clashing with this is the convention in British English that you travel *up* to a place of importance, particularly London or a university, and hence *down* to a place considered less important, such as the provinces.

downstairs, downstair *Downstair* is a rare form of the adjective. *Downstairs* is now used for both adjective and adverb: *a downstairs* (or *downstair*) *room*; *go downstairs*.

draconian This adjective, ferocious-sounding though it is (probably through the association with *dragon*), is in fact often used nowadays in a much weaker way than the purists would wish. The original *draconian punishment* was death: the word derives from *Draco,* an ancient Athenian statesman and lawgiver, whose code of laws in 621 BC prescribed the death penalty for even very minor offences.

In the spirit of Draco, the word *draconian* should be restricted today to extremely harsh laws or penalties (though not necessarily as harsh as those laid down by Draco, of course):

> The Iranian regime lost no time in enforcing the newly-enacted draconian legislation.

To brand as *draconian* any measure or punishment that you happen to think errs on the side of severity is to debase the word and reduce in a small way the potency of it that draws you to use it in the first place:

> ? Two hours' detention for neglecting your homework! If the board of governors endorses this draconian new rule, I'll take you out of that school before the meeting's over.

> ? In order to curb drunken driving the [Swedish] Government has launched a twin pronged attack, imposing draconian penalties on offenders and crippling taxes on drink.
> – Peter Dobereiner, *The Observer*

> ? One should not rejoice too soon. Censorship is not yet dead. And a hardening of political attitudes may well result in a new and even more draconian application of its apparatus.
> – André Brink, in *They Shoot Writers, Don't They?*

draft, draught *Draft* emerged in the 16th century as a variant spelling of *draught,* which probably derives from an Old Norse word akin to *draw.* In British English, the preliminary version of anything is a *draft*: *a draft of the proposed treaty* or simply *a draft treaty.* The person who makes such a version *drafts* it; if it is a legal document he or she is a *draftsman,* but if it is a sketch for a machine or structure this person is a *draughtsman* (or *draughtsperson*).

A money order is a *draft.* The transfer or special assignment of soldiers is a *draft,* and in North America military call-up is *the draft.* Helpers are *drafted* in when necessary. One drinks a *draught* of *draught* beer, and one may drive *draught* horses, which pull a *draught* or load. A current of air is a cold *draught.* The board-game is called *draughts.*

Most North Americans treat this matter more rationally. They spell all these words *draft* except for the game, which they call *checkers.*

dreadfully See AWFULLY.

dream *Dreamt* is the preferred past tense and past participle of *to dream* in British English, but is less common in American English; *dreamed* is the usual American form, and is also acceptable in British English: *I never dreamt/dreamed it would take so long.*

In British English *dreamed* can be pronounced /dreemd/ or /dremt/. In American English, *dreamed* is pronounced /dreemd/.

For a possible difference in sense between *dreamt* and *dreamed,* see -ED, -T.

dromedary See CAMEL.

drunken Standard English recognises only *drank* for the past tense of *to drink,* and *drunk* for the past participle: *I drank it; I had drunk it.* Sentences such as ✗ *I drunk it* are common in some dialects, but are considered nonstandard. The adjectival form *drunk* is generally used after a verb — *I got drunk* — whereas *drunken* is generally used before a noun: *a drunken stupor.*

However, *drunk* tends to imply a temporary state of drunkenness, whereas *drunken* is used for habitual drunkenness. So the normal order can be reversed when the meaning requires it, more commonly in the case of *drunk*: *There was a drunk man on the bus.* This is particularly true of the phrases *drunken driving/driver,* where the alternative *drunk driving/driver* has become equally, if not more, common.

due to, owing to *Owing to* and *due to,* in the sense of 'thanks to, as a result of', can both be regarded as adjectival: *The strike is owing to/due to the dismissal of a foreman; Symptoms due to/owing to malnutrition are easily identifiable.* Here *due to* and *owing to* can be considered as relating to the preceding noun in each case — *strike* and *symptoms.*

Owing to also functions on its own as a preposition, relating directly to a noun or noun equivalent that follows it (and forming with it an adverbial phrase of cause or explanation):

> Owing to the strong dollar, American tourists are flooding into Europe in even vaster numbers than usual.

Due to is also now widely used in this way, but purists still object vigorously to such use:

> ?? Due to the strong dollar, American tourists are flooding into Europe in even vaster numbers than usual.

There is no very good reason for this objection — *due to* seems to have as much or as little right to an extended grammatical function as *owing to* does — but it remains a strongly felt objection, and knowledge of it is often cited as a good test of a person's grasp of standard usage.

The difference in range between *due to* and *owing to* can be summed up in this way: *owing to* can usually replace *due to*, but *due to* cannot always replace *owing to*. You can read *due to* as 'caused by' (or 'attributable to' or 'resulting from'); and you can read *owing to* as 'because of', which is more wide-ranging. Finally, you should use *due to* only when you can answer the question '*What* is due?'

Test the acceptability of the following sentences, for instance:

a. ?? Max was barely 50, but due to an unexpected inheritance, he suddenly found himself in a position to retire.

(Unacceptable: *due to* does not relate directly as an adjective to any noun or noun phrase (apart from that immediately following it); if you try to replace *due to* by its equivalent *caused by*, it becomes clear that the construction is faulty.)

b. ?? Due to an unexpected inheritance, Max suddenly found himself in a position to retire.

(Unacceptable: *due to* can seldom be used at the beginning of a sentence — certainly not here, since it does not qualify the noun *Max*; again, the substitution of *caused by* shows how incorrect the use of *due to* is here.)

c. Max's death, due to/owing to a heart-attack, occurred on the very day that he announced his retirement.

(Acceptable: *due to* here relates directly to the noun phrase *Max's death,* and the substitution of *caused by* produces a perfectly idiomatic sentence: *Max's death, caused by a heart-attack,* occurred on .... *Owing to* would also be acceptable here.)

d. Due to a heart-attack, Max's death occurred on the very day that he announced his retirement.

(Again acceptable, as shown by the possibility of a paraphrase beginning *Caused by a heart-attack, Max's death* .... . This is one of the rare cases in which *due to* can begin a sentence correctly — though somewhat clumsily.)

e. ? Owing to a heart-attack, Max's death occurred on the very day that he announced his retirement.

(Doubtful: even though *owing to* is frequently and correctly used at the beginning of a sentence, and can usually replace *due to,* it is rather awkward when placed before the relevant noun or noun equivalent, as here, rather than after it, as in example *c.* above.)

f. ?? All the remaining first-round matches are unfortunately, due to circumstances beyond our control, postponed until further notice.

(Unacceptable: the verb *to be* does occur in front of the *due to,* but is not related to it at all; try substituting *caused by* to confirm the unacceptability of the sentence.)

The following two quotations illustrate the correct and incorrect uses of *due to*:

> Now, it is clear that the decline of a language must ultimately have political and economic causes: it is not due simply to the bad influence of this or that individual writer.
> – George Orwell, 'Politics and the English Language'

> ?? Due to what he regards as a personal plot by Hitler, 'Sir' finds himself leading a tatty company of 'old men, cripples and nancy boys' in an undercast production of 'King Lear' at the Alhambra, Bradford.
> – Philip French, *The Observer*

● *Recommendation* It is dangerous to ignore the purists' objection to the use of *due to* as a preposition. Whether it is a fair objection or not, it remains a touchstone of people's usage. Careful users of English adhere to the 'rule' — *owing to* means 'because of', *due to* means 'caused by' — and continue to frown on the breach of it by others, no matter how numerous these may be. See also FACT **2**.

E

each 1. *Each*, whether as pronoun or as adjective, is singular, and therefore all the words related to it in a sentence should be in the singular as well.

However, there is a great temptation to stray into the plural when using *each*. There are several possible reasons for this. First, *each* is often followed by *of* and a plural noun — *each of the children* — and this plural noun tends to affect the form of the rest of the sentence, and to lure the speaker or writer into adopting the plural: *?? Each of the children are searching for their coats*. A second reason might be that the singular possessive adjective *his* is perhaps inappropriate when women too are involved: the alternative *his or her* is rather awkward, and so the common-gender form *their* is resorted to. (See THEY for a detailed discussion of this problem.) A third reason is simply that *each*, like *every*, suggests 'several', and this sense of plurality might then express itself, incorrectly, in plural forms such as *they* and *their*, even when there are no girls or women involved to discourage the use of *he, him,* and *his*: *?? Each/every guardsman has to carry their own equipment, and each always grumbles as they shoulder their heavy knapsacks.*

The correct procedure, strictly speaking, is to keep the sentence in the singular throughout: *... each invariably grumbles as he shoulders his heavy knapsack*. If you want to stress the sense of plurality, then you can always reword the sentence so that it is cast entirely in the plural. Simply replace *each* and *every* with *all* (or *both*): *All the guardsmen have to carry their own equipment, and all of them invariably grumble as they shoulder their heavy knapsacks*. Similarly, the following example should either change *each* to *both*, or else be recast in the singular: *each had contrived ... to drink himself ill ... and squander his allowance*:

?? The sons had been sent to foreign universities — to Heidelberg, Cambridge, Harvard — and wherever they were, each had contrived not to attend a single lecture, to drink themselves ill, to find the nearest racecourse and squander their allowances on horses that never won.

– Anita Desai, *Fire on the Mountain*

There is a further difficulty in using *he/him/his* after *each*, apart from the possible charge of sexism, and that arises when a second clause is introduced relating to *each*. It is possible to say *Each of the students did his best*, but it sounds distinctly odd to say *? Each of the students did his best, didn't he?* And yet the alternatives are no better: *?? Each of the students did their best, didn't they?* is ungrammatical, as just suggested; *?? Each of the students did his best, didn't they?* is both ungrammatical and inconsistent. Such sentences should always be rephrased to use *all* and standard plurals throughout: *All the students did their best, didn't they?*

It seems, however, that the objection to changing from the singular to the plural in successive clauses is less applicable if the later clause has an independent grammatical structure. It is reasonably acceptable to say *Each of the students did his best, and they deserve our warmest congratulations*. The second clause is this time not in close grammatical relationship to the first — the two clauses are virtually two different sentences. And so the power of *each* cannot extend beyond its own clause to influence the grammatical form of the words in the second clause.

The same restrictions and freedoms apply to *every, everyone/everybody, none,* and similar pronouns.

2. *Each* can also be used after a plural noun: *Proposals A and B each cover about 100 printed pages*. Since *each* is grammatically subordinate here, being in apposition to the subject *proposals*, it has no influence on the form of the verb, which is dictated by *proposals* and is accordingly in the plural.

Note, however, that in the example sentence the two proposals are regarded as having similar qualities. But what if the proposals are being grouped together for the sake of contrast or differentiation? Perhaps it is then just permissible to use a singular verb: *? Proposal A and proposal B each has its own merits*. (Less jarring, though more old-fashioned, is the form *Proposals A and B are very creditable each in its own way*.) As always, it is possible to skirt this problematic choice by rewording the sentence, either moving *each* to a different position, or replacing *each* by *both* (or *all*, if there are more than two elements). Each sentence can then be cast in the plural without any suspicion of bad grammar or ambiguity: *Proposal A and proposal B both have their own merits*; *Proposals A and B cover about 100 printed pages each.* (This last sentence is preferable to *? Proposals A and B both cover about 100 printed pages*, which is slightly ambiguous: it could be taken to mean that the total length is 100 pages rather than 200 pages.)

3. If it is risky to use *each* immediately after a plural noun, it is sometimes also thought unwise to use *each* by itself immediately after a plural pronoun. Traditionally, exception is taken to such constructions as *? They each gave me a kiss*; *? She gave us each a present.* These sound fairly natural today, but are still regarded by some as very awkward. (The same is true of *both*.) It is preferable to expand the pronoun phrase into *each of them* (or *both of them* or *all of them*) and so on: *Each/both/all of them gave me a kiss*; *She gave each/all/both of us a present.*

See also BETWEEN, AMONG 4; EACH AND EVERY; EVERY; EVERYBODY; THEY.

each and every   This is a redundant and clichéd phrase, and careful users of English will avoid it: *? I want to thank each and every one of you* is a ponderous and pointless way of saying *I want to thank each of you/every one of you/all of you* or simply *Thank you all.*

Even Tiny Tim in Dickens' *Christmas Carol* knew enough to say *God bless us every one* rather than *? God bless us each and every one.*

each other, one another   **1.** There is a traditional rule that *each other* is used when two elements are being discussed, and *one another* is used of more than two elements.

> Soon, Caroline Daniel herself was in my room, removing her raincoat, apologising as she disrobed, turning for us to take in our first impressions of each other.
> — Brian Aldiss, *The Fiction Magazine*

> What stirred him was the shame and the horror which men and women could inflict upon one another in the name of money or patriotism or religion itself.
> — Michael Foot, *The Observer*

> The three children were locked in an endless game of tormenting one another. Because Gina lay down on the car-seat bed they shared, the boys ... came to edge her off

onto the dirt floor.
> — Nadine Gordimer, *July's People*

However, as with the traditional rule on split infinitives, for example, the rule about *each other* and *one another* has little to recommend it *apart* from tradition. The rule is artificial: there are few good logical or historical reasons for it (historically the phrase *either other* was used when only two elements were involved); and the meanings of the individual words provide little justification for restricting the range of the two phrases.

It has been argued that the rule at least creates a helpful distinction: it is useful to know that *We hate each other* refers to two people, whereas *We hate one another* refers to more than two. But more often than not, surely, the context will indicate whether two elements or more than two are under discussion. Perhaps because the rule has so little foundation, it is often disregarded by even the finest speakers and writers:

> *?* The two culprits were an eighteen-year-old ex-waitress named Elizabeth Jones, and an American army deserter, posing as an officer, named Karl Hulten. They were only together for six days, and it seems doubtful whether, until they were arrested, they even learned one another's true names.
> — George Orwell, 'Decline of the English Murder'

> *?* In fact, such people say, the affair that began on the evening of August 9th, 1942, in Mayapore, ended with the spectacle of two nations in violent opposition, not for the first time nor as yet for the last because they were then still locked in an imperial embrace of such long standing and subtlety it was no longer possible for them to know whether they hated or loved one another, or what it was that held them together and seemed to have confused the image of their separate destinies.
> — Paul Scott, *The Jewel in the Crown*

> *?* Hanna and Mary were not, as might be thought, alienated from one another by the apparently conflicting characters of their respective tragedies.
> — Conor Cruise O'Brien, *The Observer*

Nevertheless, even a bad rule cannot simply be ignored. If you disobey it, there are certain consequences that you must be prepared to take — in this case, the disapproval of the purists, and possibly the consequent loss of their trust in what you are saying. And this is not a small price to pay. If your object in speaking or writing is to communicate certain ideas, then obviously you should avoid provoking or even distracting your listeners or speakers. Since there is no great difficulty in observing the rule, and since failure to observe it might involve you in pedantic complications, it is as well to observe it — as a rule.

There are some interesting exceptions to the rule, however:

> The boys and the girls avoided each other, refusing to dance and clustering shyly together with friends of their own sex.

Even though the people involved here number far more than two, they are clearly being discussed in terms of two groups. *Each other* is therefore correct. In fact, *one another* would be quite misleading, since it would at first suggest that each boy avoided the other boys as well as the girls, and that each girl avoided the other girls as well as all the boys. Here is a different kind of exception:

> All the guests dutifully shook each other by the hand.

Even though everybody shook the hand of everybody else, the handshaking was presumably done in pairs each time. (See BETWEEN.) So once again, *each other* is appropriate, though *one another* is also acceptable this time.

2. There is a further difference between *each other* and *one another* — a more logical difference. (Perhaps it provided the original basis for the illogical difference discussed above.) This difference is one of *definiteness*: the phrase *each other* has a very definite ring to it, insisting that the specific elements concerned should be individually taken into account. Note how the sentence *They hated each other* might be rewritten as *(They) each hated the other*: the definite article *the* seems to be somehow implied in *each other*. (Formerly, in fact, the sentence might have been expressed as *They hated each the other*.) The phrase *one another,* however, is less definite (note the lurking presence of the indefinite pronoun *an*), and seems to make allowance for a few uninvolved elements — nonpartisan members, as it were. So it is acceptable to say *In the stampede, the horses trampled one another to death,* even when it is clear that some of the horses survived. But to say *?The horses trampled each other to death* sounds doubly odd. First because it breaks the 'rule' that *each other* should be limited to two elements; secondly, and more importantly, because it sounds so *definite* and all-embracing,

allowing of no exceptions, and therefore raising the question 'But if *all* the horses were trampled to death, how did the last surviving horse get trampled to death?'

3. Even though *one another* does allow certain elements to be exceptions, it is still best to avoid using it if it produces an odd picture in your listener's mind. There is nothing very wrong in saying *The wagons followed one another around the arena,* but it seems slightly curious to say *? The wagons followed one another down the road.* What wagon is the front wagon following? A simple rewording is preferable: *The wagons paraded down the road in a long line* or *The remaining wagons followed the lead-wagon down the road.*

Here are a few extreme cases of the misuse of *each other/one another.* First, two logical misuses:

> ✗ He was leaning forward with a heavy list, using his forearms to shore himself up. His hands lay on top of each other as if chained.
> — John le Carré,
> *The Little Drummer Girl*

Two things cannot lie 'on top of each other': it would be better to have written *one on top of the other,* or simply *clasping each other.* Similarly:

> ?? The elephants now formed into a circle, holding one another's tails and swaying to the music.

Far better to say *each holding the tail of the one in front of it.*

Then, a grammatical misuse:

> ✗ Both Mildred and her husband suspected what each other were up to.

The mistake here is in using *each other* as a grammatical subject (within its own clause). In fact, *each other* and *one another* can serve only as grammatical objects, of prepositions or of verbs (whether direct or indirect objects). The sample sentence above should be reworded to read: *She and her husband each suspected what the other was up to.*

4. In the possessive, the apostrophe comes before the *s*: *She and I tried on each other's shoes; all laughing at one another's jokes.*

One interesting problem is choosing between the singular and plural form of the noun following *each other's* or *one another's.* If each of the people (or things) involved has more than one of the items (as *shoes* or *jokes* in the examples above), then obviously the noun is in the plural. But what if only one item per person is involved? — a hat, say. *She and I tried on each other's hat/hats*: either *hat* or *hats* seems to be acceptable, though some authorities prefer the singular *hat*. Yet somehow it feels different in the case of *one another*: it sounds distinctly odd to say *? We all tried on one another's hat*. The plural form *hats* is clearly preferable here.

earthy, earthly The adjectives *earthy* and *earthly* draw on two different meanings of the word *earth*: *earthy* is related to the meaning 'soil'; *earthly* to the meaning 'the planet Earth'.

The ending -*ly* can form adjectives as well as adverbs, and *earthly* is, like *earthy*, an adjective. It has two main uses. It generally means 'relating to human life on Earth', the opposite of *heavenly,* as in *earthly woes* or *This earthly lot is all we have*. It also means 'conceivable by mortal man; possible': it is used in such negative and interrogative idioms as *no earthly reason* or *What earthly right do you have?* Perhaps it developed as a variant form of the idioms *no reason on earth* and *What right on earth do you have?*

In British English, *earthly* is sometimes, in negative sentences, used informally as a noun to mean 'a chance', as in *He doesn't stand an earthly,* where the complete sentence would be *He doesn't stand an earthly chance*.

Earthy means, literally, 'consisting of, resembling, or covered in earth' — *earth* in the sense of 'soil', that is: *His shoes were earthy from gardening*. (Note that *an earthy floor* would probably be a dirty floor; a floor simply made of earth would be an *earth floor* or an *earthen floor*.) *Earthy* is most often used figuratively, however, and means (in a negative sense) 'coarse, gross' — *His earthy jokes shocked the Ladies' Guild* — or (in a positive sense) 'down to earth, solid, forthright, sensual': *She has a strong, earthy singing voice*.

I have not seen her since, though I worked remotely for her when I translated Lina Wertmuller's Sicilian blood feud film into English. I do not know whether it was ever shown in English: it was no great success in Italian, or Sicilian, though Sophia, passionate and earthy, was as compelling as she always is.
  – Anthony Burgess, *The Observer*

The earlier meaning of earthy — 'materialistic, concerned with physical things rather than spiritual values' — has lapsed, and *earthy* now tends to have suggestions either of sexuality or of bodily functions.

Earthen, as just mentioned, can mean simply 'made of earth', but tends to mean, more specifically, 'made of potter's clay', as in *earthenware*.

In the following quotation, the contrast between *earthy* and *earthly* is neatly illustrated:

But nothing in Ronald Eyre's new production for the National Theatre alters my feeling that the play comes near to being a clever fake, as scene after scene inflates itself with a plausible mixture of colloquialism and pertinent debate only to collapse in cute theatrical effect ... The trial scene remains the best: Shaw is much better on earthly heresy than on earthy politics or divine inspiration.
  – Michael Ratcliffe, *The Observer*

The form *? unearthy* is most unlikely to occur. But *unearthly* is a very common word. It has several senses: 'not from Earth; extraterrestrial *(unearthly radio pulses)*; 'ideal, spiritual, supernatural' *(unearthly splendour)*; 'absurdly unusual or unreasonable; outrageous' *(woken at an unearthly hour)*, and above all 'unnatural, unaccountable, eerie' *(an unearthly silence)*:

Helga had developed an unearthly composure. The histrionics were over. She had entered a period of ice-cold disconnection.
  – John le Carré,
  The Little Drummer Girl

Compare FLESHY.

eatable, edible As adjectives, these two words are sometimes interchangeable: *This stew is hardly boeuf bourguignon, but it's edible/eatable*. In less colloquial contexts, *edible* tends to have a rather more formal ring to it than *eatable*, perhaps because it is derived from Latin rather than Old English roots, and because of its occasional use as a technical scientific term.

Moreover, the two words are often used in slightly different ways. *Eatable* tends to refer to food that is prepared or ready for consumption, and suggests that it is reasonably palatable: *These potatoes are just about eatable now, though they could do with another ten minutes in the oven. Edible* tends to refer to *kinds* of food that can be eaten, irrespective of their present state of preparedness: *an edible fungus*. Flour, for example, is obviously *edible,* but it is not really *eatable*.

The respective opposites are *uneatable* and *inedible*. These are more frequently interchangeable. A substance would be *inedible* either because it is poisonous — *an inedible wild berry* — or because it cannot be digested or swallowed: *Shouldn't you explain to your baby that its rattle is actually inedible?* It would also be *inedible* if it were particularly unappetising or revolting, as through being off or badly cooked. This is, in fact, the primary meaning of *uneatable*: *I can't think why that restaurant's so popular — its food is quite uneatable/inedible.* Oscar Wilde's famous definition of an English gentleman hunting a fox — *the unspeakable in full pursuit of the uneatable* — confirms that *uneatable* can also be used in the sense of 'inedible; impossible to swallow or digest'.

The corresponding adjectives relating to liquids are *drinkable* ('reasonably tasty, acceptable') and *potable* ('non-poisonous'). *Potable* now sounds very old-fashioned, however, and *drinkable* tends to cover both senses.

Note that *eatable* and *edible* both serve as nouns as well, especially when used in the plural: *Pack your eatables/edibles — we're going on a picnic!*

echelon *Echelon,* pronounced /eshə-lon/, has become a fashionable synonym for *grade* or *rank* — *The top echelons of management* — or even simply for *group*:

> Several hundred thousand would-be workers, who would have liked to go on, particularly among the older echelon who had subsisted on unemployment pay for years, had opted to retire on a lower industrial pension than if they had worked for the normal industrial spell.
> – Walter Aburn, *Daily Telegraph*

The original sense in English was 'a steplike formation of troops, in which the units are parallel but unaligned'. Hence it came to refer to similar formations of aircraft or ships, or of people within an organisation.

Another military use of *echelon* is of a subdivision within the armed forces: *the command echelon.* It is this meaning that was transferred to general use in the sense of 'a rank or level of authority in a group or organisation'.

The origins of the word suggest both a ladder (hence the senses of a formation or arrangement of units) and a single rung of a ladder (hence the senses of subdivision or rank). The French *échelon,* from which the English word was adopted, meant 'a rung of a ladder'; it comes from Old French *eschelon,* from *eschile,* 'a ladder', from Latin *scalae,* 'a ladder or stairs'.

Use *echelon* sparingly. It can sound pretentious.

economic, economical These two adjectives have different ranges of meaning. *Economic* is primarily the adjective of the noun *economics* —

as in *economic history* — or of *the economy,* as in *an economic upturn* or *grave economic problems.*

Economical is the adjective of the noun *economy,* in the sense of 'thrift'. When applied to people or organisations, it means 'careful in the management of resources, not wasteful or extravagant': *an economical housewife.* When applied to things, it means 'avoiding waste or excessive cost': *an economical detergent*; *It's more economical to buy the jumbo pack*; *an economical method of packing your suitcase.*

> Mr Hampton, adapting Graham Greene's *The Honorary Consul* of 1973, had the easier task, for the novel is economical of character and situation.
> – Patrick Gibbs, *Daily Telegraph*

The rule of thumb is this then: *economic* has to do with finance, *economical* has to do with thrift. But *economic* can sometimes be used to suggest thrift too: *It's not really economic to have a home freezer unless you buy in bulk.* The emphasis and aspect tend to be slightly different, however. *Economic* is usually used when the point of view is that of the producer, seller, lessor, and so on: *economic prices* and *economic rents* are those that enable a shopkeeper or landlord to break even or make a small profit. *Economical* is used when the point of view is that of the consumer, buyer, lessee, and so on: *economical prices* and *economical rents* are those which for a shopper or tenant represent good value.

Both *economic* and *economical* have only a single adverb between them — *economically.* This can accordingly be used in contexts where either finance or thrift is at issue. So you can speak both of *a newly independent state not yet economically viable* and of *a new furnace that burns coal very economically.*

The verb *to economise* relates to *economical* rather than to *economic.* It has two primary senses. It can mean 'to use efficiently; to save by being economical', and is then usually used with *on*: *You can economise on petrol by staying in the highest gear whenever possible.* Or it can mean 'to be frugal, to reduce expenses': *I've taken a cut in salary, so from now on we're going to have to economise.*

See -IC, -ICAL.

-ed, -t Most verbs form their past tense by the addition of *-ed* or *-d*: *climbed, hunted, seized.* Other verbs, being 'irregular', end in *-t* in the past tense (usually changing their spelling or pronunciation in the middle of the word too): *felt, meant.*

Some verbs can still take either form: *burn* produces *burnt* or *burned*; *dream* produces *dreamt* or *dreamed*. Similarly *dwell, kneel, lean, learn, leap, smell, spell, spill,* and *spoil* all offer a choice of past forms.

In general, both forms are acceptable in both British and American English, though British slightly favours the *-t* form (especially in the past participle), and American slightly favours the *-ed* form. Specifically, the forms *kneeled, burned* and *leaped* are out of favour in British English. And American English is wary of some *-t* forms — *spoilt* and *spilt* (except before a noun, as in *Don't cry over spilt milk*), and *leant, learnt,* and *spelt* are regarded in America as forms that are chiefly British. On the other hand, Americans perhaps share the British preference for *dwelt, knelt,* and *leapt.*

A few additional comments:

Some British speakers will pronounce an *-ed* form as if it were a *-t* form, notably *learned* and *spelled.*

Before a noun denoting humans, the form *learned* is pronounced with two syllables (as though *learnéd*). Its meaning is then active: 'having learnt, or knowing, much'. Thus a distinction in the pronunciation of this form is made between *a learned historian/society* and *a well-learned* (or *well-learnt*) *lesson.*

Blessed too is pronounced as two syllables if used as an adjective directly before a noun: *every blessed car in town.* So too is the phrase *the Blessed.* Elsewhere, *blessed* tends to have one syllable: *Well I'm blessed! He blessed his son.* A single-syllable pronunciation is possible for the adjective before a noun, but it would then tend to be spelt *blest: the blest Saints.* This form is now very old-fashioned if used outside religious writing.

In general, the *-t* forms are particularly likely to occur before nouns: even Americans tend to speak of *burnt toast* as well as *spilt milk.*

A distinction in meaning may sometimes be felt between *-t* forms and *-ed* forms, with the latter emphasising the duration of the action. Thus a contrast could be made between *I dreamt about her last night* and *I dreamed about her all night.* But the distinction is a very fine one.

See also BEREAVED; BURN; DREAM.

edible   See EATABLE.

-ee   There are at least two different suffixes represented by the form *-ee.* One is probably an altered form of the ending *-ie* or *-y,* and is used in such words as *bootee,* 'a baby's boot', and *townee,* 'someone from a town rather than the country, or (in Britain) from the town rather than a university in the town'.

The other *-ee* comes from the French ending *-é* or *-ée.* For a long time it has been used in English to denote a person to whom something is given: *grantee* (1491), *lessee* (1495), *mortgagee* (1584) — the words for people given a *grant,* a *lease,* or a *mortgage.*

This *-ee* ending has also been used to denote a person to whom something is done. So: *nominee* (1664), 'one who has been nominated', *appointee* (1768), 'one who has been appointed', *employee* (1822) 'one who has been employed', *trainee* (1861), 'one being trained'. Some of these words can also be analysed as if they were of the *grantee* type: 'one who has been given a *nomination,* an *appointment, employment, training*'.

Note that some of these *-ee* words have active counterparts in *-or* (*lessor*) or *-er* (*employer*).

The use of *-ee* to form words denoting people to whom something is done has created many words in recent times, few of which would pass muster in French. Among these new forms are: *evacuee* (1918), 'one who has been evacuated', *internee* (1918), 'one who has been interned', and *detainee* (1920s), 'one who has been detained, as for political reasons': *detainee* has replaced the earlier *detenu* (1803), borrowed from French and still used sometimes in Indian English.

Some of these newer formations have a decidedly humorous cast: *murderee* (1920), 'one who has been murdered (as in a detective story) by contrast with the murderer'. And many are not only humorous, but seem to have been coined on the spur of the moment. Among those attested, especially in American English, though hardly part of the core of English vocabulary, are: *holdupee, seductee, slanderee,* and *visitee.* If you are tempted to use such words or to coin others, first pause to consider whether a humorous effect is what you really want.

Another group of *-ee* words, again chiefly American, is used to refer to people who do something rather than people to whom something is done: *escapee* (1865), 'one who has escaped, as from prison', *standee* (1880s), 'one who stands when there are no seats', *returnee* (1944), 'one who has returned, as from service overseas'. Some people have criticised such words on the ground that *-ee* is properly 'passive' rather than 'active', and have urged such alternatives as *escaper, stander,* and *returner.* There is merit in this argument, but note too that these *-ee* words do have a nuance that their *-er* equivalents lack. The *-ee* ending gives them a 'perfective' meaning: an *escapee* is one who *has* escaped, not just one who is trying to escape; a *returnee* is one who *has* returned, not just one who is returning.

effect See AFFECT.

effective, efficient, effectual, efficacious These adjectives overlap in meaning, but should be distinguished. The primary sense of *effective* is 'having the intended effect, producing the result expected': *an effective technique for reprocessing waste metal*; *a bombing-raid that proved effective in halting factory production.*

> The Arts Council of Great Britain is a unique institution which has earned praise throughout the world as being as effective and impartial a method of subsidising culture as has yet been devised in any country anywhere.
> – Lord Goodman, *The Observer*

In a slightly extended sense, it means 'impressive or striking': *an effective speaker*; *an effective series of arguments in favour of shorter prison-sentences.*

> He drew her to a bench; she sat on it, then stood up in order to assert herself. She had learned that emotional scenes did not play effectively between people who were walking, so she stood still.
> – John le Carré,
> *The Little Drummer Girl*

Effective has two further important uses. It can mean 'in practice though not in theory; real and actual rather than supposed; in effect' — as though the effect were unintended this time, rather than intended: *an effective breakdown in discussions*; *She's the effective boss around here, even though Horace is officially her senior.* The adverb form is perhaps more often used: *She's effectively the boss.*

Effective means 'in effect' in another way as well: 'in force; in operation; currently being applied': *The new regulations are effective from today.*

Such regulations could be *effective* in the earlier sense as well, of course; that is, they may work smoothly and have successful results. But instead of saying *effective regulations*, you could equally well speak of *effectual regulations*, and in that way avoid the ambiguity. *Effectual* means 'producing satisfactory results, achieving the intended purpose', just as *effective* does in its primary sense: *Your intervention was timely and effec-tual/effective. Effectual* is sometimes used in the

sense of 'having the ability to achieve results, capable', and here it is probably preferable to *effective*: *He's not a very effectual father, is he?* Note the negative use here; in fact, the negative form *ineffectual* is much commoner in such contexts: *an ineffectual little man.*

> Otto and Anni had heard loud, angry voices. Schmidt had come out of the bedroom, with Arthur following him in a state of ineffectual rage ... Arthur was angry because of something Schmidt had said to the Baron; Schmidt was insulting and contemptuous by turns.
> – Christopher Isherwood,
> *Mr Norris Changes Trains*

Efficient, like *effective,* suggests desired results, but this time results that are repeatedly or continuously being produced, and in a relatively effortless and very economical way, with a minimum of waste. An *efficient engine* is one that generates a great deal of power for each unit of fuel consumed. An office manager is *efficient* if he is well-organised and capable of *effective* action in performing his duties.

> Is British industry a lost cause? The conventional wisdom is that it is inefficient, over-manned, mismanaged and, worst of all, unprofitable.
> – Tim Congden, *The Times*

Similarly, the noun *efficiency*:

> I turned to the Foreign Office for help. Help came, with all the traditional speed and efficiency. After two months my eleventh telegram struck a sympathetic chord somewhere and I received the information.
> – Lawrence Durrell, *Esprit de Corps*

Finally, *efficacious*: this has a more theoretical ring to it, and means 'capable of producing the desired effect; potentially effective'. It is unlikely to refer to humans; most often it is used in connection with medical treatment: *Acupuncture is an efficacious remedy in this case, but she refuses to submit to it.* The following passage illustrates both *efficacious* and *effective*:

> He will provide you with a prescription for tranquillisers. If you take the stipulated dose, you may feel less depressed ... After a bit, however, a puzzling effect will become apparent; the pills will begin to seem less efficacious. Returning to the doctor, you will point this out, and he will recommend a slight increase in the dose. You will be much

relieved to find that the increased dose is as effective at dealing with the depression as the old, lesser dose was. But after a bit, a puzzling effect will become apparent.

— Bernard Levin, *The Times*

Three of the four adjectives are pronounced with the stress on the second syllable. The odd-man-out is *efficacious*, pronounced /**effi-kay**shəss/. All four adjectives have an opposite form beginning with *in-*. The positive forms and their opposites all have adverbial forms ending in *-ly*. The noun *efficacy* (pronounced /**effi**kə-si/) corresponds to both *effective* and *efficacious*. Other related nouns are *effectiveness*, *efficiency*, *effectuality* (rare) and *effectualness*, and *efficaciousness*.

See also DEFECTIVE.

effeminate, effete *Effeminate* does not mean the same as *feminine* ('relating to women, womanly'). It means 'womanish, unmanly', and is almost always applied to men: *He may have an effeminate walk but he's the toughest kid on the block.*

And *effete* does not mean *effeminate,* though it is often used in this way. In fact, *effete* derives from the Latin *effetus,* which applied to women only: it meant 'exhausted and worn out by childbearing' (it is related to the word *foetus*). In English, it was originally applied to women who had passed the menopause. The proper meaning today is 'spent, exhausted, drained of vitality', but the word has become confused with *effeminate* and is now more often used to mean 'soft, decadent, over-refined, lacking vigour'. (Used of intellectual men, it can also mean 'lacking energy and efficiency'.) Here are some examples of this modern use, which is now so widespead as to be considered standard:

Since Jeremy went to Oxford, she had felt herself drifting apart from her brother. She did not know precisely who Jeremy's friends were; she merely had a sense that the boy had started to inhabit an effete and busy world which she could not penetrate.

— A.N. Wilson, *The Sweets of Pimlico*

He was small and stocky, somewhat effete, a senior advisor to the Regents on protocol who also had Imperial Court rank.

— James Clavell, *Shogun*

efficient, efficacious See EFFECTIVE.

e.g., i.e. **1.** A strangely widespread error is the use of *i.e.* in the place of *e.g.* They are not inter-

changeable: *i.e.* stands for the Latin *id est*, 'that is'; *e.g.* stands for the Latin *exempli gratia*, 'for example' (literally, 'for the sake of an example'). So *i.e.* gives a full explanation of what precedes — *The floor manager, i.e. the person ultimately responsible for security, was away at the time of the theft* — whereas *e.g.* simply introduces an example or examples of what precedes: *The people responsible for security, e.g. the floor manager, were all away at the time of the theft.* In other words, *i.e.* restates and specifies, whereas *e.g.* just exemplifies; what comes after *i.e.* is the equivalent of what comes before it; what comes after *e.g.* is much less than — just an example of — what comes before it.

✗ If life extension gets out of hand (i.e., Dracula, or the 200-year-old high lama in *Lost Horizons*), the population will be kept down only by murder, suicide or accidents.

— Peter Davalle, television review in *The Times*

2. The abbreviations are best restricted to official (or very informal) writing. In ordinary discursive or descriptive writing, and in speech of all kinds, it is far better to use the full English phrases: *that is* (or *that is to say*), and *for example* (or *for instance*). There is no longer any need ever to say or write the full Latin forms *id est* and *exempli gratia* (except, as here, in discussing the terms themselves).

3. If you use *e.g.* at the beginning of a list, do not use *etc.* at the end of it. Either one of the two is enough: the use of *e.g.* is an admission that the list of examples is incomplete, so *etc.* is clearly redundant.

4. Nowadays *i.e.* and *e.g.* are usually not put in italics (or underlined) in running text, though some old-fashioned publishers still favour italics. At the other extreme, some modern texts do away with the full stops in *i.e.* and *e.g.*, usually leaving a half-space between the two letters in each case. Sometimes even the space is dispensed with: such severe streamlining is not advisable. It results in what seem to be full and distinct words — very odd-looking words: *? ie* and *? eg.*

Equally odd-looking is a capital *i* or capital *e* at the start of either abbreviation. Try to avoid using *e.g.* or *i.e.* at the beginning of a sentence, since neither a capital letter nor a small letter would then be quite satisfactory.

Note that a comma (sometimes a dash, semicolon, or bracket) is written directly before *i.e.* and *e.g.* But as a rule there is no need for a comma immediately afterwards. Though it would not be wrong if used in that position, it would tend

to clutter the text, and is best avoided.
See also VIZ.

egoist, egotist These nouns are often used interchangeably, but there is a theoretical distinction. The *egoist* is self-seeking, selfish, obsessed with his own interests. The *egotist* is self-centred and self-important, using the word *I* a great deal, and referring everything he hears to himself. (The Latin source of both words, *ego*, means 'I'.) An *egoist* might be nasty and ruthless, or sneaky perhaps; an *egotist* might be pompous and perhaps laughable. An *egotist* is boastful; an *egoist* might deliberately avoid boasting for fear that this would jeopardise his advancement.

Related to *egoist* and *egotist* are the nouns *egoism* and *egotism,* and the adjectives *egoistic, egoistical* and *egotistic, egotistical.* The preferred pronunciation for all these forms in British English is with the first syllable pronounced as 'egg', even though the word *ego* itself can often have a long vowel sound as in 'eagle'. (In American English, however, the usual pronunciation of all the words is with /ee/.) Note how the stress changes in the adjective forms: *egotistic,* /**ega-tis**tik/, and so on.
The following example illustrates the correct use of the *-tist* form:

> The consequence in Dallas is a skyline in which each large building bawls egotistically and competingly out at the world: look at me, don't look at the other guys.
> – Julian Barnes, *The Observer*

The following examples, however, would probably have been better had *egoism* and *egoistic* been used instead:

> *?* The compilation unfolds a grimy chronicle of egotism, resentment and, above all, envy. It is — dare I say it? — the most overweening account of a meagre and loveless existence since the appearance of Peter Hall's *Diaries.*
> – John Osborne, *The Observer*

> *?* While the feminist may sometimes be a prude (she may not), the male chauvinist is really a kind of egotistical limpet who, clinging to his preconceptions, looks for the threat of equality even when the subject is not sex but humanism.
> – Kathy Gal, letter to *The Observer*

Egoist also has a specialist sense in philosophy. The ethical theory of *egoism* puts forward the view both that self-interest is the basis of morality, and that it should govern one's motives and actions. An *egoist,* in philosophical parlance, is a person who subscribes to this theory.

either 1. *Either* (like *neither*) should strictly be used only in reference to two things — neither more nor less. If there are more than two subjects, then *any* should be used instead:

> ✗ Of the three possible routes, either will serve our purposes.

Replace *either* by *any.*
2. Although suggesting plurality, *either* is in fact grammatically singular: any related verbs or pronouns or possessive adjectives should therefore also be in the singular. But it is very common to find such sentences as *?? It's hardly likely that either of my children are bothered about their appearance.* The plural forms *are* and *their* sound natural here perhaps — first, because it is true of both children rather than just one; secondly, because the plural noun *children* precedes the verb immediately; thirdly, because *their* is a common-gender possessive adjective, where the 'correct' form *his* seems to overlook girls and women, and *his or her* sounds clumsy. Nevertheless, *are* and *their* are incorrect.

The same is true of *either . . . or* constructions, where *either* is now a conjunction. If each of the two elements is in the singular, then the verb too should be in the singular:

> I shouldn't think that either Stenmark or Wenzel is going to beat that time.

It should not read *?? are going to.* Of course, if each of the subjects is itself in the plural, then the plural verb is the correct one:

> I shouldn't think that either the Mahre twins or the Bell brothers are going to cope very well with these conditions.

What if only one of the elements is in the plural, the other being in the singular? The usual advice then is that the verb accords with the element that is closer to it:

> Are either the Mahre twins or Stenmark going to be interviewed this afternoon?
> I shouldn't think that either the Mahre twins or Stenmark is going to be interviewed.
> Either the managers or the shop steward is going to have to back down.
> Either the shop steward or the managers are going to have to back down.

The first and last of these examples are preferable — *are* seems more natural than *is* — so try to keep the plural noun nearer to the verb. Even better, try to avoid the entire predicament in the first place by a slight rewording:

> Either the managers are going to have to back down, or the shop steward is.

3. Even when both subjects in an *either . . . or* construction are in the singular, a choice of verb-form may still have to be made if pronouns are involved. The priority again goes to that subject which is nearer the verb:

> Either Anthony or you are going to have to resign.
> Either I or he is going to have to resign.
> *?* Either he or I am going to have to resign.

Once again, a slight rewording will enable you to avoid the awkwardness here:

> Either I am going to have to resign, or he is.

Or simply use an invariable verb:

> Either he or I must resign.

4. Though usually used in the sense 'one of two', *either* can also be used in the sense 'each of two; both', when referring to natural pairs:

> There are lines of stalls on either side of the road.

This usage attracts criticism — even though it was in fact the original usage! If you are anxious, however, to avoid provoking (ignorant) pedants, you can always use *each* or *both* instead of *either*: *on each side of the road* and *on both sides of the road* are unobjectionable.

5. Since *either* strictly applies to two things only, the choices are properly expressed in the pattern *either A or B* — not, strictly speaking, in the pattern *?either A or B or C . . .*
And yet such a pattern is encountered extraordinarily frequently, even in the works of outstanding writers:

> *?* I would not have thought of eating a meal without drinking either wine or cider or beer.
> — Ernest Hemingway (U.S.),
> *A Moveable Feast*

More examples in a moment. It is worth pausing, however, to try to find a justification for this common usage. One suggestion is that *either* can be understood as meaning something more or less like this: 'here begins a short list of possibilities — the list is a limited one, yet complete: all the possibilities are listed, but only one of them is in fact applicable'. If this sense is acceptable, then these further examples of *either . . . or . . . or . . .*

can be considered perfectly all right; if the new definition seems a little too pat, or an entirely unjustified rationalisation, then these examples will remain unacceptable. At all events, it is advisable to avoid the *either . . . or . . . or . . .* construction when in the presence of purists. (Sometimes, too, three options are given in an *either . . . or* sequence without using *or* twice, as in the third example below.)

> *?* Like many other admirers of Shakespeare, I had for years resented that hypocrisy and that stupidity which descend upon otherwise intelligent persons when they come to discuss the bawdy element in his plays and poems. Either they tried to minimise it or they exaggerated it or they distorted by setting it in a false perspective.
> — Eric Partridge,
> *The Gentle Art of Lexicography*

> *?* Olympian . . . has come down to earth to mean either splendid, or condescending, or indifferent, or supremely calm and dispassionate.
> — Philip Howard,
> *New Words for Old*

> *?* After the success of 'The Wine Programme', Channel Four has now gone on to prove what no other channel believed: that it's possible to make a series about food without either condescension, embarrassment or Russell Harty.
> — Julian Barnes, *The Observer*

> ✗ Each of these passages has faults of its own, but, quite apart from avoidable ugliness, two qualities are common to all of them. The first is staleness of imagery: the other is lack of precision. The writer either has a meaning and cannot express it, or he inadvertently says something else, or he is almost indifferent as to whether his words mean anything or not.
> — George Orwell,
> 'Politics and the English Language'

> ✗ Those who approach human contingency with Thomistic appetites to cover every situation, either exasperate, ultimately; or they end their days in futility; or they make bad law.
> — William F. Buckley, Jr. (U.S.),
> *Execution Eve*

6. In the last two examples, the authors are guilty of a further failing — that of asymmetry. *Either* and *or* should be in grammatical balance:

the construction introduced by *either* should be parallel to the construction introduced by *or*. You should not, for example, have a main verb on one side only:

× She is either loved by the spectators or she is hated by them — no one is indifferent.

The two sides of the *either ... or ...* formula can be made parallel in one of three ways:

She is either loved by the spectators or hated by them.

She either is loved by the spectators or is hated by them.

Either she is loved by the spectators or she is hated by them.

Similarly:

× Simla was like a garden city plastered on the side of huge mountains. Either you looked down over vast precipices, or away to distant peaks with a tremendous snow-line which appeared as the ramparts of heaven.
　　　　　　　　　　　　　－ Lord Butler,
　　　　　　　　The Art of the Possible

The best way of rectifying the imbalance here would be to add another *you looked* after the *or*. One last example:

× Yet the curious fact is that Britain — and virtually Britain alone — appears, as in wartime, to have a rising market for serious fiction. We can put this down either to talent among writers or discernment among readers.
　　　　　　　－ Malcolm Bradbury, *The Times*

Professor Bradbury should, for the sake of symmetry, have inserted the word *to* after the *or*: the passage would now be properly balanced to read *either to talent ... or to discernment ...* . Alternatively, he could have said *to either talent ... or discernment ...,* though this form is rather less elegant and also slightly misleading (the combination *to either talent* might at first be misunderstood as meaning 'to one talent or the other').

See PARALLEL CONSTRUCTIONS.

7. The pronunciation of *either* is often argued about — quite needlessly.

　Both /ithər/ and /eethər/ are correct: /ithər/ is now more common in standard British English; in American English, /eethər/ predominates, and /ithər/ might be considered slightly affected.

　See also AGREEMENT; NEITHER; NOR, OR; OR; THEY; WHETHER.

eke out　The original sense of *to eke out* was 'to add to or supplement in order to extend': *He eked out his income by working as a library clerk during the evening*. The Old English source word *eacan* meant simply 'to increase'.

　Two extended senses have developed. First, 'to cause to last longer, through economising': *They eked out their emergency rations for 21 days*.

They arrived at Heathrow airport yesterday still attired in headdress and galabeyas, louse-ridden and unwashed for a month, having eked out sparse water supplies and chewed desert plants for salt.
　　　　　　　　　－ Colin Hughes, *The Times*

Here the idea is of extending a meagre supply without adding to it. This sense is widely accepted.

　The second extended sense is 'to make (a living) with great effort': *She eked out a living by serving tea to the porters*. This is so well established by idiom now that it seems pointless to object to it. Yet purists continue to condemn it, and you will be criticised if you use it in their presence.

elder, eldest, older, oldest　*Elder* and *eldest* are more restricted terms than *older* and *oldest*. First, they can apply only to people, whereas *older* and *oldest* can apply also to buildings, mountains, newspapers, customs, and so on. Secondly, they can be used in only a limited range of grammatical constructions.

　Both *elder/eldest* and *older/oldest* can be used either as adjectives — *Tony is the elder/older brother*; *Sally is my eldest/oldest child* — or as nouns: *Tony is the elder/older of the two boys*; *The eldest/oldest of my three children is Sally*.

　However, *elder* and *eldest* cannot be used as adjectives if detached from their nouns. If detached adjectives are needed, then *older* and *oldest* have to be used: *Is Tim older than Tony? No, Tony is older*; *The child who is oldest is Sally*. *Elder* and *eldest* cannot be used in these sentences. If they are detached from their nouns, then they cease to be adjectives and become like nouns themselves, preceded by *the*, *my*, and so on. *Tony is the elder*; *The eldest of the three is Sally*. *Older* and *oldest* would be equally appropriate here.

　Not that *older* and *oldest* are always equally appropriate. Where *an* or *my*, for instance, is used immediately in front, rather than *the*, then *elder* and *eldest* are preferable: *He's got family responsibilities — he is after all an elder son*; *Sally is my eldest*. *Older* and *oldest* would sound awkward in these sentences, though they are not altogether impossible. Yet another difference is that *elder* can never be followed by *than,* whereas *older* can: × *Tony is elder than Tim.*

There are a few common cases in which *elder* is used outside the context of family relationships. As an adjective, *elder* can mean 'senior' when referring to two specified people: *Mr Gray is the elder partner, I believe — not Mr Brandon.* (*Elder* probably means 'older' here, though it could mean 'senior' in the sense of 'longer-serving'. *Eldest* can be used in an equivalent way of three people or more.) An *elder statesman* is an elderly person or retired politician, usually both, who acts as an unofficial adviser.

As a noun, *elder* can be used, usually in the plural, to refer to anyone who is older than the person addressed or referred to: *That young lady has no respect for her elders and betters*; *She is my elder by a good five years. Village elders,* usually limited to men, are the elderly and influential members of a small community. A *church elder* is a parishioner, usually unpaid and a layman, who has various responsibilities in the church's affairs.

elegy, eulogy The *eulogy* and the *elegy* both originally had to do with honouring the dead. An *elegy,* /**e**lliji/, was a lament, or a song of mourning. A *eulogy,* /yōōlə-ji/, was an oration in praise of a dead person. *Elegy* comes through Latin from an ancient Greek word meaning 'a mournful poem'. *Eulogy* comes through medieval Latin from the Greek word for 'praise'.

Both words now have extended meanings that reinforce this distinction. *Eulogy* today refers to any speech of praise or written tribute. An *elegy* came to be any poem or song in the rhythm or metre traditional for laments, or any poem about man's mortality, such as Thomas Gray's *Elegy Written in a Country Churchyard.* By extension, it can be any sorrowful or serious or emotional poem. It can also refer to a sorrowful musical composition, such as Elgar's cello concerto.

Note that *eulogy* always takes the article *a* rather than *an.* The adjective from *elegy* is *elegiac* (pronounced /elli-**ji**-ak, -ik/); from *eulogy, eulogistic.*

> Bernard Levin said in a very approving review of *Alice Fell* . . . that the book didn't seem to be bitter or angry or even despairing, but that it conveyed a sort of elegiac sadness about England in the 1950s and 1960s. Did you ever think of that novel as a swan-song?
> – John Haffenden, *The Literary Review*

'London, thou art the flower of cities all!'

Never have William Dunbar's noble words been truer than now, some 500 years after they were first written — at least, as far as chess is concerned. It takes a Scot to be really eulogistic about London, but Londoners can indeed be proud of what the city has done for national and international chess during the past two years.
> – Harry Golombek, *The Times*

Elegy can be made into the verb *to elegise,* meaning 'to compose an elegy' or 'to compose an elegy for (someone or something)'; *eulogy* gives rise to the verb *to eulogise,* meaning 'to praise enthusiastically'. The *g* is soft in all forms and derivatives of both words.

elicit, illicit These words have the same pronunciation, /i-**li**ssit/, but there is no connection in meaning, function, or origin. *To elicit* is a verb, going back to the Latin roots *ex-, e-,* 'out' + *lacere,* 'to allure or deceive'. *Illicit* is an adjective, from the Latin roots *in-,* 'not' + *licere,* 'to be permitted'.

To elicit something is to bring it out or evoke it: *We tried to elicit some response from the silent fishermen.*

> In Marek Nowakowski's *The Canary,* translated by Krystyna Bronkowska . . . it is martial law in Poland which has elicited each tale, and what emerges is a black comedy about a country governed by twisted logic.
> – Roger Lewis, *The Observer*

Illicit means 'not sanctioned; illegal': *an illicit still*; *illicit love.*

See also ILLEGAL.

elision See APOSTROPHE 3.

elk, moose The *moose* is a hoofed mammal of the deer family, having the Latin name *Alces alces* (or *Alces americana*), and inhabiting the forests of northern North America. It has a broad drooping snout; the male has large flat antlers. The same creature is found in Europe and Asia, but is then called an *elk.*

The Americans, however, also use the name *elk* for a quite distinct animal — a large North American deer, *Cervus canadensis.* Outside North America this animal is therefore called the *American elk* — or it goes by its other name, the *wapiti,* pronounced /**wop**pitti/.

The word *moose* comes from the American Indian language Natick. The only possible plural of the word is *moose. Elk* comes via Middle

English from Old Norse *elgr*. The plural is *elks* or collectively *elk* — that is, when referring to elk in general or as a species, as zoologists and hunters do. *Wapiti* is a Shawnee word with the literal meaning of 'white rump'. The plural is *wapitis* or collectively *wapiti*.

See also REINDEER.

ellipsis[1] **1.** The punctuation device known as an *ellipsis* (plural, *ellipses*) is usually represented by three dots in succession (. . .), though sometimes by an indefinite number (. . . . . . .). The dots are usually called *ellipsis*, but may also be called *leaders*.

They are typically used three at a time to indicate the omission of words in a quoted passage:

The dots . . . may also be called *leaders*.

Note that each dot tends to have a space or half-space before and after.

Ellipsis is also used to indicate the omission of whole sentences. Suppose the original text is:

John pleaded desperately. He swore undying love. Finally Jane said yes.

You could quote the first and last sentence only, as follows:

a. John pleaded desperately. . . . Finally Jane said yes.

Here we have the same three dots, each surrounded by spaces . . . but this time preceded by a fourth dot — the full stop, at the end of the first sentence, which has no space before it.

Now, compare the last example with this one:

b. John pleaded . . . . He swore undying love. Finally Jane said yes.

Here, the space before the first dot shows that the first sentence is incomplete. The fourth dot is the full stop this time.

Now, consider a final example:

c. John pleaded . . . Finally Jane said yes.

Here, the three evenly spaced dots suggests to the reader that something has been omitted from the end of the first sentence — and that one or more sentences have been omitted between the first sentence and the last.

So we have three types of sequence showing three different situations:

a. abc. . . . xyz — complete sentence followed by omitted material.
b. abc . . . . xyz — incomplete sentence but no omission thereafter.

c. abc . . . xyz — incomplete sentence followed by omitted material.

This distinction, it is true, is ignored by many writers and publishers: increasingly, the tendency is to follow pattern *a*., regardless of the type of omission.

2. Ellipsis can also show the omission of one or more lines of poetry, or of one or more whole paragraphs. If a paragraph or paragraphs are omitted, three dots, either centred or else placed at the left-hand margin, sometimes replace it or them.

. . . poached salmon for lunch.

. . .

And so, another wasted day passed, I retired early and was soon asleep.

If a line or lines of poetry are omitted, the convention is to use as many dots as necessary to fill up one line:

Tyger, tyger, burning bright
. . . .
What immortal hand or eye
Could frame thy fearful symmetry?

3. Ellipsis is also used to show hesitation in speech:

I . . . um . . . er . . . well . . . that is . . . I love you.

Dashes could also be used here, but the effect of ellipsis can be to suggest a trailing off or fading away of the voice rather than sudden breaks.

4. Ellipsis is also used, to mean roughly 'etc., and so forth', in order to indicate the continuation of something (such as a mathematical series) in a way that the reader can be expected to infer:

The even numbers are 2,4,6,8(,) . . .

The reader is expected to be able to continue the series with 10,12(,) . . .

Note that the first dot is preceded by a space, and that the comma after the last specified number is optional.

5. a. Ellipsis can be used for a variety of rhetorical effects — to indicate to the reader a certain reluctance to spell things out, for instance; or to suggest a build-up to a surprise announcement or to the reversal of expectation, and so on. (A dash is often used for the same purpose.) An example of this 'rhetorical' ellipsis can be found near the start of this article:

We have the same three dots, each surrounded by spaces . . . but this time preceded by a fourth dot.

In the following example, the ellipsis serves to indicate a thoughtful pause, heralding a slight modification of the idea previously expressed:

> I thought how quickly and easily all the ties of one life could be broken and those of a new one built up ... it was sad to reflect that the new friends were probably just as transitory, and the links with them just as fragile.
> — Lynne Reid Banks,
> *The L-Shaped Room*

b. The danger in attempting rhetorical effects like this is that they will fall flat. In the following passage, ellipses are used to create brief periods of suspense — as if representing breathless pauses in speech:

> Earning that respect means keeping up the momentum ... getting down on paper the ideas whirling around in your head ... in a word, writing regularly.
> — advertisement, *The Sunday Times*

At the end of all this artificially generated suspense, the 'climax' turns out to be quite banal. The reader's reaction is one of letdown and disappointment. The text should really have been punctuated more modestly, the ellipses being replaced by a comma in each case, or by a comma in the first case, and a dash or colon in the second.

c. Some writers use ellipses at the end of a sentence instead of using a full stop, even though nothing has been omitted at all:

> Well, darling, it's getting late ... I really must end this letter ... I think of you very much ... Goodbye for now ...

This stylistic tic, characteristic of certain informal correspondence, is perhaps intended to suggest that each sentence, though complete, leaves much unsaid. The same convention, with perhaps the same implication, has been employed by gossip columnists in provincial newspapers:

> Well, so the egregious Clive Beauchamp has been seen at yet another disco with yet another sultry blonde 'business acquaintance' ... Everyone is asking when Mrs Beauchamp will find out ...

In a personal letter the effect may be amateurishly touching; in printed journalism the effect is merely amateurish. The commitment to a full stop at the end of a complete sentence may be less suggestive than this use of ellipsis, but it is more forthright and honest — full stop.

6. Look again at the example in section **5. a.** above ('quoted' from the beginning of the article):

We have the same three dots, each surrounded by spaces ... but this time preceded by a fourth dot.

In fact, the original sentence at the beginning of the article did not end at this point, and began slightly earlier than the quoted sentence here. Purists would insist that the curtailed version just quoted should therefore begin with three dots and end with three dots — and even that the capital W at the beginning should be enclosed in square brackets, since it is not a true representation of the original sentence (which had a small *w* at that point: for an example of heavy purist punctuation of this kind, see PUNCTUATION). Increasingly, however, the tendency is to take small liberties at the beginning and end of a quotation, and to restrict the three dots to the middle of a quotation. Of course, if the quoted version does not make a full sentence in itself, then dots will have to be used before or after (or both).

If each part of the quotation is enclosed in quotation marks (rather than merely indented), then even the purists are happy to omit the dots if the surrounding sentence allows it. So:

> We have here 'the same three dots', as noted above, 'but this time preceded by a fourth dot'.

No dots are needed before the *but* here, for instance: the quotation marks are enough to indicate a possible break in the quoted text.

ellipsis² See OMISSION OF VERBS.

else The possessive forms using this word are today written *anyone else's, someone else's,* and so on. If you feel it sounds awkward (*Who else's car was stolen?*), try a thorough rephrasing (*Who else had a car stolen?*) rather than the very old-fashioned possessive (*? Whose car else was stolen?*). (See -'S, -S' **6**.)

The use of *else* on its own as a coordinating conjunction is common in informal speech: *? Run, else you'll be late!* But *or else,* or simply *or,* is recommended in more formal usage.

elude, elusive See ALLUDE.

emend *To emend* is far more restricted in meaning than *to amend*. *To amend,* /ə-mend/, can have the general sense of 'to correct, or at least improve, by changing or adding to': *to amend the second chapter.* More specifically, it means 'to change or add to the wording of' (a parliamentary bill, for instance); and, in its rather old-fashioned use as an intransitive verb, 'to improve one's conduct, mend one's ways': *If you don't amend, I'll disinherit you.*

To emend, /i-**mend**/, is usually limited to the technical language of scholars, and means 'to correct and improve (a text) by critical editing': *Dr Johnson emended the available versions of Shakespeare's plays.*

You can of course *amend* a text too. The difference between *emending* and *amending* a text is based on the two ways in which a text can be considered correct. A text might be 'correct' if it is in its original, purest, or most authentic form. To restore it to this form, you *emend* it. On the other hand, the text might be 'correct' if it is in its best possible form, usually different from the original: to change it to this improved form, you *amend* it.

So an *emendation* is a change back towards an earlier state; an *amendment* is a change forward to a new and better state. *Amendments* often take the form of additions as well as corrections or alterations: the Amendments to the Constitution of the United States, for instance, include not just alterations to the original (such as the direct rather than the indirect election of Senators) but also additions to the original (such as the Bill of Rights).

Both *amend* and *emend* go back to the Latin *emendare*, 'to free from faults', from *ex-*, *e-*, 'out of' (removal) + *mendum*, 'a defect or fault'. Old French altered the Latin verb to *amender* — hence the two forms in English today.

Note the related nouns: *amendment* and *emendation*.

emigrate, immigrate   *To emigrate* is to leave a country to settle abroad. Its prefix comes from the Latin *ex*, 'out of'. *To immigrate* is to enter, and settle in, a new country: its prefix comes from the Latin *in*, 'into'. A person who *emigrates* is an *emigrant*; one who *immigrates* is an *immigrant*. (Note the spellings: one *m* in *emigrate* and its derivatives, two in *immigrate* and its derivatives).

A person who moves from one country to settle in another is obviously both an *emigrant* (from his country of origin) and an *immigrant* (to his new home). An *emigrant* from Germany who comes to Britain is an *immigrant* to Britain.

However, speakers will often say *an emigrant to Britain*, or *an immigrant from Germany* or *a German immigrant*; this is quite acceptable so long as the unspecified country is at least implicit,

as it usually is when that unnamed country is the speaker's own.

In American English the word *immigrant* occurs far more frequently than the word *emigrant*, presumably because the United States sees itself primarily as a receiving country, as 'a country of immigration'.

Immigrant, both as noun and as adjective, is occasionally used in Britain nowadays to refer to people who are not white, whether or not they were born abroad. It is true that *black* is ambiguous for this purpose (are Asians included in that term, or not?) and that *coloured, non-white,* and *non-European* may be slightly demeaning, but *immigrant* is hardly a happy or even an accurate alternative when applied to someone who was born in Leeds or London. (See BLACK.)

A contrary force is also at work in influencing the meaning of *immigrant* — the force of hospitality and assimilation. The word is often restricted to relative newcomers. Among well-disposed people, and in societies (notably the United States, Canada, and Australia) with a tradition of welcoming and absorbing foreigners, the term *immigrant* is unlikely to be used of anyone who has been settled in his new country for any length of time.

The word *émigré* (or *emigré*) is sometimes confused with *emigrant*. It originally referred to emigrants from France at the time of the French Revolution. It is the past participle of the French *émigrer,* so that its literal meaning is simply 'emigrated'. Dictionaries define both *émigré* and *refugee* as an 'emigrant who flees his country for political reasons'. But the two words have taken on connotations, in British English at least, that distinguish them from *emigrant* and also from each other.

Refugee evokes pictures of poverty and desperation. It suggests an urgent flight from danger, and huddled grouping in camps or cramped tenements in a foreign country reluctantly offering asylum. It also suggests a recent arrival or at least an unassimilated foreigner. Once again, anyone who has become successful in his new country would no longer be called a *refugee.*

Emigré has quite different associations nowadays. The *émigré*'s departure from his homeland might have been more leisurely, less urgent, than that of the *refugee.* An *émigré* probably escaped from a distant potential danger, or simply an uncongenial social or intellectual atmosphere, rather than from some immediate mortal threat.

And an *émigré* would tend to be an upper-class European, whereas *refugees* come from all societies — today from the Third World in particular. The term *émigré* strongly suggests a *cultured* emigrant. The French suffix *-é* gives the word an overtone of refinement. And since *émigrés*, often Jewish, of Russian, German, Hungarian, and other European origin, have in recent times established intellectual circles in Western Europe and North America, this overtone of cultivation has been reinforced. Artists are *émigrés*; peasants are *refugees*. The word *émigré*, especially when used adjectivally, can sound distinctly debonair: *drawn again to his favourite émigré haunts.* (In North American English this cultural differentiation between *émigré* and *refugee* is less likely to be observed. The word *refugee* brings to mind German-Jewish intellectuals and Vietnamese boat-people alike).

Finally, an *émigré*, unlike an *immigrant* or a *refugee*, is likely to retain that label throughout his life.

Note that the form *émigré* remains unchanged in English when applied to a woman: no extra *e* is added at the end as it would be if it were still a French word. When written in running text, the word need not be underlined or italicised.

The words *emigrant, refugee,* and *émigré* do not cover all the possibilities, of course. A person forced to leave his homeland by a legal decree is an *exile*. A person escaping to another country in order to evade the consequences of a crime may be called a *fugitive from justice*. A person who lives abroad in order to avoid heavy taxation at home is often referred to as a *tax exile*. An *evacuee* is someone who is sent away for his own safety — not necessarily out of a country. Since the Second World War, *displaced person* has come increasingly to be used in referring to someone ousted from his country because of political trouble. It is more neutral than *refugee* or *émigré*, suggesting neither flight nor voluntary departure. It is also rather faceless and euphemistic. By contrast an *expatriate* is typically someone living abroad voluntarily, not necessarily permanently, often for business reasons.

The verb *to migrate*, finally, is sometimes confused with *to emigrate* and *to immigrate*. *To migrate* implies a lack of permanent settlement, and a continual or repeated movement from place to place. It does not necessarily imply entering or leaving a country, and is used of birds and antelope, for example, as well as of people.

Migration, like *emigration* and *immigration,* is a widely used noun; so is *migrant,* as are *emigrant* and *immigrant*. In Australia, *migrant* is commonly used to refer to an immigrant. As an adjective too, *migrant* is in common use, far more

so than the adjectives *emigrant* and *immigrant*. You often hear of *migrant birds* or *migrant workers*: the suggestion is that they are living only temporarily in a given place, and will soon be moving on again.

eminent, imminent, immanent These words are similar in sound, but have no overlap of meaning. *Eminent* means 'prominent, outstanding': *an eminent surgeon*.

> What Amis complained of was not *how* the book was written but that it had been written at all. It lacked one vital qualification. 'He's not eminent,' Amis told the programme's presenter, Simon Winchester. 'You could take a boring account of a childhood in a Swiss village because it's Albert Schweitzer who's doing it, and that would be interesting. But Oakes isn't eminent enough.' ... Amis's law ... decrees that eminence is a prerequisite of autobiography.
> – Philip Oakes, *The Times*

Imminent means 'about to happen, threatening': *an imminent collapse*.

> This has fuelled speculation that a new clampdown on spending is imminent; some believe in weeks, rather than months.
> – David Millward, *Daily Telegraph*

> Before long it was obvious that our other arms, stuck out as they were, were in imminent danger of being torn away; so he put both arms round my waist and I tucked my elbows in.
> – Lynne Reid Banks,
> *The L-Shaped Room*

Immanent is a rarer word meaning 'existing within, inherent':

> She resisted the Hollywood professional prettifiers, who wanted to reduce her to the starlet's symmetrical banalities: beauty is not something imposed but something immanent.
> – Anthony Burgess, *The Observer*

> The sovereign power inherent in the British Crown, as exercised through Council and through Parliament, derives not from a treaty or document or compact, but from prescription, from the fact that it has been so from time immemorial — that it is immanent in the nation itself.
> – Enoch Powell, *Daily Telegraph*

Theologians use *immanent* with reference to God,

affirming that He is present throughout the universe. (Compare TRANSCENDENT.)

The Latin roots of the three words are these: *immanent* goes back to *in*-, 'in' + *manere*, 'to remain'; *imminent* to *in*-, 'towards, into' + '*-minere*', 'to project'; *eminent* to *ex*-, 'out, outwards' + *-minere*, 'to project'.

Eminent is clearly distinguished in pronunciation by its first vowel sound, but *imminent* and *immanent* are barely distinguishable by the second vowel: /imminənt/ and /immənənt/. All three words have related nouns ending in *-ence*.

emotive, emotional *Emotive* tends to mean 'causing or producing emotion' — especially, emotion as distinct from reason: *The bread shortage became an emotive issue, and riots seemed inevitable.*

Emotional can still be used in this way, though its commoner meanings — which *emotive* does not share — are rather different: 'undergoing emotion' or 'revealing emotion': *a very emotional young man, easily moved to tears*; *an emotional farewell.*

So *emotional language* would usually mean 'heartfelt language, imbued with deep feeling', though it could also mean the same as *emotive language*, 'language deliberately designed to provoke emotions' — typically feelings of anger, or an irrational and indignant response.

empathy See SYMPATHY.

-en This suffix has three principal functions: it forms plurals; it forms verbs from adjectives; and it forms adjectives from nouns.

Of the *-en* plurals, little need be said. The only three that survive in modern English are *children, oxen,* and the archaic or ceremonial *brethren,* though the form was much commoner in older English, which had *eye, eyen, hose, hosen,* and *shoe, shoon.*

The *-en* verbs are formed from one-syllable adjectives: *to cheapen, darken, quicken, ripen, sadden, sharpen, thicken, lighten, widen,* and so on. There is also the verb *to quieten,* though American English prefers *to quiet.*

This way of making verbs is not very 'productive', as the grammarians say; that is, *-en* is not continually used to make new words. Alternative ways of forming a verb from an adjective are simply to use the adjective verbally (*blind, to blind*), or to attach a prefix such as *en-* to the beginning (*large, to enlarge*). There seems to be no reason why some adjectives have selected one course and others another: we *moisten* things but

we *wet* them; a person can be either *deafened* or *blinded.*

Where there is a choice between two forms, one may be the more modern of the two. *To fat* and *to glad* are archaic synonyms of *to fatten* and *to gladden*; think of the Biblical *fatted calf*. Alternatively, one form may be chiefly in figurative use and the other be more literal: you *black* boots or someone's eye, but *blacken* a reputation; you *dampen* a shirt before ironing it, but *damp* (*down*) a fire or sound waves; you *slacken* a rope, but accuse lazy people of *slacking*; you *roughen* a surface, but *rough in* a drawing, *rough up* an opponent, and *rough it* when camping.

Adjectives too can be formed by adding *-en* to the noun: the *-en* suffix here implies 'made of' or 'like': *earthen, wooden, woollen, flaxen, silken, ashen.* In many cases, the noun alone can also be used like an adjective: *a silk dress.* The *-en* adjective tends to be more poetic and figurative than the bare form. So: *a gold watch* but *golden curls; wax candles* but *waxen pallor; lead pipes* but *leaden skies.*

encyclopaedia, encyclopedia Both spellings are perfectly acceptable, though *-pedia* is the favoured form in American English, and is becoming more widespread in British English too. The spelling in which the two vowels are fused as *æ* is very rare nowadays. The Greek roots of the word mean literally 'general education', very appropriate for the name of a comprehensive reference book.

The adjective *encyclopaedic/encyclopedic* is in common use today in the sense of 'comprehensive, embracing many subjects': *a woman with an encyclopaedic breadth of knowledge.*

endemic, epidemic These similar-sounding words are both sometimes used to describe diseases, and so the danger of confusion between them is increased.

The adjective *endemic* means 'prevalent in a particular place, restricted to one region and breaking out recurrently'. It comes from the Greek *endemos,* meaning 'native, indigenous', from *en*-, 'in' + *demos,* 'people'. It is used not only of disease but to describe anything — especially anything bad — that is prevalent or recurrent in a particular area or context, or that is native and deep-rooted: *problems endemic in an industrial city.*

I have a holy horror of COSEPI, *not* as an exotic malady, which may afflict persons of different pigmentation, in far off lands, but for precisely the opposite reason: because it is endemic among my own people, and because its ravages are all too familiar, and come too close.

– Conor Cruise O'Brien, *The Observer*

Endemic can also be used as a noun, but only in one rare and specialist context: *an endemic* is a biological term for an endemic plant or animal — one that is native to and restricted to a particular area.

Epidemic can be used as both adjective and noun; the noun is probably more common. The word, like *endemic,* also comes from the Greek: the source-words mean literally 'among people'. The noun refers to a disease that spreads rapidly among many people and then dies out: *an epidemic of cholera.*

Epidemic is also used of anything resembling a rapidly spreading disease: *There is an epidemic of mugging in our cities.*

The whole city lay under an epidemic of discreet, infectious fear. I could feel it, like influenza, in my bones.

– Christopher Isherwood,
Mr Norris Changes Trains

As an adjective, *epidemic* means 'spreading rapidly, like a disease'. It appears nowadays mostly in the overused and slipshod phrase *of epidemic proportions* — a phrase that is not only a cliché, but unacceptably loose as well — 'spreading rapidly' is not really a measure of size or extent.

In the following quotation, *epidemic* might have been replaced by *endemic,* producing a slight change in meaning:

One of the worse-hit areas was St Teresa's Gardens, a complex of Corporation flats on the southside of the city along the Grand Canal. ... Last summer the local Development Committee reckoned that unemployment was almost 60 per cent ... Heroin abuse among youngsters was epidemic. And as the number of young people with a habit to sustain increased, so did handbag snatching, muggings and break-ins.

– Eamonn McCann, *The New Statesman*

Since the Greek roots contain the word for people, *epidemic* and *endemic* should strictly speaking not be used of plagues among animals; for these there are the terms *epizootic* and *enzootic.* Only a pedant would insist on this limitation, however. *Epizootic* and *enzootic* are too rare for most people to understand.

enervate   *To enervate* is sometimes wrongly understood to mean either 'to energise, invigorate' or 'to irritate'. In fact, *to enervate* means 'to deprive of strength or energy, devitalise': *I was enervated by the oppressive heat.* It comes from the Latin *enervare,* literally 'to remove the sinews from', from *ex-,* 'away from' + *nervus,* 'a sinew or nerve'. Note that it is usually used in the present or past participle: *an enervating illness*; *feeling enervated and irritable.*

The mattresses are perfectly comfortable, and I have always found a soft bed enervating.

– Aunt Augusta, in Graham Greene's
Travels With My Aunt

From the now dark and deserted *maidan,* across which the uninterrupted currents of warm — even voluptuous — air build up an impetus that comes upon the cheek as a fairly perceptible breath of enervating rather than refreshing wind, there issues a darkness of the soul.

– Paul Scott, *The Jewel in the Crown*

Enervated tends to mean 'listless, or lethargic and inactive' rather than 'exhausted by activity'. So we might say *She was enervated by the humidity* but not ?? *She was enervated by her arduous training session.*

Enervate is also used as a bookish adjective, meaning 'drained of strength, devitalised'. The pronunciation is different, however: whereas the verb is pronounced /**enn**ər-vayt/, the adjective is pronounced /i-**nerv**ət/.

The technical verb *to innervate* (with stress on either the first or second syllable) means 'to supply with nerves' or 'to stimulate (a nerve or muscle)' — in effect, the exact opposite of *to enervate.*

The mistake sometimes made of thinking that *enervating* means 'irritating' is perhaps due to an association with 'getting on one's nerves'. Interestingly enough, the French verb *énerver,* 'to enervate', can also be used to mean 'to irritate, annoy'. In fact, the common expression *Cela m'énerve* may be translated as 'That gets on my nerves' or 'That really annoys me', but should not be translated as 'That enervates me'.

enforce   You can *enforce* a regulation, or *enforce* desirable behaviour *on* or *upon* a person, as in *The teacher enforced obedience on the children.* You cannot nowadays, correctly, *enforce* a person *to* do something or *into* doing something, as in ✗ *The teacher enforced the children into obedience*; ✗ *The teacher enforced the children to* *obey her*. Use *force*, *coerce*, or other such verbs for these constructions.

England See BRITAIN.

English round the world In 1599, a far-sighted English poet wrote these lines:

> And who in time knows whither we may vent
> The treasure of our tongue, to what strange shores
> This gain of our best glory shall be sent,
> T'enrich unknowing Nations with our stores?
>
> – Samuel Daniel, 'Musophilus'

But not even he could have guessed that in the following four centuries English would have spread from one small island and perhaps seven million speakers to become a mother tongue in every continent, the official language of the Commonwealth and the lingua franca of the world.

Other languages — Greek and Latin, Spanish and French, Turkish and Arabic — have spread beyond their original homelands in the wake of political, cultural, or religious expansion; but no language in the history of the world has spread more widely or been used more extensively than English.

The distribution of English It is difficult to put a figure on the number of English speakers in the world today. Are we to include as mother-tongue English speakers those who speak pidgins and creoles? And those who 'know' English as a foreign language — how proficient do they have to be before they are counted as 'English speakers'?

If we choose to allow fairly generous entrance-qualifications, then the worldwide community of English speakers must number at least 1000 million, almost a quarter of the world's population. If moderately rigorous standards are applied, then 700 million seems a fair figure, about half of them mother-tongue English speakers.

In terms of sheer numbers, English is rivalled or perhaps surpassed by Guoyu, the form of Mandarin Chinese promoted in the People's Republic of China as a national language, and now understood by about 800 million Chinese, four-fifths of the country's population. It is by no means the mother tongue of this number, however; and those Chinese living in communities outside China speak quite different dialects for the most part, notably Cantonese.

Next in the league table of mother tongues are Spanish (about 250 million), Hindi (about 200 million), and Arabic, Bengali, and Russian (about 150 million each).

English may be rivalled by Guoyu in respect of numbers, but in its geographical distribution and international usefulness English is in a class of its own.

There are four main categories of English in the world today: English as a mother tongue; English as a second language; English as a foreign language; and the family of pidgin and creole Englishes.

English as a mother tongue English as a mother tongue is dominated by the North Americans (about 220 million in the United States, and a further 20 million or so in Canada). What is more, the regional dialects within North America are far less diverse than they are within the British Isles. There are about 56 million English speakers in Great Britain and about four million in Ireland. Scottish English and Irish English might fairly claim to be considered separate varieties, however, as might several dialects within England itself — these are all in many ways more distinct from the 'standard' English of England than American English is. Nevertheless, 'British English' remains a convenient label, and is often used too, as in this book, to cover the varieties of mother-tongue English in Australia (about 14 million speakers), New Zealand (about three million) and South Africa (about two million).

English, ranging from standard to creole, is the sole official language of many countries in the Caribbean, and in various small islands and territories in other parts of the world.

Many other countries, though not typically having English as a mother tongue, do have a considerable number of mother-tongue English speakers nevertheless. India is the foremost example, with several million mother-tongue English speakers.

English as a second language The English of India is for the most part English as a second language. So too in the other Commonwealth countries not already mentioned, in Africa and Asia alike; and also in Pakistan, the Philippines, and various other countries. (And so too for French-speaking Canadians and for Afrikaans-speaking and many black South Africans.) In all these areas, English as a second language (sometimes as an alternative official language) enjoys great prestige, and fulfils an essential role in the educational and economic life of the nation.

It tends to be the language of much of the country's broadcasting, many of its newspapers, and often novels and other works of literature too; of secondary and higher education, the higher courts of law, and the civil service; and of international business contacts, of course.

For reasons of national pride, various Commonwealth countries have made official attempts to reduce the role of English in national life and to promote an indigenous language in its place. This policy has perhaps succeeded to some extent in Tanzania, where Swahili is widely understood. In a country such as India, however, where Hindi has to compete with so many other local languages, English has remained fairly resilient. Malaysia, after independence, attempted to promote Bahasa Malaysia as a national language, introducing it as the medium of primary education in the mid-1960s, and of secondary education in the mid-1970s. It is used to some extent in the universities too (and plans are afoot to substitute it for English in the federal and supreme courts). But the short-term effect has been a decline in examination performance, with the result that Malaysian students are now at a greater disadvantage than previously in securing university places in Britain or North America. An intensified programme of English-teaching is the planned remedy, though many educationalists, more radically, would prefer a return to the use of English as the medium of instruction.

English as a second language has traditionally been modelled on British English (understandably enough, since most of the countries using it were once part of the British Empire). The major exception is the Philippines, where American English is adopted as the model.

English as a foreign language After mother-tongue English and English as a second language, there is the category of English as a foreign language. English is easily the most widely taught foreign language in the world. All those African countries that use French rather than English as their established or official second language have a policy of teaching English as a third language. An estimated ten per cent of China's enormous population have some mastery of English. Some 51 per cent of foreign-language courses taught in the Soviet Union are English courses. Everyone is familiar with the wide range of abilities displayed by foreigners — from the enthusiastic but virtually unintelligible efforts of taxi-drivers or shopkeepers in far-flung centres of tourism, to the quiet and effortless fluency of so many Scandinavians, Dutch, Israelis, Germans, and so on.

In Europe, it has traditionally been British English that teachers have tried to teach for the most part. The tendency seems to be shifting slowly towards American English now. In Latin America, with the partial exception of Argentina,

American English is the favoured variety. The teaching of English as a foreign language, and the publication of course-books and tapes, are now considered major industries in both Britain and North America.

Two other aspects of English as a foreign language — English for special purposes, and English as a world language — are discussed below.

Pidgins and creoles The fourth category of English is pidgins and creoles. Pidgin English is a simplified language, drawing on English vocabulary (but very little on the complicated grammar of English), and used as a medium of communication between two people or communities (one of whom would, of course, originally have been English-speaking, but this soon ceases to be necessary). A pidgin that becomes a mother tongue is called a creole, and invariably acquires a more sophisticated structure. (See PIDGINS AND CREOLES.) English-based pidgins and creoles, serving many cultural and economic functions, are found throughout the British Caribbean in countries such as Barbados, Guyana, Jamaica, St Lucia, and Trinidad and Tobago; in coastal West Africa from the river Gambia to Rio Muni; and in the South Pacific, in Papua New Guinea, Samoa, the Solomons, and even parts of Australia.

Typically, the educated people in these countries speak and write standard English, at least in formal and professional contexts, either as a mother tongue or as a second language.

The spectrum of English In all countries where English is spoken, there is a spectrum or continuum, though the type of spectrum differs according to circumstances. At one end of the spectrum is always the influential 'standard' variety of English. In countries such as Jamaica and Samoa, the other end of the spectrum is creole. In countries such as Canada and Britain, the spectrum may be one of regional dialect or of social dialect. In countries such as France and China (English as a foreign language), or India and the Philippines (English as a second language), the spectrum is one of competence — with standard English as a prestige norm, and with any number of approximations to it, each affected by the pronunciation, vocabulary, and syntax of the speaker's own first language.

Although each spectrum has its unique characteristics, it is possible to make some generalisations about them. Varieties of English as a second or foreign language or in creolised form do tend to have some systematic differences from standard English.

In pronunciation, first of all, they tend to have a smaller set of vowel contrasts than either RP (the 'received pronunciation' of educated people in southeastern England) or General American pronunciation. In particular, the vowel sounds in *bit* and *beat* are pronounced alike, as are those in *full* and *fool*; diphthongs are often replaced, so that *day* might sound like *dare* and *go* like *gore*. The words *bud* and *bird* are often made to sound like *bed* (and sometimes like *bet*).

Typical consonant changes include the replacement of /th/ and /t̲h̲/ by /t/ and /d/ or sometimes by /s/ and /z̲/ — so *this thing* might sound like *dis ting* or sometimes *zis sing*. And where consonant clusters are difficult to pronounce, an extra or 'epenthetic' vowel is often inserted to break the cluster up: *school* might be pronounced as though it were *eschool* or *sechool*, and *speak* as though *espeak* or *sepeak*.

The stress system of standard English is also altered: there are fewer reduced vowels and hence fewer slurred and unstressed syllables, and there is a greater number of secondary stresses.

In vocabulary, these varieties of English all tend to draw on words borrowed from local languages, and on loan translations or 'calques' — that is, on metaphors, phrases, or compound words in the local language that are translated literally, component by component, into English. Such vocabulary items are especially common in the domains of local culture, food, clothing, and kinship.

In grammar, these varieties of English reveal many similarities: the tendency to use fewer prepositions, articles, and auxiliary verbs; the use of prepositional verbs such as *cope up with* that are not found among mother-tongue speakers; the use of unvarying question-tags: *They're just married, isn't it?*; the recapitulation of the subject: *That man he is not good*; and the non-inversion of the verb phrase in a question: *What you are doing tonight?*

English for special purposes, and English as a world language English is the international language of science, the way that Latin and then perhaps German used to be: it is estimated that two-thirds of all scientific papers today are first published in English.

Since the end of the Second World War, aircraft pilots and sea-captains on international routes have required proficiency in radio English. (Even pilots flying only within their own country tend to use international English expressions nowadays, such as *Roger, Negative*, and *How do You Read?*)

English is clearly now the language of international diplomacy, in the way that French was in the 19th century. It is the official or alternative official language of more countries than any other; it is one of the six official languages of the United Nations, and one of its two working languages (the other being French). It is also the language used by the International Olympic Committee.

It is the language of international pop culture (many young people in Europe, Japan, and so on seem to learn more English from pop records than from schoolteachers).

In some ways, then, English is already an international language — and not just among scholars, the way that Latin was during its period as an 'international' language in Europe in the Middle Ages and after. If business negotiations, or arrangements for a football match, were to be conducted between a Yugoslav and a Brazilian, say, the language of discussion would be English. It is most unlikely ever to gain official recognition as the world language, but it is as close to being one as any language ever has been. And if an official world language ever were to be adopted — in the cause of world peace, for instance — it might well be English, rather than any of the artificial world languages. (Over a dozen of these have been devised, mostly at the end of the 19th century. Esperanto is the best known and most successful: its speakers have been estimated at as many as a million, and as few as 100,000.)

English, in a simplified form at any rate, would be a fairly good choice on linguistic grounds: it has few inflections — that is, complicated changes to the form of a word according to its grammatical functions — and is free from the confusing gender-system that characterises most other European languages. Its vocabulary, with a large Latin-based component, is reasonably familiar to most western Europeans. On the other hand, its spelling is, for historical reasons, rather troublesome (see SPELLING); and its pronunciation system has subtleties of contrast that many foreigners find very difficult to master (though it has nothing to compare with the tricky clustering of consonants involved in Russian, or the tone-changes that characterise Chinese). All in all, English is a relatively easy language to acquire communicative competence in — and that is all that a world language should be expected to provide. To acquire mastery of English is another matter, of course: its large vocabulary and its vast stock of idioms (*jump the gun, to go great guns, to stick to one's guns, to spike someone's guns*) and phrasal and prepositional verbs (*to put someone down, to put someone up, to put up with someone*) are an endless headache to foreign students trying to approach full proficiency in English.

One unintended effect of the pervasiveness of English in non-English-speaking countries is the infiltration of English terms into foreign languages — a development many find distressing. Pop records, Hollywood films, and American culture generally are largely responsible for this. France in particular has long been worried by the English invasion. Over 2000 glaring English expressions have apparently been recorded in French: some are quite established now — *le weekend, le sandwich, le parking, le camping, le smoking* (a dinner jacket). Increasingly, too, *le drugstore, le gangster, le gadget, le striptease,* and *le cocktail* seem to be settling in, often, presumably, for want of an efficient French equivalent. Whether *le businessman, le bulldozer,* and *le baby-sitter* will stand the test of time is uncertain.

The late President Pompidou urged the abolition of anglicisms, and pressed for a policy of French 'linguistic integrity'. In official documents, the phrases *hot money, fast food,* and *jumbo jet* were to be replaced by French expressions instead: *capitaux fébriles, prêt-à-manger,* and *gros-porteur.* (But the Parisian public, one suspects, will continue using the English terms.)

Here are some British or American exports to other languages:
● to German: *das Baby* (fully established now), *der Bestseller, der Computer, der Teenager, das Teeshirt,* and again, *der Babysitter, der Cocktail, der Gangster.*
● to Italian: *jeans, la spray, la pop art, il popcorn, il supermarket,* and, once again, *il weekend.*
● to Spanish: *jeans* again, and *pancakes, suéter* (sweater), and the sporting terms *béisbol* (baseball), *boxeo* (boxing), and *nócaut* (knockout).

Many English words seem to be in worldwide use — the pioneers perhaps of a new world language. Some, like *cigarette, hotel, passport, post,* and *sport* might at first have been adopted internationally under French influence, but the impetus today is clearly American: *OK, jeans, Coca-Cola, program, soda, dollar,* and so on. Other 'international' terms (many from Greek, Latin, or French sources) are *airport, bank, bar, bus, camera, football, goal, golf, menu, salad, steak, stop, taxi, telephone, television, tennis, whisky.*

An independent parallel development is the coining of many scientific terms by combining Latin and Greek elements to form an International Scientific Vocabulary, with results known to specialists in many lands: *telespectroscope, polyvinyl,* and so on.

What does the future hold for World English? Some scholars are pessimistic. Dr R.W. Burchfield, when chief editor of the Oxford Dictionaries, expressed the view that some varieties of English are in danger of diverging to the point of mutual incomprehensibility — British and American English might, in 100 years time, be as different from each other as French is from Italian. English already exists in a number of *dialects*; these could become *languages* — rather in the way that Latin split into French, Italian, Spanish, and so on.

In fact, however, the evidence suggests that mother-tongue varieties of English are converging rather than diverging. With second-language varieties, it is true, English could suffer from its own success, and become fragmented in the way just suggested. But working against such a fate is the function of English as a lingua franca. Its popularity is largely because of its international intelligibility — it is the first language likely to reverse the chaos of Babel. Education and the increasingly international character of the media and communications are likely to ensure that no variety of English strays too far from a standard internationally comprehensible form.

See also AFRICAN ENGLISH; AMERICAN ENGLISH; AUSTRALIAN ENGLISH; CANADIAN ENGLISH; DIALECTS; HISTORY OF THE ENGLISH LANGUAGE; IRISH ENGLISH; NEW ZEALAND ENGLISH; PIDGINS AND CREOLES; SCOTTISH ENGLISH; SOURCES OF THE ENGLISH VOCABULARY; SOUTH AFRICAN ENGLISH; SOUTH ASIAN ENGLISH; WELSH ENGLISH; WEST INDIAN ENGLISH.

enjoy To *enjoy* is a transitive verb; that is, it takes a direct object when in the active voice: *Enjoy the party*; *Enjoy yourself at the party* ... but not — until fairly recently — simply *?? Enjoy!* This vogue use of the verb, probably imported into British English from North America, has attracted irritated criticism from careful speakers and writers. Surely it is not too much trouble for a well-wisher to use the two-word phrase *Enjoy yourself* or *Enjoy it* rather than the perfunctory *?? Enjoy*?

enormity *Enormity* is often used today in place of *enormousness* to mean 'gigantic scale, hugeness':

?? Meggie gave in, the enormity of her relief

showing in the way she sat, loosely now, relaxed.

    – Colleen McCullough, *The Thorn Birds*

?? ... fertile valleys with tall feathery trees in columns along the banks of frothing rivers, and occasionally a deep gorge of vertical granite slabs. The trees were eucalyptus, as African as the view, which was an enormity of stone and space. ...

The Patagonian paradox was this: to be here, it helped to be a miniaturist, or else interested in enormous empty spaces. There was no intermediate zone of study. Either the enormity of the desert space, or the sight of a tiny flower. You had to choose between the tiny or the vast.

    – Paul Theroux (U.S.),
    The Old Patagonian Express

Enormity is increasingly accepted in this sense in American English, but most careful speakers of British English still object to it, preferring to maintain a clear distinction between the two nouns. *Enormity* preserves something of the original sense of the adjective *enormous* — 'monstrous, abnormal, or deviant', from the Latin *ex-*, 'out of' + *norma*, 'a pattern or rule'. It has a strong moral tone, and means 'the quality of passing all moral bounds' or 'an act displaying such a quality; a monstrous offence or evil':

An outraged father called the family together and delivered a polemic on the enormity of this offense; it would get into the columns and make the family look ridiculous.

    – Arthur M. Schlesinger, Jr. (U.S.),
    Robert Kennedy and His Times.

I was in a brilliant play once, by the American author Murray Shisgal, called *Luv*. The title, spelt 'l-u-v', of course sounds like love but isn't; and the piece was about the enormities of selfishness and ruthlessness and destruction which human beings carry out in the name of love.

    – Eleanor Bron, 'Words', BBC Radio 3

By that time Shadbold had made up his mind that to take Isolde Upjohn to Paris had been a disgraceful act on Winterwade's part; an enormity aggravated by its sequel that she had proved frigid.

    – Anthony Powell,
    O, How the Wheel Becomes It!

enquiry, inquiry These nouns have traditionally been interchangeable; so too have the verbs to *enquire* and to *inquire*. However, a small distinction has for some time been developing between them, and fastidious users of English now observe it.

An *enquiry* is a request for information — a question or a set of questions. It is often used in the plural: *making a few enquiries about the price of train-tickets.* An *inquiry* has come to refer to an investigation. It is commonly used in the singular: *a court of inquiry; launched a second inquiry into the causes of the explosion.*

A few months ago, the Arts Council's music officer, Richard Lawrence, alerted by rumour, demanded a head-count of the LSO at subsidised concerts in the Barbican. Its manager, Peter Hemmings, was able to prove from its records that there had been a 91 per cent turn-out of principal players during the period under inquiry, a perfectly reputable figure.

    – Laurence Marks, *The Observer*

The respective verbs have corresponding senses, and can again be distinguished by their preferred prepositions: *to enquire about, to inquire into.* The distinction between the verbs is less frequently observed, however, than the distinction between the nouns, especially in North America, where *to inquire* is commonly used in both senses. In Britain, the spelling *to enquire* tends for some reason to occur more often.

The unrecognised figure, belonging more or less to Shadbold's own age-group, had evidently been a beauty in days gone by. There was still an elegance about her which caused several persons who had been in the congregation to enquire on the way out who she could have been.

    – Anthony Powell,
    O, How the Wheel Becomes It!

In theory, *inquiry* and *to inquire* are preferable spellings. For a start, they reflect the pronunciation more accurately: even *enquiry* and *to enquire* are usually pronounced with the first syllable as /in-/, though /en-/ is equally correct. (Note that *inquiry* and *enquiry*, usually pronounced everywhere as /in-**kwīr**-i/, are sometimes pronounced /ing-kwəri/ in North America.) And then, *inquiry* and *to inquire* fit the pattern more consistently, indicating the words' kinship to *inquisitive* and *inquisition* as well. But such arguments are surely outweighed by the more practical argument that a useful distinction has been created between the two forms and that it should be recognised and encouraged.

ensure   See ASSURE.

entomology   See ETYMOLOGY.

envelop, envelope   The verb to *envelop,* 'to surround, enclose, or wrap', is spelt without an *e* at the end. It is stressed on the second syllable, and pronounced /in-**vel**ləp, en-**vel**ləp/.

The noun *envelope,* meaning 'something that envelops, a surrounding cover or wrapping (especially for a letter)', does have an *e* at the end. It is stressed on the first syllable, and the preferred pronunciation is /**en**-və-lōp/. The variant pronunciations /**on**-və-lōp, **o**N-və-lōp/ are rather half-hearted and unnecessary attempts to reproduce the original French sound.

epidemic   See ENDEMIC.

epithet   The original meaning of *epithet* is 'a term used to characterise a person or thing' — in effect, an adjective, especially a stock adjective. In Homer's *Odyssey*, Odysseus is repeatedly called 'wily' or 'of many devices', and the sea is 'the wine-dark sea'.

The Greek *epitheton,* which reached English through Latin, meant literally 'an addition': the roots are *epi-*, 'upon' + *tithenai*, 'to put'.

By extension, *epithet* refers to a substitute name or nickname. *The Lionheart* was an epithet for Richard I, *the Great Emancipator* for Abraham Lincoln; William I is known by the epithet of (*William*) *the Conqueror,* and so on.

A more recent extension of *epithet* — and a less acceptable one — is 'a term of abuse or contempt applied to someone'; in effect, an insult, often obscene: *He went berserk, and started shouting epithets at me across the room.*

> **?** Carole [Lombard] could lay tongue to more colourful epithets than any other woman I've ever known, and more than most men. Oddly enough, you were never shocked when she swore.
> – Bing Crosby (U.S.), *Call Me Lucky*

Reserve this derogatory use for informal contexts and even there, avoid it if there is any danger of misunderstanding.

epoch-making   Used sparingly, *epoch-making* is a memorable and striking adjective for indicating the qualities of something uniquely significant or novel — something that seems to begin a new era. The invention of the modern computer was obviously *epoch-making.*

Almost by definition, there are very few things that are epoch-making. The term is debased if used to mean no more than 'exciting, original, highly impressive'. An impressive football score or pop concert might be *record-breaking* or *momentous*, but will not usher in a new period of history, and is therefore best not exaggerated into an *?? epoch-making performance.*

eponyms   See CAPITAL LETTERS **1**.

equable, equitable   Both of these adjectives go back to the Latin *aequus*, 'equal or even'. Their meanings, however, have developed from different aspects of this concept. *Equitable* means 'just and reasonable, fair', as in *an equitable arrangement about settling the debt*, or 'even-handed, fair-minded, impartial', as in *an equitable referee.*

> There were many old people in here. The old and poor who depended on the Judenrat ration. This summer the Judenrat itself, the distributor of food and even of space, had been less equitable than it had been last.
> – Thomas Keneally, *Schindler's Ark*

Equable means 'uniformly moderate, regular, steady': *an equable temperament* is a consistently calm one; *an equable climate* is a consistently mild one. Note that *equable* implies more than lack of change: it implies also the avoidance of extremes. A person who is always tetchy cannot be said to have *an equable temperament*; and a region which is unvaryingly damp and cold cannot be said to have *an equable climate.*

> 'So that's how you do your casting, is it?' she said, mustering a sceptical tone once more. 'Knock 'em over the head and drag 'em in handcuffed? That's your usual way, I suppose.'
> 'Charlie, we are surely not claiming that this is usual drama,' Kurtz replied equably, and once more left the initiative with her.
> – John le Carré,
> *The Little Drummer Girl*

equal, equally   Purists point out that if two things are equal then one cannot be more equal than the other: hence *equal* cannot be used with *more* and *most*. But sentences such as *They want a more equal distribution of wealth* are possible, with *more equal* having the sense 'more just' or 'more nearly equal'. *Most equal* is less often encountered, but is still possible in such sentences as *That's the most equal allocation of grants we could have hoped for.*

In the senses of 'adequate' and 'having the required capacities', *equal* is followed by *to*: *funds equal to the demands of the crisis*; *I felt equal to the task/equal to carrying out the task*. But the verb *to equal* is used without a preposition: *x equals y*.

Equally is often used incorrectly with *as*: ✗ *His new book is equally as interesting*. Careful usage prefers either *His new book is equally interesting* or *His new book is as interesting*. When two things are being explicitly compared, *as* is always used: *His new book is as interesting as his last one* is correct, but ✗ *His new book is equally (as) interesting as his last one* is not.

Of course, there are certain sentences where the combination *equally as* is quite acceptable, but the *as* would now be a preposition rather than an adverb: *I admire him equally as opening batsman and as spin bowler*.

Note too that if two elements are being compared after *equally*, they should be joined by *and* not *or*: *This film is enjoyed equally by children and adults* — not ✗ *equally by children or adults*.

equitable See EQUABLE.

errata The use of *errata* as a singular noun is non-standard: ✗ *An errata has been noted*; ✗ *The errata is on page 2*. The singular form *erratum* should be used here. This rule applies even when *errata* is being used in a collective sense to mean 'a list of errors': ✗ *The errata appears at the end of the book*. Change *appears* to *appear*.

escalate This vogue word is a 'back-formation' from *escalator*; that is, it is derived from *escalator* rather than being the source of it. (By contrast, *to elevate* is the source of *elevator*.)

The verb is used both transitively and intransitively — with or without a direct object. It is usually associated with prices — *the escalating cost of housing* — or war: *The hostilities are escalating*; *The Vietcong escalated their offensive*. The image of the inexorable ascent of an escalator is quite an effective one (though a cynic might point out that escalators go downwards as well), but the word added little to a language that already had the verbs *intensify*, *step up*, *magnify*, *increase*, *rise*, *raise*, *extend*, and *enlarge*. Apart from its impressive sound, *to escalate* has little to recommend it: think twice before using it.

-ese The ending *-ese* can mean 'the language of', as in *journalese* (the language typically used by journalists), *officialese* (the language of official-dom), and *computerese* (the language of computer experts). In such words, *-ese* is virtually always derogatory, and implies that the language in question is jargon-ridden and perhaps wilfully obscure, designed to baffle rather than enlighten the layman.

See also JARGON.

especially See SPECIALLY.

-ess As Western society moves closer towards equal rights for women, many needless expressions of discrimination within the English language are being prised out of acceptable usage. (See SEXISM IN THE ENGLISH LANGUAGE.) The suffix *-ess* is one of the more conspicuous victims of this purge — not in all its uses, but in many of them. It is no longer possible to append an *-ess* unthinkingly to a 'masculine' noun and simply assume that you have thereby created an unobjectionable feminine form of the same word.

The *-ess* words that are unreplaceable and unobjectionable include *duchess, heiress, lioness,* and *princess*. Others that have survived more or less unscathed are those representing a profession or status that is not the mere female version of the corresponding male profession or status. *Mistress* is hardly the exact equivalent of *master* (except in the sense of 'a schoolteacher'); or *seamstress* of *seamster* ('a tailor' — the word is now archaic anyway); or *governess* ('a nanny and tutor') of *governor*; or even *abbess* of *abbot*. A *mayoress* or *ambassadress* is the wife (or chosen female consort) of a *mayor* or *ambassador*. Now that women are more directly involved in politics and diplomacy, the appropriate term for a woman governor, mayor, or ambassador is clearly not *governess, mayoress,* or *ambassadress*, but *governor, mayor,* or *ambassador*.

Some *-ess* words remain unobjectionable so long as they are clearly understood as having a distinct historical or fictional reference — *adultress, adventuress, murderess, shepherdess, sorceress,* and *temptress*. These words are all 'loaded' in one way or another, and their historical associations make this clear to the modern user. Jael and Judith were two Biblical *murderesses,* but a woman who murders a man today is best referred to as a *murderer*. Moll Flanders was a fictitious 18th-century *adventuress,* but a lone round-the-world yachtswoman today is surely *an adventurer*. Little Bo-Peep may have been a *shepherdess,* but a woman herding sheep on a windswept moor today is a *shepherd* or perhaps a *woman shepherd*.

Other *-ess* words still surviving, though rather

precariously, are *actress, stewardess,* and *waitress,* and even *hostess* and *patroness.*

But many *-ess* words, some 400 or 500 years old, and all still freely used at the beginning of this century, are now considered patronising or demeaning — certainly unnecessary: *ancestress, authoress, conductress, editress, instructress, Jewess, manageress, poetess, proprietress,* and *sculptress.* The 'male' form (*sculptor,* and so on) or the neutral form (*poet*) is considered just as suitable for women as for men today.

The *-ess* ending labours under a further handicap — a lack of versatility: *-ess* nouns cannot function as agent nouns in the way that *-er* or *-or* nouns can. You may call the Biblical Judith *a murderess,* but you cannot easily say that she was *?? the murderess of Holofernes.* You may call Jane Austen *an authoress,* but you cannot really call her *?? the authoress of Pride and Prejudice.* You would have to call Judith *the murderer of Holofernes* and Jane Austen *the author of Pride and Prejudice.*

See also CHAIRMAN.

et al. 1. Like *etc.,* this abbreviation is very useful in its place — notably in legal documents and technical reports. In everyday writing and in speech it should be avoided.

It is short for *et alii* (or *et aliae,* the feminine form), a Latin phrase meaning 'and others' or 'and other people'. Its use tends to be restricted to human beings, therefore (even though *et al.* can also represent the neuter form *et alia,* 'and other things'). When the list is of nonhuman items, the appropriate term is *etc.*

Note that *et al.* does not mean 'and all'; it means 'and others':

> Apologies from members of the technical staff who have been called away on an emergency — Miss Wilson, Mr James, Mr Kerr, et al.

The implication of *et al.* is that some of the technical staff are absent, not that all of them are.

When *et al.* is read out, it keeps its abbreviated form (unlike *etc.)* — /et **al**/ or /et **al**/.

The phrase *et al.* is preceded by a comma if it follows a list of two or more items. If there is only one specified item, the comma is usually omitted: *Apologies from the secretaries et al.* As with *etc.,* however, it is far preferable to have at least two specified items before the *et al.,* in order to suggest how the sequence might proceed.

The abbreviation *et al.* used to represent the Latin phrase *et alibi* as well — 'and elsewhere': *inspecting the troops at Aldershot, Sandringham,*

et al. But *etc.* now tends to be used instead.

2. Use *et al.* only if it is clear to the reader what it refers to. Do not use it if it suggests ignorance or laziness on your part.

Never write × *and et al.* The *et* already means 'and'.

And do not use *et al.* at the end of a list that begins with *e.g., such as,* or *for example.*

For further details, see ET CETERA.

et cetera, etc. 1. In Latin, this idiom was written as two words — *et cetera* or *et cætera* — and meant literally 'and the remaining things'. The one word variant *etcetera* is widely used today, and is now regarded as equally acceptable. The abbreviation *etc.* usually has a full stop after it, though some writers and publishers prefer to streamline their texts by omitting the full stop unless at the end of a sentence. Either way, the word when read out should be pronounced in full. (In American English, it is sometimes read out as *and so forth.*)

The standard pronunciation is /it-**sett**rə, et-, **sett**ərə/. The commonly heard × /ek-**sett**rə/ or × /ik-**sett**rə/ should be avoided. (Not that there is ever really a need to use the word in spoken English at all.)

The various forms are no longer written in italics (except when the words themselves are being discussed, as in this article). They are fully English forms now, not simply Latin imports.

The abbreviation *etc.* is preceded by a comma if it follows a list of two or more items: *chlorine, bromine, etc.* If there is only one item, however, the comma is usually omitted: *an expert on diet etc.* Such one-item lists should be avoided wherever possible, however: at least two items should usually be specified in order to indicate how the list might continue.

2. The abbreviation *etc.* is a useful shorthand expression in technical, business, and informal writing. But it should be used only when it is clear to the reader what it refers to: *The law degree offers a range of options — public international law, constitutional law, legal history, etc.* You should avoid using it if it gives the impression that you are too ignorant or too lazy to complete the list: × *Many of the college's departments — law etc. — offer a solid professional training.*

In contexts other than technical, business, and informal writing, the use of *et cetera* and *etc.* is open to various objections. It is considered inelegant and even discourteous in formal writing: the preferable expressions are *and so on, and so forth,* and *and the like.* In speech, *et cetera* can sound pompously bureaucratic. And the charges of ignorance and laziness are once again applicable here, of course.

3. Since *etc.* means 'and the rest', it is clearly redundant to write ✗ *and etc.* Take care to avoid this common error. Avoid too the use of *etc.* at the end of a list if the list begins with *e.g., for example,* or *such as.* These already imply that your list is incomplete, and the further reminder in *etc.* is redundant: ✗ *a study of the remote Soviet regions and republics, such as Tadzhikistan, Kirgizia, etc.*

4. In Latin, the words *et cetera* mean literally 'and the remaining (things)', as in *The rodents — rats, squirrels, beavers, etc. — have incisor teeth that continue to grow throughout their life.* If we allow the Latin to dictate the English usage, we should have to disqualify *et cetera* from meaning 'and *other* things' *(apples, pears, etc.)* and 'or other things' *(As hors d'oeuvres you might be offered paté, asparagus salad, shrimp cocktail, etc.)* and 'and other *people*' *(the cultural attaché, the deputy high-commissioner, the press-officer, etc.)*

Usage, however, has long since decided that these extended meanings are quite acceptable. English is, after all, quite different from Latin. In the third case, however — a list of people — the abbreviation *et al.* is perhaps preferable. See ET AL.

5. The word *etceteras* is sometimes used as a plural noun meaning 'miscellaneous additional things':*The principal facts were clear enough, but there were a lot of etceteras that were hard to fit together.* This is acceptable in casual usage, but is best avoided in formal contexts.

ethical, moral *Ethical* (ultimately from Greek) and *moral* (ultimately from Latin) are similar in meaning in that they both have to do with the difference between right and wrong. But *ethical* now tends to refer to a system or theory of judging rightness or wrongness, whereas *moral* tends to refer to more concrete choices and to issues that arouse strong feelings: you might say that *ethical* refers to right and wrong, and *moral* refers to good and evil. The behaviour of an unscrupulous lawyer would be called *unethical*; genocide would be called *immoral*. The lawyer's behaviour is a violation of *professional ethics*; the concentration camp commandant's behaviour is a violation of *morality*.

Moral is further differentiated from *ethical* in having developed strong associations with sex and reproduction. People who are invited to name a moral problem are more likely to mention abortion than unemployment or nuclear weapons. Contraception, surrogate motherhood, prosti-tution, and genetic engineering are all said to pose *moral* problems, above all for ordinary people who think about them. For scientists and medical personnel they pose *ethical* problems as well, for these people have implicit or explicit codes of *professional ethics.*

There are other differences between the use of *moral* and the use of *ethical.* A work of art that champions good against evil is a *moral* work of art, not an *ethical* one. A medicine or drug that can be dispensed only upon presentation of a prescription is a *prescription* drug or an *ethical* drug, by contrast with one that can be sold *over the counter.* This use of *ethical* may be related to its use in describing systems of professional ethics.

Note also that just as *ethical* tends to refer to theories about right and wrong, so does *ethics.* In recent times people have talked about making moral choices on the basis of the particular characteristics of each situation in which the choice must be made: the theory that such choices depend on situations rather than on absolute principles has been called *situational ethics* or *situation ethics.* Likewise, the phrase *lifeboat ethics* has been used to name systems of thought that deal with the allocation of scarce resources as though they were seats in a lifeboat too small to hold everybody.

An *ethic,* finally, is a particular ethical theory or principle or code. The *work ethic,* for instance, extols the intrinsic value of work.

See also -ICS.

etymology, entomology These two subjects of study could hardly be further apart. But the words, being relatively rare and sounding very similar, are sometimes confused.

Etymology means 'the history of a word' or 'the study of the history or derivation of words'. The etymology of the word *etymology,* for example, is as follows: it is a learned respelling of Middle English *ethimologie,* which comes via Latin and Old French from the Greek *etumologia,* itself composed of *etumon,* 'the true sense of a word' (from *etumos,* 'true, real') + *logos,* 'a word, speech, study'.

It is interesting that in English the *etymon* of a word has come to mean not its 'true sense' but its 'earliest form'; that is, its historical source, as Greek *etumon* is of English *etymon.* Most modern language experts believe that the earliest known form, pronunciation, or meaning of a word is not necessarily more correct or better than forms, pronunciations, or meanings that have developed since.

Entomology is the scientific study of insects. The word goes back through French to the Greek verb *entɛ ːnein*, 'to cut into' (from *en-*, 'in' + *temnein*, 'to cut'): the Greek name for 'insect' is *entomon*, 'one whose body is cut into segments'. The suffix *-logy*, via French and Latin from the Greek *logos*, 'a word, speech', often means 'study', as in *biology*, 'the study of life.'

Our word *insect* itself, by the way, comes from the Latin *insectum (animale)*, 'a segmented animal', where *insectum* is the Latin equivalent of the Greek *entomon*, being the past participle of *insecare*, 'to cut into', from *in-*, 'in, into' + *secare*, 'to cut'.

If you think you are in any danger of confusing *entomology* with *etymology*, you can remember the distinction by associating the *ent-* in *entomology* with the word *ant* — one of the objects of study that *entomology* is concerned with.

eulogy See ELEGY.

euphemism *Euphemism* is the use of an inoffensive word or phrase in the place of one that is considered objectionable or too explicit. *A euphemism* is the milder word or phrase used in this way. The term goes back to the Greek source words *eu-*, 'good, well' + *phēmē*, 'speech, saying'.

'Good speech' — this is the positive side of euphemism. Civilised communication requires a sensitivity to your audience, a respect for their taboos — so long as these are not wildly unreasonable. 'Unreasonable' is a matter of opinion, of course. It is 'reasonable' to say to an employee *I am letting you go* rather than to say *You're fired*. It is more than reasonable — it is common decency — to speak of *Down's syndrome* or a *Down's baby* rather than *mongolism* or a *mongol baby*.

On the other hand, from today's vantage point, the Victorians were 'unreasonable' in their prudishness — avoiding the words *dead* and *death* where possible, sometimes referring to a piano's *legs* as *limbs*, and so on.

The line between delicacy and overcautiousness is a thin one. No one today would refer to a piano's *limbs* other than as a joke (in fact, few Victorians would have done so either). But in other contexts, favoured Victorian euphemisms still flourish — the word *rape* is often replaced in conversation and print by the imprecise word *assault*, and although *die*, *dead*, and *death* are nowadays used freely in impersonal speech and writing, people often avoid using them when consoling bereaved relatives. Undertakers in particular would never allow themselves to utter these forbidden words in the hearing of a client. They would draw on the long-established roll of euphemisms instead, such as *passed away* and *the departed*.

The word *undertaker* itself probably began life as a euphemism, as it happens. Strictly, the name should have been something like *undertaker of burials* or *undertaker of the disposing of the dead*. Ironically, the word *undertaker* — outwardly as formal and clinical as *entrepreneur* — became a taboo word in its turn, and was replaced by such terms as *funeral director* or, in America, *mortician*. This development illustrates one of the peculiarities of euphemism: since it is often the concept itself that is objectionable rather than the word as such, any new euphemism is liable to become tainted too in due course, thus necessitating a further euphemism. *Stomach* came into common use as a euphemism of *belly*, and has now itself acquired the euphemism *tummy*. *To sweat* being rather 'coarse', the verb *to perspire* came to be standard for human beings: the further euphemism *to glow* is used only jokingly still, but perhaps in due course it too will be taken seriously, and eventually supersede *to perspire*.

Some other examples: many African and Asian countries, once insensitively dismissed as *backward*, came to be referred to as *poor* or *poorer* countries (a fair description, and one that is enjoying a revival today), but this was for some reason felt to be objectionable, and was replaced by *underdeveloped*. But the negative tone of this adjective was duly detected and deplored, and the word *developing* succeeded. And this too seems now to have fallen out of favour, and has given way to *emerging*, as in *emerging nations*.

Or consider the shifting throng of terms for a common-law husband or wife, or a regular sexual partner other than one's spouse: *concubine* and *mistress* (referring only to women) gave way to *lover* and *cohabitee/cohabitant* (which could refer to men as well), but these are now old-fashioned too, or else have become taboo in turn. In their place have sprung up *partner*, *live-in friend*, *de facto* (Australian), and the American terms *spouse-equivalent*, *apartmate*, *mingles* (mixed singles), *symbiotic mate*, *biological companion*, and *POSSLQ* or *posselcue* (person of the opposite sex sharing living-quarters). And the corresponding verbs show a clear progression, one euphemism superseding another: *to live in sin*, *to live as man and wife*, *to cohabit*, *to live together*, *to shack up*.

There is nothing especially alarming in all this.

In fact, to the extent that euphemism reflects a sensitivity in human nature, it is something reassuring rather than demoralising. In three respects, however, euphemism does attract criticism. First, when it leads to imprecision: *assault* is clearly not a good substitute for *rape*; and *sexual assault*, useful as a general term, is not a good synonym of *rape*, since it might refer to *attempted rape* or various forms of molestation. Similarly, the words *lavatory* and *toilet* (themselves euphemisms originally: *lavatory* once meant 'a washing place or washing vessel'; and *toilet* was earlier used — and still can be used — to mean 'getting dressed and made up') have generated several misleading euphemisms. The main ones are: *powder-room, cloakroom,* and, in North America, *bathroom* and *restroom.* (There are also *public convenience, facilities, comfort station, loo, the geography of the house, the smallest room,* and so on.) Since a *cloakroom* can still mean 'a room where coats can be left temporarily, as at a theatre', it only creates confusion to use the word to refer to a lavatory as well.

Secondly, euphemism is objected to when it is used — as it so often is — in an inappropriate or incongruous way.

The subject is a favourite with cartoonists: a woman explorer on safari withdraws behind a bush with the explanation 'I'm just going to powder my nose'. A gaunt man on his deathbed in hospital says to his tearful wife: 'If anything should happen to me —.' And so on.

According to Fleet Street legend, a newspaper in the early 1930s printed a grisly report of a dismembered female corpse discovered in a case in the luggage office at Victoria Station. 'The woman's legs and arms had been severed from her body,' the reporter explained, and added: 'She had not been interfered with.'

And here is an example of an attempted euphemism that is laughably inadequate:

> Mr Barry Lotz, who will take over as acting editor for the time being, said Mrs Hodd had been 'not so much fired as dismissed'.
> — *The Cape Times*

Thirdly, euphemism is objected to (by both liberal and conservative people) on practical and social grounds — when words are marshalled by politicians, advertisers, economists, and bullies of all kinds to gloss over the ugly truths they have to deal with.

Advertising agents, scared of alarming potential customers by being too forthright, have become adept at churning out reassuring euphemisms: *economy* or *budget* (cheap), *outsize* or *full-figure* (fat), *adult* or *explicit* (pornographic).

Journalists sometimes jokily draw on a 'secret' code of euphemisms readily understood by all regular readers — *ruddy-faced* (drunken), *steadfast* (pig-headed), *militant* (fanatically left-wing), *outspoken* (insulting and menacing), *controversial* (extremely tiresome and unpleasant), *pert* (small and plain), *petite* (undersized), *He prefers to leave details to his subordinates* (He is ignorant about all aspects of his job).

Sociologists, psychologists, and criminologists are notorious re-phrasers: their euphemisms are condemned as 'cosmetic' (by the left wing) or 'sentimental' (by the right wing), though many laymen accept them as simply respectful and sensitive: *recidivist* (used as early as 1880 to refer to a habitual criminal), *social disease* (1918), *underprivileged* or *disadvantaged, lower-income levels, adjustment problems, educational underachievement, shrinkage* (losses through shoplifting), and so on.

The worst offenders, by common consent, are politicians, civil servants, and military and government spokesmen. The history of political and military euphemism is a long and mean one. The Roman historian Tacitus, discussing the so-called *Pax Romana*, the 'Roman peace', imagined a bitter comment that might have been made by the Pictish (British) leader Calgacus, who had been on the receiving end of this 'peace': 'They make a desert, and call it peace.' This serviceable euphemism enjoyed a 20th-century revival in the term *pacification* — often used to mean 'the suppression or elimination of hostile opposition'.

The Nazis used the clinical terms *Sonderbehandlung* and *die Endlösung* in reference to the Jews — 'special treatment' and 'the final solution', in each case spelling death.

During the American war in Vietnam and Kampuchea, bombing raids were referred to as *logistical strikes* or *close air support.* In a famous self-damning protest, an American Air Force colonel rebuked journalists in these words: 'You always write it's *bombing, bombing, bombing.* It's not *bombing!* It's air support.'

More recently, the American invasion of Grenada was officially referred to as 'a rescue mission', and President Reagan nicknamed the MX missile *the peace-keeper.*

The other side of the military coin is also cloaked in euphemism: a retreat is sometimes, in official parlance, an *exfiltration*; and the disastrous American helicopter raid to try to free the U.S. embassy hostages in Tehran in 1980 was, according to President Jimmy Carter, 'an incomplete success'.

Other euphemisms spawned by war are *take out* (to kill), *border realignment* (the seizure of neighbouring territory), and of course *liberation*, *pacification*, and *freedom fighter*.

Political euphemisms seldom escape the notice of journalists nowadays, and are given almost as much publicity as the events that prompted them. When politicians refer to *frank discussions*, journalists often put these words knowingly within quotation marks. Of all the 'cover-ups' during the Watergate scandal in the United States, the linguistic cover-ups seemed to be the reporters' favourites: *containment* was at once delightedly deciphered as meaning 'concealing information', *inoperative* as 'untrue', *I misspoke myself* as 'I lied', and so on.

More recently, President Reagan has allowed *revenue enhancements* rather than risking 'tax increases', and a government spokesman in the United States denied that Medicare (a medical aid scheme) was introducing 'a means test', but explained that it was introducing *a layering of benefits according to your income.*

In general, the appropriate name to call a spade by is *a spade.* Certainly there is no need to call it *a bloody shovel*, but it attracts just as much embarrassed attention to go to the other extreme and call it *a manual earth-mover.*

Note, finally, the distinction between *euphemism* and *euphuism*. *Euphuism* is, broadly speaking, high-flown speech or writing, consciously elegant and usually affected and overstylish. *A euphuism* is an instance of such language. To refer to a bankrupt man as being 'in a condition of ultimate financial perplexity', as Mr Micawber might have done, is to be at once *euphemistic* and *euphuistic*. Euphuism referred originally to an ornate literary style, characterised by alliteration, antithesis, and similes, used by various writers in the 16th and 17th centuries. Their model was the dramatist and prose-writer John Lyly. His two romances about the character *Euphues* typified the style.

See also JARGON.

even The sense of a sentence can be affected by the position within it of the adverb *even*.

Here are a few examples, each followed in brackets by the words that might well complete the original sentence:

1. Even I couldn't read the newspaper yesterday (so how do you expect my secretary to have done so?).

2. I couldn't even read the newspaper yesterday (— I was so busy).

3. I couldn't read even the newspaper yesterday (let alone that 200-page report you sent me).

4. I couldn't read the newspaper even yesterday (when I was only half as busy as I am today, so it's hardly likely that I would have the chance to read it today).

A problem occasionally arises, as with *not* and *only,* when idiom conflicts with logic. Sentence *2.* above might well be written when the meaning intended is that of sentence *3.* So long as the context keeps the sense clear, ambiguity is unlikely to present a real threat, and the idiomatic usage can be allowed. But the more logical positioning of *even* — as near as possible to the word or phrase it relates to — is always available, of course, and should certainly be used if the idiomatic form is in danger of being misunderstood. Purists prefer the logical form at all times.

See ONLY.

ever **1.** If used to intensify *when, what, how,* or the like in questions, *ever* follows it as a separate word: *When ever are you going to repair that window?* If used with *when, what, how,* or the like in other types of clause, to convey a collective or general force, *-ever* is locked on at the end of the word to form a single composite word: *Whenever I try to repair our window, I manage to break two others.* (See WHATEVER for further details.)

2. The use of *ever* sometimes attracts criticism in phrases such as *? the fastest cyclist ever* and *? their worst defeat ever* (in British English, *? their worst ever defeat* is also found). Far preferable, it is argued, are such forms as *the fastest cyclist on record, the fastest cyclist in history, their worst defeat yet,* and *the worst defeat they have ever suffered.*

The objection to *ever* in a simple phrase containing a superlative adjective is perhaps based on the idea that the word *ever*, unless qualified, suggests the whole of history, past and future, and that we cannot be sure that the future will not provide an even faster cyclist or still worse defeat. If the range of *ever* is somehow restricted by the tense of the verb (*the worst defeat they have ever suffered*) or by some qualifying word or phrase (in British English, *their worst ever defeat to date*), then *ever* is permissible — though redundant in the second example.

None the less, the use of *ever* in simple phrases with superlative adjectives is now a well-established idiomatic usage. There is no need to avoid it, unless you are worried about provoking the purists.

3. *Ever* is sometimes carelessly positioned, particularly in questions. Take care to place it as close as possible to the element to which it refers in the sentence. Note the difference in meaning between the following two sentences:

Do you ever think that you will see him again?
Do you think that you will ever see him again?

In the first of the sentences, the clear assumption is that you will see him again, but that you tend to avoid thinking about it. In the second sentence, it is quite uncertain whether you will see him again or not. The first construction, however, is often used when the intended sense is that of the second construction. In speech this presents little difficulty, since intonation will probably make the meaning clear. But take care, in writing, not to leave yourself open to misunderstanding by using the wrong construction.

For further details on this common problem, see ONLY.

4. In American English, *ever* can be used in informal exclamations: *Boy, was that ever good!* Such exclamations are not found in standard British English.

5. In some American English dialects, the word *every* is shortened to sound (and sometimes read) like *ever*: *? Ever time I go there I see him.* It is not standard English.

ever so This phrase, widely used in British English, is strictly colloquial: *? I'm ever so relieved*; *? I enjoyed the circus ever so much.* It is even more informal to use *ever so* by itself, without an adjective or adverb following: *? I enjoyed the circus ever so*; *? Ta ever so.* The phrase, whether used on its own or not, should be avoided in formal speech and writing.

Ever so was formerly also used in clauses of concession:

'Mid pleasures and palaces though we may roam,
Be it ever so humble, there's no place like home.
— John Howard Payne (U.S.),
'Home, Sweet Home' (1823)

(Before the late 17th century, the phrase *never so* was used instead, and can be found frequently in Shakespeare and the King James Bible.) Today, the idiomatic way of expressing such concessions would be by the use of *however* in place of *ever so*: *However humble it may be, there's no place like home.*

every *Every* (like *each*) is grammatically in the singular; all other words relating to it, therefore — not just the noun that it qualifies, but any related verbs, pronouns, and possessive adjectives as well — should be in the singular too. Strictly speaking, it is grammatically incorrect to say *?? Every single one of the doctors present were obliged to defend themselves against this accusation.* The correct form is *Every single one of the doctors present was obliged to defend himself/herself against this accusation.* The safest course, probably, is to turn the entire sentence into the plural: *All the doctors present ...* (For a more detailed discussion of the problem, see EACH 1.)

See also EACH AND EVERY; EVERYBODY; THEY.

everybody, anybody, nobody, somebody
Strictly speaking, these pronouns are singular. So too, of course, are *everyone, anyone, no one,* and *someone,* and also *everything, neither, either, a person, each, none* (sometimes), and *one,* and also the adjectives *every* and (sometimes) *any.* And being singular, they should take a singular verb (and all further pronouns and possessive adjectives relating to them should be in the singular too):

The doubts I speak of went with the job, for not everybody who joined my classes was a talented writer.
— Bernard Malamud (U.S.),
Introduction to *Selected Short Stories*

The announcement of a death rarely occasions the immediate breakdown which the movies and theatre lead us to expect. Someone informed of a disaster in solemn and understated terms tends to wonder quite consciously how he is expected to react at the time; the impact only strikes much later.
— Peter Ustinov,
We Were Only Human

All too often, however, the sentence wanders into the plural:

?? Ezra was the most generous writer I have ever known and the most disinterested. He helped poets, painters, sculptors and prose writers that he believed in and he would help anyone whether he believed in them or not if they were in trouble.
— Ernest Hemingway (U.S.),
A Moveable Feast

?? At a second hearing last week, the union argued that everyone has the right to write to their MP. This stirring defence of freedom brought forth a wonderful reply from the Corporation.

– Peter Hillmore, *The Observer*

✗ Anyone is free to walk in here, help themselves to food, eat their fill, and leave without paying — and they frequently do.

In this last sentence, *anyone* is clearly singular, and is followed by the verb *is,* yet the subsequent pronouns have been cast in the plural — *themselves, their, they.* There is clearly an inconsistency here, though neither of the chief alternatives is entirely satisfactory: *himself/his/he* (which either suggests the exclusion of women, or — in the view of many careful users of English — insults women by grouping them under male pronouns) or *himself or herself/his or her/he or she* (which can get very awkward and long-winded): *Everybody will like this book — he or she will find in it everything that he or she needs for his or her studies.* (For a more detailed discussion of these alternatives, see HE OR SHE; THEY; YOU. See also NONE.)

Everybody or *everyone* is particularly troublesome, since it suggests so strongly a plurality of people, yet is obviously singular in form. It seems far more natural to say *Everybody jumped out of their seats in excitement* than *Everybody jumped out of his seat in excitement.* Even in the present tense, when the inconsistency becomes quite glaring, it still sounds rather less awkward than the 'correct' form: *Everybody is jumping out of their seats in excitement* is easier, more natural, and in a way less misleading to say than *Everybody is jumping out of his seat in excitement.* And think of all the complications when you want to add a related clause or sentence:

?? Everybody is jumping out of his seat, isn't he?

?? Everybody is jumping out of his seat in excitement, and is raising his hands in the air, and shouting with all his might.

?? Everyone collected his hat and coat and left in twos and threes.

Surely the use of *they* and *their* is preferable to such oddities!

The obvious course of action is to avoid getting into such a tangle in the first place by simply avoiding *everybody* altogether. It is not too difficult to reword the sentences above into a form perfect in both grammar and meaning: *All the spectators are jumping out of their seats in excitement.* And if you want to avoid repeating the noun *spectators,* you could go on to say *All*

of them ... It is a pity that the simple plural pronoun *all,* used by itself, now sounds rather formal or old-fashioned: *All are jumping out of their seats in excitement.* In the following quotation, *all* is used to good effect, and matches the *they* used later in a way that *anyone* or *everybody* could not:

In the meantime, all who wish to profit from the luminous Swiftian sanity may be advised to study Professor Ehrenpreis's three volumes, starting with this one. As they read the true story of Swift's death (which, incidentally, he had written about himself in one of the most cheerful poems in the language) they will share with me perhaps a few un-Christian thoughts on Dr Johnson's brand of Christian charity.

– Michael Foot, *The Observer*

See also ANYONE.

exalt, exult   These two verbs are easily confused, being spelt and pronounced very similarly, and sometimes appearing in similar contexts. But they come from quite different sources and have distinct meanings and grammatical functions.

Exalt is pronounced /ig-**zawlt**/; *exult* /ig-**zult**/.

To exalt is typically a transitive verb, and has two main meanings: 'to elevate, raise (a person) in rank or dignity' and 'to praise highly, glorify, honour'. The source is the Latin verb *exaltare,* 'to lift up, exalt', from *ex-*, 'up' + *altus*, 'high'. The related noun is *exaltation,* which means 'elevation' or 'praise', or sometimes 'elation, spiritual delight'.

To exult is intransitive, and means 'to rejoice greatly'. It often has negative overtones, suggesting a triumph at someone else's downfall: *He exulted at/over the downfall of his enemies.* The word goes back to the Latin verb *exsultare,* a form of *exsilire,* 'to leap up, rejoice', from *ex-*, 'up' + *salire*, 'to jump'. The related noun is *exultation,* 'rejoicing'.

It is not difficult to find circumstances, especially religious ones, in which either *exaltation* (in the sense of 'praise' or 'spiritual delight') or *exultation* ('rejoicing') would seem appropriate. The following lines from a well-known carol contain the word *exultation,* but *exaltation* would not have been out of place:

Sing choirs of Angels,
Sing in exultation,
Sing, all ye citizens of Heav'n above.
'O Come All Ye Faithful',
Hymns Ancient and Modern

And in the following example, *exultation* might have been used in the place of *exaltation*:

> Henry and Leopold felt both exaltation and fear at the seriousness with which Obersturmbannführer Pavlu's party had geared themselves for their playing.
> – Thomas Keneally, *Schindler's Ark*

Note that there is no such noun as × *exultance*, which some people mistakenly form from the related adjective *exultant*.

The adjectives *exalted* and *exultant* can also approach each other closely in meaning. *Exalted* generally means 'raised in rank or position' or 'lofty, sublime, noble':

> The dedicated nineteenth-century colonial administrator had his disadvantages, but he did at least purvey the more exalted aspects of his own culture to the subject race, whether public school ethic or *civilisation française*.
> – Gillian Tindall, *The Times*

But *exalted* can also mean 'extremely excited, elated'. In this sense it is very similar to *exultant*, which means 'joyful, jubilant, triumphant': *She was exultant at the success, and spent all day in an exalted mood.*

> The rubber soles of Colonel Pomeroy went flip-flap, flip-flap on the planks as he walked eager and exultant round and round the promenade deck: every seven minutes he would pass my chair, and his exultant monologue would swell out and then decrease again.
> – Harold Nicolson, 'Miriam Codd'

Note the similarity of meaning, finally, between *to exalt* and *to extol*, in the sense of 'to praise highly'. Though both verbs are typically transitive, and formal in tone, *extol* is by far the more current, except perhaps in religious contexts. Remember that *extolling* and *extolled* have two *l*'s, *extol* only one (though in American English, *extoll* is possible).

except, excepting, excepted, except for 1. In most constructions, *except* is preferable to *excepting* and *except for* as the preposition meaning 'excluding':

> All sane adult citizens, except prisoners and peers, are entitled to vote tomorrow.

Excepting would be slightly unidiomatic here, and *except for* slightly informal, and both are best avoided. And *except* alone is appropriate when used as a conjunction, meaning 'were it not for the fact that; only' (*He would go and vote, except (that) it's raining too hard*) or 'otherwise than; for any reason, or in any way, other than' (*He won't leave the house except to go and vote*). *Excepting* and *except for* are impossible here.

Where *excepting* is the appropriate term is where the word *not, always,* or *without* comes before the preposition:

> All sane adult citizens, not excepting prisoners and peers, will be affected by tomorrow's elections.

Except would be incorrect here.

Excepting can be used without the *not, always,* or *without* in front of it if its grammatical function is that of participle or verbal noun:

> We call on all sane adult citizens to go to the polls tomorrow, excepting of course prisoners and peers. Our excepting of them is necessitated by the law of the land.

The first *excepting* here is a proper present participle, relating to the subject *We*. The second *excepting* is a verbal noun (see -ING FORMS OF VERBS).

The use of *excepted* is quite acceptable (though rather old-fashioned and awkward) whether the *not* is present or absent. *Excepted*, unlike *except* and *excepting*, is placed after rather than before the item/s mentioned:

> All sane adult citizens, prisoners and peers excepted, are entitled to vote tomorrow.
> All sane adult citizens will be affected by tomorrow's elections, prisoners and peers not excepted.

Except for should not be used, in formal contexts at least, where *except* is possible. *Except for* is rather colloquial, and should be limited to informal speech and writing — with two exceptions.

First, *except for* is the best term to use at the beginning of a sentence:

> Except for prisoners and peers, all sane adult citizens are entitled to vote tomorrow.

Secondly, *except for* is standard when the sense is 'if it weren't for'. Here the purpose is to make some qualification to an entire statement, rather than to single out any item/s for exclusion:

> The polling-station seemed quite empty except for two disconsolate officials.

Except for is often used in a slightly extended way — not so much to qualify a preceding statement as to contradict the statement:

? I could not have reached the polling-station in time except for your help.

This usage is sometimes regarded as colloquial; in formal contexts, use *but for* or *without* or *were it not for* rather than *except for*.

2. When used as a preposition, *except* (like *excepting, except for,* and *excepted*) is followed by the object-form of pronouns:

Everyone except her enjoyed the play.

It would be a mistake to use *she* instead of *her* in this example. (Things are rather more complicated with *but*: *everyone but she/her.* See BUT...)

3. The use of *except* as a conjunction, in the sense of 'unless', is no longer current English idiom though still widely known, thanks to *The Book of Common Prayer* and the Bible:

Except the Lord build the house, they labour in vain that build it: except the Lord keep the city, the watchman waketh but in vain.
        – Psalm 127:1

It survives in regional dialects, but is otherwise nonstandard — probably a contracted form of *except if*:

✕ The deal's off, except you agree to reduce the price.

It would be some improvement if *except* were changed to *except if*. But the best change would be to replace *except* by *unless*.

exceptional, exceptionable These two adjectives are quite distinct in meaning, and should never be confused. *Exceptional* can mean 'being an exception, out of the ordinary, uncommon': *With two exceptional days, the weather has been very fine this month.* More commonly the word is used in its extended sense of 'uncommonly good' — *The weather has been exceptional this month* — or in its still more refined sense 'uncommonly able; gifted': *She's an exceptional pianist for one so young.* Note, however, that, especially in American English, *an exceptional child* has come to mean 'a child who deviates from the norm in any way', and is used for the physically handicapped or the educationally subnormal as well as for the gifted. This exceptional case apart, the word *exceptional* typically has favourable associations.

The word *exceptionable* on the other hand, usually has an unfavourable ring to it. *Something exceptionable* is 'something to which exception

may be taken; something open to objection': *I find your criticisms exceptionable, and shall sue unless you withdraw them.*

Exceptionable occurs fairly infrequently: rather more common is its opposite *unexceptionable*, meaning 'acceptable, satisfactory, inoffensive': *Those lyrics are quite unexceptionable — why on earth should the censor ban them?* The opposite of *exceptional* is *unexceptional*, which can be used in three rather different ways. It can mean 'allowing of no exceptions, absolute': *an unexceptional rule*; more often it means 'in accordance with what is normal, ordinary': *unexceptional weather*; most commonly it is used in a more unfavourable sense to mean 'dull, disappointing, not coming up to expectations': *It was such an expensive restaurant, but the food was unexceptional, I'm sorry to say.* So, a plan, for example, might be both *unexceptionable* and *unexceptional*, in which case it is sound enough, but rather dull.

exclamation mark **1.** *Exclamation mark* is the usual name in British English. In American English, the usual name is *exclamation point*.

In general, the exclamation mark is rather unfashionable nowadays, and is probably used far less today than in previous times. It is rather like a rich sauce — cloying if used lavishly, and not really needed at all if the dish is already sufficiently spicy. The wording in *You're a right idiot* is explicit enough to make the sentence's meaning quite clear, regardless of punctuation; and since there is no *grammatical* need to close it with an exclamation mark, it might be best to economise on emotion here and use a full stop instead.

2. An exclamation mark is not always needed, then, to express a high degree of emotion, emphasis, or excitement.

Its most typical uses are after interjections and similar exclamations:

Hurrah! Good Heavens! Shh! Encore! For Pete's sake!

and after words expressing or suggesting loud, sharp noises:

Crash! Kapow! Boo! Yeoww!

and after certain types of exclamatory utterance, the most typical of which begin with *How, What,* or *That,* or have the form of questions (usually negative questions):

How nice you are!
What a nice person you are!
A nice person you are!

You snivelling wretch!
That such a thing should happen to me!
Long live the King!
Down with the King!
Oh for the wings of a dove!
If only I'd thought of that!
May you live forever!
Aren't you nice!
You thought I wouldn't mind!
He's over seven feet tall!

The use of the exclamation mark is especially important in expressions of the last three types, as they might otherwise be mistaken for questions or neutral statements.

Note that the exclamatory *oh* may be followed by an exclamation mark or a comma, depending on the degree of emphasis desired: *Oh! You startled me. Oh, let's forget the whole thing.* But the *O* used in direct address or in the refrains of songs and poems should stand without punctuation:

> O my sweet,
> I prattle out of fashion, and I dote
> In mine own comforts.
> — Othello, in *Othello* II i

3. Remember that although the exclamation mark is often used after imperative commands, it does not have to be. Strength of feeling is the deciding factor:

> Please write on one side of the paper only.
> Shut up!

Furthermore, when a question is used as a request, there is a range of possibilities reflecting increasing urgency and decreasing politeness:

> Would you mind opening the window?
> Would everyone wishing to visit the Doges' palace please assemble on the right.
> Would you mind not stepping on my foot!

4. The exclamation mark may be used to comment on a preceding word or phrase. Such punctuational comments, usually in brackets, are often ironic in tone. This use of the exclamation mark can be similar in effect to the use of a bracketed question mark:

> With such friends (!), I don't need enemies.

Compare:

> With such friends (?), I don't need enemies.

But many people consider it heavy-handed to use either the exclamation mark or the question mark in this way.

5. The exclamation mark may be doubled — or even trebled — for emphasis:

> Sh! Shh!! Shhh!!!
> She's won! She's won!! She's won!!!
> With such friends (!!), I don't need enemies.

Once again, use the exclamation mark sparingly, or the reader will stop taking you seriously.

6. The exclamation mark may follow the question mark and thereby reinforce it. It often adds an element of incredulity to the question:

> (Do you really mean) they want the work *tomorrow*?!

This combination of punctuation marks should be used very sparingly.

7. In chess notation, ! indicates a very good move, and !! an excellent move:

> R × P!   R × P!!

The exclamation mark may precede a question mark to indicate an interesting move that seems good but risky; if the order is reversed, with the exclamation mark following the question mark, this indicates a dubious move that looks poor but may pay off:

> R × P!?   R × P?!

8. The exclamation mark is also used in mathematics to indicate a *factorial* — that is, the product of multiplying an integer by all the positive integers below it. Thus:

> $4! = 4 \times 3 \times 2 \times 1 = 24$

For the use of exclamation marks in quotations, see QUOTATION MARKS.

9. Some typewriter keyboards do not include an exclamation mark. It is easy to make one up, however, by using the backspace key to type a full stop and an apostrophe in the same space.

exhaustive The two most important senses of the verb *to exhaust* are 'to use up' and 'to tire out'. *Exhaustive* is the adjective related to the first meaning, and should not be confused with *exhausting,* which is related to the second meaning.

Exhaustive means essentially 'comprehensive, thorough, taking everything into account, using everything up'. *Exhausting* means 'draining, extremely tiring'. So an *exhaustive* guide to usage covers all the ground; an *exhausting* guide wears you out in the reading.

When used as a present participle, it is true, *exhausting* can mean 'using everything up' as well, as in *Exhausting all other possibilities, they returned to the original plan.* But when used as a simple adjective, it remains distinct from *exhaustive*. So: *an exhausting assault course* but *an exhaustive search*.

In the following extract, *exhaustively* is a well-chosen word, suggesting that Sir Horace covered all the subjects in depth. No doubt his conversation was *exhausting* too, but that is incidental:

> So it went on. Sir Horace pursued the subjects of his nephew, education, character versus intelligence, the advantages of the late developer, the necessity of a good home background, enthusiastically and exhaustively. Jago was his chief conversational partner, though Brown now and then put in a bland, emollient word ... Indefatigably he continued to exhaust the subject of education.
> – C.P. Snow, *The Masters*

exigent, exiguous Both these adjectives come from the Latin verb *exigere,* which has two meanings: 'to demand' and 'to weigh exactly'. *Exigent* has developed from the first meaning, *exiguous* from the second.

Exigent means 'demanding, urgent, pressing'. Referring to people, it means 'demanding', as in:

> If the Prime Minister was exigent, he was also thoughtful . . . Having heard that excessive demands were being made upon me in Parliament . . .
> – Anthony Eden, *The Reckoning*

> Middleton is at his best when he writes as a translator, when he places his own gifts at the exigent service of a master.
> – Professor George Steiner,
> *The Times Literary Supplement*

Referring to situations, *exigent* means 'urgent'. This use is relatively rare: more common is the noun *exigency,* meaning 'emergency': *The flood water cut off the main road, and they were trapped — an exigency the rescuers had not anticipated.* The plural *exigencies* is still more common, and often means simply 'demands imposed by circumstances, tough requirements': *John had had an easy time at school — he was ill prepared to cope with the exigencies of army life.*

> It seemed easy to apply what I had learned in the L-shaped room to the wider field of Father's house. It was recovering — and so, more slowly, were its inhabitants — from the exigencies of the past eight months and the

past twenty-eight years.
> – Lynne Reid Banks,
> *The L-Shaped Room*

The formal word *exiguous* comes from the Latin *exigere* in its sense of 'to weigh exactly'. It means 'scanty, meagre', as if weighed out sparingly: *Food was distributed in exiguous quantities — two squares of chocolate and a dry biscuit each.*

> Only four per cent of Jackson supporters would be less likely to vote for Mondale if Jesse Jackson refused to endorse him. And if Mr Mondale still decided to play safe, he could undercut even such exiguous black opposition by choosing Mayor Tom Bradley of Los Angeles, a former policeman and a popular moderate black politician.
> – leading article, *Daily Telegraph*

The nouns derived from *exiguous* are *exiguousness* and *exiguity*.

It is interesting to note that the difference in meaning between *exigent* and *exiguous* is comparable to the difference in meaning between *exacting* and *exact* — words that also derive from the Latin verb *exigere*.

Finally, the pronunciations: note the different stresses and the different *g*-sounds: *exigent*, /**ek**sijənt/; *exigency*, /ek-**sij**ən-si; ig-**zij**ən-si/; *exiguous*, /eg-**zig**gew-əss; ek-**sig**gew-əss/; *exiguity*, /**ek**si-**gew**-əti/.

expect *To expect* used to attract criticism when used to mean 'to suppose', and still does from many purists: *?Sam's gone home already, I expect*; *?Of course she failed — what do you expect?*

> ?'A most extraordinary man, a Mr Nuttel,' said Mrs Sappleton; 'could only talk about his illnesses, and dashed off without a word of good-bye or apology when you arrived. One would think he had seen a ghost.'
> 'I expect it was the spaniel,' said the niece calmly; 'he told me he had a horror of dogs. He was once hunted into a cemetery on the banks of the Ganges by a pack of pariah dogs ...'
> – Saki, 'The Open Window'

To expect can apply only to future events, it is argued. However, the extended use of *expect* (a very old use, though it withered for some time under the blaze of criticism) is now so widespread that its acceptance into standard English, even in formal contexts, is just a matter of time. And it can be defended. If *expect* is understood as a shortened form of *expect to learn, expect to hear, expect that it will be,* or the like, then it does still refer to a future event technically, even though that future event is the discovery of a past event: *Sam's gone home already, I expect (you will tell me); Of course she failed — what do you expect (to hear)?*

That said, there is still no reason to prefer *expect* to *suppose, assume, believe, consider likely, should not be surprised to discover,* and so on. And if there are old-fashioned purists about who would object to the use of *expect* in this sense, it is best to draw on one of the many synonyms instead.

See also ANTICIPATE.

expiry, expiration The verb *to expire* has three main meanings: 'to come to an end', 'to breathe out', and 'to die'. Both *expiry* and *expiration* can be used for the first meaning (and, though rarely, for the third), but only *expiration* for the second. So: *the expiry/expiration of a contract,* but only *an expiration of breath.*

Even in the first sense of 'coming to an end', there is a slight difference that is worth preserving: *expiry* suggests a rather more automatic, long-planned, impersonal termination than *expiration: the expiry of a lease; the expiry date. Expiration* seems more considered, human, even apologetic, and is therefore often preferred in a business context, when there is a need to soften the blow of a termination: *Declining sales unfortunately mean the expiration of work contracts for more than 120 employees.*

The words go back to the Latin verb *expirare,* from *ex-,* 'out' + *spirare,* 'to breathe'.

Expiration can be pronounced with either an /i/ or an /ī/: /**ek**-spi-**ray**sh'n/ or (in British English) /**ek**-spī-**ray**sh'n/. When *expiration* is used to mean 'breathing out', its opposite is *inspiration* or *inhalation.* But because *inspiration* also means 'imaginative insight', it is better to use *inhalation* whenever there is the possibility of confusion.

extenuate 1. *To extenuate* should not be used carelessly as a synonym of *to justify* or *to excuse. To extenuate* means 'to make, or attempt to make, less blameworthy or seemingly less serious'. The Latin *extenuare* meant 'to thin out, lessen', from *ex-,* 'out' + *tenuare,* 'to make thin', from *tenuis,* 'thin'.

The proper object of *to extenuate,* then, is an abstract noun with an unfavourable sense: *guilt, offence, misdemeanour, error, brutality,* and so on: *Your poverty does not extenuate your thieving.* It is sometimes found with a more neutral

object, such as *action* or *behaviour* — *Your poverty does not extenuate your behaviour* — though the implication is clearly of *bad* behaviour.

As the two examples just quoted demonstrate, *to extenuate* is used in the same sentence-patterns and contexts as *to excuse* or *to justify,* and is often assumed to mean one or the other. But it is a much less ambitious verb than either of these: it involves only a reduction of blame, not the disappearance of blame.

Through confusion with *to excuse, to extenuate* is sometimes mistakenly used with a human object: ✗ *His deprived childhood does not extenuate that thief.* Either add the words *the guilt of* after *extenuate,* or change *extenuate* to *excuse.*

Perhaps the commonest use of *extenuate* is in the phrase *extenuating circumstances,* a technical term in criminal law. Extenuating circumstances are circumstances (existing at the time of the crime) that are considered to have influenced the accused in such a way as to make his conduct less blameworthy (from a moral, though not from a legal, point of view) than it would ordinarily be. The effect is not to alter the conviction, but to reduce the punishment. Factors that might well be regarded as extenuating circumstances are immaturity, provocation, drunkenness, absence of premeditation, and the influence of a stronger personality.

In criminal law, a common synonym for *extenuating circumstances* is *mitigating circumstances.*

2. This is not to say, however, that the verb *to extenuate* is a synonym of *to mitigate* in legal contexts. Whereas *to extenuate* is used chiefly in criminal cases, *to mitigate* is used chiefly in civil cases. It is the plaintiff's duty in a civil action to *mitigate* the loss he suffers through the defendant's wrongful act — that is, to take all reasonable steps to keep the loss to a minimum, and to refrain from doing anything that might unfairly increase it. For example, if damaged goods are sent for repair, the repairman selected should be one whose charges are reasonable — if he charges excessively, the plaintiff might not recover from the defendant the full cost of the repairs, since he had failed to mitigate his loss.

To mitigate, like *to extenuate,* goes back to a Latin verb based on an adjective — *mitis,* 'gentle, mild, soft'.

See also MILITATE.

exult See EXALT.

eyrie See AERIE.

fable   See ALLEGORY.

fabulous   Strictly, *fabulous* means 'based on or occurring in fable or legend'; so the unicorn is a *fabulous* animal. By a reasonable extension, the adjective has come to mean 'astonishing, incredible' — as difficult to believe as a fable: *a man of fabulous wealth*.

The word has now come to be used in the weakened sense of 'splendid, marvellous', especially by advertisers: *Try our fabulous new breakfast cereal*; *Win a fabulous holiday in the Far East*. And it has long been a generalised and wide-ranging term of approval, particularly among the younger generation: *That's a fabulous dress you're wearing*. But in this sense, *fabulous* and its British short form *fab* (sometimes *fabby*) have suffered from the whims of fashion, and seem less common now than they used to be. In time they are likely to be as quaint and rare as the adjective *wizard*. That is the fate of vogue superlatives: they lose their gloss through overuse, and have to be replaced.

See also ALLEGORY; FANTASTIC.

facility, faculty   *Facility* comes from the Latin *facilis*, 'easy' (from the verb *facere*, 'to do'), and means principally 'ease or fluency in doing something; an aptitude': *a facility in/with/for racket sports*. It also means 'the quality that allows something to be done or performed easily': *the facility of a simple piece of music*. The word often appears in the sense of 'something that makes things easy' or simply 'something that can be used': *sports facilities*. In this sense, the word is most often used in the plural — *facilities* refers to equipment in general, and specifically the service buildings:

The campsite has all the necessary facilities, including showers, restaurants, and shops.

As an informal euphemism, *the facilities* is often used to refer to the lavatory.

Faculty means in one sense 'the power or ability to do something specified': *He has the faculty to learn languages quickly*. This is the meaning most likely to be confused with *facility* in its sense of 'skill'. The distinction to bear in mind is this: a *facility* is the result of practice; a *faculty* is an innate power or a disposition present before the ability is exercised:

His faculty for languages was revealed by his month in Spain, during which he acquired a considerable facility with Spanish.

Each man is free to exercise his special faculty to the utmost, and every one encourages him in so doing.
— William Morris, *News from Nowhere* (1890)

Faculty can be used in a more general way, referring to any of the powers of the mind:

His body is frail but all his faculties are still sharp.
The faculty of speech is unique to man.

Faculty comes, like *facility,* from a word meaning 'easy', but in a different form. *Faculty* comes via Old French from the Latin *facultas,* 'power, capacity', itself from the Old Latin *facul,* 'easy'.

In a more specialised sense, *faculty* refers to a department at a college or university — *the science faculty* — or, as a collective noun, to the body of teachers in such a department.

However, in American English, *faculty* is used generally to mean 'teaching staff' — at secondary schools as well as at colleges and universities. North Americans speak not only of *the faculty of a college* and *faculty members* but also simply of *faculty,* in much the same way as you can speak of crew members as *crew: Ten of the demonstrators were students, and two were faculty*. In Britain these uses of *faculty* are beginning to catch on — despite criticism, especially of the last. They are still felt as strange by most speakers of British English. And in Britain you cannot yet speak of × *the faculty of a secondary school.*

fact   1. There are various idioms containing the word *fact*: *in fact, as a matter of fact, in point of fact,* and so on. There seems to be a widespread temptation to overuse these idioms in speech, resulting in a conspicuous and irritating mannerism. Added to that is our natural suspicion that someone who keeps protesting that he is telling the truth — communicating *facts* — may be lying. This suspicion is aroused above all by the boast *That's a fact*. The related idiom *Is that a fact?* — fairly common in American and South African English — is a needless ugly variant of the simple *Is that so?*

2. Equally needless and ugly (and long-winded) are the phrases *? because of the fact that, ? in view of the fact that, ? owing to the fact that, ? despite the fact that, ? notwithstanding the fact that,* and so on. The first three of these mean simply 'because' and should be reduced to that modest word; the last two are pretentious variants of *although* or *even though*.

The phrase *the fact that* is often inserted quite superfluously into a sentence, presumably because it is considered impressively elegant: *? He was forced to acknowledge the fact that his opponent was in the right*. On the contrary, it is ugly and pretentious. The sentence reads far better when worded simply as *He was forced to acknowledge that his opponent was in the right*.

3. The phrases *? the true facts, ? the actual facts, ? the real facts* and *? in actual fact* seem to be redundant. Strictly speaking, a fact is by definition true and real — otherwise it would be a lie, a speculation, or a fiction. Despite being well-established in colloquial idiom, the phrases are best avoided.

factitious, factious See FICTIONAL.

factor Among its various senses, *factor* means 'an element that actively contributes to an accomplishment, result, or process'. This sense is probably derived from the mathematical sense: 'any of the numbers or quantities that is multiplied with another to form a product'. A *factor* is, in short, a minor or contributory cause. The idea of *active* contribution is built into the word, which derives ultimately from the Latin *facere*, 'to do'. So: *The weak pound has certainly been a factor in our increased turnover*.

> Even changes that seem at first glance to have nothing to do with technology can be traced back to some technological factor that made the change possible, desirable, or both.
> – Isaac Asimov (U.S.),
> *Science Past — Science Future*

Factor is now widely used in a less precise way, and some purists dislike the generalised sense it has assumed: *There are several factors to consider here*; *They all have different factors in their upbringing* — that is, *points, features, things,* *occurrences, possibilities, components,* or the like.

There is no need to avoid using the word in this way, but do take care not to overuse it, as so many people do nowadays. And do not use it to flesh out a precise noun into a grand abstraction: *?? We must take the weather factor into consideration*. It is quite enough, surely, to *take the weather into consideration*.

Compare SITUATION.

faculty See FACILITY.

faint, feint The adjective *faint* means 'indistinct' or 'weak, lacking courage' or 'dizzy, close to fainting'. The noun means 'a brief loss of consciousness', the verb 'to lose consciousness, swoon'.

A *feint* is a misleading movement, feigned attack, pretence, or stratagem. *To feint* is to pretend to make such a movement (as in boxing): *He feinted a right*, meaning 'He pretended to throw a punch with his right fist'.

> 'Ouch! Ouf! You would, would you?' said Bob with as much avuncular bonhomie as he could force out of himself, feinting punches back at them, turning them upside down, and trying not to scream.
> – Michael Frayn,
> *Towards the End of the Morning*

The only sense in which the spellings *faint* and *feint* are interchangeable is the printer's sense of the finest line used in the printing of ruled paper, though *feint* is usually preferred here.

fantastic In most occurrences of this word today, the idea of fantasy is absent: *a fantastic film* is likely to mean 'a very good film' rather than 'a film depicting an unrealistic or visionary world'.

This abuse of a once-useful word is beyond cure. All that you can do is keep to a minimum the childish informal use of *fantastic*, choosing *remarkable, excellent, enjoyable, spectacular,* or the like instead; and to make sure, if you do use *fantastic* in its traditional senses, that there is no danger of misunderstanding. If there is, use *fantastical* instead, or any suitable near-synonym: *imaginative, bizarre, fanciful, preposterous,* or the like.

Compare FABULOUS.

farther See FURTHER.

fascination This word can cause confusion in some constructions. Consider these two sentences:

Sharks have a fascination for scuba divers.
Scuba divers have a fascination for sharks.

Which of them means that sharks fascinate divers? The first would usually convey that meaning, but the second could also (more easily in American than in British English, perhaps) be understood in that way. It is better, therefore, to avoid the possibility of ambiguity and to use a different construction. There are a number of simple alternatives:

Sharks hold a fascination for scuba divers.
Scuba divers are fascinated by sharks.
Sharks fascinate scuba divers.

fatal, fateful These two adjectives have clearly separate meanings, though the meanings can approach each other in certain uses.

Fatal means principally 'mortal, causing death', as in *a fatal accident. Fateful* means 'affecting one's destiny, important for the future': *the fateful day on which he met his future wife.* It also contains the sense of 'predetermined, destined, governed by fate' (which could be implied in this last example), but *fated* is the better word to use if this is the sense intended.

Fatal can refer to the destruction of abstract things, as well as the death of people: *It was fatal to his career, fatal to his peace of mind, and fatal to his marriage.* From this the word is extended to mean 'having a damaging result, destructive, disastrous': *He made the fatal error of asking for more.* The word has been weakened by careless informal exaggeration, and in some contexts seems to mean nothing more than 'serious' or merely 'unfortunate': *I should have known it would be fatal to get up today.*

Fateful can mean 'producing important results, having momentous consequences' — whether these are good or bad. But the word is perhaps employed more often when the results or consequences are bad. Sometimes *fateful* carries the connotation of 'ominous, foreboding doom': *the fateful sound of approaching gunfire.* When the word means 'having momentous and evil results', it comes very close to the meaning of *fatal,* in its sense of 'destructive': *Hitler's fateful assumption of the chancellorship of Germany.*

fay, fey Both of these words have meanings that carry them into the realm of the supernatural, and they are easily confused.

The noun *fay* means: 'a fairy, sprite, or elf':

 . . . tender is the night,
And haply the Queen-Moon is on her throne,

Clustered around by all her starry Fays.
 – John Keats,
'Ode to a Nightingale' (1820)

As an adjective, *fay* can accordingly mean 'relating to or resembling a fairy'. But it has another, less formal, meaning: 'pretentiously sweet or charming; arch'. It particularly applies to a person's manner, or mode of expression: *He thinks he's a good poet, but his poems are affected and sentimental and rather fay; I find these theatrical dandies to be unbearably fay.* Sometimes it is understood as something like *foppish,* suggesting languidness as well as an artificially obliging or sugary manner.

Fay comes from the Middle English word *faie,* 'one possessing magical powers', which in turn goes back via Old French to the Latin *fata,* 'the Fates' (the plural of *fatum,* 'Fate').

The adjective *fey* (also pronounced /fay/), despite having a suggestion of Fate about it as well, has its origin in a quite unconnected native word, the Old English *fæge.* Its commonest sense is probably 'whimsical, especially because interested in the supernatural'; more specifically, 'having supernatural vision, clairvoyant' or 'apparently under a magic spell, enchanted'. In Scottish English, it can mean 'fated to die soon, doomed', or 'behaving in a strange, excitable way, suggesting the approach of death'. So a romantic novel might deal with a *fey* heroine, pale and ethereal, and enfeebled by a disease from which she will never recover. No doubt this would also make her elfin in appearance or fairy-like in nature — or *fay.* Equally, a comic novel might deal with a *fey* young man, fancifully believing in supernatural powers. To some, this whimsy of his might be mere affectation, marking him as pretentiously quaint — or *fay.*

In the following quotation, *fay* rather than *fey* is probably the word that the reviewer intended:

?? Barbara Trapido (whose first novel 'Brother of the More Famous Jack' received some ecstatic notices) enamels what is essentially a fey tale of female frailty with the hardest, brightest and sharpest of surfaces, studded with jokes and aphorisms.
 – Anthony Thwaite, *The Observer*

fearfully See AWFULLY.

feasible In its strict sense, *feasible* means 'practicable, capable of being accomplished or brought about': *Modern weather forecasting techniques were simply not feasible until the development of satellite cameras.* The Old French *faisible* meant literally 'do-able', from *faire*, 'to do', from the Latin *facere*.

> All was perfectly feasible, or as good as done, and he walked in that dispensation of mind in which impossible works are in fact accomplished and mountains are moved.
> – Muriel Spark, *The Mandelbaum Gate*

The word has extended its range now, to mean 'likely or plausible' — *? not a very feasible prediction* — and 'possible': *?? Rain is likely, and even snow is feasible.* Both of these senses have attracted criticism, the second in particular. Before using the impressive-sounding but often empty adjective *feasible*, test to see whether *possible* or *probable* is the appropriate word instead.

Compare PRACTICAL.

feature As a verb, *to feature* has become a jack-of-all-trades, and has been widely criticised for taking on the tasks traditionally assigned to *exhibit, give prominence to, display, have, appear, present, affect, loom*, and so on. It is perhaps fair enough that films should *feature* well-known actors and actresses, but why should cinemas *feature* a new sound system and a non-smoking area; and why should bad luck *feature* largely in a well-known actor's life?

The noun *feature* too is overworked. It is resorted to by lazy speakers and writers when they cannot make the effort to reach for a more precise term: *? One of the features in his early career was the winning of the Atlanta Open.* Here *accomplishments, steps, triumphs*, or the like would be less vague.

Use *feature*, as both noun and verb, with caution and restraint.

feel The verb *to feel* is followed by an adjective when it describes what somebody is feeling: *Are you feeling sick?*; *I feel certain I'm right.* When it describes the extent to which, or the way in which, someone is feeling something, it is followed by an adverb: *She feels differently about him now.* Contrast *I feel strong again* and *I feel strongly about this issue.*

If you *feel bad* you can either be feeling unwell, or you can have a bad conscience: it is wrong to say *?? I feel badly about getting him fired* (= I have a bad conscience about it), though this usage is common in spoken English, especially in North America.

feint See FAINT.

female See WOMAN.

ferment See FOMENT.

fervent, fervid Both of these adjectives come ultimately from the Latin *fervere*, 'to boil or glow'. But the heat suggested by both words is of the figurative kind, referring to the fervour of passion rather than the warmth of central heating. Only in poetic or archaic usage do the words literally mean 'hot'; in general use, they both mean 'intensely enthusiastic, passionate'.

There is a small difference in tone between them, however: the use of *fervent* suggests a neutral or favourable view; the use of *fervid* suggests one that is slightly negative. If people support a cause ardently, and you like the cause and the supporters, you could describe their support as *fervent.* If you dislike the cause and the supporters, you might describe their support as *fervid* — which has slight connotations of being *feverish.* Similarly, you might well say *I fervently hope that X wins the election*, but you would be unlikely to say *?? I fervidly hope that X wins the election.*

The unfavourable associations of *fervid* are even more apparent in the related word *perfervid. A perfervid oration* is simply an extravagantly impassioned volley of words, anything but a convincing speech: its passion is of the dangerous kind that generates more heat than light.

Besides this slight difference in tone between *fervent* and *fervid,* there is also a difference in use between them. Both can be used of a *speech* or a *sentiment* or *support,* and so on, but it is only *fervent,* not *fervid,* that is commonly used of people. So you could refer to *a fervent speech* and *fervent speaker* if you were feeling neutral or favourably disposed; if you felt disapproval, however, you might talk of *a fervid speech* but probably not of *? a fervid speaker* — you would be far more likely to refer to *a wild speaker* or *an incoherent speaker.*

> *?* Chastened by the clear evidence of poor navigation and bombing accuracy in the earlier period, Harris became a fervid believer in the necessity for the indiscriminate area-bombing of cities, which later became called, without conscious irony, 'strategic bombing'.
> – Andrew Wilson, *The Observer*

The following example, having a nonhuman noun, is rather more appropriate:

> We move through a welter of fervid attractions and repulsions, shifting avant-garde alliances, bankruptcies, lurches towards

lesbianism, sudden flights to Paris and the South of France.

— John Gross, *The Observer*

Fervent, by contrast, is fairly flexible:

Censorship aims at maintaining the unity of the 'system'. In South Africa the banning of certain works has already placed some fervent disciples of the government in an unbearable situation — loyal to the politics of the government they yet find themselves constrained to defend both the aesthetics and the morality of a banned work.

— André Brink, in
They Shoot Writers, Don't They?

They did, and the blast of their first bomb threw her against the steel door . . . At first she was stone deaf, but gradually she heard the whimpering of terrified children, and the steadier but fervent voices of their mothers.

— John le Carré,
The Little Drummer Girl

festival, festivity *Festivity* tends to be a more general term, applying to any form of merry-making or celebration, and also to the atmosphere or feeling of pleasure at such an occasion. And, in the plural, *festivities* refers to the events or activities involved in the occasion.

Festival tends to be more specific, referring to a particular occasion or celebration, usually recurring annually and often of religious significance: *Harvest Festival*; *the Festival of Chanukkah*. It is also used to refer to a series of exhibitions, performances, competitions, or the like: *a film festival*; *the Edinburgh Festival*. (Curiously, *festival* as an adjective is slightly broader in range: *a festival atmosphere at the seaside on a sunny day*.)

The two adjectives *festive* and *festal* have corresponding ranges of meaning. *Festive* is again broader, and relates to *festivity* or merrymaking in general: you might be in a *festive* mood if you simply feel like celebrating joyfully. Similarly, *a festive dinner* or *a festive scene* might simply resemble a festival.

Festal relates more closely to *festival*: there actually has to be a festival for something or someone to be *festal*: *a festal costume*. The word is now rare in ordinary usage.

The words all go back to the Latin adjective *festus*, which referred to a religious festival, and could mean either 'solemn' or 'joyous'. The word *feast* comes from the same source (as does *fête*): *feast*, like *festival*, can be used of ceremonial religious occasions, in addition to its secular senses — *the Feast/Festival of the Assumption*.

few, a few 1. *Few,* without the *a*, suggests 'a small number, as against many'; *a few* suggests 'a small number, as against none'.

Accordingly, when the expectation or norm is a large number, use *few* to point the contrast: *We hired a large hall, but few spectators turned up.* When the expectation or norm is a smaller number or zero, then use *a few* to indicate the contrast: *We didn't really expect anyone at all, but a few did turn up.* (The phrases *only a few* and *just a few* are closer in meaning to *few* than to *a few*.)

Note that there is a similar distinction between *little* and *a little*: *He drinks little wine; Try a little wine and you'll feel stronger.*

2. The phrases *a good few* and *quite a few*, however odd they seem when analysed, are established idioms. But ✗ *a comparatively few*, though widely used, is unacceptable. Use *comparatively few* or *a comparative few* instead. (See RELATIVELY.)

3. *Few* and *fewer* are often used to qualify the noun *number* or *numbers* — inappropriately, since *few* already contains the idea of *number*:

?? Prospective candidates have been discouraged, and are applying in fewer numbers now than in previous months.
?? The number of flies is relatively few this year.

Numbers are *low* or *small*, not *few*.

However, the phrase *few in number*, though perhaps redundant and slightly affected, is a long-established idiom and quite acceptable:

This month's applicants are relatively few in number.

See also FEWER.

fewer, less 1. The rule, broadly, is that *fewer* refers to number, whereas *less* refers to quantity or amount. More specifically, *fewer* should be used when the noun following is plural, and *less* when it is singular. So: *fewer workers* and *less production*, *fewer opportunities* and *less opportunity*, and so on. (The word *more* is more versatile: it can be used with singular or plural nouns, and refer to number or to amount. Until the 18th century, *less* too had this same flexibility.)

It is very common in informal speech to hear *less* instead of *fewer*, especially when a contrast is stated or strongly implied, or when the plural noun (*clothes*) is inadvertently taken to be a singular mass noun (*clothing*).

✗ There were far less road accidents this year than last year.

✗ He was sighted in no less than 15 countries.

?? One needs less clothes in the summer.

✗ If all of this sounds reminiscent of Vietnam, the Administration responds that there are, after all, less than 100 American military personnel in El Salvador, and no plans yet to increase them.

— Jeremy Paxman, *The Listener*

Strictly speaking, the correct standard usage remains *fewer* in all four examples.

Sometimes, however, the 'correct' use of *fewer* before a plural noun is both clumsier and less effective than the 'incorrect' *less*:

? We want a few more buses and a few less cars.

Here, the word *less*, though not strictly correct, does serve to stress the contrast very effectively by balancing the *more* in the opening clause; and it certainly sounds better than the 'correct' phrasing would — *a few fewer cars*.

In some constructions, *less* is undoubtedly more suitable than *fewer* even though the following noun is (apparently) in the plural:

She is less than 60 years old.
They earn less than £5000 per year each.
His last jump was less than 7 metres.

In less than 10 years, most of the great banks of the Western world have exchanged the whole of their own capital and much of their depositors' money for the IOUs of South American countries.

— Lord Lever, *Time and Tide*

These expressions of measurement should really be regarded as singular rather than plural. They refer to a quantity rather than a number of individual units. Read the sentences as ... *(the age of) 60 years old, ...(a total of) £5000, ... (a distance of) 7 metres,* and ... *(a period of) 10 years,* and it becomes clear that these examples do not really break the rule. The test is whether the numerical expression can take a singular verb: if it can, then *less* is possible:

£25 is a small sum. He has less than £25.

If a singular verb is impossible, then *fewer* has to be used:

25 people are here. He invited fewer than 25 people.

A final problem: you can say *we want three*

fewer lamps, but what do you say if you have an excess of only one lamp? The first rule — that *fewer* refers to number, whereas *less* refers to amount — would suggest the form ?? *We want one fewer lamp.* The second rule — that *less* precedes singular nouns and *fewer* precedes plural nouns — would suggest the form ? *We want one less lamp.* The second of these is preferable to the first, but still attracts criticism. The best form of all is a rearrangement: *We want one lamp fewer.*
See also FEW; LESS.

fey See FAY.

fictional, fictitious, fictive, factitious, factious, fractious *Fictional* and *fictitious* are sometimes interchangeable, but in their primary senses they are distinct.

The noun *fiction* refers to imaginative literature, and *a fiction* usually to a feigned occurrence or lie. The adjective *fictional* relates chiefly to the first of these senses; the adjective *fictitious* chiefly to the second. So: *Mr Pickwick is a fictional character,* appearing in fiction (*fictitious character* is possible here, though it is no longer in common use in this sense), and *He gave a fictitious name when questioned by the police.*

Once this form has been set, it scarcely matters that individual, fictional Brits get unsympathetic treatment from their author. The form insists that *they are the ones whose stories matter,* and that is so much less than the whole truth that it must be called a falsehood.

— Salman Rushdie, *The Observer*

In a slightly extended sense, *fictional* can mean simply 'imaginary': *a solitary child, but playing quite happily with his numerous fictional friends.* Of course, *fictitious friends* are equally unreal, but they are invented with the intention of deceiving others: *The alibi collapsed when the prosecutor showed that the so-called meeting must have been with purely fictitious friends.*

Factitious is easy to confuse with *fictitious,* both through its similarity of sound and spelling, and through its related meaning. It means either 'produced deliberately for a special purpose, unnatural, artificial, contrived' — *the factitious value of gold-shares caused by heavy speculation* — or 'sham, affected, not spontaneous': *a factitious smile of welcome.* In the following quotation, *factitiously* means 'artificially, in a contrived way':

The film has two quite distinct aspects,

somewhat factitiously conjoined by Daniel's quest for purpose and identity. The first, wholly legitimate, one is the unbearably moving experience of these two children orphaned by the state.
> – Philip French, *The Observer*

The adjective *fictive* has been a very versatile word, at various times covering the senses of *fictional, fictitious,* and *factitious*. Today it is little used except perhaps with reference to fiction-writing: *He should stick to acting — his fictive gifts, if this novel is anything to go by, are very limited*.

Next, *factious* and *fractious*: *factious* is easy to confuse with *factitious*, and *fractious* with *factious* in turn. *Factious* means 'produced by or producing faction or party-allegiance': *engaged in factious in-fighting when they should be cooperating*; *a factious debate*.

Politics is really no more factious than it was at the turn of the century. It is certainly more representative of the people.
> – David Watt, 'Words', BBC Radio 3

Fractious means 'unruly, prone to violence' — *a quiet man but fractious when drunk* — or else 'peevish, irritable': *The baby grew fractious while teething*.

Anyway, it was against this background noise that I met Lindsay Anderson, the director who is consistently the critics' choice as the most fractious, hypersensitive pain in the neck in the business. He is renowned for . . . dispatching withering rebuttals of criticism and for holding the view that journalists come fairly low in the order of creation.
> – Henry Porter, *The Sunday Times*

finalise This verb has been widely criticised as a piece of needless bureaucratic jargon, serving no purpose that is not already well served by *to finish, to agree to, to conclude, to complete,* or *to put into final form*:

? It was unthinkable, in such circumstances, that they should discuss the money, even though she had thought about little else since she found the stately corpse looking out to sea. As far as she knew 'details' had not been finalised. There would be great awkwardness whatever happened.
> – A.N. Wilson, *The Sweets of Pimlico*

? On this occasion the negotiations seem to have been relatively peaceful. The Cabinet

— due to meet today to finalise matters — is reported to be very close to agreement.
> – leading article, *The Times*

? Preparations for the launch are just being finalised.

Although commonly regarded as an Americanism, and widely and freely used in North American English, the term seems to have originated in Australia.

If you are tempted to use the word, stop to ask yourself whether it really has any advantage over any of its established rivals.

finger Is the thumb a finger? In some uses of the word *finger,* the thumb is clearly included in that term: *five-finger exercise, ten fingers and ten toes, middle finger*. In other uses the thumb is clearly not considered a finger: *all fingers and thumbs; hold the shell between the thumb and fingers*.

There is no difficulty about such phrases, since the context makes the meaning quite clear in each case. The problem arises with numbering: is the middle finger your *second finger* or your *third finger*? What does *fourth finger* refer to — your ring finger or your little finger? Some people could regard it as the little finger; but the old marriage service and the modern music teaching-book alike use *fourth finger* to refer to the ring finger.

The best course of action is to avoid the problem altogether: do not refer to your fingers by their number but by their name: *thumb, index finger* or *forefinger, middle finger, ring finger,* and *little* (or sometimes *baby*) *finger*. The *little finger* is also called the *pinkie* by Scots, Americans, and South Africans.

No such problem occurs with toes — they are numbered one to five, from the big toe towards the little toe. It is not often, of course, that you need to specify a particular toe, but when you do, you would probably refer to your toes as *big toe, second toe, middle toe, fourth toe,* and *little* (or *baby*) *toe*.

first 1. There is a traditional rule that when several items or points are being listed one by one, they should be introduced by the words *first, secondly, thirdly, fourthly . . . first,* rather than *firstly* (and also *last* rather than *lastly*).

There might once have been a good reason for discouraging *firstly, secondly, thirdly,* and all the rest, leaving *first, second, third,* and so on unchallenged both as adverbs and as adjectives. But there cannot be any good reason for the present rule, which discourages only *firstly,* and there is a very good reason against it: that it creates a needless inconsistency. (Some people restore the consistency by reverting to *second* and *third* as well as *first*, rather than *secondly* and *thirdly*. There seems to be no objection to this, though it might sound slightly stiff.)

Nevertheless, even as a quaint fossil, the rule persists among purists. If you choose to ignore it, it is possible that one of your listeners or readers will choose not to.

> Just look a moment at the implications of this. First, there's the assumption that, although we are all free to make up new sentences ... there are big constraints on the individual making up new words as he goes along. Secondly, and despite this, there's the overt acknowledgment that no native speaker, however fluent and educated and well-read, is expected to know all the words of his language.
> – Sir Randolph Quirk, 'Words', BBC Radio 3

> Why was such a prodigious talent so prodigally wasted? His answer is twofold. First, Armstrong was born into the black working class, and never escaped its limitations ... Secondly, Armstrong was by temperament shy, indecisive and easily put down.
> – Philip Larkin *The Observer*

Note also that in enumerations, the phrases *first of all* and *last of all* are probably now acceptable variants of *first* and *last* throughout the English-speaking world, but *second of all, third of all*, and the like are regarded as Americanisms.

2. *First* tends to be used in a slipshod way in various expressions:

✗ The modern steam engine was first invented in 1769.

Omit the *first*. Similarly:

✗ We lived in a single room when we were first married.

This should instead read something like:

> We lived in a single room for a time just after we were married.

3. In collective expressions, *first* is today placed before rather than after a numeral: *the first two chapters* suggests chapters one and two of a single book. Reversing the elements has a separating effect: *the two first chapters* suggests chapter one of book A and chapter one of book B.
See also LAST.

fish This word has two plural forms: *fish* and *fishes*. *Fish* is far more widely used: *I don't eat fish*; *He brought home three fish*. *Fishes* is used in technical writing, usually to emphasise individual fish or species of fish: *Salmon and trout are both food fishes*.
See PLURALS.

fit, fitted In American English *fit* is sometimes used for the past tense of this verb — *This dress fit me last year* — or as the past participle: *She said it had fit last year*. British English prefers *fitted* in both these uses: *This dress fitted me last year*; *She said it had fitted last year*. Both American and British English use *fitted* in such sentences as *The dressmaker fitted the skirt carefully*, where *fitted* means 'caused to fit'.

flagrant See BLATANT.

flammable See INFLAMMABLE.

flaunt, flout *To flaunt* means 'to show off, display ostentatiously':

> Trying to get my two cents' worth into literary conversations I often used to flaunt my favourite quote from *Treasure Island*, in young Jim's account of his lone fight for the ship, Chapter XXVI: 'His blood ran over my hands as hot as tea.'
> – Basil Boothroyd, *The Times*

> Instead, there was the thrumming of the drums and drawling of the harmonium and above that the thin, high-pitched voice flaunting itself before the audience like some demented dervish of sound.
> – Anita Desai, *In Custody*

To flout means 'to scorn or treat with contempt', especially 'to show contempt for restrictions or rules by one's actions':

> If they obey the law of the land, they should go free. But if they should flout the law, they will find that their end will be at hand.
> – Lord Denning, *Time and Tide*

> Science plays God in an age of doubting,
> Morality falters before research;
> Seekers of knowledge are charged with flouting
> Rules made by nature, if not the church.
> – Roger Woddis, *Radio Times*

The two meanings are clearly distinct, yet writers and speakers are strangely tempted into using *flaunt* when they mean *flout*:

✕ The commutation of death sentences, even those with recommendations of mercy, was abandoned at a moment's notice if military objectives demanded it; rules designed to give the accused a fair hearing were flaunted; many medical officers flatly refused to recognise that shell shock represented a real psychiatric condition.
— David Hewson, *The Times*

✕ I dissent furiously from those colleagues who believe that the composer's conscious intentions are sacred. A great work of art has many faces ... But that cannot justify flaunting his intentions as they are revealed in the music.
— Peter Hayworth, *The Observer*

✕ Steaks were what the fancy cattlemen or their Chicago bosses had in mind — steaks for the tables of the rich, the bad, the beautiful, and the sleazy, who could afford to flaunt the wartime rationing laws and pay outrageous prices for prime cuts and steaks that were supposed not to be available.
— Alistair Cooke,
'Letter from America', BBC Radio 4

(Two weeks later — perhaps in response to reproachful listeners — Mr Cooke engagingly inserted a similar construction into his radio talk, this time choosing the correct word, *flout*.)

The basis for this odd confusion, apart from the words' similarity of sound, is perhaps that *flouting* often seems an ostentatious gesture — one that is flaunted.

The two words do not seem to be connected in their origins: they both emerged in the mid-16th century. *Flaunt* is possibly derived from Scandinavian sources. *Flout* probably developed as an extended sense of the Middle English *flouten*, 'to play the flute', going back through Old French to the Latin *flare*, 'to blow'.

flautist, flutist A person who plays the *flute* (the modern concert-hall version of this ancient wind-instrument) is today referred to as a *flautist* in British English. *Flutist* was formerly an acceptable variant, and remains so in American English, but in British English it now sounds archaic.

What about the player of a penny-whistle or reed-flute or any other folk instrument related to the flute? The word *flautist* is unlikely to be used then. A musician of the ancient world or a simple goatherd should be referred to as a *flute-player* instead.

Flautist is pronounced /**flaw**-tist/; in North American English, there is a variant pronunciation, /**flow**-tist/.

fleshy, fleshly A *fleshy fruit* (or *leaf*) is firm and pulpy, not fibrous. A *fleshy person* is plump. Some dictionaries now allow *fleshly* to mean 'plump' as well, but this form is best reserved for far more philosophical and psychological senses: *fleshly thoughts* are worldly thoughts, particularly about sex, in implicit contrast to more elevated, spiritual thoughts. *Fleshly delights* are typically sexual, though they might refer to the pleasure taken in food and drink.

Fleshly is seldom used to apply directly to a person. A plump person is *a fleshy person*, but it sounds rather odd to call a sensual person *? a fleshly person*.

Compare EARTHY.

floor There are often British-American differences in the way that the *floors* of a building are numbered, though there appear to be no corresponding differences in the numbering of *storeys* (see STOREY). The principal possibilities are displayed in the table below:

A	B	C
British and rare American	*Frequent American*	*Less frequent American*
Second Floor	Third Floor	Third Floor
First Floor	Second Floor	Second Floor
Ground Floor	First Floor	Ground Floor

In American English, system A may be used for residential accommodation, such as private houses or hotels; systems B and C would occur particularly frequently in commercial buildings. But it is hard to predict which system will be used where.

In North America there is the further complication that the 13th floor of a tall building is sometimes not numbered as such, in the belief that the number 13 is unlucky. It may be numbered 12A, or the numbering may proceed from 12 directly to 14.

Most other English-speaking countries and European countries follow the British system. Latin American countries tend to share the North American preferences.

A *mezzanine* floor (pronounced /**mets**ə-neen, **mezz**ə-/) is an intermediate partial storey — such as a gallery in a hotel — between the ground floor and the first floor. (It also has senses related to the theatre: in American English, the *mezzanine* is the lowest balcony of seating: in British English, it is the floor under the stage.) In some old buildings, however, the *mezzanine* is a full floor in its own right. In France, for example, an old building might have the ground floor (*rez-de-chaussée*) at street-level, above that a low *mezzanine* storey (*entresol*), and above that the 'first floor' at last (*première étage*).

See also CEILING.

flotsam, jetsam Literally, *flotsam* is wreckage or cargo that remains afloat after a ship has sunk, while *jetsam* is cargo thrown overboard or cargo or wreckage washed ashore. *Flotsam* is related in sense, and possibly origins, to *float*; *jetsam* is an alteration of *jettison*, going back to the Latin *jacere*, 'to throw'. Think of *flotsam* as that which floats, and *jetsam* as that which is thrown overboard, or thrown up on shore by the sea.

Both words, in an extended sense, can also refer to discarded miscellaneous odds and ends, or sometimes to unemployed vagrants. They are used either separately or in the combination *flotsam and jetsam*:

> 'You keep the old cow waiting, like she does me. And wait she will, don't you worry. It's not as easy as it used to be to find people so down on their luck they'd live in one of her rat-holes ...' He went on staring at me. I clenched my hands in my pockets. I felt like a piece of flotsam.
> – Lynne Reid Banks,
> *The L-Shaped Room*

> Bob tried to remember why he hadn't told her ... But he couldn't really remember the reason. It was already lost — part of the jetsam of discarded immemorabilia which disappeared astern all the time.
> – Michael Frayn,
> *Towards the End of the Morning*

flounder, founder These two verbs are easily confused. In its literal sense, *to founder* is typically used of ships, and means 'to sink': *The longboat foundered in heavy seas*; *A giant iceberg foundered the ship*. The source of the word is in fact the Latin *fundus,* 'the bottom', presumably referring to the bottom of the sea. *To founder* is also used to mean 'to collapse', as a building might, and perhaps most commonly of all, 'to stumble', as a horse might. (There is a technical sense of *founder,* both as a noun and as a verb, referring to a disease that lames horses.) In metaphorical use, *to founder* means 'to fail, weaken, or give way': *The play foundered after a week*; *The customers drifted off and his business began to founder*.

It was quite clear that Spalding's Timber Pact was going to founder in mutual mistrust once more.
> – Antrobus, in Lawrence Durrell's
> *Esprit de Corps*

> Alain, his composure foundering, breached his own code of honour and blurted, '*Mais je n'ai rien fait!*'
> – Anita Brookner, *Hotel du Lac*

To flounder also originally meant 'to stumble', but today its literal meaning is 'to move clumsily, to struggle to keep one's balance': *floundering in the dark*. It is often followed by the preposition *about* or *around*: *floundering about in the dark*. It can be used in an extended, slightly figurative way:

> So we learn ... how Elizabeth Blackwell, who was to become the first qualified woman doctor, floundered around in her youth desperately looking for 'useful' work.
> – Lorna Sage, *The Observer*

In another metaphorical use, *to flounder* means 'to go forward clumsily and in confusion, to press on or struggle hopelessly'. It is often followed by the preposition *on*: *He had clearly not learnt his lines, but he floundered on to the end of the scene.*

> Charlie flailed and rallied and flailed again with the growing desperation of the half-taught ... In her mind, as she floundered fiercely on, she saw herself in one of those improvised happenings at drama school, working her way into a part that increasingly lacked meaning for her as she advanced.
> – John le Carré,
> *The Little Drummer Girl*

The word *flounder* arose in Shakespeare's time, probably as a blend of *founder* and *blunder,* and influenced by *fling, flounce,* and similar words suggesting awkward movement.

Here is a nice example of confusion between the two words:

> ✕ The most ambitious compromise ever attempted in Northern Ireland was that of Sunningdale in 1974 (an inter-community power-sharing Executive in Northern Ireland, plus a pan-Irish Council for Ireland). That attempt is generally remembered as having floundered as a result of Protestant opposition: the Ulster Workers' Council Strike.
> – Conor Cruise O'Brien, *The Observer*

The word required was *foundered* not *floundered*.

flout See FLAUNT.

flutist, fluteplayer See FLAUTIST.

focus around See CENTRE AROUND.

fog See MIST.

foment, ferment The verbs *to ferment* and *to foment* are sometimes confused, partly through some overlap in meaning, and partly because (in British English) both words can be pronounced /fə-**ment**/. (The more distinctive pronunciations /fer-**ment**/ and /fō-**ment**/ are also possible, however.)

Either word might be used in connection with stirring up trouble: *The speech fomented/ ?fermented a riot.* But the two words are not always interchangeable, and even in this context have different meanings.

Ferment goes back to the Latin *fermentum*, 'yeast', from *fervere,* 'to boil'. It is both a verb and a noun. As a verb, it is stressed on the second syllable, and has the literal meaning 'to produce by fermentation, or to undergo or cause to undergo fermentation'. Fermentation is, of course, a chemical action such as that of yeast on sugar, making it seethe or bubble, and producing alcohol. Figuratively, *to ferment* can mean 'to generate or stir up'; it then takes a nonhuman object: *to ferment trouble in a crowd* (but probably not × *to ferment a crowd*). When used intransitively, *to ferment* means 'to be turbulent, seethe': *Trouble slowly fermented among the crowd.*

As a noun, *ferment* is stressed on the first syllable, /**fer**-ment/, and means literally 'anything that causes or undergoes fermentation', or figuratively 'agitation, commotion, or turbulence': *After the news of the assassination, the country was in a state of ferment.*

Foment cannot be used as a noun: it is a verb alone. It goes back to the Latin noun *fomentum*, 'a warm application', from the verb *fovere,* 'to warm'. Literally, *to foment* means 'to apply warmth and moisture to (the skin) by means of a poultice'. Figuratively, *to foment* means 'to excite, stir up, instigate, promote the growth or arousal of' — especially trouble or conflict. Like *ferment* it takes nonhuman objects; unlike *ferment* it should not really function intransitively — that is, without an object when in the active voice. So: *He fomented trouble,* but not ?? *Trouble fomented.* In the following citation, similarly, *fomenting* is not used strictly correctly: perhaps *fermenting* is what was intended:

?? A plot by British mercenaries to overthrow the Government of the poverty-stricken Comoro Islands in the Indian Ocean has been foiled by the arrest of three men in Australia. The attempted coup has been fomenting in Europe since early last year, and the organisation and money behind the scheme has spanned the world.
  — Peter Durisch, *The Observer*

The slight difference between *to ferment trouble* and *to foment trouble* lies perhaps in their respective sources: *to ferment* suggests seething or boiling; *to foment* suggests warming. Not that *to foment* is necessarily more favourable in tone: it suggests a more deliberate instigation than *to ferment* does, and hence a sneakiness or subversiveness, as by a political agitator.

font See FOUNT.

foot This word has alternative plural forms when it is used as a unit of measurement. In precise measurements, *feet* is formal, *foot* is informal: *The plank is three feet/foot exactly.* When the term *inches* is added, *feet* is the preferred form, even in informal usage: *He's six feet two inches.* But if the word *inches* is left out, *foot* is common in informal usage: *He's six foot two.* In hyphenated adjectives used before a noun, *foot* is the only possible form: *a six-foot plank; a six-foot-tall man.* But if the measurement goes after the verb, *feet* or *foot* can be used: *The plank was six feet long*; *The man was six foot tall.*

for Compare the following pairs of sentences:

I'd like him to stay — I don't want him to leave.
?? I'd like for him to stay — × I don't want for him to leave.
I asked for him to be allowed to stay — I didn't wish (for) him to leave.
For him to stay would be wonderful — For him to leave would be unbearable.

The second example illustrates a common error (especially frequent in American English) — the insertion of *for* in front of the noun or pronoun that comes between one verb and the infinitive of another. It is easy to see how this error arises — from the influence of such constructions as the third and fourth examples.

The *for* is fully idiomatic in the fourth example, and would remain so even if the elements were reversed: *It would be wonderful for him to stay*, and so on. In the third example, the *for* is justified as the natural preposition following the verbs *ask* and *wish*, as in *I asked for the moon, I wished for the moon*. But there is no *for* in *I'd like the moon* or *I want the moon*, and so its insertion in the second example on the list is nonstandard and should be avoided.

Note, however, that in one special type of sentence the *for* becomes obligatory — namely, the sentence that is divided into two equal parts and begins typically with *what*:

What I'd like is for him to stay — What I want is for him to stay.

In this type of sentence, the phrase *for him to stay* functions as a unit, as it does in the fourth example above.

See also BECAUSE; FOREVER; YEARS.

forbear, forebear As a general rule, the prefix *fore-* suggests 'before' (or 'in front'), and the prefix *for-* suggests 'excluded, abstaining, or prohibited' (or else 'completely').

The verb *to forbear,* 'to refrain from or hold back', is accordingly spelt without an *e*. A *forebear,* 'an ancestor', is preferably spelt with an *e*, though it is sometimes spelt *forbear,* and this is regarded as acceptable. What is no longer accepted, however, is the spelling ? *to forebear* for the verb, though it was often spelt that way in the past.

The past tense of the verb *to forbear* is *forbore: He forbore to comment*; the past participle is *forborne: He had forborne to go with them*.

Forebear was originally a Scottish word, in effect *fore-be-er,* 'one who has been before'. It used to be considered rather alien in standard English. But the English *forefather* has lost ground because of its male bias, and *ancestor* and *progenitor* sound rather formal, so *forebear* has recently gained both popularity and full acceptance.

Note that the noun, *forebear,* is stressed on the first syllable: /**for**-bair/; the verb, *forbear,* on the second syllable: /fawr-**bair**, fər-/.

forbid 1. The past tense of *forbid* is *forbade,* usually pronounced /fər-**bad**/ even though spelt with an *e* at the end. (The pronunciation /fər-**bayd**/ or /fawr-**bayd**/ is acceptable, though less common.)

The past participle is *forbidden: He has forbidden me to go*.

2. It is possible to use *to forbid* in such constructions as *I forbid you to go* or, slightly more formally, *I forbid your going*, or followed by a straightforward noun: *I forbid all departures*.

All too frequently, however, people say or write × *I forbid you going* or × *I forbid you from going*. These are not strictly correct, though the second version, probably modelled on the construction with *to prohibit,* is so common nowadays that its acceptance into standard English is probably just a matter of time.

forbidding, foreboding *Foreboding* and *forbidding* are sometimes confused. The adjective *forbidding,* from the verb *to forbid,* means 'seeming to forbid or impede, discouraging': *a forbidding appearance* or *a forbidding line-up of contestants* — either would tend to 'put you off'.

Foreboding, as the present participle of *to forebode,* means 'suggesting or indicating something unpleasant in advance — such as a premonition of a future misfortune': *Foreboding clouds threatened a storm*.

Obviously, the similarity between 'threatening' *(foreboding)* and 'discouragingly sinister' *(forbidding)* leads to some confusion. In fact, *foreboding* is only rarely used as an adjective before a noun, as in *foreboding clouds*. It is more likely to appear as a participle after a noun — *clouds foreboding a storm; feelings foreboding disaster* — or as a noun itself: *feelings of foreboding*. Here it means 'a sense of impending evil'. It can also mean 'a portent': *The owl's screech was a foreboding of death*.

Of course, *forbidding* too can be used as a participle after a noun — *a new regulation forbidding cigarette advertisements on television* — but is unlikely to be used as an ordinary noun.

Note that *foreboding* is spelt with an *e, forbidding* without.

See also FORBID.

forceful, forcible In many contexts these two adjectives are interchangeable. They can both mean 'full of force, characterised by force', especially in the sense of 'persuasive or effective': *a forceful personality, a forcible orator, a forcible reminder*. There is perhaps a slight difference of emphasis between the two words: *forcible* is supposed to be contrasted to an absence of force; *forceful* to a low level of force. So *a forcible reminder* suggests a measure of surprise, as though reminders are usually conveyed in a very easy or pleasant way rather than by means of force; *a forceful reminder* suggests impressiveness, as though this particular reminder was conveyed with more force than reminders usually are.

It also presents a forceful case for the

usefulness of art, both in the debates between the puritanical Daoud and the colonel's sister-in-law ... and in its very existence as a movie that keeps alive the tradition of Iranian cinema.

– Philip French, *The Observer*

Forcible has a further distinct meaning that *forceful* does not have; that is, 'effected through the use of force', as in *forcible entry* or *forcible expulsion*. There is a negative overtone to the word when used in this sense, which is not felt when it is used in its other sense, and which is entirely absent from the neutral or even favourable word *forceful*:

Within a few days of my going to the Foreign Office, Hitler had given us one more indication of the shape of things to come by his forcible incorporation of Austria into Germany.

– Lord Butler,
The Art of the Possible

Finally, note the rare word *forceable*. It is pronounced in exactly the same way as *forcible*, but means something quite different — 'capable of being forced', as in *a forceable lock*. Take care not to confuse the respective senses and spellings of the two words.

forensic The adjective *forensic* is used in reference to legal proceedings. *Forensic medicine* (or *medical jurisprudence*, as it is sometimes known) is the application of medical science in interpreting or establishing the facts in law cases. A *forensic scientist* is typically a scientist, employed by the police department, who tests clues for information that might be helpful in tracking down or convicting a criminal.

Because the term is usually applied to scientists or laboratories, it has come to be misunderstood as meaning 'technical', and people speak misguidedly of *?? the forensic evidence presented in court*, when what they mean is *the scientific* or *medical evidence*. Any evidence presented in court is, strictly speaking, *forensic* evidence.

In the following two extracts from a single article, *forensic* is first used incorrectly or redundantly, and then used correctly.

?? Mr Henry Bland, a Home Office analytical chemist for 18 years, believes that the assembly of defence forensic evidence on behalf of a defendant is being hindered unnecessarily. ...

A Home Office spokesman last week confirmed its officials were reviewing their policy over defence access to forensic laboratories.

– Robin McKie, *The Observer*

The word originally meant 'used in debate or argument, rhetorical': it comes from the Latin *forensis*, 'of a market or forum, public', from *forum*, 'a forum'.

forever, for ever Purists prefer to express the meaning 'for eternity, everlastingly, eternally' as two words, *for ever*: *I'll love you for ever*; *Wales for ever!*

The modern tendency to fuse these into *forever* is sure to triumph eventually, but it is worth resisting it until it is fully accepted, and to restrict *forever* to the sense 'constantly, incessantly, at all times': *She's forever complaining about her back and her feet.*

forgo, forego Generally speaking, the prefix *fore-* means 'before', and the prefix *for-* means 'excluded' (see FORBEAR).

Accordingly, *to forego* means 'to go before' — usually now occurring only in such phrases as *the foregoing information* and *a foregone conclusion* (see MISQUOTATIONS). And *to forgo* (sometimes *to forego*) means 'to give up or do without' — especially, 'to do without something one has a right to': *He was prepared to forgo his lunch break in order to finish the report.*

But Tony Camden, the LSO's chairman, points out that in a competitive business it's sometimes necessary to forgo fees, and that members cover this contingency by covenanting £10 a week to the orchestra.

– Laurence Marks, *The Observer*

The past tense of *to forgo* is *forwent*.

To forgo is increasingly being spelt *to forego*, and this variant, although still less common, is widely accepted, since the danger of confusion with *to forego* in the sense of 'to go before' is so slight.

Note that both words are stressed on the second syllable.

former, latter 1. These are very useful words in their place: they often provide the means of avoiding a long-winded and inelegant repetition of two nouns or names, and they can help to avoid ambiguity. But there is a temptation to overuse them; they sound more impressive than other pronouns such as *him*, *her*, and *it*, but that alone is no reason for preferring them.

Another drawback, especially in long sentences, is that they may force the reader to refer back to what he has already read, setting him a problem that would have been unnecessary had the writer worked a little harder.

Dr Johnson disliked the *former/latter* device: 'As long as you have the use of your pen,' he warned, 'never, Sir, be reduced to that shift.'

In the first example below, *former* and *latter* are very useful; in the second, very much less so:

> The choice is between a narrow-gauge ratchet-railway system and a wider-gauge cable-drawn funicular system: the former is cheaper but slower, the latter has the advantage of causing less ecological damage.

? The guest speakers will be Dr Anthony Franks and Mrs Sally Bowhart, MP. The former will propose the motion 'This house favours abortion on demand'; the latter will sum up for the opposition.

There are several possible objections to this second example. First, to refer to one's guests in such an impersonal way — *the former, the latter* — might be considered discourteous. Secondly, the pronouns *he* and *she* (stressed in speech) would have served just as well here, since there is no possibility of confusion in the way that there would be had both speakers been women or both been men. Thirdly, the reader or listener might well need reminding of the speakers' names: *the latter* (or *she*, for that matter) would be quite *un*economical, in fact, if it sent the reader back to an earlier part of the text to re-establish the identity of the person being referred to. Fourthly, the partial repetition of the names here would in any case not have been particularly inelegant or wasteful. It sounds less affected, and no more long-winded, to say:

> The guest speakers will be Dr Anthony Franks and Mrs Sally Bowhart, MP. Dr Franks will propose the motion 'This house favours abortion on demand'; Mrs Bowhart will sum up for the opposition.

2. Remember that *former* (in this sense) and *latter* must be used with reference to two similar items — neither more nor less. Do not use *the latter* when only one possible object is under consideration:

?? The Australians were in jubilant mood as they took formal possession of the America's Cup yesterday; and when the latter is put on display in Perth next week, the jubilation is likely to be, if anything, even greater.

As with the pretentious *the same*, *the latter* here

is doing no work that a simple *it* would not do just as well.

Similarly, do not use *the former* or *the latter* if three or more items are under consideration. *The first* and *the last* would then be needed instead:

× The semi-finalists are Borussia Mönchengladbach, Atlético Bilbao, Dynamo Bucharest, and Queen of the South. The former is clear favourite for the trophy; the latter, unfortunately, stands no more than an outside chance.

This should read *the first of these* or *the first-mentioned*, and *the last of these* or *the last-mentioned*; or better still, the full names of the two clubs concerned should be repeated.

And make sure, even when there are two similar items under discussion, that *the former* and *the latter* do clearly distinguish them.

?? The Prime Minister lived, after all, only a few yards away from the Chancellor of the Exchequer, who could easily discuss the budget with him from their respective bedroom windows; not that the latter would ever have suggested anything so undignified.

But which politician is *the latter* here referring to?

3. Note that *former* and *latter* have quite unobjectionable functions as adjectives: *a former president of the Irish Republic*; *in former days*; *in the latter part of the year*.

See also RESPECTIVE.

fortuitous *Fortuitous* is being used increasingly to mean 'fortunate' — an unfortunate development that blurs a clear distinction:

?? Finding an aggressive headmaster with new ideas was far more difficult. They made a most fortuitous choice.

> – David Niven,
> *The Moon's a Balloon*

× There used to be some validity in the description of Australia as the lucky country. But in the Seventies the succession of fortuitous circumstances ceased. The country should be brought to realise that it is no longer lucky. It has to do its own thinking and planning.
> – Michael Davie, *The Observer*

Both *fortuitous* and *fortunate* go back to a single Latin root *fors*, meaning 'chance, luck', but their meanings are traditionally quite far apart. Strictly speaking, *fortuitous* means 'happening by accident, unplanned, by chance' — no matter whether it was a desirable accident or an undesirable accident.

To believe that human personality is the result of the fortuitous interplay of atoms and electrons is as absurd as to believe that a monkey by hitting typewriter keys at random will eventually produce a Shakespearean play.

– Martin Luther King, Jr (U.S.),
Strength to Love

She felt there was between them an unexpected mutual confidence, confidence of the kind that could spring up between two strangers who found themselves thrown together quite fortuitously in difficult circumstances that might turn out to be either frightening or amusing.

– Paul Scott,
The Jewel in the Crown

The word has now acquired a hint of 'lucky chance' about it — an inevitable and fairly acceptable result of its similarity in sound to both *fortunate* and *felicitous*:

Ross's success as an editor had certain elements of the fortuitous about it; for example, it was a lucky accident that his unappeasable appetite for facts coincided with a similar appetite on the part of the public.

– Brendan Gill (U.S.),
Here at The New Yorker

Then came the valuable experience of producing Reisz's 'Dog Soldiers', still the best picture about Vietnam. The entry into direction was fortuitous. A Canadian company wanted someone to edit 'Terror Train', an exploitation quickie to cash in on the vogue for high-school horror flicks.

– Philip French, *The Observer*

But it is not acceptable to go further than this, and virtually redefine that useful word *fortuitous*, in the way that David Niven and Michael Davie do in the first two quotations above, as 'fortunate' or 'satisfactory' or 'timely'.

founder See FLOUNDER.

fount, font The word referring to a complete set of printing type is still a matter of dispute. Traditionally, the British spelling was *fount*, though pronounced /font/, and the American spelling was *font*. Many journalists and printers still favour the old British form, but it is struggling

to survive. Modern dictionaries now tend to admit *font* as an accepted variant of *fount*, and some now allow the pronunciation /fownt/ for *fount*.

Note that *fount* and *font* in this sense are only distantly related to *fount*, 'a fountain, or source' (pronounced /fownt/) and *font*, 'the water basin in a church'. This latter pair goes back to the Latin *fons*, 'a spring or fountain'. The printing *fount* and *font* go back to the Old French word for 'a casting', from *fondre*, 'to melt or cast', from the Latin *fundere*, 'to pour or melt'.

fraction Two-thirds is a fraction; so, for that matter, is four-thirds. To speak of *only a fraction of the electorate* is, strictly speaking, not a very accurate way of referring to a small part of the electorate. Idiom, however, seems to have given its blessing to this sense, though some purists will still take you to task if you risk using it in their presence.

? All the rearguard actions fought by their accountants would be likely to reduce the whopping sum by no more than a fraction. The Inland Revenue, if necessary, was going to get blood out of the Stones.

– Philip Norman, *The Stones*

See also PER CENT; PROPORTION.

fractious See FICTIONAL.

Frankenstein In Mary Shelley's novel, and in the films based on it, Frankenstein was the scientist, not the monster. This is often forgotten. If you must use the reference at all, use it correctly: ?? *Your edict is a Frankenstein that terrifies innocent citizens and will one day terrify you yourself.* The correct term here would be *Frankenstein's monster*. So too in the following quotation:

?? Hence, while the psychosis induced by the fall of Saigon has been largely exorcised the physical legacy remains. In the early 1970s we allowed to emerge in south-east Asia a political and military Frankenstein influenced from afar by its Soviet progenitors. We must bolt all the doors in the region that we can.

– Paul Johnson, *The Times*

The incorrect use is very widespread now, and many writers on usage, especially in North America, are inclined to accept it. Most careful speakers continue to shun it, however.

frightfully See AWFULLY.

frost, hoarfrost, rime   All three of these words refer to a covering of frozen water-droplets, but they are technically distinguishable.

Frost is the most general of the three terms, but it has one sense peculiar to itself — 'atmospheric conditions at or below the freezing point of water':

It seldom drops to frost in Brighton, even in January. (But it is more usual to speak of *dropping to freezing*.)
At 20 degrees of frost, work on the pipeline is halted by law. (British English only.)

The degree of severity of a frost is often conveyed by qualifying adjectives such as *light, heavy, hard, sharp, killing,* and *black*.

Ground frost is a temperature of below freezing recorded at ground level — it can harm plants even if the air temperature remains above freezing point.

Black frost refers not to the appearance of the ice-crystals (the way *black ice* might refer to its colour), but to the blackened appearance of plants damaged by the severe cold.

The usual meaning of *frost* is one that overlaps with the meanings of *hoarfrost* and *rime*: 'a deposit or covering of minute ice-crystals formed from the freezing of dew, fog, or water vapour'. This is sometimes referred to as *white frost*.

Hoarfrost is a white coating that comes from frozen dew, and often takes the form of tiny needles or whiskers of ice. This too is sometimes known as *white frost* or simply *hoar* or, in regions of North America, *white dew*. The impression of grey or white whiskers gave rise to the adjective *hoary*, meaning 'covered with greyish hair or down' — as in *hoary limbs* — or, jocularly, 'aged, very old' as in *a hoary jest*.

Rime is the coating of granular particles of ice formed from fog droplets, usually on the windward side of trees, telegraph poles, or rocks, or along telegraph wires. When these particles stick together they are popularly known as *frost feathers*.

Though fairly technical, these distinctions are probably of fairly ancient origin: all three words go back to Old English, and were probably distinguished more sharply by ordinary people then than they are in our own more comfortable times.

Frost has various extended meanings. It can refer to a person's icy manner or aloofness. In informal British English, it can mean 'a failure' — *Her latest novel is an utter frost, I'm afraid.* As a verb, it can mean 'to decorate (glass or metal) with a speckled surface'; and also, 'to dust (a cake) with castor sugar', or, especially in North America, 'to ice (a cake)': a common word for 'icing' in American English is *frosting*.

-ful   Usage now generally favours a final *-s* for the plural of nouns ending in *-ful*, as in *bucketfuls* and *spoonfuls*. Forms such as *bucketsful* or *spoonsful* are now considered somewhat old-fashioned.

full stop   1. *Full Stop* is the name usually given to this mark of punctuation in British English, but it may also be called a *stop*, a *point,* or (rarely) a *full point*. The usual American name for it is *period*. In informal British English and in some Southern dialects of American English, it may be called a *dot*.

2. **a.** The terms *full stop* and *period* may themselves be used as emphatic interjections: the effect is to discourage all further discussion, either by rejecting any modification of a preceding statement or by reinforcing that statement with a blanket or absolute version of it:

He's not just the best living British sculptor — he's the best living sculptor, period.
I'm sorry, but that's the way it is. Full stop.
No, we don't have Starking apples — in fact, we don't have apples full stop.

Minnie, at fifteen, had announced to us what her future was going to be, in no uncertain terms. She was going to marry a guy who raised horses. Period.
    – Harpo Marx (U.S.), *Harpo Speaks*

b. In both British and American English, the word *stop* may be used in the text of a telegram to indicate places where a full stop would appear if the text of the telegram were written as ordinary prose.

3. The most important use of the full stop is to end an assertion. This typically has the form of a declarative sentence, like the one that begins this paragraph, or:

The sun rises in the east.

A declarative sentence may, of course, consist of several parts:

The sun rises in the east, of course, and sets in the west.
The sun rises in the east, if I'm not mistaken.

It may even include an indirect question:

I want to know whether the sun really rises in the east.

(Do not be tempted to use a question mark here in place of the full stop.)

The full stop may also be used to end other types of sentence if they are felt to be closer in tone to assertions or requests than to questions or exclamations:

Let's dance. (suggestion)
Would you be so good as to reply by return of post. (question as polite request)
Hold the shipment until next month. (instruction or order)

But imperatives may take an exclamation mark when they are more emotionally charged:

Shut up!

Note that when an assertion serves as a title (as of a book, a pop group, or the like), it does not take a full stop: *You Can't Go Home Again* (novel by Thomas Wolfe, U.S.); *Frankie Goes to Hollywood* (Pop Group, UK).

4. It is a mistake to run together strings of words that could be separate sentences:

× In the morning they decided to swim across the lake their swimming costumes were locked in the boot of the car.

This could have had internal punctuation (for example, *lake; their* — but a comma would not be enough) or punctuation plus an appropriate connecting word (e.g. *lake; however, their*...). But it could also be made into two sentences:

In the morning they decided to swim across the lake. Their swimming costumes were locked in the boot of the car.

On the other hand, it can be a useful stylistic device to treat as separate sentences groups of words that are not ordinarily so considered:

Three o'clock. Half past three. Four o'clock. Sisters Ursula and Jane, Solomon, Gulab and the cart had not come in. Mother Morag had been up since midnight.
– Rumer Godden, *The Dark Horse*

The passage of time is emphasised by the way this text begins. Some people object, however, when this technique is used very frequently or to no obvious purpose. (See SENTENCES.)

5. A sentence may contain bracketed material:

The creditor can get a judgment against him (sometimes quite easily) and garnishee his wages (as explained on page 384).

Note that the full stop here falls outside the clos-

ing bracket, since it applies to the whole statement rather than to the bracketed material alone. Sometimes this bracketed material would be a complete sentence by itself, and would, if following a full stop and beginning with a capital, have its own full stop within the closing bracket:

The creditor can usually get a judgment against him. (Sometimes such judgments are surprisingly easy to obtain.) The creditor can also garnishee his wages. (This is explained on page 384.)

However, a complete sentence within brackets can be parenthetical within a surrounding sentence, and would then neither begin with a capital letter nor end with a full stop:

The creditor can get a judgment against him (sometimes such judgments are surprisingly easy to obtain) and garnishee his wages (see page 384).

6. Full stops are also widely used after abbreviations. See ABBREVIATIONS for a full and detailed discussion of when the full stop is and is not appropriate.

7. Another use of the full stop is after numbers and letters listing points, as in an outline or list of contents:

I. The French Revolution
    I.a. Its causes
    I.b. Its results
II. The Napoleonic Period

The full stop is often used after capital Roman numerals; small Roman numerals, Arabic numerals, and letters may take brackets instead: (ii) (a) (1)   or   ii) a) 1).

8. In British style, but not usually in North American, addresses, as on envelopes, sometimes end with a full stop and have a comma at the end of each line; they can also be indented further at the start of each line:

The Reader's Digest Association Limited,
    P.O. Box 222,
        7-10 Old Bailey,
            London EC99 1AA.

9. The full stop is written on the line. But occasionally in British English it has a variant form written above the line (·). This raised dot is used chiefly for these purposes:

● to indicate decimal places: 22·5 m.p.g.
● hence, in monetary expressions: £1·37
● in expressions of time: 9·30 a.m.

● in dates: 1·10·37 (1 October 1937).

In all these expressions, the ordinary full stop is of course equally acceptable and far more common in British English; the date could, in addition, be written 1/10/37 or 1:10:37. In American English, the corresponding punctuation would be:

22.5 m.p.g.
£1.37 (or, for dollars and cents, $1.37)
9:30 a.m.
1/10/37 (but this means 10 January 1937).

See also AMERICAN ENGLISH; QUOTATION MARKS.

fulsome The adjective *fulsome* originally meant 'abundant, copious' — in origin it is simply a compound of *full* + *some*. But it has lost that neutral sense, and should not be used as a supposedly elegant synonym for *full* or *lavish*. By Shakespeare's time the word had already developed distinctly negative associations, possibly through its apparent similarity to the word *foul*. Today *fulsome* should always be used as a pejorative term meaning 'overabundant, excessively lavish' and usually 'offensively excessive, cloying'. There is a strong suggestion of insincerity or flattery about it: *fulsome praise, fulsome enthusiasm.*

A well-meaning journalist ... wrote an impossibly enthusiastic piece about me, some five hundred lines dripping with fulsome praise.
— Vladimir Nabokov, *Speak, Memory*

'My dear Baron, do forgive me, please. I wouldn't have had this happen for the world. Did I say half-past? I did? And you've been waiting a quarter of an hour? You overwhelm me with shame. Really, I don't know how to apologise enough.'
Arthur's fulsomeness seemed to embarrass the Baron as much as it did himself.
— Christopher Isherwood, *Mr Norris Changes Trains*

? For the real Charley's Aunt I desperately needed someone of fulsome womanly beauty and immediately recognisable sexuality.
— Joshua Logan (U.S.), *Josh*

Formerly pronounced /fulsəm/, the word is now almost always pronounced /foolsəm/. The older form is probably now considered incorrect.

function Both as a verb and as a noun, *function* is overused. It goes back to the Latin verb *fungi*, 'to work or perform', and is often used nowadays as a slightly pretentious synonym of *to work* or *to perform*. Similarly, 'to operate', 'to serve', 'to act', and 'a use', 'a duty', 'a role' are all expressed in the same way, by *function*: *I don't function well in the morning*; *Her function is keeping the files in order*. A formal party will be elevated into *a function*; and 'to depend on, or result from' may be expressed by *to be a function of*, a usage adopted from mathematics: *Depression is often simply a function of fatigue.*

The word is so overworked now that some careful speakers feel driven to avoid it altogether. There is no need to go as far as that, but it is worth considering alternative wording before allowing yourself to say or write *function.*

fungus, fungous As with *mucus* and *phosphorus,* the ending *-us* is for the noun, *-ous* for the adjective. *Fungous* means 'relating to, resembling, or caused by a fungus'. So: *The mushroom is a fungus*; *Athlete's foot is a fungous disease caused by the fungus Tinea pedis.*

The two forms are pronounced identically — /fung-gəss/. They come from a Latin root, which probably goes back in turn to the Greek *spongos* or *sphongos*, 'a sponge'.

The adjective *fungal* is usually interchangeable with *fungous* and is possibly more common. It would be equally acceptable to say *Athlete's foot is a fungal disease.*

This otherwise neat picture is complicated by the fact that the noun *fungus,* like English nouns generally, can be used before other nouns. Thus *a fungous disease* and *a fungus disease* are both correct (just as *a governmental decree* and *a government decree* are). In descending order of likelihood, the forms discussed would probably be: *a fungal disease, a fungus disease, a fungous disease*. In this respect *fungus* is like *virus* and unlike *bacteria* or *bacterium*: you can say *a fungus/virus disease* or a *fungal/viral disease*, but you must say *a bacterial disease* and not × *a bacteria disease* or ?? *a bacterium disease.* The greater flexibility of *fungus* and *virus* is undoubtedly due to the similarity in pronunciation between the noun ending *-us* and the adjectival ending *-ous.*

Fungoid, finally, means 'resembling a fungus': *a fungoid disease* would be one that resembles *a fungal/fungus/fungous disease* but is not in fact caused by a fungus.

Note that the plural of *fungus* can be either *fungi* or *funguses.*

Fungi can be pronounced in any of three ways: in order of preference, /**fung**-gi, **fung**-gee, **fun-**

249

jī/. The prevailing American pronunciations are /**fun**jī, **fung**-gī/.

further, farther *Further* and *farther* are usually interchangeable, both as adjectives and as adverbs, though there are slight differences. *Further* is the more colloquial of the two and the more common in British English, especially in figurative uses such as 'further from the truth'.

Farther is rarer in British English, more poetic, and usually refers to physical distance rather than distance in time:

> And for that moment a blackbird sang,
> Close by, and round him, mistier,
> Farther and farther, all the birds
> Of Oxfordshire and Gloucestershire.
> —Edward Thomas, 'Adlestrop'

> Beyond the huts there is a stagnant water-tank on whose farther bank are laid out to dry the long coloured sarees and murky rags belonging to the black-skinned, braceleted, bare-legged women who stand thigh-high in the water, washing themselves and their clothes.
> – Paul Scott,
> *The Jewel in the Crown*

The combination of poetic overtones and the suggestion of physical distance often makes *farther* the first choice with romantic, distant place names. So: *Samarkand is farther away than we could dream of venturing.* But: *Bognor is further away than Scunthorpe.*

Some careful writers try to distinguish the two words by reserving *further* for figurative uses and *farther* for physical distances. This is not a rule, however: *farther from the truth* might sound slightly more formal than *further from the truth,* but both are perfectly acceptable. *Further* is more common, however:

> There was a direct parallel somewhere; I wasn't quite clear about it yet, but it was close; one step further in his thoughts, and he'd put it into words, words I didn't want to hear . . .
> – Lynne Reid Banks,
> *The L-Shaped Room*

There are a few meanings of *further* that *farther* cannot have. Only *further* can be used to mean 'additional' (*two further suggestions*), or 'additionally' (*I would further suggest . . .*), or 'as an addition' (*Further to my last letter . . .*), or 'moreover, furthermore' (*Further, I dislike your suggestion . . .*). And *further,* unlike *farther,* is a verb as well, meaning 'to promote, help along', and producing the noun *furtherance,* meaning 'advancement'.

G

Gaelic See CELTIC.

gamble, gambol The words *gamble* ('to bet or risk' or 'a bet or risk') and *gambol* ('to leap about, frolic' or 'a frolicking about') are usually pronounced identically. Take care to distinguish them properly by their correct spellings.

The histories of the two words are quite distinct. *Gamble* goes back through a variety of earlier forms to Old English *gamenian*, 'to sport, play', from *gamen*, 'amusement, sport'. This is also the source of the word *game*.

Gambol had the earlier form *gambade* or *gambaude*, going back via the Old French *gambade*, 'a skipping dance', to Italian *gambata*. The word *gamba* in Italian means 'a leg', and in Late Latin it meant 'a hoof'. The source of this in turn was the Greek *kampē*, 'a bend'.

Note the spellings of the other forms of these two verbs. *Gamble* has *gambled* and *gambling*; *gambol* has *gambolled* and *gambolling*, or in American English *gamboled* and *gamboling*.

> As she passed the Tibetan shawl sellers who had spread out their bright, cheap woollen ware on the street, she looked at their babies and puppies gambolling together in the middle of the street with a fine carelessness that she envied. There was a zest about them, a warmth of life's fires burning brightly.
> – Anita Desai, *Fire on the Mountain*

Although *gamble* and *gambol* are both pronounced /**gam**b'l/, the word *gambolling* can be pronounced /**gam**bə-ling/ to distinguish it from *gambling,* /**gam**-bling/.

Obviously, confusion of the two words in speech or writing can produce ridiculous effects, especially as both often take the preposition *on*.

gaol See JAIL.

gay The use of the adjective *gay* in the sense of 'homosexual' has been recorded as existing as long ago as 1935, though only as underworld and prison slang in Britain. Its spread into common idiom began after the Second World War, chiefly in American English, and it became widely established in the late 1960s or early 70s. It is now so common in this sense that many dictionaries accept it as standard — when it is used as an adjective; when used as a noun (the first such use on record is in 1953), it still tends to be labelled 'informal'. (Another slight difference between the noun and adjective uses is that the adjective *gay* readily refers to both male and female homosexuals, whereas the noun *gay* is more often used specifically of male homosexuals: *Gays and lesbians are invited to debate the new guidelines with Town Hall officials*.)

Traditionalists have been angered by the 'annexation' of *gay* by the homosexual community, and continue to use the word defiantly — though selfconsciously — in its older senses of 'cheerful, light-hearted, pleasure-seeking, brightly coloured', and so on. A typical comment is: *It was a wonderfully gay party — and I don't mean gay in its new-fangled modern sense*.

What the purists particularly object to is the apparently *deliberate* tampering with language. Of course a word can change in meaning, they concede, but it should do so slowly and *naturally* — over many years. The current sense of the verb *to surprise*, for instance — 'to astonish, amaze, or shock' — developed slowly during the 17th century out of the earlier senses, 'to see or attack unexpectedly, to catch unawares', and no one seriously objects to this 'modern' sense any longer. But, the traditionalists insist, a sudden contrived wrench of meaning is another matter. They guard their linguistic heritage jealously: meddle with it at your peril.

On the other side, the homosexual community proclaims its right to a positive name for once. The old currency of abuse — *queer, pansy,* and so on — was hurtful and humiliating.

In decrying the new sense of *gay*, traditionalists are in fact admitting its firm hold, and its power to affect the old meanings. The same thing has happened to other words. Consider *pathetic*: in its old sense of 'arousing sympathy; pitiful', it cannot easily be used in a matter-of-fact way nowadays. The new informal sense of 'inadequate, feeble, useless' — *a pathetic attempt, a pathetic candidate* — somehow washes back and colours the old sense.

This process might be called 'contamination' —

on the model of 'deterioration' (affecting such words as *crafty*, which once meant 'skilful') and 'amelioration' (affecting such words as *shrewd*, which once meant 'bad-tempered, shrewish').

'Contamination' is sometimes so strong that a word becomes a 'taboo word', and people no longer dare to use it in its original sense. But the effect is usually subtler than that: a vague self-consciousness, or a reluctance to use the word, rather than an outright shunning of it. People might still refer to *friendly intercourse between nations*, but no longer as nonchalantly as they did 200 years ago.

The word *holocaust*, formerly meaning 'a burnt sacrifice, or a massacre', now has unavoidable associations of the Nazi concentration camps, and perhaps of nuclear war (as in *nuclear holocaust*). *Bloody* has long been under such a cloud; more recently *pill, bondage*, and so on tend to be avoided if there is any possibility of mis-interpretation.

So no one in touch with current idiom can use the word *gay* unselfconsciously in its old sense of 'cheerful or merry' (though *gaily* and *gaiety* seem unaffected, and can be freely used in their old senses). That meaning has not yet been driven out, perhaps, but its frequency has certainly declined. (There are many near-synonyms, after all — *cheerful, fun-loving, in high spirits, chirpy*, and so on.) By all means preserve the old sense, but do not pretend that the new sense does not really exist, or that it has not left its mark on the old sense.

There is a converse responsibility, however: to try not to be distracted by these new overtones when coming across the word in books, plays, or films from before the 1960s.

Double entendres — double meanings — should be ignored if possible where they are unintended. They are an occupational hazard of great writers (not just the stock-in-trade of comedians), since meanings do change over the centuries. Certainly it is difficult not to be distracted from the intended meaning when Boswell quotes Dr Johnson as saying *A man who exposes himself when he is intoxicated, has not the art of getting drunk*. Yet the reader's duty is precisely not to be distracted.

The word *gay* is particularly at risk, since it was formerly so widely used. The Irish poet W.B. Yeats, in his wonderful poem 'Lapis Lazuli', written in 1936, uses *gay* as a key-word — marking an appropriate attitude to life and art. (The sense of 'homosexual' was current in underworld slang at that time, but was almost certainly unknown to Yeats):

I have heard that hysterical women say
They are sick of the palette and fiddle-bow,
Of poets that are always gay ...

All things fall and are built again,
And those that build them again are gay.

And so on. The modern sense of *gay* must not be allowed to impinge on one's reading of such lines — even if, as is almost inevitable, it does enter one's consciousness.

gentleman   *Gentleman* is used instead of *man* in only a few restricted contexts. Some fixed phrases reflect its earlier meaning, 'a man of superior social position': *a gentleman of leisure; a gentleman farmer*. Otherwise it tends to carry with it the idea of 'well-bred, well-mannered, or honourable': *He's no gentleman; a gentleman's agreement*.

Its main use nowadays is as a polite form of address: *Ladies and gentlemen, please be seated; We must now turn, gentlemen, to the main point on the agenda*. It should also be used when referring to a person in his presence, where *man* would sound rather abrupt: *Say thank you to the kind gentleman, Tommy; Please ask this gentleman to wait outside*. It should not be used by a speaker of himself: *? I'm the gentleman who called yesterday*. Use *man* or *person* instead.

See also WOMAN.

germ, bacterium, virus, amoeba, microbe
The general term for a single-celled form of life is a *microorganism* (the word is first recorded in 1880). This used to be referred to as an *animalcule* (1599), but that word is now extremely rare and old-fashioned.

Louis Pasteur (1822-95), who gave his name to *pasteurisation* (1886 — *pasteurise*, 1881), coined the word *microbe* (1881), which replaced *animalcule,* and meant the same as *microorganism*. *Microbe* came from Greek *mikros,* 'small' + *bios,* 'life'. Pasteur studied harmful varieties for the most part, and so the word came to suggest a disease-producing microorganism — the scientific name for which is *pathogen* (1880).

A similar development affected the word *germ*: it originally (1644) meant any minute organism — or the living part of a seed, as in *wheat germ*. The word comes through French from Latin *germen,* 'offshoot, sprout, foetus'. However, after biologists (following the work of the German scientist Robert Koch, 1843-1910) expounded a 'germ theory of disease', the idea sprang up in the public mind that 'germs' were bringers of disease. Used loosely in this way (to mean 'pathogenic microorganism'), *microbe* and *germ* are not scientific terms.

Bacteria (1847) is a scientific term, but is also often used loosely. Bacteria are similarly thought of as bringers of disease. (The singular, *bacterium,* is less often used.) Strictly speaking, the word *bacteria* refers to all microorganisms that exhibit both plant and animal characteristics. Many are harmless, or even essential to human life, but some are pathogens and cause serious diseases, including cholera, diphtheria, tetanus, and syphilis. *Bacterium* comes from Greek *bacterion,* diminutive of *baktron,* 'a rod'.

There are three main classes of bacteria, the best-known being *bacillus* (*c.*1879), which comprises only those bacteria that are actually rod-shaped (the name is Latin for 'a little rod'). In popular use, *bacillus* is sometimes applied inaccurately to any bacterium. The word is pronounced /bə-**sill**əss/; the plural is *bacilli,* /bə-**silli**/.

A *spirochaete* (1877 — usually *spirochete* in North American spelling) is another particular kind of bacterium: a slender, twisted structure of the order *spirochaetales.* Many spirochaetes do cause disease — they are responsible, for instance, for syphilis, relapsing fever, and yaws. The term is a scientific one, though it is not always properly used or understood by non-experts. The word *spirochaete* is pronounced /**spir**ə-keet/. It comes from New Latin *spirochaeta* (the name of the genus) from Latin *spira,* 'a coil' (Greek *speira*), + New Latin *chaeta,* 'a bristle', from Greek *khaite,* 'long hair'.

An *amoeba* (1878 — it is usually spelt the same in North America, though sometimes *ameba*) is also a single-celled microorganism, but of a different phylum from *bacteria* — that of the *protozoa* (*c.*1834). It belongs to the genus *amoeba,* and consists of one cell that is constantly changing shape. It moves by means of temporary leg-like protuberances called *pseudopodia* (1854) — 'false feet'. Some amoebae live inside animals and can produce disease: they are the cause of amoebic dysentery, for instance. *Amoeba* is pronounced /ə-**mee**-bə/; the plural is either *amoebas* or *amoebae,* pronounced /-bee/.

Virus (1599) is also a Latin word, meaning 'poison'. It refers to protein substances in the form of crystals that appear to be lifeless, until triggered into reproductive activity by contact with a living organism. They are responsible for many epidemic diseases, including polio, rabies, and colds and flu. *Virus* has a general metaphorical sense as well: it conveys the idea of a spreading poison — *the virus of fascism.*

gerunds See -ING FORMS OF VERBS.

get, got, gotten 1. An old schoolroom bugbear discourages the words *get* and *got,* regarding them as evidence of an immature or uneducated style. Certainly it is easy to overuse the words, as many an exaggerated parody has made clear:

> I got up at 6, got dressed, and left the house. I got a sandwich at the corner shop, and got the number 26 bus for Paddington in time to get the 10.10 express to Cardiff, hoping to get home before lunch. But the train got stuck just before it got to Oxford. I began to get very impatient.

Of course, what such parodies are proving at the same time is how very useful and valuable the words *get* and *got* are. By all means check your writing to make sure that you have not overused them, but do not run away from them if they seem appropriate. What can you put in place of *Get well soon,* for example, or *got married*? (To use *were married,* instead, as many people do, is to get into difficulties with ambiguity: *My parents were married in 1940* might be taken to suggest that they are now divorced.)

Even when alternative words are possible, *get* and *got* do not have to be replaced every time. Do not go to extremes and change every *get* into *arrive* or *reach (get home by midnight), become (get sick), acquire, obtain,* or *secure (get the news from the radio), possess (have got a great deal of money), suffer from (have got the measles),* and so on. If you do so, your style might be cured of 'sloppiness', but the chances are that it would end up as pretentious instead.

2. A more specific objection is to the use of *have got* in the sense of 'to own, possess'. The objection is twofold — first, that it is ambiguous; second, that it is rather slangy.

In practice, ambiguity is most unlikely to occur: the context is almost certain to make clear whether *have got* means 'have acquired' — *Since I last saw you, I've got a new bicycle* — or simply 'possess': *As you can see, I've got a new bicycle.* And even if it is not quite certain which sense is intended, the ambiguity is hardly a serious one. (See also HAVE.)

As for its level of formality, *have got* is today suitable for all except extremely formal contexts: *How many books have you got?* In ordinary British usage, it would in fact sound rather stiff to use *have* instead — *How many books do you have?* — or even archaic: ? *How many books have you?* (In American English, *have* is much commoner than *have got* in the sense of 'possess', and does not have the rather stiff tone that it does in British English.)

3. The use of *got* without the *have,* however, is nonstandard as a synonym of *possess*: ✗ *I got only three books — how many you got?* In questions, however, it is merely informal: *Got a match?*

4. Many purists again prefer *have* to *have got* before *to,* when the sense is 'must; be obliged': *You've got to do as I say* and *Have you got to go?* are considered more colloquial than *You have to do as I say* and *Do you have to go?* This preference is slightly more justified than the previous one: the *have got to* form, though quite standard in speech, is perhaps unsuitable for formal occasions. And the negative form is definitely colloquial: *You haven't got to go* is far more informal than *You don't have to go.*

Once again, the use of *got to* by itself, rather than *have got to* or *have to,* is nonstandard: ✗ *I just got to fetch my gun first.*

5. In American English, *have got (to)* or *has got (to)* is used freely, but *had got (to)* is rare and considered British. Note too that negative forms — *He hasn't got (to) work* — are rarer in American English, and perhaps in British English too.

6. *Gotten* is the old past participle of *get.* It survives in American English, but not in British English (except in the phrase *ill-gotten gains*): in British English it is regarded either as a straightforward error or as an ugly Americanism. In American English it has been criticised, but it is at least quite at home in ordinary American usage in a way that it is not in ordinary British usage.

Note that *have gotten* is never used with reference to either possession or obligation in the way that *have got* is. Americans do not say ✗ *You've gotten to do as I say* or ✗ *As you see, I've gotten a new bicycle.* Instead, *have gotten* means 'have acquired', or sometimes 'have succeeded': *Since I last saw you, I've gotten a new bicycle* and *I've gotten to learn how to ride it at last.* So American English can distinguish, as British English cannot, between the two sentences in each of the following pairs:

I've got a new bicycle (= I possess a new bicycle)

I've gotten a new bicycle (= I've acquired a new bicycle)

I've got to go to a party tonight (= I'm obliged to go)

I've gotten to go to a party tonight (= I've managed to arrange to go).

gibe, jibe, gybe, jib In British English *gibe* is the usual form of the verb or noun meaning 'taunt, jeer', though the word is sometimes spelt *jibe*:

> Bianca found herself treated, like any parvenue princess, with elaborate frontal courtesy, while the envious jibes and nicknames multiplied behind her back.
> – Philip Norman, *The Stones*

Gybe is a nautical term, also sometimes spelt *jibe*, again used as either a noun or a verb, and referring to the shift of a sail from one side of a vessel to another.

Jibe, apart from being a variant of *gibe* and *gybe*, is the usual form of the informal American verb that means 'to be in accord, harmonise', as in *His actions don't jibe with his promises.*

The origin of *gybe* may be an obsolete Dutch word *gijben*. *Gibe* probably comes from Old French *giber*, 'to handle roughly'. *Jibe* in the American sense probably comes from a different source, but its origin is uncertain. All three words are pronounced /jīb/.

Jib, pronounced /jīb/, is again a variant of *gybe*. It has a further nautical sense peculiar to itself — 'the triangular sail towards the front of a vessel'. And there are the related senses of 'the arm of a mechanical crane' and 'the boom of a derrick'.

Jib has other unrelated senses: as a verb, it can mean 'to baulk or shy': *They jibbed at giving us free tickets*; *His horse jibbed at the third fence.*

> Like Irene Shubik (Letters, 15 April), I too jibbed at your reporter's description of myself as the 'onlie begetter' of 'The Jewel in the Crown'. Paul Scott was the 'onlie begetter', and if you want to pursue this analogy, I was the godfather and Irene Shubik was indeed a most skilful midwife.
> – Sir Denis Forman,
> letter to *The Observer*

And as a noun, *jib* can mean 'an animal, especially a horse, that jibs'.

girl See WOMAN.

global *Global* originally meant 'spherical in shape', and later 'relating to things as a whole rather than in parts': *a global look at the company's training policies* (today we would speak of *an overview*).

The chief current use is 'worldwide, relating to the whole world': *a global defence strategy.*

Its impressive tone has led to its adoption by

business jargon — *a global sales campaign* — in the sense simply of 'total, comprehensive, all-out, involving all resources'. This vogue use is best avoided in general contexts.

gobbledygook See JARGON.

God, god *God* with a capital *G* refers only to the one God of the monotheistic religions — *Jehovah, Allah* — or to an underlying equivalent in other religions: *All worship God in one way or another.* All other deities take a small *g*: *the Greek god Zeus, the river god, the god of war.* So the plurals *gods* and *goddesses* always have a small *g*, except, of course, at the beginning of a sentence.

All compounds with *god* take a small *g*: *godparent* (and the associated relatives — *godfather, godson,* and so on), *godfearing, godforsaken, godly, godsend,* and even *godhead.*

In expressions such as *God bless you* or *thank God* the capital letter is retained. All other titles for the one God, as for Christ, are also capitalised: *Lord, Father, Saviour, Redeemer,* and so on. Similarly the pronouns *He, Thou,* and *Him,* standing in for God, should take a capital letter, although *thy* and *his* may or may not. The hymns in *Hymns Ancient and Modern* capitalise *Thy* and *His*; the prayers in the *Book of Common Prayer* do not.

good As an adjective *good* can follow a linking verb such as *be, become, feel, look, seem, smell,* or *taste,* to describe the actual sensation: *Exercise makes me feel good and look good*; *That roast chicken smells good!* After other verbs, *well* must be used: *She dances well*; *He can act well.* Sentences such as × *She dances good* and × *He can act real good* are often heard in colloquial English, but are unacceptable in standard usage.

Needless to say, *well* is the form to use when referring to health: *felt well after their illness*; *felt good after the party.*

got, gotten See GET.

gourmand, gourmet These two words have related but contrasting meanings. *Gourmand* is used primarily to refer to a person who eats heartily or plentifully or greedily. *Gourmet* is today used chiefly to refer to a person who is an expert or connoisseur in fine food. It is a useful distinction, and one that should be observed.

It is said (variously) that I am a health-food faddist, a vegetarian, an undiscriminating gourmand, a peevish gourmet who demands that he be served only the most exotic dishes.
– J. Paul Getty (U.S.), *As I See It*

The distinction is one that developed accidentally, however. The word *gourmet* meant 'wine taster' when it first entered English in 1820. (In its earlier French forms, it meant 'a boy servant' or 'wineseller's assistant'.) It acquired its present sense as a result of its accidental resemblance to *gourmand,* which is longer-established in English. The two words, both from Old French, appear to be quite unrelated historically.

Gourmet is pronounced more or less as in French: /**goor**-may/, sometimes /goor-**may**/. *Gourmand,* which entered Middle English as long ago as the 15th century, has traditionally been pronounced /**goor**mənd/, though increasingly nowadays the French pronunciation of /goor-**moN**/ is being used. What began as a recent affectation is rapidly becoming the standard pronunciation.

The word *gourmet* is widely used today to modify nouns in such phrases as *gourmet foods* and *gourmet cookery books.* This form too is something of an affectation, and means little more than 'fancy and expensive', as the following passage suggests:

There was nothing distinctive about Rocky Port's institutions or way of life, unless it was the frequency of gift shops selling 'gourmet' foods, outsize pepper mills, 'amusing' aprons and chef's costumes, bar equipment, and frozen croissants, 'just like in France'.
– Mary McCarthy (U.S.), *Birds of America*

Two words related to *gourmand* are the noun *gourmandise* (/goormən-**deez**/) and the verb *to gormandise* (/**gor**mən-dīz/). Note the spelling and pronunciation in each case. *Gormandise* is used as both a transitive and an intransitive verb, and means 'to eat gluttonously, gorge'. *Gourmandise,* however, is closer in sense to *gourmet* than to *gourmand*: it means 'a discriminating and refined enjoyment of good food', and there is little implication of gluttony in the word.

graceful, gracious These two adjectives are quite distinct in meaning. *Graceful* refers to movement, style, or form. It means 'effortlessly beautiful, elegant': *a graceful leap, a graceful pose, graceful proportions.*

The grotesque unnaturalness of his fluttering hands and arched back, trying to convey in movement something that could be far more precisely and indeed gracefully conveyed in speech, is the bone that sticks in my throat.

– Bernard Levin, *The Times*

Gracious refers to states of mind, to modes of life, or to the behaviour that these produce. It is a slightly old-fashioned word today. It most commonly means 'kind, sympathetic, and courteous': *a gracious deed*. The opposite is *ungracious*:

She knew me by sight and nodded ungraciously. She plainly hadn't much use for Arthur's callers. No doubt the visits of the bailiff had got the home a bad name.

– Christopher Isherwood, *Mr Norris Changes Trains*

Gracious can also mean 'leisurely and refined': *a gracious dinner, gracious living*. This sense of a style appropriate to the upper classes is more marked still in such phrases as *his gracious presence* and *her gracious smile*, where the idea of indulgence or condescension is quite clear, or *his gracious Majesty*, where *gracious* is little more than a formal indicator of respect.

The noun *grace* (apart from its religious overtones) has senses relating to both *graceful* and *gracious*. If there is any danger of ambiguity in the word, then the nouns *gracefulness* and *graciousness* are always available instead. All these words go back to the Latin adjective *gratus*, 'pleasing'.

Finally, the old-fashioned adjective *gracile*, pronounced /**gra**ssīl/ in British English: though sometimes used as a synonym of *graceful*, it strictly means 'thin or slender, in an appealing or graceful way':

It was clear that the Concorde's pilots have a good time. BA pilots who do not get to fly the gracile glamour-puss call her variously the Bionic Toothpick, the Poisoned Dart and the BAC Fuel-Converter, but would probably admit envy if pressed.

– Clive James, *The Observer*

Like *gracious* and *graceful*, *gracile* is derived from Latin, but from a source word, *gracilis*, 'slender', that appears to be unrelated to theirs.

Great Britain See BRITAIN.

Greek, Grecian *Greek* is the general adjective used of Greece, ancient or modern, and its inhabitants, and their language, culture, and church.

Grecian, pronounced /**gree**sh'n/, used sometimes to be a poetic alternative to *Greek*. The *Grecian urn* in Keats's ode, for example, would, in today's idiom, be a *Greek urn*. Today *Grecian* is usually used of things imitating the style of ancient Greece — notably in architecture, where a *Grecian pediment* or a *Grecian colonnade* might still be designed. What is Grecian today is probably not actually Greek.

A *Grecian nose* is a long straight nose extending in an unbroken line from the forehead. A *Grecian bend* was the posture, adopted by women of fashion in the late 19th century (often with the help of whalebone corsets), in which the spine was curved to emphasise the figure.

As a noun, *Greek* refers to the language (in its various forms, ancient or modern), to a person of Greek nationality or descent, and sometimes to a member of the Greek Orthodox Church. In academic circles, *Grecian* as a noun is still sometimes used to refer to a scholar or student of the classical Greek language, culture, and history — the way that the more common word *Latinist* refers to an expert in Latin.

ground, grounds In the sense 'a cause, reason, or basis', *ground* is quite suitable in the singular: *He refused to answer on the ground that he might incriminate himself*.

He would not allow them to make transatlantic telephone calls to him in Surrey, on the ground that it was cheaper to write.

– Michael Davie, *The Observer*

The modern tendency, however, is to use *grounds* here, even where there is only *one* cause, reason, or basis:

There is an official ban on the transfer of funds to prisons abroad on the grounds that this is an 'inappropriate use' of public funds.

– Ian Black, *The Guardian*

Old-fashioned purists regard this as a pointless and dubious development, but it seems now to be fully established. And when followed by *for* rather than *that*, as in *grounds for suspicion*, the plural form seems far more idiomatic than the singular.

Note that *grounds* must take a plural verb, even when it refers to only a single cause, reason, or basis: *Our grounds for suspicion are that the key has disappeared*.

grudge See BEGRUDGE.

gybe See GIBE.

H

half In certain expressions, *half* can either precede or follow *a* or *an*: *I bought a half-dozen eggs/I bought half a dozen eggs/It'll take a half-hour/It'll take half an hour.* (Note that there are no hyphens when *a/an* follows *half*.) The double use of the article, as in × *It'll take a half an hour*, is nonstandard.

When *half* is followed by a singular noun, the verb is also singular; when the following noun is plural, the verb is plural too: *Half of the cake was eaten*; *Half of the trees were cut down.*

hanged See HUNG.

hanging participle See MISRELATED CONSTRUCTIONS.

hardly 1. *Hardly* is no longer used as the adverbial form of the adjective *hard. Hard* itself is the appropriate adverb: *worked hard; didn't hit him very hard.*

2. *Hardly,* like *barely* and *scarcely,* has a negative effect on the word it relates to. To add a further negative to the sentence, therefore, is unnecessary and usually incorrect, however common it may be in dialect or nonstandard English: × *I can't hardly believe my eyes.*

The double negative here is unacceptable in standard English (see DOUBLE NEGATIVE). The correct form is either *I can hardly believe my eyes* or *I can't believe my eyes.*

3. The construction *hardly . . . when* (or *scarcely . . . when* is a very useful one:

Hardly had I put my key in the lock when the watchdog sprang at me.

(Note the inverted word order — *verb + subject* — after the initial *hardly, scarcely,* or *barely*.) A common error is to replace *when* with *than*:

× Hardly had I put my key in the lock than the watchdog sprang at me.

This is probably the result of a confusion with the following construction:

No sooner had I put my key in the lock than the watchdog sprang at me.

This construction is correct: *sooner* being the comparative form of an adverb, it can be followed by *than* — *no sooner than.* But × *hardly . . . than* is ungrammatical.

hark, hearken These are two variants of an Old English word meaning 'to listen', and are related to the verb *to hear*. The two words survive in different uses and are not interchangeable. Both are rather old-fashioned or poetic. *To hark* is mostly used in the imperative: 'Listen!'. It survives in hymns and carols:

Hark! The herald angels sing
Glory to the new born king.
— Charles Wesley, 'Christmas Hymn'

Hark at is sometimes used in colloquial or regional British English to draw attention to someone's pomposity or ridiculousness: *Hark at him! He thinks he's God's gift.*

To hark back is still in common standard use. It means 'to recall or refer to the past'. The expression comes from fox-hunting: *Hark back!* is an order to double back along the trail of the fox. It is sometimes mistakenly rendered as × *to hearken back* or, in speech, as × *to harp back* — partly because fast speech encourages this pronunciation and partly because those who reminisce tend to *harp on* about the past.

To hearken, usually occurring in the phrase *to hearken to,* is now rare. It means 'to listen to and take serious account of'. It is the standard word for 'to listen' in the King James Bible (1611). Shakespeare, however, although contemporary with this Bible, used *listen* more often; this suggests that *hearken* was by then being increasingly restricted to formal contexts.

Note that *hearken* is still usually spelt with the *e*, though *harken* is an acceptable alternative.

have 1. There used to be a theoretical distinction in British English between the structures *I haven't* (or *I haven't got*) and *I don't have* when indicating possession — the first suggesting 'at this moment', the second suggesting 'usually, generally'. The writer and scholar C.S. Lewis illustrated the difference by means of the examples *I haven't got indigestion* (= I am not suffering from indigestion at the moment) and *I don't have* *indigestion* (= I seldom or never suffer from indigestion).

There was, in theory, a corresponding difference between the structure *Have you (got) ...?* and *Do you have ...?* The usage expert H.W. Fowler used the examples *Have you coffee?* (= Have I given you your coffee yet? or Is there any coffee to drink? or Is there any coffee to use in preparing the drink?) and *Do you have coffee?* (= Are you in the habit of drinking coffee, and shall I give you some?)

It is not clear how far such distinctions were ever observed. And today they are hardly observed at all. That is a pity, perhaps, but it seems unfair to blame the Americans for the loss, as both Lewis and Fowler did.

2. The difference between American and British usage never was entirely clear-cut, and is even less so today. Consider the following sets of questions and statements:

a. Do you have any children? I don't have any children.
b. Have you got any children? I haven't got any
b.i. Got any children? children/I've got no children.
c. Have you any children? I haven't any children/I have no children.

American English clearly prefers *a.* and regards *c.* as very formal — or British. British English in the past might have favoured *c.* and regarded *a.* as an Americanism, and *b.* as informal. Today, however, *c.* sounds slightly old-fashioned or formal in British speech too; *b.* is probably the standard preference now. And the American preference *a.* now sounds more or less natural in British speech, just as the British preference *b.* is considered natural in American speech (*b.i.* is popular in informal speech in both American and British English).

In the past tense, British and American usage have clearly converged on form *a*: *Did you have any problems? I didn't have any problems.* (Forms *b.* and *c.* are still found in British English, though *c.* sounds old-fashioned: *Had you any difficulties? He had not the good looks of his brother.* But a form of *c.* is fairly common in both British and American English when *no* replaces *not*: *I had no problems.*)

In positive statements, styles *a.* and *c.* both yield the structure *I have three children.* Americans duly favour this form, whereas in British English it is formal or rather old-fashioned. The British preference is again the *b.* form, *I've got three children*, which is again acceptable though not so common in American English.

See GET.

3. In both British and American English, where the sense is 'must, to be obliged to', the forms *(do) have* and *have got* are both fully acceptable in questions and positive statements.

a. Do you have to go now?/Have you got to go now?
b. We have to go/We've got to go.
c. We *do* have to go/We *have* got to go (emphatic).

American English probably favours the first option in each pair, at least in *a.* and *c.*, but accepts the variant forms fully. But in negative statements things are slightly different:

d. We don't have to go/We haven't got to go.
d.i. We haven't to go.

Americans would distinctly prefer the first option in *d.*, probably regarding the second form as odd. And *d.i.* would not be used in American English; it is not really standard British English either, though it does occur regionally.

4. In rapid speech, or informal writing, the auxiliary *have* is contracted to *'ve* — /əv/: *He couldn't've done that.* A common mistake, made by children especially, is to write this contraction as *of*, and to pronounce it as /ɒv/ when it is expanded again: ✗ *Oh yes he could of.*

5. Traditionally, *to have* in the sense of 'to possess' should be repeated, rather than replaced by the substitute verb *to do*:

? She had a retroussé nose, just as her mother did.

This is now very common, however, in writing as well as in speech, in British English as well as in American English. Purists still insist that *to do* cannot replace *to have* here, and that the only correct form is:

She had a retroussé nose, just as her mother had.

See DO 1.

6. The verb *have* has a habit of appearing needlessly in sentences:

?? Even if she'd have realised help was at hand, she'd have been too scared to call out.

The second *have* here is correct, but the first should be omitted. Conditional sentences of this kind typically take the construction *Even if she had realised ...* rather than ?? *Even if she would have realised ....*

Another example:

? I expected to have met you here at 6 o'clock.

The sense of past time is already contained in the past tense of *expected*. There is no need to re-inforce it by using the 'perfect' infinitive: the simple present infinitive should be enough: *I expected to meet you here at 6 o'clock*. It has been argued, however, that the use of the perfect infinitive is sometimes helpful in clarifying the sense. The present infinitive can be ambiguous: *I expected to meet you here at 6 o'clock* (and I was right: here you are); and *I expected to meet you here at 6 o'clock* (yet it's now 7.30 and you've only just arrived). In speech, there would be no confusion, of course: in the first case, the stress would be placed on *expected*; in the second, on *6 o'clock*. In writing, however, confusion might result; if the perfect infinitive with *have* were used instead, only one interpretation — the second — would be likely.

Note, similarly, the ambiguity in the following sentence:

It was Felicia's duty to open the door.

Did Felicia open the door or not? If the 'dubious' perfect infinitive were used, however, the sense would almost certainly be that Felicia neglected to open the door:

? It was Felicia's duty to have opened the door.

This seems to be a case of doubtful grammar that is in some ways more helpful than correct grammar.

In other examples, however, there is no such justification for the use of the perfect infinitive. A helpful warning-sign is the presence of two *have*'s in the same clause:

?? You'd think she'd have been happy to have taken the credit for the invention.

?? Stefan really shouldn't have tried to have burrowed under the fence.

?? I should have liked to have seen more of you during your stay here.

?? After much heart-searching I have finally discovered the reason for my blunders. It is simply that I am too old for the game. ... I am much encouraged, therefore, by the following game ... in which the Dutch master, Gert Ligterink, commits a blunder I would have been proud to have made.
— Harry Golombek, *The Times*

There are too many *have*'s in each case: the last of these examples, for instance, should simply have read *commits a blunder I would have been proud to make* or else *commits a blunder I would*

be proud to have made.

Shakespeare, as usual, goes his own way:

Yet who would have thought the old man to have had so much blood in him?
— Lady Macbeth, *Macbeth* V i

But unless you can write like Shakespeare in other respects, there is no need to follow his example in this instance.

he, him, his English (like most European languages) is unfortunate in lacking a third-person singular personal pronoun (or possessive adjective) of common gender: other pronouns can refer equally to men or women — *I, we, you, they* — but in the third person singular, there is a split according to sex: *he* is male, *she* is female. How then does one refer in English to a person of unknown or unspecified sex? The traditional recommendation is to use *he*. From birth to death, it seems, the unknown human subject is expressly masculine:

Liley finds that he can make a fetus move by tickling his fetal scalp, make him grasp by stroking his palm and bring up his toes by stimulating his sole.
— Arthur J. Snider (U.S.),
The New York Post

When the child is at the table, he should be treated with the same courtesy and attention given to adults.
— Robert L. Green (U.S.),
The New York Times

But even if he doesn't want to reproduce spoken language, a writer may want to buttonhole his reader, to talk to him suddenly more directly than through the medium of formal prose.
— Dame Mary Warnock,
'Words', BBC Radio 3

Dignity lies in the patient's fight for life and in his struggle to maintain human contact, in the feeling that someone cares about him and is trying to help him.
— Dr Franklin H. Epstein (U.S.),
The New York Times

Such usage is in keeping with traditional grammar: *he/him/his* has long been understood in both official and casual English to refer to either sex in appropriate contexts (whereas *she/her/hers* is exclusively female in reference). In the words of the old legal joke, 'Man embraces Woman'. Nevertheless, some danger of misunderstanding remains: *he/him/his* is so strongly identified with the male sex that an inattentive listener or reader might well take a common-gender reference for a masculine one; and genuine ambiguity is unavoidable in such sentences as *? Every pupil of mine has individually pledged his support* — does the teacher have an all-boys class, or is it mixed?

In recent years, a further criticism has been aimed at this blanket use of *he/him/his* — a feminist criticism, that is. These masculine forms, whether or not they are taken to refer to both sexes, at least favour the male sex, and are viewed as a degrading disregard of the equal importance of women. Children, it is argued, if taught to use *he/him/his* in this way, unconsciously develop the impression that boys and men are the human norm or point of reference, and that girls and women are secondary or exceptional ('the second sex', in the translated phrase of the French writer Simone de Beauvoir).

In particular, social roles common to both sexes are instead represented as being typically male — the homeowner, the consumer, the voter, the taxpayer. The problem is made worse, if anything, by the tendency to use *she/her/hers* when referring to so-called 'female' professions, and *he/him/his* when referring to 'male' professions: *?? When a nurse discusses a case with a doctor, she must give him only the relevant details.*

But what alternative is there? Some writers strive for strict accuracy by using *he or she/him or her* and so on (see HE OR SHE), and succeed only in sounding awkward and pedantic. Most speakers unthinkingly use *they/them/their* after *anyone*, *somebody*, and so on (see THEY), only to face the accusation of using bad grammar. Attempts have been made to create a new word entirely, as a common-gender third person singular pronoun. Among the coinages have been *tey* (based on *they*), *thon* (a contraction of *the one*), *thir,* and *(s)he*. Simplest of all would be to expand the range of *it* to include human beings (as it already includes babies). But needless to say, such forms have not caught on: a pronoun is too basic an element of language to allow of much deliberate innovation in this way.

One way of skirting this impasse is to rephrase the sentence. You can avoid using a hypothetical individual (*the student, the employer, the writer,* and so on) to represent a group, and instead of generalising in the singular you can now generalise in the plural. So the second of the quotations at the start of this entry might be reworded to read:

When children are at table, they should be treated with the same courtesy and attention given to adults.

Another strategy is to change *if-* and *when-*clauses to constructions beginning *a person (who),* the *child (who),* and so on:

The child (who is) at table should be treated with the same courtesy and attention given to adults.

Sometimes, cunning editing can bypass pronouns altogether. The last of the passages quoted at the start of this entry might be rewritten to read:

Dignity lies in the patient's fight for life and struggle to maintain human contact, in the feeling that someone cares and is trying to help.

In the case of babies or foetuses (as in the first of the quotations above), *it* and *its* can replace *he/him* and *his*.

Sometimes *you/your/yours* or *one/one's* can replace *he/him/his* (see ONE; YOU), though the resulting tone can be rather condescending or hectoring (in the case of *you*) or pompous (in the case of *one*). Note that the use of *one* might not help at all in American English, which allows *he/him/his* to follow the initial *one* or *one's*. Whereas British English would insist on *But even if one doesn't want to reproduce spoken language, one may want to buttonhole one's reader*, American English might also accept *But even if one doesn't want to reproduce spoken language, he may want to buttonhole his reader*.

Another useful trick is simply to repeat the noun rather than represent it by a pronoun. The following rephrasing of the third quotation above draws on this technique and also on the use of *you* mentioned in the last paragraph:

Suppose that you are the writer, and that you don't want to reproduce spoken language. You may still want to buttonhole your reader, to talk to that reader suddenly more directly than through the medium of formal prose.

Yet another strategy: the hypothetical representative might be put forward as being specifically a man or a woman. The fourth quotation above might then be reworded in this way:

Suppose a patient is fighting for life — an 80-year-old woman with an inoperable cancer, say. For her, dignity lies in the fight for life and in her struggle to maintain human contact, in the feeling that someone cares about her and is trying to help her.

● *Recommendation* The forms *he/him/his* are still widely accepted by conservative users of English, with the backing of a long tradition, as suitable for referring to a person of unspecified sex.

But the objections to such usage are forceful and increasingly common, and it is worth making the effort to avoid it both in speech and in writing. If English is poor in its pronouns, it is rich in its flexibility, and rewording of an inappropriate construction is almost always a feasible and even simple alternative.

See also MAN; SEXISM IN THE ENGLISH LANGUAGE.

he or she English lacks a third-person singular personal pronoun of common gender — a singular *they,* as it were. The use of *he* (and *him*) to serve as one is open to two objections: first, that it is potentially misleading; and secondly, that directly or indirectly it demeans women (see HE, HIM, HIS).

As a way of meeting these objections, many writers use the compound pronouns *he or she* and *him or her* and *his or hers,* and the compound possessive adjective *his or her.* Provided that such phrases are used with restraint, they serve a good purpose; they are particularly helpful when drawing attention to the possible inclusion of women in contexts where they are usually neglected:

Following the Democratic convention, in all likelihood, Mr Anderson would produce his own candidate for Vice President ... More important would be the stature of the person who, by agreeing to make such a hazardous race, showed that he or she considered John Anderson a serious candidate indeed.
— Tom Wicker (U.S.),
The New York Times

All too often, however, the compound pronoun or adjective has to be repeated, and when that happens, its use becomes laborious, awkward, and jarring:

? Each passenger sat down in the same seat he or she had occupied before and quickly rearranged his or her face behind its previous mask of neutrality.
— Vivian Gornick (U.S.),
The New York Times

Far preferable to such clumsy phrasing is an entire rewording of the sentence, along the following lines, for example:

Each passenger sat down in the same seat as before. Each face was quickly rearranged behind its previous mask of neutrality.

(For other methods of rewording such sentences, see HE, HIM, HIS again.)

Note that the masculine pronoun or possessive adjective is usually placed before the feminine one. This is the established idiomatic usage, but the reverse order is quite permissible:

He challenged every individual in that audience to do some good thing for her or his nation.
— James Michener (U.S.), *The Covenant*

Sometimes a writer will attempt to shorten the compound phrase by replacing the *or* with a slash mark: *he/she*; *him/her*:

The average bookperson, who likes a good read and can take typos and misplaced semicolons in his/her stride, may wonder if all this fuss and money are in order for a mere work of entertainment.
— Anthony Burgess, *The Observer*

No matter what form it is cast in, the compound pronoun has to be consistently applied — you cannot wander from the singular *he/she* to the plural *their*:

✗ What an absolute travesty of justice, that those who obey the law have to pay to bring miscreants to justice. Of course the miscreant, especially if he/she is found guilty, should be required to pay for the cost of their guilt.
— D.J. Bendle, letter to *The Times*

For consistency's sake the *their* should read *his/her.* But this is again rather laborious, and it would read better if the passage were recast entirely in the plural.

● *Recommendation* For want of common-gender pronouns or possessive adjectives in English, the phrases *he or she, he/she, his or her,* and so on can be a valuable resource to the careful writer. But they are certainly not satisfactory in all circumstances, and the various alternatives should be explored wherever possible.

See also SEXISM IN THE ENGLISH LANGUAGE; THEY.

hearken See HARK.

heir apparent, heir presumptive There is a technical difference between these two terms, though they are often thought — and used — to mean the same thing.

An *heir apparent* is the person with an unquestioned and unchangeable right of succession. So, Prince Charles is the *heir apparent* to the British throne. An *heir presumptive* is the person who is at the moment in line to succeed, but whose right is merely provisional: if a candidate with a prior right is born, then this baby at once becomes the *heir presumptive* (or *heir apparent*) instead. So: Queen Victoria's first child (Princess 'Vicky') became *heir presumptive* (probably not *?? heiress presumptive*) to the throne on her birth in November 1840; but when the Queen's first son ('Bertie', later Edward VII) was born in November 1841, he immediately became *heir apparent*, and Vicky ceased to be *heir presumptive*. (Had Bertie died shortly afterwards, however, Vicky would once again — for a time — have become *heir presumptive*.)

In the United Kingdom, a woman is unlikely to be considered *heir apparent* to the throne as long as there is any possibility of the birth of a son to the monarch.

help 1. The construction *can't help but*, as in *? I couldn't help but admire her*, is common in informal English but should be avoided in serious writing. It is, strictly, a blend of two different constructions: the somewhat formal *I could not but admire her* and the (recommended) alternative *I couldn't help admiring her*. (See CAN BUT for further details.)

2. The expressions *more than you can help* and *as little as you can help* have been censured as illogical by some usage writers: *? I shall not work any harder than I can help*; *? She made as little noise as she could help, but she still woke up the baby*. What people really mean when using the expressions is 'more than you have to', 'as little as you can't help' — just the opposite of what they are saying. The expressions are well-established idioms, however, and have been used by respected stylists, including Cardinal Newman and Winston Churchill. If the illogicality of the expressions deters you from using them, you can use alternative phrasings such as *as little as possible* or *more than one has to*.

3. The pattern *to help (someone) to do something* is often shortened to *to help (someone) do something*. Both the British and the North Americans use it freely in informal contexts, as in *Help me clean the windows*; but the British sometimes resent, as an Americanism, its use by advertising copywriters: *Our product helps banish those washday blues*.

Probably two sorts of *help* are involved. In one

sort, two or more participants actually cooperate in doing something. Here, *help (me) do it* is now widely accepted as a variant of *help (me) to do it*, though some traditionalists still object to it here:

> We lost our tempers, tried to hit boys amid shouts of mirth, and wished Duffy and Sullivan would hurry up and return and help us restore order.
> – Susan Boyd, *The Fiction Magazine*

The other sort of *help* is that provided by something nonhuman, so that no actual shared effort is involved. Here, it is best to retain the *to*: *These tablets will help you to relax*. The following extract would benefit from the insertion of a *to* after *helps*:

> *?* In addition, a coherent imposed culture helps create its own counter-currents. In the long run, it tends to foster the very habits of question and criticism that bring about the end of its mandate.
> – Gillian Tindall, *The Times*

Some writers who omit *to* with these impersonal subjects, as in *? This advice will help you make the right decisions when buying property*, are perhaps trying half-consciously to suggest the sort of cosy shared relationship that is possible only when one person helps another.

hence, hither In the senses 'from this place' and 'to this place', these words are now archaic or extremely formal, and should be avoided except in legal contexts or when intending some special humorous effect.

In other senses or forms, however, both words remain in current use.

First, the phrase *hither and thither,* though slightly old-fashioned, is still commonly found: *The children scurried hither and thither in the hunt for Easter eggs.*

Also, the phrase *come hither* can still be used to suggest old-fashioned sexual allure: *She gave him a come-hither look.*

> This story was told by Svetlana, an Intourist girl with a wonderful curling lip and green come-hither eyes.
> – Bruce Chatwin, in *Great Rivers of the World*

Hence is still widely used in two senses, though it does have a rather formal ring in each case. It has no current reference to *place*, but does still refer to *time* and *cause*: first it means 'from this time': *We'll review its effectiveness six months hence*; secondly, it means 'therefore, consequently, for this reason': *The stock market is jittery just now — hence my advice to avoid shares and to buy gold instead.* In both of these sentences, *?? from hence* should be avoided: the *from* is redundant.

The compounds *henceforth* (or *henceforward*) and *hitherto* survive in formal usage, again with reference to time rather than place: *Henceforth, overtime work will command payment of time-and-a-half; a hitherto neglected masterpiece of romantic poetry.*

See also ARCHAISMS; THENCE; WHENCE.

hermeneutic, heuristic, hermetic These three difficult adjectives are becoming increasingly widespread and fashionable in intellectual contexts. Vogue words should be used very sparingly, of course, and above all correctly. Make sure not to confuse these three.

Heuristic means 'assisting the process of learning or discovery': *A heuristic computer program is part of the language course; a theory put forward purely as a heuristic device.*

> Whereas today's computers handle data or information, fifth generation computers will manipulate knowledge. Knowledge can be represented and stored as facts and practical (or heuristic) rules for its effective manipulation.
> – Garry Marshall, *The Observer*

A heuristic method of learning is one based on trial and error, in an exploratory way, using a known method to reach an unknown goal (such as keeping one hand always on the wall of a maze to find your way out). In educational theory, it is a method of teaching that allows children to learn independently through their own investigations. The word comes from the Greek *heuriskein*, 'to discover, find'. It is pronounced /hewr-**ris**tik/. The noun *heuristics* usually takes a singular verb (and is itself sometimes singular in form: *heuristic,* as in *the heuristic of Piaget*). *Heuristics* is the application or study of heuristic methods of investigation.

Hermeneutic is related to the noun *hermeneutics*, which means specifically 'the science of the interpretation of the Bible'. In philosophical usage, the word refers to interpretation in a more general way — to the art or theory of interpreting the significance in any human activity or utterance. It assumes that there is a coherent meaning behind the experience of sensations. The celebrated German philosopher Martin Heidegger (1889-1976) applied the word

to his investigations into the nature of human existence, and coloured it with his own existentialist philosophy.

> But today's Foreign Office practises a sort of *protocole de Grand Guignol* according to which the distinction between a diplomatic agent and a terrorist has become a delicate nuance requiring elaborate hermeneutics on the text of the Vienna Convention.
> – Conor Cruise O'Brien, *The Observer*

The word *hermeneutic* is pronounced /**her**mi-**new**tik/. It goes back to the Greek *hermeneutike tekhne*, 'the art of interpretation'. Like *heuristics*, *hermeneutics* is usually used with a singular verb, though if it means 'hermeneutic devices' (as in the example just quoted) rather than 'the science of interpretation', then it would take a plural verb.

The commonest meaning of the adjective *hermetic* is 'completely sealed or sealing'. The word comes from *Hermes Trismegistos* ('Hermes the thrice-greatest') — the Greek name for the Egyptian God Thoth, who was the supposed author of works of alchemy, astrology, and magic. He was said to have invented a magic seal to make vessels airtight. The word *hermetic* is today often used in its adverbial form, in the phrase *hermetically sealed*, which simply means 'airtight', or, metaphorically, 'cut-off, isolated':

> The lack of contact with the outside world and the absence of any reference to politics and changing mores suggests that these people are living in the timeless, hermetically sealed world of soap-opera.
> – Philip French, *The Observer*

Among the other senses of *hermetic* are 'relating to the occult and alchemy' and 'impervious to outside interference or influence; insulated': *She retreated to the hermetic confines of her bedroom.*

> I was agonisingly anxious to smuggle her into the hermetic seclusion of The Enchanted Hunters, and we had still eighty miles to go.
> – Vladimir Nabokov, *Lolita*

The word has also come to have a meaning in literary contexts, which adds to the confusion with the intellectual terms *hermeneutic* and *heuristic*. When it is used to describe poetry, *hermetic* means 'closed, exclusive, obscure, occult', though usually not in a negative way:

> Ms Bok has little of interest to say about the

psychological compulsion towards secrecy, and nothing at all about secrecy in art (why is it that the most enduring literature is often the most hermetic? and why do many writers who condemn State secrecy practise it in their own lives and letters?)

       – Blake Morrison, *The Observer*

Hermetic also applies to a major movement in modern Italian poetry that includes the work of the Nobel prizewinners Salvatore Quasimodo and Eugenio Montale.

Hermetic, like *hermeneutic* and *heuristic*, is pronounced with a voiced *h* — /her-**met**tik/; all three are accordingly preceded by the article *a* rather than *an*.

See also -ICS.

hiccup, hiccough *Hiccup* is the earlier form, emerging in about 1580. (The original English forms *hicket* and *hicock* probably developed as an imitation of the sound.) *Hiccough* appeared in the following century, probably on the model of *cough*, though the pronunciation remains unaffected.

Both forms are quite acceptable: *hiccup* is probably more favoured by writers today. Note the double *p* in the verb forms *hiccupped* and *hiccupping*: a single *p* used to be preferred, and still is generally preferred in North America, but it would be most uncommon in British English today.

In its metaphorical use, 'a slight hitch or delay', *hiccup* is today very much in vogue, yet it was probably used in this way as long ago as the 17th century. Both spellings are possible for this metaphorical sense too:

George Roman's production begins badly, improves at once and thereafter, apart from a few hiccups, sustains a level of clarity and intelligence which enables the central performances to flourish.

       – Michael Ratcliffe, *The Observer*

The 'Proposals' begin with a fine promise: that whatever arrangements are made following the abolition of the metropolitan county councils and the GLC, they will 'permit the continuation of existing public expenditure in that field' (i.e., the arts); adjustments in rate support grant and grant-related expenditure will take care of any hiccoughs created by the transfer of powers.

       – Joan Bakewell, *The Observer*

him, his See HE, HIM, HIS; HE OR SHE.

hire, rent, let, lease In British English, to take possession of something temporarily for a fee is to *hire* it or sometimes to *rent* it: you might hire a bicycle, or a dress suit, or a building if for a short time: *hire the village hall for a concert*. The owner of these things *hires* them *out*: *I hire out my caravan for the summer*. You *hire* or *rent* a car (though you *charter* a bus, ship, or aircraft). You *rent* a room or a building (other than for a very short time), or land, or a television set; and their owner *lets* or *rents* them to the user. A landlord, or a tenant, *leases* a building or land, under contract and for a stated period usually longer than that involved in renting.

In American English, things appear to be more fluid, with *rent* used more widely than in British English. Americans may *rent* a room from a person who *rents* rooms, and *rent* a dinner jacket for one evening where the British would *hire* it. Americans also use *hire* of people who are employed or engaged for work, as in Robert Frost's poem 'The Death of the Hired Man'.

historic, historical *Historical* means 'related to the study of history or its events' or 'occurring in or through history, or having a long history': *historical research*; *historical novels*; *historical trends*.

He offers the compendium to the future as a historical document. It was already historical when it was first published, since most of the writers were at school during the First World War, and it was felt that a revolution was already on its way in the middle Thirties.

       – Anthony Burgess, *The Observer*

Historic is sometimes used in this sense too, and has a technical sense in grammar, referring to a past-tense form of verbs in some languages. But it is most commonly used to mean 'very significant, deserving of a place in history': *Tomorrow's meeting will be a historic turning-point in relations between the two superpowers*. Used to describe historical events, it marks their importance rather than their date: *the historic signing of the Magna Carta*; *the historic battle at El Alamein*; *the historic day when treason was uncovered*. It is now overused of modern events or things to exaggerate their importance, and should be avoided except when the subject is really so important that future generations will remember it as part of history.

Ms Holmes, aged 40, the mother of two young sons, successfully complained to an industrial tribunal that the Home Office's refusal to let her work part-time amounted to unlawful sex discrimination. ... Ms Holmes's victory was hailed by the Equal Opportunities Commission as an 'historic judgment'.

– The Times

James phoned at the crack of dawn and asked me to preside over a ridiculous Press party. Shivering at the landing extension, I heard his brisk boisterous voice rattling on about the historic meeting of a famous comic and a famous bust who were going to make a film together.

– Lynne Reid Banks,
The L-Shaped Room

This last example uses *historic*, deliberately, in a very clichéd way.

A much-debated question is whether to use *a* or *an* before *historic* and *historical*. Since the initial syllable is unstressed, the *h* is sometimes not pronounced, and the word is then preceded by *an*. (This does not apply to *history*, in which the first syllable is stressed and the *h* always audible. See A, AN.)

One should not rejoice too soon. Censorship is not yet dead. ... Still, its failure is already an historical fact — provided writers continue to expose it for what it is and to fight it every inch of the way.

– André Brink, in
They Shoot Writers, Don't They?

As a rule, when the *h* is pronounced, *a* should be used; *an* is increasingly regarded as an affectation.

history of the English language It is difficult to put a date on the birth of English, but its name, and hence presumably the language itself, has been in existence for 1300 years. The earliest Germanic settlers in Britain, who called themselves *Angelcynn*, used the word *Englisc* (English) for their language when they first wrote it, around AD 700. Over the centuries this language of theirs has of course changed and developed beyond recognition, absorbing all kinds of material from outside, and is spoken today in many varieties around the world. Yet the language of the Angelcynn and our language today are really two extreme forms of a single tongue.

The history of the language is usually described as covering three stages: Old English up to about 1150, Middle English to about 1500, and then Modern English.

To get some idea of how different these stages are, compare the first two sentences of the Lord's Prayer as they were in about 850, 1400, and 1600. (Bear in mind that the language is probably a little old-fashioned in each case by the standards of the time, since written English, especially religious language, would be formal and conservative and perhaps deliberately elevated.) The approximate pronunciation is provided beneath each line.

Old English
Fæder ure,
/**fad**dər **ōō**rə/
ðu ðe eart on heofonum,
/th**ōō** thə **a**-ərt on **he**-ə-və-n**ōō**m/
si ðin nama gehalgod.
/see theen **naa**maa yə-**haal**-god/
Tobecume ðin rice.
/tō-bək**ōō**mə theen **reech**ə/

Middle English
Oure fadir
/**ōō**rə **faa**-dir/
that art in hevenes
/thaat art in **hevv**'nəs/
halewid be thi name.
/**haal**ə-wid bay thee naam/
Thi kyngdoom come to.
/thee **king**dōm k**ōō**m tō/

Early Modern English
Our father
/ə-**ōō**r **feth**ər/
which art in heaven
/hwich art in **hevv**'n/
hallowed be thy name.
/**hall**ə-wəd bee th̲ə-i ne-em/
Thy kingdom come.
/th̲ə-i **king**dəm k**ōō**m/

As these extracts show, the gap between the modern language and Old English is now so great that Old English has to be studied as if it were a foreign language.

The origins of English can be traced further back, beyond the dialects of the early Germanic settlers, to the West Germanic languages spoken by tribes in northwest Germany around the beginning of the Christian era. These West Germanic languages are in turn part of a wider Germanic group, which includes the Scandinavian languages. All of these form a branch of the Indo-European family of languages, spoken from northern India to the Atlantic coast of Europe (and now in other continents as well, of course). The clue to the kinship among all these languages — Persian, Hindi, Greek, Spanish, Gaelic, and English alike, and dozens of others — lies in the many words (in different forms) that they have in common. These words, going back to the earliest beginnings, suggest a cold land, away from the sea, where the trees lost their leaves in winter. So we find words equivalent to *snow*, *birch*, *wolf*, *honey*, and *beech*. Honey bees do not occur naturally in Asia and beech trees are not native to places much east of the Ukraine, so the likeliest source for the basic Indo-European language seems to be somewhere in Eastern or Central Europe.

What distinguishes all the Germanic languages from the other Indo-European tongues is the way that verbs can be grouped into two classes, called 'weak' and 'strong', according to the form of their past tense. The weak verbs in English are those that add a final *-ed* to form the past tense: *walk/walked*; *start/started*. In the shrinking strong class are those verbs that form their past tense and past participle by changing their main vowel sound: *bring/brought*; *drink/drank/drunk*.

The political history that underlies the development of English is this: as the Roman Empire crumbled, and the Celtic Britons were beginning to tremble under the attacks of Picts and Scots, the Roman occupiers enlisted mercenaries from the Germanic tribes on the Continent. When the Roman legions finally withdrew early in the 5th century, the Germans remained — in fact, immigration from Germany to Britain increased. Jutes, Angles, and Saxons were the principal tribes involved, with some Frisians (whose language today remains the continental language most closely related to modern English).

The Germanic tribes were no longer protectors of the British inhabitants, but their conquerors, and they soon established their own kingdoms from the Channel to the Firth of Forth. In the north were Angles, whose kingdoms were Northumbria, 'north of the River Humber', and Mercia, in the middle 'marches' of central England up to the Welsh border. To the south were the territories of the East and Middle Saxons, 'Essex and Middlesex'. The West Saxons controlled the land south of the River Thames except where the Jutes were settled in Kent.

The invaders, who called the Britons *wealas*, 'foreigners' (hence the word *Welsh*), were in turn called *Saxons* by the Britons, though they called themselves *Angelcynn*, 'the kin, or race, of the Angles' — perhaps to distinguish themselves from the Saxons remaining on the Continent. At first they also called the country *Angelcynn* too: the name *Englaland* (England) did not take over until around AD 1000.

Until recently the term *Anglo-Saxon* was used to describe both the Germanic people who settled in Britain and their language. Modern usage reserves *Anglo-Saxon* for the people and calls their language *Old English*.

The various Anglo-Saxon tribes in England had different dialects, identified by the names of the kingdoms they founded: Northumbrian, Mercian, and West Saxon. Of these, West Saxon is the most important today, since more of its manuscripts have survived, among them those of King Alfred.

King Alfred of the West Saxons, or 'Alfred the Great', is probably the best remembered Anglo-Saxon king. He was not only a soldier but a scholar, a translator, and a writer of original prose too. Here is an extract from the preface to one of his translations. It illustrates some of the particular features of Old English:

> Swa clæne hio wæs oðfeallenu on Angel-cynne ðæt swiþe feawa wæron behionan Humbre ðe hiora ðeninga cuðen underston-dan in Englisc, oððe furðum an ærendgewrit of Lædene on Englisc areccan.

> (So completely was it [learning] declined in England that very few were on this side of the Humber who could understand their service-books in English, or translate even one epistle from Latin into English.)

In this short passage we can identify some of those features that distinguish Old English from the Middle English and Modern English that developed from it.

First, the letters. The Latin alphabet was widely understood all over Europe, but 'Englisc' used some letters from the Irish Christian alphabet and others from the old runic alphabet of the Germanic tongues. The runic letters added were ƿ (*w*), and þ (*th*); from Irish came ð (also sounding like *th*) and ჳ, usually represented in print today by *g*, though it was probably used for other sounds too.

The second significant difference is in the words themselves. Old English had a wide and adaptable vocabulary which, like modern German, made new words by running together existing words. Our modern word *lord* developed from the compound *hlaf-weard* (Old English *hlaford*), 'a loaf-keeper', and *lady* from Old English *hlafdige*, 'a loaf-kneader' (*dige* is related to *dough*). *Godspell*, literally 'good news', has given us the modern word *gospel*.

Old English was capable of developing from within itself horticultural and medical terms. Medicine, for instance, was called *læce craft* —

'the craft of the physician (or leech)'. Many of these Old English words have long disappeared and been replaced by foreign words. From the passage by King Alfred we have lost several words including *ærendgewrit* (an epistle), *ðeninga* (a service-book) and *areccean* (to translate).

The core of our modern English vocabulary, nevertheless, is of Old English stock, though the spelling and pronunciation are very much altered: such pronouns as *I, me, it*; such verbs as *to eat, drink, go, have, know, love, work*; such nouns as *book, friend, home, house, wall, name, child, wife, arm, head, heart, food, milk, field, day, earth, night, sun*, and *water*.

The third difference, perhaps the most striking, is in the grammar and 'inflections', the endings of words that show their relationships with other words. Old English showed these relationships (the subjects or objects of verbs, the matching of adjectives or prepositions with nouns, and so on) by a host of inflections that indicated grammatical classifications such as those we call *nominative, genitive, masculine, feminine, neuter, strong, weak*, and many others.

For instance, around 850 the word for 'a day' had six different forms: *dæg*, 'day'; *dæges*, 'of a day'; *dæge*, 'in or on a day'; *dagas*, 'days'; *daga*, 'of days'; *dagum*, 'in or on days'. Changes in the language have cut these down to four: *day, day's, days*, and *days'* — and the last three all sound alike. So, too, adjectives, once boasting 36 different forms (12 in each of the three degrees — positive, comparative, and superlative), have changed, so that they now have only one form in each degree — for example, *smooth, smoother, smoothest*. Language change has reduced the English regular verb to its present four forms — for instance *die, dies, died, dying*; 1000 years ago the English verb had four forms in the present tense alone.

Because relationships between words were indicated by inflection there was no crucial need for related words to be positioned next to each other, and as in the passage by King Alfred a verb was often put at the end of a sentence (as in Latin, and still today in German). This complex use of inflections was breaking down throughout the Old English period, but was so well established by the strong literary tradition that the changes did not begin to appear in the written language until late in the period.

An important influence on spoken English between the 9th and 11th centuries was Scandinavian. The Northmen, as the invading Danes and Norwegian Vikings were called, settled in both the northwest and the east of England. Their language, related as it was to English, could be understood by the Anglo-Saxons, and Scandinavian words came readily into English. In particular, they contributed to the dialects of northern and eastern England. Some Scandinavian words are found in written English before the Norman Conquest (*eggs, get, sky*), though the majority are not seen in writing until a couple of centuries after the Scandinavian settlement ceased. These later words include *crooked, bath, skill, husband*, and *Thursday*.

Other Northmen, the Normans, settled in France and had become completely French-speaking by the time they invaded and conquered England in 1066. A few French words were in limited use in England before the Conquest, *bacon* and *ginger* for instance. The enormous influx from French into English after the Conquest was to alter the language vastly.

The decline of written English after the Conquest, with its replacement in official documents first by Latin and later by French, was not so swift as is often supposed. Almost a century after the Conquest some records were still being made in English, such as the Anglo-Saxon Chronicle kept at the Abbey of Peterborough until the 1150s. This document gives us an idea of how the Old English systems of writing broke down under the influence of French.

Literary activity in English, though not ceasing altogether, declined to such an extent that when English came back into general literary use in the 14th century, by this time warranting the name 'Middle English', the writing habits that had been ingrained in Old English were quite forgotten. Writers now adopted many French conventions, using *qu-* in words like *queen* or *quick*, instead of the Old English *cw-*. The French symbols *-ou-* and *-ow-* were used to represent the /-o͞o-/ sound that in Old English had been written *-u-* (*hus*, 'a house'). Changes in pronunciation, already taking place in late Old English, continued rapidly, and new spellings were adopted to represent the new sounds. Old English spellings such as *stan* and *ham* (for 'a stone' and 'a home') now became *ston* and *hom*.

French words, which had become common in spoken English, began to appear in English writing. The poet Geoffrey Chaucer, a fairly representative user of Middle English, used a high proportion of French words in his poetry. Many of these words made only a temporary appearance in English — *mappemounde* (a map of the world), for instance, and *refreyd* (cool). But many others, such as *divine* and *embrace*, have remained. By about 1400, the year of Chaucer's death, more than half of the English vocabulary consisted of French imports.

The most obvious change in Middle English was the loss of the old inflected endings. Chaucer's English is much more intelligible to the modern reader:

> With us ther was a doctour of physik,
> In al this world ne was ther noon him lyk
> To speke of physik and of surgerye
> For he was grounded in astronomye.
> He kept his pacient a ful greet deel
> In houres by his magic naturel.
> – Geoffrey Chaucer,
> General Prologue to *The Canterbury Tales*

There is little in this to baffle a modern reader.

Some of Chaucer's forms were on their way out. He still used *hath* rather than the northern form *has*, and he still used *hem* rather than *them*, though he did use the newer *they*, the Scandinavian form of the pronoun that was coming in from northern English along with *their*. He still used the 'double negative' (*ne . . . noon*), though that survived for centuries. Most striking perhaps, is that to Chaucer spelling was quite unimportant.

Englishmen in 1400 knew how to pronounce their own tongue, so the spellings, they felt, could be varied. Just as modern oddities in spelling like *plough*, *cough*, and *tough* do not really worry us today, so the alternative spellings *stream* and *streem* did not worry writers in those days, or alter their grasp of how to pronounce words.

Between Old and Middle English, it was the grammatical and vocabulary changes that were most dramatic. Between Middle and Modern English, however, it was pronunciation changes that marked the transition most strongly.

After Chaucer's time the vowel sounds, long vowels in particular, underwent a process of modification that has become known as the Great Vowel Shift. Chaucer's English may be reasonably easy to follow on the page: it would be very difficult to follow today if read aloud in the way that Chaucer would have read it. (See PRONUNCIATION; SPELLING.)

From the beginning of the 16th century there was a bursting out of activity in the language leading to many exciting changes. After Chaucer the centre of important writing moves north for a time. The great literary figures of the 15th century are Dunbar, Henryson, and other Scottish writers, whose language, though they called it *Inglis*, is clearly distinct from the English of the time and seems to warrant the term *Scots*. That is the form of language later used by James VI, who became James I of England.

It was perhaps this move of the Scottish court to London that brought about the eclipse of Scots as a true separate language. An earlier factor was the introduction of the printing press to England by William Caxton in 1476. The dissemination in print of London English hastened the use of a 'standard' English, based on the speech of London — ousting as a literary language not just Scots but the provincial dialects of England, such as that used by Chaucer's contemporary William Langland in his long poem *Piers Plowman*.

But was even London English suitable as a literary language? Throughout much of the 16th century scholars were bitterly divided over the merits of Latin and English. Innovators such as Sir Thomas Elyot and Richard Mulcaster argued fiercely that English was a truly eloquent language capable of being used for any purpose. They encouraged the building of a stock of English words adopted from Greek and Latin: *misanthrope* (1563) and *parenthesis* (1568); and *rostrum* (1542) and *meditate* (1560), for instance. Others, however, like Sir John Cheke, a Greek scholar, urged that English be kept pure and unmixed. Edmund Spenser felt that the purity of the language could be preserved by reviving old words and using words from dialect: *astound*, *belt*, *doom*, *glance*, and *surly*, for instance. On all sides, there were appeals to nationalism, patriotism, and purism.

The argument was decided, as it always is, not by the theorists but by the doers — the great writers of the time, who produced some of the finest literature in English. Shakespeare of course stands above all others as a great weaver of words. But even without a Shakespeare, the 30 years straddling 1600 would still perhaps have been the greatest age of English literature, encompassing the heyday of many other playwrights and poets — Ben Jonson, Marlowe, and Spenser among them — whose excitement in language and exuberance in writing place them in the first rank of English authors. English was now more than ever being enriched by newly coined words or compounds — *blatant* (1596), *baneful* (1593) — and by loans from other tongues: *role* (1606) from French, *rusk* (1595) from Spanish or Portuguese, *umbrella* (1611) from Italian, and so on. A sheer delight in language seemed to pervade the age, with a willingness to experiment and rejoice.

Pronunciation continued to change during the 16th and 17th centuries. Words starting with *kn*- such as *knife* and *knee* lost their first consonant, as did *wr*- words such as *write* and *wrinkle*. The old *thee/thou* forms began to decline in popularity until they disappeared from the standard language during the 18th century. The use of the auxiliary verb *do* underwent great changes: Shakespeare could use *do* for unemphatic positive declarations, as in *I do wonder*, and yet omit *do* in the negative, as in *She kisses not* — the opposite of today's usage. Numbers of strong verbs became weak. For example, *clomb* (from *climb*) gave way to *climbed*.

In the 17th century, the major movement in language was the attempt to establish rules of correctness; it was now that the first dictionaries defining the meanings of words were published, in a movement that was to culminate in the work of Dr Samuel Johnson in 1755. A number of very popular grammars of the language appeared and began to formulate rules that had never existed before, such as those governing the use of *shall* and *will*.

Minor changes in pronunciation of the language still continued. Soon after 1600 the vowel in words like *come* and *up* began to move away from its earlier pronunciation, which was like the vowel in *good* and *put*, and to take on its modern pronunciation in the southeast of England and therefore in standard English. Similarly, *last* and *bath* began to change from /last, bath/ to /laast, baath/, and the *r*-sound after vowels in words like *first* or *heard* or *hard* disappeared in the standard southeast. The old forms were retained in various dialectal areas, and in some of the new countries that were being settled by English speakers. The legacy is apparent in much North American English, for example.

Standards of 'correctness' and acceptability continued to be debated throughout the 19th and 20th centuries and are continuing today. During the first half of the 20th century, under the influence of radio, there was a strong move towards a prescribed standard speech as the most desirable one to use. This tendency was halted during the Second World War, and the academic view of language now seems to emphasise description rather than prescription — to concentrate on what the language is rather than what it should be.

In England a strong desire remains for fixing the language in its 'best' form, yet clearly English continues to change. Writers to newspapers complain furiously about developments such as the 'glottal stop', resulting in the loss of the *t*-sound in words like *butter*. The 'intrusive *r*', long noted in phrases such as *the idea(r) of it* and *China(r) and India(r)*, is now spreading into new areas such as *saw(r)ing wood* and *I saw(r) it*. Changes in grammar and vocabulary are detected and deplored by purists — the popular use of *hopefully* in the sense 'it is to be hoped', for instance.

And modern technology is likely to generate much new English vocabulary in the future.

Language is always moving and changing. The history of English is an exciting illustration of this, whether viewed in terms of its extraordinary growth during the last few decades or its deep changes over the centuries. Those few thousand *Angelcynn* and their *Englisc* gave rise to a language that is today heard all over the globe.

See also DIALECTS; SOURCES OF THE ENGLISH VOCABULARY.

histrionic   The adjective *histrionic* and its noun *histrionics* tend to recall the words *hysterical* and *hysterics*, and are sometimes confused with them. There is a certain degree of overlap in meaning, but hardly enough to blur the distinction.

Histrionic and *histrionics* are derived from the Late Latin *histrio*, meaning 'an actor'. *Hysterical* and *hysterics* go back to the Greek word *hustera*, 'a womb'. *Hysteria* or frantic behaviour was once presumably observed only in women, and thought to result from disturbances in the womb.

Histrionic originally meant 'relating to actors and acting':

> The Prince therefore survived his ordeal triumphantly. ... One of his main talents is histrionic. He worked and played with our Dryden Dramatic Society and excelled himself in their performances. This has helped him to become a national TV personality.
> – Lord Butler, *The Art of the Possible*

Histrionics originally meant 'the theatrical arts', and was used with a singular verb. The meanings of these two words have extended somewhat: today *histrionic* tends to be used in the sense 'overemotional, theatrical'; and *histrionics* means 'exaggerated emotional displays, indulged in purely for effect':

> When Miss Lapotaire talks about acting being a deeply spiritual experience, we respect the 19 years of apprenticeship that lie behind a comment that, from others, might sound histrionic.
> – Peter Davalle, *The Times*

> Helga had developed an unearthly composure. The histrionics were over. She had entered a period of ice-cold disconnection, which Charlie understood instinctively because it was something she could do herself.
> – John le Carré,
> *The Little Drummer Girl*

Note that *histrionics* is usually used with a plural verb.

Put simply, *histrionic* suggests a deliberately contrived emotional effect, whereas *hysterical* suggests loss of emotional control.

Take care not to debase *hysterical* by using it simply as a synonym for 'overexcited'.

Finally, note that it is safe to use *a* before both *histrionic* and *hysterical*, though *an hysterical...* is still used sometimes. (See A, AN.)

hither   See HENCE.

hoard, horde   *Hoard* and *horde* are sometimes confused because they sound the same and they both convey a sense of numerousness. *Hoard* comes from Old English *hord* and means primarily 'a secret store, an accumulation', whether of food, gold coins, or ideas:

> *A Bowl of Cherries* validates its title in terms of sheer profusion. Shena Mackay manages, without apparent straining, to cram into a novel of orthodox proportions a hoard of detail, not merely in placing her characters but in bedecking the outlines of the figures themselves.
> – Jonathan Keates, *The Observer*

In the plural it is used, slightly informally, to mean 'a very large amount': *hoards of time*. *Hoard* is also a verb meaning 'to store up, to accumulate'; it has a disapproving tone to it, suggesting either miserliness — *hoarding gemstones* — or a selfish precaution against shortages: *hoarding food*.

Horde comes (via French, German, and Polish) from a Turkic word *ordu*, meaning both 'camp' and 'army'. (This word was also the origin of *Urdu*, the Asian language.) It was used to refer to the tribes of Turkic nomads who migrated from northeast Asia between the 13th and 15th centuries, and threatened the civilisations of Asia and Europe.

Horde now means 'a vast and threatening army', or 'a large threatening crowd', as in *a horde of football hooligans*.

> What shape the joke should best take was further discussed. ... The idea that we should all lie on the shelves, then, when Bithel was already in bed, appear as a horde of ghosts, was abandoned as impracticable.
> – Anthony Powell, *The Valley of Bones*

Hordes are barbarous and disorganised, and overwhelm by sheer numbers (so the enemy army may be a *horde*, but our side rarely is).

However, youth and zest are never to be had on a long lease. In her newly-published memoirs Françoise Sagan subjects today's Saint-Tropez hordes to a devastating bombardment.
> – Robin Smyth, *The Observer*

More generally, *horde* can refer to aggressive groups of animals (even insects) as well: *a horde of stampeding buffalo*.

At other times, in informal contexts, *hordes* means little more than 'vast numbers':

> At Tiflis, she was handed over to a horde of her relatives and neighbours, who keened over her as if they were receiving her corpse.
> – D.M. Thomas, *The White Hotel*

> That was my introduction to Clint Eastwood. Now, looking back on his years of starring in films which return prodigious profits, it is obvious he satisfies some notion in hordes of people of how an American hero ought to look.
> – Norman Mailer (U.S.), *The Observer*

There are some colloquial contexts in which either *horde* or *hoard* might serve — *There were hordes/hoards of tiger lilies in his garden* — depending on whether the metaphor intended is 'armies' or 'secret stores'.

hoi polloi   These words, in Greek, mean literally 'the many'. Pedants therefore object to phrases such as *the celebrations of the hoi polloi,* arguing that *the hoi polloi* means 'the the many'.

But it would be quite against the natural idiom to speak of *the celebrations of hoi polloi* instead. The literal Greek meaning is not relevant to idiomatic English usage, which accepts — in fact, demands — *the hoi polloi*.

Not that there is ever much need to use the phrase in the first place. It has virtually lost its older neutral senses of 'the majority of people' and 'ordinary folk', and retained chiefly the negative and disparaging sense of 'the herd; riffraff'. If you do use the phrase, note that it takes a plural verb — *The hoi polloi are in fine spirits tonight* — and that it is often still considered foreign enough in English to need italics in printing or underlining in writing.

See also RIVER.

home   British and American English use this word in slightly different ways. When *home* means 'in one's house', and no motion or travel is involved, British English requires *at home* in formal contexts: *I stayed/I have been at home all* *day*. In American English the *at* is often dropped and this sometimes happens in colloquial British English too: *? I stayed/I have been home all day*. With the verb *to be*, however, the *at* can be dropped when referring to someone who has recently arrived, or is about to arrive, home: *I've been home an hour already*; *Is she home yet?*; *When are you due home?* And no *to* is used before *home* with verbs of motion such as *come, go, send, arrive*: *I went home early*.

Another British-American difference to note is that *home* is widely used in American English where a British person would say *house*, as when selling or buying houses or in remarks on the appearance of a house: *Luxury Homes For Sale*; *What a lovely home you have!* This is starting to happen in Britain too now; moreover, there are some long-established examples of this use of *home* in British English, notably in *stately homes*. And the expression *a mobile home* is used in both varieties.

Note also that the British expression *home from home* corresponds to the American expression *home away from home*.

honorary, honourable The American spelling of *honour* is *honor*, which reflects the Latin original. The two derived adjectives, *honorary* and *honourable* both have their own special uses. *Honorary* means 'given or done as an honour' — without remuneration, or in some cases, without the usual duties and privileges. So *an honorary degree* is conferred as an honour in recognition of achievements great enough to bypass the usual degree requirements. An *Honorary Secretary* (abbreviated as *Hon. Sec.*) carries out duties without remuneration, usually for a club or non-professional organisation. The related noun *honorarium* (plural *honoraria* or *honorariums*) refers to a voluntary fee paid, often by tradition, for services (such as certain academic functions) for which no payment is required by law or contract.

Honourable means 'worthy of honour, high-minded, honest': *Brutus is an honourable man*. *The Honourable* (with a capital H) is the courtesy title given to the children of barons and viscounts and the younger sons of earls. It is abbreviated as *the Hon*. (According to Evelyn Waugh, the young Nancy Mitford and her sisters sounded the *h* in *the Hon.*, /hon/. But this pronunciation is now rare, the *h* being silent as a rule.) The title *Right Honourable* (abbreviated *Rt. Hon.*) is a title of respect before the names of Judges of Appeal, some Privy Councillors, and some high-ranking civic officials. In the House of Commons, MPs

are referred to as *the honourable member for* ...

Note that *honorary* has no *u*, while *honourable*, in British English (though not American), does have a *u*. There is a tendency to pronounce *honorary* as though it had only one *r*: *??/on*-ri/; the preferred pronunciation is /**onnə**-rəri/; a common American pronunciation is /**onnə**-rerri/.

hopefully The use of the word *hopefully* has probably provoked more irritation in the past decade than any other controversial item of English usage.

Nobody objects to it when used in its traditional meaning, recorded as early as 1639, 'full of hope; in a hopeful way':

> To travel hopefully is better than to arrive, and the true success is to labour.
> — Robert Louis Stevenson,
> *Virginibus Puerisque* (1881)

The objections are directed against the word when it is used to mean 'it is to be hoped': *? Hopefully the fighting has stopped*. This sense is recorded as existing in 1932, and seems to be of American origin. Only in the early 1970s did it come to be widely used in Britain.

The objections to it seem to be fourfold: first, much of the British objection to it has been that it is an Americanism. Yet Americans too have fiercely criticised the new use of *hopefully*.

Secondly, people have misguidedly argued that *hopefully*, as an adverb, has the grammatical duty to modify a verb, an adjective, or another adverb, whereas in its new sense its function is instead to modify an entire sentence. The word *basically*, for instance, when used at the beginning of a sentence, is widely disliked by purists. Yet it has long been a feature of English that adverbial expressions of various kinds can be used to modify or comment on whole sentences:

> Frankly, the fighting has stopped.
> Naturally the fighting has stopped.
> Admittedly, the fighting has stopped.

Why then should *hopefully* not be accepted too?

But *hopefully* is not really on a par with *frankly, naturally, admittedly*, and similar 'sentence adverbs'. They can all be paraphrased in ways that (without resorting to *I* or *we*) use their underlying adjectival forms:

> To be frank, the fighting has stopped.
> As is natural,/It is natural that the fighting has stopped.
> As must be admitted, the fighting has stopped.

Hopefully has only one impersonal 'paraphrase':

It is hopeful that the fighting has stopped.

But this would, in most contexts, not be a true paraphrase at all of *? Hopefully the fighting has stopped*. Instead, it would usually mean 'Encouragingly, the fighting has stopped' or 'It is a hopeful sign, that the fighting has stopped'. If the word *?? hopedly* or *?? hopeably* had been used instead, (on the model of *admittedly* or *presumably*), a true paraphrase could emerge:

It is hoped/hopeable that the fighting has stopped.

Unfortunately, the words *?? hopedly* and *?? hopeably* do not really exist. (It is possible that the sentence adverb *hopefully* developed among German immigrants in America as the equivalent of the useful German sentence adverb *hoffentlich*. If only *?? hopedly* or *?? hopeably* had been available to them, they would have chosen one or other of them in preference to *hopefully*, since there is another German adverb *hoffnungsvoll* that corresponds to *hopefully* in its old sense of 'in a hopeful way'.)

There are other sentence adverbs besides *hopefully* that end in *-fully*. The commonest are *truthfully*, *delightfully*, *mercifully*, *thankfully*, and *regretfully*. *Truthfully* and *delightfully* can have a true paraphrase:

To be truthful,/It is delightful that the fighting has stopped.

Thankfully and *mercifully* cannot usually be paraphrased in this way, but they do not really have a 'false paraphrase' either in the way that *hopefully* does. So although *thankfully* and *mercifully* are condemned by purists, the condemnation is nothing like as ferocious as that which *hopefully* endures.

Regretfully, finally, is simply a mistake (an increasingly common one) for *regrettably*, which can be paraphrased:

As is regrettable, the fighting has stopped.

Regretfully is condemned, certainly, but it is a mistake that is easily eradicated, whereas *hopefully* is much more deeply rooted in people's vocabularies, and therefore much more challenging to the purists.

This rather complicated explanation of the uniquely 'wrong' formation of *hopefully* is unlikely to have occurred explicitly to most of the purists who condemn the word. But they do perhaps have an intuition of the anomaly, and this would account for their powerful feeling of unease about *hopefully* as a sentence adverb, and their extraordinarily vehement criticism of it.

The third basis for the objection to *hopefully* is the danger of ambiguity it produces. If used at the beginning of a sentence, *hopefully* (like *thankfully*) is unlikely to be misunderstood:

? Hopefully, he will pay his debts.
? Thankfully, he paid his debts.

Clearly *hopefully* and *thankfully* are sentence adverbs here rather than simple adverbs meaning 'in a hopeful spirit' and 'in a thankful spirit'.

And if used at the end of a sentence, they are also unlikely to be misunderstood, since this time they clearly function as ordinary adverbs, in their traditional senses of 'in a hopeful/thankful spirit':

He will pay his debts hopefully.
He paid his debts thankfully.

If placed in the middle of the sentence, *hopefully* and *thankfully* are perhaps ambiguous:

? He will hopefully pay his debts.
? He thankfully paid his debts.

? There is the sphere of literary and literary-philosophic essays addressed either to fellow-mandarins or, hopefully, to a general literate public.

– Professor George Steiner,
The Times Literary Supplement

But context or (in speech) intonation will usually indicate the intended sense. Besides, many unobjectionable sentence adverbs are also open to the charge of ambiguity when placed in the middle of a sentence:

? What she told me frankly can't be repeated.

The last of the standard objections to *hopefully* as a sentence adverb is, simply, that English has no need for the word. Most British people after all, got along without it until the 1970s. There was no real lexical gap for *hopefully* to fill: people used the expressions *I hope/I hope that/I hope so*; *with luck*; and *it is to be hoped/as is hoped*, and so on.

And yet, perhaps *hopefully* has an advantage over all of these. Unlike *I hope*, and so on, *hopefully* is impersonal, and might at times sound either less self-important or more self-assured. In various settings, there would be a distinct difference in tone between these two sentences:

I hope that the Chancellor will now press for a substantial rise in the base rate.
Hopefully the Chancellor will now press for

a substantial rise in the base rate.

According to the context, the first sentence might sound selfish or subjective or needlessly tentative; the second sentence, using *hopefully*, might sound confident or disinterested, and so on.

And whereas *with luck* is perfectly suitable in its place — *With luck we'll catch enough fish to save buying dinner* — in other contexts it would be far less appropriate than *hopefully*:

Hopefully, the jury will clear you on all charges.

With luck, the jury will clear you on all charges.

Finally, *it is to be hoped* and *as is hoped* and so on can be very awkward. The British usage expert H.W. Fowler, in his famous manual *Modern English Usage*, offers two examples in which *hoped* is used in expressions of this sort with 'deplorable results':

... the final arrangements for what is hoped will prove a 'monster demonstration'.

... whose self-sacrificing services for the Empire may be hoped even yet not to be at an end.

To rectify the first of these examples, Fowler recommends:

... the final arrangements for what it is hoped will prove a 'monster demonstration'.

For the second example Fowler recommends:

... whose self-sacrificing services for the Empire are not even yet, it may be hoped, at an end.

Fowler would readily admit that these versions, though now much improved, are still fairly ponderous. He wrote before the rise of *hopefully* as a sentence adverb. If he were writing today, it is possible that he would have approved the streamlining in the following versions:

... the final arrangements for what hopefully will prove a 'monster demonstration'.

... whose self-sacrificing services for the Empire are hopefully even yet not at an end.

The simplicity and (if properly controlled) clarity of *hopefully* may yet tilt the balance decisively in its favour. Certainly it has now gained the acceptance, considered or unconsidered, of many much-admired and careful users of English:

? We are here to celebrate and rejoice that this old jewel in the crown of London is to glimmer and hopefully shine sweetly and brilliantly again.

– Lord Olivier,
speech at the reopening of the
Old Vic theatre

? The hard truth which President Reagan hopefully is beginning to realise is that there is no escape from serious dialogue and negotiation with the Soviet Union.

– Dr David Owen, *The Times*

Yet the purists continue to protest, and as always, it is best to think twice before ignoring their protests.

● *Recommendation   Hopefully*, in the sense of 'it is to be hoped', is now widespread in most varieties of English, and used unreflectively by most speakers. There are some valid objections to it, but these are probably outweighed by its usefulness. Language does change; new words and new senses come and go: *hopefully* is, all things considered, reasonably qualified for admission to the ranks of standard English vocabulary.

Yet purists continue to object to *hopefully* in its new sense, and to do so with surprisingly strong feeling. Whether their case is weak or strong, they persist in it, and may well dismiss as an ignoramus or philistine anyone who uses the shameful word *hopefully* in the 'wrong' sense. If you are worried about receiving such a judgment, or about needlessly distracting your audience or reader, then you should avoid using *hopefully* as a sentence adverb. In fact, you should then consider avoiding it altogether, since your hearers and readers are likely to understand it in its new sense even when you intend it in its older sense of 'in a hopeful way'.

horde   See HOARD.

horrid, horrible, horrific, horrendous, horrifying   All of these adjectives are now widely used — or misused — in ways unrelated to their origins. Their common source is the Latin verb *horrere*, 'to tremble, bristle with fear'. *Horrid*, accordingly, used to mean 'shaggy or bristling'. *Horrible* used to mean, and perhaps should still mean, 'causing horror'.

Like so many adjectives with unfavourable suggestions, however — *dreadful, terrible, frightful*, and so on — these terms have all come to be used as general terms of disapproval, at least in informal speech and writing, and their adverbial forms are used as general intensifiers in unfavourable contexts: ? *The weather is horren-*

dous/horrid/horrible; ? *The prices are horrify-ingly/horrendously high.*

It would be easy to recommend restricting these terms to their 'proper' and original uses. The trouble is, their 'improper' uses are now so much more common that any proper use is in danger of being misunderstood. Make quite sure, if you do use any of the words in their old senses, that your meaning is clear. And before using any of them in their loose modern senses, stop to think whether some more precise or established adjective would not be better suited to what you are saying: *disagreeable*, *unbearable*, *outrageous*, or the like.

See also AWFULLY.

however 1. Take care not to write *how ever* as *however*.

How ever is an emphatic form of *how* in questions: *How ever did you do it?*

✗ Her son remarked jokingly that we ought to be grateful to van der Lubbe, because the burning of the Reichstag had melted the snow. 'Such a nice-looking boy,' observed Frl. Schroeder with a sigh. 'However could he go and do a dreadful thing like that?'
  – Christopher Isherwood,
  Mr Norris Changes Trains

However, as one word, has various distinct and mostly well-understood uses. See WHATEVER and EVER 1 for a more detailed discussion of when to use one word and when to use two.

2. *However* is used most commonly to mean 'even so, nevertheless, in spite of that': *She warned him, however, that she might later withdraw her offer.*

However has the same meaning as *but*, but is not quite interchangeable with it: *but,* unlike *however* in this sense, does not usually need a punctuation mark immediately after it; *however,* unlike *but,* can come in the middle of a clause or at the end of a sentence. (In nonstandard Australian and New Zealand English, *but* is sometimes used at the end of a sentence, but it sounds extremely odd to English speakers elsewhere: *?? It's a nice day — cold, but.*)

Since *but* and *however* are virtually identical in meaning, it is redundant to use both of them in a single clause: ✗ *But I should add, however, that there are drawbacks.* Use either one or the other, but not both. Of course, when *however* is used in any of its other senses, there is no objection to using it with *but*: *But however much you want to win, you must not cheat.*

3. Some pedantic users of English object to the use of *but* and *however* (in the sense of 'never-theless') as the first word of a sentence, on the ground that these words link two contrasting elements, and should be in the same sentence with them. Such an argument has very little to recommend it. *However* can retain its links with an earlier sentence even if separated from it by a full stop.

It is unusual, however (though not wrong), to place *however* at the beginning of a sentence, and also at the end of a long sentence. The usual position for it is near the beginning of a sentence — as in the previous sentence. More specifically, *however* is ideally positioned immediately after the word or phrase that is being held up for contrast. Consider the different emphases in the following sentences:

I, however, cannot understand why James should have voted against us (implying 'You can understand it perhaps, but I cannot').
I cannot, however, understand why James should have voted against us (implying 'I can understand some things, but this I cannot understand').
I cannot understand, however, why James should have voted against us (a general contrast).
I cannot understand why James, however, should have voted against us (implying 'I can understand why Robert should have voted against us, but not why James should').

4. Standard English still requires *however* (in the sense of 'nevertheless') to be surrounded by punctuation: a comma either side, or one comma and either a full stop or a semicolon. There is a tendency, however, to do away with the commas around *however,* in particular the comma before *however*. The previous sentence, for example, might have begun *There is a tendency however, to do away with the commas,* or *There is a tendency however to do away with the commas.* This is in keeping with the modern trend towards streamlining the text by reducing the amount of punctuation in it. (The pros and cons of this trend are discussed at PUNCTUATION.)

One argument against omitting the comma following *however* is that this would give rise to temporary ambiguity, leading the reader to assume perhaps that *however* was being used to mean 'by whatever means' rather than 'but'. A sentence beginning *However he chose to tackle the problem,* ..., for example, might be expected to continue ... *he was doomed to failure.* If it in fact continues ... *and now he has to take the consequences,* the reader is thrown into temporary bewilderment — a needless distraction that could have been avoided by placing a comma after *However*.

human, humane See INHUMAN.

hung, hanged Traditionally, pictures are *hung*, and people, when subjected to capital punishment, are *hanged*. This distinction is being eroded, but careful users still observe it. In the rough justice of the Wild West, men were *hung* rather than *hanged*, and this regional preference lingers in many English dialects.

hurricane See CYCLONE.

hyper- See HYPO-.

hyphen 1. The hyphen (-) looks like a short dash, but hyphen and dash are used very differently. Basically, the dash separates whereas the hyphen unites.

The use of the hyphen varies somewhat between British and American English, and, more significantly, from author to author and from publisher to publisher. So the following discussion is concerned with what is generally true, and offers recommendations rather than rules.

2. The hyphen can be used between a word and a prefix, suffix, or other word-element. Its main function is to prevent ambiguity or awkward-looking combinations of letters.

a. Use of the hyphen before a *suffix* is rare nowadays, but is still needed sometimes to prevent sequences of more than two identical letters: *bull-like*.

b. After a prefix or other word-element, the hyphen will be found most often:

i. When the main part of the word begins with a capital letter: *un-American*.

ii. When the main part of the word begins with the letter that ends the prefix or combining form: *pre-emptive*; *counter-revolutionary*.

iii. When the prefix is repeated: *anti-anticommunism*, *sub-subcommittee*.

iv. When the hyphen helps to prevent confusion between a new formation and a conventional one with the same prefix: *re-creation* (not *recreation*).

> The black children who watched the hut from afar and scuttled, as if her glance were a stone thrown among them, re-formed a little way off.
>
> – Nadine Gordimer, *July's People*

(In speech, the prefix of such formations generally has a stronger stress, and often a fuller vowel

sound, than the unhyphenated form.)

c. In addition, some prefixes and combining forms are particularly likely to take hyphens. These include *ex-*: *ex-wife*, *ex-directory*; and *non-* (particularly when joined to a word beginning with a vowel): *non-interference*.
See SPELLING.

3. The hyphen is also used to unite separate words into compound forms that function as a single unit. Such compound forms can also be written with spaces between their components or even as a single word with neither spaces nor hyphens:

head waiter	tax payer
head-waiter	tax-payer
headwaiter	taxpayer

American English probably uses the hyphen less often in these cases than British English does. Both British and American English tend to avoid single-word compounds that would show strings of more than three written consonants. So, whereas *boyfriend* is happily written as one word, *?girlfriend* has the awkward sequence *rlfr* and is therefore less common than *girl friend* or *girl-friend*.

Compounds that are widely used are entered in dictionaries, especially when their meaning cannot be directly inferred from the meanings of their parts. So if you are in doubt about the most common way of writing a compound, look it up in a reputable dictionary.

Despite different conventions in the hyphenation of compounds, some general tendencies can be identified:

a. If the compound consists of more than two words or elements, it is most unlikely to be fused into a single solid compound: it retains its traditional hyphens (*will-o'-the-wisp*, *mother-in-law*) or spaces (*son of a gun*).

b. On the other hand, compounds consisting of two words are increasingly being fused into a single solid word: *boardroom, boatrace, jawbone, postgraduate, standby, takeover, weekend, wellbeing, wideawake*.

c. A hyphen is often well-advised if it helps to avoid ambiguity:

> a Turkish-bath attendant/a Turkish bath-attendant
> a French-history teacher/a French history-teacher
> After finishing-school in Switzerland, she went home to Leeds./After finishing school in Switzerland . . .

Here is an amusing example of a possible

misreading caused by the omission of a hyphen:

✗ When he returned, he said there had been clear evidence of sheep rustling on the mountainside.
> – quoted in Fritz Spiegl's
> *Keep Taking The Tabloids*

This should read *evidence of sheep-rustling.*

d. Hyphens tend to be used when the latter or last word in the compound ends with a suffix, especially *-ed, -ing,* and *-er*: *hang-gliding; left-handed; awkward-looking; organ-grinder.*

e. Hyphens are usual when the compound functions as an adjective before a noun, even though it would not take hyphens elsewhere. So: *a child four years old* but *a four-year-old child; a fairy tale* but *a fairy-tale romance; free trade* but *a free-trade agreement.*

Hyphens are particularly useful when the compound has an unusual form: *a difference between 'in-order-to' actions and 'as-a-result-of' actions.*

Note that the hyphen in these constructions in writing often corresponds to a change in the stress-pattern in speech. Note too that the hyphen here is again useful in preventing confusion: there is a great deal of difference between *four year-old horses* and *four-year-old horses*, or between *a fast food-worker* (a food-worker who is fast) and *a fast-food worker* (a person who works in a fast-food factory or restaurant).

There are two important exceptions to the tendency to hyphenate compounds placed before nouns.

First, if the first element of the compound is an adverb ending in *-ly*, the hyphen is generally not used: *a widely known expert.* But if the adverb does not end in *-ly*, the hyphen is used: *a well-known expert.* And without the hyphen, the phrase *a little-known expert* would mean something rather different.

Secondly, when both or all the elements of the compound begin with capital letters, the hyphen is usually omitted: *a Northern Ireland spokesman* (but *an all-Ireland conference*).

And remember that if the compound is used after the noun, it is less likely to take hyphens: *an up-to-date report* but *a report that is up to date.*

f. Hyphens are common when the compound contains an apostrophe and has developed a figurative sense: *cat's-eye; crow's-nest.*

g. Hyphens are also frequent in compounds whose elements are coordinated, so that none is less important or subordinate: *a fighter-bomber, the secretary-treasurer; a psychological-sociological approach.*

h. Hyphens are commonly used when a compound changes its part of speech. That is in effect what happens when the compound noun *fairy tale* becomes a compound adjective in *a fairy-tale romance.* It also happens when a compound verb (verb and adverb) gives rise to adjectives and nouns. Thus *to run down*, with various meanings, yields the adjective *run-down* and a noun written *run-down* or *rundown.* Conversely, a compound noun such as *a cold shoulder* can give rise to the hyphenated verb *to cold-shoulder.* This change in function and spelling has a corresponding change, in speech, of stress or intonation.

4. When several hyphenated compounds share an element, that element need not be repeated, but the hyphens should be. So: *French-speaking and Italian-speaking* or *French- and Italian-speaking; a three-course meal or a four-course meal* or *a three- or four-course meal.*

> Pliny talked of Tuticorin; Marco Polo called it 'noble'. For centuries, it was famous as a pearl- and conch-fishing centre as well as a port.
> – Gavin Young, *The Observer*

A hyphen is sometimes used too to represent the omitted part of a solid compound — that is, a compound intended as one word rather than as hyphenated: *both micro- and macroeconomics; inter- and intranational.*

And the hyphen can stand in for the first part of the compound, not just the second: *a three-wheeled and -doored vehicle.*

> ... Arnold's insistence on allowing his craftsmen or -women to work with the original under their eyes.
> – Sir Geoffrey Keynes,
> *The Gates of Memory*

These examples show that it is occasionally possible for a hyphen to be followed or preceded by a space.

5. Compound numbers between *twenty-one* and *ninety-nine*, if they are spelt out, are written with hyphens. So: *seven hundred and forty-five* (745); *forty-five thousand and fifty-three* (45,053).

The same holds true for fractions whose numerators and denominators are between *one* and *twenty*: *three-quarters* (¾), *seven-sixteenths* (⁷⁄₁₆). For fractions whose numerators or denominators are between *twenty-one* and *ninety-nine*, each part is treated separately, with whatever hyphens are appropriate, and there are no hyphens between numerator and denominator: *seven sixty-firsts* (⁷⁄₆₁), *thirty-five ninety-eighths* (³⁵⁄₉₈). Finally, fractions whose numerators or denominators are larger than *ninety-nine* should be written as numbers rather than words wherever possible, which avoids the problem of hyphenation. Note, however, that *hundredth/s*, *thousandth/s*, *millionth/s*, and so on, can be preceded by a hyphen when they are part of the denominator of a fraction: *three six-hundredths of a second* (³⁄₆₀₀).

See NUMBER STYLE.

6. When speech is represented in writing, dashes or ellipses ('dots') are used to show hesitation between words; but hyphens are used to show the repetition of individual sounds in a word, as in stuttering or stammering:

> D-D-Damme, I don't know what you are d-d-driving at, or what you mean, but you had better g-g-go where you belong!
> – Billy, in Herman Melville (U.S.),
> *Billy Budd*

7. The hyphen is sometimes used to link the beginning and ending points of a series:

> *pages 34-63*; *the London-Paris-Bonn route*

The meaning is approximately 'to', or 'up to and including'. It can also mean 'versus': *the Liverpool-Newcastle match.*

In such constructions the dash is often preferred to the hyphen. In printing, a special 'en-dash' is often used, which is intermediate in length between a hyphen and a proper dash (an em-dash). In writing and typing, however, a hyphen serves to represent the en-dash.

8. A hyphen is used when a word has to be broken at the end of a line of print:

> They both lived a decidedly non-
> conformist life, even by the rebel-
> lious standards of the times.

When a word is broken in this way you cannot always tell whether its hyphen would be there if the word were all on one line: *non(-)conformist,* in the example above, might have been intended as a single, unbroken word. There are few hard-and-fast rules about end-of-line hyphenation that are both simple and universally accepted. Most publishers agree on the following guidelines, however:

● Never break single-syllable words at the end of a line: × *streng-ths*, × *watch-ed*.

● Generally, if there are two successive, independently sounded vowels or two successive independently sounded consonants, break the word between them: *con-tiguity, devi-ation.*

● When a single vowel forms a full syllable in the middle of a word, break after rather than

before it: *sepa-rate* rather than ? *sep-arate.*

● Avoid breaking a word after the first letter or before the last letter or the last two letters: × *a-thwart*; × *pati-o*; ? *happi-ly.*

● If a compound is already hyphenated, break it at the hyphen — *un-American* — rather than elsewhere: × *un-Ameri-can.*

● If a compound is fused into a single word, break it between the elements: *tender-hearted* not ?? *ten-derhearted.*

● If possible, avoid breaking a word if it produces a distracting unrelated word or an odd-looking syllable either side: × *ath-wart*, × *bed-raggled*, × *ex-tractor*, × *ear-nest*, × *leg-end*, × *the-rapist*, × *Beeth-oven*, × *hear-tily*, × *rear-mament.* (Several of these are disqualified anyway by one or more of the guidelines already listed, or because they are broken in the middle of syllables rather than between syllables. A good dictionary should indicate the syllable-breaks within a word.)

● If possible, avoid breaking abbreviations, numbers, dates, and names.

There is perhaps a surviving difference in practice between British and American publishers. Americans tend to divide syllables simply according to the pronunciation; the British often divide syllables according to the history and structure of the word. The word *structure*, in fact, might be divided differently: always *struc-ture* in North America, and (sometimes) *struct-ure* in Britain (the elements of the word being the suffix *-ure* and the stem *-struct-* as in *con-struct*). The trend is clearly in favour of the American system, however, and even British dictionaries now tend to use it.

Typesetting is frequently computer-controlled now. The computers are programmed with instructions on hyphenation, and the word-breaks are made automatically. The hyphenation-programs are not perfect, and many doubtful word-breaks creep into the text. Perhaps this will lead in due course to a rather more easygoing attitude to word-breaks in general. In typing and handwriting, however, it is best for the present to observe the rules outlined above.

9. Dictionaries enter word-forming elements with hyphens: *pre-, -graph, -ness, tele-, -i-*. The hyphens show the place or places where the word-forming element 'plugs in' to the word it helps to form: *pre-Cambrian, niceness, matrilineal, telegraph.* Sometimes the hyphen will appear in the final word (as it does in *pre-Cambrian*), sometimes not (as in *niceness*).

10. The interplay of these various conventions can produce some odd results: ? *unself-*

conscious; *? pre-First World War*; *? ex-Justice of the Peace*; *? the Old Bailey-Oxford Circus bus.* If the effect is intolerably odd, then the answer is either to hyphenate all the elements of the compound, or to reword the phrase altogether. So: *? a pre-First World War ambulance* might become *? a pre-First-World-War ambulance* or, preferably, *a pre-1914 ambulance* or *an ambulance from before the First World War.*

hypo-, hyper- The prefixes *hypo-* and *hyper-* come from the Greek *hupo-* and *huper-*, and mean respectively 'under, incomplete' and 'over, exceeding'. So *hypothermia* means 'excessively *low* body temperature'; *hyperthermia* means 'excessively *high* body temperature', or 'high fever'. (The *-thermia* element comes from Greek *therme*, 'heat'.) *Hypothermia* is the more common word; *hyperthermia* tends to be reserved for technical and medical uses, but *hypothermia* makes the news — especially during severe winters. Since the two terms are often pronounced similarly in British English, *hypothermia* is sometimes misspelt as its opposite — a mistake that could be very dangerous.

The spelling of the word *hypochondriac* might seem surprising in the light of the prefixes *hypo-* and *hyper-*. A *hypochondriac* exaggerates or imagines ailments, and is excessive and neurotic about them — 'hyper' about them, to use the slang term. You might therefore expect the word to be spelt × *hyperchondriac*. In fact, the word comes from the Greek term for 'a belly' — the area of the body that was thought to be the seat of melancholy (and hence of *hypochondria*). The Greek word is *hupokhondrion,* and describes the position of the belly under the cartilage of the breastbone: *hupo-,* 'under' + *khondros,* 'cartilage'.

hypocritical, hypercritical *Hypocritical* is sometimes misspelt as *hypercritical*. The two words have quite different meanings and are pronounced differently: /**hip**pə-**krit**tik'l/ and /**hī**pər-**krit**tik'l/ respectively. Unlike *hypothermia* and *hyperthermia,* however, they are not opposites, though their prefixes *hypo-* and *hyper-* might suggest that they are.

Hypercritical means 'excessively critical', especially about trivial matters. Its prefix, from the Greek *huper-,* means 'over, excessively'; *critical* goes back, through Latin, to the Greek *kritikos,* 'able to discern, critical', from *krinein,* 'to separate, choose'.

> But I am not married to radio — only living with it: a compulsive listener and, I admit, a hypercritical one (though as an occasional broadcaster I have to be careful what I criticise).
> — Fritz Spiegl, *The Listener*

Hypocritical, of course, does not mean 'insufficiently critical'. The word goes back via Old French and Late Latin to the Greek *hupokrinein* (from *hupo-,* 'under' + *krinein,* 'to separate'), which had several meanings: 'to separate gradually, answer, answer one's fellow actor, play a part'.

The words *hypocritical* and *hypercritical* were by no means parallel in development, therefore. Each began by making use of different emphases of *krinein*. *Hypocritical* now means 'playing a part, grossly insincere, feigning beliefs or feelings or virtues'.

> Accordingly, a journalist taking a high prescriptive line about correct English may seem to some as hypocritical and irritating a spectacle as Satan reproving sin.
> — Philip Howard, *New Words for Old*

Note that *hypocrite,* /**hip**pə-krit/, referring to a person who pretends in this way, is spelt with an *e* at the end; the noun *hypocrisy,* referring to such insincerity, is spelt *-sy* at the end, not *-cy*.

hysterical See HISTRIONIC.

I

-ian See -ITE, -IAN.

-ic, -ical These two suffixes are very common in the formation of adjectives. Some adjectives can exist in only one form or the other — *Gaelic, specific, ferric; spherical, numerical*. There is less flexibility now than in the past — it would be extremely old-fashioned to use *dynamical, fantastical*, and *tragical* today on the one hand, or *fanatic, hypothetic*, and *hysteric*, as adjectives, on the other. And there is slightly less flexibility in British usage than in American — Americans can still use *geologic* as well as *geological*, for instance, and say *geologic time* where British English has *geological time*.

The dominance of one form over the other seems quite arbitrary: *grammatical, phonetic, lexical, linguistic, semantic, syntactic, lexicographic/al*. One general tendency can be identified, however — *-ical* tends to be the preferred form for the adjective if the *-ic* form can be used as a noun: *logical, rhetorical, fanatical*, and *hysterical* are the standard adjectives, with *logic, rhetoric, fanatic*, and *hysteric* being the nouns. One obvious exception to this tendency is *public*, which is both adjective and noun.

Note that whether you start from *-ic* or from *-ical*, the derived adverb ends in *-ically: grammatical + -ly, phonetic + -ally. Public* is again the major exception: the adverb is spelt *publicly*. Another possible exception is *politic* ('prudent'), whose adverb, if used at all, would tend to be spelt *politicly* in order to distinguish it from *politically*, the common adverb of *political* ('relating to politics').

Despite the tendency for one form to prevail over the other, a large number of adjectives survive in both the *-ic* and *-ical* forms, with virtually no difference in meaning: *lyric, lyrical; metric, metrical; philosophic, philosophical*.

With some adjectives, however, the *-ic* and *-ical* forms have diverged in meaning. In general, the *-ic* adjective is rather more literal, suggesting an actual example of something referred to in the base element; whereas the *-ical* form is looser, suggesting a mere tendency towards that something. So *a comic actor* is one who acts in a comedy, or deliberately creates comedy; *a com-*

ical child is one who behaves *as if* acting in a comedy, and creates comedy unwittingly. Similarly, *diabolic* refers literally to the devil — *diabolic rites* — whereas *diabolical* refers only figuratively to the devil, or to devil-like things: *a diabolical liberty; diabolical malice*.

Similarly *lyrical* can be used more loosely than *lyric* can, *electrical* than *electric, magical* than *magic, mythical* than *mythic, philosophical* than *philosophic, stoical* than *stoic*, and so on. One exception, perhaps, is *cubic/al*, where the *-al* form is the one that usually refers to a cube, leaving *cubic* to refer to volume in general.

In some cases, the divergence between the *-ic* and *-ical* is so great that the two adjectives can be treated as virtually unrelated: *politic* again ('prudent, advisable') is quite distinct from *political*, and *economical* ('thrifty, or of good value') from *economic*.

See CLASSIC; COMIC; ECONOMIC; HISTORIC.

-ics *Politics is* or *politics are*? The answer is quite straightforward. Nouns ending in *-ics* should take a singular verb if they denote a specific science, art, or field of study: *Politics is very poorly taught in schools; What is Linguistics?* (the title of a book by Professor David Crystal, a British linguist and usage expert).

On the other hand, nouns ending in *-ics* should take a plural verb if they denote a set of practices, operations, activities, or qualities: *Politics are bedevilling life in the office; His verbal gymnastics make my head spin; The acoustics in this hall are very poor*.

The following quotations illustrate two correct usages — one singular and one plural — and one incorrect usage, an example of the common error of treating the academic subject as a plural:

> It also appeared that classics was taught in 75 per cent of independent schools, but in only 47 per cent of comprehensives.
>
> Even at Cambridge, classics is a shadow of its former self.
> – Professor John Vincent, *The Times*

> It was a time uniquely suited to his talents: but he took his chances. His politics were genuine enough, neither as cynical nor as

self-seeking as his detractors, then or later, made out.

– Alan Watkins, *The Listener*

✗ School prizes for English literature were kept and read throughout life. Mathematics (as distinct from English) were self-taught. There was no difficulty about this in the days before educational theorists were known.

– Professor R.F.V. Heuston, in *Lord Denning: The Judge and the Law*

Note that the choice of verb allows you to distinguish between an academic subject and the phenomena assembled or investigated by that subject: *Economics is a complex subject*; *The economics of industrial development are complex*.

Two cues might help you decide whether to use a singular or plural verb: if the complement is a singular noun, then the verb is likely to be singular too: *Politics is her favourite subject*. If the *-ics* noun is preceded by *the, these, my, vigorous*, or any other qualifying word (except *a*), then the verb is likely to be a plural verb: *His politics are quite abominable*. Not that these two cues cover all cases: in many sentences, in fact, either a singular or plural verb would be appropriate.

identify   The pattern *to identify oneself with a cause*, in the sense 'to support a cause', has been established for over 200 years. The pattern *to identify with a cause/protest/politician*, in the sense 'to support, participate in, sympathise with, belong to, or the like', is far more recent and less widely accepted: *? I really identified with that last speaker*; *? She has for years been identified with charity campaigns*. The phrases *empathised with* (or *agreed with* or *shared the views of*) and *associated with* should perhaps replace *identified with* in these two examples.

Perhaps modern psychology is to blame for this vogue use of *identify with*.

One widespread use of this modern pattern is in relation to characters in books, plays, or films: *It is easy to identify with the hero of this novel* — not just to like him, but to find echoes of one's own life in his, and to imagine oneself in his position — in a word to *empathise* with him. There used to be, and probably still is, a preference among purists for inserting the reflexive pronoun here and restoring the earlier pattern: *It is easy to identify oneself with the hero*. But modern idiom has given its blessing to the streamlined pattern, and it can be considered acceptable in all but the most formal contexts.

i.e.   See E.G., I.E.

if   **1.**   *If* is sometimes followed by the usual indicative form of the verb (*If I was ...*) and sometimes by a subjunctive form (*If I be ...*; *If I were ...*).

The difference, broadly speaking, is this: if the condition is a purely hypothetical one, or an impossible one, or at least an extremely remote one, then the subjunctive (*were*) is often used: *If my husband were a woman, he would understand my feelings a bit better*, as opposed to *If my husband was a liar, it was for my sake* or *If my husband is a liar, I'll soon catch him out*. (Note that in the middle example, the *was* actually refers to the past, whereas in the first example, the *were* is 'timeless' and does not refer to the past specifically.)

The presence of the words *would, should, could,* or *might* is a very useful pointer. If any of them appears in the sentence, then the subjunctive form may well be needed in the *if*-clause. The fixed phrase *If I were you* (or *he* or *she*), for instance, is almost always followed by *I would/could/should* or *I might* or simply *I'd*.

In the following example, the subjunctive *were* would have been preferable to the indicative *was* — the condition is very much hypothetical, as the presence of *would* suggests:

? You have chosen to violate this convention. A violation would be justified only if the Monarch was guilty of a flagrant breach of her duty to be above partisan issues.

– Dr Anthony Kenny, letter to *The Times*

In old-fashioned English, the subjunctive *be* (or *be not* in the negative) is used after *if* when the writer or speaker is being tentative or doubtful: *If this be true, we are doomed*. Other verbs can be used in the same way: *It is a hopeful sign if his temperature fall* (rather than *falls*). Modern idiom would prefer the indicative form here — *If this is true*; *if his temperature falls* — or at least the insertion of a *should*: *If this should be true*; *if his temperature should fall*.

Note that the subjunctive and past indicative forms are identical in the plural: *If our husbands were women, they would understand us better* (subjunctive), and *If our husbands were liars, it was for our sake* (indicative). (See also SUBJUNCTIVE; WAS).

2. For a simple conjunction, *if* can cause a surprising amount of ambiguity when used in senses other than the basic 'in the event that'.

If used as a synonym of *whether, if* could be misinterpreted: *? Tell me if you want an answer* might be taken to mean 'If you want me to give you the answer, you will first have to tell me something I want to know' (see WHETHER).

If used as a synonym of *although, if* could again be misinterpreted. *? I find her songs enjoyable, if slightly sentimental* could be taken to mean 'Only the rather sentimental songs appeal to me'. Note that you can say both *That statement is libellous if false* (= if it is false) and *That statement is libellous if true* (= even though it is true). Or — a different kind of misreading — *? The badger community was devastated, if not extinguished, by the tuberculosis epidemic* could be taken to mean not just 'although not extinguished', but also 'and perhaps even extinguished'.

3. When the conditional clause of a sentence begins with *if*, there is a temptation to begin the conclusion clause with *then*. This *then* should be used very sparingly, however — only in very long sentences, or when particular emphasis is required: *If you insult me, if you rob me, and if you strike me, then I might well begin to defend myself.*

In normal short conditional sentences, however, the use of *then* usually betrays an immature style, and is best avoided: *? If you swim in this stretch of the river, then you are putting yourself in danger.*

See also WHETHER.

if and when It is very seldom that this phrase really needs to be called upon. It is used in legal contexts as a failsafe formula to cover all possibilities twice over, but in ordinary usage there is no need for double protection of this kind: *if* implies *when*. If there is a doubt about something, it is enough to say *if*: *If the Prime Minister calls an early election, you'll be well-prepared for it.* If there is no doubt about something, it is enough to say *when*: *When the next election takes place, you'll be well-prepared for it.* In neither case is any benefit secured by using *if and when*.

A case could be made for *if or when,* however. Suppose you wish to remain quite uncommitted in your views about a future event, suggesting neither that it is merely hypothetical nor that it is certain to happen, you might convey a neutral tone by using *if or when*: *If or when the Prime Minister calls an early election, you'll be well-prepared for it.*

The same considerations apply to the phrases *as and when* and *unless and until*.

ilk Purists object to the modern extended senses of the phrase *of that ilk*.

The word *ilk* is of Old English origin, and is related to *like* (the preposition). In early modern English it came to mean 'same, identical', but it died out three or four hundred years ago, except in the Scottish phrase *of that ilk*. This means, strictly, 'of the place or property having the same name'. So: *Ruthven of that ilk* would refer to the owner (or clan-chief), named Ruthven, of the estate called Ruthven.

It is easy to see how the modern extended senses came about: *of that ilk* would be understood as 'of that family', or 'of that set', and hence 'of that sort'. And so such uses developed as *? I don't like hearties of that ilk, ? I love films of that ilk*, and — even more objectionable to the purists — *? I don't like supercilious hearties of his ilk, ? I'd ban him and his ilk from this club*, and so on.

? It should be in the knapsack of every journalist — certainly I shall insist on the BBC's young writers devouring it. (I would not expect MPs and their ilk to wish to improve their already perfect selves.)
— Alan Protheroe, *The Listener*

? I am very proud of my nephew — war is war, but your paper, and those of similar ilk, seem to think it would have been all right if the Conqueror had been sunk instead.
— Cynthia B. Kerre, letter to *The Observer*

Nevertheless, the extended senses and forms seem firmly established in English idiom now, and are accepted by most modern dictionaries. If you are still hesitant, however, it is easy enough to speak of *hearties of his type/breed/stripe* (*hearties of his kidney* is a very old-fashioned alternative these days, and here creates a rather bizarre mixed metaphor as well), or of *him and his like, him and his sort, him and his lot, the likes of him*, and so on.

illegal, illegitimate, illicit, unlawful These four adjectives all have slightly different ranges of meaning.

Illegal means 'against the law, specifically prohibited by law':

'I hope you don't plan anything illegal.'
'I have never planned anything illegal in my life,' Aunt Augusta said. 'How could I plan anything of the kind when I have never read any of the laws and have no idea what they are?'
— Graham Greene, *Travels with My Aunt*

It usually refers to the law of the land — *an illegal monopoly* — but it can refer to regulations, as of a sport: *an illegal hold in wrestling.*

Illegitimate has a wider range. It can mean 'not recognised by law' — *an illegitimate child.* But it also means, more generally, 'not authorised by justice, propriety, reason, or logic' — *illegitimate objections*; *an illegitimate inference from the known facts.* Both *illegal* and *illegitimate* go back to the Latin *lex*, 'law'.

Unlawful goes back to the Old English *lagu*, 'a set of rules'. The word is rather old-fashioned now, and used mainly in legal formulations such as *unlawful carnal knowledge.* It means much the same as *illegal*, but has a slightly wider reach, referring to the law of God, not just to the law of man: *Eating pork is unlawful both in Islam and in Judaism.*

Illicit comes from the Latin *licere*, 'to be permitted', as does the word *unlicensed* — and 'unlicensed' is roughly what *illicit* means:

> In one sub-division of the district, so it was rumoured, the Indian magistrate had ... fined liberals and moderates, illicitly collected revenues and hidden away money that should have been paid into the treasury.
> — Paul Scott,
> *The Jewel in the Crown*

An *illicit* activity is an activity that in some circumstances is permitted, though not in this instance: gambling, for example, or diamond-dealing. Contrast this with an *illegal* activity, which is very likely to be prohibited in all circumstances: cock-fighting is now *illegal*; poker-playing is not *illegal,* though a particular game of poker may be *illicit* if played outside a licensed gaming club. In certain Islamic countries, you might be convicted for the *illegal* sale of alcohol; in the West, you might be convicted for the *illicit* sale of alcohol if you sold homemade whisky distilled in an *illicit* still. Any sexual relationship outside marriage may be considered *illicit*, but *an illicit relationship* typically involves secrecy or deception as well:

> To any other type of tourist accommodation I soon grew to prefer the Functional Motel — clean, neat, safe nooks, ideal places for sleep, argument, reconciliation, insatiable illicit love.
> — Vladimir Nabokov, *Lolita*

Note that the positive forms *legal, legitimate,* and *lawful* are all in common use, but that *licit* is now very rare.

See also ELICIT; LEGAL.

image The word *image* suggests a picture, in reality or in the mind. Its vogue sense of 'reputation, a public impression' has attracted criticism: *Going bald is bad for my image*; *Advertisers are trying to give English wine a glamorous image.*

This sense is now well established, and useful in its way — it cannot really be replaced by *reputation.* The objection is not that it is an incorrect usage but that it is an overworked usage. Use the word sparingly.

imaginary, imaginative *Imaginary* means 'produced by the imagination, unreal, imagined'. *Imaginative* means 'having, or revealing, a strong creative imagination'. So, a fictitious companion invented by *an imaginative child* would be *an imaginary child.* A story can be both *imaginary*, if it is a made-up fiction, and *imaginative*, if it reveals a special creativity. Note that *imaginative*, though usually approving, is sometimes used ironically: *Your version of events is — how shall I put it? — somewhat imaginative.*

Take care not to use either word in the place of the other.

imbue You *imbue* something or someone *with* a quality:

> Ivory and Jhabvala deal well with the comic side. They also make the central characters sympathetic, imbuing their relationship with real feeling.
> — Philip French, *The Observer*

You cannot *imbue* a quality *into* something or someone: ✕ *They imbued real feeling into the relationship.* Use *instil* instead for this second pattern.

immigrate, immigrant See EMIGRATE.

imminent, immanent See EMINENT.

immoral, amoral These two adjectives are sometimes confused; though there is in fact a clear distinction between them.

Immoral applies to situations or activities that are contrary to normal moral standards. It means roughly 'wicked or corrupt': *Such wastage is almost immoral*; *an immoral exploitation of his friend's gullibility.* When applied to people, it often specifically suggests sexual behaviour as the object of disapproval: *In a more traditional society she would be considered a most immoral young woman.* In all these examples, the disapproving or pejorative tone of the adjective is clear.

Amoral, on the other hand, involves not a

defiance of moral standards but the kind of judgments to which moral standards do not apply. If *immoral* implies low morals, then *amoral* implies no morals. When applied to situations, *amoral* means 'outside the sphere of morality'. Theoretically, it can be neutral in tone: *I don't consider vegetarianism to be an ethical question — it's a simple, amoral matter of personal preference.* But such phrases as *an amoral person* or *amoral behaviour* are usually strongly condemnatory: people who are uninfluenced by morality are often felt to be capable of anything in furthering their own interests.

Chandler, one notes, is accusing Cain — exactly as Marlowe accuses Terry Lennox in *The Long Goodbye* — of having an amoral attitude towards murder.
— Bill Greenwell, *The Fiction Magazine*

Pierre Clergue was the priest — but also a Cathar — masquerading as a pillar of the establishment. Corrupt, amoral, ruthless, he had friends in high places who delayed, but could not finally prevent, his imprisonment for heresy.
— Andrew Sanger, *The Observer*

immune *Immune* is followed by *to* in the senses of 'resistant to (a disease)', 'not responsive, unaffected by': *immune to smallpox, immune to the attractions of city life*. When *immune* means 'legally exempt' or 'protected from risk or inconvenience', it is followed by *from*: *goods immune from excise duty*; *Few journalists are immune from commercial pressures.*

Our clergy are not immune from these self-contradictions either: Bishop Ullathorne when asked to recommend a book on humility, answered without hesitation, 'Best book on humility? I wrote it myself.'
— Sir Brian Young, quoted in *The Listener*

Sometimes, too, one can be *immune from disease*. In fact, the overlap of the various meanings has produced some confusion in the use of prepositions, as the following extracts show:

The Finns themselves are not immune from the melancholy that afflicts all northern peoples during the long, dark winter.
— Richard West, *The Spectator*

? There was no suggestion that the protesters should be immune to the normal consequences of law-breaking; nor, I think, did any of the many teachers who protested

invoke academic freedom, which was in no way at stake.
— Conor Cruise O'Brien, *The Observer*

He would have liked to exercise over Fotheringham, as over Pringle, a domination, but a certain protean acuteness, well camouflaged, made Fotheringham immune from his influences.
— Anthony Powell, *Afternoon Men*

? We're none of us immune to redundancy ...
— advertisement in *The Observer*

The verb *to immunise* is followed by *against*: *ought to be immunised against diphtheria.*

Take care not to confuse *immunity* with *impunity*. *Impunity* is more restricted in meaning, referring to exemption from punishment — *commits theft with impunity* — or, more loosely, freedom from danger or regret: *My pet leopard can be cuddled with impunity.* You can speak of *immunity from/to tetanus*, but you usually enjoy *impunity* by itself, not *from* or *to* anything.

Immune and *immunity* derive simply from the Latin *immunis*, 'exempt'. *Impunity* comes from the Latin *impunitas*, 'impunity', from *impunis*, 'not punished', from *in-*, 'not' + *poena*, 'penalty, pain', from Greek *poina*, 'punishment'.

impact The original sense of *impact* is 'a collision; the striking of one body against another'. Its Latin roots are *in-*, 'against' + *pangere*, 'to drive in'. By a natural extension, the word came to refer to the effect of the collision, whether a literal or metaphorical collision: *the impact of science on religion.* By a further and less acceptable extension, it has come to be used of any effect — in fact, as a synonym of *effect* or *influence*: *the impact of pornography on the crime figures*; *the impact of the drought on the fertility of the soil.*

This sense is probably too well entrenched now to dislodge, though careful speakers will still favour *effect* or *influence* in its place. The real worry is not so much its occasional use in the new sense, but its overuse. As a vogue word, on the lips of every other politician and advertiser and official spokesman, the word is in danger of losing all impact.

As a verb, *to impact* (stressed on the second syllable rather than the first) has been used, since 1935 or before, to mean 'to have an impact': *How has science impacted on religion?*; *inner-city areas impacted by mass unemployment.* In British English, this usage is considered an Americanism, though in North America too it is sometimes discouraged. *To affect* is generally preferable to *to impact (on)*.

impassive, impassioned See DISPASSIONATE.

imperial, imperious, imperative These three adjectives are closely related in origin, all going back to the Latin *imperare*, 'to command'. And they do share certain shades of meaning. But today they are used in quite distinct ways.

Imperial means primarily 'relating to an empire or emperor': *the imperial crown*; *an imperial decree*.

> Chinese silver poured out to pay for the opium, unbalancing the flow of trade and crippling the national economy for the next 75 years. To overcome the imperial objections — the emperor ordered 20,000 cases of British opium destroyed — and ensure perpetual free trade, Britain defeated China in the first Opium War.
> — *The Observer*

In an extended sense *imperial* means 'like an emperor, commanding or majestic': *the imperial bearing of the ladies in Gainsborough's portraits.*

> His life became an allegory of genius transcending the accidents of poverty and race; simple and modest in his personality, imperially authoritative in his work, he had by the end of his life grown into an internationally accepted symbol not only of jazz but of good will and good humour.
> — Philip Larkin, *The Observer*

And *Imperial* refers, of course, to the traditional system of weights and measures — pounds, inches, pints, and so on — as distinct from the metric system.

Imperious has a more negative tone. It means 'arrogant or overbearing', or even 'domineering or dictatorial': *a haughty and imperious manner*; *Her imperious demands almost provoked a strike.*

> She summoned a shadowy waiter with an imperious hand.
> — Anita Brookner, *Hotel du Lac*

> Her mind was upon action, and action was what she believed in. Striding to the door, she flung it open and waved imperiously for Mesterbein to return. She swung round, hands on hips, and stared at Charlie, and her big pale eyes were a dangerous and alarming void.
> — John le Carré, *The Little Drummer Girl*

Imperative means primarily 'relating to or expressing a command or plea'; in grammar, more specifically, it refers to the form or mood of a verb expressing a command or request. In a slightly wider sense it means 'abrupt, peremptory': *an imperative tone of voice that was impossible to ignore.* But it is probably used most frequently today in the sense of 'vitally necessary, crucial' or even 'obligatory': *It is imperative that we inform HQ at once*; *This is imperative repair work.*

Note two further small differences. Both *imperial* and (more commonly) *imperative* are nouns as well, each having several senses related to their adjectival senses. *Imperious*, however, cannot be used as a noun; the noun derived from it is *imperiousness*. And in pronunciation, *imperative* is the odd-man-out this time, having a short *e* — /im-**perr**ətiv/ — whereas *imperial* and *imperious* both have a long /ee/ sound: /im-**peer**-i-əl/ and /im-**peer**-i-əss/.

implement The current verb sense of this word, dating back to the beginning of the 19th century, derives perhaps from its use as a Scottish legal term, meaning 'to fulfil or carry out (a contract or obligation)'. The verb has spread very widely into general speech and writing now: people *implement* a plan, a promise, an idea, an objective. This overuse has been criticised. The simple, traditional *carry out*, *put into effect*, *accomplish*, or *complete* will often do instead — though *implement* has the virtues of being concise and being able to go with a wider range of noun objects than any of its rival synonyms.

Note that the final syllable of *implement* as verb is pronounced /-ment/, whereas the noun ends in /-mənt/.

imply, infer *To imply* and *to infer* are often confused. It is quite common to hear × *Are you inferring that . . . ?* when what the speaker means is *Are you implying that . . . ?* The words have quite distinct meanings today, though in former times they were often interchangeable. *To imply* has the primary meaning of 'to suggest, insinuate, indicate indirectly': *His condescending tone implied that I was stupid.*

> . . . a film . . . about the abortive love affair between a middle-class girl and a boy from the wrong side of the tracks. Much better than that old cliché implies, too.
> — Derek Malcolm, *The Guardian*

To infer means 'to conclude from information given':

So we have bathrooms and new pieces of kitchen equipment described ... as *clinical* ... What purist medical men infer from this meaning is that the equipment is covered with a pink-tasselled counterpane.

– Philip Howard,
New Words for Old

From the absence of further comment, it seems reasonable to infer that the line of thinking set out in the letter of the 25 is, if not generally accepted in the academic community, at least not so unusual as to call for comment.

– Conor Cruise O'Brien,
The Observer

A helpful rule of thumb for remembering the difference between the two is this: speakers or writers *imply*; listeners or readers *infer*. So, if I *imply* that you are incompetent, I say so indirectly; if I *infer* that you are incompetent, I am led to believe that you are, by what you say or do, or by what I hear about you.

Here are two examples of the all-too-common misuse of *infer* in the place of *imply*:

✕ It is startling to be asked to expand our way of appreciating the world. We've simply assumed the world is structured in the way catalogued by our concepts. Nouns are misleading representations: they infer a finality which doesn't exist. When Kleist resolves his apparent contradictions — as he does — he's telling us indirectly that all such contradictions are made by us.

– Professor Idris Parry,
BBC Radio 3

The apology, slipped into press copies last night, says the reference to Grant 'may be seen as inferring that he acted with less than professional competence and integrity in the incident described'. Implications are unreservedly withdrawn.

– PHS, *The Times*

Both *imply* and *infer* are also used when referring to the logical connection between one thing and another. *To imply* can mean 'to have as its logical or inevitable conclusion; lead to or include inescapably', as in *The effect implies the cause*; *Does poverty imply squalor?* And generally speaking, *to infer* means the same as *to deduce*. There is a technical difference, however: *to deduce* is to reach a conclusion by *deduction*, a logical operation from first principles; *to infer* (and rarely, *to induce*) is to reach a conclusion

by *induction* (or *inference*), the process of reasoning from observable evidence. (See DEDUCTION.)

Note the spelling: *inferred, inferring,* but *inference*. And *inference* differs further in having its stress on the first syllable rather than on the second.

Imply and *infer* both go back through Old French to Latin roots: *imply* to the same source as the word *implicate*, the Latin verb *implicare*, 'to interweave or enfold', from *in-*, 'in' + *plicare*, 'to fold'. *Infer* goes back to the Latin *inferre*, 'to bring in, introduce, deduce', from *in-*, 'in' + *ferre*, 'to bear'.

important The words *more important* can be used as a connecting phrase, as in *We need helpers, and, more important, we need funds.* There is the tendency to add a *-ly* ending, by analogy with adverbs such as *luckily, significantly, thankfully*: *? ... and more importantly, we need funds.* This usage is especially common in American English, but has become widespread in British English too. It has attracted criticism here: *more important* is short for *What is more important*, and needs no alteration.

See also HOPEFULLY.

impractical, impracticable See PRACTICAL, PRACTICABLE.

improvement When something has improved, we say there has been an improvement *in* it: *There has been a marked improvement in the patient's condition.* However, when two things or people are being directly compared, the better one is said to be an improvement *on* the other: *This year's model is a definite improvement on last year's.* Here, *on* means 'over'.

impunity See IMMUNE.

in so far as This phrase is often written nowadays as *?insofar as* (two words). Many purists object to this .fused form, and it is advisable to go along with their preference for the four separate words.

in spite of See DESPITE.

in the event This is a useful alternative to such phrases as 'in the end' or 'as it happens':

McEnroe was odds-on favourite. In the event, he did win, but it was not without a titanic struggle.

The phrase is used in a quite different sense too, to indicate a future possibility rather than a past occurrence:

> In the event of a rail strike, you will have to take the inter-city coach to work.

This is reasonable, but often the phrase is no more than a supposedly impressive version of the simple 'if':

> ? In the event (that) the coach service joins the strike, you will have to take the car.

This construction is regarded by some as an Americanism — especially when the *that* is omitted. It is fairly widespread in British English now, though purists still prefer to use *of* and a verbal noun after *in the event*:

> In the event of the coach service's joining the strike, you will have to take the car.

(See -ING FORMS OF VERBS.) But the best form of all remains the straightforward unpretentious *if*:

> If the coach service joins the strike, you will have to take the car.

Note, however, that the construction *in any event* — 'in any case' — does not seem to have attracted criticism.

inasmuch as 1. Some publishers and experts prefer the partly fused form *inasmuch as*; others insist on the four separate words *in as much as*. Both can be accepted as standard (unlike ? *insofar as,* which is still on the borderline). The forms *insomuch as* and *in so much as* are now rather old-fashioned.

2. The phrase *in as much as* has been criticised as being either pompous or ambiguous. It is pompous when used in its modern sense of 'since or because':

> ? I can hardly be held responsible, in as much as I was on the other side of the Atlantic when it happened.

A simple *since* or *because,* or even a colon or dash, would be less affected than *in as much as* here.

And the phrase is ambiguous in that its modern sense competes with the older sense of 'in so far as, to the extent that':

> ? Miriam's enjoyment of the opera was spoiled in as much as she had to crane her neck all evening to see past a pillar.

On one interpretation (*in as much as* = 'because'), Miriam probably had a very disap-

pointing evening; on the other interpretation (*in as much as* = 'to the extent that'), Miriam probably had a reasonably enjoyable evening. The ambiguity, in other words, is not a trivial one. It could have been avoided by using *since* or *because* on the one hand, and *to the extent that* or *in so far as* on the other, in place of *in as much as.*

In view of these two criticisms, it is perhaps best to relegate *in as much as* to your 'passive' vocabulary, and to avoid using the phrase altogether in speech and writing.

Note, finally, that the variant ✗ *in as much that,* though quite common nowadays, is incorrect.

inconceivable See UNTHINKABLE.

inculcate You can *inculcate* ideas, information, or qualities *in* or *into* a person, as in *The teachers inculcated a sense of responsibility into the children.* You cannot, correctly, *inculcate* a person *with* ideas, information, or qualities, as in ✗ *The teacher inculcated the children with a sense of responsibility.* Use *imbue* for this second construction.

index The plural of *index* is *indexes* if you are referring to an alphabetical listing of the contents of a book or journal: it is *indices* only if you are referring to symbols in mathematics, economics, and related fields.

Indian The range of this word, as both adjective and noun, varies from context to context.

The term can refer to a citizen or inhabitant of the Republic of India. If the reference is prior to 1947 (when the Indian subcontinent was partitioned into India and Pakistan at the time of independence), *Indian* would refer to an indigenous inhabitant of the entire subcontinent — the peninsula south of the Himalayas, today incorporating Pakistan, India, and Bangladesh, and also the Himalayan countries of Nepal and Bhutan. Pakistanis and Bangladeshis are sometimes still loosely referred to as 'Indians', though they might object to the term. So too with Sri Lankans, and Malaysians (Malaya used to be part of the 'East Indies').

Indian can also apply to the descendants of indigenous inhabitants of India or these other countries, whether living in Britain, the Seychelles, South Africa, or the like. In British English, *Indian* in this sense is now being increasingly replaced by *Asian*. (See ASIAN.)

By a historical accident, *Indian* also applies to

the descendants of the original inhabitants of America (North or South) and the West Indies. (The Inuit, or Eskimos, are never referred to as Indians, however.) When Christopher Columbus reached the Americas, he apparently concluded that he had found an outlying part of Asia, and therefore called the local people *Indios*, Spanish for 'Indians'.

Some confusion naturally results: *an Indian drum*, in the absence of a clarifying context, could refer to a drum from India or from Canada, say. To avoid such confusion, and also out of courtesy, the *Indians* of America are increasingly referred to in a more precise way: *Amazon Indians*, for instance, or — for those in the United States and Canada — *American Indians*, *Amerindians*, *Native Americans*, or *Aboriginal Americans*. The British English term *Red Indian* is no longer widely used, and might in any case be considered offensive.

There is one other theoretical ambiguity: someone from Jamaica, in the West Indies, is a *West Indian*; someone from Bombay, in west India, might be called a *West Indian* too. This is not very likely, and it would certainly be extremely ill-advised in view of the confusion that might result.

See also BLACK.

Indian English See SOUTH ASIAN ENGLISH.

indicative See SUBJUNCTIVE.

indict, indite *Indict* and *indite* are pronounced the same way: /in-**dīt**/. However, they mean quite different things. Take care not to confuse their spellings.

To indict once meant 'to proclaim' but now means 'to accuse of, or to charge with, a crime'. *An indictable offence* is an offence that could result in a criminal charge. An *indictment* is a document bringing charges, or the act of charging or state of being charged:

> But once the criminal trial is over the civil bankruptcy proceedings in Detroit concerning the De Lorean Motor Company are expected to resume. There is also still the possibility of a criminal indictment of De Lorean in Detroit on fraud and/or tax charges.
> — Adrian Hamilton, *The Observer*

All these words are extended from their specific judicial uses to general ones, as in *He indicted the government for not spending enough on welfare.*

One can tell that it has honestly never occurred to him that verse is not the same thing as prose, that poetry used to be an art which had certain affinities with music. What an indictment of the English theatre! What a neglect of the shining example of John Gielgud!
> — John Wain, *The Listener*

Note that you say *indict for*, but *accuse of* and *charge with*.

To indite means 'to put into words, compose, set down in writing' — as you might a speech or a poem. It is a rather archaic word now, and seldom used. Even rarer is the noun *inditement* referring to a composition, something written down or drawn up. It is possible to *indite* an *indictment* (if you draw up an accusation) and also to *indict* an *inditement* (if you charge someone's composition, for example, with misleading its audience).

Both *indict* and *indite* go back through Anglo-French to the Latin *indicere*, 'to proclaim', from *in-*, 'towards' + *dicere*, 'to say'.

indifferent 1. The preposition that usually follows *indifferent*, and its related noun *indifference*, is *to*:

> I am indifferent to her advances.
> It's a matter of indifference to me.

> These disputes surface time and again in *British Sign Language*, probably to the annoyance of those readers (almost certainly the majority) who are completely indifferent to the touchiness which linguists are inclined to display.
> — Professor Roy Harris,
> *The Times Literary Supplement*

When the object of this indifference is hypothetical or disputable, then *as to* tends to be used with *indifferent*, and *towards* with *indifference*:

> She seems quite indifferent as to the consequences of her betrayal.
> By this oversight the playwright reveals his utter indifference towards the moral implications of the plot he is concocting.

The distinction is not always easy to draw: a woman might be indifferent *as to* the consequences of her betrayal, but she would be indifferent *to* the *evil* consequences of her betrayal — since *evil consequences* are known and real, whereas mere *consequences* are unspecified and still perhaps hypothetical or abstract.

The prepositions *about* and *for* are often used colloquially, but are best avoided in formal contexts:

? I'm indifferent about money.
? All I see is his complete indifference for my feelings.

These prepositions are probably borrowed from similar idioms such as *unconcerned about, couldn't care less about,* and *complete disregard for.*

2. The meaning of *indifferent* or *indifferently* has undergone deterioration in the last century or two. The various neutral or positive senses have faded, leaving the field clear for the more negative senses.

One of the old senses, 'disinterested, impartial, having no preference one way or the other', has virtually been driven out now by the related sense 'uninterested, apathetic'. A sentence such as *The judge listened indifferently to the evidence* would today suggest a bored, inattentive judge rather than an open-minded impartial one.

Another old sense, 'not mattering one way or the other; or average, neither good nor bad', probably gave rise to the more negative sense of 'fairly bad, mediocre', only to be completely supplanted by it. The phrase *an indifferent performance* today suggests not an average performance but a below-average performance, and *an indifferent result* suggests a mediocre or poor result rather than an unimportant result.

Meanings come and go, and the fading of these two old meanings, however regrettable, does at least reduce the danger of ambiguity. But the triumph of the two surviving senses does not mean that ambiguity has disappeared entirely, since these two senses remain in competition with each other.

Consider the sentence *? The judge summed up indifferently.* It is true that this is no longer likely to be understood as referring to a fair and impartial summing-up, but it remains ambiguous nevertheless — was the judge bored and apathetic when summing up, or was he delivering a rather incompetent and uninspired summing-up?

Use *indifferent* and *indifferently* with caution, then; make sure that its meaning is clear to your reader or audience.

indiscriminate See DISCRIMINATING.

indite See INDICT.

individual The use of the noun *individual* to mean simply 'a person' has been established for a long time, though it tended in the past to be confined to humorous or scornful utterances: *Who is that unkempt individual over there?* This use is now considered irritatingly quaint by some writers, but it remains reasonably acceptable. *Individual* is an indispensable term when any one person is contrasted with a group: *the individual's right to dissent*; *History cares little for the fate of the individual so long as the human race survives.*

The objection to *individual* is to its use in contexts that have no such saving grace: *? I arrested a number of individuals on charges of being drunk and disorderly.* What is wrong with *people* here?

indoor, indoors *Indoor* is the adjective: *indoor fireworks. Indoors* is the adverb: *to stay indoors.* Compare OUTDOOR.

induction See DEDUCTION.

industrial action It seems strange that industrial action has come to imply a state of inactivity at the place of work, referring as it does to strikes, overtime bans, boycotts, or working to rule. A foreigner who is well versed in English but unfamiliar with the finer points might be hopelessly puzzled by the following news report:

> Leaders of the National Graphical Association (NGA) decided last night that there will be no return to industrial action in the six-month-old dispute with Mr Eddie Shah's Messenger Group newspapers and no more mass picketing of the plant at Warrington, Cheshire.
> The NGA national council, meeting in Bedford, agreed, however, that it would continue the dispute despite the withdrawal of TUC support for industrial action in contravention of the Government's labour laws.
> – Paul Routledge, *The Times*

The phrase has a parallel: *political action.* A trade union involved in a dispute may take political action, putting its case to Parliament and to the nation's opinion makers; and it may combine this with industrial action, bringing pressure on employers directly by calling the workforce out on strike. Even so, *industrial action* is sometimes unnecessarily vague, and has a bureaucratic ring about it. It is better to talk of a *strike*, an *overtime ban*, a *boycott*, or a *work-to-rule*, if only one of these techniques is being discussed.

Industrial action is not used in American English: a near-equivalent there is *job action.*

inept, inapt These two adjectives are very closely related, having the same pair of meanings in common; but the meaning that is primary in one is very much secondary in the other, and vice versa. So although interchangeable in theory, the two words are in practice very rarely equal alternatives in any one context.

Inapt is the common term for the sense 'inappropriate, unsuitable' — *an inapt candidate for the job of interior decorator, an inapt remark to make at a funeral*; and *inept* is the usual term for 'incompetent; awkward or foolish': *an inept interior decorator*; *an inept attempt to comfort the bereaved.*

Inapt and *inept* have identical roots — the Latin *in-*, 'not' + *aptus,* 'fit, suitable' (from *apere,* 'to fasten'). The difference is that *inapt* is a compound of the derived elements in English, whereas *inept* comes from *ineptus,* a compound that already existed in Latin. So *inapt* has the opposite *apt,* but there is no equivalent word × *ept* to serve as the opposite of *inept.*

Inapt can be replaced by *unapt,* and it should be when the further sense of 'unlikely or disinclined' is intended: *She is unapt to award high marks even to her best students.*

The related nouns are usually *inaptness* and *ineptitude,* though the forms *inaptitude* and *ineptness* are also possible. The only possible noun for *unapt,* however, is *unaptness.*

See also LIKELY, APT, LIABLE, PRONE.

inequity, iniquity *Inequity* means 'inequality, injustice, or unfairness', or 'an instance of injustice': *the inequity of the country's distribution of wealth*; *To single me out for punishment was a gross inequity.*

Iniquity means 'wickedness, immorality', or more often 'a sin or immoral act': *The red light district was a den of iniquity.*

'Edwina Crane,' Mrs White said, 'has obviously missed her vocation. Instead of wasting her time in the missions and thumping the old tub about the iniquities of the British Raj and the intolerable burdens borne by what her church calls our dark brethren, she should have been headmistress of a good school for girls, back in the old home counties.'
– Paul Scott,
The Jewel in the Crown

Both words go back to the same Latin roots: *in-*, 'not' + *aequus,* 'just, equal'.

The adjective from *inequity* is *inequitable,* meaning 'unjust'. The adjective from *iniquity* is

iniquitous, meaning 'wicked'. All four words are stressed on the second syllable.

The truth is damning enough. But I feel that she exaggerates the iniquitous folly of George III's ministers, which is a trifle worrying.
– Professor John Kenyon,
The Observer

infamous, notorious *Notorious* means 'widely known for being something that is regarded unfavourably': *a notorious womaniser.* It is also loosely used, not always with the approval of the purists, as a casual synonym of *well-known*: *the notorious facts of the case; the notorious Ralph Nader, champion of the consumer and foe of the giant corporations.* In either case, the sense 'well-known' is important: the word goes back to the Latin *noscere,* 'to become acquainted'.

Infamous can be used in much the same ways, but the emphasis is more on the wicked aspect (of something that in itself need not be bad) than on the well-known aspect: *an infamous temper*; *an infamous deed.* The sense is often 'deserving a bad reputation' rather than 'having a bad reputation'. A modern extension of this meaning, deplored by many careful speakers, is simply 'impressive, quaint, intense': *? You'll enjoy my partner's infamous sense of humour.* This development follows a typical pattern — the weakening of a powerful word: *wicked* is another example — but it should not be encouraged.

infer See IMPLY.

infinite, infinitely *Infinite* and *infinitely* go back to the Latin roots *in-*, 'not, without' + *finis,* 'an end' — they suggest limitlessness or endlessness, whether of time, space, love, charm, or the like.

To reduce *infinite* or *infinitely* to suggesting merely a very large quantity, proportion, distance, or the like, is to debase the words somewhat, though the development is a natural one, and widespread.

? The so-called Fourth Man was reputed to have done infinite harm to British national security.

? The current chairman is an infinitely more effective negotiator than his predecessor, but then he has had infinitely more opportunities.

Such uses of *infinite* and *infinitely* are virtually standard idiom now, though they do still jar with the purists. What does *infinite harm* mean? And how can one person have *infinitely more* opportunities than his predecessor (unless that predecessor had no opportunities at all, in which case even one opportunity is *infinitely more,* mathematically speaking)? It would be sharper and no less idiomatic to speak of *incalculable harm, vastly more effective,* and *considerably more opportunities.*

infinitive The infinitive is the basic form of a verb, used with or without *to.* It is 'uninflected' — that is, lacking the modifications such as *-ing, -s,* and *-ed* that indicate a verb's grammatical function. (See VERBS.)

The infinitive can be the subject or complement of another verb: *To understand* (subject) *is to forgive* (complement); or it can feature in a wide variety of other grammatical patterns. In each of the following sentences, the second verb is in the infinitive: *She hopes to go; They might agree; He's unlikely to succeed; What is the next train to arrive?; All I did was touch it; Here is a spoon to stir it with; They persuaded him to retire.*

There are three possible pitfalls in using the infinitive: first, using it where the *-ing* form of the verb is needed; secondly, producing a 'misrelated infinitive' or a 'dangling infinitive', incorrectly or insufficiently attached to the rest of the sentence; thirdly, inappropriately using the 'split infinitive'.

The first kind of error appears in this sentence: × *The habit of small builders to take on too much work is very trying.* Here, the noun *habit* actually requires to be followed not by the infinitive *to take* but by the construction *of taking.* Perhaps the writer of such a sentence is unwilling to use two *of*-phrases one after the other, or perhaps he is misled by the model of a construction such as *the tendency of small builders to take on too much.* (See -ING FORMS OF VERBS **2**.)

The 'misrelated infinitive' appears in such sentences as ? *To reach the top, an early start is essential.* Strictly, it is not the *start* that is going to reach the top. Although such constructions are widely and unreflectively used, purists prefer them to be rephrased: *To reach the top, one must start early,* or *It is essential to start early if one is to reach the top.* (See MISRELATED CONSTRUCTIONS.)

A 'split infinitive' occurs when another word is inserted between *to* and a following infinitive, as in *to critically evaluate our situation.* This practice has long been frowned on, though for rather flimsy reasons. There are certain phrases, as in *We expect costs to more than double,* where it is almost impossible not to split the infinitive. (See SPLIT INFINITIVE.)

inflammable, inflammatory, flammable The adjectives *inflammable* and *flammable* are not opposites. They both mean 'highly combustible, tending to catch fire easily and burn rapidly'. The older word is *inflammable*: you can think of it as consisting of *inflame* + *-able.*

The problem is that the prefix *in-* might be regarded as serving a negative function (as in *invisible* or *inadequate*) rather than an intensifying function (as in *invaluable*). The dangers of such a misunderstanding in factories and school laboratories are obvious. The unambiguous word *flammable* is helpful in reducing the risk — it is recorded as long ago as 1813, though it is only relatively recently that its use in technical writing and warning signs has become widespread. To complement it, the word *nonflammable* was devised as well, in 1915, with the meaning 'not flammable, not easily set alight'.

In figurative uses, however, *inflammable* remains the only correct form. It means either 'easily aroused to strong emotion, passionate' — *a politician with an inflammable temperament* — or 'likely to get out of control, dangerously volatile', as in the rather hackneyed phrase *an inflammable situation.* The word *inflammatory* has the corresponding sense of 'arousing strong emotions'. Thus: *an inflammatory speaker* but *an inflammable audience.*

> The sentence is typical of a flood of illiterate and inflammatory leaflets from the Socialist Workers Student Society, inciting the students of North London Polytechnic to crime.
>
> – Roger Scruton, *The Times*

> He did not really want to excite any sort of passion in his friends, or linger in their minds under some inflammable aspect. A very boring guest or a very entertaining one could provoke all sorts of undesirable feelings in people — revulsion, heart-quickenings, murderous attachments, the sort of emotions that had always led to trouble at school and university, and they led to international incidents as well.
>
> – Muriel Spark, *The Mandelbaum Gate*

> Cheap brandy may be both *inflammatory* (figuratively) and *inflammable* (in the literal sense).

inflict You can *inflict* something unpleasant *on* or *upon* a person, as in *The commander inflicted heavy taxation on the villagers.* You cannot, correctly, *inflict* a person *with* anything, as in ✗ *The commander inflicted the villagers with heavy taxation*. Use *afflict* instead for this second construction.

informant, informer These two nouns are sometimes used interchangeably. But they do have distinct uses and overtones, *informer* being much less favourable than *informant*. The verb *to inform* can mean either simply 'to tell' or 'to provide incriminating information'. *Informant* is linked to the first meaning; *informer* can be linked to the second.

An *informant* is a person who discloses information: *She asked a passer-by when the bus was due, and her informant turned out to know her name*. *Informer* can be neutral in this way, though usually only in informal speech. An *informer* tends today to be someone who discloses information in exchange for money — such as a criminal who betrays his companions to the police. The connotations are unpleasant, so do not use *informer* if you mean *informant*. When police spokesmen or newspapers refer to 'our informant', however, they are no doubt often using a euphemism for *informer*.

The word *informant* has recently been overshadowed by its fashionable synonym *source*. This is a strange development — the shift from a precise term to a more diffuse one with several rival meanings. Some careful users of English deplore the rise of *source*, but its prevalence means that *informant*, in this sense, has become a rather rare and perhaps old-fashioned word now. In linguistic research, however, *informant* remains the standard term for a person who provides information to the researcher.

infringe Formerly, *to infringe* was mainly used as a transitive verb (that is, a verb taking a direct object, or used in the passive), in the sense 'to violate': *to infringe the rules*. Today it is often used intransitively, in the sense of 'to intrude or trespass': *to infringe on our civil rights*. Perhaps this intransitive use is due to the word's resemblance to *impinge*. The modern sense, together with the use of *on* or *upon*, has been criticised by some writers on usage, who prefer the verb *to encroach* in such contexts.

Both uses seem to be fully established now, and accepted by modern dictionaries. But to those of the old school, the modern intransitive use still has a slovenly air about it.

infuse You can *infuse* a quality *into* a person, as in *The teacher infused enthusiasm into his class*.

You cannot, correctly, *infuse* a person *with* a quality, as in ✗ *The teacher infused his class with enthusiasm*. Use *imbue* instead for this second construction.

Infuse is also used quite legitimately like *pervade*, as in the following example:

Swift loved them both; the Journal to Stella and the poem to Vanessa are there to prove it. The same delicious playfulness infuses them both.
— Michael Foot, *The Observer*

-ing forms of verbs 1. *'possessive before a verbal noun'*. English verbs form nouns with the suffix *-ing*, which are thus identical to their present participles: *spring was coming* (participle); *the coming of spring* (noun). In traditional (Latin-based) grammar, such a noun is called a *gerund*; a simpler and better term is *verbal noun*.

The underlying subject of a verbal noun is, in traditional usage, put in the possessive form:

Elinor was prevented from making any reply to this . . . by the door's being thrown open, the servant's announcing Mr Ferrars, and Edward's immediately walking in.
— Jane Austen, *Sense and Sensibility*

Note the three uses of - 's. Here is another example of the possessive before a verbal noun:

Everybody wanted to touch Arthur. A rain of hand-claps descended on his wincing shoulders. An ill-timed attempt to hoist him into the air nearly resulted in his being pitched headlong over the banisters.
— Christopher Isherwood,
Mr Norris Changes Trains

Note the wording: *nearly resulted in his being pitched headlong* — *his* rather than *him*.

But such phrases are very often constructed in a different way, with the subject simply placed before the verbal noun without being put in the possessive — the verbal noun seems almost to be functioning as a participle:

? Mother dislikes John watching so much television.

? His visits were conditional upon the *African Queen* being fit to travel.
— C.S. Forester, *The African Queen*

? The indications seem to me to point to the Government appealing to the country in November.
— Anthony Eden, *The Reckoning*

? This had . . . clearly ante-dated the

troublesome incident in a manner to disclaim any possibility of Winterwade being in the running for co-blame.

> – Anthony Powell,
> *O, How the Wheel Becomes It!*

? However, Lord Gowrie is already shifting his ground. On Merseyside he talked of the Government being prepared to help local authorities who show themselves willing to fund the arts.

> – Joan Bakewell, *The Observer*

Grammar-conscious users of English regard this uncertain noun-participle usage as unacceptable. In the first example, they would point out, what Mother dislikes is not *John* but *John's watching so much television*: to use *John* rather than *John's* is momentarily misleading. And Forester should have written *the African Queen's being fit*; Eden, *the Government's appealing*; Powell, *Winterwade's being in the running*, and so on. However, the construction without the possessive has evolved naturally within the structure of English. It occurred as early as the 18th century and is now prevalent in everyday speech and very widespread in writing, though it is avoided in two patterns: first, at the start of a sentence — almost everyone would write *His leaving town was a surprise* rather than ?? *Him leaving town was a surprise*. Secondly, if an *of*-phrase follows: *We enjoyed his parodying of the Minister*. No competent speaker would use *him* here.

Note too the old-fashioned 'absolute' construction: *At last, he being fit to travel once more, we left the town*. The *-ing* noun is here preceded neither by *him* nor by *his*, but by *he*.

In general, however, when both *his* and *him* are usable, it is better to side with the purists, in formal contexts at least, and use the possessive form. (In informal contexts, where the possessive form tends to sound affected, the purists' rule is more of an embarrassment than a help.)

In some specific cases, however, the possessive form is awkward, unidiomatic, or downright impossible. The cure can be worse than the disease. Here are several sentences, ranging from the easily though inelegantly 'curable' to the totally 'incurable':

? The possibility of him leaving town was a surprise.

Pronouns such as *him*, unlike names and common nouns, are slightly less comfortable when put in the possessive in mid-sentence.

Other pronouns would be more awkward still if recast into the possessive form:

? The possibility of someone arriving was very exciting.

? You can depend on something turning up.

It seems odd to speak of *someone's arriving* and *something's turning up*. Similarly:

? The possibility of the table being genuine was very exciting.

? The question of beauty being truth has been widely debated.

Inanimate nouns and abstract nouns would not take easily to the possessive form in these constructions (and are generally used less often with an -*'s* or -*s'* ending: see -'S, -S'). Next:

? She did it without her brother or sister knowing.

If you added an -*'s* to *sister*, you would probably feel the need to add one to *brother* as well. Similarly:

? She did it without the acting head of department knowing.

Longer noun phrases are unwieldy enough as it is: to add an -*'s* at the end would make things still worse.

Some noun phrases simply cannot take a possessive form such as -*'s*:

? She did it without either of us knowing.

And some noun phrases or noun clauses are so complicated that the addition of an -*'s* at the end would seem laughably inadequate:

? There is no chance of a satisfactory solution to this vexatious problem ever being found.

? The convenor would be outraged at the merest suggestion of any delegates involved leaking information to the press.

? True, he was influenced by the Murphys and their philosophy of living well being the only revenge; he needed a lot of money.

> – Anthony Burgess, *The Observer*

? Such bankruptcies are the inevitable result of the laws specifically designed to protect the small trader being bypassed on a technicality by the giant corporations.

It would be an outrage on idiom to try to 'cure' these examples by a construction such as ✗ *the merest suggestion of any delegate involved's leaking information to the press*.

The obvious course, in the face of these difficulties, is to shrug off the purist's rule, and accept that idiom allows — or demands — the contravention of the rule. But if you still feel worried about such open defiance, the way out of the impasse is, as always, to change the construction entirely, doing away with the verbal noun and the dilemma it generates.

Try changing the *of* to a *that* or *when* in some of the examples, and then using a full relative clause rather than a verbal noun:

> There is no chance that a satisfactory solution to this vexatious problem will ever be found.
> The conference chairman would be outraged at the merest suggestion that any delegates involved might leak information to the press.
> Such bankruptcies inevitably occur when the laws specifically designed to protect the small trader are bypassed on a technicality by the giant corporations.

Finally, remember that, with the *-ing* form of a verb, the noun-function and participle-function often fade into each other rather than being clear-cut:

> I watched Joe cooking onions.
> I watched Joe cooking for us all.
> I was surprised at Joe cooking for us all.
> I was surprised at Joe's cooking for us all.
> I enjoy Joe's cooking.

In the last sentence, *cooking* is of course a full and independent noun by now. In the first sentence, *cooking* is purely a participle. The middle three sentences show how *cooking* moves gradually across from its participle-function to its noun-function.

The presence or absence of the possessive form is important in two ways. First, it allows the reader to distinguish separate meanings by distinguishing between a full noun (*cooking* = 'food that has been cooked') and a verbal noun (*cooking* = 'being occupied in preparing food'). To say *I marvelled at Joe's cooking* would usually be understood to mean 'I admired the quality of the food that Joe prepared'. If, however, I intended to express the idea 'I was amazed that Joe was preparing the food', it would obviously be less ambiguous to say *I marvelled at Joe cooking* (even if the purists were to frown at this).

Secondly, and more subtly, the use or omission of a possessive allows for a shift of focus. In the sentence *I heard Joe's singing*, the focus is on the *singing*: what I heard was *singing*. In the sentence *I heard Joe singing*, the focus is equally on *Joe* and *singing*: I heard *Joe* and I heard *singing* too.

Or consider, in the following quotation, how different the effect would be if the second *them* were changed (or 'corrected') to *their*:

> I have sat with them round their camp fires and heard them laughing.
> – Evelyn Waugh, in *Noblesse Oblige*

● *Recommendation* When the *-ing* form of a verb functions as a noun, any noun directly in front of it should, according to a traditional rule, take the possessive form. In formal contexts, the rule should be observed wherever possible. But in some constructions the possessive would sound awkward or is simply impossible: you may (or must) then ignore the rule, or else — if that feels unsatisfactory — you should reconstruct the sentence in such a way as to avoid the problem altogether.

Bear in mind that a rigorous adherence to the rule often results in stilted, affected, or unidiomatic language. It might also result in ambiguity, as in *I marvelled at Joe's cooking*. Remember too that it is not always clear when an *-ing* form of the verb is a verbal noun and when it is a participle: the freedom to use or to disregard the possessive in such cases is an important stylistic tool, allowing a modulation of emphasis (as between *I heard Joe singing* and *I heard Joe's singing*).

2. *-ing vs the infinitive.* **a.** The choice between an *-ing* form of a verb (*I had the idea of leaving home*) and the simple infinitive form without *-ing* (*? I had the idea to leave home*) is chiefly a matter of idiom rather than of rules. Most constructions seem to have their own rules: *I thought of leaving home*; *I planned leaving/to leave home*; *I determined to leave home*; *I made plans to leave home* but *I had plans of leaving home*. So no helpful generalisations can really be drawn up. A few pieces of advice are possible, however.

First, be on the alert. It might seem natural to say ✗ *She has a penchant, inherited from her father, to read other people's letters.* A moment's thought should indicate that *for reading* rather than *to read* is correct here: you say *a penchant for cigars* or *a penchant for letters*, so the correct form is likely to be *a penchant for reading letters*.

Secondly, when testing for the correct form, try omitting any material that interrupts the construction: ✗ *a penchant, inherited from her father, to read other people's letters* may sound natural enough, but the simple unadorned construction, ✗ *a penchant to read other people's letters*, sounds rather less so, and might alert you to the mistake. Another, fairly common example:

✗ *She is certainly capable, given the right opportunities, to make a success of her career*. Omit the middle phrase, and the mistake at once becomes clear.

Thirdly, make sure that you are not being wrongly influenced by some other construction: perhaps it was the analogy of *a tendency to read other people's letters* that prompted the mistaken form ✗ *a penchant to read other people's letters*. Similarly, the faulty construction ✗ *She has dedicated herself to restore her father's reputation* is possibly based on the model of *She has promised herself to restore her father's reputation*.

Fourthly, if you are in doubt, the chances are that the *-ing* form is the correct one: it is more common than the infinitive form.

Finally, if you remain in doubt, consult a good dictionary. It will often direct you to the appropriate form.

b. Some verbs allow either the *-ing* form (usually without a preceding preposition) or the simple infinitive form (usually preceded by *to*): *I planned leaving/to leave home*; *I began speaking/to speak* (but only *I finished speaking*). In these examples, there is only a very slight difference in meaning between the two forms in each case.

With some verbs, however, the difference in meaning is considerable: *I stopped speaking* vs *I stopped to speak*, or *She remembered going there* vs *She remembered to go there*.

3. There is a tendency in American English to drop the *-ing* from various adjectival forms: *rowboat* for *rowing boat* (*rowboat* is in fact a long-established form, but is no longer idiomatic in British English); *swim suit* for *swimming suit* (*swimming costume*), and so on. In British English, such streamlining is beginning to occur too, but it is generally discouraged: ? *wash powder* is still considered an informal version of *washing powder* (as it happens, Americans almost always say *washing powder*), but the American *spark-plug* has now clearly superseded *sparking plug* in British English.

See also WANT 2.

ingenious, ingenuous, disingenuous The qualities suggested by the adjectives *ingenious* and *ingenuous* have changed since the early days of the two words — they are no longer such impressive qualities as they were.

Ingenious, which once meant 'of highest intellect', now means merely 'having or showing cleverness in an inventive way; cunning':

New inventions, each with incalculable effects on American society, poured out of ingenious American minds.
— Isaac Asimov (U.S.),
Science Past – Science Future

Baskerville constructs an elaborate theory based on Apocalyptic predictions, using Occam's razor to cut through the obstacles set by both the intractable material and the jealous manoeuvring of the monks. The dazzlingly ingenious *dénouement* reveals the minor interstices that still linger in his deductions.
— Philip Lloyd Bostock,
The Literary Review

Ingenuous, once 'noble, honest', now means 'innocent' or even 'unsophisticated, naive':

He had a dangerous charm, on the surface so ingenuous that one thought he couldn't be aware of it.
— Catherine Gaskin, *Edge of Glass*

Stephen Brook is the latest eager, ingenuous Englishman to volunteer for the city's accidents, abrasions and venereal scars. He set out in the autumn of 1982 on a tour of New York's kink-ridden culture, and has written funnily and endearingly about his exploits.
— Peter Conrad, *The Observer*

Ingenious derives, via French, from the Latin *ingeniosus*, from *ingenium*, 'inborn talent, skill'. *Ingenuous* comes from the Latin *ingenuus*, 'native, noble, free-born, honest, frank'.

The noun *ingenue* or *ingénue*, /aN-zhay-new, -noo/, is the feminine form of a French adjective meaning 'innocent, unsophisticated'. In English it means 'an inexperienced or ingenuous young woman':

Included in the party are Professor Aronnax [and] his daughter, a kittenish ingénue, all corkscrew curls and maidenly simpers.
— S.J. Perelman (U.S.),
The Road to Milltown

It is used most often of a character in a play or film, or the actress playing such a character. The masculine equivalent *ingenu* or *ingénu* (pronounced in the same way) is rare in English.

The noun *ingenuity*, originally the noun from *ingenuous*, now serves as the noun form of *ingenious* alone. (The noun currently corresponding to *ingenuous* is *ingenuousness*.)

An examination of the figures demonstrates all too clearly that, however much time and energy and ingenuity may be expended (and there is a great deal of skill and ingenuity within the Arts Council), their new decisions must necessarily involve the withdrawal of support for a number of worthwhile establishments.

– Lord Goodman, *The Observer*

Disingenuous, in a way the opposite of *ingenuous,* means 'devious or crafty, not straightforward, dishonest':

In supposing this method of using the Winterwade Diary for disingenuous ends would discompose Isolde Upjohn no misjudgment could have been greater on Shadbold's part.

– Anthony Powell, *O, How The Wheel Becomes It!*

It often seems to mean 'feigning ingenuousness, acting as though ingenuous':

The fact is that sponsorship monies come out of the companies' advertising and publicity budgets (and as such are set against tax). If the director of ABSA thinks advertising expenditure is not directed to selling products, then it is he who is being naive — or disingenuous.

– Sir Roy Shaw, letter to *The Observer*

'What is it, exactly, that you export and import?'

He took it quite calmly. His smile was disingenuous and bland.

'My dear boy, what, in my time, have I *not* exported? I think I may claim to have exported everything which is — er — exportable.'

– Christopher Isherwood, *Mr Norris Changes Trains*

inhuman, inhumane *Inhumane* is the opposite of *humane,* which usually means 'merciful, compassionate, kind'. *Inhumane,* then, means 'cruel, lacking in pity or compassion': *inhumane prison conditions — locked up, three to a cell, for 23 out of every 24 hours.*

Inhuman, being the opposite of *human,* is at once more intense and more wide-ranging than this. To be *inhuman* is to lack all essentially desirable qualities of humankind: to be *inhumane* is to lack one such quality, admittedly an extremely important one — compassion.

When referring to acts of cruelty, *inhuman* suggests something not merely unkind, but lacking all moral restraint: *inhuman prison conditions — no room even to sit down, sadistic guards, and arbitrary executions.* *Inhuman* means 'not human' in more general ways too — especially in the sense of 'not of ordinary human form or type': *The inhuman appearance of Frankenstein's creation.*

Both words derive from Latin *humanus,* via Old French and Middle English. *Humanus* is akin to *homo,* the Latin word for 'a man'.

iniquity See INEQUITY.

initiate You can *initiate* a person *in* or *into* something, as in *The teacher initiated the children into the mysteries of long division.* You cannot, correctly, *initiate* something *into* a person, as in ✗ *The teacher initiated the mysteries of long division into the children.* Use *instil* instead for this second pattern.

inquiry See ENQUIRY.

insidious, invidious Both of these adjectives suggest the idea of causing harm, but they are used in different contexts, and should not be confused.

Insidious means 'spreading or working harmfully in a subtle or stealthy way'. It comes from the Latin word for 'ambush', *insidiae,* and suggests an unseen danger: *an insidious cancer* spreads invisibly. The word also means 'intended or seeking to trap with guile, wily, treacherous': *an insidious argument*; *insidious brainwashing by propaganda.*

Streets that follow like a tedious argument
Of insidious intent
To lead you to an overwhelming question . . .
– T.S. Eliot (U.S.), 'The Love Song of J. Alfred Prufrock'

I suspect it's all part of the changing style of radio, and some pessimists say it's an insidious process of turning the BBC into a kind of national local radio station.
– Fritz Spiegl, *The Listener*

The adverb *insidiously* is particularly common; it is used to mean 'by spreading stealthily', or simply 'by stealth'.

Invidious is related to *envious*; both come from the Latin *invidia,* 'envy or malice'. The word means 'likely to cause ill will, offensive', as through a real or imagined injustice or insult: *He was bound to resent that invidious comparison between him and his elder brother.*

Is this the best Truemanism of the cricket season? It was spotted by so many people that it would be invidious to single out anyone for the usual fiver, so my apologies and thanks to all who reported this splendid remark.

– Simon Barnes, *The Times*

An *invidious* clause in a contract is likely to provoke a sense of being wronged; it might be *insidiously* inserted by someone trying to secure an unfair advantage for himself.

inspiration See EXPIRY.

instantly, instantaneously *Instantly* means 'at once, immediately, straight away': *Do it instantly!* *Instantaneously* means 'completed within an instant, taking an imperceptibly short time to occur': *It happened instantaneously, before he'd realised the danger.*

It is easy to see how the two adverbs can be confused: *They liked each other instantly* (at once) and *They liked each other instantaneously* (within the passing of an instant) could mean effectively the same thing.

Sometimes the same context yields different meanings, however: *They both arrived instantly* means 'They arrived immediately', but *They both arrived instantaneously* may imply 'They arrived at the same instant, virtually simultaneously, within a moment of each other'.

instil You can *instil* a quality *into* a person, as in *The tutor instilled a sense of responsibility into the class.* You cannot, correctly, *instil* a person *with* a quality, as in ✗ *The tutor instilled the class with a sense of responsibility.* Use *imbue* or *inspire* instead for this second construction.

The standard American spelling is *instill*.

instinctual, instinctive The standard and traditional adjective from *instinct* is *instinctive*, whether referring to animals or humans. *Instinctual* seems to have been popularised by psychologists, and some usage experts have dismissed it as a needless variant.

Instinctive seems to serve both in general and specific contexts:

Julie Walters and Ian Charleson as the lovers appear to have transcended performance altogether and entered into a realm of instinctive behaviour that embraces not merely the accents and appearances of love, but its heart and muscle too.

– Ros Asquith, *The Observer*

He started violently at the sound of my voice; so violently, indeed, that his nervous recoil hit me like repercussion. Instinctively I took a pace backwards ...

... I kept hurrying forward in an instinctive desire to get away from our pursuer, then slowing down, lest we should leave him altogether behind.

– Christopher Isherwood,
Mr Norris Changes Trains

Instinctual tends to be used in general contexts. It would be a possible, though unnecessary, replacement for *instinctive* in the first quotation above. The passages from the Isherwood novel, however, refer to specific actions or wishes; *instinctually* and *instinctual* would not really be appropriate here.

insure See ASSURE.

intensive Do not use *intensive* where *intense* will do — that is, in most general contexts: ✗ *intensive pain*; ✗ *making intensive efforts.*

Intensive has to do with the concentration of resources in a small area. It suggests quality, whereas *extensive* suggests quantity. *Intensive farming* is aimed at securing the highest yield regardless of cost. It is often *labour-intensive* — that is, 'making heavier use of labour than machinery'. You might speak of *an intensive course of study* (a 'cram' course) but *an intense period of study* (deep and devoted). If you mean nothing more than 'extreme', then *intense*, not *intensive*, is the word to use.

interface Where two surfaces meet, or where in a computer system two circuits are linked, the boundary between them is an *interface*. This is a useful term in technical contexts or in relation to systems of ideas; it has come to be used as a verb too in such settings.

Unfortunately, however, it has also become a much-derided vogue word, used pretentiously as an alternative to *relationship, meeting-place, contact, interaction*, or the like: ? *The government-science interface is now increasingly moral and political rather than merely financial.*

? By ranging back and forth along the Christian-Moslem interface from the eighth to the fourteenth centuries, he covers a great deal of ground and is invariably entertaining.
– Carlo Gébler, *The Literary Review*

As a verb, *to interface* is attested since 1964. It

is appropriate when referring to computers, but elsewhere it smacks of affectation and jargon: *? Government policy must interface with the needs of the general public.*

internecine This adjective, when used today, tends to suggest quite distinctly the idea of in-fighting or quarrelling within a single group:

? If the Labour party does not cease this internecine squabbling, and turn its united energies to opposing the Tories, it will once again be thrashed at the polls.

? We know, for example, that it distressed Frau Schindler that her son, like his father, was a negligent Catholic. But it cannot have been too internecine a household. From the little that Oskar would say of his childhood, there was no darkness there.

   – Thomas Keneally, *Schindler's Ark*

In this sense of 'carried on within a nation or organisation, fratricidal', *internecine* has still not found full acceptance with the purists. For one thing, it detracts from the earlier meanings; for another, it misrepresents the Latin roots of the word. Finally, it is a needlessly showy word: *internal* would have been just as suitable in the first example above, *quarrelsome* or *hostile* in the second.

Even in its stronger sense of 'mutually destructive; ruinous or fatal to both sides', *internecine* fails to find favour with the purists:

? That internecine madness called the American Civil War retains its fascination for cultural historians.

? It is little more than a decade since serious urban terrorism in civilised western societies began; before that, there was nothing to worry about, apart from the internecine wars of Chicago gangsters, a brief flurry by the IRA just before the Second World War, and the random actions of those who were collectively known as anarchists.

   – Bernard Levin, *The Times*

Perhaps the main objection is the etymological one. In the original Latin word, the root *inter-* did not mean 'between or mutual' (Dr Johnson assumed mistakenly that it did); it served simply as an intensifier, suggesting 'thoroughly'. The Latin verb *necare*, 'to kill', was elaborated into *internecare*, 'to slaughter or massacre'; hence the noun *internecio*, 'a massacre, extermination', and the adjective *internecinus*, 'of or relating to extermination; extremely destructive'. This was

its original sense in English:

Lawless adventurers ... would wage an internecine struggle with the aboriginal tribes in their neighbourhood.

   – George Bowen
   (governor of Queensland, Australia),
   letter (1861)

When *internecine* retains this sense — 'characterised by slaughter or carnage' — purists give it the nod of approval at last:

The irony is that the battle of Verdun, internecine though it was, in the larger view had little effect on the development of the war.

Even here, however, the word is no more than an impressive-sounding substitute for *bloody*, *costly*, *disastrously destructive*, or the like. It seems, then, that there is seldom any call to use the word at all.

The standard pronunciation today is /intər-**nee**-sīn/. In American speech, it is also pronounced /intər-**ness**-een/ and /in-**tern**ə-seen/.

into, in to, in 1. Take care not to write *in to* as one word when the two words have separate functions. As one word, *into* is a preposition: *The waiter poured the wine into the glasses*; *The magician turned the wine into milk*.

With *in to*, the *in* is an adverb (related to the verb before it) and *to* is the marker of a following infinitive, or a preposition introducing a following word or phrase: *We were invited in to inspect the wine*; *The chairman led us in to the wine-tasting contest*.

Compare ONTO, ON TO.

2. The modern sense of *into*, 'interested in or involved with', is strictly informal: *? I'm into vegetarianism these days*; *? James is getting into karate apparently*. This use is quite unsuited to formal speech and writing, though it seems quite fashionable in much modern journalism:

? The Romanians, who were into sports medicine before we had ever heard of it, asked us on the morning of the game whether they could test our fitness.

   – Clem Thomas, *The Guardian*

? We may ask ourselves why Mr Pond bothers us with this boring nonsense. The answer, I suppose, is that Chris is into the business of job creation — his own and the 12 other people employed by the Low Pay Unit.

   – Auberon Waugh, *The Spectator*

3. There is still a preference for *into* over *in*

when movement is suggested: *She swept into the hall*; *He put my article straight into the dustbin.* In the first of these examples, the use of *in* rather than *into* would change the meaning considerably; in the second, the meaning would remain much the same, but the sentence would lose some of its effect (and possibly some of its acceptability too). Not that *in* has to be limited, as some pedants argue, to referring to position rather than movement.

intransitive See TRANSITIVE.

invaluable Do not make the mistake of thinking that *invaluable* is the opposite of *valuable*, in the way that *invalid*, for instance, is the opposite of *valid*. On the contrary: *invaluable* (like *priceless*) means 'very valuable, indispensable'. There is a Latin prefix *in-* of intensity, as well as the one of negation.

> Hill Samuel's Trevor Swete believes that the decision to issue a dummy or 'red herring' prospectus a month before the formal document proved an invaluable way of informing the City about Jaguar. It gave stockbrokers considerable time to analyse prospects.
> – Gareth David, *The Observer*

inveigh, inveigle These two verbs are quite different in sense. It is the similarity of their spelling, and sometimes of their pronunciation, that lies behind the occasional confusion between them.
Inveigh, pronounced /in-**vay**/, means 'to give vent to angry censure, protest vehemently, rail'. It is used with *against*: *He inveighed against the incompetence of the travel agency.*

> 'An indignant Aberdonian', Jack Webster, was accorded the accolade of an article in the *Opinion* slot, to inveigh against 'transparent shallowness'.
> – Bill Greenwell, *The Literary Review*

The word derives from the Latin *invehere*, 'to carry in, sail into, assail, attack'.
The noun from *inveigh* is *invective*, going back to the same Latin verb, via *invectiva oratio*, 'abusive speech'.
Inveigle is pronounced /in-**vayg**'l/ or /in**veeg**'l/: the first of these is the more common pronunciation (though it increases the likelihood of confusion with *inveigh*). The word means either 'to entice or win over by deceit, flattery, or persuasion' — *He inveigled me into joining his plot* —

or 'to make (one's way) or obtain (something) by cajolery': *He inveigled his way into the private club*; *He inveigled my last fiver out of me.*

> Ashley said 'Good-bye', very softly, caught up from the table the wide felt hat she had inveigled from Rhett and walked into the dark front hall.
> – Margaret Mitchell (U.S.),
> *Gone with the Wind*

The noun from *inveigle* is *inveiglement*. *Inveigle* is related to the French word *aveugle*, 'blind', and goes back to the Medieval Latin origin of that word, *ab*, 'out of' + *oculis*, 'eyes'.
Note that *inveigh* and *inveigle* are spelt with an *ei* (as in *neighbour*, *weigh*), not with an *ie* (as in *believe*, *reprieve*).

inverted word order Unlike German or Latin, English today is by and large an 'uninflected' language — that is, there are very few word endings to indicate the grammatical function of a word. Most of the grammatical information comes from the position of a word in a sentence: so, the normal word-order in English statements is Subject — Verb — Object and/or Additional information (such as adverbial or adjectival expressions).
The acrobat caught the net is clearly different in meaning from *The net caught the acrobat,* and *Boy loves girl* from *Girl loves boy*. In other languages, it would be possible to express the two ideas in each pair simply by changing the word endings rather than by changing the word-order. Take Latin: *Puer puellam amat* (Boy loves girl); *Puerum puella amat* (Girl loves boy).
When the customary English word-order is changed, a danger of misunderstanding arises. 'Poetic' word-order can be very confusing: *? The son the father slew.* Who killed whom? Or consider this well-known line from Thomas Gray's 'Elegy Written in a Country Churchyard':

? And all the air a solemn stillness holds.

Is the air holding the stillness or is the stillness holding the air? We are thrown into confusion by the shifting of the verb *holds* from the middle of the sentence to the end.
Of course, some change in the normal pattern is permissible and often desirable. A long text would be very monotonous if all its sentences were constructed on the same grammatical pattern. Inverted word-order does more than add variety and rhythm to a text, however: it helps to create a number of effects — dramatic, ironic, and so on:

Suddenly the door flew open.
(more dramatic than the 'normal' word-order, which places the adverb at the end of the sentence: *The door flew open suddenly*)
Handsome he's not.
(ironic or emphatic in a way that the usual word-order *He's not handsome* is definitely not)
I want to cross the ocean blue.
(more poetic or wistful than the simple *blue ocean*)

Sometimes, too, a departure from normal word-order can help to make a sentence fit smoothly into its surroundings. It is normal to say:

Chapter 1 makes several proposals, including at least one that is highly controversial.
The author says more about that proposal in chapter 3.

But you can easily construct a context in which another word-order is at least as appropriate:

Chapter 1 makes several proposals, including at least one that is highly controversial.
About that proposal the author says more in chapter 3.

A similar effect could be achieved by making the second sentence passive:

Chapter 1 makes several proposals, including at least one that is highly controversial.
That proposal is discussed more fully in chapter 3.

These last two examples illustrate the English tendency to begin a sentence with 'given' information that is already known, and to place 'new' information at the end.

One particular form of inverted word-order raises difficulties of style and usage in English — that is, the placing of a verb before the subject of a clause.

1. In English, the subject typically comes before the verb in statements — *James loves Julie* — and after the verb (or between the two parts of the verb) in yes-no questions: *Does James love Julie?*

Inverted word-order of this kind can occur in sentences other than yes-no questions, but it does not always sound so natural. When it occurs in commands, it may be archaic or regional, or simply informal:

Hear ye the word of the Lord!
Come here, you!
Help, somebody!

Likewise in exclamations it may be old-fashioned:

What a piece of work is a man!
Such loneliness must I suffer!

— though it is still current in certain relatively fixed expressions:

Long live the Queen!
May you always be happy!

2. With statements, things are rather more complicated. In certain constructions, it is quite natural for the subject to follow the verb (or to come between the parts of the verb group) — especially when that verb is the verb *to be*:

There are two symphonies and two violin concertos in tonight's programme.
Included in tonight's programme is a specially commissioned violin concerto by Wolf Blamire.
Among the scheduled works tonight are Beethoven's third symphony and a new violin concerto by Wolf Blamire.
More interesting still is the new Blamire violin concerto.

Take care to use a plural verb when the subject is plural:

× After the interval is Beethoven's third symphony and a concerto by Wolf Blamire.

Strictly speaking, the *is* here should be replaced by *are*.

When the subject is a particularly long and complicated one, you might well want to get the adverb and verb out of the way beforehand:

Over the crest of the hill (there) galloped a hundred-strong herd of those magnificent wild ponies that I had heard so much of but had never previously seen, let alone photographed.

If the standard word-order of Subject — Verb — Adverbial had been attempted here instead, the sentence would sound extremely awkward. This illustrates the principle of 'end-weight': in English, long, 'heavy' constructions tend to come at the end (and since they usually contain 'new' information, they are in keeping with that principle too).

3. There are other good reasons for inverted word-order in a statement — linking it to a previous statement for example, as in such expressions as *Neither can he* or *So do I* or *Out of this grew an entirely new philosophy* or *Next comes the backlash*.

In other cases, inversion is used because some deliberate emotional, rhetorical, or dramatic effect is being sought:

Lovingly did he kiss her.

Pop goes the weasel.
Full many a glorious morning have I seen.
Came the dawn.
And into the room marched — Sgt Hob!
Only by persevering can you expect to attain
success.

Never in the field of human conflict was so
much owed by so many to so few.
— Winston Churchill,
Speech in the House of Commons

Inverted word-order applies to passive verbs, as
in this last example, just as it does to active verbs.

4. Note that the inverted word-order in
statements (subject following verb) almost always
occurs when the adverbial element is placed at the
beginning of the sentence: *Lovingly did he kiss
her*; *Nor can I reveal anything*. But the early
adverb does not as a rule *force* this type of
inverted word-order — it is quite possible to say
Lovingly, he kissed her. However, when this
element is negative (*never, nor, not only, in no
circumstances, in neither instance*; and also
scarcely, hardly, barely, least of all), then the
word-order does have to be inverted. We cannot
say × *Nor I can reveal anything*; × *In no circumstances you must open this cupboard*;
× *Scarcely the alarm had sounded*, and so on.

The words *only* and *rarely* are particularly
interesting in this connection. *Only* takes
inversion when its meaning is negative:

Only in this way can you succeed (= In no
other way can you succeed).

But not when it is attached to the subject:

Only you can succeed.

And not when it has other meanings, such as
'but':

You want to succeed, only in this particular
way you cannot.

Rarely usually requires inversion, in contrast to
sometimes:

Rarely have I seen anything so beautiful.
Sometimes I have seen beautiful things.

Here, *rarely* means 'not often'. But *rarely* can
mean 'now and then — even though not often',
and in this meaning it does not require inversion:

Often he goes to French films, sometimes he
goes to Italian films, and rarely he goes to
American films.

5. Inversion is also possible in certain types of
conditional clause:

Had I known ... (= If I had known ...)
Were I free ... (= If I were free ...)
Should you see him ... (= If you should
see him ...)

6. In general, beware of using inverted word-
order. It is necessary in questions; and in
statements, it does help to bind various clauses
or sentences into a tight relationship. It also adds
variety and style to a long prose text. But as with
all spices and seasoning, it is most effective when
used sparingly. To invert the word-order of every
third or fourth sentence is like adding a spoon
of salt for every two or three spoons of soup.

7. More specifically, there are certain constructions where inverted word-order — though traditionally adopted — today sounds affected and
should be avoided.

a. The order Adverb — Verb — Subject is
common, though slightly old-fashioned, when
some emotional effect is wanted, as discussed
above: *Lovingly did he kiss her*. But if no such
emotional or dramatic effect is called for, such
inverted word-order sounds faintly ridiculous:

? Slowly and subtly does the storyteller unwind
the plot.
? Forcibly is it brought home to the audience
just how malevolent Iago really is.

b. After *as*, and *that*, and in comparisons
generally, an inverted word-order is still found
in official writing. It sounds very stilted even
there, and all the more so in less formal writing:

? Bear in mind that this year's overheads cost
the company almost twice as much as did last
year's.
(preferably: *as last year's did* or simply *as
last year's*)
? Accordingly, we find ourselves, as do most
of our sister-companies, in the unhappy
position of having to withhold the dividend
this year.
(preferably: *as most of our sister-companies
do*)
? At least we can still afford to keep more
plants open and more workers on the payroll
than can either of our two chief rivals.
(preferably: *than either of our two chief
rivals can*)

One excuse for this inverted word-order is that
the subject of the clause after *as* or *then* might
be so long and complicated that the verb would
lose all its impact if left until the end. Consider
the inverted word-order in this sentence:

? However, we are obliged to undertake certain closures and redundancies, as would be any enterprise that has to cater in a time of recession for a clientele at once very specialised and notoriously volatile.

Of course, if the verb *would be* were moved right to the end it would hardly improve the elegance or comprehensibility of the sentence. But it is not necessary to go that far to avoid inverted word-order. The verb does not have to follow the *complete* subject — it is enough if it follows the main part of the subject. So:

> However, we are obliged to undertake certain closures and redundancies, as any enterprise would be that has to cater in a time of recession for a clientele at once very specialised and notoriously volatile.

c. As suggested earlier, there are various conjunction-like adverbs that frequently come at the start of a sentence or clause and require an inverted word-order to follow: *So do I, Nor can I reveal anything,* and so on. But when various other conjunction-like adverbs are followed by this inverted word-order, the effect is one of archaism or affectation. Among such adverbs and adverbial phrases encouraging a stilted inversion of the word-order are *above all, all the more, especially, in particular, rather,* and *yet*:

× Half the crew was ill; half was threatening to mutiny; yet did the captain stubbornly refuse to turn back.
(substitute: *yet the captain stubbornly refused*)
? If it is wrong to resent an injury, all the more is it wrong to resent a favour.
(it would be better to move *all the more* into the middle of the clause, and avoid the inverted word-order: ... *it is all the more wrong to resent a favour*)
?? You ought not to read much significance into that remark; rather should it be seen as a momentary aberration.
(again, move *rather* into the middle of the clause: ... *it should rather be seen* ...)

8. One special type of inverted word-order in written English occurs after direct speech:

'No, you cannot,' said Mrs Robinson.

Certain modern writers, notably Graham Greene, dislike this convention, and insist on retaining the usual word-order:

'No, you cannot,' Mrs Robinson said.

This blanket objection seems needlessly strict.

In three specific cases, however, inversion should be avoided. First, when the subject is a pronoun rather than a noun:

? 'No, you cannot,' said she.

This now sounds almost laughably old-fashioned.

The second case is all too modern, in the view of many purists; that is, when the presentational material comes at the start of the sentence:

? Said Mrs Robinson: 'No, you cannot.'

Associated with American news-magazines in particular, this rather awkward structure is now fairly common in the journalism of Britain and other English-speaking countries as well. Avoid using it unless you are quite sure that it is in keeping with the style of the publication or acceptable to your readers.

The third case concerns verbs more specialised or complex than the simple *said, continued, laughed, replied, wrote,* and the like:

? 'No, you cannot,' admonished Mrs Robinson.
? 'No, you cannot,' went on Mrs Robinson.

In each case the usual word-order should be restored: ... *Mrs Robinson admonished,* ... *Mrs Robinson went on.*

invidious   See INSIDIOUS.

invite   As a noun meaning 'an invitation', *invite* has been recorded as existing in English since as early as 1659. Yet it is still under something of a cloud. The reason is that it seems to duplicate the work of *invitation,* whereas most other nouns derived unchanged from verbs — *a command, a request,* even *a commute* — have the field to themselves; true, the noun *commandment* exists, but it hardly has the same meaning as the noun *command.* So the nouns *command* and *request* are completely acceptable. Even the noun *commute* (attested only since 1954) is not considered vulgar in the way that the noun *invite* sometimes is, though *a commute* is as informal in tone as *an invite.*

The noun *invitation* is safer than the noun *invite* in all circumstances. Use *invite,* if at all, only for special effects, such as assuming the stance of a plain-spoken, unpretentious person impervious to the lure of high society: *They'll be sending us an invite to the May Ball next.*

Note that the noun *invite* is stressed on the first syllable, unlike the verb. This in keeping with a common pattern: *object,* and *record,* for instance, similarly vary their stress.

involve This word attracts criticism when used in a loose or imprecise way: *? everyone involved in the demonstration* (= taking part in); *? The police did not wish to get involved* (= to be drawn in); *? There were allegations that undue violence was involved* (= was used); *? a number of countercharges involving obstruction and provocation* (= of).

The word tends to be extremely uninformative. A sentence such as *John Bradshaw was involved in the trial of Charles I* hardly says much about the nature of the involvement. It does not even tell us which side Bradshaw took; it would be far more helpful to specify that Bradshaw was president of the court that tried the King.

Use *involve* only when its sense is rather sharper. The Latin roots provide a helpful reminder: *involvere* meant 'to enwrap', from *in-*, 'in' + *volvere*, 'to roll or turn'. There is a distinct idea of close interconnection — logical implication, legal entanglement, or deep concentration: *The Minister was heavily involved in the scandal*; *completely involved in his studies. Involved* also means 'intricate or complicated', sometimes 'overcomplicated and confused', and, more informally, 'having a romantic or sexual relationship'.

In parts of southern England, *involve* is pronounced /in-**vōlv**/. This can sound affected to many ears, and is often — perhaps unfairly — considered non-U.

Irish English The history of the English language in Ireland seems to be as complicated as the history of the English people in Ireland — and rather less precise. It is still uncertain exactly when and how spoken English ousted Gaelic as the dominant language, though the outlines at least of its fluctuating fortunes are clear enough.

English was not, in fact, the first Germanic language spoken in Ireland: that honour goes to Norse. There were Viking settlements in the east and south of Ireland from the 9th century until 1150, when the Anglo-Normans, speaking Old English by now, took control of them. Old English was closely related to Norse, so the transition — for those who wished to speak the language of the occupying power — would not have been difficult to make.

By 1250, about three-quarters of Ireland was divided into shires, on the English system, and under English control. The language used in all large settlements was now English.

English authority began to decline in the 14th century, however. Attempts at enforcing anglicisation were largely unsuccessful. Laws might be passed — the Statutes of Kilkenny, in 1366, insisted on the use of English throughout Ireland and on the adoption of English surnames — but the common people ignored them, and went increasingly their own Irish way. By 1500, the country had reverted largely to Gaelic.

The English reconquest of Ireland began about 1550 under the Tudors. By the time of Queen Elizabeth's death in 1603, the English had achieved, in the words of Sir John Davies, 'an universall and absolute conquest of all the Irishrie'.

Throughout the 17th century, settlements of English and Scottish 'planters' expanded, creating a new and distinct community of English speakers within Ireland, marked out from the native population by culture (Anglo-Saxon), religion (Protestant), and language (English).

From that time on Gaelic lost ground increasingly to English, and today there is virtually no Irish person who speaks Gaelic alone. Perhaps 200,000 speak it, together with English, as one of their mother tongues; and efforts are being made to preserve and restore Gaelic: all children in the Republic of Ireland, and most Catholic schoolchildren in Northern Ireland, now study Gaelic at school.

'Irish English' is a rather misleading term. In fact, there are four more or less distinct types of English characteristic of Ireland: standard English (the language of schools, the churches, the media, and most written transactions), Anglo-Irish, Ulster Scots, and Hiberno-English. The account here will concentrate on the last three. Anglo-Irish is the variety spoken by Protestants in Eire, and Ulster Scots the variety spoken by Protestants in Ulster (that is, the six counties of Northern Ireland plus Monaghan, Cavan, and Donegal); Hiberno-English is the variety spoken by Catholics throughout Ireland.

There is, as you would expect, considerable overlap in these three varieties, since they have co-existed in Ireland for over three centuries. In pronunciation, for example, all three varieties retain the *r*-sound after vowels: in words like *park* or *beer*, for instance, the *r* is distinctly sounded by Irish speakers (as it is by Scots and most North Americans, but not by speakers of RP — the 'received pronunciation' of educated people in southeast England).

In addition, /ay/ occurs instead of /ee/ in words such as *key* and *sea* (though this pronunciation is discouraged in schools and is therefore receding). The prevalence of this pronunciation in the Britain of the 17th and 18th centuries is apparent from the following couplet:

Here thou, great Anna! whom three realms
obey,
Dost sometimes counsel take — and
sometimes tea.
> – Alexander Pope,
> *The Rape of the Lock*

Words ending in *-old* are pronounced to rhyme
with *owl*, so *hold* and *howl* are homophones (that
is, they sound identical). Words such as *glance*
and *bath* have the short *a*-sound of *glad* and *bad*;
and words such as *full* and *good* have the long
oo-sound of *rude* and *mood*, so *pull* and *pool* are
homophones. In addition, the *h* is sounded (as
in Scottish English) in words beginning with *wh-*,
so *which* is pronounced /hwich/, thus
distinguishing it from *witch* /wich/, whereas RP
and many other accents fail to distinguish between
these two words.

In vocabulary, all three varieties retain several
English words in their 17th-century sense. The
verb *to annoy* can still mean 'to make anxious,
worry'; *bold* can mean 'naughty'; *to cog*, 'to
cheat'; *delph*, 'crockery'; and *to doubt*, 'to believe
or suspect':

> I'm annoyed the poor child is not well. I
> doubt he has the cold.

In grammar, earlier structures also appear in the
conversation of most Irish speakers. Indirect
questions often retain the inverted word-order of
the original question:

> He asked would you have a match.
> She was wondering will we come.

Double or triple negatives are used for emphasis
— *I never said nothing to nobody* — and irregular
verbs sometimes retain the past tense or past participle forms of the 17th century: *climb-clum*; *dig-
digged*; *write-writ*.

A combination of the double negative and a
17th-century verb form could produce in Ireland
a sentence like *She never writ nothing*, closely
paralleling the concluding couplet of
Shakespeare's sonnet 116 (written about 1590):

> If this be error, and upon me proved,
> I never writ, nor no man ever lov'd.

Anglo-Irish Anglo-Irish developed from the
speech of the 17th-century English settlers,
especially those from the west and northwest of
England. Accordingly, it preserves several 17th-
century peculiarities of pronunciation,
vocabulary, and grammar.

In pronunciation, words like *salt* and *cough* contain the same vowel sound as *saw* (as in American

English too); there is a tendency to pronounce
with to rhyme with *pith*, and /garss/ is still
occasionally heard for *grass*.

In vocabulary, earlier and dialectal forms of
English are still found. These include *lap* for
wrap, hough (/hokh/) for *hock* ('a fetlock') and
fashion for *behaviour*.

In grammar, there is a tendency to avoid continuous tenses, preferring *The kettle boils* to *The
kettle is boiling*, and *The beast lows* to *The cow
is lowing*.

Ulster Scots Ulster Scots developed from the
speech of Scottish settlers. It has many features
of pronunciation, vocabulary, and grammar in
common with those of southwest Scotland,
though many are now unique to Ulster Scots,
either having died out in Scotland, or else having developed independently in Ireland.

In pronunciation, the *r* after vowels, as in *park*
and *beer*, is not only sounded but also trilled. And
the consonant clusters *tr* and *dr* are often pronounced /thr/ and /t͟hr/ (a feature that Ulster
Scots shares with Northern Hiberno-English), so
that *try* is pronounced /thrī/ and *dry* /t͟hrī/.

The vowel in *down, ground*, and similar words
is often the Scottish /ōo/ rather than the RP
/ow/, producing sentences that sound like *He
bent doon to the groon*. (The /ōo/ sound of RP,
as in *two* or *mood*, becomes slightly shifted in
turn, producing a vowel similar in quality to the
u in French *vu*.)

In vocabulary, Ulster Scots retains many words
and senses of Scottish origin (some adopted from
French during the 'Auld Alliance'):

ashet a large plate (from the French *assiette*)
burn a stream
but-and-ben a small house
dishabels, /dishə-b'ls/ untidy, scruffy (from the
French *déshabillé*)
jeg to prick
wee small.

A more obscure list, also known in parts of
Scotland, would include:

boke to vomit
drooth thirst
dwam dizziness, temporary loss of balance
hogo a bad smell (from the French *haut goût*)
lift to steal
hoke to poke around, search for
skite to splash
skunder (noun or verb) distaste; to sicken
thole to endure.

In grammar, *nae* is used to indicate negation —
He shouldnae go for he disnae like her—and *aye* is

used, as in Scotland, to mean both *yes* and *always*:

> She was aye thrig (She was always neat and tidy)
> Aye, wasn't she (Yes, she was indeed).

In Ulster Scots, as in many other working-class varieties of English, there is a strong tendency to reduce the number of verb forms in the language, producing, for example:

> He went oot and he woulda went oot at any time.
> Will you give me the money? No, I give it to you yesterday.
> I seen your father this morning.

Hiberno-English Hiberno-English is the mother tongue of over 70 per cent of the population in Ireland. It has developed from the English used by people whose ancestral mother-tongue was Gaelic, and it shows the influence of Gaelic in pronunciation, vocabulary, grammar, and idiom. There are two main sub-varieties: Northern and Southern Hiberno-English. Their differences are due to the dialect differences in the original Gaelic of the two areas, and also to the strong Scottish influence on Northern Hiberno-English.

In pronunciation, the *r* after vowels, as in *park* and *beer*, is typical in Gaelic too, and may have reinforced its retention in Anglo-Irish and Ulster Scots pronunciation.

There is a marked breathiness in the pronunciation of the consonants *p, t* and *k*, a breathiness that has been described as 'the peat in the voice'.

In Southern Hiberno-English, the two sounds of *th* are realised as a dental /t/ and /d/ rather than as /th/ and /th̲/, so *thin* sounds like *tin*, and *then* like *den*. Northern Hiberno-English, like Ulster Scots, keeps the /th/ or /th̲/ pronunciation in words like *thin* and *then* but extends it to words containing the combinations *tr* and *dr*, so *try* and *dry* become /thrī/ and /thrī/. The phrase *three trees* therefore sounds like *tree trees* in Southern Hiberno-English, and like *three threes* in Northern.

In vocabulary, Hiberno-English is marked by the retention in modified form of many Gaelic words:

backy (Gaelic: bacach) lame
clobber (Gaelic: clabar) mud
graw (Gaelic: gradh) love, affection, a crush
keeny (Gaelic: caoineadh) a cry or lament due to a death
twig (Gaelic: tuig) to understand.

In grammar, Hiberno-English has many 'verb forms and constructions available to it that are not found in standard English. So, in addition to *He's tired*, for instance:

> He biz tired (He's regularly tired)
> He diz be tired (He's regularly and habitually tired)
> I'm afther seeing him and him as full as a shuch (I've just seen him and he was as drunk as can be — *shuch*, pronounced /shukh̲/, comes from the Gaelic *sruth*, 'a river').

A great many constructions and turns of phrase derive from Gaelic equivalents. Gaelic, for instance, does not have individual words for 'yes' and 'no'. Questions are answered by re-using the verb of the question, and this tendency has been carried over into Hiberno-English:

> Would you be wanting a drink? I would, to be sure.
> Have you heard the latest? I have not.

And 'foregrounding', a widely used stylistic device in Gaelic, is a feature of Hiberno-English:

> It's mad in the head you are.
> It's tired I am of this trummicky (awkward) business.
> It was dead she was.

It is probably at the level of idiom that Hiberno-English is most clearly differentiated from Anglo-Irish and Ulster Scots. In Hiberno-English, as in Gaelic, a distinction is made, for instance, between being full of food — *as full as a trout* — and full of drink: *as full as a shuch*. Speakers delight in similes translated from the Gaelic —

> as fat in the forehead as a hen (unintelligent)
> as mean as get out
> as often as fingers and toes (many times)

— and in Gaelic-based proverbs that often take time to unravel:

> An inch is a dale (a large amount) in a man's nose (Don't talk about what you nearly did)
> There's a truth in the last drop in the bottle (Is it *the* truth or a whisky truth?)

Irish English and World English The reconquest of Ireland during the 16th and 17th centuries coincided with the most vibrant period of the English language — the period that included Shakespeare and his contemporaries. It was this English that the Irish adopted and adapted, and in many respects the English of modern Ireland is far closer to that rich heritage than the English of modern Britain is. Irish English has always had, and continues to have, an unmistakable exuberance — an exuberance that has found expression in the language of the plays of Sheridan, Goldsmith, Oscar Wilde, J.M. Synge, George Bernard Shaw, Sean O'Casey, and Samuel Beckett; in the prose writings of Jonathan Swift, Edmund Burke, James Joyce, and Iris Murdoch; and in the poetry of Thomas Moore, W.B. Yeats, and Seamus Heaney. The Irish contribution to English literature has been proportionally greater than that of any other English-speaking nation.

But it is not only their literary talents that the Irish have shared with the world. The thousands of Irish people deported to the colonies between the 17th and the 19th centuries helped to spread English to the West Indies, the Americas, and Australia; and the missionary zeal which took so many Irish priests and nuns to Africa left a linguistic imprint on African English.

To World English, the Gaelic language (whether from Ireland or Scotland or jointly) has bequeathed a wealth of terms from *brat* to *brogue, spree, smithereens, leprechaun,* and *whiskey galore.*

What the future holds is unclear: local differences may be smoothed out and a drift develop towards a standardised Irish English. But it will remain a distinctly Irish English: neither American nor British influence is likely to encroach on Ireland's linguistic independence.

ironic, sarcastic An *ironic* remark or effect implies a twofold view of things — a literal meaning and a different intention. It comes from a Greek word meaning 'pretended ignorance, or saying the opposite of what is meant'. Used gently, irony conveys amused mockery or banter:

> Mr Richard Harvey is going to be married, but it is a great secret and only known to half the neighbourhood, so you must not mention it.
>
> — Jane Austen, letter (1796)

Ironic is used of life as well as of language: *Isn't it ironic that so many doctors take drug overdoses?* Some critics dislike this loose sense of *ironic* or *irony.* Use it sparingly. If the oddity is an extremely unimportant one, it probably does not deserve to be graced with the imposing adjective *ironic:* it is no more than *odd.*

Ironical is a variant of *ironic,* used mostly in direct reference to people: *an ironical critic.*

> He was a man who looked across a gulf at his fellow beings. An intelligent person in that position becomes extremely ironical. ...

There was a streak of coldness.
> — Sir Stephen Spender, *The Observer*

Dramatic irony again involves a double view — it refers to a tense situation in a play, when the audience knows of some important detail or danger that the character is ignorant of.

Socratic irony refers to the teaching technique, used by the philosopher Socrates, of pretending to be ignorant of a truth in order to induce a pupil or opponent to work it out and accept it for himself.

Irony is sometimes confused with *sarcasm.* Certainly irony is a major weapon in the armoury of sarcasm, but it does not have to be biting in the way that sarcasm does. *Sarcastic,* whether applied to people or remarks, suggests a cruel and taunting ridicule. It goes back to the Greek verb *sarkazein,* literally 'to tear the flesh', hence 'to bite one's lips in rage' or 'to speak bitterly'. The cutting or wounding intention of sarcasm is often conveyed by irony — saying something opposite or irrelevant to what is intended. To say *Congratulations!* to someone who has dropped a plate would be to make a sarcastic remark. Here is another example of sarcasm:

> One couldn't help feeling that many were about as interested in the treasures they guard as a teetotaller is in the *Oktoberfest.*
>
> — Judy Froschaug, *The Times*

irregardless See REGARD 3.

irregular verbs See -ED, -T; VERBS 1.

-ise, -ize 1. Which spelling is to be preferred: *dramatise* or *dramatize, Africanise* or *Africanize*? The preference in this book is for *-ise* (and hence *-isation, -isable,* and so on), though such publishers as Oxford University Press, Cambridge University Press, and *The Times* now opt for *-ize.* The *-ise* ending is similar to that used in French, *-iser;* the *-ize* ending reflects the original Latin ending *-izare,* based on the Greek *-izein.*

Appeals to a word's history to account for a preferred spelling carry little weight. The *-ise/ -ize* ending is affixed not just to Greek roots (*organise, ionise*) or Latin roots directly (*fossilise*) or indirectly (*utilise*), but also to purely French roots (*gormandise*), Spanish roots (*cannibalise*), proper nouns or adjectives derived from them (*pasteurise, Americanise*), and so on. And the ending might be added at different points in the development of a root (*memorise, memorialise*), or change its form as it moves from language to language: *to baptise* derives from Middle English *baptizen*, from old French *baptiser*, from late Latin *baptizare*, from Greek *baptizein*. There is no clear guide in all this to a choice between *-ise* and *-ize* in modern English.

In American English, *-ize* is the only standard form for most words (hence the preference, among many British writers, for *-ise*!); *-ize* is also a better rendering of the pronunciation. Again, however, this is not a very convincing argument in its favour, since many verbs pronounced /-īz/ are spelt only *-ise*, the usual variant of *-ize* being unavailable. This brings us to the one spelling principle that is relevant here: when the suffix is added to a root that is itself a full word, both *-ise* and *-ize* are possible: *union* produces *unionise/unionize*, *civil* produces *civilise/civilize*, and so on. *To advertise* (where only *-ise* is possible, though Americans occasionally allow *-ize*) is the one exception (the stem being the older verb *to advert*, not the derived British colloquial noun **ad**vert). Note that the obverse of this principle does not hold good: in *utilise/utilize* or *baptise/baptize*, both spellings are possible, even though the element before the suffix is not a self-contained word as it stands.

As for the verbs that take only *-ise* (and those that take only *-ize*), the *-ise* (or *-ize*) is usually not a suffix as such, but part of the base word. The verbs that take only *-ize* are very few: the commonest are *capsize, prize, seize*, and *size*. Of the verbs that take *-ise* only, the commonest are these: *advertise, advise, apprise, arise, chastise, circumcise, comprise, compromise, despise, devise, disguise, enfranchise, excise, exercise, improvise, merchandise, prise open* (though *prize open* is possible in American English), *promise, poise, praise, raise, revise, rise, supervise, surmise, surprise, televise*.

Though some of these are occasionally found spelt *-ize* in American English, *-ise* is really the only acceptable form in World English. But hundreds of other verbs can be spelt with either *-ise* or *-ize* in British English: *anaesthetise/ize, bowdlerise, crystallise, idolise, Hellenise, jeopardise, legalise, modernise, realise, sterilise...*

Within this open-ended list, the choice is yours — though changing fashions may push you in one direction or the other. The one obligation is consistency: if you choose *-ize* to begin with, stick with it throughout (except for those words that take only *-ise*). If you use *-ize* for a verb, use *-ization* for the corresponding noun, *-izable* for the adjective, and so on — *civilize, civilization, civilizable* — and if you use *-ise* for a verb, use *-isation* and *-isable*: *civilise, civilisation, civilisable*.

Remember, too, that if you opt for *-ise*, you will make very few mistakes, since far more words allow only *-ise* than allow only *-ize*. However, your spelling will then be marked as British rather than American or 'mid-Atlantic'.

2. The rules are rather stricter in the case of the ending *-lyse* (also of Greek origin), as in *analyse, catalyse*, and *paralyse*. This is the only acceptable British spelling, though *-lyze* predominates in American English (*analyze, catalyze, paralyze*), and is now occasionally encountered in Britain too: a recent British book on English grammar was called *Analyzing English*. However, the related nouns are always spelt with *-lysis* in both varieties — *analysis, paralysis* — since the pronunciation of these nouns uses /s/ rather than /z/.

3. Careful users of English have long rallied against the tendency — particularly common in American English, and in the jargon of sociologists, bureaucrats, advertising agents, and so on — to create new verbs ending in *-ise/-ize*. The temptation is to append the suffix to any noun or adjective at hand, instead of taking the trouble to think of an appropriate established verb: *to accessorise, to capsulise, to martyrise, to prioritise, to routinise, to therapise*. The verb *to finalise* is the best-known case. (See FINALISE.) It often does no work that is not already done by *to end, to finish*, or *to complete*. *To finalize* (or *finalise*) has been in existence for over 60 years, and has been in widespread use for over 20. It is too late to banish it, but easy enough to boycott it. Other well-established *-ise* words are subjected to equal disapproval: *to conceptualise, to destabilise, to glamorise, to itemise, to moisturise*, and *to tenderise*. Unfortunately, it is not always easy to paraphrase these verbs.

The verb *to pressurise* is particularly interesting. British English can use it both literally (as in *a pressurised cabin*) and figuratively (*to pressurise someone into doing something*). American English generally discriminates, using *to pressurize* literally (*a pressurized cabin*) but *to pressure* figuratively (*to pressure someone into doing something*). Both verbs are apparently of relatively recent origin: *to pressure* is attested since 1938, *to pressurise* since 1940.

Some coinages are useful, of course: *to denationalise* (or *to privatise*), *to hospitalise, to personalise, to politicise, to computerise, to containerise, to decimalise, to publicise*. These are not as a rule ousting any established verb, but serving instead to fill a lexical gap — making the language more efficient in representing a concept by a single word rather than a complicated phrase. Even when a new word serves this purpose, however, it is sometimes so ugly that it is best avoided: *to comprehensivise, to concertise, to decriminalise, to defamiliarise.*

it **1.** Make sure, when using *it* or any other pronoun, that your reader or listener knows exactly what you are referring to.

? In frustration, he struck at the hoe with his axe, and it broke across the shaft.

Which was it that broke — the axe or the hoe? Again:

? Its budget is likely to dominate the first day's discussion at the conference of the general council of the Theosophy Society.

Whose finances — the conference's, the council's, or the society's?

This last example illustrates another common failing — the use of *it* (or some other pronoun) earlier in the sentence than the noun it refers to. Although such sentences are occasionally clear and effective, all too often the reader is kept waiting impatiently, holding the thread in his hand and trying to learn where it belongs.

? Now that it has established itself as so dependable, as well as symbolic in all sorts of ways, the Concorde is obliged to remain in service despite its economic impracticability.
? Since it has a quite different chemical structure and mode of operation from the bacterium, the virus is unaffected by antibiotics.

In each case, the long first clause remains incomprehensible until the relevant noun (*Concorde, virus*) at last appears in the second clause — at which point the reader or listener has probably lost the thread after all, and has to return to the beginning of the sentence and approach it once again. The remedy, as a rule, is simply to transpose *it* and the noun:

Now that Concorde has established itself as so dependable, as well as symbolic in all sorts of ways, it is obliged to remain in service despite its economic impracticability.

But the cure sometimes has an unfortunate side-effect — confusion once again over which noun the *it* refers to:

? Since the virus has a quite different chemical structure and mode of operation from the bacterium, it is unaffected by antibiotics.

Does the *it* here refer to *virus* or *bacterium*? Probably to *virus*, but some possibility of misinter-

pretation persists. The original sentence is at least better than this, but there is still a way around it: the proper remedy would be to reverse the two clauses of the original example —

The virus is unaffected by antibiotics, since it has a quite different chemical structure and mode of operation from the bacterium.

2. *it is X that.* One useful way of emphasising or 'marking' a word or phrase in a sentence is by placing it after the words *it is* or *it was* at the beginning of a clause, and by following it with *that, which,* or *who* (or sometimes no relative pronoun at all), and then the rest of the sentence. Instead of using a loud voice or italics for emphasis —

But the accident happened on *Wednesday,* and I'm always out of town on Wednesdays

— you can use the *it is X that* construction for variety or as a more elegant alternative:

But it was on Wednesday that the accident happened, and I'm always out of town on Wednesdays.

Similarly:

It's the tax concessions that attract so many expatriate writers to Ireland.
It was Abraham Lincoln who said you can't fool all of the people all of the time.
It's a Ford Capri (that) he drives, not a Ford Cortina.

He is also very experienced and has some genuine achievements to his name. It was he more than anyone, except Mr Trudeau himself, who was responsible for the successful outcome of that interminable wrangle over the 'patriation' of the Canadian constitution.
— Tim Heard, *Daily Telegraph*

Such 'clefting' raises several points. First, relative pronouns other than *that, which,* and *who* should not really be used in the pattern. So it is wrong, or at least of doubtful acceptability, to say:

? But it was on Wednesday when the accident happened.
? It is on Table Mountain where this particular wild flower is found.

Change *when* and *where* to *that.*

Secondly, the form of the verb that follows *that* takes its cue not from the *it* but from the noun or pronoun after the *is.* So: *It is I who am asking* the favour, not × *It is I who is asking the favour.* (However, *It is me who is being asked the favour.*) Similarly, the verb after *that* will be in the plural if the noun before *that* is a plural noun. Even though the subject of the sentence is *it* and might seem to call for a singular verb in the subordinate clause too, it is wrong to say:

× It's the tax concessions that attracts so many expatriate writers to Ireland.

Change *attracts* to *attract.*

Thirdly, *that* is slightly preferable to *which* in the construction, even though *which* is widely used. Somehow, *that* sounds more natural and idiomatic. (See THAT.)

Fourthly, if a preposition is involved, it is best placed in the first clause — the *it was* clause. Do not hold it back until the subordinate clause, as in this example:

? But it was Wednesday that the accident happened on

or

? But it was Wednesday on which the accident happened.

Restore the preposition *on* to the main clause:

But it was on Wednesday that the accident happened.

Lastly, there is a tendency to use the *it is X that* construction far too often. Do not use it simply as a supposedly elegant flourish — it will only sound pompous. Reserve it for contexts where some special emphasis is needed.

3. A similar construction is the use of the passive voice after *it*:

It is reported from Zaire that a coup has been thwarted.
It is suspected that the wolf is now hiding in a nearby copse.

This 'impersonal' use of the verb is helpful when the reporter is unknown, for example, or when the suspicion is a very widespread one, or when it is necessary for the writer or speaker to keep a distance from the view or claim expressed. But the construction is very much overused. The social sciences in particular draw on it as a favourite jargon expression — ? *It is hypothesised that* . . . ; ? *It was assumed that* — to convey a sense of spurious scientific objectivity. *Who* is advancing the hypothesis? *Who* assumes? It sounds far less pretentious, surely, to spell out what you mean: *Some experts have hypothesised* . . . , or *I assumed that* . . .

4. A related construction is represented by such examples as:

It is surprising that he should have come so late.
It would be wonderful if you could come to the party.

Remember that the use of this 'dummy' *it* is equally appropriate at other places in the sentence:

I consider it surprising that he should have come so late.
I'd like it very much if you could come to the party.

See also ITS, IT'S; IT'S ME.

italics *Italics,* or *italic,* or the *italic* typeface, acquired its name in a peculiar way. The sloping type was first used in 1501, by the Venetian printing house of Aldus Manutius, in an edition of Virgil that was dedicated to the land of Italy. (The Latin word was *italicus,* from the Greek *italikos.*)

The ordinary typeface is known as *roman*: this entire sentence, for example, is printed in roman, except for two occurrences of the word *roman,* which are printed in italics.

In handwritten or typewritten text, italics are represented by underlining.

Italics are often used for decoration or to be eye-catching, as in advertisements or chapter-headings. As with all unusual or attention-getting habits in writing, italics should be used sparingly if they are to retain their effect. Needless use leads to familiarity, and thence to contempt.

Italics can take a singular or plural verb: *Italics is/are needed here.* (See -ICS.)

1. a. Italics are used for the titles of self-contained publications (written works that are separately published, rather than being part of a collection) and of most works of art in other media:

Tolstoy's *War and Peace* (novel)
Wagner's *Tristan und Isolde* (opera)
Newsweek (magazine)
The Mirror (newspaper)
Osborne's *Luther* (play)
Michelangelo's *David* (sculpture)
Picasso's *Guernica* (painting)
Eisenstein's *Battleship Potemkin* (film)

A major exception is the Bible, whose name is printed in roman, as are the names of its books (John 16:43) and its major divisions: the Old Testament, the New Testament, the Pentateuch. Other sacred scriptures may also be treated in this way: the Koran, the Torah.

A distinction is often made between long poems, which might be published on their own, and short poems. Titles of long poems are referred to in italics; titles of short poems are enclosed in quotation marks:

Eliot's *Four Quartets*
Eliot's 'Gerontion'

A distinction is also made between titles of books and titles of short stories, articles, or chapters in books:

Chomsky's *Aspects of the Theory of Syntax*
Chomsky's 'Remarks on Nominalization'

The result is that the same title can be referred to in different ways:

Jerzy Skolimowski's film *The Shout* was based on Robert Graves's story 'The Shout'.

A distinction is also often made between the names of works of music, which are italicised, and their descriptions, which are often simply in roman:

Beethoven's *Eroica Symphony*
Beethoven's Symphony No. 3

b. Note that the -*s* suffix in the plurals of such italicised titles is sometimes shown in roman:

examining three *Newsweek*s.

c. Italics are also used when referring to the names of vehicles —

the *Brighton Belle* (train)
the *QE II* (ship)

— but not when using their trade names:

a Ford Cortina.

d. Italics are also used to refer to court cases:

the case of *Regina* v *Smith*

The *v* of *versus* is usually printed in roman.

e. An interesting problem concerns the use of the word *the* — is it part of the title? Sometimes it is and sometimes it is not. The periodical now known as *New Scientist* was originally called *The New Scientist*. When *The* (or *A*) is part of a title, some people prefer to leave it out when it sounds awkward. Thus you can have either:

Shakespeare's *The Tempest*

or

Shakespeare's *Tempest*

See A, AN **5** and THE **4** for further details.

2. Italics are used when referring to words, letters, and figures as such:

The word *numinous* is beautiful
the name *Socrates*
Some people do not pronounce their *h*'s.
Is that number *205*?

(Note the way the plural, *h*'s, is written.)

This use of italics makes it possible to distinguish between such pairs of sentences as:

Socrates has eight letters

and

Socrates was a Greek philosopher

— and also between

Is that number *205*? (or did you say *206*?)

and

Is that number 205? (or 206? — I've lost count)

3. a. Italics are used for words and phrases from foreign languages that are felt to be not yet established in English:

(French) *coup de maître,* 'masterstroke'
(German) *Gleitzeit,* 'flexitime'

Note that when such expressions are 'glossed' (that is, given a brief definition or translation) the gloss generally appears in single quotation marks or brackets.

It is not always easy to decide when such expressions have become a part of the English language. It is easy to imagine coming across a sentence like:

Her coup d'état was a real *coup de maître.*

The phrase 'coup d'état' here is familiar enough to be printed in roman. This decision might depend on the type of writing involved. A literary critic, addressing other literary critics, might write of:

the familiar topoi found throughout the essay.

The same literary critic, addressing a wider public, might prefer to write of:

the familiar *topoi* (well-known traditional rhetorical devices) found throughout the essay.

Contrast this treatment of foreign terms with the treatment of variant, dialectal, or deviant English terms — here quotation marks instead are used:

They all got medals, or what some people would call 'gongs'.
We got trapped in a lift in New York — I mean an 'elevator'.
I can't warm to 'hearties' like the Beauchamp twins.

b. Italics are used too for the technical names of plants and animals — a particular type of scientific Latin:

The horse (*Equus caballus*) has affected the course of history more than any other animal.
The lilac (*Syringa vulgaris*) has several medical uses.

A typical technical name of this sort will consist of two parts: the genus (capitalised) and the species. When groups of higher rank are named, they are traditionally put in roman. The Reader's Digest *Great Illustrated Dictionary* defines one sense of *man* as:

A member of the genus *Homo,* family Hominidae, order Primates, class Mammalia, characterised by erect posture and an opposable thumb; especially, a member of the only extant species, *Homo sapiens*, distinguished by the ability to communicate by means of organised speech and to record information in a variety of symbolic systems.

4. In ordinary writing, italics play an important role in showing that a word, a phrase, or a part of a word or phrase is to be given special emphasis — for the sake of urging the reader to reflect on it, for example, or as indicating a contrast:

She wondered if the best way would be to yank him down, hard, and hope that she could pull him right through the rotten gutter. But then the whole gutter could possibly rip free of the roof — and *then* what? she thought. She saw them both swept off the fire escape and falling. But she knew no one could actually go up *on* the rain gutter and pull the child out.
— John Irving (U.S.),
The World According to Garp

Consider this simple example:

She left on *Thursday*

(as distinct from Wednesday). Such emphasis in writing corresponds to various devices of pronunciation and intonation in speech, and can often clarify what would otherwise be an ambiguous sentence. Thus the normal interpretation of:

I only saw her on Thursday

would be 'I didn't see her on any other day' (see ONLY). However, if you write:

I only *saw* her on Thursday

you are implying that you did not speak to her.

Traditionally, this use of 'emphatic' italics (or underlining) has been discouraged by schoolteachers, editors, and purists generally. It is considered the easy way out. It is preferable to restructure the sentence and allow word-order to convey the proper emphases. The commonest emphasising device is the 'it is' construction:

It was on Thursday that she left.

But it is not always possible to use it. Sometimes, italics are the least objectionable form of emphasis. It is certainly no improvement to reword

I only *saw* her on Thursday

as

?? My only contact with her on Thursday was a visual one.

5. In dictionaries, italics are used for a variety of purposes — for instance, marking parts of speech (*n.* = 'noun'), labels (*Informal*; *Nonstandard*; *Astronomy*; *Chiefly U.S.*), and various comments on usage (*Often capitalised*).

In addition, many dictionaries and other language books (including this one) use italics when giving examples of a usage point or specimen sentences illustrating a word in context.

6. The interplay of all these conventions can produce difficulties: it sometimes happens that a word or phrase deserves to be italicised on two or three different counts. The name of a ship or aircraft, for instance, should be in italics; and a film title should be in italics: what about the name of a ship or aircraft as part of a film title? As it happens, the films *Raise the Titanic* and *The Flight of the Phoenix* simply ignore the problem, and that is perhaps the best approach to it.

Nevertheless, it is a pity that the role italics have of setting a word or phrase off from its context cannot really be maintained if that context itself is in italics. With quotation marks, subdivisions are possible, by shifting from single quotation marks to double quotation marks and back again. But to alternate between italics and roman might not work, since the roman part might simply blend into the surrounding roman context:

? Have you read *A Study of Dante's* Inferno by Professor Lowe?

Other solutions are possible, less uncompromising about the rules, but at least less confusing as well:

Have you read *A Study of Dante's* **Inferno** by Professor Lowe?
Have you read 'A Study of Dante's *Inferno*' by Professor Lowe?
Have you read *A Study of Dante's 'Inferno'* by Professor Lowe?

and once again the simplest (and likeliest):

Have you read *A Study of Dante's Inferno* by Professor Lowe?

-ite, -ian When used with reference to humans, the Greek-based suffix *-ite* and the Latin-based suffix *-ian* (or *-an* or *-ean*) share a few shades of meaning. They can both indicate, for instance, a native or resident of a specified place — a *Guernseyite*; a *Liverpudlian* — and a member of a people or family: the *Ammonites*; the *Martians*. (The *-ite* ending also indicates an adherent of an idea or way of life: a *socialite*. And the *-ian* ending can indicate an expert or specialist in a specified subject: a *mathematician*.)

One other sense that the two suffixes share is 'a believer in or follower of': *Pre-Raphaelite, neo-Darwinian, a Christian, a Bennite*.

What determines whether *-ian* or *-ite* is used? Partly, considerations of sound seem to be at work: *? Friedmanian* is more difficult to pronounce than *Friedmanite* (referring to the American economist Milton Friedman). In fact, the use of *-ian* often requires a change in the stress or pronunciation of the base word: **Dar**win but *Dar**win**ian*, **Liver**pool but *Liver**pud**lian*, **Shaw** but **Shav**ian. The addition of *-ite*, however, leaves the base word unaffected. Compare the derivatives of **Wag**ner: *Wag**ner**ian* (the usual form) and **Wag**nerite (as in George Bernard Shaw's book *The Perfect Wagnerite*). Admirers of the novelist Jane **Aus**ten were always **Aus**tenites (now often *Janeites* or *Janites*) rather than *?? Austenians* — presumably for reasons of euphony.

But it goes deeper than that: there does seem to be something slightly more negative about the *-ite* ending, a suggestion of an unjustified cult following rather than a genuine ideological movement, or of a distortion of the original theories rather than a consistent continuation of them.

So, a *Chomskyan* or *Chomskian* (noun) is an adherent of the deservedly renowned linguistic theories of Professor Noam Chomsky, and a *Chomskyan theory* (adjective) is one in keeping with the letter or spirit of these theories. The word

Chomskyite, on the other hand, suggests either that the person is a rather rebellious or heretical disciple of Chomsky, or that Chomsky is unjustifiably celebrated and does not deserve a following at all. And a *Chomskyite theory* suggests a theory that might have been sparked off by Chomsky's ideas but has now strayed far from the orthodox *Chomskyan* view of things. (Other suffixes are possible too. A lukewarm proponent of Chomsky's ideas might be called a *Chomskyoid*. An ardent disciple might call himself a *Chomskyist*: *-ist* is a much more respectful suffix than *-ite* or *-ian*, implying the existence of a full and coherent system of thought — *Chomskyism* — for people to believe in or follow.)

There is a third possible basis for the choice between *-ite* and *-ian*: quite simply that *-ite* has recently, within the last 40 years perhaps, become more popular than *-ian*, especially for a noun.

Any of these three reasons could account for the following distribution: *Churchillian* but *Gaitskellite* (Hugh Gaitskell was the leader of the British Labour Party from 1955 to 1963); *Reaganite, Thatcherite, Nasserite, Bennite, Powellite, Hawkite*; *Hitlerian* formerly, today often *Hitlerite*; *Jamesian* and *Leavisite*, referring to champions or imitators of the novelist and critic Henry James (1843-1916) and adherents of the approach to literary criticism of the late Dr F.R. Leavis (1895-1978).

its, it's The misuse of the apostrophe in *it's/its* betrays an uncertain grasp of the finer points of English. Used with an apostrophe, *it's* is always an abbreviation of 'it is' or 'it has': *It's good to hear that it's been dealt with at last.*

Its, without the apostrophe, is the possessive form of the pronoun *it* — the equivalent of *my*, *her*, *their*, *our*, and so on: *The curtain has lost one of its rings.* It is very difficult to use *its* other than in front of the noun it refers to; anything else sounds very awkward: *? This can't be our dog's bone, but perhaps that bone there is its.*

Its is a relatively new addition to English. Although it first appeared in about 1600 (originally spelt as *it's*!), it had to share the field for some time with *it* and *his*. Shakespeare uses them all. Here is an example of *his* for *its*:

This day I breathed first; time is come round,
And where I did begin, there shall I end;
My life is run his compass.
— Cassius, in *Julius Caesar* V iii

His remained a rival of *its* throughout the 17th century. The King James Bible of 1611 uses *his* frequently:

Ye are the salt of the earth, but if the salt have lost his savour, wherewith shall it be salted? It is thenceforth good for nothing, but to be cast out, and to be trodden under foot of men.

– Matthew 5:13

Gradually, however, *his* became restricted to the masculine possessive.

See also -'S, -S'.

it's me   A few old-fashioned purists continue to object to this widespread phrase. According to the schoolroom rule (based on Latin grammar), the verb *to be* requires the subject-form of the pronoun in such constructions:

? 'Who's there?' — 'It is I.'
? Oh no, it's not *he* again, is it?
? I don't know who was responsible, but it wasn't we.

Yet such constructions sound intolerably affected — they may represent correct grammar, but they are far from good idiom, and would raise a laugh of ridicule rather than a compliment, if used in ordinary conversation or writing.

It sounds natural only in such patterns as *It was X who Y.* So: *It wasn't we who broke the window.* But even here, the object-form *us* is still probably more idiomatic. Note, by the way, that the verb can change according to the form of the pronoun used: *It is I who am responsible,* but *It's me who is responsible.*

What all this reveals is the danger of trying to transfer a Latin rule to English grammar. French, which is actually descended from Latin, has no such rule: instead, French has a third form for its pronouns — *C'est moi, c'est lui,* and so on rather than × *C'est je,* × *C'est il,* or × *C'est me,* × *C'est le,* and so on. The English object-forms — *me, him, them,* and so on — are related to these French forms in other ways; so if we took French rather than Latin as our model, then it might in fact be considered correct to say *It's me, It wasn't us,* and so on.

But English does not need to take its rules from any other language anyway. Its system and its idiom are peculiar to itself. Idiom prefers *It's me* to *It is I.*

The colloquial expression *That's me* is established as an informal idiom: '*Hey, are you Dr Deadrock?*' — '*That's me.*' It would be quite inappropriate to change this to × *That's I.* It would, of course, be equally inappropriate to use the expression in a formal setting:

?? 'How do you do: you are Dr Deadrock, I believe?' — 'That's me.'
?? 'Dr Livingstone, I presume?' — 'That's me.'

The phrase *That's right* is stylistically more neutral, neither too casual nor overformal.

See also BETWEEN YOU AND I; PRONOUNS.

-ize   See -ISE, -IZE.

J, K

jail, gaol These variant spellings are equally acceptable in British English, both as the noun meaning 'prison' and as the verb meaning 'to imprison'. *Jail* is the far commoner form, however, and in American English the only acceptable form. *Gaol* might well die out in British English too in due course, partly through the danger of confusion with the word *goal*.

The difference in spelling is due to the slightly different routes the two forms took on their way from Vulgar Latin into English: two forms developed, the Old French *jaiole* and the Norman French *gaiole*, and both passed independently into Middle English.

These forms in turn go back ultimately to the Latin adjective *cavus*, 'hollow', which is the source of the words *cage* and *cave* as well.

Note that derivatives and compounds too can take either spelling: *gaoler* or *jailer*, *gaolbird* or *jailbird*, and so on.

jargon The word *jargon* tends to be used in an impatient or dismissive way nowadays: *Enough of that jargon — just tell me what you mean in plain English*. This pejorative use is likely to take over completely in time to come, and would be authorised in this by the origins of the word *jargon*: in Middle English, *iargoun* or *gargoun* meant 'meaningless chatter, gibberish' (it is still sometimes used in this sense), and in Old French *jargoun* or *gargon* referred to the twittering of birds. But at the moment the word *jargon* still has a neutral sense — just as jargon itself has a legitimate positive function.

That function is to make communication more efficient between members of a professional or social grouping. *Jargon* refers to the specialised vocabularies of such groups — technical expressions or 'terminology' that may be incomprehensible to laymen (either because the words themselves are quite unfamiliar, or because they are being used in a quite unfamiliar sense) but that are valued shorthand counters of communication to insiders. Consider this sentence, for instance, from an American computer magazine:

The relocatable machine-code program is turned into an executable, absolute machine code by the linker, CLINK, which also merges the user's program with previously compiled program files (such as the standard C function library) if necessary.

– Christopher Kern (U.S.), *Byte*

However opaque this statement might seem to the layman, it represents a clear and economical exposition of facts to a computer specialist. Similarly scientists, soldiers, publishers, philosophers, dressmakers, and doctors all use some special vocabulary among themselves: if physicists were barred from using *quark* or *black hole* in their discussions and had to spell out their meaning in simple jargon-free language whenever they spoke or wrote, they would achieve scarcely any exchange of ideas at all. Wine-experts are easily mocked, with their extended uses of *finesse, breed, elegance*, and so on, but they might argue that these are in fact the simplest terms available — it is the concepts, not the words, that are complicated, and this is no fault of the connoisseur. Lawyers too rely (in theory) on their particular jargon, especially in drawing up contracts and other documents, to establish exact definitions and close all loopholes.

There are several interesting points to note here. First, much of this jargon consists of familiar words, though used in unusual ways: *code, breed, black hole*, and so on. It is certainly 'friendlier' to outsiders than technical language involving unfamiliar words — a technical term for *black hole*, for instance, might be the forbidding phrase *high-gravity post-stellar lacuna*.

Note, next, that the distinction between jargon and slang is a subtle one. Why do we refer to *medical jargon* but *hippie slang*, when they are both in-group specialised vocabularies, often unintelligible to outsiders? There seem to be three differences: a high-status group, particularly a professional group (doctors, say) is credited with a jargon, whereas a lower-status group or subculture (dockworkers, or teenagers) might be credited with slang. Then, jargons tend to be formal, and slang to be informal. And jargons tend to consist of words for new or technical concepts (*black hole*, referring to a collapsed star), whereas slang often consists of words for very familiar concepts (*stoned*, for 'drunk or drugged').

Another important point to note is that, within the limits just discussed — technical shorthand — jargon is not only unobjectionable but also clearly indispensable. The trouble is, jargon does not remain within these limits. It strays beyond them in at least four directions.

First, it is used between 'insiders' not just for the purpose of efficient communication but with ulterior motives too: as self-congratulatory and mutually reassuring; as a way of impressing or browbeating one another; and, more sinister, as a kind of elitist private code — to exclude outsiders from the magic circle and to limit public comprehension of its 'secrets'.

Secondly, jargon may be used by an insider to impress, browbeat, or bamboozle an outsider.

Thirdly, jargon is often adopted by laymen and used among themselves, to the detriment of clear communication.

Finally, a quasi-jargon is devised and used by groups (notably bureaucrats, businessmen, and politicians) that have no need of special technical vocabularies, to the detriment not just of clear communication but of the English language as well.

About the first abuse of jargon — its overuse among insiders — a famous economist has had this to say:

> Complexity and obscurity have professional value — they are the academic equivalents of apprenticeship rules in the building trades. They exclude outsiders, keep down competition, preserve the image of a privileged or priestly class. The man who makes things clear is a scab. He is criticised less for his clarity than for his treachery.
>
> – J.K. Galbraith (Canadian),
> *Wall Street Journal*

Such acts of 'treachery' are increasingly common nowadays, thank goodness. One literary critic or art expert might well attack a rival's vocabulary, not just his judgment: words like *ambivalent, engaged* (or *engagé*), *deconstruction, textuality*, and so on are to some critics indispensable tools of their trade, but to others merely showy and needless academic jargon.

A particularly striking example of academic demystification can be found in a well-known work of sociology. The author takes some of his colleagues to task (specifically, for their 'grand theory' rather than their use of language), and 'translates' a few jargon-ridden passages for our

benefit — a definition of sociology, for instance, as dealing apparently with

> that aspect of the theory of social systems which is concerned with the phenomena of the institutionalisation of patterns of value-orientation in the social system, with the conditions of that institutionalisation; and of changes in the patterns, with conditions of conformity with and deviance from a set of such patterns, and with motivational processes in so far as they are involved in all of these.
>
> – Talcott Parsons (U.S.),
> *The Social System*

The plain-worded rewriting of this passage reads:

> Sociologists of my sort would like to study what people want and cherish. We would also like to find out why there is a variety of such values and why they change. When we do find a more or less unitary set of values, we would like to find out why some people do and others do not conform to them. (end of translation)
>
> – C. Wright Mills (U.S.),
> *The Sociological Imagination*

Here is (part of) another passage in need of translation:

> A 'value-orientation' aspect ... concerns, not the meaning of the expected state of affairs to the actor in terms of his gratification-deprivation balance but the contents of the selective standards themselves. The concept of value-orientations in this sense is thus the logical device for formulating one central aspect of the articulation of cultural traditions into the action system.
>
> ... Expectations then, in combination with the 'double contingency' of the process of interaction as it has been called, create a crucially imperative problem of order. Two aspects of this problem of order may in turn be distinguished, order in the symbolic systems which make communication possible, and order in the mutuality of motivational orientation to the normative aspect of expectations, the 'Hobbesian' problem of order.
>
> The problem of order, and thus of the nature of the integration of stable systems of interaction, that is, of social structure, thus focuses on the integration of the motivation of actors with the normative cultural

standards which integrate the action system, in our context interpersonally.
– Talcott Parsons (U.S.),
The Social System

The laconic translation reads as follows:

People often share standards and expect one another to stick to them. In so far as they do, their society may be orderly.
– C. Wright Mills (U.S.),
The Sociological Imagination

Clearly not all insiders are happy about preserving the cosy masonic character of unintelligible jargon.

As for the second abuse of jargon — its use by insiders to outsiders — note the following warning:

It is reasonable to insist that all members of all professional groups must be intelligible to people outside. A doctor who can only talk like a textbook may leave you in serious doubt as to your state of health. A clergyman who can only address his congregation in the difficult terms which theologians use among themselves might not succeed in his professional duty of saving souls.
– Christopher Sykes,
in *Noblesse Oblige*

Lawyers are traditionally condemned, perhaps unfairly, for blinding their clients with — not science exactly, but verbiage ... their *hereinafters* and *parties of the first part*. Their excuse is, as mentioned earlier, that their wording alone is capable of sealing the legal loopholes. Increasingly, however, lawyers are having to admit that simpler wording is possible. Some large American law firms now employ editors to revise the wording in letters sent to clients, and even advise on the wording of contracts. In Britain, the City Council in Bradford boldly decided to experiment with 'plain English'. In consultation with a lawyer, a group of 'non-experts' — a journalist, a librarian, teachers, and so on — redrafted the rule books. The results were fascinating. Not only did the revised version appear to keep all sealed loopholes sealed; it also, allegedly, succeeded in sealing some loopholes that in the original version had been left open. Here is an example of the changes made — taken from the Council's 'Standing Orders for Contracts'. First, the original passage in 'legalese':

After expiration of the period specified in the public notice, invitations to tender for the contract shall be sent to not less than four of the persons who apply for permission to tender, selected in the manner determined by the appropriate Committee, Special Sub-Committee, College Governing Body or an Officer referred to in 3(1) above generally or in relation to a particular contract or category of contracts or, if fewer than four persons have applied and are considered suitable, to all such persons.

Here now is the passage after redrafting into 'plain English':

After the closing date at least four contractors, chosen by the appropriate Committee, Special Sub-Committee, College Governing Body or appropriate Officer, must be asked to tender. If there are fewer than four, all those considered suitable must be asked to tender.

Not only is this new version much easier to understand, but it also alerted the council to a weakness in the standing order; namely, that the 'appropriate ... Officer' might, acting on his own, use improper criteria in deciding which contractors are 'suitable' — that the original rules were not tight enough to guard against corruption. (Whether the new version has really closed this loophole, as the drafters of it claimed, is open to doubt.)

The wider moral here is surely this: that even in specialised contexts, jargon should be kept to a minimum if outsiders are likely to confront it. The *Journal of Plasma Physics* is one thing — few non-scientists will ever have to grapple with its contents — but Bradford City Council's 'Standing Orders for Contracts' is another: it is largely intended for the inspection of non-lawyers. It is aimed at builders, plumbers, and other contractors.

Jargon, then, has a tendency to find its way from insiders to outsiders, and insiders should provide for this contingency. *The British Medical Journal* has been widely complimented for doing just this: it has a deliberate policy of excluding jargon wherever possible, and the result is a far more elegant and intelligible but no less precise and informative prose than that of most other professional or scholarly journals.

Mystifying an outsider with jargon is bad enough. Using jargon to mislead or manipulate him is even more reprehensible. A doctor who tells a patient, concerned about his oily skin, that he is suffering from *epidermal seborrhoea*, is in effect telling him simply that he is suffering from an oily skin — fobbing him off with an 'explanation' that explains nothing. A salesman who subjects an uninformed customer to a bombardment of unexplained jargon terms — *Dolby, woofer*, and *tweeter*, for example — and induces him to spend far more than he wants to or needs to, is abusing not just his position but the English language as well.

Just how insidious and manipulative jargon can be is borne out by a recent court case in the United States. An American government health-insurance scheme, Medicare, is required to meet only a part of a client's claim. In the past, clients who disputed the benefits awarded would receive a form letter — so jargon-ridden and confusing, apparently, that they often simply dropped their complaint, finding it too troublesome and bewildering to pursue. Medicare was finally taken to court in New York in 1984. A federal judge, U.S. District Judge Jack B. Weinstein, duly ordered the United States government to rewrite the Medicare form letters in plain English instead of 'bureaucratic gobbledygook'.

Earlier, in 1979, a law was passed in New York requiring landlords, estate agents, building societies, and the like (on pain of a token $50 fine) to word their loan agreements, leases, and other contracts in language that could be understood by the layman.

Official concern in Britain about the dangers of jargon surfaced many years ago. In 1948, Sir Ernest Gowers was commissioned by the Treasury to write a guide to official English — hence his books *Plain Words* and *The ABC of Plain Words*.

More recently, the Rayner Report urged simplification of official forms. The Civil Service College now runs courses on simplifying reports, forms, and other documents. Building societies, insurance companies, county councils, and so on are also now changing their old habits.

The third abuse of jargon — its adoption by outsiders — is a favourite subject of satirists: the pseudo-intellectual slipping on a linguistic banana-skin of his own making, the office-boy trying to impress his employers with a few of their own favourite phrases, ever so slightly misused ... these are traditional figures of fun.

Two of the most glaring examples of adopted jargon today are sociological jargon and psychological jargon — sociologese and psychobabble, as they have been called.

Sociologese permeates journalism and fashionable conversation to such an extent today that many speakers have virtually ceased to notice it. One amazing reminder of its prevalence is the 'buzz-phrase generator' — a set of three columns

(or discs) of sociological vogue words that can combine into a huge number of meaningless but impressive-sounding jargon phrases. The first and second columns list adjectives, and the third column nouns. Here is a very abbreviated version of the buzz-phrase generator:

column 1	column 2	column 3
divergent	compensatory	dysfunction
elitist	diagnostic	polarisation
operational	empirical	quotient
supportive	socio-economic	synthesis
viable	unstructured	validation

By combining these items in different ways, the user can produce such euphonious phrases as *supportive compensatory dysfunction* and *operational diagnostic quotient*.

Whereas sociologese afflicts users of American and British English alike, psychobabble is clearly an American disease, but it is beginning to infect British English too. (The term *psychobabble* was coined by the American writer R.D. Rosen in 1977, but the phenomenon goes back much further than that.)

Given the partiality of most people for engaging in critical self-reflection and for gossiping about their friends (and more recently, for engaging in 'self-improvement'), it was probably inevitable that the language of modern psychology would eventually seep into everyday speech. By the 1940s, many laymen were freely (and often inaccurately) spicing their conversation or diary-notes with the Freudian terms *complex, repression, sublimation, projection*, and so on.

In the decades that followed, dozens of additional terms from the jargon of psychologists were co-opted by nonprofessionals, and almost always debased in the process. The clinical term *paranoid*, for example, began to be used as a popular synonym for *suspicious* or *worried*, and *schizophrenic* for *undecided*.

Here is an example of the kind of writing that emerged from this absorption of jargon — a piece of film criticism aspiring to the style of a psychotherapist's casebook:

> The fusion of conflicting tendencies in the figure of the monster in horror films has the dream process of condensation as its approximate psychic prototype.
> — Noel Carroll (U.S.), *Film Quarterly*

The American infatuation with the language of psychology took an even more extreme form. In about the mid-1960s, American laymen began inventing their own pseudopsychological terms — *uptight, hang-up, to swing with, personal space, where you're coming from*, *laid back*, and so on. Ironically, some professional psychotherapists, perhaps in an effort to 'relate' better to their patients, even began to incorporate these same coinages into their own vocabularies. And so the wheel of jargon turned full circle. The result has been a victory neither for psychology in particular nor for meaning in general.

Those who cherish the English language continue to fulminate against these atrocities, but to little avail. In 1977, a devastating satirical novel appeared in North America, couched entirely in a pastiche of psychobabble. It was widely read — and its message widely disregarded. Here is a typical sentence from the book:

> Right away they'd flashed on how much their trips were alike, because he, too, had just split from a paranoid psychotic and was presently giving first priority to getting his head together.
> – Cyra McFadden (U.S.), *The Serial*

How 'hip' young middle-class people, in North America and elsewhere, could continue to talk this kind of nonsense after seeing it so savagely satirised is difficult to comprehend — but they could, and they did, and all too many of them still do.

This elevation of slang terms or vogue words into a kind of jargon leads neatly to the fourth abuse of jargon identified earlier: the needless creation of jargon-terms by groups traditionally lacking in them. In one respect this tendency is understandable and forgivable: if a professional or social grouping has coalesced only quite recently, it might be tempted to adopt all sorts of measures to reinforce its fragile group identity — a qualifying examination, a uniform, an oath of loyalty perhaps . . . and of course a language of its own.

A long-established profession — the profession of *lawyer*, *doctor*, *architect*, or the like — is secure in its group-identity. A profession lacking this centuries-old tradition — the profession of *businessman* notably, or *estate agent* or *management consultant* or *advertising executive* — lacks the accompanying self-confidence and cohesiveness too. The emergence of a special language, a jargon, is perhaps a natural result of the new profession's anxious floundering for cohesion and public respect. The new jargon serves as a kind of identifying mark or in-group badge.

The linguistic techniques that go into building this jargon are varied: distinctive words are borrowed or coined (*glitch* and *snivitz* — a technical hitch or mishap, as in a computer); old words are given new senses (*dawn raid* — a surprise purchase on the stock exchange of a large share in a company); old words are combined into new compounds (*bounce-back* — a review and change of tactics by an advertiser); buzz phrases are generated by the omission of prepositions (*consumer feedback, the industry-academia interface*); nouns are converted into verbs (*Let's round-table that idea*), and so on. And many of the terms in the new jargon are simply loanwords from older jargons.

Business jargon in particular is a hotchpotch of borrowings from other jargons, not just those of accountancy and technology — *feedback*, *input*, *mode*, *parameter* — but also those of war, sports, and gambling: *bargaining chips, baseline, eye on the ball, goals* and *own-goals, hard-hitting, impact, sure bet,* and *target*.

People in the world of showbusiness also now unthinkingly use a jargon of their own: *bankable* (referring to an actor so popular that his presence alone will guarantee the film's success), *indie* (an independent film producer), *pancake* (a disc of wood on which an actor stands to make him appear taller), *skeds* (schedules), and so on.

The world of espionage has produced such jargon terms as *wet work, to demote maximally, to negotiate,* and *to take out* (all referring to killing); *cannon, mole, sleeper, spook,* and *willie* (all agents of one kind or another), and *biographic leverage* (material used for blackmail). Many of these terms are also euphemisms, as *to liquidate* once was.

There is another, more sinister, reason for the devising of a new jargon — to obscure meaning. Jargon, while ostensibly introduced for the sake of refining or clarifying or pinpointing one's meaning, is often valued precisely for its inherent lack of precision. Politicians, bureaucrats, advertisers, and salesmen of various kinds are the great culprits here. Bureaucrats sometimes seem to succeed according to their ability to avoid giving offence. They managed to shirk direct responsibility by using devices also found in scientific writing: resorting to the passive voice (*Orders were given for ten consignments to be delivered* instead of *I ordered ten consignments*) or abstractions and impersonal statements: *A review of the available facts by the department concerned has determined that . . .* 'Officialese' of this kind used to blight official forms, memoranda, and other documents. Things are much better now than they used to be, though still far from being jargon-free.

Politicians, civil servants, and military

spokesmen have become adept, when hard pressed to explain their policies or defend their actions, at sending up a smoke-screen of new jargon terms or euphemisms, sometimes specially invented for the occasion. Some of the finest moments in the witty BBC situation comedy *Yes, Minister* are those in which bureaucratic jargon is satirised. Here is a fine example:

(Sir Humphrey Appleby): '... We've just heard from the Special Branch that your protection is being withdrawn ... The police have suffered an acute personnel-establishment shortfall.'
(The Rt. Hon. James Hacker, MP): 'What?'
'They're short-staffed ... They overheard a conversation ... to the effect that in view of the somewhat nebulous and inexplicit nature of your remit, and the arguably marginal and peripheral nature of your influence on the central deliberations and decisions within the political process, there could be a case for restructuring their action-priorities in such a way as to eliminate your liquidation from their immediate agenda.'
... 'Well, what does it mean in English?'
'Well, Minister, it means — that you're not really important enough for it to be worth assassinating you.'

In real life, the most celebrated examples of such verbiage seem to come out of the United States. In the early 1970s, for instance, a White House aide announced that an earlier statement issued by the administration should now be considered 'no longer operative'. Translation: it had been wrong — or untruthful. And in 1983, Admiral Wesley L. McDonald, of the U.S. Navy, reluctantly admitting the navy's ignorance of events in Grenada just before the American landing on the island, phrased it in this devious way: 'We were not micromanaging Grenada intelligence-wise until about that time frame.'

And American military euphemisms are notorious: *air support* (bombing raids), *anticipatory retaliation* (a surprise attack), and so on. Perhaps the most celebrated jargon-monger or English-mangler in recent American history was Alexander Haig. During his period of office as U.S. Secretary of State he became a favourite source of quotations for journalists. Here is a reasonably typical example: 'Because of the fluctuational predisposition of your position's productive capacity as juxtaposed to government standards, it would be momentarily injudicious to advocate an increment.' Haig was simply — simply? — turning down a sub-

ordinate's application for a pay increase.

So distinctive and consistent was Haig's use of English that the term *Haigspeak* was coined to refer to it. There was an allusion here (not really an apt one) to the term *Newspeak* used by George Orwell in his novel *1984* to refer to the insidious language policy of the fictional government — a policy designed to abolish the power of independent thinking in people by progressively restricting freedom of language. Old words were impoverished: *equal* and *free*, for instance, were purged of all their political connotations. And new words of a precise, clinical kind were introduced: *crimethink*, for instance, or the adjective *doubleplusungood*, which is more a mathematical formula than a heartfelt, finely tuned expression of disapproval.

Much of today's thoughtless political sloganeering and propaganda seems to aspire to the condition of Newspeak. Governments, no matter how oppressive, will refer to themselves as *democratic*. Opponents of their rule are *terrorists, traitors, bandits,* and so on, whereas the secret police tend to be *the forces of law and order*. From the other side come such slogans as *running dogs, puppets of Moscow/Washington, fascistic hyenas, the reactionary boss-class*, and so on. One man's *terrorist* is another man's *freedom fighter*.

It is not only those involved in politics who use jargon to manipulate thinking or to mask the true state of affairs. Advertisers, estate agents, and public relations officers have their repertoires of jargon phrases (constantly renewed, since the public is always catching up) to obscure reality. The PR-officer of a company might refer to a project as *in abeyance* when he means *virtually unrevivable*. An advertiser might refer to *statu-esque* women when he means *enormously overgrown* women or to *economy-size* when he means *small*. An estate agent might say *sun-drenched* when he means *too hot in summer* and *a renovator's dream* when he means *falling down*.

It should be clear by now to what extent needless jargon has infected our language. Fortunately, official awareness of it is increasing — and official discouragement of it is too. Then there are unofficial organisations devoted to monitoring and combating it; and newspapers and magazines have taken to publicising the more outrageous specimens of jargon; finally, careful users of language can guard themselves against its abuses.

The official steps taken to check the plague of jargon have been discussed earlier. The unofficial organisations include the Plain English Campaign in England, and in America the Committee on

Public Doublespeak (a committee of the U.S. National Council of Teachers of English). Both of these organisations award annual prizes — either for the best-written most jargon-free document of the year, or for the worst-written most jargon-ridden document of the year. In 1983, for example, the American organisation's third (booby) prize went to a firm of accountants which in its inventory of a client's building had listed the fire alarms as 'combustion enunciators'.

The publications that have taken to highlighting jargon include the *Washington Star,* which in its regular feature 'Gobbledygook' quotes selected passages of current officialese. And many of the extracts quoted in the 'Pseuds Corner' column in the British satirical magazine *Private Eye* exemplify sociologese, psychobabble, the jargon of literary criticism or art history, and so on at their worst.

As for defending yourself against the allure of jargon, keep in mind these obvious truths.

If jargon has 'always' been used in a particular context, that is no justification for its continuing to be used there. Even if business letters have traditionally used such formulas as *inst., prox., ult., please send same, your esteemed favour,* and so on, that is no reason for you to use such 'commercialese' in business letters today.

Even if a text is drafted by 'experts', it might still be worded more simply and intelligibly without loss of accuracy.

If a text sounds 'impressive', this is no guarantee that it is any more reliable than a straightforward, more modest version would be.

When confronted by a jargon word or phrase, careful users of English tend automatically to apply the following commonsense tests to determine its acceptability. Does it really convey a meaning? Could it be replaced by a simpler unspecialised synonym or paraphrase? Is it being used for any purposes other than clear communication, and if so, are those purposes legitimate? If everyone were to apply these simple tests to their choice of words, a great deal of the needless jargon now current would disappear overnight.

See also SLANG; VOGUE WORDS.

jejune The Latin adjective *jejunus* means 'fasting or hungry; barren, unproductive; meagre'. In English *jejune*, pronounced /ji-jōōn/, originally meant 'going without food'; also 'barren', as in *jejune farming land.* But these senses are obsolete. The correct surviving sense is 'deficient, scanty, unsatisfying, insipid, meagre': *jejune words and empty phrases; That is a quite jejune excuse.*

Words are a bit like clothes. For one thing they're subject to fashion. Last year's word which seemed apt or witty at the time may now seem jejune or vulgar, dated.
— Dame Mary Warnock, 'Words', BBC Radio 3

Perhaps through association with *juvenile* or the French word *jeune*, 'young', *jejune* has come to acquire the sense of 'young, unsophisticated, callow, childish': *? a jejune attempt to impress his editor*; *? Do stop your jejune antics.* This sense is well established now, but purists continue to object to it. There is in any case no need to use it when so many other serviceable and less pretentious adjectives — *puerile, callow, immature, inexperienced, juvenile,* and so on — are available.

jetsam See FLOTSAM.

jib See GIBE.

judicial, judicious These two adjectives are easily confused, though since the 17th century their primary meanings have been quite distinct. Both go back to the Latin noun *judex*, 'a judge'.

Judicial refers chiefly to legal proceedings — the courts, judges, and judgments: *judicial chambers, a judicial survey.*

Our colleague on the *Sunday People* had been exonerated by the Press Council for writing in her column that an actress had 'little piggy eyes'. It was a moment of keen and necessary judicial wisdom: for where would our great profession be without the constitutional right to slag off anyone who gives us the pip?
— Julian Barnes, *The Observer*

Judicious refers to judgment in the psychological not the legal sense — the mental capacity of comparing, evaluating, and making decisions. *Judicious* means 'having or showing sound judgment; prudent and wise': *a judicious choice; a judicious withdrawal.* It is often used in a rather wry, ironic way:

He was astonishingly fastidious ... A massage-roller occupied another fifteen minutes daily of his valuable time, and then there was a thorough manipulation of his cheeks with face cream (seven or eight minutes) and a little judicious powdering (three or four).
— Christopher Isherwood, *Mr Norris Changes Trains*

This distinction is clear enough. But a difficulty emerges with a possible second sense of *judicial* — 'judge-like': *ended the chapter with a judicial summing-up*. Judges are supposed to be impartial and fair – in a word, *judicious* — so people may assume that *a judicial summing-up*, in this sense, is also a *judicious* one. If you want to stress the *judiciousness* of the summing-up and avoid ambiguity, call it *judicious*.

junction, juncture A *junction* is a joint or meeting-point. *Juncture* means much the same, but in ordinary English usually appears only in the phrase *at this juncture*. This is a figurative use: it ought to mean 'at this conjunction of events' and imply a point of crisis. However, the phrase is now most often used to mean 'at this moment', which robs it of its power.

Conjunction is sometimes used simply as an elaborate way of saying *junction*. It is often more appropriate in figurative uses, while *junction* has its own range of literal uses. So: *a junction of power lines*, but *a conjunction of ideas*.

In the various general senses so far discussed, *juncture* has the advantage that it can stand alone; *junction* and *conjunction* need to be completed by *of* . . . .

Junction does of course have a special meaning, referring to a meeting of roads or railway lines. *Conjunction* has a scientific sense in astronomy, and the specialised sense of a link-word in grammar: *and* and *but* are *conjunctions*, bringing words, phrases, or clauses together. (See CONJUNCTIONS.)

just 1. As an adverb, meaning 'very recently', *just* is used with the present perfect form of the verb: *He has just left the house*. In American English, it is often used with the simple past tense — *?He just left* — though this is probably still considered informal there. Its increasing use in this way in British English is regarded as nonstandard.

However, if *just* is understood in the sense of 'only', a simple-past-tense verb may be required: *She just got in a few minutes ago/She got in just five minutes ago*.

2. Like *only* and various other adverbs, *just* requires careful positioning within the sentence to avoid ambiguity. Consider the different meanings of the following four sentences:

She just managed to finish question three in time (— how could she have had time for question four?).
She managed to answer question three just in time (— ten seconds later the bell rang).
Just she managed to finish question three in time (— all the other candidates failed to finish it).
She managed to finish just question three in time (— she had to leave questions one and two unfinished).

In the first two examples, *just* means 'barely, by a narrow margin'; in the third and fourth, *just* means 'only, merely'. In spoken English, different intonation will indicate the intended meaning. In written English, however, ambiguity is possible. The likeliest danger is that a writer who intends the last sense will word it as the first — and thereby make himself liable to misunderstanding. (See ONLY for a more detailed discussion.)

3. One modern use of *just* (or *exactly*) has attracted considerable criticism — its use in introducing or emphasising direct or indirect questions:

?Just what do you think you're doing?
?Exactly how he plans to raise the money is not relevant to our discussion.

Such sentences are common and established nowadays, and can probably be accepted as standard idiom. The criticism should be aimed not at their occasional use, but at their overuse — an irritating and extremely widespread fault of style.

Note that it is redundant to combine *just* and *exactly*, whether in sentences such as those above —

✗ Just what exactly do you think you're doing?

— or in more traditional constructions:

✗ He stands just exactly six foot in his socks.

See also JUST NOW.

just now 1. Take great care when using this phrase that your meaning is quite clear. *Just now* has an extraordinary set of meanings: 'at this very moment': *I'm afraid he's speaking on the other phone just now*; 'only a moment ago': *She left the office just now — you'll catch her if you run*; and, in Indian and South African English, 'in the very near future, shortly': *We'll have lunch just now — I must write a letter first*.

In certain constructions, ambiguity is quite possible, and unless the context indicates the intended meaning, you should reword the sentence: *?But they cost £5 just now*, for example, could be changed to either *But they cost £5 at the moment* or *But only a moment ago they cost £5*. And if an Indian or South African is present (either speaking or listening) the sentence

? He's leaving just now is a likely source of confusion: it should be changed to either *He's leaving at this very moment* or *He's leaving in a short while from now.*

2. A separate problem is the choice of verb form — simple past or present perfect — to be used with *just now.* The choice seems to depend on the position of *just now* in the sentence:

For simple past:

She left the office just now.
? She just now left the office.

For present perfect:

She has just now left the office.
?? She has left the office just now.

When *just now* comes at the end of the clause or sentence, its meaning and function seem close to those of *a moment ago,* which favours the simple past.

When *just now* comes in the middle, its meaning and function seem close to those of *just* alone, which favours the present perfect. (See JUST **1.**)

karat See CARAT.

kerb See CURB.

kind of See SORT OF.

kindly The word *kindly* can be both adjective and adverb, and it is possible (though hardly common or advisable) to combine these tv〉uses in a single sentence: *Kindly people behave kindly.*

As an adverb, *kindly* has come to have the added sense of 'please', perhaps developed from the expression *Be so kind as to*: *Kindly take your seats* ('Be so kind as to take your seats'). *Kindly* in this specialised sense can be combined in a single sentence with *kindly* in its more ordinary adverbial sense, 'in a kind way': *Kindly treat her kindly.* (Once again, the example illustrates what is possible rather than what is typical or advisable.)

The problem arises when these uses of *kindly* are blended — the word is positioned in the sentence as though it meant 'in a kind way', but the intended sense is clearly 'please':

?? Passengers are kindly requested to move to the front of the lift.

A number of preferable formulations are possible:

Passengers are politely requested to move to the front of the lift.
Passengers are kindly to move to the front of the lift.
Kindly move to the front of the lift.
Please move to the front of the lift.

The last of these is best, combining politeness, clarity, and idiom in the most satisfactory way.

K.O. See O.K.

L

laden See LOADED.

lady See WOMAN.

laid, lain See LIE.

lama, llama The *llama* with two *l*'s is the South American domesticated animal, a ruminant mammal of the camel family and genus *lama* (with one *l*). The name comes via Spanish from Quechua, the language of the Incas, still spoken by South American Indians today.

The lama with one *l* is a Buddhist monk of Tibet or Mongolia: the name comes from Tibetan *bla-ma*, 'superior one'. The word can be spelt *lhama*, although this is no longer common. The highest priest of the lamas is the Dalai Lama (*Dalai* is a Mongolian word, here meaning 'great'). His title is capitalised; that of ordinary lamas is usually not. The most common English pronunciation of both *llama* and *lama* is /**laa**mə/.

Both Hilaire Belloc and Ogden Nash wrote poems about the *llama/lama* spelling problem. Memorise Nash's poem, and the danger of misspelling will evaporate.

> The one-l lama,
> He's a priest.
> The two-l llama,
> He's a beast.
> And I will bet
> A silk pajama
> There isn't any
> Three-l lllama.
> — Ogden Nash (U.S.), 'The Lama'

languid, languorous Although these words have a common source (Latin *languere*, 'to languish') and some overlap of meaning, they also have connotations peculiar to themselves.

Languid tends to have the more negative sense. It means 'drooping, sluggish, listless, lacking in energy': *The languid lady lay all afternoon on her chaise-longue.*

> He certainly does not seek to palliate their failings. James III emerges as languid and indecisive, probably acclimatised quite early to a life of elegant idleness, and not inwardly ambitious of sovereign power.
> — Professor John Kenyon,
> *The Observer*

However, *languid* may also have the pleasant meaning of 'agreeably relaxed and free from tension', as in *a languid and tranquil feeling*.

> I kneel over the boy, bringing the light close to his face, and shake him. His eyes open languidly and close again. He sighs, his rapid breathing slows.
> — J. M. Coetzee,
> *Waiting for the Barbarians*

Languorous sometimes shares this second meaning. But it has the additional meaning of 'gracefully slow-moving': *the languorous walk of the giraffe.*

> No more beautiful people exist in the world than the languorous, able Chinese-Polynesians of the South Seas.
> — James A. Michener (U.S.),
> *The Covenant*

The nouns *languor* and *languorousness* correspond more or less to the adjectives *languid* and *languorous* respectively. The noun *languor* can mean 'physical or mental lassitude, sluggishness' or 'a soft wistful atmosphere or feeling', and also 'oppressive silence'. *Languorousness* would tend to be used in the sense of 'physical grace shown by slow sensuous movements'.

Note the spellings of these various forms, and their preferred modern pronunciations: *languid* /**lang**-gwid/; *languorous* /**lang**-gərəss/; *languor* /**lang**-gər/.

last 1. Old-fashioned writers who prefer *first* to *firstly* when listing several points or items (see FIRST) sometimes also urge the use of *last* rather than *lastly*.

This traditional preference is now so little observed (far less so than the equally irrational preference for *first* over *firstly*) that it can be regarded as obsolete, and safely ignored.

2. Like *first* again, *last* tends to be placed before a numeral rather than after it in collective expressions. If referring to chapters six, seven, and eight

of an eight-chapter book, for example, you should speak of *the last three chapters*. When the elements are reversed, there is a separating rather than collective effect: *the three last chapters* suggests that you are referring to the last chapter of three distinct books.

3. Where *last* might be ambiguous, use *latest* or *final* instead. Unless the context makes it clear, a phrase such as *her last novel* or *the last issue of the magazine* is ambiguous, and should be reworded as *her latest novel* or *her final novel* according to the meaning intended, or *the latest issue of the magazine* or *the final issue of the magazine*.

Some ambiguous phrases might have to be reworded in a different way: *the last time I saw him* cannot be reworded by the use of *latest*: instead, you might say something like *the time I last saw him*. (The risk of ambiguity in the original expression is very slight, however, and rewording would seldom be necessary.) A phrase such as *in the last two chapters* might be reworded as either *in the final two chapters* or *in the preceding/previous two chapters* depending on the sense intended.

4. The expressions *? second last, ? third last,* and so on, though very commonly used in British English, attract criticism from purists. Similarly, *? third farthest, ? second worst,* and so on. The recommended rewording is *last but one* or *next to (the) last, farthest but two,* and so on. (For *? second last* and *? third last,* the synonyms *penultimate* and *antepenultimate* are also possible, though they are rather formal and available only as adjectives, not as adverbs. So they cannot usually be used in the common position after verbs: *She finished last but one*; *? She finished second last*; *?? She finished penultimate.*)

Certainly there does seem to be a logical confusion in such expressions as *second last,* but one that is difficult to identify precisely. Perhaps the odd sound of these phrases is due to our feeling that the ordinal numbers (*first, second, third*...) can move in only one direction along a scale such as *good-bad, early-late,* or *near-far.*

But not all scales are so obviously one-directional. What about *large-small* or *fast-slow*? It is natural to say *second largest* or *third fastest,* but is it then odd to say *second smallest* or *third slowest*? Possibly, but certainly not as odd as *? second worst* or *? third last.*

Even these phrases, however, could be defended on the ground that they are long-established idioms. Current English has to balance logic or grammar on the one side against idiom on the other, and in this case, it might well be argued,

the purists are putting far too much weight on to the logic argument.

Not that the alternative wording is always completely natural either. When the *last but one* construction is used as an adverbial phrase, or as an adjectival phrase after the noun, it is not too awkward perhaps: *He was/came last but one.* But when it is used as an adjectival phrase surrounding the noun, it sounds very strained: to say *? He got the worst result but two* sounds far less idiomatic than the 'illogical' *? He got the third worst result.* (Worst of all is *?? He got the worst but two result* — avoid this word-order.)

The only way out of this impasse would be to restructure the sentence in such a way that the adjectival phrase follows the noun: *His result was the worst but two.*

● *Recommendation* The phrases *? second last, ? third worst,* and so on are well entrenched within English idiom. The purist objection to them persists, however (though not, perhaps, to *second lowest, third slowest,* and so on, and certainly not to *second best* or *third best*); if you are worried about provoking the purists, you should use the alternative wording *last but one, worst but two,* and so on. And if this sounds too awkward, as it probably will if a noun falls in the middle of the phrase, try restructuring the sentence to reposition the noun in front of the phrase.

See also LAST BUT NOT LEAST.

last but not least This particularly common and thoughtless cliché occurs in other forms as well — *last not least* and *last but by no means least.* Apart from its rhythm, the phrase has nothing to recommend it. After all, no one is going to assume that the last-mentioned person or item is the least important, and to protest against such an assumption is therefore self-defeating — why draw attention to the possibility that the person or item might be insignificant? It is a curious compliment — either patronising or unflattering, and certainly reflecting poorly on the person or thing being spoken about. It reflects poorly on the speaker too, suggesting that he cannot take the trouble to search for more precise words to express his meaning.

Shakespeare, as always, could get away with it (as could Edmund Spenser just before him, and Alexander Pope after him, in other well-known lines):

Let each man render me his bloody hand:
First, Marcus Brutus, will I shake with you; . . .
Yours, Cinna; and, my valiant Casca, yours;

Though last, not least in love, yours, good
Trebonius.
> – Antony, in *Julius Caesar* III i

> Now, our joy,
> Although our last, not least; to whose young
> love
> The vines of France and milk of Burgundy
> Strive to be interess'd; what can you say to
> draw
> A third more opulent than your sisters?
> – King Lear, in *King Lear* I i

Perhaps it was Shakespeare, then, who set the
lamentable fashion.

late 1. *The late president* is a polite way of saying *the (recently) dead president*. It is often used
also as a way of saying *the former president* or
the ex-president, but it is best not to use it in this
way: the momentary ambiguity in a sentence such
as *The late president and his wife will attend the
opening ceremony* is quite macabre.

2. When *late* means 'recently dead', it cannot,
of course, be used of those dead a long time. But
how long is 'a long time'? Though some may still
talk of *the late James Mason* (who died in 1984),
no one would talk of × *the late William
Shakespeare* and few if any of ?? *the late
Winston Churchill.* Perhaps the safest guide is to
restrict *late* to people who have died so recently
(or are so unprominent) that some reader or
listener may not be aware that they are dead.

3. Avoid such constructions as × *the widow of
the late Mr Kaye.* The reference to a *widow*
already indicates that the person mentioned is
dead — it is superfluous to use *the late* as well.

latter See FORMER.

laudable, laudatory These two adjectives are
clearly distinguished by their endings, but they
are still often confused.

Both come from the Latin verb *laudare*, 'to
praise'. *Laudable* means 'deserving praise,
praiseworthy': *a laudable attempt in the competition. Laudatory* means 'giving praise': *a
laudatory speech about the prizewinner*. The pronunciation of both words is **/lawd-/**, not
× /lowd-/.

In some contexts, *laudable* is a rather un-
enthusiastic description, 'damning with faint
praise', because of its formal tone: *His attempt
was laudable but misguided.*

Laud as both noun and verb, meaning 'praise'
or 'to praise', is now even rarer than *laudable* and
laudatory. As a verb, it occurs most often in the
expression *lauded to the skies*. As a noun, it can
still be found in hymns:

> All laud we would render: O help us to see
> 'Tis only the splendour of light hideth Thee.
> – Hymn: 'Immortal, invisible,
>   God only wise',
>   *Hymns Ancient and Modern*

lawful See LEGAL.

lay See LIE.

lead, led The common noun and verb is
pronounced /leed/ and spelt *lead*: *to lead a
discussion*; *to take the lead.*

The heavy metal is also spelt *lead*, but is pronounced /led/: *heavy as lead*; *a lead weight*. The
two words come from two distinct Old English
source words.

The past tense and past participle of *to lead* is
led, /led/. A common careless error is to spell
this too as *lead*, on the model of the spelling of
lead the metal: × *I've lead a dog's life.*

leaders See ELLIPSIS.

leading question In a court of law, the judge will
frown on a lawyer who asks a leading question
— a question suggesting its own answer — since
this is in effect putting words into the mouth of
the witness. *So you actually saw the accused put
poison in the cup?* is a leading question because
the witness is being led to the answer required.
What did you see the accused do next? is not a
leading question, because the answer is not built
into the question.

Outside the police stations and courts, the term
leading question has come to be used inaccurately
and somewhat vaguely to mean any question that
is embarrassing to answer, or even one that is particularly pointed. A football manager will decline
to answer a reporter's query about the line-up for
Saturday's game, saying simply that ?? *That's a
leading question.* Strictly speaking, it is not: it is
an unwelcome question, or a tricky question, or
an unfair question, or an unduly probing question. Leave *leading questions* to the lawyers (to
talk about, that is, not to indulge in).

Here are two examples, one of correct use, the
other of the dubious modern sense:

> The most likely explanation is that Foster
> was fed the damning details of the offences
> ... in the form of leading questions by police
> officers who saw him and that he then
> adopted the story and made it his own.

If this is what did happen it underlines the dangers of putting leading questions, especially to suspects who are mentally handicapped.

— leading article, *The Guardian*

?? Yet Beaverbrook ... had pressed the case for aid to Russia and, like Aneurin Bevan, had dared to ask leading questions about British strategists who had grossly underestimated Russian staying power and who persisted in minimising whenever they could the importance of the struggle on the Eastern front.

— Ian S. Wood, *History Today*

lean In British English the past tense and past participle of *to lean* can be *leant* or *leaned*, with *leant* being slightly more common. North American English generally uses *leaned*.

See -ED, -T.

leap The past tense and past participle of *to leap* can be either *leapt* or *leaped*. *Leapt* is more common in British English; *leapt* and *leaped* are about equally common in North American English. In British English it is possible to pronounce *leaped* as either /lept/ or /leept/.

In the English-speaking world as a whole, the written form *leaped* seems more common than the written form *leapt*.

See -ED, -T.

learn In British English the past tense and past participle of *to learn* can be *learnt* or *learned*. In the rest of the English-speaking world *learned* is the more common form, overwhelmingly so in North American English. (See -ED, -T.)

Be careful not to confuse *learned* (pronounced as one syllable, /lernd/ or in British English /lernt/) with the adjective *learned* (pronounced as two syllables, /lernid/): *a learned professor*.

The use of *to learn* to mean 'to teach', as in × *My teachers didn't learn me anything*, is unacceptable in standard English.

leave, let In idiomatic use, the verb *to leave* is increasingly replacing the verb *to let*, as in ? *to leave be* for *to let be* and ? *to leave go* for *to let go*. Most such uses of *leave* for *let* have not yet been accepted into formal English. But the idiom *to leave alone*, in the sense of 'not to interfere with', has now become a standard English substitute for *to let alone*.

Note that both *leave alone* and *let alone* have other meanings. *To leave alone* retains its earlier sense of 'to leave in solitude':

> Other refuge have I none;
> Hangs my helpless soul on Thee;
> Leave, ah! leave me not alone,
> Still support and comfort me.
> — Hymn: 'Jesu, Lover of my soul',
> *Hymns Ancient and Modern*

(Note the contrast then in the sentence: *He left her alone in the jungle, but the wild animals let her alone*.)

And *let alone* (possibly *leave alone* too, though this is regional) can be used as a fixed phrase to introduce the least likely of a group of possibilities: *I didn't get to see the Vice-President or even the Treasurer, let alone the President*.

Even the politically divisive factor of a woman Prime Minister did not produce a gender gap, let alone one on the American scale.

— Carol Thatcher, *Daily Telegraph*

The sentence is usually negative; if not, it should at least have some negative feel to it.

This was the first time I had ever taken a fully rigged sailing ship, without an engine, into an anchorage, let alone without any notion of the currents or the state of the tide.

— Tim Severin, *The Sinbad Voyage*

The following example, lacking any negative sense in the construction preceding *let alone*, sounds distinctly odd:

× Physically, few cities have changed more radically in a lifetime: there are cab-drivers still on the road who remember the building of the Lincoln Memorial, let alone the Jefferson.

— Jan Morris, in *Travels*

Instead of *let alone* here, which is close in sense to *still less*, the author should have written *and even*.

led See LEAD.

legal, lawful, legitimate There is a great deal of overlap in meaning among these three adjectives, though each of them does have at least one special sense that is absent from the others.

All three of them have the basic meaning of 'authorised by, or recognised by, or conforming with the law or regulations': *a perfectly legal/lawful/legitimate move in chess*.

I really believe she would have opted for the

Chamber of Horrors rather than have had no image made of her at all. A bizarre thought, for my aunt was not of a criminal temperament, even though some of her activities were not strictly legal. I think that the childish saying, 'Finding's keeping', was one of her ten commandments.

– Graham Greene,
Travels With My Aunt

At its best, the LSO's musicianship is superb, but there have been recurrent allegations of moonlighting by orchestra members who legitimately drop out from time to time to do more lucrative commercial work.

– Laurence Marks, *The Observer*

No one has ever explained why it should be supposed that anyone would want to pay to bring over here a middle-aged woman who was not actually his wife: by this device, however, very many families have been permanently sundered and not a few men lawfully settled here have been induced to leave.

– Professor Michael Dummett,
The Observer

Not that these words are interchangeable in all such contexts: *lawful*, for instance, is rather old-fashioned now, except in certain technical combinations such as *his lawful wife*, *lawful access*, *going about her lawful business*, and *on all lawful occasions*.

From this core common meaning, the three adjectives begin to diverge. *Legal* alone has the general sense of 'concerning or relating to lawyers and the law': *the legal profession*, *legal documents*, *legal advice*. *Lawful* is often used in reference to moral or divine law: *Is it lawful for a Christian to take up arms in the cause of liberty?* And *legitimate* has several senses not covered by *legal* or *lawful*: 'born in wedlock' — *a legitimate child*; 'conforming to logic' — *a legitimate deduction from the premises*; and, particularly widespread nowadays, 'fair and justified': *legitimate grounds for complaint*.

It says they would reveal that *all* Argentine warships had been declared legitimate targets for attack from 2 May — and not just the Belgrano, whose sinking with the loss of 368 lives was subsequently justified on the ground that it threatened the safety of the fleet.

– Andrew Wilson, *The Observer*

It was wrong to find much of Kubrick's 'A Space Odyssey' boring. If ennui can be a legitimate object of modern film, so the grim cultivation of antipathy may be in order in the new fiction.

– Anthony Burgess, *The Observer*

Note too that *legitimate* is also a verb, meaning 'to justify, establish as legitimate': *He tried to legitimate his seizure of power by reference to the late king's will.*

How do I know this? Why, because I have been watching Channel 4's new experiment, *Case on Camera*, in which His Honour ... has been conned into legitimating a farcical notion borrowed from American television. This is the idea of staging 'real' legal proceedings in a TV studio.

– John Naughton, *The Listener*

As a verb it is pronounced /li-**ji**tti-mayt/, whereas the adjective is pronounced /li-**ji**tti-mət/. *To legitimate* is seldom used in the context of making a child legitimate; the verb more commonly used today in this sense is *legitimise* or perhaps *legitimatise*: *By marrying his mistress at last, he legitimised three daughters at a stroke.* *To legitimise* can also be used as *to legitimate* is — 'to justify, account for, establish as legitimate':

They used a girl, which was common sense considering Yanuka's proven appetites, and they gave her a guitar, which was a nice touch because these days a guitar legitimises a girl even if she can't play it. A guitar is the uniform of a certain soulful peaceability.

– John le Carré,
The Little Drummer Girl

When a political leader hints at retirement he risks undermining his authority and opening up a can of worms. Speculation about the succession is legitimised and the contenders are set free to marshal their forces and demonstrate their virility.

– Ian Waller, *Sunday Telegraph*

The nouns derived from these three adjectives are *legality*, *lawfulness*, and *legitimacy*.

Note, finally, the term *legalistic*. It usually has an unfavourable tone today, suggesting as it does an overprecise, nitpicking adherence to or insistence on a set of regulations or a moral code — a concentration on the letter rather than the spirit of the law.

See also ILLEGAL.

less, lesser *Less* is the comparative form of *little* or *a little*, and is used before singular nouns only:

Drink less coffee. Before plural nouns, *fewer* should be used instead: *Drink fewer cups of coffee*. (See FEWER.)

When used as an adverb (modifying an adjective), *less* can be preceded by the indefinite article *a*: *on a less unhappy occasion*; *on less unhappy occasions*. But as an adjective, *less* cannot as a rule be preceded by *a*: some alternative adjective would have to be used after *a*, such as *lower, smaller* — or *lesser*. So: *Give him less responsibility*; *Give him a smaller/lesser responsibility*.

Less as an adjective can be used before a noun or after the verb — *He feels less guilt than she does, even though her guilt is less than his* — and as an adverb can be used after a verb or before an adjective: *He feels the cold less than she does*; *It is less likely than ever*.

Lesser is far more restricted. It is used occasionally in a set phrase: *the lesser of two evils*. As an adjective, it can be used only directly before a noun — *the Lesser Antilles, lesser brethren* — and as an adverb, it is used directly in front of an adjective, usually combining with it by means of a hyphen: *a lesser-known poet*.

Lesser is a 'double comparative', meaning 'less serious or impressive than the other/s': *a lesser authority*. It should not be used in the sense of 'less numerous, less extensive, less bulky, or the like': ✗ *a lesser sum of money*, ✗ *a lesser yacht*. Use *lower, smaller, less powerful*, and so on.

let¹ The negative form *let's not* has widespread currency in both British and North American English: *Let's not quarrel over it*. *Don't let's* is largely British; ✗ *Let's don't* is to be found in American English, but is considered nonstandard.

Let is followed by pronouns in their objective form: *Let Jane and me/him/us decide*, not ✗ *Let Jane and I/he/we decide*.

Such constructions as *? Let's you and me try again, shall we?* are informal. However, the alternative, *Let you and me try again, shall we?*, seems awkward, and it is better to be informal than awkward. If you want to avoid both informality and awkwardness, you can reformulate: *Let's try again, you and me, shall we?*

See also BETWEEN YOU AND I; LEAVE.

let² See HIRE.

level The noun *level* is now a vogue word, badly overused: *? The matter was apparently debated at Cabinet level*. Why not simply say *The matter was apparently debated by the Cabinet*? And why speak of *? temperature levels* rather than *temperatures*?

Not that *level* is always inappropriate: it is difficult to replace *at grass-roots level* and *at the highest levels*, for instance. Furthermore, a phrase like *various levels of management* has a suggestion that the distinctions are unofficial, whereas *various grades of management* suggests formal rankings. On the whole, however, the noun *level* is more often than not superfluous. Test it each time you are tempted to use it, and dispense with its services if it is not earning its keep.

liable See LIKELY, APT, LIABLE, PRONE.

licence, license *Licence* is the noun; *to license* is the verb — hence, *a dog licence, to license a gun, licensed premises*. Compare *practice* and *practise*. (In American English, however, *license* usually serves for both noun and verb, as does *practice*.) To remember the spellings, think of *advice* (noun) and *advise* (verb), where the difference in pronunciation provides a clear guide to the spelling.

Though *licensed* is generally considered the correct spelling throughout the English-speaking world, it could be argued that *? licenced* is equally acceptable. A *licensed establishment* is one that has been *licensed*; a *licenced establishment* would be one that has a *licence*. Since *-ed* can be added to nouns (*hatted*) as well as to verbs (*boiled*), both *? licenced* (from the noun *licence*) and *licensed* (from the verb *to license*) are possible in principle — though *licensed* is better in practice.

lie, lay In nonstandard English, both British and American, the verb *to lay* is often used for *to lie* (and occasionally *to lie* is used for *to lay*). But in standard English the two words are kept quite distinct.

To lay is almost always transitive, having a direct object (or being used in the passive voice), except in two particular cases discussed later. The primary meaning of *to lay* is 'to cause (something or someone) to lie down, to place (something or someone) in a stationary or reclining position': *Please lay the fish knives to the right of the butter knives*.

> Lay your sleeping head, my love,
> Human on my faithless arm.
> — W.H. Auden,
> 'Lay your Sleeping Head, My Love'

There are certain phrases in which the verb *to lay* is used in an extended sense: *to lay the table; to lay a ghost; to lay the blame on someone; Now I lay me down to sleep,* and so on. And in two exceptional cases, the verb *to lay* can be used intransitively without any overt direct object at all, as in *The hens won't lay until the storm subsides* and *The ship is laying aft.* So *to lay* has become a standard way of saying 'to lay eggs', and in its special nautical sense it means 'to drift or float in a certain position'.

To lie means primarily 'to recline, to be positioned on a flat surface, or to move into such a position'. *To lie* is always intransitive in standard English, and takes no direct object.

The verbs *to lay* and *to lie* are often confused, as in these examples:

× Rosemary begins to have dreams and these are wonderfully inventive cinematically: she lays on her bed, eyes closed, but head tilted upward, the camera tilts up to the blank wall above which dissolves into terrors.
    — Julian Jebb, *The Listener*

× Gardeners better at laying down than laying lawns perhaps weren't introduced early enough to the joys of drilling and hoeing.
    — Julia Watson, *The Observer*

The chief reason for this confusion between the two verbs is that the past of *to lie* is *lay*: *We lay in the grass all morning.* However, the forms of the two verbs are otherwise distinct: *lie, lay, lain, lying, lies*; and *lay, laid, laid, laying, lays.* (Note that there is no such word as × *layed* and that there is a regular verb *to lie*, meaning 'to tell a lie', which is not related to the verbs discussed here, and whose forms are simply *lie, lied, lied, lying, lies.*)

Here are some typical problems:

Nonstandard or Regional	Standard
× Let it lay	Let it lie
× Lie it along the wall	Lay it along the wall
× He laid down on the grass	He lay down on the grass
× Lie the baby on the bed	Lay the baby on the bed
× He was laying on the grass	He was lying on the grass
× Your papers have laid there for weeks	Your papers have lain there for weeks
× When were the railway lines lain?	When were the railway lines laid?

One possible reason for the modern tendency to use *to lie* instead of *to lay* (as in some of the examples above) is the sexual innuendo, imported from America, in the word *lay* (as in *to get laid*,

meaning 'to have sexual intercourse'). Another possible reason is 'hypercorrection': in order to avoid the prevalent nonstandard use of *to lay* for *to lie*, as in × *let it lay*, speakers overcompensate by using *to lie* in cases where *to lay* would have been appropriate.

The use of *to lay* for *to lie* is still very common, however, and is slowly approaching acceptability in standard American English. Many pop song lyrics use it for instance: *Come and lay down by my side* (from Kris Kristofferson's 'Help Me Make It Through The Night'), or *Lay, lady, lay; lay across my big brass bed* (from Bob Dylan's 'Lay, Lady, Lay'). And in American English, the form *? to lay low* seems to be a fully acceptable variant of the idiom *to lie low,* meaning 'to remain in hiding or inconspicuous'. In formal British English, however, such uses should still be avoided.

The noun forms of the two verbs are sometimes confused in the phrase *the lie of the land.* The form *?? the lay of the land* is nonstandard in British English, though once again it now appears to be standard in American English.

Some controversy has surrounded the British word *lay-by* since its appearance in about 1939. Some people argued that it should be *lie-by* (or even *lie-bay*), since the car *lies* there. But the motorist, after all, *lays* his car there, so the objection does not really stand up. (In fact, the original *lay-by* was probably on a canal, allowing one vessel to be *laid up* while the other moved past.) No such defence can be made, however, of the word *layabout,* meaning 'a loafer'. (Compare the old form *lie-abed.*) But the word, which appeared about 1932, is well-established now.

It is worth noting that there seems to be a tendency in modern British and American English to replace *to lay* (and *to set*) by *to put*; so *Put the book on the table* is nowadays more likely than *Lay/Set the book on the table.* Note too, finally, that in British English *to lie* very commonly has a further sense that it very seldom has in American English; that is 'to occupy the stated position in a competition': *the team that is now lying fifth.*

lifelong, livelong *Lifelong* means 'lasting a lifetime': *his lifelong commitment to painting.* It is best spelt as one word, rather than with a hyphen in the middle. It comes, obviously, from *life* and *long*, and is pronounced accordingly: /līf-long/.

What we do not know, and may not know for some time to come, is the way the Gorbachevs are thinking — they and what must be a host of their contemporaries in fairly high and responsible positions. Are they so coloured by their lifelong environment and corrupted by their rivalries that they are incapable of launching any radical attempt to make the Soviet Union work and bring it back into the brotherhood of nations?

– Edward Crankshaw, *The Observer*

A staunch, opinionated, lifelong Republican, she lived through most of the traumas of twentieth-century Ireland and knew many of its leading characters.

– John Naughton, *The Observer*

Livelong has nothing to do with life. The first syllable comes from the Old English word *leof*, meaning 'love'. In Middle English this became *lef*, 'dear', and was used as an intensifier, like 'very', to strengthen adjectives. *Lefe* + *longe* became a standard combination, producing the modern *livelong*. This is pronounced /**liv**-long/, and means 'seemingly long in passing, complete, whole'. The word is rare nowadays. It appears chiefly in the phrase *(all) the livelong day*.

Fountains and wells, ever since the scriptural days, have been noted gossiping places in hot climates, and, at the well in question, there is a kind of perpetual club kept up during the livelong day by the invalids, old women and other curious do-nothing folk of the fortress who sit here on the stone benches under an awning.

– Washington Irving (U.S.), *Tales of the Alhambra*

light The past tense and past participle of *to light* can generally be either *lit* or *lighted*: *I lit/lighted my pipe.*

In pity a cigarette was given to Paolo, other cigarettes were lighted, the smoke frailed upwards like the thin prayer of a very old imam.

– Anthony Burgess, *Devil of a State*

When *to light* means 'to guide or provide with light', *lighted* may be more frequent than *lit*: *I was lighted along the corridor by candles; Candles lighted/lit the way.*

Before a noun, *lighted* is the usual form: *a lighted cigarette*; 'A Clean, Well-Lighted Place' (the title of a short story by Ernest Hemingway). But *lit* is sometimes used as an adjective too, especially when there is a preceding adverb. So *a clean, well-lit place* is also possible.

lightning, lightening *Lightning* is the noun referring to electric flashes in the sky. It is often misspelt as *lightening*, with an *e* — which means something different. *Lightening* is the present participle of the verb *to lighten*, and therefore means 'making lighter' in various senses: *the lightening of his load*; *the lightening of her cares*; *bicarbonate of soda for lightening your cakes*; *lightening her hair with bleach*; *the lightening of the room as the sun rose.*

The adjectival sense of *lightning*, 'extremely quick', as in *a lightning journey* or *a lightning move*, developed by analogy with the speed of a flash of lightning. Its spelling remains unchanged, without the *e*.

I wondered what part M. Janin's secretary (he insisted, several times, on this title) played in his lightning researches.

– Christopher Isherwood, *Mr Norris Changes Trains*

A possible source of confusion is this: the verb *to lighten* can mean 'to give off flashes of lightning'. So although you write *thunder and lightning*, you could write *It was thundering and lightening*. This usage is very old-fashioned now, however.

The difference in pronunciation of these two words, if there is one, is an almost imperceptible neutral vowel sound in *lightening*, /**līt**'ning/, as against *lightning*, /**līt**-ning/.

like[1] 1. A standard test of a good grasp of English grammar is the correct use of *like* and *as*. The temptation is to use *like* as a conjunction, whereas it should, according to a traditional rule, be used only as a preposition (that is, introducing only a noun or noun equivalent, rather than a clause). When *like* is used as a conjunction, it is usurping the place of a rightful conjunction such as *as* or *as if* or *as though*:

?? Children today don't obey orders unthinkingly like they did thirty years ago.
?? He treats his wife like a cat treats a mouse.

In each case here, *like* should be replaced by *as* or *in the same way as* or *in the way that*, or the like. (But it is quite acceptable to say *He treats his secretary like a slave*: *like* is here being used as a preposition, and introduces a mere noun.) Again:

?? He went on preaching every Sunday like nothing had happened.

– William Faulkner (U.S.), *Light in August*

?? Humphrey was closing the gap in the polls and it looked like the campaign of '68 would be another cliffhanger.
    – William Safire (U.S.),
    Before the Fall

In both of these quotations, *like* should have been replaced by *as if* or *as though*. (Worst of all is the phrase *like as if*, which is sometimes used by careless speakers, either in an attempt at emphasis or perhaps because they are unsure whether to use *like* or *as if*: they are not solving the problem by using both — ✕ *He resumed work like as if nothing had happened*.) Again:

?? Like Noël Coward said, only mad dogs and Englishmen go out in the midday sun, and, brother, was he right.
    – S.J. Perelman (U.S.), *Vinegar Puss*

This should, strictly speaking, read *As Noël Coward said* . . . .

Some of the examples above illustrate two particularly common idioms containing the conjunction *like* — *it looked like* . . . and *like (I) said*. Widespread though they are, and widely accepted though they are in casual speech, they should still be avoided in more formal usage. Of course, *(it) looks like* is perfectly acceptable if *like* is used as a preposition rather than a conjunction (and introduces a noun or noun equivalent, rather than an adverbial clause):

This painting is supposed to be a sunset, but it looks like a poached egg.
Her new house is just like where she used to live.
You look like the cat that got the cream.

The examples discussed so far are fairly clear-cut. The choice between *like* and *as* is not always so simple, however. Sometimes, it is difficult to decide whether you are dealing with a conjunction (in which case you must usually use *as*) or with a preposition (in which case *like* is acceptable). And in some contexts, even when you are dealing with a conjunction, *like* may be preferable to *as*.

Consider the following three examples:

? They conjured up ever more lurid pictures of the Matson children going through their money like Sherman to the sea.
    – Dorothy Parker (U.S.),
    'Little Cuties'

She went through her opponents like a knife through butter.

?? Step backwards, looking intently at the roots of the girl's hair, like in the films.
    – Stephen Potter, 'Anti-Woo'

To a greater or less degree, idiom surely sanctions these uses: *like* cannot (except in the third example, perhaps) simply be replaced by *as* or *as if*. Yet some purists would still feel unhappy with these examples. They might point out that, even though the group of words following *like* in each case lacks an explicit verb, there is an implied verb: the clauses are, in effect, *like Sherman (went) to the sea*, *like a knife (goes) through butter* and *like (they do) in the films*. So *like* is once again being used as a conjunction in all three sentences, and is, strictly speaking, incorrect.

This analysis is really too severe, however. Although it is often a fair grammatical test to supply any missing words to a construction, it is not fair in testing for the acceptability of *like*. Idiom clearly allows *It looks like rain*, even though the 'full' form ?? *It looks like it's going to rain* is not strictly acceptable and should be corrected to *It looks as if it's going to rain*. Similarly, there is nothing wrong in saying *She moves very slowly, like you* or *She moves like a snail*. But if you supply the missing word, mentally or explicitly, then *like* would be incorrect: ✕ *She moves very slowly, like you do*, and ? *She moves like a snail does*. In both of these sentences (more obviously in the first than the second), *as* is preferable to *like*.

A useful rule of thumb seems to emerge, then: if you can replace *like* with *as* or *as if/as though*, then *like* is wrong; it is only right when *as* and *as if/as though* sound impossible.

Unfortunately it is not always easy to decide when *as* is impossible. Consider the following sentences:

✕ He dances superbly, like his father used to.
He dances like his father.
He dances, like his father.
? He dances like his father used to.
✕ He dances, like his father used to.

In the first and last of these sentences, it is obviously possible to use *as* in the place of *like*, and *like* is therefore wrong. In the second and third of the sentences, it is obviously impossible to use *as*, so *like* is quite correct. The fourth sentence is open to dispute: it is perhaps possible to use *as* in the place of *like*, but it sounds slightly awkward.

In borderline cases like this, careful users will be divided: some will allow *like*, even though it is clearly being used as a conjunction, because it sounds more natural than *as*; others, though conceding this, will still insist that *like* cannot be used as a conjunction, and that it should be replaced by a phrase like *as elegantly as* or *(in) the way (that)*: *He dances (in) the way (that) his father used to.* But how would they reword the sentence *He looks like his father used to*?

And note the negative form *unlike*: since there is no form × *unas*, *unlike* tends to be the negative equivalent of *as* as well as *like*, and does seem to be acceptable as a conjunction sometimes. The sentence *He won again, as when he played last time*, for instance, has an acceptable counterpart in *He lost, unlike when he played last time.*

A reminder and a warning, finally. The reminder is that *like,* as preposition, has many valuable uses. In short comparisons, for example, *like* is the appropriate word to follow a verb and precede a noun: *She moves like a snail*; *It went like clockwork*; *They live like pigs*; *Joan sings like an angel.* (After adjectives and adverbs, however, *as*, not *like*, would usually be used in comparisons: *She moves as slowly as a snail*; *smooth as clockwork*; *as squalid as a pigsty*; *singing as beautifully as an angel.* But *like* is possible after an adjective or adverb if a comma separates them: *She moves slowly, like a snail.*)

The warning is against changing *like* to *as* in such constructions. To do so might change the meaning very considerably: *He worked like a slave* means something quite different from *He worked as a slave.* Or compare the sentences *He spoke as a novice (communist/foreigner/ bishop)* and *He spoke like a novice (communist/foreigner/bishop)*: in the first, he *is* a novice, in the second, he is speaking *as though he were* a novice — speaking very nervously perhaps — whereas he is in fact not a novice at all.

● *Recommendation* Except in informal contexts, avoid the common mistake of using *like* as a straightforward conjunction: if a verb follows, in other words, avoid *like* in favour of *as* or *as if/as though.* Even if the verb is unstated, avoid *like* if *as* or *as if* can be used instead.

Take care, however, not to go to the opposite extreme by 'correcting' *like*, as preposition, to *as*: it is unnecessary and sometimes even misleading to do so.

2. Since *like* functions as a preposition, pronouns that follow it have to be in the object form, not the subject form. So: *Sally, like John and me, adores the opera.* Do not 'correct' this to read × *Sally, like John and I, adores the opera.* It is only after conjunctions that pronouns take the subject form: *Sally adores the opera, as I do* or *Sally likes the opera as much as I (do).*

3. *Like* is often used to introduce an example: *The better wines, like claret, will naturally cost more.* There is a traditional objection to the use of *like* here, especially when more than one example is cited: *? The better wines, like claret and a good burgundy, will naturally cost more.* It is argued that *like* should here be replaced by *such as.* One possible basis for the objection to *like* is that it can (perhaps should) mean 'resembling', and therefore precisely does *not* include the examples that follow it. The objection seems rather old-fashioned now — *like* has long been used to mean 'for example; such as' — but it is worth heeding if you are addressing purists: certainly there is no loss of accuracy or elegance, and there might be a gain in keeping your audience's feathers unruffled.

When *like* follows a relative clause rather than a single noun or noun phrase, it again attracts criticism, the preference being for *as* (plus a verb): *? Wines that are more highly priced, like claret, can be kept in your cellar for years without deteriorating.* Although not really incorrect, *like* might sound rather awkward here: the phrase *like claret* could be changed to read *as claret is.*

Neither of the objections just raised applies to *unlike*, however. There is no suitable negative form of *as* or *such as*; and although it might be possible to say *Wines that are more highly priced, as Algerian and Yugoslav wines are not, can be kept ...*, it is certainly more clumsy and ponderous than the simple *Wines that are more highly priced, unlike Algerian and Yugoslav wines, can be kept ...*

4. There is a risk of ambiguity when using *like* in negative sentences: *? You never complain like your mother.* Is this the equivalent of *Like your mother, you never complain* or *You never complain in the way that your mother does*? If it means the first, word it that way; if it means the second, word it that way. But take care not to word it in the ambiguous way just mentioned.

5. *Like* is still sometimes used as an adjective similar in meaning to *alike: as like as two peas in a pod.* And one of the most fascinating things about the word is the way it retains some features of adjectives or adverbs even when used as a preposition. For example, it can be intensified by *very* or *too.* Polonius agreed with Hamlet that the cloud looked *very like a whale*, and older people might still say, quite naturally, *It may look very like porridge but it tastes too like glue for me* and *He sounds/sings very like his father* (just as everyone would say quite happily *It tastes very similar to glue*).

Yet such constructions as *very like his father*

sound distinctly odd to the modern ear. Current idiom favours *He sounds/sings very much like his father.* Compare the following constructions: *very much in the news*; *very much in debt*; *very much under the weather*; *very far under the surface.* So, some ordinary prepositions can be intensified too, and the change from *very like his father* to *very much like his father* is an effort to make prepositional *like* conform to the pattern of these other phrases.

6. *Like* is often used in conversation as a kind of automatic punctuation mark, the way that *you know* and *sort of* and *um* often are:

× Like I was just walking along the road, like, minding my own business, like, when up runs this, like, police dog, and just jumps at me, like.

× You know, some guy's been working all his life in a steel mill. He wins a quarter of a million dollars and he's like 60 years old and they show him with tears running down his face. There's something very disturbing about that. It's like people are hungry and struggling and coming up and banging on the door trying to get in out of the cold. Then they throw money at you and that'll kill you just as quick. Pennies from heaven, but each one weighs like 100 lbs.

– Tom Waits (U.S.),
quoted in *The Observer*

It can sometimes be helpful in speech as a way of giving emphasis, or of qualifying assertions (*this like police dog* might, like *this sort of police dog,* mean 'this dog that resembled a police dog but was probably not actually a police dog'). But usually it serves only as a mindless pause-filler, allowing the speaker to think out his next clause before proceeding. It hardly needs pointing out that *like* used in this way is inappropriate in formal speech and impossible in writing (except in written dialogue).

7. *Like* is sometimes used in dialect or colloquial English to mean *likely:*

?? She's like to scream if you don't feed her right away.
?? Like as not he'll be back in five minutes begging for your forgiveness.

In standard formal English, *like* is not acceptable in this sense: *likely* or *as likely* must be used in its place.

8. *Like* is used as a noun as well:

? Have you ever heard the like of it?
? I have no sympathy for the likes of them.

Such usages are considered informal by many careful users of English. In formal contexts, they should be reworded to read:

Have you ever heard anything like it?
I have no sympathy for people like them.

However, *like* is quite acceptable as a noun when used in the phrase *and/or the like*:

The writers' union welcomes journalists, copy editors, proofreaders, and the like.

(The meaning of this phrase is similar to that of *etc.*: see ET CETERA.) And of course, the other word *like* (= desire) can be used as a noun, especially in the phrase *likes and dislikes.*
See also LIKE[2]; SUCHLIKE.

like[2] **1.** The verb *to like* is often followed by a sequence of two elements — a noun or pronoun and then an infinitive form of another verb:

I should like you to drive me there.
She says she would like Simon to become her marketing manager.

A common usage, particularly in American English, is to insert *for* between *like* and the noun or pronoun:

?? I'd like for you to drive there.
?? She says she would like for Simon to become her marketing manager.

The *for* is unnecessary here, and sentences containing it are not accepted as standard English.
However, with *what*-constructions such as *What I'd like is . . . ,* the *for* will usually appear, and is acceptable: *What I'd like is for you to drive me there.*
For further details, see FOR.
(Note that in one of the examples above, the form *I should like* is used in preference to *I would like.* This is, in most of British English, the more correct form. See SHOULD.)

2. The past tense of *would like* or *should like* is *would have liked* or *should have liked.* The infinitive form that follows should not be couched in a past-tense form as well:

?? I should have liked you to have driven me there.
?? He would very much have liked to have become her marketing manager.

The simple present infinitive is all that is needed:

I should have liked you to drive me there.
He would very much have liked to become her marketing manager.

For further details, see HAVE **6**.

3. Note the difference in the structures following *to like* and *to dislike*. The verb following *to dislike* must be in the *-ing* form: *I dislike leading when I dance.* You cannot say ✗ *I dislike to lead when I dance.* The verb following *to like* may take either an *-ing* form or a *to*-infinitive: *I like leading when I dance*; *I like to lead when I dance.* However, many speakers of British English regard the *to*-infinitive in such constructions as sounding distinctly American, and would prefer the *-ing* form. (It is from an American popular song, after all, that the example *I like to lead when I dance* comes.)

But this is not the whole story: with *would like* and *should like* the *to*-infinitive is preferred in both British and American English, especially when a specific future event is being discussed: *I'd like to ski tomorrow.* The form *I'd like skiing . . .* has a distinctly theoretical ring to it: the sentence would probably continue *if someone would teach me how* or *if only I didn't always get so cold.*

likely When used as an adjective, *likely* has a number of subtly different senses: *a likely excuse*; *even though we tried phoning all the likely shops*; *Rain is (quite/very/most) likely*; and so on. Note, in the last of these examples, that a qualifying adverb such as *quite* or *very* is possible but not essential — *likely* as an adjective can stand by itself.

When *likely* is used as an adverb, however, British idiom usually demands the qualifying word as well: *He will very/quite/most likely call again this evening.*

> . . . the misgiving that De Lorean was being made a victim of legal entrapment. And if that contention came to be proved, De Lorean would very likely go free.
> — Alistair Cooke,
> 'Letter From America', BBC Radio 4

The unqualified form — *? He will likely call again this evening*; *? He would likely go free* — is perfectly acceptable in much of American English and in spoken English in Scotland and Ireland, but is unidiomatic in standard British English. Insert *extremely, quite, most, more*, or the like; alternatively, change the construction — *He is likely to call again this evening*; *It is likely that he will call again this evening* — or substitute *probably* for *likely*: *He will probably call again this evening.*

See also LIKELY, APT, LIABLE, PRONE.

likely, apt, liable, prone These four words have subtly distinct meanings and can appear in slightly different grammatical constructions from one another. All four words express probabilities of various kinds.

Likely is best reserved for specific probabilities, whether these are desirable or undesirable:

> She's likely to do very well in her French-grammar paper.
> She's likely to hit you if you tell her that.

Likely is here followed by the infinitive form of the verb with *to*. It can also — unlike the other words listed — be followed by *that*:

> It's likely that she will hit you if you tell her that.

For *general* probabilities, *apt* is preferable:

> She's apt to do better in exams than in class-tests.
> She's apt to break windows when provoked.

It is best to keep *apt* for general contexts, and *likely* for specific ones. To reverse these would be to produce slightly awkward or informal sentences:

> ?? She's apt to hit you if you tell her that.
> ? She's likely to break windows when provoked.

> ?? Since there are no survivors of the Harappa culture and no Easter Islander now speaks or reads the old tongue, there is no key to this unusual script, nor is there apt to be.
> — Charles Berlitz (U.S.),
> *Native Tongues*

There is perhaps a further limitation on the use of *apt*. *Apt* means primarily 'inherently inclined': *She's apt to break windows when provoked*; *Windows are apt to break when struck with a steel chair.* More dubious is the meaning 'likely owing to circumstance; incidentally inclined': *? Windows are apt to break when she gets in one of her tempers.* Perhaps *likely* is slightly preferable in this case.

(Note that if *apt* is followed by *that,* it takes on a quite different meaning — no longer 'probably, inclined', but something like 'appropriate or just' instead: *It is apt that she should have cut herself — she's always breaking windows.*)

Liable can be used for specific or general probabilities, but, strictly speaking, only when these are undesirable probabilities. And when the infinitive follows, these probabilities should be undesirable for the subject of the sentence (rather than generally undesirable or undesirable for the object of the sentence).

?? She is liable to do very well in her French-grammar paper.
(This is a pleasant or desirable probability.)

? She's liable to break windows when provoked.
(This is an undesirable probability, but just generally undesirable, or undesirable for the object *windows,* rather than undesirable for the subject *she*.)

She's liable to lose her job if she breaks windows here.
(Here the probability is undesirable for the subject, and *liable* is therefore appropriate.)

Liable is often used when the undesirable probability affecting the subject is really no more than the prospect of embarrassment or being considered slightly eccentric:

She's liable to start showing off her French at the least excuse.

He made no secret of his false teeth, told everybody who was interested all about them, and was liable to take out his plate to show you how splendid it was.
— Cole Lesley,
The Life of Noël Coward

This is probably quite in order, though *apt* would still be slightly preferable here.

Note that, in the examples listed so far, *liable to* is followed by the infinitive of a verb. It can also be followed by a noun, in which case it means 'susceptible to'. This time, the undesirable probability need not threaten the subject of the sentence, but can be generally undesirable:

She's liable to fits of temper.

(When followed by *for*, *liable* means 'responsible, legally obliged': *liable for military service*.)

The word *prone* could be used in the previous example equally appropriately: *prone to fits of temper*. But *prone* cannot always replace *liable*: it cannot be used of a *specific* probability and it cannot be followed by the infinitive with *to*:

× She's prone to lose her job if she breaks windows here.

But it can — unlike *liable* — be followed by *to* + the *-ing* form of the verb:

She's prone to losing jobs — thanks to her explosive temper.

See also LIKELY; PRONE.

likewise In standard English, *likewise* is supposed to behave like *similarly*: *Go and do likewise/similarly*; *Her speech, and likewise/similarly her manner, upset me*. In constructions such as the preceding one, the *and* is sometimes omitted before *likewise*, but purists disapprove: ? *Her speech, likewise her manner, upset me.*

Likewise can occur in at least one position where *similarly* cannot really fit, and where *and* cannot be omitted: *Her speech, and her manner likewise, upset me.*

limited This is now widely used as a synonym of *small, little, few, rare, inadequate*, or the like: ? *a candidate of limited qualifications*; ? *a very limited income*; ? *limited intelligence*.

There is, it is true, a delicately ironic understatement in *limited* sometimes. But for the most part, something is *limited* because some limits have been set, as in *Funds are limited because of the cutbacks*. If you mean no more than 'small' or 'few' or 'little', why not simply say *small* or *few* or *little*?

litany, liturgy Since both these words have to do with religious services, they are sometimes confused. *Litany* comes from a Greek word meaning 'prayer, supplication', and is the form of prayer in Christian services in which the clergyman leads the congregation in a series of requests and responses, asking forgiveness for sins. It is used metaphorically in one of two ways. It can mean 'a repetitive sequence of questions and answers', as in:

No sooner had the Princess of Wales stepped off the plane than the press began their litany of interrogation.

Or it can mean 'a repetitive recitation or list or series of errors or troubles':

And the conclusion he reaches is that America now has an 'underclass', lost populations expected, even encouraged, to dispose of themselves with junk, poison and Saturday-night specials. I asked Bellow how he had assembled this litany of depredation. Did he trudge round the jails, the hospitals, the projects?
— Martin Amis, *The Observer*

Last week's bomb blast was only the latest incident in a litany of IRA terror outside . . . Northern Ireland. In the last 12 years more than 80 people have died and 1,300 have been injured in a campaign of violence to 'bring

it all back home' to Britain.
— *Newsweek* (U.S.)

Liturgy is a more general term: the original Greek means 'public or divine duty'. It is the ritual form of worship in any religion. In Christianity it often refers more particularly to the service of Holy Communion in Orthodox churches, or to the Anglican form of worship contained in the 1629 *Book of Common Prayer*.

Metaphorically, *liturgy* refers to ritualistically repeated and unchanging language, especially when used for unthinking praise:

But in the liturgy of the conventional wisdom, the praises of price competition are still vigorously sung.
— J.K. Galbraith (Canadian),
The Affluent Society

literally Poor word! It could hardly state its meaning more clearly — 'in a strict sense, exactly according to the letter'. And yet it is now widely used as an intensifier in assertions that are figurative or metaphorical — precisely *not* literal. To say *She literally worked 12 hours a day for six days in a row* is presumably an accurate reflection of reality. To say × *She literally worked 24 hours a day seven days a week* is presumably not the literal truth: why then suggest that it is?

The *literal* sense of a phrase such as *to bleed to death* is 'to die through loss of blood', as in *The victim of the blast did not die immediately, but bled to death before help arrived*. A figurative sense of *to bleed to death* might be 'to go bankrupt through inefficiency or wasteful business practices', as in *The company slowly bled to death under the deplorable management of my brother-in-law*.

To suggest that the figurative sense might be the literal sense, merely for the sake of emphasis, as in × *The company literally bled to death under his management*, is to abuse language as blatantly as it is possible to do. Yet the temptation has proved irresistible to great writers, competent journalists, and the man in the street alike. Sometimes, *literally* can perhaps be taken to mean 'as it were' or 'so to speak', and accepted as a succinct synonym of these phrases:

? But there was a change in Gatsby that was simply confounding. He literally glowed; without a word or a gesture of exultation a new well-being radiated from him and filled the little room.
— F. Scott Fitzgerald (U.S.),
The Great Gatsby

? In a community where facial tics were commonplace, his were exceptional; they literally pursued each other across his face like snipe.
— S.J. Perelman (U.S.)
Baby, It's Cold Outside

In the next example, however, the idea of intensity could more appropriately be conveyed by *really* than by *literally* — though once again *really* could not be meant in a literal way:

× Bonnie Berman is one of America's top models and the present hit of the season. She works constantly for the leading fashion magazines, struts down the catwalks of multi-millionaire designers and literally rakes in the money being photographed for major advertising campaigns.
— Sally Brampton, *The Observer*

The following amusing extract shows how misusing *literally* can lead to downright absurdities:

Sir Brian Young ... quoted a letter from a vicar who, on his retirement, had been described by the parish magazine as 'literally a father to every child in the parish'. 'Still the practice goes on,' Sir Brian said. 'When Mrs Thatcher appeared on French television, a reporter said admiringly, "There on the screen was the Prime Minister literally seducing her interviewer." ...'
— *The Listener*

One particularly effective and quite acceptable use of *literally* is when both the literal and metaphorical senses apply. A millionaire who began his business-life selling second-hand clothing might be described as having *gone literally from rags to riches*. Here is a striking example of this clever play on words:

For such people, the vast verse epic 'Pantaloon' which he completed after a quarter of a century's work and of which only four parts have so far found a publisher, has remained literally a closed book. But distinguished voices have shared the author's confidence in its worth.
— Robert Kee, *The Observer*

literature *Literature* refers primarily to creative writing of excellent artistic quality, or at least aiming at high quality. By extension, it can refer to the written work of scholars or researchers: *all the medical literature on the subject of AIDS*.

Towards the end of the last century, it acquired a broader sense that some purists found, and still find, objectionable: 'printed material of any kind, especially for a political or publicity campaign'. Certainly there is something odd about using the same word to refer to a holiday brochure and *King Lear*, but *literature* does at least fill a lexical gap: no other single word seems available for 'written and printed material'. Nevertheless, in formal contexts *literature* is best reserved for the more elevated kind of writing.

liturgy See LITANY.

livelong See LIFELONG.

loaded, laden *Loaded* is the past tense and past participle of *to load*: *We loaded the goods onto the lorry*; *The goods were loaded onto the lorry*. *Laden* is an adjective meaning 'heavily weighed down', and it has a slightly more poetic feel to it than *loaded*: *The table was laden with good things to eat*; *a heavily laden table*.

> After him trod a scared young man in a white coat, laden with a duplicate of the now celebrated scuffed grey suitcase complete with its Scandinavian Airline Systems labels.
> – John le Carré,
> *The Little Drummer Girl*

So: you might speak of *a gun loaded with ammunition* and of *a pack animal laden with ammunition*.

loan Except for one special use as a verb, *loan* should be restricted to being used as a noun. In the usual senses — referring to the temporary giving of one's money (whether at interest or not) or possessions to another — the correct verb, in current British English, is *to lend*. In American English, however, *to loan* is an acceptable synonym. Its increasing use in British English is frowned upon by careful speakers and writers. ??*Can you loan me ten pounds till payday?*

The one special sense in which *to loan* is usually countenanced in British English is 'to transfer (something valuable) formally, especially to an institution':

> Professor Sythe has loaned his priceless collection of Ming-dynasty vases to the Victoria and Albert Museum for the duration of its current exhibition.

The use of *loaned* in the following quotation is perhaps justified in view of the alleged high value of the object in question:

> The First Edition of *Lady Addle Remembers*

(Methuen 1936) is now a collector's piece. When first loaned it by Leo Maguire some years ago I was threatened with a terrible fate if I failed to return it.
> – Hugo Vickers,
> *The Literary Review*

As it happens, *to loan* was in past centuries a perfectly proper verb in the more general senses too in England, until it was driven out by *to lend*. But the return of *to loan* to British English today cannot be justified as a revival: instead, the word should be regarded as an intrusive Americanism, and its invasion resisted.

loose, lose, loosen The words *loose* and *lose* with their distinctive pronunciations — /lo͞os/ and /lo͞oz/ respectively — are unlikely to be confused in speech or meaning, but are sometimes confused in spelling. *Loose* is both the adjective meaning 'slack, not tight', and the verb meaning 'to let loose, release'. *Lose* is a verb only, meaning 'to mislay, fail, be deprived of, not win', and so on.

Loose and *loosen* (/lo͞os'n/) are more easily confused. Broadly, the verb *to loose* means 'to undo or set free' (the opposite of 'to fetter, tie-up, or imprison'), and *to loosen* means 'to make looser' (the opposite of 'to tighten'). A prisoner who is *loosed* from his chains is set free; one whose chains are *loosened* is merely made more comfortable in his captivity.

To loose is a much rarer verb than *to loosen*, and now sounds slightly archaic (it is common in the King James Bible). *To let loose, to undo,* and *to set free* are far more likely in current everyday use.

> Mine eyes have seen the glory of the
>   coming of the Lord;
> He is trampling out the vintage where the
>   grapes of wrath are stored;
> He hath loosed the fateful lightning of
>   His terrible, swift sword;
> His truth is marching on.
> – Julia Ward Howe (U.S.),
> *Battle Hymn of the Republic*

> And behold there was a woman which had a spirit of infirmity eighteen years, and was bowed together, and could in no wise lift up herself. And when Jesus saw her, he called her to him and said unto her, Woman, thou art loosed from thine infirmity. And he laid his hands on her: and immediately she was made straight, and glorified God.
> – Luke 13:11-13

lot, lots Phrases such as *a lot of money* and *lots of people* are perfectly acceptable in informal contexts but should be avoided in very formal speech and writing, where expressions such as *a great deal of* and *a great many* are more appropriate. In the following extract, *lots* seem to jar slightly, perhaps, in its relative informality:

> Last year I wrote *The Closing Chapter*. I so called it because it was the closing chapter of my judicial life. But it was not the end of my activities. Since my retirement I have done lots of things. My appearances on television have been so frequent that taxi-drivers and passers-by recognise me.
> – Lord Denning, *Landmarks in the Law*

loud *Loud* and *loudly* are often interchangeable: *Don't shout so loud/loudly! Loudly* is, however, the usual form found in more formal speech and writing, and in sentences where the idea is not simply volume of sound, but clamorous and insistent noise: *They protested loudly.*

The construction *Say it loud and clear* seems more idiomatic than *Say it loudly and clearly*, though both are correct.

lubricious This adjective, pronounced /loo-**brish**əss, lew-/, is related by origin to *lubricant* and *lubrication* — all go back, directly or indirectly, to the Latin *lubricus,* 'slippery'.

Lubricious, however, is today almost always used in the quite different sense of 'lewd, rude, lascivious, or salacious': *a lubricious novel, a lubricious comedian.*

> And the daughter would blush and bridle, thus inviting lubricious speculation on the part of the elderly gentlemen who would, Edith was sure, be in relatively constant attendance on the mother.
> – Anita Brookner, *Hotel du Lac*

Perhaps the word has a rather formal ring to it: *this lubricious age of licentiousness and diseased imagination.*

In its former senses of 'slippery' and 'elusive', *lubricious* is scarcely ever used nowadays. And its variant forms *lubricous* and *lubric* are scarcely ever used either.

Note that *lubricant,* as a noun, is often used in the figurative sense of 'someone or something that reduces difficulty or conflict': *The lubricant of alcohol eased the flow of conversation. To lubricate* can be used similarly in a figurative way.

Lubricious has the related nouns *lubriciousness* and *lubricity*; to *lubricate* and *lubricant* have the related noun *lubrication* and the related adjective *lubricative* (/loo-brik-ətiv, **lew**-, -kaytiv/).

luxuriant, luxurious These two adjectives are quite distinct in meaning. They are derived from the Latin noun *luxus*, meaning either 'abundance' or 'sumptuous comfort': *luxuriant* relates to the first of these senses, *luxurious* to the second.

Luxurious means primarily 'lavish, characterised by luxury': *a luxurious waiting-room, luxurious tastes.*

> Bayer inhabited a large untidy flat on the top floor of one of the shabbier houses beyond the Zimmerstrasse. It was certainly a striking enough contrast to what Arthur called the 'camp of the enemy', the padded, sombre, luxurious hotel we had just left.
> – Christopher Isherwood, *Mr Norris Changes Trains*

> Later, my companion and I toured the new galleries, a luxurious experience on the new carpets and among many of the landmarks of modern art.
> – Michael Davie, *The Observer*

Luxuriant is sometimes used in this sense too — quite mistakenly. What it really means is 'growing abundantly, profuse, flourishing' — *luxuriant vegetation; luxuriant hair* — or conversely 'producing abundantly, fertile': *luxuriant soil, a luxuriant scalp. Luxuriant* has very active associations, in other words, while *luxurious* sounds quite passive by contrast.

> There was a continuous garden in front of them, going down to the water's edge, in which the flowers were now blooming luxuriantly, and sending delicious waves of summer scent over the eddying stream.
> – William Norris, *News from Nowhere*

> His wig struck a daring, more luxuriant note. It was composed of glossy, waved locks, which wreathed themselves around his temples in tropical abundance.
> – Christopher Isherwood, *Mr Norris Changes Trains*

Both *luxurious* and *luxuriant* have slightly extended senses, and it is here that some overlap of meaning occurs. *Luxurious* can mean 'indulgent, excessive': *luxurious idleness, luxurious dreams.* And *luxuriant* can mean 'fertile or prolific' in a figurative way, equivalent perhaps to 'florid or exuberant': *a luxuriant literary style; luxuriant powers of invention.* So you could speak of both *a luxuriant imagination* (great creativity) and *a luxurious imagination* (an over-elaborate, unpractical, self-absorbed mental life).

The verb *to luxuriate*, though applicable to both adjectives, is today understood as being closer to *luxurious*; it is sometimes used to mean 'to grow profusely, proliferate' — *the creepers luxuriating on the jungle floor* — but it usually means 'to enjoy or indulge oneself, bask or revel': *luxuriating in the applause*; *luxuriating in a hot pine-scented bath*.

The noun *luxury* today corresponds only to *luxurious*, no longer to *luxuriant*. The noun relating to *luxuriant* is *luxuriance*. *Luxurious* has as its nouns not just *luxury* but *luxuriousness* as well: *Luxuries and necessities*; *the luxury of staying at a luxurious hotel*; *the luxuriousness of the hotel*.

Luxury, it is worth noting, is now being used not just as a noun but as an adjective too: *luxury bath soap, luxury food, a luxury suite*. The phrase *de luxe*, adopted from French, is now also in wide use; when placed before the noun, it means 'luxury, luxurious': *the de-luxe model of the new sports car*; when placed after the noun, it tends to be informal, and means 'outstanding of its kind, *par excellence*': *If you do that once more, I'll give you a hiding de luxe*' — that is, a hiding to end all hidings.

The preferred pronunciations are these: *luxury,* /**luk**-shəri/; *luxuriant,* /lug-**zewr**-iənt, -**zhoor**-/; *luxurious,* /lug-**zewr**-i-əss, -**zhoor**-/; *luxuriate,* /lug-**zewr**-i-ayt, -**zhoor**-/.

-ly 1. Adjectives can usually be converted into adverbs by the addition of the suffix *-ly*: *flat, flatly*; *intense, intensely*. Sometimes small adjustments have to be made to the spelling: *dry, drily*; *subtle, subtly*; *terrible, terribly*; *terrific, terrifically*.

Not all adjectives can take the *-ly* ending in this way, however. Sometimes, the sound would be too ugly: *?? terrifiedly* (though *distortedly* is acceptable) — the adverbial sense must then be conveyed in a roundabout way (not *?? roundaboutly*): *in a terrified fashion/way/manner*; *in terror*, or the like.

2. Adverbs constructed in this way cannot as a rule take *-er* and *-est* to indicate the comparative and superlative degrees: *?? He fought bravelier than we expected.* Use *more* and *most* instead: *He fought more bravely than we expected.* However, if an adverb ends independently in *-ly* — without having been built from an adjective — it can take *-er* and *-est*: *He arrived earlier than we expected.*

Words such as *? quicklier* and *? slowlier* present special problems. They undoubtedly do

occur, but some people object to them. The alternatives are *more quickly/slowly*, which are unexceptionable, and *quicker, slower*, which are simple but have attracted criticism from those who object to the use of *quick* and *slow* as adverbs. So the various possibilities are:

? He arrived quicklier than expected.
? He arrived quicker than expected.
He arrived more quickly than expected.

3. The *-ly* ending sometimes characterises adjectives as well as adverbs. In some of these adjectives, the *-ly* is not really a suffix at all, but part of the root: *early* again, *ghastly, holy, jolly, silly*, and so on. In others, the *-ly* is clearly a separate element: *cowardly, deadly, deathly, friendly, ghostly, heavenly, leisurely, lovely, masterly, princely, scholarly, sisterly, untimely. Kindly* can be both adjective and adverb: *A kindly person behaves kindly.* (In general, *adjective + -ly* yields an adverb: *pleasant + -ly*; and *noun + -ly* yields an adjective: *father + -ly*. Unfortunately, there are exceptions — *good + -ly* yields the adjective *goodly*, for example; similarly, *deadly*.)

Two-syllable adjectives, of both kinds, can usually take *-er* and *-est*: *deadlier, friendliest, likelier* (though *more* and *most* are also usually acceptable). But if the adjective is of three syllables or longer, *more* and *most* have to be used instead: *more cowardly, most scholarly*.

4. Some *-ly* adjectives, especially those that refer to periods of time, are adverbs too: *an early bird, arrives early*; *an hourly/daily/weekly rate, paid hourly/daily/weekly*; *an only child, only halfway there*; *a deadly poison, deadly serious*. (Note that *deadly* is an adverb only by virtue of modifying an adjective: it cannot be used to modify a verb.)

Other *-ly* adjectives of the first type identified above — *holy, jolly,* and so on — can usually be converted into adverbs by the addition of a further *-ly*: *cavorting jollily*; *What thou wouldst highly, That thou wouldst holily* (*Macbeth* I iv). (Note the spelling change: the original *-ly* becomes *-li-*.)

Most *-ly* adjectives of the second type — *cowardly, princely,* and so on — cannot easily be converted into adverbs by taking a further *-ly* suffix. It sounds unacceptably odd to say *?? withdraw cowardlily* or *?? speaking scholarlily*. Use a roundabout phrasing instead: *spoke in a scholarly way*. In the following passage, the author is clearly playing knowingly, and provocatively, with the dubious form:

'What did they do before?' asked Mrs Covendry. She was a compact plump woman

who spoke queenlily. She seemed to Lydgate like a publican's wife.
   – Anthony Burgess, *Devil of A State*

5. Take care not to use *-ly* adjectives as adverbs unless the word really does serve both functions (as *early* and *deadly* do). It is a common mistake to say, for instance, ✗ *He walked leisurely down the street* (though it was perhaps acceptable in Shakespeare's time), or ✗ *He played it masterly*: the correct form is *He played it in a masterly way/fashion/manner*. (See MASTERLY.)

6. If possible, avoid using *-ly* in successive words. The juxtaposition sounds very awkward: *?The second statue was removed comparatively quickly.* It would sound better to say *removed comparatively fast/soon* or *removed more quickly*. Similarly, *?It was probably simply dislodged* would sound better as *It was perhaps simply dislodged* or *It was probably just dislodged*.

7. A common error is the insertion of a hyphen between the *-ly* adverb and the adjective following it: *??a nearly-new car, ??a quickly-realised aim*. There is no need to link the adverb to the adjective in this way, since it could not possibly refer to the noun following. However, if the adverb could be taken as referring to a noun — in other words, if the adverb could be taken for an adjective — then the hyphen should be used: *a deadly-dull silence* (this is slightly different from *a deadly dull silence*); *an early-rising young executive* (this is very different from *an early rising young executive*).

The same applies to adverbs without the *-ly* suffix: *a fast-rising young executive*. However, such adverbs are sometimes followed by a hyphen even when there is no danger of ambiguity, and this does seem to be acceptable (though not always necessary): *a much-esteemed politician*; *a soon-ended ordeal*.

8. Three important points to remember:

First, not all adverbs end in *-ly*: *He ran fast*; *He was hard hit*; *He was hit hard* (contrast *He was hardly hit*); *He drove there direct* (contrast *He drove there directly*). *Quick* and *slow*, as discussed earlier, can be adverbs as well as adjectives, but some people object to their adverbial use in such phrases as *?Drive slow*.

Secondly, some *-ing* adjectives can be used adverbially to pre-modify adjectives: *a boiling hot day*; *a spanking new car*.

Thirdly, some constructions require adjectives rather than adverbs — the idioms *to aim high*, *to cost someone dear*, *to loom large*, and *to stand firm*, for instance. It is a common mistake to be 'too correct' by producing such phrases as: ✗ *It tastes/smells deliciously*. Use the adjective instead: *It tastes/smells delicious*. It is perfectly correct to say *I feel bad/good*, though some speakers distinguish between *I felt bad* (= ill, sad) and *I felt badly* (= regretful) *about the incident*. (See ADJECTIVES **4**; FEEL; SMELL.)

See also DIRECT; FIRST.

M

machinations Although deriving from the Latin *machina*, 'a contrivance or machine', the word *machinations* now means something quite different from *machine*. It is related to the verb *to machinate* meaning 'to plot'. So *machinations*, almost always used in the plural, means 'a hostile intrigue or conspiracy, or devious manoeuvrings': *foiled his machinations to wrest the leadership from her.* It is pronounced /**mac**ki-**nay**sh'nz/; sometimes /**mashi-nay**sh'nz/.

> On the question of academic standards, it must be emphasised that there are many serious and conscientious students who enrol in good faith. The tragedy is that their work is disturbed and their qualifications are in danger of devaluation by the machinations of the highly politicised minority.
> – Caroline Cox, *Daily Telegraph*

madam, madame The distribution of these two terms is fairly complicated. *Madam* is a polite form of address used in speaking or writing to a woman, especially a married or elderly lady. In everyday speech it is now rather old-fashioned – a pity, since there is no real substitute in English in the case of a woman whose name you do not know: *Could I see your ticket please, Madam?* sounds very formal; *Could I see your ticket please, Lady/Mrs?* and *Could I see your ticket please, Miss?* sound informal to the point of rudeness, though *Miss* is more acceptable in American English (and reasonably acceptable in British English too when addressed to a young woman or to a schoolmistress by a child).

In formal settings, however, where *Madam* is used before the woman's official position, the formal ring to the word is usually quite appropriate: *Madam Chairman, ladies and gentlemen.* Similarly, in official letters, *Madam* (usually with a capital M) has the correct level of formality: *Dear Sir or Madam.* In all such cases, it is almost impossible to use the word in the plural: strictly speaking, *Mesdames* (pronounced /may-**dam**/ or /may-**daam**/) is correct, but it sounds and looks rather pretentious today.

When used as an ordinary noun rather than as a term of address, *madam* has two further senses:

'a woman who owns a brothel'; and informally in British English, 'a bossy or impudent girl or young woman', especially in the phrase *a little madam.* In both these senses, the plural is *madams* and is perfectly acceptable.

Madame, with the *e* on the end, retains the original French spelling (*ma dame* means 'my lady'), and usually a French-like pronunciation as well, /mə-**daam**/. The plural is always *mesdames*. In French, *madame* is the equivalent of the English *Mrs* and *Madam*. In English it tends to be used as a courtesy title, instead of *Mrs*, when addressing important foreign women, especially diplomatic or artistic VIPs: *The Thai ambassador and Madame Vitakomantri photographed with their two children in the embassy garden*; *and then the Rachmaninoff piano concerto no. 3, as performed by Madame Postnikova.* It is also much favoured by women in various occupations who like to give the appearance of being foreign: *Madame Robinson & Co., milliners to the nobility.*

> Madame Sosostris, famous clairvoyante,
> Had a bad cold, nevertheless
> Is known to be the wisest woman in Europe,
> With a wicked pack of cards.
> – T. S. Eliot (U.S.), 'The Waste Land'

In fashionable environments, women might also find themselves affectedly addressed in the third person as *Madame* (or sometimes in British English as *Madam*): *Would Madame care for a cocktail before ordering her meal?*

Madame is often used, like *madam*, to refer to a female brothel-keeper. Strictly speaking, however, *madam* is the only correct form.
See also MRS; WOMAN.

Mahomet See MUHAMMAD.

major In Latin *major* meant 'greater', and many careful users of English still insist that the word should be used only when there is some implied comparison. A *major* road and a *major* film are *major* relative to other roads and films; it is wrong to call them *major* if they are simply important in their own terms.

Whether or not this analysis is helpful and correct, the word is certainly overused: any statement by a political leader tends to be *major*; there are *major* questions; all too many artists are *major*; accidents are *major* if they are anything more than trivial, and so on. Do think twice, before using *major*, whether some other adjective would not serve even better: *chief, serious, principal, fundamental, important*, or the like.

The phrase *?the major portion* has also often been criticised, as a pompous and unnecessary way of saying *the greater part*.

majority, minority 1. Each of these nouns has various subtly different senses. Depending on which sense is used, the word will take a singular or plural verb:

> The government's majority, when the House divided, was 62.
> Only a minority of MPs return to their constituencies every weekend during the parliamentary session.
> Most of the backbenchers will endorse the cabinet's recommendation, but a minority is/are likely to abstain in the voting.

In the last of these examples, *is* would be used to stress the unity of the group in question, *are* (especially in British English) to stress the individuality of the group's members. (See PLURALS Part II)

2. Depending on the sense intended again, the use of *greater* or *greatest* with *majority* is either quite acceptable or redundant:

> This government has a greater majority than any other since the war.
> × The greater majority of constituencies are in effect deprived of their MPs' presence except during a recess.

3. Note the ambiguity in such phrases as *?a majority of ten* and *?a small minority*. The first of these could mean either that the majority party numbers ten altogether or that the majority party has ten more members than the opposition (say, 60 members on a 110-man council).

?A small minority could refer to an opposition grouping that has very few members, or to one that has almost as many members as the majority. Exactly the same two meanings could be attributed to *?a large minority*. Clearly, these two phrases are best avoided altogether, and phrases such as *?a majority of ten* and *?a minority of two* used only with the greatest of caution.

4. There are other ambiguities in the word *majority*. In elections, it can be used to mean 'the difference in number between the votes for the

winner and those for the runner-up'. On the other hand, it can mean 'the difference in number between the votes for the winner and those for all the other candidates combined'. In opinion polls, similarly, the *majority* might refer simply to the largest group favouring a certain response, or it might be used only if that group is greater than 50 per cent of the total. In American English, *plurality* tends to be used for the first of these senses in each case, thus avoiding the ambiguity. In British English, *plurality* is seldom used in this sense, and writers or speakers have to struggle to make the distinction clear:

> The Democrats ... have been watching the polls. A big majority of Americans thinks of Lebanon as the most present danger in foreign affairs. And a literal majority wants the Marines brought home now.
> – Alistair Cooke,
> 'Letter from America', BBC Radio 4

A *big majority* might here refer to 40 per cent of those polled — perhaps the next largest response (Central America, say) was offered by only 28 per cent of those polled, for instance. A *literal majority* (or *overall majority*) refers to over 50 per cent of those polled. In theory, an American audience could have been given this information more economically — by the use of *plurality* in the first case and *majority* in the second.

5. Avoid using *majority* and *minority* when referring to a single item:

> × The majority of the concert was very poorly performed.
> × You're exaggerating — only a minority of the magazine consists of advertisements.

Majority and *minority* should here be replaced by *more than half/less than half* or *the greater part/only a small amount* or the like.

Majority and *minority* should be used only when referring to several items:

> The majority of concerts are very competently performed.
> Only a minority of magazines can afford to turn down advertisements.

malicious, malignant, malevolent These adjectives are all based on the Latin root *malus*, 'bad, evil', or *malē*, 'ill, badly', and convey the sense of evil-doing or harmfulness. But the meaning is slightly different in each case.

Malevolent has the added Latin root *velle*, 'to wish', and retains this sense of 'wishing harm, ill-disposed': *a nasty, resentful little man, malevolent but powerless; a malevolent sneer.* (Formerly it also meant 'having an evil influence' – *malevolent stars* – but this sense has fallen out of use.)

The expression 'Great Cat Massacre' will attract the indignant concern of cat-lovers as well as the malevolent curiosity of cat-dislikers, two big divisions of the human race.

> – Professor John Weightman,
> *The Observer*

Malignant is a more forceful term, suggesting great ill-will — 'actively evil in nature', 'extremely harmful or dangerous', and so on: *a coldly malignant persecution of his old enemy.*

I couldn't see many people; most of the lights had been turned off, and we happened to be sitting in the patch of light thrown by one small lamp. All round were people in the gloom — an audience of attentive and potentially malignant strangers.
I thought: *These are just the first hundred, for the rest of my life — strangers who'll know, who'll find out, who'll try not to react but who will react.*

> – Lynne Reid Banks,
> *The L-Shaped Room*

It does still preserve some hint of evil intentions as well, whereas with the related adjective *malign* it is the evil effects that are being suggested above all.

And she remembered the landing in London, more alone than she had ever been in her life; and the smell of English sadness that greeted her even on the runway, reminding her of what it was that had turned her towards radical solutions in the first place: the malign sloth of authority, the caged despair of the losers. There was a luggage handlers' go-slow and a rail-strike.

> – John le Carré,
> *The Little Drummer Girl*

Malignant has a technical sense in medical contexts, roughly 'threatening to life, likely to spread, virulent': *a malignant tumour* (in contrast to *a benign tumour*). *Malign* is not used as a technical term in this way.
As a verb *to malign* is fairly common; it means 'to slander, spread ill-willed reports about': *If that magazine maligns me again, I'll sue for libel.*

He began work on this biography of his father 36 years ago, soon after Wells's death, as an act of revenge on his mother, Rebecca

West, who in his view had deliberately set out to malign Wells, 'spreading spiteful slanders and untruths', blackening the name of the father in public, and privately pursuing the son with unabated malice almost from the cradle until she died last year.

> – Hilary Spurling, *The Observer*

Note that *malign* and *malignant* seem rarely to be used of people: you are much more likely to speak of a *malicious* or *malevolent* person than of a *? malign* or *? malignant* person.
Malicious, like *malevolent*, can mean 'wishing to cause harm', and also 'produced by or resulting from such a wish': *malicious rumours.*

A day or two later, I happened to see Fritz in the street. From the pleasure with which he greeted me, I knew at once that he had something extra spiteful to tell me. For a quarter of an hour he chatted gaily about bridge, night clubs, and his latest flame, a well-known sculptress; his malicious smile broadening all the while at the thought of the tit-bit which he had in reserve.

> – Christopher Isherwood,
> *Mr Norris Changes Trains*

Malicious also has a special legal sense, referring to an unjustified plan of action, usually criminal, by which harm to others will be caused: *malicious intent.*

The fact that Mr Jameson may not have much cared for what they said about him did not make it libellous. He had to establish that the words complained of were written with a malicious intent.

> – Robin Lustig, *The Observer*

The noun *malice* occurs in legal contexts, in the phrases *malice aforethought* and *malice prepense.*
A rare and very literary adjective, finally – *maleficent* or *malefic*. This means 'producing evil or harm' or 'having an evil nature': *maleficent arts.* The Latin roots are *malē* once again, and *facere*, 'to do or make'.
Note that all the adjectives mentioned (and also the verb *malign*) are stressed on the second syllable. The noun *malice,* however, has its stress on the first syllable. Other related nouns are *maliciousness, malignance* or *malignancy, malignity, malevolence,* and *maleficence.* Note also that in *malign,* /mə-**līn**/, the g is not pronounced, but in *malignance, malignancy,* and *malignity,* it is.
See also BENEVOLENT.

man The noun *man* is used in over a dozen senses. The two major meanings are these:

1. 'an adult male human being, as distinct from a woman or a child': *Three men and two women were wounded in the crossfire.*

2. 'any human being; a male or female person, especially an adult, as distinct from an animal or god': *In ancient times, men feared thunder — some still do.*

The distinction between *man* as male and *man* as human generates considerable confusion — and criticism. Interestingly enough, the earlier sense of *man* is probably the neutral one, 'a human being'. That was its meaning in Old English, where it was applied equally to both sexes. (Similarly, the word *girl* originally referred to boys as well as girls.)

There were other words for a male adult alone and a female adult. *Wer* meant 'a male human being', and also 'a husband'. *Wif* meant 'a female human being', and also 'a wife' — this fused with *man* or *mann* ('a human being') to become *wīf-mann*, hence *wimman* or *wummon*, hence *woman*. And gradually, *man* drove out *wer*, and developed its specifically male sense.

The two basic senses of *man* managed for some time to exist on equal terms side by side. Consider one of Hamlet's speeches — *man* is first used in its neutral sense of 'a human'; the second *man* is specifically male (or is reinterpreted as being so, after the contrasting word *woman* is introduced):

What a piece of work is a man! How noble in reason! How infinite in faculty! ... And yet, to me, what is this quintessence of dust? Man delights not me; no, nor woman neither.
– Hamlet, in *Hamlet* II ii (?1598)

By the 18th century, the male sense of *man* had become dominant. When the neutral sense was used, writers tended to specify that both sexes were intended:

There is in all men, both male and female, a desire and power of generation.
– David Hume,
Political Discourses (1752)

It would be wise to follow this example today, when the male overtones of *man* are stronger than ever (as psychological studies have proved). The neutral sense has passed, in common usage, to *human, people*, and so on. Nevertheless, *man* is still used in the neutral sense when humans are being contrasted, implicitly or explicitly, with animals.

Take care, however, not to lay yourself open to misunderstanding, and not to change meanings in midstream without making it clear that you are doing so. Hamlet at least made his senses clear, but in the following passage, the shift in sense is unannounced and therefore unacceptable:

? As for man, he is no different from the rest. His back aches, he ruptures easily, his women have difficulties in childbirth, all because he has struggled up upon his hind legs without having achieved a perfect adjustment to his new posture.
– Loren Eiseley (U.S.), *Natural History*

The more common warning nowadays is against the sexist use of *man*. It is no longer advisable to use *man* freely and unthinkingly to refer to humans or human adults in general: the male overtones persist, even when the word is used neutrally, and women understandably object to the implied belittlement or disregard of their role. The following quotations, for example, are unlikely to make women readers feel properly appreciated:

The American once was a man bound to his country and his fellows by a common belief in something, not yet realized, that he loved. Now he is a man — or there are those who tell him he is a man — bound to his country and the rest by a common hatred of something looming that he fears.
– Archibald MacLeish (U.S.),
The Atlantic Monthly

To this land came the huddled masses of Europe, pushing West to this plain beside the ocean which nature had blessed with a climate in which all man had to do was to plant and water and then watch as the fruits of the earth blossomed.

Man wished to show what he had found to the world, so in 1932 he invited Olympians to this plain beside the ocean.
– Christopher Brasher, *The Observer*

Some traditional formulas cannot easily be eradicated, it is true — *one man, one vote*; *man overboard*; *the man in the street*, and so on, though substitutions are possible: *the average person*, say, or *the ordinary citizen*. And some terms that have been tampered with should have been left alone: *mankind* has associations that *humankind* cannot hope to match; *man-hours* has a conciseness that *worker-hours* lacks. The substitution of *-person* for *-man* in such compounds as *chairperson* and *spokesperson* has been a widespread but not entirely satisfactory experiment in getting rid of the in-built sexism in the language of the professions. (For a detailed discussion of this question, see CHAIRMAN.)

See also -ESS; HE; SEXISM IN THE ENGLISH LANGUAGE; THEY.

manically, maniacally Both these words convey some idea of insanity. *Manically* comes from the adjective *manic*, and means 'in a crazily hyperactive way': *She whirled through the housework, manically scrubbing and polishing.*

> The night of our arrival they have checked with their extensive files and with Interpol in Paris, and found we are harmless spectators. Just the same, we see them manically gabbling into their walkie-talkies as we walk by them, talking.
> – Edward Steen, *Sunday Telegraph*

Maniacally comes from *maniac* or *maniacal*, and means 'with insane enthusiasm or frenzy':

> There had been the moment when Ila Das babbled maniacally about mixed doubles at the Vice-Chancellor's badminton party.
> – Anita Desai, *Fire on the Mountain*

The words *maniac*, *maniacal*, and *maniacally* are not used as technical terms in psychiatry. But *manic* is: *a manic-depressive* illness is one characterised by alternate *manic* and depressive phases.

Take care with the pronunciations: *maniac* is /**may**ni-ak/, but *manically* like *manic* has a short *a*: /**man**nik-li/; and *maniacally* like *maniacal* is stressed on the second syllable: /mə-**nī**-ək-li/. The source of all these words is the Greek *mania*, 'madness'.

manner See SORT OF 4.

mantle, mantel Both words derive from the Latin *mantellum*, 'a cloak'. A *mantle* can still refer to a cloak, or it can refer to any covering – *a mantle of coarse woollen cloth; a gas mantle; a mantle of ivy.* It is also used metaphorically, when referring to a person's job or status: *Tennyson assumed Wordsworth's mantle as Poet Laureate.* Finally, the noun *mantle* has technical senses in physics, anatomy, geology, and zoology.

Mantle is also a verb meaning 'to cover' — *Snow mantled the mountains* — or 'to become covered with colour, as by a blush': *Her face mantled.*

A *mantel* is a shelf over a fireplace, also known as a *mantelpiece*. The *mantel* can refer to the whole surround of a fire. The spellings *mantle* and *mantelpiece* are also possible, but they are not common and it is best to avoid them.

many, much 1. *Many* and *much* tend to sound fairly formal in simple positive statements: *He has seen many plays during his stay in London; She has spent much time here.* If you want a rather more relaxed and informal tone, use *a lot of* instead: *He has seen a lot of plays; She has spent a lot of time here.* Another way of reducing the slight stiffness might be by adding *a great* before *many*: *He has seen a great many plays.*

Many and *much* sound all right, however, in negative constructions, or conditional clauses, or questions, and so on: *He has not seen many plays; Have you seen many plays?; She hasn't spent much time here; If he's seen many plays, ask him which he recommends.*

A number of other words and phrases show this same aversion to simple positive statements — and show it to an even stronger degree. The word *any,* for instance, is quite wrong in such a sentence as × *He has got any friends* (though it is correct in *Any friend of yours is a friend of mine.*) The correct form is *He has got some friends.* But *any* is suitable in a variety of other constructions: *He hasn't got any friends; Has he got some/any friends?; If he's got any friends, they're welcome too.*

2. The expression *many a...*, as in *? Many a gambler has lost his shirt in that club,* takes a singular verb and pronoun, Although obviously plural in sense, it is grammatically singular. (Compare MORE 2.)

The expression is little used nowadays. It has a distinctly old-fashioned ring to it. So too has the form *many are the...*, as in *? Many are the gamblers who have lost their shirts in that club.* The modern idiomatic form would be *Many gamblers have...* or *There are many gamblers who have...* or *A great many gamblers have...*

One related idiom does seem to have survived however — *Many's the man who...* So: *Many's the man who has lost his shirt in that club.* Note that the sentence is cast in the singular throughout, and that *man* alone is fully suitable here: if the word *gambler*, say, (or *woman*) were used in its place, the sentence would once again sound rather old-fashioned.

massive Try to keep this adjective linked to the idea of *mass* — bulkiness or solidity: *a massive stone plinth.* It has become a vogue synonym for *big* or *large*, and for *impressive*, much to the dismay of many purists: *massive cutbacks in public spending; a massive heart-attack; a massive* *achievement*; *a massive attempt to find a cure*; *a massive victory*.

There are adjectives in English that are likely to express your meaning more accurately and more freshly: *sweeping*, *grand*, *imposing*, *glorious*, *overwhelming*, *vigorous*, or the like. This is not to outlaw all uses of *massive* that go beyond referring to physical size. It is just to caution against unthinkingly following fashion, and overusing and thus weakening a once-useful adjective.

masterly, masterful The noun *master* has two basic senses: 'the man in charge' – *Who is the master around here?* – and 'a person (male or female) of great skill, an expert: *a master of the backward somersault*. The adjective *masterful* corresponds to the first of these senses; the adjective *masterly* to the second.

Masterful has two slightly different aspects, one favourable, one unfavourable. It can mean simply 'powerful, commanding': *his masterful presence on the rostrum*; *a masterful president*. But it can also mean 'high-handed, domineering': *a masterful husband*. *Masterly* means 'very skilful, practised, expert', and can once again apply both to people and to things: *a masterly portrait*; *a masterly violinist*; *a masterly production of Hamlet*.

As for Noël Coward's attempt to impersonate Edith Sitwell, never can the Master have been less masterly. There is a far better Sitwell parody available.
– John Gross, *The Observer*

Outwardly all might be the same but the interpretation had altered: his masterly efficiency was nothing but cold heartlessness, his authority was only tyranny in disguise.
– Anita Desai, *Games at Twilight*

In former times, both adjectives had both meanings and were freely interchangeable. Today, the distinction is a fairly clear one, but some overlap remains between the two, and both adjectives can sometimes be fitted into the same combination: *masterly piano-playing* means 'excellent pianoplaying'; *masterful piano-playing* suggests piano playing that shows complete domination of both instrument and music. Nevertheless, such phrases as *masterful piano-playing* have been criticised, and *masterly* is recommended here instead. In the following quotation, *masterly* would surely have reflected the writer's intention more accurately:

? So here he was doing it. It was a technically masterful performance, the product of many

years experimentation, which could — by tradition — be interpreted as this year's leadership bid.
– Michael White, *The Guardian*

The criticism also applies to the adverb *masterfully* as in ? *She's playing the backhand volley masterfully today*.

? He is, needless to say, not a type that is easily found, let alone encouraged, in the Soviet Union today. In 50 years, the country has lurched from the youthful passions that Stalin exploited so masterfully to a regularity that is middle class in all but name.
– *The Observer*

But here *masterfully* cannot easily be replaced because the adjective *masterly* appears to have no adverb form. When you want to use *masterly* as an adverb, you have to use the phrase *in a masterly way*. (See -LY.)

Note that the abstract noun *mastery* can be used in ways corresponding to both *masterful* — *mastery of the seas* — and *masterly*: *displayed the utmost mastery in his conducting of the orchestra*. With slight modifications, this is true too of the verb *to master* — *She soon mastered her opponent*; *still mastering the art of horsemanship* — and the adjective *master*: *the master switch*; *a master thief*; *She is a master lexicographer*.

materialise The use of this verb to mean 'to happen' or 'to turn up' — *The promised holiday never materialised*; *I waited an hour but he failed to materialise* — still attracts criticism as unnecessarily longwinded. However, it has become firmly established in all styles of spoken and written English, and needs to be avoided only in the most formal contexts.

To materialise can also mean 'to assume material form, to become real' — *The ghost materialised before our eyes* — or 'to invest with material form, to make real': *By building that house, she at last materialised her dream*.

Compare TRANSPIRE.

mathematics *Mathematics* takes a singular verb when it means the academic subject or science: *Mathematics is my worst subject*; *Mathematics was studied by the ancient Greeks*. It takes a plural verb when it refers to the mathematical figures or calculations involved in a particular estimate or project: *If my mathematics are correct, you owe me £50*; *The mathematics of setting up in business are very complicated*. (See -ICS.)

mawkish, maudlin Both these adjectives mean 'sentimental' and have a disapproving tone to them. They can usually be used in identical combinations: *a mawkish/ maudlin love story*; *Stop being so mawkish/maudlin – everyone's children get measles*. But there is a slight difference in the kinds of sentimentality suggested by the two words.

Mawkish is related to the word *maggot*, both words deriving from a Middle English word *mathek*, which comes from Old Norse. In some of its various forms the word also acquired the sense of 'a whim, a peculiar idea', perhaps because of the strange movements of maggots, or because whims were thought of as being like maggots in the mind. The form *mawk* had a further extended sense, 'a whimsical or fussy person'. *Mawkish* originally meant 'nauseating or nauseous; causing squeamishness or feeling squeamish', perhaps because of the association with maggots, or perhaps because the commonest whim of a fussy person was that he or she was ill (or perhaps because a fussy person tended to make others ill). It then came to mean 'having a nauseating taste' and then simply 'having a weak, sweetish taste; bland'. The word has now lost these senses, though it retains some suggestion of them. A *mawkish* play, for example, is sentimental in a weak, sickly, insincere, cloying way, like a diet of thin sugar-water, causing the heart to flutter.

A *maudlin* play, in slight contrast, is sentimental in a tearful way, and is likely to produce enthusiastic bouts of weeping – gushing, in both senses – in a susceptible (and maudlin) audience rather than the heartwarming, cosy feeling that a *mawkish* play generates. The word *maudlin* derives from the name of *Mary Magdalene*, who was so often shown in early paintings of Biblical scenes as shedding tears of penitence.

As a rule of thumb, think of *mawkish* as referring to sickly sentimentality and *maudlin* as referring to tear-jerking sentimentality.

> Who wants to admit to writing lines like 'Delay and disappointment could not flatten/The ardour of Lieutenant P. Mountbatten'; or 'In Africa, George had a four month spell/The Queen and the Princesses went as well.' There are so many mawkish lines and gruesome rhymes ('chintz' with 'prince', and 'she' with 'C of E') that a pop song by Abba is skilful by comparison.
> – Peter Hillmore, *The Observer*

> Graham Swift is a young writer, but, as he has shown in his novels *The Sweet Shop Owner* and the outstanding *Shuttlecock,* he has an authority — of style, characterisation, grasp on life — that is wholly free from maudlin self-exposure or faux-sophisticated self-concealment.
> – Alan Hollinghurst,
> *The Times Literary Supplement*

Maudlin has the extended sense (lacking in *mawkish*) of 'slightly drunk, in a silly and tearfully emotional way': *She was maudlin by now, and was starting to tell the barman the sad story of her life*.

The pronunciation of *maudlin*, /**mawd**lin/, is quite different of course from that of its source, *Magdalene*, most often pronounced /**mag**də-lin/. But *Magdalen College* (Oxford) and *Magdalene College* (Cambridge) are now pronounced exactly like *maudlin*.

may, might 1. As a request for permission, *May I . . . ?* is the standard formula — *May I smoke?* (*Can I . . . ?* is probably more commonly used, but is still frowned on by purists.) It is sometimes possible to use *Might I . . . ?*: the tone is slightly different then, either more tentative — *Might I ask you a favour?* — or more firm: *Might I suggest, my friend, that we look at these figures again?*

2. Both *may* and *might* can be used when referring to present or future possibilities. *May* suggests a serious possibility and *might* a remote possibility:

> Oh dear, it looks like I may miss the last train.
> Just in case, bring your sleeping-bag — you might miss the last train.

3. When referring to past possibilities, only *might* should be used after a main verb in the past (like *were warned* below):

> The last time we came here, we were warned that we might miss the last train.

It is a common error, especially in British English, to use *may* instead of *might* in such constructions.

4. *May have* and *might have* are used to express past possibilities: *may have* suggests that this possibility is still alive; *might have* suggests that the possibility no longer exists. A common error, especially in British English, is to use *may have* where *might have* is the appropriate form:

> ?? She may have lived if doctors had heeded the warning signs.
> ?? Keegan was perfectly positioned, and may have scored yet again had he not been fouled.

At least the meaning is clear here, though the grammar is faulty. But sometimes the grammatical error can lead to ambiguity or give a quite false impression. Suppose the last of the examples had stopped after the word *again*:

Keegan was perfectly positioned, and may have scored yet again.

Out of context, this appears to mean that Keegan did perhaps score a goal (but that the referee disallowed it). If the intended sense was that Keegan had a chance of scoring a goal but failed to do so, then *might have* would be the correct wording — the faulty use of *may have* in its place could easily mislead the reader.

See also CAN.

maybe Written as one word, *maybe* means 'perhaps' and tends in British English to be restricted to informal contexts: *Maybe you're right*. It is occasionally found at the end of a clause or sentence, when it is less informal and is also stressed on the last syllable: *It could go wrong, maybe* (/may-**bee**/), *but it's worth the risk*. As two words, *may be* is appropriate for formal contexts. It is often followed by *that*: *It may be that he will reconsider*.

In North American English *maybe* is more widespread than it is in British English, though it still retains a whiff of informality. However, North American English tends not to use *maybe* at the end of a clause or sentence in the way that British English can.

me Until about thirty years ago, grammarians taught that the correct answer to the question *Who is there?* was *It is I*, not *It's me*. They pointed out that the verb *to be* has no object, so that any pronoun following it should be in the subjective form. Today, however, *It is I* sounds careful to the point of being pedantic, and objective forms of the pronouns (*me, him, her, us, them*) are acceptable in all but extremely formal contexts. The subjective forms *I/he/she/we* can be used in formal contexts where there is a following clause, as in *It was he who complained*, though current idiom would probably again favour *It was him who complained*. (For further details, see IT'S ME.)

Following *than* or *as*, subjective forms of the pronoun are used in formal writing — *John is bigger than I* — and objective forms in informal contexts. If the construction continues, the subjective form must be used in standard English whether written or spoken, formal or informal: *John is bigger than I am*. (See THAN.)

When an *-ing* form of a verb follows the pronoun, there is the problem of choosing between an objective form of the pronoun (*me, him, us*, and so on) and a possessive form (*my, his, our*, and so on). Purists insist on the possessive form, in such sentences as *I remember your doing that*. But the objective form — *I remember you doing that* — has become normal in informal usage, and is often heard in formal contexts too. Sometimes it helps avoid ambiguity: *I remember you acting in Macbeth* means 'I remember that you acted in that play', whereas *I remember your acting in Macbeth* could be taken to mean 'I remember the quality of your acting'. (For further details, see -ING FORMS OF VERBS.)

See also PRONOUNS.

mean In the sense of 'to intend', the verb *to mean* has three possible constructions: you can mean *to* do something, you can mean *somebody to* do something, or, in more formal contexts, you can mean *that* somebody *should* do something: *I meant to tell him*; *I meant you to tell him*; *I meant that you should tell him*. A construction using *for* is sometimes found in American English, but is considered nonstandard there too just as it is in British English: × *I didn't mean for you to tell him*.

meaningful *Meaning* comes in many forms: the cryptic utterances of a soothsayer may be meaningless nonsense or they may be *meaningful* — that is, 'having meaning'. So too, a *meaningful glance* is a glance that conveys a message.

But *meaning* can also refer to values — importance or efficiency, for instance. So *meaningful negotiations* suggests negotiations that may have important results. The word *meaningful* has become so fashionable in this sense, however, that it is now often derided as a cliché (and sometimes even used as a joke, as in a *meaningful relationship*, often a euphemism for a *love affair*).

Try to reach for a less shop-soiled adjective when you want to express the importance of something — *far-reaching, serious, promising*, or simply *important*.

means *Means* in the sense of 'financial resources' takes a plural verb: *Her means are sufficient to support her and her children*. In the sense of 'a method or way', it takes a singular verb when preceded by *a, any, each*, and so on, and a plural verb when preceded by *all, several, such, many*, and other plural markers: *A means of solving the problem has yet to be found*; *Several new means of communication are now available. The means* can be followed by a singular or plural verb, depending on the meaning intended: *The means of travel is for you to decide* (singular); *The means of travel available are numerous and cheap* (plural). (See PLURALS.)

meantime, meanwhile *Meantime* is used principally in the phrases *in the meantime* and *for the meantime*. *Meanwhile* is used principally as an adverb, standing on its own: *Meanwhile, reinforcements had been sent up.* Some speakers, for example in Scotland, regularly do just the opposite, and use *meantime* as an adverb, and *meanwhile* as a noun: *in/for the meanwhile*. Outside Scotland too, *meantime* can frequently be found instead of *meanwhile* in casual speech and writing, but it is not recommended in formal usage:

? Meantime, those children's older sisters, 'teenagers' already, were preparing for the lives their mothers led.
　　　　　　　– Ann Shearer, *The Guardian*

media The word *media,* referring to newspapers, television, radio, and so on, is a plural noun — the Latin plural of *medium*, as in *the medium of television*. (*Medium* in the sense of 'a person who conducts a seance and claims to communicate with spirits' has a different plural — the regular *mediums*.)

Since the various media are nowadays so often considered together (for their joint political bias, say, or common immorality, or combined effects on society), they are often thought of as a single entity — in much the same way as the various newspapers are lumped together as *the press*. And as a result, the term *the media* is treated as grammatically singular rather than plural:

× The media is showing its usual prurient interest in the private lives of public figures.

The *is* should be changed to *are*, and *its* to *their*. Similarly:

× The media in the Arab world has been upsetting some Western — not least British — applecarts.
　　　　　　　– Bob Crew, *The Guardian*

× *Russell Davies.* How the media handles sport.
　　　　　　　– cover headline, *The Listener*

× And it's not only the media that leaves men stranded, it's the whole lifestyle. Men during divorce have fewer friends to confide in.
　　　　　　　– Helen Franks, *The Observer*

It is probably only a matter of time before this widespread usage becomes accepted as standard English — the way that *agenda* has become acceptable as a singular noun in place of *agendum*. But until that time arrives, treat *media* as a plural noun.

A further mistake, arising out of the previous one, is the use of *media*, as a singular noun, to refer to a single *medium*:

× Some historians believe that without the media of radio to spread Nazi ideas, Hitler would never have come to power.

Though *media* is best regarded as a plural noun, it is, like *data*, difficult to use when counting or quantifying is called for. For instance, it sounds very awkward to say:

?? Two media were for her and one was against.

It also sounds awkward to quantify *media* in other ways:

? Most media were for her.

If you really need to convey such ideas, you could use a bridging or 'partitive' expression:

Three of the media were for her and two were against/Three branches of the media ...
Most of the media were for her.

See also DATA; PLURALS.

melt The past tense of the verb *to melt* is *melted* — *The sun melted the ice* — but in British English *melt* is often heard in casual speech and regional usage.

Molten, an adjective form, is mainly used before nouns. It differs from *melted* in that it applies only to substances that melt at a very high temperature. People say *molten rock*, but *melted ice cream*. Note that *molten* is never spelt with a *u*.

mendacious, mendicant *Mendacious* is a rather formal adjective meaning 'lying, untruthful, or untrue': *a mendacious child, a mendacious statement*. It should not be confused with *mendicant*, which means 'begging': *mendicant friars who depended on charity to survive*. *Mendicant* is also a formal noun meaning 'a beggar' or 'a member of a mendicant order of friars'.

Mendicant comes from the Latin *mendicare*, 'to beg', which has its root in *mendum*, meaning 'a physical defect' – beggars were usually crippled. *Mendacious* comes from the Latin *mendax*, probably also related to *mendum*, since a lie too is a fault or defect.

The political joke is a short sharp shock against a given target. In Russia the mendacious press is often its victim . . .

Napoleon looks up from a copy of *Pravda:* 'If I'd had a newspaper like this, nobody would ever have heard of Waterloo.'
– George Mikes,
English Humour for Beginners

The nouns *mendacity* and *mendicity* are even more dangerously similar than their related adjectives. *Mendacity* (or *mendaciousness*) of course means 'lying', especially 'habitual lying and deceit': *He was renowned for his mendacity and was always mistrusted.*

The hero of the thriller is one who enters unknown territory . . . . His vulnerability presumably imposes on your sympathy; his mendacity presumably should repel it. So he needs a kind of politics to justify his demands on that sympathy.
– Owen Dudley Edwards,
The Listener

A *mendacity* can be simply an elaborate synonym for 'a lie':

The world's most accountable police service is entitled to feel very angry when its members are likened to the Gestapo and compared with the Polish and South African police — especially when the author of such mendacities is a man who denies his own union members the right to a secret ballot.
– Eldon Griffiths,
quoted in the *Daily Telegraph*

Mendicity or its more common variant *mendicancy* refers to the state of being a beggar, or the habit of begging, or the existence of a begging class: *Mendicity is rife in the slums.*

Note, finally, these two pronunciations: *mendacious*, /men-**day**shəss/; *mendacity*, /men-**dass**əti/.

mercifully See HOPEFULLY.

meretricious To use the word *meretricious* when you mean *meritorious* would be a grave blunder.

Meritorious is a laudatory adjective — 'having merit, deserving praise or a reward': *a meritorious service to his country.* The Latin verb *merere*, which underlies the word, meant 'to earn or deserve', and this gave rise to the Latin adjective *meritorius*, 'deserving money'.

The Latin *merere* is also the basis of *meretricious*, but the intermediary Latin word this time is *meretrix* (and hence *meritricius*), which meant 'a prostitute'. *Meretricious* could in fact formerly mean 'of or like a prostitute'. Today it means 'superficially attractive, insincere, or vulgarly conspicuous': *meretricious ornamentation, a meretricious argument.*

According to an unnamed Minister, the BBC has jeopardised its case for an increase in the present licence fee by showing 'The Thorn Birds'. Decoded, his remarks mean that this soap opera is a load of meretricious rubbish which is not worth a fraction of the £600,000 the BBC is said to have paid for it.
– leading article, *Daily Telegraph*

Note that the second vowel of *meretricious* is an *e*, not an *i* as in *meritorious*.

metaphor, simile, metonymy, synecdoche *Metaphor* has both a broad and a narrow sense. In its broad sense, it refers to figurative language generally, and embraces simile, metonymy, and synecdoche. In its narrower sense, it is differentiated from these, and denotes an implicit, unstated comparison between an item under consideration and a more-or-less unrelated item that has one or two incidental similarities: *the evening of his life,* for example, or *My brother is a mad dog.* (This means that my brother is irrational and unpredictable, and behaves extremely violently when he loses his temper: the comparison goes only so far — the metaphor does not require my brother to have four legs and a tail as well.)

In a *simile* the comparison is made explicit, being clearly indicated by a prefatory word or phrase such as *like, as,* or *in the way that: My brother is like a mad dog*; *My brother will turn on you just as a mad dog would.*

Here are two famous similes from a single book:

I turned to Aunt Agatha, whose demeanour was now rather like that of one who, picking daisies on the railway, has just caught the down express in the small of the back. . . .

I'm not lugged into Family Rows. On the occasions when Aunt is calling to Aunt like mastodons bellowing across primeval swamps . . . , the clan has a tendency to ignore me.
– P.G. Wodehouse,
The Inimitable Jeeves

In *metonymy* and *synecdoche*, the two elements of the comparison are fused, and only the related item — not the item under discussion — is actually mentioned. In *metonymy*, the item under discussion is replaced by something closely associated with it (whereas in a metaphor, in the narrower sense, the elements of the comparison are not directly associated): *the Crown* is used in the place of *the monarchy,* for instance, or *the law* for *the police.*

In *synecdoche,* the item under discussion is replaced by something referring to one of its parts, or by something that it is a part of — in other words, by a wider, more inclusive term or a narrower, less inclusive term: in *a fleet of 80 sail,* the word *sail* stands in for *sailing ships;* obversely, *Newcastle* might stand in for *Newcastle United Football Team.*

Metaphor goes back through Old French and Latin to the Greek *metaphora,* 'transference', from *metapherein,* 'to transfer', from *meta-,* 'involving change' + *pherein,* 'to bear, carry'.

Simile is Latin in origin, the neuter form of the adjective *similis,* 'similar'.

Metonymy comes through Late Latin from the Greek *metonumia,* 'substitute naming', from *meta-,* 'involving transfer' + *onoma,* 'a name'. It is pronounced /mi-**ton**nimi, me-/.

Synecdoche comes through Latin and Greek from Greek roots meaning 'to take up, or understand, with another' — *sun-,* 'with' + *ex,* 'out of' + *dekhesthai,* 'to take, receive'. It is pronounced /si-**nek**-dəki/.

metaphors and similes Figurative language is not just an adornment to speech and writing. It is often essential to communication. Conveying a complex idea from one mind to another can be virtually impossible without recourse to some image or analogy. And it is probably central even to thought itself. William James, the American philosopher, pointed out almost 100 years ago that 'pure similarity' comes before 'abstraction': abstract ideas arise only as a result of similes and metaphors. 'The primeval man,' James continued, 'will say, not "the bread is hard" but "the bread is stone".'

Our everyday language is riddled with metaphors — so deeply embedded that they are all but unnoticeable: *the arms of a chair, the legs of a table, a sparkling personality,* and so on. Concealed within the etymology of hundreds of Greek- or Latin-based words are metaphorical beginnings: the verbs *to consider* and *to contemplate* for example, are related to *sidereal* ('to do with stars, stellar') and *temple* (the Latin verbs both originally referred to the meditations and observations of augurs or soothsayers).

If these are 'dead' metaphors, many others can be described as half-dead: *hawk-eyed, breathing*

down one's neck, an open-and-shut case, financial liquidity, a blockbuster novel, and so on.

Depending on the definition you choose, *metaphor* can be thought of as embracing *simile,* or as being distinguished from it. (See METAPHOR, SIMILE, METONOMY, SYNECDOCHE.)

Both similes and metaphors (in the narrower sense) raise several dangers and give rise to several usage points. Discussion of these tends to concentrate on metaphors — people speak of *mixed metaphors* rather than *mixed similes* — but the warnings and criticisms apply equally to similes.

1. bewitchment. Poetry thrives on figurative language. So too, unfortunately, does propaganda: to speak of *rivers of blood* is far more stirring or scaring than to speak merely of *civil unrest.* Take care not to abuse metaphoric language in this way, or to be manipulated by it. To *compare* a reality to something quite different is not to *convert* it into that reality. To give a dog a bad name (or to call a man *a mad dog*) is not in itself reason enough to hang him. As the French poet Paul Valéry warned, in his *Introduction to the Method of Leonardo da Vinci:*

> The folly of mistaking a paradox for a discovery, a metaphor for a proof, a torrent of verbiage for a spring of capital truths, and oneself for an oracle, is inborn in us.

2. cloying imagery. Figurative language bewitches in a simpler way: the beauty of it and the cleverness of it (often the specious beauty and the irritating cleverness) may 'inspire' writers and speakers to indulge in far more of it than they ought to. The language becomes rich — too rich — with ingenious metaphors and euphonious similes, often at the expense of meaning itself: all sauce and no meat. And so far from becoming ever more striking, the language begins to decline in effectiveness: when *everything* in a meal is piquant, nothing stands out as piquant any longer. Ornateness is useless unless there is a basis of plainness to show it up. The particularly florid styles of writing, such as *euphuism* (discussed at EUPHEMISM) are by no means the most successful or best-loved styles in English literature.

Here is a typically overspiced example:

> *?* Perhaps Mrs Thatcher's aim is that he should act as a lightning conductor, because one of the problems of having sacked or exiled all of the 'wets' is that there are no longer any scapegoats around to blame.

Lord Whitelaw has few illusions about his new job. He sees himself as a behind-the-scenes man who can offer a friendly word of advice to a colleague in trouble and is able to provide the odd spot of Ministerial muscle to back up the Prime Minister's press secretary Bernard Inghams.

But he knows that he will be able to do little to pre-empt the next banana skin or defuse such interesting personality clashes as the recent one between Chancellor Nigel Lawson and Energy Secretary Peter Walker.

– Adam Raphael, *The Observer*

Even a single image can be overworked. To ring the changes once or twice may be effective and amusing enough, of course:

Mr Lawson's statement was clearly intended to shiver the timbers of his Cabinet colleagues and put the wind up the backbenchers seated behind him.

– Ian Aitken, *The Guardian*

Until the Okhai Group stepped in with a £3 million offer for the ailing James Keiller and Son, by then an untended subsidiary of the multinational Nestlé, jam seemed to have had the last pips squeezed out of it. Nestlé had shut down many of the Keiller lines, marmalade production took place only a few days a month and it looked as though the bitter fruits of recession would result in the death of a firm that was identified with Dundee.

– Lindsay Mackie, *The Observer*

But take care not to be carried away. If you choose to compare a dying man to a guttering candle, for example, every elaboration on this image marks a further risk:

?? The fire of life burnt very low now. His consciousness dimmed and brightened, as a dying flame might surge and subside. The wick was all but burnt out, yet the vital fire clung to it and would not quit. It was not a calm death: he blazed and writhed and sputtered. It was painful to watch. Yet the doctor stayed his hand: who would wish to snuff that valiant taper rather than let it burn itself out?

3. *clichéd metaphors and similes.* Such overextended imagery comes from trying too hard, putting too much thought into your wording. Another danger is not giving enough thought to the wording — and trotting out stale images that dull rather than enliven the description: *dead as a doornail, playing your cards right,* and so on. These no longer evoke an image in the mind of the reader or listener, though they might provoke a yawn.

See also CLICHÉS.

4. *half-heartedness.* The reverse of an excessively bold use of figurative language is a needless timidity — a failure to see the metaphor or simile through, out of fear of overdoing things. If you speak of a *gulf* between the managers and the workers, you are committed to that metaphor for a time. The appropriate resolution is the *bridging* of that gulf, or perhaps the *narrowing* of it: it sounds extremely tame to abandon the metaphor and speak instead of ? *ending the gulf.* Similarly, it sounds odd, when you think about it, that salesmen or civil servants should be congratulated for ? *passing a target* or ? *reducing a bottleneck.*

5. *mixed metaphors and similes.* A succession of metaphors or similes drawn from different fields of comparison sometimes produces an incongruous or ludicrous effect. There are many celebrated examples that make the point without need of comment:

× We stand on the abyss — let us march forward together.
× You are sitting on the fence and burying your head in the sand.

Mr Ian Smith, when Prime Minister of Rhodesia, was reported to have said: × *Are we going to sit back and take this lying down?* And the film-producer Sam Goldwyn, a notorious (and possibly quite deliberate) language-mangler, apparently once complained that × *Every director bites the hand that lays the golden egg.* Similarly:

× West Berlin is an oasis of democracy in a sea of communism.

– John Hosken, *The Listener*

A former head of the British Civil Service sidestepped a question, during an interview, with these words:

× That's an invitation to cock my leg over a wild goose and go off into a mare's nest.

– Lord Bancroft, BBC Radio 4

× Braudel does not allow us to forget that there are no easy recipes for staying at the top of the greasy pole, once one has got there.

– Lord Beloff, *Daily Telegraph*

Perhaps the most famous example of bizarrely mixed metaphors is attributed to an 18th-century Irish politician:

✗ Mr Speaker, I smell a rat; I see him forming in the air and darkening the sky; but I'll nip him in the bud.
  – attributed to Sir Boyle Roche, quoted in *The Oxford Book of Quotations*

Another 18th-century example, this time from a judge, later to be Lord Chief Justice of England; convicting a butler of stealing wine, the judge apparently said:

You burst through all restraints of religion and morality, and have for years been feathering your nest with your master's bottles.
  – Lord Kenyon, quoted in George A. Morton and D.M. Malloch, *Law and Laughter*

Even 'dead' or 'half-dead' metaphors can become embarrassingly active when mixed inappropriately:

✗ So let me look at the roots of a few sacred cows.
  – Sir John Donaldson, *New Law Journal*

✗ For the contents of Mr Heseltine's memorandum, whatever else they were, were themselves highly deceitful. A fast one was being pulled over the eyes and ears of the good old British public.
  – Professor Anthony Clare, *The Listener*

?? Even if this target is wildly optimistic, it provides considerable leeway for at least doubling Soviet oil exports to the West.
  – Steve Vines, *The Observer*

Of course language lends itself to confusions of all kinds — malapropisms (*the pineapple of success* = 'the pinnacle of success'); spoonerisms (*Sew me to my sheet* = 'Show me to my seat'), and so on. 'Mixed idioms' are very common:
✗ *pays the consequences* ('pays the price' + 'takes the consequences'); ✗ *playing a major contribution* ('playing a major role' + 'making a major contribution'); ✗ *by far and away the best* ('by far' + 'far and away'); ✗ *rose and cheered as to a man* ('as one man' + 'to a man'). There is a certain inventive freshness about linguistic confusions of these kinds, and many commentators have suspected that 'Goldwynisms' or 'Whitelawisms' were coined calculatedly rather than accidentally. 'Mixed clichés' can be very striking in their grotesque way:

✗ green behind the ears
✗ Save your breath to cool your bacon
✗ to kill two birds in one bush

✗ You can't have your pound of flesh and eat it
✗ throwing a sponge in the works
✗ A nudge is as good as a wink to a blind bat
✗ skating on the thin edge of the wedge
✗ The scheme seemed as safe as a house on fire.

Comedians use clashing imagery as part of their stock-in-trade. And good writers sometimes playfully mix their metaphors or idioms to witty effect, or to prod clichés back into life:

Earlier in the year the Justice Department had more or less dropped the case, saying that an FBI inquiry had uncovered 'no credible evidence of wrongdoing'. Now the House sub-committee has poured oil on these smouldering embers by strongly challenging that finding.
  – Harold Jackson, *The Guardian*

When we Woosters put our hands to the plough, we do not readily sheathe the sword.
  – P.G. Wodehouse, *Right Ho, Jeeves*

Such mischievous juggling with language can be delightful in experienced hands. But inexperienced jugglers tend to make fools of themselves. As a rule, examine your idioms and figures of speech within any sentence to check that they are all consistent with one another. If they are not, think twice before proceeding: for every mixed metaphor that works successfully in context, there must be hundreds that simply fizzle, clang, jar, or blush.

Note finally, however, that not all changes of metaphor entail 'mixed metaphors'. The usual limit is a single sentence. Once a new sentence or (to be quite safe) a new idea has begun, there is no reason why you should not draw on a new image — with the proviso that you are not thereby overspicing your writing with figurative language generally.

6. inappropriateness. Pause to consider before lighting on any particular metaphor or simile. A man who has broken both arms in an industrial accident would not welcome the advice to *throw the book at his employers*. A man whose house has just burnt down would be only half-pleased to hear that his insurance-claim was proceeding *like a house on fire*.

This inappropriate choice of simile or metaphor is particularly likely when the simile or metaphor has become absorbed through common use into standard English idiom and apparently lost all its original metaphoric force: *a flood of protest, a fiery speech,* and so on — these no longer evoke images in the mind of floods or fires. None the less, the metaphoric core remains, and reveals itself at the most unfortunate moments. You may never think twice about using the idiom *to jump to conclusions* — until the moment when you warn a man in a wheelchair against jumping to conclusions. Similarly, the metaphor in *spate* (which can still mean 'a flood') remains asleep in such phrases as *a spate of bankruptcies in the City, a recent spate of misfortunes,* and so on, but it wakes up suddenly when you speak of the *? recent spate of droughts around the world.*

Here are some more examples. A football manager reputedly once confessed to reporters:

✗ Smith's knee is still a bit of a headache for me, but he'll be playing.
— quoted in Fritz Spiegl's
Keep Taking the Tabloids!

✗ Crash courses are available for those who wish to acquire their pilot's licence in the minimum possible time.

The inappropriateness sometimes results not from a too-distant metaphor but rather from a too closely related one — what has been referred to as 'an unconscious pun':

A reader who telephoned Cambridge University's Department of Anatomy was told that, because of Easter, the switchboard is operating on a skeleton staff.
— *The Times*

A police spokesman once apparently made the following statement to the press:

✗ A hole has appeared in the road. Fife police are looking into it.
— quoted in Fritz Spiegl's
Keep Taking the Tabloids!

?? Lord Bauer ... lives in Montagu Square, near Marble Arch, in a ground floor flat. A housekeeper serves coffee from a silver coffee pot. Lord Bauer is full of beans; slim, neatly dressed, gregarious.
— Michael Davie, *The Observer*

To which the obvious footnote is: 'Coffee beans?' See also CLICHÉS.

meter, metre In British English, these spellings are sometimes confused. (No such problem arises in American English, since the form *meter* is correct for all senses.)

A meter is an instrument for measuring or regulating, such as *a gas meter* or *a parking meter*. *To meter,* the verb, is, accordingly, to measure or regulate with a metering device. But the unit of length, *the metre,* is spelt *-re.* So is the *metre*

that is the rhythmic pattern of poetry. The distinction is confused by the specific types of line in poetry, such as *pentameter* (a line having five stresses), which are spelt *-er.*

All of these words go back, through French or Latin, to the Greek *metron,* 'a meter or measure'.

Note that the adjective from *metre,* the unit of length, is *metric,* as in *the metric system* or *a metric mile.* The adjective *metrical* means 'relating to verse metre' or 'relating to measurement in general'.

Compounds with *-meter* tend to be stressed on the syllable immediately before *-meter,* and the first *e* of *-meter* is reduced to the neutral vowel /ə/: ba**rom**eter, ther**mom**eter. Compounds with *-metre* tend to be stressed on their first syllable, and the first *e* of *-metre* remains /ee/: **cen**timetre, **mil**limetre. A controversial case in this regard is *kilometre,* which by analogy with other *-metre* compounds should be stressed **kil**ometre, but is often stressed *? ki***lom**etre, apparently on the mistaken model of such *-meter* compounds as ba**rom**eter and ther**mom**eter. This faulty analogy is probably strengthened by the fact that there is an *-o-* in *kilometre* rather than the *-i-* of *centimetre* and *millimetre.*

meticulous Many writers on usage have noted the strange popularity of this adjective, and its slightly careless use as a substitute for *scrupulous* or *punctilious*: *? Try to be a little more meticulous about keeping your files up to date.* The original sense was 'scared, timid', the main Latin root being *metus,* 'fear'. But when the word was revived in the last century (needlessly, in the view of some critics), it was in the sense of 'painstakingly careful and precise' or 'excessively concerned with details, overscrupulous'. There is still perhaps a slightly negative ring to it, in other words, a suggestion of hairsplitting or nitpicking. A purist would consider it an unsuitable word for a compliment, and urge *conscientious, scrupulous,* or *accurate* instead. In the first of the following quotations, *meticulous* is used, dubiously, in a complimentary way; in the second, it is used more appropriately, in the sense 'precise to a fault':

? And whereas the others called her Mum, or Ma'am, Clancy called her Miss Crane. She was herself meticulous in the business of getting to know their names and dignifying them with the prefix Mister.
— Paul Scott,
The Jewel in the Crown

Minute by minute throughout the hours the

prisoner discoursed on the massacre without mentioning the word, covering all aspects of every question addressed to him with the meticulous undiscriminating reflex of a computing machine.

– Muriel Spark,
The Mandelbaum Gate

It is worth remembering the element of fear still lurking in the word: *a meticulous man* is conscientious to a fault through fear of failure or criticism. Nevertheless, the word is now widely used with a neutral or even favourable tone, and in all but extremely formal contexts it is safe to use the word in this looser way.

metonomy See METAPHOR.

metre See METER.

microbe See GERM.

might See MAY.

migrate, migrant See EMIGRATE.

militate, mitigate These two words are often confused: some people say ✕ *to mitigate against* when what they mean is *to militate against*. The intransitive verb *to militate* comes from the Latin *militare*, 'to serve as a soldier', from *miles*, 'a soldier', so it usually conveys a sense of fighting against something. It means 'to serve as strong evidence or as a powerful influence', and usually occurs with *towards* or *against* as in *Mutual suspicion militates against a reconciliation.*

It is the reluctance of the British to take baseball seriously which militates against acceptance of a fine story like 'Alibi Ike', which is about a professional baseball player.
– Anthony Burgess, *The Observer*

The transitive verb *to mitigate* means 'to soften, or reduce the severity of', as in *The appeals tribunal mitigated their earlier harsh views of the rioting.* Or in:

To the ordinary man in fact, the pealing of bells is a monotonous jangle and a nuisance, tolerable only when mitigated by remote distance and sentimental association.
– Dorothy L. Sayers, *The Nine Tailors*

Mr du Cann, MP for Taunton, urged Mr Jopling to devote his energies in the long term to getting the agreement replaced by a price mechanism.

'Until that time, the worst effects of the present arrangements must be mitigated,' he said.

– William Weekes,
Daily Telegraph

To mitigate comes from the Latin verb *mitigare*, from *mitis*, 'gentle, mild'.
See also EXTENUATE.

million See BILLION; NUMBER STYLE.

minimal, minimise The Latin *minimus* meant 'least, smallest'. In English, *minimal*, like *minimum*, should strictly be used only of the smallest possible amount or degree.

You are not the sort of woman of whom men are afraid, hysterics who behave as though they are the constant object of scandal or desire, who boast of their conquests and their performance, and who think they can do anything so long as they entertain their friends and keep a minimal bargain with their husbands.
– Philip Neville, in Anita Brookner's
Hotel du Lac

Minimal is now widely used in the loose sense of 'very small, insignificant or negligible' — *a minimal return on investment* — and this sense, though dubious to purists, is safe to use in all but the most formal contexts.
To minimise, correspondingly, means literally 'to reduce to the smallest possible amount or degree': *He minimised his losses.* By extension, it has come to mean 'belittle, play down, depreciate': *Her husband always tries to minimise any success she achieves*; *I don't wish to minimise his contribution, but* ... This seems a fair enough usage. In the earlier sense, the word is now used loosely to mean simply 'to reduce': *? He minimised his losses as best he could.* Purists object to this weakened sense, and criticise the use of adverbs such as *greatly* or *somewhat* when applied to *minimise*. Use *reduce* or *lessen* instead if you have to qualify the verb in this way: *He greatly reduced his losses.*

minority See MAJORITY.

misquotation A great many of the most familiar 'quotations' and allusions from the Bible, literature, and films are in fact inaccurate versions of the original. The popular version is usually so well established that there is no point in correcting it in line with the true version. Only a pedant would quarrel with the phrases *the sweat of your brow* or *by the skin of my teeth,* and point to the correct wording in the King James Bible in support of his objections: *In the sweat of thy face shalt thou eat bread* (Genesis 3:19) and *I am escaped with the skin of my teeth* (Job 19:20). And the phrase *a parting shot* is now firmly established in its own right, and can no longer be considered a malapropism or misuse of *a Parthian shot* (Parthian horsemen were renowned for turning in the saddle as they fled, and showering arrows on their pursuers).

There is another consideration, often neglected by those who are swift to pounce on a misquotation: it may be at least as good as the original. Any misquotation that has the vigour to find its way into the popular mind, and lodge there, clearly has a certain right to survive. It could be argued that *Tomorrow to fresh fields and pastures new* is even more effective a line — in its sound-pattern and imagery — than John Milton's original wording, *Tomorrow to fresh woods and pastures new.*

Nevertheless, it is at least worth being aware when and how the common form departs from the original.

Here is a list of the most frequent culprits (printed in italics), together with the accurate versions in each case. First, some more Biblical misquotations:

Esau sold his birthright for a mess of pottage.

> And Esau said to Jacob, Feed me, I pray thee, with that same red pottage; for I am faint ... And Jacob said, Sell me this day thy birthright ... and he sold his birthright unto Jacob. Then Jacob gave Esau bread and pottage of lentiles.
> — Genesis 25:30-34

> ... Esau, who for one morsel of meat sold his birthright.
> — Hebrews 12:16

to go the way of all flesh

> And, behold, this day I am going the way of all the earth.
> — Joshua 23:14

> Now the days of David drew nigh that he should die; and he charged Solomon his son, saying, I go the way of all the earth: be thou strong therefore, and shew thyself a man.
> — I Kings 2:2

a cloud no bigger than a man's hand

> Behold, there ariseth a little cloud out of the sea, like a man's hand.
> — Elijah, in I Kings 18:44

Pride goes before a fall.

> Pride goeth before destruction and an haughty spirit before a fall.
> — Proverbs 16:18

Of the making of books there is no end.

> Of making many books there is no end; and much study is a weariness of the flesh.
> — Ecclesiastes 12:12

The lion shall lie down with the lamb.

> The wolf also shall dwell with the lamb, and the leopard shall lie down with the kid; and the calf and the young lion and the fatling together; and a little child shall lead them.
> — Isaiah 11:6

a voice crying in the wilderness

> For this is he that was spoken of by the prophet Esaias, saying, The voice of one crying in the wilderness, Prepare ye the way of the Lord.
> — John the Baptist, in Matthew 3:3

A prophet is without honour in his own country.

> But Jesus said unto them, A prophet is not without honour, save in his own country, and in his own house.
> — Matthew 13:57

Vengeance is mine, saith the Lord.

> Vengeance is mine; I will repay, saith the Lord.
> — Romans 12:19

Money is the root of all evil.

> For the love of money is the root of all evil.
> — I Timothy 6:10

Some quotations are occasionally attributed to the Bible, when in fact they come from quite unrelated sources. *The Assyrian came down like the wolf on the fold*, for instance, was in fact written by Lord Byron, in his poem 'The Destruction of Sennacherib' (1815). The story, but certainly not the wording, is from II Kings 19:35.

God tempers the wind to the shorn lamb sounds as though it might come from the Book of Proverbs. In fact, it was written by Laurence Sterne in his novel *A Sentimental Journey* (1768). The quotation, put in the mouth of the character Maria, is a translation of a popular proverb written in French in 1594 by Henri Estienne.

Another saying that sounds as though it might come from the Book of Proverbs is: *Spare the rod and spoil the child*. In fact, it was the poet Samuel Butler who wrote this, in his satirical poem *Hudibras* (1663-78). He was, it is true, alluding to the King James Bible — Proverbs 13:24 reads *He that spareth his rod hateth his son*, and Proverbs 24:13-14: *Withhold not correction from the child: for if thou beatest him with the rod, he shall not die. Thou shalt beat him with the rod, and shalt deliver his soul from hell.*

Finally: *What is truth? said jesting Pilate; and would not stay for an answer.* Although alluding to the Gospels, the wording is Francis Bacon's, from his essay, 'On Truth' (1625).

And a common misquotation from *The Book of Common Prayer* (1662) is:

Speak now or forever hold your peace.

> Let him now speak, or else hereafter forever hold his peace.
> — the marriage service

Here is another saying mistakenly ascribed to the Bible, and misquoted as well:

Cleanliness is next to godliness.

> Cleanliness is indeed next to godliness.
> — John Wesley, *Sermons*

And note the commonly mistaken punctuation in this well-known line:

God rest you, merry gentlemen.

> God rest you merry, gentlemen.
> — anonymous, Christmas carol

Next Shakespeare, perhaps even more prolific a source of quotations — and hence misquotations — than the King James Bible. *Hamlet* in particular:

flat, stale, and unprofitable

> How weary, stale, flat, and unprofitable
> Seem to me all the uses of this world.
> — Hamlet, in *Hamlet* I ii

There are more things in heaven and earth Than are dreamed of in your philosophy.

> There are more things in heaven and earth, Horatio,
> Than are dreamt of in your philosophy.
> — Hamlet, in *Hamlet* I iv

the thousand natural ills that flesh is heir to

> To die: to sleep;
> No more; and, by a sleep to say we end
> The heart-ache and the thousand natural shocks
> That flesh is heir to, 'tis a consummation
> Devoutly to be wish'd.
> — Hamlet, in *Hamlet* III i

hoist by his own petard

> For 'tis the sport to have the enginer
> Hoist with his own petar.
> — Hamlet, in *Hamlet* III iv

(Shakespeare used the earlier form *petar*, referring to the small bomb used to break down a gate.)

Alas, poor Yorick: I knew him well.

> Alas, poor Yorick; I knew him, Horatio;
> a fellow of infinite jest, of most excellent fancy.
> — Hamlet, in *Hamlet* V i

One last example from *Hamlet* — not a misquotation so much as a common misuse. When Hamlet says

> It is a custom
> More honour'd in the breach than the observance
> — Hamlet, in *Hamlet* I iv

he is referring to carousing, a custom that he considers undesirable — one that it is honourable to neglect. Today people tend to quote the words when lamenting a desirable practice that is no longer observed.

To continue with some misquotations from other Shakespeare plays:

O Romeo, Romeo! wherefore art thou, Romeo?

> O Romeo, Romeo! wherefore art thou Romeo?
> — Juliet, in *Romeo and Juliet* II ii

(The comma before the last *Romeo* makes all the difference: the *wherefore* does not mean 'where'; it means 'why'.

Juliet is lamenting the obstacle to the fulfilment of her love for Romeo — that he happens to be the son of her father's enemy.)

The devil can quote Scripture for his own purpose

and:

a goodly apple rotten at the core.

The devil can cite Scripture for his purpose.
An evil soul, producing holy witness,
Is like a villain with a smiling cheek,
A goodly apple rotten at the heart.
— Antonio, of Shylock, in
The Merchant of Venice I ii

(But Antonio was probably citing, in his own words, two well-known sentiments of the time.)

All that glitters is not gold.

All that glisters is not gold,
Often have you heard that told.
— Morocco, reading the scroll, in
The Merchant of Venice I viii

(Again, however, the proverb is an old one, going back to Aristotle in ancient Greece, and cited by Chaucer, Spenser, and many others. After Shakespeare, Dryden cited the proverb in the version used today, in 'The Hind and the Panther', 1687.)

to gild the lily

To be possess'd with double pomp,
To guard a title that was rich before,
To gild refined gold, to paint the lily,
To throw a perfume on the violet,
To smooth the ice, or add another hue
Unto the rainbow, or with taper light
To seek the beauteous eye of heaven to garnish,
Is wasteful and ridiculous excess.
— Salisbury, in *King John* IV ii

Discretion is the better part of valour.

The better part of valour is discretion; in the which better part I have saved my life.

— Falstaff, in
King Henry IV part 2, V iv

(But Falstaff is himself just producing one

version of a traditional piece of wisdom.)

a poor thing, but mine own

A poor virgin, sir, an ill-favoured thing, sir, but mine own.
— Touchstone, speaking of his betrothed, in *As You Like It* V iv

Cry havoc, and unleash the dogs of war.

And Caesar's spirit, ranging for revenge,
With Ate by his side come hot from hell,
Shall in these confines with a monarch's voice
Cry 'Havoc!' and let slip the dogs of war.
— Mark Antony, in *Julius Caesar* III i

screw your courage to the sticking-point

But screw your courage to the sticking-place,
And we'll not fail.
— Lady Macbeth, in *Macbeth* I vii

make assurance doubly sure

Then live, Macduff: what need I fear of thee?
But yet I'll make assurance double sure,
And take a bond of fate: thou shalt not live.
— Macbeth, in *Macbeth* IV i

Lead on, Macduff...

Lay on, Macduff;
And damn'd be him that first cries, 'Hold, enough!'
— Macbeth, in *Macbeth* V vii

such stuff as dreams are made of

We are such stuff
As dreams are made on; and our little life
Is rounded with a sleep.
— Prospero, in *The Tempest* IV i

Finally, a misuse again, rather than a misquotation — the common phrase *a foregone conclusion*. This is used today to mean 'something that is bound to happen in the future; a future certainty'. What Othello meant by it, however (in *Othello* III iii), was 'something that has already happened; a past event', *foregone* meaning 'gone before': he is quite convinced that Desdemona has already been seduced by Cassio.

Next, a selection of misquotations from the works of writers since Shakespeare:

Death, be not proud, though some have called thee so.

> Death be not proud, though some have called thee
> Mighty and dreadful, for thou art not so.
> – John Donne, *Holy Sonnets* (c. 1620)

the last infirmity of noble minds

> Fame is the spur that the clear spirit doth raise
> (That last infirmity of noble mind)
> To scorn delights, and live laborious days.
> – John Milton, 'Lycidas' (1637)

Tomorrow to fresh fields, and pastures new.

> At last he rose, and twitch'd his mantle blue;
> To-morrow to fresh woods, and pastures new.
> – John Milton,
> 'Lycidas' (the last two lines)

I could not love thee half so much, Loved I not honour more.

> Yet this inconstancy is such,
> As you too shall adore;
> I could not love thee (Dear) so much,
> Lov'd I not honour more.
> – Richard Lovelace, 'To Lucasta,
> Going to the Wars' (c. 1650)

He that consents against his will, Is of the same opinion still.

> He that complies against his will,
> Is of his own opinion still.
> – Samuel Butler, *Hudibras* (1663-78)

When Greek meets Greek ...

> When Greeks joined Greeks, then was the tug of war!
> – Nathaniel Lee,
> *The Rival Queens* IV ii (1677)

Music has charms to soothe the savage beast.

> Music hath charms to soothe the savage breast.
> – William Congreve,
> *The Mourning Bride* I i (1697)

Hell hath no fury like a woman scorn'd.

> Heav'n has no rage, like love to hatred turn'd,

> Nor Hell a fury, like a woman scorn'd.
> – William Congreve,
> *The Mourning Bride* III viii

A little knowledge is a dangerous thing.

> A little learning is a dang'rous thing;
> Drink deep, or taste not the Pierian spring:
> There shallow draughts intoxicate the brain,
> And drinking largely sobers us again.
> – Alexander Pope,
> *Essay on Criticism* (1711)

Rule Britannia, Britannia rules the waves; Britons never shall be slaves.

> Rule, Britannia, rule the waves;
> Britons never will be slaves.
> – James Thomson, *Alfred* II v (1740)

First catch your hare — attributed to Mrs Beeton.

> Take your hare when it is cased.
> – Mrs Hannah Glasse,
> *The Art of Cookery
> Made Plain and Easy* (1747)

Far from the maddening crowd

and:

They kept the even tenor of their way.

> Far from the madding crowd's ignoble strife,
> Their sober wishes never learn'd to stray;
> Along the cool sequester'd vale of life
> They kept the noiseless tenor of their way.
> – Thomas Gray, 'Elegy Written in
> a Country Churchyard', (1742-50)

The best-laid plans of mice and men Go oft astray.

> The best laid schemes o' mice and men
> Gang aft a-gley.
> – Robert Burns, 'To a Mouse' (1785)

Eternal vigilance is the price of liberty — attributed to Thomas Jefferson.

> The condition upon which God hath given liberty to man is eternal vigilance.
> – John Philpot Curran,
> in a speech in Dublin (1790)

Water, water, everywhere, and not a drop to drink.

Water, water, everywhere,
Nor any drop to drink.
    – Samuel Taylor Coleridge, 'The Rime
        of the Ancient Mariner' (1798)

kind hearts and coronets

'Tis only noble to be good.
Kind hearts are more than coronets,
And simple faith than Norman blood.
    – Alfred, Lord Tennyson,
    'Lady Clara Vere de Vere' (1832)

The law is an ass.

'If the law supposes that,' said Mr
Bumble ... 'the law is a ass, a idiot.'
    – Charles Dickens,
    Oliver Twist (1837-8)

Consistency is the virtue of small minds.

A foolish consistency is the hobgoblin of
little minds, adored by little statesmen
and philosophers and divines.
    – Ralph Waldo Emerson (U.S.),
    Self-Reliance (1841)

It just growed.

'Do you know who made you?' 'Nobody,
as I knows on,' said the child, with a
short laugh ... 'I 'spect I grow'd.'
    – Topsy, in Harriet
    Beecher Stowe (U.S.),
    Uncle Tom's Cabin (1852)

*Theirs not to reason why, Theirs but to do or
die.*

and:

*Cannons to the right of them,
Cannons to the left of them.*

Their's not to make reply,
Their's not to reason why,
Their's but to do and die:
Into the valley of Death
Rode the six hundred.

Cannon to right of them,
Cannon to left of them,
Cannon in front of them
Volley'd and thunder'd.
    – Alfred, Lord Tennyson, 'The
    Charge of the Light Brigade' (1854)

(Several details here: first, Tennyson's
strange use of the apostrophe in *Their's*

– he must have intended the sense
'Theirs *is* not to reason why' or 'Their
duty *is* not to reason why', since the
possessive pronoun *theirs* is spelt without
an apostrophe. Secondly, Tennyson
wrote *to do and die,* not *to do or die*
though *do or die* was a common phrase
then, as now; it had, for example,
appeared earlier in poems by Robert
Burns and Thomas Campbell. Then,
Tennyson chose the collective form
cannon rather than the usual plural
cannons. Finally, he wrote *to right of
them* and *to left of them,* not *to the right
of them* and *to the left of them.*)

*It is a far, far better thing I do than I have
ever done before.*

It is a far, far better thing that I do, than
I have ever done; it is a far, far better rest
that I go to, than I have ever known.
    – Sydney Carton's thoughts,
    while he is awaiting execution,
    in Charles Dickens's
    A Tale of Two Cities (1859)

*Power corrupts; absolute power corrupts
absolutely.*

Power tends to corrupt and absolute
power corrupts absolutely.
    – Lord Acton, letter to Bishop
    Mandell Creighton (5 April 1887)

Home is the sailor, Home from the sea.

Home is the sailor, Home from sea.
    – Robert Louis Stevenson,
    'Requiem' (1887)

'Elementary, my dear Watson!'

'Excellent!' I cried. 'Elementary,' said he.
    – Dr Watson, of Sherlock Holmes,
    in Sir Arthur Conan Doyle's
    'The Crooked Man' (1894)

*They shall not grow old as we that are left
grow old.*

They shall grow not old as we that are left
grow old.
    – Laurence Binyon,
    'For the Fallen' (1914)

Peace in our time.

I believe it is peace for our time ... Go

home and get a nice quiet sleep.
> – Neville Chamberlain,
> address from 10 Downing Street
> (September, 1938)

blood, sweat, and tears

I would say to the House, as I said to
those who have joined this Government,
'I have nothing to offer but blood, toil,
tears and sweat'.
> – Sir Winston Churchill, House
> of Commons speech (13 May 1940)

We are the masters now.

We are the masters at the moment — and
not only for the moment but for a very
long time to come.
> – Sir Hartley Shawcross,
> speaking of the Labour Party,
> House of Commons (April 1946)

Finally, some 'quotations' that never were said
or written in the way commonly supposed, or that
at least are commonly misattributed.

Voltaire, for example, is credited with the statement (in French presumably) *I disapprove of what
you say, but I will defend to the death your right
to say it.* This fine credo was in fact written by
his British biographer 'S.G. Tallentyre' (the pen-
name of E. Beatrice Hall) either as a summary
of Voltaire's beliefs or as something that Voltaire
might have said.

Marie Antoinette's reputed response to the Paris
bread riots of 1788 — *Let them eat cake* — is a
very unfair invention. Most historians agree that
she would never have said it. In fact, she made
large private donations to relieve the poor.

Napoleon is sometimes thought to have said (in
French), *God is on the side of the big battalions.*
This sentiment has in fact a long tradition, going
back to the Roman historian Tacitus, and
repeated in one form or another by Frederick the
Great, Voltaire, Madame de Sévigné, Boileau,
and Gibbon. A similar remark also attributed to
Napoleon is *Providence is on the side of the last
reserve*, which may be what he did in fact say.

The Duke of Wellington denied having said *The
Battle of Waterloo was won on the playing fields
of Eton.* He was, as it happens, an unremarkable
sportsman when at school there.

The survival of the fittest is usually assumed to
have been coined by Charles Darwin. In fact, it
was his contemporary, Herbert Spencer, who
invented the phrase (in his book *Principles of
Biology*, 1864-67), which Darwin acknowledged

to be accurate and convenient. In the context, *fittest* meant 'best suited (to the circumstances)',
not, as people often suppose, 'strongest'.

The saying *Go west, young man* is often
attributed to Horace Greeley, editor of the New
York *Tribune*. He did apparently write, in an
editorial, 'Go west, young man, and grow up with
the country.' But after the saying became
popular, he acknowledged his source: John Bab-
sone Lane Soule, who had written it in 1851 in
another newspaper.

Mark Twain is often credited with the remark
*Everybody talks about the weather, but nobody
does anything about it.* But the editorial in *The
Hartford Courant*, in which the remark appeared
in 1897, was probably written by Charles Dudley
Warner (a collaborator of Twain's on *The Gilded
Age*).

Film stars are frequent victims of such
misrepresentation. Mae West, for instance, did
not say *Come up and see me some time.* She
apparently did say — in the film *She Done Him
Wrong* (1933) — *You know, I always did like a
man in uniform. And that one fits you grand.
Why don't you come up some time and see me?*

And W.C. Fields apparently did not say *Anybody who hates children and dogs* (or *dogs and
babies* or *small dogs and children*) *can't be all
bad.* The writer Leo Rosten claims to have said
it, of Fields, when introducing the misanthropic
actor at a Hollywood banquet in 1938.

Greta Garbo was supposed to have said *I want
to be alone* in her early days in Hollywood, but
insisted that what she actually said was *I want to
be let alone.* After the phrase had caught on,
however, it was used in the film *Grand Hotel*
(1932).

The line *Play it again, Sam* was not in fact said
in the film *Casablanca* (1942). Ingrid Bergman
said *Play it, Sam. Play 'As Time Goes By'*, and
Play it once, Sam, for old time's sake. And Humphrey Bogart said *You played it for her. You can
play it for me ... If she can stand it, I can. Play
it!* The popular version is an understandable
paraphrase on the part of imitators, but incorrect.

And it was the impersonators of James Cagney,
not Cagney himself, who first used the phrase
You dirty rat! But in *Blonde Crazy* (1931) Cagney
does call someone a *dirty double-crossing rat*.

Perhaps it is imitation or impersonation of this
sort that generates and perpetuates most misquotations. If the wording is recognised as typical
or appropriate, then it will probably catch on,
whether it is in fact accurate or not. The allure
of misquotations lies precisely in their ability to
ring true, to capture the spirit of the original, if

not the letter. Most of the misquotations mentioned in this article will probably, therefore, stand the test of time more firmly than the words that they distort.

misrelated constructions 1. Notice the peculiar wording of the following sentences:

× Quietly descending the stairs, a loose tile tripped him up.
?? On opening the door, Sally's gaze at once fell on the corpse.
× Wide-brimmed and furry, the prince raised his hat and waved it at the crowd.
× A brilliant but outrageous comedian, Lenny Bruce's sketches both amused and unsettled his audience.
?? When making up prescriptions, some tablets have to be divided into four.
× Born in Thailand, I was amazed that Wutichai fits so well into English society.
× As Prime Minister, I should like to ask you a question about your cabinet reshuffle.
× Like most cars with four-wheel drive, I find the new Audi handles excellently on rough surfaces.
× Having observed the sequence so far, it should be obvious how it continues.

Grammar requires that opening phrases such as these should — with certain exceptions — relate to the first noun or pronoun or other noun equivalent that follows. Each of the examples just cited displays a conflict between this requirement and the intended meaning. The opening phrase in each case (except the last) is known as a 'misrelated modifier' (or 'misrelated adjective/participle/phrase').

Clearly it was not the loose tile that quietly descended the stairs, or Sally's gaze that opened the door. No prince is wide-brimmed and furry, sketches are not comedians, and tablets do not make up prescriptions. I was not born in Thailand, nor am I Prime Minister, or a car with four-wheel drive. (Note that an introductory *on* or *when*, as in two of the examples listed above, is sometimes considered to improve the construction slightly.)

In the last example, the impersonal clause *it should be obvious* is preceded by a participle (*Having observed the sequence so far*) that relates grammatically to nothing at all, but seems simply to be 'hanging' or 'dangling' in mid-air: hence the name 'hanging participle' or 'dangling participle' (or 'detached/disconnected/suspended/unrelated/unattached participle').

Various remedies are possible, according to the

structure of the opening phrase in each case. The correct noun or pronoun can be moved forwards:

Like most cars with four-wheel drive, the new Audi handles excellently on rough surfaces, I find.

The correct noun or pronoun might not appear in the sentence at all, in which case it will have to be introduced:

A brilliant but outrageous comedian, Lenny Bruce devised sketches that both amused and unsettled his audience.

When the correct noun or pronoun is introduced in this way, the main clause might change from active to passive or vice versa:

When making up prescriptions, you will sometimes have to divide tablets into four.
Quietly descending the stairs, he was tripped up by a loose tile.

The main clause might have to be altered in other ways:

As Prime Minister, could you please answer a question about your cabinet reshuffle?

Sometimes the opening phrase rather than the main clause should be altered in form:

As Sally opened the door, her gaze at once fell on the corpse. (Here the opening phrase has been expanded into an adverbial clause.)
On her opening the door, Sally's gaze at once fell on the corpse. (Rather awkward.)
Sally having opened the door, her gaze at once fell on the corpse. (Rather old-fashioned or formal.)

Or the opening phrase could be moved to the middle of the sentence, to a position immediately following the noun or pronoun it relates to:

The prince raised his hat, wide-brimmed and furry, and waved it at the crowd.

In the case of the dangling participle, finally, the missing subject must be introduced, either by changing the impersonal main clause into a personal clause, or by expanding the dangling phrase into a full clause:

Having observed the sequence so far, you should easily see how it continues.
Now that you have observed the sequence so far, it should be obvious how it continues.

It has to be said that the misrelated phrase has a long and distinguished history, and that — so long as the meaning was clear and unambiguous

— it was not really regarded in past centuries as a grammatical error:

✕ 'Tis given out that, sleeping in mine orchard,
A serpent stung me.
> – The ghost of Hamlet's father,
> in *Hamlet* I v (c. 1600)

? Far from the madding crowd's ignoble strife,
Their sober wishes never learn'd to stray.
> – Thomas Gray,
> 'Elegy Written in a Country
> Churchyard' (1750)

(It is possible that this sentence is correctly constructed, but Gray probably intended the opening phrase to relate to an implied *they,* rather than to *their sober wishes.*)

✕ Uncommonly conscientious for a seaman, and endued with a deep natural reverence, the wild watery loneliness of his life did therefore strongly incline him to superstition.
> – Herman Melville (U.S.),
> *Moby Dick* (1851)

Such sentences would not get past an alert editor today: in the last of them, for instance, the proper subject *he* would somehow have to be introduced.

Here are some recent examples of misrelated phrases. Obviously newspaper sub-editors are not as alert as they might be:

✕ Selling at prices ranging from £200 to £1,000, retail sources believe the mobile modules could become as popular as personal computers.
> – Julian Allason, *The Observer*

It is the *mobile modules,* not the *retail sources,* that sell at the specified prices. Similarly:

✕ Naturally, I tried to find out more about Myerscough-Walker. As well as a prolific perspectivist, I knew he had been an architect who had designed an unusual Modern Movement house in 1937.
> – Gavin Stamp, *The Times*

The *prolific perspectivist* is presumably Myerscough-Walker, and not — as the grammar implies — Gavin Stamp the reporter.

✕ Stepping off the Hong Kong plane in Bangkok, the Third World greets you with a smack of hot wet air and a tug on the sleeve.
> – Tony Partington, *The Times*

It is not the Third World that steps off the plane, but 'you' or the writer.

Having locked up Miss Tisdall so that we all might sleep more easily in our beds, I trust that the custodians of our peace are sleeping more easily in theirs.
> – Professor Anthony Clare,
> *The Listener*

Now that they have locked up . . . would have been preferable.

2. Here now are three rather less clear-cut examples of misrelated constructions:

? As authors of this book, allow us the occasional lapse.
? Barbados only just defeated Trinidad, handicapped by a spate of recent injuries.
? Children, this food must not be eaten without washing first.

The first of these sentences seems at first glance to be quite in order: the first noun or pronoun of the main clause is *us,* and *us* is clearly what the opening phrase relates to. The problem is that the main clause is an imperative, and imperatives can be thought of as beginning with an implied *you*: *As authors of this book, (you must) allow us the occasional lapse.* And in that case, the opening phrase is misrelated: grammatically it relates to *you,* whereas the intended meaning requires it to relate to *us.* Purists would therefore urge the recasting of the sentence — along the following lines, for example:

Allow us, as authors of this book, the occasional lapse

or:

As authors of this book, we ask you to overlook the occasional lapse.

The second of the dubious sentences — *?Barbados only just defeated Trinidad, handicapped by a spate of recent injuries* — is open to the charge of ambiguity. Which team is handicapped by a spate of recent injuries — Barbados or Trinidad? The sentence should be reworded to make the meaning clear. If the injury-prone team is Barbados, you could say:

Barbados, handicapped by a spate of recent injuries, only just defeated Trinidad

— or perhaps:

Barbados only just defeated Trinidad, being handicapped by a spate of recent injuries.

(The insertion of the *-ing* participle, *being* or *having been,* has the effect of attaching the phrase unambiguously to the subject of the main clause

— in this case *Barbados*.) On the other hand, if the injury-prone team is Trinidad, the sentence might be reworded as:

Barbados only just defeated Trinidad, which was handicapped by a spate of recent injuries.

The comic potential of ambiguously positioned phrases of this kind has always been gratefully exploited by comedians. Groucho Marx had this to say, for example, in a Marx Brothers film:

One morning I shot an elephant in my pyjamas. How he got into my pyjamas I'll never know.
— George S. Kaufman (U.S.)
and Morrie Ryskind (U.S.),
Animal Crackers

The humour of misrelated constructions is more often unintentional than intentional, however:

✕ Sinyavsky . . . is a small man, aged 58, rather hunched, with a white beard and, usually, a gentle and humorous demeanour. He wore a brown cardigan and an open-necked grey shirt, speaking only in Russian.
— Michael Davie, *The Observer*

Surely the shirt spoke English as well as Russian, one reader retorted.

Note that misrelated phrases can be adverbial phrases too — a phrase, in other words, can relate to the incorrect verb as well as to the incorrect noun. Another inadvertently comic quotation illustrates this. Lord Olivier is quoted as saying of Sir Ralph Richardson:

✕ He wanted to play *Anthony and Cleopatra* very badly. I said, 'Ralph, you can't play Anthony . . .' . . . in my mind it spelt out the difference between us.
— Lord Olivier, BBC Radio 4

To which one might retort: surely Sir Ralph wanted to play it very well. What Lord Olivier should have said is *He wanted very badly to play Anthony and Cleopatra* or *He very badly wanted to play Anthony and Cleopatra*. Here the adverbial phrase *very badly* is correctly related to the verb *wanted*. In the actual version, *very badly* is, through its poor positioning, incorrectly related to the verb *to play*.

The third of the dubious sentences cited — *? Children, this food must not be eaten without washing first* — is also open to the charge of ambiguity. Is it the food that has to be washed, or the hands of the children eating the food? It

seems that only a major rephrasing of the sentence can get rid of the ambiguity.

In some similar constructions, ambiguity is avoided simply because only one interpretation makes sense: *The next exercise should be done standing up.* The participle *standing up* obviously relates to an implied object *you* or *one*. (An *exercise* cannot stand up.) But in the sentence *? The bottles should be stored standing up,* a possible ambiguity is once again present — *standing up* referring either to *bottles* or to an implied *you* or *one,* referring to the person who will store them. Usually the context will make clear which meaning is intended in such sentences, but even then, it is perhaps advisable to avoid all possibility of misunderstanding by rephrasing the sentence into a completely unambiguous form — such as *You should stand up rather than crouch when storing the bottles* on the one hand, or *When you store the bottles, ensure that they are standing upright.*

Similarly the sentence *? You'll never find a policeman just walking here in the park* should, for the sake of absolute clarity, be reworded considerably: on the one hand, *If you want to find a policeman, you'll have to look outside the park*; on the other, *Policemen don't have time to go walking about in parks.*

3. The prohibition on misrelated or dangling phrases allows certain exceptions. Three types are especially important:

● so-called 'absolute constructions', which have subjects of their own:

Sally having opened the door, her gaze at once fell on the corpse.
That said/That being the case, we can go on to the next point.
All things considered, he's a fool.

Note that *having opened the door* is grammatically related to *Sally* rather than to *her gaze.*
● constructions that function as 'sentence adverbials' — that is, that comment on the main sentence or link it with other sentences:

Speaking frankly, he's a fool.
To be frank, he's a fool.
Simply stated, he's a fool.
To sum up, he's a fool.

● constructions with participles or participial phrases that function as prepositions or conjunctions:

Considering his age, he's very fit.
Considering that he's past 80, he's very fit
According to her, he's very fit.

Other obvious examples include *owing to, provided that, regarding, concerning,* and *excepting.* No one would expect *owing to* to 'relate' directly to some subject in the main clause. And such forms as *during* and *pending* are felt to be purely prepositional in modern English, not verbal at all.

Consider these further examples of the various types:

> Given all these uncertainties, it is not surprising that a lot of people should yearn for linguistic simplification and should try to make words less endlessly complex than they are.
> — Professor John Weightman, 'Words', BBC Radio 3

> Barring accidents, we shall arrive shortly before noon.
> Seeing you're ill, the performance will have to be cancelled.
> Speaking of firearms, the Kalashnikov has apparently undergone modifications recently.
> Failing that, I'll take the smaller version.

Other constructions of various types that are fully acceptable even though apparently 'misrelated' are *allowing for exceptions, broadly speaking, strictly speaking, putting two and two together, putting it simply* or *put simply, taking everything into account, using the term loosely, coming down to details, assuming, supposing, granting* or *granted, depending on,* and *excluding* (and also perhaps *come to think of it, come to that,* and so on). If you said *There were ten commanders, not counting the sergeant,* not even the most pedantic purist would object by asking 'Who is not counting the sergeant?'

A handful of phrases are still on the borderline between the status of (literal) participles and the status of (figurative) prepositions or conjunctions: *based upon, judging (from), referring to,* and *having said (that).*

Purists might still object to such sentences as:

> ? Having said that, kippers nevertheless remain a valuable and nutritious breakfast-food.

(Kippers do not speak, it might be argued.)

> ? Judging from previous analyses, this new star cluster is likely to have a high carbon content.

> ? Judging by the first episode, the half-hour plays, adapted by Bleasdale from his Scully novels, are in a more genial humour than his painfully, sometimes tearfully funny 'Boys

from the Black Stuff'.
> — Geoffrey Nicholson, *The Observer*

Until these borderline participles are fully accepted as standard prepositions or conjunctions, however, it is best to relate them properly to a subject in the main clause, or else to reword the idiom altogether — to *That said* or *If previous analyses are relevant* or *If the first episode is anything to go by* in the examples above. If left misrelated or dangling, they are still liable to objection.

One *-ing* form that has come in for special criticism is *following,* since it lends itself to ambiguity:

> ? Following several new leads, police have made a number of arrests.

The ambiguity here is based on the word's meaning as much as on its position: since about 1926, *following* has been used as a preposition meaning 'after, subsequent to'. So in the specimen sentence, there is some doubt about whether the police made their arrests *by following* the leads or simply *after receiving* the leads. (However, the prepositional 'after'-interpretation is far more likely if the sentence is rephrased as *Police have made a number of arrests following several new leads.*) This is not to suggest the abandonment of *following* as a preposition, just to point out its danger and urge caution in the use of it.

● *Recommendation* Take care to avoid the common errors of misrelating phrases and letting participles dangle. Certain phrases are permitted by idiom to remain detached from any particular subject in the main clause. The various borderline candidates, however, should be treated with more caution: if exception is likely to be taken to their misrelated use, then take the simple precaution of relating them to a proper subject in the main clause, or else of rewording them entirely.

See also AMBIGUITY; INFINITIVE; -ING FORMS OF VERBS; NON SEQUITUR.

Miss, Mrs, Ms   These three titles are all abbreviations of the word *mistress,* just as *Mr* is an abbreviation of *master.* Five centuries ago a male head of household was addressed as *Master,* a female as *Mistress.* Both words go back through Old French to the Latin *magister,* 'a master, head of a household, or teacher'.

Master came to be abbreviated as *Mr* and pronounced /**mis**-tər/. *Mistress* was abbreviated in two ways: as *Mrs,* pronounced /**mis**siz/, and as *Miss.*

Mrs had two different uses in the 17th and 18th

centuries. It was used before the name of a married woman, as it is today. But *Mrs* (like *Mistress* too) was also used to distinguish an adult woman, even when unmarried, from a child:

> His only sister Mrs Grizzle ... was now in the thirtieth year of her maidenhood.
> — Tobias Smollet,
> *Peregrine Pickle* (1751)

It was not until the 19th century that *Miss* and *Mrs* were strictly distinguished in meaning and used as marks of marital status:

> The Miss Gaskells were staying with them.
> — George Eliot, *Letters and Journals*

The 20th century brought yet another change in courtesy titles for women. A third abbreviation of *mistress* was introduced: *Ms*, pronounced /miz/. Like *Mr*, *Ms* abbreviated its parent word by first and last letters only. Also like *Mr*, *Ms* did not indicate marital status.

Ms may have been first introduced as early as the 1930s. But it was only with the advent of computerised mailing lists in the 1960s that *Ms* came into very wide usage. Some early computers were programmed to combine *Mrs* and *Miss* when they encountered a woman's name without a title — some to *Mrss*, others (more efficiently and productively) to *Ms*.

By the 1970s, the use of *Ms* had become a subject of controversy, in the United States particularly.

In December 1971, the preview issue of the U.S. magazine *Ms* was published. *Ms* provided this rationale for the new title:

> For more than 20 years, *Ms* has appeared in secretarial handbooks as the suggested form of address when a woman's marital status is unknown; a sort of neutral combination of *Miss* and *Mrs*.
>
> Now *Ms* is being adopted as a standard form of address by women who want to be recognised as individuals, rather than being identified by their relationship with a man. After all, if *Mr* is enough to indicate 'male', then *Ms* should be enough to indicate 'female'.

Throughout the 1970s, the battle raged, and although *Ms* has clearly triumphed over its opponents, pockets of resistance continue to this day.

Those opposing *Ms* argue that we have got along without it for centuries, that the word is ugly, that the spelling is unfortunate (*Ms* can also stand for *manuscript*, though *MS* is the more usual form), and that it is *not* neutral: for one thing, it makes a statement, uninvited, about one's view of the world and women's status; for another, it is used far more often of unmarried women than of married women; and finally, it has not replaced *Mrs* and *Miss*, but simply added a third option, so it is far from being the equivalent of *Mr*.

In reply, those favouring *Ms* argue that this 'statement' is heard only by those who are zealous to hear it, and that in time *Ms* will be used as widely by married women as by unmarried women, and might even drive out *Miss* and *Mrs*; that its spelling and pronunciation are irrelevant; and that its novelty reflects women's changed role in modern western society. Furthermore, although *Ms* may be a new form it is not a new sense: in the 17th and 18th centuries, as mentioned above, *Mrs* served the same purpose, referring to adult women regardless of their marital status. Above all, the primary motive for the introduction of *Ms* remains as strong as ever: women, like men, should not have to announce their marital status (and to be judged according to it, whether that judgment is conscious or unconscious) every time they give their name.

The fact remains, however, that *Ms* is contentious. Some women might still object to being referred to by it; on the other hand, some unmarried women will object to being referred to as *Miss*, and most unmarried women (and even some married women) will object to being referred to as *Mrs*.

Caution is needed. Use the title a woman prefers if you know her preference. If you do not know her preference, try to find it out. Failing that, it is sometimes possible to avoid using a title altogether, relying instead simply on her first name and surname (or sometimes on the surname alone, as with a man). In some circumstances, this would of course be inappropriate or discourteous, and you will then have to take your chances. And the chances are that a married woman who has adopted her husband's surname (no longer a universal practice) can still safely be called *Mrs*. But do use her first name rather than her husband's first name: to refer to a woman as *Mrs James Keegan* rather than *Mrs Janet Keegan* is very old-fashioned now in most settings. The chances are, too, that unmarried women between the ages of 20 and 60 can most safely be referred to as *Ms*. So too with a woman whose marital status is unknown, and a married woman who has retained her maiden name. Unmarried young women still in their teens, and elderly unmarried women who have through the decades been addressed as *Miss*, are perhaps still best referred to as *Miss* rather than *Ms*.

Ms seems laughably inappropriate for those who are long dead. Elizabeth Barret Browning, if she has to have a title at all, is *Mrs Browning* and Jane Austen is *Miss Austen*.

Note, finally, that British English by and large omits the full stop after *Mrs* or *Ms*, whereas American English seems still to prefer it.

See also CHAIRMAN; CHRISTIAN NAME; MADAM; SEXISM IN THE ENGLISH LANGUAGE; WOMAN.

mist, fog, smog These words tend to be used fairly indiscriminately, but there are certain technical distinctions. *Mist* is in effect, a low cloud, a mass of fine droplets of water in the atmosphere, near the ground, limiting visibility to between about half a mile and a mile (between one and two kilometres).

In *fog* these droplets of condensed water vapour tend to carry particles of dust and smoke in suspension; light is thus further obscured, and visibility limited to about half a mile or less (less than one kilometre).

Both *mist* and *fog* have several related senses, technical and nontechnical, as well as extended or metaphorical senses, as in *lost in the mists of time* or *a fog of rhetoric*.

Smog, a word coined in 1905 as a blend of *smoke* and *fog,* refers to a thick yellow cloud over a built-up area: the condensation of water vapour in the air is promoted by soot particles, and sulphur dioxide in the air combines with the condensed droplets to form the typically acrid atmosphere of dilute sulphuric acid.

mistrust See DISTRUST.

mitigate See EXTENUATE; MILITATE.

mixed metaphors See METAPHORS AND SIMILES 5.

moat See MOTE.

mobile See MOVABLE.

Mohammed See MUHAMMAD.

momentous, momentary, momentarily, momently Among the senses of the noun *moment* are 'a short period of time' (*I'll be with you in a moment*), 'the present time' (*He's busy at the moment*), 'a period of time, or an event, of particular significance' (*His arrival was a great moment for me*), and hence 'significance in general; importance' (*Your opinions on this matter are of no great moment*).

It is to the last of these senses that the adjective *momentous* is related — 'outstandingly important; having serious implications or consequences': *a momentous alliance that altered the entire course of the war.*

> He noticed that he spent a lot of time gossiping about two things: molecular biology and the human brain; ... and went into molecular biology as being the one about which he knew a fraction more than nothing. So he found himself on a momentous path, one which turned into a highway with the arrival in Cambridge of his collaborator.
> – David Wade, *The Times*

Momentary, on the other hand, is related to the first of the senses listed above. It usually means 'lasting only a short time': *a momentary loss of concentration*; but it can also be used (though rarely is nowadays) to mean 'present at every moment' — *in momentary fear of being exposed* — and also 'at very short notice': *He had to make a momentary decision.* Contrast the rare *a momentary decision* — one made on the spur of the moment — with *a momentous decision,* one that has important and far-reaching effects.

These three senses of *momentary* give rise to three corresponding senses of the related adverb *momentarily.* Only the first of these is strictly acceptable, however — 'lasting for just a moment; very briefly': *He momentarily lost concentration.*

> Winterwade ... contrived to join the army, a commitment from which age and some minor physical disability (flat feet or something of the sort) could at least momentarily have absolved him.
> – Anthony Powell, *O, How the Wheel Becomes It!*

The second sense of *momentarily* is objected to by purists — 'at every moment; from moment to moment': *? He was afraid of being exposed momentarily.* Note the ambiguity in this example — an ambiguity that would be avoided if the word *momently* had been used instead. *Momently* has only this one sense, and is far preferable in such contexts for that reason. (Best of all, of course, are the more common expressions *from moment to moment* and *at every moment.*)

A third sense of *momentarily* is less acceptable still: 'in just a moment; very soon; immediately'. It is very common in informal American English — *Dr Barnes will see you momentarily* — but should be avoided in formal speech and writing.

We must leave. Now. I should warn you that my mother may return momentarily. If I see her again, I'll regress horribly. We must dash.

> – Ignatius, in
> John Kennedy Toole (U.S.),
> *A Confederacy of Dunces*

All the words discussed derive from the Latin *momentum,* 'movement', from the verb *movere,* 'to move'. Note the stress in each case: in *momentous,* the stress falls on the second syllable; in all the others, on the first. In some regional pronunciations, however, and frequently in American English, *momentarily* takes a slight stress on the third syllable: *?*/**mo**mən-**terr**əli/. Purists disapprove of this, preferring to slur the third syllable, and leave all the stress on the first: /**mo**mən-trəli/.

month See YEAR.

mood See SUBJUNCTIVE.

moose See ELK.

moral See ETHICAL.

more 1. Four schoolroom warnings. First, the comparative degree of an adjective or adverb can be expressed by placing *more* in front of the word, or attaching *-er* to the end of it. But it is redundant to use both: × *A more prettier child I never have seen*; × *He was much more sadder than even the Mock Turtle.* Similarly the forms × *more superior,* × *more inferior,* × *more major,* and × *more preferable* are all redundant. Shakespeare (like Elizabethan English generally) is above such rules, as usual:

> Then poor Cordelia!
> And yet not so; since, I am sure, my love's
> More richer than my tongue.
> – Cordelia, in *King Lear* I i

Secondly, *more* tends to be used only with longer words — single-syllable words, and many two-syllable words, should take *-er* to form the comparative: × *He was more sad than even the Mock Turtle.* Use *sadder* instead.

Some words can take either *more* or *-er*: *an unkinder man, a more unkind man*; so too can many compound adjectives: *a kinder-hearted man; a more kind-hearted man.* But not × *a more kind man* or × *a more sad man.* Shakespeare goes his own way again; Mark Antony in *Julius Caesar* speaks of *ingratitude, more strong than traitors' arms,* whereas we would today say *ingratitude, stronger than traitors' arms.*

However, if two adjectives (rather than two nouns) are being compared with each other, then *more* is needed even for single-syllable words: *I wouldn't call him gruff — he's more sad than gruff.* Similarly, when the appropriateness of the adjective is being denied: *She's no more poor than Jackie Onassis is!* — meaning 'To call her poor is hardly suitable'. But: *She's no poorer than I am* — 'I am just as poor as she is'.

Thirdly, *more* and *-er* are used when comparing two and only two elements; if there are three or more, then *most* and *-est* are needed: × *Which of these four candidates seems the more promising to you?* Use *most,* not *more.*

A common construction nowadays is *one of the more ...* or *one of our more ...* : *? one of the more interesting younger poets.* Before using this construction, ask yourself why you are not saying *one of the most* instead: *one of the most interesting younger poets.* If you cannot answer this question convincingly, use *one of the most.*

Fourthly, adjectives that already suggest completeness or perfection should not usually be modified by *more* or *-er*: *? The sky is even more cloudless today than yesterday*; × *an even more universal truth.* (See ADJECTIVES; VERY.)

2. *more than one.* This noun phrase is plural in meaning, but singular in form, and takes a singular verb and singular pronouns:

> More than one actor owes his success to Byrd Theatrical Agents Inc.
> I know a handful of actors, and I can assure you that more than one is living below the poverty line.

But if a plural noun is inserted between *more* and *than one*, then a plural verb or pronoun is needed:

> More actors than one owe their success to Byrd Theatrical Agents Inc.

3. *three/four/five times more.* Note the ambiguity in the following sentences:

× Traffic accidents occur five times more frequently in January than in June.
× This year's profits are five times more than last year's.
× This painting is five times more expensive than that one.

Suppose there are 1000 accidents in June, what is the figure for January — 5000 or 6000?

Presumably 5000 was intended in each case, but the *more* suggests 5000 plus the original 1000. The sentences should have been worded differently: *occur five times as frequently in January as in June*; *profits are five times last year's* (or *5000 dollars more than last year's*); *This painting is five times as expensive as that*.

4. *many more*. Note the possible ambiguity that often arises when this combination of words is used: *? There were many more threatening developments in store for us*. In speech, a different stress pattern would distinguish between the two possible senses here, and in writing, the context might do so too — 'many developments even more threatening than the previous one' or 'many further developments of the same threatening kind as the previous ones'. But even if the context does indicate the correct sense, it is still worth rewording the sentence.

For the first sense, insert an *even* between *many* and *more*; for the second sense, change the *more* to *other, further*, or *additional*.

5. *the more*. In certain constructions, *more* is preceded by *the*: *Which twin is (the) more intelligent?*; *Which is the more intelligent of the twins?*; *The more, the merrier*; *I think (the) more highly of her for changing her mind*. In the third and fourth of these examples, the *the* functions as a kind of adverb, meaning 'by that much' or 'to that extent'. It is obviously indispensable in the third example, and very useful in the fourth in giving emphasis and introducing the explanation.

But *the* is often used needlessly before *more* (or *less, better, older*, or the like), perhaps simply because it sounds sophisticated. It should not be used unless there is some reason or explanation for whatever is *more*:

× It may be slightly odd that he's late, but it's the more worrying that he hasn't even phoned to reassure us.

Omit the *the* here: the first part of the sentence does not explain why things are *more worrying*. In the following example, however, it does, and accordingly the *the* (or *all the*) is correct:

He's not always punctual, but he is always extremely considerate, so it's (all) the more worrying that he hasn't phoned to reassure us.

A good warning sign of an unnecessary *the* is the presence of the word *than* in the sentence:

× Her assistance was the more valuable than if it had come an hour earlier or an hour later.

Omit the *the*. Similarly:

× He lives none the more flashily than he did before winning the pools.

Change *none the more* to *no more*.

Moslem See MUSLIM.

most **1.** Four traditional and obvious warnings to begin with. First, if you express the superlative degree of an adjective or adverb by adding *-est* to the end of it, do not use *most* as well. Shakespeare did so, it is true:

> For Brutus, as you know, was Caesar's angel:
> Judge, O you gods! how dearly Caesar lov'd him.
> This was the most unkindest cut of all;
> For when the noble Caesar saw him stab,
> Ingratitude, more strong than traitor's arms,
> Quite vanquish'd him.
> — Mark Antony, in *Julius Caesar* III ii

But language changes, and those who write less ably than Shakespeare have less excuse for a redundant construction of this sort.

Secondly, single-syllable adjectives and adverbs — and often two- or even three-syllabled ones — should take *-est* rather than *most* when cast in the superlative: *the kindest man I know* and *the ugliest man I know* rather than × *the most kind man I know* and *? the most ugly man I know*. But *the unkindest man* and *the most unkind man* are perhaps equally acceptable; a similar versatility is possible in many compound adjectives: the *most kind-hearted man* and *the kindest-hearted man*.

Thirdly, *most*, like *-est*, should be used only when three or more elements are being compared: × *Which of the two twins do you consider the most handsome?* Since there are only two elements in the comparison here, it should read *consider the more handsome*.

Fourthly, *most* cannot usually be used with adjectives or adverbs that already suggest completeness or perfection: × *the most unique statue of all*.

See ADJECTIVES; VERY.

2. As an intensifier used before simple adjectives or adverbs, *most* tends to sound very formal or old-fashioned nowadays, and should usually be avoided in favour of *very*: *? I am most grateful for your help*; *? She is a most honest woman*; *? She waited most patiently for the lawyers to arrive*.

As a rule, if *most* is followed by a simple adjective, it should be preceded by *the*, not *a*, and indicate the superlative degree rather than simply a great degree: *She is the most patient woman I know*, but not *? She is a most patient woman*.

However, if the adjective is formed as the present participle of a verb, then *most* is often fairly suitable as an intensifier: *She is a most amusing woman*. Even here, however, *very* would sound rather less stiff. (See VERY again.)

3. *Most* should not be changed to *mostly* when serving as an adverb of degree meaning 'to the greatest extent':

Those most affected by the new regulations are the farmers.

It is common, but nonstandard, to use *mostly* here instead.

Mostly should be restricted to the senses 'almost entirely' and 'usually':

a whole crate of oranges for one dollar, but they were mostly rotten.
I mostly avoid the city centre, except on Sundays.

4. As an alternative to *almost, most* is often heard in informal English and various regional dialects, especially in the United States: *Most everyone was there.*

Smiley said all a frog wanted was education, and he could do most anything — and I believe him.
— Mark Twain (U.S.),
'The Celebrated Jumping Frog of Calaveras County'

This construction is of course not appropriate for formal usage.

mote, moat A *mote* is a speck, particularly a speck of dust. The word is of Old English origin. A *moat* is a ditch, typically filled with water, surrounding something, such as a medieval castle or modern zoo enclosure. It originally referred to an embankment or mound, derived as it is from the Old French *mote* or *motte*, 'a clod or hill'.

motivation In psychology, *motivation* refers to any mental force or process, conscious or unconscious, that arouses and directs action towards the achievement of a desired aim. It has acquired an extended sense in industrial psychology: the inducement or incentive to employees to work hard.

It is entirely wrong for the nation, or for them, that the people we rely on to educate our children should have no career prospects or motivation.
— Philip Merridale, quoted in *The Guardian*

But *motivation* has come to be used more loosely, as a grand-sounding synonym for *cause* or *reason* or perhaps *motive*: *? I wonder what her motivation was in breaking the windows?* So too with the verb *to motivate*: *? What could have motivated her to turn nasty like that?*

This transfer of psychological language into everyday speech will not impress anyone but the gullible.

movable, mobile *Movable* and *mobile* are not usually interchangeable. *Movable* means 'capable of being moved (through some external force or decision)'; *mobile* means 'capable of moving (through internal or inherent characteristics)'. So furniture and feast-days may be *movable*; circulating libraries and energetic faces are *mobile*; an ambitious working-class boy or girl may be *upwardly mobile*.

Occasionally, something may be referred to by either adjective, depending on the emphasis intended. A mechanical crane is *mobile* — its structure is specifically designed to enable it to move. But some small cranes are also *movable*, notably those fixed to vehicles that can be transported from place to place, for repairing street lights, for instance.

The tongue is *a mobile organ* when regarded as producing movement under its own muscular power; and *a movable organ* when regarded as subject to the control of the brain.

mow The past participle of *to mow* is usually *mowed*, but *mown* is frequently used in British English and sometimes in North American English: *I have just mowed/mown the lawn*. The correct form to use as an adjective, before the noun, is always *mown*: *A mown lawn looks very nice; new-mown hay*.

Mrs, Ms See MISS.

much See MANY; VERY.

much more, much less *Much more* and *still more* are used to show that what applies to one thing applies even more emphatically to another: *Even the juniors should receive some sex education, much/still more the seniors. Much less* and *still less* express the converse idea; what is denied about one thing is more emphatically denied about the other: *Not even the seniors receive any*

369

sex education, much/still less the juniors.

It is a common error to use *much less* or *still less* in sentences that are not grammatically negative (even though the sense might be negative). Here *much more* or *still more* is required. Note the structure of the following three sentences — the first and second are correct, the third is wrong:

> It was not possible even to keep the fire under, much less (= even less possible) to put it out.
> It was impossible even to keep the fire under, much more (= even more impossible) to put it out.
> ✗ It was impossible even to keep the fire under, much less to put it out.

The following quotations illustrate the correct use of *much less* and *still less*:

> There was condescension and, in some cases, pity in their expressions and attitudes that he could not bear to see directed at his fellow fair-heads, much less at his own wife. He turned and almost raced back to the boarding house.
> – Anita Desai, *Games at Twilight*

> Pace Protheroe, I could not bring myself to speak (as people on the BBC now do all the time), still less to write, about someone 'hosting' a chat show or 'guesting' in a concert.
> – Fritz Spiegl, *The Listener*

And this next quotation illustrates a faulty use of *much less*:

> ✗ By the time Prudence Shadbold drove up to the cottage he had made up his mind to attempt recovery of the Winterwade Diary from Jason Price, but paralysis of the will prevented any coherent plan, much less active steps to achieve that end.
> – Anthony Powell,
> *O, How the Wheel Becomes It!*

Expanded, this would read: ✗ *much less did it prevent active steps*, whereas the intended sense is in fact *much more did it prevent active steps*.

The same rule applies to *most of all* (grammatically positive sentences) and *least of all* (grammatically negative sentences):

> A busy doctor, most of all one with so many political commitments, is unlikely to spend very much time with his children.
> No busy doctor, least of all one with so many political commitments, is likely to spend very

much time with his children.

If you are still in doubt about whether to use *much/still more* or *much/still less*, remember that the useful expression *let alone* can usually replace either of them correctly:

> It was not possible even to keep the fire under, let alone to put it out.
> It was impossible even to keep the fire under, let alone to put it out.

mucus, mucous The noun is *mucus*; the adjective is *mucous,* meaning 'like, or consisting of mucus'. Both forms are pronounced /mew-kəss/.

Mucus comes directly from the same word in Latin. *Mucous* comes from the Latin *mucosus,* but the adjectival ending -*ous* is perfectly familiar to us from other words such as *dangerous*.

Note that the first word in the phrase *mucous membrane* is spelt preferably with the *o*: the word needed here is the adjective rather than the noun (though nouns can often serve as adjectives: see FUNGUS).

muffin, crumpet, tea cake, scone These cakes are distinguishable by their shape, taste, and consistency; one rough distinction is the raising agent used in the baking. Yeast produces a more bread-like cake, such as a crumpet; baking powder produces a spongier cake, such as a scone.

The distinctions are complicated, however, by a difference in meaning between *muffin* in British English and *muffin* in American English. A North American muffin is raised by baking powder: it is a light, round breakfast cake or snack made with flour, milk, and butter, sometimes unsweetened, and made in a special muffin pan. A British muffin is made with yeast, and is cooked in a special muffin ring on a baking sheet or griddle on top of the stove. It is small, round, thick, doughy, and flat-topped, and is cooked on both sides.

A *crumpet* is made with yeast, and is distinguished from muffins and tea cakes by having holes in the top and being cooked only on one side. It is made in a crumpet ring on a griddle or baking sheet. Like the British muffin, it is often reheated by toasting, and served with butter.

Confusingly, the Americans have a breakfast cake very like a crumpet, and call it *an English muffin.* It is a stranger to the English breakfast-table.

A *tea cake* is rather like a muffin and is also made with yeast, but is slightly more rounded on top than either a crumpet or a muffin, and often contains currants.

A *scone* is made with baking powder. It is smaller than a crumpet, muffin, or tea cake, and has a pale yellow colour. Both the pronunciations /skon/ and /skōn/ are acceptable, but some people regard /skon/ as socially preferable, /skōn/ being a non-U attempt at refinement. (The village in Scotland — hence the *Stone of Scone* in the coronation chair in Westminster Abbey — is pronounced /skōn/). The word *scone* comes from the Dutch *schoonbrood*, 'fine white bread', from Middle Dutch *schoonbroot,* (from *schoon,* 'beautiful, bright' + *broot brood*, 'bread').

See also PANCAKE; U and NON-U.

Muhammad, Mohammed, Mahomet *Muhammad* and *Mohammed* are the commonest forms in English of the name of the prophet of Islam. *Mahomet* lost ground some time ago to *Mohammed*, but this in turn is now on the decline: today the spelling *Muhammad* is favoured by most writers and newspapers as being a more accurate and respectful rendering.

As a personal name, *Mohammed* is still a widely used spelling in English for various historical figures and for living people.

See also MUSLIM.

Muslim, Moslem These are two rival English forms of the term for a believer in Islam. The word comes from Arabic and means literally 'one who surrenders (to God)'. It is related to *Islam*, which means literally 'submission, surrender'.

The form *Moslem* is still perhaps the more widespread, but its use is on the wane. *Muslim* is preferred by scholars and by most Muslims themselves, and is regarded as the only correct form by members of the 'Nation of Islam', the 'Black Muslims'. One other variant, little used, is *Muslem*.

Muslim is pronounced /**mōōss**-lim, **mōōz**-lim, **muz**-lim/; *Moslem* /**moz**-lim, **moz**-lem/.

The word *Mohammedan* (or *Muhammedan* or *Muhammadan*) is no longer an acceptable substitute. It is offensive to most Muslims because it implies the worship of the Prophet rather than of Allah (God).

Even more out of date is the noun *Mussulman*, a Turkish form adapted into English but now quite archaic.

Muslim, Moslem, Muhammadan, and *Mohammedan* are adjectives as well as nouns. *Islamic* is a related adjective, and is in common use, though never applied to people: *the Islamic republics, Islamic art, the Islamic way of life.*

See also MUHAMMAD.

must 1. The verb *must* has two chief meanings, connected with 'likelihood or assumption' and 'necessity or obligation'. Likelihood or assumption is expressed in a sentence such as: *If you didn't have any breakfast you must be hungry; You must be joking!* North Americans often like to replace this *must* by *have to* or *have got to*. The second of the examples just given (though not the first) might be rephrased: *You have to be joking!/You've got to be joking!*

The standard opposite of this sense is *cannot* or *can't*, as in *If you've just eaten a steak, you can't be very hungry*, but North American English, and some regional varieties of British English, often use *mustn't* (or *must not*) here.

The second chief use of *must* is to express the idea of something 'necessary' or 'obligatory'. This idea has two opposites: that of 'not necessary' and that of 'prohibited'. So the sentence *I must leave early* has two kinds of negative form. On the one hand, *I needn't leave early* or *I don't have to leave early* (= It is not necessary). On the other hand, *I mustn't leave early* (= It is prohibited) or *I can't leave early.*

The past forms of *must* also vary, of course, according to the sense and construction:

> If you hadn't had any breakfast, you must have been hungry.
> You had to be joking!
> If you had just eaten a steak, you couldn't have been very hungry.
> I had to leave early.
> I didn't have to leave early.
> I couldn't leave early.

2. *Must* as a noun is still slightly informal, and has become something of a vogue word too: *That new production of The Tempest is a must.* Perhaps it is still best to avoid it in formal contexts; and in informal contexts, it should be used sparingly if at all.

In North American English, *must* is sometimes used as an adjective too: *That's a must film.* This usage is uncommon in British English, and would be considered even more informal than the noun use of *must.*

mutual, reciprocal, common 1. *Mutual* and *mutually* indicate a specific kind of relationship — a kind of mirror-relationship, almost always between two elements, in which the first does to the second or feels towards the second exactly what the second does to or feels towards the first:

> Literary intellectuals at one pole, at the other scientists ... Between the two a gulf of

mutual incomprehension.
— C.P. Snow, *The Two Cultures*

The signs for 'good' and 'bad' in Britain mean 'male' and 'female' in Japan. Furthermore, British Sign Language and American Sign Language differ to such an extent as to be considered mutually unintelligible.
— Professor Roy Harris,
The Times Literary Supplement

At that moment I could have embraced him. We had referred to the thing at last, and our relief was so great that we were like two people who have just made a mutual declaration of love.
— Christopher Isherwood,
Mr Norris Changes Trains

Africa could claim an older civilisation than most, not to mention an active if disastrous role in the Crusades. And nobody in Europe had questioned its equal status until mutual respect was destroyed by the slave trade.
— Geoffrey Nicholson, *The Observer*

Since only two elements are usually involved in the relationship, it is not strictly correct to speak of ? *our mutual enemy,* × *a decision mutually agreed upon*; ? *a mutual rival,* and so on. These imply the existence of a third or unequal element. The correct word here might be *jointly, together* (*a decision jointly/together agreed upon*), or *common* (*our common enemy*).

The problem is that *common* is ambiguous: *our common friend* could be taken to mean 'our unsophisticated, bad-mannered friend'. It would be better to refer to *the friend we have in common* or simply *the friend we share*.

However, *mutual* in the world of insurance does mean 'in common' (*unit trusts* are called *mutual funds* in America), and the phrase ? *our mutual friend* is so widespread now as to be almost idiomatic. Strictly speaking, however, *mutual* should govern only an abstract noun or nonhuman noun — *our mutual friendship, our mutual bombardment* — never a human noun: ? *our mutual admirer.*

It is not very helpful, by the way, to appeal to the authority of Charles Dickens to justify the phrase ? *our mutual friend.* The title of his novel *Our Mutual Friend* is based on a favourite phrase of one of the characters in the book — a character who is not a particularly careful user of English. In the following example, *common* should be used instead of *mutual*:

× As outgoing chairman of the Jowett Society

(for the best undergraduate philosophers) she appointed him her successor: they discovered a mutual love of committee plotting over his mother's home-made biscuits, and were married in 1949.
— *The Observer*

Mutual love means 'love for each other'. The word is not only wrong in the extract; it misleads the reader momentarily, and makes him backtrack to establish the intended meaning.

2. Since *mutual* and *mutually* already imply a two-way action or attitude between two elements, you should avoid using any other words in the same sentence that convey the same idea. A sentence like × *The twins have a mutual contempt for each other* is quite redundant: you should say either *The twins have a mutual contempt* or *The twins have a contempt for each other.*

Similarly, such words as *rivalry* and *exchange* already imply a two-way relationship. It would be redundant to speak of × *our mutual rivalry for the trophy,* and × *a mutual exchange of prisoners*: omit the *mutual.* Another danger sign is the word *share* or *shared* — it would be best to avoid using *mutual* in the same sentence: × *They share a mutual distrust*; × *They have a shared mutual disdain.* In the following quotation, *mutual* is probably superfluous on this basis:

? The two cats, Lord Jim and Gentleman Brown, maintained their mutual running warfare, which if one abandoned the other would take up.
— Anthony Powell,
O, How the Wheel Becomes It!

3. The adjective *reciprocal* has a rather wider range than *mutual. Reciprocal* can almost always be used in place of *mutual,* but not the other way round. *Reciprocal* can, like *mutual,* refer to the two-way relationship considered from both sides (*mutual* regards these two sides jointly, *reciprocal* separately or alternatively). *Reciprocal* can also, unlike *mutual,* refer to the two-way relationship from only one side. So, if Max betrayed Doris and then Doris betrayed Max in revenge, we can say:

The mutual betrayal of Max and Doris enabled the police to arrest both of them.
The reciprocal betrayal of Max and Doris enabled the police to arrest both of them.
The reciprocal betrayal of Max by Doris enabled the police to arrest him as well.

— but not:

× The mutual betrayal of Max by Doris enabled the police to arrest him as well.

Again: *our mutual/reciprocal favours*, but only *his reciprocal favour to me*. A *mutual* action (or attitude) has to be taken (or held) by two people, animals, things, or groups. A *reciprocal* action can be taken by two parties, or by one alone in response to an equivalent action by someone else.

The greater flexibility of *reciprocal* is easier to remember if you think of the related verb *to reciprocate*:

She lent me money when I was in need, and years later I was able to reciprocate (the favour) by standing bail for her.

myself Purists object to the use of *myself* as a substitute for *I* or *me* in formal style: *? They've invited Mr Jones and myself to the talk*; × *Mr Jones and myself will be at the talk*; *? The house is owned jointly by my brother and myself.*

? The next day a dogged and worried Maisky came to a meeting with the Chiefs of Staff and myself.
— Anthony Eden, *The Reckoning*

We were sitting at a peculiar lightweight collapsible construction, designed and built by my elder brother and myself so that, while eating, we could pay full attention to ... the television set.
— Andrew Hislop, *The Observer*

With *herself* and *oneself*, however, the reflexive form is often stylistically preferable to a simple *her* or *one*: *The relations between one's parents and oneself*; *She showed me her photo of George and herself.* And in the following sentence, surely *of myself* is better than the weak *of me*: *I beg to move an amendment in the names of my right honourable friend and myself.*

Something else that attracts criticism is the use of *myself* with *I* for added emphasis, as in *? I can't say I know him myself*, or *? I myself never go near the place. Myself* here is felt to be unnecessary, and in careful writing it should either be avoided altogether, or replaced by an alternative expression such as *for my part*. The commonest alternative *personally* — as in *? I personally never go near the place* — has, however, been subjected to much the same criticism. (See PERSONAL.) The emphatic use of *myself* is now in very wide use, despite the criticisms, and is likely to gain full acceptance in due course.

Note that the purists object to this use of *myself* because they consider it unnecessary. Sometimes, however, similar constructions use *myself* to make or emphasise a contrast, and such use is perfectly acceptable: *Some people believe in Father Christmas, but I've never seen him myself.* In speech you could stress *I've* and so make the contrast clear without using *myself*. In writing you could italicise *I've*; if not, the word *myself* is important here for the purpose of contrast. So too is *herself* in the following quotation:

And whereas the others called her Mum or Ma'am, Clancy called her Miss Crane. She was herself meticulous in the business of getting to know their names and dignifying them with the prefix Mister.
— Paul Scott, *The Jewel in the Crown*

Myself is also perfectly acceptable when it means 'by myself, unaided'. It cannot be omitted then. So there is an important difference between the fully acceptable *I did it myself* (= I did it all by myself) and the sometimes dubious, though widespread, *? I myself did it* (= I did it).

The same considerations apply to other pronouns ending in *-self*. (See SELF for further details.)

N

name In British English, a child is named *after* someone. In North American English, it is also possible to use *for*: *He was named for his late grandfather.*

See also CHRISTIAN NAME.

nationalisation, naturalisation *Naturalisation* is the process by which an immigrant becomes a citizen of his new country of residence. *Nationalisation* is the transfer of an industry or business or public service from private ownership to state ownership. It was formerly sometimes used to mean 'naturalisation' too, but this confusing use has now fallen away and should be avoided.

The verbs *to naturalise* and *to nationalise* have corresponding senses, but the grammatical constructions that they typically appear in tend to be quite different. *To nationalise* is a transitive verb; that is, used with a direct object or in the passive voice: *Attlee's government nationalised the coalmining industry in 1946. To naturalise* can be used transitively in this way – *The Home Office agreed to naturalise her despite her criminal record; They were/got naturalised in 1973*. But it can also be used intransitively (that is, always in the active voice and without a direct object): *After five years' residence, he could naturalise at last. To naturalise* has a few other senses – 'to adapt', 'to acclimatise', and so on.

In their past participle form, the two words typically appear in the following combinations: *a naturalised Briton; a nationalised industry.*

Note that the opposites of *nationalisation* and *naturalisation* are *denationalisation* and *denaturalisation*. But the noun *privatisation* is now a common synonym of *denationalisation*, especially in British English. In their economic senses, the words *denationalisation* and *denationalise* are recorded as being current in 1921, *privatisation* in 1959, and *privatise* in 1969.

Other related or derived forms tend, of course, to have very different meanings from those discussed here – *nationalist, nationalistic*, and *nationalism*, and *naturalist, naturalistic, natural*, and *naturalism*.

naturally See OF COURSE.

nature Lazy and pompous speakers and writers use this word carelessly to pad out their sentences: *? an artist of an enigmatic nature*; *? reports of a rather technical nature*; *? His reputation is of a dubious nature*. It is far more efficient to attach the adjective directly to its appropriate noun: *an enigmatic artist*; *rather technical reports*; *His reputation is dubious*.

The word *description* has the same curious appeal: *? an artist of an enigmatic description*. If any abstract noun is really needed here, use the traditional *type, kind, sort*, or *variety* instead. Best of all, keep your language tight, and avoid circumlocution of this kind altogether.

See also CHARACTER; SORT OF.

naught, nought *Naught* is an old-fashioned word for 'nothing' that still survives in a few idiomatic phrases, and in poetic or archaic or religious language. *To set at naught* means 'to consider as being of little or no importance': *He set the dangers of the voyage at naught. To bring to naught* (or *to come to naught*) is sometimes used to mean 'to produce no results' (or 'to come to nothing'): *All his efforts came to naught.*

> If thou must love me, let it be for naught
> Except for love's sake only.
> — Elizabeth Barrett Browning,
> *Sonnets From the Portuguese*

> I tell you naught for your comfort,
> Yea, naught for your desire,
> Save that the sky grows darker yet
> And the sea rises higher.
> — Our Lady, in G.K. Chesterton's
> 'Ballad of the White Horse'

Naught comes from Old English *nawiht*, 'nothing', from *na*, 'no' + *wiht*, 'a creature, thing' (also the source of the common adjective *naughty*). A regional variant of it, both in British and American dialects, is *aught* or *ought* (the result of a slurring process whereby *a naught* came to be *an aught*).

More commonly, however, *aught* or *ought* is the opposite of *naught*, and means 'all' or 'anything'. In this sense, it derives from Old English *auht* or *awiht*, 'anything', from *a*, 'ever' + *wiht*, 'a thing'. It occurs in regional dialects (it can be pronounced /owt/ as well as /awt/) — *didna give me aught* — and in the standard phrase *for aught I know.*

In British English, the variant form *nought*, with an *o*, is reserved for the figure *0* or zero: *One million, written in figures, has six noughts*. In American English, however, the form *naught* is preferred even in this sense.

In the following quotation, the reporter or typesetter should really have spelt the phrase *set at naught* with an *a* rather than the *o*:

If orders of the court are seen to be set at nought in this way, openly and repeatedly defied by such a body with impunity, where is the rule of law?

> — Mr Justice Nicholls,
> quoted in *The Guardian*

nauseous *Nauseous* properly means 'sickening, nauseating, causing nausea' (hence 'repulsive or offensive'). It is widely used nowadays (especially in North America), and widely accepted, in the reverse sense, 'suffering from nausea, nauseated'. (It was used in this sense in the 17th century, then died out, to be revived only in the 20th century.) Someone who says *I am nauseous* is probably complaining that he is feeling sick; a purist might pretend to understand him as saying that he is sickening, and retort: *Yes, you are nauseous when you misuse words in that way.*

But this loose sense is too well established now to be considered a misuse any longer:

Ochiba felt faint and nauseous and she wondered if it was her *karma* to be buried in the rubble today.

> — James Clavell, *Shogun*

To avoid any chance of ambiguity, you can always use the words *nauseated* (or *ill, bilious, sick*) and *nauseating* (or *sickening*) instead.

Nausea and *nauseous* have an interesting origin: they go back through Latin to the Greek *nausia*, 'seasickness', from *naus*, 'a ship' — the source too of the word *nautical*. From the same line of inheritance, interestingly enough, comes the word *noise*: seasickness was probably often associated with a noisy confusion on shipboard.

Compare NOSTALGIA.

nautical, naval *Nautical* goes back to the Greek words *nautes*, 'a sailor', and *naus,* 'a ship'. It means 'to do with ships, shipping, seamen, or navigation': *nautical miles*; *nautical charts*. *Naval* comes from the Latin word for a ship, *navis*, but means specifically 'to do with a navy — its equipment, personnel, operations, and customs': *a naval battle*. It can also mean 'having a navy': *a great naval power*. What is *naval* is often also *nautical*, but what is *nautical* is not necessarily *naval*.

Take care not to misspell *naval* as *navel*, which refers to one's 'belly button'.

nearest See NEXT.

need *Need* as a verb is used in two different ways in standard English. It can be a full verb, taking an *-s* ending in the third person, followed by *to*, and having a past tense: *He needs to go*; *He needed to go*; *Does he need to go?*, and so on.

Need can also be an auxiliary verb, with no endings and no *to*: *He need not go/He needn't go*; *Need he go?*; *Need he have gone?*

The full-verb construction is more frequent, since the auxiliary can be used only in negative sentences or questions (as above) or in sentences (such as those that follow) with some negative implication:

Americans, after all, come forward to embrace the foreign TV-man so welcomingly that all he need do is stand there and occasionally put out his foot.

> — Julian Barnes, *The Observer*

The negative implication here is apparent in this paraphrasing: *that he need do nothing more than stand there.* Similarly:

Scott, the England Captain, spoke of the good spirit which has been built up in the four tour games, reminiscent of so many past tours when England has disappointed at home yet compensated abroad. One need think only of South Africa in 1972, New Zealand the following year and Argentina in 1981.

> — David Hands, *The Times*

This can be paraphrased as: *One need do no more than think of . . .*

In sentences that offer a choice, North Americans often prefer the full verb where the British would use the auxiliary. If the above two writers had been American or Canadian, they might have chosen to write *all he needs to do* and *one needs only to think.*

What is important is not to mix the full verb with the auxiliary. Say either *Need we go?* or *Do we need to go?* but not ✕ *Do we need go?* Say *No one needs to go* or *No one need go* but not ✕ *No one needs go.*

Note, finally, the different implications of the two past forms *I needn't have gone* (auxiliary) and *I didn't need to go* (full verb). The first of these implies that I did in fact go; the second leaves it open whether I went or not.

Need enters certain other fixed constructions and phrases that must be got right if they are to be used at all. The passive forms are either *This needs to be changed* (full verb) or *This needs changing* (auxiliary); only in regional dialects is it usual to say *This needs changed*. The idiom *if need be* can be used in past- as well as present-tense constructions (though there is the very literary past-tense form *if need were*): *He said that if need be we had to risk our lives*. The expression *needs must*, or *must needs*, has only those two possible forms. It is used ironically, of a stupid unnecessary action: *If you must needs argue about politics, go and do it in the kitchen!*

negligent, negligible Both these words derive from Latin *negligere*, 'to neglect' (from *neg-*, 'not' + *legere*, 'to choose'). In fact, *negligent* has much of the sense of *neglectful*: 'careless, heedless, lacking proper care or attention'. But *negligent* carries a suggestion of physical accident, and has stronger legal overtones than *neglectful* does: *a negligent driver* is more culpable than *a neglectful driver*; *negligent parents* are probably the indirect cause of physical injury in their children, whereas *neglectful parents* fail in their duty to feed, shelter, and tutor their children adequately. On the other hand, *negligent* does have a weaker sense as well, 'careless in a nonchalant or easy-going way': *negligent in his dress*; *Negligent of the opinion of other people, he acted with his usual flamboyance.*

Negligible means something quite different. Literally, it means 'capable of being neglected', or more specifically, 'so small or trivial as not to be worth taking into account': *His car needed major repairs, but the damage to my car was negligible*; *The amount of material wasted is negligible — it's a very efficient process.*

> Roma would have suffered more if Dalglish, plainly diminished by the aftermath of his desperate facial injury, had not been almost negligible against them.
> – Hugh McIlvanney, *The Observer*

Note the spelling with *-ible*; the original form *negligeable* borrowed straight from French was once common, but has now disappeared.

Also borrowed from the French, by the way, is the word *negligée* (/**neg**gli-zhay/ — or /**neg**gli-**zhay**/ in North America), referring to the loose, flimsy gown of a woman, which means literally 'neglected'.

Negro See BLACK.

neither 1. *Neither* (like *either*), whether as pronoun or as adjective, is used in reference to *two* things – neither more nor less. If there are more than two subjects, then *none*, *no*, or *not* should be used instead: ✗ *Three possible choices occur to me, but neither will be entirely suitable*. Replace *neither* by *none* or *not one* or *no choice*.

2. *Neither* suggests a zero quantity; strictly speaking, therefore, it has neither a singular reference (one) nor a plural reference (more than one). Nevertheless, since *either* is grammatically singular, and since *neither* is usually interpreted as *not either* (rather than as *not both*), *neither* is regarded as grammatically in the singular as well: any related verbs, nouns, pronouns, or possessive adjectives should therefore also be in the singular.

> She cannot stand dolls. Rigid human effigies provoke 'sheer, utter horror' and neither of her daughters has ever been allowed such toys.
> – Bryan Appleyard, *The Times*

But it is very common to find such sentences as ✗ *Neither of my colleagues are prepared to give up their holidays*. The plural forms *are* and *their* sound natural here perhaps – first, because what is said applies to both colleagues rather than just to one; secondly, because the plural noun *colleagues* is placed immediately in front of the verb and therefore encourages a plural form; thirdly, because *their* is a common-gender possessive adjective, whereas the 'correct' form *his* seems to disregard women (*her* would be used only if both colleagues were women), and *his or her* is rather laborious. All the same, *are* and *their* are not strictly correct.

The same is true of *neither . . . nor* constructions. If each of the two elements is in the singular, then the verb too should be in the singular: *I'm sure that neither Mr Bentley nor Dr Cutler has any objections to my plan*. It should not read ✗ *have any objections*.

> ✗ Today he wore his tweed suit from Austin Reed. He stood like a squire amidst the swaying weeds. Summer was ending now, and grass choked the flowerbeds. Neither he nor his wife were proficient in gardening but that did not stop the pride.
> – Deborah Moggach,
> *The Fiction Magazine*

Of course, if each of the two subjects is itself in the plural, then it is correct to use a plural verb: *I'm sure that neither the Bentleys at No. 42 nor the Stevensons at No. 45 have any objections to my plan.* If one of the subjects is in the plural, and the other in the singular, then the verb should again be in the plural: *I'm sure that neither the Stevensons at No. 45 nor Dr Cutler at No. 43 have any objections to my plan; Neither they nor I are going to take this matter any further.* Both these sentences are fairly clumsy, however. The first would benefit from re-ordering the subjects so that the plural *Stevensons* came after the singular *Dr Cutler.* The second sentence would benefit from a thorough rewording: *They are not going to take this matter any further, and neither am I.*

Rewording is often advisable, even essential, when additional pronouns or possessive adjectives are involved, especially when confusion over the sexes arises: *?? Neither Mary nor John knows what he wants or how to change his mind.* A complete rephrasing is necessary here. (See THEY.)

3. Even when both subjects in a *neither ... nor* construction are in the singular, a choice of verb-form may still have to be made if pronouns are involved. The priority would then go to that subject (whether pronoun or not) that is nearer the verb: *Neither Simon nor you have grounds for complaint; Neither you nor he has grounds for complaint.*

> Neither Professor Prawer nor I have been guilty of distortion. B. Burgoyne (Letters, July 6) is mistaken in describing Freud's comment on an Expressionist portrait as 'joking and bantering'.
> – Sir Ernst Gombrich, letter to
> *The Times Literary Supplement*

Once more, rewording will get rid of the awkwardness here: *You don't have any grounds for complaint, and neither does he,* and so on.

4. Since *neither* applies strictly speaking to two elements only, the pattern *? neither A nor B nor C* would seem to be a very doubtful one. Even the most stylish and careful of writers sometimes adopt it, however:

> *?* Her daughter enjoyed a most uncommon degree of popularity for a woman neither young, handsome, rich, nor married.
> – Jane Austen, *Emma* (1816)

> *?* We should historically expect to find *elephant* to be Indo-European or Semitic or Hamitic, rather than, say, Burmese: and, in the fact, the source is neither Burmese nor Malayan nor Chinese. But no more is it

indigenously Sanskrit.
> – Eric Partridge, *A Charm of Words*

> *?* The General said these things in a manner entirely free from any of those implied comments which might be thought inseparable from such a chronicle of events. This is to say he was neither shocked, facetious nor caustic. It was evident that the situation interested rather than surprised him.
> – Anthony Powell, *At Lady Molly's*

It is a long-established usage, and regarded as acceptable by many authorities. Certainly it is considered less objectionable than *either A or B or C*, but it is perhaps still best avoided, if only so as not to provoke the purists.

5. Surprising though it may seem, many people still tend to use *or* instead of *nor* in *neither ... nor* constructions.

> ✗ My best chance would be to rap the ball so firmly that neither the left or right break could really take effect.
> – Jack Nicklaus (U.S.),
> *The Greatest Game of All*

6. The passage just quoted displays a further common error – that of asymmetry. *Neither* and *nor* should be in grammatical balance, the construction introduced by the one being parallel to the construction introduced by the other. Not only should *or* be *nor* in the quotation, but the word *the* should then be inserted after the *nor* to match the one after the *neither*. Similarly:

> ✗ He is neither in favour of the arms race nor of simple nuclear disarmament.

In order to restore the balance here, either move *in favour* to a position in front of *neither*, or insert an additional *in favour* immediately after *nor*:

> He is in favour neither of the arms race nor of simple nuclear disarmament.
> He is neither in favour of the arms race nor in favour of simple nuclear disarmament.

7. *Neither* can be used, with the sense 'and not' or 'but not', to link two clauses. Take care in such cases not to think that it automatically takes a corresponding *nor*. Consider, for example, the following rather old-fashioned exchange: *'You haven't brushed your hair yet!' 'Neither has Ian or Mary – why single me out?'* The *or* is correct here: it would be incorrect to replace it by *nor* (the *neither*, as it happens, could easily be replaced by *nor*), though it could be replaced by the phrase *nor has*.

In such cases *neither* can be preceded by *and* or *but*: *But neither has Ian or Mary*. In informal British English, though not in American English, *nor* can also be preceded by *and* or *but*: *And nor has Ian or Mary*. Here American English allows only *Nor has Ian or Mary*.

8. *Neither* on its own should not be used in sentences that are already in the negative. It is wrong to say ✗ *There was no food left, and nothing to drink neither*. Although such a construction would have been quite common even in the last century, today we have to use *either* instead.

Children often use *neither/either* as an intensifier when making a negative counterclaim to contradict some assertion or accusation. The correct form here is *either* rather than *neither*. ✗ *'I gave the bat back to you yesterday!' 'You didn't neither!' 'I did too!'*

9. The pronunciation of *neither* — both /nīthər/ and /neethər/ are correct: /nīthər/ is now more common in British English, and /neethər/ in American English.

See also COMMA **1.a**; EITHER; NO 3; NOR; THEY; WHETHER.

never *Never* is the negative adverb referring to the whole of history or the part of history implied: *It has never snowed in this valley before*; *You never turn up on time*. It can also refer to a specified period: *I never fell ill once last year*; *I'd never kissed her until last night*. What it cannot refer to, in standard English, is a single occasion: ✗ *I waited for you, but you never turned up*. Here the simple *not* is required: *I waited for you, but you didn't turn up*.

Children are particularly prone to use *never* in the place of *not* or *didn't*: ✗ *'I never took your bike yesterday.' 'You did.' 'I never.' 'I saw you.' 'You never.'*

In certain contexts, it is permissible to use *never* for emphasis in the way that children (usually incorrectly) do, rather than for referring to a period of time: *Never fear*; *That will never do*; and even *I never thought I'd be hearing from you again*, or *Well I never!*

See also EVER SO; NOT.

New Zealand English The kind of English spoken in New Zealand is often thought to resemble Cockney speech quite closely. Yet the British immigrants, during the major immigration of the mid-19th century, were from all parts of the United Kingdom, by no means predominantly from London. The Cockney influence, if there really is one, was probably transmitted by Australians, many of whom travelled across the Tasman Sea to settle in New Zealand.

Whether Cockney-like or not, Australian English was almost certainly the main influence on the development of a distinctive New Zealand English. To an outsider a New Zealander and an Australian sound much the same, and it might make good linguistic sense to refer to 'Austral English', embracing both countries. A great many features alien to British and American varieties of English are common to Australia and New Zealand. (See AUSTRALIAN ENGLISH.)

But native speakers tend, of course, to notice the differences rather than the similarities. New Zealanders consider their English a distinct variety, just as Canadians consider their English distinct from American English. Nothing irritates a 'Kiwi' more than being mistaken for an 'Aussie'.

Within New Zealand, with its history of settled communities, there is some slight regional variation of accent and vocabulary — more so than in Australia, where the population has traditionally been very mobile. But the New Zealand regional variation is far less than that of Britain. Far more marked is the social variation of speech patterns — speakers vary (as they do everywhere) according to their social, economic, and educational status and aspirations. New Zealand English may reasonably be divided into 'broad', 'general', and 'conservative' — the last of which sets out to model itself on standard British English.

Pronunciation Perhaps the most noticeable single feature that marks both New Zealand and Australian English is the long /aa/ sound of the vowel in such words as *start*, *part*, and *father*. The vowel is said to be 'fronted' because it is produced with the tongue further forward in the mouth than is the corresponding British English vowel. In words such as *dance*, *chance*, *plant*, and *sample*, Australians sometimes replace it with the short vowel /a/, pronouncing it in a way that is close to American English. New Zealanders, however, never do this.

Another characteristic of New Zealand English is the sound of the 'short' vowels — those found in *pan*, *pen*, and *pin*. A New Zealander's *pan* may be heard by an Englishman as *pen*; his *pen* as *pin*; and his *pin* as something like *pun* — really /pən/, with the neutral vowel sound, or 'schwa', as heard in the second syllable of *father*.

Since New Zealanders do not differentiate between /i/ and /ə/, especially in unstressed syllables, they tend not to distinguish between *matted* and *mattered*, or *batted* and *battered*. A news commentator got into hot water during a visit by the Queen to New Zealand when, reporting that she had 'chatted' to the Prime Minister, he said something that sounded to English ears like 'chattered'. Australians too would fail to differentiate the words in these pairs, but New Zealanders often go a stage further, and use /ə/ instead of /i/ even in stressed syllables. Many Australians, on the other hand, have developed a very clear /i/ in stressed syllables, almost an /ee/ sound, giving rise to mock spellings such as *Seedney* for *Sydney*. Whereas an Englishman would pronounce Prince Philip's name in keeping with its spelling, an Australian would say it as though it were spelt *Philup* or *Pheelup*, and a New Zealander as though it were *Phulup*.

Another sure way to tell a New Zealander is to listen for the word *yes*. It is often given two distinct syllables: /**yee**-əss/ or even /**ee**-əss/.

The loss of distinction between /i/ and /ə/ is an example of the simplification of a sound system. An even more striking example is the approach of the /air/ vowel sound to the /eer/ vowel sound, so that *share* sounds like *sheer*. Many New Zealanders sit on a 'cheer' just as readily as they cheer at a football match. This particular change, however, seems to carry some mild social stigma, and has been known to worry parents from the more affluent suburbs when they notice it in their children's speech.

But not all the changes in New Zealand pronunciation have involved simplification. There is at least one typical New Zealand pronunciation that has added a distinction not found in British English: the addition of a schwa to such words as *grown*, *thrown*, and *mown*. This results in the pronunciations /gr**ō**-ən, thr**ō**-ən, m**ō**-ən/. But the change does not affect *groan*, *throne*, and *moan*; New Zealanders distinguish these word-pairs in pronunciation as well as in spelling, whereas in British English they sound alike despite being spelt differently.

In intonation too, New Zealand usage differs from British usage. When a New Zealander asks a question that calls for a straight 'yes' or 'no' answer, his or her intonation will rise continuously, as it does with Australians. In addition, New Zealanders, perhaps to a greater extent than Australians, often give this same rising intonation to a statement. A sentence such as *I went down the road to the stables* might accordingly sound like a question, giving the strong impression that there is more discourse on the way. It it not uncommon for visitors to New Zealand to stand politely silent, waiting for the next bit of a conversational exchange that has in fact already finished.

Vocabulary New Zealand English has in common with Australian English many terms or senses different from those used typically in Britain: *paddock* (fenced-in land of any size) and *station* (a stock farm), for instance. Similarly *footpath* (a pavement), *theatre* (a cinema), and *gumboots* (wellingtons), though these are sometimes used in this way in Britain.

Many familiar Australian colloquialisms occur readily in everyday conversation in New Zealand, including *bludger* (a sponger), *cocky* (a farmer — usually on a small farm), *crook* (sick, out of order, or broken), *goodday* (hello), *hooray* (goodbye), *lolly* (a sweet), *maggoty* (bad-tempered), *pommy* or *pom* (an English person) and *rubbish* (to criticise — now used in Britain too).

Other familiar Australian colloquialisms, however, such as *cobber* (a companion or mate) and *dinkum* (genuine), would sound slightly out of place in New Zealand unless they were being deliberately used to suggest Australian usage.

New Zealand English has borrowed a fair number of words from the Maori language. The word *Maori* itself originally meant 'ordinary, usual', and was adopted by the early settlers to denote both the indigenous population and the language; and *pakeha*, pronounced /**paa**ki-haa/, the term used to refer to any European, seems to have Maori affiliations, though its exact origin remains a matter of speculation.

Kiwi, now the standard familiar term to denote a New Zealander, is one of the many borrowed Maori names of native birds. Others include *moa*, *takahe*, *tui*, and *weka*. There are similar borrowings from Maori of tree names — *kauri*, *rata*, *rimu*, *totara* — and names for other plants: *raupo*, *toi toi*, *tutu*.

Coinages from English roots include *waxeye* and *fantail* to refer to some unusual small birds. English words with modified senses include *section* (a plot of building land, or a garden) — which contrasts with the Australian equivalent *block* — and *bush*, which in New Zealand usually implies dense forest rather than the sparse scrub that the word suggests to an Australian.

One delightful extended sense still occasionally encountered in New Zealand is *zambuk*, meaning 'a person who gives first-aid at a sporting event'. The derivation is obvious to those of the older generation, but most young New Zealanders today have probably never heard of the ointment of the same name.

Two other words apparently restricted to New Zealand usage are *bach* — pronounced like *batch*

— the word for a holiday cottage (it once referred to the kind of shack inhabited by a bachelor), and *crib*, the equivalent of a *bach* in Otago, a province in the South Island of New Zealand.

To a New Zealander, the word *football* always suggests rugby, whereas it usually suggests soccer in England, and either rugby or Australian Rules football in Australia.

The invention of the *jet boat* in New Zealand, with the subsequent success of this shallow-water power-craft, has contributed a term to the stock of international English; and the Melanesian, Polynesian, and Maori word *mana* (authority, charisma, prestige, or influence) seems to be increasingly widespread.

Grammar As with Australian English, there are very few differences of grammar between New Zealand English and British English, especially in educated speech.

A few tendencies can be noted, however: the increasing disuse of *shall* and *should* after *I* or *we*, for example, and the survival or revival in speech of the construction *She usedn't to work* as against the usual British form nowadays, *She didn't use to work*. (In formal written usage, the standard construction is always *She used not to work*.)

For the most part, however, a New Zealander would be recognised by his accent, and — in writing — sometimes by his vocabulary. The likelihood is that these distinguishing characteristics will remain much as they are, neither intensifying nor slackening, in the near future, with the balance continuing between the forces of linguistic assimilation (through travel, foreign broadcasts, and so on) and linguistic isolation (based on distance and national pride).

newspaper English Newspapers are in the front line in the defence of good written English — or the attack on it. Much modern journalism sets excellent examples of style and usage for its readers. Many of the serious papers run regular features — not too solemn or scholarly — on developments in language, and open their letters pages to debates on knotty points of grammar, language-teaching in schools, and so on.

At the other extreme, much journalism is riddled with clichés, grammatical errors, abuses of old words, and monstrous modern coinages. The idea, presumably, is to make the language of the articles or features both easy to understand and excitingly colourful. The effect, in the end, is to diminish understanding, by doing away with the need for the reader to do any thinking for himself — the way that muscles weaken if not allowed to do any exercise, or taste is dulled if subjected to spices only. And so far from being exciting and colourful, such writing soon becomes depressingly familiar: where everything is garish, nothing stands out.

Here are examples of the two styles at their best and worst:

In the English language there are many mansions, cellars, cupboards, departments, and registers; from Strine to Sociologese. The two great registers are written and spoken English, which are almost two different languages. You have only to listen to a tape-recorder of yourself speaking, or to read a transcript of an unscripted talk to see the difference. Oral English is unbuttoned, ungrammatical, catachrestic, and full of pauses and cottonwool fillers such as 'You know what I mean' to give oneself time to work out what one is going to say next. It is to written English what, in the wardrobe, jeans and a T-shirt are to the old fish-and-soup white tie and tails.

Very few people speak as they write; and they tend to be sages. I am told that Bertie Russell and Bernard Shaw spoke in the same sort of structured way that they wrote.

– Philip Howard, *The Times*

★ EYES DOWN, folks, for the first day of a fabulous Bingo game that can bring you MORE than ONE MILLION POUNDS.

We're playing Game 194, the last on your red Bingo card. Your numbers are on the left. Check them off and you could get rich double-quick by winning ...

OUR GAME JACKPOT — a fabulous £40,000.

PLUS A GOLDEN KEY to your very own treasure chest in our ONE MILLION POUNDS open-the-box bonanza.

★ Yes, folks, Sun Bingo is twice as nice now we've GUARANTEED a £1 million pay-out in ADDITION to our regular prize of £40,000. ...

★ When this last game has been completed, ALL the winners will be invited to London for the most sensational event of the century. In front of them will be an exact number of boxes to match the total of Golden Keys. Each winner will step forward and open the box with the number which corresponds to their key.

★ One of the boxes will contain a monster cheque for a guaranteed £1 million — placed there earlier by a mystery celebrity. So one reader is GUARANTEED to become a magic millionaire.

— The Sun

In between these two very different styles lies a use of English that is usually accepted and respected by language-experts for what it is — a clear and concise vehicle for direct and economical reporting. Its admirers draw attention to its efficient streamlining of grammar and (at its best) its closeness to everyday spoken English. Here is an example of this simple yet robust style:

Ringo the loyal Labrador muzzled up to his old master and licked a smile back onto Bill Knapp's wrinkled face.

The pensioner had spent a dismal weekend worrying about how he was going to save his pet from being put down.

Two court decisions had gone against him but yesterday Mr Knapp, 72, vowed: 'I'll take my case all the way to the House of Lords if I can.'

The death sentence — first imposed by Hastings magistrates in November and upheld by Lewes Crown Court on Friday — was the dog's penalty for biting four people who went to his owner's aid when he fell on his way home from the pub.

Mr Knapp pleaded that Ringo was only trying to guard him.

— Daily Mail

Only a pedant would dismiss this use of language out of hand. Certainly it is better than the old-style 'journalese', which, in addition to its sensationalism and superficiality, tended incongruously to use complicated, long-winded, and pompous sentences, and inflated vocabulary.

Even in the British press, where there is a widely accepted division between the upmarket 'quality' newspapers and the 'popular' tabloids, the borders between the various styles are not very clearly demarcated. The quality papers, for instance, often use clever word play in their headlines, whereas the equivalent papers in North America and Europe retain the tradition of purely informative, almost solemn, headlines.

Most of the criticism directed against newspaper English these days is in fact directed — not always fairly — at the popular press. 'Tabloid English' can in fact be crisp, vibrant, and efficient. Unfortunately, it can also be flabby, mindless, and extremely irritating. Here are some of its characteristics, some good, some bad.

Headlines Headline writers on a newspaper are pulled in two directions: they want to convey maximum information, but they have to do it in minimum space. For a start, verbs, articles, prepositions, and so on tend to be left out of headlines, much as they are in telegrams: *Heir in murder probe*; *Lead banned from paint*. The simple present tense is widely used — *Poland mourns slain priest* — instead of the past tense or present continuous (*mourned* or *is mourning*). Nouns are used as adjectives — *Germ war secrets leak row* (a recent front-page headline in the *Daily Mail*); *Bread riot death toll tops 1000*. And a vocabulary of snappy shorthand synonyms develops: including the words *probe*, *to ban*, *to slay*, and *to top* used in the above examples.

There is another convention in the British press — even the serious papers, as mentioned above, often light-heartedly join in it: the use of punning, alliterative, teasing, or facetious headlines. Sometimes the effect is witty and welcome: *Whisky exporter on the rocks*; *The end of the world* (a headline announcing the relegation of the Scottish soccer team from contention in the World Cup). Sometimes it is laboured: *Shipmakers on crest of a wave*; *Musicians' union strikes a sour note*. Sometimes it is just irritating: *Cat show's purrfect prizewinner*; *Luscious ladies in lucky legs contest*.

On the whole, the serious papers do not allow 'headline language' to spread from the headline to the report or article itself. The tabloids, to a greater or lesser extent, do use headline language in the text: *probe*, *to ban*, *to seize*, and *to top* are transferred from the headline (where they are valued for their brevity) to the body of the report — where they are valued for their supposedly punchy and exciting effect and their up-to-date feel.

The irony is that, through overuse, they have lost most of their punch, and that many are anything but up-to-date: *to seize*, for instance, sounds extremely old-fashioned in speech, yet is freely used in newspapers that boast of their modern and colloquial English style. Some of the dozens of other *un*colloquial tabloid-terms are listed below.

Cramped wording Another characteristic of headline language has penetrated into the news-story itself — that is, the build-up of key words side by side: *The Belgravia porn-club rumour is the subject of an official Scotland Yard probe*, for example. This piling up of syntax is in fact more tedious to sort out than the looser structure of a more traditional piece of reporting: *The allegation that there is a pornography club in Belgravia is to be investigated officially by the Metropolitan Police*.

Description of people One special case of cramped wording is the description of a person in a news report — of a bank robbery, for example. If the person is named Susan Wykham, is 27 years old, lives in Troybridge, and works as a bank-clerk, she might be introduced as *27-year-old Troybridge bank-clerk Susan Wykham* or *Troybridge bank-clerk Susan Wykham (27).* (Note the typical omission of the article *a* or *the*.) Suppose she has been recently married (as though that were relevant) and has blonde hair and a good figure (as though that were relevant): she might then be referred to as *Newly wed Troybridge bank-clerk, fun-loving shapely blonde Susan Wykham (27).* By contrast, a traditional report — less 'interesting' perhaps, but surely more elegant, and probably easier to follow — might begin simply: *Susan Wykham, a 27-year-old bank-clerk from Troybridge.*

Another tendency of tabloid headlines is to refer to politicians and celebrities by pet forms of their first names: *Maggie, Willie, Shirl,* and so on.

Vocabulary In their quest for 'readability' — that is, in trying to make topics or events seem more interesting or more understandable than they really are — journalists have developed a kind of tabloid vocabulary. The terms tend to be short, catchy, and graphic — a *hike*, for instance, meaning 'an increase'. They sometimes involve the rejuvenation of old-fashioned words: *to anger, to seize, to reign*; sometimes a distortion of the proper sense: *to slam* in the sense of 'to criticise', or *geriatric* in the sense of 'old'; occasionally a genteel affectation: *accord, overly.* Catchy and varied they may be, perhaps more than offsetting the loss of accuracy they entail, but one boast of theirs surely cannot be sustained — that they reflect spoken English more truly than the quality papers do. Who really uses the words *slay* or *a price-hike* in conversation (except in 'tabloid' broadcasting, such as some sports commentaries or pop-music programmes)? Here are some more examples of tabloid-terms:

The idea of an increase — in crime, prices, or the like — is conveyed by the many other 'vivid' terms besides *hike*: *an explosion, a leap, to rocket, to soar, a surge,* and *to up* (wages). And the idea of a decrease might be conveyed by *a cut, to hurtle, to plummet, to plunge, to tumble,* and *to slash.*

Criminals may *grab* or *snatch* a payroll, or *gun down* a rival.

The police may *probe* the crime, then *swoop* or *pounce, seize* the suspects, *hold* them, and *quiz* or *grill* them, and generally *clamp down* on lawlessness.

Politicians may hold *talks* and reach *a pact* or *accord*, or *do a deal*; more commonly they *clash with, rap,* or *give a tongue-lashing to* their opponents, and *slam, hit out at,* or *lash out* at their opponents' mistakes — and *whitewash* their own.

A company may be forced to *shed* or *axe* some of its staff. The workers have to face the *chop*, or *cuts*, while managers may *quit* or *go* or *bow out.*

A sportsman (or team) may *clash with* a rival, make a *bid* for the title, be *hammered*, face a *crunch* or a *ban*, have his *hopes dashed* and his chances *sunk, scuppered,* or *torpedoed.*

A woman may be *sultry, petite, statuesque, shapely,* or a *supergran* or *supermum.*

A man may be *dashing, bronzed, lean, muscular, balding,* or *paunchy*; and a man or woman could be *cheeky, shell-shocked,* or *famed.*

An event reported in the tabloid press may be a *spree, bonanza,* or *miracle,* or it may be part of a *saga,* or it may be a *headache,* a *drama,* or involve *horror* or *tragedy.* A fire is likely to be a *blaze,* a campaign a *crusade,* and a heart transplant a *swap* — even though the donor of the heart never gets one in exchange.

Any group of three people is a *trio* (or a *troika* if they are Russian), and any person or organisation who inspects or monitors anything is a *watchdog.*

Among the other tabloid-terms — archaic, hackneyed, misused, affected, contrivedly waggish or slangy as the case may be — are:

barrier a difficulty or obstruction
bombshell a surprise
critical critically ill
to gag to censor
jab an injection
leak the publication or disclosure of confidential information
over concerning, in connection with, in protest against, and so on (*downing tools over their working conditions*)
overly over (*an overly loving Mum*)
to pledge to promise
to quaff to drink
supremo a person having complete authority
top victorious or leading
to top to exceed
to vow to promise
to wed to marry, or to get married to

And here are some of the clichéd phrases that jaded newspapermen heedlessly pepper their writing with:

alive and well and living in Ibiza/clover/sin

amid tight security
carbon copy
crisp banknotes
a licence to cheat/starve/print money
love-nest
mercy dash
Monopoly money
office romeo
sickening thud
to sip tea
sleazy suburb
tug-of-love baby
whirlwind romance
Whitehall mandarin

To conclude, here are the versions, from two British daily tabloids, of the same news story. The first version shows the strengths of tabloid prose. It is lean, light, and lucid:

The NUM profits by sick pound

Daily Mail Reporter

The plunging pound has made £850,000 for the miners' union.

The NUM has £4·63 million frozen in a Luxembourg bank account by court sequestrators. The money, moved out of Britain in the autumn to escape seizure, is in bonds valued in dollars.

The dollar was then 1·30 to the pound — but now the rate is 1·12 and the bond's value has gone up by some £850,000. Interest payments are likely to have increased the profit still further.

Union officials cannot touch the cash until all outstanding fines and legal costs have been paid.

The following version, by contrast, shows many features of the unacceptable face of tabloid prose: the use of loaded or subjective wording (*hiding union funds abroad*, *stashed away*, *salted away*), the typical use of 'punchy' tabloid-terms (*makes a million*, *plunge*, *plummeted*), the attempts at dramatisation (*legal battle*), and so on:

SCARGILL MAKES A MILLION

Profit on shaky £

SUN EXCLUSIVE
— By CHARLES RAY

ARTHUR SCARGILL has made £1 million for the miners by hiding union funds abroad.

The reason is the pound's plunge against the dollar — which Mr Scargill boasts is caused by his own pit strike.

The NUM has £4.63 million stashed away in a Luxembourg bank, mainly in dollars.

When the switch was made — probably last September — the £ was worth about 1.30 dollars.

Now it has plummeted to 1.12.

BATTLE

So if the cash was turned back into pounds today, it would be worth around 25 per cent more, including the interest.

One financial expert said last night: 'It's been a good investment for the union.'

An international legal battle is now being fought over the return of the money to Britain.

Altogether the NUM salted away £8 million abroad to prevent the seizure of its funds by High Court sequestrators.

See also CLICHÉS; JARGON; PREPOSITIONS OMITTED; VOGUE WORDS.

Newspeak   See JARGON.

next, nearest   In the sense 'coming directly after in time or sequence', *next* can be ambiguous. There is no ambiguity about referring on Tuesday to *next Friday*, but if it were said on Thursday, a time reference of eight days hence would usually be intended; and if said on Wednesday, there would often be uncertainty over which Friday was in question. *This* is commonly used as a way out of the problem: *this Friday*, meaning 'the Friday of this week'.

Next and *nearest* are sometimes interchangeable, as in *Pull in at the next/nearest petrol station*. However, *next* always indicates direct succession in a series, whereas *nearest* is used more generally to indicate the closest possible proximity, as in time, space, or kinship.

Note that *near, nearer, nearest*, and *next* can be used as prepositions, without *to*, to indicate close proximity in space. However, the use of *next* as a preposition now sounds either informal or old-fashioned: *the house next the baker's*.

We were already through the soup and fish when Crawford came into hall. He slipped into the seat next mine, but before he sat down called up the table to Winslow.
— C.P. Snow, *The Masters*

Current idiom favours *next to* here.
See also AMBIGUITY 3.

nice *Nice* has changed its meaning in an extra-ordinary way over the centuries. It goes back to the Latin *nescius*, 'ignorant', from *nescire*, 'to be ignorant of' (from *ne-*, 'not' + *scire*, 'to know'). In Old French, *nice* meant 'silly', and it entered Middle English in that sense too, though it also acquired the meanings 'shy' and 'naughty, wanton'.

It later came to mean 'difficult to please, demanding', and hence, 'subtle; discerning or sensitively critical': *a nice distinction*; *a nice appreciation of piano music*.

> Admittedly Swinburne's masochism certainly seems relevant to the English thriller, though how far this relates to a Tory concept of ideal society is a nice point.
> – Owen Dudley Edwards,
> *The Listener*

This is the sense that purists like to restrict the word to today.

The history of *nice* so far is largely one of 'amelioration': that is, it has acquired more favourable senses and overtones as the years go by. Its development into a wide-ranging term of approval was quite natural therefore. It came to be used to mean 'attractive': *a nice dress*; 'kind or well-mannered': *a nice man*; *a nice compliment*; 'sexually modest or virtuous': *a nice young lady, mindful of her reputation*.

> We passed lots of Basques, with oxen, or cattle, hauling carts along the road, and nice farm houses, low roofs, and all white-plastered.
> – Ernest Hemingway (U.S.),
> *The Sun Also Rises*

Hemingway might have chosen a more telling word than *nice* here. *Nice* is far too widely used nowadays. A *nice* egg, a *nice* piece of toast with *nice* marmalade, and a *nice* cup of tea can all make a contribution to a *nice* breakfast. Small wonder that stylists look down on *nice* as a 'lazy' word.

True enough, *nice* does sometimes seem the appropriate word for expressing generalised mild approval. But if you want sharper characterisation, try to think of a more precise alternative whenever you are tempted to use *nice*. The toast can be *crisp*, the egg *tasty*, and so on. In other contexts, adjectives such as *pleasant*, *agreeable*, *amusing*, and *interesting*, might suggest themselves as appropriate. English is not yet so impoverished that approval or admiration has to be expressed by just one word.

The expressions *coming along nicely* or *doing very nicely for himself* and *nice and hot* or *nice and friendly* are widely used in everyday speech, but are not really suitable for formal contexts.

nicety *Nicety* does not mean 'niceness' in the sense of 'pleasantness' or 'kindness'. It can mean 'niceness' in the sense of 'subtlety' or 'refinement' or 'fastidiousness': *the nicety of a diplomatic exchange*.

> ... watched her as she walked primly away across the square, holding her skirts at the curbs with ladylike nicety.
> – Thomas Wolfe (U.S.),
> *Look Homeward, Angel*

But it is seldom used in such a general way nowadays. It usually has a more specific reference, particularly with the meaning 'a subtle point, detail, or distinction': *I can't accept that objection — it's a mere nicety*. It is perhaps most often used in the plural: *He left the niceties of spelling to his secretary*.

> Kennedy, who could not imagine letting legal niceties halt the search for a kidnapped child, grew heated.
> – Arthur M. Schlesinger, Jr (U.S.),
> *Robert Kennedy and His Times*

While anti-terrorist officers sped up the motorway to inspect the crates, the Home Office, the Foreign Office and the Cabinet Office were consulted about the diplomatic niceties of breaking into the crates.
> – *The Observer*

> But before World War Two the pattern of thrillers was highly anti-democratic. There was a decided cult of lynch law, with greatest admiration being reserved for the hero who brushed aside the niceties of democracy and civil liberties. This may have been owed to the British Empire tough soldiers, with short shrift for niceties and contempt for civilians.
> – Owen Dudley Edwards,
> *The Listener*

In colloquial usage, *niceties* has the extended sense of 'polite formalities, used as a gesture of courtesy': *Never mind the niceties – let's get down to business*.

The phrase *to a nicety* means 'with the utmost care and precision, exactly': *He timed the shot to a nicety, and the boat exploded in a ball of fire*.

no 1. The phrase *or no* still occurs in sentences such as *I'll do it whether you like it or no*. It is a traditional usage, and has a rather old-fashioned ring to it, but is quite acceptable as a variant of the more modern form *or not*.

2. The idioms *to say no* and *to say yes* are well established, requiring neither a capital letter for *no* and *yes* nor quotation marks around them: *He didn't actually agree, but he didn't say no either.* It would not really be incorrect to write ... *he didn't say 'No' either,* but it is unnecessary. Similarly: *I won't take no for an answer.*

It is nowadays quite common to hear *no* or *yes* between an optional *that* and a report of someone's words:

He said (that) no, he would not budge an inch.
He said (that) yes, the question was still negotiable.

Such sentences seem to violate the traditional rules for reported speech in English, but they do not appear to have attracted criticism — yet. The *no* or *yes* can be omitted without change of meaning, though perhaps with some loss of emphasis.

3. In many sentences, a single subject may extend over two or more clauses. If that subject contains the word *no,* make sure that you intend this negative sense to apply to the later clause or clauses as well as to the opening clause. It is a common error to assume that the subject reverts to a positive sense when applying to the later clause or clauses.

× No orders will be given special attention, but will have to wait their turn and be processed in the ordinary way.

This reads: *No orders ... will have to wait their turn ...* — clearly the very opposite of the intended meaning. To rectify the sentence, the word *all* should be inserted after *but,* to introduce the later clauses.

The same mistake occurs with related negative words such as *none, not,* and *neither ... nor.*

no one See ANYONE.

no question The noun *question* has many meanings, two of them being 'doubt' and 'possibility'. Compare:

There's some question (= doubt) as to his honesty.
I'm afraid there's no question (= possibility) of my changing my mind.

Or consider the phrases *beyond question* ('undoubtedly') and *out of the question* ('impossible').

The danger of ambiguity arises in the phrase *no question*. It can mean either that something is certainly true (no doubt), or that it is certainly false (no possibility). There are three common forms: *no question that, no question of,* and *no question but* (or *no question but that*). Only the last of these is unambiguous: it can only mean 'no doubt that':

If Robert Maxwell didn't exist, then there's no question but we diarists would have to invent him.
– Peter Hillmore, *The Observer*

There is no question but that particle physics is a British invention.
– Professor Abdus Salam,
New Scientist

(The *but* here is rather old-fashioned: see BUT 6.)

But *no question that* and (less often) *no question of* are ambiguous: ? *There's no question that I'm going to return the fee*; ? *There's no question of his making 50 runs by tea.*

? Even after I'd recovered to some extent, I felt awful and looked worse. There could be no question this time of wine having caused it.
– Lynne Reid Banks,
The L-Shaped Room

(Most people would probably interpret this as meaning that there is *no doubt* that wine caused the narrator's illness. In fact, as the book makes clear, the point is that there is *no possibility* that it was wine that caused her illness: what she is suffering from is morning sickness.) Again:

? There is also no question that such films are being rented or traded by children.
– leading article, *Daily Telegraph*

(The context, as it happens, indicates that there is *no doubt* that children are renting or trading these films.) If there is any danger of misleading the reader or listener, even for a moment, avoid the constructions *no question of* and *no question that.* English has a wealth of alternative ways of phrasing the same idea — including *no doubt* and *no possibility.*

noisome *Noisome* is sometimes mistakenly associated with *noisy.* In fact it means 'offensive, disgusting': it comes from Middle English *noyesum,* from *(a)noy,* 'annoyance' + *-some.* The offence is almost always to the nose rather than to the ear — *noisome* now usually means 'foul-smelling': *a noisome rubbish dump.*

We sat in a tiled hall, two steps below street level, drinking our mint tea — or, rather, Fatima drank hers while I let mine cool in the glass. It was a noisome beverage.

– Evelyn Waugh,
Work Suspended and Other Stories

Apart from the claustrophobic proximity of the buildings to one another, and the noisome cloying stench of rubbish and assorted decomposing matter, it was the heaving manifestation of organic life in all its forms that most struck Morgan about Nkongsamba.

– William Boyd, *A Good Man in Africa*

The word can also mean 'harmful or dangerous' — *That noisome substance is corrosive* — but this sense is far less common.

Noisome is pronounced /noy-səm/, although some people, again by analogy with *noise* or *noisy*, pronounce it × /noyz-səm/. The noun from *noisome* is *noisomeness*. Both words are rather formal or literary, and fairly rare.

non- 1. Some writers prefer to keep a hyphen between *non-* and the base word; others — preferring a more streamlined appearance, and noting such long-established forms as *nonsense* and *nonconformity* — prefer to fuse *non-* and the base word into a single unbroken word where possible: *nonperson, nonviable.*

In certain combinations, however, it is advisable to retain the hyphen. When the base word begins with a vowel, for instance, there is a danger that the syllable-break might be momentarily misread: *? nonevent,* for example, might be read initially as × *none-vent* rather than as the fashionable new noun *non-event.* Some similar combinations, on the other hand, are now well established as single words: *nonentity,* for example.

The hyphen should also be retained where the base word begins with an *n-* — *non-nutritive* — or a capital letter: *non-Russian.*

2. As a negative prefix, *non-* is particularly useful for creating a neutral opposite of a word. The other negative prefixes such as *in-* or *un-* often create a more forcefully negative and disapproving opposite: *inhuman, unprofessional, unscientific* and so on. The simple, neutral opposites of *human, professional,* and *scientific* are, accordingly, *nonhuman, nonprofessional,* and *nonscientific.* Being *non-American* is quite different from being *un-American.*

There is an unfortunate trend, however, to overwork this useful prefix — either creating an alternative opposite where the original is quite neutral

(*nonapplicable* for *inapplicable, nonessential* for *inessential*) or creating a new negative opposite where none is needed in the first place (*nontransparent* for *opaque; nonpresence* for *absence,* and so on). Avoid the needless creation of such words, however fashionable a tendency it may be.

non sequitur Pronounced /**non** sekwittər/, a *non sequitur* is essentially a statement that has little relevance to what has gone before. A particularly irritating form of this common logical and stylistic error is illustrated in the previous sentence: the syntax suggests that the opening phrase expresses the *cause* of what is said in the main clause, as in *Pronounced unfit for human consumption, the consignment of imported pork was sold as pet food.* In the opening sentence of this article, however, there is no such causal connection between the two pieces of information — the pronunciation and the definition. The information should have been imparted in two separate sentences, or at least in two clauses linked by *and.*

The commonest breeding-grounds of *non sequiturs* include captions to pictures in newspapers and magazines, brief biographies in dictionaries or encyclopaedias, and 'arresting' opening sentences in news reports. Here are two further typical examples:

? Born in Alabama in 1913, Jesse Owens won four gold medals at the 1936 Olympic Games in Berlin.
? Worn around the neck as a good luck charm, this small jade figurine — called a *tiki* — was believed to house the spirit of an ancestor.

In other contexts, *non sequitur* can refer to a reply that seems to have no bearing at all on the question; or to a logical inference that is falsely drawn from the premises or evidence. The literal meaning of the Latin words *non sequitur* is, in fact, 'it does not follow'.

none The schoolroom tradition is that *none* takes a singular verb. But things are not as simple as that. It is not altogether correct to say that *none* is a contraction of *not one* or *no one* (which certainly do take a singular verb). The word originated in Old English as *nan,* a fusion of *ne an,* 'not one'; but the form *no* ('not any') itself came later — as a contraction of *none.*

Since nobody demands that *no* should be restricted to singular constructions, it seems odd that such a demand is so often made of *none.* Nevertheless, certain rules regarding *none* are still worth observing.

The best course is most easily summed up in the

following set of guidelines.

The pronoun *none* can be understood as the equivalent of various distinct phrases — *not one*, *no one*, *no people*, and *not any*. When it is understood as *not one*, it is in the singular and should take a singular verb:

> Some readers don't get this message at all; that appears to be Mr Kinnock's case. Professor Crick does get the message, though quite faintly, but he receives such a variety of other messages as well that none of them seems to convey anything in particular.
> – Conor Cruise O'Brien,
> *The Observer*

It is very common practice, however, to regard *none* ('not one') as a plural: *? Are you telling me that out of 15 players, none are prepared to sign a new contract?* Strictly speaking, this should read *none is prepared to sign.* Similarly:

> ?? When he went to the library to find a book on the subject before going backpacking in Europe, the librarian had assured him there were none.
> – Sue Arnold, *The Observer*

Here, the item referred to is singular (*a book*) and *none* should be understood as the singular *not one* in keeping with this, and given a singular verb: *there was none.*

The singular verb should also be used where *none* is understood as *no one,* as in the famous line by the 17th-century English poet John Dryden: *None but the brave deserves the fair.*

But in certain constructions, *none* is properly understood as *no people,* and a plural verb would then be correct, and has always been considered so. The English poet Andrew Marvell, writing at much the same time as Dryden, composed this famous couplet:

> The grave's a fine and private place,
> But none, I think, do there embrace.
> – Andrew Marvell,
> 'To His Coy Mistress' (1652)

Again: *None but the nurses deserve a salary increase*; *There are none so blind as those who will not see.* If the singular were wanted throughout in this last sentence, *none* would best be replaced by *no one*: *There is no one so blind as he who will not see.*

None can also be understood as *not any,* and again a plural verb might be the only appropriate form: *I was sure we still had some eggs, but there are none in the fridge.* To say *?? but there is none in the fridge* not only sounds pedantic, but seems

to be grammatically incorrect as well.

The choice is evenly balanced where *none* can be understood as either *not one* or *not any*:

> The seven boats set out a week ago, and so far none of them has/have returned.

> I have never used the words attributed to me in 'Pendennis's' concluding 'witticism' last week. None of my neighbours possess cats. May I suggest you barbecue your columnist?
> – Denis Healey, letter to *The Observer*

In this last example, although *possess* is a rather formal word, the context as a whole is relatively informal and the plural form *possess* is acceptable. More formal contexts might favour the singular *possesses* instead (and would probably change *cats* to *a cat* as well).

See also NO 3.

none the less   *None the less* is increasingly found written as one word, especially in American English, on the model of *nevertheless*. It seems that *? nonetheless* is now nearly accepted.

None the less, many writers and publishers still insist on the three-word spelling.

non-U   See U AND NON-U.

nor, or   **1.** *Neither* is followed by *nor* (not *or*) in *neither ... nor* constructions: *I am neither involved nor even interested in that scheme.* But when the first phrase is introduced by *not, never, no,* and so on, then the alternative phrase can usually be introduced by *or* or *and not* as well as *nor.*

In fact, many authorities frown on the unthinking use of *nor* in such sentences as *? I'm afraid he is never free on Wednesdays nor on Thursdays* and *? I am not involved nor even interested in such a scheme.*

> ? He opened Ma's letter. He could not make head nor tail of most of it.
> – Muriel Spark,
> *The Mandelbaum Gate*

> ? There seems to be no rhyme nor reason in names, why one takes and not another, or why, having taken, a name should vanish and be replaced.
> – Marghanita Laski,
> 'Words', BBC Radio 3

The argument against such usage is that the negative force of *not, never,* or *no* persists throughout the sentence, and to add *nor* is simply to add a superfluous further negative in each case.

It is perhaps best to limit the use of *nor* in such sentences to contexts where a strong negative emphasis is intended. In place of *nor* in the examples above, it would usually be advisable to write *or* or *and not*.

However, *nor* is essential when the negative alternative is a quite separate clause, since here the negative force of the original clause is not carried over to the new verb: *I am not involved in that scheme, nor is my brother.* When the alternative is a clause, but without being fully independent (usually because it shares the subject of the first negative clause), then *or* and *nor* are both acceptable, though perhaps *or* is still preferable: *That scheme does not involve me at all, or/nor even interest me.*

Sometimes the negative force of the first clause is expressed by a word such as *hardly* or *slightly* or *seldom* or *little*. Take care in such cases to ensure that the second phrase or clause is fully negative as well. Often, a simple *or* is insufficient: × *I'm hardly involved in that scheme at all, or much interested in it.* This should read ... *and not much interested in it*; or ... *and hardly interested in it*; or ... *nor much interested in it.*

Similarly, the *not, no,* or *never* of the first clause may apply not to the main verb (as it does in *I am not involved in that scheme*), but to some other element (as in *I have had no involvement in that scheme*). In these circumstances again, the second clause might require some negating introduction of its own — a simple *or* might not be adequate: × *I have had no involvement at all in that scheme, or even shown any interest in it.* This should read ... *nor even shown any interest in it*, or simply ... *or interest in it.*

2. In informal British English (but not American English), the phrases *and nor* and *but nor* are often found: *I'm not involved in that scheme, and nor is my brother.* (In more formal contexts, *and nor* might be inadvisable.) Strangely enough, however, the alternative *and neither* is fully acceptable in both British and American English: *I'm not involved in that scheme, and neither is my brother.*

3. There is no objection to beginning a sentence with *nor*, though the old and needless schoolroom prohibition on using *and* or *but* at the start of a sentence sometimes discourages writers from using *nor* as the first word too. In fact, the use of *nor* at the beginning of a sentence is often an economical and very effective way of linking that sentence to the previous one:

In all Gower batted for seven hours ... Nor, on a day of heroes, should Vic Marks be forgotten. As a batsman he has grown up two years in the last fortnight.
— Scyld Berry, *The Observer*

See also COMMA **1. a**; NEITHER **7**.

normalcy, normally Warren G. Harding, who became President of the United States in 1921, called for a return to *normalcy* in his Presidential campaign — breathing new life into a word that had been little used since it was first recorded in 1857. It has never gained full acceptance in British English, and in North America, where it is increasingly used, it is regarded by some purists as badly formed and hence nonstandard. With the established and correctly formed noun *normality* available, there seems to be no need to use *normalcy* at all.

Take care too with the word *normally*. It is too often used as a synonym of *usually* or *frequently*: ? *We normally take Oak Street if we want to get to the Town Hall.* Strictly, it is closer in sense to *typically*, and means 'as is the norm or pattern': *The leg normally jerks forward when the knee is tapped at this spot.* The Latin word *norma*, from which it derives, meant originally 'a carpenter's square, or a pattern'.

Northern Ireland See BRITAIN.

nostalgia, nostalgic *Nostalgia* originally meant 'homesickness', referring specifically to an acute form of longing for one's home that expressed itself in actual psychological or physical illness. *Nostalgia* is a New Latin term that entered English in 1780, but was coined in 1678 by Swiss medical writers, on the model of the German *Heimweh* ('home-pain'), from the Greek roots *nostos*, 'a homecoming, a return home' + *algos*, 'pain'.

By extension, the word has come to refer to any wistful or sentimental longing, in particular for times past: *a shiver of nostalgia for the country-dances of her youth.*

Tolkien had long dreamt of returning to Oxford. Throughout his war service he had suffered an ache of nostalgia for his college, his friends, and the way of life that he had led for four years.
— Humphrey Carpenter, *Tolkien*

Pedants might still object to this looser usage, but it is now so firmly established that many dictionaries have promoted it to the primary sense, relegating 'homesickness' to the status of a secondary definition.

Nostalgic has developed in the same way, but

it has gone further, into regions of meaning where it surely does not belong — referring to any allure, memory, or desire, whether painful or not. One helpful warning-sign of a dubious use is the application of *nostalgic* to the thing that causes nostalgia rather than to the person who experiences nostalgia: *? a nostalgic little country inn*; *? the sweetly nostalgic smell of rosewater*. When you want to apply the idea of yearning or reminiscence to a thing rather than to a person, you should try to find an adjective other than *nostalgic* — something along the lines of *old-fashioned, touching, memory-stirring*, or *heart-rending*.

Various other nouns and adjectives have extended their range in this way, with greater or lesser acceptance. For instance, *claustrophobic* used to be applied only to people suffering from claustrophobia; it is now used also of rooms inducing claustrophobia: *a claustrophobic prison cell*.

Conversely, *soporific* and *nauseous* were formerly applied to things, not to people: *a nauseous/soporific play*. Today, *nauseous* is, in American English at least, used freely of people — *I felt nauseous after watching that play* — and so too, though rather less acceptably, is *soporific*: *? That play made me quite soporific*.

See also NAUSEOUS.

not　**1.** Care is needed in positioning *not* within a sentence. As with *only* and *even,* there is the occasional conflict between the logical position and the idiomatic position. Usually, the adverb *not*, like *never,* relates to the sentence as a whole, and is placed between the auxiliary and infinitive parts of the verb:

We shall not fly the flag.

However, when *not* is a distinguishing adverb, contrasting one element in the sentence to another, then the grammatically 'logical' position for it is directly before the element it relates to:

We shall fly not the green flag but the blue one.

Unfortunately, such a sentence sounds peculiarly stilted. The more common way of putting it — the idiomatic way — is to keep the *not* in between the auxiliary and infinitive parts of the verb, even though it is not here intended to negate that verb or the sentence as a whole:

*? We shall not fly the green flag but the blue one.

Neither construction is perfect. The logical form

is awkward and unnatural; the idiomatic form is not logically and symmetrically constructed. (See PARALLEL CONSTRUCTIONS.)

Here are some more examples of the idiomatic but illogical form:

*? When one watches some tired hack on the platform mechanically repeating the familiar phrases — *bestial atrocities, iron heel, ... stand shoulder to shoulder* — one often has the curious feeling that one is not watching a live human being but some kind of dummy.
　　　　　　　　　　　　– George Orwell,
　　　　　'Politics and the English Language'

The 'logical' wording would be ... *one is watching not a live human being but some kind of dummy*. Similarly:

*? But for my money the most arresting revelation so far did not come from the Reith lectures proper, but from the preliminary interview he gave to Mary Goldring, on Radio 4.
　　　　　　– Lord Bruce Gardyne, *The Times*

The words *did not come* should ideally be replaced by *came not*.

In some cases, unfortunately, the remedy is worse than the ailment. In the following quotation, the writer has carefully placed his *not* in the 'grammatical' rather than 'idiomatic' position ... only to produce a quite unintended sense. There is a great difference between *trying not to make a point*, which the writer wrote, and *not trying to make a point*, which is what he meant.

*?? The mindless yelling that now arises from the Labour benches is of more significance. It is significant because it is different in its nature from the noise of the past. It is trying not to make a point but to deny a hearing.
　　　　　　– Alan Watkins, *The Observer*

One solution is to avoid the impasse altogether, by taking a slightly different route, such as:

It is not trying to make a point; it is trying to deny a hearing.
We shall not fly the green flag; we shall fly the blue one.

A combination, in other words, of idiom on the one hand, and logic and symmetry on the other.

The idiomatic form cited earlier — *? We shall not fly the green flag but the blue one* — may be 'illogical', but at least its meaning is clear. Other 'miswordings' are more dangerous, however, in that they open the door to ambiguity. One common construction in which *not* is dangerously misplaced is the sentence containing *because*:

? The restrictions were not imposed because of the danger of food-riots.

? The Turk did not favour the Jew because he preferred him to the Christian; on the contrary ... But the Jew stood alone and could be treated alone.
　　　– James Michener (U.S.), *The Source*

? I don't like Croft's novels because they happen to be intellectually demanding.

The sense dictated by grammar here is that I dislike Croft's novels (a comma after *novels* would reinforce this sense), and the text might be expected to continue ... *I read only for relaxation, and prefer thrillers.* But the intended sense might have been quite different: that I *do* like Croft's novels, but the reason for my liking them has nothing to do with the intellectual challenge of them. The text might continue ... *I like them because they're fun.* If so, then the original sentence should be reworded, with the *not* shifted to its correct position in front of the relevant element:

I like Croft's novels, (but) not because they happen to be intellectually demanding.

Here are some more examples of ambiguity created by the misplacing of *not.* Consider, first, two traditional constructions that are glaringly open to misinterpretation — or would be if their intended meaning were any less well-known:

? All is not lost.
? All that glisters is not gold.

The more logical rendering of the ideas here would be:

Not all is lost.
Not all that glisters is gold.

Similarly:

? Every man is not a manipulative oppressor of women.

On the face of it, this is a general statement about *every man,* and could be reworded as:

No man is a manipulative oppressor of women.

But the speaker, unless he were more ignorant of the world than he should be, probably meant something different:

Not every man is a manipulative oppressor of women.

2. There are other, subtler dangers of positioning *not* incorrectly within a sentence. If a single *not* is required, for instance, to extend over more than one clause or phrase or word, it must be positioned in such a precise way that it is permitted grammatically to reach across to the later element or elements. Compare these two sentences:

× There is little chance of being selected for the expedition if you have not studied first aid and are experienced in survival techniques.

There is little chance of being selected for the expedition if you have not studied first aid and gained experience in survival techniques.

In the second sentence, the *not* transfers easily from the clause *have ... studied first aid* to the clause *(have) gained experience in survival techniques,* because the two clauses are of the same grammatical structure: the later clause implicitly picks up the introductory words *have not* from the earlier clause, to read *(have not) gained experience.* In the first of the examples, however, the two phrases are of different structure: *have ... studied* and *are experienced*; the reading that is wanted is *if you are not experienced,* but the reading actually produced by the grammar is *if you are experienced.* (See also NO 3, PARALLEL CONSTRUCTIONS.)

3. The converse danger, of course, is that *not* might grammatically reach across to apply to a later element where it is not intended to:

? If you do not leave this house at once and continue bothering me, I shall inform the police.
? You are not going to phone anybody, but to listen very carefully to what I say.

Grammatically, the first sentence can be understood in two ways: either *If you ... continue bothering me* (the intended meaning), or *If you do not ... continue bothering me* (the unintended meaning). The second sentence, according to the grammar, can in theory be read in a way quite the opposite of the one intended: *You are not going ... to listen very carefully.*

The remedy in each case is either to reverse the clauses (so that the *not* is now part of the second clause and therefore cannot be understood as part of the other clause), or to add extra words in front of the second clause to indicate that the *not* is no longer applicable:

If you do not leave this house at once, and *if you* continue bothering me, I shall inform the police.
You are not going to phone anybody, but

you are going to listen very carefully to what I say.

4. Another source of difficulty is the omission of *not* in favour of *un-, im-,* and so on. The following sentence is correct and unambiguous (note the careful positioning of the *not*):

We are likely not to vote against but to abstain.

If you attempt to use *unlikely* to convey this sense, you produce the following very misleading sentence:

? We are unlikely to vote against but to abstain.

According to the grammar, this reads, in theory, *We are unlikely ... to abstain,* which is the opposite of the meaning intended. Similarly:

? I was unimpressed, as the critics were, with his performance.

As it stands, this implies that the critics were unimpressed too. But if the intended sense is that the critics were impressed, then the sentence should begin *I was not impressed ...*

5. When *not* occurs in sentences containing contrasting elements, it can be part of either the first element or the second:

I want you to fly not the green flag but the blue one.
I want you to fly the blue flag, not the green one.

Note that when the *not* is part of the second element, it tends to have a comma in front of it; when the *not* is part of the first element, it is no longer customary to place a comma in front of it. A comma is still possible in front of the *but* that introduces the second element, though the modern tendency to streamline punctuation would tend to discourage that comma too.

I come to bury Caesar, not to praise him.
I come not to bury Caesar but to praise him.
I come not to bury Caesar, but to praise him.

6. The word *not* seems to tempt speakers and writers into making strangely simple-minded statements:

? I advise you not to offer too low a price.
? Could I have some milk in my tea — but not too much, please.
? The importance of this discovery should not be underestimated.
? You should not be unduly worried.
? It is a good security system, but its effec-

tiveness should not be exaggerated.

All such sentences state the obvious. Of course you should not offer too low a price. (It would be better to say *I advise you not to offer a very low price*). Of course a thing should not be exaggerated — exaggeration is almost by definition something that should be avoided. (It would be better to say *... but its effectiveness is easily exaggerated.*) And so on.

Try to avoid such banalities, no matter how common and apparently idiomatic they may be.

7. Avoid if possible using *not* after *unless*; otherwise the result will almost certainly be difficult for your reader or audience to unravel: *? Don't do that unless you haven't enough time to do anything else.* The intended meaning here is probably 'Do that only if you haven't the time to do anything else'. It would be better to word your sentence in the same or a similar way. (See DOUBLE NEGATIVE.)

See also NOT UN-.

not about to   See ABOUT 2.

not only ... but also   When used to introduce parallel constructions, *not (only)* and *but (also)* must each be followed by the same kind of item:

We saw not only the secretary but the chairman too (two objects).
We not only saw the chairman but spoke to him (two verbs).
Not only I but also Sylvia spoke to him (two subjects).
We spoke not only to the secretary but to the chairman (two prepositional phrases).

To word these in a way that spoils the parallel structure would be an error of style and of grammar:

✗ We not only saw the secretary but the chairman too (one verb, one noun).

In the following examples, *not only* and *not merely* have become misplaced:

✗ A high fat diet does not only increase the risks of CHD but also that of other disorders, such as high blood pressure, certain cancers and obesity.
— Annabel Ferriman, *The Observer*

This should read *A high fat diet increases not only the risks of CHD but also that of other disorders* (two objects). Another correct version of this sentence would begin: *A high fat diet not only increases the risks of CHD but also increases the risk of other disorders* (two verbs). Note that in the original sentence the construction × *does not only increase* was incorrect.

× His mistresses became matter not merely for Court gossip but had names which every housewife in the country knew.
– Peter Brent, *The Edwardians*

This should be rearranged to read: *His mistresses not merely became matter for Court gossip but had names which every housewife in the country knew* (two verbs).
See PARALLEL CONSTRUCTIONS.

not so much ... as 1. The correlative conjunctions *not so much* and *as* (or *not as much* and *as*) form a useful idiom, occurring in such sentences as:

Carter was not so much an incompetent president as an unlucky one.

A common tendency is to replace *as* with *but*, producing a faulty sentence:

× Carter was not so much an incompetent president but an unlucky one.

This is probably the result of a confusion with the construction:

Carter was not an incompetent president but an unlucky one.

2. Take care to keep the constructions parallel. The phrase or clause following *not so much* should be of the same structure as that following the *as*:

His problem was that he suffered not so much from poor judgment as from poor advice.

or:

His problem was not so much that he suffered from poor judgment as that he suffered from poor advice.

If these two approaches are fused, however, the symmetry between the constructions would be lost, and the sentence would lose its correct balance:

× His problem was not so much that he suffered from poor judgment as from poor advice.

Here one element has a verb, and the other does not. The necessary symmetry has been lost, and the sentence lapses into a stylistically and grammatically faulty structure.

See PARALLEL CONSTRUCTIONS.
3. The phrase *not so much* is often used in combination with *more* rather than *as,* as in the title of a former BBC television comedy programme *Not so much a programme more a way of life.* Such jocular constructions are now well established in informal usage — but the grammar remains faulty, and unacceptable in formal English.

not un- The construction *not un-* (or *not im-*, *not dis-*, and so on) — as in *not displeased at the outcome* or *a not unwelcome bonus* — has attracted a great deal of criticism. It is argued that it marks a cowardly avoidance of the positive adjective, and contributes to a weak, blurry, euphemistic text. George Orwell dismissed it in these words:

It should ... be possible to laugh the *not un-* formation out of existence ... One can cure oneself of the *not un-* formation by memorising this sentence: *A not unblack dog was chasing a not unsmall ɾabbit across a not ungreen field.*
– George Orwell,
'Politics and the English Language'

This all seems rather unfair. Orwell's examples are ridiculous: the *not un-* construction is used only with adjectives that already have established opposites formed with a negative prefix (such as *possible-impossible* or even *worried-unworried*). The phrase × *not unblack* is odd because the word × *unblack* itself would be odd.

It might be argued, moreover, that the *not un-* construction enriches rather than impoverishes the language — that it refines the adjective rather than blunts it. There is surely a difference worth preserving between the phrases *happy with the result* and *not unhappy with the result.* The tendency of British English to avoid bold statements and to hedge its bets by qualifying every claim does not necessarily reflect any weakness or lack of commitment. Perhaps it marks an admirable prudence, flexibility, and desire for accuracy.

'Dead Zone' is like a 'Twilight Zone' TV-special — thin, unduly protracted, though not unentertaining — and, for a Cronenberg film, surprisingly restrained in its gore and violence.
– Philip French, *The Observer*

There are dangers, of course, in using the construction, but these are the same dangers in using any construction: the dangers of overusing it and of using it ambiguously. Since it is a conspicuous construction, it is advisable to use it only seldom and with caution. And since it is a contentious construction, make sure that it really is doing the work it should — securing an effect that a more straightforward wording would not secure.

Two of the most useful effects are, as it happens, at odds with each other — hence the danger of ambiguity. On the one hand, the *not un-* construction has a fine-tuning effect, as suggested earlier: *not unhappy* thus means 'reasonably happy; contented'. On the other hand, the *not un-* construction can be used for ironic understatement (another speciality of British English): *not unhappy* would then mean 'extremely happy; ecstatic'. Consider the different interpretations, then, of a simple sentence such as:

? Speaking as team manager, I am not altogether unhappy with the result.

Perhaps the manager was speaking about a goalless draw at a home game — a satisfactory though not really pleasing result, in other words. Perhaps, however, he was speaking about a 7-0 triumph over the league leaders — a spectacular result.

In this instance, the context would of course make clear whether the sentence was aiming at modulation or understatement. But without any clues from the context, such a sentence would be ambiguous. Make sure that your intended meaning comes through unambiguously when using the *not un-* construction.

notorious See INFAMOUS.

nought See NAUGHT.

nouns 1. A noun names a thing, person, place, quality, or act. These are all nouns: *house, story, Peter, Devonshire, income tax, statesman, sand, weather, botany, happiness, flock, committee, jump.*

A noun can also be identified by the part it plays in a sentence. It can be the subject of a verb, as *house* is in *The house needs painting.* It can be the object of a verb, as *story* and *Peter* are in *I believed his story* and *I'll ask Peter.* It can be the object of a preposition, as *Devonshire* and *income tax* are in *a farm in Devonshire* and *Charge it against income tax.* It can stand in the relationship called 'apposition' to another noun, showing that they both refer to the same person or thing. In *Gladstone, the famous statesman,* the noun *statesman* is in apposition to *Gladstone.*

There are several kinds of noun. An ordinary *count noun* or *countable noun,* the commonest

type, can form plurals — *three houses, two men* — or can be used with *one* or *a/an: a story, an excuse.*

But many other nouns cannot be used in these ways. This may be because the noun in question is a *mass noun,* which typically names 'stuff' rather than 'a thing'. *Sand* and *weather* are mass nouns: you cannot usually speak of *a sand* or *two weathers.* Or it may be because the noun is not a *common noun* such as *house* or *sand,* but a *proper noun,* which names a single particular person or thing and begins with a capital letter. You cannot usually speak of *a Peter* or *two Devonshires* (though special contexts would make such phrases possible).

Common nouns can be divided into *concrete nouns* — naming things or people that you can see, hear, touch, taste, or smell, such as *trousers, policeman, cat, toffee* — and *abstract nouns,* for things that you cannot perceive directly with your senses, such as *botany, worry, education, diabetes.* Concrete nouns are mostly count nouns, and abstract ones are mostly mass nouns, but not necessarily so. In the following sentence, *education* appears to be at once a count noun and an abstract noun: *She received a good education.* (See ABSTRACT NOUNS.)

Some nouns can behave in more than one way. *Cake* is a count noun in *I ate three cakes,* but a mass noun in *Have some more cake. Uncle* is a common noun in *both my uncles,* but a proper noun, or name, in *You'd better ask Uncle.*

Nouns such as *committee, flock,* and *crew* refer to a group of people or things. They are called *group nouns.* (See also COLLECTIVE NOUNS.)

2. A *compound noun* is formed when two or more words are used to name something, as with the example *income tax.* It is typically formed by joining two (or more) nouns: *cat's-eye, hairbrush, houseboat, tape measure, post office, Trades Union Congress.*

The words that make up a compound noun do not have to be nouns themselves, however (though at least one of the elements is usually a noun). What matters is that the unit functions as a noun: *bypass, print-out, yellow fever, boiling point, half-truth, man in the street.*

As the examples show, some compound nouns are written as separate words, some are hyphenated, and some are written as one word. There are no consistent patterns; dictionaries vary in their practice: should it be *postoffice, post-office,* or *post office*? The only safe advice here is to accept the authority of some good dictionary and follow it consistently, noting that British dictionaries (following the example of British publications generally) use considerably more hyphens than American ones do.

Some compound nouns form their plural in an irregular way: *mothers-in-law*, *courts martial*, *menservants*. (See PLURALS for a discussion of this subject.)

In general, the longer a compound has been accepted as a single unit, the more likely it is to have passed from the stage of separate words through the intervening hyphen stage to the point of being joined up; and the further it has gone in this process, the more likely it is to be pronounced as one word, with one stressed syllable: we say (and spell) *blackbird* as one word, but *black hole* as two, because the first has been longer established as a compound.

Although *black hole* remains two words, it qualifies for entry as a compound noun in the dictionary because it now represents a single idea — not merely a hole that is black but a region in space caused by a star collapsing under its own gravitational force; just as a *blackbird* is not simply any bird that is black, but a particular kind of black thrush with an orange beak. Where a combination of words means no more than the sum of its parts, it will not appear in the dictionary at all. *Christmas tree* appears as a dictionary entry because it means more than a tree that grows at Christmas; but *Christmas traffic*, being merely the sort of traffic that occurs at Christmas time, will not be shown. In general, if a combination does not appear in a good large dictionary, you can assume that it is not really a compound noun (it means no more than the sum of its parts), and that it should accordingly be written as two words.

3. *Christmas traffic* is a typical noun-noun combination, a formation very common in everyday English: *railway station*, *street map*, *television set*, and so on. Such combinations help to make the language more economical and efficient. But they can be overused. Sometimes it is worth considering whether the first noun could be replaced by a true adjective. Why should a *home computer* not be a *domestic computer*, or a *noun phrase* a *nominal phrase*?

The use of very long noun-noun-noun strings is characteristic of newspaper language — *Tourist Holiday Coach Crash Disaster* — and of the titles of public bodies: *World Health Organisation*. In ordinary running prose, however, such noun-sequences have a clogging effect: *our tea import requirements* would be better referred to as *the tea we need to import*. The formation sometimes becomes quite incomprehensible to the layman. Consider this example:

a proposed Bristol rocket powered delta-wing prone pilot interceptor
> – label for an exhibit,
> RAF Museum, Hendon

Who but an expert could say whether *Bristol* refers to *rocket* or *interceptor*, and whether the adjective *prone* refers to *pilot* or *interceptor*? (See NEWSPAPER ENGLISH; PREPOSITIONS OMITTED.)

Nouns used like adjectives before other nouns in this way are called 'attributive nouns'. One interesting characteristic of them is they may have a special form, used only in this position. A note worth *five pounds* is a *five-pound* note; the trousers of one's *pyjamas* are *pyjama* trousers; a table for playing *billiards* on is a *billiard* table. This feature is particularly common in American English, which can have *sport car* as well as *sports car*, and prefers *account executive* to the British *accounts executive*. It occasionally creates confusion where a true adjective also exists. A firm calling itself *Perennial Specialists* presumably sells flowering *perennials*, but the title might well suggest a firm of specialists who go on for ever. (In speech, differing stress patterns would distinguish the two meanings.)

Note too that a compound noun or noun combination is more often hyphenated or fused into a single word when it is used attributively, like an adjective: *a Christmas-tree effect*.

4. A long-established way of forming nouns is by the process technically known as 'conversion': the use of a word belonging to one part of speech, such as an adjective or verb, to make a word of another part of speech, such as a noun. We made the noun *a fall* from the verb *to fall* in the 13th century, the noun *a natural* from the adjective *natural* in the 16th, and the noun *a daily* from the adjective (or adverb) *daily* in the 19th. Criticism is sometimes directed against such converted nouns as *the royals*, *an invite*, *the locals*, and *a quote* — yet these all date back a surprisingly long way: to the 15th century, 1659, 1824, and 1888 respectively.

Nouns formed from adjectives are often plural in function: *the rich* and *the deaf* are rich people and deaf people, with no singular. A few nouns, however, formed from the past participles of verbs, can refer to either one person or more than one, according to the context: *The accused was/were found guilty of manslaughter*; *The bereaved was/were standing by the grave*; *The deceased left the money to his wife/to their wives*. And some ordinary adjectives can be plural or singular, too: *Are the good* ('those who are good') *happier than the bad* ('those who are bad')*?*; *The* *good* ('that which is good') *is sometimes just not worth defending against the bad* ('that which is bad').

nubile   Applied to adolescent girls or young women, this adjective is freely used today in the sense of 'physically attractive, or sexually alluring', usually with either a leering or a waggish tone: *? the tantalising sight of his neighbour's nubile daughter.* Some purists object to this meaning, but the damage seems past mending and the word is now fully established in this sense. The meaning that the purists wish to restrict the word to is 'ready for marriage, of marriageable age'. Strictly then, even an extremely ugly young woman could claim to be *nubile.* But to use the word in this 'correct' way nowadays would only cause confusion.

This sense is closer to the word's source (though that alone is not enough to disqualify the newer sense from acceptance). *Nubile* comes through French from Latin *nubilis*, 'marriageable', from *nubere,* 'to take a husband, get married'.

number   When preceded by *the*, *number* takes a singular verb: *The number of people now out of work has grown.* When preceded by *a* or *any*, it usually takes a plural verb: *A number of people have applied*; *A large number of candidates were turned down.* (See PLURALS Part II.)

number style   When should a number be expressed in words, and when in figures?

Rules vary from publisher to publisher. For your own purposes, consider the different effects of the two forms. Numbers expressed in figures stand out; numbers spelt out in words recede into the middle distance, along with all the other words in a sentence. Figures are emphatic; their spelt-out equivalents are not. Figures give the appearance of being precise, accurate, crisp — and sometimes informal. Numbers expressed in words convey an air of approximation — or of formality.

Contrast, for example, an office memo announcing a staff meeting and an engraved invitation to a church wedding. The company memo might announce the meeting at *10.30 am on 27/7/83.* The invitation might announce the wedding ceremony *at half past ten on the twenty-seventh of July in the year of Our Lord one thousand nine hundred and eighty-three.* These two forms mark the extreme limits of number style — figure style and word style.

Figure style   This is the style used in business and technical writing and in journalism, since most of the numbers in this material represent important information that should stand out. Here are the key rules:

1. Spell out numbers from one to ten inclusive, but use figures for all numbers above ten: *About 75 people attended the introductory lecture, but only 23 registered for the course.* (Some publishers place the limit at 9, some at 12.)

2. If a sentence or paragraph contains related numbers and some are above ten and some below, practice varies. Some publishers stick steadfastly to rule 1: *We need only eight to 13 volunteers.* Other publishers put all the related numbers in figures: *We need only 8 to 13 volunteers to keep the three day-care centres operating during the summer months.* The number *8* is in figures, since it is paired with *13*, but *three* remains spelt out, since it is not related to the number of volunteers.

3. Large numbers of more than a million can be expressed all in figures; or in a mixed form: *6,800,000* or *6.8 million.* (See BILLION.)

Word style   This style is used in writing that is formal, literary, or nontechnical, where not many numbers are used, and where figures might look obtrusive and distracting:

1. Spell out numbers from one to a hundred inclusive.

2. Spell out round numbers above a hundred that can be written in one or two words. A hyphenated compound like *thirty-eight* is considered one word; thus *thirty-eight thousand* or *thirty-eight million* falls within the two-word limit.

3. Large numbers over a million that would require more than two words if spelt out can be expressed all in figures or in the mixed form again: *6,800,000* or *6.8 million.*

4. If there is a clash between the preferred styles of related numbers, practice varies: some publishers stick to the rules regardless: *a target of three million units, but sold only 1,682,544.* Other publishers would bring these numbers into line, expressing them both in figures: *Despite predictions that we would sell more than 3,000,000 units, we sold only 1,682,544.*

Your choice of style should depend on the effects you are aiming for (and the policy of the publication, if one is involved). Will the material contain numbers that should stand out for emphasis or easy reference? If so, choose the figure style. Are the numbers not especially significant, or is the writing somewhat formal (though not technical)? If so, choose the word style.

More important than the choice itself is the consistency in implementing it. If you choose the figure style for a particular occasion, then write *the 15th of May* (or *15 May*) rather than *the fifteenth of May*; both forms are 'correct', but the former would be more appropriate in view of your general choice of style.

Some number expressions call for special handling, regardless of which basic style you have chosen. Here are some guidelines for dealing with these expressions.

Mostly figures Even if you are following a word style, certain number expressions almost always require the use of figures. In such cases even the numbers from one to ten are expressed in figures.

1. *dates.* There is a variety of possible styles:

7 October 1978	(this is now the standard form in British publications and those of several other countries)
October 7 1978	(this is the commonest form in the USA and Canada and is still used by some British publications)
7/10/78	(these styles of representing
7.10.78	7 October 1978 are common
7·10·78	in Britain and other English-speaking countries — even Canada — but not in the USA)
10/7/78	(this is the U.S. style for 7 October 1978)
78.10.7	(this is the style now recommended by the International Organisation for Standardisation. It is being increasingly adopted, in technical, manufacturing and banking contexts, in Europe and South Africa)

In view of the possible confusions over a date written as *7/10/78*, it is perhaps best to avoid it except in informal writing.

In more explicit writing of the date, there are several possible forms: *the 7th of October* (emphatic or informal) and *the seventh of October* (more formal); or *October 7th, 1978*, or *7th October 1978* (these last two are not standard for formal American writing).

2. *the time.* Most publications now favour the form *2 o'clock* over *two o'clock*. Another modern tendency, not yet so widespread, is to omit the full stops in *a.m.* and *p.m.*: *3.40 am*. To avoid the danger that the abbreviation will be read as the common verb *am*, some publishers omit the space as well: *3.40am*.

On the Continent, the 24-hour clock is widely used in timetables. The International Organisation for Standardisation recommends the forms *08 00* and *16 30* — to be read as *eight hours* (not *eight hundred hours*) and *sixteen hours thirty* (not *sixteen-thirty hours*). These conventions are being adopted in technical contexts, but have made almost no headway in everyday use.

3. *money.* Use figures to express specific amounts: *£2; £24.50* or *£24·50; about £600; £37.5 million* or *£37·5 million; 50 pence worth; 50p worth* (in statistical or in informal material). Use words to express indefinite amounts — *millions of pounds* — and isolated references where figures would be too prominent: *not worth two cents*; *a story called 'Simon and Sara and a fifty-pence piece'*.

4. *technical numbers.* Use figures to express percentages, ratios, measurements and proportions: *an 8.4 per cent increase; a 60-40 split; a surcharge on packages of more than 10 pounds; 6 parts of gin to 1 part of vermouth.*

5. *abbreviations and symbols:* for example, *7pm; 4 × 6m; No. 1; 25°C; 5lb 2oz.*

6. *scores, votes,* and *numbers used as in arithmetic:* for example, *an 8-to-5 victory; a majority of only 59 votes; count backwards from 10 to 1; multiply by 3.1; divide by 2.*

7. *pages and chapters:* for example, *chapter 3, ch 3, p 6, pp 4-8.*

8. *age.* There is a tendency to use a number when specifying the age of a young child: *a 6-year-old boy; a child of 3.* The spelt-out forms are still quite acceptable, however.

Mostly words Some types of number expressions almost always require the use of words (even if you have chosen to follow a figure style).

1. *At the beginning of a sentence*, spell out any number as the first word of a sentence, and also any related numbers that follow it: *Eight to fifteen per cent of the voters are undecided.* If the spelt-out number requires more than two words or if figures are preferable, try to reword the sentence: *Between 8 and 15 per cent ...*

2. *indefinite numbers:* for example, *hundreds of men; thousands of women; tens of millions of hungry people.*

3. *straightforward fractions that stand alone* (without a whole number preceding them). So: *one-third the usual time; three-quarters of the student body*; but: *less than 2½ inches of rain* (the whole number precedes the fraction); *a ¾-inch pipe* (a technical measurement); *multiply by ⅜* (a number used as a number), and *sacrificed 7/17 of their holdings* (too long and complicated to be spelt out neatly).

4. *in dialogue and direct quotations* (except for such things as year dates): '*She earned five thousand pounds in 1955,*' he said.

A few technical guidelines finally:

1. When expressing numbers in figures, use commas to set off thousands, hundreds of thousands, and so on, in numbers that run to more than three digits: *1,435,647.* The comma is now often omitted in a four-digit number: *1250.* Never use commas in page numbers (*page 1518*), year numbers (*2001*), or similar expressions.

Instead of the comma, a thin space is now often used when metric measurements are given — *23 021km* — and on the Continent, a full stop is sometimes used for this purpose in expressing sums of money: *38.561.238 Frs.*

Note that in the Continental system too (also in operation in South Africa), the decimal point is replaced by a comma: *220,5m; DM26.381,55.*

2. When expressing amounts in whole units of currency (*£56*) or time on the hour (*7am*), do not add noughts (? *£56.00*; ? *7.00 am*) unless such expressions are displayed together with others that include real sub-units, as in a column of numbers where a consistent appearance is important:

£56.00	7.00pm
£27.25	8.15am

However, a nought before a decimal point can be useful to show that no whole numbers are involved: *0.5.* Remember, too, not to combine *£* with *p* or *$* with *c*, or the like: it is correct to write *25p, £3,* and *£3.25,* but not × *£3.25p.*

3. To form the plurals of figures, just add -*s: during the 1980s, the '80s, the 80s; temperatures in the 20s.* The use of the apostrophe-*s* — *the 1860's; in the low 20's* — is permissible, but is now used less and less frequently. (See -'S, -S'.)

4. When expressing numbers in words, hyphenate all compound numbers between 21 and 99, whether they stand alone (*twenty-five*) or are part of a larger number (*twenty-five hundred*). But do not hyphenate other parts of a spelt-out number: *sixty thousand; eighty-five million.*

Fractions too are almost always hyphenated: *three-quarters; seven-tenths.*

5. When saying or spelling out round numbers between 1100 and 1950, people tend to use hundreds only, not thousands and hundreds: *1500 metres/feet/people* is represented as *fifteen hundred*; and *1550* probably as *fifteen hundred and fifty.* But *1567,* say, would tend to be *one thousand five hundred and sixty-seven* (note the absence of commas — this is the most economical style). Of course the year *AD 1567* is referred to

by hundreds: *fifteen hundred and sixty-seven* or simply *fifteen sixty-seven.*

6. To form the plurals of spelt-out numbers, follow the standard rules for adding -*s* or -*es: ones; twos; thirds; sixes; eighths; twenties; hundreds; hundredths; millions.*

7. In expressions such as *twenty 8-page brochures* and *six 4-room flats,* put one of the numbers in words and the other in figures for the sake of clarity. As a rule, spell the first of the numbers, unless the second number will make a much shorter word: *2000 eight-page brochures.*

8. In a sequence of numbers (*during the years 1980-1985; on pages 348-356*) a hyphen may be used to replace the word *to.* (Abbreviations of such hyphenated sequences are possible: *1980-85.*) However, if the sequence begins with the word *between,* use *and* rather than a hyphen: *between 1980 and 1985,* not × *between 1980-1985.* If the sequence begins with the word *from,* use *to* rather than a hyphen: *from page 348 to page 356,* not × *from page 348-page 356* or × *from pages 348-356.*

Upper-case Roman numerals are used after names and titles: *Louis XIV; Tom Vandibs III.*

9. *Roman numerals.* Lower-case Roman numerals are generally used to number the pages of the introduction to a book: the eighth page of the introduction will typically bear the number *viii* rather than *VIII* or *8.* Capital Roman numerals may also be used to number the chapters or appendices of a book, the stanzas of a poem, the acts of a play, or other major divisions of a written work, though Arabic numbers sometimes serve these functions too. A typical reference would be *Hamlet III iv 145* — that is, Act III, scene iv, line 145.

Some periodicals use Roman numerals for their volumes; others use Arabic numerals. Both of the following forms, for example, are common and correct:

New Literary History Volume XV No. 3; Spring 1984

The Historical Journal Volume 27 No. 2; June 1984.

A combination of Roman and Arabic numerals is often used for the sections of an outline:

I	Introduction: Genre and Literary History.
II.1	The novel: from Defoe to Dickens.
II.2	The novel: from Dickens to date.
III	Poetry.
IV.1	Drama: Shakespeare and before.
IV.2	Drama: After Shakespeare.

O

O, oh *O* is little used today. It serves to introduce a direct address, usually in poetry or song lyrics or religious writing: *O my fair warrior*; *O Carol*; *Hear, O Israel*. It is always capitalised, and is usually not followed by a comma. It is used either directly before the subject to which it refers — *O Best Beloved*; *O happy band of pilgrims* — or directly before an imperative form of the verb (the subject 'you' being implied or else following explicitly): *O come all ye faithful*.

O can also be used in the refrains of poetry, or to fill out a line: *Green grow the rushes, O*.

Oh introduces exclamations or expresses a reflective pause or an emotion. It is not capitalised (except at the beginning of sentences). It is followed by a comma when a pause is intended — *Oh, I meant to tell you . . .* — or it can be followed by an exclamation mark when pain or surprise is expressed: *Oh! Horrors! He's dead!* But it can do without punctuation when no pause is wanted: *Oh what a lovely war!* Similarly, punctuation is omitted in set exclamatory phrases — *Oh dear, what can the matter be?*; *Oh me, oh my, I hope that little lady comes by* — and in the phrases *oh for* and *oh to* expressing a wish: *Oh for the wings of a dove*; *Oh to be in England*.

Oh can also be used in literary or rhetorical contexts before requests or appeals: *Oh, say, does that star-spangled banner yet wave . . . ?* It is also used to introduce a call or summons: *Oh John, come here for a moment, will you?* Contrast such a direct address with the more literary one introduced by *O*: *Be merciful, O prince!*

In a few phrases, *O* can be used to replace *oh*, especially in American English: *O my! O dear!*

objective, subjective 1. As adjectives these two terms have established meanings in philosophy and medicine — *objective and subjective sensations* — and in grammar. From the philosophical sense, several rather looser uses have developed in each case, generally distinguishing material, external, observable reality from mental, internal impressions and speculations: *Your jealousy is purely subjective — there is nothing in objective reality to warrant it*. Such uses are now quite established.

But the words tend to be used more loosely still.

On the borderline of acceptability are the use of *objective* in the sense of 'free from prejudice or personal interest, uninfluenced by emotion or speculation', and the use of *subjective* to mean 'subject to such prejudice, personal interest, emotion, or speculation': *Put your own feelings to one side, and try to be objective in discussing my proposal*.

More loosely still — and on the wrong side of the borderline — *objective* and *subjective* are often used as pretentious and supposedly impressive synonyms of *fair, honest*, or *accurate*, and *distorted, dubious*, or *personal*: ? *Please give me an objective assessment of the value of these antiques*; ? *Don't let your subjective views affect your appreciation of the play*.

In general, *objective* and *subjective* are overused vogue words, and should be avoided if one of their simpler, and more accurate, synonyms will serve instead.

2. *Objective* as a noun, apart from its philosophical, grammatical, and optical senses, used to occur chiefly in military contexts: *We've gained this strategic hill — the river is our next objective*. From this sense of 'the goal of a military operation', *objective* extended its range to refer to any goal: *Our objective is a five per cent increase over last month's sales*. This is now accepted as standard, though some purists consider that *object* (or *goal*) is the better word here. And they dislike *objective* even more when it is followed by a verbal construction: *Our objective is to increase sales by five per cent*. Again, *object* (or *intention*) is urged in preference.

Certainly *objective* can sound slightly affected — a merely stylish variant of *object* — but in other respects the criticism of it seems old-fashioned and unfair.

oblique See SOLIDUS.

oblivious *Oblivious* goes back to the Latin verb *oblivisci*, 'to forget', and originally meant 'lacking all memory of something, forgetful': *oblivious of her long-lost brother's features*. Today it is more commonly used to mean 'unaware, unmindful, not conscious' — *oblivious of the danger she was in* — though some purists have objected to this usage. In either sense, *of* is the standard preposition.

The preposition *to*, however, is now widely used instead of *of*, especially with inanimate nouns: *? She was oblivious to the danger she was in.* This usage is also likely to be accepted in time, but the objections to it are still fairly vigorous, and it should be avoided in careful writing.

observance, observation Three of the primary meanings of the verb *to observe* are 'to watch, survey, notice', 'to remark or state', 'to follow, carry out'. The noun *observation* relates to the first two of the senses, and the noun *observance* to the third.

So *observation* means either 'looking, watching, noticing, surveillance' — *The poet's acute observation was the source of his power*; *The patient is now under observation* — or a comment or remark: *She was renowned for her witty and astute observations.*

Observance means 'the attending to and carrying out of a duty or rule or custom': *observance of the laws*; *the observance of the university's traditions.* An *observance* may also be the duty or rule or custom itself: *religious ceremonies and observances.*

obsolete, obsolescent Both these words go back to the Latin *obsolere*, 'to be old'. *Obsolete* means 'out of date, out of use, no longer current'. A piece of machinery of outmoded design or a word no longer in use may be *obsolete* – 'already grown old'.

> 'This stinking plane's never going to get to the Middle East,' he snarled ... 'It's got stinking straight wings, John!'
> 'All right — it's got straight wings! What's wrong with straight wings, for God's sake?'
> 'Because they mean it's just a cartload of old scrap-iron! It's obsolete!'
> 'Obsolete? How can it be obsolete when it's jet-propelled?'
> 'For God's sake, John — stinking jets have been around for a hundred stinking years! They were new when you were a kid — but that's a long stinking time ago now.'
> – Michael Frayn,
> *Towards the End of the Morning*

The word is used typically of inanimate things – and only humorously of people.

Obsolescent means 'becoming obsolete, growing old, on the way to being out of date'. So machinery that is increasingly being replaced by more modern machines, or words that are now

rare but not extinct, may be *obsolescent*.

The *-scent* ending is from the Latin present participle, with the sense '-ing', as in *crescent. Crescent*, as it happens, has a now obsolescent sense of 'increasing, growing'. (A *crescent moon* is waxing – 'getting larger'; from this developed the sense of the curved shape, as in croissants and concave terraces.)

The noun is *obsolescence*:

> The hold of the Greeks on our thinking is due to their pre-emptive generation of the basic equipment of Western speech. Despite the supposed obsolescence of the classics, we have no choice but to be Hellenists.
> – Frederic Raphael, *The Listener*

The phrases *built-in obsolescence* and *planned obsolescence* are now in common use. They refer to the designing of manufactured products deliberately to ensure that they do not last — in order to maintain the market for replacements.

In American English, *to obsolete* is sometimes found being used as a verb, meaning 'to make obsolete, or to replace', as in *New technology obsoletes this old equipment.* Though recorded as existing since 1640, this use of *obsolete* is still opposed by many.

occasion *Occasion* can mean 'a reason; grounds': it is then followed by *for* when introducing a noun or the *-ing* form — *this is an occasion for merriment/rejoicing* — or by *to* when introducing a verb: *I have had occasion to complain in the past.*

When *occasion* means 'an opportunity', it is followed by *to* on introducing a verb: *I would like to take this occasion to thank our host.*

Compare OPPORTUNITY.

oculist, optician, optometrist An *oculist* is a qualified medical doctor who specialises in the treatment of diseases of the eye. The term goes back to the Latin word for 'eye', *oculus*. Note that the word has only one *c*, not two as in *occult*.

An *oculist* is also known as an *ophthalmologist* or sometimes an *ophthalmic surgeon*, from the Greek word for 'eye', *ophthalmos*. The *ophth-* in *ophthalmology* and its derivatives is pronounced /ofth-/. Despite its tricky spelling and pronunciation, the title *ophthalmologist* is becoming increasingly popular with doctors, especially in North America, perhaps because *oculist* has been adopted by people who are not qualified doctors.

An *optician* specialises in lenses and glasses. The word comes through French from the Medieval

Latin *optica*, 'optics, the scientific study of light and vision', which goes back to the Greek *optos*, 'visible'. A *dispensing optician* makes and sells glasses according to the prescription of an oculist or ophthalmic optician. An *ophthalmic optician*, more highly trained, is qualified to test sight and prescribe glasses as well.

An *ophthalmic optician* is also, especially in North America, called an *optometrist*, a person qualified in *optometry*, 'the measuring (that is, the testing) of eyes'.

of   1. A common mistake, especially among children, is the use of *of* instead of *have*: × *I could of danced all night*. The confusion is no doubt due to the identical pronunciation in spoken English of *have* and *of*: an /əv/ sound common to *I could have danced* and *a pound of dates*. Even worse is × *if you'd of been here,* which means × *if you'd have been here,* which is still wrong: the correct form is *if you'd been here.*

2. The use of *of* in such sentences as ? *He always plays darts of a Friday evening* is now current only in dialect. In standard English it sounds somewhat old-fashioned: *on Friday evenings* is the idiomatic way of expressing it today.

3. *Of* is sometimes incorrectly omitted or needlessly inserted in certain simple constructions: you can say *a dozen eggs* but not, in formal English, × *a couple eggs* — the correct form is *a couple of eggs.* (See PLENTY 1.)

Obversely, *of* should be omitted from the sentences × *It was not too good of a shot* and × *How big of a house are you looking for?* And × *What colour of a dress?* should become *What colour dress?*

4. In longer sentences, *of* is again often wrongly omitted or inserted, but for different reasons. Writers and speakers might simply feel that a sentence is too complicated, and insert an *of* in order to 'simplify' it. On the other hand, if there is already an *of* or two in the sentence, another, necessary, *of* might simply be left out as being 'ugly' or 'repetitive'. And so on. Consider these examples:

× It is difficult to detect the difference between a petrol sample refined in the usual way from crude oil and of one obtained by the complicated 'Sasol' system from coal.

Here the *of* is inserted presumably in order to mark off the second element under discussion and set it apart from the first; but it is grammatically impermissible, and should be omitted. Similarly:

× I have now taken legal advice on our pro-

posed method of assessing and paying the lease, and of the freeholder's refusal to consider it.

The second *of* here is incorrect. The writer probably wanted to insert a preposition at that point — in order to take up the thread again of a rather complex sentence — and chose the preposition *of* because that was the last preposition he had used. But the grammatically appropriate preposition is *on*, not *of*: *taken legal advice . . . on the freeholder's refusal.* (See PARALLEL CONSTRUCTIONS.) Here now is a different kind of oversight:

? The junta's announcement was duly followed by the banning of independent newspapers and the organisation of protest movements.

There is an ambiguity here: was it *the organisation of protest movements* that emerged, or *the banning of . . . the organisation of protest movements*? If the former, the sentence should read *. . . and by the organisation . . .*; if the latter, it should read *. . . and of the organisation . . .* In fact, the latter meaning was almost certainly the one intended: the omission of a crucial *of*, however, probably out of fear that the sentence was in danger of being swamped by *of*'s, resulted in a far more serious danger — that of being misunderstood. Here now is another example of a missing *of*:

× They spoke to each other in French, the rudiments of which they both had a grasp.

Another *of* is needed here: *. . . in French, the rudiments of which they both had a grasp of,* or *. . . in French, of the rudiments of which they both had a grasp.* The single *of* in the sentence cannot serve both *grasp* and *which*. The writer obviously disliked the idea of using two *of*'s in the same clause: in that case, he could perhaps have said *. . . in French, of whose rudiments they both had a grasp.* (See WHO 1., WHICH 2.)

5. Of course, not all omissions of *of* are incorrect. There are two common ways of streamlining a construction by doing away with the *of*. The phrase *the theories of relativity,* for instance, might be reworded as *the relativity theories*; and the phrase *the theories of Einstein* might be reworded as *Einstein's theories.* In some cases, either form may be possible: *the theories of the Bow Group* might be reworded as *the Bow Group's theories* or *the Bow-Group theories.*

All of these forms are standard idiom today, but such revision is not always acceptable, and the *of* cannot be eliminated in all cases. (For the restrictions and the dangers, see -'s, -s' and PREPOSITIONS OMITTED.).

of course This innocent-looking and common phrase, when slipped into statements, produces a variety of subtle and intriguing effects. All too often it is used either unthinkingly or deviously — and has accordingly attracted considerable criticism.

There is an intuitive objection to it: if something is a matter *of course,* then why mention it at all? And if it is not a matter *of course,* then why call it one?

But language does not work that way — of course; it is a system, but not (of course) a completely logical system.

Here are some typical uses of *of course,* followed by explanations of their tone and function:

The white king cannot take the pawn, because he would then of course be moving into check.

(apologetic: 'I have to state the obvious just in order to make my account complete, or because it is a necessary link in the chain of a logical argument that I am spelling out.' To use *of course* here is not to insult the reader's intelligence; in fact, to omit the *of course* might be to insult the reader's intelligence.)

? The white king should not take the pawn, of course, because black would then advance his rook to QB4 and in two or three moves seriously erode white's defences down the central file.

(conspiratorial: 'I address myself to the initiated: it's obvious to *us*, isn't it?')

? I've read all your novels of course, and am very pleased to meet you at last.

(flattering: 'How could I fail to read such important works?')

We're all open-minded people, of course, but let us not flinch from scrutinising these new philosophies with full critical rigour.

(clearing away irrelevance: 'Our open-mindedness is immaterial to our duty now.')

? I'm a very open-minded person, of course, but I do find these new philosophies a lot of hocus-pocus.

(deceitful: 'I am not an open-minded person — hence my automatic disapproval.')

Of course you feel bitter — it's only natural.

(sympathetic: 'Don't feel guilty about feeling the way you do.')

Well of course if you use 250-watt bulbs you're going to blow a 3-amp fuse eventually.

(patronising or contemptuous: 'If you *will* do stupid things ...')

? Antony and Cleopatra would have spoken to each other in Greek, of course, though it was not Antony's native language.

? The other Orient, the Orient of the mind or of fantasy, is best represented by the sly little 'Odalisque' of Ingres. Ingres, of course, never visited the East, and would have considered the opportunity to do so, had it presented itself, as utterly beneath his dignity.

– Anita Brookner,
The Times Literary Supplement

(superior: 'Few people realise this — but to superior people like me it's second-nature to know such things.')

? We understand your problem. Of course we do. But put yourself in our position.

(wheedling or seductive: 'Accept our good faith — or even agree with us — in our refusal to oblige you.' *Of course* is used in this way, with a falling intonation, mainly in British English. The ploy is often successful, but it can antagonise a more strong-willed listener.)

?? Cardinal Mezzofanti had a reading knowledge of 164 languages, but he was of course surpassed by Sir John Bouring, sometime governor of Hong Kong, who could read over 200.

(outrageous: 'The very reverse of *of course* — this is an extremely esoteric piece of information; I'm certain you had no idea of it.')

Several of these uses are dubious, and the last in particular should be avoided. In general, stop to think before you write *of course* and limit its frequency in your conversation. In many people it represents an irritating conversational tic, much like *you know* or *um* or *actually.*

The same caution should be observed with words and phrases resembling *of course,* such as *clearly, naturally, obviously, needless to say,* and *as you know.*

off of This complex preposition is common in colloquial American English and in some British dialects: ✕ *I can't get the top off of this bottle.* It is nonstandard: *off* alone should be used here. The complex preposition *off of* is even less excusable when it supplants the simple *from*, and the simple preposition *off* is hardly better: ✕ *I borrowed the car off (of) my neighbour.*

official, officious As an adjective, *official* means primarily 'relating to office or a position of authority': *official duties*. It can also mean 'formal or ceremonial' — *an official banquet* — and 'authorised, based on proper authority': *official permission*.

The adjective *officious* suggests the opposite of proper authority. It means 'interfering, over-helpful, fussy': *an officious waiter*. The word has a distinctly negative or disapproving tone.

In its second sense, now little used, *officious* is again almost the opposite of *official*: in the language of diplomacy, *an officious statement* is an unofficial statement, a casual or unauthorised report that is not to be interpreted as official policy.

often Many people believe that the *t* in *often* should be pronounced because it is there in the spelling. The pronunciation /offtən/ is, however, far less commonly heard than /off'n/. The U (upper-class) pronunciation /awf'n/ now sounds rather old-fashioned, and is very uncommon among the younger generation.

The comparative and superlative forms *oftener* and *oftenest* are acceptable in standard English, but the compound forms *more often* and *most often* are more often used.

oh See O, OH.

O.K., okay The term *O.K.* originated in the United States about 150 years ago — how it originated is still a subject of much scholarly argument — but it cannot be regarded as an Americanism any longer. It is at home in most varieties of English today, and in many languages other than English as well.

The term is still restricted to informal usage, however, and it is unlikely that it will ever graduate to acceptable formal English (except in commercial usage, where it is used in various grading systems).

The form *O.K.*, with full stops, is still the commonest, though *OK* is bound to overtake it soon. The expanded form *okay* is preferable when the term is used as a verb — *She vetoed one or two of the details, but okayed the plan as a whole* (or *O.K.'d* or *OK'd*) — and also perhaps when the

adjective comes before the noun: *He's an okay guy — you can trust him.* (Contrast *That guy's O.K. — you can trust him.*) As an interjection, as an adverb, and as a noun, *O.K.* is the usual form: *O.K., I'll do it*; *It's working O.K. now*; *I'm just waiting for the O.K. from the control tower.*

The slang expression *K.O.*, 'to knock out' or 'a knockout', presents many of the same spelling problems. When used as a verb it is often spelt *kayo*: *I kayoed him in the third round* (or *K.O.'d* or *KO'd*).

okra, bhindi, lady's finger, gumbo These words refer to the tropical plant *Hibiscus esculentis*, or to its small, green, gummy, carrot-shaped pods, or to dishes made from the pods. The scope of each word is slightly different.

The word *okra*, pronounced /ōkrə/, comes from a West African language. It refers to the whole plant, or to its pods as used in cookery, or to a particular dish thickened with the pods — a soup or stew popular in Africa, the Caribbean, and the Southern United States. In the United States this dish is known as *gumbo* or *gombo*, a word originating in Louisiana French, in turn from a West African word, again introduced by slaves. This word *gumbo* can be used to refer to the plant or the pods as well. It is used too to refer to a type of sail, and to a dialect or creole spoken in Louisiana and the French West Indies.

Bhindi is the Hindi word for the okra plant or its pods, as used in Indian dishes.

Lady's fingers refers to the pods, raw or cooked. The term *ladies' fingers,* however (note the different spelling), refers to a completely unrelated plant, the kidney vetch.

older, oldest See ELDER.

omission of verbs The efficient functioning of English — of any language at all, in fact — relies to a great extent on the economical use of words. Not everything needs to be laboriously spelt out: two or more ideas may be grouped together. So, for example, the two ideas 'John is guilty, and Mary is guilty too', can be expressed in a variety of simpler ways: *John and Mary are guilty*; *John is guilty, and Mary is too*; *John is guilty, and Mary too.* Such omission of a word or words — *ellipsis,* as it is called — is not always so straightforward, unfortunately. Suppose the sentence were ⁇ *John is guilty, and his sisters too.* We cannot really 'understand' the omitted word *is* in the second part of the sentence, since this would produce the clause ✕ *his sisters is too.*

Nevertheless, some authorities consider the sentence acceptable: idiom seems to allow this leeway to the verb *to be* and the verb *to have* — provided that the sentence is fairly short, and that there is no change of tense halfway through.

Elsewhere, when a word would change its form if repeated, it should not be omitted. Verbs other than *be* and *have* should be repeated if they change from singular to plural or vice versa.

?? If John flees, and his sisters too, that would be further proof.

It would be far better to insert the plural verb *flee* (or the plural substitute verb *do*) after *sisters* here.

More unacceptable still is the omission of a verb when the tense changes in the course of the sentence. It is fine to say *No prisoner can or will escape,* but not to say:

✗ No prisoner has ever or will ever escape.

This should read:

No prisoner has ever escaped or will ever escape.

Similarly:

✗ Security here has always been very tight, and always will.

This should read:

Security here has always been very tight, and always will be.

Make sure too that the verb is repeated if idiom requires a different form to follow it in each case:

✗ No prisoner has ever tried, let alone succeeded, in escaping.

This should read:

No prisoner has ever tried to escape, let alone succeeded in escaping.

Finally, the verb should not be omitted if ambiguity might result:

? I trust John more than Maria.

The two possible meanings of this sentence are made clear once the missing words are restored:

I trust John more than I trust/do Maria.
I trust John more than Maria does.

See also PARALLEL CONSTRUCTIONS; SENTENCES; THAN 1.; THAT 3.

on the contrary, on the other hand *On the other hand* means 'however; from another point of view':

John was rich; his sister, on the other hand, was poor.

On the contrary typically means 'rather; quite the opposite':

John was not rich; on the contrary, he was poor.

Note that *on the other hand* seems to suggest a contrast between two different ideas (John as rich, his sister as poor), whereas *on the contrary* suggests a contradiction of a single idea — or rather, the reinforcement of that contradiction (John as not rich; i.e., John as poor).

It used to be possible — and perhaps still is — to use *on the contrary* in the same way as *on the other hand*, to mean simply 'however', so long as it was placed in the middle of the clause rather than at the beginning. So whereas it would be quite wrong to say:

✗ John was rich; on the contrary, his sister was poor

— it might be possible to say:

? John was rich; his sister, on the contrary, was poor.

This is not recommended, however: *on the other hand* is available and should be used here.

on to, onto 1. Some writers, publishers, and grammarians object to the one-word form *onto*. But if it serves simply as a preposition, meaning 'to a position on', *onto* would seem to have as much right to be a single word as *into* does.

They jumped onto the roof of the car.
They jumped into the boot of the car.

Purists, for some reason, still prefer *on to,* in British English, and if you want to avoid provoking them, use the two-word form by all means. Often enough, it will be possible and advisable to leave out either the *on* or the *to*: *imposing their views on (to) us*; *got slowly (on) to his feet.*

Where *on to* has to be kept unfused is where *on* expresses the idea of 'continuity', or where *to* is part of the infinitive, or both:

Keep right on to the end of the road.
He went on to fame and wealth.
He went on to succeed.

In each case the *on* clearly belongs more closely to what precedes than to what follows. Consider how the *on* and *to* might be separated by other words: *Keep right on (and you will come) to the end of the road.* Accordingly, it would be wrong to fuse the *on* and *to* when they do happen to be side by side.

A simple test is pronunciation: if the *to* is very weak, the spelling is likely to be *onto*; in *on to,* both words are pronounced clearly and distinctly, and there can even be a slight pause between them.

2. *Onto* has the modern sense of 'in contact with, in communication with': *The radio operator promised to get onto headquarters directly.* This is probably accepted as standard English now, though would not be suitable for the most formal contexts.

Possibly deriving from this sense is the colloquial sense of 'within reach of, on the trail of' — *? These latest experiments suggest that I'm really onto something* — or 'aware of the true nature of': *? She's onto his schemes.* Such constructions remain restricted to informal usage.

one **1.** The indefinite personal pronoun *one,* meaning 'a person, anyone', is a useful word in many ways, but it begins to sound affected if overused: *? If one wants to succeed, one needs to overcome one's scruples in dealing with one's rivals.*

There are various ways of rewording such a sentence: *If a person/anyone wants to succeed, he needs to overcome . . . ; If people want to succeed, they need to overcome . . . ; If you want to succeed, you need to overcome . . .* (see EVERYBODY; HE; THEY; YOU).

If you do begin a sentence with *one,* however, then stick to it. In British English, it is not really acceptable to switch pronouns in midstream:

✗ One can be sure only of one thing, and that is that [human nature] will never cease to have a surprise in store for you.
— Somerset Maugham,
'A Man With a Conscience'

In American English, this is fairly acceptable, and it is almost fully acceptable to slip from *one* into *he, him,* and *his* — but once again, not in British English:

✗ Maycomb's proportion of professional people ran high; one went there to have his teeth pulled, his wagon fixed, his heart listened to, his money deposited, his soul saved, his mules vetted.
— Harper Lee (U.S.),
To Kill a Mockingbird

✗ Ultimately such seeking becomes the subject matter of fiction. Observing, reading, think-

ing, one invents himself . . . In essence, one doesn't teach writing; he encourages talented people . . . One pays for free thought in the wrong cause . . . if it falls like a hammer blow on the head as one is attempting to work out his fiction.
— Bernard Malamud (U.S.),
Introduction to *Selected Stories*

The following example shows an extraordinary mixture of pronouns: *one* is lumped together with *they, you,* and *I:*

✗ I suppose every writer feels there is something they would like to say — that's on the tip of one's tongue — about one's experience and understanding of the world. Then you finish something, and realise it's still there — unsaid, waiting to be said. In that way, I am just as ambitious: to get it said.
— Michael Frayn,
quoted in *The Observer*

Of course, if *one* is used as a pronoun referring to a specific person, then it is not a mistake to use *he* and *his* afterwards:

The three brothers inherited £10,000 each: one spent his share on a plot of land, and he soon became a successful farmer; the second deposited his share in a bank . . .

2. *One* can sound even more affected if used in the place of *I* or *we.* Public figures and upper-class people generally in Britain, out of a mistaken sense of modesty perhaps, often try to avoid first-person pronouns and adjectives, only to fall into such awkward statements as *? One's work schedule can really exhaust one, so of course one is always looking forward to one's holidays.* How much more elegant, and how much friendlier, to use *I, me,* and *my* in such sentences!

Here is another example:

My uncle Giles . . . was a relation: a being who had in him perhaps some of the same essence that went towards forming oneself as a separate entity. Would one's adult days be spent in worrying about the Trust?
— Anthony Powell,
A Question of Upbringing

3. Where *one* is used in the sense of 'a person or thing of a type already mentioned', there is a traditional restriction regarding its use. The plural form *ones* should preferably not be used directly after *these, those,* or *many,* or directly after numbers (*two, four,* and so on): *Do you want* *these crayons as well as those* is considered stylistically better, especially in American English, than *?Do you want these crayons as well as those ones?* There is no such problem in the singular: *Do you want this crayon as well as that one?* is perfectly all right. And when an intervening adjective is present, the objection to *ones* falls away too: *Do you want these crayons as well as those red ones?*

4. Increasingly, *one* is being used to refer to something that has *not* been explicitly mentioned previously: *Nice one, Cyril* (referring perhaps to a goal in a soccer match). In the following example, the first *one* is used in place of the unstated noun *question*:

?So how can those inside the national camp now want to join forces with the suspect and unpatriotic people who are outside that camp? Likud has an answer to that one. The Government of National Unity it has in mind is one which would be dominated by 'the ideology of Likud'.
— Conor Cruise O'Brien,
The Observer

This peculiar idiom has very little to recommend it: it smacks of laziness, and can be vague or even ambiguous; many people find it irritating. Use the precise word or phrase that you mean in the first instance; *one* is a suitable replacement only when you want to repeat the word or phrase — the second *one* in the quotation above, for instance, is helpful in saving the writer from having to repeat the cumbersome phrase *Government of National Unity*.

5. The construction *one of those who* or *one of the Xs that* often presents the writer or speaker with a problem: does the verb that follows go into the singular or the plural? — *She is one of the finest artists that has/have ever exhibited here.* The answer is — the plural: *who* or *that* refers not to *one,* but to *those* or *the Xs.*

The above example could be reworded to read *Of all the artists that have exhibited here, she is one of the finest* — and the verb forms become clear. The following quotations illustrate the correct and the incorrect forms.

I have not abandoned literature; nor shall I do so, for I am, after all, one of those who think that the divorce between language and literature should never have taken place.
— Eric Partridge,
The Gentle Art of Lexicography

Raymond was one of those rare people who not only derive great pleasure from organising

events, but also are forlornly bad at doing it.
— Ian McEwan, *First Love, Last Rites*

× Herbert Morrison, the Home Secretary who decided to release the Mosleys, is one of the few men who comes out of the affair with some credit.
— A.J.P. Taylor, *The Observer*

× If you are one of those listeners who is alternately worried and puzzled by the state of modern English, or who writes to the Pronunciation Unit, or to *Speak Out!*, Dick Leith's perspective will interest, explain and perhaps even reassure.
— Professor David Crystal,
The Listener

The following quotation is a further good example of the correct usage. In two successive sentences, the phrase *one of the mysteries* is used. In the first of the sentences, *one* is the subject of the verb that follows (and the verb is accordingly in the singular). In the second sentence, however, the word *mysteries* is the subject of the verb that follows (and the verb is accordingly in the plural):

One of the mysteries of our time is the sight of fat wallets and overfed infants as more and more go on the dole. It is one of the mysteries which confront Ms Bainbridge on her travels.
— Anthony Burgess, *The Observer*

6. The construction *one in two/three/four ...* (or *one out of two ...*) also poses a problem — can the verb go into the plural, or must it go into the singular? — *One in five babies suffer/suffers from serious parental neglect.* The experts differ here. Some feel that the plural form (*suffer*) sounds more natural and is in a way more logical, since obviously thousands of babies are under discussion.

Nevertheless, the grammar of the sentence does strictly require the singular form (*suffers*), since the subject *one* is singular: *Only one in three of the workers is satisfied with his pay and conditions,* rather than *? Only one in three of the workers are satisfied with their pay and conditions.*

? Only one in five of the young people who have applied to take up Youth Training Scheme places in the Armed Forces have been accepted, according to figures released yesterday by the Ministry of Defence.
— Barrie Clement, *The Times*

? Divorces, which before the Second World

War numbered between 5,000 and 10,000 annually, now top 170,000, one in every three marriages ultimately break up and seven of every ten of these involve children.
— Professor Anthony Clare, *The Listener*

But the problem can be avoided by rephrasing the sentence. Such constructions are all rather awkward in any case, and would almost always benefit from rewording.

The first two examples above read and sound better when worded as *One baby in five suffers from serious parental neglect* and *Only one worker in three is satisfied with his pay and conditions.*

In the third example the second *have* can become *has.* Or the whole sentence could be re-cast, perhaps as *Only twenty per cent of the young people who have applied . . . have been accepted . . .* (See PER CENT; PLURALS Part II.)

7. A common but faulty construction is: × *one of the greatest, if not the greatest, Xs . . .* : × *She is one of the greatest, if not the greatest, artists to exhibit here.*

× *El Cid . . .* remains one of the finest, if not the finest, epics ever made. The roles of the eponymous hero and his Chimène seem to define Charlton Heston and Sophia Loren.
— Gavin Millar, *The Listener*

The plural *epics* here is suitable for *one of the finest,* but not for *the finest,* which requires instead the singular *epic: one of the finest epics, if not the finest epic, ever made.* (See PARALLEL CONSTRUCTIONS.) It is perhaps acceptable to leave out *epic* in this reworded version, so long as *epics* remains in front of *the finest: one of the finest epics, if not the finest, ever made.*

See also ANYONE; EACH OTHER.

one another See EACH OTHER.

only **1.** In the placing of *only* in a sentence, idiom is in conflict with logic. The idiomatic usage, when modifying the predicate of a sentence, is to place the *only* between the subject and the verb: *I only drink water; She can only see you for five minutes.* The 'logical' usage, on the other hand, is to position the *only* as near as possible to the word or phrase it relates to, usually just next to it: *I drink only water; She can see you for only five minutes/for five minutes only.*

The objection to the idiomatic usage is that it can be ambiguous and misleading. The purist might argue that saying *I only drink water* amounts to saying *I never wash — the only thing I ever do with water is drink it.*

The proponent of idiomatic usage would counter by saying that only an overingenious fool would give a simple sentence such a complicated meaning; that the shifting of *only* produces a stilted, unnatural-sounding, and sometimes discourteous sentence; that in spoken English no ambiguity is possible, since intonation directs the listener to the intended meaning; that many common idioms *cannot* be recast in the purist's 'logical' form — *In what can only be described as a massacre . . .* ; *She only laughed louder; I can only say that I disagree* — and that in any case, the idiomatic form *is* perhaps grammatical, since there is in fact a subtle grammatical rule justifying it.

That rule would be something like this: in spoken sentences, where the *only* is placed, as usual, before or within the verb group, it applies to whatever part of the sentence is most strongly pronounced. In the case of a written sentence (disregarding any context), the *only* will be taken to apply to the part of the sentence that would be most strongly pronounced if the sentence were read out in the most neutral way. That part of the sentence is typically the last important phrase in it. So, take the following written sentences:

John only writes.
John only writes sonnets.
John only writes sonnets on Sundays.

Only will be taken to apply to *writes* in the first, to *sonnets* in the second, and to *on Sundays* in the third. Suppose you wanted, instead, to make the third written sentence imply that John does not write *limericks* on Sundays: you could then re-word it in a number of different ways. You could write:

John writes only sonnets on Sundays.

Or, to be absolutely clear and idiomatic (though somewhat long-winded), you might write:

The only poems John writes on Sundays are sonnets.

Or else you might write:

John only writes *sonnets* on Sundays.

(This use of italics corresponds to a stress in speech. It is often considered a sign of an inflexible or immature style, however, and should as a rule be avoided when alternative wordings are available, as in the other two versions above.)

To take another example: consider the sentence *I swam seven lengths.* If *only* were introduced into the sentence, it would most probably relate to *seven lengths*. The sentence might then be worded in any one of three ways:

a. I swam seven lengths only (rather awkward and unnatural, but unambiguous).

b. I swam only seven lengths (slightly formal still, perhaps; again unambiguous).

c. I only swam seven lengths (the most idiomatic and natural way of expressing it, though not the most logical).

The purist's objection to sentence *c.* is that it could be misunderstood. Without cues from intonation (when spoken) or context (when written), the sentence might be taken to mean any of the following:

i. I only *swam* seven lengths (I didn't use the canoe).

ii. *I* only swam seven lengths (the other swimmers couldn't manage that many).

iii. I swam only *seven* lengths (I couldn't manage any more).

The proponent of the idiomatic rule would insist that sentence *c.* could be understood only in sense *iii.*, and that senses *i.* and *ii.* would in ordinary English be expressed by different sentences. Sense *ii.*, in which *only* relates to the subject *I,* would be expressed by either of the following sentences:

d. Only I swam seven lengths.
e. I alone swam seven lengths.

Sense *i.*, in which *only* relates to the verb *swam,* would be expressed by a drastically recast sentence, such as:

f. I covered the seven lengths solely by swimming.

A few further points to note in the argument between the idiomatic and the 'logical' wording: first, it seems that the misplaced *only* attracts criticism only when it is positioned just before the verb or within a complex verb group, but not when it is in other 'illogical' positions. Consider these three sentences:

g. I only like Riesling with fish.
h. I like Riesling only with fish.
j. I like Riesling with fish only.

The third sentence here is certainly logical, but sounds rather pedantic. The second is just as 'illogical' as the first — a computer might assume it referred to Riesling *with*, but not *on*, fish. Fortunately, people know more about language than computers do, so nobody objects to the second sentence. But if nobody objects to the second

sentence, why should anybody object to the first? After all, everybody knows that all three sentences express the same basic idea.

Then, the minds of purists might be put at rest by the consideration that *only* is often put before a verb for reasons of rhythm. English likes a sentence rhythm based on the alternation of stressed and unstressed syllables. This rhythm is maintained in sentence *g.* (**only like**) and perhaps in sentence *h.* (**on**ly with **fish**), but not in the 'correct' sentence *j.* (with **fish on**ly), where two stressed syllables come together.

Finally, there is more to language than the literal meaning of the propositions it expresses. As linguists have pointed out, a sentence with *only* placed before a verb can be more modest and polite than one with *only* in another position. The sentence *I can only lend you a pound* sounds somewhat more cordial than the 'correct' but brusque *I can lend you only a pound*: the first version, but not the second, can be paraphrased as 'The only thing I can do (alas!) is lend you a pound.'

The following two quotations illustrate the debate between the idiomatic and the purist views of *only.* Paradoxically, the more conservative approach is taken by a British Labour MP, Ian Mikardo, and the rather more liberal view by a British Conservative MP, the late Angus Maude. First, Mr Mikardo's version of the purist view, which was provoked by the wording of a subsection of a parliamentary Bill. The controversial wording was as follows:

'An authorisation may only be given under Section One above for a period not exceeding seven days.'

Mr Mikardo objected:

Only should not stand after the word *may* but should appear after the word *above* ... The phrase *Drink to me only with thine eyes* contains a perfect example of the right use of the word *only,* because it says *Drink to me only with thine eyes* and not *Drink to me with a pint of bitter!* Had it said *Only drink to me with thine eyes,* as is the formulation in the clause, that would mean 'Only drink to me but don't wink at me with your eyes'. The word *only* qualifies the phrase that immediately follows it, and it is in the wrong place on this occasion.

   – Ian Mikardo, in the minutes of a
Commons Select Committee considering
the Police and Criminal Evidence Bill

(In fact, Mr Mikardo should have spotted that

Drink to me only with thine eyes is ambiguous. The *only* could be taken to refer to the word or phrase that immediately precedes it, as well as to the one that immediately follows it. In addition to Mr Mikardo's interpretation, the line could mean 'Drink to me only, and not to anyone else'.)

A more liberal view, favourable to the idiomatic usage, was voiced by Mr Maude in the course of a radio broadcast:

> I did — and still do — question my father's puristic dictum on the placing in a sentence of the word *only*. Of course it's perfectly true that if you say to someone, *I can only lend you a pound,* you are talking nonsense. There are all sorts of other things you can do, such as not lending him anything, or walking away, or sending for the police or even punching him on the nose. Still, I don't think many people would actually say, *I can lend you only a pound.* In writing, perhaps; in speaking, no.
>
> — Angus Maude,
> 'Words', BBC Radio 3

Here is a selection of quotations bearing out Mr Maude's idiomatic preference:

> The direct conflict of opinions . . . could only be settled, if at all, between the President and myself.
>
> — Winston Churchill,
> *Triumph and Tragedy*

> Once upon a time Aristotle, who only pronounced upon nature when he was sure of the truth of his statements, asserted *natura non facit saltis,* thus upholding the unbroken chain of causality. 'Nature does not do anything in jumps.'
>
> — Lawrence Durrell,
> *The Fiction Magazine*

> Answer, 'Yes, I must say I like to be able to taste the botanicals, which means I like the taste of gin, I suppose. Of course, a lot of people only like the effect.'
>
> — Kingsley Amis,
> *The Art of Drinking*

> He is surely one of the most remarkable figures whom even that great college has produced. His affection for Oxford is only rivalled by Oxford's for him.
>
> — Lord Blake, *The Times*

> Some of his best work, lyrical as well as musical, can only be known to a generation, like mine, which saw the shows — in Lon-

don, on Broadway, even in Manchester try-outs.
>
> — Anthony Burgess, *The Observer*

> These simple paradoxes once had an arresting ring to them, now they seem so glib as to be entirely divorced from truth. The fact remains, however, that clichés only became clichés because they were based on recognisable truth.
>
> — Peter Ustinov,
> *We Were Only Human*

> The trouble, Mr Goldwyn, is that you are only interested in art and I am only interested in money.
>
> — George Bernard Shaw, quoted in
> Philip French's *The Movie Moguls*

And here is another selection of examples, this time favouring Mr Mikardo's careful and logical positioning of *only*:

> Khrushchev, under Stalin, was a comic bit-player who emerged in his true colours only after the tyrant's death and at a very late stage in his own career.
>
> — David Watt, *The Times*

> If the Greeks can defeat Denmark in Athens then England can go through to the last eight of the European Championship in Paris next year . . . the fact remains that England can go to Paris only by courtesy of the sons of Hellene.
>
> — Peter Corrigan, *The Observer*

> Some families, deprived of food and water for days, managed to survive only with the help of emergency rations from the United Nations.
>
> — Shyam Bhatia, *The Observer*

> American intelligence had intercepted a message from the Libyan government ordering its London embassy to fire on the demonstrators. British officials said only that they had received no 'specific' warning prior to the shooting.
>
> — *Newsweek* (U.S.)

> Quine the Swine. Guilty of killing Quilty. Oh, my Lolita. I have only words to play with.
>
> — Vladimir Nabokov, *Lolita*

All the quotations above are acceptable on one basis or the other — the idiomatic or the puristic approach. The idiomatic constructions are not really ambiguous; the puristic constructions are not especially stilted or ungainly. This next example uses first an idiomatic 'incorrect' *only*, then a purist's *only* — also sounding perfectly idiomatic.

> Parents on governing bodies are useless if they can only think about Tommy's problem areas; they work only if they're prepared to spend long afternoons agonising over the school boiler or the inspectorate in their own child's last hot summer term.
> – Katharine Whitehorn, *The Observer*

Sometimes, however, the purist will stray into an unacceptably awkward construction, and the idiomatic writer will stray into unacceptable ambiguity. Here is an example of the purist approach taken to extremes:

?? Lampreys are a good fish. The fleshier, richer, more mackerel taste distinguishes them from eel. Red wine and leeks are just what they need to set them off. The very similar lampern are found on only fishermen's tables, robed in parsley sauce.
– Jane Grigson, *The Observer*

(It would be far preferable idiomatically to move the *only* to a position immediately before or after the word *found*. And if this goes against your purist nature, the *only* could be moved to after *tables*. But it is unacceptably jarring in its present 'correct' position.)

And here, conversely, are some examples of thoughtless idiomatic usage that does veer into ambiguity, and might well be misunderstood, at least temporarily:

? At any rate I will only send you a guinea with which to rebuild your college if you can satisfy me that you will use it to produce the kind of society, the kind of people that will help to prevent war.
– Virginia Woolf, *Three Guineas*

(The reader probably realises that the *only* is not intended to relate to *send*, and duly assumes that it relates to *guinea*, only to realise later that its proper place is before the *if*-clause.)

? Think of those dozens of English poets who only chanced on the inspired lyric two, maybe three, at most six times during the course of their lives.
– Paul Bailey, *The Observer*

(The reader initially takes the *only* to apply to *chanced* — as though *the inspired lyric* were in each case a fluke. It would be far less confusing were the *only* shifted to a place just in front of

the phrase it does in fact relate to: *two, maybe three, at most six times*.)

? It will not do to argue that Scott was attempting only to portray the British in India, and that such was the nature of imperialist society that the Indians *would* only have had bit parts.
– Salman Rushdie, *The Observer*

(The natural idiomatic position of the first *only* here is before *attempting*. This would certainly have been misleading, and so the writer has shifted the *only* — but he has not shifted it far enough. It now appears to relate to *portray*, where it once again causes the reader momentary confusion. The correct position for *only* is directly in front of *the British*, which is what it does in fact relate to. The second *only* is in the standard idiomatic position — just before the verb *have had* — though a purist would shift it to the more logical position just before the noun phrase *bit parts*.)

× The Constitution requires that anyone chosen by the President to fill a cabinet post ... must be questioned at hearings of an appropriate Senate Committee, since all such nominees can only be confirmed in the appointment with the advice and consent of the Senate.
– Alistair Cooke, 'Letter from America', BBC Radio 4

(A classic case of the misleading positioning of *only* — though the text was written for broadcast, not for print, and the intonation of the sentence when spoken made it clear what the author intended. With *only* in its present position, the sense seems to be that nominees cannot be disputed or rejected by the Senate, only confirmed. The true meaning, of course, is almost the opposite: that the Senate has full power to reject a nominee. The correct wording would involve shifting the *only* to the position in front of the *with,* so that the text would now read ... *all such nominees can be confirmed in the appointment only with the advice and consent of the Senate.*)

The same considerations apply to *merely,* and sometimes to *solely* as well. They also apply to *even* and *just,* though few people object to putting *just* before a verb: *I just want to borrow two dollars* sounds natural, whereas *I want to borrow just two dollars* might sound distinctly odd.

● *Recommendation* The idiomatic positioning of *only* — detached from its referent — is appropriate in ordinary speech and relaxed writing, so long as no dangerous ambiguity is caused. The more logical positioning of *only* favoured by the purist is appropriate in formal contexts, so long as it does not sound jarringly unnatural.

Sometimes *only* may be unsatisfactory in any position. You would then have to rephrase the sentence drastically to convey the right meaning and emphasis.

2. *Only* as a conjunction is a useful word, more or less equivalent to *but* or *except that*: *You're always saying you love me, only you never show me any real affection; We were planning a picnic, only it suddenly turned very chilly.*

It is still slightly casual or colloquial, however, and is best avoided in strictly formal contexts. Note that there is no need for a comma after *only,* though there is always a comma (or semicolon, colon, dash, or full stop) before it. If there is any danger of ambiguity, however, the comma after *only* should be inserted: *? Everyone seems to like me, only you never show me any real affection.* This might be taken to mean 'You are the only person who never shows me any real affection'. If the *only* is intended to mean 'but' here, it should have a comma after it, and preferably a semicolon in front of it. In fact, when *only* follows a semicolon, colon, dash, or full stop, it should be followed by the comma in turn.

> When you think of the unhealthy amount of sugar even in things like baked beans, ... then you realise that the man who makes a scene because his 'morning picked mushrooms' came out of a tin is someone we truly need. Only, if the food fusspot is to be considered necessary, he must not just stop at taste.
> — Katharine Whitehorn, *The Observer*

(Note the idiomatic but 'illogical' position of *just* in the last sentence.)

3. The combination *only too* is increasingly popular, and is useful in the right place:

> A full-scale war between the neighbouring states now looks only too probable.
> He has a martyr-complex, and is only too willing to lay down his life for some cause or other.
> That habitual criminal may feign penitence, but he is only too ready to steal or defraud again.

In each case, the *only too* carries a hint of excess or disproportion.

Unfortunately, *only too* is now being used in a looser way, and is approaching very closely the meaning of *very* or *extremely:*

? No need to thank me — I'm only too glad to be of service.
? He's only too willing to lend you money.

If you stop to think about it, you can see that these sentences, if understood literally, contain an insult rather than a reassurance. In formal contexts at least, this careless use of *only too* should be avoided: the sentences would read more convincingly if they were worded *very glad* or *quite willing* instead.

A useful hint is that *only too* is more appropriate when it can be replaced by *all too (A full-scale war ... looks all too probable)* than when it cannot be, as in ? *I'm only too glad* (very glad) *to lend you money.* The hint is an apt one because *all too* has negative connotations, whereas *very* is neutral.

See also AMBIGUITY; NOT ONLY.

opportunity There are two possible constructions after *opportunity*. You can have an opportunity *to* do something, or an *opportunity for* (doing) something: *This is an ideal opportunity to further your career*; *This is an ideal opportunity for furthering your career.*

Compare OCCASION.

opposite As a noun, *opposite* is followed by *of* — *The opposite of good is bad* — though *to* is sometimes heard in casual speech. As an adjective, it can be followed by *to* or *from*: *His ideas on the subject are opposite to mine/from mine.*

Opposite can also be used as a preposition: *the house opposite mine.* Here it would also be correct, though less common, to have *the house opposite to mine.*

optician See OCULIST.

optimism, optimistic, pessimism, pessimistic
Optimism and *pessimism* refer primarily to states of mind or dispositions — the human tendency to look on the bright side of things or to expect the best possible outcome, and the opposing tendency to take a gloomy view of things or to expect the worst possible outcome. The words refer also to various philosophical theories — that we live in the best/worst possible world, or that the world is getting better/worse continuously.

Optimistic and *pessimistic* have corresponding adjectival senses, chiefly 'expecting a favourable outcome, having a hopeful outlook' and 'expecting an unfavourable outcome'.

The four words are today widely used in extended senses. Purists tend to object to these uses: the words are often only impressive-sounding synonyms of *cheerfulness* or *gloominess*, for instance: *? plunged into a mood of blackest pessimism*; or of *hopeful*, *lack of hope*, or the like: *? We are optimistic that help is on its way*; *? There is no cause for pessimism*; or of *encouraging* or *discouraging*: *? optimistic signs of a recovery*; *? a pessimistic report of a breakdown in negotiations*; or of *overestimated* or *over-hopeful*: *? a wildly optimistic forecast*.

On the other hand, there are circumstances in which the extended senses of *optimistic* and *pessimistic* are more appropriate than any alternative. You might well call a medical report *encouraging*, but you would hardly want to call it *gloomy*. Besides, a *gloomy medical report* is in a way ambiguous: it could refer either to a patient's present condition or to the likely outlook of his illness. A *pessimistic medical report* not only is an appropriate phrase stylistically, but also focuses on the future course of the patient's illness.

As for *optimistic*, it is difficult to imagine any substitute for it in the following quotation:

With no expectation of substantially increased funding from central Government, the Arts Council has turned its hopes towards local authorities, issuing 'challenges' to them to match its funding, at least in part, whether from their own resources or from locally raised funds. These challenges are proving hopelessly optimistic. Local authorities — notoriously modest in their support for the arts — now have a legitimate excuse for not cooperating.

– Joan Bakewell, *The Observer*

For want of a suitable replacement for *optimistic* here, the entire construction would have to be changed, to something like *These challenges are proving impossible to meet* or *People have shown themselves very reluctant to take up these challenges*. The author perhaps had both interpretations in mind, and found the word *optimistic* a succinct means of conveying them.

That said, it is still always worth checking your own use of *optimism*, *pessimistic*, and so on. They often sound rather affected, and should not be allowed to oust *hopeful*, *discouraging*, or the like if these words properly represent the sense you intend.

optimum, optimal These words are now in fashionable — and incorrect — use as synonyms

of *best*. Their meaning is subtler than that: they refer to the best possible or best available in the given conditions; 'most advantageous, or most favourable' is the standard definition:

The optimal exposure, given that you haven't got a suitably fast film, is one-tenth of a second.

Optimum is a noun as well as an adjective; it means 'the most favourable condition, degree, or amount' — for the efficient functioning of a machine, the flourishing of a plant, and so on. It does not mean 'maximum': a helicopter might carry a *maximum* of 300 litres of petrol, but the *optimum* — balancing the extra weight involved in carrying fuel against the risk of running out of fuel — would almost always be less than the *maximum*.

The plural of *optimum* can be either *optima* or *optimums*.

optometrist See OCULIST.

or 1. If *or* connects two or more singular nouns as the subject of a clause, that subject remains singular and requires a singular verb:

He is such a light sleeper that even a dripping tap or distant birdsong or the creaking of the roof is enough to wake him up.

It has become a cliché to say that laughter and tears are not entirely incompatible, while many's the bad play in which hero or heroine passes the same reflection about love and hatred.

– Peter Ustinov,
We Were Only Human

— *is*, not *are*. Here is an example of the common mistake — using the plural verb instead of the singular:

× All the summer weeks of their first meeting she had felt in a state of complete liberation from guilt. Moral or social censure were meaningless.

– Muriel Spark,
The Mandelbaum Gate

Of course, if *and* rather than *or* links singular nouns, they become jointly a plural noun, and require a plural verb.

If all the nouns connected by *or* are plural nouns, then a plural verb is needed, of course. But suppose the nouns are a mix of singular and plural — the standard advice then is that the verb follows the lead of the noun nearest to it:

Even dripping taps or distant birdsong is enough to wake him up.
Even distant birdsong or dripping taps are enough to wake him up.

2. Similarly, when *or* connects pronouns, it is the pronoun nearest to the verb that determines the form of that verb, in theory at least:

? You or he is responsible for this!
? Are you or he responsible for this?

Such constructions are not very elegant, however, and in practice the structure is likely to be unravelled a bit:

One of you is responsible for this!
Are you responsible for this, or is he?

3. A further problem occurs when *or* combines a singular male noun and a singular female noun. Consider the complications in a passage such as this:

Each boy or girl must stretch his or her right hand forward before he or she makes his or her first step to the right.

To change *his or her* to a simple *his* is impossible here, though it has been recommended after *everyone, anyone,* and other general pronouns. And to change *his or her* to *their* might be considered ungrammatical. It is best to avoid the problem altogether, if possible — by casting the whole sentence in the second person, for example: *You must stretch your right hand forward* . . . .
For a more detailed discussion, see HE OR SHE; THEY; YOU.

4. As with *and, or* can be replaced by a comma between any two elements in a list, usually with the exception of the last two. So, it is just as correct to say *A, B, C, or D* (the last comma is optional) as to say *A or B or C or D,* and it is more natural to say so (unless you want to secure some special emphasis by using *or* each time).
This is only true, however, if *A, B, C,* and *D* all have the same status in grammar. Suppose the four elements are not equal alternatives, however: there may be only two main elements, and one of these may be divided in turn into three sub-elements as in the following sentence:

✗ She could resign, go mad, run away, or she could grit her teeth and carry on working.

What is needed here is an extra *or* before *run away,* to distinguish the three grammatically equivalent elements *resign, go mad,* and *run away* from one another, before distinguishing all of them as a group from the gramatically (and

practically) different element *she could grit her teeth and carry on working.*
Sometimes, for special effect, the *or* is omitted entirely from a sequence, resulting in the pattern *A,B,C,D*:

In those examples I have scamped, not distorted, the evidence. One could discourse for an hour, two hours, a day, on the ramifications of English *cow* or those of Latin *uidēre*. But I'm no sadist.
— Eric Partridge,
A Charm of Words

5. *Or* can be used freely as the opening word of a sentence. Such use has not attracted the blanket criticism, even from pedants, that the use of *and* has when it begins a sentence. Or so it seems. And any such blanket criticism would be quite wrong-headed.
6. *or* vs *nor.* Take care, in *neither ... nor* sentences, not to use *or* mistakenly for *nor*:

✗ She was on a treadmill, neither wanting to work so hard or able to stop working so hard.

In certain other negative sentences *or* is an acceptable alternative to *nor*:

She did not want to continue working so hard nor/or stop working so hard.

But make quite sure that the negative force of the first part is properly transferred, by grammatical parallels, to the second part; if not, *nor* rather than *or* must be used:

✗ She could see no end to the work, or bear to do any more of it.

In the first clause, the word *no* relates not to the verb *see,* but to the noun *end,* and so it cannot be extended to the verb *bear* in the second clause: the *or* should therefore be changed to *nor,* or else the structure of the first clause should be changed:

She could see no end to the work, nor bear to do the work.
She could not see an end to the work, or bear to do the work.

See NOR for a further discussion of this danger.

oral See AURAL.

ordinance, ordnance, ordonnance An *ordinance* is a decree, statute, or enactment: *municipal ordinance no. 23.* The word can also refer to a religious rite, especially Holy Communion, and to any long-established custom.

Ordnance is military weaponry: artillery and ammunition. (The British Ordnance Survey maps were originally drawn up by the artillery department of the army.)

Ordonnance is an old variant of *ordinance*. It developed into a formal word for the systematic arrangement of a literary or artistic composition or architectural plan. The poet Coleridge spoke of the difference *between the ordonnance of poetic composition and that of prose.*

The words all go back to the Latin *ordo*, 'order or arrangement'. Their pronunciations are hardly distinguishable, though in theory *ordinance* has an /i/ after the *d*, *ordonnance* an /ə/, and *ordnance* no vowel sound at all. *Ordonnance* can also be pronounced in a French way, especially when referring to decrees in French history.

orient, orientate　The word *orient* comes from the Latin *oriens*, meaning 'rising'. It is applied to the quarter of the earth (or heavens) from which the sun appears to rise, and often means 'the countries of the East'. When the noun refers specifically to countries, rather than generally or poetically to the East, it is spelt with a capital *O*: *the increasing economic strength of the Orient.*

The phrase *orient pearl*, referring to a particularly high-quality and brilliant pearl that comes from the East, has given rise to an adjectival sense of *orient*, especially in poetry — 'shining, brilliant'. (This is reinforced by the original Latin association with the rising sun.) The dominant meaning of the adjective *orient* is still 'eastern', however, though the word is seldom used in this way. *Oriental* is the usual adjective.

The verb *to orient* originally meant 'to place facing east', and applied especially to the building of churches along an east-west axis, as though directed towards the Holy Land. This was extended to mean 'to place anything in a particular relation to any point of the compass', as in *The swimming pool was oriented north to south.* Figuratively, it means 'to familiarise (a person) with new circumstances', or 'to guide in a particular direction': *Once oriented to the mysteries of college life, you will feel quite at home*; *She oriented her behaviour towards whatever subculture seemed to be in vogue.*

To orient is often used in the pattern *to orient oneself*, which means 'to get one's bearings' or 'to put oneself in the right position, or in a favourable relation to a goal or context': *She oriented herself by a familiar landmark.*

In its past participle form, *oriented*, it is widely used today to mean 'inclined towards, interested in': *? He was very much arts-oriented, but his parents insisted that he study medicine.*

I hesitate to vulgarise this splendid Tawney prose but what this means in the deplorable modern vernacular is that Labour's campaign should be more customer-oriented.
– David Watt, *The Times*

As this citation makes clear, the usage is often frowned on as a lazy and inelegant shortcut. It does have the virtue of conciseness, but in formal contexts it is best replaced by a paraphrase such as *specialising in*, *inclined towards*, *concentrating on*, or the like.

The noun from *to orient* is *orientation*. It covers all the senses of the verb, referring to the positioning of a building, to self-adaptation, to introductory instruction, and so on.

A common variant of the verb *to orient* is *to orientate*. This is a back-formation; that is, it derives from the noun *orientation* rather than giving rise to it. (This does not mean that it is incorrect — many perfectly respectable words in English are formed in this way: *to laze* is a back-formation from *lazy*, *to edit* from *editor*, and so on.) In British English, *to orientate* is a very common form of the verb, especially when used without a direct object — *China is now orientating strongly towards Europe* — and as a past participle: *correctly orientated at last*; *not exactly work-orientated.* In American English, however, *to orientate* is now less current than to *orient*, and may even be considered nonstandard.

The opposite of *to orient/orientate* is *to disorient/disorientate*. This means 'to lose or cause to lose one's bearings', either literally — one's sense of direction or location — or figuratively, referring to one's sense of self: *He remained quite disoriented/disorientated for months after the operation.*

Note the preferred pronunciations: *orient* as noun and adjective, /**aw**ri-ənt/; as verb, /**aw**ri-ent/; *oriental*, /**aw**ri-**en**t'l/; *orientate*, /**aw**ri-en-tayt, -ən-/.

orotund　See ROTUND.

ostensible, ostentatious, ostensive　All these adjectives go back to the Latin verb *ostendere*, 'to show, display'. *Ostentatious* means 'openly on display, pointedly conspicuous':

> ... that fear of seeing a revolution provoked by the ostentatious frivolity and extravagance of the highest classes.
> – Philip Magnus, *Edward VII*

The bower-birds of language outside the

specialist vocabulary pick up the pretty new word to decorate their discourse with. They tend to come from politics, journalism, and the other ostentatious professions.
– Philip Howard, *Weasel Words*

I was just about to ring again when I became aware that an eye was regarding me through the peep-hole in the door. How long it had been there, I didn't know. I felt embarrassed and uncertain whether to stare the eye out of its hole or merely pretend that I hadn't seen it. Ostentatiously, I examined the ceiling, the floor, the walls; then ventured a furtive glance to make sure that it had gone. It hadn't.
– Christopher Isherwood,
Mr Norris Changes Trains

Applied to people, *ostentatious* often means 'attention-seeking, showing off, pretentious'. It suggests displays of wealth or self-glorification: *an ostentatious life of lavish parties.*

The ideals of chivalry inspired almost all the secular literature of the age. Its greatest practitioners were ostentatiously feasted by kings, and showered with praise, medals and riches.
– Jonathan Sumption,
Sunday Telegraph

The related noun is *ostentation*:

Imagine me, reader, with my shyness, my distaste for any ostentation, my inherent sense of the *comme il faut,* imagine me masking the frenzy of my grief with a trembling ingratiating smile while devising some casual pretext to flip through the hotel register.
– Vladimir Nabokov, *Lolita*

Note the spelling of *ostentatious* or *ostentation*: three *t*'s, no *c*.
Ostensible means 'outwardly appearing to be so, alleged to be so; apparent':

'The Hypochondriac' is typical. The narrator is a doctor ... The ostensible motivation of the story is to explain the case of a young man who pesters him endlessly with imaginary complaints, of which he finally dies.
– Alan Hollinghurst,
The Times Literary Supplement

Ostensible usually implies deception – possible deception or certain deception according to the context. The statement *His ostensible intentions were honourable* suggests duplicity but does not

insist on it, whereas in the following example a clear contrast between assertion and actuality is being drawn:

The ostensible purpose of the meeting was to plan how the campaign for the last three weeks would be handled and that was hardly discussed at all.
– Arthur M. Schlesinger, Jr. (U.S.),
Robert Kennedy and His Times

The adverb *ostensibly* seems to be much commoner than the adjective *ostensible*: *The detective taped the suspect's voice while ostensibly talking about gardening.*

Then the warnings began, like the advance creakings of a seastorm in the rigging. The first came from Ned Quilley, a phone call much earlier in the day than was his custom, ostensibly to return one she had made to him the day before. But she knew at once it was something Marjory had ordered him to do the moment he got into the office.
– John le Carré,
The Little Drummer Girl

Do not confuse *ostensibly* with *ostensively*. *Ostensive*, in keeping with the Latin *ostendere*, means 'demonstrative' in the sense of 'showing by direct example'. An explanation of the word *red*, for instance, if printed in red ink would be an *ostensive* definition – showing what it describes; and to define the verb 'to point' ostensively, you would simply point. So: *The missionary's behaviour was ostensively a lesson in selflessness* is a compliment – he practises what he preaches; *The missionary's behaviour was ostensibly a lesson in selflessness* is not a compliment at all — it suggests motives that are actually selfish although they do not appear to be so.

other   See EACH OTHER.

other than   1. In the phrase *other than,* the word *other* is usually an adjective or pronoun:

He wants any paint other than that.
At no time was his recital anything other than quite magnificent.
Other than John, no one was there.
She is other than I thought.

Strictly speaking, *other than* should not be used when *other* would have to function as an adverb:

?He wants it painted in any way other than diagonally like that.

?At no time did he play other than magnificently.

These constructions are now well-established as standard idiom, however; it may be fully 'correct', grammatically speaking, to use the adverb *otherwise* rather than the adjective *other,* but the sentences then sound less idiomatic:

?He wants it painted in any way otherwise than diagonally like that.

?At no time did he seem to play otherwise than quite magnificently.

If you want to be both 'grammatical' and idiomatic, you will often have to choose a third structure:

He wants it painted any way except diagonally like that.

At no time did he play less than quite magnificently.

2. *Other than* is correct in such sentences as:

The cooking had no fault other than that the peas were overdone.

He made no sound at all other than an occasional grunt of satisfaction.

In both examples, *other* functions as an adjective qualifying *fault* and *sound.*

However, the following sentences are open to criticism because in them *other* no longer functions as an adjective:

?The peas were overdone; other than that, I cannot fault the cooking.

?He made no sound at all, other than emitting/to emit an occasional grunt of satisfaction.

The use of *other than* in these last two examples has by now become a well-established idiom. It does attract the criticism of some purists, but much less criticism than that which surrounds the dubious uses of *due to.* (See DUE TO.) However, if you wish to oblige the purists, replace *other than* with *apart from*: *apart from that*; *apart from emitting an occasional grunt.*

3. The combination *other ... than* is often replaced, in informal usage, by the combination *other ... but* or *other ... except,* especially in negative constructions:

?The child had no other shoes but those.

?She could do no other except submit meekly to his criticisms.

?Why do all other children except ours know how to tie their own shoelaces?

Widespread though such sentences are, they are still not accepted as standard: formal usage requires *other ... than.* Alternatively, leave out *other* altogether in favour of *but* or *except*: *no shoes but those*; *all children except ours.*

See also EACH OTHER; OTHERWISE 1.

otherwise **1.** *Otherwise,* as an adverb, is often used, after *and* or *or,* in combination with another adverb:

The members of the expedition set off reconnoitring, and after three hours each of them had — accurately or otherwise — drawn a map of the valley and returned to base.

This pattern has been extended, and, especially in British English, *otherwise* is now commonly found in combination with an adjective, noun, or verb instead of an adverb. Purists object to this development.

?Each member of the expedition succeeded in drawing a map — sophisticated or otherwise — of the valley.

?Each member of the expedition — whether cartographer or otherwise — was assigned to reconnoitre and map the valley.

?All the maps, sophisticated and otherwise, were exhibited at the reunion.

?All members of the expedition survived, whether they succeeded or otherwise in drawing a map.

These constructions are now so well-established, however, that they can be regarded as standard idiom, whether strictly grammatical or not. In fact, the more 'grammatical' version is far less acceptable idiomatically — the substituting of *other* for *otherwise*: ? *... succeeded in drawing a map — sophisticated or other — of the valley*; ? *Each member — whether trained cartographer or other — was assigned ...,* and so on. This sounds extremely old-fashioned. (And it cannot be used when *or otherwise* is used with a verb: *succeeded or not* is appropriate here.)

The telling objection to *otherwise* in the constructions is on stylistic grounds rather than grammatical grounds: the use of *otherwise* after *and* or *or* tends to sound flippant, or affected (as though the user would not stoop to using the simple word *not*), or lazy (as though the user could not be bothered to think of a proper antonym). Here are some possible rewordings of the examples above in a way less open to these criticisms:

Each member of the expedition succeeded in

drawing a map — sophisticated or rudimentary — of the valley

(or simply: *sophisticated or not*).

All the members of the expedition — cartographers and non-cartographers — were assigned to reconnoitre and map the valley

(or simply: *cartographers and others*).

All the maps, sophisticated and unsophisticated alike, were exhibited at the reunion

(or simply: *All the sophisticated and unsophisticated maps ...*).

See also OTHER THAN.

2. A more extreme criticism of the phrase *or otherwise* is that it is often inserted where there is no need to state any alternative at all. From an appropriate use of the phrase — as in

It is the navigator's duty to be aware that the flight is on schedule or otherwise

— it is all too easy to fall into an uneconomical, unnecessary use of the phrase:

? It is the navigator's duty to know whether the flight is on schedule or otherwise.

In the first example, the omission of *or otherwise* would be misleading — it might suggest that there is no alternative. In the second example, however, the word *whether* is enough to make it clear that there are at least two possibilities. It would be a slight improvement to say: *to know whether the flight is on schedule or not,* but the simplest and most efficient wording of all is to leave the alternative unstated — simply: *to know whether the flight is on schedule.*

3. When *otherwise* is used as a conjunction meaning 'or else' or 'if not', it must not have the *or* in front of it:

× We'd better get going before daylight, or otherwise they'll be on our trail.

Omit the *or*.

ought *Ought* is followed by *to* and another verb: *You ought to wear a raincoat in this weather.* In negatives and questions it becomes *You ought not to wear it/You oughtn't to wear it*; *Ought you to wear it?*; *Oughtn't you to wear it?* (formally, *Ought you not to wear it?*; very formally, *Ought not you to wear it?*).

Some people, however, are reluctant to use these negative and question forms. Americans, in particular, often prefer to use *should*: *You shouldn't wear it*; *Should you wear it? Shouldn't*

you wear it? This is perfectly correct, although *should* expresses a somewhat weaker moral obligation than *ought*, and so may be less appropriate in such injunctions as *You really ought not to/should not treat him like that.*

When *ought* introduces another verb, the *to* must come in between. A recent tendency is to omit the *to*, as in *?? You ought wear it.* This is quite nonstandard. In negative sentences and questions, however — *? You oughtn't wear it*; *? Ought you wear it?* — the omission of the *to* is fairly widespread, especially in American English, where it is perhaps on its way to acceptability.

To can be left out, however, at the end of a sentence: *Shall we write and thank them? We really ought (to).* It is easy to forget the *to* when *ought* is combined with another verb: *?? He ought and could have mentioned it.* The correct form is *He ought to and could have mentioned it* or *He ought to have mentioned it, and he could have.*

Other nonstandard usages, though common in some dialects, are: *?? You didn't ought to wear it*; *?? He hadn't ought to*; *?? Did I ought to wear it? ?? He really did ought.*

outdoor, outdoors *Outdoor* (or *out-of-door*) is the adjective: *outdoor exercise. Outdoors* (or *out-of-doors* or *out of doors*) is the adverb: *to go outdoors/out-of-doors/out of doors for fresh air.*

Compare INDOOR.

outside The phrase *outside of* (like *inside of*) occurs in British English sometimes and in American English often. In British English the *of* should not be used if it can be omitted, so *?? Don't mention this outside of these four walls* should be *Don't mention this outside these four walls.* However, when *outside of* means 'except for', the *of* is often indispensable: *Outside of her, there's no one qualified for the job.* Here *outside* cannot be used: *outside of* is acceptable, though an alternative wording such as *except for* is usually available.

Compare EXCEPT.

outstanding The two commonest meanings of this adjective are 'exceptionally good' (*an outstanding poet*) and 'not yet settled' (*an outstanding debt*). If attached to certain nouns, *outstanding* might be understood in either of these senses, and ambiguity could theoretically result: *? There were several outstanding decisions*; *? We have two outstanding projects.* This word order, however, is far likelier to be used when the sense is 'exceptionally good'; in the sense 'not yet settled', *outstanding* tends to be placed after the noun: *There were several decisions outstanding*; *We have two projects outstanding*. In fact, the adverb *still* would commonly be inserted here, at least in sentences in the present tense, and this would make the sense even clearer: *There are three cases still outstanding for court B*.

If the *still* is omitted, however (and some would say it is tautologous and should be omitted), and if the word-order favours both interpretations equally, then ambiguity does occur: *? Three of the five by-election results are outstanding*. The context might clarify the meaning, of course. If not, choose another form of words: *Three of the results are of exceptional interest* or *Three of the results are uncertain*.

over 1. Some meticulous users of English used to object to the word *over* in the sense of 'more than, or greater than', as in *We collected over £50; They had to walk over ten miles*. There was no good reason for this objection then, and there is none now: it can be safely ignored.

2. *Over* has become something of a jack-of-all-trades preposition, especially in modern journalism: *a walkout over an unfair dismissal; The Minister was criticised over his handling of the incident; She was worried over the delay; a reduction over last year's figures*. In these four examples, *over* should be replaced by *based on* or *provoked by, for, about*, and *on* or *from*. *Over* has a very wide range of meanings as it is, but it cannot be used to indicate every kind of relationship. Unless you want to keep your meaning vague, do not use *over* in the constructions just listed. And do not throw it heedlessly into a sentence to save yourself the trouble of finding a sharper and more appropriate preposition.

overall This word has a strange attraction for writers and speakers. Many critics have pointed out how it has taken to ousting established terms such as *total, complete, absolute, whole*, or *generally* — *? our overall impression; ? an overall defeat; ? my qualified approval overall* — and how it is often used quite superfluously: *? the net profits overall; ? an overall increase of*

21 per cent; ? the overall outcome.

This is not to say that *overall* could, or should, always be replaced. Consider these sentences:

Despite several early victories, the team suffered an overall defeat.
Overall, we were impressed with her performance.

As an adjective in the first example, *overall* seems just right: the defeat is not necessarily *total, complete*, or *absolute*. As an adverb in the second example, *overall* cannot really be replaced by *generally* or *all in all* or *on the whole*, which all seem less generous and imply stronger reservations.

But do use *overall* sparingly. Choose one of the traditional synonyms where appropriate — *total, inclusive, primary, by and large*, and so on. And make sure that if you do use *overall*, it is not just serving some purely decorative or slightly emphatic purpose, but is really contributing to the sense of the sentence.

overly The use of this word to mean 'excessively' is common in North American English and Scottish English, as in *She has been overly cautious*. It has attracted criticism in other varieties of English as an unnecessary development, the same sense being adequately expressed by the element *over-*, as in *overcautious*, or by a word like *excessively*. The usage is becoming more widespread, particularly in negative sentences — *He was not overly concerned* — but it has not yet found acceptance in formal speech and writing.

? The editors have selected 207 from Forster's 15,000 letters (about 1½% of the total) and nearly smothered them in overly detailed, distracting and disproportionate annotations.
    – Jeffrey Meyers, *New Statesman*

overseas, oversea *Oversea* is a rare form of both the adjective and the adverb. *Overseas* is now used for both: *overseas students; to travel overseas*. Only *overseas* can be used after a preposition: *visitors from overseas*.

owing to See DUE TO.

P

pace 1. The preposition *pace,* pronounced /**pay**-si/ or /**paa**-chay/, has nothing to do with the common noun and verb *pace,* 'a step' or 'to step'. The preposition is usually in italics, reflecting its Latin source: in Latin it means more or less 'with peace to . . . ' or 'with the permission of . . . '; in English it is used before a person's name or role when his opinion is being respectfully rejected:

> A week, *pace* Harold Wilson, is not really a long time in politics.
> Like Lincoln Steffens, I too have visited the Soviet Union — it may or may not represent the future, but it certainly, *pace* Mr Steffens, does *not* work.
>
> As time passed, agreement gradually emerged about who was and who was not a great artist, for instance (*pace* Kingsley Amis) Picasso.
> – Michael Davie, *The Observer*

2. Like many unabsorbed Latin terms, *pace* can seem rather affected in writing and intolerably so in speech. True enough, there is no concise English equivalent, but a more leisurely wording may often be more suitable than the high-flown Latin preposition. In many contexts it might, for example, be better to say something along these lines:

> A week, despite what Harold Wilson said, is not really a long time in politics.
> Harold Wilson's remark may have been witty but it was far from wise — a week is *not* a long time in politics.

There is, of course, a further objection to *pace* — and to its various alternatives: that is, an objection to 'name-dropping' in the first place. The objection is twofold: on the one hand, to the showing-off involved — as if the writer is preening himself on his wide knowledge of quotations and opinions; on the other hand, to the insult to the reader's intelligence — as if the reader would not have recognised the remark without the writer's help. A more cunning writer would omit the source — simply:

> A week is *not* a long time in politics.

In that way, he would either flatter the reader and create an intimacy with him by implying that they share a sophisticated understanding of these things, or else intrigue the reader with these mysterious allusions.

3. The preposition *pace* is dangerous too in that it is often misused or misunderstood. Because it is used in the same pattern as that of *according to,* it is sometimes taken as a synonym of that phrase:

> ✕ The proper study of mankind, *pace* Alexander Pope, is Man.

In fact, *pace* means just the opposite — 'in contradiction of; despite the views of':

> The proper study of mankind, *pace* Alexander Pope, is not Man but God.

Pace is sometimes misused in a subtler way to mean 'despite the example of' rather than 'despite the opinion of':

> ✕ But you can hardly expect a heavyweight champion (*pace* Gene Tunney) to be an intellectual as well.

The sense intended here would be properly expressed by something along these lines instead:

> But you can hardly expect a heavyweight champion (notwithstanding the example of Gene Tunney) to be an intellectual as well

or

> But you can hardly expect a heavyweight champion to be an intellectual as well — even if Gene Tunney managed to be both.

One alarm signal, warning of a faulty usage, is the presence of *pace* before a noun that refers to a thing rather than a person:

> ✕ The accused is at heart a very gentle person, *pace* the brawl in the pub last night.

For *pace,* read *despite.*

> ✕ A week, *pace* Harold Wilson's opinion, is not really a long time in politics.

This should be either . . . *notwithstanding /as against/despite Harold Wilson's opinion . . .* or

simply ... *pace Harold Wilson* ...
● *Recommendation* Use the preposition *pace*
only when referring to a person, not a thing; even
then, use *pace* only when that person is responsible for the *opinion* you are disputing, not when
he is an *example* of some claim you are disputing;
and even then, use *pace* only very sparingly.

pair *Pair* is followed by a verb in the singular
when the components are being considered as a
unit: *This pair of shoes is not for sale.* A plural
verb is used when the components are considered
as separate individuals: *The pair of them are
working together more harmoniously now.* (See
PLURALS Part II.)

When *pair* follows a numeral other than *one*,
the plural is standard — *six pairs of shoes* —
though the singular is used in informal and
dialectal speech: *six pair of shoes.*

palpable According to its origins, *palpable*
should mean 'perceptible by touch, tangible,
feelable': *A hit, a very palpable hit*, says the judge
of the duelling scene in *Hamlet*. The Latin verb
palpare meant 'to stroke or touch' — hence the
medical technique of *palpation* or *palpating*, in
which the doctor feels or presses parts of the
patient's body.

The word is nowadays, however, very seldom
used in this earlier sense, except — curiously
enough — when combined with *almost*: *The cat's
hostility to us was almost palpable.* It tends instead to be used in an extended, more figurative,
rather abstract way, suggesting the idea of 'real
not imaginary; considerable, obvious, easily perceived or recognised': *The cat's hostility to us was
palpable.*

We examined the drawings, which, incidentally, happened to be the most palpable
forgeries, and clucked dutifully.
— S.J. Perelman (U.S.),
Westward Ha!

But there is something else in the McGovern
Spirit, and it is quite palpable here in Miami.
It is the sense of absolute, total self-
righteousness.
— William F. Buckley, Jr (U.S.),
The New Religion

The doubt raised by such usages is not about the
correctness of the sense, but about the appropriateness of the tone. *Palpable* often sounds
inflated or pretentious, a vogue word or fancy-
sounding substitute for *glaring, obvious, clear-
cut, noticeable*, or the like. Use it sparingly.

panacea A *panacea*, pronounced /**pan**ə-**see**-ə/,
is more than a remedy: it is a remedy for
everything, a universal cure. It goes back to the
Greek roots *pan*, 'all' + *akos*, 'a cure'. The
medical panacea was one of the goals of the
alchemists. Today, *panacea* is used in a more
metaphorical way, referring to a cure for social
rather than bodily ills: *The monetarists believe
that tight control of the money supply is the
panacea for our economic problems.*

Three cautions: first, since a panacea is a very
wide-ranging cure, the word should not be used
in relation to any specific disease, literal or
metaphorical: you should not speak of ✗ *a
panacea for baldness* or ✗ *a panacea for inflation*. The appropriate word here would be *cure*
or *remedy*.

Secondly, since *panacea* already contains the
notion of universality, it is tautologous to speak
of ?? *a universal panacea.*

Thirdly, *panacea* is almost always used
disparagingly or dismissively. It is your opponents
who are always proposing panaceas; your own
proposals are always modest and realistic.

**pancake, drop scone, griddle cake, Scotch
pancake** In British English, a *pancake* is a thin,
flat cake made of batter and fried on both sides
until brown, and usually rolled up around a sweet
or savoury filling. It is the equivalent of a French
crêpe, though crêpes tend to be even thinner than
English pancakes. In American English, the word
pancake can refer to the same thing, but it usually
refers to a thicker, fluffier, sweeter, pancake,
rather like a large *griddle cake*. This American
pancake is served flat, not rolled.

In American English there are several synonyms
for the typical American flat pancake, notably
a *flapjack* and a *griddle cake*. But *flapjack* in
British English is used to refer to the sweet,
crunchy biscuit made from rolled oats, syrup, and
butter; and a *griddle cake* is much smaller in
Britain than in America: a small, thick, flat
pancake made by dropping a spoonful of batter
onto a hot cooking surface such as a griddle. It
can be eaten hot or cold.

The *griddle cake* is also known in British English
as *a girdle cake* (especially in Scotland), *a Scotch
pancake,* or *a drop scone*.

Regional dialects in America have a host of
names for the typical American pancake, whether
thin or thick: *flannel cake, flatjack, slapjack, hot
cake, batter cake, flippumjack, fritterjack,
gandy* or *gandie, jumpover, leatherbread,
splatterdab,* and *stack cake.*

See also MUFFIN, CRUMPET, TEA CAKE, SCONE.

pandit See PUNDIT.

parable See ALLEGORY.

paradigm This noun remains valuable as a term in grammar, psychology, and philosophy. In general contexts, it has become a vogue word, being favoured — for its impressive look or sound, and usually for no other reason — over *model, standard, pattern, framework,* or *example.* So: *His career is a paradigm of political opportunism* (= a typical example); *Her life is a paradigm of civic virtues* (= an excellent example; a model worth imitating), and so on. Where possible, choose a less pretentious term such as *pattern* or *example.*

Note the pronunciation: /**par**rə-dīm/. The adjective *paradigmatic* is pronounced /**par**rə-dig-**mat**tik, -dīg-/. The Greek roots are *para-,* 'alongside' + *deiknunai,* 'to show'.

Note the overlap between *paradigm* and *paragon: paragon* means 'a perfect model, an unsurpassed example': *She is a real paragon of civic virtues. Paragon* almost always applies to humans, and *paradigm* usually to things.

paragraphs A paragraph is a distinct division of a piece of writing. It expresses some thought or point relevant to the whole, but is to some degree complete in itself. As far as punctuation goes, it begins on a new line, even where this means leaving most of the previous line empty. It is often marked by being 'indented' from the edge of the page. And in typing, an extra line of space is often used between paragraphs. In the punctuation of dialogue, each new speech or speaker should begin a new paragraph.

Paragraphing provides resting-places for the reader. There are no rules on how often these resting-places should occur. In much light journalism and advertising, almost every sentence seems to start a new paragraph. In more serious writing, a paragraph can last for a page or more. Most paragraphs contain at least three sentences, but an occasional one-sentence paragraph is refreshing to the eye and the attention.

If a single topic needs a good deal of space to develop, it may be made more digestible to the reader by breaking it up into more than one paragraph. But the converse is not true: two topics that have nothing in common should be discussed in two separate paragraphs, no matter how short those two paragraphs may be.

In planning an extended piece of narrative, description, or exposition, you could begin by jotting down the topics for successive paragraphs.

If appropriate, each topic may appear in the final text as an actual 'topic sentence', often at the beginning of its paragraph. The paragraph then develops the topic, amplifying, explaining, or justifying it with further details and examples. Where the paragraph builds up evidence towards a conclusion, however, the topic sentence may well come at the end.

Good writers try to make a smooth transition between one paragraph and the next. Paragraphs may be linked by such simple signals as *Moreover, Alternatively, For example, In these circumstances, Above all, In conclusion.*

> Just as the sentence contains one idea in all its fullness, so the paragraph should embrace a distinct episode; and as sentences should follow one another in harmonious sequence, so paragraphs must fit on to one another like the automatic couplings of railway carriages.
> – Winston Churchill, *My Early Life*

See also SENTENCES.

parallel constructions If you have two or more related ideas to convey, they are often most effectively presented when constructed according to a single pattern. The pattern can be very simple:

> The more, the merrier.
> I came, I saw, I conquered.

The elements might be linked by a conjunction:

> Speech is silver, but silence is golden.

Or 'correlative conjunctions' might be used as a frame in which to pattern the elements:

> Either you must leave, or I must leave.

The pattern need not be identical within each element. Part of one element can be omitted; it is 'understood', as if carried over from the other element:

> Either you must leave, or I must (= I must leave).
> To err is human — to forgive divine (= to forgive is divine).
> Rise above rather than bow beneath your fate (= Rise above your fate).

Parallel constructions are not restricted to *parts* of a sentence, and not restricted to two elements. Whole sentences, or even paragraphs, can be constructed on the same pattern, and the elements can be more than two in number:

> If Wagner had not been a composer, he

might still be remembered today — as a second-rate philosopher. If Rousseau had not been a philosopher, he might still be remembered today — as a second-rate composer. If Uncle Edgar had not been a relative of ours, we might still have heard of him — as a saloon-bar composer and the town's homespun philosopher.

Parallel constructions, then, come in a great variety of sizes and shapes. These are all subject to an overriding and obvious rule (sometimes a rule of grammar, sometimes of style): if elements are presented as parallel, then they must be parallel — their structures must be properly matched.

Here are some examples that contravene this rule. First, a simple failure of style.

⨯ She is stubborn, selfish, and has a sharp temper.

The three elements are not symmetrical here, and should not be organised as though they were. Either rearrange them so that they no longer pretend to be equally weighted —

She is stubborn and selfish, and has a sharp temper

— or make them symmetrical in structure:

She is stubborn, selfish, and quick-tempered.

Now to those failures of symmetry that involve mistakes of grammar as well:

⨯ Not only is that a very unfair statement, but also quite untrue.

The structures following *not only* and *but* (*also*) should match each other closely. In this example, however, the *not only* element contains a verb, whereas the *but also* element does not. The sentence can be reconstructed in such a way that both elements have a verb, or that neither element has:

That statement is not only very unfair, but also quite untrue.
Not only is that a very unfair statement, but it is also quite untrue.

Here is another example of a poorly arranged *not-only* construction:

⨯ By writing a story in the form of a computer program, one can not only change the ending, but just about everything else too.
— Julian Allason, *Daily Telegraph*

Next, consider this faulty construction:

⨯ The actors were criticised both by their friends and their enemies.

Again, the correlative conjunctions *both* and *and* demand matching constructions. Yet here the *both*-phrase contains the preposition *by*, whereas the *and*-phrase lacks it. The two elements can, theoretically, be brought into parallel in either of two ways:

The actors were criticised both by their friends and by their enemies.
? The actors were criticised by both their friends and their enemies.

The second version here remains unsatisfactory, however, since it introduces an ambiguity into the sentence: *both their friends* could be taken to suggest that the actors have only two friends.

Here is another example of a *both-and* construction that fails to keep the two elements parallel:

⨯ In the incident agents wearing carnival masks and armed with sub-machine guns battered down a bedroom door in the hotel ... The service both failed to warn the hotel management and the police of the planned exercise.
— Tony Duboudin, *The Times*

A simple test for many parallel constructions is this: if a part of one element has been omitted as 'understood', try inserting the 'understood' element and see if it really fits; alternatively, leave out the second of the elements and see if the sentence still makes sense.

⨯ She is as talented, if not more talented than, any of the male riders in the team.

The two related components are not properly matched: to match *more talented than*, the earlier phrase should read *as talented as*. To see how the syntax has gone wrong, leave out all the parenthetical words between the two commas. The need for an extra *as* at once becomes apparent. (See AS GOOD OR BETTER THAN.)

Similarly:

⨯ More than half the cars in Brazil now run on alcohol, and the number is rising. Performance is comparable — or slightly better — than that of a petrol car, and can be as much as a 10 per cent improvement.
— Sue Baker, *The Observer*

For the sake of symmetry, and syntax, a *to* should be added after *comparable*, and the sentence should be repunctuated: *is comparable to — or slightly better than — that of a petrol car.*

A slightly different example:

✕ The avoidance of tax was the sole or one of the main purposes of the transaction.

This should read: *was the sole purpose or one of the main purposes.* As it stands, the sentence reads: ✕ *was the sole ... purposes.*

✕ When a Scots appeal comes to the Lords strong efforts are made to ensure that one, if not both, Scottish Law Lords will sit. But of course other things never are equal.
— Alan Paterson, *The Law Lords*

This is easily remedied: simply add *of the* before *Scottish Law Lords*, and balance is restored. Similarly:

✕ A problem with which Skeat was faced was whether ... to accept only material written in phonetic systems, which would mean rejecting lists made by collectors who had not, or could not, use them.
— K.M. Elisabeth Murray,
Caught in the Web of Words

This should read: *collectors who had not used them, or could not use them.* As it stands, the sentence reads: ✕ *collectors who had not ... use them.* Similarly:

✕ If the leading actor falls ill, the play will not be performed and the audience given a refund.

The intended meaning here, presumably, is that the audience *will be* given a refund. These words should have been expressed explicitly. The 'understood' words from the first element, if inserted in the supposedly parallel construction, would produce this quite misleading reading: ✕ *the audience will not be given a refund.*

Two examples now of a preposition that is assumed to be appropriate to both parallel elements but is in fact appropriate to only one:

✕ To be fair, he wasn't alone in his ignorance. A recent report from Brunel University's Department of Government let the cat smartly out of the bag: 'Many British employers still think that the best graduates come from universities and remain ignorant or uninterested in what the more vocationally orientated polytechnics and colleges have to offer.'
— Susanna Frayn, *The Observer*

This should read: *remain ignorant of or uninterested in. ...* Similarly:

✕ It was only a few weeks ago that Mrs Thatcher was expressing her admiration and interest for the King of Tonga because he had 'progressed from being a Prime Minister to becoming a monarch ...'
— Peter Hillmore, *The Observer*

This should read: *her admiration for and interest in the King.*
Here is a subtler kind of error:

✕ I may be a bad writer, but I am better than Howard Tucker when it comes to fabricating or lying. Being uncommitted to verifiable fact, as his kind of writer is, I can indulge in the free fancy that often turns out to be the truth.
— Anthony Burgess, *Earthly Powers*

The narrator's intention here, apparently, is to contrast himself, an imaginative or fanciful writer, with a realistic writer such as 'Howard Tucker'. The implied parallel is between a writer 'uncommitted to verifiable fact' and a writer 'committed to verifiable fact'. Yet the word *committed* appears nowhere in the text. The narrator should have said *Not being committed to verifiable fact, as his kind of writer is, I can indulge ...* The word *committed* is now 'understood' at the end of the phrase *as his kind of writer is*. But as the text stands, the only word that can be 'understood' in that position is *uncommitted* — which is quite the reverse of the sense intended.
Consider, next, this doubly poor sentence:

✕ A judge, both then and now, did not have completely free choice in the selection of their itineraries.
— Fenton Bresler, *Lord Goddard*

First there is a failure of agreement: the subject of the sentence is singular — *A judge* — yet the sentence refers to *their itineraries*: this should read *his itinerary* or *his or her itinerary*. More to the point, there is a failure of symmetry: *both then and now* is a phrase that invites trouble, since *then* usually calls for the past tense, and *now* for the present. The passage needs rewording:

A judge did not then, and does not now, have completely free choice ...

Perhaps if the phrase *both then and now* had been changed to *then as now*, the use of the past-tense verb alone might have been allowed to pass unchallenged.
To turn finally to a rather subtler violation of parallelism. There is something wrong with each of the following sentences:

✕ She heard him laugh and, unable to restrain

himself a moment longer, to open the door.

× She hopes to become interested in Amazonian birdlife and eventually in writing a book on the subject.

× In as much as the problem remains unsolved and that time and funds are short, let us turn our attention to other matters.

What is wrong is that each sentence begins with a construction of one type and then shifts to a construction of another type. The correct versions of the sentences are:

She heard him laugh and, unable to restrain himself a moment longer, open the door.

She hopes to become interested in Amazonian birdlife and eventually to write a book on the subject.

In as much as the problem remains unsolved and (as) time and funds are short, let us turn our attention to other matters.

In the first two sentences, the original error was caused by 'contamination' from an intermediate construction. The *to* of *unable to restrain himself* prompted the writer to produce *to open the door*, but the correct construction depends not on *unable* but on *heard*: *She heard him laugh and . . . open the door.* The *in* of *interested in Amazonian birdlife* prompted the phrase *in writing a book*, but the correct construction depends not on *interested* but on *hopes*: *She hopes to become interested . . . and eventually to write a book . . . .* In the third sentence, the mistake has a different basis. The *that* of *that time and funds are short* has been introduced not because it appears in an intervening construction, but simply because the use of *In as much as* at the beginning of the sentence has been forgotten.

This sort of error — changing horses in midstream, as it has been called — is traditionally referred to as *anacoluthon*. It was observed and studied even in classical times. The remedy is to plan your sentences properly, and to keep in mind that each part should fit properly into the structure of the whole.

See also AGREEMENT.

parameter   This once obscure mathematical term has risen quickly to the status of a vogue word. Technically a parameter is a measurable quantity or factor that goes into determining a system, event, or mathematical expression. So, among the parameters affecting the flight of a Frisbee are launch, spin, speed, and wind.

Partly through association with *perimeter*, perhaps, *parameter* (usually in the plural form *parameters*) is now widely used in general contexts to refer to a boundary, limitation, or constraint: *?? We are well within the parameters of our budget*; *?? I'm still feeling my way around the parameters of my new job.*

It is also used in the sense of 'a characteristic or defining feature; a touchstone': *?? one of the parameters of democracy.*

The word may sound impressive, but it tends to obscure rather than clarify meaning. It is difficult to imagine any nontechnical context where *parameter* would be more suitable or intelligible than every established synonym: *limit, border, restraint, determinant, definition, outline, range, scope,* and so on.

paranoid, paranoiac   *Paranoia* is a serious mental disorder in which the sufferer experiences delusions of persecution or grandeur. The word comes from the Greek *paranoos,* 'demented', from *para-,* 'beyond, out of' + *nous,* 'mind'. A sufferer from paranoia is usually referred to as a *paranoiac.* This form also used to be the adjective commonly chosen in referring to a sufferer, but it is being replaced by *paranoid,* and some now consider *paranoiac* to be altogether unacceptable as an adjective. Others, however, prefer it as the technical adjective (except in the name of the psychiatric condition *paranoid schizophrenia*): *paranoiac* should refer to acute sufferers, they argue, while *paranoid,* with its *-oid* ending (as in *humanoid*), should be reserved for those who merely resemble real sufferers.

Eliot knew his wife well enough to realise that it would take a great deal of time before she was convinced that he would not change his mind about the separation and, in her highly anxious state, her paranoiac fears once more came to the surface: she accused both Virginia Woolf and Ottoline Morrell of having affairs with her husband.

— Peter Ackroyd, *T.S. Eliot*

Whatever distinctions the experts may care to make, *paranoid* and *paranoiac* are both acceptable for ordinary purposes, and both can be adjectives and nouns, with *paranoid* more likely in humorous uses, as in the legendary cry *Help! The paranoids are after me!* The layman's one responsibility is not to reduce these terms to sloppy vogue words: if a person is simply touchy or suspicious, why refer to him or her as *paranoid* or *paranoiac*? The words *touchy* and *suspicious* are always available, and they are, after all, what you mean. Similarly, *paranoia* should not be used unthinkingly for *anxiety* or *suspiciousness*.

?? That men need a study or a shed, that teenagers probably encourage what their mothers regard as their indefensible mess on purpose to keep her out, is understood. Less appreciated is the paranoia of the family woman who in one sense possesses the whole house, but in another sense possesses none of it.

– Katharine Whitehorn,
The Observer

?? Garp suspected most people to whom his wife and children were drawn; he had an urgent need to protect the few people he loved from what he imagined 'everyone else' was like. Poor Mrs Ralph was not the only victim perhaps slandered by his paranoid assumptions.

– John Irving (U.S.),
The World According to Garp

parentheses See BRACKETS.

parley, parlay The slightly informal word meaning 'a conference' or 'to negotiate' is spelt *parley*. The word *parlay* is used chiefly in American English. Both can be pronounced /**par**-li/; *parlay* can also be pronounced /**par**-lay/.

Parlay can be a verb or a noun. The verb means 'to bet (an original wager and its winnings) on a subsequent event' — the British equivalent is *to double up*. It is also extended to mean 'to manoeuvre (an asset) to great advantage': *He parlayed his good looks into a theatrical career.* The noun refers to a bet or series of bets made with the original wager and its winnings — what in British English is called an *accumulator*. The word comes from the French *paroli*, referring to a bet of this kind as used in the game *faro*; the word was borrowed from Neapolitan Italian, which derived it from *paro*, 'like', from the Latin *par*, 'equal'.

Parley is also either a noun or a verb. As a noun, it refers to a discussion or negotiations, especially between enemies. The verb has two meanings, 'to confer or debate', and, informally, 'to speak (a foreign language)': *? Do you parley the lingo?*

Parley comes from French *parlé*, past participle of the verb *parler*, 'to talk', and goes further back to roots in Late Latin and ancient Greek.

participles An English verb has two participles: its *present participle*, formed with *-ing*, as in *He's singing*; and its *past participle*, which is formed with *-d* or *-ed* for regular verbs — as in *We've finished* — and in various other ways for irregular

verbs, as in *broken biscuits*, or *very badly built*.

There are three common problems with participles: first, the tendency to produce a 'misrelated participle', incorrectly attached to the rest of the sentence; secondly, the stylistic fault of beginning too many sentences with a participle; thirdly, making the wrong choice between *me* and *my* or between *John* and *John's* before an *-ing* form.

The misrelated participle appears in such sentences as × *Working at my desk, the sudden crash startled me.* The participle *working* is misrelated here: it cannot be the crash that was working, though the structure of the sentence seems to imply that it was. The sentence should be rephrased: *Working at my desk, I was startled by the sudden crash* or *While I was working at my desk, the sudden crash startled me.* (See MISRELATED CONSTRUCTIONS.)

Note that it is perfectly legitimate to begin a sentence with a participle, so long as it is properly attached like an adjective to the subject of the sentence or in a few other special circumstances (see MISRELATED CONSTRUCTIONS again). There is nothing wrong with *Working at my desk, I was startled by the sudden crash*, or with *Startled by the sudden crash, the dog crawled under the sideboard*; but the device should be used sparingly. It is better not to produce a repetitiously structured text such as this:

? Believed to be the oldest working sculptor in the world, Ambrose Lightfeet has just celebrated his 98th birthday. Described as 'the Michelangelo of Leighton Buzzard', Mr Lightfeet has recently completed a gigantic equestrian statue of the Mayor.

And avoid using an opening participle as a device to link two unrelated ideas into a single sentence: ?? *Born the ninth of ten children, Jeremiah was a millionaire by the age of 30.* (See NON SEQUITUR.)

The choice between *He doesn't like me whistling* and *He doesn't like my whistling* depends on whether you interpret *whistling* as a sort of adjective attached to *me*, or as a sort of noun to which *my* is attached. When there is doubt, it is safer to use a possessive form here, such as *my* or *John's* rather than *me* or *John*. The possessive form is not always possible, however. (For more about this complicated subject, see -ING FORMS OF VERBS.)

particular, particularly 1. *Particular* has several senses: 'exceptional', as in *of particular importance*; 'choosy or fussy', as in *very particular* *about her food*, and so on. When used in its more general sense of 'specific or special', and attached to a noun, *particular* serves to set that thing apart, and contrast it to other things of the same type:

He had gone to the same pub without fail every Wednesday night for as long as anyone could remember, but on that particular Wednesday night he failed to appear.

But *particular* is often used when it has no such distinguishing function, serving instead only as a vague form of emphasis:

No particular place to go.
Are you doing anything particular right now?
? Not at that particular moment.
? I'm sorry, officer — I don't remember anyone answering that particular description.

In formal (and more efficient) usage, the *particular* would be left out in the third and fourth examples, and possibly in the first two as well.

2. Take care to position *particularly* correctly in a sentence. Consider how the meaning changes when the adverb is shifted:

He doesn't particularly want to eat out tonight.
He particularly doesn't want to eat out tonight.

partly, partially These two adverbs, although sometimes interchangeable, usually have slightly different meanings, and appear in different phrases. There are a number of guidelines to help in deciding which to use. *Partly* is usually found in two contexts: first, when discussing some physical object and emphasising the part as opposed to the whole: *a sculpture partly of scrap metal*; secondly, when the sense is 'to some extent': *partly to blame*; *the delay was partly due to engine trouble*.

I have tried to keep staleness out of the Wexford novels and the series characters fresh. It is partly for this reason that I write the other books and give myself a rest from Wexford for a year or two.
— Ruth Rendell, *Bookcase*

Partially, by contrast, is usually used when referring to a condition or state rather than a physical object, and it tends to emphasise the whole rather than the part. It means roughly 'to a limited degree; not fully': *She is partially blind now*.

After the end of the war, Abdul, partially

cured in both lungs, returned to Palestine.
— Muriel Spark,
The Mandelbaum Gate

The Press Council has partially upheld a complaint about a *Mail on Sunday* article on the life and violent death of actor Peter Arne.

— *The Observer*

It seems, moreover, that *partially* has to be used immediately in front of a verb, an adjective, or another adverb: it cannot easily be used directly before any other part of speech: ? *The accident was partially my fault*; × *It was partially because of the heat that he fainted*; × *I owe my success partially to my agent's stubbornness*. In each of these sentences, *partly* is the correct adverb to use.

All the examples so far listed are fairly clear-cut. But when there is an adjective immediately in front, and when it refers neither to a physical object nor specifically to a condition or state, then the choice is not so easy. The rule of thumb is this: when it is the parts rather than the whole that are under consideration, then *partly* is the adverb to use.

Consider the case of an opera production. Suppose the soprano strained too hard, and her singing sometimes became shrill and off-key. A reviewer might write: *Her singing was partly shrill and off-key*. That is, some of the notes (parts) were shrill and off-key. He would not write ?? *Her singing was partially shrill and off-key*, since this would suggest that singing can be slightly off-key, whereas really there are no half-measures — a note is either off-key or it is not off-key.

This suggests another guideline, not entirely reliable but still fairly useful: *partly* tends to refer in large measure to the noun, even though grammatically it modifies the adjective; *partially* refers mainly to the adjective.

Suppose, for example, that the opera was not a total disaster. The reviewer might sum it up either as *a partly disappointing production* or *a partially disappointing production*. If only a few aspects of the production were disappointing (the soprano's singing, the costumes, and the set, for example), but everything else was very good (the other singers, the staging, the orchestra, and so on), then the reviewer would write *a partly disappointing production*; that is, parts of the production were disappointing, while other parts were quite up to standard. On the other hand, if most of the aspects of the performance were slightly unsatisfactory (if all the singers and musicians followed the soprano in being occasionally off-key), then the reviewer would write *a partially disappointing production*; that is, the production as a whole fell slightly short of the expected standards. Perhaps, in these examples at least, *partly* can be translated as 'in parts'; *partially* as 'in part'.

> There was another long pause and then he said unsteadily, 'All right.' He sounded far away, as if he had partially covered the mouthpiece with his hand.
> – Lynne Reid Banks,
> *The L-Shaped Room*

Again, if you said *The house is partly built*, you would be suggesting that some parts of the house were completed, and some either incomplete or not even begun, whereas if you said *The house is partially built*, you would be suggesting that many or most of the parts are already underway, but that few of them perhaps have actually been finished.

Here is another guideline: the distinction between *partly* and *partially* is similar to the distinction between 'some' and 'not all': so try reading *partly* as 'somewhat', and *partially* as 'incompletely'. The difference then between *a partly successful operation* and *a partially successful operation* would be this: *partly successful* has, as its point of reference, the idea of non-success, a zero quantity of success; *partially successful* has, as its point of reference, the idea of total success. Perhaps *partly successful* is an optimistic way of putting things, and *partially successful* is a more pessimistic way.

The distinction remains a very fine one, however, and the various guidelines listed above remain just that — only guidelines, not infallible rules.

Note that *partially* has two other senses, both little-used nowadays, and not relevant here: 'affectionately, with favour or partiality', and 'in a biased way, not impartially'.

passed, past *Passed* is the past tense and past participle of *to pass*: *We passed the garage*; *The crisis has passed*.

For all other uses — adjective, preposition, adverb, and noun — the word is *past*. So: *the past three weeks*; *The crisis is past*; *We drove past the garage*; *went hurrying past*; *remembering the past*.

Confusion sometimes arises between the adjective *past* and the participle *passed*. Compare:

> The night was past. (adjective)
> The night has passed. (past participle)

Because of the long time already passed (= that has passed), we can do nothing.

> Time present and time past (= that is past)
> Are both perhaps present in time future.
> – T.S. Eliot, 'Burnt Norton'

passive See ACTIVE AND PASSIVE.

patent When the word is used in a general, non-technical sense, as in *Her insincerity was patent for all to see*, or *a patent of respectability*, the preferred pronunciation is /**payt**'nt/. When the sense is legal or official, as in *letters patent* or *He took out a patent for his invention*, the *a* is preferably short, /**patt**'nt/. Americans have no such problems: they tend to use the short *a* in all cases.

pathetic In recent years, *pathetic* has come into wide use in informal speech in the sense of 'worthless, feeble, laughably inadequate'. A football manager might complain of his team's *pathetic performance*. This usage has not yet worked its way into formal standard English, but it has already affected the traditional sense of *pathetic* — 'arousing sympathy or sadness'. To say that Margot Fonteyn gave *a pathetic performance* in *Swan Lake* might, unfortunately, be to court misunderstanding. (See also PITIFUL.) So long as the traditional sense of *pathetic* survives, it is better to restrict the modern, unfavourable sense to informal contexts.

Take care not to confuse *pathetic* (and the noun *pathos*) with *bathetic* (and *bathos*), referring typically to an anticlimax or letdown: *a bathetic ending to an impressive speech*.

peninsula, peninsular Take care not to spell the noun *peninsula* with an *r* on the end, and take care not to omit the *r* when spelling the adjective *peninsular*.

A *peninsula* is a projection of land almost entirely surrounded by water. (It comes from Latin *paene*, 'almost' + insula, 'an island'.) *Peninsular* (like *insular*) is its adjective, as in *the Peninsular War* of 1808-14, fought in the Iberian Peninsula between British troops and Napoleon's French forces.

penny The change to decimal currency in the United Kingdom in 1971 raised several linguistic problems for British English. Chief among these is the question of how to pronounce the conventional abbreviation *p*, as in *10p*. Immediately following decimalisation, to speak of 'tenpence' was ambiguous: it was unclear whether this meant ten 'old' or ten 'new' pence. The forms *old pence* and *new pence* have now largely died out as people have become familiar with the new system, and the abbreviation *p*, pronounced /pee/, has become the dominant form. However, many people dislike it, and prefer the form *pence*. Certainly in formal styles, *pence* is the form to use. Restrict *p* to informal use.

When used in isolation *pence* is pronounced /penss/. In combination, it used to be pronounced /-pənss/ — for example *tenpence*, /tenpənss/. Since decimalisation this pronunciation has been giving way to /-**penss**/, even when the word occurs in combination: *tenpence* is now usually pronounced /ten-**penss**/.

In British English, *penny* still survives in set phrases like *He hasn't got a penny to his name*. It ought to survive also in expressions like *a one-penny coin*, but here it seems to have been mostly replaced by *pence* or *p*: *? a one-pence coin*; *a one-p coin*. In American English a *penny* is a coin worth one cent, so Americans might say: *It cost ten cents and I paid with ten pennies because I didn't have a dime*. In older British usage this would have been like saying: *It cost a shilling and I paid with 12 pennies because I hadn't got a shilling piece*. Nowadays you would be more likely to hear: *It cost five pence and I paid with five pennies because I hadn't got a five-pence piece/five-p coin*. The expression *a five-penny piece/coin*, though correct, is now very seldom heard.

per There is a tendency to use this preposition needlessly, presumably because its Latin sound is thought to be impressively sophisticated. Certain formulas do demand *per*: *kilometres per hour* and *miles per gallon,* for example. And if a double ratio is being expressed, *per ... per* is always needed: *32 feet per second per second*; *an average of 70 lb per person per year*. But there is nothing better about *? six pints per week,* say, than *six pints a week* — except perhaps in official documents or statistical reports.

Per annum or *per year* is sometimes necessary in official contexts again — *17 billion dollars per year on defence* — but elsewhere *a year* is preferable: *We go to four or five concerts a year on average.*

And *per day* sounds distinctly odd in the phrase *? three times per day*. The idiomatic wording is *Take two teaspoonfuls three times a day.*

Per, like *via,* is also sometimes used as an affected alternative of *by*: ✗ *Are you going per hovercraft or ferry?* ✗ *The package you*

requested is being sent per motorcycle courier.*

And *per* is quite unnecessary in the jocular phrase ✗ *as per usual*. The combination *as per* is used rather more seriously, but no more appealingly, in commercial jargon, to mean 'according to': *? We await delivery as per instructions*. If you mean 'according to', then say or write *according to.*

per capita Purists object to this phrase as it is commonly used in English today. Literally it means 'by heads' — hence its original use in legal terminology, in the sense of 'counting by heads' or 'divided according to the number of individual people involved':

> The reward was distributed *per capita* to all those members of the public who gave the police crucial information.

Today the phrase is almost always used to mean 'per head; per person' instead — a meaning that should strictly be expressed as *per caput*. But accurate Latin is beside the point — the phrase is now so well-established in its modern sense that there is no possibility of dislodging it:

> Absenteeism among transport workers has now fallen below two days a year *per capita*.

Of course, there is no need to use the phrase at all, when the single terms *per man, per worker,* and so on are available. In some official and technical contexts, however, *per capita* is established in certain standard formulas, and is virtually unavoidable there:

> Which country has the world's highest per capita GNP?

> Thailand is a net exporter of rice, her industry is expanding rapidly; overall prosperity, measured in terms of per capita income, is three times that of India.
> – Gillian Tindall, *The Times*

Make sure, if you do use the phrase, to avoid redundancy; if the word *average* appears in the sentence, for example, it is unlikely that *per capita* will be needed as well:

> ✗ For the average transport worker, absenteeism has now fallen below two days a year *per capita*.

per cent, percentage 1. It is sometimes argued that since *per cent* comes from the Latin *per centum*, a term used in legal documents, it ought properly to be written *per cent.*, with a full stop, to show that it is an abbreviation. This form is very rare nowadays, however, and seems pedantic; and in any case it may be that *per cent* is from the French *par cent* and not an abbreviation at all.

North Americans have taken to writing it as one word, *percent*, but this is still considered incorrect in British English.

2. North Americans tend also to use *percent* as a noun: *? A small percent of the income goes into insuring the property.* But the noun from *per cent* should be *percentage*: *What percentage of the price is profit?*

3. *Percentage* is increasingly being used, incorrectly, to mean 'a *small* percentage, a small number', as in × *Only a percentage of the workers accepted the government's offer.* The percentage could as well be 99 per cent as 2 per cent. (See also FRACTION; PROPORTION.)

4. There is a long-standing objection to the use of *per cent* and *percentage* to express proportions greater than 100 out of 100. The objection has little to be said for it; *per cent* can be understood as 'on a hundred' as well as 'in a hundred'. So a book bought at £10 and sold for £30 makes a 200 per cent profit on its original cost.

5. Percentages are valuable for expressing complicated and precise proportions and fractions. But there is little point in using percentages where simple fractions are clearer. A *third* is usually preferable to *33⅓ per cent* or *33⅓%*, a *quarter* to *25%*, and *half* or *a half* to *50%*. *Percentage* is also overused in contexts where *number*, or *fraction*, or *proportion* is intended. Avoid *percentage* where possible and use these instead.

6. Percentages usually take a plural verb if the related noun (whether stated or implied) is in the plural: *Ten per cent of the samples were substandard.* Even *one per cent* tends to take a plural verb — *One per cent of the samples were substandard* — though it could be argued that the subject here is *one*, and that the verb should therefore be the singular *was*.

When the related noun is in the singular, a singular verb is needed: *Ten per cent of the wool was substandard.* Note too the singular verb in the following sentences: *Ten per cent is the average commission*; *Ten per cent is a very low mark.* There is an implied subject here in each case: *(A commission of) ten per cent* or *(A mark of) ten per cent* — hence the singular verb. (See PLURALS Part II.)

7. *Percentage* has acquired a further sense fairly recently — 'advantage; a slight gain or benefit' — that is now in common use, especially in North America: *? There's no percentage in working so hard.* It remains a colloquial usage, and should be avoided in formal contexts, with the possible

exception of sports journalism, where it seems to have become a standard technical term, even in British English:

> Now even the best of their heirs, such as Liverpool, respond to a major final by soberly calculating the percentages like men seeking to pass an exam.
> – Hugh McIlvanney, *The Observer*

In this extended sense, *percentage* has even come to be used as an adjective, meaning roughly 'relying on small gains rather than profitable risks; safe rather than spectacular':

> It may be that de Wet Ras, the Orange Free State stand-off who can kick the leather off the ball, might have served them better by playing a percentage game.
> – David Hands, *The Times*

perceptibly, perceptively Be careful not to confuse these two adverbs. *Perceptively* means 'intelligently, in a manner showing insight and good judgment': *She criticised the paintings very perceptively.* *Perceptibly* means 'noticeably' or even 'glaringly, obviously': *He is perceptibly balder than when I last saw him five years ago.*

The adjective *perceptible* is in danger of being overused and misused nowadays. It occurs most often in such a phrase as *a perceptible difference*, and what it should mean here is simply a 'visible' or 'observable' difference; it should not be taken to mean a 'considerable' or 'huge' difference, as it is often apparently intended or understood to mean.

See also PERSPICACIOUS.

peremptory A *peremptory* command is one that admits of no discussion. The Latin verb *perimere*, from which it derives, means 'to remove completely'; hence the Late Latin *peremptorius*, 'removing all discussion; decisive'. A *peremptory* manner is that of a person given to peremptory decisions or commands — an overbearing or imperious manner.

By association with *perfunctory*, perhaps *peremptory* has come to be thought of as meaning 'abrupt', even though a *peremptory* manner can in theory be slow and painstaking; and by a further extension (or corruption, as some purists believe) it has come to be used in the sense of 'sudden', even though a *peremptory* decision or command might in fact have been long and well thought out. If you mean no more than 'abrupt' or 'sudden', then say *abrupt* or *sudden*. *Peremptory* is more than a grandiose synonym for these two terms.

Note that *peremptory* can be stressed on the first or second syllable: second-syllable stress is now more common in British English, and overwhelmingly preferred in North America.

perfect Purists point out that anything that is *perfect*, in the sense 'flawless, complete in all respects', must be absolutely so, and that it is therefore incorrect to use qualifying words such as *more*, *most*, *so*, and *very*.

?? Earlier this month I was in Sussex for the weekend and went to evensong — surely the most perfect Anglican service — in Crowborough.
  – Russell Twisk, *The Listener*

It is quite permissible, however, to speak of one thing as being *more nearly perfect* than another. (See ADJECTIVES; VERY, MUCH.)

When *perfect* is used more loosely to mean 'excellent', the use of such words as *more*, *so*, and *most* is acceptable: *The weather couldn't have been more perfect*; *That's one of the most perfect specimens I've seen.* The American Constitution speaks of forming 'a more perfect union' among the people of the various states.

Tripping over some young fool's trailing skate, I took off, sailed high, and fell with my body so perfectly arched that my upper thighs were the first part of it to hit the ice.
  – Clive James, *The Observer*

period See FULL STOP.

permit In its most common meaning of 'to allow', *to permit* can be used in two ways: you *permit* something, or you *permit* somebody *to* do something: *The law permits smoking here*; *The law permits patrons to smoke here.* In its more formal meaning of 'to make possible', *permit* can be used with or without *of*: *The wording permits (of) only one interpretation.* Be careful not to confuse these different constructions: it is wrong to write × *The law permits of smoking here.*

perquisite See PREREQUISITE.

-person See CHAIRMAN; SEXISM IN THE ENGLISH LANGUAGE.

personal, personally These words are useful in their proper place, but are often used where they are really quite superfluous.

Among their correct uses are the following.

First, they confirm that the person mentioned was in fact the one who acted or suffered directly, rather than acting or suffering indirectly through a representative or substitute. In this sense, it functions much like *myself, herself, themselves,* and so on:

The manager sometimes conducts a personal inspection of the assembly line.
She seldom trusts the cook to get the sauce béarnaise right, and as a rule insists on making it personally.

Secondly, *personal* and *personally* are used when referring to a person's private concerns or possessions, as contrasted with those of his work, public office, or the like: *personal effects*; *no personal interest in the decision*:

The Minister denies that he stands to benefit personally from the award of the contract to Global Enterprises.

Note the possible sources of ambiguity here: in a sentence such as ? *The chairman is personally interested in the sale of the subsidiary,* the word *personally* can be understood in either of the two senses just outlined; and in a sentence such as ? *James wanted to discuss it with the chairman personally,* the word *personally* could be taken to refer (in the first of its senses) either to *James* or to *the chairman.*

Thirdly, *personally* can be used to highlight a contrast: *You may not think so, but personally I rate that restaurant second to none.*

By extension from this last usage, *personal* and *personally* have come to be used more loosely, simply in an attempt to give some emphasis to the sentence as a whole:

?? Mary has strong reservations — she personally takes the view that it's considerably overpriced.
? You want my opinion? Personally, I consider it a bargain.
? If you want to know how I personally feel about it, you can read my letter of resignation.
? My personal opinion is that it's a bargain.
? He's a man of great personal charm./ He's a personal friend of mine./ He paid a personal visit to the hospital.
?? The vicar makes a point of shaking hands personally with all his parishioners as they leave the church.

? One big reason why Mrs Thatcher and the Irish Prime Minister, Garret FitzGerald, are planning to meet personally is that it's getting more difficult to communicate by telephone.

– Peter Hillmore, The Observer

In the first two and last three of these examples, *personal* or *personally* can be omitted, without seriously weakening the element of contrast or insistence. In the remaining two examples, the emphasis could be conveyed in a different way. In speech, it would be enough to stress the *I* or *My*. In writing, the surrounding context would probably establish the necessary contrast in the first place; if not, the sentences might be prefaced by *But* or *On the other hand,* or a slight change of wording could be made: ... *how I for one feel about it* ..., or the like.

See also MYSELF; PARTICULAR.

personal pronouns See PRONOUNS.

personnel *Personnel*, borrowed from the French, has been established in English for well over 100 years. It probably referred originally to the body of people employed by the army or navy. This involved not just soldiers, but civilians too: cooks, purchasers, and so on — the human counterpart of *materiél*, the equipment and supplies used by the army and navy.

More generally, *personnel* applies to the body of people working in any large public institution — a hospital, for instance — and can refer to the employees collectively of large private organisations too. (*Personnel* also refers to the division or department, within such an organisation, concerned with the recruitment and well-being of its employees.)

Nevertheless, the word can sometimes still be justly criticised — as a needlessly affected synonym of *staff, workers, work force,* or simply *people*. When referring to merely a small group of employees, or to workers individually, *personnel* is best avoided: *?? We need to hire two more personnel for the typing pool.* Strictly *personnel* indicates an indefinite (and large) group of people.

Personnel can be used with a singular or plural verb: traditionalists prefer the singular, though this does sound rather stiff nowadays.

Finally, take care with the spelling and pronunciation of *personnel*. Unlike *personal*, it has two *n*'s, and is stressed on the final syllable as well as on the first.

perspicacious, perspicuous These two adjectives are easy to confuse. *Perspicacious* suggests insight and sensitivity; *perspicuous* suggests clarity or lucidity. *Perspicacious* means 'having good powers of judgment and discernment; shrewd': *a perspicacious mind, a perspicacious counseller.* *Perspicuous* can mean 'expressed clearly': *a perspicuous sermon*; or, rarely, 'expressing clearly': *a perspicuous preacher*; or 'clearly comprehensible':

The usual vogue word is not one whose meaning is easily perspicuous to the average man, who has to work it out as best he can.

– Philip Howard, Weasel Words

A simple guideline is to think of *perspicacious* as 'very understanding' and *perspicuous* as 'clearly understandable'. *Perspicacious* is usually used to refer to people, sometimes to their faculties; *perspicuous* is usually used to refer to things, only rarely to people. But the distinction is not an easy one to retain: a *perspicuous* explanation will help somewhat, but even then you have to be reasonably *perspicacious* to grasp it.

Two other similar-sounding adjectives, *perceptive* and the rarer *percipient*, are very close in meaning to *perspicacious*, and not at all to *perspicuous*.

She sometimes appears frivolous but is in reality very profound. Heaven knows how many *soustextes* the percipient critic will find here. Even odd throwaway lines have large resonance.

– Anthony Burgess, The Observer

The corresponding nouns are *perspicacity* (or *perspicaciousness*), *perspicuity*, *perceptiveness* or *perceptivity*, and *percipience*.

His first meeting with Miss Vaughan now came back to him, fused with subsequent meetings here in the green courtyard. He saw them all with that total perceptivity of his which might have made a poet of him, given the missing element.

– Muriel Spark,
The Mandelbaum Gate

See also PERCEPTIBLY.

perverse, perverted *Perverse* is easily confused with *perverted*. Both go back to the Latin elements *per-*, 'completely' + *vertere*, 'to turn', and both retain some idea of turning away from the correct course; but they tend now to be used in quite distinct ways.

Perverse broadly means 'obstinately contradictory; taking or persisting in a course different from what is reasonable or right or required; contrary': *The child was perverse and argumentative*; *A perverse impulse made her shut the door in her boyfriend's face.*

> In his relationship with Biggs, even a grim sort of satisfaction to Stringham might be suspected, one of those perverse involutions of feeling that had brought him into the army in the first instance.
> – Anthony Powell, *The Soldier's Art*

> We walked into the 'wilderness', and I mentioned Winslow. Roy frowned. We were both uncomfortable; we shared a perverse affection for him, we had not liked to watch his fall ...
> – C.P. Snow, *The Masters*

> But Gray is a good novelist, however much he at times perversely rejects the gift, and what he tells us we have to believe.
> – Anthony Burgess, *The Observer*

Perverted is the past participle of the verb *to pervert*, which means 'to misuse, distort, or debase':

> I have always maintained that the chief function of any holder of that office is to pervert the course of justice if he can, and to reduce it to a preposterous and incomprehensible shambles if he can't.
> – Bernard Levin, *The Times*

Perverted nowadays usually means 'corrupt; deviating from correct behaviour or beliefs; morally deformed': *He has a perverted sense of humour — he thinks suffering is funny.* In the following quotation, written 50 years ago, *perverted* now seems an unsuitable word in the context: *perverse* would be the appropriate choice today.

> ? The bowler hat was either a novice at his job or exceedingly bored with it. He made no attempt at concealment; stood staring at us from the middle of a pool of lamplight. A sort of perverted sense of courtesy prevented me from looking over my shoulder to see if he was following; as for Arthur, his embarrassment was only too painfully visible.
> – Christopher Isherwood, *Mr Norris Changes Trains*

A perverted person is especially one whose sexual instincts deviate from what is considered normal behaviour. The noun *pervert* refers to such a person. Note that the noun and verb forms of *pervert* are pronounced differently, the verb as /pər-**vert**/; the noun as /**per**-vərt/.

The abstract noun that relates to *perverse* is *perversity* or *perverseness*, meaning 'contrariness': *He acted out of perversity — he had no good reason for doing it.* Related to *perverted* is the noun *perversion*, 'distortion, or a moral or sexual deviation': *The verdict was a perversion of justice*; *a pornographic film with appalling scenes of perversion.*

pessimism, pessimistic See OPTIMISM.

phenomenon, phenomena, phenomenal
1. Virtually all modern dictionaries now recognise as standard English the use of *phenomenal* in the sense 'extraordinary, outstanding, remarkable' — *a phenomenal success*; *a woman of phenomenal insight.*

> My next bullet caught him somewhere in the side, and he rose from his chair higher and higher ... to a phenomenal altitude, or so it seemed, as he rent the air.
> – Vladimir Nabokov, *Lolita*

> The phenomenal demand for home-computer software was demonstrated this Christmas as stores around the country sold out of both games and home computers.
> – David Dawson, *The Listener*

The noun *phenomenon* is also widely accepted in the senses of 'an extraordinary, extremely significant, or unaccountable fact or occurrence; a marvel' — *A quadruple somersault on the trampoline is no longer the phenomenon that it would have been in 1950* — and 'a person or organisation of outstanding achievement or extremely unusual qualities':

> Houdini was a phenomenon not just of suppleness and ingenuity but of physical strength as well.

> The abrupt downfall of one of the most powerful and respected labour leaders in the country made the Rackets Committee overnight a national phenomenon.
> – Arthur M. Schlesinger, Jr (U.S.), *Robert Kennedy and His Times*

Phenomenon is even used today, without causing any comment, in the very diluted sense of simply 'something puzzling or slightly peculiar or unusual':

> Warts can be ordered off the skin by hypnotic suggestion. Generations of internists and dermatologists, and their grandmothers,

for that matter, have been convinced of the phenomenon.

– Professor Lewis Thomas (U.S.),
The Medusa and the Snail

Little more than a generation ago, however, purists deplored and shunned such usages, insisting on limiting *phenomenon* and *phenomenal* to their original more or less philosophical senses, 'a thing or event perceptible to the senses, whether real or not', and 'known or derived through the senses, rather than through thought'. (The ultimate root is the Greek verb *phainein*, 'to show or reveal'.) Yet the extended meanings are not especially recent: Dickens's *David Copperfield*, for instance, recorded how he *thought Mr Barkis a phenomenon of respectability*.

The warning today is not against using the words in their extended senses — that battle, if it ever was waged or worth waging in the first place, is long since lost. The warning is rather against overusing the words, and thereby weakening their effect: if everything worth noting is *phenomenal* (or *great* or *unreal* or any other predictably recurrent and voguish intensifier), then all sense of contrast is lost and nothing is truly *phenomenal*. Use the words sparingly.

2. *Phenomenon* takes the Greek plural *phenomena* when used in its original philosophical sense. In its modern extended sense of 'a marvel' or 'a prodigy', *phenomenons* is also possible (and is probably preferable when applying to human beings):

... his executive directors at Harris Queensway, the carpet and furniture group that has become one of the retailing phenomenons of the past decade.

– Lindsay Vincent, *The Observer*

Nowadays the singular is sometimes expressed as × *phenomena*, and the plural as × *phenomenas*. This is perhaps due to a false analogy with Latin-based words such as *arena* or *formula*. Unlike *stamina, insignia, agenda*, and *regalia* — also originally plurals — *phenomena* is most unlikely ever to be accepted as the standard singular form.

See also CRITERION; DATA; MEDIA; PLURALS.

phosphorus, phosphorous The chemical element is *phosphorus*, which exists in three forms — white (or sometimes yellow), red, and black. *Phosphorous*, with an extra *o*, is the related adjective.

In British English both words are pronounced /**fos**fərəss/, but in North America the pronunciations /foss-**faw**rəss/ and /foss-**fō**rəss/ can also be used for the adjective *phosphorous*.

The word *phosphorus* goes back to the Greek *phosphoros*, 'light-bearing': white *phosphorus* is *phosphorescent*; that is, it gives off light when exposed to air or incident radiation.

The noun *phosphor* refers to any substance that can be made to give off light by such exposure to radiation. So white *phosphorus* is a *phosphor*, but not all *phosphors* consist of *phosphorus*.

See also FUNGUS; MUCUS.

phrasal verbs See VERBS 5.

phrases To grammarians a *phrase* is a sequence of words that form a grammatical unit; particularly a sequence not containing a verb, or with a verb only in the infinitive or the *-ing* form or the past-participle form.

A common kind of phrase is the *prepositional phrase*, consisting of a preposition and a noun or noun equivalent: *in the morning*; *over the hills*; *without me*; *after waiting a week*. Such phrases do the work of a single adverb: instead of saying *Go without me* you could say *Go alone*.

Another sort of *adverbial phrase* is *every day* in *Go there every day*; you could replace it by *Go regularly*. *Very much easier* is an *adjectival phrase* in *He found it very much easier*. *Where to go* is a *verbal phrase* in *Tell them where to go*.

But the term *phrase* is sometimes used more broadly, to allow for the ideas of *noun phrase* and *verb phrase*. A *noun phrase* consists of a noun or noun equivalent together with all its attendant adjectives and relative clauses. An example is *the big new refrigerator which stood in the corner of the kitchen*. And a *verb phrase* can have not only an infinitive or *-ing* verb or past participle, but a full finite verb, with any of its attendant auxiliaries: *has been collected*; *may have understood*; *would prefer to stop*. Sometimes the term *verb phrase* is extended to cover the whole 'predicate' (see SENTENCES). In the sentence *John may have seen her yesterday*, the words *may have seen her yesterday* might be considered a verb phrase.

pidgins and creoles A *pidgin*, or *pidgin language*, is a makeshift language that develops to permit simple communication between two peoples (or more) who have no language or dialect in common. Typically a pidgin would arise for the purpose of trade contact; the word *pidgin* is probably based on the Chinese pronunciation of *business* (hence too the British idiom *That's your* *pigeon,* meaning 'That's your business' or 'That's your affair').

A *creole,* or a *creole language,* is a pidgin that has developed into a mother tongue. It is estimated that some 60 million people around the world speak creoles or pidgins for everyday purposes.

The processes of pidginisation must be as old as travelling itself. They are found in all simplified communication systems, and include such features as:

● speaking slowly and loudly and using frequent repetitions.

● using gestures.

● a simplification of pronunciation — by fusing different vowels (in Jamaican creole, *rat* and *rot* are both /raat/) and different consonants (the English consonants /th/ and /th/ tend to be pronounced /t/ and /d/); and by separating certain consonant combinations (in Melanesian pidgin, *clear* is pronounced /kə-**li**-a/ and *stone* /sə-**tōn**/.

● a simplification of vocabulary — specifically, the use of a single form to cover a variety of related words: this includes a preference for the base form (or most emphatic form) of nouns, pronouns, verbs, and negative terms. So:

— *man* serves for *man, man's, men,* or *men's;*

— *go* for *go, goes, going, gone,* and *went* (tenses are indicated by adverbs instead: *bye and bye, now, tomorrow,* and so on);

— *me* for *I* or *me;*

— *no* for *no, nor, not, none,* or *neither.*

Similarly, a base form might be duplicated to indicate the intensive (*bikbik* means 'very big' in English-based Atlantic pidgins and creoles) or to generate the word for a related concept (*tingktingk* means 'a thought or opinion').

● a simplification of syntax — notably the use of short sentences with rigid word order, usually Subject-Verb-Object; a question is indicated by intonation rather than a change of word order.

There are two types of pidgins:

1. *restricted pidgins,* which serve minimal communication needs:

Come see. Fine dress. Dress fine. Cheap. No dear. You want? Me get. Okay price. Okay price?

These pidgins tend to be unstable and short-lived. One recent example was the 'bamboo' English used by Americans and Koreans during the Korean War.

2. *elaborated pidgins,* which develop in multilingual communities and are expanded because of their value as lingua francas. These languages are capable of fulfilling all the linguistic aspirations of a people, from proverbial wisdom —

Troki wan fait bot i sabi sei i han shot (Tortoise wants to fight but he knows his arms are short)

— to biblical parable —

Bot di papa bin tok sei: Ma pikin, yu dei wit mi ol taim an ol ting wei a getam na yu on. Bot i gud med wi glad foseka dis yu broda bin don dai an i don wikop fo dai agen. (But the father said: My son, you are with me always and everything that I have is yours. But it is good for us to rejoice because your brother was dead and he is alive again.)

— to the language of administration, as in multilingual Papua New Guinea where the pidgin is used in parliament and many schools.

Restricted pidgins can be heard in most ports and tourist resorts, where the local people master enough words and structures of the visitors' language to allow elementary communication. Elaborated pidgins are found in multilingual areas such as Africa and the South Pacific. They undoubtedly began as restricted pidgins, but proved so useful that they soon outgrew that limited role.

A creole would tend to have more linguistic sophistication still: it has to be capable of describing all reaches of human experience and emotion, and therefore usually draws on a wider vocabulary and might evolve a more elaborate grammar too. But in general, a creole and an elaborated pidgin are differentiated not by their linguistic characteristics but by their sociological functions: a creole is a mother tongue, the first language of its speakers, whereas an elaborated pidgin is a secondary language, usually acquired after (though sometimes alongside) a traditional vernacular language.

A pidgin or creole acquires, and expands, its vocabulary in a variety of ways.

For a start, it draws — though to a small extent, no more than 20 per cent — on the vocabulary of the native vernacular languages. Typically, these terms refer to local flora, fauna, geography, and culture: Atlantic varieties have *akara* (a beancake), *mboma* (a snake), and *ngombi* or *zombi* (a spirit), for instance; Pacific varieties have *kapul* (a tree kangaroo) and *tultul* (a leader). It is relatively unusual to find basic core-vocabulary items represented by terms of native origin: two such rarities should be mentioned, however — the Jamaican creole word for both 'food' and 'to eat', *ninyam* or *nyam,* which derives from a West African language, probably Twi; in some Pacific varieties, the word for 'meat' is *abus,* probably derived from Tolai.

A more important source of pidgin or creole words is the 'base' language (English, French, Portuguese, or the like) — accounting for up to 80 per cent of the vocabulary: *ai* (eye), *bring, fut* (foot or leg), *go,* and *kam* (come) are common to both Pacific and Atlantic English-based varieties of pidgin and creole.

Such base words are often manipulated to extend their range — the word *grass,* for instance, is used by many English-based pidgins in naming various things that grow outwards from a surface: the term 'hair' is *grass-bilong-head,* and a 'moustache' is *mows-grass (mouth + grass).*

There are a number of processes involved here. 'Compounding' of base words produces *bigman* (= an important person), *daiman* (= a corpse — from *die + man*), and *sweetmot* (= to flatter, or flattery — from *sweet + mouth*).

The process known as 'reduplication', as mentioned earlier, serves to intensify a word (*bikbik,* in some Atlantic creoles, meaning 'very big'), to create a new word (*benben,* in some Atlantic creoles, meaning 'crooked' — from *bend + bend*), or to distinguish two words that might otherwise sound the same (*sansan,* in Atlantic creoles, means 'sand', distinguished from *san,* 'the sun').

Finally, 'calques' or 'loan translations' — the translation, element for element, of a native compound or phrase based on a metaphor: *kukim nos* (*cook + nose*), 'to kiss, became intimate', is probably such a loan translation, from a Papua New Guinea language. Similarly, *tai han* means 'stingy' in some Atlantic varieties, and *plenti han* means 'centipede' in some Pacific varieties — from *tie + hand* and *plenty + hand* respectively. Some further examples are listed below.

Pidgins and creoles have probably existed throughout history, wherever trade or conquest has taken place. The oldest well-recorded pidgin is a medieval language that was actually called *Lingua Franca.* It was based on French and Italian dialects and came to be used, by traders and crusaders alike, in the Middle East. Pidgins proliferated in the 15th century when Europeans began to explore and exploit the entire planet. After the voyages of discovery, pidgins began to spring up along the trade routes, and creoles to develop (among native labourers or imported slaves) in colonial plantations. The base language might be Portuguese, Spanish, Dutch, French, or English: one theory suggests that the true base is an early Portuguese pidgin (in turn derived from *Lingua Franca*) which was the first to gain a foothold in Africa, India, and the Far East, and was therefore partially adopted, with modifications, by Dutch, French, Spanish, or British traders and sailors. In fact, nearly every European-based creole does contain a variety of Portuguese roots, as in *pikin* or *pikinini,* 'a child', and *savi,* 'to know'.

As to English-derived pidgins and creoles, there are, broadly speaking, two families: one found in or bordering the Atlantic, the other in the Pacific. The Atlantic Family comprises a range of pidgins along the West African coast, and closely related creoles in Sierra Leone and Liberia, in Guyana and Surinam, in all the Caribbean islands with historical links with Britain, in Nicaragua and Belize, and in Florida and the Sea Islands along the coast of Georgia and South Carolina. (Black American English shares many similarities with Atlantic pidgins and creoles.)

The Pacific Family comprises a range of related pidgins and creoles in Australia among Aborigines, in Papua New Guinea, the Solomon Islands and Vanuatu, and, to a lesser extent, in Samoa and Fiji. All of these varieties resemble the China Coast Pidgin English, once very widely used by European and Chinese traders and merchants, and may well be offshoots from it.

In their core vocabularies, Atlantic and Pacific English-based varieties overlap considerably, since the bulk of their vocabulary is derived from English. Their vocabularies have two main points of difference — first, the element derived from native roots: Atlantic varieties, with their historical links to the slave trade, draw many items from African languages, whereas Pacific varieties reflect Pacific influences and environment — consider again the examples *mboma* (= a snake — Atlantic) and *kapul* (= a tree kangaroo — Pacific). The second lexical divergence between the Atlantic and Pacific families is in their loan translations; like *tai han* and *plenti han,* mentioned earlier, the following examples, though superficially similar, would not be understandable across the family-divide:

Atlantic
big ai (big eye) greed/greedy
drai ai (dry eye) brave
man han (man hand) the right-hand side
tai fes (tie face) a frown
wuman i bele (woman's belly) a carrier-bag or holdall

Pacific
big mows (big mouth) conceited
drai bon (dry bone) tough
grass bilong paul (grass belong fowl) feathers

nek bilong singsing (neck belong song) a
melody
nos bilong kanu (nose belong canoe) a prow

More specifically, there are three characteristics
of Pacific pidgins and creoles that immediately
distinguish this family from Atlantic varieties:
1. the use of *long/bilong* as locative and
possessive prepositions:

Mi stap long Mosbi (I live in Port Moresby)
han bilong mi (my hand/arm)

2. the marking of some adjectives by the suffix
-pela (from the word *fellow*):

bikpela big
longpela long
waitpela white

3. the marking of transitive verbs by the suffix
-im (from *him* or *them*):

bai mi oraitim em (I'll fix it)

Such differences are well illustrated by juxtapos-
ing translations of 'The Three Little Pigs' in
Cameroon Pidgin (Atlantic) and the standard
pidgin of New Guinea (Pacific), sometimes
known as Tok Pisin (literally 'Talk Pidgin'):

Cameroon
Di tri smol swain
Long taim bifoa tudei, tri smol swain liv fo
bush. An som waildog tu dei fo dis bush. I
sabi kil plenti bif, an i go laik fo kil dis tri
smol swain.

Tok Pisin
Tripela liklik pik
Bipo tru, tripela liklik pik i stap long bush.
Na i gat wanpela waildok tru em i stap long
dispela bush. Em i sabi kilim plenti abus, na
em i laikim kilim dispela tripela pik.

The majority of English-related pidgins and
creoles coexist with standard English, which
usually remains the language of education and
government. Accordingly, we find in many communities a spectrum of dialects, ranging from the
local pidgin/creole to perfect standard English.
This phenomenon, often referred to as a 'post-
creole continuum', can be illustrated by the
following sentences from Cameroon:

Di tu man pikin kam wan taim
Di tu boy dem kam wan taim
Di tu boys dem come at once
The two boys came at once.

As more and more speakers are educated in the
standard medium, the pidgin/creole will drift

towards and increasingly resemble the standard
variety. This has already happened to Black
American English.

In the past, pidgins and creoles were often
despised as 'bastardised lingos' and 'inferiority
made half articulate', largely because they were
spoken mainly by indentured labourers and
ex-slaves. Linguists have since shown that
pidginisation is inevitable in language contact of
this kind, and that the simple structures that
characterise these makeshift languages have much
to teach us about the nature of language in
general, and language-learning strategies. It is
heartening to note that many young pidgin- and
creole-speakers are now exploiting the flexibility
of their languages for literary purposes. Plays,
stories, poems, and political satire have recently
appeared in both the Atlantic and the Pacific
regions, and many writers have found that these
varieties (easy enough, after a little initial effort,
for English speakers to understand) are better
suited than standard English to express the
nuances of local culture.

See also AFRICAN ENGLISH; WEST INDIAN
ENGLISH.

pitiful, pitiable, piteous These three adjectives
all share the basic sense of 'arousing pity or sympathy', and they are accordingly often
interchangeable.

Perishing cold, wringing wet, their clothes
clogged with mud and eyes reddened by
woodsmoke, they squat doggedly round the
missile base: a pitiful, evidently painful and
apparently permanent reminder to the people of Newbury that something is up.
– Hilary Spurling, *The Observer*

Minnie had been encouraged to feel like a
member of the family and is asked to come
back ten years later, only to find herself a
pitiable figure who still can't get in to this
family which paradoxically no longer exists:
the father has been found dead, and the sons
have spent a long time in America.
– Emma Tennant,
interviewed in *The Literary Review*

Piteous might have served here just as well. The
three words can also share a second sense, the
pejorative or disapproving sense of 'arousing
disdain, contemptible, despicable' – either
because very small, as in *a pitiful/pitiable/
?piteous score*, or because very poor in quality,
as in *a pitiful/pitiable/piteous performance*.

I might have easily found ... creatures far

more fascinating than Valeria. My choice, however, was prompted by considerations whose essence was, as I realised too late, a piteous compromise.

– Vladimir Nabokov, *Lolita*

It is interesting to note that the word *pathetic* has much the same two meanings – the positive one of 'arousing pity' and the negative one of 'arousing contempt'. (See PATHETIC.) Note too the danger of ambiguity produced by these two senses, in such phrases as *a pitiful excuse* and *a pitiable sight*: in the absence of any clue from the context, it is unclear whether the tone of such phrases is sympathetic or scornful. And even when the context is provided, the sense can remain uncertain:

Among other things, the novel is a chronicle of Emily's success. In the course of four years, Emily rises to such a highly paid position as a star dancer in London that she is able to transform Alfred, who has been brought to a pitiful condition — gnawing cauliflower stems for sustenance and chattering in Piccadilly. It is when he becomes most monkey-like that Emily shimmers out of the Ritz and offers him a new life.
– Paul Theroux (U.S.),
The Literary Review

Pitiful has a third sense, very little used now, of 'feeling or showing pity, merciful, compassionate'. *Piteous* too formerly had this meaning, but has now lost it altogether.

The three words are sometimes distinguishable by their distribution: one or another may be favoured in certain combinations or contexts. *Pitiable* and *piteous* are perhaps distinguished from *pitiful* in being preferred when the context suggests suffering, misery, or wretchedness: *a pitiable hovel, piteous surroundings, pitiable urchins, a piteous groan. Pitiful* is perhaps more appropriate in non-human contexts: *the pitiful ruins of a once-proud castle*.

plain, plane   A common spelling problem, this. One way of keeping them distinct in your mind is to remember that *plain* has many senses as an adjective but only one nontechnical sense as a noun, whereas *plane* has many noun senses but only one nontechnical sense as an adjective. The problem is that the single noun sense of *plain* and the single adjective sense of *plane* are very close in meaning: a *plain* is a flat, treeless stretch of land; the adjective *plane* means 'flat', especially in the phrase *a plane surface*.

The adjective senses of *plain* include 'clear', 'pure', 'straightforward', 'ordinary', 'unattractive', and so on. The noun senses of *plane* include 'a geometrical surface', 'a level of development', 'an aeroplane', 'a carpenter's tool', and so on. *Plane* is also used as a verb, 'to smooth or remove with a carpenter's plane'. Here the two words are used almost side by side:

Once they came by train and buggy to find fame and fortune in Hollywood; now they come by bus and plane because this plain beside the Pacific Ocean still represents the golden grail for many Americans.
– Christopher Brasher, *The Observer*

Both *plain* and *plane* come from the same Latin base word, *planus*, 'level or flat'. The *plane* of *plane tree* is a quite different word, coming from an ancient Greek source.

plaintiff, plaintive   Take care not to confuse and misspell these two words. The noun *plantiff* refers to the person or organisation that brings legal action in court — the opponent of the *defendant*, against whom the action is brought. *Plaintive* is an adjective, meaning 'sounding sad or expressing sorrow, mournful, melancholy': *the plaintive song of the curlew*.

The sky grew darker and darker as the morning wore on. By the time the coffee came round it was like a winter evening ...
'Bob!' said Dyson plaintively. 'Will somebody for God's sake put the lights on?'
– Michael Frayn,
Towards the End of the Morning

Both these words go back via Middle English to the Old French *plaintif,* from *plainte,* 'a lamentation'. This word comes in turn from the Latin *planctus,* past participle of *plangere,* 'to strike (one's breast), lament'.

Another English derivative of this Latin verb is the adjective *plangent* (pronounced /**plan**jənt/), which is used almost exclusively of sounds — repeated striking sounds, as of waves on a shore; or loud reverberating sounds, as of church bells; or sad, twangy sounds, as of an oriental stringed instrument. In this last sense, *plangent* is virtually a synonym of *plaintive*.

The noun related to *plangent* is *plangency*; the noun related to *plaintive* is *plaintiveness*.

platform   In American usage, *platform* is quite acceptable in its modern political sense: the set of policies that a party or candidate puts forward to appeal to the electorate. Each of the individual policies in a platform is called, appropriately enough, a *plank*. The written version of an American party *platform* is what in British English is called a party's *manifesto*.

The entry into British English of *platform* in its political sense is still resisted by some purists, however, though acceptance is just a matter of time. The word does seem to fill a lexical gap: *He emphasised his anti-nuclear platform during the election campaign, and this might well account for his poor showing.*

plausible This adjective originally meant 'deserving applause' or 'acceptable', going back as it does to the Latin verb *plaudere*, 'to applaud'. The idea of acceptability remains in the modern sense — 'believable, apparently convincing or valid': *a plausible excuse.*

> Even where we know, from a comparison with other sources, that Snorri Sturluson's facts are considerably inaccurate, his account is always eminently plausible.
> – Magnus Magnusson,
> Introduction to *King Harald's Saga*

> Our destination was ... Lepingville, somewhere near a hypothetical hospital. That destination was in itself a perfectly arbitrary one (as, alas, so many were to be), and I shook in my shoes as I wondered how to keep the whole arrangement plausible, and what other plausible objectives to invent after we had taken in all the movies in Lepingville.
> – Vladimir Nabokov, *Lolita*

There tends to be at least a tinge of doubt when *plausible* is used, as these examples show in different degrees. When *plausible* is applied directly to people, that doubt is very much to the fore:

> He was a fast-talking, plausible, well-dressed man, and might have fooled others, but Joanna was not taken in.

> I found him a plausible, attractive rogue, all nervous energy and wit.
> – Thomas Flanagan (U.S.),
> *The Year of the French*

Here the idea of deceptive appearances is fairly strong. *Plausible* here would mean 'superficially impressive, but arousing the suspicion that one is putting on an act'.

plenty 1. There is a common temptation to leave out the *of* in such sentences as *We've got plenty of eggs* and *There's plenty of fruit in the bowl*

still. Among children for example, or in certain dialects and regional varieties such as South African English, the *of* is regarded as superfluous, and omitted, on the model of *We've got a dozen eggs*; *There's enough fruit in the bowl still,* and so on.

Nevertheless, the standard usage remains *plenty of X/Xs,* rather than *?plenty X/Xs,* and the omission of the *of* is considered unacceptable in formal contexts.

2. A common informal use of *plenty,* especially in American English, is in the sense of 'very' or 'sufficiently, quite': *?She's plenty rich all right*; *?A five-hour speech is plenty long enough for me, thank you.* Naturally, such constructions are hardly suited to formal speech or writing.

3. The forms *plenteous, aplenty,* and *in plenty* sound rather affected today, even in very formal contexts, and are best avoided unless you are aiming specifically for some archaic or jocular effect. Instead of *?a plenteous supply of champagne* and *?Bankruptcies were plenteous last month,* use a *plentiful supply* and *Bankruptcies were plentiful.* And instead of *?champagne aplenty* and *?There were bankruptcies in plenty,* say simply *plenty of champagne* and *plenty of bankruptcies;* or if these then sound too informal, you could say instead *a large amount of champagne* and *a large number of bankruptcies.*

pleonasm See TAUTOLOGY.

plurality See MAJORITY 4.

plurals The plural forms of English nouns can be a source of considerable perplexity, not just to foreigners but quite often to native English speakers as well.

Part I: plural-forms The regular written plural for English nouns is formed by adding *-s* or *-es* (*hugs, kisses*). In speech, the plural is formed by adding to the base word the sound /s/ as in *ships,* /z/ as in *shoes,* or /iz/ as in *glimpses.* (These rules apply not just to the plurals or nouns, but also to the *-s* forms of verbs: all five examples so far cited could be verbs as well as nouns. Much of what follows applies to verb-forms too, not just to plurals.) These plural forms are very productive, and speakers who encounter a word they do not know will happily apply them.

● *plurals in -s.* Most nouns (or words functioning like nouns) just add *-s: pens* and *pencils, sharps* and *flats.* This includes words with a silent *e* on the end: *traces, smudges, shades, oozes.* There is no apostrophe before or after the *s.* Note that the final consonant of the singular form may change its pronunciation in the plural: *house*, /howss/, but *houses*, /**how**ziz/; *mouth*, /mowth/, but *mouths* /mow**thz**/.

● *plurals in -es.* The suffix *-es* is regularly added to nouns ending in *s*, *x*, *z*, *ch*, *sh* (but not usually *th*, which takes a simple *-s*): *bosses*, *boxes*, *buzzes*, *beeches*, *bushes*.

So much for the regular formation of simple plurals in English. What follows is a discussion of difficult plurals, and often 'irregular' plurals.

But first, an important general consideration: a noun that normally takes an irregular plural — *ox*, *oxen*; *corpus*, *corpora* — can sometimes take a regular plural — *oxes*, *corpuses* — if used in a special way. For example, *corpus*, when used as a technical term to refer to a collection of quotations needed in the preparation of dictionaries, tends to be pluralised by lexicographers as *corpuses* rather than *corpora*. And *ox*, if used metaphorically to mean 'a clumsy person', might acceptably take the plural *oxes*. Similarly *louse*, used as a term of abuse, might pluralise as *louses* rather than as *lice*. The plural of *life* is *lives*, but the plural of *still life* is *still lifes*. The plural of *half* is normally *halves*, but someone wanting two half-pints of beer in a pub may well order two *halfs*. The plural *mouths*, as just pointed out, has the irregular pronunciation /mow**thz**/, but *loudmouths* is likely to keep the 'unvoiced' *th*-consonant of the singular: /**lowd**-mowths/.

Other examples of this 'irregular regularity' are mentioned in the discussion that follows. Note that other areas of grammar display it too: the past-tense form of the verb *to put*, for instance, is usually the irregular *put*, but the related verb *to input* often has the regular *inputted* as its past tense and past participle. Once again, an unusual or irregular function is associated with an unusually regular form.

Here now is a survey of difficult plurals.

The -s ending ● *words ending in -y.* Words ending in a consonant + *y* such as *lady*, *baby*, and *gypsy* change *-y* to *-ies* in the plural: *ladies*, *babies*, *gypsies*. The only important exception to this rule is proper nouns, which can form a plural simply by adding *s*: *the two Germanys, both Sallys*.

Note that there is no apostrophe in any of these plural forms. If the word is both plural and possessive — that is, it means 'of/belonging to several/many' — the apostrophe goes at the end of the word, as in *ladies' room*. (If the sign on the door appears as *ladies'* it could be intended as an abbreviation of *ladies' room* or *ladies'*

lavatory but it is more likely to be a mistake — the form *ladies* corresponds to *gentlemen*; *ladies'*, with an apostrophe, corresponds to *gentlemen's*.)

Words ending *-quy* also change *-y* to *-ies* in the plural: *soliloquies*, *obloquies*, and *colloquies*.

All other words ending with *vowel* + *y* simply add *s*, so: *bays*, *jockeys*, *decoys*, *guys*, *buoys*, and so on. Thus British English has a useful contrast between *storey/storeys* and *story/stories*. The only exception to this rule is *money*, which has the specialised plural *monies* as well as a regular plural *moneys*. Elsewhere, when the plural *-ies* appears to be formed from any *-ey* word, it can be explained away as the plural of a variant singular without the *-e*: so *flunkies* is the plural of *flunky* rather than of *flunkey*: similarly, *fogies*, *bogies*, and *phonies*.

● *words ending -f or -fe.* Some words ending in *-f* or *-fe* change their ending to *-ves* in the plural, but some end simply in *-s*. A few words allow a choice.

First, changing *-f* to *-ves*: *calf/calves*; similarly, *elves*, *halves*, *loaves*, *scarves*, *leaves*, *selves*, *sheaves*, *thieves*, *wolves*. And *-fe* to *-ves*: *life/lives* (but *still lifes*), *knives*, and *wives*.

Secondly, free variation: *dwarfs* or *dwarves*; *hoofs* or *hooves*; *wharfs* or *wharves*.

Finally, the simple addition of *-s*: *beliefs*, *cuffs* (and all double *-f* words), *(hand)(ker)chiefs*, *oafs*, *roofs*. Most *-fe* words follow suit: *carafes*, *safes*, *fifes*, and so on.

● *words ending in -i.* It used to be possible to add *-es* to form the plural of some words ending in *-i*: the plural of *taxi* used commonly to be *taxies*. This is now very rare; the safe and simple rule is that words ending in *-i* just add *-s*: *taxis*, *alkalis*, *borzois*, *Kiwis*, *Maoris*, *rabbis*, *skis*.

Take care not to pluralise *-i* words that are already plural, such as *bacilli* (the Latin plural of *bacillus*) or *libretti* (the Italian plural of *libretto*). But sometimes a plural form comes to be regarded as a singular, and it can then be repluralised by adding an *-s*: *Three salamis please* (= three sausages); *We stock green, red, and wholemeal spaghettis* (= three kinds of spaghetti).

● *words ending in -o.* Some *-o* words take *-es* to form the plural, and some simply take *-s*. A few guidelines:

1. When the final *-o* is preceded by a vowel (or *y*), the word takes *-s*: *arpeggios*, *cameos*, *duos*, *embryos*, *radios*, *studios*, *trios*, and all words ending in *-oo*: *coos*, *cuckoos*, *kangaroos*, *tattoos*, *zoos*.

2. If a word is 'clipped' or 'apocopated' — *photo*, for instance, being the shortened form of *photograph* — it takes *-s* in the plural: *photos*;

similarly *dynamos, hippos, pros, rhinos, stereos, typos, videos.*

3. All proper names ending in *-o* simply add *-s: Neros, Paulos, Romeos, Lotharios.*

4. Most other *-o* words seem to be quite flexible, and can accept either *-s* or *-es* to form their plural. There is usually a preference, however, indicated in the following list: *bravoes, buffaloes, commandos, frescoes, ghettos, halos, mangoes, mottoes, mulattos, porticoes, provisos, stuccoes, tobaccos, volcanoes, zeros.*

Of those remaining *-o* words that virtually insist on one form or the other, the lists are not entirely random: *-oes* words seem more common and everyday; *-os* words more specialised or exotic.

-oes: *cargoes, dominoes, echoes, goes, heroes, innuendoes, Negroes, potatoes, tomatoes,* and probably *torpedoes.*

-os: *albinos, altos, armadillos, broncos, dittos, egos, escudos, Eskimos, espressos, generalissimos, infernos, major-domos, quangos, stilettos.*

A very rough rule of thumb is this: the less familiar and more 'un-English' an *-o* word looks, the likelier it is to take a simple *-s* in the plural. (See also the section on Italian plurals below).

● *words ending in -s.* A noun ending in *-s* presents a number of problems. Can it be pluralised at all? If so, how? If not, does it take a singular or plural verb?

1. a. Some nouns ending in *-s* already function as plurals, taking a plural verb, and thus cannot be pluralised: *banns* (*The banns were published yesterday*), *entrails, genitals, pants,* and *trousers* (*These trousers are too large for me*). Similarly: *alms, binoculars, contents, dregs, glasses, goods, jinks, premises* (*These premises are for sale*), *proceedings, proceeds, remains, spectacles,* and *victuals.*

And so too *scissors* (*These scissors are blunt*), *calipers, pliers, shears, tweezers, pincers, compasses, scales.* The plural of *scissors* tends to be *pairs of scissors,* just as an alternative singular is *a pair of scissors.* An alternative for *tweezers,* especially in American English, is *tweezer.* Compasses and *scales* have the flexibility of both *scissors* and *tweezers:* they would pluralise as *pairs of compasses/scales,* and have the singular forms *a pair of compasses/scales* and the simple *compass* or *scale.* (Note that *forceps* does not follow this general pattern. See the following paragraph.)

b. Conversely, some nouns appear to be plural in form but take a singular verb — games such as *billiards, dominoes,* or *skittles,* for instance (*Skittles is my favourite pastime;* but of course,

Six skittles are broken), and some diseases: *Rabies is spreading. Biceps, triceps,* and *forceps* are singular nouns — *This forceps is broken* — but are often, mistakenly, used with a plural verb. The plural of *biceps* is *biceps* or *bicepses;* the plural of *forceps* is now usually *forceps,* though it used to be *forcipes* (/**for**-sipeez/): the commonly heard plural × *pairs of forceps,* like the singular × *a pair of forceps,* is not strictly correct.

A noun ending *-ics* tends to take a singular verb if it refers to the subject itself — *Economics is not an exact science* — but can be regarded as plural if used in an extended sense: *The economics of a ski-holiday are more complicated than you think.* (See -ICS.)

Four oddities, finally: *innings* (in cricket), *mews, molasses,* and *news* all take singular verbs. The plurals of *innings* and *mews* are again *innings* and *mews,* though ? *inningses* and ? *mewses* are often heard. *News* used to allow a plural verb as well — Queen Victoria apparently complained that *The news from the Crimea are bad* — but no longer. In baseball, *inning* is the singular form, *innings* the plural.

c. Next, those *-s* words that can take either a singular or a plural verb: *barracks, bellows, gallows, headquarters, stocks, waterworks,* and *whereabouts,* for instance: *The waterworks is/are just up the road.* The plural of such words is identical to the singular (except that *gallows* allows *gallowses* as well as *gallows*) but this time takes only a plural verb, of course: *The waterworks of both London and New York are due for modernisation.*

Some names of diseases have this flexibility too — *Measles is/are more dangerous than people realise* — though the singular verb is perhaps preferable. (See also MEANS; WOODS.)

2. Most nouns ending in *-s* (apart from those ending *-us* and *-sis*) simply add *-es* to form the plural: *lenses, successes, trellises, the Joneses.* Even *gas* and *bus* usually pluralise as *gases* and *buses;* similarly *yeses, alases,* and so on.

3. a. Words ending *-us,* if of Latin origin, vary between *-uses* and *-i* for the plural. (For a fuller set of rules, see the section on Latin plurals below.)

b. Words ending *-sis* almost always pluralise as *-ses: analysis/analyses; basis/bases.* Similarly *amanuenses, axes, catharses, crises, diagnoses, ellipses, geneses, hypotheses, metamorphoses, neuroses, oases, synopses.* Such words entered English from Latin or New Latin, usually going back to Greek words or roots.

A few other *-is* nouns can follow this pattern:

mantis and *pelvis* can pluralise as *mantes* and *pelves*, though *mantises* and *pelvises* are more common.

4. a. Some nouns ending *-es* (from Greek or Latin; and pronounced /-eez/ or /-iz/) remain unchanged in form when pluralising: *one series*; *ten series*. Similarly *litotes, sorites, species*, and *superficies*.

b. Similarly, some nouns borrowed from French and having a silent final *-s* remain unchanged in spelling when pluralising: *one corps, ten corps*. Similarly, *Beaujolais, chamois*, and *Charolais*. However, the pronunciation does change (in English, though not in French): *corps*, for instance, is /kor/ in the singular, but /korz/ in the plural.

Irregular forms **1.** *changing the middle vowels.* A handful of words in English change the vowel in the middle for the plural. So: *foot* becomes *feet*: *goose* becomes *geese*; *louse, lice*; *man, men*; *mouse, mice*; *tooth, teeth*. Compounds ending with any of these forms typically change in the same way. So: *women, fieldmice, woodlice, eyeteeth, forefeet*, and so on. *Tenderfoot* can pluralise as *tenderfeet*, but *tenderfoots* is more appropriate and probably more acceptable.

Note that several words ending *-man* are not compounds of the common English noun *man*, and that they pluralise with a simple *-s*: *caymans, dragomans, humans* (despite some association of meaning), *ottomans, talismans, Turkomans*.

Note too that the plural of *mongoose* (not directly related to *goose*) is *mongooses*. Yet *titmouse* (a bird), though not directly related to *mouse*, does pluralise as *titmice*.

The six base forms just listed are the only ones that change their middle vowels in this way. The models of *mouse* and *goose* do not oblige *grouse* to pluralise as × *grice*, or *moose* to pluralise as × *meese*.

2. *-en.* Three English words form their plural in *-en*, all in slightly different ways: *ox/oxen, child/children, brother/brethren* (archaic or specialised: the usual plural is now *brothers*).

3. *zero-plural.* A few nouns that could easily add *-s* to pluralise can nevertheless keep the singular form when pluralising. The word *counsel*, referring to a barrister or advocate, remains unchanged in the plural: *Counsel are conferring.* Similarly, *Cannon were perched on the hill* (though *Cannons* would be more common today). The commonest types of word that pluralise in this way are names of peoples — *Apache were here* — and names of animals: *Fish are returning to the Thames.* (For further details, see the section on 'peoples and animals' below.)

Foreign plurals ● **Latin plurals** The problem in pluralising Latin words is twofold: not only to know what the correct Latin plural would be, but also to know whether a Latin plural is wanted at all in preference to an anglicised form.

1. *words ending in -us.* Many singular nouns ending in *-us* pluralise by changing the *-us* to *-i* — *alumnus* becoming *alumni*, for instance; *bacilli* and *stimuli* are other uncompromising examples. The following forms also favour *-i*, though *-uses* is possible: *colossi, fungi, gladioli, humeri, nimbi, radii*. Note that the *-i* here is traditionally pronounced /-ī/ rather than /-i/ in English: *nimbi*, for instance, is pronounced /**nim**-bī/.

Cacti and *cactuses* seem to be equally common at the moment — so too *hippopotami* and *hippopotamuses*. Other *-us* words have probably gone over to favouring *-uses*, though the *-i* form is still acceptable: *abacuses, crocuses, discuses, eucalyptuses, focuses, uteruses*, and probably *narcissuses*. *Arbutuses*, like *circuses*, seems to be the only acceptable plural form. Many such words go back to Greek roots, their Latin form being medieval or New Latin.

If a noun ending *-cus* is pluralised as *-ci*, the *c*-sound can be softened in pronunciation: *abaci*, /**abb**ə-sī/; *croci*, /**crō**-sī/. *Disci* and *foci* can be pronounced with either a hard or a soft *c*: /-k-/ or /-s-/.

Note the difference in meaning between *genii* (= guardian spirits) and *geniuses* (= brilliantly talented people).

Not all Latin-based *-us* nouns would take an *-i* plural in Latin, and accordingly they never take one in English. Usually these are 'fourth-declension' Latin nouns, which in Latin keep the *-us* ending unchanged in the plural. English occasionally follows suit, allowing *apparatus, hiatus*, and *nexus*, for instance, to remain unchanged in the plural. But the usual practice in English today is to add *-es* to form the ending *-uses*: *apparatuses, hiatuses, nexuses; censuses, consensuses, foetuses, impetuses*; similarly, *prospectuses, sinuses, statuses*.

The irregular Latin *callus* and *virus*, and the New Latin *octopus* and *platypus*, again simply take *-es* to form the plural in English (though some dictionaries do enter *octopi* as an alternative plural).

The English nouns *ignoramus, omnibus, quietus*, and *rebus* are all irregular Latin formations (based on a verb, or on the dative or ablative case of the noun), so again *-i* is impossible (the plural ✗ *ignorami* is only a joke): *-uses* is the plural form in each case.

Another category of Latin *-us* nouns formed its Latin plural not in *-i* but in *-era* or *-ora*. A few of these survive in English: *corpus/corpora*, *genus/genera* (compare *femur/femora*). The plural of *opus* should be *opera*, but *opuses* is usually used to distinguish the two musical terms.

2. *words ending in -um*. Some neuter Latin nouns ending in *-um* have been adopted unchanged into English, and form their plurals in both Latin and English by changing the *-um* to *-a*: *addenda*, *bacteria*, *curricula*, *data*, *desiderata*, *errata*, *media*, *ova*, and *quanta*. *Agenda* and *pudenda* too (*agenda* so much so that it is now established as a singular noun, with the plural *agendas*), though singular *-um* forms of these two words are now rarer in English than the plural forms.

Memoranda, *scrota*, and *strata* still favour the *-a* ending, though *memorandums*, *scrotums*, and *stratums* are possible. The plural of *medium*, in several of its senses, can be either *media* or *mediums*; but only *media* is used when referring to means of mass communication such as radio and television, and only *mediums* is used when referring to people who allegedly communicate with the spirits of the dead.

In many other *-um* nouns, however, the anglicised *-ums* ending seems to have edged out the Latinate *-a* form: *aquariums*, *auditoriums*, *compendiums*, *consortiums*, *craniums*, *crematoriums*, *encomiums*, *fulcrums*, *gymnasiums*, *honorariums*, *maximums*, *modicums*, *sanatoriums*, *rostrums*, *vacuums*, and possibly *millenniums*, *referendums*, *stadiums*, and *ultimatums* too.

The following end only in *-ums* in English: *albums*, *antirrhinums*, *asylums*, *decorums*, *delphiniums*, *forums*, *geraniums*, *harmoniums*, *laburnums*, *magnums*, *museums*, *nasturtiums*, *pendulums*, *petroleums*, and *premiums*. And the following *-ums* plurals could not even in theory take *-a* instead, since the singular form in each case is not by origin a Latin neuter noun in the nominative: *conundrums*, *factotums*, *locums*, *quorums*, and *vellums*.

Note the slipshod tendency to regard certain *-a* plurals as singular (and often to 'pluralise' them as *-as*): *candelabra*, *data*, *media*, *phenomena*. What is an accepted and established development in the case of *agenda* is dubious or quite non-standard in other *-um/-a* words:

✗ I started to read, belatedly, Thomas Keneally's *Schindler's Ark*. Here, again, one is struck by the infectious quality of deceit, for

prewar Germany and Austria were ideal culture plates for this particular bacteria to proliferate. In such societies, those with a gift for deception flourish.

> – Professor Anthony Clare,
> *The Listener*

? Of the two the latter is more terrifying. At night she patrols the corridors, flourishing a candelabra and listening for me.
> – Ron Butlin, *The Fiction Magazine*

(See DATA; ERRATA; MEDIA; STRATUM.)

3. *words ending in -a*. Latin feminine nouns ending in *-a* typically took the ending *-ae* in the plural, and so do several such words adopted into English: *alumnae*, *larvae*, *vertebrae*; similarly *algae* and *minutiae*, though the singular forms of these two are extremely rare. Note that the *-ae* here is traditionally pronounced /-ee/ rather than /ī/ in English: *larvae*, for instance, is pronounced /**lar**vee/.

Many *-a* words have alternative plurals: *-ae* or *-as*. The more technical the context, the likelier an *-ae* ending; the more general the context, the likelier an *-as* ending: so research scientists might speak of *chemical formulae*, but journalists would probably speak of *chemical formulas* (and certainly of *political formulas*). The list of flexible nouns of this kind includes *amoeba*, *cicada*, *lacuna*, *placenta*, *tibia*, *trachea*, *verruca*. Note that *antenna* takes the plural *antennae* when referring to the sensory organs of insects or crustaceans, but *antennas* when used, as in American English chiefly, to refer to a radio, radar, or television aerial.

Many English *-a* nouns, though derived from or through Latin, never end with *-ae* in the plural, always taking a simple English *-s* instead. Sometimes they are simply too well assimilated into English — *areas*, *arenas*, *chimeras*, *hyenas*, *ideas*, *orchestras*, *plethoras*, *tiaras*, *villas*. Sometimes they are New Latin in origin — unknown in classical Latin, and thus lacking a tradition of an *-ae* plural: *aspidistras*, *japonicas*, *manias*, *neuralgias*, *phobias*, *silicas*, *utopias*, *dahlias*, *magnolias*. (These last two named after botanists called *Dahl* and *Magnol*.) But the New Latin *flora* and *fauna* (from the names of Roman goddesses) can take either an *-ae* or *-as* plural (though since they are usually used as collective nouns, the plurals are rare).

Of course, there are scores of *-a* words in English that do not come directly from Latin, and could not possibly take the Latin plural ending *-ae*. The following, for instance, are Italian in origin (they would be pluralised with *-e* instead of -*a* in Italian, but almost always take -*s* in English): *aria, coda, diva, loggia, pizza, regatta, stanza, tuba, vista*, and, in a distorted form, *harmonica*. All the following words, from various other languages (as far apart as Spanish and Sanskrit) again pluralise with a simple -*s*: *bonanza, mantra, pagoda, panda, puma, sciatica, siesta, sofa, tapioca, veranda, zebra*.

The nouns *carcinoma, dogma*, and *stigma*, even though entering English through Latin, revert to their Greek origins when pluralising in technical contexts, and take the Greek -*ata* ending rather than a Latin ending. (See the section on Greek plurals below.)

Various other English -*a* words, though derived from Latin or through Latin, do not represent Latin nominative feminine singular nouns, and cannot therefore take -*ae* in the plural: hence *agendas* and *operas* once again, *commas, dramas, insignias, propagandas, quotas*, and *subpoenas*.

4. *words ending in -x.* The Latin plural ending -*ices*, for nouns ending -*ix* or -*ex* in the singular, is now confined mostly to formal or technical contexts. In more general or informal use, the anglicised -*ixes* or -*exes* is more common: *appendices* or *appendixes*; *apices, apexes*; *codices, codexes*; *cortices, cortexes*; *helices, helixes*; *indices, indexes*; *matrices, matrixes*; *radices, radixes*; *vortices, vortexes*. Analogously, *cruces* or *cruxes*, and *calyces* or *calyxes*.

Note that the two plurals each of *appendix* and *index* tend to be used in different ways. Books usually have *appendices* (very occasionally *appendixes*), but surgeons remove the *appendixes* of their patients. Books also have *indexes* (probably not ? *indices*), but inflation and unemployment are *indices* of economic problems (very seldom ? *indexes*).

Several -*x* words, derived through Latin or New Latin but originating in Greek, take a Greek plural ending -*ges* (pronounced /-jeez/), though a simple English -*es* suffix seems to be always acceptable too, and is far commoner today in general contexts: *coccyxes, coccyges*; *phalanxes, phalanges*; *sphinxes, sphinges*; *syrinxes, syringes*.

Not all -*ix* or -*ex* nouns can take an -*ices* ending, of course: if the word did not exist in that form in Latin, it will obviously not take a Latinised plural ending. Hence the regular English plurals *circumflexes, complexes, duplexes, fixes, flexes, prefixes, reflexes, suffixes*, and so on. And trade names such as *Perspex* and *Pyrex* would similarly take a simple -*es* in the plural.

● **Greek plurals** **1.** *words ending in -a.* Several Greek-based English words ending in -*a*

sometimes take the Greek ending -*ata* in the plural even if entering English through Latin or New Latin. But they usually have a simple -*s* plural form as an alternative. So: *carcinomas* or *carcinomata*; *dogmas, dogmata*; *miasmas, ? miasmata*; *schemas, schemata*; *stigmas, stigmata*; *stomas, stomata*; *traumas, traumata*. The more formal or technical the context, the more likely the -*ata* ending; the more informal or general the context, the more likely the -*s* ending.

2. *words ending in -on.* The Greek plural for -*on* words is -*a*: hence, in English as in Greek, *criteria, ephemera*, and *ganglia*, for instance. So too *phenomena*, though the anglicised plural *phenomenons* can be used in the extended non-philosophical senses of 'extraordinary events' or 'extraordinary people'.

•Some -*on* nouns can take either plural ending: *oxymora, oxymorons*; *automata, automatons*. And some seem so at home in English that they now take the -*s* plural exclusively: *electrons, lexicons, neutrons, protons*, and *skeletons*.

There is another group of -*on* words that pluralise only in -*s* — either the relevant Greek plural would not in fact be -*ata*, or the word, though apparently Greek in form, did not exist in ancient Greek: hence *canons, cotyledons, demons, mastodons, nylons, pylons, siphons*.

Avoid once again the common trap of regarding the -*a* form as singular — ✗ *a criteria*, ✗ *a phenomena* — and repluralising it as -*as*: ✗ *several criterias*, ✗ *many phenomenas*. (See CRITERION; PHENOMENON.)

3. *words ending in -is.* As discussed above, many Greek-based words (entering English through Latin) that have the singular ending -*is* change this to -*es* (pronounced /eez/) in the plural: *crises, ellipses, nemeses, prognoses, syntheses*, and *theses*. On the whole, this plural formation does not sound pedantic in English even in informal use: it seems easier and somehow more natural to say -*es* than -*ises*.

Some -*is* nouns take the plural -*ides* in Greek, and this is sometimes carried over into English too (and pronounced /-ideez/). But outside technical contexts, the English plural ending -*es* is usually used instead. So: *irises* or *irides*; *proboscises, proboscides*. The plural of *aphis* (New Latin, not really of Greek origin at all) is *aphides*, but the forms *aphid* and *aphids* are far commoner.

4. Three unusual Greek-based plurals finally. The plural of *cyclops* is *cyclopes* in Greek, and sometimes in English too, though the English variants *cyclopses* and *cyclops* (the same as the singular) are more likely. The Greek plural of *necropolis* — *necropoleis* — is seldom used in English: *necropolises* is commonest, and *necropoles* and *necropoli* are also found. The word *atlas*, in its rare architectural sense of 'a figure of a man used as a masonry column to support an entablature' (the male equivalent of *caryatid*), has the plural *atlantes*; in its other senses, *atlas* has the regular plural *atlases*.

● **Italian plurals** Italian nouns ending in -*o* or -*e* typically change to -*i* in the plural, and this -*i* ending is sometimes adopted in English too. If a word retains very strong Italian associations, -*i* tends to be the only acceptable plural: *mafiosi*, *palazzi*. Words of more general application have -*s* as an alternative: *ciceroni*, *cicerones*; *dilettanti*, *dilettantes*; *libretti*, *librettos*; *soli*, *solos*; *tempi*, *tempos*. Note that it is -*s* rather than -*es* that is added.

Nouns ending -*io* tend to favour a simple -*s* in the plural, since the -*i* ending would be awkward in English: hence *adagios*, *arpeggios*, *seraglios*.

Italian words ending in -*a*, which would end in -*e* in the Italian plural, almost always end in -*s* in English: *pizzas*, *loggias*, *prima donnas*. The exception is *lasagne*, from *lasagna*, which like *spaghetti* is not generally recognised as a plural by English-speakers.

● **French plurals** French nouns ending in a vowel cluster such as -*ou*, -*ieu*, or -*eau* typically take an -*x* in the plural in French — the *x* being silent, so that the plural form usually sounds indistinguishable from the singular.

In English, things are more flexible: an -*s* can usually be used as an alternative to the -*x*, and when the -*x* is used, it can be silent or sounded as /z/ (the -*s* ending is always sounded this way): so the plural of *adieu* in English can be *adieus* or *adieux*; similarly with *bijous*, *bijoux*; *chateaus*, *chateaux*; *flambeaus*, *flambeaux*. Note that all these examples are still felt to be markedly French. Nouns that are more at home in English would strongly favour the anglicised -*s* ending nowadays — *beaus*, *bureaus*, *portmanteaus*, *plateaus*, *tableaus*, *trousseaus* — though the -*x* form is still permissible. Note that *purlieu* is an English formation (though from a Norman French source), quite unrelated to the French *lieu*: the plural is *purlieus*, an -*x* form being impossible.

Obversely, in *jeux d'esprit*, the -*x* form alone is possible, since it occurs in the middle of a French phrase (this -*x* is not pronounced).

A noun that might cause trouble is *Bordeaux* (a wine from the region around the French town of Bordeaux). The plural is unchanged in spell-

ing, in both French and English, but in English would change its pronunciation by adding a /z/ sound at the end.

A final pair of tricky French plurals sometimes used in English: *mesdames* and *messieurs*, from *madame* and *monsieur*. (Compare *Messrs*, the plural form of *Mr.*) Note that the first part of the word changes, as well as the second part, in each case.

● **other foreign plurals** Hebrew accounts for a few unusual plural endings in English: the plural of *kibbutz* is *kibbutzim*. *Cherub* and *seraph* can take either the Hebrew or the anglicised plural: *cherubim*, *cherubs*; *seraphim*, *seraphs*. (*Cherubim* is usually used of the angels; *cherubs* of the decorative chubby child-angel figures in paintings, or of innocent-looking children.) In the past, the plural forms *cherubim* and *seraphim* were incorrectly taken for singular forms, and further 'pluralised' as × *cherubims* (or sometimes × *cherubins*) and × *seraphims*.

The plural of *fellah*, 'a peasant or farmworker in Arab countries', is usually *fellahin*, as in Arabic.

When a word is clearly still a foreigner in English — if it is italicised, for instance, to mark its foreignness — the plural used should, if it is known, be that of the appropriate foreign language. If the Spanish word *señor*, for example, were wanted in its plural form in an English text, the correct Spanish plural *señores* would be the one to use.

Compounds Many compound nouns (whether hyphenated or open) consist of a noun first and an adjective second: *heir apparent*. The plural of the compound should be created by pluralising the noun: *heirs apparent*, *knights errant*, *battles royal*, *princes regent*, *Lords spiritual*.

Sometimes, however, the adjective is taken for a noun, and the second word rather than the first is pluralised — to the dismay of purists. Purists still insist on *courts-martial*, and *poets laureate*, but the variants *court-martials*, and *poet laureates* are well-established now, and probably more frequent. And *sergeants major*, still favoured by purists, has surely been overtaken by *sergeant majors*. More informal compounds add the -*s* at the end: *lady bountifuls*, *prince charmings*.

In contrast to *sergeant major*, the compound *major general* is now regarded as consisting of two nouns (the first here functioning like an adjective — the reverse, in other words, of the standard pattern) and therefore pluralises as *major generals*. Other two-noun compounds pluralise similarly: *judge presidents*, *lieutenant* colonels, *Lord Mayors*, *Lord Chancellors*, *Lord Lieutenants*, and *Attorney Generals* sound correct, though *Lords Chancellor* is sometimes recommended, and *Lords Lieutenant* and *Attorneys General* seem to be the official plural forms (at least in Britain). Note too *Lords Chief Justice* and the double plural in *Lords Justices of Appeal*.

With longer compounds, it is again usually the dominant noun-element that takes the plural form: *lilies of the valley*, *masters-at-arms* (from *master-at-arms*), *daughters-in-law*, *Chancellors of the Exchequer*.

If there is no obvious noun-element, or if the compound is so familiar that it is virtually a single, unbreakable word, the *-s* typically goes at the end: *forget-me-nots*, *will-o'-the-wisps*, *gin-and-tonics*. Likewise *teaspoonsful* (although *teaspoonsful* and similar formations are still possible) and *handfuls*, and *handouts*, *send-ups*, and *tip-offs*.

A few compounds, however, even if tightly knit, pluralise both elements; *manservant* pluralises as *menservants*, *woman golfer* as *women golfers*. There are many idiomatic compounds that exist only in the plural, with both nouns having the *-s* ending: *rights and wrongs*, *ups and downs*, *pros and cons*, *ifs and buts*.

Proper nouns With few exceptions, the names of people and places take a regular *-s* or *-es* ending in the plural, however tempting it might be to give them an irregular plural. So, *the Gladstones* and *the Disraelis*; *the Thackerays*, *Trollopes*, and *Dickenses*; *the Dulleses* and *the Kennedys*. Similarly, as already mentioned, *the two Germanys*, *both Sallys*, *the three Marys*, and so on. (Possible exceptions are *Ptolemies*, *Mercuries*, and the American mountain ranges the *Alleghenies* and the *Rockies*.)

When two or more people share a name and a title, pluralise one or the other, but not both: *the Misses Halliday* or *the Miss Hallidays*. If the title is shared but not the name, the title can be pluralised or just repeated: *Messrs Farnham and Scott* or *Mr Farnham and Mr Scott*. Pluralising the title tends to be more formal, in both of the cases just discussed. Other pluralised titles are *Mrs* (plural of *Mrs*) or *Mmes* (plural of *Mme* or *Mrs* — seldom used); *Mss* or *Mses* (the plurals of *Ms* — seldom used); and *Drs*.

Peoples and animals When several humans and several animals are under discussion, they can be thought of in one of two ways: either collectively, as an undifferentiated group, or individually. The 'collective' plural of the names of peoples often

keeps the same form as the singular: *In 1900 there were still Apache in these hills*. Contrast the 'individualised' plural: *Three Apaches are approaching the camp*. Similarly *Xhosa* or *Xhosas*; *Ainu*, *Ainus*; *Inuit*, *Inuits*; and so on. The collective plural is little used nowadays, having a slightly demeaning tone to it. The modern tendency would be to add the *-s* even when referring to the people in a very general 'collective' way: *In 1900 there were still Apaches in these hills*.

Note, however, that some national or group names cannot take an *-s* when pluralising — notably, those names ending in *-ese*: *A Japanese steps forward*; *There were Japanese in these hills*; *Three Japanese are approaching*. Similarly *Burmese*, *Chinese*, *Maltese*, *Portuguese*, and so on. False singulars like × *Chinee* should not be used.

Note too that some national or group names can be used only as noun-like adjectives in the plural — notably, those ending in *-ish*: *The British are approaching*. Similarly *Danish*, *Irish*, *Scottish*, *Swedish*, and so on (with *Danes*, *Scots*, and *Swedes* as available alternatives).

With animal names, there are several categories. First, some animal names cannot take an *-s* when pluralising, and simply retain the singular form: *A deer darts forward*; *There were deer in these hills*; *Three deer are approaching*. Similarly *bison*, *grouse*, *moose*, *sheep*, and *swine*. Note that *cattle* can be used only as a plural.

Other animal-names that generally take a zero-plural in this way do allow an *-s* plural occasionally. The usual zero-plural occurs when a group of the animals is referred to collectively: *He collects tropical fish*; *We caught haddock*. When individual animals are referred to, either the regular or the irregular plural may be used: *four buck* or *bucks*; *five elk* or *elks*; *six pike* or *pikes*, *seven trout* or *trouts*. When different types of the animal are referred to, there is a stronger tendency to use the regular plural: *the haddocks of the Old World and the New World*. The word *fish* tends to be used in its regular plural form *fishes* when the reference is to different species or classifications: *studying the development of the ganoid fishes*. The names of specific types of fish are often used in this way: *All the mackerels belong to the family Scombridae*.

Thirdly, there are those animal names that typically take an *-s* plural, but that occasionally take a zero-plural when considered collectively, as by scientists or game rangers. Compare the common *Tigers still inhabit the surrounding forests* and the rare *There is evidence that tiger still survive in the forests*. Note that the singular as well as the zero-plural is possible in such contexts: *There is evidence that tiger still survives in the forests.* Perhaps the majority of undomesticated animals follow this pattern: *bears, bear; ducks, duck; eagles, eagle; hares, hare; lions, lion; lobsters, lobster; quails, quail; squirrels, squirrel; turtles, turtle.*

Finally the animal names that virtually always pluralise with an *-s.* The more familiar or common the animal, the likelier it is to avoid the zero-plural — it is almost impossible, for example, to say: *?? There is evidence that dog still survive in the desert.* The only standard plural is *dogs.* Similarly *birds, cows, cuckoos, chickens, larks, moles, parrots, rats, sparrows,* and so on. A distinction is made between 'domestic' ducks and wild ones: only the wild ones can pluralise as both *ducks* and *duck.* Likewise, *cat* has the plural *cats* only, but *wildcat* can yield both *wildcats* and *wildcat.*

Numbers and quantities A word indicating a number or quantity, even when it is singular in form, can often take either a singular or plural verb according to context: *A dozen is quite enough; A dozen have been invited.*

And it often has two plural forms: a zero-plural — *Two dozen are expected* — or an *-s* plural: *Dozens are expected.* The difference in general is this: when a specific quantity is indicated, the zero-plural is used; when a rough or unspecified figure is intended, or in colloquial exaggerations, the *-s* plural is used: *five million dollars; millions of dollars; Millions of people have been invited.* Similarly *score* or *scores; hundred, hundreds; thousand, thousands; billion, billions.* One minor exception in British English — in formal contexts, the form *millions* is sometimes used to indicate a specific quantity: *In addition, two million pounds have been allocated to legal aid, and three millions to overseas aid.* In American English, only *three million* would be used here.

In some contexts, a spelt-out number can readily take a regular plural: *How many sixes did you score?*

When numbers are written as numbers, the tendency nowadays is simply to add an *-s* at the end, rather than *-'s: the 1960s; well into his 80s.* (See *-'S, -S'.*)

Unique entities Even apparently unpluralisable nouns can often be pluralised: *How can our team compete with the Liverpools or the Manchester Uniteds?*

The name of a unique entity is put forward as an example (of football teams, in this case) or type, thereby being stripped of its uniqueness and made susceptible to being pluralised. The construction should perhaps be avoided in the most formal contexts, but is widely acceptable elsewhere:

> This was a juke box with a built-in film — the forerunner of the video cassette, really. And there they were — the Louis Armstrongs, the Fats Wallers, the Duke Ellingtons, the Nat King Coles, the marvellous Mills Brothers playing and singing away at their sweet and singular music.
> – Mary Kenny, *Daily Mail*

Abbreviations, letters of the alphabet, symbols, numerals, and so on The tendency nowadays is to add a simple *-s* at the end when pluralising these, though *-'s* is still fairly common. So the abbreviations *MP* and *VIP* would preferably be pluralised as *MPs* and *VIPs;* similarly words not usually used as nouns: *whys and wherefores.*

If a word is being discussed in its role as word, it is usually put in italics, and if it is pluralised the *-s* or *-'s* ending can be left in roman type to distinguish it:

> There are too many *that*'s in your last paragraph.

Perhaps the apostrophe is best retained here, to make the distinction even clearer.

Similarly, the apostrophe tends to be used when single letters or symbols are pluralised, or where confusion might otherwise result:

> Dot your *i*'s and cross your *t*'s.
> A series of *?*'s pockmarked the text.
> There are too many Mrs's and not enough Miss's here.
> I should prefer *an*'s to *the*'s in this text.

(See *-'S, -S'* for a more detailed discussion.)

Note, finally, that nouns do not ordinarily take an apostrophe in the plural. It is a common mistake to insert one before the *s:* × *peach's 50p for six;* × *tomato's 23p* (or × *tomatoe's 23p*). The correct form is simply *peaches* and *tomatoes.*

Part II: agreement — singular and plural A singular subject takes a singular verb; a plural subject takes a plural verb.

1. Unfortunately, it is not always obvious, at least in British English, whether a subject is singular or plural. Do you say *The jury was convinced* or *The jury were convinced,* for instance?

The word *jury* is a 'group noun' — that is, it is singular in form but often has a distinctly plural sense. Other examples are *audience, cabinet, chorus, committee, couple, crew, crowd, group* itself, *jury*, *majority*, *NATO*, *pair*, *proportion*, *public*, *regiment*, and *team*. Sometimes even *Labour* (meaning 'the Labour Party'), *England* (meaning 'the England football team', for instance), and *village* can function as group nouns and take a plural verb (*The village are up in arms*). And so of course can 'collective nouns': *congregation*, *flock*, *pride* (of lions), and so on.

In many contexts, a group noun can take either a singular or a plural verb. Purists would tend to favour the singular, but the plural is probably more common in British English nowadays. In the following pair of quotations, *number* takes a singular noun in the first, and a plural noun in the second. It could easily have been the other way round:

> They argued that it did not work: that for all the elaboration of the laws, and the ruthlessness with which they were applied, an ever-increasing number of blacks was in fact settling within and around the cities.
> – Dan Jacobson, *The Guardian*

> The record number of fringe candidates seem likely to have even less effect on the result than usual.
> – Simon Hoggart, *The Observer*

Here are two more examples of group nouns with singular verbs that could just as well have been plural:

> A regiment of personal robots is preparing to invade British homes. Equipped with synthetic voices and mounted on wheels ...
> – Julian Allason, *The Observer*

> The committee of Privy Councillors was concerned that chairmen of companies which donate to Conservative Party funds, who are honoured for their contribution to industry rather than for political services, could be suspected of receiving peerages or knighthoods for unacknowledged political reasons.
> – Peter Hennessy, *The Times*

And here, on the other side, are a few more examples of group nouns with plural verbs that could just as well have been singular.

> The occasion had ... filled Wembley to capacity ... The audience were raucous but essentially good-natured as blue mingled amicably with red.
> – Ronald Atkin, *The Observer*

> We seem to be seized with diary mania ... The public seem to have an insatiable

appetite for the genre. Newspapers cannot wait to serialise the revelations.
> – Sir Roy Strong, *The Times*

> If the Conservatives are no longer the Nobs' party, Labour are in danger of becoming the Yobs' party.
> – Alan Watkins, *The Observer*

Not all contexts allow the group noun a free choice between a singular verb and a plural verb, however. First of all, if words or phrases such as *they*, *these*, *one another* or *such people* are used elsewhere to refer to the mass noun, then clearly the group noun should take a plural verb. In the following two extracts, for instance, the plural verb could not really be replaced by a singular verb (North Americans would tend to reformulate the sentence in the first example and say *the members of the party*):

> On the way to the French border the party stop over at an underworld safe-house in Madrid, where they stumble across a sweaty middle-aged Australian crook (superbly played by Bill Hunter) and his sexy Spanish mistress (Laura del Sol).
> – Philip French, *The Observer*

> Viewed merely from a humanist standpoint, it was remarkable. A group of total strangers were acknowledging in front of one another their bereavement and their feelings.
> – Sue Limb, *The Observer*

The use of *they* and *one another* in the same sentence as the group noun (*party*, *group*) virtually necessitates a plural verb. The following two quotations ignore this guideline, and an uncomfortable inconsistency results — the presence of *they* and *is/was* together in the same context:

> ??If the staff is united in their determination to keep the work within the NHS — and they usually are — and if the tenders are handled fairly and objectively, then Ruocco thinks the in-house tender should win.
> – Francis Beckett, *New Statesman*

> ??A group of left-wing leaders was already considering what to do if Benn survived in Bristol. They had in mind a deal: if Benn stood down against Kinnock, they would back him for the deputy.
> – Peter Gillman, *The Times*

This points to a more general guideline: if the group noun is used in a collective, undifferentiated way, suggesting a single entity, then it should perhaps take a singular verb — *The jury has retired* — though a plural verb is still usually possible. On the other hand, if the group noun is used in an individualising way, suggesting a number of distinct components or members, then it should take a plural verb: *The jury are still exchanging ideas*; *The jury are in disagreement*.

But American English, as suggested earlier, strongly favours the singular: *The jury was convinced*. Rather than use a plural verb, Americans would tend to reformulate the sentence. They would try to avoid saying *The jury are still exchanging ideas* or even *The jury are arguing among themselves*, and would say instead *The members of the jury are* . . . .

2. a. Just as an apparently singular subject (*the jury*) can take a plural verb, so an apparently plural subject (*two full houses*) can sometimes take a singular verb:

Two full houses at the Dominion is testament to the enduring loyalty of his audience, and Martyn repaid it.
— Mick Brown, *The Guardian*

Two aficionados of Dumas's famous prisoner, one admittedly madder than the other, living in the same council block is perhaps stretching the imagination too much.
— Jonathan Mantle, *The Listener*

The singular verb is acceptable here because the subject, despite appearances, clearly refers to a single concept. The opening words can be understood as (*the fact of*) *two full houses* and (*the idea of*) *two aficionados* — in this way the subject can be interpreted as singular, and the singular verb justified. Similarly:

Two weeks is a long time in politics.
Eight kilometres is too far for novice hikers.
Five dollars isn't enough for a square meal these days.

If the subjects are understood as (*a period of*) *two weeks,* (*a distance of*) *eight kilometres,* and (*the sum of*) *five dollars,* then the singular verb in each case is seen as quite acceptable.

b. Another kind of singular subject that appears, for a moment, to be plural is exemplified in the sentence *My son and heir is 16 today.* Despite the distracting presence of an *and,* the subject is clearly singular, as though it were written *my son-and-heir.* Similarly: *Her pride and joy is the rockery.* Not all compound subjects are so clear-cut unfortunately: is the phrase *fear and trembling,* for instance, singular or plural in function? Here are two other borderline cases — on

balance, the singular verb is probably less acceptable than a plural verb would be:

??This obsession . . . brought him respect but also fear. The charm and drive was real, but it could all be a little tough.
— Caroline Moorhead, *The Times*

?Fire and smoke on board an aircraft is a serious emergency — yet the crew spent a crucial four minutes and 21 seconds confirming that the warning was genuine and not spurious.
— Peter Durisch, *The Observer*

See AND 2. for further details.

c. Even when the *and* clearly indicates a plural subject rather than a compound subject, it is sometimes ignored, and a singular verb is mistakenly used in place of a plural verb.

??This catch-all phrase and the very wide discretion it gives the Home Secretary is criticised by some lawyers.
— Michael Davie, *The Observer*

The *is* should strictly speaking be *are.* However, *is* could be defended perhaps on the ground that the *and*-element is parenthetical or very subordinate, and not really a full part of the subject of the sentence.

3. Although the presence of *and* in a subject usually makes it a plural subject, the presence of *or, nor, together with, like,* or *as well as* does not. A common mistake is to assume that if a subject has two or more elements, it must be plural. Not so:

✗ Holloway, as well as Harrison, give a comic performance in the classic British tradition.

Change *give* to *gives* (or else change *as well as* to *and* in order to create a plural subject). Similarly:

✗ Neither the plaintiff nor the defendant seem pleased with the judgment.

This should be *seems,* not *seem.* (See EITHER; NEITHER.)

But note that when *or* or *nor* separates the elements of a complex subject, the verb will be singular or plural according to the element nearest to it. So:

Even rain or distant footsteps or birdsong is enough to wake me.
Even rain or birdsong or distant footsteps are enough to wake me.

See OR for further details.

4. Two other common types of error, or 'failure of agreement', are exemplified in these sentences:

× Essentially, man's aggressive energies is the basis of Art.

× Man's aggressive nature, redirected by sensitive minds into peaceful channels, underlie all Art.

The first mistake is based on an overhasty reversal of subject and complement: the natural form of the sentence is *The basis of Art is man's aggressive energies*. But the two noun phrases cannot simply be switched about. The verb should change too, since the subject has changed from singular to plural. In times past, the simple switch was apparently possible: *The wages of sin is death*. But today (assuming that the word *wages* could still be used at all in the same sense), the sentence would have to be rephrased: *The wages of sin are death* or *Death is the wages of sin*.

The second mistake — the use of a plural verb after a singular subject — is due to the distraction (or attraction) of the plural nouns in between. The sentence should read *Man's aggressive nature ... underlies all Art*. The intervention of the words *minds* and *channels* misleads the writer into assuming that a plural verb is required. Here are some further examples:

× It will be some time before the proof of the benefits of the programme are accepted.
— Lord Vaizey; 'Letter from London', BBC World Service

× This feeling is underlined by her conviction, widely shared, that the sale of council houses have been an important success during her term of office.
— Michael White, *The Guardian*

× The sense of a buried world, of which glimpses can only be uneasily caught, have the true whiff of that human history of hell of which the Western traveller has so little experience or comprehension.
— Elaine Feinstein, *The Fiction Magazine*

× There are good grounds for believing that many hundreds, perhaps thousands, of sensitive documents passed through Miss Tisdall's hands, and the confidentiality of their contents were at all times respected.
— Professor Anthony Clare, *The Listener*

× The constant interplay between the academic lecture and the 'elite' essay on the one hand, and the presentation of the same or closely related material and signatures by the media — the quality papers, the weeklies, the radio-talk — on the other, have produced hybrid forms.
— Professor George Steiner, *The Times Literary Supplement*

In the last example, despite all the *and*'s and all the plural verbs, the subject of the sentence is singular, *interplay*, and the verb should therefore be *has* not *have*.

In the following examples, by contrast, the authors remain admirably undistracted by the thicket of plural nouns, and correctly choose a singular verb to correspond to the singular subject:

For the moment, though, the simple combination of antique home movies (preferably shot abroad) cut together with present-day reflections from their now elderly participants never fails to fascinate.
— Julian Barnes, *The Observer*

The financial strength of both the debtors and the banks is now firmly interlocked. The questionable value of the banks' claims upon the developing countries represents a challenge to their solvency.
— Lord Lever, *Time and Tide*

5. A final type of common error of agreement: in inverted word-order, when the subject follows the verb, the speaker or writer tends to begin with a singular verb, and realises too late, if at all, that the subject he wants is plural:

× Into the room walks Professor Wilkins and his wife.

?? On the left wing of the Royalist army opposite Fairfax was George Goring, Sir Charles Lucas and the Northern Horse.
— C.V. Wedgwood, *The King's War*

?? Whenever we have a simple difference of opinion, why is there always an argument, accusations, tears, and sulking.

Strictly speaking, *walks* should be *walk*, *was* should be *were*, and *why is there* should be *why are there*. The last of the examples could, however, be defended: the phrase *there is* is sometimes considered an unvarying idiomatic formula applicable to singular and plural subjects alike, especially when the noun directly following is in the singular. (For further details, see THERE IS.)

See also AGREEMENT; NONE; ONE **5**; SORT OF **2**.

plus When *plus* is used as a preposition to mean 'together with, in addition to', the following verb agrees with the noun that precedes *plus*, and can therefore be singular or plural: *Her experience plus her qualifications makes her an obvious choice for the post* (singular subject and verb); *Savings plus interest total £2,500* (plural subject and verb). (See PLURALS Part II.)

Plus has now come to be used as a conjunction too, meaning 'and': *? He's handsome, plus he has a good job.* This usage is about 20 years old now, but has still not found full acceptance in standard English. Restrict it to casual speech and informal writing. (See CONJUNCTIONS.)

point In informal English, the noun *point* is often followed directly by the *-ing* form of a verb:

> *? There's absolutely no point complaining to me, lady.*

Formal usage requires the insertion of the preposition *in*:

> There is no point in complaining to me, madam.

point of view 1. The phrase *point of view* is valuable in its proper place, but it tends to be used far too often in inappropriate surroundings.

First, it should not be used as a supposedly elegant substitute for *view/s* or *opinion/s,* especially when the opinions are specific:

> ✗ If your point of view conflicts with hers, can't you just agree to differ?
> ✗ It is my considered point of view that interest rates will fall by at least two points by December.

A simple *view* or *opinion* should replace *point of view* in both of these examples. Compare the correct use, as in *His point of view is broadly conservative.* Here *view* and *opinion* could not be substituted, since their range is not general enough.

Secondly, *point of view* is often enrolled to create extremely (and needlessly) complex prepositions:

> ?? Our current rate of progress is quite inadequate from the point of view of meeting the deadline.

It is much simpler and more elegant to say: *quite inadequate for meeting the deadline,* for example, or *quite inadequate in view of the deadline* or *quite inadequate if we are to meet the deadline.* Again:

> ?? These recruits appear quite ill-equipped from the point of view of active combat.
> ?? These recruits appear quite ill-equipped from the active-combat point of view.

Use instead the simple *quite ill-equipped for active combat.*

2. Objections are sometimes raised to the use of *viewpoint, standpoint,* and *angle* as alternatives to *point of view.*

Angle is perhaps still not fully acceptable: there is a slightly colloquial tone to it, as in *? not really suitable from my angle* or *? virtually heretical from the Vatican's angle,* that is inappropriate to very formal usage. But *standpoint* (a loan translation from the German Standpunkt) and *viewpoint* (a reasonably elegant fusion of *standpoint* and *point of view*) are now so well established and convenient that they can be regarded as standard English — though they should, like all abstract or technical or modish terms, be used sparingly. They are especially useful as variants of *point of view* when the sentence suffers from a surplus of *of*'s:

> From the viewpoint of the ecology of the Isle of Mull, the current increase in tourism is a threat rather than a blessing.

This is awkward enough, but at least it is better than *? From the point of view of the ecology of the Isle of Mull . . .*

Of course, a quite different word or phrase might be the best of all: *As for the ecology of the Isle of Mull . . . .*

politic This adjective, in its common present-day usage, has a quite different sense from *political,* though the two words were originally just variants. Certainly the notion of *politics* is bound up in the common origin of the two words, which is found in the Greek *polis,* 'a city'.

A political decision is one connected with *politics* (whether national politics, office politics, or the politics — or so-called power-game — of a marriage); *a politic decision* is simply a wise or prudent one, a decision based on *policy,* in the sense of wise or prudent principles. Many *political* decisions are far from *politic.*

Politic does retain the sense of 'political' in one phrase still: *the body politic.* And it does have other, less positive shades of meaning: 'shrewd' or even 'cunning and unscrupulous'. But its usual meaning is the laudatory one of 'prudent, judicious'.

Note that *politic* is stressed on the first syllable, *political* on the second.

In forming the adverb, *politic* differs from most words ending in -*ic*: *music(al)* produces *musically*, *terrific* produces *terrifically*, and so on. *Politic* (like *public*) simply adds -*ly*: *a politicly swift retreat*. This helps to avoid confusion with the adverb from *political*: *a politically damaging retreat*.

See -IC, -ICAL.

politics See -ICS.

pore, pour No one confuses the *pores* of the skin with *pouring rain*, but the verb *to pore* as in *to pore over a book* is sometimes misspelt as the more common verb *to pour*. Perhaps the reason for this is the assumption that a metaphor is somehow involved, by which the reader is thought to pour attention over the book. What *to pore over* really means is 'to ponder or examine', a sense far removed from that of *to pour*, 'to flow or cause to flow'.

The two verbs are perhaps connected in origin: the Middle English form of both was *pouren*. The noun *pore* has a quite different source, the Greek *poros*, 'a passage'.

potential, potentiality As nouns, both of these words refer to an inherent capacity for development, or to something that has this quality. The words are related to *potent*, and share with it the idea of power, though in their case still latent. The difference between them is more a matter of the different constructions they typically occur in than of any easily identifiable difference in meaning.

The words are used in various ways: with *the*; with *a*; without either article, as mass nouns; and in the plural. Here are some typical usages:

Women have the potential for far greater political influence.
This production has potentialities, but it needs to be tightened up throughout, and recast in the third act.
That young soprano has great potential.

Potential has technical senses in grammar, physics, and electronics, and can of course be used as an adjective too.

pour See PORE.

practical, practicable *Practicable* means essentially 'capable of being done or put into practice, workable, feasible': *It was not practicable to move the bed in without taking the door off its hinges.*

I always think that the danger with any group of men like a college is that we tend to get on each other's nerves. I believe that everyone, particularly the unmarried fellows, ought to be compelled to spend three months abroad each year. And also — and this I do suggest to you all as a practicable proposition — I think we ought to set for ourselves an almost artificially high standard of manners and behaviour.

– Crawford, in C.P. Snow's
The Masters

Practicable can also mean 'usable, reasonably suitable and efficient': *a rough but practicable road*; *a practicable implement for the purpose*. There is clearly some overlap with *practical,* but the two adjectives can and should be kept distinct.

The most important meanings of *practical* are these:

—'carried out in practice, involving action rather than thought' (the opposite of *theoretical*): *a practical joke*; *the practical application of your discovery*; *a practical examination in the laboratory after the written paper*.
—'suitable for the purpose, and functioning well': *Season tickets are very practical.*
—(of things) 'suited or adapted to actual conditions': *a practical suggestion* — that is, one which takes account of the circumstances and their restrictions and demands.
—(of people) 'efficient, sensible, down-to-earth, capable of putting ideas into effect, skilled at actually doing things': *Mary is a very practical person* — *John has grand ideas for redesigning the living room, but she is the one who actually builds the bookcases.*
—'in effect, virtual': *a practical disaster.* (The adverbial form is more common here: see PRACTICALLY.)

The second and third of these senses seem to be illustrated in the following passage:

Nightingale seemed to be satisfied or to have lost interest. Brown's explanation was that he was enough open to reason to realise that he could go no further; for his own practical ends, it was sensible to stop. Brown did not let us forget Nightingale's practical ends: 'He may be unbalanced,' said Brown, 'he may be driven by impulses which I am sure you understand better than I do, but somehow he manages to give them a direction. And that concerns me most. He wants some very practical things, and he's going to be a confounded nuisance.'

– C.P. Snow, *The Masters*

The contrast between *practicable* and *practical* can be clearly seen in this sentence: *A practical person knows the difference between what is practicable and what is not.* Note that *practicable* cannot ordinarily be applied directly to people, whereas *practical* clearly can be. And consider the difference between a scheme that is *not practicable* (or that is *impracticable*) — it is impossible, and simply cannot be put into practice — and a scheme that is *not practical* (or that is *impractical* or *unpractical*): it is theoretically possible, and could be put into practice, but only at a cost in time, money, or effort that makes it hardly worth while.

Note finally the opposite forms just mentioned — *impracticable, impractical,* and *unpractical. Impracticable* is certainly preferable to *unpracticable* nowadays. But about *impractical* and *unpractical* there is considerable argument. Some authorities prefer one, some the other. Some use *unpractical* when referring to people, and *impractical* when referring to things. Some use *unpractical* to mean 'slightly unworkable' and 'slightly unskilled', and *impractical* to mean 'completely unworkable' and 'completely unskilled, utterly ham-fisted'. Such distinctions are not widely recognised however; the tendency is clearly towards *impractical* in all senses and in all circumstances, though *unpractical* is still fighting a rearguard action:

> During that extravagant year 1947-48, August to August, lodgings and food cost us around 5,500 dollars; gas, oil and repairs 1,234 and various extras almost as much; ... this modest *rentier* spent around 8,000 dollars, or better say 10,000 because, unpractical as I am, I have surely forgotten a number of items.
> — Vladimir Nabokov, *Lolita*

practically This is the adverbial form of *practical*, and shares its range of meanings (see PRACTICAL above). However, its commonest senses today are 'in every important respect, in practice, in effect, virtually' and 'very nearly, almost'. These two senses seem to be very close, and many sentences can be understood in both ways: *? His business is practically bankrupt* can mean that it has in practice ceased trading (though formal bankruptcy proceedings have not yet been completed), or it can mean that it is nearly bankrupt but not quite, and that it could still rally and survive.

Both of these senses are sometimes criticised, though the first of them is now widely accepted.

The second sense — 'very nearly, almost' — is widely used but remains unacceptable to careful speakers and writers, both because it creates ambiguity, as in the example just mentioned, and conversely because it very often ends up meaning almost the opposite of 'in practice, in effect'. To say *?? I practically succeeded* when you mean *I did not succeed (but I nearly did)* is an absurd distortion of the original sense of *practically*. Use *nearly* or *almost* instead.

It is interesting to note that the phrase *for all practical purposes* seems to share with *practically* the sense of 'in effect', but not the questionable sense of 'almost'. *For all practical purposes, I succeeded* implies, unambiguously, a genuine (though perhaps unrecognised) success.

practice, practise *Practice* is the noun, *to practise* is the verb. Compare *licence* and *license*. (In American English, however, *practice* usually serves for both noun and verb, as does *license*.) To remember the spellings, think of *advice* (noun) and *advise* (verb), where the difference in pronunciation provides a clear guide to the spelling.

A further danger of misspelling is possible when the two forms are used adjectivally: *a practice match,* but *a well-practised player.*

precedence, precedent A *precedent* is an event, decision, or the like that will serve as an example or model in later cases. Typically, a judge's decision might be a precedent that other judges will take into account in similar trials in the future. But precedents are set in other contexts too: *If I renew your contract, I shall be setting a precedent, and all the other labourers will expect a new contract too.*

> For him the precedents for suicide had been set in his scholarly childhood, when his father had read to him in Josephus the account of the Dead Sea Zealots' mass suicide on the eve of capture by the Romans.
> — Thomas Keneally, *Schindler's Ark*

Precedent can be an adjective as well as a noun, though it is now old-fashioned: *My claim was precedent.* A common derivative is *unprecedented*, meaning 'unheard of, unique, original': *an unprecedented lapse of concentration by Borg.*

Precedence, unlike *precedent*, is an uncountable noun: whereas you can speak of *a precedent* or *five precedents*, you cannot usually use *a* or *five* before *precedence. Precedence* shares with *precedent* the core idea of 'going before': both words share the Latin roots *prae*, 'before' + *cedere*, 'to go'. But *precedence* (sometimes *precedency*), suggests priority in importance or status rather than in time: *Sooner or later, money takes precedence over love*. More specifically, *precedence* refers to the ceremonial order of rank, observed especially on formal occasions: *A duke has precedence of a marquis, and a baron gives precedence to an earl*.

Note the prepositions: *to take/have precedence over* (or, more formally, *of*), and *to give precedence to*. As a noun, *precedent* may be followed by *of* — *the precedent of staying for a year* — or *for*: *There is no precedent for doing that*. As an adjective, if used after a verb, *precedent* takes the preposition *to*: *My claim was precedent to hers*.

Both *precedence* and *precedent* as noun can be pronounced /**press**-/ or /**preess**-/ — /**press**-/ is slightly preferable. As adjective, *precedent* usually shifts the stress to the second syllable: /pri-**seed**'nt/.

precipitate, precipitous These adjectives are related in their origins: both can be traced back to the Latin *praeceps*, 'headlong or headfirst' (from *prae*, 'before' + *caput*, 'a head'). But they now have distinct uses.

Precipitate primarily means 'rushing headlong, going pellmell', as in *The enemy scattered in a precipitate retreat*.

Secondly, it means 'sudden, abrupt':

> The pain was minimal, the ordeal so quickly over it might hardly have been; in spite of the stitches she had to have because his entry into the world had been so precipitate, Maggie felt wonderful.
> — Colleen McCullough,
> *The Thorn Birds*

Thirdly, *precipitate* means 'too sudden, too hasty, without due consideration, rash':

> It is impossible to estimate how much revenue the Getty interests lost because of my precipitate decision.
> — J. Paul Getty (U.S.), *As I See It*

Note that there is a verb *precipitate* too — it can mean 'to hurl', 'to fall', 'to cause to happen prematurely', and so on:

> The IRA Godfathers believe, and probably with good reason, that each new attempt at a political solution, followed by the failure of that attempt (a failure which the IRA will help to precipitate), brings the idea of British withdrawal from Northern Ireland a little

further up the agenda.
> — Conor Cruise O'Brien,
> *The Observer*

The pronunciation of the verb is different — usually /pri-**sip**pi-tayt/, whereas the adjective is usually /pri-**sip**pi-tət/.

And *precipitate* can be used as a noun too, usually in connection with chemistry. It refers to the solid particles that are separated out of a solution or suspension. It can be pronounced in either of the ways just listed.

The noun *precipitation* has various senses, among them the technical meteorological reference to any fall of water from the air, such as rain, snow, dew, and sleet. It is not an accurate synonym of *rain* alone, though it is often used in place of *rain* in a jocular or facetious way.

There is the rare word *precipitant* too (pronounced /pri-**sip**pi-tənt/), which as an adjective can replace *precipitate* in any of its senses, and as a noun means 'any substance that causes precipitation'. *Precipitantly* can also be used instead of the adverb *precipitately*.

The adjective *precipitous* has a quite different sense from *precipitate* and the related words just discussed. *Precipitous* refers primarily to terrain, and means 'like a precipice' (or 'having many precipices'), or 'extremely steep':

> For the next two years he would be campaigning in rough country, against tribesmen familiar with it, and often established in precipitous strongholds.
> — Mary Renault,
> *The Nature of Alexander*

> But meanwhile I had said goodbye to my elephant Sadu and my father had obtained a new job in the hills. It was to maintain a small mountain railway, the one that runs in the most precipitous fashion, sometimes upon gradients of one in three, up the rampart of Himalayan foothills until it arrives at Darjeeling, the terminus; after which, mules and horses carry the traveller onwards into Tibet.
> — Lawrence Durrell,
> *The Fiction Magazine*

Precipitous may also suggest falling or plunging down a steep place: *the river's precipitous plunge*.

Figuratively, *precipitous* is used of dramatic, often disastrous, declines or plunges; the adverb *precipitously* is most likely to occur in this sense: *The company's profits have dropped precipitously in the last three years*.

There is a danger of confusion between the words *precipitate* and *precipitous*. Be careful not to use *precipitous* in such phrases as ✗ *a precipitous decision*. The correct form is: *a precipitate decision*.

In the following quotation, the author or narrator has made the mistake of using *precipitously* for *precipitately*:

> ✗ When he'd gone I tried to make myself presentable for work. I was beginning to realise just how ill-managed was the move I'd so precipitously made. I'd brought a few clothes, my sponge-bag, my make up — and nothing else. No food, no linen, no clothes-hangers even.
> — Lynne Reid Banks,
> *The L-Shaped Room*

predicate The verb *to predicate* has several meanings — 'to imply or connote', 'to proclaim or declare', 'to ascribe or attribute' (as in *The poet predicated natural aggressiveness of mankind* — note the preposition *of* here). It is little used in any of these senses nowadays (except perhaps in the last sense, in the study of logic).

But one sense in which it is all too often used is 'to base or establish (an idea, belief, statement, or action)':

> The president predicates his policy on the 'proofs' provided by the Think-tank that he himself set up.
> The Senate's fears were predicated upon legends of previous emperors, and how corrupted they had become after their elevation.

> That's the second question which is predicated on a series of assumptions which are yours rather than mine.
> — Joseph Heller (U.S.),
> quoted in *The Times*

(Note the preposition *on* or *upon* here.) There is nothing incorrect in such sentences; there is something slightly pompous about them. *To predicate* has become a vogue word, a fancy substitute for the more familiar verbs *to base*, *to establish*, and *to found*.

Take care not to mistake *predicate* for *predict*, or *predication* for *prediction*, or *predicable* for *predictable*: ✗ *The child's ruses were quite transparent and predicable and I soon put a stop to them*. The word needed here is *predictable*.

The Latin source words of *predict* and *predicate* are ultimately the same, though they were taken up in different ways: *predict* goes back to *prae*, in the sense of 'before' + *dicere*, 'to speak';

predicate goes back to *prae*, in the sense of 'in front of, in public' + *dicare* (a variant form of *dicere*), 'to proclaim, make known'.

For the use in grammar of the noun *predicate*, see SENTENCES.

predicative See ADJECTIVES 1.

prefer, preferable 1. Avoid adding a redundant *more* or *most* to *preferable* or *prefer*:

> ✗ Perhaps violent sports were necessary and more preferable than the other things human beings could do to each other.
> — Shirley MacLaine (U.S.),
> *Don't Fall Off the Mountain*

> ✗ You can take the lilac or the beige — whichever you find the more preferable.
> ✗ I prefer this brand of toothpaste the most.

This common mistake is perhaps due to a confusion of two distinct constructions: in the second of the examples above, between *whichever you find preferable* and *whichever you find (the) more attractive*; and in the third example, between *I like this brand the most* and *I prefer this brand to the others*.

2. If both elements of the preference are mentioned, the preposition usually setting them apart is *to*:

> She preferred Thackeray to Dickens.
> They seem to find gossiping preferable to studying.
> I'll take the beige in preference to the blue.

But note this construction:

> She showed a preference for Thackeray over Dickens.

The temptation to model the first three of these examples on the fourth, by replacing *to* by *over* (or *above, before,* or *instead of*) is not very strong nowadays: just as well, since these prepositions are considered not strictly acceptable. The use of *than* (as in ✗ *She preferred Thackeray than Dickens*) is quite nonstandard. Yet *to* is not always satisfactory. Suppose the first element is a verb in the infinitive — *I prefer to foxtrot ...* — how does the sentence continue? The various options are all unacceptable in different ways:

> ✗ I prefer to foxtrot to to waltz.
> ✗ I prefer to foxtrot to waltz.
> ✗ I prefer to foxtrot to waltzing.

Clearly some change is needed. The verbs could be changed to the *-ing* form, or to nouns:

I prefer foxtrotting to waltzing.
I prefer the foxtrot to the waltz.

Alternatively, *prefer* can give way to other constructions:

I like to foxtrot more than to waltz.
I had/would sooner/rather foxtrot than waltz.
I like to foxtrot rather than to waltz.
I choose to foxtrot rather than (to) waltz.

The problem arises when *prefer* is retained but mixed with these other patterns:

?? I prefer to foxtrot than (to) waltz.
?? I prefer to foxtrot more than to waltz.
?? I prefer rather to foxtrot than to waltz.
I prefer to foxtrot rather than (to) waltz.

The first of these constructions is fairly common now, but still considered nonstandard. The last of the constructions is even more common, and is widely regarded as acceptable (though some purists do still object to it). But where the rejected element of the preference is not an infinitive, *rather than* should not be used as a substitute for *to*. The temptation to use it is very strong, however, especially in long and complex sentences, in order to reinforce the contrast between the two elements:

? Anybody in his right mind would prefer paying an extra one per cent tax on his income rather than risking a breakdown in essential security and medical services.

Strictly speaking, *rather than* should here be replaced by *to*.

● *Recommendation* The only fully acceptable pattern is to *prefer X to Y*, but it is not always possible, and the temptation then is to use *prefer X than Y* or *prefer X rather than Y*. The first of these should be avoided; the second now sounds so natural that it can be safely used in speech and informal writing. In formal usage, however, it is still best avoided; use instead any of the various alternative constructions: *had/would rather X than Y, would sooner X than Y, choose X rather than Y,* and so on.

3. Note that *preferable* is stressed on the first syllable, not the second, and is spelt with only two single *r*'s; likewise *preference*; but *prefer* doubles its final *r* in the verb forms *preferred* and *preferring*.

prefixes and suffixes   These are word elements, attached respectively to the front and end of a base word or element to form a new word. The word *antidisestablishmentarianism*, for instance, is built up from the base word *establish* with two prefixes (*anti-* and *dis-*) and three or four suffixes.

A third type of 'affix' is called an *infix*, and occurs in the middle of a word. In English, infixes are used to link two elements into a single word; the *-o-* in *meritocracy*, for example, is an infix, linking the two elements *merit* and *-cracy*.

Note that *-cracy* here is usually regarded in dictionaries as a *combining form* rather than as a *suffix*. Combining forms are word elements that seem more self-sufficient than affixes, and that have a more concrete meaning.

Note that some words containing affixes cannot survive without them: the base form by itself may have ceased to be an acceptable word, or may never have been one in the first place. So, *dilapidated, disgruntled, dishevelled, disparage, distraught, inept, uncouth, unkempt,* and so on cannot really be stripped of their prefix — except in jest. P.G. Wodehouse, for instance, used the word *gruntled* in a jocular way in his writings. (These prefixes tended, in any case, to be attached to the base form very early in the word's development — when still in Latin, Old French, or Old English). The forms *trepid* and *gainly* do still seem to be current, but occur far less frequently than *intrepid* and *ungainly*.

Note, conversely, that some affixes and combining forms may take on a life of their own and become independent words. You might, for instance, express distrust of all *isms* and *ologies*.

Finally, note that the use of affixes and combining forms in coining new words sometimes attracts criticism: among the coinages objected to are *disbenefit, diseconomy,* and even *unsober*. The short-cut involved here is often regarded as a sign of laziness rather than thrift. On the other hand, many such coinages clearly perform a useful function by *naming* an important concept that previously could only be *described*. For example, in the complex political world of today, *non-aggression pact, deselection, disinformation,* and *destabilisation* are extremely economical ways of expressing complicated ideas. And of course, the playful use of affixes and combining forms in generating satirical terms or nonce-words (that is, words devised for a particular context, and intended to be used on that one occasion only) is a legitimate device for creating a light-hearted style: *eco-food, nonproblem, peacenik, underwhelmed, unfavourite,* and so on.

Speciesism is thinking that the human species is in any way superior to the animal ... I dare say the GLC is already making arrange-

ments for an anti-speciesist grant.
　　– Mary Kenny, *Sunday Telegraph*

The Gridiron Club, bastion of Sloane Rangerdom, is more conservative in its attitudes and correspondingly more adamant in its rejection of women.
　　– Alison Payne, *The Guardian*

See also -ED,-T; -EE; -EN.

prepared Constructions such as *I am prepared to forgive you this time* and *He is not prepared to give me a reference* have been criticised for a needlessly loose use of *prepared*. They are well established now, however, and it is only in very formal contexts that they need to be avoided. The forms *is willing to*, *refuses to*, and so on would then be used instead, with *prepared to* restricted to contexts that actually imply making preparations: *We are prepared to mobilise at a moment's notice*; *Are you prepared to leave as soon as I've finished my dinner?* The danger is, of course, that these 'correct' uses will be misunderstood as meaning *willing to* rather than *ready to*. One unfortunate effect of the loose sense is to introduce ambiguity. Take care that your meaning is clear, whether you use the word in its strict or its loose sense.

prepositions 1. A preposition shows the relationship of a noun, or a noun equivalent, to the rest of the sentence. It may, for instance, answer the question Where? as in *He sat at/on/beside/under the table*; or When? as in *They arrived before/after breakfast*. It may express direction, as in *to/from/towards/via Leeds*; or possession, as in *a horse of mine*.

Sometimes a short phrase is used in the same way as a single preposition: the opposite of the one-word preposition *behind* is the three-word phrase *in front of*. Similar constructions are *by means of*, *in accordance with*, *with regard to*, *as for*, *in view of*.

Prepositions often occur in set combinations with some particular verb, noun, adjective, or adverb. The more familiar of these combinations are obvious enough: we say *by mistake* but *on purpose*, we are *fond of* things, and we travel *by train* but *on foot*. Many people, however, have difficulty in choosing the right preposition to 'go with' a word or construction that they may not have used before: one acts *in support of* (not *for*) someone else, and seeks *revenge on* (not *of*) him or her. The following example illustrates the problem:

✗ The accused was known for his passionate interest for Germany, his admiration of Hitler, and his collection of Nazi war medals and other memorabilia.

The phrase *interest for Germany*, which suggests that Germany was interested in the accused, should have been *interest in Germany*. The *for* was perhaps influenced by the *for* of *known for*, or by the model of a synonymous phrase such as *passion for*.

2. A good many of these errors arise by such an analogy with a similar phrase. One is *fond of* children, but we speak of a *fondness for* (not *of*) them. One *shows a dislike of* small dogs, but *takes a dislike to* the neighbours. One acts *in view of* new information but *with a view to* new successes. The police may *charge* someone *with* manslaughter, but the suspect is arrested on a *charge of* manslaughter.

Often there is more than one possible choice. Preparations might be *adequate to* or *for* a party. You might ask a question *apropos* the party or *apropos of* the party. To *conform to* or *with* a custom is to observe it. You might *replace* an old hat *by* or *with* a new hat. A man can either *tyrannise*, or *tyrannise over*, his clerk.

Usually, however, the choice of prepositions is not a free one. The context, or the intended sense, necessitates the use of one preposition rather than another. When a person *admits* or *admits to* something, he or she confesses it: *He admits (to) having stolen the jewels*. When something *admits of* something, it permits it: *The facts admit of only one explanation*. To *start on* papering the kitchen is to start doing it, but to *start by with* papering the kitchen is to deal with it first, before going on to the other projects, such as tiling the bathroom perhaps.

One *connives with* a person, but *at* a wrongful action. If something *consists of* something else, it is made up or composed of it: *The United Kingdom consists of Great Britain and Northern Ireland*; if it *consists in* something, it has it as a basis: *The beauty of the city consists in its ancient buildings*. (See CONSIST IN.)

If we say that something is *covered in* something else, we refer to its state: *a face covered in spots*; if we say it is *covered with* or *by* something, we refer to the result of the action: *a desk covered with/by a large cloth*. One is *disgusted at* an action, *with* a person or action, *by* a person, thing, or action. Well-known things are *familiar to* people, and the people are *familiar with* them. We say *free of* tax or disease, meaning merely that there is no problem, but we keep a garden *free from* weeds when we actually prevent them from growing.

If one is *possessed of* something, one owns it: *possessed of a sharp tongue*; but if one is *possessed with* or *by* something, one is controlled by it: *possessed with sudden rage*. A person could be very *susceptible to* flattery or disease, but a theory is *susceptible of* an interpretation. You may feel *sympathy* (compassion) *for* a person, but you would be *in sympathy* (agreement) *with* a point of view.

The choice may, of course, be between a preposition and some word that is not a preposition at all. *According to* is a preposition, and means 'depending on': *Pay them according to the work they do*. But *according as*, meaning 'depending on how or whether', is a conjunction and introduces a full clause: *Promote them according as they do well or badly*.

In many cases, particularly where usage is changing, one preposition rather than another is to be preferred for serious writing. Here is a brief list:

> an *affinity between/with* (not *to/for*)
> to *brood on/over* something (not *about*)
> *consequent on* something (not *to*)
> to *die of* something (better than *from*)
> to *forbid* someone *to do* something (not *from doing*)
> to *prevent* someone *from doing* something
> to *prohibit* someone *from doing* something
> *identical to* something (not *with*)
> *oblivious of* something (better than *to*)
> to *prefer* something *to* something else (not *than*)
> *junior/senior/inferior/superior to* someone or something (not *than*)

3. Take care not to omit an essential preposition.

> ✗ In regard to whom you spoke, you should have been more discreet.
> ✗ He is interested in what you are interested.

In the first of these examples, a further *to* is needed after *spoke*; in the second, a further *in* after *interested*. What prompted the omission in each case was the distracting presence of the same preposition elsewhere in the sentence. If you find it ungainly to have two identical prepositions so close to each other, or if you are worried about ending a clause with a preposition, try to reformulate the sentence:

> As for the person to whom you spoke, you should have been more discreet.

> He is interested in the same things that interest you.

See PREPOSITIONS ENDING A SENTENCE; PREPOSITIONS OMITTED.

prepositions ending a sentence One of the most troublesome and illogical 'rules' of English grammar is the traditional prohibition on ending a sentence with a preposition. (The Latin roots of *preposition* do, it is true, suggest that it should be 'placed in front of' another word — in the *pre-* position.) As generations of ironic schoolchildren have put it, 'Never use a preposition to end a sentence with.'

The shadow of the schoolroom is amusingly reinvoked in this extract:

> 'So if Raschid has anything to say perhaps he had better say it to me. Not that I think he will. I know Raschid of old and Raschid knows me, and Raschid, though a fool, is not such a fool as to try anything on that he can't get away with.' He thought for a moment and amended this statement. 'With which he can't get away.'
> – Anthony Burgess, *Devil of a State*

The trend was probably begun by John Dryden in the 17th century, and encouraged by Edward Gibbon in the 18th. But as actually formulated by Bishop Lowth in the 18th century, the 'rule' went no further than to recommend avoiding where possible the use of a preposition at the end of a sentence (and the end of a clause too, for that matter). Instead of saying *Which unit did you serve in?*, you would have been urged to bring the preposition forward and say *In which unit did you serve?*

The basis for this 'rule' was Latin grammar, in which a preposition always precedes its noun or pronoun, and cannot come after it. And certainly the gain in elegance can be enormous when the Latinate construction is used: the previous sentence, for example, contains the phrase *in which*, and would be far clumsier if worded instead as *?? The basis for this 'rule' was Latin grammar, which a preposition always precedes its noun or pronoun in.*

However, English grammar is not Latin grammar: in English a preposition *can* come after its noun or pronoun, and this flexibility is in fact part of the character and strength of the language.

Not only is it possible for the preposition to be placed at the end of a sentence; it is also very often the natural place for it, as in questions and exclamations: *Which flight did they book you on?*

sounds natural and idiomatic; so does *What a fine mess you've got us into!* But *? On which flight did they book you?* sounds stilted, over-formal, even pretentious. And × *Into what a fine mess you've got us!* is virtually impossible.

In relative clauses, the shift of a preposition from the end to the middle or beginning usually means an increase in formality and stiffness: compare *This is the book I was telling you about* with *This is the book about which I was telling you.* The shift of preposition is particularly awkward when the preposition is separated by more than two or three words from the word it relates most closely to: a sentence such as *It's the kind of book that even after months of study one can reach only a vague understanding of* can hardly be rephrased as *?? It's the kind of book of which even after months of study one can reach only a vague understanding.* And it sounds extremely awkward to rewrite *That all depends on what you're involved in* as *?? That all depends on that in which you're involved* (let alone *?? on in what you're involved*). The following quotations too could not easily be twisted to conform with the rule:

None the less, for all the squalor and gore, felicities of syntax are what the book aspires to be full of.
　　　　　　　　 – Martin Amis, *The Observer*

Geoffrey Robertson, who has been an inquisitor in Granada's hypothetical cases, pressed magistrates and clerks a good deal harder, one was entertained to see, than they are used to or altogether care for.
　　　　　　　 – Nancy Banks-Smith, *The Guardian*

Not only is it often very awkward to shift the preposition from the end of a sentence; it is sometimes impossible to do so. *What are you complaining for?* (meaning 'Why are you complaining?') cannot be rephrased in the way that *What are you complaining about?* can be. Idiom does not allow the elements of *what for* to be reversed. And in short sentences involving passive or infinitive clauses, the final preposition cannot be moved forward, except by completely redrafting the sentence:

Everything was accounted for.
You'd better get that cough seen to.
It's not worth worrying about.
That portrait is very pleasant to look at.
He's impossible to reason with.
She's not easy to talk to.

And where there are several phrases or clauses in a sentence, all having a similar structure, it can be very misleading or even downright ungrammatical to transfer the one 'objectionable' preposition. It is both misleading and ungrammatical, for example, to change the sentence

She spoke vehemently against the new regulations and whatever had motivated them and whatever they might be used for

into

?? She spoke vehemently against the new regulations and whatever had motivated them and for whatever they might be used.

It is usually possible to move the preposition towards the front of the sentence when it comes at the end of a relative clause: *Joan was the editor I spoke to* can be changed to *Joan was the editor to whom I spoke;* similarly *It's made of glass that you cannot see through* can be changed to *It's made of glass through which you cannot see* (see WHICH 1).

The combinations *speak to* and *see through* in these examples can be split without any difficulty. But some verb-preposition combinations cannot be separated so easily, especially those that have a figurative rather than a literal sense.

The combination *see through,* for example, can be understood in a different way — a more figurative way — as meaning 'to penetrate and understand': *She tells lies that even a child could see through.* This sentence would sound very unnatural indeed if rephrased as *?? She tells lies through which even a child could see.* And if *see through* is used as a verb-adverb combination rather than a verb-preposition combination, meaning 'to persist with and complete', then it is quite impossible to shift *through* (an adverb now, no longer a preposition) from the end of a clause or sentence to the middle or beginning: *It's an ordeal that you must see through* cannot be 'corrected' into × *It's an ordeal through which you must see.*

Winston Churchill revealed the absurdity of trying to split such prepositional or phrasal verbs artificially, when he apparently made the ironic comment, 'This is the sort of English up with which I will not put.' (But note that *up* is an adverb here, not a preposition. The 'rule' would permit ... *with which I will not put up* — still ungainly, but better than Churchill's version.)

It is true that some prepositions are consistently more idiomatic when placed at the beginning of their clause or sentence — *during* and *throughout* are good examples: *Throughout/During which century did the Industrial Revolution take place?* It would sound most unnatural if these prepositions came at the end of the sentence: *?? Which century did the Industrial Revolution take place during/throughout?* (There is, of course, no such restriction on placing *in* at the end of the sentence, however: *Which century did the Industrial Revolution take place in?*) The restriction often applies to compound prepositions: *with regard to, in exchange for, out of respect for, in defiance of, owing to, because of,* and so on:

> *?* They proposed a new regulation, which the opposition benches immediately began shouting in protest against.

It would be preferable to say:

> They proposed a new regulation, in protest against which the opposition benches immediately began shouting.

Note, finally, that certain prepositions can be used immediately after their noun or noun phrase, without any verb in between:

> She married him, notwithstanding her father's protests = She married him, her father's protests notwithstanding.
> It's the same all over the world = It's the same all the world over = It's the same the whole world over.
> They are harvested all through the year = They are harvested all the year through.

The sentences here ending with a preposition are once again standard idiomatic English, and defy the disapproval of pedants.

● *Recommendation* A preposition should be placed where it sounds appropriate. In some relative clauses, and in many formal questions, the appropriate place for it is the beginning or middle of the sentence. In other relative clauses, and in informal questions, the end of the sentence is appropriate. In many short statements, it is impossible to place the preposition anywhere other than at the end.

Disregard, in other words, any blanket rule outlawing prepositions at the end of sentences. If you are liable to encounter the disapproval of purists, you might want to avoid provocation by recasting 'objectionable' sentences where possible. But you are within your rights not to, and if the purists do take you to task, you could always retort 'Your criticism is hardly worth responding *to*'.

prepositions omitted 1. Since its earliest days, English (in common with other Germanic languages, far more so than the Romance languages) has commonly allowed alternative close-packed constructions to the fuller constructions containing prepositions. Instead of saying *a display of gymnastics,* you can say *a gymnastics display,* simply reversing the two nouns and dropping the *of.* Instead of saying *the performance of the gymnast* you can say *the gymnast's performance,* involving a similar procedure but with the addition of *-'s.*

Such rewordings are not always possible. The use of *-'s* or *-s'* is traditionally limited to nouns referring to humans or animals — *John's coat; the donkey's hat* — and a variety of idiomatic expressions: *an hour's wait, at arm's length,* and so on. The acceptability is not always easy to assess: *the book's publication* seems to be just as idiomatic as *the publication of the book;* but *? my new book's publication* is certainly less idiomatic than *the publication of my new book.* The phrase *? the bridge's inauguration* is on the borderline, but *?? the bridge's opening* is not really acceptable, and should be replaced by *the opening of the bridge.* (For further details, see *-'S, -S'.*)

The omission of prepositions without a compensating *-'s* or *-s'* is rather more complicated. Underlying it, more often than not today, is the influence of the newspaper and news-magazine. Headlines in particular (like telegrams) have to pack maximum information into minimum space — and challenge traditional grammar in doing so, omitting not only *a, the,* and *is,* but also *of, in,* and other prepositions. An expression such as *journey time,* for instance (instead of *the time of the journey*), is an obvious product of the space-saving newspaper age — and perhaps a useful one. But far too many new compounds of this sort are being generated by the press, and careful users of English are understandably dismayed at the trend.

Not that such omission of prepositions is a recent development (though the surging increase in it certainly is). Throughout the history of English, nouns have been used like adjectives: no one objects to the word *gravestone,* for instance, insisting that the correct form should be *the stone of a grave.* An enormous number of old everyday words or phrases in English are compounds of two nouns: *newspaper* itself, *bedside, hearth-rug, doorway, garden path, peachblossom, horsefly, street-corner,* and so on. Here are the titles of some poems by Robert Browning, all written more than 120 years ago: 'By the Fireside', 'Cavalier Tunes', 'Christmas-Eve', 'Easter-Day', 'A Forest Thought', 'Garden Fancies',

'Home-Thoughts from Abroad', 'Madhouse Cells', 'Queen-Worship' (and also some doubtful uses of the *'s*: 'Earth's Immortalities', 'The Flower's Name', 'Time's Revenges').

Note that long-established compounds tend today to be spelt as single words — *gravestone, horsefly* — though some might commonly retain a hyphen: *street-corner*. More recent compounds tend to remain as two words — *journey time, space race* — but if this noun phrase in turn is used as an adjective, modifying some other noun, then a hyphen is inserted: *journey-time reductions*; *a space-race expert*.

The omission of *of* and other prepositions from noun phrases obviously cannot be condemned out of hand. But think twice before streamlining a preposition out of existence: *journey time* might be a useful modern formation, and *journey's end* is a fully established idiom, but *?? journey distance* and *?? at journey's outset* are far from elegant and would be unlikely to gain acceptance in standard English even if they came into common use. Above all avoid unbroken strings of nouns — all except the last serving as adjectives. Newspaper headlines provide extreme examples, of course:

?? Panelbeater-firm tax-evasion conspiracy allegation: Government Committee investigation promise scandal.

Even as a headline this seems excessive (though better than *?? Tax-dodge pact charge probe pledge cover-up*); it could never occur in ordinary speech and writing. Some of the combinations are quite acceptable, as it happens — *tax-evasion* and even *tax-evasion conspiracy*. But whereas *panelbeater* is obviously unobjectionable, *?? panelbeater-firm* is very doubtful: *a firm of panelbeaters* would be the way to phrase it in ordinary prose, and *?? investigation promise* would become *a promise of an investigation,* and so on. But the jargons of politicians and sociologists, bureaucrats and businessmen, have been infected by the special language of headlines, and together they seem to make up a campaign to eliminate *of* and other prepositions altogether.

?? Productivity-levels maintenance coupled with a five-per-cent overtime-pay reduction and the predicted ten-per-cent export sales increase should raise dividend hopes and effect very soon a substantial stock-market-valuation rise.

In extreme cases, such language becomes ambiguous or quite incomprehensible. A woman whose husband has been injured by a bomb might be referred to as a *Bomb Wife* in newspaper headlines. If the bomb was planted by the IRA, the headlines or caption might read *? IRA Bomb Wife* — quite ambiguously. The word *bomb* could be understood as a verb here, and a casual reader might get the impression that the wife herself was the victim of an IRA bomb. Such constructions should of course be avoided all the more in ordinary speech and writing.

See also OF 4; PREPOSITIONS.

2. A preposition does not usually need to be repeated if it applies to two elements in the sentence: *The typical PA is characterised by conscientiousness and lack of ambition*. An additional *by* could have been placed before *lack* here, but is not necessary. Sometimes, however, if the preposition is not repeated, ambiguity might result: *? The typical PA is characterised by lack of ambition and conscientiousness*. The omission of a repeated *by* in front of *conscientiousness* here has resulted in the possibility of an unintended and unflattering interpretation of the sentence.

See also AMBIGUITY 5, 6; PARALLEL CONSTRUCTIONS.

3. In a few expressions, a preposition may be considered indispensable on one side of the Atlantic, but be acceptably omitted on the other. British English, unlike American, now allows *to agree a new policy* as well as *to agree on a new policy*. American English, unlike British, allows *to protest the new policy* as well as *to protest at/against the new policy*.

One American habit, increasingly being adopted in British English (though far from being accepted as standard British English, and sometimes still criticised in American English too) is the omission of *on* before days of the week: *?? Let's meet Friday at 12*; *?? Fridays I leave early*. Until such sentences are more at home in British English, restore the *on* before *Friday* or *Fridays*.

prerequisite, perquisite A *prerequisite*, as the word suggests, is 'something required beforehand' — a precondition, in other words: *Success is not a prerequisite of happiness, but it certainly helps*.

A resurgence of brand loyalty has also appeared. As a prerequisite to taking a new job, some executive secretaries specify the type of word processor which they will need.
— Rita Marshall, *The Times*

The preposition following *prerequisite* can be *of*, *to*, or *for*.

Prerequisite can be used as an adjective too, however, and the appropriate preposition then is to: *Creativity is prerequisite to computer programming.*

A *perquisite* is a special advantage or privilege, a fringe benefit incidental to your salary — a perk, in short (literally: the word *perk* is an informal abbreviation, dating from about 1824, of *perquisite*). A *perquisite* may well be your rightful due, written into your contract — for example, the use of a company car. But most perquisites are unofficial and are simply *regarded* as being your rightful due — the right to make a reasonable number of personal telephone calls at work, for example.

> He did not like to tell his colleagues to stop passing on their unwanted perquisites, because occasionally they involved free airline trips abroad, which he and his department accepted.
> — Michael Frayn,
> *Towards the End of the Morning*

Perquisite has two further minor senses: 'a tip or gratuity' — *He gave the valet a miserly 50 pence as a perquisite* — and 'something claimed as an exclusive right': *Foxhunting has become the perquisite of the upper classes.* The last sense is frowned upon by some critics as an unnecessary or incorrect substitute for *preserve* or *privilege.*

The pronunciation of *prerequisite* is /**pree**-**rek**wizit/, sometimes /pri-**rek**wizit/; *perquisite* is pronounced /**perk**wizit/.

See also REQUIREMENT.

prescribe, proscribe The verbs *to prescribe* and *to proscribe* are sometimes confused, particularly since it is possible to pronounce both /prə-**skrib**/. The pronunciations /pri-**skrib**/ and /prō-**skrib**/ are also used, and help to make a distinction. Take care to spell and use these words correctly, since their meanings are quite different — almost exact opposites, in fact.

To prescribe means 'to order, direct, advise, lay down as a rule, or appoint'. It can be used with or without an object. It also means, in medical language, 'to issue (a prescription), or to advise (a treatment)': *The doctor prescribed an anti-depressant.*

> The British Medical Association is to debate its attitudes to prescribing contraceptives to girls aged under 16 at its annual meeting in Manchester next month.
> — *The Times*

Prescribe comes from the Latin *prae-*, 'before' + *scribere*, 'to write'.

To proscribe comes from the Latin *pro-*, 'in

front of, publicly' + *scribere*, 'to write'; *proscribere* in Latin originally meant 'to publish in writing', and was used particularly when publishing the name of a person as an outlaw and announcing the confiscation of his property. In current English it means 'to forbid by law' or, more generally, 'to condemn, prohibit, or outlaw'. So a doctor might *prescribe* exercise but *proscribe* smoking. *Prescribed books* on a syllabus would be those set for study; *proscribed books* would be those prohibited or banned by censors.

An easy way to remember the difference is this: when you *prescribe* something you issue a *prescription*; when you *proscribe* something you place it under a *prohibition* (or *proscription*).

The related adjectives are *prescriptive* and — rather rarer — *proscriptive*. The two are juxtaposed in the following quotation:

> While national differences have been reduced by a shared technology, and the corners of the earth communicate by satellite, 'nationality' is increasingly potent, both prescriptive and proscriptive. Those Martian observers must gape at Earthmen cowering behind their nuclear-defended walls.
> — D.J. Enright, *The Observer*

Prescriptive is more commonly contrasted with *descriptive*, particularly in linguistics: *prescriptive* is used of a grammar that lays down rules for correct usage; a *descriptive* grammar simply analyses language as it is used, without ruling on whether any particular usage is correct or incorrect.

present When used before a noun, the adjective *present* often finds itself in phrases and sentences that have a pompous ring to them: *Present circumstances will not permit it; at the present time; the present posture of events.* It should not be too difficult to reword such constructions: *We cannot do it; now; as things stand.* These are less formal phrasings perhaps, but far more efficient.

The old-fashioned phrase *the present writer* (= I or me) is nowadays widely criticised as an attempt to pass off a personal style as somehow impersonal and objective. Here is a recent example of a similar phrase, written by — of all people — an expert on modern usage:

> ?The first-class critic, like the first-class artist, is always to some extent ahead of his times. The editor of an internationally famous art magazine confessed to the present author that quite frequently he found himself unable to understand the articles written by

one particular expert on contemporary art.
— Kenneth Hudson, Introduction to
The Dictionary of Diseased English

presently *Presently* once meant 'immediately', but its chief current meaning in standard English is 'soon, after a short time', as in *Presently she got up and left the room.* Even here it is a rather old-fashioned word to use.

Presently has a second meaning, 'now, at present', as in *? He's presently unemployed.* This sense too was once standard in British English, though it died out three or four centuries ago. It has remained, or become, established in American English and Scottish English, however, and in many English dialects, but it still attracts criticism in standard British English, where *currently* or *at present* is preferred.

One obvious difficulty in having these two senses is the danger of ambiguity. Does the sentence *? I am presently starting on a new career* mean 'I am about to start' (standard World English) or 'I am in the process of starting' (American and Scottish usage)?

Despite the attempts by writers on usage to fend off the Scottish and American influence, the controversial sense, 'now, currently', seems to be, if anything, more common than the traditional sense, and it should eventually gain complete acceptance. The following example shows how respectable the controversial sense has become:

? India hopes to be self-sufficient in oil before the end of the century and the fields off Bombay presently provide 60 per cent of production.
— Leonard Bushkoff,
The Times Higher Education Supplement

Here, to restore the balance, is an example of the standard usage:

Freddy could be heard moving about and creaking his bed as he sat, presumably taking off his shoes since a shoe-like thud on the floor, dropping dead-weight with tiredness, was followed presently by another.
— Muriel Spark,
The Mandelbaum Gate

prestigious The modern senses of this word — 'conferring prestige' (*a prestigious prize*) and 'enjoying prestige, renowned' (*a prestigious author*) — used to raise the hackles of pedants. The latter sense especially was objected to, and sometimes still is, though the position of *prestigious* as the adjective of *prestige* is now secure.

In this country, he would have a knighthood and the Mastership of a Cambridge college. In the United States he has to make do with regular columns on scientific topics in prestigious journals.
— John Naughton, *The Observer*

But perhaps the most striking effect of co-education has been in those colleges which were formerly all female. Whereas it is quite prestigious to be a woman in a predominantly male college, the corollary does not hold true.
— Alison Payne, *The Guardian*

The objection to *prestigious* was on etymological grounds: the word's origins, in French and Latin, suggest conjuring and illusion, and should, allegedly, retain something of this sense. (Curiously enough, the word *prestidigitation*, which still means 'the dexterity of a magician or juggler; sleight of hand', comes from quite different and unrelated Latin roots.) Yet the sense of *prestigious* as 'involving illusion, magic, or trickery' seems quite archaic now. The writer of the following extract (poorly worded in other ways) has to strain to revive that earlier sense of *prestigious*:

The Acorn Computer World Chess Championship semi-finals now in progress at the Great Eastern Hotel in Liverpool Street, London, are the most prestigious chess events held in this country since the International Team Tournament (later the Chess Olympiad) of 1927.

I use the word prestigious both in its modern and derivative senses, since it needed little less than a conjuring trick to have them played here after the dead-ends resulting from disagreement between the Soviet Chess Federation and the World Chess Federation President.
— Harry Golombek, *The Times*

It is strange that the objections to *prestigious* have been so much more vehement than the objections to *prestige*, which has the same association, in its origins, with magic and juggling. Yet its use in the sense of 'prominence, influential status, renown' seems to have been more or less acceptable even to those most intensely opposed to the corresponding sense of *prestige*. The probable reason for this disparity was that *prestigious*, unlike *prestige*, is considered an Americanism (though it is not in fact of American origin). *Prestigious*, like *hopefully* and the split infinitive, is one of those controversial usages in which the arguments in favour are far more persuasive than the arguments against, and which many careful users nevertheless avoid precisely because they are so controversial. The debate over *prestigious* has diminished, however (whereas the debates over *hopefully* and the split infinitive continue quite vigorously), and it is more or less safe to venture the occasional *prestigious* without provoking or distracting your listener or reader.

Should you wish to avoid the remote risk, however, you have a wealth of near-synonyms to choose from: *highly valued, esteemed, powerful, high-status, renowned, admired, influential*, and so on. The rare adjective *prestigeful* is not recommended, but you can use the word *prestige* itself before a noun —*a prestige job*. (The ultra-pedantic would probably object to this too, however.)

> The Export Credits Guarantee Department is facing the prospect of a politically sensitive £500 million debt renegotiation with Mexico over Britain's largest prestige contract in Latin America. Mexico's £2 billion Sicartsa steel plate mill project ... is now likely to be substantially delayed or even cancelled.
> – Adrian Hamilton, *The Observer*

Note the change in pronunciation from *prestige* to *prestigious*: /press-**teezh**/ or (in British English) /**press**-teezh/, and /press-**tij**əss/ or /press-**tiji**-əss/. *Prestige* is sometimes used with a *j* sound too, **?** /press-**teej**/, or even (in British English) **?**/**prest**ij/ as in *vestige*, but these pronunciations are rare and dubious.

presume See ASSUME.

presumptuous, presumptive The adjective *presumptuous* has a strongly negative tone, and means 'excessively bold; audacious; impudent and self-confident to the point of arrogance': *How presumptuous of her to think we might want her as guest of honour!*

> However I am getting ready to be astonished that the reticent British, to whom the investigative psychiatrist is still seen as a presumptuous busybody, should be so much more forthcoming than their American counterparts.
> – David Wade, *The Times*

Note the spelling: there is a middle *u*; in the past, the word could also be spelt ✗ *presumptious* (based on the Latin form, whereas *presumptuous* comes through Old French) and it is still often — incorrectly — spelt this way today, on the

model of the noun *presumption*. In pronunciation too, the preferred form takes the middle *u* into account, /pri-**zum**-tew-əss/, though the last two syllables can be fused as /-chəss/ or /-shəss/.

In the past, once again, the adjective *presumptive* was used in the sense of 'presumptuous' (and vice versa, as it happens), and is today often used — quite incorrectly — in this sense. The surviving senses of *presumptive* are 'providing a basis for a belief' — *Such presumptive evidence is not enough: we need proof* — and 'based on a presumption or probability': *a presumptive conclusion.*

See also HEIR APPARENT.

pretence, pretension, pretentiousness *Pretence* has the general meaning of 'an act of pretending or feigning' — referring to a false appearance or an act intended to deceive: *He made a pretence of doing his homework.*

Pretension relates to a rarer sense of the verb *to pretend*, and means 'an unsupported claim'. It is often used in the plural: *I have no pretensions to being a chess player.*

Pretentiousness usually refers either to a gaudy or ostentatious display, or to an appearance of having qualities, especially intellectual qualities, that are not really present: *Such pretentiousness, using all those French phrases in his speech.*

These distinctions are useful, but not really binding. *Pretence* is sometimes used in the sense of 'pretension' and 'pretentiousness', and *pretension* is sometimes used in the sense of 'pretentiousness', as in this quotation:

> For Larkin, as for many other English essayists, humour is a conservative rather than anarchic force. It can be harnessed effectively to literary criticism, whenever the most appropriate form of that criticism is the debunking of pretension.
> – Martin Walker, *The Literary Review*

Note the spelling: the *c* in *pretence* (often *s* in American spelling) becomes an *s* in *pretension*, and a *t* in *pretentiousness*.

Finally, compare the word *pretext*, 'a professed or ostensible purpose, but usually not the true purpose': *His pretext in coming here was to discuss business, but I think he was really wanting to cadge a free meal.*

prevaricate, procrastinate The verb *to prevaricate* is used alarmingly often in inappropriate contexts, where *procrastinate* was clearly the word intended.

To procrastinate means 'to delay or put off

doing something': *If she procrastinates any further, she'll miss the deadline.* The original Latin verb *procrastinari* was more specific in its meaning — 'to move forward to the following day; to put off until tomorrow', from *pro-*, 'forward' + *crastinus*, 'of tomorrow', from *cras*, 'tomorrow'.

Prevaricate sounds fairly similar to *procrastinate*, and also shares with it a suggestion of irresponsible evasion. But there the overlap ends: *to prevaricate* strictly means 'to stray from the truth, to speak evasively, to mislead deliberately or quibble'. In short, if you *prevaricate* you are virtually telling a lie (though a milder synonym such as *equivocate* or *temporise* is more in keeping with the tone). So, to accuse someone of *prevaricating* when he is simply *procrastinating* is not only to misuse the English language but to imply an unwarranted insult as well.

The idea of deviation from the truth is vividly embodied in the origin of *prevaricate*. It comes from the Latin *prevaricari*, 'to walk crookedly, deviate from one's course; collude', from *prae-*, 'before, beyond' + *varicare*, 'to straddle', from *varus*, 'stretched, bent, knock-kneed'. (In medical English, *varus* can be used as a technical name for 'knock-knees'.)

The following quotations illustrate the correct and incorrect senses of *prevaricate*. In the second of them, the writer has fallen into the trap: the word needed was surely *procrastinated*, not *prevaricated*.

At first she hesitated and prevaricated, telling little, flustered stories about having stupidly misunderstood something Boo had said, but he soon put a stop to that.
— Gillian Tindall, *The Fiction Magazine*

✗ Pedroza tried every trick to relieve his aching legs: every time he went back to his corner he chewed ice, forgot his gum shield . . ., and was late coming out round after round. . . . Now McGuigan was . . . quickly out at the bell and on one occasion was almost standing on top of Pedroza as he prevaricated.
— Srikumar Sen, *The Times*

prevent, preventive, preventative 1. The verb *to prevent* originally meant simply 'to come or go before', from the Latin *prae-*, 'before' + *venire*, 'to come'.

It is used in this sense in *The Book of Common Prayer* (1662): *Prevent us, O Lord, in all our doings with thy most gracious favour*, meaning *Precede us* . . . .

The poet John Milton similarly used *prevent* to mean 'come before', in a poem in which he imagines reaching the Christ child before the three wise men do:

See how from far upon the Eastern road
The star-led wizards haste with odours sweet,
O run, prevent them with thy humble ode,
And lay it lowly at his blessed feet.
— John Milton,
'Ode on the Morning of
Christ's Nativity' (1629)

In general usage the verb *to prevent* has now taken on the very different sense of 'to stop, hinder'. The formally correct pattern is *to prevent X's doing*, as in *John prevented Mary's leaving*. Note the *-'s* after Mary. Slightly less formal, though now widely accepted, is the pattern in *John prevented Mary from leaving*. But the pattern in which neither the possessive form nor the *from* appears is still considered dubious, widespread though it has now become: *? John prevented Mary leaving*.

? About two months ago, . . . he began attending each lecture and obtained a High Court injunction preventing other students impeding him.
— Stephen Cook, *The Guardian*

Either an apostrophe or the word *from* should have been added after *students* here.

2. The adjectives *preventive* and *preventative* mean 'thwarting, averting'. The two are different forms of the same word, but the preferred form is *preventive*. (Many authorities regard *preventative* as an unnecessarily long and pompous variation. However, it has caught on, and finds a place in dictionaries.)

Mr Barney Hayhoe, Minister of State at the Treasury, said in an exclusive interview last week that there would be a 'modest increase' in preventive controls on passengers and freight.
— Shyam Bhatia, *The Observer*

Applied to medical procedures, *preventive* or *preventative* means 'averting illness or damage', as distinct from curing or repairing: *preventive medicine*. The following newspaper extract uses the form *preventative* in this sense:

Leonard was examined on Monday by a doctor and 'his left eye passed', said a source close to Leonard. But the doctor found the need for preventative surgery for the other eye and told Leonard he could wait until after the bout or have it done immediately.

The boxer wanted to get it over with.
— *The Times*

Each form can also be used as a noun, but again *preventive* is preferable. *Preventative*, however, seems to be the more common form when referring to a contraceptive device.

principal, principle The spellings of these two words are often confused, although their meanings are quite different.

Principal as an adjective means 'ranking first in importance, chief': *my principal objection to your theory; the country's principal export.* The primary forms of a verb are called its *principal parts.* As a noun, *principal* has several senses — 'the head of a college', 'the lead actor or musician', 'the basic sum of money owed or invested', and so on.

Principle is always a noun, and refers to any basic law, premise, moral standard, policy, quality, or process: *a blatant opportunist without any moral principles at all; in defiance of all known principles of science; the principle of jet propulsion.*

There is a related adjective, *principled*, meaning 'guided by principles', and usually being commendatory in tone when applied to a person. It can also mean 'based on principles; considered; not arbitrary': *There can be no principled objection to their plan.*

The phrase *in principle*, finally, means 'in theory; having regard to an idea but disregarding its practicability': *In principle it would be fun to go, but I don't see how we can get there.*

prise, prize The verb meaning 'to lever (open) with force' can be spelt in either of these ways in British English; *to prise* is probably more common, and certainly more helpful in distinguishing the word from the other words spelt *prize.*

'Are you some kind of an artist?'
'No,' I said.
'I can see you're revelling in your mystery-woman act. Never mind; I'll prise it out of you eventually.'
— Lynne Reid Banks,
The L-Shaped Room

(In American English, however — which usually favours -*z*- over -*s*- — *to prize* is far more common.)

To prise/prize goes back to the Old French *prise,* 'a lever', originally 'seized', the past participle of *prendre,* itself from the Latin *pre(he)ndere,* 'to seize'.

It is interesting that the verb *to pry* as in *to pry open,* which is an Americanism, arose through the mistaking of *prise* for a third-person singular form, as if it were *pries.*

A new word *pry* thus arose to rival the established *pry,* a noun or verb referring to inquisitive searching.

Prize is the only possible spelling for the noun meaning 'a reward or an award' and its related adjective, and the verb meaning 'to value highly'. Both the noun and the verb go back, along different routes, to the Latin *pretium,* 'a price, value, or reward' — the noun is related to *price,* and the verb to *praise.*

There is another distinct word *prize,* meaning 'something seized, such as booty', or 'the act of seizing'. It derives from the same sources as *to prise* does, but can be spelt only in the one way, with a *z.*

pristine The Latin adjective *pristinus* means 'original', and that sense is the core meaning of the English *pristine*: 'in its primitive or original state'; hence 'uncorrupted, still in a state of original purity'. There is a definite suggestion of antiquity about it. An archaeologist might stumble across a *pristine* urn from pre-classical times: that is, an undamaged urn, in the same perfect condition now as when it was made thousands of years ago.

The choice, after all, is not between a country that has been influenced by a more powerful one, and a country in a pristine state. In practice, there are no pristine countries left: the Noble Savage has long been extinct.
— Gillian Tindall, *The Times*

Perhaps by a misunderstanding of the common association of *pristine* with the idea of purity, people have come to think of *pristine* as meaning 'absolutely pure or perfectly clean': *? The cleaning lady restored my messy flat to a pristine condition.* This is, in the view of most purists, an unacceptable extension of the word's meaning.

Pristine is best pronounced /**priss**-teen/, though /-tīn/ is possible. Americans often put the stress on the second syllable.

privation See DEPRIVATION.

proclivity, propensity Since these words sound similar, and both mean something like 'a tendency, leaning, or inclination', it is easy to assume they are always interchangeable. But they do have different connotations and tend to be used in different contexts.

Propensity goes back to the Latin *propensus,* 'hanging downwards, inclined', from *pro-,* 'forward, down' + *pendere,* 'to hang'. It means 'a strong natural leaning or preference': *A propensity for football prompted him to choose a college with a well-known team. Propensity* can be used with the words *to, towards,* or *for.*

Proclivity comes from the Latin *proclivitas,* from *proclivus,* 'sloping forward', *pro-,* 'forward' + *clivus,* 'a slope or hill'. It too means 'an innate or inherent inclination', but unlike *propensity* it has the connotation of a strong leaning towards something secret or dubious. We would tend to speak of *strange sexual proclivities* on the one hand, and *academic and artistic propensities* on the other; but the phrases *? sexual propensities* and *? academic proclivities* are unlikely combinations.

> Her outwardly Quakerish demureness conceals an appetite for unsought adventures and a proclivity for emotional disasters.
> – Anthony Thwaite, *The Observer*

Proclivity, like *propensity,* can be used with the word *for,* possibly also *to,* but probably not *? towards.*

procrastinate   See PREVARICATE.

prodigy, protégé   A prodigy is a marvel — an act, object, event, or person so rare or extraordinary that it inspires wonder in people. Applied to humans, *prodigy* means 'a person with exceptional talents or powers'. It is commonly used in the combination *a child prodigy.* The word also used to refer to an omen or portent, derived as it is from the Latin *prodigium,* meaning 'a prophetic sign, or a marvel'.

Protégé has a quite unrelated origin: in French it means literally 'protected', or 'one who is protected' (going back to the Latin roots *pro-,* 'in front' + *tegere,* 'to cover'). The idea is of a person, often young, who is under the protection or sponsorship of another, more influential, person: *A protégé of the cardinal, he owes his training, career, and general welfare entirely to that generous sponsor.*

A girl or woman whose welfare is promoted in this way is a *protégée,* spelt with an extra *e* on the end. Both forms are usually pronounced /protta-zhay/, though Americans often stress the last syllable as well as the first.

programme, program   *Programme* is the usual British spelling: *a theatre programme, a pro-*gramme *of reform. Program* is the usual American spelling, but is also used in British English in connection with computers: *a word-processing program.*

Compare DISC.

prohibit   The verb *to prohibit* has two possible constructions: you *prohibit* something, or you *prohibit* somebody *from* doing something: *The law prohibits the carrying of firearms*; *The law prohibits civilians from carrying firearms.* Take care not to confuse the constructions of *prohibit* and *forbid:* you can *forbid* somebody *to* do something, but you cannot *prohibit* somebody *to* do something; *The law forbids civilians to carry firearms,* but not × *The law prohibits civilians to carry firearms.* Similarly, do not follow the British model of the construction for the verb *to stop: The new law will stop you doing that,* but not × *The new law will prohibit you doing that.* But it is fine to say *The new law will prohibit your doing that.*

prolific   The primary sense of this adjective is 'producing abundant offspring or fruit': *a prolific pear tree.* The word goes back to the Latin *proles,* 'offspring' + *facere,* 'to make'.

By extension, the word means 'producing abundant works or results', and is often applied to writers, artists, and craftsmen: *Crime writers are among the most prolific of authors.*

The word is sometimes transferred from the producer to the product — from the writer, for instance, to his writings: *?? a prolific output of novels.* This seems to accord with the way English and other languages extend the senses of their adjectives: *a thoughtless person,* for instance, can utter *thoughtless words.* But the transferred use of *prolific* still attracts criticism (unlike the transferred use of *thoughtless*): it is advisable to speak of *an abundant output* or *a large output* rather than *?? a prolific output.* Until *prolific* gains wider acceptance in its transferred use, reserve it for the sense 'producing abundantly'.

prone, supine   Both these words mean 'lying down', but *prone* means 'lying face down', and *supine* means 'lying on one's back'.

> We went sailing and swimming ... ; we ate every meal together, and lay prone on the stone piers, reaching shoulder-deep into the water to catch the scarlet starfish, which petrified with fury when we lifted them out.
> – Lynne Reid Banks,
> *The L-Shaped Room*

Daniel and the local were talking about him, the white man, as he stood there holding the radio and trying to get some other station; talking over him as people talk over the supine man in his hospital bed.

　　　　　　　　　　　　– Nadine Gordimer,
　　　　　　　　　　　　　July's People

Prone comes from the Latin *pronus,* meaning 'bending or leaning forward'. *Prone* also has the meaning 'tending or liable' (typically in reference to something undesirable) as in *accident-prone* or *prone to catch colds.*

Prone to is followed either by a noun, as in *prone to mischief,* or by an infinitive as in *prone to misbehave.* Do not use the present participle, as in *? prone to misbehaving.* There are cases, however, when the noun that follows *prone to* is a verbal noun that looks like a present participle, and the *-ing* form is then of course quite acceptable:

　　Good my lords,
　I am not prone to weeping, as our sex
　Commonly are; ... but I have
　That honourable grief lodg'd here which
　burns
　Worse than tears drown.
　　　　　　　– Hermione, in Shakespeare's
　　　　　　　　　The Winter's Tale II i

Supine comes from the Latin *supinus,* 'lying on one's back, bent backwards'. Figuratively, it means 'lethargic, passive, reluctant to act against': *industry's supine response to stricter government controls.*

　She watched the television again all evening in fact, doing *The Times* crossword simultaneously to persuade herself that she was not being entirely supine.
　　　　　　　　　　　– Michael Frayn,
　　　　　　　　　Towards the End of the Morning

One way of remembering which word is which is to think of *supine* as containing the word *spine* — thus suggesting lying on one's back — and to think of *prone* as closer to *front,* thus suggesting lying face downwards.

Both words are sometimes confused with *prostrate*, which means lying down in either position, with the added suggestion of being thrown down or collapsing.

See also LIKELY, APT, LIABLE, PRONE; PROSTATE.

pronouns　A pronoun is a word that is used as a substitute for a noun or noun phrase, and that refers to a person or thing understood from the

context. Pronouns are traditionally divided into several classes.

First, *personal pronouns:* these indicate the speaker, the person or people spoken to, or the person or thing spoken about.

	subject	possessive	object
first person	I	my, mine	me
(speaker)	we	our, ours	us
second person	you	your, yours	you
(spoken to)			
third person	he	his	him
(spoken of)	she	her, hers	her
	it	its	it
	one	one's	one
	they	their, theirs	them

(The forms *my*, *our*, *your*, and so on that precede a noun are often called *possessive adjectives*. See ADJECTIVES. The old second-person forms — the singular *thou, thy,* and *thee,* and the plural *ye* — are now largely restricted to religious contexts or regional dialects.)

Some common grammatical errors arise over confusion between the subject forms *I, we, he, she,* and *they* (not the others)*,* and the corresponding object forms *me, us, him, her,* and *them.*

For instance, if the pronoun is connected by the verb *to be* to the subject of the sentence, it too should, strictly speaking, be in the subject form, though the temptation is to use the object form: *? It may have been me who broke it.* It should strictly be *I* not *me* here. (See IT'S ME.) Similarly, the common error made by children, × *John and me want our prize,* and the widespread constructions *? He runs as fast as me/faster than me.* (See AS; THAN.)

Those who are aware of these dangers often err in the opposite direction, however, producing such faulty constructions as × *He discussed it with my wife and I,* and × *That's good news for we teachers*, where *me* and *us* are required.

× The Government were looking for a stick with which to beat the BBC because *Panorama* had pointed out that some Conservative Party members were considerably more right-wing than Mr Gummer would wish you or I to know.
　　　　　　　　– Sir Denis Forman, *The Listener*

(See also BETWEEN YOU AND I; COLLECTIVE NOUNS; ME.)

There are two other dangers in the handling of personal pronouns: that of using them inconsistently; and that of failing to make clear which noun they refer to.

The danger of inconsistency is illustrated in

these examples:

?? We were worried because one felt so helpless.
× If one tries to switch on the radio you get a nasty shock.

The first example would be improved by changing *one* to *we*. The second example should have either *one tries* and *one gets,* or *you try* and *you get,* but not a mix of the two as it has at present. (In American English, however, *one tries* could be followed by *he gets*.)

The second danger — of uncertain reference — particularly affects the use of *they* and *it*:

× Only a few students have done any statistics before reaching university. They mostly have to begin the subject from scratch.

This second sentence seems to refer to those students who *have* done some statistics, which is nonsense. Similarly:

?? We made some more tea, because it was cold.

Was the tea cold, or the weather?
William Cobbett wrote in 1819: 'When I see too many *its* on a page, I always tremble for the writer.'

Uncertain reference can affect the other pronouns too. *He* and *she* can present difficulties, in such sentences as ?? *He told him that he must help him to move his car.* Plainly, this will not do, but it is hard to correct without some clumsiness. Avoiding pronouns may clarify the meaning but it produces an awkward style: ? *George told Andrew that Andrew must help George to move George's car.* Such a sentence had better be completely recast: *George had to move his car, and he told Andrew to help him.*

For the sake once again of making the reference clear, it is often better not to let a personal pronoun come before the noun to which it refers: ? *In view of her tender years, I should advise Mary to wait another term or two.* This would be better if reworded to read *In view of Mary's tender years, I should advise her to wait another term or two.*

The other classes of pronoun are:
● *demonstrative pronouns*: *this, that, these,* and *those.*
● *reciprocal pronouns*: *each other* and *one another.*
● *relative* and *interrogative pronouns*: *who, whom, whose, which, what,* and *that,* with their expanded forms *whoever, whatever,* and the like.
● *indefinite pronouns*: an indeterminate list in which most grammarians would include *any,*

anybody, anyone, anything, some, somebody, someone, something, none, nobody, no one, nothing, everybody, everyone, everything, as well as *each, both, all, many, either, neither.*
● *reflexive pronouns*: *myself, ourselves, yourself, yourselves, himself, herself, itself, oneself, themselves.* There is also the strange form *ourself,* used especially after the 'royal *we*' of a single sovereign: *We find ourself well pleased.*

Only the last two sets, the indefinite and reflexive pronouns, merit any further comment.

Some indefinite pronouns raise the problem of whether they should take a singular or a plural verb. It is quite common today, for instance, to treat *none* as a plural when it means 'not any of a group': *None of my cardigans match this dress.* However, purists might argue that the singular should be used even here: *None of my cardigans matches this dress.* (See NONE.)

Either and *neither* are still best treated as singular, at least in formal writing: *Neither of us is interested.* However, there is a good deal of controversy about the use of *he, him, his,* and so on with an indefinite pronoun treated as singular: *Anybody is welcome to eat his fill/their fill/his or her fill.* (See EITHER; EVERYBODY; NEITHER; NONE.)

Reflexive pronouns are used with verbs, or with prepositions, that refer back to the subject of the sentence: *I hurt myself; to talk to oneself.* They are also used for emphasis, as in *I'll post it myself.* Be careful not to confuse these two functions, as happens when a verb can be used either with or without an object ? *I'll advertise myself* might mean either that the advertisement will be about me, or that I shall see to the advertising personally.

Avoid too the common use of a reflexive pronoun as a variant of a personal pronoun: × *The letter was addressed to my wife and myself.* Why not simply *my wife and me*? (See MYSELF; SELF.)
See also AMBIGUITY 4.

pronunciation Almost every European language has a wide range of accents, varying from place to place and from social class to social class. Pronunciations can also change slightly from century to century, and even from decade to decade. English has the added disadvantage of pronunciations that all too often are quite out of keeping with the words' spellings. No wonder foreigners struggle to gain full competence in English.
Accents Show the word *butter* to a middle-class person from the southeast of England, and he will pronounce it roughly as /**butt**ə/. A farmer from

the west of England would sound the final *r*, /**but**-tər/. An Australian might have a harsher final vowel, /**butt**-u/. Someone from the north of England would have a gentler first vowel, closer to /**bōot**-ər/. A North American might sound the *t* rather like a *d*, /**bud**dər/, whereas a Cockney might manage to avoid sounding the *t* altogether — /**bu**-ə/, with a 'glottal stop' between the vowels.

Or take the phrase *sadly turned around*, /**sad**li turnd ə-**rownd**/ in the pronunciation-system of this book. In a heavy accent from Scotland, the phrase might sound, to some speakers, something like /**sud**lay **tu**-rənd ə-**rōnd**/; from the West Indies as /**saad**li tornd ə-**rungd**/; from South Africa /**sed**-lee tōond ə-**re**-und/; from New York /**see**-ədli toynd u-**rownd**/; and from the very upper crust of English high society, /**sed**li tarnd ə-**rīnd**/. And the word *buy* might be heard as /bay/ if spoken by someone from Belfast, /boy/ if spoken by a working-class Londoner, and /baa/ if spoken by someone from the North of England, from South Africa, or from the southern United States.

What all this variety of accents means is that there cannot really be such a thing as 'uniform English pronunciation'. What most British textbooks and dictionaries (and those of other English-speaking countries outside North America) rely on is *Received Pronunciation* or *RP* — the pronunciation of well-educated, middle-class or upper-class people, typically (though not exclusively) from southeastern England.

This is not to say that a London lawyer's pronunciation is more 'correct', taken as a whole, than that of a shopkeeper in Glasgow, a beekeeper in Sydney, or a fireman in New York. In fact, RP is in some ways a very unhelpful system: for one thing, it tends — unlike Scottish and most American accents — to omit the *r*-sound (as in *secure* or *worm* or *butter*) unless the written *r* is followed by a spoken vowel (as in *buttering* or *butter it*); for another, it reduces the vowel in many unstressed prefixes and suffixes to an indistinct ə-sound, and sometimes even eliminates it completely. Consider the word *consider*, for instance: in the north of England, the *o* would be clearly sounded, /kon-**sid**dər/, whereas in the south, in RP, it would be reduced: /kən-**sid**dər/. And in *secondary*, the *a* tends to disappear altogether in RP — /**seck**ən-dri/ — whereas a common American pronunciation would give it a distinct value: /**seck**ən-derri/. In RP, the word *observatory* would typically be pronounced /əb-**zerv**ə-tri/, the two *o*'s and the *a* (and the first *r* too) all losing their distinctive quality. A full-

blooded Welsh or West Indian accent, by contrast, would represent the written form far more faithfully, giving each vowel a generous and distinct value.

Nevertheless, RP remains the basis of dictionary pronunciation outside North America, and is used, unless otherwise indicated, in this book.

Not that RP is entirely uniform within itself. Many words have more than one accepted pronunciation: *often* can be /**off**'n/, /**awf**'n/, or /**off**-tən/; the word *photolithograph* probably has 16 different acceptable pronunciations, since each syllable except the first can be pronounced in either of two ways.

On the other hand, some pronunciations of individual words are clearly 'wrong', or at least 'less acceptable' than others. To pronounce *meringue* as ✗ /**mer**ring-gew/ is 'wrong' (no reasonably well-educated speaker would pronounce it that way, other than jokingly); to pronounce *respite* as ?? /ri-**spīt**/, on the model of *despite*, is 'nonstandard' (fairly common, but most educated speakers would agree that it is better avoided); to pronounce *controversy* with the stress on the second syllable is now 'acceptable' in RP (it is extremely widespread even among very well-educated speakers), but the older pronunciation, with the stress on the first syllable is still 'preferable'.

Development　Pronunciation changes over time as well as over distance and social class. Most large-scale changes take centuries to complete, but for individual words the common pronunciation may change surprisingly fast. Consider the following list. RP-speakers aged about 75 or over would have been brought up to pronounce each word with a distinctly different stress or vowel-value from that current among most other RP-speakers today.

spelling	former pronunciation	usual pronunciation today
acoustic	/a-**kow**stik/	/ə-**kōo**stik/
armada	/aar-**may**də/	/aar-**maa**də/
demonstrate	/də-**mon**strayt/	/**dem**mən-strayt/
hygiene	/**hī**ji-een/	/**hī**-jeen/
launch	/laanch/	/lawnch/
rabies	/**ray**-bi-eez/	/**ray**beez/
rationale	/**rash**ə-**nay**li/	/**rash**ə-**naal**/
sonorous	/sə-**naw**rəss/	/**sonn**ə-rəss/
supine	/sew-**pīn**/	/**sōo**pīn/
syndrome	/**sin**drə-mi/	/**sin**-drōm/
vagary	/və-**gair**-i/	/**vay**gəri/

Going further back in time, about 150 years, we would find the common educated pronunciation of *balcony* to be /bal-**kō**ni/, of *hospital* to be

/**aw**spit'l/ of *obliged* to be /ə-**bleejd**/, and of *virtue* to be /**var**tew/.

Further back still in the history of the language, slow changes have been identified that affected not just individual words but individual sounds — and hence the entire class of words containing such sounds. In the 15th century in particular, between Chaucer and Shakespeare, the set of changes known as the Great Vowel Shift was taking place. Shakespeare might well have found it easier to understand our accents today, 400 years later, than Chaucer's accent, 200 years earlier. Consider the different vowel sounds probably current at these different points in history (the spelling, of course, would be different too):

	Chaucer's pronunciation	Shakespeare's pronunciation	Received Pronunciation today
wife	/wif, weef/	/wayf/	/wīf/
mouse	/mo͞oss/	/mōss/	/mowss/
name	/naamə/	/ne-em/	/naym/
home	/hawm/	/ho-om/	/hōm/

Alongside the Great Vowel Shift another interesting change was occurring — we might call it the Small Consonant Loss. Many consonants, retained in the written word, disappeared from the spoken word — the *w* of *sword*, the *b* of *climb*, the *t* of *castle*, the *k* and *gh* of *knight*, the double *d*-sound in *ladder*, and so on.

In early modern English, *wind* ('moving air') was pronounced with a long *i*, the way *to wind* ('to twist') is today. And in the 18th century, *tea* was pronounced /tay/, at least among educated Englishmen. We know this from the rhymes used in verse at the time:

Blow, blow, thou winter wind,
Thou art not so unkind
As man's ingratitude.
 — Amiens, in Shakespeare's
 As You Like It II vii

Here thou, Great Anna! whom three realms obey,
Dost sometimes counsel take — and sometimes tea.
 — Alexander Pope,
 The Rape of the Lock

Wind ('moving air') is a particularly interesting example, since it has come full circle: in Old English, it would have been pronounced with a weak *i* as it is today. As Old English evolved into Middle English, weak vowels in front of a double consonant tended to become long, strong vowels or diphthongs: *blind*, for instance, was pronounced /blind/ in Old English, rhyming with *pinned*, but became /blīnd/, as it is today, in about the 11th century. However, the weak vowels did not change if followed by a triple consonant: hence the difference, surviving to this day, between the *i* in *child* and the *i* in *children*. In Shakespeare's time then, *wind* ('moving air') was pronounced /wīnd/, whereas *windmill* and similar compounds retained the short *i*, as in *children*. At some point during or after Shakespeare's time, the pronunciation of *wind* must have reverted to a weak *i*, through the influence of *windmill* and so on.

These few examples, drawn from a great number of pronunciation 'laws', illustrate how changeable pronunciation is over time. And it continues to change. In London, for instance, the *l*-sound in *bell, milk*, and so on is more and more being 'darkened' into a *w*-sound, and the *t* at the end of *packet, start*, and so on is increasingly being reduced to a 'glottal stop' — virtually soundless. In general, some old variants are dying out: *lather* and *ant*, for instance, are now settling down into /**laa**th͟ər/ and /ant/, whereas formerly they could also be acceptably pronounced as /**lath**ər/ and /aant/. The words *graph* and *plastic* are still holding on to their alternative forms, /graf/ and /**plaa**-stik/, though these are unlikely to survive for very much longer.

Spelling vs pronunciation The spelling combination *al* can be pronounced in six or seven distinct ways, according to the word containing it: *calculate*, /al/; *halt*, /ol, awl/; *chalk*, /aw/; *half*, /aa/; *salmon*, /a/; *halfpenny*, /ay/. You can find further examples of this asymmetry at the article SPELLING, and also some account there of the historical reasons for such inconsistency.

But the tendency today is towards reuniting spelling and pronunciation. And it is almost always the pronunciation that changes to conform with the spelling, not the other way round. *Waistcoat* was once widely pronounced very differently from the more 'accurate' pronunciation of today (the old pronunciation /**wes**-kət/ can still be heard in some regions of North America and in parts of Britain). A similar speak-as-you-spell influence is today at work on such words as *fortune* and *actual* (the *t* is increasingly being pronounced as a *t* rather than as a *ch*), and *controversial* and *species* (which are following *omniscience* in having the central *s* or *c* pronounced as an *s* rather than as a *sh*). Increasingly, letters once neglected or slurred are now sounded distinctly: the first *a* of *extraordinary*; the first *i* of *medicine*; the *t* of *postpone* and *dustbin*; the *h* in *annihilate, forehead*, and *philharmonic*, and the *th* of *clothes* (now /klōthz/ rather than /klōz/). The combination /hw/ is being consciously reinstated in *where, wheel*, and so on by some speakers whose parents and peer-group use plain /w/: they thus rejoin many Scots, Irish, and Americans who never lost it. Some purists are not at all happy about these developments (except perhaps the last), regarding them as symptoms of increasing ignorance.

It could be argued, however, that these developments are symptoms of increasing education. If you tend to 'speak as you spell', this is evidence that you know how to spell. It was the surge in working-class education last century that perhaps underlies the trend towards 'accurate' pronunciation today.

One further broad pronunciation change: the decline of the sound /ew/, or /yōo/, into a simple /ōo/, possibly under American influence. The words *lute* and *include* formerly had the *y*-sound — /lewt/, /in-**klewd**/ — in RP, but now more commonly do without it: /lōot/, /in-**klōod**/. The words *lewd* and *absolute* are still evenly divided, it is true, and the *y*-sound is retained — unlike in America — after the letter *n*: *nude* and *nuclear* are very seldom heard without their *y*-sound in RP, except for parts of London. *Sue* and *suit* too, are evenly divided, though *assume* perhaps tends to hold on to its *y*-sound more tenaciously. The American influence, if that is what is responsible, seems irresistible, however, and it may be only a matter of time before Londoners, New Zealanders, and so on are saying /nōod/, /ə-**sōom**/, and /**nōo**-kli-ər/ just like a native New Yorker.

Stress   Other types of change identified in recent times involve the stress pattern of words. The Germanic languages generally stress their words near the front; the Romance languages generally stress their words near the end, if at all: English, being a Germanic language at root, but with a large Romance contribution (especially Norman French, French, and Latin) in its vocabulary, has always had a very varied pattern of stresses.

One modern tendency is to move the stress closer to the front of a word, in keeping with the Germanic pattern. Many late borrowings from French, for example, have been distorted into the Germanic mould: **bu**reau, **cou**pon, **cam**ouflage, and so on. As these became naturalised into English, and lost their feeling of Frenchness, so they came to be stressed on the first syllable rather than having a late stress or being evenly stressed as in French. And many words long established in English have, in the past 150 years or thereabouts, shifted their stress from the second

syllable to the first — *compensate, defect, demonstrate, equerry, quandary* — or are on the way towards doing so in British English: *contribute, distribute*, and *research*.

Note that most of these examples have three syllables each. The new stress pattern — stress on the first syllable — now conforms to the general rhythmic pattern of three-syllable words: **dis**cipline, **li**brary, **pho**tograph, **tele**phone, **per**sonal, and so on. With four- and five-syllable words, however, the general rhythmic pattern is different, the stress falling on the second or third syllable: *li**bra**rian, pho**to**graphy, photo**graph**ic, tele**phon**ist, perso**nal**ity*, and so on. It is not really unusual to have the stress on the first syllable alone — **ad**mirable, **cap**italist, **dif**ficulty, **dis**ciplinary — but it does sound more awkward having three or four unstressed syllables in a row at the end in this way. So another tendency has developed — an opposite tendency — of moving the stress on to a later syllable (or at least adding an extra stress on a later syllable): increasingly we hear disci**plin**ary or **disci**plinary. Similarly, *ap**plic**able, con**trov**ersy, hos**pit**able, **necess**arily*, and tem**por**arily (the last three being standard in American English) are perhaps more common now in British English than the old first-syllable stress, though purists still prefer the old form. And *la**bor**atory* and *me**tall**urgy* have long since won the battle for a mid-syllable stress in British English; in American speech the older pronunciations — **lab**oratory, **met**allurgy (and also **con**troversy) — remain quite unchallenged.

What underlies these tendencies is the principle that stressed and unstressed syllables should alternate: one finds this principle observed even in such a word as **pho**tograph, whose last syllable (although not fully stressed) has a rhythmic beat (and a full vowel quality) that its second syllable lacks. This principle is basic to the rhythm of English speech as a whole, in which the time from one stressed syllable to the next is kept roughly the same regardless of how many unstressed syllables intervene. Other languages (Spanish, for example) give about the same time to each syllable, stressed or unstressed. English is said to be a 'stress-timed language' and Spanish a 'syllable-timed language'. A stress-timed language must see to it that there are not too many unstressed syllables between two stressed ones, since little extra time will be given to them. The ideal rhythm for such a language would be **tum**-*te*-**tum** or *te*-**tum**-*te*.

Many two-syllable words are subject to a different historical tendency: if the word has both a noun-sense and a verb-sense, there is a tradition of differentiating them — the noun being stressed on the first syllable, the verb on the second. Notice the two possible stress patterns in the words *accent, compress, conflict, contest, convert, convict, discount, escort, extract, import, increase, insult, present, record, suspect,* and so on. This development is still at work today. It can be seen in the increasing — but not yet universal — preference for stressing such verbs as *ally, commune,* and *incline* on the second syllable, leaving the first-syllable stress to the noun in each case.

Guidelines It is unnecessary — and probably impossible — to set out a full list here of 'the laws of English pronunciation'. But a few suggestions and warnings may be useful.

1. *American influence.* American pronunciation is inevitably influencing British pronunciation, but careful speakers generally discourage this infiltration as best they can. Among the forms discussed above, American influence is possibly responsible for **nece***ssarily* and **tem***porarily* — and perhaps for the nouns **de***fect* and **re***search* too; and it is threatening the *y*-sound in *nude, assume,* and *nuclear.* And the tendency to 'voice' the *t*-sound — turning *butter* into /**bud**dər/, for instance — is almost certainly modelled on American speech. (On the other hand, the reduction of *t* to a glottal stop — turning *butter* into /**bu**-ə/ — is a purely British innovation, and shows that British accents are still independent of American accents.)

A blanket ban on American pronunciations is as pointless as a blanket ban on American words: **de***fect* (as noun) is now fully established, and so far from doing any harm, has in fact created a useful distinction in sound between the noun **de***fect* and the verb **de***fect* (compare again **im***port*/ **im***port,* **pro***test*/**pro***test,* **record***/record,* and so on). On the other hand, the feeling against American influence is strong. And this linguistic protectionism has to be respected up to a point. In general, avoid Americanised pronunciations until they are firmly rooted in your own community.

2. *intrusive and residual sounds: p,t,k,g.* Certain words and phrases require some agility to pronounce. In regional accents, the difficulty is resolved by adding a sound that is not justified by the word's spelling or the history of its pronunciation.

Consider the intrusive *p*-sound that is increasingly heard between *m* and *th*: *? some(p)thing, ? warm(p)th.* Or the intrusive *t* between *n* and an *s*-sound: *? fen(t)ce, ? dan(t)ce, ? in(t)cident.* It seems over-pedantic to condemn these, even though it does mean that fewer people now

distinguish such pairs as *mince* and *mints* in speech.

Similar to this in effect (though not in cause) is the retention or revival in some varieties of British English of a /g/ (or /k/) in the pronunciation of *ng* when standard English has dropped it: *? The thing(g) is this; ? something(k).*

3. *the 'intrusive r'.* Perhaps the commonest, and certainly the most notorious, of these unwarranted sounds is the *'intrusive r'* — though here the fault (if it is one) is committed by many speakers traditionally considered the best — aristocrats, newsreaders, and classical actors alike.

When two vowel sounds occur in direct succession, the transition between them is often difficult to make. A common, though nonstandard, way of easing this transition is to insert an *r*-sound between the two vowels. This usually occurs between words — × *law(r)and order* — but can now also occur in the middle of a word: × *draw(r)ing.* Careful speakers frown on this practice: clear and deliberate sounding-out of syllables is a far better way of avoiding slurring the adjacent vowels.

Note that it is perfectly acceptable, on the other hand, to sound the *r* in the phrase *father(r)and son,* even though the *r* is usually not sounded by RP-speakers in the word *father* on its own. Since the *r* really does belong to the phrase this time, it is quite standard to invoke it as a 'linking *r*' in order to ease the changeover. Consider the sentence × *Jamaica(r)is far(r)away*: the first *r*-sound is intrusive and nonstandard; the second *r*-sound is a legitimate transition.

4. *intrusive vowel-sounds.* The counterpart of this problem is the difficult transition from one consonant to another. The temptation here is to slip a short vowel sound — /ə/ — between the two consonants, as in × *disast(ə)rous,* × *encumb(ə)rance,* × *suff(ə)rage,* × *ath(ə)lete,* × *strugg(ə)ling,* × *umb(ə)rella* — nonstandard in each case. (The first three 'mispronunciations' suggest that the speaker would probably misspell the words as well.)

5. *neglected sounds.* The converse mistake is neglecting letters that deserve to be sounded. The most obvious of these is the *h* at the beginning of a word: do not 'drop your aitches' (or add aitches where they do not belong). Music-hall comedy may thrive on it — × *Heven a ungry orse heats honly alf a eap of ay* — but ordinary conversation does not. It is, however, quite acceptable to drop the *h* in unstressed pronouns and auxiliary verbs (except at the start of a sentence): *Tell 'im what do; Some 'ave finished already.* (Remember that the *name* of the letter

h, paradoxically, does not contain the *sound* /h/: it is *aitch*, not *haitch*!)

The *h* is not alone in being 'dropped' by careless speakers. Take care too not to omit the first *r* of *February*, the first *c* of *Arctic*, the first *l* in *vulnerable*, the second *t* of *instincts*, and perhaps the *g* of *recognise* (the omission of this *g* is so common in British English, though not in American English, that it will probably become acceptable in due course). And do not let *stand up* and *going to* and *want to* slip lazily into × *stan' up* and × *gonna* and × *wanna*, or *length* and *strength* into × *lenth* and × *strenth*, or *geometry* and *geography* into × *jometry* and × *jography* (though *?sorta* is perhaps a legitimate weak form of *sort of*). Similarly, be careful not to drop an entire syllable from *authoritative, deteriorate, government, library, particularly*, and so on.

6. *foreign words and names.* When a borrowing from French, say, looks and feels quite at home in English, then it should usually be pronounced in a fully English way: in *enclave* and *envelope*, for instance, it is probably better to pronounce the first syllable /en-/ than the Frenchified /on-/; *chiffon* and *chagrin* have the clear English endings /-on/ and /-in/, not the nasalised French endings /-oɴ/ and /-aɴ/ (though the French *sh*-sound at the beginning has not given way to an English *ch*-); similarly *baton* is pronounced /**batt**'n/ in preference to /**bat**-oɴ/. *Nonchalant* is simply /**non**-shələnt/ in British English; *liqueur* and *amateur* are best pronounced /li-**kewr**/ and /**amm**ə-tər/ rather than taking a Frenchified /-**er**/ ending. And it sounds very affected to begin *questionnaire* as /**kest**-/ rather than /**kwest**-/, and to pronounce the first and last syllables of *insouciant* as /aɴ-/ and /-yoɴ/. There are some inconsistencies, of course: the words *charade* and *marinade* look equally at home in English, yet only *marinade* has become properly integrated into the English pronunciation system — /**marri**-nayd**/**; *charade* remains /shə-**raad**/ in British English as a rule, the anglicised /shə-**rayd**/ being used mainly in North America.

Not all French borrowings are fully absorbed, however. Some still openly declare their foreign origins by appearing in italics — *jeu d'esprit*, for example — and their pronunciation remains close to the French version (the final *t* is silent; the *r*, however, would be sounded in the English rather than French style). Others such as *chic, détente*, and *coup d'état* still look vaguely French, and feel slightly specialised: they retain an essentially French pronunciation. Others may look English — *debut*, say, if you omit the accent over the *e*

— but the change from a fully French pronunciation (a silent *t*) to a fully English one (a sounded *t*) is too great a leap, and so the essentially French pronunciation persists. And *entourage* remains stubbornly /**on**toor-**aazh**/.

The borderline cases are (of course) the problem: *chauffeur, confidante, cul-de-sac, niche, penchant, restaurant*, and *valet* still have a foreign look about them, but they are well-established English words by now. On balance, the anglicised pronunciation seems to be preferred: /**shō**fər/ rather than /shō-**fur**/; /**konf**i-**dant**/ rather than the Frenchified /-**do**ɴ/ or the American /-**daant**/; /**kul**-də-sak/ rather than /**kōōl**-/; /**nich**/ rather than /**neesh**/; /**vall**it/ rather than /**val**lay/. But the preference is a very slight one, and with *garage, penchant*, and *restaurant*, the Frenchified /**garr**-aazh/, /**po**ɴ-shoɴ/, and /**rest**ə-roɴ/ still have the edge, perhaps, in British English, over /**garr**ij/, /**pen**chənt/, and /**rest**ə-ront, -rənt/.

One fairly important difference has been noted between British and American pronunciation of French-based words: Americans sometimes stress the last syllable (apparently more in keeping with the original French) where the British would move the stress to the next-to-last syllable: Americans tend, for instance, to say *bal***let** and *recher***ché**, whereas British pronunciation favours **bal***let* and **recher***ché*.

The pronunciation of Latin words in English is generally in keeping with the 'old-fashioned' teaching of Latin sounds rather than the 'modern' system. (The 'old-fashioned' sound-system, prevalent in schools and universities until perhaps 50 years ago though discredited since the mid-19th century, treated Latin almost as if the words were English rather than foreign; the 'modern' system treats Latin — its vowels at least — more like French or Italian.)

So: *via*, following old-style pronunciation, is /**vī**-ə/ not /**vee**-ə/. Plurals ending in *-i* and *-ae* are pronounced /ī/ and /ee/ rather than the other way round: so, *fungi* is preferably /**fun**-gī/, and *algae* is preferably /**al**-jee/.

As for place names (and up to a point, people's names too), you will seldom when speaking English need to pronounce the major ones in a foreign way. Foreign cities (and historical characters) that have for centuries been known to English-speakers and discussed by them have acquired English names — *Florence* for the Italian *Firenze, The Hague* for the Dutch *den Haag, Moscow* for the Russian *Moskva, Vienna* for the German *Wien*, and so on. Sometimes, these anglicised names tend to change only the pronunciation of the original, leaving the spelling the same as in the local language since it happens to conform to English spelling patterns. So *Paris* is spelt the same way as in French, *Madrid* as in Spanish, and so on — but this is no reason to pronounce them /pa-**ree**/ and /ma-**threeth**/, any more than we should refer to Florence as /fee-**rent**-say/ (let alone as /flo-**ren**-chay/!).

Of course, only an outrageous snob would, when talking English, pronounce *Paris* and *Madrid* in the foreign way. Yet less prominent places have lost their English pronunciation in the last 50 or 60 years. Perhaps this indicates a new tolerance of foreigners and respect for their towns and countries — the result of tourism presumably, rather than diplomacy.

	former English pronunciation	standard English pronunciation today
Buenos Aires	/**bew**-i-nōz airz/	/**bwen**oss **air**iz, **bway**noss ī-riz/
Majorca (in Spanish, *Mallorca*)	/mə-**jawr**-kə/	/mə-**yawr**-kə/
Marseilles (in French *Marseille*)	/maar-**saylz**/	/maar-**say**/
Sofia	/sə-**fī**-ə/	/**sō**fi-ə, so-**fee**-ə/

The familiar **Him***a***layas** are slowly becoming the /hi-**maal**-yəz/, the Polish town of *Lodz* (really *Łódź*) is in danger of becoming /**wōoch**/, and so on. Certainly there are political reasons sometimes for respecting a foreign state's preference for the pronunciation (or even spelling) of a place name: Kenya has urged the pronunciation /**ken**-yə/; *Peking* has become *Beijing* (as part of a general change in the way Chinese is transliterated and pronounced) to most English-language newspapers, and is pronounced /**bay-jing**/; the prophet of Islam *Mohammed* is now in British publications widely spelt in the officially approved form *Muhammad*, pronounced /mōo-**hamm**əd/ (and *Moslem* has become *Muslim*, usually pronounced /**mōoz**-lim/).

For the rest, however, there is no need to be ashamed of the long-established English versions of foreign names and place-names: there is really no need to attempt to say *Teheran* as /**tekh**-raan/, Calcutta as /**kal**-kuttə/, or *Mexico* as /**mekh**i-kō/ (the Spanish, after all, tend to spell the country *Méjico*). And continue pronouncing *Don Juan* and *Don Quixote* in their traditional English way of /**don jōo**-ən/ and /**don kwiks**ət/ rather than attempting a full-throated or even half-hearted

Spanish version.

7. *proper names in English-speaking countries.* It is courteous, not to say prudent, to establish the correct pronunciation of the names of people, towns, institutions, and so on. For historical reasons, the pronunciation often diverges quite sharply from the spelling. To take a few obvious examples: London's river *Thames* is pronounced /temz/; the 17th-century diarist Samuel *Pepys* pronounced his surname /peeps/; the common Scottish surname *Campbell* is pronounced /**kam**bəl/; the economist John Maynard *Keynes* pronounced his surname /kaynz/; and the American presidents *Roosevelt* and *Reagan* are referred to as /**rōz**ə-velt/ and /**ray**gən/.

The BBC, through its own pronunciation unit, has various internal lists of tricky names and their pronunciations, and has even published *The BBC Pronouncing Dictionary of Proper Names*. It is worth consulting if you are in doubt. Or else, for the pronunciation of better-known people and places, try a good encyclopaedic dictionary such as the Reader's Digest *Great Illustrated Dictionary*.

Here are just a few names that you might be led into mispronouncing: first, some old British surnames:

Beaulieu	/**bew**li/
Cholmondeley	/**chum**li/
Cockburn	often /**kō**-bərn/
Dalyell	/dee-**el**/
Featherstonehaugh	often /**fan**-shaw/
Menzies	in Scotland, often /**ming**-iss/ or /**meng**-iz/
Rievaulx	often /**rivv**əz/
Ruthven	/**rivv**ən/
St John (as first name)	/**sinj**ən/
Wodehouse	/**wōod**-howss/

Then, some place-names:

Cherwell (river in Oxford)	/**char**wəl/
Chiswick (London suburb)	/**chiz**zik/
Des Moines Iowa, USA	/də **moynz**, də **moyn**/
Greenwich	/**grinn**-ij, **grenn**-, -ich/
Kirkcudbright (area of Scotland)	/kir-**kōo**bri/
Michigan	/**mishi**-gan/
Southwark	/**suth**ək/
Warwickshire	/**worrik**-shər, -sheer/

Worcester	/wŏŏstər/
Caius College, Cambridge (full name: Gonville and Caius College)	/keez/
Holborn Circus, London	/hōbərn/
Magdalen College, Oxford and Magdalene College, Cambridge	/mawdlin/
Marylebone Road, London	/marri-ləbən, marli-bən/
Notre Dame University, Indiana, USA	/nōt-ər daym/

Here now is a list of words whose pronunciations often produce mistakes or at least doubts. Note that when a word is given two or more acceptable pronunciations, without comment, the first of these is the one favoured and recommended. Remember too that this is a guide to British rather than North American pronunciations, though North American differences are discussed now and then.

abdomen /ab-dəmən/ has now widely replaced the traditional /ab-dōmən/ with its second-syllable stress.

absinthe /ab-sinth, ab-saNth/; the second, Frenchified pronunciation is not obligatory.

abyss /ə-biss/; stressed on the second syllable, not on the first as *abbess* is.

academician /ə-kaddə-mish'n/; only in American speech can the first syllable take a stress: /ackədə-mish'n/.

accomplice, accomplish the middle syllable can be /-kum-/ or /-kom-/.

acerbic /ə-serbik/: the first *c* is soft, the second hard.

acumen /ackew-mən/ is now far commoner than the traditional /ə-kewmən/ with its second-syllable stress.

adieu /ə-dew/ is the accepted English pronunciation, despite its difference from the French.

adults /addult, ə-dult/: the former is preferred in British English, the latter is the main pronunciation in American English; /add'lt/ is a common regional variant.

adversary /advər-səri, -sri/; /-serri/ is regional or American; note the stress on the first syllable — do not model it on *anniversary*.

aegis /eejiss/; not /ī/ as in *high jump*.

aeon /ee-on, ee-ən/: both are acceptable; but do not pronounce it like *eye on*.

aesthete /eess-theet/; the variant /ess-/ is American; ?/ayss-/ is dubious. But /ess-/ or /iss-/ (without stress) can begin *aesthetic*.

aficionado the *c* is usually pronounced *sh*, /ə-fish-yə-naadō/, but /-fiss-/ instead of /-fish-/ in the middle is also accepted; note the ending is /-naadō/, not ×/-naydō/.

again /ə-gen/ is heard slightly more often than /a-gayn/: both are fully acceptable, but /ə-gin/ is a regionalism.

against /ə-genst/ and /ə-gaynst/ are both acceptable, the former occurring more often; /ə-ginst/ is a regionalism.

aged /ayjid/, with the last syllable pronounced, is the adjective referring to old age (as in *Help the Aged* or *very aged*), but use /ayjd/ in *aged wine* and *someone aged 40*.

agent provocateur /azhoN prə-vockə-ter/: the first word is not pronounced like *agent*.

ague /ay-gew/ — two syllables, unlike *plague*.

albumen, albumin traditionally stressed on the second syllable, /al-bew-mən/, but now often stressed on the first: /al-bew-mən/. The words can be differentiated by ending *albumin* with a sharper /-min/ sound. (See separate entry.)

ally /al-ī/ for the noun; /ə-lī/ is now usual for the verb.

almond the *l* should be silent, though increasingly it is being sounded; however, in *almandine*, the *l* must be sounded.

alms, almoner the *l* should be silent, though it is heard in regional speech.

alter ego /altər eego/ or /eggo/; preferably not the same as the verb *to alter*.

amateur /ammə-tər/ is the most usual; /-ter/, /-tewr/, and ?/-chər/ are also heard.

amen /aa-men/ and /ay-men/ are both acceptable, the former being preferred in British English, the latter in American.

amenities /-meen-/ in the middle is slightly more usual, but /-men-/ is also acceptable.

analogous /ə-nalləgəs/, with a hard *g*, is more correct; the *j*-sound is often used, on the model of *analogy*, but is less acceptable.

anchovy the stress should be on the first syllable: /an-chəvi/. Second-syllable stress, ?/an-chōvi/, though common regionally, is best avoided.

Antarctic do not forget to sound the first hard *c*.

Antigua this Caribbean island should be pronounced /an-teegə/; there is no *y*- or *w*-sound in the name.

antiquary the stress is on the first syllable; /anti-kwəri/, not on the second.

apartheid the word is Afrikaans in origin, and should strictly be pronounced /ə-part-hayt/; however, /ə-part-hīt/, with the *ei* sounded /ī/ on the model of German, is a very common pronunciation outside South Africa, and attracts little criticism now. What is not acceptable is the omission of the *h*-sound, and the pronunciation /d/ rather than /t/ for the last consonant.

apothegm/apophthegm both forms are pronounced /**app**ə-them, app**ō**-/.

apparatus /**app**ə-**ray**təss/ and /-**raa**təss/ are both acceptable, the former being slightly preferable today; /-**ratt**əss/ is regional, especially in North America.

applicable either the first or second syllable can take the stress: the first is favoured by traditionalists, the second is now more commonly used.

apposite /**app**ə-zit/: the final syllable has a *z*-rather than an *s*-sound, and a short *i*, not /ī/ as in *sight*.

apricot /**ay**pri-kot/ rather than /**app**ri-/, which is a common regionalism.

a priori two acceptable pronunciations: /ay prī-**awr**ī/ is established, but a recent trend towards a more continental pronunciation of Latin phrases in English has given a boost to /**aa** pree-**awr**ee/.

aquatic rhymes with *attic* or *static*; it is regional or dubious when rhyming with *idiotic*.

archipelago /**ar**ki-**pell**əgō/; a *k*- not a *ch*-sound at the beginning.

Arctic do not forget the first hard *c*.

Argentine /-teen/ and /-tīn/ are both acceptable, though *Argentina* is always /-**teen**ə/. However, *argentine*, with a lower-case *a*, and meaning 'silvery' (or referring to a silver metal or a small fish), should always be /-tīn/ rather than /-teen/.

aristocrat /**arr**istə-krat/; the main stress on the first syllable rather than on the second is considered correct in British English, but second-syllable stress prevails in American English.

Arkansas /**ark**-ən-saw/ for the U.S. state; the last two syllables are pronounced very differently from *Kansas*.

art nouveau /**ar** noo-**vō**/; the *t* in *art* here is usually silent.

asp the short *a* as in *aspen* or *aspic* is usual; the pronunciation rhyming with *grasp* is now rare in British English.

ate in British English, /et/ is more usual and standard, but /ayt/ is also acceptable: the reverse in American English, where /et/ is regarded as chiefly British or nonstandard.

atrophy /**attr**ə-fi/; not ×/ay-/ at the beginning, and not ×/fī/ at the end as in *terrify*; and the middle syllable must not be stressed or mispronounced on the mistaken model of *trophy*.

attribute /**attr**ibewt/ for the noun; /ə-**tribb**əwt/ for the verb.

aural /**aw**-rəl/; the use of ʔ/**ow**-rəl/ to distinguish it from *oral* is well-intentioned but remains dubious.

bade traditionally pronounced /bad/ rather than /bayd/, though both are acceptable.

banal /bə-**naal**/ is now the most common pronunciation, although /**bayn**'l/ is also considered acceptable; /bə-**nal**/ is regional.

bankruptcy the *t* is usually silent, and this is quite standard.

bas-relief /**baa**-ri-**leef**/ and /**bass**-/ are both acceptable.

bathed, bathing *bathed* is the past tense and past participle, and *bathing* the present participle, both of the verb *to bath* and of the verb *to bathe*; the pronunciation distinguishes between the meanings; from *bath*, /**baa**thing, baatht/ (or regionally, and in North America, /**bath**ing, batht/); from *bathe*, /**bay**thing, baythd/.

been /been/ and /bin/ are both acceptable in British English, often varying according to context. In American English, /bin/ prevails and /been/ is considered chiefly British.

behemoth /bi-**hee**moth/ is the usual pronunciation; stress on the first syllable is quite common in American English, however.

beloved /bi-**luvv**id/ is preferable to /bi-**luvd**/.

blancmange /blə-**moNzh**/ is better than the anglicised /-**monj**/; do not sound the -*nc* of *blanc*-.

boatswain the alternative spellings of this word are *bo's'n* and *bosun*, and they indicate how it should best be pronounced: /**bō**-s'n/.

bona fide /**bōn**ə **fīd**i/ is usual, /**bonn**ə/ is sometimes heard; but *fide* is never pronounced like *side* in Britain, though it is usual in North America.

booth the word rhymes with *soothe*, rather than *tooth*. This latter form is regional or North American.

bouquet this should be stressed on the second syllable, and /**boo**-/ is preferred to /bō-/ for the first syllable: /boo-**kay**/ ideally. First-syllable stress is regional or nonstandard.

breeches referring to trousers, /**brich**iz/ is the usual pronunciation; not like *breaches*.

brochure now usually anglicised to /**brō**-shər/, though a more Frenchified pronunciation is possible: /brə-**shoor**/; a common American form is /brō-**shoor**/.

brusque the *u* sounds like the vowel sound in *hook* or in *whose* but not as in *husk*, though this is a common regional pronunciation and the standard North American form.

buffet the pronunciation /boŏffay/ is preferred for the refreshment counter; ?/buffi/ is regional or nonstandard. And /buffit/ is best reserved for the word meaning 'to strike' or 'a blow'.

bulwark /boŏl-wərk, -wurk/: the *w* is retained, unlike in *rowlocks* and *coxswain*.

bureau preferably stressed on the first syllable, /bewr-rō/, though often stressed on the second.

burgh this Scottish form of *borough* is pronounced just as *borough* is — /burrə/. A widespread regional variant in North America is /burrō/.

Byzantine most variants are acceptable: stress on the first syllable, /bizz'n-tīn, -teen/ or on the second /bī-zantīn, bi-, -teen/.

cadaver traditionally, this word rhymes with *waver*: /kə-dayvər/; now it is more often pronounced /kə-daavər/, sometimes /kə-davvər/.

cadaverous despite the variations in the word *cadaver* (see above), *cadaverous* is better as /kə-davvə-rəss/ than as /kə-daavə-rəss/.

cadre /kaadər/; the pronunciation /kaddri/ is chiefly North American.

capitalist the stress is on the first syllable, /kap-pitəlist/. Second-syllable stress is nonstandard.

Caribbean stressed usually on the first and third syllable /karri-bee-ən/; /kə-ribbi-ən/ is not favoured in British English, although it is used by West Indian speakers of English.

catacombs /kattə-koōmz/ is slightly preferred to /-kōmz/, though this too is quite acceptable.

caviar/caviare today commonly /kavvi-aar/ in British English, though /kavvi-ar/, with the main stress on the final syllable, is more traditional, and favoured in North America.

celerity the initial *c* is soft, as in *celery*: /si-lerrəti, sə-/.

centenary three possibilities, perhaps in this order of preference: /sen-teenəri, sen-tennəri, sentin-əri/. A common North American variant is /sentə-nerri/.

centrifugal it is best to stress this on the second syllable: /sen-triffewg'l/; /sentri-fewg'l/, also acceptable, is becoming increasingly common.

centripetal as above: /sen-trippit'l/ is slightly preferred to /sentri-peet'l, -peet'l; the ending is never pronounced like *petal*.

ceramic(s) /si-rammik(s)/ is much more usual than /kə-/, though experts prefer the /kə-/.

cervical /ser-vīk'l/ is slightly preferred to /ser-vik'l/.

chagrin the standard British English pronunciation used to be /shə-grin/; today it is /shag-grin/, though North Americans still say only /shə-grin/. It is unnecessary to use a more

Frenchified pronunciation.

chamois say /sham-waa/ for the mountain antelope; the plural, though unchanged in spelling, can be pronounced /sham-waaz/; but say /shammi/ for the soft leather made from the chamois's hide.

chancre /shang-kər/ — a *sh*-sound at the beginning; not like *canker* or *chance*.

chassis /shass-i, -ee/; not a *ch*-sound as in *chase* (though North American pronunciation allows it); and the final *s* is silent. The plural, unchanged in spelling, adds a /-z/ sound at the end.

chastisement /chastiz-mənt/, stressed on the first syllable, is the traditional preference; /chas-tīz-mənt/, with the stress on the second syllable, is also acceptable and probably now more common.

chemotherapy /keemō-therrəpi/ is perhaps preferred to /kemmō-/ as in *chemistry*, though this is becoming very common.

chiaroscuro /ki-aarə-skoor-ō, -skewr-/; not a *ch*-sound as in *charming*, but *k*- as in *Chianti*.

chic /sheek/ rather than /shik/, which is acceptable but rarer.

chimera/chimaera /kī-meer-ə, ki-/, not *sh*- as in *shimmer*.

chiropodist /ki-roppədist/ or /shi-roppədist/, not ×/chi-/.

cicerone /chichə-rōni/ or /sissə-rōni/ not ×/kik-/ and not ×/-ōn/ at the end as in *telephone*.

cinch the first *c* is soft as in *cinnamon*, not hard as in *clinch*.

circa /sur-kə, -kaa/; the first *c* is soft, no longer hard as it probably was in Latin.

clandestine various acceptable combinations are possible here: the stress can be on the first or second syllable, and the last syllable can be /-tin/ or /-tīn/. Perhaps the best, and commonest, form is /klan-dess-tin/.

clangour the *ng*-sound is preferably as in *anger*: /klang-gər/; /klang-ər/ as in *hanger* is also possible.

cliché /kleeshay/; it is chiefly the Americans who stress it on the second syllable: /klee-shay/.

clientele all three syllables have two possible pronunciations: /klee-, klī-/ (the second here is best avoided), /-ON-, -ən-/, and /-tel, -tayl/. Perhaps the best combination is /klee-ON-tel/.

clique /kleek/, like *pique*, rather than /klik/, which is regional or nonstandard.

clothes the pronunciation /klōz/ as in *to close*, is today considered more informal than /klōthz/, though it used to be fully standard.

coccyx /kok-siks/.

codify more usually /**kō**di-fī/, as if beginning with *code*; sometimes /**kod**difī/, as if beginning with *cod*.

coiffeur the most usual standard pronunciation is /kwa-**fer**/; /kwaa-/ and /kwo-/ are also acceptable, but not ×/kwo-**fewr**/.

colander /**kul**-in-dər/ is perhaps slightly preferable to /**kol**-/.

combat the stress is always on the first syllable for the noun or adjective, /**kom**-bat, **kum**-, -bət/; for the verb, the stress can be on either syllable: /kəm-**bat**, **kom**-bat, **kum**-/.

commandant /kommən-**dant**/ has long been accepted; /-**daant**/ is now sometimes heard; do not place the stress on the second syllable in imitation of *command*.

communal first-syllable stress is slightly preferable to second-syllable stress, though both are quite standard: /**kom**mew-n'l, kə-**mewn**'l/.

commune the noun is stressed on the first syllable: /**kom**mewn/; the verb is now usually stressed on the second: /kə-**mewn**/.

comparable the standard pronunciation is /**kom**pərə-b'l/, with the stress on the first syllable. Regional variants have the stress on the second syllable: /kəm-**parrə**-b'l, kom-**pair**-əb'l/.

compilation the second syllable should sound like *pill*, not like *pile* on the model of *compile*.

composite stress on the first syllable, /**kom**pə-zit/, and usually a short *i* in the last syllable rather than /ī/ as in *site*. In regional pronunciation, especially in North America, the stress sometimes goes on the second syllable.

conch /kongk/ used to be the standard pronunciation, though it has now been largely replaced by /konch/.

conduit /**kon**-dit/ is now the most common standard pronunciation; /**kun**-/ and /-dewit/ are possible variants; /-doo-it/ and /-dwit/ are regional.

confidant pronounced either /konfi-**dant**/ or the Frenchified /konfi-**doN**/. In North America /konfi-**daant**/ is possible. All options are different from the adjective *confident*: /**kon**fi-dənt/.

congeries /kon-**jeer**-eez, -**jerri**-, -iz/; note the soft *g* and the stress on the second syllable — unlike *conga* and *Congo*.

conjugal the stress should be on the first syllable, /**kon**-jŏog'l/; second-syllable stress is regional or nonstandard.

Connecticut the U.S. state is pronounced /kə-**nett**i-kət/, the middle *c* being silent.

constable /**kun**-stəb'l/ and /**kon**-/ are both established.

consummate the verb has the stress on the first syllable: /kon-sə-mayt, -su-, -sew-/; with the adjective, a second-syllable stress is slightly preferred: /kən-**summ**ət/. Even when the first syllable is stressed, the adjective should still be distinguished from the verb by its final syllable: /-mət/ rather than /-mayt/.

contrary in all senses /**kon**-trəri/, except the adjective sense, 'wilfully contradictory', which can be stressed on the second syllable: /kən-**trair**-i/.

contrast the noun is stressed on the first syllable: /**kon**-traast/; the verb on the second: /kən-**traast**/.

contribute /kən-**trib**-bewt/; purists object to a British tendency to shift the stress to the first syllable; *contribution*, however, has stresses on the first and third syllables.

controversy originally (and still in American English) stressed on the first syllable; increasingly there has been a shift towards stress on the second; traditionalists still prefer /**kon**trə-versi/. (See separate entry.)

contumely preferably three syllables, not four; and preferably stressed on the first syllable: /**kon**-tewm-li/. Similarly, *contumacy* is best stressed on the first syllable, but *contumacious* has stresses on the first and third syllables.

conversely the stress can go on first or second syllable, the second being slightly preferable.

Copenhagen /**kō**pən-**hayg**ən/ is correct. Despite Danny Kaye's pronunciation in the song, ?/**kō**pən-**haag**ən/ is not recommended: it is a misconceived attempt to imitate the Danes, who in fact spell their capital *København*, and pronounce it something like /**kerb**'n-**hown**/.

corps preferably /kor/; the plural, unchanged in spelling, is usually pronounced /korz/ in English. (See separate entry.)

corpuscle there is a slight preference for stress on the first syllable: /**kor**-puss'l/; but second-syllable stress is acceptable too: /kawr-**puss**'l/.

courtesan /**kor**ti-**zan**/ — contrast *courtesy* below; the stress on the final syllable is optional.

courtesy /**kurt**ə-si/ is the most usual; /**kort**ə-si/ is possible in British English.

Coventry /**kovv**'ntri/ and /**kuvv**'ntri/ are both possible.

covert /**kuvv**ərt/ is standard; ?/**kō**-vert/, on the model of *overt*, is regional or nonstandard or American.

coxswain /**kok**-s'n/ is the common naval form; /**kok**-swayn/ is just possible too.

coyote /kī-**ōt**i/ is now the most common pronunciation.

crochet the commonest standard pronunciation is /**krō**-shay/, though North American pronunciation usually shifts the stress to the second syllable.

croquet either /krō-kay/ or /krō-ki/; a North American variant allows the stress on the second syllable instead: /krō-**kay**/.

cucumber stressed on the first syllable; second-syllable stress is nonstandard.

cul-de-sac /**kul**-də-sak/ is the common preference; /**kōōl**/ is more Frenchified, as is a stress on the /**sak**/.

culinary /**kul**li-nəri/; in North American English, /-**nerri**/. Note that ?/**kewl**li-/ is not recommended.

cumulus /**kew**mew-ləss/, similar to *accumulate*.

cupola always stressed on the first syllable, which sounds like the first syllable of *Cupid*; so: /**kew**-pələ/. The commonly heard ×/kew-**pō**lə/, modelled on *polar* or *pianola*, is nonstandard.

daemon /**dee**mən/ is usual, though /dī-/ is also used with this spelling.

dais /**day**-iss/ is usual, though /dayss/ like *dace* is also possible, but preferably not ?/**dī**-əss/.

data /**day**tə/ is the usual pronunciation, but /**daa**tə/ is possible. (See separate entry.)

debacle/débâcle /day-**baak**'l, di-/; the *day*-pronunciation should be used if the word is spelt with an acute accent over the *e*.

debris/débris /**day**-, de-, -bree, -bri/; note that the stress is on the first syllable in British English, though usually on the second in North America. See *debacle* above.

debut/début /**day**-bew, deb**bew**/; again the stress is on the first syllable in British English, on the second in American. See *debacle* above.

debutante/débutante /**deb**bew-taant, **day**bew-, -tont, -tant/. See *debacle* above.

decade /**dek**kayd/ is slightly preferable to the pronunciation that sounds like *decayed*.

decanal stress on the second syllable: /di-**kayn**'l/; first-syllable stress, as in *deacon* or *decadent*, is regional or nonstandard.

decorous usually stressed on the first syllable, /**deck**ə-rəss/, like *decoration*, even though *decorum* is always stressed on the second.

deity /**dee**-əti/ has been standard for longer than /**day**-əti/, though both are acceptable.

deleterious /**delli**-**teeri**-əss/; also /**dilli**-, **deeli**-/ but not ?/-**tairi**-/.

deliberate the adjective is pronounced /di-**libb**ə-rət, -rit/; the verb ends /-rayt/.

demise /di-**mīz**/ is preferred, though /di-**meez**/, like *chemise*, is acceptable.

demonstrable purists prefer the stress to be on the first syllable, though the commoner second-syllable stress is quite acceptable.

denigrate /**denn**i-grayt/ is preferred, with the first syllable like *denim*; /**dee**-nīgrayt/ is very rare.

denouement/dénouement /day-**nōō**-moN/; in North American speech the stress can be on the first and third syllables instead.

depot /**depp**o/ in British English; /**dee**pō/ in North America.

Derby, derby the English town, horserace, and cheese should all be pronounced /**dar**bi/; the American horserace and hat are pronounced /**der**bi/.

desideratum the fourth syllable used to be pronounced like *ray*, and still can be, but the most usual pronunciation now is /di-**zidd**ə-**raa**-təm/, or with the *s* soft: /-**sidd**ə-/.

despicable /di-**spick**ə-b'l/ is now more usual, but stress on the first syllable is still favoured by purists: /**dess**-pikə-b'l/.

desultory stress on the first syllable /**dess**'l-tri/; do not model the stress on *sultry*; note the soft *s*, as in *insult*: /**dezz**'l-/ is regional.

deteriorate in careful speech all the syllables should be pronounced: /di-**teeri**-ə-rayt/; not ×/di-**teeri**-ayt/ — do not forget the second *r*.

detour /**dee**-toor/; the stress on the second syllable is less acceptable.

detritus /di-**trī**təss/, not like *detriment*.

devolution /**dee**-və-**lōō**sh'n/ is now more usual, though /**de**-və-**lew**sh'n/ used to be.

dilemma /di-**lemm**ə/ is the usual pronunciation; /dī-/ as in *dilate* is possible.

dinghy the pronunciation /**ding**-gi/, with a hard *g*-sound, is preferred to the common pronunciation rhyming with *stringy*.

diocesan /di-**oss**-iss'n, -iz'n/; only in North American speech is stress on the third syllable possible.

diphtheria /difth-/ and /dipth-/ are both acceptable.

diphthong /dipth-/ is now acceptable, as well as /difth-/.

disastrous /di-**zaa**strəss/; do not pronounce it with an extra syllable as if it were spelt ×*disasterous*.

dishabille traditionally the word ends with an *l*-sound, /**diss**ə-**beel**/, but the Frenchified pronunciation /**diss**ə-**bee**/ now seems more popular. Do not pronounce the first syllable as *dish*.

disparate stress on the first syllable, /**diss**-pər-ət/, in contrast to *disparity*, which is stressed on the second syllable, /diss-**parr**əti/, like *clarity*.

disputable both /diss-**pew**-təb'l/, stressed on the second syllable like *immutable*, and /**diss**-pewtəb'l/, stressed on the first syllable like *reputable*, are acceptable.

dispute /diss-**pewt**/, traditionally stressed on the second syllable for both the noun and the verb; this is still preferred to the increasingly common British stress on the first syllable for the noun: /**diss**-pewt/.

dissect /di-**sekt**/ and /dī-/ are both acceptable, the former being slightly preferable.

distribute the stress should be on the second syllable, like *to attribute*, and not, like *an attribute*, on the first: so /di-**strib**bewt/; the wish to shift the stress in British English no doubt arises from association with *distribution*.

doctrinal /dok-**trīn**'l/; the variant /**dok**-trin'l/ is chiefly North American.

doge this should be /dōj/ with a *j*-sound as in *dodge*; × /dōzh/, with the softened ending as in *mirage*, is common but incorrect.

doldrums /**dol**-drəmz/, as in *doll*, is the usual pronunciation; but /dōl-/, as in *dole*, is quite acceptable, and spreading.

dour this should be pronounced /door/ to rhyme with *poor*, though a regional variant, particularly in North America, is /dowr/ as in *flour*.

doyen stress the first syllable: /**doy**-ən/ ideally, though the Frenchified /**dwī**-en/ is possible. But do not nasalise the second syllable as in French, and do not stress it as you would in the feminine form *doyenne*, /doy-**en**/.

droll rhymes with *roll*, not with *doll*.

dynast, dynasty the pronunciation of these with the first syllable like *dine* used to be possible in British English but is now chiefly a North American pronunciation; /**din**-əst(i)/ is now the preferred British pronunciation.

ebullient /i-**bul**-iənt/ is the established pronunciation, the second syllable rhyming with *gull*, and preferable to a second syllable sounding like *bull*, though this too is now probably acceptable. The last two syllables can be run together as /-yənt/.

economic /eekə-**nom**mik/ is longer established, but /eckə-/ is also possible.

economy /i-**kon**nəmi/ is the only standard pronunciation.

ecumenical /eekew-**men**nik'l/ is the traditional pronunciation, but /eckew-/ is now also accepted.

Edwardian /ed-**wawr**di-ən/ is usual, but the old-fashioned variant /ed-**waar**di-ən/ is also used, and is common in North America.

e'er sounds like *air*, not *ear*.

egregious the first *g* is hard, the second soft: /i-**gree**-jəss, -ji-əss/.

either /**ī**thər/ is slightly more common in British English than /**ee**thər/, but less common in North America. (See separate entry.)

elegiac /elli-**jī**-ak, -ək/, not × /-**jee**-/ in the middle or × /-**ik**/ at the end. In North American English the stress can be on the second syllable.

elixir /i-**lik**-sər/; preferably not ? /-**eer**/.

empyreal several possibilities here: /em-pī-**ree**-əl/ is perhaps best, but /empi-**ree**-əl/ and /em-**pirri**-əl/ are also acceptable.

encephalography /en-seffə-**logg**rəfi/; note the stress, unlike *encephalogram*, /en-**seffələ**-gram/, which is stressed on the second syllable. In both cases, the second syllable can take a hard rather than soft *c*.

encyclical /en-**sik**klik'l/ has now clearly taken over from ?/en-**sīk**lik'l/ as the preferred pronunciation.

endemic /en-**dem**-ik/ as in *academic*; not × /-**deem**-/ as in *anaemic*.

ennui /oN-**nwee**/; the word is not yet sufficiently at home in English to lose its French pronunciation.

envelope /**en**-və-lōp/ is slightly preferable to /**on**-və-lōp/, which is no more than a half-hearted attempt at a French pronunciation.

ephemeral /i-**femm**ərəl/ is slightly preferable to /i-**feem**-/ as in *female*.

epicurean should be pronounced /eppi-**kewr**-ee-ən/; stressing the word on the third syllable is less acceptable, though very common.

epitome four syllables: /i-**pitt**əmi/.

epoch /**ee**-pok/ is standard; /**ee**-pokh/, common in Scotland, and /**epp**ək/, often heard in North American speech, are less acceptable.

equitable stressed on the first syllable, /**ek**witəb'l/; second-syllable stress, as in *equivalent* or *acquitted*, is nonstandard.

ersatz usually /**air**-zats/ or /**er**-zats/, reversing the *s* and *z* of the spelling; the ending /-saats/ is also possible.

esoteric /ess-ə-**terr**ik/ is standard, but /eess-/ and /-ō-/ are also acceptable.

et cetera Do not sound the first *t* as if it were a *k*: × /ek-**settr**ə/ is often heard, but is quite nonstandard.

evocation /**ev**-/ as in *every* is longer established, but /**eev**-/ is now a common variant.

evolution /**evv**ə-/ and /**eev**ə-/ are both acceptable.

exacerbate these are the possible standard pronunciations: /ig-**zass**ər-bayt, ik-**sass**ər-, eg-, ek-/; note the soft *c*, and the stress on the second syllable.

execrable /**eks**i-krəb'l/; do not place the stress on the second syllable as in *executive*.

exigency the stress on the first syllable, /**ek**-sijən-si/, is marginally preferable to the widespread second-syllable stress, /ig-**zij**-ən-si/, though this too is accepted as standard.

expatiate /ek-**spay**shi-ayt/, like *patience* in the middle, not sounding the *t* as in *patio*.

experiential /ik-**speer**-i-ensh'l/ as in *experience*, rather than ?/-sperr-/ as in *experiment*.

expiatory traditionally this is stressed on the first syllable alone: /**ek**spi-ətəri, -aytəri/; an additional stress on the third syllable is increasingly common, /**ek**spi-**ayt**əri/, and is now considered acceptable.

explicable purists prefer the stress on the first syllable, though it is now more usual — and quite acceptable — to stress the second syllable instead.

exquisite stress on the first or second syllable is acceptable: /**ek**skwizit/ or /iks-**kwizz**it/; the first pronunciation now sounds slightly precious (or too exquisite).

extempore /ek-**stem**pəri/; there is no need to latinise the final syllable into ?/-ray/.

extraordinary it is more usual, and slightly preferable, to slur both of the *a*'s, and to stress the second syllable: /ik-**strord**'n-ri/. But it is quite possible to retain both *a*'s in a weak form, and to stress the first and third syllables: /**ek**-strə-**ord**'n-əri/. Various combinations are acceptable, but the regional /-erri/ ending is best avoided outside North America.

fait accompli /**fayt**ə-**kom**-plee, **fett**ə-, **koN**-, -plee/; the plural *faits accomplis* is pronounced the same as the singular.

fakir can be pronounced on the first or second syllable: /**fay**-keer, **faa**-, **fack**-/ or /fə-**keer**/. The pronunciation /**fay**kər/, though also possible, might be confused with *faker*, and is best avoided.

falcon best is /**fawl**-kən/, though /**fol**-/ and even /**faw**-/ are acceptable; /**fal**-/ is regional, though standard in American speech.

farrago /fə-**raa**-gō/ has now replaced /fə-**ray**-go/ as the commonest pronunciation.

febrile the standard pronunciation used to be either ?/**fee**-bril/ or ?/**feb**ril/, but now /**fee**-brīl/ rhyming with *mile* is the accepted pronunciation.

February purists like the word to be pronounced fully: /**feb**brōō-əri/ rather than /**feb**bew-ri/; the ending /-erri/ is common in North American speech.

fecund /**feck**ənd/ and /**fee**-kənd/ are both acceptable.

femme fatale /**fam**-fə-**taal**/ is the only proper pronunciation; ?/**fem**-/ as in *feminine*, and ?/-**tal**/ as in *talisman*, though common, are less acceptable.

femur /**fee**-mər/, not /-mewr/ as in *mural*. The plural *femora* can be /**fee**mərə/ or /**fem**mərə/. The adjective *femoral*, however, should be /**fem**mərəl/.

fetid/foetid /**fett**id/ and /**fee**tid/ are both acceptable, the former slightly likelier for the spelling *fetid*, the latter for *foetid*.

fiat this Latin word for a decree or ruling is best pronounced /**fī**-ət/, though /**fee**-ət/ is more common and is quite acceptable, as are the endings /-at/ and /-aat/.

fifth in standard pronunciation, the second *f* should be heard.

figurative, figurine these can follow *figure* in beginning simply /**figg**ər-/, but it is slightly preferable to say /**figg**ewr-/. *Figurine* has an optional further stress on the last syllable; *figurative* should not be stressed on the second syllable.

figure /**fig**-gər/ and /**fig**-yər/ were once both standard in English, but now the second of the two pronunciations is heard mainly in North American English.

film the standard pronunciation is a single syllable: /film/. The regional variant ?/**fil**'m/, common in the north of England, South Africa, and so on, is best avoided.

finance traditionally /fi-**nanss**/, with the stress on the second syllable (though /fī-**nanss**/ has long been an acceptable variant); the now common stress on the first syllable, /**fī**-nanss/, is more recent.

flaccid /**flas**-sid/ seems to have overtaken /**flak**-sid/ as the most common pronunciation of this word; purists still insist on the *ks*-sound, however.

(pâté de) foie gras /(**pat**tay də) **fwaa graa**/.

forbade the second syllable is preferably pronounced like *bad*, though /-**bayd**/ is also acceptable.

forecastle best pronounced /**fōk**-s'l/ and sometimes spelt as pronounced: *fo'c's'le*.

forehead traditionally /**forr**id/, like *horrid*; but many people nowadays favour the regional /**for**-hed/, especially in North American English.

formidable the stress is preferable on the first syllable, though accepted on the second.

forte the musical term is pronounced /**for**-tay/ or /**for**-ti/. In the sense of 'something at which one excels; one's strong point', *forte* has both these pronunciations too, and a third possibility as well: /fort/. The best in both senses remains /**for**-tay/.

forthwith the second *th* (like the first) is

preferably soft as in *kith* rather than hard as in *writhe*.

fortune traditionally the second syllable is pronounced precisely: /-tewn/; the pronunciations /**for**-chōōn/ and /**for**-chən/ are now more usual, however.

foyer the pronunciation has moved further from the French /fwa-**yay**/, and is now usually /**foy**-ay/, or the more dubious ? /**foy**-ər/.

fracas the *s* is silent in British English, /**frack**aa/ (the pronunciations /**fray**-kəss/ and /**frack**əss/ are often heard in North American English); the plural (in British English spelt the same as the singular) is pronounced /**frack**aaz/ in English. (In North America, the plural is *fracases*.)

frequent the adjective has the stress on the first syllable, the verb on the second. To stress the verb on the first syllable is a common regionalism, but is not recommended.

frontier stressed on the first syllable in British English, and usually on the second in North American English; the stressed vowel is preferably /u/, as in *front*, though /o/ as in *font* is also acceptable.

fructify, fructose /**fruk**-/ as in *truck* is slightly preferable to /**frōōk**-/ as in *crook*; the *-ose* in *fructose* is either like *morose* or like *nose*.

fulminate preferably rhymes with *culminate* — having a *u* as in *up*; the common pronunciation beginning like *full* is also acceptable.

fulsome the first syllable is always pronounced like *full*, although it was once standard to rhyme it with *gull*. (See separate entry.)

fungi, fungicide the traditional pronunciations are /**fun**jī/ and /**fun**ji-sīd/, but /**fung**-gī/ or perhaps /-gee/ and /**fung**-gi-sīd/ are increasingly used, on the model of *fungus*.

furore preferably three syllables, with the stress on the second: /fewr-**raw**-ri/. The commonly heard ? /**fewr**-or/ is best avoided, unless the word is spelt *furor*, as it often is in North American English.

Gaelic the traditional and perhaps preferable pronunciation is /**gay**-lik/; /**gal**-ik/ is also acceptable — but it could be confused with *Gallic*, meaning 'from Gaul'; the pronunciation /**gaa**lik/, like *garlic*, is regional.

gala traditionally /**gay**lə/, and still that way for the miners' festival; but the swimming competition is now usually /**gaa**lə/.

gallant the stress on the first syllable is accepted for all senses: /**gal**-ənt/; but in the sense of 'attentive to women, chivalrous, courteous', stress on the second syllable is also possible: /gə-**lant**/; but /gə-**laant**/ is a regionalism or else an affectation.

garage /**garr**-aazh/ and /**garr**-ij/ are the two accepted pronunciations in British English, the former being slightly preferred; note that the stress is on the first syllable in each case, though in North American English commonly on the second; in British speech this second-syllable stress is often considered an affectation.

garrulous /**garr**ə-ləss/ is slightly preferable to /**garr**ew-ləss/.

gaseous both the pronunciations /**gass**i-əss/ and /**gay**si-əss/ are established and acceptable; /**gay**zi-əss/ is also sometimes used now; ? /**gay**-shəss/ is doubtful.

genre /**zho**Nrə/; there is no acceptable pronunciation more anglicised than this.

genuine the last syllable rhymes with *inn*: /**jen**new-in/; only in North American English can it ever rhyme with *wine*.

genus traditionally sounds like *gene* at the beginning, though the plural *genera* is pronounced very much like *generous*; the pronunciation /**jen**nəss/, increasingly common, is also acceptable.

geometry /jee-**om**-/: do not fuse the first two syllables into × /**jom**-/.

gewgaw traditionally pronounced /**gew**-gaw/; sometimes /**gōō**-gaw/ is heard.

geyser for the hot spring, /**gī**zər/ and /**gee**zər/ are both acceptable; for the hot-water heater, only /**gee**zər/.

gibber /**jib**bər/ is usual but /**gib**bər/ as in *gibbon* is also accepted; similarly *gibberish* favours /j/ but allows /g/.

glacial traditionally this is /**glay**shi-əl/ or /**glay**sh'l/, rhyming with *racial*; /**glay**-si-əl/ is now also accepted, and /**glass**i-əl/ too — see *glacier* below.

glacier /**glass**i-ər, **glay**si-/ — note the *s*- sound; in North American English /**glay**-shər/ and even /**glay**-zhər/ are sometimes heard; see *glacial* above.

glazier The *z* can be either /z/ or /zh/.

glower in the sense of 'to frown or scowl', shares their vowel: /**glow**-ər, glowr/, to rhyme with *power*. See also *lower* below.

golf /golf/ normally; /gof/ and /gawf/ are now old-fashioned.

gooseberry /**gōōz**-bəri, -bri/. The first syllable sometimes resembles *goose* in regional English, but ideally, the vowel is that of *good*, and the *z*-sound that of *choose*.

government /**guv**vərn-mənt/ is preferred by careful speakers, retaining the sound of the first *n*.

graph /graaf/ is now commoner than /graf/, though purists prefer the latter.

gratis traditionally pronounced /**gray**-tiss/; these days /**graa**-tiss/ is more usual, and /**grat**tiss/ is also heard.

greasy /**gree**-si/ is now common, but in the past the word tended to follow the pattern of *easy* and *queasy*, having a hard *z*-sound, /**gree**-zi/, and this is still used and accepted.

Grenada the Caribbean island is pronounced /grə-**nayd**ə/; it sounds similar to *grenade*. Do not use the long /aa/ sound in the middle as in the Spanish city of *Granada*.

Gruyère the French pronunciation of this Swiss cheese, with the *u*-sound as in the French *tu*, is unnatural in English; the English approximation of it is either /grōō-**yair**/ or /gree-**yair**/; both are acceptable. Rather less acceptable is to stress either form on the first syllable.

guerrilla/guerilla the standard pronunciation is identical to that of *gorilla*, /gə-**rill**ə/. Attempts to differentiate by pronouncing the first syllable /ge-/ or /gye-/ tend to sound affected.

gunwale the alternative spelling is *gunnel*, which indicates the pronunciation; the word rhymes with *funnel*.

gyroscope /**jīr**-ə-skōp/; the *g* is soft, as in *gypsy*.

hagiography /**haggi**-**oggr**əfi/; /**hay**ji-/ is possible in North America.

halcyon /**hal**-si-ən/, not × /**hawl**-/.

half-past in careful speech, the *f* should be pronounced.

harass, harassment stress on the first syllable in *harass*, /**harr**əss/, was the only accepted pronunciation in Britain until the 1970s, when a second-syllable stress began to spread: /hə-**rass**/ and /hə-**rass**-ment/; this is still doubtful: /**harr**-əss/ is recommended.

harem all sorts of pronunciations are acceptable: /**hair**-əm, **haar**-eem, hə-**reem**/ are all standard, as are other combinations of these syllables.

hectare /**hek**tair/ rather than ? /-aar/ as in French; rhyming with *care* rather than *car*.

hedonist the first syllable as in *heed*, not as in *head*.

hegemony the two common rival pronunciations, /hi-**gemm**əni/ and /**heji**-məni/, are both perfectly acceptable. Less advisable, though common in North American speech, is /hi-**jemm**əni/.

heinous /**hayn**əss/, rhyming with *Janus*, is best; rhyming with *Venus* is also possible; rhyming with *highness* is nonstandard.

herb /herb/; only in American speech is the *h* silent.

Herculean /**her**-kew-**lee**-ən/, modelled on the stress in *Hercules*, is encroaching on the traditional pronunciation /her-**kew**li-ən/, rhyming with *Julian*.

heroin pronounced /**herr**ō-in/, just like *heroine* — not ? /**herr**oyn/.

hiatus /hī-**ayt**əss/: not × /hēē-/.

Hiroshima /**hirr**ə-**sheem**ə/, with stresses on the first and third syllables, is the preferred pronunciation, but /hi-**rosh**imə/ is also accepted.

homeopathy /**hom**-/ and /**hōm**-/ are both acceptable; stressed most strongly on the third syllable: /**hom**-i-**opp**əthi/.

homosexual the element *homo* is from the Greek word for 'alike, same', not from the Latin for 'a man': so purists prefer /**hom**-/ to /**hōm**-/ as the first syllable. But the trend is against them: /**hōm**-ə-**sek**-sew-əl/ is perhaps the most favoured form today. Several variants are possible, using a combination of these elements: /**hom**-, -ō-, -shoo-, -shwəl/.

hors d'oeuvre /awr-**derv**/; the plural is either pronounced and spelt the same, or pronounced with a /-z/ on the end if spelt *hors d'oeuvres*.

hospitable traditionally the stress is on the first syllable, as in *hospital*, and this is still slightly preferable; but second-syllable stress is perhaps now more common, and perfectly acceptable.

housewife the old-fashioned pronunciation /**huzz**iff/ is now used only for the word meaning 'a pocket container for sewing equipment'; otherwise /**howss**-wīf/; note that *housewifery*, however, is still pronounced /**howss**-wiffəri/.

hover /**hov**vər/ and /**huv**vər/ (like *cover*) are both acceptable.

hydraulic /hī-**draw**lik/ is traditional, but /hī-**drol**lik/ is now often heard, and is quite acceptable.

ideology /**īdi**-ollaji/ like *idea* is slightly preferred to /**iddi**-/ like *idiot*.

idyll /**idd**il/ is slightly preferable to /**ī**-dil/, though both are acceptable.

ignominy stressed on the first syllable: /**ig**-nə-mini/; a regional alternative, especially in North America, is /ig-**nomm**ini/, stressed like *economy*. This second-syllable stress is best avoided.

illustrative traditionally stressed on the second syllable, /il-**lust**rətiv/, but this is now rare except in North American English; the usual British pronunciation today is /**illə**-strətiv/, stressed on the first syllable, though /**illə**-stray-tiv/ is also possible.

imbroglio /im-**brōl**-yō/; the *g* should not be pronounced.

impasse the first syllable can be /im-/ or /am-/, the second should be /-paass/; /-pass/ is regional; the stress can be on either syllable; perhaps the best combination is /**am**-paass/.

impious /**im**-pi-əss/ with the stress on the first syllable; contrast *pious*.

importune the traditional preference was for /im-pawr-**tewn**/, sometimes with the stress on the third syllable alone; but second-syllable stress has long been an acceptable option too, and is now probably more common: /im-**por**-tewn/.

impotent stressed at the beginning, /**im**pətənt/, like *competent*; contrast *potent*, /**pōt**'nt/.

inchoate the *ch* is pronounced /k/; the stress can be on the first or second syllable; the final syllable too is variable; the best combination perhaps is /in-**kō**-ayt/.

inherent /in-**heer**-ənt/ is the traditional pronunciation; /in-**herr**ənt/ is an acceptable variation.

innovative /**inn**ə-vaytiv, **inn**ō-, -vətiv/; note that the stress of *innovate* does not shift forward onto the *o* the way it does in *interrogative*; but *innovatory* offers a choice — the stress can go on the first syllable alone, or on the first and third syllables as in *elementary*, or on the second syllable alone as in *derogatory*.

insouciance /in-**soo**-si-ənss/ is the accepted anglicised pronunciation of the French; if you want a Frenchified pronunciation, attempt it wholeheartedly, rather than changing just one syllable here or there.

integer /**in**tijər/; note the soft *g*-sound.

integral stressed on the first syllable: /**in**tigrəl/; second-syllable stress is regional or North American.

interdict /**in**tər-dikt/ is preferred, but /**in**tər-dīt/ like *indict* is also acceptable. These pronunciations, with the final syllable unstressed, apply to the noun; in the verb, the final syllable is stressed.

internecine /**in**tər-**nee**-sīn/ is the accepted pronunciation; /-**nayss**-, -**ness**-, -seen, -sən/ are regionalisms, especially in North America, as is the stress on the second syllable. (See separate entry.)

interpolate /in-**ter**-pə-layt, -**pō**-/; note the stress on the second syllable.

interstice /in-**ter**-stiss/; do not add a vowel to the end, as in *hyperbole*, on the mistaken model of *ecstasy*.

intestinal second-syllable stress is traditionally preferred, /in-**test**in'l/, but /**in**tes-**tīn**'l/ is now more common and quite acceptable.

intricacy this should be stressed on the first syllable /**in**-trickəsi/.

invalid stress on the second syllable for 'not valid'; on the first when referring to someone who is ill — traditionally in British English this has been pronounced with the last syllable as /-leed/, and remains usual for the verb sense, but for the noun and adjective, /-lid/ is probably more common nowadays.

inveigle /in-**veeg**'l/ is the longer established pronunciation, but /in-**vayg**'l/ like *inveigh* has become accepted, and is now more common. (See separate entry.)

inventory stress on the first syllable rather than the second; not like *invention*.

iodine the last syllable is variable: /-deen, -dīn, -din/, and the second syllable can be /-ə-/ or /-ō-/. The best British version is perhaps /**ī**-ə-deen/.

Iran /i-**raan**/ rather than ? /i-**ran**/; *Iranian* is usually /i-**rayn**iən/ but sometimes has /ī/ at the beginning, like *Irish*; so does *Iran* in North American speech sometimes.

irascible /i-**rass**ə-b'l/ is usual, but /ī/ at the beginning is still accepted; note that the *c* is not pronounced hard.

irrefutable it is possible to stress this either on the second syllable, as with *irregular* and *disreputable*, or on the first and third, as with *irretrievable*.

irreparable should be stressed on the second syllable; the *-repar-* in the middle is as in *reparation*, not as in *repair*.

irrevocable should be stressed on the second syllable, /i-**revv**əkə-b'l/, not on the first and third as the base word *revoke* might suggest.

issue the second syllable can be like *shoe* or *sue* — both are acceptable.

January purists prefer all the syllables to be pronounced, though the ending is commonly slurred into /-ewri/, like *fury*; and in regional or North American speech, it is often expanded to /-ew-erri/.

jejune /ji-**joon**/; no French *j*'s are involved. (See separate entry.)

jewellery as the North American spelling *jewelry* suggests, the standard pronunciation is /**joo**-əl-ri/; ? /**jool**-ri/ is doubtful, and ? /**joo**ləri/ regional or nonstandard.

jubilee the third syllable can take an extra stress, but it is best to stress the first syllable alone.

junta /**junt**ə/ is the standard anglicised pronunciation of this word; but the Spanish /**khoont**ə/ and in-betweens such as /**hoont**ə/ and /**joont**ə/ are also used.

kilometre stress on the first syllable is the traditional British pronunciation: /**kil**-ə-meetər, -o-/; the common alternative American second-syllable stress, /ki-**lomm**itər/, is spreading, however.

kinetic traditionally /kī-**nett**ik/ as in *kind*, but increasingly pronounced with a short *i*, as in *kin*;

the second syllable always has a short *e*, so ×/-**nee**tik/ is nonstandard.

knoll rhymes with *roll*, not with *doll*.

kudos /**kew**-doss/; the American variant /**kew**-dōss/ is nonstandard in British English.

laisser faire/laissez faire /**less**ay/ is slightly preferable to /**lay**say/.

lamentable stress on the first syllable is the traditional and standard British pronunciation, but stress on the second is common and acceptable.

largesse /**lar**-jess/, the traditional pronunciation, is now perhaps less common than the second-syllable stress: /laar-**jess**/; the Frenchified /lar-**zhess**/ is also acceptable.

lasso now usually /la-**soo**, lə-/ in British English, though /**lass**-ō/ used to be standard.

lather /**lath**-ər/ is traditional, but /**lāath**ər/ is now standard; not ×/**lay**thər/.

leeward /**lee**-wərd/ is a common and accepted pronunciation, but the nautical pronunciation /**loord**/ is also possible.

length this should be pronounced /leng-th/, but /lengk-th/ is a slightly dubious variant; ×/len-th/ is nonstandard.

Leyden/Leiden the town is pronounced /**līd**'n/, like *lied* at the beginning, not like *laid*.

liaison /li-**ay**-z'n, -zon/, or the French /-zoN/; the first syllable is never /lī/ as in *liable*.

library strictly, three syllables, /**lī**-brəri/, though /**lī**bri/ is also acceptable; the common North American pronunciation /**lī**brerri/ is nonstandard in British English.

lichen /**lī**kən/, as *liken*, and /**lich**ən/, as in *kitchen*, are both accepted.

lien /**lee**-ən/ is best; ?/leen/ like *lean*, and ?/**lī**-ən/ like *lion*, are dubious, though these were both standard formerly.

liqueur the French would say roughly /li-**ker**/, but in English the pronunciation /li-**kewr**/ is now standard and preferable.

liquorice traditionally and preferably ends with /-riss/, though /-rish/ is now acceptable too.

longevity /lon-**jev**-/ is traditionally correct, though /long-**jev**-/ is now common; ×/long-**gev**-/ is nonstandard.

longitude the *j*- rather than *g*-sound is traditional here, though /g/ is acceptable now and far more common in British English.

loth/loath the *th* is unvoiced and the word rhymes with *both* in either spelling; preferably not like *loathe*.

lower/lour the verb 'to look sullen, or glower' rhymes with *power*; only the comparative of *low* rhymes with *slower*.

macabre /mə-**kaa**-brə/ is longer established than /mə-**kaa**-bər/, though both are acceptable.

machination /**mack**i-**nay**sh'n/ is the traditional pronunciation, although /**mash**i-/ is now widespread. (See separate entry.)

macho a *ch*-sound in the middle like *match*, though *machismo* may be pronounced /-**chiz**-/ or /-**kiz**-/ in the middle.

macramé /mək-**rāā**mi/ is the accepted anglicised pronunciation; the Frenchified /**mack**rə-may, -may/ is also acceptable.

magazine preferably /**magg**ə-**zeen**/, though the final syllable can be left unstressed, as it commonly is in North American speech.

maladroit /**mal**-ə-**droyt**/; do not try to make the last syllable sound French.

malign /mə-**līn**/ with a silent *g*, unlike *malignant*.

malinger the *g* is hard as in *linger*, not soft as in *impinge*.

mall in most uses the word is pronounced /mawl/; in the names of certain streets, such as *The Mall* or *Pall Mall* in London, and in the game *pall-mall*, *mall* is pronounced /mal/.

malmsey /**maam**zi/ like *alms*, not an *aw*- or *awl*-sound as in *palsy*.

mandatory traditionally stressed on the first syllable, /**man**də-təri/, rather than on the second, /man-**day**təri/, though both are acceptable now in British English.

manifold pronounced like *man*, not like *many*: /**man**ni-**fōld**/.

margarine the *g* is now usually soft, to sound like *Marjory*, though originally it was hard as in *Margaret*.

marigold like *marry*, not *Mary*: /**marri**-gōld/.

marinade /**marri**-nayd/; not a Frenchified /-naad/ as in *facade*.

massage /**mass**-aazh/ is best — the stress on the first syllable (an American variant allows it on the second), and the *g* sounded /zh/ as in *mirage*; /**mass**-aaj/ is also acceptable, however.

masseuse /mass-**urz**/ is the correct pronunciation, still close to the French; anglicised versions of the second syllable are dubious, and best avoided.

matrix the first syllable is like *mate*, /**may**triks/, in all uses of the word except possibly the specialist printing term, which can be pronounced /**mat**triks/.

matutinal two possible stress patterns here: /**mattew**-**tīn**'l/ and /mə-**tewt**in'l/.

mausoleum stress on first and third syllable: /**maw**-sə-**lee**-əm, -zə-/; do not model it on *linoleum*.

mauve /mōv/ to rhyme with *stove*; the vowel is not like in *Maud*.

mayor in Britain, /mair/ is the favoured pronunciation; in the United States, South Africa, and elsewhere, however, /**may**-ər/ is more common, and considered quite acceptable.

medicament the stress can be on either the first syllable, /**med**dikə-mənt/, or on the second: /mə-**dikk**ə-mənt/.

medicine /**med**-s'n/ and /**med**di-sin/ are both acceptable.

metallurgy in British English, the stress is usually on the second syllable, but the preferred American form — first-syllable stress — is also acceptable.

métier since the French accent-mark is retained, the Frenchified pronunciation /**may**ti-ay/ is slightly preferable to the anglicised /**met**ti-ay/.

mezzanine /**mezz**ə-neen/ is traditional, though /**met**sə-neen/ is closer to the original Italian; both are fully acceptable; the last syllable should not be sounded like *nine*.

midwifery the traditional pronunciation is /**mid**-wiffri/; the second *i* is always as in *whiff* (except in North American speech, where /mid-**wī**fri/ is possible); the stress can be shifted from the first to the second syllable.

migraine /**mee**-grayn/ is the standard British pronunciation, /**mī**-grayn/ is a common variant, and standard in North American English.

migratory traditionally and preferably stressed on the first syllable, /**mī**-grə-təri/, rather than on the second, though this too is acceptable.

milieu /**meel**-yer/ is standard; /meel-**yer**/, slightly Frenchified, is also acceptable.

minutiae /mī-**new**-shi-ee/, mi-: note the various vowel- and consonant-differences from the noun *minute*; note too that the last syllable is /-ee/ rather than /-ī/.

miscellany the *c* is silent; the stress should be on the second syllable in British English, though first-syllable stress, standard in North America, is accepted too.

mischievous /**miss**-chivəss/, not ✕ /miss-**chee**vəss/ let alone ✕ /miss-**chee**vi-əss/.

mocha the traditional pronunciation /**mō**kə/ is now largely restricted to North American speech; common usage favours /**mock**ə/; the *ch* is always pronounced like a *k*.

momentary stress on the first syllable, /**mō**mən-təri/, as in *moment*, not as in *momentous*.

monetary the preferred pronunciation is /**mun**ni-tri/; /**mon**ni-tri/ is also acceptable.

moor /moor/ and /mor/ are both acceptable, varying according to the region.

moussaka/mousaka usually pronounced /moo-**saak**ə/ in English, though some people pronounce it closer to the Greek: /moo-sa-**kaa**/.

Ms /miz/ and /məz/ are both possible.

Munich /**mew**nik/; not a /kh/ sound on the end as in *loch* — the German name of the city is, after all, quite different: *München*.

municipal stress should fall on the second syllable: /mew-**niss**ip'l/; **?** /**mew**-ni-**sipp**'l/, on the pattern of *municipality*, is regional or nonstandard.

nadir what used to be the standard pronunciation is discouraged: **?** /**nay**-dər/; it is now /**nay**-deer/ or /**nad**deer/.

naive two syllables: /naa-**eev**, nī-/. The spelling may have anglicised, but the anglicised pronunciation **??** /nayv/ is still very doubtful.

necessarily the doubly stressed /**ness**ə-**serr**əli/ is now acceptable, though British purists still insist on the traditional /**ness**ə-sərəli/.

neither In British English, /**nī**thər/ is usually preferred to /**nee**-thər/, though both are acceptable. But in American English, /**nee**-thər/ is standard. (See separate entry.)

nephew both the pronunciations /**nev**vew/ and /**nef**few/ have long been accepted in British English; in North American speech, only the *f*-form tends to be heard.

niche /nich/ is the standard anglicisation, but the Frenchified /neesh/ is also acceptable.

nougat the standard pronunciation is /**noo**-gaa/, as in French; /**new**-gaa/ is an unnecessary 'improvement'; /**noo**-gət/ and /**nug**gət/ are regional.

nuance /new-**ɒnss**/; alternatively, stressed on the first syllable; the Americanised **?** /noo-/ is dubious.

nuclear /new-/ at the beginning; ✕ /noo-/ is nonstandard in British English; ✕ /**noo**k-yə-lər/ is nonstandard in both British and North American speech.

obdurate this can be stressed either on the first or on the second syllable: /**ob**-dewrət/ or /ob-**dewr**ət/; the first-syllable stress is slightly preferable.

obligatory the preference is now for stress on the second syllable: /ə-**bligg**ə-tri/; traditionally a first-syllable stress was possible, but it is now rare: /**obblig**ə-təri/; what is unacceptable is an additional third-syllable stress, with ✕ /-**gayt**-/ in the middle.

octave /**ok**-tiv/ is the traditional pronunciation for all senses; /**ok**-tayv/ is just possible, but is common only for the ecclesiastical sense, 'the eighth day after a feast day'.

octavo /ok-**tay**vō/ is the standard pronunciation, **?** /ok**taa**vō/ is best avoided.

o'er /or/ or /**ō**-ər/; **?** /ōr/ and **?** /oor/ are regional or dubious.

off /awf/ tends to sound old-fashioned or American; /off/ is now more common; both are acceptable.

often a silent *t* is preferable, though it is acceptable to sound the *t*; as with *off*, the /**awf**-/ pronunciation was standard but now sounds old-fashioned or American.

onerous beginning like *honour* rather than like *owner*, though both are acceptable.

ophthalmic /ofth-/; the common ?/opth-/ is not really standard.

opus /**op**pəss/ and /**ō**pəss/ are both acceptable.

oral /**aw**-rəl/ is alone acceptable, despite its unfortunate coinciding with *aural*; ?/**ō**-rəl/ and ?/**orr**əl/ are regional or nonstandard.

oregano in British English /**orr**i-**gaan**ō/ is standard; in North American speech, the common form is /aw-**regg**ənō/, which is closer to the Spanish.

otiose the traditional pronunciation is /**ō**shi-**ō**ss/, but it is now common and acceptable to pronounce the *t* as /t/ and to pronounce the last syllable as /-**ō**z/.

overt traditionally stressed on the first syllable: /**ō**-vərt/; stress on the second syllable is now also common and accepted: /ō-**vert**/.

oyez traditionally /**ō**-yess/, stressed on the first syllable, but second-syllable stress, and the endings /-**yez**/ and /-**yay**/ are also acceptable.

pace (Latin) the traditional pronunciation is /**pay**-si/, but /**paa**-chay/ as in Church Latin is perhaps more common now. (See separate entry.)

paella /pī-**ell**ə/, or else like the Spanish /pa-**el**-yə/ or /pa-**ay**-ə/.

panegyric /**pan**ni-**jirr**ik/; the form ?/-**jīr**-ik/, as in *gyrate*, is dubious.

paprika the word can be stressed in either of two ways — on the first syllable, /**pap**prikə/, or on the second: /pə-**preek**ə/; the second is the only possibility in American English.

paradigmatic /**parr**ə-dig-**matt**ik, -dīg-/; the *g* is sounded, unlike in *paradigm*, /**parr**ədīm/.

parsimony stressed on the first syllable: /**par**-si-məni/; the remaining vowels are weak, unlike the *i* of *simony* or the first *o* of *parsimonious* (though North American speech does allow this /**ō**/ as a variant).

participle the main stress should be at the beginning of the word: /**parti**-sipp'l/; traditionally, it is also possible to leave out the first *i* in pronunciation, though this is now fairly rare; the common second-syllable stress, ?/**paar**-**tiss**ip'l/, is less favoured.

pasty meaning either 'pale' or 'like paste', the word is pronounced /**pay**sti/; this pronunciation used to be possible for the word meaning 'a small pie', along with the pronunciation /**pas**ti/, which is the favoured current form; /**paas**ti/ is now sometimes also heard.

patent /**payt**'nt/ for most senses in British English, but /**patt**'nt/ is preferred for legal and technical senses, such as the protection of inventions. In American English, /**patt**'nt/ is used for all senses. (See separate entry.)

patrial /**pay**tri-əl/ is much better than ?/**patt**ri-əl/; similarly *patriarch*; but *patricide* is the reverse.

patriot /**pay**tri-ət/ and /**patt**ri-ət/ are both acceptable.

paucity /**pawss**əti/, with a soft *s*-sound in the middle.

pejorative /pi-**jorr**ətiv/ is the most common pronunciation, though the traditional /**peej**ə-rətiv/, stressed on the first syllable, is also still acceptable.

penchant the Frenchified /**poN**-shoN/ and the anglicised /**pen**chənt/ are both acceptable; if the French form is used, keep the stress on the first syllable still.

peremptory the stress can be on either the first or second syllable.

perhaps the usual full form is /pər-**haps**/, but it is quite acceptable to reduce this to a single syllable: /**praps**/.

periphrasis stress on the second syllable: /pə-**riffr**ə-siss/; contrast *periphrastic*: /**perri**-**frast**ik/.

pharmaceutical /**farm**ə-**sew**-tik'l/ is traditional; /-**soo**-/ in the middle is now common; note the soft *c*.

phthisis the most common pronunciation does not sound the *ph*: /**thī**-siss/; /**tī**-siss/ is also possible; the pronunciation with *ph* can still be heard, however: /**fthī**-siss/, or even the traditional /**fth**ississ/; *phthisic* by contrast is usually pronounced /**tizz**ik/.

physiognomy the *g* is silent: /**fizz**i-**onn**ə-mi/.

pianist the stress is slightly better on the first than on the second syllable: ideally, /**peer**-nist/.

piano a long /aa/ in the middle now sounds rather old-fashioned; the short /a/ is more common and quite acceptable.

picture traditionally this could be /**pik**-tewr/, but /**pik**-chər/ is now standard; ×/**pich**ər/, just like *pitcher*, is fairly common, but nonstandard.

piquant this is usually pronounced /**peek**ənt/; the more Frenchified (and affected?) pronunciations /**peek**oN/ and /**peek**aant/ are also heard; avoid /**pik**wənt/, though it is heard in North American speech.

piquet traditionally, this card game is /pi-**ket**/ though /pi-**kay**/ is now common; either way, the stress is on the second syllable, unlike *picket*.

piracy /**pīr**-əsi/ with the first syllable as in *pirate*; do not model it on *conspiracy*.

placebo /plə-**see**-bō/; but in the Roman Catholic service for the dead, it can be /plə-**chay**-bō/; the *c* is never pronounced /k/ as in *placate*.

plaid, plait both have a short *a*: /plad/ and /plat/; the use of /ay/, making the words sound like *played* and *plate*, is regional, being common in Scotland, for instance (and the latter in North America).

plastic a short *a* is preferred, /**plas**tik/, but /**plaa**stik/ is also acceptable.

plebeian /pli-**bee**-ən/, not ×/-**bay**-/, and not stressed on the first syllable.

plebiscite /**plebb**i-sīt/ or /**plebb**i-sit/: both endings are acceptable.

plethora /**pleth**ərə/ is correct, the stress being on the first syllable.

pogrom this is originally a Russian word and was traditionally stressed on the second syllable as in Russian: /pə-**grom**/; these days, a first-syllable stress is more usual: /**pog**-rəm/ or /**pog**-rom/; all three are quite acceptable.

poignant preferably pronounced /**poyn**-yənt/, though /**poy**-nənt/ and even /**poyg**-nənt/ are possible.

polemic /pə-**lem**mik, po-, pō-/; the *e* is short, as in *academic*, not /ee/ as in *anaemic*.

police /pə-**leess**/, not ×/po-/ or ×/pō-/, and not slurred into ×/pleess/.

poltergeist /**polt**ər-gīst, **pōlt**ər-/; the *g* is hard.

pommel /**pumm**'l/ is the traditional and preferred pronunciation, but /**pomm**'l/ is also acceptable.

posthumous the *h* is silent: /**post**ew-məss/; the first syllable is not as in *post* but as in *possible*.

postpone /pəs-**pōn**/ is traditionally as acceptable as /pōst-**pōn**/: it is not necessary to sound the *t*.

pot-pourri the stress in British English falls on the first and second syllables (in American English it can fall on the first and third), and the first syllable is pronounced as in French: /pō-**poo**ri/; do not sound the *t*.

precedent for the noun, /**press**i-dənt/ is best, though /**pree**-si-/ is also acceptable; only in the adjective does the stress go on the second syllable, as in *precede*. (See separate entry.)

premature the first syllable can be /**prem**-/ or /**pree**-/, and the final syllable /-**tewr**/ or /-**choor**/, but preferably not /-**toor**/ as sometimes in North American speech; and the final syllable can take a secondary stress. Perhaps the best form is /**premm**ə-tewr/.

premier /**premm**i-ər/ in British English; in North American English, /**preem**i-ər/ and /pri-**meer**/ are also possible, but are best avoided in British speech.

prerogative do not omit the first *r*.

presage as a noun, /**press**ij/; as a verb, either this or /pri-**sayj**/.

prescience /**press**i-ənss/ or /**presh**i-/ rather than ?/**pree**si-/.

preterite /**prett**-ər-it/; not ×/**preet**-/ and not ×/-īt/.

prima facie /**prīm**ə **fay**-shi-ee/ is the traditional pronunciation; also possible is /**fay**-si-ee/; the final syllable is today commonly omitted.

primarily should be stressed on the first syllable: /**prī**-mərəli/; the form ?/prī-**merr**əli/ is regional or nonstandard in British English, but the standard form in North American speech.

pristine traditionally rhyming with *mine* but now more usually rhyming with *teen*: /**priss**-teen/; only in North American English can the word be stressed on the second syllable.

privacy /**priv**vəsi/ is generally preferred these days, but /**prī**-vəsi/ remains an accepted variant, and is standard in North American speech.

privy as both adjective and noun, /**priv**vi/ rather than ?/**prī**-vi/.

probity the first syllable was traditionally as in *probably*, but can now be only as in *probe*: /**prō**bəti/.

proboscis the *c* is silent: /prə-**boss**iss/.

process /**prō**-sess, -siss/; regionally, and widely in North America, /**pross**-ess, -əss/ is also heard. In the rare verb sense of 'to move as if in a procession', the stress shifts to the second syllable.

progress the verb is stressed on the second syllable: /prə-**gress**/; the noun is stressed on the first syllable: /**prō**gress/; it is now chiefly a North American pronunciation to say /**prog**-rəss/.

prohibit, prohibition the *h* is sounded in *prohibit*, but can be omitted in *prohibition*.

project the *o* should be short: /**proj**-ekt, -ikt/. The /ō/ as in ?/**prō**-jekt/ is common in many regions, and in Australian English, but is not fully standard.

promenade /**promm**ə-**naad**, -naad/ is accepted for all senses: /**promm**ə-**nayd**/ should be used only with reference to a square dance or country dance.

pronunciation note the vowel change from verb to noun: *pronounce/pronunciation, announce/ annunciation, denounce/denunciation, renounce/renunciation* — so no /-ow-/ sound in *pronunciation*.

prosody a short *o* in the first syllable, and a soft *s*: /**pross**ədi/; the common pronunciation ?/**prō**zədi/, on the model of *prose*, is doubtful and best avoided.

proven /**prōō**v'n/ is usual; /**prōv**'n/ is a scholarly pronunciation, except in the phrase *not proven*, a verdict in Scottish courts of law, where /**prōv**'n/ is standard. (See separate entry.)

proverb /**prov**vərb/; not ×/prō-/, except in a technical sense in linguistics.

proviso /prə-**vīz**ō/; not ×/-**veez**ō/ as in *visa*.

pulverise /pul-/, as in *dull* rather than *pull*.

Punjab the best pronunciation is /**pun**-jaab/; the second syllable can be left unstressed; to pronounce the first syllable /**pōōn**-/ is less favoured, and to pronounce the second syllable ?/-jab/ is dubious.

pyramidal traditionally stressed on the second syllable: /pi-**ram**mid'l/.

quaff traditionally rhymed with *staff*; today more commonly rhymes with *doff*; to rhyme it with *gaff* is regional or nonstandard.

quagmire /**kwog**-mīr/ is perhaps the more common pronunciation now, but /**kwag**-/ is also accepted.

qualm either /kwaam/ rhyming with *calm* or /kwawm/ rhyming with *storm*, but the *l* should always be silent.

quarter /**kwawr**tər/ is the standard pronunciation; ?/**kawr**tər/ is still not accepted by purists.

quasi traditionally /**kway**-zī, -sī/, but /**kwaa**-/ and /-si, -zi/ are also possible.

questionnaire /kest-/ was traditionally standard, but now sounds rather affected; it is preferable now to pronounce the first two syllables as *question*.

quiche /keesh/; the humorous pronunciation ×/kwich/ is wrong in three ways.

quiescent the beginning of the word is like *quick*, not like *quiet*: /kwi-**ess**'nt/.

rabid the first syllable is preferably as in *rabbit*, despite the pronunciation of *rabies*.

rabies this often used to be pronounced with three syllables, /**ray**-bi-eez/, but this is now rare; /**ray**-beez/ or /-biz/ is standard today.

racism /**ray**ssiz'm/; the first syllable sounds like *race*. The commonly heard ?/**ray**shizm/, modelled on *racialism*, or *fascism*, is not recommended. (See separate entry.)

rapport the *t* at the end, once sounded in the anglicised pronunciation, is now no longer heard; /ra-**por**/ or /rə-**por**/ is usual.

ratiocinate /**ra**tti-ossi-nayt/ in British English; not like *ratio*.

recess both the noun and the verb are preferably stressed on the second syllable, /ri-**sess**/, though

first-syllable stress is often heard, especially on the noun.

recidivist /ri-**sidd**i-vist/; the word is stressed on the second syllable and the *c* is soft, as in *recipient*.

recognise missing out the g-sound is widely condemned, though so common as to be virtually acceptable today in British English.

recondite the stress can acceptably be on either the first or the second syllable: /**reck**ən-dīt/ or /ri-**kond**it/; the first of these two pronunciations is perhaps more usual.

reconnaissance stressed on the second syllable: /ri-**konn**i-s'nss/; do not be led astray by the stress-pattern of *reconnoitre*.

record /**reck**awrd/ (noun); /ri-**kord**/ (verb); /**reck**ərd/ is chiefly a North American pronunciation, though it is quite often heard in British English in phrases such as *record sleeve*.

regime/régime the *g* retains its French sound /zh/, the sound in the middle of *pleasure*. If the accent is written over the first *e*, pronounce the word /ray-**zheem**/; if not, /ri-/ or /re-**zheem**/ is just as good.

regimen in contrast to *regime*, *regimen* is fully anglicised, pronounced like *regiment* without the *t*. Do not stress the last syllable.

remembrance only three syllables; do not pronounce it as if it were spelt ×*rememberance*.

Renaissance both anglicised and Frenchified pronunciations are possible: /ri-**nay**ss'nss/ or /**renn**ay-sonss/, for instance. This French final syllable can be given an additional stress, and in North American speech is sometimes pronounced /-**zonss**/. (See separate entry.)

renascence a short *a* in the stressed middle syllable, /ri-**nass**'nss/, is perhaps slightly preferable, though /ri-**nay**ss'nss/ is more usual and quite acceptable. But the Frenchified pronunciation of *Renaissance* cannot be used for *renascence*. (See separate entry.)

renege /ri-**neeg**/ is the traditional pronunciation; /rə-**nayg**/ or /-**neg**/ are also widespread and acceptable.

repatriate /ri-**patt**ri-ayt/ is now usual in British English; /ri-**payt**ri-ayt/, once common, is now chiefly a North American pronunciation.

reportage two acceptable versions: /ri-**port**-ij/ and the Frenchified /**repp**awr-**taazh**/.

reprimand the chief stress is on the first syllable for the noun, /**repp**ri-maand/, and on the final syllable for the verb: /reppri-**maand**/.

reputable stress on the first syllable, /**repp**ewtə-b'l/; unlike *disputable*, it cannot take the stress on the second syllable.

research stress on the second syllable is

preferable: /ri-**serch**/; /**ree**-serch/ is chiefly North American.

respite   stress on the first syllable traditionally, /**ress**-pit/, but /**ress**-pīt/ is also accepted; not stressed at the end — **??**/ri-**spīt**/, on the model of *despite* — except in regional accents.

restaurateur   more or less /**ress**-torrə-**tur**/, with the final syllable slightly Frenchified; note that there is no *n* as there is in *restaurant*, so the pronunciation is not ×/-tə-ron-/ or ×/-tə-roN-/.

reveille   /ri-**vall**i/, /rə-/, and /-**vell**i/ are acceptable; the pronunciation is nothing like the French /re-**vay**/; /**revv**əli/ is common in North American speech.

ribald   /**ribb**'ld/; **?**/**rī**-bawld/, with the second syllable like *bald*, is dubious or regional.

ricochet   /**rick**ə-shay/ is the most common pronunciation, but /**rick**ə-shet/ is also acceptable; if the past tense is spelt *ricocheted* it is pronounced /**rick**ə-shayd/; spelt *ricochetted* it is pronounced /**rick**ə-shettid/; it is also possible to stress the word on the /-**shay**, -**shet**/ syllable.

robust   this should be stressed on the second syllable: /rō-**bust**/; first-syllable stress is less favoured.

room   /rōōm/ and /rŏŏm/ are both fully acceptable.

Roquefort   /**rok**-fawr/ or sometimes /**rock**ə-fawr/; a common North American pronunciation is **?**/**rōk**-fərt/; ×/**rock**ə-fawrt/ is nonstandard.

rotund   stress on the second syllable: /rō-**tund**/ or /rə-**tund**/; first-syllable stress is regional or nonstandard. (See separate entry.)

route   /rōōt/, except in military use and in regional English, especially U.S. regional English, when it is sometimes /rowt/.

rowlock   /**roll**ək/ or /**rull**ək/, rather than **?**/**rō**-lok/.

sacrilegious   /**sack**ri-**lij**əss/, like *sack* and *religious*, even though the spelling corresponds to neither word.

sadism   /**say**diz'm/; /**sadd**iz'm/ is now rare; *Sade* in *the Marquis de Sade*, whose name is the source of the word, is pronounced /saad/.

salivary   traditionally the stress was on the first syllable, /**sali**-vəri/, and purists still favour this. But second-syllable stress, /sə-**līv**əri/, is now established and acceptable.

salmonella   /**sal**-mə-**nell**ə/; the first *l* is sounded, unlike in *salmon*.

sang-froid   /soN-**frwaa**/ like the French, or, also acceptably, /**sang**-/, but do not pronounce the *d*.

sanguine   /**sang**-gwin/; not /-gwīn/ as in *wine*;

and do not neglect to sound the hard *g*.

satyr   /**satt**ər/; in North American speech /**say**-tər/ is also possible; note the difference from *satire*: /**satt**īr/.

Saudi   preferably /**sow**di/; /**saw**di/ is possible.

sauna   /**sawn**ə/ is usual; /**sown**ə/ is possible.

scabrous   /**skayb**-rəss/; /**skab**-/ is chiefly North American pronunciation. (See separate entry.)

scallop   this is preferably pronounced /**skoll**əp/, rhyming with *wallop* (and can sometimes also be spelt *scollop*); the pronunciation rhyming with *gallop* is dubious.

scarify   /**skarr**i-fī/ is traditional, like *clarify*; /**skair**-/ is also used, but the word is closer in meaning to *scar* than to *scare*, and the first pronunciation helps to avoid confusion. (See separate entry.)

scenario   /si-**naar**-i-ō, se-, sə-/; but **?**/-**nair**-/ is regional or nonstandard. (See separate entry.)

schism   traditionally /**siz**'m/, but /**skiz**'m/ is now catching on, perhaps being easier to understand.

schizophrenic   now usually /skitsō-**fren**-ik/ rather than **?**/-**freen**-/.

scone   an endless subject of debate, this; both /skon/ and /skōn/ are acceptable, but /skon/ is regarded as more nearly correct. The Scottish village of *Scone* is pronounced /skōōn/, and so too is the stone in the coronation chair.

scourge   /skurj/; like *urge*, not *gourd* or *scour*.

secretary   do not neglect to sound the first *r*; /**seckr**ə-tri/ and /**seckr**ə-təri/ are accepted; **?**/**seckr**ə-terri/ is common in North American speech, but is considered dubious in British English.

secretive   /si-**kreet**iv/, once standard, is now rare, except in the sense of 'exuding' or 'concealing'; /**see**-krətiv/ is now the common standard pronunciation for the sense of 'keeping secrets'.

semiotic(s), semiology   /seemi-/ or /semmi-/; only in North America is it also possible to say /seemī-/ or /semmī-/.

seraglio   /si-**raali**-ō/; the *g* is silent.

sheikh   /shayk/, like *shake*; the form **?**/sheek/, rhyming with *week*, is common but dubious.

simony   /**sī**-məni/; in North America /**simm**əni/ is also possible.

simultaneous   /sim-/ as in *similar*; /sīm-/ is chiefly a North American pronunciation.

sinecure   preferably sounds like *sign* at the beginning, though a sound like *sin* has long been a common alternative.

skeleton, skeletal   /**skell**i-t'n, -t'l/; the regional ×/**skell**ing-tən/ and the distorted ×/skə-**leet**'l/ are nonstandard.

sleight of hand   the same as *slight*, not *slate*.

sloth   rhymes with *both*; the form rhyming with *cloth* is regional or North American or nonstandard.

slough   /slow/, rhyming with *cow*, for the ditch, as in the 'Slough of Despond'; /sloo/ only in North America; but /sluf/ when referring to the snake's shed skin or the verb meaning 'to shed'.

sojourn   both syllables have variants: /soj-ərn, suj-, -urn/. The stress is on the first syllable, though North American speech allows second-syllable stress instead, and also a long /ō/ vowel: /sō-**jurn**/.

solder   /**sold**ər/ is preferable to /**sōld**ər/; regional pronunciations, especially in North America, include /**sodd**ər/ and /**saw**-dər/; these were once favoured in British speech too, but are now very old-fashioned.

sonorous   stressing the word on the second syllable, /sə-**naw**-rəss/, was formerly widespread; more common today is first-syllable stress: /**sonn**ə-rəss/ or /**sōn**ə-rəss/; all three are acceptable.

sophomore   /**sof**-fə-mawr/ in British English; the Americans, who use the word more often, tend to leave out the middle syllable.

sotto voce   /sottō-vōchi/.

Soviet   /sō-vi-ət, -vyet/ and /sov-i-ət, -yet, -yət/ are acceptable; /sō-/ is slightly more usual.

species   a /sh/ sound in the middle, rather than a ?/s/ sound; usually /**spee**-sheez/ but /**spee**-shiz/ is also possible; /**spee**-shi-eez/ used to be possible too, but has died out.

specious   /**spee**-shəss/, not like *special*; and note the /sh/ sound in the middle. (See separate entry.)

spinach   /**spinn**ij/ is standard, /**spinn**ich/ an acceptable but unnecessary 'correction'.

spontaneity   /spontə-**nee**-əti/ is an older standard pronunciation, and preferred by purists, but /spontə-**nay**-əti/ is probably now more common.

stabilise   the first syllable can sound like *stay* or like *stab*.

stanch, staunch   *stanch* is probably better and more common as /staanch/ than /stanch/; *staunch* is either /staanch/ or /stawnch/. (See separate entry.)

stasis   /**stay**-siss/, not ×/**stass**-/ or ×/**staass**-/.

status   /**stay**-təss/; the pronunciation /**statt**əss/ is common in North America.

status quo   as above, with /kwō/.

stereotype   both /**steer**-/ and /**sterr**-i-ə-tīp/ are possible.

stevedore   /**stee**-və-dawr/; the word has three syllables.

stigmata   there is a slight preference for stress on the first syllable, /**stig**mətə/, though second-syllable stress is acceptable and very common: /stig-**maat**ə/.

strafe   the standard pronunciation used to be /straaf/, but now /strayf/ is more common, and is considered quite acceptable.

stratum   traditionally this was /**stray**-təm/; now /**straa**-təm/ is usual; in North American speech /**statt**əm/ is also possible.

strength   the best pronunciation is in accordance with the spelling, /streng-th/; an intrusive *k*-sound is very common, and more or less acceptable, /strengk-th/; a common tendency is to reduce the *ng*-sound to a simple *n*, ×/stren-th/, but this is best avoided.

strophe   /**strō**fi/ like *trophy*; do not reduce it to a single syllable.

strychnine   /**strik**-neen/; it is mostly in North America that /-nīn/ or /-nin/ is used.

suave   /swaav/ and /swayv/ are both acceptable; /swaav/ is now the more usual.

subpoena   /səb-**pee**-nə, sub-, səpee-nə/: all are acceptable.

subsidence   /səb-**sīd**'nss/ and /**sub**-sidənss/ are both acceptable.

substantial   /səb-**stansh**'l/ and /-**staansh**'l/ are both possible, though the latter can sound slightly affected.

succinct   the *cc* is pronounced as in *success*, so: /suk-**singkt**/.

suffragan   a hard *g*, unlike *suffragette*: so, /**suffr**əgən/.

supine   /**soo**-pīn/ is usual; but /sew-**pīn**/, different in two ways, is also still possible.

surety   /**shoor**-əti/, with three syllables.

surveillance   /sər-**vayl**ənss, sur-/: it would be pretentious today to pronounce it as in French.

sward   /swawrd/, not like *sword* or *hard*.

swath   /swawth/ or /swoth/; not like *bath* or *Kathy* or *swathe*.

swathe   /swayth̲/, like *bathe*.

sycophant   /**sick**ə-fənt, -fant/ is preferable to /**sīk**ə-/ and far better than ?/**sīk**ō-/.

symbiosis   /simbi-**ōsis**/ and /simbī-/ are both acceptable.

synod   ideally /**sinn**əd/, though /**sin**-od/ is also possible.

syringe   traditionally stressed on the first syllable, but more commonly nowadays on the second: either is acceptable.

systole   /**sis**-təli/, ending like *hyperbole*, not like *casserole*.

taciturn   the *c* is soft: /**tassi**-turn/.

temporarily   ideally, /**temp**ə-rərəli/; stress on the first syllable, and five syllables altogether; common variants involve either omitting the third syllable, or (especially in North America) stressing it — both of these are best avoided.

timbre the anglicised pronunciation /**tim**-bər/ is not much favoured; the Frenchified /**tam**bər/ and the French /taʌbr/ are more common.

tirade /tī-**rayd**/ is recommended; /ti-**rayd**/ is also acceptable and established; /ti-**raad**/ is also used, in imitation of the French; ?/**tīr**-ayd/ occurs too, but the first-syllable stress here is not recommended.

tissue /**tish**oō/ and /**tiss**ew/ are both acceptable.

tonne /tun/, or sometimes /ton/ to distinguish it from an old *ton*; either way, do not add a second syllable.

topsail /**tops**'l/ is the nautical pronunciation, but /**top**-sayl/ is also acceptable.

torte /**tort**ə/ is closer to the German, but /tort/ is also acceptable, and probably more usual.

tortilla /tawr-**tee**-yə/: the *ll* retains a Spanish *y*-sound.

tortoise /**tor**-təss/ is preferred; /**tor**-toyz/ is regional.

tournedos the *s* remains silent, as in the French: /**toorn**ə-dō, **tur**-/.

tourniquet /**toor**-ni-kay, **tor**-, **tur**-/, ending like *croquet* and *parquet*; the final *t* is sometimes sounded, especially in North American speech, but this is best avoided.

towards /tə-**wawrdz**, toō-/ are both standard; so is the monosyllabic /tordz/, though it is now slightly old-fashioned.

trachea /trə-**kee**-ə/ in British English; /**tray**ki-ə/ is sometimes used in North American speech.

trait the final *t* is silent according to traditionalists: /tray/; but /trayt/ is now very common, and can be considered acceptable.

trajectory the stress can be on the first or second syllable: /**traj**ik-tri, -təri/ or /trə-**jek**təri/; the second is now more usual.

transferable /**transs**-fər-əb'l/ stressed on the first syllable and /transs-**ferr**əb'l/ stressed on the second are both possible; and the first syllable can be pronounced /**traanss**-/.

transparent /transs-**parr**ənt/ is probably the commonest pronunciation, but the first syllable can also be /**traanss**-, **tranz**-/, and so on, and the second syllable can be /-**pair**-/.

trauma /**trawm**ə/ is now more common than /**trowm**ə/; ?/**trōm**ə/ is dubious, and should be avoided. (See separate entry.)

travail preferably stressed on the first syllable, for both noun and verb; stress on the second syllable is increasingly common, but is essentially a regional or North American form.

traverse stress on the first syllable is traditional,

though second-syllable stress is also acceptable and is increasingly common.

trefoil /**tref**-oyl/ is now standard; the variant forms /**tree**-foyl/ and /tri-**foyl**/ are rare.

triptych /**trip**-tik/, with a *k*-sound at the end, is preferable to /-tich/.

troll the word for a Norse demon can be either /trōl/ or /trol/; the various meanings of the verb are usually pronounced /trōl/; in the phrase *to troll along*, however, it is usually pronounced /trol/.

trompe l'oeil the nearest anglicised equivalent to the French would be something like /**trawmp loy**/.

turbine /**tur**-bīn/ and /**turbin**/ are both standard; the former, being unambiguous, is slightly preferable.

tureen /tə-**reen**, tewr-, toō-/: all acceptable.

turquoise /**tur**-kwoyz/ is now the most usual perhaps, but /**tur**-koyz/ is also common and acceptable; /**tur**-kwaaz/ is possible too, imitating the French pronunciation, and even /**tur**-kwawz/ is acceptable.

Tutankhamun/Tutankhamen the first (and preferred) form is pronounced /toō-təng-kaa-**moōn**, -**moōn**/; the second /toō-təng-**kaa**-men, -tang-, -mən/.

twelfth neglecting to sound the *f* is common, but regarded by purists as slipshod.

ultra vires traditionally /**ultr**ə **vī**reez/; but /**oō**ltraa **veer**-ayz/, in keeping with a full Latin pronunciation, is now quite common.

ululate /**yoō**-lew-layt/; the first syllable /**ull**-/ is regional, and quite common in North American speech.

umbilical /um-**bill**i-k'l/ and /umbi-**līk**'l/ are both accepted.

umbrella there is no /-ə-/ between the *b* and the *r*; the word has three syllables, not four.

unprecedented the second syllable can be pronounced /-**press**-/ or /-**preess**-/, the former being slightly preferable; the *un-* can be either stressed or unstressed.

Uranus traditionally, the stress is on the first syllable, /**yoor**-ənəss/, but second-syllable stress is probably more common nowadays, and is considered acceptable too: /yoor-**rayn**əss, yoō-/.

urinal first- and second-syllable stress seem to be equally acceptable in British English; first-syllable stress prevails in North America.

usage a soft *s* as in *no use* is slowly superseding the traditional *z*-sound as in *using*.

Utah /**yoo**-taa/ is standard, though the local pronunciation is /**yoo**-taw/.

vade mecum traditionally /**vay**di **meek**əm/; but

the modern liking for a full Latin pronunciation has brought /vaa-day maykōōm/ into more common use.

Van Gogh the proper Dutch pronunciation is something like /**fun khokh**/, but it sounds pretentious in English conversation: the usual British pronunciation is /**van gokh**/; the *Van* is sometimes unstressed, and the *Gogh* sometimes pronounced /**gof**/ or, in North America, /**gō**/.

vase preferably /**vaaz**/; /**vawz**/ is now old-fashioned and rare; /**vayz**/ and /**vayss**/ are chiefly American.

vehemence /**vee**-ə-mənss/; the *h* should be silent, though it is often heard in regional speech.

vehicle /**vee**-ik'l/; the *h* is silent, except in regional speech. However, in the adjective *vehicular*, the *h* is sounded as the stress shifts to the second syllable.

veld/veldt spelt either way, this word can be pronounced with an *f-* or a *v*-sound at the beginning: /felt, velt/; the *f*-sound is truer to the original Dutch or Afrikaans. Note that the final consonant is always pronounced as a *t*, not a *d*.

venison the *s* is traditionally hard, like *z*, and the middle *i* silent: /**venz**'n/. But /**venni**-z'n/ and /**venni**-s'n/ are also acceptable.

verbatim /ver-**bay**-tim, vər-/; the Latinised /-**baa**-/ has not gained wide acceptance.

Verdun /ver-**dun**/ in English; the French say /vair-**daN**/.

veterinary strictly, five syllables in all: /**vett**ər-innəri/; but the word is more frequently now concertinaed to /**vett**'n-ri/ or /**vetrin**-ri/; a common regional and North American ending is /-**erri**/.

via /**vī**-ə/ is the accepted pronunciation; the Latinised ✗ /**vee**-ə/ is nonstandard or regional.

vice versa /**vī**-si **ver**-sə/ is preferred by dictionaries, but /**vīss ver**-sə/ is now probably more common.

victuals pronounced /**vitt**'lz/, rhyming with *skittles*; quite unlike its spelling; *victualler*, similarly, is pronounced /**vitt**'l-ər/.

viscid the *c* is silent or soft, as in *ascent* or *visceral*: /**vissid**/; yet *viscous* is pronounced /**viskəss**/.

volte-face /**volt faass, fass**/ is standard, with a short *o* in the first part; the /**ō**/ sound, as in *both*, is common but not recommended.

voluntarily should be stressed on the first syllable alone, /**vollən**-tri-li/, rather than on the third as well, ❓/**vollən-terr**əli/, though this is an acceptable pronunciation in North American speech.

vulnerable take care not to omit the first *l*:

/**vuln**-ərəb'l, -rəb'l/.

wassail the first syllable can be either /**woss**-/ as in *wasp*, or /**wass**-/ rhyming with *mass*; the second syllable can be /-ayl/ or /-'l/.

Wednesday /**wenz**-di, **wedd**'nz-, -day/: the first *d* is not obligatory, though purists prefer to sound it.

were usually now rhymes with *her* (when unstressed, it is simply /wər/); the pronunciation that rhymes with *hair* is now very — rare.

with /with/ is standard, with the th voiced; the unvoiced ❓/with/ is regional or dubious.

wont as in *as was his wont*: it is better when sounded as *won't* rather than as *want*.

year /yeer/ and /yer/ are both standard.

yoghurt now usually /**yogg**ərt/ in British English, though /**yogg**oort/ is also acceptable; in some other varieties — American and South African, for instance — /**yō**-gərt/ is standard.

zoology /zō-**oll**əji/ is the traditional pronunciation, though /zōō-**oll**əji/ is now more common.

propensity See PROCLIVITY.

proper nouns See CAPITAL LETTERS 1; NOUNS.

prophecy, prophesy Keep these two words distinct, in both spelling and pronunciation: the noun *prophecy,* 'a prediction or revelation', is spelt with a *c*, and pronounced /**proff**ə-si/; the verb *prophesy*, 'to predict, or speak as a prophet', is spelt with an *s*, and pronounced /**proff**i-sī/. These spellings are also correct in American English, though Americans will sometimes spell the noun with *-sy*. They will not, however, pronounce it like the verb.

The words go back to the Greek roots *pro-* 'before' + *phanai,* 'to say', just as the word *predict* comes from the Latin roots *prae-* + *dicere,* with the same senses.

proportion A speaker trying to sound impressive will reach for the word *proportion* sooner than make use of the simpler *part, much,* or *most* — possibly through confusion with *portion*: ❓*A large proportion of the country's inhabitants devote only a small proportion of their time to the opera.* This would be better expressed by saying that *most* of them do not devote *much* of the time to that pursuit.

Proportions is often used as an impressive-sounding synonym of *size* or *extent*: ❓*A man of your proportions should be able to defend himself*; ❓*a violent earthquake of enormous proportions.*

It is better to keep *proportion* and *proportions*

for contexts in which there is a strong feeling of ratio, of a part viewed in relation to other parts or to the whole: *The proportion of the voters supporting the Minister's policies has dwindled over the past few years.*

See also FRACTION; PER CENT.

proportional, proportionate These two adjectives have precisely the same primary meaning: 'being in proportion, forming a relationship with other parts or quantities'. The difference, if there is one, lies in their preferred grammatical constructions: *proportional* tends to be used directly in front of a noun — *a proportional amount* — whereas *proportionate* tends to be used after a noun or verb (such as the verb *to be*) and in front of the preposition *to*: *profits proportionate to the sum invested.*

Each of the words has a secondary sense, however, and here a distinction can be made. *Proportional* means 'relating to proportions' in general, as in the common political phrase *proportional representation*. *Proportionate* means 'of similar intensity, analogous', as in *a punishment proportionate to the crime*. Where the relationship between the items is one of quality rather than quantity, in other words, *proportionate* is perhaps the better term to use.

Much the same applies to the corresponding adverbs *proportionally* and *proportionately*:

Blacks should register and vote in elections ... Mr Brittan, Home Secretary, said yesterday during a tour of Brent, North-West London, which has proportionally the highest black population in Britain.
– Ian Glover-James, *Daily Telegraph*

Many of the glimpses indicate that the élite's attachment to the governing ideology is increasingly perfunctory; and that popular resentment at the élite's privileges — among all those shortages — is increasing proportionately.
– Conor Cruise O'Brien,
The Observer

Note too that *proportional* is also used as a noun, in mathematical idiom. It means 'any of the quantities in a proportion'. And *proportionate* can be used as a verb (the final syllable changing from /-ət/ to /-ayt/).

As for the opposites, *disproportionate* and *disproportionately* are far more common than *disproportional* and *disproportionally*. Strictly speaking, they mean simply 'not proportionate/ly, out of proportion':

In her later life, Helen would spare herself considerable unhappiness by refusing to feel guilty; in her later life the whole business with Michael Milton would more often make her angry than it would make her sad — because she was strong enough to believe that she was a good woman, which she was, who'd been made to suffer disproportionately for a trivial indiscretion.
– John Irving (U.S.),
The World According to Garp

But if unqualified, *disproportionate* and *disproportionately* almost always imply an unduly great quantity or excessive severity: *a disproportionate outburst*; *a disproportionate fine*; *She punished us disproportionately* — these all indicate an overreaction, an intensity beyond what was called for.

It seemed to get worse, not better, as the days passed. I felt a sense of unreality, as if I had been left alone in a condemned house ... Ludicrous things comforted or upset me. It was a disproportionate relief to find the pilot light in the bathroom Ascot still burning.
– Lynne Reid Banks,
The L-Shaped Room

If the proportion is in the other direction, this has to be spelt out: *His reaction was disproportionately mild.*

proposition The word *proposition* has various long-established senses — a suggested plan or business offer, a subject for discussion in a debate, a statement used in logical or mathematical analysis, and so on. It has, fairly recently, acquired two further senses that purists refuse to admit into standard English.

The first such sense is, roughly, 'any matter or person requiring special handling; any problem or prospect or enterprise or project or opponent or colleague considered abstractly':

? Is that hotel a paying proposition, do you think?

? Macleary, his right ankle still heavily bandaged, is a very doubtful proposition for the team's semi-final against Manchester on Saturday.

? As an opening bowler, Holding is about as formidable a proposition as any batsman would care to face.

? Don't think your viva voce exam is just a formality: it's known to be a tough proposition at times.

? Social work will remain an unattractive

proposition for job-hunters until the salary system is revised.

? The kind of guard dogs which the vet will no longer go near could be made a totally uneconomic proposition; they're in the position of man traps, which hurt without trial or argument, and which even the savage nineteenth century eventually banned.
     – Katharine Whitehorn, *The Observer*

Proposition, used in this way, has become a vogue word, and illustrates the annoying tendency to abstraction found in so much modern speaking and writing. (See ABSTRACT NOUNS; VOGUE WORDS.) If used at all, it should be kept strictly for jocular or informal contexts.

The second new use of *proposition*, more commonly as a verb than a noun, is in reference to a sexual invitation. *To proposition* a man or woman is to make an offer of sexual intercourse, often, though not necessarily, involving an exchange of money, and certainly not accompanied by a *proposal* of marriage! The word is well on its way to full acceptance, and can be found in police reports and court records, but it has still not quite crossed into standard idiom, and is once again best reserved for informal speech and writing.

proscribe See PRESCRIBE.

prostate, prostrate The *prostate* is a gland in male mammals that secretes the seminal fluid.

Its name was coined by Greek anatomists, from words meaning 'to put in front': the gland is positioned under and in front of the bladder. Note the spelling — only one *r* — and take care not to confuse the word with *prostrate*, which as an adjective (stressed on the first syllable, as *prostate* is) and as a verb (stressed on the second syllable) means 'lying face down', 'to lay (oneself) face down', 'to abase (oneself) in reverence, pleading, or the like', and so on. It comes from the Latin *prostratus*, 'thrown forward' (from *pro-*, 'down before' + *sternere*, 'to stretch out or throw down').

Here is an example of its typical adjectival use:

Mrs Thatcher ... can hardly be expected to refrain from jumping up and down, heels foremost, on the prostrate body of the post-conference Labour Party.
     – Bernard Levin, *The Times*

Prostrate, as an adjective, has the extended sense of 'physically or emotionally exhausted; incapacitated'. From such phrases as *prostrate*

from fatigue and *prostrate with grief*, the word *prostrate* must have acquired these overtones in its own right:

As the work in rehearsal is a version of 'The Tempest', why do events on stage resemble a circus? What has reduced the protagonist to a prostrate condition by the end of the first act? And what is his relationship to the drama he observes?
     – Peter Heyworth, *The Observer*

See also PRONE.

protagonist The Greek word *protagonistes* meant literally 'the first actor' (in a performance of a Greek tragic drama). The English form *protagonist* thus at first meant 'the leading character in a play — or novel, or other literary work':

I brought it on myself like the tragic protagonist of a Greek play.
     – Woody Allen (U.S.), *Side Effects*

Novelists often use novelists as the protagonists of novels because novel-writing is the trade they know best, but they usually go out of their way to avoid the imputation of self-portraiture.
     – Anthony Burgess, *The Observer*

Even in this 'pure' sense, *protagonist* has attracted the attention of usage experts on two grounds. First, the phrases ✗ *chief protagonist*, ✗ *principal protagonist*, ✗ *leading protagonist*, and so on are considered tautologous — the adjective is superfluous in each case, since *protagonist* already carries that notion:

✗ He had resolved to take the chief protagonists across the sea towards the West at the end of the book.
     – Humphrey Carpenter, *Tolkien*

This quotation is guilty of the second alleged misuse too — the use of the plural *protagonists* in reference to a single literary work: theoretically, there can be only one protagonist in any one play, novel, epic poem, or the like. Here is another example:

? Philip was caught on the wrong foot while fuddled with wine; Alexander acted like Alexander; it was one of those situations where hidden fires, which the protagonists have been containing, are released by shock.
     – Mary Renault,
     The Nature of Alexander

This second 'misuse', however, is one that it

would be rather pedantic to protest at nowadays.

More recently, *protagonist* has been subjected to more justifiable criticism. From its original limited definition, it has extended its meaning in two directions — one being a legitimate extension, the other probably not. The first new sense, a fair and natural expansion of the word beyond technical contexts into general use, is 'any leading or principal figure', notably a person who initiates a political policy or is prominent in propounding a philosophical doctrine — a *prime mover* in current journalistic idiom:

> Dr Henry Putlow, the protagonist of the treasury's proposed new accounting system, began his career as an auditor with Stevenage House.

> The birthplace of these ideas was nineteenth-century England, and their principal source and protagonist was Herbert Spencer.
> — J.K. Galbraith (Canadian),
> *The Affluent Society*

(If the adjective *principal* is intended to apply to *protagonist* as well as *source*, then there is a redundancy in the sentence. But in itself, *protagonist* in this extended sense is quite acceptable.) A possible association of *protagonist* with such words as *provenance, proposer, propagator, promulgator,* and *promoter* must have helped to spread and reinforce this meaning.

Protagonist is even more closely associated in sound and origin with the word *antagonist*, and it is this association no doubt that gave rise to the second, still looser, new sense of *protagonist*, 'a proponent or champion of some cause; a supporter or partisan; one who fights or campaigns in favour of something' — the opposite of an *antagonist*:

?? She is a staunch protagonist of the militant 'Left-Handers Lib' movement.

?? A major rift threatens the party: protagonists of the transport workers' strike are losing ground to opponents of it, and rebellious backbenchers are calling on the shadow cabinet to modify its official views on the dispute.

?? For a time I was canvassed to be the First Secretary-General at the United Nations. ...
Mr Trygve Lie was an enthusiastic protagonist on my behalf.
— Anthony Eden, *The Reckoning*

Here the notion of a leading or principal influence has been lost, leaving nothing more than a sup-

posedly impressive synonym of *advocate* or *supporter* (in the first example), *proponents* or simply *those in favour* (in the second), and *campaigner* or *champion* (in the last). In all the examples, the word *protagonist/s* should have yielded to these more established — and less controversial — terms. The new usage is, however, extremely common now, and its 'antagonists' are fighting what seems to be a lost cause: nevertheless, even if surrender is inevitable, there is no need to go right over to the enemy and adopt his habits actively.

One probable reason for the dubious balancing of *protagonist* and *antagonist* is the mistaken assumption that the roots of the prefixes are *pro-* and *anti-*, that is 'for' and 'against'. They are not: they are *proto-* and *anti-* — *protos* being the Greek word for 'first', hence 'most important'. There is a further asymmetry: the Greek noun *agonistes* (deriving ultimately from the verb *agein*, 'to lead or drive'), could mean either 'a fighter' or 'an actor': the former sense was represented in *antagonist*, the latter in *protagonist*.

● *Recommendation* When used in discussing plays or other literary works, the word *protagonist* should not be prefaced by *leading, primary, principal,* or any similar superfluous adjective. But there is no longer any need really to avoid speaking of two or more *protagonists* in any one play, novel, or the like.

And *protagonist* no longer has to be restricted to these literary contexts at all. The word is now quite acceptable in the sense of 'a leading or principal figure in some cause; a prominent endorser'.

But in its still looser usage, referring to any supporter or campaigner, no matter how minor, *protagonist* is best avoided, even though this new sense seems firmly established. It is especially to be avoided when (as in the quotation from Anthony Eden above) the object of the support is another human being: you can (if prominent enough) be a protagonist of a policy or ideology, but not really of a person.

protégé See PRODIGY.

protestation The noun *protestation* is sometimes used as though it meant the same as the noun *protest*: 'a declaration of disapproval or dissent; an objection'. This is commonly regarded as a misuse — a waste of the distinct meaning of *protestation*, simply (and misguidedly) for the sake of a longer word.

The difference between *a protest* and *a protestation* can be clarified by a look at the verb *to protest*, which underlies them both. *To protest* means primarily 'to state or affirm formally and solemnly (something that is in doubt)': *She protested her innocence.* The Latin verb *protestari* meant 'to declare in public', from *pro-*, 'forth, in public' + *testari*, 'to be a witness, or make a will'. The common meaning of *to protest* as 'to express strong objection, disagreement, or annoyance' is limited in British English to the intransitive use of the verb — *We protest!* — or to the phrase *to protest against* (or *about* or *at*). To say *They protested the introduction of cruise missiles into Britain* is an Americanism; in British English, it should be *They protested against the introduction of cruise missiles into Britain* (which is equally correct in American English).

Protestation, then, is the noun related to the transitive verb *to protest* in its primary sense, and means 'a formal statement or emphatic declaration': *His protestations of love swept her off her feet.* (Singular and plural are often, as in this example, virtually interchangeable.) Here are two further examples:

> Bamford Smales and his wife and the chief were together a few minutes longer, standing about now, smiling, exchanging remarks about the need for rain again; thanks, and protestations of pleasure at meeting.
> – Nadine Gordimer, *July's People*

> We can even learn to sleep longer, simply by going to sleep again on morning awakening. Most people can easily sleep another 1-1½ hours at this time, despite protestations that they cannot do this — simply by turning over and going back to sleep.
> – Jim Horne, *The Guardian*

Protest is the noun related to the intransitive verb or to the phrase *to protest against*, and means, as we have seen, 'a declaration of disapproval or dissent; an objection': *The angry workers organised a protest.* In the following quotation, *protestation* is passable, but *protest* would probably be even closer to the writer's intended meaning:

> He spends some time demonstrating that the first poem in that book, '1887', is ironical in its conclusion . . . but omitting Housman's indignant protestation that this was an utter misreading.
> – Philip Larkin, *The Observer*

Note the difference in stress and pronunciation between the verb *to protest* — usually /prə-**test**/ — and the noun: /**prō**-test/. *Protestation* can be pronounced /**prō**-tess-**taysh**'n/ or /**prott**-iss-

taysh'n/. *Protest*, /**prō**-test/, can also be used like an adjective, to describe another noun, as in *a protest march* or *a protest song*.

The useful idiom *under protest* means 'against one's will and in the face of one's objections': *Very well, officer, I shall come with you, but under protest.*

proved, proven In British English the preferred past-participle form of the verb *to prove* is *proved*, the same as the past-tense form: *He has proved his point*; *I was proved right.* The alternative form *proven* is mainly restricted to formal or literary usage: it can be found in legal contexts, in particular, and survives in the Scots law verdict of *not proven*. (The standard pronunciation is /**prōo**v'n/, though /**prō**v'n/ is often used, particularly in reference to the law.)

In North American English the reverse is true, and *proven* has now probably overtaken *proved* as the most frequent past-participle form: *He has proven his point.* When the past participle is used adjectivally before the noun, *proven* is preferred in both varieties of English: *a candidate with a proven record of excellence.*

provided that 1. The *that* can be omitted — *You can go provided (that) you return by nightfall* — though it is perhaps better retained. And the form *? providing* or *? providing that*, though very common in informal spoken English, is still not fully accepted as standard, and is best avoided in writing.

> *?* Her own authorization to lend money extended to a million dollars in any one instance, providing two other officers in the branch concurred.
> – Arthur Hailey (U.S.), *The Moneychangers*

> *?* The *lucent* example shows that, providing both the form and the meaning of a word agree, the sound need not exactly agree.
> – Eric Partridge, *A Charm of Words*

2. Do not use *provided that* as an elegant substitute for *if*. Compare the following three sentences:

> He threatened to prosecute us if our dog spoilt his garden.
> He used to get very angry if our dog went into his garden.
> He promised to stop complaining if we kept our dog on a lead.

The sentences seem to resemble each other closely

in structure, yet only in the last of them could the *if* be replaced by *provided that* (in the first, the *if* could be replaced by *in the event that*, and in the second, by *whenever*). It is only the last sentence that really lays down a condition; the first two sentences simply set out events (theoretical or actual) and the consequences of them. Use *provided that* only when a condition or demand or requirement is involved. One useful test for the correctness of any use of *provided that* is to check that it can be replaced by *on condition that*. If it cannot, then it is incorrect, and you should use *if* instead.

As it happens, such conditions are usually stipulated only for favourable (or neutral) events. So *provided that* seldom occurs if the main clause deals with negative or purely unfavourable consequences. You can say *I'll succeed, provided that I keep my head* but you would not ordinarily say *?? I'll fail, provided that I lose my head.* Similarly, it is fine to say:

> Pressure and volume remain in perfect inverse proportion, provided that the temperature remains constant.

But it sounds very strange to say:

> ?? Pressure and volume will not remain in perfect inverse proportion, provided that the temperature changes.

See also MISRELATED CONSTRUCTIONS.

prudent, prudish, prurient, puritanical The adjective *prudent* comes from the Latin *prudens*, 'wise, having foresight', going back to the roots *pro-*, 'beforehand' + *videre*, 'to see'. (Hence too our words *provide* and *provident*.) *Prudent* can in fact mean 'showing foresight and care'.

> The brakes were relined, the waterpipes unclogged, the valves ground, and a number of other repairs and improvements were paid for by not very mechanically-minded but prudent papa Humbert, so that the late Mrs Humbert's car was in respectable shape when ready to undertake a new journey.
> – Vladimir Nabokov, *Lolita*

More specifically, it means 'practical, exercising good judgment or common sense'; or 'provident or careful about one's own interests, or about one's conduct'; or 'circumspect, discreet'.

The noun *prudence* refers to the state or quality of being prudent (and it also means 'careful management, economy').

I gave up the task, returned the advance to the publisher (except for the agent's 10 per cent) and determined thereafter to keep away from lexicography. I admired Partridge's courage the more for my own cowardice, glossed as prudence, and the admiration continues posthumously.
> – Anthony Burgess, *The Observer*

The adjective *prudential* means 'based on or marked by prudence' – often a misguided notion of prudence. It can, in other words, have negative overtones. So: *Her prudent preparations saved them in the emergency*; but *His prudential warnings stifled their sense of adventure*.

The words *prudish* and *prude* have little to do with the word *prudent*. The Old French *prudefemme*, 'a virtuous woman', gave rise in French and then in English to the shortened form *prude*, now meaning 'a person over-concerned with being or seeming proper, especially about sex'. *Prudish* accordingly means 'having an excessive regard for propriety, modesty, or morality, especially that of others; prim, and often disapproving'.

> Churchill had already had a shower and came out stark naked to meet the President. Roosevelt was a shy and somewhat prudish man, obviously quite embarrassed. Churchill noticed this and reassured him: 'The Prime Minister of Great Britain has nothing to conceal from the President of the United States.'
> – George Mikes,
> *English Humour for Beginners*

Both *prude* and *prudish* can of course now apply to men as well as women: *He/She is too prudish to enjoy such an outspoken play*. The related nouns are *prudery* and *prudishness*.

It is a serious mistake to confuse *prurient* with *prudent* or *prudish*. In fact, the meaning of *prurient* is almost the opposite of that of *prudish*. *Prurient* means 'obsessively interested in improper matters, especially sexual matters': *a prurient little man haunting the sleazy clubs of the city*. It also means 'characterised by, or arousing, such an interest': *prurient thoughts*; *prurient stories in the scandal sheets*.

> The best of the book is the vivid picture it paints of the social and cultural climate of the nineties and after, in particular the frenzied terror of homosexuality that was so widespread (and which now lingers only in the prurient swineries of *Private Eye*); the worst is the astonishing profusion of illiteracies.
> – Bernard Levin, *The Observer*

Prurient comes from the Latin *pruriens*, the present participle of *prurire*, 'to itch, or be lascivious'. (There is in English the medical term *pruritis*, /proor-rītəss/, referring to a severe and persistent itching of the skin.) The noun from *prurient* is *prurience* or *pruriency*. *Prurient* is usually pronounced /**proor**-i-ənt/: take care not to omit the first *r*.

Puritanical is sometimes used to mean something like *prudish*. The Puritans of the 16th and 17th centuries were a group of English Protestants who sought the simplification – or purification – of the ceremonies and creeds of the Church of England. They regarded luxury and pleasure as sinful. So a *puritan* (with a small *p*) or a *puritanical* person is, by extension, likely to be morally strict and censorious, and to frown on luxury and idle pleasures:

> To see how absurd the notion of satiation is we only have to ask ourselves whether we would have any difficulty in spending, say, double our incomes. A few puritanical souls might wrinkle their noses in horror at the thought of such a thing, but most of us can very easily imagine that there are goods and services we might wish to buy with the extra money.
> – Matthew Symonds, *Daily Telegraph*

In particular, *puritan* and *puritanical* apply to those who disapprove of most sexual activity or expression – and so approach *prudish* in meaning. (All three words today have a distinctly unfavourable tone.)

> 'In a bedroom he did other things than sleep,' she said. 'You are the proof.' I began to understand why my parents had seen so little of Aunt Augusta. She had a temperament my mother would not have liked. My mother was far from being a puritan, but she wanted everything to be done or said at a suitable time.
> – Graham Greene,
> *Travels With My Aunt*

Puritan and its derivatives *puritanical* and *puritanism* come from the Late Latin *puritas*, 'purity', from the Latin *purus*, 'pure'.

Purist (like *puristic* and *purism*) also comes from Latin *purus*. It overlaps with a rarer sense of *puritanical* – 'seeking simplicity'. A *purist* is someone who practises or urges strict correctness or basic simplicity, as in style or most commonly in language. It has no connection with moral purity. So: *She was a purist in the kitchen, and refused to use frozen pastry*; *Her painting was*

puristic, adhering to a classical simplicity; *Purists say 'I hope' rather than 'hopefully'*.

psychobabble See JARGON.

psychological moment This phrase originated in German, was borrowed by French, and from there adopted into English. Its meaning changed *en route*: the original idea was of a psychological *momentum* — the power of the mind, mental influence. In French and in English, however, it was understood as referring to a key point in a patient's treatment — a time of maximum susceptibility or cooperation, when his mental state is most likely to produce the desired response. And with this sense it was adopted into wider use, typically when referring to attempts at persuading someone to do something:

> 'What I now merely ask you is this: would you, or would you not, be prepared to spend a few days in Switzerland this Christmas, at one or other of the winter sport resorts?' ...
> He was watching my face, shrewdly and covertly, in its various phases of astonishment. At what he evidently considered to be the psychological moment, he added:
> 'All expenses would be paid, of course.'
> – Christopher Isherwood,
> *Mr Norris Changes Trains*

This distortion of the original meaning is natural and acceptable; the phrase did fill a lexical gap, providing a name for a new concept. But the phrase gradually came to be used too loosely, as a fancy substitute for *a dramatic moment* or *the exact moment* or *a turning point*:

> ?? On the far side of the closed rear door crouched Jeff, breathless from his recent exertions, panting whispered admonitions in the ear of his co-conspirator. Red Hoss was impatient to lunge forward. He wanted to surge in right now. But Jeff held fast to him. Jeff could sense a psychological moment, even if he could not pronounce one.
> – Irvin S. Cobb (U.S.),
> 'Hark! From the Tomb'

> ?? At the psychological moment the prosecuting counsel produced his final devastating piece of evidence.

> ?? Reinforcements arrived at the psychological moment, just as the besieged commander was about to raise the white flag.

In these last two examples, *at the psychological moment* is filling no lexical gap, but rather driving out such established — and idiomatically preferable — phrases as *at the crucial moment* and *in the nick of time.* If you must use the pompous phrase *psychological moment* at all, use it only when discussing psychology or the techniques of persuasion.

punctuation 1. The purpose of punctuation is, above all, to make the meaning of a written passage clear. It is not just an optional frill: it is essential to the accurate exchange of written information, just as — in speech — intonation is a major clue to meaning. Punctuate negligently, and you will communicate inefficiently and probably misleadingly. Ambiguity thrives on careless punctuation (see AMBIGUITY 7).

Punctuation has four specific functions:
● to end or round out: *Who says so? The boss does. How amazing!*
● to introduce: *He has one response to every request — blunt refusal.*
● to separate: *Those who can, do; those who can't, teach.*
● to enclose and set apart: *You, my fine fellow, are in serious trouble. 'I'll kill you,' he snarled.*

All these functions serve the higher purpose of punctuation — to clarify the writer's meaning. Punctuation does this in a variety of ways. Sometimes it shows that the writer intends one form of a word rather than another:

These are my daughters (= These people are my daughters).
These are my daughter's (= These things belong to my daughter).
These are my daughters' (= These things belong to my daughters).

Sometimes it shows that the writer intends one structure rather than another — and the difference can be important. The following sentence has a non-restrictive relative clause (see RESTRICTIVE AND NONRESTRICTIVE CLAUSES):

My sister, who lives in Chicago, is 21 today.

It implies that I have only one sister. Contrast the sentence:

My sister who lives in Chicago is 21 today.

It has a restrictive relative clause, and implies that I have more than one sister.

Punctuation can show which words go together to form a unit: the phrase *three-year-old horses* refers to an indefinite number of horses that are three years old. The phrase *three year-old horses* refers to three horses, each of which is one year old.

Punctuation can also show which words go together to make a phrase or clause. Note the difference that the placing of a comma makes in the following pair of sentences:

I notified Jeremy, and Pat and Winslow reported to base.
I notified Jeremy and Pat, and Winslow reported to base.

If the comma were omitted altogether, it would be impossible to determine which meaning was intended.

A famous example of the importance of commas is the following apocryphal pair of sentences:

King Frederick says Voltaire is an ass.
King Frederick, says Voltaire, is an ass.

In the first sentence, *Frederick* goes with *says*, and Voltaire is the ass. In the second sentence, *says* goes with Voltaire, and Frederick is the ass. That vast difference in meaning is conveyed by the simple presence or absence of commas.

All of this follows from well-recognised principles of punctuation — principles that can be regarded as rules and applied almost mechanically. Unfortunately, punctuation cannot be reduced completely to a system of rules. Its effective use requires an ability by the writer to put himself in the position of his readers and anticipate any likely difficulty or misunderstanding of theirs. Take the sentence:

? As Martin Luther Albert Finney was a great success.

It is not exactly incorrect, but it might well cause readers a moment of puzzlement before understanding dawns. It might seem momentarily to refer to someone called *Martin Luther Albert Finney* or to someone called *Martin Luther Albert.* The author's intention would have been immediately clear, however, if he had taken the trouble to insert a single comma:

As Martin Luther, Albert Finney was a great success.

Here are two more examples of 'false starts':

As soon as he learnt that there was only one course of action remaining to him.
However much has been written on this subject.

A comma after *that* and *However* would have saved the reader his momentary disorientation. Here is another, subtler, example:

? In the great variety of English sentences, long

499

and short, complicated or simple, these situations are not always clear-cut and require judgment on the writer's part.

> – Harrison Platt, Jr (U.S.),
> 'Guide to Usage', in
> *The American College Dictionary*

The subject *these situations* is followed by two predicates — one negative and one positive. The shift from one to the other would be much easier to follow if an extra comma were introduced to divide them:

> . . . these situations are not always clear-cut, and require judgment on the writer's part.

This example suggests another principle that is worth bearing in mind: if a sentence is hard to punctuate, re-formulation may be desirable as well as, or instead of, re-punctuation:

> . . . these situations are not always clear-cut, and they require judgment on the writer's part.

The insertion of *they* into the sentence is a great aid to clarity.

2. Punctuation can serve other purposes besides simply distinguishing meanings. It can also produce delicate effects of style. The difference between these two phrases —

> an intelligent, beautiful woman

and

> an intelligent beautiful woman

— is very subtle indeed: perhaps the comma induces the reader to pause momentarily, and reflect upon each of the adjectives separately. A more obvious example:

> The aims of writers and publishers of all sorts are clarity and suitability to the general style. If these two aims are achieved, consistently, the punctuation is good.
> – Harrison Platt, Jr (U.S.),
> 'Guide to Usage', in
> *The American College Dictionary*

The two commas in the second sentence do not alter the truth of the sentence one way or the other, but they do produce an interesting change of effect. It is as if the sentence read:

> If these two aims are achieved, and achieved consistently, the punctuation is good.

The word *consistently* has greater prominence with the commas than it would have without them, and almost becomes a clause on its own.

3. So some aspects of punctuation are rule-governed, and some are matters of judgment and taste. The judgment and taste in question are by no means always those of the writer. Publishers, newspapers, and magazines tend increasingly to impose 'house styles' on everything they print, and much punctuation is changed or eliminated in the transition from manuscript to print.

However, in those matters of punctuation that are variable, two general tendencies can be discerned. They are usually called *heavy punctuation* and *light punctuation*. In simple terms, *heavy punctuation* is the tendency to use as many different marks as possible and to use them as much as possible. Its aim is to keep the interpretation continuously under the author's control and to force the reader's attention on to even relatively small units of text, such as phrases or even single words. *Light punctuation* gives more scope for the reader to sort things out for himself: it risks some confusion and ambiguity for the sake of a text that flows quickly.

One tendency in light punctuation is to use the hyphen as little as possible. Light punctuators will tend to write compounds open (*head waiter*) or solid (*headwaiter*) rather than hyphenated (*head-waiter*). Another, perhaps more important tendency, involves the use of commas. Light punctuators will tend to use commas instead of brackets, dashes, and semicolons, and will tend to use the comma itself as little as possible. They will write

> an intelligent beautiful woman

rather than

> an intelligent, beautiful woman.

They will write

> apples, peaches and pears

rather than

> apples, peaches, and pears.

Both styles of punctuation can still be found on both sides of the Atlantic, though even the heaviest of punctuation nowadays seems light by comparison with that of past centuries, just as capital letters are used far less today than they were in times past. And the drift towards lighter punctuation seems to be continuing.

In general, heavy punctuation may be appropriate to the serious discussion of complex ideas, but it can seem ponderous. Light punctuation may be appropriate for journalism and fast-moving fiction, but it can lead to misunderstanding and actually slow the reader's progress by forcing him to read a confusing passage several times. The aim in this book, which tries to entertain as well as to enlighten, is to follow a middle course and to provide a model that can be used by most writers in most circumstances.

4. When quoting from other texts, a writer has the basic duty to reproduce that text accurately. The one small degree of leeway traditionally allowed him is in the matter of punctuation conventions. Not, of course, that he can change the punctuation at will — from heavy punctuation to light punctuation say — any more than he can change difficult words in the original text to simpler words. What he is permitted to change — in the view of many publishers, anyway — is the punctuation convention: if the quoted text, for instance, used double quotation marks, the writer may silently (that is, without explicitly acknowledging it) change these to single quotation marks in line with the practice of the surrounding text. Many publishers similarly allow spelling changes — from *-ize* to *-ise*, for instance — in order to achieve a standardised style throughout the text as a whole.

Rather more dubious punctuation changes are those at the start and end of a quoted passage. Suppose that the text is a very long and complicated sentence, but that you want to quote just a portion from the middle of it. It is clearly tempting to begin that quoted portion with a capital letter and to end it with a full stop, even though these did not appear in the original. Many publishers allow this liberty; others, more pedantic, refuse to allow it, and insist that any such changes must be explicitly acknowledged, typically in the following way:

> The committee stated, in their report: '[T]hese acts are clearly outrageous, but that is irrelevant: what we have to determine is whether they are illegal ...'

A more permissive writer or publisher would omit the square brackets and use a full stop rather than the dot-dot-dot of the ellipsis.

Or consider this pair of extracts (quoted here exactly as they appear in the original text) from a famous British law journal:

> Dixon J. concluded comprehensively that "[a]rguments founded upon such Charters and Statutes are sufficiently answered by a reference to ... [Moore's] paper and to the relevant parts of such works as *McKechnie, Magna Carta* ... and *Holdsworth, History of English Law* ..."

> ... the examiners, who had earlier observed that they had investigated "the crime of murder," concluded *inter alia* that "[Samuel] Crookes [*scil.* intentionally] shot Linley with an air gun. ... [H]e died from the effects of the injury ..."
>
> – David R. Mummery,
> *The Law Quarterly Review*

This abundance of dots and square brackets is hardly pleasing to the eye. In the first extract, a less meticulous writer or publisher would have allowed lighter punctuation within the quotation: he would for a start have omitted the square brackets around the *a* of *arguments* (or retained the capital *A* of the original), then omitted the ellipsis before [*Moore's*], since the square brackets adequately indicate a break in the text, and finally replaced the ellipsis at the end with a single full stop.

In the second extract, the quotation marks could have been distributed differently — arranged in such a way as to make all the dots and square brackets unnecessary:

> ... the examiners, who had earlier observed that they had investigated "the crime of murder," concluded *inter alia* that Samuel Crookes had intentionally "shot Linley with an air gun," and that Linley had "died from the effects of the injury."

Note, finally, that the punctuation here is still not in accordance with the style of punctuation used generally in this book. (The policy here is to use single rather than double quotation marks, and to place punctuation outside the closing quotation mark if that punctuation is part of the surrounding text rather than actually belonging to the quoted words.) Suppose that the rewritten extract above had appeared in exactly that form in the law journal, and that the extract had been chosen for inclusion in this book. It would then have appeared in the following form:

> ... the examiners, who had earlier observed that they had investigated 'the crime of murder', concluded *inter alia* that Samuel Crookes had intentionally 'shot Linley with an air gun', and that Linley had 'died from the effects of the injury'.

Single quotation marks have now replaced the double marks, and two of the commas and the full stop have been shifted to a position outside the quoted phrases. Liberties have clearly been taken in 'reproducing' the earlier passage, and purists will shudder at them. But the trend is on the side of the liberties here, not the purists.

5. The various punctuation marks are discussed individually in their due alphabetical place. See: BRACKETS; COLON; COMMA; DASH; ELLIPSIS; EXCLAMATION MARK; FULL STOP; HYPHEN; ITALICS; PARAGRAPHS; QUESTION MARK; QUOTATION MARKS; SEMI-COLON; SOLIDUS; SQUARE BRACKETS.

pundit, pandit *A pandit*, best pronounced /**pun**dit/, is a Hindu scholar of the Brahman caste. The word is Hindi, from the Sanskrit *pandita*, 'a wise man, a scholar', originally from a Dravidian language. It was the pandits who first taught the Europeans Sanskrit, and informed them about Indian culture in general. In India the word is used as an honorary title for a learned man, as in *Pandit Nehru*.

The British, using the spelling *pundit*, brought the word into general use, applying it, sometimes slightly disapprovingly or mockingly, to anyone setting up as an expert or specialist: *the contradictory recommendations of the pundits*.

> The pundits of popular psychology have much to answer for. Before we all discovered psychoanalysis, literature was enjoyed not only as entertainment but as a colourful, uncodified source of self-knowledge. Now our curiosity is more likely to be fed by pseudo-scientific, predigested pap.
> – Carol Rumens, *The Observer*

In its older, more restricted use — referring to a Hindu scholar — the word should retain its original spelling, *pandit* (though it should be pronounced like *pundit*):

> The ceremony itself ... would go on for hours, in accordance with the Vedic rites. He sat next to his bride, facing the sacred fire on the other side of which the pandit sat. ... The pandit was intoning mantras. Incense was thrown on the flames of the fire.
> – Paul Scott,
> *The Jewel in the Crown*

puritanical See PRUDENT.

purposely, purposefully *Purposely* means 'on purpose, intentionally': *He purposely dawdled so as to miss the train.*

> But my uncle always blamed the World Press for purposely fostering the desire to 'win at any price', and for aggravating isolated affairs into international incidents.
> – B.L. Kentish,
> letter to *The Observer*

Purposefully usually adds a nuance to this, to suggest 'in a determined way, as if influenced by a strong purpose': *He marched purposefully out of the room.*

> The hilltop smelt of thyme and was a special place for Joseph. He had looked for it on the map and led Charlie to it with an air of moment, first by car and now on foot, climbing purposefully past rows of wattle beehives, through glades of cypress trees and stony fields of yellow flowers.
> – John le Carré,
> *The Little Drummer Girl*

The rarely-used *purposively* (pronounced /**pur**pəss-ivli/ in British English) means 'with a particular purpose', as in *Their strategy was purposively organised.*

In the following example, the interviewee has used *purposefully* when it would have been slightly preferable to use *purposely*:

> My chief aim was to make the novel rather like a high-tech modern building, where all the plumbing is purposefully shown on the outside. The anatomy was put on the outside, to show all the things that Freudian analysts and social workers would think had happened.
> – Emma Tennant,
> interviewed in *The Literary Review*

Q

qua This Latin word, used in English as a preposition, is pronounced /kway/ or sometimes /kwaa/, and means 'considered as' or 'in the role of':

> The rights of a human being qua person may be different from the rights of a human being qua citizen.

Qua does not mean 'as regards', as it is often taken to mean. So the following sentence is wrong:

> ✗ The situation qua agriculture is better than the situation qua industry.

More subtly, *qua* has a narrower meaning than *as*. The following sentence is wrong too:

> ✗ After a successful career qua stockbroker, she began an even more successful career qua missionary.

What is missing here is the necessary idea of an *aspect* of the subject, or a *point of view*.

Note that *qua* is not followed by *a* or *an*.

Finally, remember that *qua* is a rather formal word and may not be appropriate in all circumstances. Although *qua* cannot always replace *as*, *as* can usually replace *qua*:

> The rights of a human being as person may be different from the rights of a human being as citizen.

question See NO QUESTION.

question mark 1. The question mark is put at the end of a direct question:

> Are you well?
> How are you?
> Do you want coffee or tea?
> Do you want coffee or do you want tea?

It is not used in an indirect question:

> She asked how I was.
> She asked if you wanted coffee or tea.

The question may be added to a sentence as a 'tag':

> You're well, aren't you?

Such 'tag questions' are of various types, but usually take question marks whether their intonation is rising or falling. Sometimes, however, they may take exclamation marks:

> The weather is wonderful, isn't it!

The question may not have the typical form of a question:

> He said *what*?

It may even have the form of a declarative sentence:

> He said *that*?
> He came on the 14th of June?
> Surely that's wrong?

An important problem occurs with questions that function as requests. These come in various degrees. First, a tentative request for permission (spoken with a rising tone at the end, just like a straightforward question):

> Could I have another piece of cake?
> Would you mind very much if I closed the window?
> I wonder if I might ask you to open the door for me?

Here a question mark seems appropriate, even in the last example, which is constructed like a statement rather than a question.

Second, a rather more confident request (spoken without a rising tone), expecting action, rather than a spoken reply, by way of response:

> Could I have another piece of cake, please (?)
> Would you open the door for me (?)

Here the suitability and unsuitability of the question mark are evenly balanced.

Next, a 'request' that is spoken in a flat tone, like an instruction, and functions as a piece of advice rather than as a request.

> Could you pass me that piece of cake, please.

> Would everyone wishing to visit the Doge's palace please assemble on the right.

Here a question mark would be very unlikely.

Finally, a sarcastic sneer, though still in the structure of request:

> Would you mind not spitting cake in my face when you talk.
> Would you open the blasted door.

A question mark seems quite inappropriate here. An exclamation mark is far more likely.

2. Questions do not have to be in the form of a complete sentence:

> What? Yes? Over there? Why not come tonight? Coffee? Coffee or tea?

Such questions might take the form of split-off parts of a longer sentence, each part having a capital letter and ending with a question mark:

> Do you want coffee? Or do you want tea?
> What will happen if it rains? If the match is cancelled? If the train is late?

Conversely, a question may be embedded in a larger sentence:

> Which way forward? were the words on everyone's lips.

There may even be a series of questions so embedded:

> A story that answers the questions What?, Where?, and When? may still leave other important questions unanswered.
> Who knows about editing the book?, proof-reading the book?, printing the book?

When the parts of such a series do not begin with a typical question word (such as *what*), the whole series may have only one question mark:

> Who knows about editing the book, proof-reading the book, printing the book?

And the series should have only one question mark if the sub-questions are numbered or lettered:

> Who knows about (a) editing the book, (b) proofreading the book, (c) printing the book?

3. A question mark may be used after a quoted question (see QUOTATION MARKS):

> She asked, 'How are you?'
> 'How are you?' she asked.

But remember, it should not be used after an 'indirect' or reported question:

> She asked how you were.

She wondered how you were.

It can sometimes be used when a verb of thinking follows a question:

> How are you now, I wonder?

But it should not be used when such a verb 'reports' a previous question:

> How were they, I wondered.

'Indirect questions' are in effect statements rather than questions, and take full stops not question marks:

> I asked them whether they were now fully recovered.
> One question remains to be answered, and that is how he acquired the gun.

4. The question mark can be used to express doubt about a fact:

> Geoffrey Chaucer (1340? – 1400)
> Geoffrey Chaucer (?1340 – 1400)

(In the first example, only the date of birth is considered doubtful; in the second, both dates are put in doubt.) It can also express doubt, often ironic, about a characterisation:

> With such friends(?), I don't need enemies.

But many people would regard as heavy-handed the use of the question mark in this last example.

In this book, as in many other books about language, the question mark is used to show that an example is dubious. So, because many people object to the last example, we might put an additional question mark in front of it:

> ? With such friends(?), I don't need enemies.

5. The question mark may be doubled, or even trebled, for emphasis:

> Can they really have meant *that*??
> With such friends(??), I don't need enemies.
> ?? With such friends(???), I don't need enemies.

Do not overdo this, or readers will stop taking you seriously.

The question mark can also be reinforced by an exclamation mark. When this happens, the exclamation mark usually follows the question mark, except in the chess notation discussed below:

> They want the work *tomorrow*?!

A special punctuation mark called the 'interrabang' or 'interrobang' has been invented for this purpose:

> They want the work *tomorrow*?

— but it is hardly ever used.

Remember that it is advisable to be very sparing in the use of the combined question mark and exclamation mark.

But note that ?, ??, ?!, and !? are well-known conventions of chess notation. The first indicates a mistake, the second a blunder, the third a dubious move that looks poor but may work, and the fourth an unusual move that seems good but is risky:

R×P?   R×P??   R×P?!   R×P!?

quick   In informal contexts, *quick* is often used as an adverb interchangeably with *quickly*, particularly in spoken commands and with verbs of motion: *Come quick/quickly! It'll dry quicker/more quickly in front of the fire. Quick* is also standard in some set phrases — *to get rich quick* — and some compound expressions: *quick-setting cement, quick-frozen foods.* Apart from these phrases, more formal speech and writing usually favours the form *quickly.* (See ADVERBS; -LY.)

quit, quitted   The verb *to quit* has two past-tense forms: *quit* and *quitted.* British usage is now tending to follow American practice, and increasingly favouring *quit* rather than *quitted: She quit her job last week.* (Older speakers — though not in North America — would often use *quitted* here.)

Quitted is still very much alive in formal or literary sentences, however: *She has quitted these shores.*

So much for *to quit* in the sense of 'to leave'. It can also mean 'to stop': *She has quit smoking.* (Here *quitted* cannot be used.) Many British speakers dislike this use, regarding it as chiefly American. It is best to avoid using *quit* in this way in formal contexts.

quite   1. *Quite* has two senses that are virtually opposite: 'somewhat, fairly' and 'totally, completely'. The first sense was once objected to by purists but is now fully established in standard English. It tends to occur with 'gradable' adjectives (adjectives that can be modified by *more, less,* and *very*): *a quite pleasant afternoon.* In the sense of 'totally, completely', on the other hand, *quite* tends to refer to 'absolute' adjectives (adjectives that cannot be modified by *more, less,* and *very*) — a *quite impossible request* — or at least to adjectives that suggest extremes: a *quite outstanding performance*; a *quite exquisite brooch.* (A similar distinction applies when *quite* refers to verbs or adverbs.)

Ambiguity remains a threat, however, since some adjectives can fall either side of the divide. Consider the sentence *? The bottle is quite full* — is the bottle full to the brim, or only, say, two-thirds full?

In speech, a different intonation in each case is likely to distinguish the two senses; in writing, greater caution is necessary: if the context does not make clear which sense is intended, then the word *quite* should be replaced by *fairly* or *absolutely* or the like.

2. There is, furthermore, a problem about how strongly *quite* intensifies a gradable expression it modifies. And the problem is made worse by differences between British and American English.

Is *quite good* nearer in meaning to *very good* or to *fair*? In written British English the phrase can have either meaning, but is perhaps now more likely to have the second, weaker, one. In written American English the phrase is more likely to be interpreted in the first, stronger, way. In spoken British English, intonation can make the meaning clear. Spoken with a lively intonation that rises and then falls, the phrase has its stronger meaning: *quite* **good**! Spoken with a more restrained intonation that falls and then rises, the meaning is weak and almost dismissive: (It's) **quite** *good* (— but I've seen better). In spoken American English, as in written American English, *quite good* is likely to have a meaning close to that of *very good*, and does not really take the second intonation pattern. In general, then, the meaning of such expressions as *quite good* is likely to be stronger in American than in British English.

Note also that two common constructions in British English are very rare in American English. First, *I quite liked the performance* (where *quite* modifies a verb); secondly, *'It'll do more harm than good.' 'Quite.'* (Here *quite* is a one-word response of agreement.)

3. The combination *quite a* or *quite an* — originally an Americanism — is used in two senses, one indicating quantity, the other indicating quality. First, quantity — an indefinite though considerable quantity: *quite a few, quite a large number, quite a while.* Such phrases still have a slightly informal ring to them, though they are generally now regarded as standard English.

Secondly, *quite a/an* is used to indicate quality — remarkable quality: *Quite a film! That was quite an accident.* The combination *quite some* can be used here instead of *quite a/an.* Either way, the usage remains distinctly informal.

4. Note the different constructions that *quite* takes when used before an adjective on the one

hand and a noun on the other:

> That was quite interesting (= fairly).
> That was quite needless (= absolutely).
> That was quite a display.

When a noun and adjective are used together in a sentence, then the constructions are as follows: Where *quite* means 'fairly', both are acceptable:

> That was a quite interesting display.
> That was quite an interesting display.

Where *quite* means 'absolutely', only the one construction is fully acceptable:

> That was a quite needless display.

Avoid saying:

> ?? That was quite a needless display.

quixotic *Don Quixote* is the aged, impractical, idealistic hero of a satirical chivalric romance (1605-15) by the Spanish writer Miguel de Cervantes, a contemporary of Shakespeare.

Quixotic, an adjective derived from this character, means 'enthusiastic and well-meaning, but absent-minded; romantic; unpractical; given to unreachable ideals'. A man tinkering in his garage at a perpetual-motion machine could be described as *quixotic*. There is a certain sense of charm and indulgent affection about the word, or there should be: *Don Quixote* is one of the best-loved characters in fiction, perhaps because we all, deep down, are tempted to tilt at windmills no matter how hard-nosed and realistic we are on the surface.

But *quixotic* is often used today with a hostile tone, in the sense of 'absurd' or 'dangerously foolish': *? I wish you'd stop harping on this quixotic idea of a ski-trip — you know we can't afford it*; *? a tiresome old lady in a quixotic old hat*. If you mean no more than 'foolish' or 'absurd' or 'ridiculous', say *foolish* or *absurd* or *ridiculous*.

Quixotic is pronounced /kwik-**sot**tik/. *Don Quixote* is traditionally, in English, pronounced /don **kwik**-sət/. If you are tempted to try a Spanish pronunciation, as most Americans are, /don ki-**hō**-tay/, you might reflect that Spaniards today tend to spell the name *Don Quijote*.

quotation marks 1. Quotation marks are also called, informally, *quote marks* or *quotes* and, especially in British English, *inverted commas*. In handwriting and printing a clear distinction is made between those at the beginning of quoted material (', ") and those at the end (', "). On a typewriter keyboard no such distinction is

possible: single quotation marks are represented by an apostrophe (') and double quotation marks by a special symbol equivalent to a double apostrophe (").

2. In handwriting, typing, and American printing, double quotation marks are normal (single quotation marks being used to enclose quotations within quotations). In British printing single quotation marks are nowadays more common. There is perhaps a gain in elegance and economy in this, but it does have one disadvantage — the closing quotation mark is identical to an apostrophe, and the reader might therefore momentarily think that he has reached the end of a quoted passage when in fact what he has seen is only an apostrophe:

> Stacy always spoke bitterly of 'that damn' high-falutin' ship's steward O'Reilly', who had first laughed at his rustic manners and then cheated at cards.

For better or worse, however, single quotation marks are dominant in British printing; they are used in this book, for example, and the following discussion will be based on them unless otherwise stated. But it should be emphasised that they are very rare in American printing, and that double quotation marks are still fighting a rearguard action in Britain and other English-speaking countries. The London *Times* and its supplements, for instance, still favour double quotation marks.

Where single quotation marks are standard, the role of double quotation marks is to enclose quotations within quotations. So:

> She asked, 'Did he say "alimony" or "palimony"?'

If there are ever quotations within quotations within quotations, you simply go on alternating between single and double quotation marks:

> She asked, 'Did he say, "The word 'palimony' is horrible"?'

3. The main purpose of quotation marks is to enclose material that is brought into a text from outside it, such as the words used by other people or by the author himself in other circumstances. For such material the author does not take direct personal responsibility at the moment of writing.

Note that other languages, notably French and German, sometimes have different conventions from those described here. Note too that English itself has not always had these conventions: the King James Bible, for instance, does not use quotation marks at all. And many modern authors — James Joyce and Alan Paton, to name two very different kinds of novelist — dispense with quotation marks in various works, commonly using a dash instead to introduce direct speech.

4. a. Quotation marks are used to enclose direct quotation, as in the examples above, by contrast with indirect quotation — that is, quotation paraphrased by the author:

> She said, 'What have I done?' (direct quotation)
> She asked what she had done. (indirect or reported quotation)

It is a common blunder — or a common act of dishonesty — to blend these two conventions:

> ✕ She admitted that she had 'bent the rules once or twice, but this only put her on a par with all her colleagues'.

Surely the words actually spoken by her would have been '. . . this only put *me* on a par with all *my* colleagues'. The writer should either have used the exact wording, or else have closed the quotation after *twice.*

b. Note that the words *yes* and *no* are not usually put in quotation marks unless they are part of a direct quotation:

> The government have said no to our demands.
> She said, 'No, you cannot.'

c. The words that introduce, present, or comment on direct quotation may come before, after, or in the middle of the quoted words. This 'presentational material' is usually set off from the direct quotation proper by commas:

> She wrote, 'No, you cannot.'
> 'No,' she wrote, 'you cannot.'
> 'No, you cannot,' she wrote.

d. If the quoted passage has more than one paragraph, a peculiar convention is adopted by most publishers: opening quotation marks are used at the beginning of each paragraph, as if to remind the reader that he is still reading quoted material; but closing quotation marks are used only where they would naturally occur — at the end of the quoted material:

> 'I'll tell you one thing,' Burns said, 'you'll have no trouble finding a publisher for this book.
> 'And I'll tell you something else,' he went on: 'it'll be a bestseller.

> 'And I might as well add, while I'm about it, that it'll be the first of many.'

5. The wording within quotation marks is in principle almost identical to the wording of the original text. In the sentence *'No,' she wrote, 'you cannot'*, the *you* has a small *y* rather than a capital, accurately reflecting the original quotation. And if the original text had consisted of two sentences — *No, you cannot. It's impossible* — this too would be apparent in the punctuation:

> 'No, you cannot,' she wrote. 'It's impossible.'

The capital *I* of *It's* is retained in the quoted version, as it was in the original wording.

The punctuation of the quoted version, however, cannot in practice always be identical to that of the original:

a. The full stop of the original is replaced by a comma in the quoted version if the presentational material follows it — as in this example once again.

> 'No, you cannot,' she wrote.

b. Or suppose the original text had been punctuated with a semi-colon rather than a comma in the middle — *No; you cannot.* If presented as direct quotation, with the presentational material coming in the middle, the semi-colon would now be displaced to a position outside the quotation marks, its position inside the quotation marks again being taken by a comma instead:

> 'No,' she wrote; 'you cannot.'

Note the position of the semi-colon now.

The same applies to a colon or full stop, as in this example again:

> 'No, you cannot,' she wrote. 'It's impossible.'

But the question mark and exclamation mark are different — they remain true to the original text by appearing within the quotation marks:

> 'Well, you cannot!' she wrote. 'It's outrageous.'

The dash is more versatile: it can appear outside or inside the quotation marks, and if inside can appear within the first set or the second set. The likeliest location for it is inside the second set of quotation marks, as follows:

> 'You simply cannot,' she wrote, '— it's out of the question.'

c. If you want to quote only part of the original

wording, omitting some words in the middle, you can do this by replacing the omitted words with an ellipsis — the 'dot-dot-dot':

'No, . . . impossible,' she wrote.

See ELLIPSIS for further details.

d. Suppose, conversely, that you wanted to quote more than the original — to add an explanation, for instance. You can do this by enclosing the added material within square brackets.

'No, it [the plan to travel to Athens] is impossible,' she wrote.

See SQUARE BRACKETS for further details.

In general, avoid the 'dot-dot-dot' and square brackets when you can. If they occur more than once or twice, they clutter the text and distract rather than help the reader.

6. *the comma — inside or outside the quotation marks.*

In the examples so far, the comma that ends or interrupts a quoted passage has always fallen within the quotation marks — just to the left of the closing quotation mark.

In American English, this holds good throughout: a comma (or a full stop) never comes directly after the closing quotation marks — it always falls just within them.

In British English, things are more complicated. The comma usually falls within the quotation marks if followed by presentational material such as *he said, Jesse replied,* or *she wrote*:

'No, you cannot,' she wrote.

Some purists object even to this, arguing that the original text did not have a comma after *cannot,* and that the quotation should therefore not have one either. They prefer the more 'logical' order:

? 'No, you cannot', she wrote.

Logical it may be, but it is now very rare. Fashion favours the placing of the comma *before* the closing quotation mark here.

However, when the quoted material is followed by something other than *he said, she wrote,* or the like, then the comma — in British usage — usually comes *after* the closing quotation mark:

But I hate the word 'palimony', and use it as little as possible.

(The American usage here would be to place the comma within the quotation marks — double quotation marks of course. The American convention is perhaps beginning to influence British usage: the national British Sunday newspaper *The*

Observer, for instance, tends to place all commas — and full stops — within the closing quotation mark.)

In British usage, it is possible for the comma to come after the quotation mark even though the quotation is followed by *she wrote*:

Although she said on the phone 'Yes, you can', she wrote 'No, you cannot' in her letter.

The reason for this reversal is that the *she wrote* applies not to the first quoted passage but to the second.

7. *the full stop — inside or outside the quotation marks.*

The original text might well have a full stop, but this is no guarantee that the quoted version of it will have one. As shown earlier, the full stop might be converted into a comma:

'No, you cannot,' she said.

Or it might be omitted altogether if it occurs in the middle of a sentence:

She said 'No, you cannot' and she meant it.

The full stop will also be omitted if a 'stronger' punctuation mark — the question mark or exclamation mark — is required by the surrounding sentence:

Did she really say 'No, you cannot'?
To think that she said 'No, you cannot'!

But when the quotation comes at the end of an ordinary declarative sentence, a full stop is obviously needed. Does it go inside or outside the closing quotation mark/s?

In American English, the rule is the same as that for the comma: The full stop always falls just within — to the left of — the closing quotation marks.

In British usage, it is more complicated once again. The rule is as follows.

The full stop will fall within the closing quotation mark only if two conditions are both met:

a. The quoted words ended with a full stop in the original (or at least can stand on their own as a complete utterance deserving a full stop in their own right).

b. The quoted words are preceded by a punctuation mark. So:

Mary Magpie said, 'You should try to be perfect in an imperfect world.'
'Listen to me,' Mary Magpie said. 'Try to be perfect in an imperfect world.'

This holds good even when the quoted sentence

is interrupted by the presentational material:

'You should try,' Mary Magpie said, 'to be perfect in an imperfect world.'

Note — in keeping with the rule — that if only half the sentence is directly quoted, then the full stop would fall outside the quotation mark:

Mary Magpie urges us 'to be perfect in an imperfect world'.
One ought to try, Mary Magpie said, 'to be perfect in an imperfect world'.

And if the quoted words are not directly preceded by a punctuation mark, then the full stop would again, as a rule, fall outside the quotation mark:

My motto is 'Try to be perfect in an imperfect world'.

Note the difference that a preceding punctuation mark can make. If a colon were inserted after *is* in the previous example, then the full stop would probably go back inside the closing quotation mark:

My motto is: 'Try to be perfect in an imperfect world.'

8. *the question mark and exclamation mark — inside or outside the quotation marks.*

With the question mark and exclamation mark, British and American usage are at last in agreement. The question mark and exclamation mark are placed strictly where they logically belong.

If the quotation, considered alone, demands a question mark or exclamation mark, then it gets one — within the closing quotation mark/s. But if it is the surrounding sentence that demands one, then it is placed outside the quotation marks:

She said, 'Do you still love me?'
Did she say, 'I still love you'?

Note, in the two examples just quoted, that a full stop might have been expected at the very end of the first sentence, and directly after the word *you* in the second sentence. It is omitted, however, because the 'stronger' question mark (or exclamation mark) in each case makes the full stop unnecessary. A comma also sometimes disappears when a question mark or exclamation mark is in the immediate neighbourhood, as in the following example:

'Shut up!' she said.

But where the surrounding wording is not presentational material (*he wrote, she said,* and so on), then a comma can exist near a question mark or exclamation mark:

She said 'Shut up!', but I continued shouting.

A further problem: what if both the quotation and the surrounding sentence require a question mark or exclamation mark? The best course here is simply to assign one to each:

Did she say, 'Do you still love me?'?
To think that she said 'Shut up!'!

Some authorities would omit the second question mark and second exclamation mark here, regarding them as impermissible, in the way that it is impermissible to place a full stop at the end of the following example, even though 'logically' the surrounding sentence requires one:

She said 'Shut up!'

But this rule surely applies only to the full stop, not to the question mark or exclamation mark. It is obviously impossible, for instance, to omit the final question mark from this example:

Did she really say 'Shut up!'?

9. Not all direct quotations are enclosed in quotation marks.
a. An allusion, even one that accurately quotes the original, no longer takes quotation marks if it has passed into general idiomatic usage:

He had to support four children, his hostages to fortune, and therefore could not risk losing his job.

(The phrase *hostages to fortune* occurred originally in an essay by Francis Bacon, in turn echoing the Roman poet Lucan.)

Ever since Queen Medbh and her Dun Cow, people have enjoyed getting dismal about Ireland. Things fall apart once again in *The Railway Station Man*, not least the heroine's yellowing teeth.
— Jonathan Keates, *The Observer*

(The words *Things fall apart* are the opening words of the poem 'The Second Coming' by W.B. Yeats.)
b. Even when the author is identified, the quotation might not take quotation marks if it is well known and if it is integrated into the surrounding text:

It is the heart of winter now, but we remain in good spirits. Can spring be far behind? as Shelley rhetorically asked. We are assured of better days, and soon.

c. The dialogue of a play dispenses with quotation marks. A colon after the speaker's name is enough to mark off his words:

Apemantus: Beast!
Timon: Slave!
Apemantus: Toad!

— Shakespeare,
Timon of Athens IV iii

d. A similar practice is often adopted in the published reports of official proceedings. In fact, any long quotations can generally be introduced by a colon, indented from the surrounding text, and freed of quotation marks (as is the practice in this book):

Simons goes on to say:
There are seven types of ambiguity, according to some ...

10. The distinction has already been made between direct quotation and indirect or reported quotation. It is imporant to note that direct quotation and indirect quotation may be combined for literary effect. When this is done, the punctuation conventions of each type should be observed:

He thought, 'I shall never escape.' The crocodiles would eat him.

11. Direct quotation generally requires a presentational verb such as *say*.
a. Remember that far more verbs can assume this role after direct speech than before it:

She said, 'Come here.'
'Come here,' she said/urged/pressed.

b. The presentational material is sometimes 'inverted' — that is, the verb comes before the subject:

'No, you cannot,' said Mrs Robinson.

See INVERTED WORD ORDER **8** for a more detailed discussion.
12. In all the examples so far, the quotation marks have in effect been saying, 'These words are not my words now: they are other people's words, or my words in other circumstances.'
This use of quotation marks can be extended to serve as a kind of 'authorial disclaimer': to indicate that the words are used in a special way. (Hence the expression 'in inverted commas', as in *After a few drinks, he gets very — friendly ... in inverted commas.* You might even crook your fingers in the air to suggest the shape of inverted commas when you use words that call for them.) In the first sentence of this paragraph, for example, the words *authorial disclaimer* are in

quotation marks to show that they constitute a technical term — or perhaps only to show that the phrase is not ideal, but the best term available. Note that italics is sometimes an alternative to such quotation marks.

This use of quotation marks may serve to distance the author in any of several ways from the words quoted:

God preserve me from such 'friends'! (= the word is inappropriate and is being used ironically)

a certain 'je ne sais quoi' (= the words are foreign: italics would be more usual here)

impossible to get 'snout' (= the word belongs to a different level of language from the rest of the text; in this case, slang)

Accused 'tried to bribe judge' (= allegedly: newspaper headlines use inverted commas as shorthand to indicate allegations or rumours).

The use of quotation marks and italics in such cases is important evidence that lexicographers use when deciding whether to label a dictionary entry as slang, foreign, or the like.

Two warnings: first, take care not to overuse quotation marks for such functions as irony or apologising for an inadequate word. It can be very irritating to the reader to see quotation marks scattered over the page unless they are truly serving the purpose of quotation.

Secondly, it is usually enough to use the quotation marks only once when indicating your authorial disclaimer: subsequent uses of the word or phrase can do without the quotation marks. The phrase *authorial disclaimer,* for example, has no quotation marks in the previous sentence, since it has already appeared in them once, near the start of this section.

13. Unfortunately, the use of quotation marks discussed above has led to a common and ludicrous error: the attempted use of quotation marks simply to give emphasis. A greengrocer, for instance, might display a sign reading:

× 'Fresh' Tomatoes.

He is presumably trying to say that they are really fresh. But educated readers could argue that it conveys just the opposite impression: that the tomatoes might be considered fresh by some, but are not really so. It is just like:

God preserve me from such 'friends'!

Such quotation marks indicate irony, not reinforcement. For emphasis, use italics, underlining capitalisation, exclamation marks — any thing but quotation marks.

14. Single quotation marks have another special use — a rather technical one, but common in books about language or philosophy, including this one. It is the use of quotation marks to enclose a gloss, or interpretation, of an expression. The expression being glossed will often appear in italics:

The French word *chien* means 'dog'.

Compare:

The French word *chien* is synonymous with *dog*.

The first sentence talks about a word and its meaning. The second sentence talks about two words.

Note that such glossing is often done in single quotation marks even by Americans — who would, however, put the full stop to the left of the final quotation mark here, as always.

15. Quotation marks distinguish certain kinds of title from the surrounding text. Nowadays a fairly clear distinction is made between those titles that are in quotation marks and those that are italicised; the distinction is the same in Britain and America. The titles in quotation marks tend to be of relatively short works, or parts of longer works. They include the titles of articles, chapters or parts of books (except for the Bible), brochures or pamphlets, lectures, short stories, short poems, short pieces of music, and, in general, single radio and television programmes. Italicisation is used for the titles of longer works, such as periodicals, books, plays, longer musical works such as operas, and sometimes radio and television series and serials.

The names of paintings are also usually italicised.

So you might refer to:

the article 'New Light on Old Bones' in *New Scientist* (article in periodical)
Tennyson's 'Ulysses', Homer's *Odyssey,* and Joyce's *Ulysses* (shorter poem, long poem, and novel)
the television series 'M.A.S.H.' based on the film *M.A.S.H.*

Other names, such as those of ships, space capsules, and railway engines (but not horses, or hotels, for example), are sometimes enclosed in quotation marks, though the tendency today would probably be to use italics instead.

R

racism, racialism Both words refer to the belief that some races — particularly one's own — are inherently superior to others; and also to discriminatory practices based on this belief. Some writers have sought to draw a distinction between *racism* as a scientific theory and *racialism* as racial prejudice, but the two words appear to be used indiscriminately.

Racialism (1907) is the older word, *racism* (1936) probably commoner today (certainly so in American English):

> Racial segregation is enforced by law in most areas of South African life, as is the racial classification of children at birth. A person's classification determines for ever his or her political, social and economic rights. This would seem to be a classic definition of racism.
> – Michael Hornsby, *The Times*

Note the difference in the pronunciation of the *c* in the two words: *racialism,* /**ray**sh'l-izm/, but *racism,* /**rays**sizm/.

racket, racquet Tennis, squash and badminton have traditionally been played with a *racket*, so spelt. And the game *rackets* is traditionally so spelt. The spellings *racquet* and *racquets* which are now so common were introduced by association with the French word *racquette*, and were long felt to be quite incorrect. *Racquet* is now very well established in British English, however, and is a useful option because it distinguishes the item of sports equipment from the other meanings of *racket* (which always have this spelling): 'a din or clamour', 'a shoddy or dishonest business', or, informally, 'any business or job'.

> Mid-twentieth century ideas concerning child-parent relationship have been considerably tainted by the scholastic rigmarole and standardised symbols of the psychoanalytic racket, but I hope I am addressing myself to unbiased readers.
> – Vladimir Nabokov, *Lolita*

Nevertheless, the North Americans manage with just the one spelling, *racket*, for all meanings. (Compare CHECK.)

raise, raze To *raze* means to tear down. Take care not to misspell it as *raise*, which means the opposite, 'to lift up'. However, *raze* can be spelt *rase*, though this form is rarely seen today. *To raze* comes from the same Latin root word as *erase*, but means 'to level', not 'to wipe out'.

> The fact that the forest is being razed to provide new crops and a different way of life must be evidence of another side to the argument, even if a wrong-headed one.
> – Richard Last, *Daily Telegraph*

A common phrase is *to raze to the ground*. See also RISE.

rarely, seldom In careless or informal speech, *ever* is commonly used for emphasis after *rarely* or *seldom* — ✗ *I rarely ever go there* — but in formal contexts the *ever* is considered redundant, and should be avoided. Combinations such as *seldom if ever* and *rarely or never* are, however, perfectly acceptable: *I rarely if ever travel by train*; *She seldom or never left the house alone*.

rat race *Rat race*, or *rat-race*, refers to the fiercely competitive, and often unpleasant, struggle for power or promotion, or simply survival, that commonly occurs in urban society: *disillusioned with the academic rat race*. It has become a vogue phrase, too popular to retain its sharpness. Use it sparingly.

There is some dispute about the origin of the expression. Some authorities attribute the metaphor to the study of animal behaviour: in some experiments, rats are timed as they try to master the pattern of a maze; in others, they are perhaps forced to keep walking or running on a treadmill. Other authorities feel that the term has more connection with the rats which raced blindly on in pursuit of the Pied Piper of Hamelin.

rather 1. *Rather* is a favourite British adverb, with its ability to moderate verbs and adjectives into very controlled or even understated expressions of feeling: *I rather liked that concert — didn't you think it was rather good?*

But not every verb or adjective is appropriate for such tranquillising treatment. Some verbs and adjectives refer to extreme conditions — *to flummox, to overwhelm, gorgeous, freezing,* and so on. The weather might be *rather cold,* but it cannot really be *? rather freezing.* So when someone says *? I rather adored that concert — didn't you think it was rather splendid?,* he is either being jocular or speaking bad English. Or perhaps he is simply being very 'British' — keeping his feelings on a tight rein — and sounding quaint and rather peculiar as a result.

2. Note that *I'd rather . . .* is the contraction of *I had rather . . .* as well as *I would/should rather . . .* There is perhaps a slight difference in these forms: *had rather* used usually to express a real preference: *I had rather go to the beach tomorrow than have lunch at your parents';* and *would rather* used usually to express a very hypothetical preference: *I would rather be President of the United States than Prime Minister of the United Kingdom.*

This distinction is all but dead now; in fact, the *had rather* form is all but dead. A sentence such as *I had rather resign than apologise to him* has a very old-fashioned ring to it: this use of *had* is in fact an archaic one, occurring also in the expression *had better* but not found in other constructions; yet many purists still prefer *I had rather resign* to *I would rather resign* or *I should rather resign.*

This preference is even more marked when a full clause follows the *rather: I had rather you resign at once.* However, *had* is not possible at the beginning of a question: here, *would* must be used: *Would she rather resign at once? Would you rather I resigned?*

3. The phrase *rather than* is often followed by a pronoun. This can be either in the subject form or in the object form according to its role in relation to the rest of the sentence. So, *I invited him rather than her.* But: *He, rather than she, happened to be on my guest-list.* (See THAN 1.) In informal English, however, *her* would tend to follow *rather than* regardless: *?? He, rather than her, happened to be on my guest-list.*

Of course, the element that comes before *rather than* has priority over the element that follows it. So: *You, rather than she, are my guest — are,* not *is,* since the verb takes its cue from the first element *you,* not from the second element *she.*

4. Note that *rather than* can be understood in two slightly different senses: 'in preference to' and 'and not; instead of'. A slight ambiguity is sometimes possible, therefore. The sentence *? I take the bus rather than the train* would usually be understood as 'I never take the train: I take the bus', but it could also be the equivalent of

I'd rather take the bus than the train — that is, 'I take both the bus and the train, but I prefer the bus'.

When *rather than* is used to contrast two verbs (rather than two nouns, say, as in the last example), a subtle distinction is sometimes observed. When the sense is 'in preference to', the verb directly after *rather than* should remain in the simple infinitive form:

> He will resign rather than accept the new pay offer.
> He resigned rather than accept the new pay offer.
> Rather than accept the new pay offer, he resigned.

However, when the sense is 'instead of', the verb directly after *rather than* can take the infinitive or the *-s* or *-ed* or *-ing* form:

> He will reject rather than accept the new pay offer.
> He rejected rather than accepted the new pay offer.
> Rather than accepting the new pay offer, he rejected it.

5. Take care not to use *rather than* in place of *than* after *more, simpler, harder,* and so on.

✗ He finds it simpler doing the sums in his head rather than looking for a pencil and paper.

Either omit the *rather* here, or say simply *He does the sums in his head rather than looking for a pencil and paper.*

6. When *rather* begins a new sentence or clause, the word-order following it is sometimes inverted. (See INVERTED WORD ORDER **6.c.**)

? It was neither a matter of dismissal nor a matter of resignation, strictly speaking; rather was it a question of early retirement.

This use of *rather was it . . .* now sounds very old-fashioned, and should be avoided. It is smoother, perhaps, than saying *rather, it was . . . ,* but no smoother than saying *it was rather . . . .*

7. In South African and West African English, *rather* is often used to mean 'instead' or perhaps 'in preference':

? 'I don't feel like swimming — let's play football rather.' 'No, let's rather go to a film.'

This is not standard usage elsewhere. Either use *instead* (or perhaps *preferably*) or change the construction to *I'd rather: I'd rather play football; Let's go to a film instead.*

When used in the sense of 'somewhat', *rather*

requires careful positioning. There is no problem when the word it relates to is a verb or adjective:

> She's rather irritating.
> She rather irritates me.
> She irritates me rather.

(This last example, and to some extent the second example too, are chiefly British rather than American idiom.)

But when *rather* relates to a noun, it demands a peculiar construction:

> She's rather a fool.

The temptation is to keep this structure even when an adjective is added:

?? She's rather an irritating fool.

Strictly speaking, the adjective *irritating* here requires *rather* directly in front of it again. So the correct construction is:

> She's a rather irritating fool.

Note also a curious difference between the singular and plural forms. Whereas you can say both:

> She's a rather irritating fool

and:

> They're rather irritating fools

you can say only:

> She's rather a fool

not:

× They're rather fools.

Instead, you would have to say:

> They're rather foolish.

raze   See RAISE.

re   This preposition should be kept strictly for official use or legal documents or for the opening words of a business letter — or for very informal writing such as holiday postcards. In this extract from a novel, for example, it is used in a chatty letter:

> Have you found an agent or anyone to act for you *re*: The Book? I believe it's a necessity. There's a woman I've heard of called Billie Lee; I hear she's very good and 'knows everyone' in the publishing world.
> – letter, in Lynne Reid Banks's
> *The L-Shaped Room*

In all other writings, and always in speech, the word *about* or *on* or possibly *concerning*, or a phrase like *with reference to*, should be used instead. Out of its proper environment, *re* looks and sounds extremely pretentious:

?? In your recent leading article re genetic engineering, you seriously misrepresent my views.

?? A date has been set for the new round of negotiations re border security.

Perhaps it is a mistaken notion about the origin of *re* that prompts people to use it so loosely. It is not an abbreviation of *referring to* or *regarding*: it is a contraction of the Latin phrase *in re*, 'in the matter of'.

The most common acceptable role for *re* is to introduce, at the start of an official letter, the subject of discussion, in order to help the reader to get his bearings directly:

> Dear Mrs Hathwaye,
>   *re*: My application for a rates rebate.
>   I enclose, as you requested by phone yesterday, both the doctor's certificate and my current rates bill ...

The punctuation here is very variable. The colon after *re* can be omitted, as can the full stop at the end of the line. And *re* itself need not be in italics.

Note the pronunciation of *re,* in case you ever have to pronounce it (and the only time you should need to is when dictating an official or business letter): /ree/ and /ray/ are both acceptable, /ree/ slightly more so.

Compare PACE.

real, really   1. *Real* has become something of a vogue word, a fashionable substitute for *important*, *pressing*, *threatening*, and so on:

? In one aspect, I feel, this ludicrous exercise in political propaganda does real harm. This is by generating a disbelief which is not easy to distinguish from cynicism or callousness.
  – Auberon Waugh, *The Spectator*

? Chronic unemployment is a very real problem throughout the developed world.

Many careful speakers find this usage irritating. One warning sign, as in the second example above, is the use of *very, more, most,* and so on in front of *real*. In more restricted use, *real* is an 'absolute' adjective: something is either real or it is not — there are not really degrees of realness, as the use of *very, more,* and *most* would imply. (See ADJECTIVES; UNIQUE; VERY.)

2. *Real* has also attracted criticism when used to qualify nouns that apparently need no qualifying: *? the real facts of the matter* (what other kind of facts is there?), *? a real shambles*, and so on. But sometimes *real* does perhaps earn its keep in such constructions, by acting as an intensifier of the noun — the way that *really* often works in a sentence. To say *My son is a real disgrace* seems no worse than to say *My son is really a disgrace*.

3. *Really*, as it happens, is all too frequently overused in this way, especially in excited, informal conversation:

?? He was really being pushed around, and at last he got really cross, and really started getting his own back. He really made a nuisance of himself, and the whole project was really getting into a mess as a result ...

Take care, in more formal settings, to use *really* more sparingly than this.

4. And avoid using *really* in this way in metaphorical contexts. The clash between the metaphor (where the words are not intended literally) and the word *really* can be a jarring and sometimes ludicrous one: *? He really went to town during his deep-sea fishing expedition, and returned with a record catch.*

To Spinoza's brilliant and closely argued work, *The Problems of Philosophy* served as an easy introduction. One can really get one's teeth into something when one tackles Spinoza's *Ethics*.

– Eric Partridge,
The Gentle Art of Lexicography

Compare LITERALLY.

5. The standard pronunciation of *really* is /ree-ə-li/; the pronunciation *?*/rair-li/ can sound affected, and causes a needless confusion with the word *rarely*; and ×/reeli/ is considered nonstandard.

6. *Real* has various uses in dialects — *It was real kind of him* (= really, very) — and slang: *? Is that guy for real* (= to be taken seriously). A recent offshoot is the slangy use of *unreal*: *?? That concert was unreal* (= very good/bad); *?? We're so tired — it's unreal* (= you wouldn't believe it). All of these uses are of course inappropriate for formal speech and writing.

realism, realistic, unrealistic *Realism* has several senses in psychology, the arts, and philosophy, usually suggesting a loyalty to everyday experience and external reality, as opposed to the abstract, the romantic, and the idealistic.

Realistic is the adjective: the negative, in these specialised contexts, is usually *nonrealistic*.

By a slight extension, *realistic* is used in general contexts to suggest a down-to-earth no-nonsense view of the world, and *unrealistic* to suggest a pipe dream. Unfortunately, the words have now become buzzwords, debased by journalists, politicians, and trade-union spokesmen into mere indicators of approval or disapproval. When two people disagree, you can be sure that each considers his own policy *realistic* and the rival policy *unrealistic*. What is really meant is that his own policy is *good, sensible, practical*, or the like, and the rival policy *bad, imprudent, stupid, unworkable*, or the like.

The words are so overused now, are trotted out so automatically in interviews and speeches, that a careful user of English raises an eyebrow whenever he hears them, suspecting that the speaker is ranting rather than thinking. Take care not to use the words unthinkingly in this way: if you mean 'possible', say *possible* rather than *realistic*; if you mean 'common sense' or 'cooperation', try not to say *realism* instead; if you mean 'risky' or 'difficult to implement' or 'unacceptable', say what you mean rather than saying *unrealistic*.

reason **1.** The correct construction is *The reason is that* ... A common error, particularly in long sentences, is to use the construction × *The reason is because* ...

× The reason for the slow decline in the value of the pound against the dollar is because American interest rates are being kept needlessly and artificially high.

× The reason why 'South' *seems* such a wonderful word is because we had the word 'North' to begin with.

– Thomas Wolfe (U.S.),
The Web and the Rock

× Most people don't make the unspoken assumption that the only reason you are tearing into them is because you think they and their notions are worth saving. They tend to assume you are being rude on purpose.

– Lord Vaizey,
'Words', BBC Radio 3

There is an unacceptable mix of constructions here: on the one hand, *The reason ... is that*; on the other *The pound is declining ... because* ... Similarly, × *The reason is owing to/thanks to ...*, × *The reason is by virtue of/on account of ...*, and so on. In all of these, the word *reason* already contains the idea of 'because, owing to', and to spell it out again is not to give emphasis but to create a tautology.

The same criticism applies to the construction *Why ... because*: × *Why the pound is declining is because ...* Again, use *that* rather than because.

2. Another construction — more widespread and less obviously objectionable — is *? The reason why ...*

? The reason why the pound is declining in value against the dollar is that American interest rates are being kept so high.

? Then there is the critical matter of ... that indefinable 'bond' which is wayward, elusive and the reason why one child, sometimes for no apparent reason, will become a favourite.
— Judy Froshaug, *The Times*

Purists regard this structure as rather dubious too, however: again it is slightly redundant — the word *reason* already suggests the notion of 'why'. (Tennyson's lines are a different case — *? Their's not to reason why, Their's but to do and die*: here *reason* is being used not as a noun but as a verb, meaning 'to consider or question', and is quite acceptably followed by *why*.)

Many careful speakers and writers prefer to use *that* or *for* in the place of *why* here: *The reason that the pound is declining in value is that ...* or *The reason for the pound's decline in value is that ...* Nevertheless, idiom seems to be welcoming *? the reason why* into standard English just as it allows the equally redundant phrases *the place where* and *the time when*. It is just a matter of time before *? the reason why* acquires the same full acceptability.

rebound, redound *To redound* means primarily 'to have an effect or consequence; contribute', and occurs especially in such idioms as *redound to one's advantage*. In such contexts, it is sometimes wrongly replaced by *rebound*. But *redound* has developed a second meaning, 'to return or recoil', which is very close to that of *rebound*:

The Mayor's insistence on harsh new penalties for traffic offences redounded/ rebounded on his own head, when he himself was heavily fined for speeding.

Redound goes back to the Latin verb *redundare*, 'to overflow', from the noun *unda*, 'a wave'. (This meaning survives partially in another derivative, the adjective *redundant*, which means

'superfluous').

To rebound means either 'to bounce back' or 'to recoil and do harm', and goes back through the French *rebondir*, 'to bounce or resound', further back through Latin to the Greek *bombos*, 'a buzz'. The English verb to *resound* (from the Latin *resonare*) is therefore doubly easy to confuse with *rebound* in turn. A noise which *rebounds* (off the walls) may also *resound*. By extension, *to resound* has come also to mean 'to be extolled or become celebrated': *His success resounded through Paris*. Here *rebound* would, of course, be inappropriate.

In the following quotation, *to rebound* is used simply in the sense 'to bounce back':

There can be no doubt that in 1980 and 1981 British industry earned very low profits even by its own previous standards. But there can also be no doubt that in the last three years corporate profits have rebounded vigorously. Indeed, company finances at present are in excellent shape.
— Tim Congdon, *The Times*

And here, *to rebound* is used to mean 'to recoil and do harm':

But I am convinced that all the talk about sexual equality and women's liberation has rebounded on women. It is not the men who run the risk, it is the women, and they should do more to protect themselves.
— Dr Robert Yule, quoted in *The Times*

reciprocal See MUTUAL.

recount, re-count In this pair of words, as in many other such pairs, a hyphen makes all the difference to meaning and pronunciation. *Re-count*, /**ree-kownt**/, with a hyphen means, as a verb, 'to count again', and as a noun, 'a further count': *to re-count the votes*; *demanded a re-count*. *To recount*, /ri-**kownt**/, means 'to narrate': *recounted his adventures to the spellbound children*. Take care not to use the wrong word inadvertently through the incorrect inclusion or omission of the hyphen.

The two words in fact go back to a common source in Old French, *re-*, 'again' + *conter* or *compter*, which meant both 'to count' and 'to narrate' (and which goes back in turn to the Latin *computare*, 'to think or calculate together' — whence our words *compute* and *computer*).

Interestingly enough, the common word *tell*, a synonym of *recount*, also used to mean 'to count' as well as 'to narrate': the idea survives in the word *teller* — as in a *bank teller,* or *a teller* who counts votes in a legislative assembly — and also in the expression *to tell one's beads.*

recourse See RESOURCE.

recrudescence This noun is widely used today in a neutral or even favourable tone, much like *revival* or *rekindling* or *renascence* or *renewal*: *? The remarkable recrudescence of British chess is admirably borne out by last year's second place in the world men's team championship.* In the past, the word was restricted to undesirable outbreaks: people spoke of the recrudescence of a disease or danger or criminal tendency. The same was true of the verb *recrudesce* — pronounced /ree-krōō-**dess**, reckrōō-/ — meaning 'to break out anew after a dormant or inactive period'. It comes from the Latin *recrudescere*, from *re-*, 'again' + *crudescere*, 'to get worse', from *crudus*, 'harsh, raw', and suggested a reopened wound or chafed flesh. The sense of an *unpleasant* revival is clear in the word's origin, and purists are alarmed to see how the sense of *recrudesce* and *recrudescence* has been weakened or neutralised or improved.

The linguistic process of 'amelioration', or 'elevation', is both common and natural, it is true: the word *shrewd*, for example, used to mean 'mischievous, ill-tempered, or dangerous' (like *shrewish*) but slowly, through amelioration, came to acquire its modern favourable tone. (The opposite process — 'deterioration', or 'pejoration' — can be illustrated by the similar word *crafty*, which used to mean 'wise or knowledgeable', but now has a slightly negative tone.) But such changes in the meaning or tone of a word are conceded only when the process is a very gradual one. Those who observe the change during their own lifetime are inclined to oppose it, and it can be unwise to go against their wishes in such matters. In a generation or two, the weakened sense of *recrudesce* or *recrudescence* will probably be accepted unhesitatingly by even the most careful of speakers, but its time has not quite yet arrived.

redound See REBOUND.

redundant Until fairly recently *redundant* was quite restricted in its use. It means 'more than is necessary or natural'. (In its origins it has the idea of overflowing: the Latin roots are *re-*, *red-*, 'back, backwards' + *undare*, 'to overflow', from *unda*, 'a wave'.) *Redundant* used to apply mainly to a particular word in a sentence or phrase that was superfluous and produced a tautology. In the sentence *She was also the winner of the second race too*, either the word *also* or the word *too* is redundant, as the two words here cover a single meaning. *Redundant* is used in economic contexts too, of things that are no longer serviceable:

I had retired from the bank two years before with an adequate pension and a silver handshake. There had been a takeover by the Westminster and my branch was considered redundant.
— Graham Greene, *Travels With My Aunt*

With the increase of unemployment in Britain, *redundant* came to be used of a worker who becomes unemployed because his job has been eliminated — perhaps through reduction of staffing or the closure of a factory: *Because of the decrease in export orders, the company has made 100 warehousemen redundant.* This usage is restricted to British English: to North Americans it sounds distinctly odd.

The modern sense has now become more general, and the word *redundant* is developing into a vogue word — used in the place of *superfluous*, *unnecessary*, or even *irrelevant*: *? Now that the children have left home three of the bedrooms in the house are redundant.*

See also TAUTOLOGY.

refer The use of *refer back* to mean 'to direct to a source of information' has attracted much criticism, as *back* is unnecessary in such cases: ✗ *I referred her back to a recently published work on the subject. Back* should be used only when a second act of referring is involved: *I referred her back to the passage she had quoted earlier.*

reflexive verbs See VERBS 4.

refute This verb is widely used today in a weak sense that irritates careful users of English. The proper meaning is 'to prove (a statement, allegation, or argument) to be wrong':

She refuted the shareholders' charge by producing the company's audited accounts to confirm her own figures.

To refute can also have a human object, though it is seldom used in this way nowadays:

She refuted the shareholders by producing audited accounts to confirm her figures.

(The word *confute* might be used here as well, though it too is rare, and rather more formal than *refute*.)

The weakened sense of *refute*, still considered unacceptable, is 'to deny, oppose, reject, challenge, contradict, dispute, protest at, repudiate':

? I refute any suggestion that I've been negligent — I challenge you to give one single example of negligence.

The sense of 'proof' inherent in *refute* is clearly absent here. Any of the synonyms listed above would have been more acceptable. The following two quotations actually draw attention to their own dubious usage, by choosing the 'synonym' *challenge* or *deny* after first using *refute*:

? In this space, a fortnight ago, I sought to refute Mr Neil Kinnock's view that 'Nineteen Eighty-Four' couldn't ever happen anywhere, 'any more than anyone has ever lived in Lilliput or Brobdingnag'. Challenging that, I suggested that hundreds of millions of people, mainly in what are called 'the Socialist countries', 'live today under political conditions quite closely comparable to the essentials of Orwell's picture'.
— Conor Cruise O'Brien,
The Observer

? Many computer industry experts believe that Sinclair's plans are wildly unrealistic, an allegation Sinclair totally refutes.

He also denies that Sinclair Research has abandoned plans for a stockmarket flotation next year.
— Steve Vines, *The Observer*

The Latin source of the word, *refutare*, means 'to drive back', hence 'to disprove, demolish by argument'. It would be a pity if the word were to lose the sense of *decisive* counter-argument that seems to be its heritage. Resist the watered-down usage that is now so widespread: you can *deny* a charge without being able to *refute* it.

regard 1. *Regard,* as noun or verb, occurs in many idiomatic phrases, some of which need an additional *-s*. So: *to have regard to* (to take into account), *to have regard for* (to show consideration for), *with regard to* (concerning), and *without regard to* (without taking into account); and *as regards* (concerning), *give one's regards to* (to greet), *kind regards* (used when ending a letter).

Take care not to add the *-s* where it is inappropriate to do so, as in the commonly heard × *with regards to*.

2. One sense of the noun *regard,* 'a particular point or respect', is sometimes considered nonstandard:

? In certain regards, she is a very good choice.

Purists prefer *respect/s* to *regard/s* here, though there seems little basis for the preference.

3. Where *regard* certainly cannot match *respect,* however, is in the formation *irrespective.* The faulty formation × *irregardless,* though often heard, is quite unacceptable: it is probably a blend of *regardless* and *irrespective.*

4. Also criticised occasionally is the use of *regarding* (as well as *respecting* this time) as a preposition meaning 'about, concerning':

? I want to talk to you regarding this proposal of yours.

Certainly it should be used sparingly, but once again a blanket prohibition of it seems unjustified. (See also RE.)

5. There are a further three prepositions based on *regard* and having the same meaning of 'about, concerning': *with regard to, in regard to,* and *as regards.* Of these, only *in regard to* is ever seriously queried, sometimes being considered a less acceptable variant of *with regard to.* But all three of these compound prepositions need to be used with caution: they may sound more impressive than *about* or *in,* but they have very little advantage when it comes to the meaning or even the rhythm of a sentence. They are helpful as occasional substitutes, but the temptation to overuse them must be firmly resisted.

Perhaps their most useful role is at the beginning of a sentence, where *about* would be inappropriately brusque:

With regard to the proposal you put forward yesterday: there are one or two points I should like you to clarify.

Elsewhere, they are in danger of sounding rather affected:

? He seems to have no thoughts in regard to my proposal one way or the other.

About would be preferable here.

Sometimes these compound prepositions simply encourage lazy or sloppy wording:

? The actors were disappointed as regards the size of the audience, and the audience in turn felt that the performance was poor with regard to vitality and humour.

Far from sounding impressive, such a sentence sounds merely puffy, ponderous, and pompous — more style (and bad style too) than content.

(Still, it is perhaps preferable to saying *audience-wise* and *humour-wise*: see -WISE.) A sharper and simpler way of saying the same thing is:

> The actors were disappointed that the audience was so small, and the audience in turn felt that the performance lacked vitality and humour.

6. The verb *to regard,* meaning 'to consider in a specified way', is normally followed by an *as*; the verb *to consider* can do without the *as,* or sometimes takes *to be* instead. So:

> I regard it as (being) a brilliant but flawed masterpiece.
> I consider it (to be) a brilliant but flawed masterpiece.

An extremely common set of errors is to get these patterns mixed up: ✗ *to consider the idea as cowardly,* ✗ *to regard it to be my duty,* and so on. The omission of *as* after *to regard* occurs especially in two sets of circumstances. First, with inverted word-order:

✗ No matter how clever you may regard yourself, you'll never get the better of me.
✗ This is in fact a private road, not the public thoroughfare that you and your brother seem to regard it.

The preposition *as* (or the phrase *as being*) should be inserted after *yourself* and *it.* (Better still, use *consider* instead of *regard* in both sentences.)

Secondly, the *as* is often omitted when another *as* happens to occur in the sentence in some other role; the temptation then would be to drop the *as* of *to regard as* in order to avoid a clash or ugly repetition:

✗ I regard this masterpiece as brilliant as *Don Giovanni.*

The first *as* here belongs to the phrase *as brilliant as*; the verb *regard* has lost its own *as,* in other words, and this has to be replaced — with the following result:

? I regard this masterpiece as as brilliant as *Don Giovanni.*

Clearly this combination of two *as*'s side by side is inelegant to the point of unacceptability. But that is no excuse for simply leaving one of them out. Various solutions are possible. First, a *being* could be inserted:

> I regard this masterpiece as being as brilliant as *Don Giovanni.*

Alternatively, the sentence could be restructured,

or the verb *to regard* could be dropped in favour of the verb *to consider*:

> I regard this work as a masterpiece as brilliant as *Don Giovanni.*
> I regard this masterpiece as equal in brilliance to *Don Giovanni.*
> I consider this masterpiece as brilliant as *Don Giovanni.*

See also CONSIDER 1.

regretfully See HOPEFULLY.

reindeer, caribou The reindeer and the caribou are really one and the same animal: *Rangifer tarandus,* a large shaggy-muzzled deer living in arctic regions and, unlike other deer, having antlers in both sexes. *Reindeer* is the name given to the animal in Greenland and Northern Europe and Asia; *caribou* is the North American name. *Reindeer* comes via Middle English from Old Norse *hreindyri*: *hreinn,* 'a reindeer' + *dyr,* 'an animal'. *Caribou* is Canadian French, probably borrowed from one of the Algonquian languages of the North American Indians.

The pronunciations are /**rayn**-deer/ and /**karri**-boo/. The plurals of *reindeer* is *reindeer*; of *caribou, caribous* or collectively *caribou.*

The only other difference is that reindeers of the Old World are domesticated and used as dairy and draught-animals, while the New World caribous are not. So Father Christmas's sleigh is always drawn by *reindeer.*

See also ELK.

relation, relative, relationship The people to whom we are connected by descent, marriage, or adoption are our *relations* or *relatives*:

> At Tiflis she was handed over to a horde of her relatives and neighbours, who keened over her as if they were receiving her corpse.
> – D.M. Thomas, *The White Hotel*

> The affection in which the dolphin is held is easily explained, and the sympathy for its cousin the porpoise even more so; they look sufficiently like us to stir fellow-feeling, without the uncomfortable suspicion, which the apes generate, that they actually are our relations.
> – Bernard Levin, *The Observer*

The form *relations* would have been just as appropriate in the first of these examples, and *relatives* just as appropriate in the second. But the two forms are not always perfectly interchangeable:

we tend to speak, for some reason, of *rich* or *poor relations*, but *elderly relatives*.

The fact or degree of being connected with these people is a *relationship*:

What's the relationship between Sophie and Paul? They're first cousins, are they?

Relationship is also used of other kinds of human connection: *an uneasy relationship*; *a platonic relationship*. Since the mid-1960s *relationship* has been used as yet another euphemism for a love affair, just as *relations* is used as a euphemism for sexual intercourse.

If the connections are specified, they tend to be called *relations* instead: *business relations*; *the relations between landlord and tenant*. Here *relations* means 'dealings'. And in more abstract or nonhuman connections, *relation* is often preferred to *relationship*: *the relation between poverty and crime*.

Since *relation* has this wide range of senses, it is better to use one of the other terms if there is any danger of ambiguity. The sentence *? We have no banking relations* might mean that there are no money transactions between us, or it might mean that no uncles, aunts, or cousins of ours are bankers.

relative pronouns See PRONOUNS.

relatively, comparatively These words are now frequently used as substitutes for *fairly, somewhat,* or the like — to tone down an adjective or adverb, or blur the outlines of a statement: *? Help arrived comparatively soon*; *? This discovery was relatively recent.*

? Dr Blue, whose learning, no doubt, was infinitely inferior to his reputation, assured me it was a virus infection, and when I alluded to her comparatively recent flu, curtly said this was another bug, he had forty such cases on his hands.
    — Vladimir Nabokov, *Lolita*

Purists object to this imprecise use, pointing out that *relatively* and *comparatively* would seem to suggest some *related* element, some *comparison,* at least implicitly. It is fully idiomatic to say *Kazuo is relatively tall for a Japanese,* since there is here an implied comparison between Kazuo and a typical Japanese. From such uses, it was a short step to the careless sense of 'somewhat, fairly' — but a dubious step, and one that cannot yet be regarded as acceptable: *? Kazuo is relatively shy* is confusing because it implies a *related* element or comparison without giving any indication what

it might be. It would be far preferable if reworded as *Kazuo is fairly shy*.

The same considerations apply to *relative* and *comparative*: *? The show was a comparative success*; *? a relative lack of confidence.*

Note the spelling of *comparatively*: the third vowel is an *a,* not an *i* as in *comparison.*

renaissance, renascence Both spellings are correct, but the French version, *renaissance*, is longer-established. *Renascence* is an anglicised version, and oddly enough, often tends to look slightly affected.

With a small *r* the word can refer to any rebirth or revival, particularly a cultural revival: *a religious renascence/renaissance*. With a capital *R*, it usually refers to the flowering of European culture that began in Italy in the 14th century.

The words go back through French, Old French, and Latin to the Latin source words *re-*, 'again' + *nasci*, 'to be born'.

Renaissance can serve as an adjective — *Renaissance paintings* — but *renascence* cannot.

The usual pronunciation in British English, for either spelling, is /ri-**nay**ss'nss/. *Renaissance* can also be pronounced the French way: /**ren**nay-soNss/ or /rennə-**soN**ss/. And *renascence* can also be pronounced /ri-**nass**'nss/.

Take care not to make the common spelling mistake of doubling the first *n*.

rent See HIRE.

repellent See REPULSIVE.

repercussion This noun, particularly in its plural form, has become a fashionable and grand-sounding synonym of *result* or *consequence*: *?? It is still too early to assess the repercussions of the latest round of peace talks.* This has been criticised as a needlessly and unacceptably loose use of the term. Bear in mind its origins: the word is related to *percussion*, its Latin roots being *re-* 'again, back' + *per-*, 'intensely' + *quatere*, 'to strike' — the *repercussion* of a rifle is, strictly speaking, its recoil.

A reasonable development of the word was the sense of 'a questionable or undesirable effect or influence': *The repercussions of the breakdown in the peace talks are too horrible to contemplate.* But used in a neutral or favourable way, as in the earlier example, *repercussions* seems to contribute nothing, other than a certain pretentiousness, that any of the established terms *result, effect, influence, upshot,* and *outcome* cannot rise to.

repertoire, repertory A *repertoire* is the stock of songs, music, plays, operas, or the like that a player or company is ready to perform. By extension, it refers to the range of accomplishments of a person or group: *Her repertoire of ideas is vast — she comes up with a new project every day.*

Although *repertory* is used in these ways too, its traditional meaning is 'a storehouse, or a stock of things': *a repertory of bygone fashions.* Its commonest use today is as an adjective in the phrases *a repertory theatre* or *a repertory company* (often contracted to *rep*) — one presenting a *repertoire* of plays for a limited season.

repetitious, repetitive These adjectives are both related to *repetition*; but *repetitious* tends to be more derogatory, suggesting needless or tedious repetition, whereas *repetitive* tends to be neutral, referring for example to work on an assembly line, without necessarily criticising it.

In the following quotation, *repetitive* would have been a better choice than *repetitious*:

? But now she giggled, partly with relief that the quiet repetitious tap-tap at the door which had eventually wakened her, was only Freddy's.

— Muriel Spark,
The Mandelbaum Gate

And *repetitious* would be better than *repetitive* in the examples below:

? Members of the circle know what to expect and, in any case, the jokes soon become repetitive, follow a pattern and become boring.

— George Mikes,
English Humour for Beginners

? I still think that the idea of 'Mozart in Palm Springs' is a good one, and no doubt I'm hopelessly literal minded, but an hour and a half of ambiguous tooting, repetitive, semi-audible speech and a few period costumes didn't seem to take it very far.

— Dave Gelly, *The Observer*

replace See SUBSTITUTE.

repulsive, repellent *Repulsive* is much the more forceful of these two adjectives. Both of them mean 'causing aversion or great dislike, disgusting, offensive' (also 'able or tending to drive off'), but *repulsive* conjures up an image of physical recoiling, whereas *repellent* suggests simply keeping your distance. Many nouns can be used with either adjective: *a repellent/repulsive young man*; *repellent/repulsive ideas*, and so on. But where a sense of horror is present, the likelier choice is *repulsive*: *a repulsive grimace, a repulsive disfigurement, a repulsive stench.*

I had preserved in the alcohol of a clouded memory the toad of a face. In the course of a few glimpses, I had noticed its slight resemblance to a cheery and rather repulsive wine dealer, a relative of mine in Switzerland. With his dumbbells and stinking tricot, and fat hairy arms, and bald patch, and pig-faced servant-concubine, he was on the whole a harmless old rascal.

— Vladimir Nabokov, *Lolita*

Instead of being the Good Losers the British ought to become the Nasty Winners; instead of sophisticated self-mockery they ought to learn repulsive competitiveness; instead of the endearing understatement they must get into the habit of wild exaggeration; instead of the enchanting ability of laughing at themselves they ought to learn taking themselves seriously.

— George Mikes,
English Humour for Beginners

A straight sermon shows what dreadful novels he could have written. One sees really how very simple his ideas are, and rather repellent to me as I am. I once wrote that Christianity was the greatest disaster ever to befall the West, so you can see how happy I am with these sermons.

— Gore Vidal (U.S.),
BBC Radio 3

Both words are derived from the Latin *re-* + *pellere*, 'to drive back'.

The adjective *repugnant*, often preferred to *repellent* and *repulsive*, comes from the Latin *re-* + *pugnare*, 'to fight back, or fight against'. It is perhaps slightly milder than *repellent* and *repulsive*, and suggests a rather more intellectual dislike. Things that are against your principles, tastes, or values are sometimes said to be *repugnant* to you.

The suggestion that the 'shrine' was an 'independent' republic outside the jurisdiction of Nigeria was repugnant to the authorities, and they also suspected that Kalakuta was a centre for marijuana.

— Cameron Duodu, *The Observer*

And Barbara fumed against Ruth's totally womanly solicitude combined with her totally repugnant human theories, and against the total misunderstanding.

> – Muriel Spark,
> *The Mandelbaum Gate*

Repugnant has the additional sense, little used nowadays, of 'inconsistent or contradictory'. *Repellent* has the further sense of 'impervious or resistant' to a specified substance: *a water-repellent fabric*. And *repulsive* has a specialised sense in physics, 'opposite in direction': *a repulsive force*.

The related verbs are *repugn*, *repel*, and *repulse*. *To repugn* (pronounced /ri-**pewn**/) means 'to oppose, to be opposed'. It is little used today. *To repulse* is once again stronger than *to repel*: *We repelled the invasion* sounds distinctly less of a triumph than *We repulsed the invasion*: in the first case, we simply withstood the invaders, warded them off; in the second case, we drove them back, defeated them. In personal relations, you would be *repelled* by someone if you found him overbearing, conceited, or generally unlikeable. You would be *repulsed* by him only if he actively rebuffed you or rejected your offers. The chairman can *repulse* you and *repel* you, but his ideas or policies (or photographs) can only *repel* you; they cannot *repulse* you (though you might find them *repulsive*). *To repulse*, in other words, cannot really be used in the same metaphorical way as *to repel* can, and it is less versatile than its adjective *repulsive*.

Note finally that *repellent* and *repulse* can both be used as nouns — *an insect repellent*; *a rude repulse of my offer* — and that the spelling *repellent*, for both noun and adjective senses, is far more common than, and far preferable to, the spelling *repellant*.

request As a noun, *request* can be followed by *for*: *Her request for a rise was turned down*. As a verb *request* has two possible constructions: you can request something *of* or *from* somebody, or you can request somebody *to* do something: *They requested help of/from the authorities*; *They requested the authorities to help them*. The verb (unlike *to ask*) cannot usually take *for* in correct usage: × *They requested the authorities for help*; × *They requested for the authorities to help them*. A *for* is permissible, however, when the sentence is of this pattern: *What they requested was for the authorities to help them*.

requirement, requisite, requisition A *requirement* is essentially a need or a condition, a *requisite* is the thing that is needed, and a *requisi-*tion is principally an order to obtain a thing that is needed. *Requirement* is often used in the plural, with almost no change in meaning, in the sense of 'a need' — *the government's budget requirements*; *This should meet your requirements* — or in the sense of 'a condition': *Do you meet the requirements for exemption from duty?*; *He failed to fulfil the requirements for college entrance*.

Requirement is also used in the sense of 'the thing needed', and can often be used in the place of *requisite*: *Intelligence is not the only requirement/requisite for the appreciation of poetry — concentration and imagination are also necessary*.

> He raises himself above every other midfield player in Britain because he meets so many of the basic requirements of his position so superlatively well, because he competes with such wonderfully sustained vigour, has an innate understanding of the geometry of the game that keeps him constantly aware of where the killing positions are and possesses the devastating quickness to arrive in those spaces at the deadliest moment.
>
> – Hugh McIlvanney, *The Observer*

However, when 'the thing needed' is a physical object (rather than an abstract quality such as imagination), then *requisite* is definitely preferable: *hairbrush, soap, and other toilet requisites*. Note that *requisite* can also be used as an adjective: *hairbrush, soap, and other requisite articles*. The pronunciation of *requisite* is /**rek**wizit/.

Requisition, finally, may sometimes be used to mean 'a thing needed, a necessity', just as *requisite* and *requirement* do. But it more commonly refers to a written claim or request, such as a demand issued by a military unit to a village to hand over food supplies, or a formal request by one government to another for the extradition of a criminal.

> Mitchell failed to date his letters; failed to submit the draft contract until one month *after* sending the office copy entries; proposed exchange four days after the draft contract had been received; and failed to reply to requisitions.
>
> – PHS, *The Times*

Note that *requisition* can also be used as a verb: *requisitioned food supplies from the village*; *requisitioned the village for food supplies*.

See also ACQUIREMENT; PRE-REQUISITE.

resin, rosin *Resin* is the more general term. *Resins* are substances exuded by trees, typically yellow or brown and translucent, sticky when soft, and shiny and brittle when hard. There are many different kinds, with a wide range of industrial applications including the manufacture of varnish and adhesives. The word *resin* is now also applied to synthetic substances, such as epoxy, that resemble natural resins.

The form *rosin* is a medieval variant of *resin,* but the word has a more restricted meaning today. *Rosin* is a particular type of resin, made by removing the turpentine from pine-tree resin. Its chemical derivatives are used as waterproof sealants, and for rubbing on the bows of stringed instruments to create suitable friction between them and the strings.

resound   See REBOUND.

resource, recourse, resort   There is a danger of misusing one or other of these nouns, since they can all suggest turning for help. *Resource* and *resort*, of course, have several other senses as well, as in these phrases: *mineral resources, mental resources, financial resources, all available resources, a woman of cunning and resource* (or *resourcefulness*); *a popular place of resort, a holiday resort.*

Recourse, however, is limited (except for a technical legal use) to the following two senses: first, 'turning to some source for help; applying to a person or thing for aid or security' — *had recourse to the courts*; and then, by extension, 'the person or thing from whom such help is expected': *Her only recourse was the police.*

> In applying the law to industrial disputes, a fine judgment is required. Too eager a rush to the courts may provoke solidarity among the strikers; too delayed a recourse to law may encourage public contempt for its apparent irrelevance.
> — leading article, *Daily Telegraph*

Resort has also these two senses, and *resource* has, more or less, the second of these senses, 'something that can be used for help or support', or perhaps 'an action or measure adopted when in difficulties': *My usual resource is simply running away.*

The danger is not so much of using the words in an incorrect sense, as of using the words in the wrong idioms. The commonest correct forms are these: *to have recourse to, without recourse to*; *a simple resource, as a last resource* or *resort*; *in the last resort*, and, using *resort* as a verb, *to resort to* and *without resorting to*. So: *She*

resorted to tears; *Keep your judo-skills as a last resource*; *In the last resort, you can always sue him*; *I hope to pay you back without resorting to a bridging loan from the bank.*

The words' origins are these: *resort* derives from the Old French verb *resortir*, 'to go out again, or to go back'; *resource* goes back through Old French to the Latin verb *resurgere*, 'to rise again, or to surge back'; *recourse* goes back through Old French to the Latin *recurrere*, 'to run again, or to run back'.

respective, respectively   These are helpful words in their place, but are all too often used needlessly (and occasionally incorrectly) in an effort to sound impressive.

The words are properly used when referring to people or things considered individually and (where applicable) in the order mentioned:

> After dinner, he invited his three daughters into his study to discuss their respective school reports with him.

The use of *respective* here indicates that each daughter was expected to discuss her own report alone; without *respective,* the sentence might suggest that each girl was being invited to discuss all three reports.

> Clubhouses for boys and girls are situated in the camp's northeast and southeast corners respectively.

Without *respectively* to guide the reader here, the sentence would probably have been understood as meaning that the two clubhouses were much the same — each intended for children of either sex (as distinct from adults). The presence of *respectively* is doubly informative: first, it makes clear that one clubhouse is for boys only, and the other is for girls only; secondly, it explains which is which.

A similar example, though a slightly more controversial one:

> ? The Historical Society's three annual bursaries were last night awarded to Estelle Rory, Murray Ernst, and Simon Peltiar, to help them pursue their research into ancient Greek warfare, the development of plainsong, and Victorian childrearing practices respectively.

Respectively again serves two functions here: first, it indicates that each student is investigating only one of the topics mentioned, not two or all three; secondly, it correlates the two lists, explicitly assigning the first-mentioned topic to the first-mentioned student, the second to the second, and so on.

It might be felt, however, that the use of *respectively* here betrays excessive cautiousness. After all, it is virtually unthinkable that any one student might be researching more than one of the three very different subjects; and it is most unlikely that any reader would assume that the two lists were in different sequences.

Conversely, it might be felt that *respectively* is a lazy device of the writer's, invoked so as to force the reader to do the work of matching the two lists — work that the writer, had he been more diligent, would have done himself, along the following lines perhaps:

> The Historical Society's three annual bursaries were last night awarded to three students to help them pursue their research: Estelle Rory (ancient Greek warfare), Murray Ernst (the development of plainsong), and Simon Peltiar (Victorian childrearing practices).

Worded in this way, the announcement saves the reader the trouble of glancing back and forth three times to identify each student's area of research.

Here is an example of *respectively* where caution has been taken to ridiculous limits:

?? The Professor of French Literature, the Dean of the Dental School, and the Chairman of the Law Faculty have all raised their respective departments from modest academic backwaters into internationally acclaimed centres of research during the past ten years.

Why *their respective departments*? — it is hardly likely that the Professor of French Literature has made a major contribution to the world of dentistry. If any adjective were needed here at all, *various* would be far more appropriate.

Other words or phrases that *respective* or *respectively* sometimes mistakenly replace are *both* and *each other's*.

× He won medals in the 100 metres and the long jump respectively.
× The New Republic Party and the New Initiative Party respectively have issued statements dissociating themselves from the racist policy-document published by the Phalange.

Respectively here is saying no more than *both,* and saying it wrongly. Use *both* instead, though in a different position in the sentence.

× The All Blacks and the Wallabies are hoping to take advantage of their respective weaknesses in defence.

What this literally means (bearing in mind that *respective* implies staying in the same sequence) is that the All Blacks are hoping to take advantage of the All Blacks' weaknesses, and the Wallabies are hoping to take advantage of the Wallabies' weaknesses! Presumably this is just the opposite of the intended meaning: instead of *their respective weaknesses,* say *each other's weaknesses,* and the correct meaning emerges.

Sometimes *respective* or *respectively* seems to be quite redundant, not simply a mistaken substitute for some more appropriate adjective or adverb:

× Each of the prizewinners received his respective trophy last night directly from the hands of the League chairman.

There seems to be no alternative adjective here: *respective* should simply be omitted. One warning sign in that example was that it was worded in the singular: *respective* and *respectively* almost always occur in association with plural subjects, verbs, possessive forms, and objects.

● *Recommendation* Always stop and think before using *respective/ly*. All too often, the word will prove to be no more than a redundant ornament, contributing nothing to the sense of the sentence containing it. If it can be omitted without affecting the meaning, then it should be omitted. It is not simply an affectation — it can be a dangerous affectation. The word is sometimes used quite wrongly as a supposed synonym of *various* or *both* or *each other's*; so far from sounding impressive, then, it falls doubly flat.

Reserve *respectively* for contexts where it does genuinely serve to disentangle the meaning or save a sentence from ambiguity.

See also FORMER.

restive *Restive* would seem to be a convenient fusion of *restful* and *restorative*: in fact, its meaning is almost the very opposite, much closer to that of *restless*. However, there is a distinction between these two words as well. Strictly speaking, *restive* means 'resistant to control or discipline; unruly; disobedient'.

> Mark's admission that he was used by Cementation is expected to increase pressure dramatically on Mrs Thatcher from restive colleagues for her to now simply explain her own role in the affair.
> – *The Observer*

Restless means broadly 'without quiet or rest'; more specifically, 'deprived of rest', and hence 'unsettled, agitated, uneasy'. A horse loose in a field could be *restless* and fidgety; but a *restive* horse is one defying attempts to control it.

In some contexts, the ideas of restlessness and resistance to control come very close, so a confusion is not surprising. In the sentence *Susie was restive/restless and would not behave in class*, the word *restive* might be intended if her disobedience is being stressed, and *restless* if the meaning intended is 'fidgety, unsettled'. But to say *?? She was restive and bored and paced about her empty room* would be to force the sense of *restive* beyond what is acceptable. So too, probably, in the following quotations:

> *?* 'I will tell you now what he liked *best* in the house', said Nanda Kaul, lowering her eyes on Raka who was growing restive, finding this luncheon too tiresomely drawn out.
> — Anita Desai,
> *Fire on the Mountain*

> *??* Later, when I replayed the tape of this interview, Ballard's voice was eerily underscored by two distinct sound-effects: the premonitory surge of airliners as they banked for Heathrow; and the poppings and squawkings of Ballard's swivel chair. He writhed as he talked, partly through natural restiveness, and partly through the difficulty of recalling these times. The memories cannot be assimilated, or purged.
> — Martin Amis, *The Observer*

Surely *restlessness* was the word intended here. In origin, *restive* is quite unrelated to *restless*. *Restive* goes back through the Old French *restif*, 'unwilling to move, resistant to moving, stationary' (the opposite of *restless*!) to the Latin verb *restare* 'to keep back', from *re-*, 'back' + *stare*, 'to stand'. *Restless*, on the other hand, like *restful*, comes from pure Old English roots: *reste* and *leas*.

restrictive and nonrestrictive clauses 1. These are two kinds of *relative clause*, doing the work of an adjective in a sentence. (See CLAUSE.)

A relative clause may simply give some information about the noun it relates to; or it may actually define that noun — make it definite, restrict it, set it apart from all other nouns.

An example of the second kind is found in the sentence *The family that prays together stays together*. In this sentence the relative clause *that prays together* is known as *a defining clause* or

a restrictive clause, since it defines or restricts the type of family being discussed. It is obviously an essential part of the meaning, and cannot be left out of the sentence.

An example of the first kind of relative clause, the kind that simply gives some information about the noun, occurs in the sentence *The family, which is the basic unit of human society, is losing its appeal.* The relative clause here, *which is the basic unit of human society,* is known as *a nondefining clause* or *a nonrestrictive clause*: it gives some information about the family, but does not define or restrict the type of family being discussed. It is an incidental rather than an essential part of the sentence: it could be enclosed in brackets, or even left out altogether, without affecting the meaning of the sentence too drastically.

Here are the two model sentences again:

a. *restrictive clause*: The family that/which prays together stays together.
b. *nonrestrictive clause*: The family, which is the basic unit of human society, is losing its appeal.

There are two important differences to note here. First, the nonrestrictive clause is enclosed within commas (or by pauses in speech), whereas the restrictive clause usually has no commas (or pauses) either side of it. The commas in sentence *b.* indicate that the nonrestrictive clause is incidental (even optional or dispensable) — to be considered separately from the noun *family* that it relates to. The absence of commas in sentence *a.* indicates that the restrictive clause is an inherent part of the sentence's meaning, and crucially affects (restricts, defines) the sense of the noun *family* that it relates to. (Of course, a restrictive clause may accidentally find itself next to a comma that is present for some other reason, as in *The family that prays together, he said, stays together*, or in *I'm looking for something, not too expensive, I hope, that I can wear at Ladies' Day*.)

The second difference between the two model sentences is that the restrictive clause in sentence *a.* is introduced by the relative pronoun *that* (or *which*), whereas the nonrestrictive clause in sentence *b.* is introduced by the relative pronoun *which*. *That* cannot usually be used to introduce a nonrestrictive clause. *Which, Who, Whom, Whose*, and so on, can be used to introduce restrictive and nonrestrictive clauses.

A restrictive clause can often do without any pronoun to introduce it: *The man I love is six feet tall*. The condition is that the subject of the restrictive clause (*I*, in this example) is not the subject of the sentence (*The man*). Note, however, that nonrestrictive clauses cannot usually occur without a pronoun of some kind: *David, whom I love, is six feet tall.*

Note the difference between the following two sentences:

My brother who lives in Perth is a dentist.
My brother, who lives in Perth, is a dentist.

In the first of these, which has a restrictive clause, the implication is that I have more brothers than one, and that I am here identifying or defining the one I mean. In the second example, the implication is that I have only one brother. The word *father* could replace *brother* in the second example, but not in the first.

The distinction between restrictive and nonrestrictive clauses may be brought out most clearly by two examples of what not to do. In the first, an important comma has been omitted, turning what was presumably intended as a nonrestrictive clause into a restrictive one:

× His pride and pleasure come in understated comedy — like *California Suite*, in which he played the antique-dealer husband of Maggie Smith who turns out to be a closet gay.
– Alexander Walker, *High Life*

The absence of a comma before *who* here makes it sound as if Maggie Smith has had several antique-dealer husbands, the one in question happening to be homosexual. (The sentence is poorly constructed too: the *who*-clause could be read as referring to *Maggie Smith*, whereas it really refers to *husband*. Ideally the sentence should read: ... *in which he played Maggie Smith's antique-dealer husband, who turns out to be a closet gay.*)

In this second example now, a pair of unwanted commas has turned a restrictive clause into a nonrestrictive one:

× The Vatican newspaper, *Osservatore Romano*, yesterday condemned horoscopes and said Roman Catholics, who believe that stars can predict the future, commit religious deviation.
– *The Times*

This sounds as if all Roman Catholics commit religious deviation, and that they all, incidentally, believe in astrology.

2. The terms *restrictive* and *nonrestrictive* are almost always used in connection with relative clauses, of the kind just discussed. But the terms can apply to other constructions — notably to 'appositional' words, phrases, and clauses. (*Apposition* is the construction in which one

noun, or noun phrase or clause, is placed after another to explain it, and has the same grammatical function in the sentence.)

In the following two sentences, the appositional phrase *the actor* is restrictive in one case and nonrestrictive in the next:

James Caan the actor is a distant relative of mine.
James Caan, the actor, is a distant relative of mine.

In the second of these examples, *the actor* is more or less incidental to the sense of the sentence. In the first, it is an essential explanation of the identity of *James Caan*, the subject of the sentence.

Now compare the following three sentences:

The fact, which we discussed yesterday, is irrelevant.
The fact (that/which) we discussed yesterday is irrelevant.
The fact that we discussed it yesterday is irrelevant.

The first example has a relative clause — a nonrestrictive clause that is introduced by *which* (not by *that*). The second example has a relative clause — a restrictive clause that can be introduced by *that* or *which* (or by nothing at all). The third example has an appositional clause — a restrictive clause that is introduced by *that* (not by *which*). The *that* here has a different grammatical function, however: it is a conjunction now rather than a relative pronoun. So too in the following example, which (in apparent contravention of the rule) has *that* introducing a nonrestrictive clause:

Parkinson's law, that work expands to fill the time available, needs some qualification.

Do remember that *that* is a conjunction here, not a relative pronoun, and that the clause is appositional, not relative. If there were more than one *Parkinson's law* the sentence might read: *Parkinson's law that work expands ...* — without the commas this time. The *that* is still a conjunction, the clause is still appositional, but it is now restrictive rather than nonrestrictive.

See also THAT; WHICH; WHO.

result A result can be good or bad: the word on its own usually gives no indication of which of the two is implied or intended.

Recently, however, a new sense of *result* has crept into British English (especially with reference to sport) — 'a successful or decisive result'. A football manager might complain: *? I* *was counting on a result, but all we could manage was a draw.* This extended use of the word is best restricted to informal contexts.

revenge, vengeance These two nouns have different overtones today. *Vengeance* suggests large-scale retribution for an original offence or injury that was probably serious and unprovoked: *Vengeance is mine, saith the Lord.*

> Before her eyes, one cropped tentacle curled sideways and down, as if in the throes of death. A primitive joy went through her, a sense of vengeance, of a wrong righted.
> – Patricia Highsmith (U.S.),
> *Slowly, Slowly in the Wind*

Revenge, on the other hand, sometimes suggests retaliation for an injury or provocation that was possibly trivial or even imaginary; and the word always carries a strong sense of malice:

> Revenge is an act which you want to commit when you are powerless and because you are powerless: as soon as the sense of impotence is removed, the desire evaporates also.
> – George Orwell, 'Revenge is Sour'

> So, halfway across the Atlantic, he turned to his police escort and said: 'When we arrive, there are a couple of things I'd like to talk to you about.' For the first time, a Mafia boss had decided to wreak his revenge on his enemies legally.
> – Robin Lustig, *The Observer*

The idiom *with a vengeance* means 'forcibly or furiously' or 'excessively' or 'emphatically, intensely':

> There were a number of long hard struggles and quite a number of sudden deaths and brevities of the sweet and twenty nature. This was chess for everyman, with a vengeance.
> – Harry Golombek, *The Times*

Associated with the noun *vengeance* is the verb *to avenge* (and the adjective *vengeful*); associated with the noun *revenge* is the verb *to revenge* (and the adjective *revengeful*). There is a corresponding difference — though a very slight one — in the feel of the two verbs. *To avenge* is more objective, and suggests a just motive and the righting of wrongs; *to revenge oneself* is more dubious, and suggests a vindictive motive and the settling of scores.

As this passage moves in and out of high seriousness, it uses the grandiose words *vengeance* and *avenged*, and the less grand word *revenge*:

Gage has had no choice but to taste his dish of revenge late in life. He was a child when his mother died, and he was taken straight to America as a result of her sacrifice. By the time he was of age to consider, let alone savour the matter, he was Greek only by birth. Then there was the question — would his mother have wanted vengeance? Would she, like Antigone, have accepted death as the price of her defiance, or would she, like Hecuba, have shrieked for her shade to be avenged?
> – Christopher Hitchens,
> *The Literary Review*

The primary difference today between the two verbs, however, is not so much in meaning as in grammatical usage. *To revenge* is typically used reflexively; that is, in the pattern *to revenge oneself*: *They revenged themselves on workmates who had reported them for pilfering.*

> And he takes Emma away from the family home in an affluent Houston suburb to live the miserable existence of a minor academic in the middle-west.
> To revenge herself on the philandering Flap, Emma takes up with an unhappy bank clerk (John Lithgow) in darkest Iowa.
> – Philip French, *The Observer*

The form ✗ *to avenge oneself* is not really standard: the proper forms are *to be avenged* or *to avenge*:

> ✗ To her surprise, she heard herself enumerating aloud for Kurtz — or was it for Joseph? — her rows and rows of early lovers and all the stupid reasons she had invented for going to bed with them ... Men to prove her power, men to avenge herself against other men, or against other women.
> – John le Carré,
> *The Little Drummer Girl*

> Those who held that there would have been little or no rioting if it hadn't been for the rape and the steps taken to avenge it believed that the men the Deputy Commissioner had ordered to be arrested on the morning of the 9th August were the right ones to have arrested.
> – Paul Scott,
> *The Jewel in the Crown*

To avenge can be used with either personal or nonpersonal objects: *Orestes avenged his murdered father Agamemnon; Orestes avenged the murder of his father Agamemnon.* And having done so, he *was avenged* at last. This form *to be avenged* is perhaps the commonest.

> You are not permitted to kill a woman who has wronged you, but nothing forbids you to reflect that she is growing older every minute. You are avenged 1440 times a day.
> — Ambrose Bierce (U.S.),
> *Epigrams*

In principle, the adjective *revengeful* corresponds to *revenge*, and *vengeful* to *vengeance*. In practice, however, the distinction between the adjectives is observed even less than that between the nouns — *vengeful*, as the commoner term, tends to be used arbitrarily to refer to justified or unjustified reprisals:

> There was the famous dispatch of a Mme Lacour in Arles, southern France, at the close of last century. An unidentified bearded six-footer, who, it was later conjectured, had been the lady's secret lover, walked up to her in a crowded street, soon after her marriage to Colonel Lacour, and mortally stabbed her in the back ... By a miraculous and beautiful coincidence ... a cranky Italian in the house nearest to the scene set off by accident some kind of explosive he was tinkering with ... The explosion hurt no one (except that it knocked out the game Colonel Lacour); but one lady's vengeful lover ran when the others ran — and lived happily ever after.
> — Vladimir Nabokov, *Lolita*

In the following quotation, however, the author has carefully chosen *revengeful*, as more suited to a sense of vindictiveness:

> Social classes are on the move and classes on the move are always bloody awful: desperate, bitter and paranoid if they move downwards, power-hungry, gloating, revengeful and self-conscious if they move upwards.
> — George Mikes,
> *English Humour for Beginners*

reverent, reverential, reverend 1. *Reverent* and *reverential* both mean 'showing reverence', but *reverent* implies more clearly that the reverence is deserved and genuinely felt. Compare the two following extracts:

> In the twilight room we dedicated a grateful, reverent moment to Arthur's memory.
> — Christopher Isherwood,
> *Mr Norris Changes Trains*

> When he bent that famous craggy face and strong jaw down from its natural elevation to the level of ordinary human beings it was not to advance any opinions or tell any anecdotes of his own. It was purely to bring his ear reverentially into line with the mouth of whomever was speaking.
> — Michael Frayn,
> *Towards the End of the Morning*

(Note that *whomever* is an incorrect 'improvement' of *whoever* here: see WHO.)

By contrast, *reverend* means 'deserving reverence': *a saintly and reverend old man*. The word is now mostly limited to being used as a title for clergymen below the rank of dean.

2. *Reverend*, when used of clergymen, is often abbreviated to *Rev.* or sometimes *Revd.* The title should correctly be used in combination with a first name or an initial, or with Mr or Dr: *(The) Rev. P. Jones*; *(The) Rev. Peter Jones*; *(The) Rev. Mr/Dr Jones*. It is becoming common to write simply *Rev. Jones* and to speak of *Reverend Jones*, perhaps by analogy with *Father Jones* for a Catholic priest:

?? A diary of a present-day Parson Woodforde or Rev. Kilvert would therefore have to wait for a period. One is I hope, being written somewhere, for such diaries are the true and rarest jewels of the art, a chronicle of the ordinary.
> — Sir Roy Strong, *The Times*

This is still considered wrong in the Anglican Church in England and in high Protestant churches elsewhere. Other churches, however, especially in America, seem to regard it as fully acceptable:

> Jean's best friend at Laurel was the daughter of the minister of the conservative Presbyterian Church of the Covenant, the Reverend Bird. Some years later, when Jean Struven married James Harris, the Reverend Bird officiated at the ceremony.
> — Diana Trilling (U.S.),
> *Mrs Harris: The Death
> of the Scarsdale Diet Doctor*

Reverend is a useful and reasonably respectful way of addressing a clergyman whose name or status you do not know. But it is again considered dubious to refer to a known clergyman as just *the Reverend*, as is implied in the following example:

> 'Do you know,' she asked Appleby gravely, 'that nobody has been so nice to me as the Reverend here?' This appeared to be her way

of referring to Rixon.
— Michael Innes, *The Long Farewell*

review, revue A *review* is an inspection or examination of something. It may take the form of a military inspection, a legal examination of a verdict, or a published assessment of a book, play, art exhibition, film, or the like. (The magazine in which such assessments appear may also be called a *review*.)

A *revue* is an entertainment consisting of dancing and of songs and sketches, often satirical:

Revue, of the acid and astringent European kind, has been one of his interests and, indeed, he'd hoped there might have been a London audience for 'the kind of social and moral comment that is familiar in Germany or France'.
— Robert Ottaway, *Radio Times*

Revue is sometimes spelled *review*, but this may cause confusion, and is best avoided.

Review of course is also widely used as a verb, *to review a book*. (In North America, students *review* for an examination — in British English, the equivalent is *to revise*.) *Revue* is unlikely to be used as a verb. Both words can be used like adjectives in front of another noun: *a revue sketch*, *a review article*.

ribbon, riband The common word *ribbon* developed in the early 16th century as a variant of *riband*, which goes back to the Old French *riban*, and possibly further back to the Germanic word *band*. Note that *riband* has only one *b*. It is pronounced like *ribbon* with a *d*-sound at the end — /ribbənd/.

Riband is now archaic in general use, but is still current in specialised contexts, such as in sport and heraldry. A first prize is sometimes *a blue riband* in British English, notably the Blue Riband awarded for the fastest Atlantic crossing by an ocean liner. (It has been suggested that this form was preferred because the similar word *ribband* — with two *b*s, and based simply on the fusion of *rib + band* — is a nautical term, referring to the beam that holds the ribs of a ship in place during construction.) The prize was last given in 1952, and with the passing of the prize the word has been less on the lips of the general public. It is *a blue ribbon*, however, that is the badge of honour for members of the Order of the Garter; it was also the identifying badge formerly worn by certain teetotallers. And the Derby, the major flat race in the British horseracing calendar, is still sometimes called *the Blue Ribbon of the turf*.

right 1. As an adverb, *right* has many senses — 'straight, directly' (*He went right to the heart of the matter*), 'immediately' (*I'll be right down*), 'completely, thoroughly' (*The rain wet us right through*), and so on. What is often overlooked is that it can also mean 'accurately, correctly' as well (*He guessed right*; *Serves you right!*). Of course, the adverb *rightly* exists too, but the adverb *right* survives alongside it. Their distribution is roughly as follows: if the adverb follows the verb it refers to, then *right* is usually preferable; if the adverb comes before the verb, then *rightly* is usually more appropriate. Here then are some typical uses:

He guessed right.	He rightly guessed that I'd bowl a googly.
If I remember aright/ right/rightly …	I can't rightly remember
You're not using the softpedal right.	You rightly used the softpedal during the legato, but you kept it down too long.
She did quite right to report her suspicions.	She quite rightly reported her suspicions at once.

2. One other adverbial sense of *right* is now considered archaic or dialectal in British English, but remains common in colloquial regional American English — that is, 'extremely, very, thoroughly, greatly':

You'll be right glad you changed your mind.
He was right sorry to have missed you.
They had a right good laugh about it afterwards.
Let's get together again right soon.
We had a right old time at the fair.

Right is found serving this intensifying function frequently in the King James Bible, and still occurs in ceremonial or very formal language: *a right royal occasion*. It is preserved above all in certain formal titles: *the Right Reverend Dr Hermanus*; *the Right Honourable*.

3. This intensifying function of *right* seems quite redundant in the combinations *right this minute* and *right now*: *Tidy your room right this minute, or you get no dinner*. There are, after all, no degrees of *this minute* or *now*. But the phrases are established idiom, and convey a sense of urgency that *this minute* or *now* on their own can-

not match. They are really no more objectionable than the equivalent idiomatic phrase *right away*.

4. *Right* has so many meanings that ambiguity is a frequent danger. It is not only in comedy sketches that the following typical exchange might take place:

'I turn left at the next corner then?'
'Right.'
'I thought you said left.'

There is, accordingly, an increasing tendency to use the word *correct* instead of *right* to indicate assent or agreement in conversation — an awkward though necessary precaution. *Right* remains unchallenged, however, as an interjection indicating sudden comprehension:

'Then all you have to do is multiply by 100, and there's your answer.'
'Right!'

5. The interjected *right?* is widely used nowadays, especially by young people, as a kind of spoken punctuation-mark, sprinkled intermittently into the conversation in the way that *um* or *you know* might be. Needless to say, it would be quite inappropriate in formal speech:

?? You tie the string into a loop, right?, and put it over the two pins. Then stretch the loop like this, right? — with your pencil, right? — so it forms a triangle, right?

Perhaps this *right?* just represents a pause in thought, allowing the speaker a moment to choose his words; but perhaps it is also a way of checking the listener's comprehension: it is spoken with a rising intonation, like a question, and seems to be inviting some response from the listener, such as a nod or grunt of understanding, or else a worried frown.

It has been suggested that the origin of this mannerism is the German *nicht?* ('not so?'). This was apparently anglicised by German Americans into *right?*, which established itself in American English before infecting British English.

Careful speakers, on both sides of the Atlantic, tend to avoid the expression.

rise, arise, raise, rouse, arouse In general, *to rise* and *to arise* are intransitive verbs (they do not take a direct object, and cannot be used in the passive), and *to rouse* and *to arouse* are transitive verbs. And in general, *to rise* and *to rouse* are used in a literal way, and apply to people or animals; *to arise* and *to arouse* are used in a more figurative and abstract way. In tabular form, their general distribution is this:

	transitive	intransitive
literal, animate	rouse	rise
figurative, abstract	arouse	arise

To raise, in its contrary way, spoils the pattern. It is transitive (like *rouse* and *arouse*), but usually applies literally (like *arise* and *arouse*). Here are some examples of all these verbs in common contexts:

I rise at dawn; My batman rouses me at dawn; The general raised an army in three weeks.
The cake took half an hour to rise; He raised the cake above his head.
A hot wind arose; The temperature rose; The hot wind raised the temperature.
Strong feeling arose; Feelings rose; The news aroused/raised strong feeling.
A mood of optimism arose; Expectations were aroused/raised.

More specifically, *to arise* is no longer widely used in the sense of 'to get up from a lying, sitting, or kneeling position' (as in *Arise, Sir Godfrey* or W.B. Yeats's line *I will arise and go now, and go to Innisfree*). It is now used chiefly in the sense of 'to come into existence; become apparent; result': *Opportunities always arise*; *Doubts arose at once*.

Similarly, *arouse* is now seldom used in the sense of 'to wake from sleep'; it is used chiefly to mean 'to bring into existence, or to provoke or excite': *It aroused my suspicions*. It usually refers to an immediate and brief response: *His views arouse interest/fear/criticism*. By contrast, *to rouse* implies a deeper, stronger response, and takes as its object a human (or animal) rather than an abstract noun: *His views roused me to anger/action*.

To arouse has another current sense as a transitive verb with a personal object: 'to awaken sexual feelings in'. So there is a doubly good reason for not saying ✕ *My batman arouses me in the morning* when you mean *My batman rouses me in the morning*.

To rise and *to rouse* (with *to raise*), though generally intransitive and transitive respectively, are sometimes used the other way round, especially in technical senses. The intransitive use of *to raise*, for instance, is well-established in card-games: *Joyce bid, Nick passed, and then I raised*. And *to rouse* is used intransitively of game animals, and means 'to start from cover': *The stag roused*. (Its original sense, in fact, was 'to startle (game) out of hiding', from Middle English *rowsen*, which was used of game animals and meant 'to shake one's feathers or body'. To *rise,* and hence *arise,* are from Old English roots; *to raise* is of Norse origin.)

Note that *rouse, arouse,* and *raise* take regular verb forms, but that *rise* and *arise* are irregular: *a/rise, rose, risen.*

In dialects, especially American dialects, there is a great deal of crossing of division-lines: *to raise* is sometimes used intransitively: *The cake has finally raised.* Or the past participle of *rise* may be rendered as *rose* (or *riz*) rather than *risen: The cake had rose after ten minutes.*

Rise is frequently used as a noun as well; *raise* too can be used as a noun. In the sense 'an increase in salary or wages', the preferred term in British English is *a rise;* the alternative, *a raise,* though fairly common now throughout the English-speaking world, is still regarded by purists as an unwelcome Americanism. So too, sometimes, is the use of the verb *to raise* when applied to animals or children (as opposed to plants); the traditional term is *to rear: I was reared by an aunt; They rear pigs and goats.* The variant *to raise* seems to go in and out of fashion in British usage, but is well enough established to be accepted as standard.

American purists make quite a different distinction here. For them, one *rears children* but *raises animals. To raise plants/crops* is, however, acceptable universally, and *to raise children* is in fact a very widespread construction in American English.

A final British-American difference: what in British English is called *self-raising flour* is referred to as *self-rising flour* in American usage. Each is perfectly well-formed, being understood respectively as 'raising itself' (transitive) and 'rising by itself' (intransitive).

river Many geographical names are derived from the name of the geographical feature itself. Both *Sahara* and *Gobi* actually mean 'a desert' in the local languages, so it is superfluous, strictly speaking, to say ? *The Sahara Desert* or ? *The Gobi Desert.* Similarly *Lake Chad* and *Lake Nyasa* (now *Lake Malawi*) both mean literally 'Lake lake'. ? *Mount Fujiyama* means literally 'Mount Fuji mountain' — those in the know therefore speak either of *Fujiyama* or *Mount Fuji.*

Rivers seem most susceptible to being named after the local word for 'a river': *Avon* takes its name from an ancient Celtic word for 'water' or 'a river' (as do the rivers *Wear, Wye, Ouse, Usk, Exe, Dore,* and *Wey*), so the several rivers called *the River Avon* have in theory tautologous names. *Nile, Niger,* and *Ganges* all probably mean 'a

river' as well. The Soviet river known as the *Don* (as also the British rivers so named), immortalised in the novels of the Nobel laureate Mikhail Sholokhov such as *And Quiet Flows the Don,* probably takes its name from an ancient Indo-European word for 'a river'. The river *Danube* seems to contain the roots both of *Don* and *Avon,* so to speak of *the River Danube* is in effect to be doubly guilty of redundancy.

A specific usage problem is the placement of the word *river* in the name of a river: we say *the Colorado River* but *the River Thames;* and *the River Rhine* but *the Yellow River.*

The rules seem to be these: British rivers generally have the word *river* in front of the name: *the River Tyne, the River Trent.* (There are many exceptions: *the Helford River, the Lymington River, the East Dart River.*)

Rivers in other English-speaking countries generally have the word *river* after the name: *the Colorado River, the Limpopo River, the Murrumbidgee River.*

The rivers of countries outside the English-speaking world are less consistent: in South America, for instance, there is *the Amazon River* (though *the River Amazon* is possible) but *the River Plate.* And the Nile, though more commonly *the River Nile,* is sometimes referred to as *the Nile River.*

European rivers usually conform to the British pattern, having *river* before the name: *the River Weser, the River Seine.* (Many of them, however, are almost always referred to by their name alone, without the use of *river* before or after: *the Loire, the Po, the Rhone:* compare *the Humber* in England, and *the Ganges* in India.) Asian rivers, on the other hand, seem to conform to the other pattern: *the Mekong River, the Yangtze River* (now the *Chang Jiang*), *the Yalu River, the Yellow River.*

Two rather more specific clues: first, rivers named after people or places tend to have the word *River* at the end of their names wherever they are: *the Hudson River, the Lymington River.* (This perhaps accounts even for the form *the Amazon River,* named in the fanciful belief that the legendary Amazons might dwell on its banks.) Secondly, rivers whose names include colours and compass points also tend to have the word *River* postponed: *the East Dart River, the Red River, the Yellow River.*

Note, finally, that speakers of American English can generalise the typical pattern of American river names, and may speak of *the Danube River* as well as of *the River Danube.*

On the question of using a capital *R* for *river*

in such names, usage is divided. An increasing tendency is to use a small letter, but the capital has much to be said for it. *River* does often seem to be a full part of the name, and the capital letter reduces the chances of ambiguity: the capital *R* in *the River Thames* marks this as an official name; the small *r* in *the London river* would mark this as a sobriquet — a merely informal name for the Thames.

road See STREET.

rococo See BAROQUE.

Roman numerals See NUMBER STYLE.

rosin See RESIN.

rotund, orotund *Rotund* primarily means 'round, spherical, plump'. It comes from the Latin *rotundus*, 'rounded', from *rotare*, 'to revolve', from *rota*, 'a wheel': *a jovial, rotund, and red-faced little man.*

Orotund comes from the Latin phrase *ore rotundo*, literally 'with round mouth', which has been fused into one word. When referring to utterances, *orotund* generally means 'with full voice, clear- or strong-voiced': *He was a classical actor of the old school, with orotund delivery and grandiose gestures.* When referring to language, *orotund* can also mean 'imposing, dignified', or — with negative overtones — 'pompous, overblown': *His orotund phrases were hardly appropriate for his audience of restless and fun-loving schoolboys.*

Antrobus leaned forward and said with portentous triumph: 'He wrote good English in those days.' Then he sat back and stared impressively at me down the long bony incline of his nose. He allowed the idea to soak in. Of course what he meant by good English was the vaguely orotund and ornamental eighteenth-century shift which was then so much in vogue. A sort of mental copperplate prose.
— Lawrence Durrell, *Esprit de Corps*

Reluctantly, Brown rang up the Tutor's house. He was sure it was an error of judgment not to wait for Nightingale — whom he wanted to bind to the party. On the other hand, he had had trouble bringing Chrystal 'up to the boil'. He did not choose to risk putting him off now. He rang up, his voice orotund, confidential, cordial; from his replies, one could guess that Jago was

welcoming us round without a second's delay.
— C.P. Snow, *The Masters*

The word can be extended metaphorically to refer to styles other than language:

In the bar of the Hotel Cracovia, in fact, Oskar had already seen Gebauer hand over forged papers to a Jewish businessman for a flight to Hungary . . . it was certain, in spite of this act in front of Toffel, that he was no abominator of the tribe. Nor were any of them. At Christmas 1939 Oskar found them simply a relief from the orotund official line.
— Thomas Keneally, *Schindler's Ark*

The two adjectives are not quite so distinct in meaning, however. *Rotund*, probably through association with *orotund*, has also come to mean 'dignified in speech or grandiloquent in style'. *He delivered his address in rotund tones.* Many people now prefer *rotund* to *orotund* in this sense, finding *orotund* to be rather formal, pedantic — or simply orotund:

The general was accompanied in the discussion by Vladimir Zagladyn, first deputy head of the International Department of the Central Committee, a man of rotund phrases and features, peering owlishly through glasses, who is a key figure in the formulation of Soviet foreign policy.
— Donald Trelford, *The Observer*

How capably he had managed it, I thought. He had not pressed Jago on any one of us. Chrystal had been undecided, but patiently Brown drew him in. With Chrystal, with me, with Nightingale, he had waited, talking placidly and sensibly, often rotundly and platitudinously, while our likes and dislikes shaped themselves. Only when it was needed had he thrown in a remark to stir one of our weaknesses, or warm our affection. He had given no sign of his own unshakable resolve to get the Mastership for Jago.
— C.P. Snow, *The Masters*

Note the pronunciations. The preferred pronunciation of *rotund* is with the stress on the second syllable: /rō-**tund**, rə-/. *Orotund*, on the other hand, is always stressed on the first syllable: /**o**-rō-tund, **aw**-/.

round See AROUND; CENTRE AROUND.

rouse See RISE.

rural, rustic Both of these adjectives derive from the Latin *rus*, 'the country', and refer to country life as opposed to city life. But they have different overtones, and are usually used in different contexts.

Rural is the more general and neutral word, meaning 'of or relating to the country, country people, country life, and farming': *the rural environment, rural pursuits.*

> Ted Kotcheff's last film, 'First Blood', brought the Vietnam war back home to complacent rural America in the shape of an angry veteran driven beyond endurance by provocative cops.
> – Philip French, *The Observer*

Rustic carries the added suggestion of simplicity or even crudeness: *rustic charm.*

> By a paradox of pictorial thought, the average lowland North American countryside had at first seemed to me something I accepted with a shock of amused recognition because of those painted oilcloths which were imported from America in the old days to be hung above washstands in central-European nurseries, and which fascinated a drowsy child at bed time with the rustic green views they depicted — opaque curly trees, a barn, cattle, a brook, the dull white of vague orchards in bloom, and perhaps a stone fence or hills of greenish gouache.
> – Vladimir Nabokov, *Lolita*

> Schindler laughed at that. A wide, toothy, almost rustic laugh. 'Thank you very much, my friend,' he told Stern.
> – Thomas Keneally, *Schindler's Ark*

Sometimes *rustic* seems to lose its associations with the country almost entirely, and is used to mean 'quaint' or 'lacking in sophistication': *a delightful rustic cottage on 44th Street.*

> Trendy split-level duplex gone to seed, she recorded automatically, noting the tasteful open-tread staircase, the rustic minstrel gallery and the handcrafted iron balustrade. One English-style fireplace with mock coals in painted canvas.
> – John le Carré, *The Little Drummer Girl*

Rustic can be used as a noun as well, usually with some 'country' overtones. It can in principle mean simply 'a rural person', one living in the country rather than in a town, and probably working in farming or in country crafts. But it is far more likely to mean 'a country bumpkin' — both rural and naive.

S

-'s, -s' **1.** *the 'possessive'.* The so-called *possessive* in English is formed by adding -'s, or simply an apostrophe, to the end of the noun.

There are two important qualifications to this apparently innocent statement. First, that -'s and -s' are often used to express relationships other than possession. Secondly, that possession (and these other relationships) cannot always be expressed by -'s and -s'.

a. The typical function of the apostrophe is to indicate possession — *the girl's left shoe*; *the shark's tail.* But consider these phrases: *the teams' rivalry*; *the waiter's tip*; *the reviewer's savage criticism.*

It is not as if rivalry really 'belongs' to the teams — 'possessive' is not quite the right word (grammarians prefer the term 'genitive'). But you can still say *the rivalry of the teams.* You cannot, however, easily say *? the tip of the waiter* — it would be more natural to say *the tip for the waiter.* As for *the reviewer's savage criticism,* it would be ambiguous to say *? the savage criticism of the reviewer.* That can mean either *the savage criticism by the reviewer* (the 'subjective genitive') or *the savage criticism directed against the reviewer* (the 'objective genitive').

b. In general, -'s and -s' occur only with human or animal nouns: *John's views, the dogs' pedigrees* (some pedants object even to this use of the apostrophe with animal nouns). It is perhaps not fully acceptable when used with plant or inanimate nouns: *? the tree's branches, ? the monument's inscriptions* (but *its branches* and *its inscriptions* are acceptable). Purists prefer *the branches of the tree* and *the inscriptions on the monument,* though the apostrophe is now so common that full acceptance is just a matter of time.

Certain inanimate nouns have such strong human associations that even a pedant would allow them to end in -'s or -s': *London's theatres*; *the Concorde's maiden flight*; *the sea's cold embrace*; *the BBC's latest cutbacks,* and *Wednesday's child.* And other inanimate nouns are entitled to their -'s or -s' by virtue of long-established idiomatic expressions: *to her heart's content, a ship's steward, for heaven's sake, five pounds' worth, the razor's edge, out of harm's*

way, and so on. Expressions of time, in particular, are allowed by idiom to take -'s or -s' almost as freely as human names are: *six weeks' holiday, yesterday's men, tomorrow's headlines.*

Obversely, certain human nouns are sometimes too complicated to take an apostrophe, and should take *of, by, made by,* or the like, to express 'possession'. It is all right to say *the King of Sweden's powers* (though in the past the wording had to be *the King's powers of Sweden*) and it is slightly more concise than *the powers of the King of Sweden.* But consider this example:

?? The director of the Industrial Safety Research Centre's annual report is published today.

This would read far better if worded along these lines:

The annual report drawn up by the director of the Industrial Safety Research Centre is published today.

The expanded form should also be used when too many -'s or -s' words threaten to pile up side by side and create an ugly sound and possible misunderstanding: *?? the president's children's nanny's husband's suicide.* It would be better to say: *the suicide of the husband of the president's children's nanny.*

2. *apostrophe-s* vs *s-apostrophe* vs *simple s.* The rules for possessives are these:

a. the apostrophe comes before the *s* if the noun is singular: *one scientist's theories*; *John's views*; *Jones's school-report.*

b. the apostrophe comes after the *s* if that *s* serves to make the noun plural: *the scientists' theories*; *the boys' opposing views*; *the Joneses' new car.*

c. the apostrophe comes before the *s* if the noun is already plural without the *s*: *the women's opposing views.*

d. possessive personal pronouns ending in *s* take no apostrophe at all: *its, ours, whose, theirs,* and so on. Indefinite pronouns (except for *each*) do take an apostrophe: *anyone's, either's,* and so on. (See section **8** below for more details.)

3. *nouns ending in -s* (or -*x*, -*z*, -*nce*, -*ese*, and so on). The cottage where Keats lived is *Keats's* *cottage*; similarly *Marx's study*. The house where Dickens lived is probably *Dickens's house*, though formerly it might have been *Dickens' house*; similarly *the Chinese's office*. (North American English is slightly more conservative perhaps: *Keats' cottage* and *Dickens' house* are readily available to Americans and Canadians.) The villa where *Onassis* lived is probably *Onassis's villa*, though it could be *Onassis' villa*; similarly *Velasquez's studio/Velasquez' studio*.

Again, *the boss's party, the chorus's performance* (formerly also *the chorus' performance*), and *the brontosaurus's skull* (also *the brontosaurus' skull*).

In other words, the modern tendency, when constructing a possessive, is to add *-'s* to all singular nouns ending in *s,* though the longer the word, the likelier it is that a simple apostrophe, without the *s,* will be acceptable: *Zeus's thunder* but *Euripides' plays*.

Many longer nouns are unlikely to be spoken with the extra /əz/ syllable at the end, and are therefore unlikely to be written with the *-'s* rather than with the single apostrophe: the more commonly used forms would probably be *Jesus' disciples, Aristophanes' comedies, Berlioz' 'Symphonie fantastique', Sir Robert Menzies' term of office*, and *the amanuensis' desk*. If the last syllable takes a stress, however, the *-'s* is preferable: *Inverness's beauty spots* (contrast *Hastings' beauty spots,* which is likelier than *Hastings's beauty spots*). But there are no binding rules — it is really a matter of what seems appropriate to the ear, and hence what is appropriate for the pen.

4. *the disappearing apostrophe.* The *-'s* ending often seems to indicate a noun rather than a possessive adjective: *I'm staying at my aunt's* (= aunt's home); *Will you be passing the greengrocer's?* (= greengrocer's shop).

Many proper names came to be referred to in this familiar way as well: *Barclay's* (Bank), *Pears'* (Cyclopaedia), *Boot's* (Chemists), *Beecham's* (Powders). It is perhaps for this reason — the apparent uselessness of the apostrophe — that the apostrophe was eventually dropped from many such terms, so that the official name is now *Barclays Bank, Pears Cyclopaedia, Boots, Beechams Products*.

Note too that many place-names where you might expect *-'s* end in fact with a simple *s*: *St Albans* (Hertfordshire, England), *St Andrews* (Fife, Scotland), *Regents Park, St Pancras Station*. On the other hand, *St David's* (Dyfed, Wales), *St James's Park*, and so on. Two adjacent stops on the Piccadilly line of the London

underground are *Barons Court* and *Earl's Court*! Always check in a good atlas or road-map to ensure that you are spelling a place-name correctly.

5. *noun phrases and the possessive.* Some noun phrases can take the *-'s* quite happily: *the King of Spain's daughter*. As pointed out earlier, however, certain more complex noun phrases cannot really take the *-'s*:

?? the director of the Industrial Safety Research Centre's annual report.
✗ the man who knew too much's disappearance.

They should instead take *of, by*, or the like: *the disappearance of the man who knew too much*.

Here are some other examples of noun phrases that should take the expanded form, or at least limit their use of the apostrophe to particularly favourable conditions:

?? 'Spandau Ballet''s latest LP
?? 'Spandau Ballet's' latest LP.

It is better to write:

the latest LP from 'Spandau Ballet'

— or perhaps:

? *Spandau Ballet*'s latest LP (note that the *-'s* is not in italics)

— or simply:

Spandau Ballet's latest LP.

Again:

? the owl and the pussycat's pea-green boat.
?? the owl's and the pussycat's pea-green boat.

It would be preferable to write:

the pea-green boat of the owl and the pussycat.

Traditionally, there is a difference between *the owl and the pussycat's voyages* and *the owl's and the pussycat's voyages*. The first suggests 'the voyages taken together by the owl and the pussycat', the second suggests 'the voyage/s taken by the owl and the separate voyage/s taken by the pussycat'. Compare *Gilbert and Sullivan's operettas* and *Gilbert's and Sullivan's shirts*. None of these phrases is recommended, of course: the expanded *of* form is preferable in each case.

Some further examples of the misused apostrophe:

✗ Uncle Tom Cobbley and all's opinions.
? every Tom, Dick, and Harry's opinions.

535

? the world and his wife's opinions.

Use *the opinions of . . .* in preference in each case. Again:

?? the member for Slough's (Conservative) question to the Prime Minister.

?? Mrs Pat Hartley (née Charmiane)'s wedding-ring.

?? the arctic fox's (*Alopex lagopus*'s) highly-valued fur.

Use *of* in each case.

? Dr Thacker, the headmaster's, sudden announcement.

?? Dr Thacker's, the headmaster's, sudden announcement.

The first of these is preferable to the second, and if the commas are left out is probably quite acceptable — it is then as if you have a single subject *Dr-Thacker-the-headmaster,* and the *-'s* is quite appropriate. To be on the safe side, however, it would be better to use the expanded form with *of* or *by*:

the sudden announcement by Dr Thacker, the headmaster.

6. *two special cases.* First, the possessive of *someone else, anybody else, who else,* and so on. It is quite acceptable nowadays to say:

These shoes are someone else's.
These are someone else's shoes.
I'd prefer anybody else's company to yours.
Who else's prize still remains uncollected?

There is a traditional objection to attaching *-'s* to *else,* since *else* is not a noun, and pedants might still try rewording the examples above, especially the first and last:

? These shoes are someone's else.
? Whose prize else still remains uncollected?

These old-fashioned and rather stilted versions are hardly an improvement on the modern idiomatic sentences: the pedant's objection to the modern idiom can safely be ignored.

Secondly, the expression *for goodness' sake,* and related idioms. The *-'s* is usual in such phrases — *for pity's sake, for heaven's sake, for Pete's sake,* also *for Alice's sake, for Mike Morris's sake,* and so on. But if the noun ends in *s* (or an *s*-sound) and the phrase is a set idiomatic phrase, then the *-'s* is not usually used. Add an apostrophe alone, or (if the last letter is not actually *s*) leave the noun as it is: *for goodness' sake, for Jesus' sake, for conscience sake.*

7. *the double possessive.* We speak of *a friend of mine.* But suppose he is my brother's friend instead: is he *a friend of my brother's* or *a friend of my brother?* Both are correct; the first is perhaps slightly more common and idiomatic, even though it appears redundant, indicating the possessive both by *of* and by *-'s.*

The double possessive would never, however, be used of inanimate nouns: *the wind's whistling* or *the whistling of the wind,* but not × *the whistling of the wind's,* × *the maiden flight of Concorde's,* or the like.

Note that in the double possessive the first element is usually indefinite (it begins with *a* or *any*) and the second element is always definite (it begins with *the, this, my,* or the like, or is a proper name). So, it is acceptable to say:

a child of the artist's is posing for a picture

— but not:

× The child of the artist's is posing for a picture.
× Any child of an artist's will make a good model.

(However, if the first element is already very familiar, then it can be definite rather than indefinite: *this country of ours; That shoulder of McEnroe's is playing up again.*)

Note too that the double possessive should not be used if the pronoun *that* happens to be in front of the *of*: × *a hairstyle very different from that of Genevieve's;* × *a growl as frightening as that of a tiger's.* The correct form is either *a hairstyle very different from that of Genevieve* or *a hairstyle very different from Genevieve's;* similarly, *as that of a tiger* or *as a tiger's.*

8. *possessive pronouns.* **a.** Note that possessive pronouns that end in *s* do so without any apostrophe: *its, ours, hers, his, yours, theirs, whose.*

Its coat changes from brown to white as winter approaches.
Victory is ours.
I'm entitled to my opinion and you to yours, but I'm not sure the neighbours are entitled to theirs.

The possessive of *who* (and *which*) is *whose. Who's* is a contraction of *who is,* just as *it's* is a contraction of *it is.*

'Who's at the door?' — 'It's John again.'

(See ITS; WHO.)

b. Indefinite pronouns do take *-'s,* however:

another's, anybody's, either's, no one's, someone's, and so on:

It is no one's business but hers.
The one is always living in the other's pocket.

The exception is *each*: no *-'s* is possible here — use *of each* instead. Compare:

Each one's wounds were quickly bathed and bandaged.
The wounds of each were quickly bathed and bandaged.

The only possible plural possessive among indefinite pronouns is *others'*:

The others' gifts were not as nice as yours.

Two thorny problems are the possessive forms of *whoever* and *anyone/nobody at all*. Of the possible possessive forms of *whoever* — *whoever's book, whose ever book,* and *whosever book* — the last is the best. (Remember that *who's* is not a possessive, but the contraction of *who is*.) Similarly, the best possessive form of the rare *whosoever* is *whosesoever*.

As for pronoun phrases ending in *at all,* there are two possible possessive forms: *anyone at all's book* and *anyone's book at all*; or *This book is no one's at all* and *This book is no one at all's*. Both forms are acceptable, though there is perhaps a slight difference in emphasis. But such phrases are somewhat ungainly, and it would usually be more elegant to reformulate them: *a book belonging to anyone at all*; *This book belongs to no one at all*.

9. *the apostrophe-s in plurals.* In a few cases the plural of a word might be indicated by *-'s*. In this book, for example, we might say something like:

Note that *reference* has only two single *r*'s, whereas *referred* doubles the final *r* of *refer*.

Similarly: *mind your p's and q's*; *dot your i's and cross your t's*. And contractions of common nouns might take an apostrophe before the *s* when plural:

lettuces — 10p each; cauli's — 18p each; mush's — 20p a quarter.

But by and large, even the most peculiar nouns, even invented nouns, can take a simple *s* when plural, though it is not always advisable.

assorted presidents, PMs, and other V.I.P.s.
the 1940s.
the whys and the wherefores.
his charming old-fashioned way of speaking,

full of *my dear sir*s and *far be it from me*s.

Note that the *s* following *sir* and *me* is not in italics as the rest of the phrase is in each case. If it were in italics, then an apostrophe would probably be inserted before the *s* each time, first to make it clear that the typical phrase is *my dear sir* rather than *my dear sirs,* and secondly, to avoid the very peculiar-looking word *mes*.

Above all, the apostrophe must not be used when a simple *s*-plural is standard and long-established. The following market-stall sign displays some all too common mistakes:

✗ lettuce's — 10p each; potato's — 5p a pound; tomatoe's — 14p a pound.

See also PLURALS.

10. *ambiguity.* Since *-'s* or *-s'* can indicate various relationships other than possession, there is the danger that a single 'possessive' phrase could be understood in two different ways. Consider the phrase *? the artist's portrait*. Does this mean *the portrait by the artist* (such as *Monet's portrait* of Renoir) or does it mean *the portrait of the artist* (such as *Renoir's portrait* by Monet)? Unless the context makes clear which sense is intended, you should avoid the *-'s* convention and spell out your meaning explicitly.

A further source of ambiguity is this: an *-'s* phrase has only one *a* or *the*: *the chef's hat*. The expanded form, however, has two articles: *the hat of the chef* or *a hat of the chef*. (Similarly, *a chef's hat* = either *a hat of a chef* or *the hat of a chef*.)

If you want to make your meaning absolutely clear, it may therefore be necessary to use the expanded form. The sentence *The chef's hat fell in the soup* could imply 'so he had to go bareheaded the whole evening', or it could imply 'so he had to put on one of his spare hats'.

In practice, the second implication would probably be expressed by a different sentence: *One of the chef's hats fell in the soup*. Note, however, that this too is theoretically ambiguous: it could refer to one hat of several owned by the chef, or it could refer to a hat or (the hat) belonging to one of the several chefs. Once again, if there is any danger of being misunderstood, abandon the *-'s* form and use the expanded form instead.

11. *avoiding the problem.* Sometimes the ambiguities of the possessive are built into the structures in which it is used. Suppose you have a dictionary useful in teaching English as a foreign language — is it *a learner's dictionary* (= a dictionary for the learner) or *a learners' dictionary* (= a dictionary for learners)? Both interpretations are possible, and both *learner's* and *learners'* appear in the titles of at least one such book. Similarly, a teacher-training college can be called, with equal plausibility, *a teacher's college* or *a teachers' college*. It is not surprising, therefore, that for many years the pedagogical faculty of Columbia University in New York has been called officially *Teachers College,* avoiding the problem of *-'s* vs *-s'* by rejecting the apostrophe altogether.

Similarly, in Britain, you find the *Citizens Advice Bureau, Sports Council, Parks Department,* and so on. A grammatical analysis of such phrases would characterise the first word in each case as a 'noun modifier' — a noun serving as an adjective, as in *trades union, drinks machine, arts degree,* and the like. This is an admirable solution — the only trouble being that it might be taken as indicating not linguistic sophistication but simply ignorance of the rules of punctuation.

12. *-'s indicating contraction.* *-'s* is the standard contraction, attached to the end of a word, of *is* (*John's here*); *has* (*He's arrived at last*); and *us* (*Let's go then*). But it is considered nonstandard when used as a contraction of *does*: ? *What's he want to do now?*

See also APOSTROPHE; -ING FORMS OF VERBS.

sabotage English adopted the noun *sabotage* from French in the 1890s, and had begun using it as a verb, too, by 1912. The term refers to the deliberate damaging of property or disruption of routine and productivity, as by enemy agents or dissatisfied workers.

It has now come to be used more loosely — to the dismay of purists: the noun, for example, is used to mean 'any underhand action designed to defeat or frustrate a project; deliberate subversion'; the verb occurs in such contexts as ? *The managers have sabotaged the negotiations by refusing to reinstate the sacked supervisor.*

To sabotage in this sense may have a dramatic ring to it, useful in political sloganeering; but in most contexts it is nothing more than a fashionable synonym of *spoil, ruin, destroy, frustrate, jeopardise, obstruct, thwart,* or various similar verbs. It has become a vogue word, and should be used very sparingly in its new extended sense: use it, if at all, only when referring to damage that is done deliberately out of spite.

Sabotage goes back to the French *sabot,* 'a boot or clog'; the derived verb *saboter,* 'to clatter shoes', came to mean 'to work clumsily or botch', and hence 'to wreck deliberately'. It was this last sense that the derived noun *sabotage* adopted.

In English, the word retains a French-style pronunciation of the last syllable, /**sabb**ə-taa<u>zh</u>/; a slightly anglicised form is possible, /-taaj/, but there is no fully anglicised pronunciation as there is with *garage.*

salubrious, salutary, salutatory *Salubrious* means 'good for physical health or well-being, wholesome' and in an extended sense, 'clean, respectable': *a salubrious spot for a holiday*; *a none-too-salubrious nightclub.*

Salutary (note the spelling: *-ary* not ✕ *-ory*) means 'producing an improvement or cure, favourable to recovery, or morally beneficial': *a salutary experience* (it teaches you a lesson) or *a salutary rest* (you come back feeling healthier).

> Ex-wife, ex-lover, and their household prepare with some trepidation to listen in to C. Gordon Glover's latest radio play, *Farewell, Helen*, which makes good use of the copy Gordon has gained from this experience. Life in the WRENS appears a salutary escape from the misery of the Bristol household, despite the dreary details of camp life.
>
> – James Fenton, *The Times*

> It is salutary to be reminded of the price which literature (and society) pay when '*logos* and language begin to go their separate ways'.
>
> – Professor George Steiner, *The Times Literary Supplement*

Both *salubrious* and *salutary* come from the Latin *salus,* meaning 'health'.

Salutatory means 'welcoming, having to do with greeting': *His salutatory wave attracted my attention as the train pulled in*. It is related to *salute* and *salutation*: all three derive from the Latin *salutare* 'to greet', which again goes back to *salus,* 'health'.

Note the stress in *salutary* and *salutatory*. In British English, *salutary* is pronounced /**sal**-yoo-tri/; *salutatory* usually has a stress on both the first and third syllables: /**sal**-yoo-**tay**təri/.

same *Same* or *the same*, is still sometimes used as a pronoun, in legal and commercial contexts, to mean 'the persons or things just mentioned': *Our order for the consignment is enclosed — we hope to receive same next week.*

As business jargon declines, this use of *same* is declining as well (and so too with *said* and *such*: *the said consignment; The order for such is attached*). Outside business and legal contexts, *same* and *the same* should not be used in this way at all except as a joke or for special stylistic purposes. In the following extract, for instance,

Kipling used it to convey the effect of legal drafting:

Lair-Right is the right of the Mother. From all of her year she may claim
One haunch of each kill for her litter, and none may deny her the same.
— Rudyard Kipling,
The Second Jungle Book

The same can be used as an adverb meaning 'in the same way': *These two words are spelt the same.* To use *same* as an adverb without *the*, however, is not acceptable in formal usage, though common in everyday speech: *?? He goes to work by train, same as I do.*

When *same* is joined to a following word or phrase, it uses *as* of course as the link: *Her dress is the same colour as mine.* When *same* is joined to a following clause, there is a temptation to omit the *as*, or to replace it by *that* or *which*: *? She is wearing the same dress (that) she wore yesterday.* This construction is very common in informal English, but formal usage still requires the *as*: *She is wearing the same dress as she wore yesterday.*

sanguinary, sanguine These two adjectives are both stressed on the first syllable, and both go back to the Latin *sanguis*, 'blood'. *Sanguinary* means 'bloody', and so can be applied either to events involving bloodshed — *a sanguinary battle* — or to people, in the sense of 'bloodthirsty': *a cruel and sanguinary tyrant*.

Then we have Iran before the expulsion of the Shah, the tremendous boom of luxury and spending before the bubble burst and the sanguinary reign of the Ayatollah took over.
— Anthony Powell, *Daily Telegraph*

Sanguine initially meant 'blood-coloured' or 'ruddy', as in *a sanguine complexion* or *a sanguine sunset*. But it is now much more often used in a sense that developed from medieval physiology. It was believed that the body contained four liquids or humours that governed temperament: blood, phlegm (hence *phlegmatic*), yellow bile (choler), and black bile (melancholy). A predominance of blood over the other humours produced a *sanguine* temperament, which was cheerful, energetic, or bold. The word is still sometimes used with these overtones:

At the Loughborough University Sleep Laboratory we carry out work on sleep deprivation, not on animals but on humans. The great advantage here is that we can com-municate with our volunteers (animals cannot volunteer) and convey to them that they will not be harmed and that their wellbeing is of paramount importance. We can achieve sleepless but sanguine subjects, not otherwise stressed.
— Dr Jim Horne, *The Guardian*

However, *sanguine* came to develop a more modern sense — 'confident, hopeful, optimistic' — and it has for some time now been used more commonly in this way:

The microbe is so very small
You can hardly make him out at all;
But many sanguine people hope
To see him through a microscope.
— Hilaire Belloc,
The Bad Child's Book of Beasts

And, more recently:

Stern, however, wasn't one of the sanguine ones. He didn't presume the legislation would soon achieve a plateau of negotiable severity. For these were the worst of times.
— Thomas Keneally, *Schindler's Ark*

sarcastic See IRONIC.

sate, satiate, saturate These three verbs are very close in meaning. *To sate* is to satisfy fully or even indulge excessively — a person, or his appetites or desires, or oneself. *To satiate* is much the same, except it is perhaps likelier than *sate* is to have the sense of excessive indulgence, and sometimes even carries the suggestion of nausea: *satiated with candy floss*. Both verbs are used almost exclusively of humans or animals. And they are probably used most often in the past participle form, and in contexts of food and drink: *satiated with bread and beer*. They can, however, refer to any psychological appetite, repeated experience, and so on: *sated by war and bloodshed; satiated with ballet-music*.

Reagan (or his advisers) may have sensed that this alliance with the technology of marketing might be the unmaking as well as the making of the New Religious Political Right. At some stage the technology of superficial persuasion has to satiate the audience.
— Geoffrey Ahern, *Daily Telegraph*

To saturate has few such restrictions. In its most common sense of 'to wet thoroughly, soak', it can be used of inanimate objects and people alike: *First saturate the flannel in vinegar; This drizzle is going to saturate us if we don't find shelter soon*. It has the extended senses of 'to fill', 'to charge or supply to the maximum', and so on — *a room saturated with the smell of incense*; *to saturate the market with a new commodity*; *a film saturated with menace* — and several technical uses as well, referring to the chemical strength of a solution, the strength or vividness of a colour, the degree of magnetism in a metal, the amount of water vapour in the air, the level of military bombardment, and so on.

The three verbs seem to have three different origins: *saturate* goes back to the Latin *satur* 'full', *satiate* to the Latin *satis*, 'enough', and *sate* (possibly influenced by *satiate*) from the Old English *sadian*, 'to fill'. All three of these source words, however, go further back to a single prehistoric Indo-European root.

Note the related nouns: *satedness*, *satiation* or *satiety*, and *saturation*. And note the change in pronunciation from *satiate*, /**say**shi-ayt/ and *satiation*, /**say**shi-**aysh**'n/, to *satiety*, /sə-**tī**-əti/, sometimes /**say**shi-əti/.

says See INVERTED WORD ORDER **8**.

scabrous The adjective *scabrous* has nothing directly to do with *scabs* or *scabies*, being derived from a quite different source. (The adjectives relating to the two skin conditions are *scabby* and *scabious* respectively.)

The original and literal sense of *scabrous* is 'roughened with small projections, rough to the touch, scaly (though not with scabs)', but it is still occasionally used in this sense, with the added suggestion of 'shabby or scruffy':

We climbed to the top ... We were both panting as I unlocked the scabrous door and switched on another 40-watt dangling bulb.

I hadn't seen the room at night before. It was infinitely depressing. The bulb threw a mean, chilly light on the shoddy, shabby furniture and by its plentiful shadows increased the day-time impression of dirty walls and dark, unloved corners.

– Lynne Reid Banks,
The L-Shaped Room

However, *scabrous* is nowadays more commonly used in the more figurative sense of 'indelicate or salacious, indecent': *Rochester's scabrous verses*. Applied in this way to a piece of writing, *scabrous* could formerly mean 'rough, unpolished, harsh, unharmonious', but would now have a distinct connotation of 'risqué' — if not downright 'indecent'.

Raven's account of a drinking match at Deolali Transit Camp in India between the present Secretary of State for Northern Ireland and 'Spotty' Duvell is a masterpiece of comic writing which deserves comparison with A.G. Macdonnell's cricket match in *England their England* — or perhaps its scabrous tone would place it more happily alongside the very best of Tom Sharpe.

– Rupert Morris, *The Times*

The very idea of a concentration camp or of a human stud-farm is like a scabrous daydream of a lonely lover. Most dreams lose their charm when they become reality, and these are no exceptions.

– Peter Ustinov,
We Were Only Human

Scabrous can also mean 'difficult to handle tactfully; thorny', though today it seldom is used in this way: *a scabrous problem to resolve*.

The confusion with *scabby* is complicated by the occasional use of *scabby*, in informal contexts, to mean 'low, debased, vile', as in *a scabby trick*.

Scabrous comes from the Latin *scabrosus* or *scaber*, 'rough or scurfy'.

Scabious goes back to the related Latin noun *scabies*, 'roughness, itch', from *scabere* 'to scratch'.

Scabby, however, like *scab*, has a quite different source, going back to the Old Norse *skabbr* (though ultimately this does share a common Indo-European root with the Latin words just mentioned).

Scabrous is commonly mispronounced. In fact, it should have an *ay*-sound: /**skayb**-rəss/. *Scabious* too has this *ay*-sound. Both words are often pronounced, particularly in North American English, with a short *a*-sound, again on the model of *scabby*.

scant, scanty, skimpy, scarce, sparse, spare All these adjectives suggest a small or insufficient supply. But there are differences among them, both in meaning and in use.

Scant is a rather formal word, seldom being found in everyday English except perhaps in certain set phrases such as *scant praise*, *paid scant attention*, and *scant regard for my feelings*. Its meaning in such phrases is 'insufficient, inadequate'. Note that when used in this sense it tends to refer to abstract nouns, and has to be used directly in front of such nouns, not after the verb *to be*: ✗ *Her regard for my feelings was scant*. In a slightly different sense, *scant* means 'barely, only just', or even 'not quite': *We covered a scant two miles before the engine seized up.* Finally, *scant* can mean 'inadequately supplied with'; it is virtually never used in this sense any longer, except in the phrase *scant of breath*, a deliberate reference to *Hamlet.*

Scanty is less old-fashioned than *scant*, and less restricted in use; it can occur before or after the noun, and tends to apply to concrete nouns: *a scanty harvest this year*, *scanty living space*, *a scanty bathing suit.* The meaning in each case is 'noticeably small or brief, meagre'. *Skimpy* has just the same sense, and can be used in much the same contexts, although it has a slightly more jocular or informal ring to it. It is also less likely than *scanty* to be used when referring to room or time: *scanty living space* is more likely than ? *skimpy living space.*

Scarce means 'difficult to find; uncommon or infrequent': *Oranges are scarce at this time of year.* (The use of *scarce* as an adverb meaning 'scarcely' is very literary or old-fashioned today: *She was scarce three days old at the time*).

Sparse means 'thinly distributed, scattered, not dense': *The vegetation was very sparse as a result of the drought*; *a sparse population.*

> Their meetings during this period were sparse and businesslike, usually elaborately planned car pickups. Sometimes he took her to out-of-the-way restaurants on the edge of London ...
>
> – John le Carré,
> *The Little Drummer Girl*

Spare suggests a bare but adequate minimum, a healthy lack of excess. It is used either in the sense of 'lean, thin' – *spare of build yet very strong* – or in the sense of 'very economical, unadorned, meagre': *a spare prose style.*

scarcely   See HARDLY 3.

scarify   The verb *to scarify* has nothing to do with the more common verb *to scare*, though it is often misused to mean *scare.*

> × Technology is another goad, and it pushes adventurers in at least two directions. Fixed-object parachutists can succeed in their scarifying dives, most of the time, because new square-shaped, directional chutes allow them to guide their descent away from the buildings and cliff faces from which they jump.
>
> – *Time* (U.S.)

In fact, it means 'to make small incisions, lacerate or cut', as in *scarifying the skin during vaccina-*

tion. It can also mean 'to break up the surface of', as in *scarifying the topsoil before sowing*, and has acquired the figurative meaning 'to wound with severe criticism': *cruelly scarified by brutal reviewers.*

> Three times, in getting together material for this gloomy travelogue, Hills was admitted to Uganda. He had some credit with the new regime, having been jailed by Uganda's former tyrant Idi Amin. ... Now that he has published his scarifying verdict on Obote's Uganda, he is scarcely likely to go back a fourth time.
>
> – Richard Hall, *The Observer*

To scarify is derived ultimately from the Greek *skariphos*, 'a stylus', used for scratching lines when writing or drawing. *To scare*, by contrast, comes from Scandinavian. So too does *to score*, which through its sound and meaning ('to cut or notch') might seem to be related to *scarify.* And *to scar*, which also would seem to be related, again has a quite different origin, the Greek *eskhara*, meaning 'a fireplace' and hence 'a burn-mark or scab'.

Scarify is pronounced /**skar**ri-fī/, sometimes /**skair**i-fī/.

scenario   The word *scenario* came into English from Italian (where it meant 'scenery, or the stage'), probably from *libro scenario*, 'a stage book' — a brief plot outline from which Italian actors used to improvise the action and dialogue. (The Italian word goes back to the Latin *scaena*, 'a stage or theatre', from Greek *skene*, 'a tent'.) In English, *scenario* used to be chiefly used in the sense 'a short outline of a dramatic or literary work'. It then came to have virtually the opposite sense in the film world, referring to the detailed form of a story prepared for cinema or film production — in other words, the screenplay or the script used in shooting the film.

In the 1960s *scenario* moved into more general use, to mean 'a possible or planned project' or else 'an imagined or expected state of affairs or chain of events' — the idea being that the projected events were thought of as following in sequence, in much the same way as the scenes in a film-script do.

> The USSR could invade the Sa'udi oilfields tomorrow. So, of course, could the USA — and contingency planners on both sides of the Iron Curtain regularly update their scenarios for doing precisely that.
>
> – Robert Lacey, *The Kingdom*

He told MPs that his forecast 'implies the need for some net increase in taxes . . .' But even this gloomy scenario is dependent on economic growth of 3 per cent next year.

– Victor Keegan, *The Guardian*

Some critics dislike this meaning, and condemn *scenario* as a vogue word. Yet it does seem to fill a lexical gap. The idea of 'a hypothetical chain of events' is not quite covered by *scene*, *circumstance*, or *situation*. Use *scenario*, then, if it suits your purposes precisely, but try to use it sparingly.

The preferred pronunciation is /si-**naar**-i-o/; the form **?** /-**nair**-/ is regional or nonstandard.

Note the spelling of the plural: *scenarios*.

scone See MUFFIN.

Scots, Scotch, Scottish A person from Scotland likes to be referred to as a *Scot*. The nouns *a Scotsman* and *a Scotswoman* are rather more formal. *A Scotchman* and *a Scotchwoman* are not accepted by Scots, and are sometimes regarded as offensive. Collectively, people from Scotland are *Scots*; *the Scottish* is possible, but *the Scotch* is again unacceptable, even though it was widely used by Scots themselves in the 18th and 19th centuries. (In the United States, however, the term *Scotch-Irish*, attested since 1744, is still widely used to refer to Protestant immigrants from Ulster and their descendants.)

Of the corresponding adjectives, *Scots* and *Scottish* are used of people: *a Scots/Scottish lawyer*. In some combinations, only *Scots* is possible: *Scots law*, *the Scots Guards*. *Scottish* is the adjective commonly used in the sense 'located in or relating to Scotland': *Scottish Universities*, *Scottish newspapers*. *Scotch* is usually limited to products originating in or associated with Scotland: *Scotch whisky*, *Scotch broth*, *Scotch wool*. (Scots themselves call their national drink *whisky* rather than *Scotch whisky* or *Scotch*.)

The variety of English spoken in Scotland is called *Scottish English* if fairly close to the standard English of southern England. There are, or were, various dialects diverging markedly from standard English, however, and any of these is known as *Scots*.

Scottish English Scottish English is the variety of standard English spoken in Scotland. Its pronunciation, vocabulary, and grammar have all been strongly conditioned by the two other languages already spoken in Scotland before standard English was introduced there: Gaelic and Older Scots (also known as Lowland Scots).

History Gaelic was introduced into Scotland by Celts from Ireland around AD 600, and was for centuries the native tongue of the Highlands and Islands of northern and western Scotland. English began to gain a foothold in these areas only when it was introduced into schools in the mid-18th century. However, Gaelic is still the first language of many thousands of inhabitants of the islands and the Highland Region.

Older Scots developed from northern English dialects and lowland dialects (from AD 700 there were Anglo-Saxons living in the lowlands of southern Scotland). It was the language used at the Scottish court and in Scottish literature up to the time of Mary, Queen of Scots (16th century).

However, with the unification of the crowns of Scotland and England in 1603, Scots began to give way to standard English as the language of writing, and subsequently the educated classes began to use a form of standard English, coloured by their native Scots, as their spoken language.

The Scots tongue survived in the lowland dialect known as Lallans, which was used by Burns, and still survives in the features of dialect found in southern and eastern Scotland, in both rural and working-class urban areas. A number of modern writers, such as Hugh MacDiarmid, have used dialect in their writing in a conscious attempt to revive Scots as a national language.

Today most educated Scots speak Scottish English; that is, standard English with a distinctive Scottish accent and some striking differences of vocabulary and variations in grammar.

Pronunciation The most distinctive feature of Scottish English is its pronunciation. The following list indicates some differences in pronunciation (and traditional spelling) between broad Scottish and standard southern English:

ain, /ayn/ own
auld, /awld/ old
frae, /fray/ from
gie, /gee/ give
hame, /haym/ home
haud, /hawd, hod/ hold
heid, /heed/ head
lang, /lang/ long
licht, /li<u>kh</u>t/ light
mair, /mairr/ more
sae, /say/ so
sic, /sik/ such
toon, /tōōn/ town
wha, /hwa/ who

An important difference between Scottish English and RP (the 'Received Pronunciation' of educated people in southeastern England) is vowel length. Scottish English has fewer diphthongs than RP, which means in effect fewer and shorter vowel sounds. So a Scot would tend to pronounce the following pairs of words identically, with the same short vowel:

Sam, psalm — /sam/
tot, taught — /tot/
pull, pool — /po͞ol/

Conversely, words pronounced identically in RP are sometimes distinguished in Scottish English by the lengthening of a vowel:

greed — /grid/; agreed — /ə-**greed**/
booze — /bo͞oz/; boos — /bo͞oz/

The reason for the differentiation here is this: the simple forms *agree* and *boo* all end with a vowel sound, which has to be a long vowel. And it remains a long vowel even when an inflectional ending (*-d, -s*) is added to the word.

Unlike RP-speakers, Scots pronounce the letter *r* wherever it occurs in a word. This means that they distinguish between pairs such as *sawed,*/sod/, and *soared,*/so-rrd/, or *baa,*/ba/, and *bar,*/ba-rr/, which are identical in RP. And some pairs of words that are distinguished in RP by different vowel sounds are distinguished in Scottish English by the sounding of the *r*, the vowel sounds being identical:

bee — /bi/; beer — /bi-rr/
bay — /bay/; bear — /bay-rr/
hut — /hut/; hurt — /hu-rrt/
so — /so/; sore — /so-rr/
too — /to͞o/; tour — /to͞orr/

In keeping with the fondness for the *r*-sound, many Scots transpose the *r* and *e* in such words as *modern, pattern,* and *lantern,* producing /**mod**-rən/, /**lan**-trən/, and so on.

Other sounds more common in Scottish English than in RP are the /kh/ as in *loch* and *nicht* (night), and the aspirated /hw/ at the beginning of words such as *which, where,* and *whale.*

Finally some individual words that are pronounced differently: *length* and *strength* have /n/, not /ng/, in Scottish English (and in much American speech too); the verb form *says* is pronounced /sayz/ rather than /sez/; certain monosyllabic words in RP seem to have virtually a second syllable in Scottish English: *girl,* /gə-rr'l/; *film,*/fill'm/; and *burn,*/bə-rr'n/. The th sound in *though*, which in RP is hard or voiced, /thō/, in Scottish English is soft or unvoiced, /thō/. And southern urban dialects tend (as in Cockney) to substitute a 'glottal stop'

(a tiny pause of silence) for *t* in words such as *bitter* or *might*, though this is considered non-standard by most Scots speakers.

Vocabulary The vocabulary of Scottish English reflects both its Gaelic and Germanic (Anglo-Saxon) roots, and also the distinct historical and cultural development of the Scots people. Many items of vocabulary are known and recognised as typically Scottish by speakers of English in other countries: everyday words such as *ay* or *aye* (yes; always, ever), *bonnie* (pretty), *bairn* (child), *canny* (thrifty; shrewd), *kirk* (church), *plaid*, and the adjective *wee* (small); words associated with Scottish culture and society like *Hogmanay* (New Year's celebrations) and *laird* (landowner); and geographical terms such as *burn* (stream), *brae* (hillside), *firth* (estuary or inlet), *glen* (valley), *loch*, and *mull* (a promontory). From Gaelic are derived *whisky, clan, ceilidh* (pronounced /**kay**-li/ — a social gathering), and *Sassenach* (pronounced /**sass**ə-na<u>kh</u>/ and referring to an English person: from the Gaelic form of *Saxon*); as well as many placename elements: *ard-* (high), as in *Ardrossan* or *Ardnamurchan*; *blair-* (plain), as in *Blair Atholl* and *Blairgowrie*; *inver-* (estuary), as in *Inverness* and *Inverary*; and *strath-* (valley), as in *Strathpeffer* and *Strathclyde.*

Other terms that have passed into standard English are now so assimilated that the non-expert might be quite unaware that they have their origins in Gaelic — *bog, slogan* — or in Scottish forms: *gruesome, kerfuffle, raid, rampage,* and *stalwart.*

Scottish English has certain strong affinities with American and Canadian English (and other national varieties outside Britain). Scots, Americans, and South Africans, for example, all recognise *pinkie* (little finger), and use *folk* or *folks* to mean people or relatives, as in *How are your folks?* Scots and Americans say *janitor* for 'caretaker', and sometimes *infirmary* for 'hospital'.

Some familiar English words have extended or different senses in Scottish English: *loaf* can mean 'bread' — *a slice of loaf* — and *piece* can mean 'a slice of buttered bread': *a piece and jam.*

There is a number of everyday Scottish English words that would not be understood at all by English speakers outside Scotland — *rone* (drainpipe), *outwith* (outside), *sort* (to mend), *dreich* (pronounced /dree<u>kh</u>/ — dreary), *haar* (sea-mist — used along the east coast of Scotland). Some other dialect words still found in speech and writing are:

braid broad
dwam a daze or daydream

dicht, /di̱ht/ to wipe

dub a puddle

een eyes

feart afraid

fleg a fright (used in the northeast of Scotland)

fou, /fo͞o/ drunk

gang to go

gey, /gī, gay/ rather, very

glaikit, /**glay**-kit/ foolish, simple

greet to cry or weep

keek to peep

laverock a lark

loon a youth

lum a chimney

maun, /mawn, mon/ must

quean, /kween, kwīn/ a girl

redd up to tidy up

sark a shirt

speir, /speer/ to ask, pry

sweir, /sweer/ reluctant

unco, /ung-kō/ very

yin one

There are also a number of common expressions used in Scottish English and not in standard English: *to go the messages* (= to go shopping); *Is that you away then?* (= Are you about to leave?); *Where do you stay?* (= Where do you live?; also found in South African English); *It's not yours — it's mines* (= it's mine); *the back of 6 o'clock* (= after 6 o'clock); *He gave me a row* (= He scolded me).

Scottish dialect is rich in traditional idioms half-familiar to outsiders, and only half-understood by them: *Lang mae yer lum reek* (used to convey best wishes, especially at New Year — literally, 'Long may your chimney smoke'; it is now used chiefly self-consciously); *to dree yer weird* (= to endure your fate, especially ill fortune — again, this is little used nowadays except in a jocular way); *Dinnae fash yersel* (= Don't vex yourself; don't get upset); *to wet yer thrapple* (= to wet your throat; have a drink); *Haud yer wheesht* (= Hold your tongue; keep quiet); *auld lang syne* (= the good old days; the past — the literal meaning is 'old long ago').

Where Scottish institutions differ from those in England, different words too are used. The Scottish legal system, for example, uses terms such as *procurator fiscal* (public prosecutor and coroner), *advocate* (barrister — also in South Africa, again), and *provost* (mayor or chief magistrate); and the old Scottish education system had *dominie* (schoolmaster), the *tawse* (belt, the Scottish equivalent of the cane), *academy* (fee-paying

day school), and *dux* (top pupil).

The close historical association between Scotland and France, the Auld Alliance, has introduced several words of French origin into Scottish English, notably some traditional cookery terms: *ashet* (a serving plate, from *assiette*), *gigot* or *jigot* (pronounced /**jig**-ət/ — a leg of lamb; from the French *gigot*); possibly also *haggis* (according to one theory, from *hachis*, 'minced meat') and *collop* (a slice of meat; possibly from *escalope*).

Grammar There are many slight grammatical differences between Scottish English (and also that of Northern Ireland) and the standard English of England: the use of *will* instead of *shall*, for instance, especially in first-person questions: *Will I call you back?*

There is a preference for the full, uncontracted *not* in negative sentences; where southern English would use *He won't be long* and *Don't you understand?*, Scottish English prefers *He'll not be long* and *Do you not understand?* (in broader dialect, *He'll no be long* and *Dinna ye understand?*).

The verb *to have* (to experience) is used slightly differently in Scottish English; in both the present and past tense it can contract — *He'd a bad day at work* (= He had a bad day at work) — and it does not need to be used with the verb *do* in questions and negatives: *Had you a bad day at work?* (= Did you have a bad day at work?).

Certain verbs that in standard southern English seldom take the present continuous form, are quite happy to do so in Scottish English (as in Indian English and much of Irish English): *I'm wanting a ticket to Fife.*

Yet in questions requires the present perfect tense in standard southern English — *Have you fetched your coat yet?* — but in Scottish English, as in American English, it can be used more freely, and often follows the past tense: *Did you fetch your coat yet? Yet* also has a wider range in Scottish English, covering the sense of 'still' in positive statements: *She is crying yet* (in southern English, *She is still crying*).

Not that usage is uniform across the country, of course: the speech of working-class people in Glasgow and Edinburgh, for example, has several interesting grammatical features thought of as incorrect by other Scottish speakers; for instance, the use of *for* before the infinitive, as in *?? I'm away for to buy a new hat*, and the double negative in *?? He shouldnae never hae went*.

seasonal, seasonable The adjectives *seasonal* and *seasonable* are often confused. Their senses are quite distinct, however. *Seasonal* is the term with the general meaning of 'relating to the season or seasons'; more specifically, 'dependent on or varying with the season or seasons': *a seasonal adjustment to the unemployment figures*; *seasonal fruits*. Casual farm-work may be *seasonal*; that is, available only during certain seasons. Many farm-workers are accordingly *seasonal labourers*. Strawberries are *seasonal*, and hayfever is *seasonal*, too.

> 'Oh, Charlie, what *have* you been up to?' Mrs Ellis said, speaking very low because she feared the phone might be tapped. 'The police came for a whole morning about you, three of them, and none of us are allowed to say.' ... One of their seasonal checkups, she told herself. The Discreet Enquiry brigade, barging in with hobnailed boots to top up her dossier for Christmas. They had done it periodically ever since she had started going to the forum.
> – John le Carré,
> *The Little Drummer Girl*

> The new year has brought seasonal cheer to the world economy. From round the world a stream of official statistics and reports are appearing, all reinforcing the message that the longest and deepest of the postwar recessions has run its course.
> – Lionel Barber, *The Sunday Times*

(Note the faulty use of *are* here, rather than *is*: see AGREEMENT; PLURALS Part II.) *Seasonable*, on the other hand, means 'suitable for the season; as expected, given the season'. It occurs most often in the phrase *seasonable weather*. So in Britain, damp and windy weather in March is perfectly *seasonable*, though far from pleasant.

> I cannot see what flowers are at my feet,
> Nor what soft incense hangs upon the
>   boughs,
> But, in embalmed darkness, guess each
>   sweet,
> Wherewith the seasonable month endows
> The grass, the thicket and the fruit-tree wild.
> – John Keats,
> 'Ode to a Nightingale' (1819)

Note that *seasonable*, unlike *seasonal*, has an opposite form — *unseasonable*: snow in the middle of summer would be quite *unseasonable*. There is an extended but not very common sense of *seasonable*: 'happening at the right time, opportune, timely', as in *a seasonable word of advice*; *a seasonable loan of £500*.

secession See CESSION.

seldom See RARELY.

self, -self The use of *self* to mean 'me' — as in *a living wage for self*; *sold to self three boxes*; *book a room for wife and self* — may be suitable in commercial (and joking) contexts, but is inappropriate elsewhere.

Some careful speakers object to the use of *myself, yourself, himself*, and so on when no emphasis is required, as in *? I myself don't like carrots*, and also as substitutes for *I* or *me*, *you*, *he* or *him*, and so on, as in × *Pearce and myself will lead the attack* or ?? *The decision was taken by the manager and myself*.

> ?? This direct conflict of opinions ... could only be settled, if at all, between the President and myself.
> – Winston Churchill,
> *Triumph and Tragedy*

For a more detailed discussion of these objections, see MYSELF.

self-deprecation See DEPRECATE.

semicolon 1. a. The semicolon (;) is typically used between clauses that might have been separate sentences. The clauses are closely connected in thought or meaning:

> The sun shone; the children played.
> (= The sun shone and the children played.)

> Designers and musicians have been threatening to take over Shakespearean productions for some time now; here they do it, with encouraging results.
> – Robert Cushman, *The Observer*

Note that the semicolon is not followed by a capital letter here.

The use of the semicolon between two independent clauses serves to emphasise or add weight to the second clause:

> So you say; but how can I be sure you will keep your word? (The choice of semicolon rather than comma here emphasises the tone of mistrust.)

This use of the semicolon can be especially handy when the clauses that it links happen to contain commas:

> The sun, a bright yellow ball, shone; the children, happy as always, played.

When two parallel clauses are joined by a semicolon, a comma can be used to represent a missing element in the second of them:

> Antony loved Cleopatra; Romeo, Juliet.
> (= Antony loved Cleopatra; Romeo loved Juliet.)

b. The preceding principle is a description, not a rule: the clauses linked by a semicolon can often be punctuated in other ways. They can be separate sentences:

> The sun shone. The children played.

If you feel that there is a logical relation between the clauses, or if they have similar structures, a colon can be used:

> The sun shone: the children played.

If the clauses are as short as these, they may be linked by a comma only, especially in British English:

> ? The sun shone, the children played.

Many people still object to such a 'weak' form of punctuation, however.

c. Semicolon and conjunction are not mutually exclusive: both can be present in formal, deliberate style:

> The sun shone; and the children played.

But here a comma, or no punctuation at all, would be more likely:

> The sun shone (,) and the children played.

2. a. Although the conjunctions *and*, *but*, and *or* are preceded by a semicolon only in certain circumstances, other conjunction-like words or phrases (especially the mobile ones — really adverbial expressions — such as *none the less, however,* and so on) tend to take a semicolon (if not a full stop) in front of the clause they appear in:

> They tried hard; however, they failed. / They tried hard; they failed, however.
> They tried hard; nevertheless, they failed. / They tried hard; they failed nevertheless.
> They tried hard; all the same, they failed. / They tried hard; they failed all the same.

This general use of the semicolon can be contrasted with the options available before *but*:

> They tried hard but they failed.
> They tried hard, but they failed.
> They tried hard; but they failed. (very deliberate)

b. The semicolon is also used before adverbial elements that are not mobile and that introduce explanations or exemplifications:

> They tried hard; that is, they worked all day and all night.
> They tried hard; for example, they worked at weekends.

(Similarly, if *i.e.* or *e.g.* had been used in these examples, they would have had a semicolon before, and probably a comma after.)

If the introductory element is omitted, the semicolon should be replaced by a colon:

> They tried hard: they worked all day and all night.
> They tried hard: they worked at weekends.

3. As mentioned above, the semicolon can be used to link clauses that contain commas, and it can also be a weightier, more deliberate, alternative to the comma. Here are other examples of its use to punctuate stretches of text where commas are also used:

> The group consisted of John Smith, B.A., M.A.; Mary Jones, M.A., Ph.D.; and Fiona Forthright, M.D., Ph.D.

This example might attract criticism on the ground that only a simple string of similar elements is involved, with no internal hierarchy among its constituents. But in the next two examples, the semicolon helps to establish real internal sub-sets:

> On the table there were knives, forks, and spoons; cups and saucers; and plates, bowls, and glasses of all kinds.

This hardly fits in with Nicolson's view of the English character. The English national characteristics are, according to him: good humour, tolerance, ready sympathy, compassion; an affection for nature, animals, children; a fund of common sense; ... a dislike of extremes, of over-emphasis and boastfulness; a love of games; diffidence; shyness; laziness; optimism.

> – George Mikes,
> *English Humour For Beginners*

4. In some dictionaries, the semicolon is used between definitions or translations that are further apart in meaning than those separated by commas. However, other dictionaries use semicolons between near-synonymous definitions or translations, and use commas only *within* definitions. For example, the definition of the word *boisterous* in the Reader's Digest *Great Illustrated Dictionary* reads:

1. Rough and stormy; violent and turbulent.
2. Loud, noisy, and unrestrained.

Sense *1.* has two near-synonymous definitions separated by a semicolon. Sense *2.* has one definition, which contains two commas.

However, even dictionaries that use semicolons between definitions generally use commas between the glosses in etymologies. So, in its etymology of *boisterous,* the *Great Illustrated Dictionary* has:

[Middle English *boistres*, variant of *boist(e)ous*†, rude, fierce, stout.]

senior citizen The phrase *senior citizen* is now widely used as a term for 'an elderly person'. The phrase has been criticised as an unnecessary euphemism. It could be taken to imply that getting old is bad or embarrassing, and might even be used as a way of avoiding addressing the problems of society's care (or lack of care) for the aged.

sensitive, sensible One common sense of *sensible* is, to risk a pun, 'having common sense'. When used in this way, it is unlikely to be confused with *sensitive*, meaning 'having delicate feelings', 'easily affected', 'capable of perception', and so on. *Sensible* used to have these meanings too, though they have now fallen away. But one of its surviving senses does overlap slightly with *sensitive*: compare *She is sensible of your disapproval* with the more current *She is sensitive to your disapproval*. Even here, the distinction is still fairly easy to draw: both adjectives refer to an emotional consciousness, but *sensible* stresses the consciousness, whereas *sensitive* stresses the emotion or feeling. Note too that *sensible* in such contexts is a rather old-fashioned word now, that it typically is followed by the preposition *of* (whereas *sensitive* takes the preposition *to*), and that it cannot (unlike *sensitive*) be used directly in front of a noun: the phrase *a sensible woman* would be used only in referring to an intelligent woman, not in referring to an observant or vulnerable woman.

The problem really arises with the noun forms — *sense, sensibility, sensitivity*. The noun that best corresponds to *sensible* is simply *sense* (or *sensibleness*, though this is little used); the noun *sensibility* is much closer in meaning to *sensitive*! Jane Austen's novel *Sense and Sensibility* bears this out: Elinor (representing *Sense*) is the *sen-*

sible heroine; Marianne (representing *Sensibility*) is the *sensitive* heroine, who tends to overreact.

This is not to say that *sensibility* is an exact synonym of *sensitivity*. *Sensibility* primarily suggests the possession of fine perceptions — *the poet's sensibility* — or of delicate feelings: *a gentleman of sensibility and compassion*; *a comedian who offended our sensibilities with his bad language*.

I didn't go there because I don't like to go. Because it upsets me to go. The disorder in that office is terrible. It depresses me. It offends a person of my sensibilities to see such entire lack of method.

> – Arthur Norris,
> in Christopher Isherwood's
> *Mr Norris Changes Trains*

Sensibility can also be used in a broader sense — almost synonymously with *worldview* or even *consciousness*:

What a gap stretched between Robinson Crusoe — the last novel of human isolation without loss of identity, without alienation — and Kafka's Castle in which the new sensibility had been mercilessly exposed to view. The new departures in scientific thought had unsettled and indeed had even ruptured both syntax and serial order; the signal of course had long been given.

> – Lawrence Durrell,
> *The Fiction Magazine*

In the first two of these senses, *sensitivity* can be used as well, but it is more likely to occur when the stimuli or impressions prompting these delicate feelings and fine perceptions are being explicitly discussed as well: *In matters of art and music he has great sensitivity, but he's beastly to his wife.*

He was, however, on friendly terms with a living statesman, the Liberal Prime Minister, Asquith, whom he recalls in an attractive brief memoir. MacCarthy's sensitivity to the life of his times inspires one of his best short pieces, 'The First World War,' which juxtaposes his memories of London.

> – Professor Bernard Bergonzi,
> *The Observer*

Sensitivity has a far wider range of meaning than *sensibility*: *the sensitivity of the skin, the sensitivity of a photographic plate, the sensitivity of the stock-market*, and so on. However, *sensitivity* is seldom used in the sense of 'a tendency to react readily to criticism; touchiness'. The preferred noun here is *sensitiveness*. The following quotation neatly illustrates the difference:

> Others cluster round him; Daphne Manners
> — whose clumsy delicacy Susan Wooldridge
> movingly caught in a performance of intense
> precision and poignancy — an upper-class
> girl uneasy in the Raj community because of
> her sensitivity, and Ronald Merrick, a lower-
> class man uneasy in it because of his sen-
> sitiveness. Clutching his swagger-stick as if
> it were a talisman to ward off feelings of class
> discomfiture, Tim Pigott-Smith brings out
> the way Merrick is a man trying to exorcise
> a sense of social inferiority by exercising a
> sense of racial superiority.
> — Peter Kemp,
> *The Times Literary Supplement*

The opposite forms, *insensitive* and *insensible*, once again fail to correspond exactly to *sensitive* and *sensible*. *Insensitive* can mean 'lacking physical sensation or sensitivity' and 'lacking delicate feelings and responses', but it is used most often in the slightly extended sense of 'hurtfully tactless; thoughtless and hence cruel': *How insensitive you are, talking about suicide in that cavalier way when Paul is still so depressed.*

Insensible can mean 'unaffected or indifferent' — *insensible to the cold*; *insensible to my cries of pain* — or 'unaware': *I am not insensible of your anxiety* (note the different prepositions, according to the sense). It can no longer be used to mean 'unintelligent or irrational', even though 'intelligent' is the commonest meaning of *sensible*. And conversely, two very common meanings of *insensible* are not related to any current meanings of *sensible*: *insensible* can mean 'unconscious' — *He was knocked insensible* — and 'imperceptible, scarely visible': *an insensible change in temperature.*

sensual, sensuous These two adjectives both refer to the enjoyment of physical sensations. Both originally meant simply 'sensory'; that is, 'relating to the senses'. But they have diverged from this meaning, and from each other too in a way.

Both *sensual* and *sensuous* are often used in combination with the noun *pleasures*. Until recently, *sensuous pleasures* was the more general term:

> He ... refused to give up alcohol and tobac-
> co, which had become his only sensuous
> pleasures.
> — Peter Quennell, *The Wanton Chase*

But *sensual* is now perhaps more usual in such contexts:

> John Ruskin, the critic and champion of the
> Pre-Raphaelites, implied that the appropriate
> goal for painting was to take its 'proper place
> beside literature'. Indeed, the word, the plot,
> the narrative, the programme, remained
> paramount, and sensual delight and pleasure
> in the properties of paint second best.
> — Marina Vaizey, *The Sunday Times*

Sensuous has been tending increasingly towards the more refined sense of 'sensitive' — enjoying or providing fine sensations:

> Two recent paintings by Michael Andrews,
> in particular 'Melanie and Me Swimming' —
> in which a man holds up a little girl, both
> figures suspended in a blackness which
> merges water with sky — convey an enviably
> sensuous approach to the everyday world.
> — Lucy Ellmann (U.S.),
> *The Times Literary Supplement*

Today's *sensuous pleasures* are more likely to be music and painting than tobacco and alcohol. Tobacco and alcohol may now be regarded as *sensual pleasures* instead, which are earthier and coarser than *sensuous pleasures*. The words are easily confused when sensations perceived and enjoyed through the sense of touch are being described. *Sensual* often takes over the province of touch, even when the implications of coarseness or earthiness are no stronger than in the word *luxurious*:

> The light was amber-brown in vast, dark
> chambers shuttered from young light, where,
> in great walnut beds, the glorious women
> stirred in sensual warmth their lavish limbs.
> — Thomas Wolfe (U.S.),
> *The Web and the Rock*

> It's not Western motherhood that she now
> focuses on — it's the motherhood of Third
> World patriarchal societies, and their sensual
> absorption in babies and family life.
> — Minette Marrin, *The Observer*

Sensual has, however, developed a suggestion of excess, of too much physical enjoyment, and has come to mean 'self-indulgent, intent on or implying physical gratification'. In particular, it has become associated with sexual pleasure, probably because of the similarity in sound of *sensual* and *sexual*.

> Gay claims that social conditions created 'a
> family of desires and anxieties', a laboratory

site for neuroses. By the end of the book we have returned to a social situation in which the middle class shielded their sensuality from prying eyes.

– Phyllis Grosskurth, *The Observer*

She read Michel's letters first because she felt she owed him the attention. There were a dozen, and they varied from the frankly sensual and passionate to the brief and authoritarian.

– John le Carré,
The Little Drummer Girl

The distinction between *sensual* and *sensuous* becomes much clearer when the adjectives are applied to people rather than to pleasures. A *sensuous poet* is responsive to sensation, enjoying the beauties of art and nature and trying to convey them in his poetry (his *sensuous* poetry). He may or may not be a *sensual man*; that is, one who indulges in the more basic physical pleasures. *Sensual* is also used to indicate signs of such indulgence: *a sensual swagger, a sensual leer.*

The man was tall and fair, and his face was striking — the planes sharp, the mouth a straight deep line, but sensual.

– Catherine Gaskin, *Edge of Glass*

It is interesting to note a small difference in the meaning of *sensual* as it applies to a man or to a woman. *A sensual man* would be regarded as self-indulgent, unduly interested in sexual gratification; *a sensual woman* would be regarded as arousing sexual interest, as being 'sexy', not simply as interested in sexual gratification.

In the following example, the word *sensual* would surely be more appropriate than *sensuous,* which sounds very much like a euphemism in this context:

?? Hollywood is good at doing that sort of thing. Its proficiency at transforming little Connie Ockleman of Brooklyn into sultry, sensuous Veronica Lake was proved by the success of the venture.

– Veronica Lake (U.S.), *Veronica*

Sensuous has two common derivatives — *sensuously* and *sensuousness. Sensual* has many more: not just *sensually* and *sensualness,* but also *sensuality* (which can mean 'excessive devotion to sensual pleasures'), *sensualise* and *sensualisation, sensualism* (which can refer to the philosophical doctrine that the good is the same thing as the pleasurable), and *sensualistic* and *sensualist* (which can mean 'a person devoted to sensual pleasures').

sentences A sentence is a complete and independent grammatical unit consisting of a word or group of words. A full sentence, such as *The door was open*, consists usually of a 'subject' (the topic that the sentence is about) and a finite verb or verb phrase, the 'predicate', that tells us something about the subject. A sentence need not contain more than this, but it may have more than one 'main clause', as with *The door was open and I went in*, or one or more 'subordinate clauses' in addition to the main clause, as in *The door was open when I arrived*. (See CLAUSES.)

That is how a grammarian defines a sentence. Another way, perhaps more accurate, is simply by its punctuation. Sentences begin with a capital letter and end with a full stop, an exclamation mark, or a question mark.

A third approach would be to say that a sentence conveys some complete message, such as a statement, a question, a command, or an exclamation.

Sentences without full verbs The schoolroom rule that 'every sentence must have a full verb, and stand on its own as a complete utterance' is perhaps a good rule for schoolroom writing. But not for all writing. Effective style will not submit to arbitrary restraints of that kind. If a short verbless sentence or 'sentence fragment' is best suited to convey the message — as the second sentence of this paragraph is — then that is the sentence to use.

A verbless sentence is fairly common in answer to questions — *Of course not*; *Very well* — and sometimes in questions themselves: *What now? How so? The upshot?*

It is often used as a brief punchy introduction to some important statement: *To business. ... So much for that objection. ... In conclusion, a warning. ... And yet.*

It can be strikingly effective as a supplement, qualification, or contradiction of a statement:

He looks 90 years old. Perhaps older.

She says she overslept. My eye.

Brother Gianni keeps the keys to the catacombs, and eyes all visitors with suspicion. A kind of subterranean Quasimodo.

Criticism as a profession is losing, has lost, much of its respectability. Pity, that, and a sad thought for the coming year.

– Frank Delaney, *The Listener*

Many 'sentence fragments' are, in effect, subordinate clauses of a complex sentence, detached from the main clause and presented as a separate unit for the sake of greater emphasis:

And so my dear brother is gone. But not forgotten.
They advised me to sell up and move to Dublin. Which is what I did.

(The last sentence here, or sentence fragment, does have a full verb, but would not ordinarily be able to stand on its own as 'a complete utterance'.)

Finally, verbless sentences and sentence fragments can be used for deliberate dramatic or descriptive purposes:

The light retreats slowly, the wind drops, the birds return to their nests. Twilight and silence. A star quivers into view. Then another, and another. Until the whole night sky is ablaze.

Sentence fragments, including verbless sentences, achieve their effects by means of contrast with self-sufficient sentences that do have full verbs. As with all unconventional stylistic devices, sentence fragments need to be used with care. If they are to stand out from their background, they cannot also be the background at the same time. If overused, the sentence fragment draws attention to itself and can become an irritating mannerism. Used sparingly, it can be a great aid to the effective imparting of ideas or atmosphere; and that is sufficient justification of it, whatever the schoolroom view may be.

Sentence style There can be no cut-and-dried advice on the best length for sentences: so much depends on the purpose of the passage, and its intended audience or readership. Sentences in children's reading-books and in the less intellectual newspapers are usually kept short. And a short, crisp style is appropriate for written instructions:

After you plug your iron in the first time, a little smoke may be emitted from the sole plate. This reaction is quite normal and disappears after a short time. Allow two minutes for the iron to heat to the required temperature setting.

In general, a good stylist will vary sentence length, and not attempt longer sentences than he or she can structure (and punctuate) properly. The reader may lose the thread if a subject is separated from its verb, or a verb from its object, by too many subordinate clauses.

The kind of sentence should vary too. The writer must be aware of the many ways of building sentences. Children, when writing, often string together a series of main clauses with *and*: *I got up and cleaned my teeth and had breakfast and then I went to school*, and so on. Obviously, a more sophisticated writer will use subordinate clauses to break up such a monotonous sequence; yet subordinate clauses can be just as monotonous if limited to a single pattern: *This is the dog that worried the cat that killed the rat that ate the malt ...*

Stylists have distinguished three types of sentence: the close-knit *periodic sentence*, in which the thought develops with a gradual heightening of suspense until the main point is reached at the end; the *balanced sentence*, in which those parts that correspond or contrast in meaning are made to match each other in form; and the *loose sentence*, in which each element is added as it occurs, with little attempt at structuring.

Here are examples of each. First the periodic sentence:

When I consider all that I've done for you, without any thanks, and all that I've had to put up with from you, without any justification, and when I think how different it would have been had I married Mary instead of you, I could die of regret.

Here is a balanced sentence:

You may think that she has a simple and happy life, but I happen to know something of its complexities and sadness.

Here, finally, is a loose sentence. There would have been no effect of incompleteness if it had ended at the word *last* or the word *fatigue*:

We reached our destination at last, not without difficulties and considerable fatigue, bearing in mind the poor roads and bad weather.

sentiment, sentimentality *Sentiment* implies sincere or delicate feeling, and is a neutral or favourable term; *sentimentality* by contrast has distinctly negative overtones, and suggests excessive, affected, or tearful emotion, quite out of proportion and needing to be brought under the control of reason. Contrast the tones in the following two quotations:

'Take care of your little self,' she said, fixing her young blue eyes on me. The 'little' touched me; sentiment was unusual from her.

– Lynne Reid Banks,
The L-Shaped Room

... a pervasive streak of silliness. It is not that he knows no economics. He is awash with sentimentality: about Nye and Byron, the Celtic nations and the last war.

— Alan Watkins, *The Observer*

Sentimentality tends to be used in a general way, very seldom in the plural: *a recital that betrayed her sentimentality. Sentiment* is unlikely to be used in this simple way any longer: the phrase *a man of sentiment*, meaning 'a man of refined feeling, a sensitive man', now sounds very old-fashioned. If used in a general way at all, *sentiment* is likely to be qualified by an adjective: *a decision influenced by anti-American sentiment.* Usually, however, *sentiment* is used in a more specific way, often in the plural (though without any real feeling of plurality): the sense might be 'an attitude' — *an appeal to your patriotic sentiments* — or 'the emotional effect or intellectual message of a book, film, or the like' — *a beautifully written story, but its sentiments are dangerous* — or, slightly informally, 'an opinion': *You've heard what we think — what are your own sentiments?*

Sentimental is, theoretically, the adjective for both *sentiment* and *sentimentality*, but it almost always has the negative tone of *sentimentality* nowadays: *a sentimental love-story*; *Stop being so sentimental.*

And like Donal Davoren ... , Yeats is at times a foolishly sentimental nationalist, 'poet and poltroon, poltroon and poet'.

— Tom Paulin, *The Observer*

In three common phrases, however, *sentimental* retains the neutral tone of *sentiment*. The first is *sentimental reasons*, meaning 'reasons influenced by emotional rather than intellectual considerations': *He kept his old watch for sentimental reasons.* The second is *sentimental value*, meaning 'the importance attached to an object by its owner because of fond associations rather than monetary worth': *How cruel that thief was – he won't get £5 for that old clock of mine, but to me its sentimental value is incalculable.* The third phrase is *a sentimental journey*, immortalised by Lawrence Sterne in the title of a book (published posthumously in 1768) based on his travels in France and Italy. A popular song of the 1940s gave further currency to the phrase, which nowadays is used to refer to a journey made for emotional reasons, notably the nostalgic associations of the places visited.

sequence of tenses See TENSE 2.

serial, series The difference between these two nouns, when referring to literature or drama, is that a *serial* is a slowly unfolding tale, presented in instalments, whereas a *series* is a set of self-contained episodes, stories, or books, connected by common characters, theme, or format. Thus, *Dallas* and *Coronation Street* are television *serials*, whereas *Minder*, with a new story each week, is a *series*. Most of Dickens's novels were first published as *serials* in magazines, with a new instalment of the story each issue. Sir Arthur Conan Doyle wrote a *series* of Sherlock Holmes stories.

Series is always a noun, and takes the same form in singular and plural. *Serial* can be both noun and adjective.

Series has a wide range of other meanings too, of course: in sport, mathematics, grammar, electronics, and geology. *Serial*, as an adjective, has specialised senses in music and computing. Both words go back to the Latin *series*, from *serere*, 'to join'.

session See CESSION.

sewage, sewerage *Sewage* is the waste material carried away by water in sewers or drains. *Sewerage* is sometimes used in this sense too, but it is more commonly, and preferably, used to refer to the *system* or method of removing sewage, or simply to the network of sewers and drains. So: *There was a leak of sewage into the street*, and *The sewerage in this town needs improving.* Since *sewerage* implies a system, it is really redundant to speak of *? a sewerage system*. It is better to refer to *a sewage system*; similarly, *a sewage farm*.

It is quite common to hear the first syllable pronounced as /sōō-/ in both words; but traditionally, British English slightly prefers /**sew**-/, with its *y*- sound.

sexism in the English language Tennis commentators at Wimbledon — both male and female — speak of the *men's* championship and the *ladies'* championship. They compare the progress of the British *men* with that of the British *girls*. Discussing the singles finals, they refer typically to *McEnroe* and *Connors*, and to *Chrissie* and *Martina*. The scoreboard lists *McEnroe* and *Connors*, and *Mrs Evert-Lloyd* and *Miss Navratilova*.

Whether these distinctions serve to demean women, or patronise them, or elevate them, is a matter of opinion. But they clearly do set women apart, treat them in a different way, where there is no apparent need (except that of convention) to do so.

Western society is changing a great deal in its view of the role of women; the equal-rights movement has brought about not just practical changes but changes in thinking as well. And in the wake of these, language has been changing too, though rather more slowly: English remains strongly coloured by beliefs of the past. (Language is like that. We continue to speak of *the four corners of the earth* and of the sun as *rising* and *setting*, even though we know that the earth is round, and that it goes round the sun and not vice versa.)

Language reflects current beliefs too, not just those of the past, and residual sexism within English can be an indication of sexism in people's actions and attitudes. Some feminists go further, and argue that sexist language is in some way a *cause*, rather than simply a *result*, of sexist thinking and behaviour. The inequalities fossilised within English, they insist, are responsible for perpetuating the attitudes underlying them. Accordingly, they urge the introduction of new neutral terms to replace the old sexist terms — *humankind* for *mankind, chairperson* or *chair* for *chairman*, and so on.

They have achieved some successes, certainly. Many reputable newspapers throughout the English-speaking world have adopted *Ms* as an addition to, if not a replacement of, the traditional forms *Miss* and *Mrs*. On a much larger scale, the federal government in Australia decided in 1984 to expunge all sexist references from the statute books. Over 50,000 words in hundreds of parliamentary Acts will apparently have to be altered. 'Masculine' words such as *seaman* and *chairman* will be replaced — by *mariner* and *convenor* or *president*, for instance. And sentences will be restructured in order to avoid having to use *he, him*, and *his* to refer to both men and women.

But these policies can go only so far. They cannot force changes in people's speaking and writing habits, though they can influence these habits slowly. Even if English-speakers had an official academy (the way French-speakers do) to monitor and advise on the use of language, they would largely ignore its recommendations (just as French-speakers do). English technical and scientific vocabularies are standardised from time to time, but no large-scale language-planning and standardisation (of the kind undertaken in Indonesia, Malaysia, or the Philippines, for instance) would be tolerated in most English-speaking countries.

Gender It might perhaps be argued that English has far less in-built sexism than many other languages. Most European languages have (and even Old English *had*) gender-systems for nouns, pronouns, adjectives, and even the articles *a* and *the*: German has three forms for the singular *the* — masculine *der*, feminine *die*, and neuter *das*. In English, gender is hardly ever a problem: apart from the occasional crossing of boundaries — referring to a baby as *it* or a ship as *she* — the assignment of gender is quite regular and very simple.

English is often criticised for having to use *he* when referring to a person in the abstract, regardless of sex: *Any patient is free to bring his complaint to me if he feels aggrieved*. Yet many other European languages are apparently even worse off: English at least has a 'sexless' third person pronoun in the plural — *they: All patients can bring their complaints to me if they feel aggrieved*. On the other hand, Italian, for example, has to choose between *tutti i malati* ('all the patients' — masculine) and *tutte le malate* ('all the patients' — feminine). The feminine form is chosen only if every single patient referred to is female; but if even one of 20 patients is a man — the remaining 19 being women — then the masculine form takes priority.

Yet it would be quite wrong to conclude from all this that other European languages are more 'sexist' than English. Precisely because they are so gender-marked, they tend to dissociate gender and sex. When a Frenchman refers to a boat (*une barque*) as *elle* he is unlikely to be thinking of it as a woman — he is simply following the grammatical demands of his language — whereas an English-speaker referring to a boat as *she* is using a metaphor, and probably is intending a comparison between his boat and a woman. Similarly, for an Italian to refer to a predominantly female group of patients as *tutti i malati* is not to demean women: the 'masculine' form here is masculine in gender only — it is unlikely to be specifically associated with men as distinct from women. (Nevertheless, in 1984, the French Minister for Women's Rights, Mme Yvette Roudy, complained about her title *Madame le Ministre*, suggesting that the 'masculine' article *le* here was evidence of sexism in the French language.)

The symptoms of sexism in language Sexism in language is usually divided by linguists into 'active' and 'passive' sexism. Passive sexism involves taboos and 'avoidance behaviour' — the avoidance by women of certain kinds of language, notably swear-words and sometimes technical terms and political discussion. (These last two taboos represent a hangover from the days when technology and politics were considered the exclusive domain of men.)

But although 'passive sexism' may lead to observable differences between the language of women and the language of men, English is less culpable in this respect than certain other languages. In Japanese, for example, women have traditionally tended to choose the politer verb forms, and to use longer, less abrupt, more respectful sentence-patterns (though this is apparently changing). And some tribal peoples seem to have secret jargons, and sometimes virtually separate dialects, for all-male conversation and all-female conversation.

Active sexism takes various forms:
1. language used of women is often 'marked'; that is, it is different from the neutral, 'unmarked' form that is used of men (*actor* vs *actress*, for instance, or *author* vs *authoress*, or *judge* vs *woman judge*).
2. feminine words or forms can have pejorative meanings or associations (*spinster* — contrast *bachelor*).
3. certain 'masculine' words or expressions have no feminine equivalents (*masterful, masterly*) and vice-versa (*old maid*). And the 'masculine' words are more likely to have connotations of skill or power.
4. several 'neutral' words that apply to both men and women are in fact masculine in form (*mankind*).

To discuss each of these in detail:
1. *marked language.* The clearest example of 'marked' language for women is the set of titles *Mr, Mrs, Miss.* Just as it is the tradition for a married woman to wear a wedding ring, whereas her husband might well not, so a married woman has been traditionally distinguished from an unmarried woman by the title *Mrs* as opposed to *Miss.* The man of course is addressed only by one form, whether married or not. The neutral *Ms* form has now been fairly widely adopted, in the effort to correct what is regarded as unfair discrimination.

Feminine suffixes are also used to 'mark' language, as in the pair *actor/actress.* The masculine form is also the 'neutral' form, in that it can be applied to men and women; the suffix *-ess* marks out the actor as a woman. Not that the distinction is unimportant here — in the acting profession, jobs are seldom interchangeable between the sexes; the problem is rather the asymmetry — that women are assigned a 'marked' form, whereas men are not, suggesting that it is normal for men to act but unusual for women to (and so it was in times past). In other cases, such as *author/authoress* (see section **2.b.** below),

the feminine suffix is not necessary, and is often objected to as demeaning.
2. *pejorative feminine words.* **a.** Consider the following list:

bachelor *vs* spinster
to father *vs* to mother
old dog *vs* old bitch
barman *vs* barmaid

Bachelor suggests freedom — it has a debonair and adventurous ring to it; *spinster* suggests age, loneliness, dullness. (So much so that the phrase *bachelor girl* is now used of unmarried young career women.) *To father* implies 'to create'; *to mother* implies 'to nurture', and sometimes, disparagingly, 'to smother'. To call a man an *old dog* is probably to pay him a wry compliment; to call a woman an *old bitch* is to be extremely insulting. *Barman* merely denotes a job, *barmaid* can suggest a bosomy physique. (Perhaps *bargirl* is the more neutral equivalent, but *girl* suggests a lower status here than *man* does. The properly symmetrical term would be *barwoman*, but it is hardly ever used. At least the American term, *bartender*, can in theory be used to refer to either a man or a woman.)

For some people, interestingly enough, *lady* has become an objectionable term. As with *gentleman* and *man*, it can serve merely as a polite equivalent of *woman*. (*Who's that lady over there?*, one might ask, especially if she is in earshot, as opposed to the blunter *Who's that woman over there?*) However, it is now considered better by some to refer to a female dentist, for instance, as a *woman dentist* than as a *lady dentist*, which allegedly trivialises her professional status (see WOMAN).
b. The feminine suffixes *-ess, -ette, -enne* (as in *comedienne*) are seen by some people as unnecessary and even in some cases demeaning:

author   authoress
poet   poetess
sculptor   sculptress

(And yet these *-ess* forms have been established for hundreds of years — dating back to the 15th, 16th, and 17th centuries respectively.) The use of the *-ess* suffix today implies, some people feel, that female authors, sculptors, and so on are deviations from the standard, and thus in some way inferior. Why use a feminine form at all, if the neutral (or masculine) form can refer to both men and women?

The difference between *waiter* and *waitress*, *steward* and *stewardess*, or *bus conductor* and *bus conductress*, however, does not carry any pejorative overtones; but then these are occupations of relatively low status. (Yet feminists prefer *flight attendant* to *steward/stewardess*. And although you might shout *Waiter!* in a restaurant to attract the waiter's attention, you might not so readily shout *Waitress!* to attract the waitress's attention.)

There is of course a world of difference between the sphere of influence of a *governor* (of a state, province, prison, or the like), and that of a *governess* in a private house. The feminine form has in this case taken on a less important meaning. In these days of greater equality between the sexes, however, when the possibility exists of a female administrator of a state, she would obviously also be called a *governor*, as the sense of the female form is now too restricted. (See the article -ESS for a more detailed discussion.)

The *-ette* suffix, as used in French, indicates not just feminine but diminutive as well. (The diminutive sense is quite apparent in English in such terms as *caravanette*, *kitchenette*, and *maisonette*.) When applied in English to people, the *-ette* suffix often purports simply to denote the feminine — *usher/usherette* — but the 'diminutive' association remains — an *usherette* is smaller, and hence less important, than an *usher*. Similarly, though with greater justice, *drum majorette* sounds distinctly insignificant alongside *drum major*. The suffix *-ette* has become a common means of disparagement: to call a young female student an *undergraduette* is almost always to diminish her; to call a young female journalist a *hackette* is to add an extra twist to the insult inherent in the term *hack*.

3. *lack of feminine/masculine equivalents.* Consider *master/mistress*. In the sense of 'a schoolteacher', the two words are equivalent in tone and range, differing only in the sex-reference; in their other senses they are far from parallel: *He was a past master in the art of deception* would, in the case of a woman remain *She was a past master . . . .* And although *postmaster* has a feminine equivalent in *postmistress*, there is no corresponding equivalent of *postmaster general*. And there are no feminine equivalents of many other compounds or derivatives: *mastermind, masterstroke, masterpiece, masterful, master key, mastery*.

Mistress, in the sense of 'a married man's female lover', has no masculine equivalent from the same root; traditionally society saw the relationship as one-directional — a man took a mistress, not vice versa (a woman these days simply takes a *lover*).

The traditional dominance (or despotism) of the man is seen in such expressions as *ladies' man*,

to womanise, wife-swapping, and *wife-beater*: there is no corresponding feminine term for any of these. The traditional concentration of political and economic power in the hands of men is reflected in such terms as *kingdom* and *son and heir* — again, there is no exact idiomatic feminine equivalent.

Traditionally, certain jobs have been performed by men, and others by women. This is sometimes reflected in the names of these jobs: *dustman, fireman, hangman*, and *milkman* (*milkmaid* is of course an archaic word for the female farm-worker who milked the cows); *midwife* and *charwoman* (and also *nanny* and *nurse*). None of these has a precise opposite-sex equivalent. However, now that roles are changing, and there is more flexibility in employment, solutions have to be found. One solution is simply to use the original form as a 'neutral', applying to men and women alike:

? She's a milkman.
? Mary works as a dustman.

Alternatively, *-man* is sometimes changed to *-woman*:

> She wants to be a policewoman when she grows up.
> Molly has been voted businesswoman of the year.
> We now have a postwoman instead of a postman.

Traditionally feminine jobs can be preceded by 'male', or again used as neutral forms:

> He's a (male) nurse.
> He's a (male) midwife.

In some cases an entirely different word is adopted to skirt the problem:

> He/She's a cleaner (rather than *charwoman*, or ✗ *charman*).

Considerable effort is now being devoted, in English and other languages, to developing 'sex-neutral' (and 'age-neutral') occupational titles, and these efforts sometimes have official support.

Other jobs or professions traditionally monopolised by men — *surgeon, barrister, MP, magistrate* — are not marked as specifically male (in the way that *dustman* and *milkman* are), and are apparently sex-neutral. They would seem, therefore, to present no equivalent problem. During the transitional period when women first took to entering these professions, there was a natural tendency to use the word *woman* as a modifier when there was any chance of misunderstanding:

a woman surgeon, a woman judge. Now that women are well-represented in most such professions (though often still far from equally represented), it would seem unnecessary to specify *woman* before the name of the profession. Yet the precaution sometimes is still necessary, since in the popular imagination *a surgeon* or *a barrister* still tends to be male.

It is natural enough to speak of a *woman judge*; but what title could be used when a woman judge attains one of the senior judicial positions in the United Kingdom — *Lord Chief Justice*, for instance (as it is currently known), or *Master of the Rolls* or a *Lord Justice of Appeal*?

In the United States, the legal system faced and dealt with a similar problem a few years ago. In 1980, the nine (male) judges of the US Supreme Court stopped referring to themselves as *Mr Justice X* — the official title and mode of address since the early 19th century. They became simply *Justice X*, thereby accommodating Sandra Day O'Connor when she became the first woman member of the Supreme Court in September 1981.

Certain words and expressions that apply only or mainly to women reflect society's traditional views on woman's status and nature: *maiden aunt*, *old maid*, *to henpeck*, and *wifely*. An unmarried woman can be a cause for comment, an unmarried man is less likely to be; *nagging* is associated with women far more than with men, and so on. (True enough, the word *househusband* has recently been coined as the equivalent of *housewife*, for a man who stays at home while his wife goes out to work, but it is not as yet extensively used. Nor is the 'neutral' term *homemaker*.)

Note too that even some sex-neutral adjectives have slightly different meanings when applied to men and to women. An *imposing* man is obviously an impressive and admirable man; an *imposing* woman is probably a daunting and unsympathetic woman — a 'battle-axe'. (See SENSUAL.)

Finally, note the lack of commonly used opposites for *old woman* and *misogynist*. If we refer to someone as an *old man*, we are talking about his age or status; if someone (in particular, a man) is called an *old woman*, the meaning is very different. And whereas hatred of women is firmly incorporated in the language by the word *misogynist*, its opposite *misandrist* is so rare as to suggest that hatred of men scarcely exists. (The word *misanthrope* or *misanthropist* refers to a person who hates mankind — humankind — in general rather than men specifically.)

4. 'neutral' masculine words. When a neutral term is required, English has usually employed the masculine form: *to master, man, spokesman, layman, chairman, mankind, he/his* (*Any patient is free to bring his complaint to me ...*). These forms are objected to by some feminists on the grounds that they are not in fact neutral terms, but distinctly masculine, and hence that they subconsciously reinforce the dominant role played by men in our society. There has been much discussion about the use of *he* to mean 'he or she', and *man* to mean 'men and women'. (See HE, HIM, HIS; HE OR SHE; MAN; THEY, THEM, THEIR; YOU, YOUR, YOURS.) Psychological studies confirm the 'maleness' of *he* and *man*: when people are asked to draw pictures based on sentences in which *man* and *he* are used neutrally, they tend overwhelmingly to draw pictures of men and boys.

Yet the alternatives are all unsatisfactory in one way or another: *he or she* is awkward; *they* is considered by purists to be bad grammar; *you* can be hectoring, and so on. Some writers, desperate to redress the balance, have taken to using *she* as the neutral pronoun (or to alternating *he* and *she*):

> Essentially, a linguist needs to fill two kinds of gap. On the one hand, she must push back our knowledge of the language to a point prior to that of our first written records. On the other hand she must bridge the gaps between documents.
>
> – Jean Aitchison,
> *Language Change: Progress or Decay?*

'Baby and Child' is written from your baby or child's point of view because, however fashion in child-rearing may shift and alter, her viewpoint is both the most important and the most neglected.

> The book looks at what is happening within her, from the moment of birth until the time when you launch her into the wider world of school.
>
> – Penelope Leach, *Baby and Child*

> Yet, unless a judge regularly selects clerks who remain total ciphers — a prospect that would cause us to wonder about the judge or the quality of her judicial output — there is a substantial risk.
>
> – Professor Harlon L. Dalton (U.S.),
> *The Yale Law Journal*

On the other hand, some feminist writers see no reason to distract the reader's attention from more important matters, and accept the traditional male/neutral *he* and *his* as including women. The following passage, written by a leading black feminist woman writer from the southern United States, displays a resolute lack of concern with the minutiae of pronoun-forms:

> But this view of a strictly private and hidden existence, with its triumphs, failures, grotesqueries, is not nearly as valuable to the socially conscious black southern writer as his double vision is. For not only is he in a position to see his own world, and its close community ... but also he is capable of knowing, with remarkably silent accuracy, the people who make up the larger world that surrounds and suppresses his own.
>
> – Alice Walker (U.S.),
> *The Fiction Magazine*

Avoiding sexist language For those who are concerned with the sexist implications of *he/his*, *chairman*, and so on, there are three different ways of challenging the traditional forms.

● replacement by truly 'neutral' forms:

mankind	— humankind
chairman	— chair
spaceman	— astronaut
snowman	— ? snow sculpture
manhole	— ? utility tunnel
foreman	— supervisor
manned by	— staffed by
fireman	— fire fighter

This is a satisfactory method so long as it uses unobjectionable existing words and does not sound too contrived. Sometimes a 'neutral' term is devised in a playful spirit:

> But in her new novel — her first for seven years — Ms Carter has at last hit on means of bringing together her various tastes and subjects. The result is a mistress-piece of sustained and weirdly wonderful Gothic that's both intensely amusing and also provocatively serious.
>
> – Valentine Cunningham,
> *The Observer*

But sometimes the 'neutral' term is so forced and unnatural as to sound just silly, as this amusing recollection makes clear:

> Once a month we ran a live phone-in programme with the Governor of Texas in the studio answering questions from the public. We had a group of people assigned to answer the phone and vet the calls, and as I wasn't directly involved with the programme that night I volunteered to man one of the

phones. The producer carefully put me right on my use of the term 'man', telling me that they don't 'man' phones, they 'person' them. So I went off to person the phone.

> – Kate Turkington, quoted in
> *The Star* (Johannesburg)

Person as a neutral form has been much discussed, especially in connection with the notorious *chairperson*. The major problem, apart from the ugliness of the word, is that it is *not* used indifferently of men and women, but is usually applied to women. So it merely draws attention to the users' view of sexual politics (as, to some extent, does the use of the term *Ms*). Another problem is the tendency for *-person* to have the prissy *-persons* as its plural, rather than the plainer *-people*. (See CHAIRMAN.)

● use of female opposites in job titles such as:

spacewoman
saleswoman
horsewoman
postwoman

These would seem to be acceptable alternatives to the masculine versions, though some feminists would argue that such 'marking' is demeaning. In jobs where the woman's role is different from the man's, as often in the police force, the feminine form is less controversial; *policewoman* and *WPC* (Woman Police Constable) are certainly established in their own right.

Feminists are rightly contemptuous of the 'chauvinist' claim that the word *-person* is itself sexist, embracing as it apparently does the masculine word *son*. In fact, the two words are quite unrelated in origin. But feminists cannot dismiss quite so lightly the retort that *woman* too retains a masculine tinge, embracing as it does the word *man*: the original Old English form was *wīf-mann*, from *wīf*, 'wife' + *man*. As it happens, the root-word *man* probably meant 'a person' here rather than 'a male adult human being'. But, equally, *man* can also be understood today as 'a person' or 'people in general' — throughout the history of the language it has retained this meaning. (See MAN.) Yet feminists persist in objecting to its use in this sense.

● creation of new terms such as:

herm	('her or him')
per	('person', 'he or she')
s/he	('she or he')
wm	(pronounced /ŏŏm/, meaning 'him or her')
peep	('singular' of *people*: hence *cowpeep, police-peep, chairpeep*).

New words do sometimes arise and oust old words — but very rarely can they oust words as common and deeply rooted as *she, he, him, her,* and so on. (See ITS.) And they are even less likely to do so if they are unnatural, artificial-sounding coinages. Any attempt at a contrived foisting of new pronouns on the language seems bound to fail, unless the English-speaking world begins a drastic new policy of dictating, rather than simply observing and occasionally nudging, the development of its language.

One last minor technique is worth mentioning: reversing the traditional sexual hierarchy by reversing the usual sequence of elements within a phrase: *he or she* becomes *she or he, husband and wife* becomes *wife and husband*. Feminist writers are increasingly drawn to this reversal, as a good-humoured and temperate reminder that English allows at least some leeway between sexist phrasing and unacceptable rephrasing.

In conclusion: where the spirit of the language allows it, try to avoid discriminatory wording. It is not always easy to strike a balance between the linguistic sensitivity of men (and women) and the personal feminist feelings of women (and men). Given an appropriate audience or readership, and an appropriate context, you might favour *woman* over *lady*, substitute *Ms* for *Mrs* or *Miss* (see MISS), and use unmarked or neutral forms such as *author, sculptor,* and *astronaut*. Above all, consider whether and to what degree you and other people are influenced by traditional assumptions enshrined in language or built into its very structure.

shall, will The choice between these two verbs (and between their past forms *should* and *would*) is a very complex one. The traditional rules, in the English of England at any rate, are these:

1. *In statements (and exclamations)*:
— *shall* is used after *I* or *we* to indicate future time;
— *will* is used after *I* or *we* to indicate determination, intention, a promise, an assurance, and the like;
— with the second and third persons, both singular and plural, (*you, he, she, it, they, Peter, the dog*) it is the other way round.
So:

I shall meet you in Newcastle at 6.30 as usual (also: I shall be meeting you . . . ; I shall have met you . . .).
James will meet me in Newcastle at 6.30 as usual.
We will take the car tonight, whether you like it or not.
They shall have the car, whether you like it or not.
I will win the case, I promise you: rest assured, you shall see justice done.

According to a famous apocryphal story, a drowning man shouted *I will drown, for no one shall save me,* only to be politely ignored by the Englishmen on shore — they assumed that he intended to commit suicide (*I will drown*), and was determined to fight off all rescue attempts (*no one shall save me*).

Unfortunately, the language is simply not as neat as that today, and probably never was. In Scotland and Ireland, and probably in North America, the distinction was never widely acknowledged in the first place, let alone observed — the word *shan't* is almost never heard there, for example. Australia, New Zealand, and South Africa may pay lip-service to the English of England, but on this question are even less rigorous than England is. And in England, the attention paid to the rule today is little enough.

In Winston Churchill's classic expression of determination and assurance during the Second World War, the emphatic *we will* might, for instance, have been expected. Instead:

? We shall fight on the beaches, we shall fight on the landing grounds, we shall fight in the fields and in the streets, we shall fight in the hills; we shall never surrender.
— Winston Churchill, speech in the House of Commons, June 1940

In a later speech during the war, Churchill did use the emphatic *we will* in accordance with the rule. He preceded it, however, with an unemphatic *? I will* that is in defiance of the rule.

? Here is the answer which I will give to President Roosevelt . . . Give us the tools, and we will finish the job.
— Winston Churchill, radio broadcast, February 1941

Lord Denning, in his judgments, virtually always used *I will*, whether in emphatic or unemphatic contexts.

✗ It will enable the court to avoid an erroneous construction of the Act; and that will be for the good of all. So I will proceed to consider them in this case. . . .

The statements made in committee disposed completely of counsel for the respondent's argument before us. It is just as well that you should know of them as well as me. So I will give them.

– Lord Denning, 'Davis v Johnson',
The All England Law Reports

The exceptions to the rule, and the common contraventions of it, can be summed up as follows:

First, in informal usage — both in spoken and increasingly in written English — the contraction *'ll* is commonly used, and the choice between *shall* and *will* is thereby avoided. (Note that the negative contraction *'ll not,* as in *They'll not be staying tonight,* is chiefly British English (especially Scottish), and *shan't* occurs chiefly in the English of England; the World English form is *won't.*)

Secondly, the use of *shall* and *will* is probably not the commonest way of expressing future time even in formal English, and is a very uncommon way of expressing determination, intention, or assurance. *The president will fly to Camp David tonight* might just as easily be worded *The president is going to fly to Camp David tonight* or *The president is flying to Camp David tonight.* And the emphatic *He shall do it* might just as easily be represented in speech as *He **will** do it* (stressing the *will*) or in writing (according to the context) as *He must do it* or *You cannot stop him doing it.*

Thirdly, *shall* and *will* have other functions and meanings, and these tend to interfere with the smooth implementation of the rule. *Shall* can indicate obligation or compulsion — especially in legal contexts — in the first person as well as in the second and third:

The fine shall not exceed £50.
You shall complete payment within three years.
According to section 3, I shall be answerable only to the directors themselves.

Shall is also the form used — in both second and third person as well as first — in many very formal or archaic constructions after *if, that,* or *lest*:

If you shall ever change your mind, come and see me again.
I am worried lest he shall resort to some desperate measure.
His majesty desires that you shall report this matter to the minister.

(For further details of such constructions, see SHOULD. The modern idiom would of course simply omit *shall* in all three of these sentences, or use *should.*)

Will, especially in British English, can indicate inference or assumption — *That will be Simon ringing*; *That will have been Simon* — and repeated or habitual action: *We will sit for hours at a time just staring into space*; *Boys will be boys.* In indirect commands, especially military commands, *will* tends to be used, rather than the emphatic *shall*: *You will assemble at 1800 hours for embarkation*; *The fourth brigade will advance ten kilometres.* (The regular verb *to will* — referring to choosing, decreeing, influencing, bequeathing, and so on — is not relevant here: it works quite differently, having for example the past form *willed* rather than *would: I willed her death.*)

2. *In questions:*
a. Questions in which advice or an instruction is sought, or which make a suggestion:
— *shall* is used before *I* or *we*;
— *should* (sometimes *shall*) is used before *he*, *she*, *it*, *you*, *they*, *the cat*, *Mary*, and so on.

What shall I/we do?
Shall we dance?
Shall I open the window?
(Shall)/Should James open the window?

Again, the English of Scotland, Ireland, and sometimes North America fails to oblige. In North America (and increasingly in England too, perhaps), people may prefer the form *Should I open the window?* In Scotland and Ireland, people tend to say *Will I open the window?* — a construction that sounds very strange to the ear of an Englishman.

Some North Americans observe the following distinction: if the person being addressed is included in the *we, shall* is used in invitations — *Shall we dance?* — and *shall* or *should* in suggestions: *Should/Shall we go and visit your mother this evening?* If the person being addressed is excluded from the *we,* then *should* tends to be used (though *shall* is also possible): *Should we put the keys under the mat, lady?*

b. Questions posing a request:
— *will you* or *would you*:

Will you let me know as soon as you hear any news?
Would you give me a hand, please?

c. Questions in which a prediction is sought that does not depend on the speaker or the subject of the sentence:
— *will* is used in all persons:

What will I/we need?
Will they betray us?

Will I pass my driving test?
Will they betray us?

d. Questions in which information about the future is sought that depends at least partly on the speaker or the subject of the sentence:
— *shall* for *I* and *we,* and formerly for *you* as well;
— *will* for the third person, and today for the second person too:

When shall we meet again?
How (shall)/will you approach this problem?
(*Shall* combines with *you* more easily in yes-no questions than in *wh*-questions.)
Why will he oppose our suggestion?
(Shall)/Will you resign?

The Scots and Irish would say *When will we meet again?*, and North Americans also use *will* more often than *shall* here. (Note that North Americans do tend, however, to observe a distinction between *should* and *would* in one particular pair of rhetorical questions: *How should I know?* and *How would you/he/they know?*)

Note the advantage of the form *Shall you*: it indicates unambiguously a question rather than a request: *Shall you join us tomorrow?* The form *? Will you join us tomorrow?,* on the other hand, is ambiguous: it can mean 'Inform us — yes or no?' (question) or it can mean 'Please do join us' (request or invitation). However, if the progressive form *be + -ing* is used after *Will you,* then the ambiguity dissolves — the intention is clearly a question not a request: *Will you be joining us tomorrow?*

● *Recommendation* In informal usage, the contraction *'ll* is quite adequate, and the choice between *shall* and *will* is thereby avoided. Even in formal English, a variety of alternative expressions is available — *must, is going to, is determined to, presumably,* and so on: the need to choose between *shall* and *will* is therefore much less common than is generally supposed.

Where a choice has to be made, it is worth testing yourself by trying to follow the rules outlined earlier — not just in order to oblige the purists, but also in the effort to preserve a small but useful distinction of meaning in our language.

The minimum set of guidelines is this (at least for speakers in England, Australia, New Zealand, South Africa, and other countries where the model is the English of England):
Will is the common form, but *shall* should be used in most first-person questions: *Shall I go? When shall we go?*
Shall is also available in various other construc-

tions: in descending order of importance, they are as follows —
● in indicating legal or official requirements: *The applicant shall submit three copies*;
● in first-person statements that simply indicate future time: *I shall go*;
● in questions (as distinct from requests) expecting a *yes/no* answer in the second person as well as the first — especially where the answer depends on the action of the subject of the question: *Shall you visit him?*;
● in second- and third-person statements where the intention is to indicate the speaker's determination, command, or assurance rather than simply to indicate future time: *You **shall** go! They shall not pass!*
See also SHOULD.

shambles Many purists regret and discourage the weak modern sense of this word, 'a scene of disorder or wreckage; a mess': *? Tidy your room — you've left it in a shambles.*
Originally a *shamble* was a table or market stall, typically one on which a butcher's meat was displayed for sale. The word was later used of a slaughterhouse, and by extension came to refer to a place or scene of carnage. The most recent extension — from the scene of bloodshed to a scene of mere untidiness — has understandably distressed many careful speakers. It has drained a vigorous and valuable word of its — blood. For better or worse, however, the change has taken place. All that the careful speaker can do today is take care not to overwork the word, in the way that many journalists tend to do.
Note that *shambles,* although originally the plural of *shamble,* is now a singular noun:

The shambles on the M4 yesterday evening — it involved 93 vehicles, and has so far cost 13 lives — is to be the subject of an official investigation by the Department of Transport.

The adjective *shambolic,* meaning 'hopelessly disorganised, or inept', probably began life as a facetious and slangy formation, but seems to have quickly gained acceptance into standard British English. It would still not be appropriate in very formal contexts, however.

should, would The choice between *should* and *would* is not always a straightforward one. The traditional rules (which may never have been a faithful reflection of existing practice) are in some respects similar to those governing *shall* and *will,* but there is no exact overlap. (See SHALL.)

1. The basic rule applies only to certain uses of *should* and *would* (and whether it applies even to them is disputed): *should* is used with *I* and *we*; *would* is used with second and third person subjects — *you, he, she, it, they, James, the dogs,* and so on.

a. *Should* and *would* are used as the equivalents, in indirect or reported speech or in past-tense constructions, of *shall* and *will*:

> I thought I should come second or third, but I never expected to win.

> I thought he would come second or third, but I never expected him to win.

> His uncle rallied him from time to time on his silence, and I reflected how much I should dislike to travel with Mr van Hoorn.
> – Christopher Isherwood,
> *Mr Norris Changes Trains*

In informal English, both spoken and written, the contraction *'d* (less often written *'ld* nowadays) would be used in these sentences: *I thought I'd/he'd come second ...* So the need to choose between *would* and *should* is averted. (The negative contraction *'d not,* as in *I thought that he'd not do badly,* is chiefly British English; the World English forms are *wouldn't* and *shouldn't*.) Where the contraction is not used, the chances are that *would* rather than *should* would be used in both of the sentences. The rule requiring *should* after *I* or *we* is not recognised in Scotland, Ireland, or North America, and nowadays is hardly recognised in England either, or in those countries where England provides the model.

There is in fact a good argument against the rule; namely, that this future-in-the-past use of *should* clashes with the far more common ethical sense of *should,* 'ought to', and produces ambiguity as a result:

> ? It was obvious that we should report him to the police.

Most people would understand this to mean 'it was obvious that we ought to report him'. But a purist might have intended it to mean 'It was obvious that we were going to report him', and thereby have laid himself open to misunderstanding. Had he followed the prevailing idiom and said

> It was obvious that we would report him to the police,

his meaning would have been clear and unambiguous.

b. *Should* and *would* are used in conditional constructions.

i. First, in the main clause:

> If we persevered, we should meet our quota.
> If you persevered, you would meet your quota.
> If you had persevered, you would have met your quota.
> I should be a liar were I to give you any such assurance.

Again, the prevailing idiom would tend to disregard the rule, and would consider *would* after *I* and *we* as acceptable as *should*.

A typical mistake of children is to write *would of* instead of *would have*:

> ✗ If you'd asked her, she would of said yes.

Note that the *should/would* or *should have/would have* appears in the main clause not the *if*-clause of ordinary conditional sentences: *If you had tried harder, you would have succeeded.* A fairly common variant, though considered nonstandard, has *would (have)* in the *if*-clause as well:

> ✗ If you would have tried harder, you would have succeeded.
> ✗ If you would try harder, you would succeed.
> ✗ If only she would have discussed it with me first!

ii. In some conditional sentences, the *if*-clause can appropriately take a subjunctive or 'conditional' verb: this time, *should* rather than *would* is the correct form, for second- and third- as well as first-person subjects:

> If I should die, think only this of me ...
> If you should leave him, he will/would kill himself.
> Should they attempt another assault, send for reinforcements.

(These constructions are all fairly old-fashioned now, and would probably be rephrased today as *If I die, If you ever leave/left him,* and *If they attempt*.)

iii. However, an *if*-clause can sometimes be used as a polite request or instruction (always in the second person), and here *would* not *should* is once more the correct verb:

> If you would care to follow me, ladies and gentlemen, the musicians are ready to begin their recital in the drawing-room.

> If you would be so good as to put this slide under the microscope and tell me what you

think it is, please ...

iv. The form *I should* (or *I would*) in the main clause can be used as a means of giving advice or a warning, especially in southern British English. The *if*-clause is sometimes left unstated:

I should dress warmly (if I were you).
I should behave myself if I were you.

I would and *I'd* are perhaps equally idiomatic here. (Some speakers can even go so far as to say *? I should behave yourself,* but here, though the meaning is clear enough, the mixture of *I* and *yourself* is too strange for standard idiom.)

c. *Should* and *would* can be used to indicate courtesy or moderation:

My wife would be only too happy to oblige.
Would you help me with this bolt, please?
I should be honoured to meet your mother.
I should be delighted to see you home.

A slight danger of ambiguity is again present here. The last of the examples, for instance, could just possibly be interpreted as 'I ought to be delighted to see you home (but I'm not)'.

Pronunciation and stress make misunderstanding unlikely, however; if *should* means 'ought to' here, it will be pronounced /shŏŏd/ and stressed; if it means 'would', it will be pronounced /shəd/ and left unstressed. So *should* remains reasonably idiomatic here, though *would* is probably found more often — all the more so when the courteous wording introduces a refusal rather than consent or acceptance:

I would be delighted to see you home, but unfortunately I'm due at a meeting in five minutes.

d. *Should* and *would* are often used with verbs indicating desire or reluctance:

I should like to propose a toast.
I should prefer to put it off until next week.
Would you care for a cigarette?
You wouldn't want to eat there, believe me.
I should jolly well hope so.
We should be most reluctant to implement that suggestion.
They would be most reluctant to implement that suggestion.

Should remains reasonably idiomatic in first-person constructions here.

One peculiarity: consider the common expressions *I'd rather* or *She'd/You'd rather* (or *sooner*), as in *He'd rather be in Philadelphia than here* or *I'd sooner die.* For the second and third person, the preferred expansion is usually *He/You/They would rather.* But in the first person, *I had rather* is just as likely as *I would rather.* (For a slight difference in usage between these two forms, see RATHER **2.**) But *?? I should rather* sounds quite unidiomatic today. The expansion of *I'd better* or *She'd/You'd better,* as in *I'd better own up,* is *had better* for all persons: *I/You/They had better own up.* You cannot use *would* or *should* here.

Note the past tense of a sentence such as *I should like to meet her* or *They would prefer not to go.* Either the main verb or the infinitive can be couched in the past: *I should have liked to meet her* or *I should like to have met her.* It is excessive — and probably unacceptable — to couch both parts in the past:

?? I should have liked to have met her.
?? They would have preferred not to have gone.

(For further details, see HAVE **6.**)

e. *Should* (and *would*) can be used to indicate uncertainty or tentative opinion. The expressions considered here are in the first person singular only:

I shouldn't have thought so.
I shouldn't be at all surprised.
I should imagine that they'll sign the treaty early next week.

Should is still quite idiomatic here, though *would* sounds equally correct. One instance where *should* cannot be used after *I* is the colloquial expression *I wouldn't know.* The interrogative form, however, can use either *would* or *should,* probably favouring the original rule: *How should I know? How would you/she/they know?* There is a tendency to keep this particular *should/would* distinction even in North American English.

f. *Should* and *would* are used in negative or exclamatory constructions, as a protest of indignant denial. Only first-person subjects are concerned here (singular or plural). According to the traditional rule, therefore, *should* is the correct form:

We shouldn't dream of inconveniencing you.
To think that I should ever do such a thing!

To many people, however, the use of *should* in such sentences seems so old-fashioned or stilted as to be virtually unacceptable. Modern idiom would probably prefer *wouldn't* and *would ever* in the above examples.

2. *Would* and *should* are not always in competition. In certain contexts, only one is possible.

a. In subordinate clauses generally expressing

561

wishes or emotional reactions — after verbs such as *propose*, *intend*, *be eager*, and *it is a pity* — *should* (or *shall*) is often used. It can sometimes be omitted, but it cannot be replaced by *would*:

> It was his dying wish that we should get married.
> I am sorry that you should have taken it that way.
> I am amazed that you should take it that way.
> It is disgraceful/surprising/natural that Mary should worry about him.

In nonstandard American English, especially in New York, *should* is sometimes heard in a clause after the verb *to want*: × *I want you should listen very carefully to me*. This is not used (and should not be used) in British English.

b. *Should* has various senses absent from *would*, and is therefore often correctly used with second- and third- as well as first-person constructions. Among the shades of meaning indicated by *should* are:

● duty, necessity or strong probability:

> You should always check your rear-view mirror before setting off.
> Your parents should have arrived by now.

● anticipation or assumption:

> The meeting should be over in half an hour, at this rate.
> Your parents should be here at about 10.30.

● condition or contingency (see section **1. b. ii.** above):

> Should he so much as move, blow his head off.
> If you should ever change your mind, come and see me again.

● surprise or indignation:

> Who should bump into us at the theatre but your parents!
> That he should do such a thing! (see **1. f.** above).

c. Conversely, *would* has various senses absent from *should*, and is therefore often used uncontroversially in first-person constructions as well as second- and third-. Among the shades of meaning indicated by *would* are:

● habitual action:

> As a child, I would gaze at the stars for hours every night.

● stubbornness (chiefly British English):

> I would go and back the wrong horse, fool that I am!
> I would discuss politics with the barber! (Compare: I should discuss politics with the barber.)

● irony or cynicism:

> So, I would appear to be under arrest again.

● conjecture about the past (chiefly British English):

> That would have been John on the phone last night.

d. In clauses of purpose, *should* used to be preferred for second- and third- as well as first-person subjects:

> I worked overtime in order that the project should finish on schedule.

Today, however, *would* is probably considered equally acceptable. (Neither is in fact as idiomatic as *could*.)

● *Recommendation* The choice between *should* and *would* is not one that you will have to make very often. Each word has several uses peculiar to itself, and no confusion is possible there. Even where both forms are possible, the contraction *'d* — in informal speech and writing — averts the need to choose between them.

In those cases where a choice between *should* and *would* has to be made, the traditional rule (in the English of England) is that *I* and *we* take *should*, and that *he/she/it/you/they/the newspapers/Joe*, and so on take *would*. However, *should* is increasingly being displaced by *would* in first-person constructions of this kind, and it cannot be considered a serious mistake to go along with that trend. Purists continue to champion *should* of course, but in some constructions at least — such as ? *I shouldn't dream of disturbing him* — the *should* seems almost laughably old-fashioned. And the casual *I wouldn't know* is an unchangeable idiom now. In general, the best guide is a respect for the traditional rules, moderated by a good ear.

In the *if*-clauses of conditional sentences, *should* and *would* are acceptable only in certain circumstances (*If I should die . . .*; *If you would step this way, please . . .*), and their use in other *if*-clauses can lead to mistakes: ?? *If you would have arrived sooner, you would have missed the train.*

And in the past tense of sentences such as *He would like to thank you*, use *have* either with the main verb or with the infinitive, but not with both: *He would have liked to thank you* is better than *?? He would have liked to have thanked you.*

shrimp, prawn, scampi, langoustine *Shrimps* and *prawns* are hard to tell apart, but they are different creatures: they are classified under the same suborder, but belong to different sets of genera.

There are a number of fine distinctions between the two creatures but the only infallible test (covering all species of both genera) if you have an unidentified prawn or shrimp on your plate is this: observe the shell around the creature's head — that of a prawn has a long, leaf-like, toothed 'nose-piece' or projection at the front; in the shrimp this projection is very short. Shelled prawns and shrimps are likely to be indistinguishable — though as a rule of thumb, shrimps are smaller, with flatter bodies.

Scampi are large prawns. In English, the word is used of the shellfish when cooked — usually fried in batter — rather than when live. There is no singular form of the word.

Langoustines are *Dublin Bay prawns* — large prawns often served as scampi — and also known as *Norway lobsters*.

In North America and South Africa, the *hors d'oeuvre* is commonly called *shrimp cocktail*. In most other English-speaking countries, including Britain and Australia, it is usually called *prawn cocktail*. This is probably a case not of different ingredients (either dish may well include either creature) but of different names for the same thing. It has been claimed, however, that the typical North American shrimp is bigger than the typical British shrimp, and indeed almost as big as the typical British prawn. This would account for the rough equivalence of the American *shrimp cocktail* and the British *prawn cocktail*.

In American English, the collective plural *shrimp* is widely used: *Shrimp for sale*; *Let's have shrimp for dinner*. Elsewhere the ordinary plural is more likely to be used: *Let's have shrimps for dinner*.

Shrimp is probably of Germanic origin. *Scampi* is an Italian word. *Prawn*, or *prayne* as it was spelt in Middle English, is of unknown origin. *Langoustine* is a French word, the diminutive of *langouste,* 'the spiny lobster', which probably goes back to the Latin *locusta,* 'a lobster or locust'.

shrink The verb *to shrink* has two past tenses, *shrank* and *shrunk*: *shrank* is the form used in the meanings 'to recoil' or 'to flinch', while *shrunk* is more commonly used of fabrics contracting: *He shrank away from me*; *The shirt shrunk in the wash*. The past participle is always *shrunk*: *Your shirt has shrunk in the wash*. The form *shrunken* is now restricted to adjectival use, before the noun, in such phrases as *a shrunken head* or *the shrunken figure of an old man*.

Compare LIGHT; MELT; SINK.

sic This is a Latin word meaning 'thus, so'. In official or academic writing, it is often found, in brackets, within or after quotations. It is particularly useful in assuring the reader that the quoted words are faithful to the source — especially where some detail of the quotation may be unexpected or unlikely.

When quoting an old text, for example, you might want to indicate that a peculiar spelling is in fact the spelling in the original, and not a transcription error of your own:

> In his youth, John Donne was — as his famous contemporary euphemistically put it — 'a great visiter (*sic*) of ladies'.

And when quoting a modern text, you might want to confirm an odd wording:

> The causes of obesity in North America, according to Dr Owen, are not purely environmental: 'There is a genetic factor at work, the survival of the fattest (*sic*) among the early settlers ...'

Surely, the reader might think, Dr Owen was talking about *the survival of the fittest*? But no, the *sic* here is an assurance that the quotation is accurate, and that *fattest* is in fact (as a moment's reflection will show) the word intended and used by the author quoted.

Today, however, *sic* more commonly serves other less honourable purposes. Where it was once used primarily to indicate some intended though unusual detail of the original author's, it is now widely used to indicate instead some unintended error of the author's (or of the printer's!):

> Among the puffs on the back cover is the following comment on her previous book: 'The humour is as international as Sunday jogging and speaks eloquently for that great urban middle-class which has gobbles (*sic*) up the goodies which the consumer society has on display, but still feels the aching void inside.'
> – Richard Boston, *The Observer*

The reviewer here perhaps feels a duty to quote

accurately, but it does seem rather pedantic. Surely there would have been no harm in silently correcting the passage.

Sometimes the *sic* is used for the purposes of ridicule:

Mr Mali's misguided complaint continues: 'On 31 June (*sic*) last year, I underwent an emergency appendectamy (*sic*) at the North-western Clinic', and he goes on to allege that the hospital staff had at first refused to take his symptoms seriously, 'making flippant remarks, winking at one another, and generally trivialising (*sic*!) my views and my distress'.

There is a patronising and know-all air about the various uses of *sic* here: the date is irrelevant, and has been quoted, it seems, purely in order to score a point; the misspelling of *appendectomy* is again probably a printer's error and might have been silently corrected instead of gleefully repeated. As to Mr Mali's allegation — of neglect on the part of the hospital staff — the *sic* here appears to sneer at it, as if saying that nothing could be more ridiculous than the idea that the hospital staff should ever trivialise a patient's distress. It would have been far more courteous (and far more persuasive) to take issue with Mr Mali's allegation and dispute it respectfully, than to dismiss it contemptuously in the way that the reporter has done. To use *sic* in this imperious way is indeed to trivialise a person's views.

Note the form — (*sic*) — used in the quotations here: italics, and round brackets. This is probably the commonest form used. Some publishers, however, use ordinary roman typeface instead of italics, and some prefer square brackets to round brackets.

● *Recommendation* Use *sic* to reassure the reader that an unlikely quotation is in fact correctly worded. When an error occurs in a quotation, and there is a danger that the error may be attributed to you, then a *sic* is again a fair precaution. But use the word sparingly. And use it fairly; it should not be used as a rhetorical device that puts down a quoted writer by demonstrating his grammatical errors or scoffing at his views.

significant The core sense of this adjective is simply 'having or conveying meaning': *a significant but still undeciphered panel of hieroglyphics*; *a significant walkout by the negotiators*. It can also mean 'having a hidden meaning, suggesting a meaning': *She threw me a significant glance*. Doctors often use the word in the phrase *a significant change in the patient's condition*; that is, a

change that affects the original outlook or treatment. Yet today the phrase would probably be understood as referring simply to an *important* change — since *significant*, like its synonym *meaningful*, has become a kind of modish substitute for *important*, *serious*, or *valuable*: *? a significant new playwright*.

? Venice, the enemy or the envy of the British imagination for centuries past, is now recreated in our half-bankrupt, sponsorship-maintained Royal Academy in *The Genius of Venice 1500-1600*, the most significant exhibition of Renaissance art for decades and, considering its extraordinary loans, a show that can never be repeated in our lifetimes.

– Tim Hilton, *The Observer*

Curiously, *insignificant* in the sense of 'unimportant, trivial' has not attracted the same kind of criticism. It seems quite acceptable to speak of *an insignificant playwright* (or *exhibition* or *obstacle*).

silicon, silicone These quite distinct scientific terms have come to be widely used in everyday speech and writing, and are in danger of being confused. *Silicon* is an element (just as ne*on* and carb*on* are: note the common *-on* ending). It is hard and non-metallic, and is the main ingredient of sand. It is used in transistors and computer chips (hence the *silicon chip*); its name was adopted informally for the centre of the microelectronics industry in California, *Silicon Valley*, and hence for that in Scotland, *Silicon Glen*.

Silicone is a compound, including carbon, silicon, and oxygen. (Compounds with oxygen often end in *-one*, as *acetone* does.) It is a plastic, used for artificial limbs, for the lining of non-stick pans, for cosmetic surgery, and for many industrial purposes.

Note that the words differ in pronunciation as well as spelling: *silicon* is usually pronounced /**si**lli-kən/, sometimes /**si**lli-kon/; *silicone* is pronounced /**si**lli-kōn/.

similar *Similar* is an adjective. It can be followed by *to*, but not *as* or *with*: *Your handwriting is similar to mine*; *The building is of a similar design to Westminster Abbey's*. It is incorrect to say: ✗ *The building is of a similar design as Westminster Abbey*. (The model here is probably *the same as*.)

Similar cannot be used as an adverb; sentences such as ✗ *You write similar to me* are unacceptable in formal standard English. Strictly speaking, *similarly* should be used here. If it feels awkward, rephrase the sentence: *Your handwriting is similar to mine.*

And do not write × *Her new book is well-written, similar to her last one* when you mean *Her new book is well-written, like her last one.*

The opposite of *similar*, *dissimilar*, is subject to the same rules and restrictions. Again, say *dissimilar to*, not × *dissimilar from* on the model of *different from.*

simile See METAPHOR; METAPHORS AND SIMILES.

simplistic *Simplistic* is not just a grandiose synonym of *simple*, though it is so often used that way that you might be forgiven for thinking it is. It means 'oversimplified' or 'oversimplifying': a person with a *simple* philosophy of life is admirable; a person with a *simplistic* philosophy of life sounds like a superficial or complacent person. News reports are sometimes criticised as *simplistic* — that is, as unrealistically limited or shallow in their analysis of a complicated issue.

In the following helpful quotation, *simplistic* and *simple* appear in conjunction, and the contrast between them is quite clear:

> She ... tends in any case to endorse the liberal but simplistic view of the Greenham women as noble, simple, pure and *right*, crusading against opponents who are choleric, stupid, violent and *wrong*.
> – Hilary Spurling, *The Observer*

Here is a slightly dubious example:

> ? The unadorned idea of humble men doing essential linguistic work by adding to the language, as Chesterton says, 'new symbols and new circumstances' is too simplistic, as was the notion, a couple of decades later in the Thirties, that writings by and about proletarians would revive literature.
> – Roy Fuller, *The Listener*

The combination ? *too simplistic* here seems tautologous: it would have been correct to use *too simple* or else *simplistic* alone, but ? *too simplistic* is rather too much.

Finally, a more or less clear-cut example of the fashionable, but ill-advised use of *simplistic* as meaning no more than 'simple':

> ?? The Soviet Union has had an anti-satellite capability, however simplistic and easy to counter, since the 1960s. It could easily be upgraded.
> – leading article, *Daily Telegraph*

since See AGO.

sink The verb *sink* has two past tenses, *sank* and *sunk*; *sank* is by far the more common; moreover, *sunk* is slightly informal: *He sank/ ? sunk to his knees*; *The battleship sank/ ? sunk an enemy vessel.* The usual past participle is *sunk*, as in *He has sunk into a depression.* The form *sunken* is now restricted to adjectival use in front of the noun, in such phrases as *sunken treasure* or *sunken cheeks* — that is, 'hollow cheeks'.

Compare LIGHT; MELT; SHRINK.

situation The careless use of *situation* has been widely criticised. In the sense 'a state of affairs or set of circumstances', *situation* (to a lesser extent, *position*, too) is a vogue word *par excellence*, resorted to by speakers and writers either in the attempt to sound impressive or in order to avoid the trouble of finding a sharper way of expressing their thoughts: *? a no-win situation, ? my financial situation, ? ongoing situations, ? in the present situation, ? in a classroom situation*, and so on. So far from sounding impressive, such hollow phrases have become the object of mockery. The pompous phrase *in the present situation* can often be replaced by a simple *now*, and *in a classroom situation* by *in the classroom.*

Not that *situation* has to be shunned in all contexts. In its other senses, it is seldom overused, and remains unobjectionable, notably in the senses of 'location or position' — *the situation of the castle above the lake* — and 'a job': *looking for a situation to suit his talents.* And in the sense of 'a state of affairs', *situation* can still be extremely useful: *a hypothetical situation; how such a dangerous situation arose.*

> In some obscure way I wanted to punish myself, I wanted to put myself in the setting that seemed proper to my situation.
> – Lynne Reid Banks,
> *The L-Shaped Room*

> We who write for newspapers are not precisely in Scheherazade's predicament but we are better placed than most people to understand it. We have to look at any given situation not only in terms of its intrinsic nature (as far as ascertainable) but also in terms of its entertainment potential.
> – Conor Cruise O'Brien,
> *The Observer*

Where *situation* is objectionable is where it is just used to pad out some simple concrete idea into a flabby and pretentious abstract phrase:

?? I was in a learning situation this week. I came here not knowing what Buster's form was and not knowing how Colin would react.
— Paul Hutchins,
quoted in *The Times*

?? Their scrummaging is very solid, largely due to the Argentine prop Rodriguez, but for all the improvement in the support of their extremely tall line-out jumpers, one can still detect a vulnerability in their feed and also in the ruck and maul situations where they are still not properly organised.
— Clem Thomas, *The Observer*

The writers here apparently meant no more than 'I was still learning things this week' and 'also in rucks and mauls'. And that is what they should have written.

See also ABSTRACT NOUNS.

skimpy See SCANT.

slang *Slang* itself must have begun life as a slang word (and the verb *to slang*, meaning 'to insult', might still be considered slangy if not quite slang). Its origin is uncertain, but it seems likely that it developed in underworld slang from the word *language* or the French form *langue*. It is recorded as far back as 1756 (and must have been in use long before), but did not appear in Dr Johnson's famous dictionary published in the previous year.

The concept, however, goes back much further than the 18th century. Plato, well over 2000 years ago, complained that the Greek ruling classes were using terms once associated exclusively with slaves, soldiers, and artisans — in other words, that, they had adopted slang terms and were threatening the purity of the standard idiom.

Attitudes towards slang Until very recently, Plato's disapproval was echoed in the views of most writers on language. They felt that the availability of slang discouraged people from mastering standard idiom, and in fact threatened to infect standard idiom. Today, by contrast, slang is widely recognised as capable of being extremely lively, unpretentious, and inventive (though it can often be vague, trivial, dull, euphemistic, and overworked), and as serving a useful social function. Slang has been particularly admired for its vivid use of metaphor:

Keats never put into a sonnet so many remote metaphors as a coster puts into a curse.
— G.K. Chesterton,
'A Defence of Slang'

In the same essay, Chesterton put forward the view that 'All slang is metaphor, and all metaphor is poetry'.

Linguists and sociologists also now acknowledge that slang can be a very efficient way of communicating your thoughts and feelings — and this communicative function is, after all, the primary purpose of all language. For a start, most slang terms are simple and concrete, rather than abstract and complicated: metaphor often underlies the slang term, producing a sharp, immediately accessible image, and usually a train of emotive associations too. The term *loanshark*, for instance, meaning 'a moneylender', is effective and appealing both through the easily visualised image of a shark and through the associated ideas of cruelty and inescapability.

Similarly, to call someone a *gasbag* is a striking and unambiguous characterisation of him. (Not that standard English is necessarily deficient in such power: it would be just as striking to call that person a *fool* — a word, incidentally, that in its origins means much the same as *gasbag*. The Latin *follis*, from which *fool* derives, meant 'a bellows'. Metaphor underlies much of standard English too, not just of slang.)

Furthermore, slang terms tend to spring from, and reflect, real everyday experience. They often have an up-to-date colour about them that is lacking in the pallid, long-established standard terms. If you speak of your *hassles* or *hang-ups*, you will almost certainly convey your idea — and your feelings — more vividly than if you spoke of your *doubts, pressing demands, personal fears and anxieties*, or the like.

Finally, the communicative power of slang can derive from its shock effect. A consistently level tone is, precisely, monotonous. Language needs the occasional change of pitch. Effective language is more than precise language: it involves interaction between speaker and listener, or writer and reader. The audience's interest tends to wane, and has to be revived from time to time. A well-placed slang term is often as effective in startling people back into attentiveness as a joke or dramatic pause or sudden rhetorical flourish would be.

In the wake of these more positive attitudes to slang, linguists and sociologists and psychologists now accept slang as a subject worthy of serious academic study. Slang dictionaries, though they have existed for centuries, are now both more popular and more scholarly than ever before. And conventional dictionaries now make a point of including slang terms or senses, so long as these are in fairly wide use and appear not to be too transitory.

Above all, slang is now used copiously in contexts where it might formerly have been discouraged — in films and the theatre, sometimes in fiction and written journalism, occasionally even in broadcasting and in parliament:

Modern Popes, because of the bloody-mindedness of the loony Left and Right in the Church, have little to smile about.
– Desmond Albrow, *Sunday Telegraph*

Mr Dale Campbell Savours (Lab, Workington) asked him to comment on the 'outrageous statement by the Governor of Oxford Prison that offenders should be duffed up by the police'.
– parliamentary report, *Daily Telegraph*

Perhaps if Boycott had been able to persuade himself to take the occasional rum or two, he might have been able to get his act better together off the field.
– David Miller, *The Times*

I have occasionally suspected that HM Treasury flipped its departmental lid when it gave its blessing three short years ago to Section 30 of the Wildlife and Countryside Act.
– Lord Bruce-Gardyne, *Sunday Telegraph*

Identifying slang Of course, the decision to label or classify an item as *Slang* in a dictionary is to some extent an arbitrary decision. There are no hard-and-fast dividing lines between the various levels of language: acceptability is a continuum rather than a set of compartments. Even the choice of imposed levels varies from dictionary to dictionary: a typical range, but by no means a universal one, would be *Formal* or *Literary*, *Standard*, *Informal* or *Colloquial*, *Slang*, *Vulgar* or *Obscene* or *Taboo*, and *Nonstandard*. But whether a word is *slang* or merely *informal*, or *taboo* or merely *slang*, or *slang* or *nonstandard*, is not something that can be determined by rules: an informed decision would take into account the word's frequency, the contexts in which it occurs, the people who use it, the way these people feel about it when they use it, and the likely persistence or changeability of these attitudes. But in the end, the label is a matter of personal judgment by the dictionary-maker. And the label is nothing more than a label: the danger is that the label will affect or even determine people's view and use of the word, whereas it should be the

other way around. Call one plant *a wild flower* and another *a weed*, and people will regard them in very different ways.

For the purposes of discussion here, the divisions of *Informal*, *Slang*, *Vulgar*, and *Nonstandard* can be ignored. The important distinction is between words felt as fully acceptable (or too stilted) in standard, conventional, or formal settings, and words felt to be doubtful or inappropriate in such settings. Most adult speakers, regardless of their level of education, have this intuitive grasp, and can choose the appropriate vocabulary — just as they can choose the appropriate clothing — for the occasion. (If caring people do err, as at formal occasions, it tends to be on the side of over-formal language rather than of informality.)

The social distribution and social value of slang Almost everyone uses some slang sometimes, and some people use a great deal of slang a great deal of the time. Those who do not go to offices or seldom find themselves in formal situations, and those who spend more time with close friends than with business associates and mere acquaintances, use the most slang. Students and young people tend to use slang abundantly: they are receptive to new ideas and words, they regard some old ideas as new, and so devise new words to fit them, and — most important perhaps — they may want to establish their individuality and independence by using terminology that older people have not yet adopted.

People of all ages use slang to appear 'with it'. Most adults do not want to be considered old fogies; and both young and old like to be recognised as people with an awareness of the latest ideas, attitudes, and fads. Many older people have a youthful outlook — or at least want others to think they have — and therefore often adopt a good deal of new slang too.

This projection of personality is an important part of language. And your use of slang is an especially helpful indicator of your personality. It directs the listener to your social status and your in-group connections, and also, more tellingly, to your feelings and attitudes (or rather, to the feelings and attitudes you are adopting for the occasion) towards the listener himself (relaxed? respectful?) and towards society in general (conservative? resentful? nonconformist?).

The sources and varieties of slang terms A number of factors — psychological, sociological, and linguistic — lie behind the development and persistence of slang.

Some terms seem to be the result of sheer exuberance: people take a simple and natural joy in something they have mastered, whether it is carpentry, windsurfing — or the English language. And this joy in command over one's language often expresses itself in a creative delight in playing with words, experimenting with new sound-combinations and grammatical distortions, ascribing new senses to old terms or inventing new terms for old concepts, and so on. The onomatopoeic zest in such slang terms as *pizzazz*, *slob*, or *to zap*, and the metaphorical imaginativeness of *ticker* (a heart) or *clinch* (a long, loving kiss or embrace) or, more recently, *to graze* (to eat food in a supermarket in order to avoid paying for it) — these are almost certainly the brainchildren of inspired, high-spirited members of the public simply in love with their language.

Two other psychological motives seem to be at work in inspiring the invention of slang terms. The first is the urge to soften the blow of a refusal, a piece of bad news, an unpleasant description, a shameful admission, or the like. The slangy phrase *No can do* (perhaps borrowed from pidgin English) probably acquired its popularity through being a relatively soft and apologetic way of declining a request. And many slang euphemisms seem to have been prompted by a sense of delicacy or concern: *a so-and-so*, *to total* (to wreck a car beyond repair in an accident), *to have had one over the eight* (to be drunk).

The opposite human tendency — towards envy, resentment, aggression, and intolerance — gives rise to another set of slang terms, the debunking and bitter euphemisms and nicknames that far outnumber the gentle and mollifying ones just discussed: *sky pilot* (a clergyman), *stinking* (drunk), *dago* (a foreigner, expecially one of Latin origin), and so on.

The major sociological factor in the origin of slang is in-group identity. Perhaps the chief source of slang terms is 'cant', the private or secret vocabulary of various groups outside the social and economic mainstream — gypsies, gamblers, tramps, thieves, hippies, and so on. Once their cant terms permeate into wider public use, they become slang (and usually cease to be cant — the original users abandon them now that they can no longer claim exclusive right to them; some examples are listed below). Cant originates, it seems, partly as a kind of rebellious breaking away from the majority (who speak the standard form of the language) and partly out of the common though often regrettable human desire to set oneself apart in a distinct group. Cant is a way of enforcing loyal membership to this group, and of generating a cosy feeling of belonging within

it — a kind of badge or code: those who wear the badge or know the code are one's fellows; those who do not are outsiders.

The sociological and psychological reasons underlying slang are perhaps both simpler and deeper than those just mentioned. At its crudest, a slang term might, it has been suggested, be coined by criminals for the simple purpose of confusing the police. It may be for that reason that underworld slang has such a quick turnover — as soon as it becomes too widely known, it no longer serves its purpose. At the other extreme, slang may be subject to primitive psychological promptings and taboos: the ancient fear of naming something explicitly (*death*, for instance) for fear of bad luck; or a residual shame — or conversely, a defiant or boastful frankness — when discussing sex, drunkenness, money, and the other common coin of ordinary life, the blunt and material rather than refined and spiritual aspects of the daily round.

The detailed linguistic origins of slang are many and varied. Here are some of the processes commonly identified:

● compounding — as in *lowdown* or *has-been*,
● clipping — *pro*, 'a professional' or 'a prostitute'; *perv*, 'a pervert'; *to psych* or *psyche*, 'to affect psychologically'.
● abbreviations and acronyms — *snafu*.
● onomatopoeia — *pow*, *wham*, *zap*.
● analogy — *crash out*, 'to sleep'; *pickled*, 'drunk'.

Then, various forms of word-play, including:
● nonsense reduplication — *heebie-jeebies*.
● backslang — *ynnep*, 'penny' spelt backwards; *knurd*, 'drunk'; *slop*, 'police'; *yob* (from *boy*).
● rhyming slang: this favourite form of slang apparently developed among Cockneys in about 1840, and quickly found its way from there to Ireland and Australia (it remains virtually unknown in the United States, though Australians did apparently introduce it in California at the time of the gold rush). Back in Britain, it became fashionable with the Teddy Boys after the Second World War, and has become a source of facetious catchphrases among educated people today. Well-known examples are *trouble and strife* (wife), *God forbids* (kids), and *apples and pears* (stairs).

Finally, borrowings from other vocabularies:
● loanwords from dialects or foreign languages — *vamoose*, *savvy*. (Of course, other languages borrow from English to produce slangy terms of their own, such as *le gangster*, *le hold-up*, and *le racket* in French.)
● adoptions of the specialised terms (cant or jargon terms) of various social or professional

groups: from trades and professions — *premmie* (a premature baby), *to OD* (to take an overdose of medicine or drugs); from soldiers and sportsmen — *chopper* (a helicopter), *to play ball* (to cooperate); and from popular subcultures and the world of crime — *groovy*, *downer* (a mood of depression, or a depressant drug), *beak* (a judge), and *putting the boot in*.

Of course, much slang remains confined to a particular group or profession, without permeating into general use. Note that the slang of a special group is not the same thing as its jargon. The word *clavicle* is medical jargon, perhaps: a technical, and perhaps unnecessarily fancy, term for 'collarbone'; the expression *FLK* is a medical slang term, standing for 'funny-looking kid'. To the outsider, the distinction between slang and jargon may not always be clear: he might find them equally unintelligible.

Some slang terms are the product of more than one of the linguistic processes just outlined: the jokey word *titfer* results from the clipping of *tit-for-tat*, rhyming slang for 'hat'. Similarly *china* is a clipping of *china plate*, rhyming slang for 'mate', and *loaf* (as in *Use your loaf!*) a clipping of *loaf of bread*, 'head'. And *shrink*, meaning 'a psychoanalyst', is a clipped form of *headshrinker*, itself originating through the process of analogy.

Remember that slang is not just a matter of single words (*naff*) or distorted meanings (*cracked*, 'mad'). It can involve word-elements (*-nik*, for instance, as in *nogoodnik*) or longer expressions (*Keep your hair on*), and it can be based also on deviant stress (*positively*), pronunciation (/**ay**-rab/), and grammar (*We was robbed*; *He talks weird*).

The stability of slang Slang, like any other aspect of language, is subject to change. Some slang terms, it is true, manage to resist the ebb and flow of fashion, and retain more or less the same level throughout the centuries. Chaucer, 600 years ago, used the terms *to booze* (to drink liquor) and *bones* (dice) in an apparently slangy way. Thackeray used the expression *Tell it to the marines* in his novel *Vanity Fair* (1848). The word *dough*, in the sense of 'money', has similarly been American slang for more than 130 years.

But in general, the fate of slang words is an unhappy one. On the one hand, they might simply fade out of fashion, as *square* (conventional) is doing, or has done, in Britain, and *neat* (impressive) in the United States, and *bonzer* (very nice) in Australia. Sometimes slang terms might disappear from view entirely: *fizz* used to be a slang word for 'face', being a clipping of *physiognomy*; *tomato* used to be a slang term for

'a young woman', the way that *bird* is today in Britain, and *chick* in the United States.

On the other hand, slang terms might lose their vagabond waywardness and become domesticated into respectable standard idiomatic usage. *Hijack*, for instance, has risen very quickly through the ranks from its slang origins in the 1920s to its fully standard status today. The old sexual associations in the music terms *jazz*, *jive*, *swing*, and *rock and roll* have long since been forgotten. *Bogus*, *rowdy*, and *rollicking* were still considered slang in the early years of this century.

In the 18th century, Jonathan Swift and Dr Johnson denounced a variety of words and phrases that today seem perfectly respectable. Swift objected to the slangy vulgarity of *sham*, *banter*, *mob*, *uppish*, *bamboozle*, *speculations*, and *to the tune of*. Dr Johnson railed against *budge*, *coax*, *shabby*, *nonplus*, *squabble*, *dodge*, *stingy*, *tiff*, *touchy*, *width*, *job*, *fun*, *cajole*, *fuss*, *conundrum*, *gamble*, *simpleton*, and *frisky*. Other words once frowned upon and now fully standard, are *joke*, *bet*, *flog*, *jilt*, *cheat*, *bored*, *prig*, *slump*, *club* (in the sense of 'a society or meeting-place'), *dwindle*, *flout*, *glib*, *simper*, *swagger*, *blizzard*, *racketeer*, and *trip* (in the sense of 'a journey').

Some very familiar standard terms in the Romance languages are derived not from the standard Latin term but from the slang of Roman legionaries. The Latin words for *head*, *leg*, and *horse*, for instance were *caput*, *crus*, and *equus*. The French and Italian words, however, are *tête* and *testa*; *jambe* and *gamba*; and *cheval* and *cavallo* — deriving instead from the Latin words *testa*, meaning 'a pot', *gamba*, 'a hoof', and *caballus*, 'a nag, or useless old horse'. These were the slang terms used by Roman soldiers to refer to their own head, leg, and horse; hence their adoption, as the standard terms, into French and Italian.

Another possibility is that a term will move in the opposite direction, from respectability into slanginess. A character in a Shakespeare play might use *cocksure* in an apparently conventional and unslangy way, for instance. The word *ain't* used to be the correct and fully acceptable contraction of *am not*. The modern slang phrase *by the skin of one's teeth* occurs, in a slightly different form, in the Book of Job in the King James Bible, and so on.

If western society continues the trend towards a greater frankness in speech, more modern attitudes, the breaking down of class barriers, and so on, the outlook for slang is a bleak one. Slang relies to a large extent on its shock effect and on its deviance from standard idiom. If everything becomes 'acceptable', and everyone becomes unshockable, then much of the basis of slang will disappear. Language will be the poorer.

slash See SOLIDUS.

slay The usual past-tense form of this verb is *slew*, and the past participle is *slain*. However, in the slang meaning of 'to overwhelm', *slayed* is used for both the past-tense and past-participle forms: *The comedian went out and really slayed the audience.*

In its literal sense of 'to kill violently', *slay* is now very old-fashioned. It has been revived by newspapermen, however, especially in the United States, as a supposedly dramatic and eye-catching synonym of *kill* or *murder*. It is certainly not appropriate for ordinary speech or writing.

sledge, sled, sleigh These are all vehicles that slide on snow or ice. All three forms derive from Dutch words. In British English *sledge* is the commonest form, both for a small downhill toboggan and for a larger vehicle pulled on the level by dogs, horses, or reindeer. In American and Canadian English *sled* is preferred for the smaller vehicle and *sleigh* for the larger, particularly when it has seats and is pulled by a horse.

slow In informal usage *slow* is often used as an adverb interchangeably with *slowly*, especially in spoken commands and with verbs of motion: *Go slow/slowly; Eat slower/more slowly. Slow* is also the standard form in some fixed phrases: *a go-slow, the trains are running slow today*; road signs: *Dead Slow*; and some compound expressions: *slow-moving traffic, a slow-acting drug.* Outside of these idioms, the preferred form in more formal speech and writing is always *slowly.*

Compare QUICK. See also ADVERBS; -LY.

smell The past-tense and past-participle form of the verb *to smell* is *smelt* in British English, with *smelled* a perfectly acceptable and only slightly less common alternative. In American English, however, *smelled* is the preferred form.

When the verb means 'to have a particular smell', it is followed either by an adjective or by a descriptive phrase beginning with *of, like,* and so on: *It smells spicy; This room smells of damp.* (These adjectives or descriptive phrases can themselves be modified by an adverb: *It smells very spicy; This room smells strongly of damp.*) However, when *to smell* means 'to stink', it can either stand alone, or be followed by an adverb

describing how badly something smells: *This meat is beginning to smell*; *The drains smelt appallingly in the hot weather.*

All three of the following forms are possible, therefore, with slight differences of emphasis:

> It smells strong (neutral in tone).
> It smells strongly of fish (neutral, and specific).
> It smells strongly (negative in tone).

smog See MIST.

so 1. Clauses introduced by *so that* or *so* express either purpose or result. Purpose: *He filled the tank so that he could drive all the way without stopping.* Result: *The tank was full, so he drove all the way without stopping.*

There is a slight idiomatic preference in British English for *so that* to indicate purpose, and *so* to indicate result; it is possible to use them the other way round, though some careful users regard the simple *so* as unacceptably casual in clauses of purpose; conversely, *so that* in clauses of result can sound rather too formal.

Note that in clauses of result, there is a comma before the *so*, unlike in clauses of purpose. This distinction is worth observing, as ambiguity or actual misunderstanding might otherwise result: *He had filled the tank (,) so he could drive all the way without stopping.*

Note too that when *so* begins a sentence, it is usually wrong to follow it with a comma: ✗ *So, they all rolled over and one fell out.* Omit the comma, unless it introduces some incidental or parenthetical wording: *So, as you know, they all rolled over and one fell out.*

In clauses of purpose, *so that* can be replaced by *in order that,* but it would be nonstandard to replace it with *so as:* ✗ *He filled the tank so as he could drive all the way without stopping. So as* has to be followed in standard English by the infinitive, not by a clause: *He filled the tank so as to be able to drive all the way without stopping.* Here, *so as to* could be replaced by (*in order*) *to.* In fact, some purists still object to *so as to,* arguing that the *so as* part is redundant.

2. The phrase *doing so* or *to do so* is a useful way of avoiding having to repeat a verb phrase: *You can hire a car over the weekend as well, though if you do so you will have to pay a surcharge.* (Here, *if you do so* could also be expressed simply as *if you do.*) The *do so* replaces *hire a car over the weekend.*

Such replacement is not always appropriate, however. For one thing, the original verb has to be in the active voice; verbs in the passive cannot be followed by *to do so:* × *Cars can be hired over the weekend as well, though if you do so you will have to pay a surcharge.*

Then, it is best if you keep the verb forms parallel. It is perhaps possible to rewrite the original example as *? You can hire a car over the weekend as well, though doing so will involve a surcharge* — but it is not as elegant or well-balanced. (Note also that here it is impossible for *doing* to be used alone: *doing so* must be used.)

And if the verb-forms are the other way round, the sentence becomes unacceptable: × *Hiring a car is possible over the weekend, though if you do so you will have to pay a surcharge.* If the original verb is in the *-ing* form, then the symmetrical form *doing so* has to follow: *Hiring a car is possible over the weekend as well, though doing so will involve a surcharge.*

Above all, make sure that *to do so* reflects the sense you want: × *You have learnt almost nothing the whole term, and I am now going to force you to do so.* A close inspection will reveal the absurdity in such a sentence. Again: × *Slow though they were to do so, they were finally reconciled to their loss.* This should read: *Slow though they were to become so . . .*

3. The use of *so* as a simple intensive, in the sense of 'very', is widely used in conversation — *I am feeling so tired* — but should be avoided in formal speech and writing: *I am feeling very/ extremely tired* is more appropriate in such contexts. However, there is nothing informal about *I have never felt so tired (before),* which is a different construction — a shortened form of *I have never felt so/as tired as this.*

4. *So* can be used in such sentences as *You can stay the night if you so wish/desire,* though it would be just as correct to say *You can stay the night if you wish (to).* However, *so* should not be used in such sentences as *?? You can have as much money as you so wish/desire.* Say *. . . as you wish/desire/want* instead.

See also AS; SUCH; VERY.

so-called This compound adjective used to mean principally 'thus named, though not really entitled to the name':

> This so-called erotic masterpiece is no better than any other pornographic novel sold in sleazy bookshops.

> Tottenham Hotspur face a big enough threat from Anderlecht, the holders of the trophy, but their so-called supporters who will travel along unofficial paths to Brussels could

prove an even larger menace.
> — Stuart Jones, *The Times*

But increasingly it is being used in a neutral sense: the *so-called truth drugs,* or:

> Edward Teller, the so-called father of the H-bomb, is still hard at work on various defence projects.

The earlier ironic function is often served by *self-styled* or *soi disant* instead, though these tend to be used only of humans.

If you want to use *so-called* in its original ironic sense, do not hammer the irony home by adding inverted commas to the noun as well: × *this so-called 'erotic masterpiece'* is overdone. Use either *so-called* or the inverted commas, but not both.

Note that *so-called* tends to be hyphenated only when it precedes the noun it qualifies. If used after the noun (either with or without irony), it is written as two words: *all his various friends, so called.*

> The truth drugs — so called because of their property of encouraging confessions from captives — are of recent origin, and are not really covered by the Geneva convention.

social, sociable The noun *society* has, among its many senses, the rather old-fashioned one of 'companionship, the company of other people', as in *a man who enjoys society.* It is to this sense of *society* that the adjective *sociable* is related. *Social* refers to *society* in its more general senses. So: *social classes, social studies, social services, social values, man as a social animal.* The word is hardly ever used today to refer specifically to people, whereas *sociable* is often so used: *not a very sociable tour-guide, is he?*

The danger of confusion arises in those contexts where either *social* or *sociable* could be used: *a social/sociable evening, a social/sociable club, social/sociable circles.*

In each case, *social* tends to classify the noun, whereas *sociable* tends to describe it. A *social evening* is one classified as an evening spent with other people, in contrast to a solitary evening; although a *social* evening, it would not be described as a *sociable* evening if the people were stiff and unfriendly.

Similarly, any *social* circle that is not your own might strike you, the outsider, as being not at all *sociable.* In the following quotation, the first *social* should be *sociable* (the second is correct, though *sociable* too would have been possible):

× Toby kept nagging at me to be more social.

He was determined that I must meet this Mavis who shared the house with us. I tried to discourage Toby's social enthusiasm, because the more people I got to know, the more would have to be told, sooner or later, about the baby.

— Lynne Reid Banks,
The L-Shaped Room

Unsociable is the opposite of *sociable* and means 'not disposed to seek the company of others, not companionable, reserved': *He's an unsociable character — he keeps himself to himself. Unsociable* can also mean 'not conducive to social exchange': *an unsociable atmosphere.*

Unsocial, however, is not exactly the opposite of *social* as defined above. It is used mainly in British English, and means 'not compatible with or conducive to a full social life': *The night shift means working unsocial hours.* This is now perhaps its only common use.

The word more nearly opposite in meaning to *social* is *antisocial*, which can be defined as 'opposed to or interfering with the general welfare of society, or contravening its principles and customs': *the antisocial behaviour of criminals.* The adjective has come to be used more loosely to describe anything offensive or upsetting to other people; *antisocial behaviour* is often applied to such relatively minor offences as smoking. Less justifiably, some speakers now use *antisocial* to mean the same as *unsociable* — simply 'unfriendly and reserved'. This is to blur a useful distinction: a gang of hooligans may be *antisocial* without being *unsociable* among themselves; a recluse is *unsociable* but not likely to be *antisocial* since in his isolation he does not disturb outside society.

Note that *antisocial* is usually spelt as one word, without a hyphen.

The rarely used *asocial* (/ay-sōsh'l/) overlaps slightly in meaning with *unsociable* and *antisocial* but really has a distinctive sense of its own. It means 'ignoring or avoiding the society of others' (similar to *unsociable*) or 'being inconsiderate of others; self-centred' (similar to *antisocial*). The blanket definition of *asocial* might be 'taking no account of or interest in society or sociability'.

Both *social* and *antisocial* are overused. *Social* would sometimes be better omitted from such phrases as *social welfare, social justice, social revolution.* The nouns here are usually powerful enough to stand on their own. *Social* has become a vogue word suggesting democratic motives and carrying a built-in favourable tone.

Of course, *social* should not be omitted if it does make a genuine distinction, as when social welfare is contrasted with personal welfare, social justice with the justice of the courts, or social revolution with political revolution. But do ensure that *social* is serving a proper purpose in this way, rather than simply imparting a fashionable buzz.

The looseness of the use of *antisocial* has already been touched on. If you want to use the word precisely, save it for serious, socially damaging or criminal practices. Not for friends who miss a party.

sociologese See JARGON.

solidus 1. This punctuation mark, represented by a diagonal stroke (/), is pronounced /**sol**li-dəss/; its plural is *solidi*, /**sol**li-dī/. The *solidus* may also be called the *slant*, the *slash (mark)*, the *oblique* (in British English), the *bar*, the *virgule*, the *diagonal* (in American English), or the *stroke.* The term *stroke* is used especially when reading out a written text: the written words *section A/54* might be read out as 'section A stroke 54'.

2. a. The solidus is commonly used to separate alternatives:

Everyone must do as he/she thinks best.
You need strength and/or speed to win.

(But see the separate entry on AND/OR.)
It is often used in this way in this book:

loth/loath (this means that the two forms are regarded as acceptable spelling variants of a single word).
Susie was restive/restless and would not behave in class (this means that each of these words might be appropriately used in this particular sentence).

New formations are possible by the use of the solidus: one product of the move to avoid sexism in language is the formation *s/he*, an even more economical way than *he/she* or expressing the idea 'he or she, as the case may be':

Everyone must do what s/he thinks best.

b. The solidus may also come before an optional element: *vowel/s.* It is here the equivalent of a pair of brackets: *vowel(s).* The meaning in each case is 'either vowel or vowels'.

3. In expressions of time, the solidus can separate successive units:

1972/1973 1972/73 August/September
the weekend of 18/19 January

A dash or hyphen can be used instead, and is usual when the units are *not* successive.

1972-1975 1972-75 August-November

The solidus can also be used in writing dates:

1/12/72

A very important difference between British and American English is that the example above would mean 'the first of December, 1972' in British English but 'January (the) twelfth, 1972' in American English. British English uses the order day/month/year; American English, the order month/day/year.

4. The solidus is frequently used in writing fractions:

½ ¾ ⅛

It is also used in the symbol representing percentage: %.

5. The solidus is often used to indicate subsections, as in legal documents:

section A/54

This is especially true when the heading of the subsection includes numbers.

6. The solidus is often used instead of the word *per*:

16 ft/sec. 73 km/hr

(This expression would be read out as '16 feet per second' not as × '16 feet stroke second'.) However, the expressions *mpg* and *mph* use *p* rather than the solidus.

The solidus is also used in some abbreviations, notably in a/c, 'account', and c/o, '(in the) care of': *a/c Professor J. Brock, c/o The Red Lion Trust Company.*

7. When successive lines of poetry are written as a single line, the solidus is used to indicate the line-break of the original:

The castled crag of Drachenfels/Frowns o'er the wide and winding Rhine.

— Lord Byron,
Childe Harold's Pilgrimage (1812-18)

8. When the pronunciation of a word is being represented, it is often enclosed in solidi, as at the beginning of this article:

solidi, /**solli**-dī/.

Many dictionaries use round brackets, however, to enclose their pronunciations:

solidus (**solli**-dəss)

Note too that some dictionaries use the solidus in the headline at the top of a page:

precocious/predict

These two words are the first and the last entered on that page, and the solidus again, as in *1974/5*, stands for the word *to*.

some **1.** The modern use of *some* (or *quite some*) in understated exclamations — as the equivalent of 'very much' or 'very impressive' — was probably an Americanism at first, but is now quite at home in colloquial British English:

It takes (quite) some training to play the piano like that!
That was some performance!

Despite Churchill's famous wartime boast *Some chicken — some neck!,* the usage remains slightly informal.

Some is also used in exclamations in a slightly different sense — in a dismissive way rather than an admiring or boastful way:

Some hero! — he ran off as soon as the shooting started.

Some here indicates scornful or amused disbelief, as if to say 'That's not what I'd call a *hero*'.

2. *Some* also appears, especially in American English, as an informal form of *somewhat* or *to some extent*:

? She thought about him some, but not for long.
? It sure would help some if we could use your cart.

In questions and negative statements, *any* would be used as the equivalent colloquial term:
? *Would it help any if I lent you the car?* Note that some Americans can even say *He's some better now* (He's somewhat better now) — the equivalent, after all, of the perfectly familiar negative and interrogative forms *He isn't any better, He's no better,* and *Is he any better?*

3. *Some* can be used before a number to mean 'approximately, an estimated': *Some 250 Sherman tanks were involved in the action.* Note that it should be used only before a round figure. It seems very odd when used before a figure that appears to be exact — ? *Some 248 Sherman tanks . . .*

4. *some of us.* Is this pronoun phrase in the first person or the third person? Should you say *Some of us waste our money* or *Some of us waste their money*? It probably depends on whether the speaker (or writer) is one of those who wastes his money or not. If he is, he would use *our*; if not, he should use *their*.

someone See ANYONE.

someplace This adverb is an Americanism that has failed to gain much acceptance in British English. Since *somewhere* is a perfectly suitable and untroublesome word, there seems no need to replace it. Even in North America, *someplace* remains relatively informal. The same considerations apply to *anyplace* and *anywhere*.

Somewheres is another American version of *somewhere* — dialectal or nonstandard.

sometime, sometimes, some time, some times
1. Besides its present function as an adverb meaning 'occasionally, now and then', *sometimes* used to be an adjective in the sense of 'former' as well. Here is an example from Shakespeare:

Farewell old Gaunt; thy sometimes brother's wife
With her companion grief must end her life.
— the Duchess of Gloucester,
in *Richard II* I ii

This use is now obsolete. Today, the *-s* is dropped for this meaning: *the sometime Bishop of Birmingham; Mr Dubois, sometime Chairman of this society.* (Note that the word *one-time,* rather less formal but used in the same way, is hyphenated, whereas *sometime* is not: *a one-time boxing champion.*)

2. This sense of *sometime* is the only fully acceptable sense of the word today, and is found chiefly in British English. But it is used in several other ways as well. It is sometimes used to mean 'occasional', for example: *? His sometime sportiness took the form of a game of squash every two months.* This use is very dubious, and in any case might lead to confusion with the sense of 'former': *? She's a musician and sometime dancer.* (This should mean 'and was a dancer in the past'; the danger is that it might be taken to mean 'and is also, though only occasionally, a dancer'.)

As an adverb meaning 'once, formerly', *sometime* is now archaic:

They flee from me that sometime did me seek,
With naked foot stalking in my chamber.
— Sir Thomas Wyatt,
'The Lover Showeth How He Is Forsaken of Such as He Sometime Enjoyed' (*c.*1535)

And the word is obsolete as a substitute for *sometimes*:

Sometime too hot the eye of heaven shines,
And often is his gold complexion dimm'd;

And every fair from fair sometime declines,
By chance, or nature's changing course untrimm'd.
— Shakespeare, Sonnet 18:
'Shall I compare thee to a summer's day?'

As an adverb, *sometime* is now widely used to mean 'at an indefinite time in the future, one day, someday' — as in the invitation attributed to Mae West, *Come up and see me sometime* — or to mean 'at any indefinite or unstated time': *It happened sometime during the last decade.* Some purists object to these uses, arguing that the word is here a shortened version of *at some time* and should accordingly be written as two separate words: *I saw him some time last year; Let's get married some time.* However, the fused form is now generally accepted in all but the most formal contexts.

3. *Some time* as two separate words does have meanings not shared by *sometime.* Whereas *sometime* (or *some time*) as an adverb suggests an indefinite time in the future or past, *some time* as a noun phrase suggests a particular (though unstated) time: *Please name some time when you'll be free for an appointment tomorrow.* (This distinction applies also to *someday* and *some day.*) And *some time* can also mean 'an indefinite length of time': *They got married some time ago*; or 'a portion of time': *He spends some time working at home, and some in the library*; or 'quite a long time': *It'll take some time to heal, I'm afraid.*

4. *Some times* means of course 'some occasions': *Some times are better than others.* But informally, it tends to mean 'some good occasions': *We've had some times together!*

See also SOME 1.

soporific Strictly, *soporific* means 'sleep-inducing', from the Latin *sopor*, 'sleep' + *facere*, 'to make': a sleeping pill is a *soporific* drug, and you might call a sermon or lecture *soporific* if it is extremely dull.

The word is often used today in a different sense, as a grand-sounding synonym of *drowsy* or *sleepy*: *? He suppressed a soporific yawn.* This is probably too well established now to try to combat, but many careful users still consider the extended sense incorrect. At all events, it is rather pompous: use *sleepy* or *drowsy* instead if that is what you mean.

Compare NAUSEOUS; NOSTALGIA.

sort of 1. Phrases such as (*a*) *sort of, type of,* and *kind of* should usually be followed by a simple singular noun. It is a common error to insert the article *a* or *an* in front of the noun: ✗ *I drive a Morris Minor — what sort of a car do you drive?* This should read: ... *what sort of car do you drive?*

However, there is one case where the article *a* or *an* is permissible. Suppose you are interested not in the classification but in the quality of the object, then *a* or *an* might make your meaning clear. If you said, for instance, *What kind of scientist is he?*, the answer might be *A nuclear physicist* or *A biochemist*. But if you wanted instead an assessment of the scientist's ability (as an employer might, when requesting references relating to a job-applicant), you could say: *What kind of a scientist is he?* — to which the answer might be *An outstanding one* or *A below-average scientist*.

2. The construction *this sort of thing* is a common one in English, as are *that kind of, this type of, that breed of,* and so on. Such phrases are often needlessly cast in the plural — ? *I like these sorts of car* — when the singular is quite sufficient: *I like this sort of car*. Only when more than one *type* is at issue should the plural form be used: *It's difficult to choose between the Jaguar and the Daimler — I like both these sorts of car*. If it is simply a matter of several *instances* (of a single type), then the plural is inappropriate. If you want to convey a sense of plurality, and to use a plural verb, then the phrase can be recast into *cars of this kind*.

When the plural has to be used, it can be formed in various ways, not all of them very elegant.

One dubious plural is formed by pluralising the second noun only — ? *this sort of cars*: ? *The new XL and XG are the sort of cars we tend to regard as unnecessarily ornate*. If you do form the plural in this way, remember that any verb that follows it directly should go into the singular, since the subject *sort* remains grammatically singular itself:

✗ The point of a four-channel system is not to get an equal four-way audience split; indeed if Mr Isaacs finds his current five per cent shooting up suddenly, it will probably be a sign that the wrong sort of programmes are being introduced.
— Julian Barnes, *The Observer*

This should read: *the wrong sort of programmes is being introduced*.

The second way of pluralising, slightly preferable, is to cast all three elements of the phrase in the plural — the *this* or *that* if there is one, and both the nouns: *these sorts of cars*; the

wrong sorts of programmes.

Best of all is to pluralise the *this* or *that* if there is one, and the first of the nouns alone: *these sorts of car*; *the wrong sorts of programme*.

Why writers and speakers should find these plural forms insufficient is a mystery, but apparently they do, and perversely choose to pluralise the *this* or *that* and the second of the nouns: ✗ *these sort of cars*.

This sort of construction is glaringly illogical, yet it has an enduring fatal attraction, going back to Shakespeare and beyond, and is found both in conversation and in straightforward journalism.

✗ It is three o'clock, and your sister is not used to these sort of hours.
— Sir Thomas Bertram, in
Jane Austen's *Mansfield Park*

✗ It is best to leave those sort of people out of serious matters.
— Somerset Maugham, *Ashenden*

✗ When they charge £2.40 for three portions of tiny roast potatoes, you know you're into £18-£20 a head territory. At these sort of prices, the only children likely to be there are American micro-brats.
— Stan Hey, *The Times*

✗ These sort of comparisons delight Nadine Gordimer and fill her novels with jostling impressions, some specifically South African, others universal.
— Anne Barnes, *The Times*

Avoid this sort of mistake at all costs.

3. The phrases *(a) sort of* and *(a) kind of* are often needlessly inserted in speech, and sometimes in writing too: ? *I've got a sort of pain in my left foot*.

As a meaningless tag in conversation, *sort of* rivals *you know*: ? *He got me in a headlock, sort of, but I twisted out of it, sort of*.

As an adverb meaning 'in a way, somewhat, to some extent', *sort of* or *kind of* is very common nowadays:

The speaker let fly with some remarks about his chief Republican tormenter, Bruce Caputo of New York, for which he sort of apologised to the House last week.
— Joseph Kraft (U.S.),
The Boston Globe.

Such usage is considered informal. Like *a sort of pain,* it suggests laziness on the part of the user, as if he could not be bothered to find the precise word he needs.

It has to be said, however, that *sort of* and *kind of* do sometimes fit a context where no other phrase will really do: the irony in the quotation above comes from the use of *sort of,* and is enough to justify the deliberate informality. *Sort of* and *kind of* are also useful in indicating an unavoidable inaccuracy and apologising for it: *It's sort of jelly-like in texture.* And they can also be justified as ways of refining your meaning: *We work as curators in the national museum — sort of civil servants.*

Nevertheless, the phrases remain stubbornly informal in tone, and are best avoided in formal contexts. A simple rewording of your sentence should dispense with the need for such phrases.

Note that when *sort of* and *kind of* are merely expressions of vagueness, they are always singular in form: *these sort of red things* (= 'these red-dish things': *sort of* here relates to the adjective *red*).

There is a difference, then, between this accept-able, though informal, construction, and the apparently identical yet unacceptable × *these sort of red things* (= 'red things of this sort': *sort of* here relates to the noun *things*). This construc-tion, as has been suggested, should be changed to *this sort of red thing* or *these sorts of red thing/s.*

4. The informal phrase *all sorts of* is often heard — *The challenger has got himself into all sorts of difficulty* — and is quite acceptable in appropriately informal contexts. So is the phrase *all kinds of.* But the equally common phrase × *all kind of* is no longer acceptable — × *into all kind of difficulty.* As with *these kind of,* it is considered illogical, and should be avoided. The correct form is *all kinds of.* However, the phrase *all manner of* is a long-established oddity that remains a fully acceptable English idiom.

source See INFORMANT.

sources of the English vocabulary English belongs to the Indo-European family of languages, a family that includes most European languages and several Asian languages: Persian, Hindi, Bengali, and so on. All of these seem to have descended from a single ancestor — an ancient lost language, Proto-Indo-European, now partly reconstructed by scholars.

It was probably spoken 5000-7000 years ago by a farming people somewhere in Central or Eastern Europe. It probably broke up into several dialects, and as various tribes began to migrate, so these dialects spread across Europe and Asia,

changing their form slightly wherever they went.

English belongs to the Germanic branch of Indo-European, and began about 1500 years ago as Old English or Anglo-Saxon — in effect, the dialects of the Angles, Saxons, and other Germanic peoples who had served as Roman mercenaries in Britain. They took over after the Romans withdrew, and increased their numbers through waves of settlers or invaders from the continent. (See HISTORY OF THE ENGLISH LANGUAGE.)

The English vocabulary was later enriched from many other sources: from the Norse of the Viking invaders; from Norman French after the Norman conquest; from Latin and Greek during the Renaissance and again during the modern technological age; and from the imported cultural fashions of Italy, France, and Holland from the 16th or 17th century onwards.

But all of these languages are Indo-European languages, so the bulk of the English vocabulary really goes back to a single common source, even though it has descended by such a variety of routes. The words *cow* and *beef*, for example, which sound so different and followed such different paths on their way into English, can in fact be traced back to a single root-word in Proto-Indo-European.

The English vocabulary has drawn on languages from outside Europe as well — a legacy of the trading contacts and colonial relations that Britain and other European powers have had with other peoples and cultures around the world.

See the map opposite for a list of words from this extraordinary variety of sources.

South African English · The English language was probably heard on the South African coast as early as the 16th century — spoken by British seafarers during the age of exploration.

It was not until 1820, however, that the first large-scale settlement of English speakers took place — 4000-5000 British settlers beginning a new life in the Eastern Cape. Before that, the Euro-pean presence in the Cape had been overwhelm-ingly Dutch — a settler-community stretching back to 1652, when the Dutch had established a refreshment-station in the Cape for ships sailing to the East.

The Cape, and later South Africa as a whole, came under British rule, and it was not until 1961 that the country became an independent republic outside the Commonwealth. English is one of the country's two official languages (the other being Afrikaans), even though a mere ten per cent of the 30 million inhabitants speak English as a

WORDS FROM OTHER LANGUAGES

FRENCH *often from Latin*

Old French
anguish
battle
beauty
beef
chapel
charity
courtesy
damage
debonair
delight
dinner
feast
flower
forest
govern
joy
liberty
marriage
mercy
miracle
navy
parliament
peace
people
pleasure
power
prayer
prince
prison
privilege
reign
religion
repent
riches
saint
soldier
state
tower
verdict
very
vessel

Early French Modern
ballet
brochure
corduroy
espionage
etiquette
group
naive
police
rendezvous
reprimand
ricochet
soup
verve

*19th and
20th century*
camouflage
chic
cliché
compere
détente
elite
garage
gourmet
liaison
menu
prestige
quiche
suede

French phrases
à la carte
bête noire
coup d'état
cul de sac
esprit de corps
fait accompli
hors d'oeuvre
noblesse oblige
nouveau riche
savoir faire
tour de force

DUTCH
boss
brandy
clink
coleslaw
cruise
decoy
deck
dock
drill (bore)
easel
etch
foist
gin
groove
hoist
keelhaul
kit
landscape
loiter
luck
maelstrom
schooner
skates
sketch
skipper
sledge
sleigh
sloop
splice
splinter
split
spool
trigger
waffle
wagon
yacht

ANGLO-SAXON
answer
be
begin
cheerful
child
clock
do
fast
fly
freedom
go
happy
hand
heart
help
house
kill
light
life
love
merry
night
old
pain
sad
ship
stone
sorrow
thing
think
time
twelve
upwards
us
wealth
wedding
where
who
work
year

NORSE *through
the Viking invaders*
anger
are
ask
bag
clumsy
crooked
die
egg
freckles
get
give
husband
knife
law
leg
neck
odd
ransack
rotten
sister
sky
slaughter
take
they
ugly
weak
window

**SCANDINAVIAN
LANGUAGES**
fjord
geyser
lemming
mink
ombudsman
rug
saga
ski
smorgasbord
walrus

LATIN *often via French*
accommodate
admire
album
alias
alibi
animal
apparatus
area
art
candidate
capable
census
circus
civil
community
compute
convent
create
culture
dental
dictator
divine
education
elect
essence
estimate
exit
experiment
focus
fortune
forum
frigid
genius
glory
grand
honour
hospitality
interim
invention
justice
lens
library
literature

luxury
manufacture
manuscript
medium
miser
moral
municipal
nation
nature
orator
pagan
perfect
persecute
province
public
quality
quasi
republic
science
series
specimen
splendid
squalor
stupid
tedium
tradition
tribe
vacuum
verbatim
via

Latin phrases
ad nauseam
bona fides
curriculum vitae
quid pro quo
sine qua non
status quo
sui generis
terra firma

*Modern
formation*
penicillin

ITALIAN *usually
from Latin*
arcade
balcony
bandit
brigand
bronze
cameo
caprice
caress
cartoon
casino
cello
colonel
corridor
dilettante
duet
espresso
fiasco
gazette
gelatine
grotto
incognito
infantry
influenza
malaria
manifesto
pastel
piano
picturesque
regatta
replica
salami
scenario
sentinel
sonata
sonnet
spaghetti
squadron
stanza
stiletto
studio
traffic

HUNGARIAN
coach
goulash
hussar
paprika
sabre

YIDDISH
*from Hebrew or
early German
sources*
bagel
chutzpah
nosh
schlock
schmaltz
schmuck

GERMAN
blitz
carouse
delicatessen
dollar
glockenspiel
kindergarten
lager
loafer
nickel
noodle
poodle
rucksack
seminar
snorkel
spanner
swindle
waltz
zinc

CZECH
howitzer
pistol
robot

RUSSIAN
balalaika
borscht
commissar
knout
mammoth
pogrom
samovar
vodka

GREEK
academy
alphabet
anarchy
athlete
atom
automatic
character
chorus
climax
cycle
cynic
democracy
diagnosis
drama
echo
eclipse
emphasis
energy
hero
history
hysterical
idea
irony
machine
music
myth
ocean
orchestra
parallel
philosophy
physical
planet
poet
politics
rhythm
sceptical
school
technical
theory
tone

*Modern
formations*
astronaut
polystyrene
schizophrenia

CHINESE
ketchup
kowtow
kung fu
lychee
sampan
silk
soya
tea
typhoon
wok

JAPANESE
bonsai
futon
geisha
harakiri
judo
kamikaze
karate
kimono
origami
rickshaw
saki
shogun
tsunami
tycoon

GAELIC
bard
blarney
bog
brat
brogue
cadge
galore
leprechaun
loch
plaid
shamrock
slogan
smithereens
sporran
spree
Tory
trousers
whisky

INUIT
(Eskimo)
anorak
igloo
kayak
parka

**AMERICAN INDIAN
LANGUAGES**
chipmunk
hickory
moccasin
moose
papoose
pecan
possum
powwow
raccoon
skunk
squaw
tepee
terrapin
toboggan
tomahawk
totem
wigwam

AZTEC
avocado
cocoa
chilli
chocolate
coyote
tomato

WELSH
coracle
corgi
eisteddfod
flannel
flummery

**CARIBBEAN
LANGUAGES**
barbecue
cannibal
canoe
cassava
curare
hammock
hurricane
maize
papaya
potato
tobacco

**SOUTH AMERICAN
LANGUAGES**
alpaca
cashew
cayenne
coca
condor
cougar
guano
guava
jacaranda
jaguar
llama
petunia
piranha
poncho
puma
quinine
tapioca
tapir
toucan
vicuna

PORTUGUESE
often from Latin
albatross
albino
auto da fé
brocade
cobra
corral
creole
dodo
marmalade
mandarin
pagoda
palaver
piccaninny
port (wine)
rusk
zebra

SPANISH *often from Latin*
aficionado
alfalfa
alligator
anchovy
armada
bonanza
booby
bravado
cafeteria
canyon
cask
cigar
cockroach
desperado
fiesta

grandee
lasso
macho
marijuana
mosquito
mustang
picaresque
patio
plaza
ranch
rodeo
siesta
sombrero
stampede
tornado

AFRIKAANS
aardvark
apartheid
boer
commandeer
commando
kop
kraal
rand
spoor
trek
veld
wildebeest

**AFRICAN
LANGUAGES**
banana
banjo
chimpanzee
cola
guinea
hoodoo
juju
okra
tango
tote
voodoo
yam
zombie

TURKISH
bosh
caviar
coffee
horde
kebab
kiosk
ottoman
pilau
yoghurt

PERSIAN
bazaar
candy
caravan
check
divan
jackal
jasmine
lemon
lilac
magic
orange
paradise
scimitar
shawl
spinach
taffeta
talc
tulip
turban

ARABIC
admiral
alcohol
algebra
alkali
arsenal
artichoke
assassin
carafe
cipher
cotton

crimson
gazelle
ghoul
harem
hazard
jar
lute
magazine
masquerade
mattress

monsoon
racket
saffron
sash
sherbert
sofa
syrup
tariff
zenith
zero

MALAY
amok
bamboo
batik
caddy (for tea)
compound
(buildings)
cockatoo
gingham
gong
kapok
launch
(motorboat)
orangutan
paddy
sago
sarong

**PACIFIC
LANGUAGES**
kiwi
mana
moa
taboo
tattoo
(on skin)
ukulele

**ABORIGINAL
LANGUAGES**
boomerang
dingo
budgerigar
kangaroo
koala
kookaburra
wallaby

HINDI
*often from
Sanskrit*
bandana
bangle
bungalow
cheetah
chintz
chit
cot
cushy
dinghy
dungarees
juggernaut
jungle
kedgeree
loot
pyjamas
shampoo
thug
toddy
veranda
yogi

**SOUTH INDIAN
LANGUAGES**
*(especially Tamil
and Malayalam)*
catamaran
cheroot
coir
mongoose
mulligitawny
pariah
teak

mother tongue (with Afrikaans representing another 12 to 15 per cent). Its importance, culturally and economically, is far greater than this figure would suggest, however. It is by far the commonest second language, and is widely used as a lingua franca by speakers of other languages.

Alongside 'South African English' (the variety of English used as a mother tongue chiefly by white South Africans), other varieties of English are used in South Africa — Afrikaans English (English spoken, as a second language, by Afrikaners), Cape Coloured English, and varieties spoken by South African Indians and by Africans with mother tongues such as Sotho, Xhosa, and Zulu. The white English-speaking population of nearby African countries, through Zambia and Zimbabwe and up the east coast, have speech patterns so closely related to those of South African English that they are usually considered to be part of the same linguistic community.

Standard written English in South Africa is much the same as that of Britain — thanks to the long and crucial influence of Britain in South African administration, education, and culture. In spoken English, however, there are a number of distinctive South African features in pronunciation, vocabulary, and syntax. These are mostly due to the influence of other South African languages, in particular Afrikaans, but partly also due to the type of English spoken by the early settlers.

Pronunciation The distinctive pronunciation of English-speaking South Africans with their flat vowels (technically, 'raised' vowels) and sharp consonants is immediately recognisable to anyone who has had any previous exposure to it. There is of course a whole range of intensity within the general South African English accent. There is not much geographical variation, except that speakers from rural areas and small towns tend to have a 'broader accent' — that is, a more marked regional accent; for the most part, it is social status and education that determine the breadth of a person's accent. Among the more conspicuous characteristics of South African English pronunciation are the following.

The consonants /p, t, k/ are rather sharper, more explosive, than those of southern British English, and the *r* — when it is sounded at all — is often rolled. Some 'voiced' consonants become almost 'voiceless' (probably through the influence of Afrikaans) in a broad South African accent (except at the beginning of a stressed syllable): the *b* sounds more like a *p*, the *z* like an *s*, and so on: the name *David* might be pronounced

something like /**day**-fət/. And the combinations /ty/ and /dy/ are commonly simplified to /ch/ and /j/, so that *tune* and *dune* sound like /chōōn/ and /jōōn/.

As for vowels, the /aa/ sound converges on /aw/, so that *bar* and *bore* are often impossible to distinguish. The diphthongs /ī/ and /air/ are reduced to the vowels /aa/ and /e-e/, so that *tight* sounds like the British *tart* (which in turn, if spoken by a South African, might sound like the British *taught*), and *barely* sounds something like the British *belly*.

In common with Australians and New Zealanders, South Africans tend to raise the tongue for the vowels /a/ and /e/, so that *bat* sounds, to the British ear, like *bet*, and *bet* like *bit*; they also tend to lower the /i/ sound, so that *bit* sounds something like /bət/, and they tend too to lengthen the final vowel in such words as *sorry* and *candy* and some of their derivatives from /i/ to /ee/ — *candied* therefore sounds rather different from *candid*, whereas in the Received Pronunciation (RP) of southeastern England they are indistinguishable.

Southeastern England shares with South Africa (and Australia and New Zealand) the tendency not to pronounce a written *r* before another consonant or at the end of a word, so that *sword* sounds just the same as *sawed* (in most of North America, Scotland, and Ireland, the words would usually be differentiated by the presence or absence of the *r* -sound). South African English goes further, however, in tending not to pronounce a written *r* at the end of a word even when the next word begins with a vowel: in British English, *four or five* would usually be pronounced /**fawr** aw **fīv**/; in South African English, the *r* remains silent: /**faw** aw **fīv**/ (or probably /**faw** aw **faav**/).

Vocabulary It is in vocabulary that South African English differs most extensively from other varieties of English.

Some terms have entered World English — *apartheid, the bush, commandeer, commando, laager, spoor, trek,* and *veld*, for instance. A large number of words peculiar to South African English refer to plants, animals, terrain, cooking, and so on, and have no exact equivalents in other varieties of English. Even so, many of them are likely to be understood by non-South Africans: *wildebeest,* and *springbok*, for instance, and *aardvark*, of course, renowned as the first full noun in many dictionaries and the first entry in many encyclopaedias.

The chief source of loanwords in South African English is of course Afrikaans (or earlier Dutch)

— all those listed, in the previous paragraph, for instance, and also *biltong* (salted sun-dried meat), *boer, boerewors* (a spicy sausage), *braaivleis* (a barbecue), *dorp* (a country town or village), *kloof* (a ravine), *koppie* (a small hill), *lekker* (nice), *stoep* (a veranda), *vlei* (a marsh or lake).

The second major source is Bantu languages: *bonsella* (a small gift), *donga* (a dry river bed), *indaba* (a conference or discussion), and the like.

From the Khoisan languages (of the Khoi-Khoin and San people, known to Europeans as the 'Hottentots' and 'Bushmen' respectively) comes *dagga* (cannabis), *gnu, quagga* (an extinct wild ass), and *gogga* (any insect).

Three other sources reflect various aspects of South African history: from Malay, probably, came the cookery-terms *babotie* (a dish of curried mincemeat), *sosatie* (a skewer of curried meat), and also *sjambok* (a taut whip). From Indian languages came such cookery terms (increasingly familiar in Britain now, but long-established in South Africa) as *biriani* (a spicy rice dish), *masala* (a mix of spices), and *samoosa* (a fried savoury pastry). From Portuguese came *bredie* (a stew), *mealie* (corn on the cob), and *pawpaw* (papaya), and also *piccanin* (a small child — the word is used in Australia too, and in pidgin languages elsewhere).

Some terms are loan translations or half-translations or folk-etymology translations from Afrikaans (or Dutch): *stinkwood* (from *stinkhout*), *outspan* (from *uitspan*, 'to stretch out, unyoke, break one's journey'), *poegeyed* ('drunk', from Dutch *poechai*, 'a fuss'), *to hold thumbs* (used when expressing a hope or wishing someone luck — the equivalent of *to keep one's fingers crossed* — probably derived from the corresponding expression in Afrikaans, originally perhaps from German or French).

A few South African English words (as in Australia) follow American rather than British vocabulary — *chips* (potato crisps), *freeway* (a motorway), *pantihose* (tights), and *yield* (the equivalent of 'give way' in traffic signs) — but the American influence is still proportionally insignificant compared with the British.

A small number of words and phrases have been coined in South Africa from English roots — by far the best-known is *concentration camp* (coined by the British during the Boer War). A more typical example is *tackies* (gym shoes, plimsolls).

A number of terms common in South African English might surprise or confuse an English-speaker elsewhere — the word might seem strangely outdated or contrived, or the sense might seem slightly distorted. (Some of the following examples may be found in one or two other varieties of English — *globe* and *station wagon* are common in Australian usage, for example, and are still occasionally used in British English — but none is common to all standard varieties of English.) Many South Africans still refer to the cinema as *the bioscope* and to the radio as *the wireless*; and everyday terms include *butchery* (a butcher's shop), *cookie* (a cupcake, or fairy cake), *globe* (a light bulb), *granadilla* (a passion fruit), *station wagon* (an estate car), and *traffic circle* (a roundabout). Then there are the different or additional senses of *coloured/s* (referring to people of mixed-race birth or descent), *gown* (a dressing gown or bathrobe), *just now* ('in a little while; soon'), *location* (a township for a specified race group), *mason* (a bricklayer), *pass book* and *reference book* (an identity document), *rather* ('instead'), *robot* (traffic lights), and *so long* ('in the meantime').

Most striking of all, perhaps, are the peculiarly South African uses of *man, shame,* and *no. Man* is used when addressing someone in a familiar way — the person addressed being either male or female:

> You women always take so long to get ready — can't you hurry up, man?

Shame is often used by itself to express sympathy or sentimental admiration:

> 'I've just had a tooth out.' 'Shame.'
> 'Look at my beautiful baby.' 'Ah, shame.'

No can be used neutrally, and sometimes even seems to indicate the positive rather than the negative:

> 'How are you feeling?' 'No, I'm very well, thanks.'
> 'Are you feeling better?' 'No, I'm really fine, thanks.'

Grammar South African English still follows British usage closely. But there are a few traditional exceptions, mostly in informal speech. (Again, any of these might be found too in American, Australian, or Indian English, say, but none is considered standard idiom across the range of World English.)

With is sometimes used adverbially: *Are you coming with?* (probably influenced by the Afrikaans form; it is also common in American dialect).

This last example could be analysed in a different way — as leaving out a word (*me* or *us* or the like). The omission of a word or word-element that standard British English would consider essential is a common South African peculiarity: *But has he got (any)? She lectures (to) me in history; I'm going to the baker('s) shop; Be careful of the barb(ed) wire; I beg yours?* ('I beg your pardon?').

In requests, the negative is often used where standard British English would favour the positive: *Won't you do me a favour?*

The adverb *also* is preferred to *too* as the final word in a sentence: *He's going to do that also.*

The unvarying question *Is it?* is used widely in informal speech — the equivalent perhaps of *really?* in British English:

'She turns 22 in May.' 'Is it?'
'Oranges are going up in price.' 'Is it?'

(This is a characteristic common, in informal use, to several other national varieties of English.)

Some of the more extreme deviations often cited by linguists are in fact extremely rare: one notorious example, *He threw me over the hedge with a rock* ('He threw a stone at me over the hedge' — modelled on Afrikaans structures) is quite nonstandard, and is most unlikely to be said, other than jokingly, by anyone whose mother tongue is English.

Trends and conclusion Since South Africa became a Republic and left the Commonwealth in 1961, speakers of South African English have tended to rely increasingly on local models of usage. The chief result seems to be a general drift towards a more marked South African pronunciation, so that speakers of South African English and speakers of Afrikaans English are likely to become indistinguishable. This trend has been reinforced by the increased contact that English speakers have with Afrikaans and Afrikaans English — thanks to such factors as the introduction of television (Afrikaans and English share a single channel); the cultural boycott of South Africa by British radio, television, and stage actors; the presence of many Afrikaans teachers in English-medium schools; longer military service; and in general a greater integration within the white community.

Language use in South Africa reflects many of the country's contrasts and conflicts. The Soweto unrest of 1976 was sparked off by black schoolchildren's protesting against the official attempt to substitute Afrikaans for English as the medium of instruction. English remains the favoured lingua franca within the country, despite the very small proportion of those who use it as their mother tongue. Part of its appeal is its usefulness in contacts with the outside world, and this guiding and monitoring factor is likely to keep the continuing development of South African English under restraint — well within the mainstream of World English.

South Asian English Approximately one fifth of the world's people live in South Asia — perhaps 750 million in India, about 90 million each in Bangladesh and Pakistan, and about 17 or 18 million each in Sri Lanka and Nepal. (Burma, with its population of between 35 and 40 million, is also sometimes included in surveys of South Asian English.) This enormous population sustains a diversity of cultures and religions and also at least four distinct language families, embracing well over a thousand distinct languages. In such a linguistically complex area, English is of enormous value as a link language and lingua franca.

English began to be established in the Indian subcontinent almost 400 years ago, in the trading stations of the East India Company. In the centuries of British domination, from about 1600 to 1947, the influence of the alien language never waned. And it continues today, as one of the official or administrative languages in most of the countries of the region, and often as the language of higher education, the higher courts of law, and the media. British English remains the favoured variety and model, though American words and expressions are penetrating South Asia almost as steadily as they are penetrating other varieties of English throughout the world.

Naturally enough in such a large area and diverse population, there is not just *one* English but a continuum, ranging from standard international English, indistinguishable in the written medium from the British standard, through a range of forms influenced by the speakers' mother tongues, to pidgins like 'Butler English'. The description here will concentrate on the standard end of the spectrum, and, as far as possible, on widespread features that straddle social and regional differences.

Pronunciation The distinctive South Asian English accent is produced by a 'retroflex articulatory setting' — that is, the jaw is kept loose, and the tip of the tongue habitually curls towards the roof of the mouth. This affects all speech, but especially the consonants /t,d,s,z,l,r,n/.

Many English words beginning with *p*, *t*, and *c/k* are pronounced in British and American English with an accompanying breathiness — *pin* sounds slightly like /p-hin/. In South Asian English, however, this breathiness or 'aspiration' is seldom reproduced — with the result that words such as *pin*, *tin* and *con* sound to British and

American ears like *bin*, *din* and *gone*. Since thousands of English words are distinguished by initial *p* or *b*, *t* or *d*, and *k* or *g*, the possibility of confusion is considerable.

Many South Asian speakers do not distinguish between /v/ and /w/ or between /n/ and /ng/; so *vine* and *wine* are often homophones (that is, are pronounced identically), and so are *sin* and *sing*. And /th/ and /th/ tend to be sounded as /t/ and /d/ — so *thought* can sound just like *taught*, and *heather* like *header*.

Consonant clusters beginning with *s* are often prefixed or (in Kashmir especially) broken up by an *i*-sound — 'ispeak', 'ischool', 'istate', or 'sipeak', 'sichool', 'sitate'.

There are fewer vowel contrasts than in RP (the 'received pronunciation' of educated people in southeastern England) — *jar* and *jaw* are often homophones, as are *not* and *gnat*. On the other hand, vowels are less frequently reduced to the neutral ə-sound, so that *about*, for instance, tends to be pronounced /a-**bowt**/, with the *a* as in *hat*, rather than /ə-**bowt**/ as in RP.

The stress-pattern in South Asian English is different from that of British English and other varieties. The tendency is to give equal stress to all syllables; when the stress-timed pattern of mother-tongue English is attempted, the wrong syllable is sometimes stressed: *at***mos***phere*, **beg***in-ning*, *def***in***itely*.

Vocabulary Many familiar English words are derived from Indian languages — *bungalow*, *jungle*, *veranda*, *curry*, *gymkhana*, and *pyjamas*, for instance. Within South Asia itself, a great many other local words are used in everyday English conversation and writing:

acha a term of agreement
charpoy a string bed
chowkidar a night watchman
dacoit a robber
dhobi, dhobi walla a laundryman
gherao a protest demonstration usually involving the siege of an office or building; or to take part in such a protest
goonda a hooligan or irresponsible person; and also used as an insulting adjective
jhuggi a squatter settlement
-ji used as a suffix to indicate a term of respect: *Mamaji, Daddyji, Gandhiji*
maidan a parade ground or esplanade
mali a gardener
mela a fair, or a festive occasion

The words *bandh* and *hartal* refer to kinds of general strike; a *lakh* and a *crore* refer to large quantities — 100,000 and ten million respectively.

Local foods (the lentils *urad* and *moong*, for instance) and items of clothing (*choli*, *dhoti*) naturally have local names.

Many English terms favoured in South Asian English sound archaic or extremely formal to mother-tongue English speakers: *demise* instead of *death*; *to felicitate* rather than *to congratulate*; *to do the needful*, *miscreant*, *How is your good self?*

Sometimes a standard English phrase is tightened into a compound: *key-bunch* (a bunch of keys) or *milk bottle* (a bottle of milk); *pindrop silence*; *age-barred* (barred by age).

Many other terms, though formed from English words or word-elements, are virtually incomprehensible to the outsider, being either obsolete in other varieties of English or of purely local coinage:

airdash to fly from place to place
cooling glasses sunglasses
co-brother one's wife's sister's husband
co-daughters-in-law the wives of brothers
cutpiece an oddment of cloth
derecognise to withdraw recognition from
demit to resign
deputant a representative
dissentment dissent
duck's egg zero: *That goonda teacher is always giving me duck's eggs.*
eve-teasing teasing girls
fair out to make a fair copy
finger chips potato crisps served as a snack
footmat a doormat, or mat to wipe one's feet on
half pant short trousers, shorts
ice-candy ice lolly
jack support, influence: *You can do nothing if you have no jack.*
native place home town
on seat in one's office
out of station away from one's office
ownership flats private flats, owner-occupied
preponement the bringing forward of an event
quarter-plate a side plate
sit on somebody's neck to keep a close watch on somebody
standing seat standing room
undertrial a person, usually a prisoner, awaiting trial
wheat complexion a fair complexion

Grammar Grammatical competence in English varies in South Asia (as in other regions where English is used as a second language) with the speaker's education. Generalisations are therefore difficult to make. The following patterns, however, occur fairly widely.

The 'progressive' tenses, with the *-ing* form of the verb, are often used in South Asian English where standard British English does not permit them:

I am not knowing the answer now.
He is hearing the noises very often.

Many other modifications of the British English verb-system are commonly heard. Here are some typical examples:

But I have sold you one last month.
He is waiting here since 12 o'clock.
If you will get here in time, she will see you.

The standard English constructions *There is X* and *There are X* are sometimes inverted:

What shall we eat? Eggs are there; rice is there; beans are there.

And inversion also occurs in indirect questions:

She asked me when are you coming home.

On the other hand, there is a tendency not to invert the subject and predicate in direct questions:

What you will do when you go home?
Where he has gone?

As for nouns, the singular-plural system is often used in a different way, and 'partitive phrases' (*a piece of wood*) are often reduced to the key noun (*a wood*):

You can eat fruits if you are hungry.
Please buy me two breads (= two loaves of bread).

The is frequently omitted when the reference is known to the listener:

We have just seen new hotel.
They have gone to pictures.

And *one* is preferred to *a/an* when the reference is specific:

I lived with one very kind lady.

Many speakers use *isn't it?* as an unvarying tag after a yes/no question:

You have recently married, isn't it?
They would like to attend, isn't it?

Finally, prepositions are often used differently — altered, inserted, or omitted:

Pay attention on what I am saying.
He voiced out a strong opinion.
Throw the leftovers (= Throw them away).

Trends It would be wrong to think of South Asian English simply as a 'deviation' from British English. It has evolved into a distinctive and standard variety in its own right, as well-suited to its environment as Irish English and American English are to theirs.

Asian writers, in their generous contribution to World English literature in the last few decades, have forged an idiom that, while still fully comprehensible to other speakers of English, is clearly more capable than British English of expressing Asian culture and experience.

South Asians or their descendants who live in English-speaking countries have a complex view of the use of language. Immigrant parents, in Britain at least, tend to encourage their children to acquire 'good English' and at the same time to retain or acquire proficiency in their mother tongue (usually Bengali, Gujerati, Hindi, Punjabi, or Urdu) and the culture it represents. Research has shown that these first- or second-generation children become adept at 'code-switching' — shifting easily not just from their home language to English, but also from one variety of English to another, from standard British English in school, say, to various forms of South Asian English when talking to recent immigrants. How long this versatility will continue is uncertain. The experience of the large and long-established South Asian communities in South Africa suggests that a tightly knit social grouping moves only very slowly but inevitably towards the linguistic norms of the surrounding society.

spare, sparse See SCANT.

speciality, specialty A product, pursuit, subject, or service that one specialises in, or is particularly adept at, is a *speciality* in British English and a *specialty* in American English: *Jugged hare is the speciality of the house*; *Professor Fairfax's speciality is Norse mythology*.

In both British and American English, a distinguishing characteristic is a *speciality*, and a legal agreement kept under seal is a *specialty*.

specially, especially These two adverbs are often used incorrectly, especially *specially*.

Specially means 'in a special way' or, more commonly, 'in this particular way, or for this particular purpose, and no other; expressly, specifically'. It is more or less the opposite of *ordinarily* or *generally: specially trained dogs; arranged the meeting specially.*

Especially, means 'to a great extent, extremely',

or 'in particular, above all': *I dislike motorbikes, especially noisy motorbikes.*

Especially is probably the commoner word (or should be, except that *specially* is often mistakenly used in its place). And *especially* is a more versatile word. *Specially* tends to apply only to verbs: *She danced specially to please me. Especially* applies to adverbs (*She danced especially gracefully*), adjectives (*an especially graceful dancer*), and verbs (*I especially dislike motorbikes*), and even seems to govern nouns (*I dislike all bikes, especially motorbikes; All of them are fools, Nicholas especially*).

In some contexts, either adverb can be used: *She danced especially for me/She danced specially for me.* Perhaps even here there is some slight difference in meaning: *especially for me* suggests: 'for me above all; more for me than for others'; *specially for me* suggests 'for me alone; exclusively for me, and for no one else'. (Of course, *She danced specially for me* can be understood in quite different way too — 'She danced for me in a special way'.) Fortunately, the word order if nothing else usually sets the two adverbs apart and makes the choice clear: *He came especially late to annoy me; He came late specially to annoy me.*

A similar distinction used to apply to the corresponding adjectives *special* ('distinct, out of the ordinary, specific') and *especial* ('particular, very great, outstanding'). But *special* is now widely used (and more or less fully accepted) in phrases where formerly only *especial* was suitable: *my special friend, a special talent for irritating me, done with special verve, for the special benefit of those who don't already know. Especial,* in other words, has fallen almost totally out of use, except in very literary contexts.

specious, spurious The adjective *specious* is quite different in meaning from the noun *species*. (The adjective that retains the sense of *species* is *specific*.) *Specious* and *species* do, it is true, go back to the same Latin word *speciēs*, 'outward appearance', from *specere*, 'to look at'. But they soon went their separate ways: the Latin *speciēs* developed an extended sense, 'a particular type'; and a derived Latin adjective *speciosus* emerged, meaning 'having a fine outward appearance, good-looking'. The word *specious* entered Middle English in this sense. But it began to develop an unfavourable meaning: associations of insincerity and false appearance clung to the word, and today it means 'seemingly attractive or authentic or convincing, but not really so; deceptive': *a specious excuse, specious flattery.*

To those who produce the time-honoured and specious argument that people should not pay for what they themselves do not want, there are a dozen answers. The simple one is that this philosophy would ensure the disappearance of many vital public services.
— Lord Goodman, *The Observer*

In 1963 again *confrontation* was the specious contranomer and lying vogue word that President Sukarno selected to describe what Indonesia was doing to Malaysia. It sounded impressive. What it actually meant was intimidation, guerrilla warfare, arson, loot, murder, and confiscation.
— Philip Howard, *Weasel Words*

The word is pronounced /**spee**shəss/.

The adjective *spurious*, pronounced /**spew**ri-əss/, means 'invalid, not authentic or genuine in origin, counterfeit': *a spurious claim to the title; a manuscript formerly attributed to Erasmus but now regarded as spurious.*

Exactly who first had the idea of hiring Hell's Angels as a security force, no one can remember now. The idea did possess a glimmering of logic. Previous rock concerts in the San Francisco area had found it better to invite the Angels than to risk their arrival, unbidden, in a spirit of antagonism. Giving them spurious official status had proved an even better emollient.
— Philip Norman, *The Stones*

I don't think he'd want to be remembered, anyway, as an ideas man. When he was didactic, it was in the blunt manner of a popular, secular preacher who wanted us to use our common sense, not be taken in by the spurious, to cherish the beef and pudding tradition of an old England he looked at with the ambiguous eyes of a George Orwell.
— Anthony Burgess, *The Observer*

In 1979, for example, a leading scientist received his rehabilitation dossier. It was as thick as a London telephone book. Every charge since 1951 had been reinvestigated and judged spurious. A brilliant student from a rich Shanghai family who obtained a PhD from Yale, he had been assumed to be a spy for having voluntarily returned to China to serve the new communist state.
— Jonathan Mirsky, *The Times*

The word comes from the Latin *spurius*, meaning 'illegitimate, born out of wedlock' (and can be used with this sense in English too, though it very seldom is nowadays).

The two adjectives can often be used in the same combinations: *a specious/spurious resemblance*; *specious/spurious reasoning*. There is very little, if any, difference in sense here. Perhaps *specious* has a slightly greater tone of disapproval to it, suggesting merely superficial beauty and the deliberate adoption of an appealing outward appearance in order to deceive. *Spurious* has perhaps less hint of deliberate deception about it: a person may, in good faith, promote a *spurious* claim or argument or antique, and its worthlessness in each case, when proved, may come as a complete surprise to him.

To put it another way, *specious* emphasises the contrast between good appearance and bad reality, whereas *spurious* just indicates that the reality is false, without implying anything about the appearance.

The related nouns are *speciousness* and *spuriousness*.

spelling English spelling has a reputation — especially among schoolchildren and foreigners — for being extremely difficult. Note, for instance, the variety (and inconsistency) of pronunciations that the spelling-combination -*ough*-can have: *bough, cough, dough, ought, tough, through, hiccough* /**hik**kup/, *borough*, and *lough* /lo<u>kh</u>/.

Obversely, note the great number of spelling-combinations that can be used to represent the sound /ō/: *dough* again, *so, sew, low, owe, oh, toe, tote, boat, soul, brooch, yeoman, bureau*, and *faux pas*.

Students of language have a story about how to spell 'fish'. Start with *gh* as in *tough*, then take *o* as in *women*, and for the final *sh*-sound use the *ti* from *lotion*. You end up with the nonsense word *ghoti*. They then cap the story by pointing out that *ghoti* can be completely soundless: pronounce the *gh* as in *dough*, *o* as in *foetus*, *t* as in *castle*, *i* as in *cushion*.

How did this inconsistency come about? Many of the spelling peculiarities are fossils within the complicated history of English. Primarily a Germanic language (that of the Angles, Saxons, and Jutes, who continued to arrive and settle in Britain after the end of the Roman occupation), English developed under a succession of further linguistic invasions and influences. The Norse of the Vikings in the ninth and tenth centuries was followed by Norman French in and after 1066. Then came the Latin and Greek of Renaissance scholars, the French and Italian of fashionable

Enlightenment Europe, especially in the 18th century, the Indian and African languages of the colonial period, and so on. Adapted into English, a foreign 'loanword' (such as *calm* or *champagne*) might quickly fall into line with the English sound-system and yet retain its foreign spelling. And a variety of written forms might converge in pronunciation (like *sea* and *see*). Hence our heritage of discrepancies today.

Coupled with that is changing pronunciation within English itself — notably the large-scale change between the 14th and 16th centuries (between Chaucer's lifetime and Shakespeare's) known as the Great Vowel Shift. Of course, spelling changes too occur over the centuries, but they are not synchronised with pronunciation changes. At most points in history, certain glaring irregularities would have been evident, as they are today. Here are just two examples to show how things change: the words *life* and *house* were generally spelt *lyf* and *hous* by Chaucer, and were pronounced /leef/ and /hōōss/ by him; Shakespeare's pronunciations would probably have been /layf/ and /hōss/; today, the standard pronunciations are /līf/ and /howss/.

Further small factors: after the Norman conquest, Norman scribes, unfamiliar with English, would sometimes 'frenchify' Anglo-Saxon words. During the Renaissance, well-educated writers or printers might insert silent letters into words to indicate their Latin source: a *b* was introduced into *doubt* and *debt*, for example (which had come into Middle English from Old French without a *b*), to mark them as derivatives of the Latin *dubitare* and *debitum*; a *p* was introduced into *receipt* (also into *conceit* and *deceit*, though it has now disappeared again) to acknowledge its derivation from the Latin *recipere*; a *g* was stuck into *deign*, though not into *disdain* (both ultimately from the Latin *dignus*, 'worthy'), and so on. Such 'corrections' were sometimes quite inappropriate: an *s* was introduced into both *island* and *aisle* by association with *isle* (which is derived from Latin *insula*), whereas *aisle* derives in fact from the Latin *ala*, via Old French *aile*, and *island* from Old English *igland* or *īland*. And through false analogy, the *gh* was inserted into *delight* (from the Old French *deleitier*, from Latin *delectare*) and *tight* (from Old Norse *thettr*), because of their apparent similarity to *light* and *night* (where *gh* is historically justified, since it was sounded in Old English).

Before that, in the early days of printing, compositors might spell a word in several different ways in order to 'justify' the lines (align the line-endings on the printed page). Consistency was not really regarded as a great virtue in those days: Shakespeare apparently spelt his own name in several different ways, as the mood took him. One theory is that standardised spelling in printed texts began to be taken in earnest only after the Civil War in England (1642-50). A torrent of propaganda pamphlets came off the presses during the war, all so urgent that printers could no longer justify the lines perfectly — and the need for variant spellings thus fell away.

At all events standardisation in spelling did come to be regarded as something desirable. In France, it was done quite brutally in the 17th century — by the decrees of the Académie Française. John Dryden, and then Jonathan Swift, urged comparable 'fixing' of English spelling. Dr Johnson did too, at first, and even though he later decided that language could not be forced in this way, his famous *Dictionary of the English Language* (1755) was responsible, more than any other single factor, for establishing standard spelling in Britain.

Meanwhile, across the Atlantic, a slightly different standardised spelling established itself, defended partly on grounds of logic and partly by appeals to linguistic nationalism (why should America automatically follow Britain in spelling, any more than in any other area?). This American spelling was heavily influenced by the spelling-books and dictionaries of Noah Webster (1758–1843). Not that the emergent American standard was wildly different from the British standard; in fact many American spellings (such as *color* for *colour*) had been used widely in Britain in earlier times.

Both British and American spelling, however, were — for the various historical reasons just discussed — quite out of keeping with pronunciation. Calls for 'reform', both before and after Dr Johnson, were inevitable, the most famous reformer (though far from the most radical one) being George Bernard Shaw.

How much more convenient it would be, it was argued, if there were always one spelling corresponding to one sound — foreigners could pick up the language far more easily, children could learn to read without a struggle, and the common embarrassment of a misspelt word would virtually disappear.

As long ago as the 16th century, various reformers tried to link writing to pronunciation by devising systems of phonetic spelling. But such attempts, however well-intentioned, were doomed to failure, just as any comparable scheme today would be quite impracticable. For one thing, there are 44 or 46 distinct sounds in standard English

(including diphthongs) — twice the number of sound-forming letters in the alphabet (bearing in mind that *q*, *c*, and *x* are superfluous, since their sounds can be represented by other letters). To introduce new symbols, as the 16th-century reformers tried to do, is in many ways to make spelling more complicated rather than easier (though ITA — the Initial Teaching Alphabet, widely used in primary schools in the 1960s — did apparently help children to learn to read more quickly). In any case, as the grammarian Richard Mulcaster noted in 1582, to use the same letter to represent different sounds is no worse a linguistic offence than to use a single word to represent different senses.

Furthermore, pronunciation is after all very variable in English — not just across regional, national, and class boundaries (*whose* accent would form the basis of a pure phonetic spelling system?), but through time as well: our pronunciation is not just utterly different from Chaucer's or Shakespeare's — it is also perceptibly different from our grandparents' and even our parents'. A fixed phonetic spelling might soon be out of keeping with pronunciation, even if it matched the way we (or some of us) spoke when the system was introduced.

Or it might be argued that natural development is (very slowly) bringing sound and spelling together in any case: *baulk*, *salve* (as in *to salve one's conscience*), and *solder* now commonly have the *l* pronounced in British English, whereas it tended until recently to be silent. *Often* increasingly sounds the *t* in British English. *Service* and *virtue* were pronounced /**sar**-viss/ and /**var**-tew/ as late as the 19th century; and *join* was pronounced /jīn/ in the 18th. It is as if nature is taking her own course in all this: there is no need for us to speed things up artificially.

Another consideration: the spelling of a word, as hinted earlier, tells a great deal about its history and its relationship to other words (including its own derivatives). The spelling *knight* might appear to be a ludicrous representation of the sound /nīt/, but it harks back to a distant time when the *k* and *gh* were indeed sounded. And to those who know German, it indicates a relationship with the modern German word *Knecht* ('a boy' or 'a servant'), and suggests how the sense of *knight* has 'ameliorated' (improved) over the centuries. To take a simpler example: the adjectives *pious* and *impious* are clearly closely related as opposites; but their pronunciations are now very different, /**pī**-əss/ and /**im**pi-əss/: if their spelling were reformed to reflect their pronunciation, then their close linguistic kinship would cease to be obvious. Spelling reform would even obscure the relationship of *photograph*, *photography*, and *photographic*.

As for the alleged difficulty caused to foreigners — it is surely easier for a Frenchman to understand (and to spell) the word *centre*, which retains its original French appearance, than it would be if the word were spelt *senta* instead (though it is *center* in American English). Existing spelling, then, preserves a great deal of information about a word's history (and hence about its meaning) that would be lost if phonetic spelling were introduced.

The strongest argument of all against a drastic revision of English spelling is this: our current troublesome spelling system at least enables us to read the writing of times past. Suppose a new set of symbols were introduced tomorrow — how would a child brought up on them be able to read an old copy of Dickens when he grew up, or even the sleeve-notes of a Beatles record, say? Quite simply, he would have to learn the old spelling system anyway (for the purpose of reading at least, if not for writing), so the great reform would founder at once. Dr Johnson was surely right to urge his readers, in the introduction to his great dictionary, 'not to disturb, upon narrower views, or for minute propriety, the orthography [spelling] of their fathers'.

Spelling and handwriting do change, of course (old manuscripts are difficult for us to read, and Shakespearean spelling does take a bit of effort to master), but to accelerate these natural shifts by one great reforming leap would be to open up a huge and needless chasm between now and then.

So we are stuck with our peculiar spelling system, and must make the best of a bad job. And it is not really such a bad job after all: even to speak of the English spelling 'system' is to admit that English spelling is far from random. There is, in fact, a great deal of consistency in it: words from similar sources tend to behave in similar ways, and the value of letters varies according to context with a certain regularity.

There are exceptions to the rules, of course, but — more importantly — there are the rules: most of us could, after all, make a fair guess at the pronunciation of a word, even a nonsense word, that we had never seen before . . . even one containing *-ough*! Or, to return to the joke spelling of *fish* as *ghoti*, it is easy to see why the problems it presents can never occur in practice: *gh* cannot be pronounced like an *f* if it is at the beginning of a word; it is only in the word *women* that *o* has the sound /i/, and it is only when there is a vowel following (as in *satiate* or *nation*) that *ti*

has the sound /sh/.

To conclude, here is a summary of the often neglected virtues of our spelling system:

● It allows us to read the literature of our past with relative ease.

● It allows us to read material produced throughout the English-speaking world: even the differences between British and American spelling do not stop Americans from reading British books or British people from reading American ones.

● It reminds us of the connection between related words: the *n* of *autumn* is silent, but it reminds us that *autumnal* has an *n* that is pronounced.

● It is one of the very few European spelling systems based on the Roman alphabet that uses no special letters or accents (like the ç or è of French or the ö or ß of German), and so can be printed using only 26 letters, plus punctuation marks.

Some modern linguists have even claimed that English spelling comes close to being an ideal representation of the sound system of our language. We need not go as far as that in its praise, but neither should we be so concerned with its faults as to lose sight of its virtues.

See also PRONUNCIATION.

The rules of English spelling The following set of rules provides a guideline to some of the regularities of English spelling — regularities that are ultimately far more striking than the inconsistencies. The rules as set out are not watertight, and they are far from complete. Some rules are so complex that, true to the old joke, it is easier to learn all the spellings individually than to learn the rules governing them. The rules determining which adjectives end in *-ible* (*dispersible* and *responsible*) and which in *-able* (*dispensable*), for instance, are too intricate to be worth formulating.

Where rules are lacking, there are two resources always available: first, analogy (a rough guide at best: it helps to direct the speller from *ghost* to *ghastly* and *aghast*, say, but not from *responsible* to *dispensable*), and secondly, of course, a good English dictionary.

● **-ae-** *and* **-oe-.** These vowel combinations are now seldom written or printed as single characters — æ, œ. Furthermore, they are increasingly being replaced by a single *e*, even in British English. The trend is as follows:

For words of Greek derivation, *-ae-* and *-oe-* in the middle of a word are now rare in American English — *paleography* and *encyclopedia* for example, are preferred to *palaeography* and *encyclopaedia* in the United States; three important exceptions are *aeon*, *amoeba*, and *archaeology* which still remain more popular there than *eon*, *ameba*, and *archeology*.

At the beginning of a word, *oe-* has given way to *e-* in American English — *estrogen* is far more common than *oestrogen* (the reverse of British English), though *Oedipus* remains unchanged; *ae-* has survived rather better: *aesthetics* persists in American English alongside *esthetics*, and *aerobics* is the only acceptable form in World English.

Words of Latin origin usually converted their *ae* to *e* early in the history of English: *equal* from the Latin *aequalis* or *aequus*, for instance.

When the *-ae* came at the end of a word, as a Latin suffix, it usually remained unchanged, and is in little danger of being changed now: *algae*, *aqua vitae*, *vertebrae*.

Many words once spelt with *ae* or *oe* have by now fully normalised the spelling to a simple *e*: *phenomenon*, for instance, was once spelt *phaenomenon*, and *pedagogy* and *ecumenical* have now virtually driven out *paedagogy* and *oecumenical*. Similarly, *penology* and *pederast* are now the clearly preferred forms. In some cases, the rivalry persists in British English, but the simple *e* is surely winning: *homeopathy* vs *homoeopathy*, *medieval* vs *mediaeval*. In other cases, the rearguard action of the *ae* forms is surprisingly strong: *encyclopaedia* and *archaeology* — but it is just a matter of time before *encyclopedia* and *archeology* overtake them. In British English even stronger resistance comes from *gynaecology*, *paediatrics*, *diarrhoea*, and *oestrogen*: they show no sign of yielding to the American alternatives, *gynecology*, *pediatrics*, *diarrhea*, *estrogen*. Likewise *manoeuvre*, with its French appearance and its double difference from the American *maneuver*. The word *foetus* is interesting in that as a Latin word its spelling should really be *fetus*. There is thus less resistance in Britain to the spelling *fetus* than to other spellings involving *e* instead of *oe*.

Regarding the pronunciation of *ae* and *oe* in Greek-based words: the combination *aer* is generally /air/ — *aerobics*. Before a vowel, *ae* and *oe* are /ee/ generally in British English and often in American English: *Aeolian*, *palaeolithic*, *homoeopathy*. Before a consonant, *oe* is generally /ee/ in British English but /e/ in American English: *Oedipus*, *oestrogen*. The tendency here to pronounce the words /e/ in American English is no doubt related to the tendency to replace *oe* by *e* in the spelling. As for the pronunciation of

ae before a consonant, it is hard to give a general rule, and a dictionary must be consulted in individual cases.

● **-ise** *vs* **-ize.** American spelling favours *-ize* overwhelmingly; British usage is divided, though the trend seems to be towards *-ize* too.

There are arguments in favour of each side, but in the end, the choice is your own — subject to a few qualifications. First, if you are writing for publication, then use the style favoured by the publisher. Secondly, be consistent: if you choose the spelling *civilize*, then use a *z* too in *realize*, *civilization*, and so on. Thirdly, remember that some words do not offer the option: *capsize* can take the *z* only; *compromise*, *supervise*, and many others can take the *s* only.

For a fuller list of such words, and for a more detailed discussion of the *-ise/-ize* question, see the separate article -ISE, -IZE.

● **-re** *vs* **-er.** It is well known that North American spelling often regularises the *-er* ending, whereas British usage has retained the French *-re* ending of *centre*, *theatre*, *litre*, *sombre*, *mitre*, *fibre*, and so on.

All that needs mentioning here, then, is an alert to the exceptions.

First, Americans tend to retain the *-re* ending in some special cases — *macabre*, *timbre* — and particularly after hard *c* (and sometimes hard *g*): the *c* is in danger of being pronounced soft, as an *s*, if followed directly by an *e*. So: *acre*, *lucre*, *massacre*, *mediocre*, *ogre* (though the American spelling is *meager*).

Secondly, there are certain regional irregularities in North America. In Canada, for instance (possibly because of French influence), and sometimes in the United States too, the tendency is to spell *theatre* with a *-re* ending.

Thirdly, many words in British English end in *-er* without any choice in the matter, and they are not all as obvious as *number*. Consider *sober*, *neuter*, *beleaguer*, and *diameter*. Take care not to 'correct' these spellings into an *-re* ending.

● **-our** *vs* **-or.** One of the most widely known distinctions between British and American spelling is the *-our/-or* ending. British English usually favours the French-based ending *-our*: *ardour*, *clamour*, *colour*, *endeavour*, *favour*, *fervour*, *honour*, *humour*, *labour*, *odour*, *savour*, *succour*, *valour*, *vapour*, and *vigour*. American English omits the final *u* here generally, apparently preferring the Latin-based ending *-or* in all the words above. (There are one or two such words, however, such as *glamour*, where Americans tend to retain the *u* more often than not.)

Two warnings: first, there are many words spelt

-or even in British English: the obvious ones are the agent nouns — *author, executor, governor* (formerly *governour*), *mayor, professor, victor,* and so on (*saviour* is the only important agent noun to retain the *u,* and frequently retains it in American English too) — and various well-known common nouns such as *anchor, equator, error, motor, sector,* and *tenor;* less well known, and often misspelt, are *pallor, torpor,* and *tremor.*

Secondly, -our words lose the *u* when compounded with the suffixes -ous, -ation, -ise (or -ize), and -ist. These are Latinate suffixes (originally -osus, -atio, -izare, and -ista), and with these endings -our words revert to their Latinate form, which has no *u.* So: *vigour* but *vigorous, valour* but *valorous, humour* but *humorous.* And *colour* but *coloration, vigour* but *invigoration, vapour* but *evaporation.* Similarly, *vaporise, deodorise,* and *glamorise;* and *humorist* and *rigorist* (*colourist* is an exception in British English).

Derivatives with -ite, -able, and -y on the other hand, retain the *u* in British English. They are considered to be formed directly from English words, and have no Latin original: *favourite, Labourite, favourable, honourable, armoury, savoury,* and so on. (In American English, *savoury* is sometimes found alongside *savory.*)

For other differences between British and North American spelling — *mould/mold; defence/defense,* and so on — see AMERICAN ENGLISH.

● **-or** *vs* **-er.** The suffix -or is the Latin version of the English -er and so tends to be used with words of Latin derivation: hence, *author* vs *writer, orator* vs *speaker.* Curiously, -er is used also with some words of Greek derivation: *astrologer, photographer.* Verbs coming through French tend again to take the -or ending: *conqueror, governor, surveyor.*

Generally, if the base verb ends in -ate, the agent noun takes -or: *agitator, demonstrator, escalator, illustrator, incubator, navigator, originator, refrigerator, speculator, translator,* and so on (exception: *debater*). Similarly, most stems in -ess take the -or ending: *aggressor, assessor, confessor, oppressor, possessor, predecessor, professor, successor,* and so on (but, of course, *dresser, hairdresser*). Similarly, most stems ending in -ct: *actor, benefactor, collector, conductor, director, instructor, projector, reflector,* and so on (exceptions: *perfecter, respecter*).

Where there is a choice between forms, -er is often used when a person is referred to, and -or for a mechanical device (even when the stem is Latin). For example, *a conveyor belt* but often

a conveyer of good news; an adaptor for a plug but *a good adapter to new circumstances; a resistor in a circuit* but *a resister of change; a distributor in an engine* but *a distributer of charity.*

The endings -or and -er also distinguish legal and ordinary use. In legal documents the following words, for instance, might take -or, though they take -er in other contexts: *assign, assure, consign, devise, mortgage, oblige, pay, promise, settle, vend.* Some such words have found their way into general use with -or, because their meaning is predominantly legal, such as *abettor* and *juror* (but note the different endings of *solicitor* and *barrister*).

● **i** *before* **e.** The familiar spelling-rule '*i* before *e* except after *c*' applies when the vowel sound is /ee/ and only /ee/. So: *thief, piece, grief, fiend* — and *receive, ceiling, conceit,* and so on. The best-known exception is *seize.*

As for words that contain different vowel sounds, however, the rule is not necessarily valid. The *i* does come before the *e* in *friend* and *sieve,* for example, but not in *their, heir, neighbour, inveigh, weigh.* And the following words, though they can be pronounced with /ee/, have alternative pronunciations too, and are therefore not subject to the rule: *neither* and *either* (/ī/), *heinous* and *inveigle* (/ay/), and *weir* and *weird* /ee-ə/.

● *doubling consonants.* Certain consonants are doubled when the conditions are appropriate — particularly *b, d, m, n, p, r, s, t.* Words ending in a single such consonant after a single written short vowel, and stressed on the last syllable (including single-syllable words), double this consonant when the -ed and -ing endings are added. So: **fit**, *fitted, fitting;* re**gret**, *regretted, regretting.* Note that various other suffixes beginning with a vowel (including -y) have a similar effect: *fittish, fitter, regrettable, bidden, occurrence, batty, robber* (but *preferable, transferable, conference,* and so on represent slight exceptions).

The major set of exceptions concerns the nouns *bus, gas,* and *plus:* the preferred plurals are *buses, gases,* and *pluses,* though the double -s is possible. The verbs *to bus* and *to gas* have different tendencies: *to bus* again is exceptional in favouring the single *s: buses, busing, bused.* (The double -s may be more common in the United States, where *bussing* is a live issue in educational policy.) But *to gas* usually reverts to the rule (almost always in American English) and doubles the *s: gasses, gassing, gassed.*

Another possible exception is a word ending in a silent consonant: *crocheted, ricocheting* (though in British English the root words are not strongly stressed on the final syllable in any case).

When the vowel-sound before the final consonant is represented by a double letter (*oo*, *ou*, and so on; and also *aw*, *ir*, and so on), the doubling does not occur: *appeared*, *crooner*, *deaden*, *pawning*, and so on.

When the suffix begins with a consonant, doubling does not occur: *spotless*, *equipment*, *droplet*, and so on.

And when the base word is not stressed on the final syllable, the final consonant again usually remains undoubled: note, accordingly, the difference between the single *n* of **hap**pening and the doubled *n* of *begin*ning; and contrast **whim**pered and *concur*red, **lim**iting and *commit*ting, **chor**used and *concus*sed.

There is a fair amount of variation here, however: *bayoneted-bayoneting* and *bayonetted-bayonetting* are equally acceptable (perhaps because the stress is mobile). So too are *combated-combating* and *combatted-combatting* (though only *combatant* is possible). *Biases-biased-biasing* and *focuses-focused-focusing* are the usual forms, though a double consonant is sometimes used. *Benefited-benefiting* is the standard form, though American English allows a double *-t* (but only *benefiter* seems possible). Conversely, the preferred forms are *worshipped-worshipping-worshipper* and *kidnapped-kidnapping-kidnapper*, though American English here seems to allow a single *p* as an alternative. Both British and American English insist on *handicapped-handicapping-handicapper* and *hobnobbed-hobnobbing* exclusively.

There are two further refinements to this rule (that an unstressed final syllable in the base word means an undoubled final consonant). First, the rule holds true even if the stress shifts in the derived word: **frig**id yields *frig*idity — a single *d*, since in the base-form the final syllable was unstressed. Secondly, however, if the final unstressed syllable represents a full word that is part of a compound word, then the final consonant is doubled: **horse**whip, for instance, is not stressed on the final syllable, but since the final syllable is *whip*, which yields *whipped*, the past form of *horsewhip* is spelt *horsewhipped*.

Finally, note that final *l*, *c*, and *g* are special cases, and have their own rules — see below.
● *double* **l**. In American English, the *l* can be double or single according to the general rules above. For British English, the rules are slightly more complicated.

In a word ending in a single vowel + *l*, the final *l* is doubled (whether the last syllable is stressed or not) before the suffixes *-ed*, *-ing*, *-able*, *-or*, *-er* (for the agent noun), and *-y* — *travelled*, *grovelling*, *uncontrollable*, *jeweller* (American English would allow these, but prefers *traveled*, *groveling*, and *jeweler*). One interesting exception is *unparalleled*, where the final *l* is not doubled, though in *parallelled* and *parallelling* it often is (but not in American English, as a rule).

However, if the suffix is *-ise/-ize*, *-ish*, *-ism*, or *-ist*, the final *l* is usually singular in both British and American English: *moralise*, *royalist*, *devilish*. The *l* also remains single before *-er* (comparative) and *-est* — *level*, *leveler*, *levelest* — except after *-ful*: *painfullest*.

Note the different effects of the two *-er* endings: *leveler*, 'more level'; *leveller*, 'a person or machine that levels'.

If the vowel preceding the *l* is a long vowel or represented by two letters, then the *l* is not doubled: *toiled*, *unfurling*. Note, however, the exceptional spellings *woolly* (preferred even in American English) and *woollen* (*woolen* in North America).

Certain verbs with a stressed final syllable pose a problem: is the ending in the base form a single *l* or a double *l*? British spelling favours a single *l*, American a double *l*: *appal*, *enthral*, *extol*, *fulfil*, *instil* (in each case, the final *l* would be doubled in American spelling). *Expel* and *dispel* have a single *l* in both British and American spelling, and *befall*, *forestall*, and *install* have a double *l* in both (*instal* is a possible variant in British English). (Before *-ed*, *-er*, and *-ing* suffixes, all these words double the *l*, in accordance with the rules above: *appalled*, *fulfilling*, *dispelled*, *installer*, and so on.)

Note that *install* drops one *l* (only in British English) when *-ment* is added: *instalment*. Compare the lost *l* in *almost*, *chilblain*, *skilful* (though usually *skillful* in American English), and so on. Note too that *dullness*, *fullness*, and so on are sometimes spelt *dulness* and *fulness*, though fashion is now against the single *-l*.
● *the* **-ly** *suffix*. The suffix *-ly*, when added to a base word to produce an adjective (*leisurely*, *shapely*) or an adverb (*gladly*, *safely*), usually leaves the spelling of the base word unaffected: *safe* + *-ly* = *safely* (exceptions: *duly* and *truly*).

The problem arises with words ending in an *-l* sound: *cruel*; *agile*; *shrill*; *able*.

The first two types remain unaffected; the last two types, however, lose their final letter. So:
— words ending *vowel* + *-l*: the base word is unaffected: *cruel* + *-ly* = *cruelly*; *cool* + *-ly* = *coolly*; *doubtful* + *-ly* = *doubtfully*; *foul* + *-ly* = *foully*.

— words ending *vowel* + *-le*: the base word remains unchanged: *agile* + *-ly* = *agilely*; *sole* + *-ly* = *solely* (exception: *whole-wholly*).

— words ending in double-*l*: only two *l*'s in a row are possible. So: *shrill* + *-ly* = *shrilly*; *dull* + *-ly* = *dully*; *droll* + *-ly* = *drolly*.

— words ending *consonant* + *-le*: the *-le* simply changes to *-ly*: *able* + *-ly* = *ably*; *credible* + *-ly* = *credibly*; *single* + *-ly* = *singly*; *ample* + *-ly* = *amply*; *subtle* + *-ly* = *subtly*. Even *supple* yields *supply*, despite the confusion this creates with the noun or verb *supply*, 'a store' or 'to provide'. Some dictionaries, however, allow *supplely* as a variant.

● *prefixes.* In compound words, the spelling of the base word remains unaffected by the addition of a prefix: so *dis-* + *satisfied* produces *dissatisfied* (two *s*'s) and *dis-* + *able* produces *disable* (one *s*). Similarly, *overreact* (two *r*'s) but *overeager* (one *r*); *unnatural* but *unerring*.

The compounding might well go all the way back to Latin, but the principle remains the same: *innovate* (*in-* + *novus*, 'new') and *inundate* (*in-* + *unda*, 'a wave'); *imply* and *immigrate*, and so on.

Note that *il-* and *ir-* compounds always have a double *l* or double *r* because these prefixes always precede roots that start with *l* and *r* respectively: *illiterate, irradiate.*

Prefixes such as *co-*, *re-*, *anti-*, *non-*, and *by-* are sometimes joined solidly to the base word, and sometimes separated from it by a hyphen. Dictionaries and publishers differ in their preferences, so no clear rules can be given.

The trend, however, is clearly against hyphens. Most writers seem to prefer *antiestablishment* and some even prefer *? antiAmerican* to the hyphenated forms. But *anti-imperialism* should retain its hyphen, since the presence of two *i*'s side by side here would be disconcerting (though it occurs in *taxiing* and *skiing*).

This points to the one useful guideline here: if the omission of the hyphen would cause confusion, then retain it — *by-election* and *co-worker* usually keep their hyphens, since without them the words might appear momentarily to read *bye-lection* and *cow-orker*. *Co-respondent* keeps its hyphen so as to avoid any chance of confusion with *correspondent*. *To re-form*, meaning 'to form again or reshape', has a hyphen in order to distinguish it from *to reform*, 'to improve'. Similarly *re-creation* and *recreation*.

This guideline is no more than a guideline, however. Practice is far from consistent. It is right that *by-election* should keep its hyphen, but it is strange that *by-product* should stubbornly keep its hyphen too, rather than following the example of *bypass* and *bystander*. And on the other hand, *coincidence* (which could momentarily be read as *coin-cidence*), being so long-established, does without its hyphen, and so too, usually, do *cooperate*, *coopt*, and even *preeminence* — though not *re-examine*. (See HYPHEN for more details.)

● *mute* **e.** The letter *e* is often silent ('mute') in English, determining the sound of other letters rather than representing a sound itself. Its commonest such function is to indicate a long vowel or diphthong (a fusion of two vowel sounds): *mat* has a short *a*, but add an *e* at the end, and the *a* is changed into the diphthong of *mate*. If the short vowel is to be retained in longer forms, then the final consonant has to be doubled: *matted*, *matting*.

A traditional spelling problem is whether to retain the mute *e* when adding suffixes to the stem: *like* produces *likeness*, but does it produce *likable* or *likeable*? The simplest set of rules is this.

1. When the mute *e* follows a consonant (excluding *w* and *y*):

With suffixes beginning with a consonant (*-ness*, *-ment*, and so on), the mute *e* is kept — *likeness*, *lifelike*, *confinement*;

Before *-ing*, *-ish*, *-ism*, *-ise/-ize*, and *-ist*, the mute *e* is usually dropped — *likewise*, of course before *-ed*, *-en*, and *-er* (and *-or*), since a double *e* would affect the pronunciation: *liking*, *thriving*, *liner*, *mauvish*, *absolutist*;

Before *-y*, the *e* is preferably dropped — *joky*, *spiny*, *shady*, *mousy*, *grimy*.

The trickiest decision occurs when the suffix is *-able* or *-age*: dictionaries differ among themselves and publishers have different preferences, so no clear-cut recommendation can be made. The general movement, however, seems to be towards dropping the *e*: *likable* being favoured over *likeable*, and *lovable*, *movable*, *sizable*, *unmistakable*, and *usable* over their respective variants; *clearage*, *dosage*, *dotage*, *storage*, and *usage* are the only appropriate forms. The great exceptions are *acreage* (the only acceptable form), and *saleable* and *mileage*, which are generally preferred to *salable* and *milage*.

These rules are subject to three broad exceptions: one, when the mute *e* follows a *c* or *g*, special rules apply (see above); two, when the suffix is *-ly* special rules apply (see above); three, when confusion with some similar word threatens to distort the pronunciation, the alternative form is preferred. So: *routeing*, *probeable*, and *holey* retain their mute *e* in order to avoid confusion with *routing*, *probable*, and *holy*.

2. When the mute *e* follows a vowel or *w* or *y*:

a. For *-ue*: the *e* is usually dropped before suffixes: *continuing, continual, continuance, continuable, continuation, continuity, burlesquing, suing.* But note *gluey* (though *gluily* drops the *e*) — probably because ✗ *gluy* would tend to be mispronounced as /glī/, on the model of *guy*. Note too that American English allows, as alternatives, *glueing* and *queueing*, whereas British English almost always insists on *gluing* and *queuing. Cliquish* drops the *e*, though *cliquy* and *cliquey* are both acceptable.

Again, when the suffix begins with a consonant, the mute *e* tends to remain: *issueless, accruement* (but *argument* loses the mute *e* of *argue*).

b. For *-oe*: the *e* is retained before suffixes — *canoeist, hoeing, shoeable, tiptoeing* — though of course there is no double *e* in *hoer, shoed*, and so on. *Oboist* is an exception.

c. For *-ie*: *to die, vie, lie,* and *tie* become *dying, vying, lying, tying* (though *dieing* is correct for the other verb *to die*, 'to cut or stamp with a die-tool'). *Hie* leads to both *hieing* (slightly preferred in British English) and *hying* (slightly preferred in American English). Also *sortieing* and *stymieing* (*stimying*, is possible too in British English, probably because the base form can be spelt *stymy* as well as *stymie* in British English).

d. For *-we*: *owe* produces *owing; awe* produces *aweing* in British English, and *awing* in American English. Note: *awful* but *awesome*.

e. For *-ye*: *to dye* produces *dyeing* (to drop the *e* would confuse it with the *-ing* form of *to die*), but *dyable; to eye* produces *eyeing* or *eying*, the former now being preferred to the latter.

● *words ending* **-y.** The usual pattern for verbs ending in a consonant + *y* is *dry, dries, drying, dried, driable; pity, pities, pitying, pitied, pitiable.*

The agent noun from such verbs usually ends in *-ier: trier* and *crier*. But although *drier* and *flier* are possible as nouns (and the commonest spellings of the comparative adjectives), *dryer* and *flyer* are probably the more usual noun forms.

Adjectives are erratic: *dry, drier, driest, drily* or *dryly, dryness, dryish*. But *sly* and *spry* retain the *y* throughout: *sly, slyer, slyest, slyly, slyness, slyish*.

Verbs ending in *-oy, -uy,* and *-ay* retain these combinations throughout: *destroy, destroys, destroying, destroyed, destroyer; relay, relays, relaying, relayed, relayer*. But *lay, pay,* and *say* (and verbs that contain them, such as *inlay, repay,* and *gainsay*) take *-aid* in the past form: *repaid, gainsaid*.

Note the spellings *laity, gaiety, clayey*.

Words ending in *-ey* tend to keep the *-ey* regardless of the suffix: *surveying, surveyor, surveyable*. But *gluey*, once again, reverts to *gluily, gluier, gluiest*.

● *hard and soft* **c** *and* **g.** In most combinations, the letters *g* and *c* are usually sounded hard — /g/ and /k/ rather than /j/ and /s/ — and tend to change to their soft form only when followed by an *e* or *i/y*. So: *allegation* but *allege, tic* but *entice; grand* but *gerund, garish* but *gyrate, rag* but *rage. Margarine* should, strictly speaking, be pronounced with a hard *g* — even though nowadays it usually has a soft /j/ sound; similarly *analogous* and *tautologous* should have a hard *g* but are often heard as /-jəs/. The undoubted exceptions are *gaol*, /**jay**-əl/, and *algae*, almost always pronounced /**al**-jēē/.

The obverse of the rule does not hold good. It is true that *c* and *g* tend to be soft *only* when followed by *i/y* or *e*, but it is not true that *c* and *g* are always soft when followed by *i/y* or *e*: consider *baccy, begin, Celt, get, gift, soccer.*

And there are various qualifications to the rule: in words and names of Italian origin, *c* is pronounced /ch/ before *e* and *i: cello, Leonardo da Vinci*. In words and names of German origin, *g* is always hard; *lager, Gesundheit, Luger*.

The combination *-gg-* is always hard (except in *exaggerate*, the British pronunciation of *suggest*, and certain words of Italian origin, such as *arpeggio*). So, *ragging* as against *raging, hugger* as against *huger*. And *-dg-* is always soft (unless the *d* and *g* belong to different base words in a compound, as in *headgear* or *mudguard*): so *judgment* is just as acceptable as *judgement* — in fact, slightly preferable to it nowadays, especially in American English. (Likewise *abridgment, acknowledgment,* and *fledgling,* though *knowledgeable, unbridgeable,* and so on remain preferable to *knowledgable, unbridgable,* and so on — overwhelmingly so in American English.) Note too the English place-names *Edgware* and *Edgbaston. Manageable*, on the other hand, has to retain the *e* in order to keep the *g* soft; similarly *salvageable* and *noticeable*.

Note that the *-ing* form of *to age* can be spelt *ageing* or *aging*. The verbs *to singe* and *to swinge* retain their *e* before *-ing* — *singeing* and *swingeing* (in order to avoid confusion with the *-ing* forms of *sing* and *swing*) — though *hinging* is regular. Elsewhere the *e* is dropped consistently — *enraging, privileging, icing* — since the *i* of *-ing* ensures that the *c* or *g* remains soft.

Where a final *c* or *g* is hard, on the other hand, it has to be adjusted before *-ing* or *-ed* or *-er* or *-y* is added, or else it would be softened by the vowel following it. The *g* is doubled — *rag-*

ragged-ragging; the *c* becomes *ck*: *picnicked*, *mimicking*, *panicky*, *trafficker*. (In the past, the base form sometimes ended *-ck* rather than *-c*: *musick*, *physick*.) Possible exceptions occur where a consonant rather than a vowel precedes the final *c*: *talcing/talcking*; *arced/arcked*. The forms without the *k* are preferable, and *disced* — as in *a disced bone* — is probably the only acceptable form (*disked* in American English, which has the base form *disk*).

Though not exhaustive, the rules just set out do cover the majority of spelling problems typically encountered by people when writing. Here now is a long list of words that are tricky to spell and commonly misspelt. Anyone who masters this list, and becomes fully familiarised with the set of rules, can consider himself or herself an expert at spelling.

aberration one *b*, two *r*'s, like *err* — not like *abbess* or *oration*.

abominable no *h* the way that *abhorrent* has.

abscess *-sc-*, not like *recess* or *absence*.

abysmal with a *y*, unlike *dismal*.

abhorrent *abh-*, not *ab-* as in *abominable*.

abyss one *b* and a *y*; not like *abbess* or *amiss*.

accelerate two *c*'s, one *l*.

accessory, accessary see separate entry.

accommodate double *c* — unlike *recommend* — and double *m*.

acoustic begins *ac-*, not *acc-* like *accuse*.

acrylic note the *-yl-* in the middle, like *dactylic*, not *cyrillic*.

acquaintance remember the *c* before the *qu*, as in *acquit* or *acquire* — not like *aquarium*; ends with *-ance*, like *maintenance*, not *dependence*.

ad nauseam ends *-eam*; not ✗ *ad nauseum*, on the mistaken model of *ad absurdum* or *ad infinitum*.

addendum three *d*'s altogether: begins *add-*, like *addition*.

adjourned with a *d* before the *j*, like *adjoining*; *-jour-* as in *journey*.

advice, advise see separate entry.

aerie, eyrie see separate entry.

affidavit double *f*; ends in *-t*, unlike *David*.

aficionado no double letters — not like *affection*, *success*, *colonnade*.

ageing/aging both acceptable, the former slightly preferable in ensuring a soft *g*.

agoraphobia *agora-,* not *agri-* the way *agricultural* is.

aisle do not forget to write the silent *s*, and do not confuse with *isle*.

albumen, albumin see separate entry.

aligned only one *l* — not like *allied*; the simple form is *align*, quite unlike *line*.

alliteration a double *l*, but the *t*'s are separate — like *allude* and *literature*, not like *letter*.

amanuensis no double *n*; like *manual* not *mannerism*; and no double *m* either.

analgesic *-es-*, not *-aes-* the way *anaesthetic* is in British spelling.

ancillary only one *i* — not ✗ *ancilliary*; a double *l*, and ends *-ary*, not like *celery*.

anorexic *ano-*, not *ana-* the way *anabolic* is.

Antarctic do not forget the first *c*, even if you slur it when speaking.

antirrhinum two *r*'s, then an *h*, as in *catarrh*.

aplomb note the silent *b*, as in *plumber*.

apostasy *-asy* like *ecstasy*; not *-acy* the way *democracy* is.

apparatus two *p*'s, as in *apparent*.

Apennines only one *p*: *A-* + *-pennines* — contrast *Appalachians*; double *n* in the middle, unlike *peninsula*.

appurtenance *-pur-*, despite *appertain*; two *p*'s in both.

aqueduct *aque-*, not *aqua-* the way *aqualung* is.

archetypal *arche-*, not *archi-* the way *architecture* is.

Arctic note the first *c*, often slurred in speech.

artefact/artifact the former spelling is traditionally preferred, but is giving way to *artifact* both because of the influence of *artificial* and because the North Americans far prefer the *-i-*.

asinine no double letters, unlike *ass* or *inner*.

asphalt no *ash-* or *-felt* in the spelling: *asph-* as in *asphyxiate*.

assassin double *s* throughout.

assiduous double *s* — no *c* as in *acidic*.

assimilate double *s*, one *m*, one *l*.

assonance double *s*, then single *n*'s; like *assorted* and *sonorous*; compare *dissonance*.

asthma despite the pronunciation, which sometimes has the *th-* before the *s* or ignores it entirely, the spelling is *-sth-* as in *aesthetic*.

attenuate double *t*, single *n*, as in *attentive* and *tenuous*.

Attila two *t*'s; one *l* — like *Attic* and *Milan*.

auger, augur see separate entry.

aural, oral see separate entry.

aye/ay both are acceptable: *aye* is probably less confusing and more common, especially when repeated in *aye aye*.

bacillus one *c*, two *l*'s.

balmy, barmy see separate entry.

balustrade one *l*, and a *u* in the middle; not like *ballet* or *banister*.

banister a single *n* is preferable, though a double *n* is acceptable; the first four-minute miler was Roger Bannister — double *n*.

bankruptcy do not forget the *t*, often slurred in speech: *bankrupt* + *-cy*.

bated, baited the expression is *with bated breath* (a variant of *abated*). The word *baited* has to do with luring or tormenting: *a baited fish-hook*; *She baited her opponent*.

battalion two *t*'s as in *battle*; one *l*, unlike *stallion*.

baulk, balk see separate entry.

behove, behoove see separate entry.

beleaguer do not forget the *u* after the *g*, as in *league*; not *-geur* or *-gre*.

benefited only one *t*, unlike *fitted*, or *committed*; the reason for the single *t* here is that its syllable is unstressed.

bequeath no *e* on the end, unlike *breathe*; but the past is *bequeathed*.

berserk note the *r* before the *s*, unlike *beside* or *besiege*.

biased the single *s* is preferable, though a double *s* is also acceptable.

bicycle first the *i*, then the *y*: *bi-* + *cycle*.

bilious only one *l* (unlike *billion*) — related to *bile*.

bizarre single *z*, double *r*.

bludgeon *d* before the *g*, like *cudgel* not *pigeon*.

bogy, bogie, bogey all three forms can be used of the hobgoblin; in the extended form, *bogeyman*, *bogyman*, and the American *boogieman* are used. The railway coach or tank wheel is a *bogie* or *bogy*. The score in golf is a *bogey*.

bourgeois *-geois* on the end; the *e* is to soften the *g*; *bour-* as in *bourbon*, not *boer-* or *boor-*.

breech, breach see separate entry.

Brittany double *t*, unlike *Britain*.

Buddha double *d*, single *h*.

bulrush one *l* as in *bulwark*, not two as in *bull*.

buoy not ✕ *bouy*; hence *buoyant* and *buoyancy*.

bureaucracy watch the vowels, exactly as in *bureau*: first the *u*, then the *eau*, the reverse of *beautiful*.

bursar *-ar* as in *pulsar*, not *-er* as in *purser*; compare *bursary*.

cadaver *-er* on the end, not *-re* as in *macabre*.

caddy, caddie see separate entry.

cajole no *d* as in *cadge*.

calendar a *calendar* tells you the date; a *calender* is a machine for smoothing paper or cloth; another word *calender* refers to a kind of Muslim holy man.

calibre one *l*, not like *callous*; ends *-re* in British English, *-er* in American English.

callipers the double *l* is preferred in British English, a single *l* in American English; only one

p, unlike *nippers*.

camaraderie *-ara-* as in *parade*, not like *camera*.

camellia one *m*, two *l*'s; not like *Amelia* which has only one *l*.

camouflage single *m*, followed by *ou*.

candelabra *-dela-* not *-dla-*, and not *-dle-* the way *candle* is.

canon, cannon see separate entry.

canvas, canvass see separate entry.

carcase/carcass both forms are acceptable, though in American English only the latter is.

Caribbean one *r*, two *b*'s.

caricature no *h* as *character* has; and not ✕ *-tuare*.

cartilage *-age*, as in *silage*, not *-ege-* as in *sacrilege* or *privilege*; only one *l*, unlike *spillage*.

catarrh note the *rrh*, as in *haemorrhage*.

catechism only one *t*; and no *r* as *caterwaul* has; ends *-chism*, like *masochism*.

caviar/caviare both are fully acceptable.

censor, censure, censer see separate entry.

changeable keeps the *e* of *change* in order to keep the soft *g*-sound.

check, cheque see separate entry.

chilblain no double *l* the way *chill* has; and ends *-ain*, not *-ane* as in *bane*.

chilli/chili both forms are fully acceptable, as is the rare *chile*. British spelling slightly favours *chilli*; American favours *chili* or *chile*. The South American country is *Chile*.

cholesterol not *chlorest-*; and do not forget the second *e*.

chord the combination of notes in music is a *chord*, with an *h*. But do not be tempted to add an *h* to *vocal cords*.

chrysalis with an *h*, unlike *crystal*.

cider/cyder *cider* is preferable; *cyder* is still acceptable in British English, but not in American English. Note that it ends *-er*, not *-re*, in British as well as American spelling.

cinnamon a double *n*, followed by an *a* — very different from *cinema*.

cipher/cypher *cipher* is traditional; *cypher* is a possible variant, perhaps more common for the noun than the verb.

cirrhosis *-rrh-* in the middle, as in *haemorrhage*.

claustrophobia *claustro-*, not ✕ *clostro-*; and note the *o* before *-phobia*, not *a* as in *agoraphobia*.

clayey *-yey*.

cluster *-er*, not *-re* as in *theatre*.

coccyx a *-cc-* in the middle, followed by a *y*.

cocoon two single *c*'s, no *-cc-*; and the first vowel is *o* not *a*.

colander a single *l*, and ends *-der*, not *-dar* the way *calendar* does.

collateral a double *l*, as in *collect*; a single *t*, unlike *latter*.

colonnade one *l* as in *column,* but *-nn-* unlike *serenade* or *promenade*.

coloration the American spelling, and the preferred spelling in British English too, though *colouration* is also just possible here.

colossal no double *l,* but a double *s*.

colosseum like *colossal, -loss-* in the middle. The Roman amphitheatre can also be spelt *Coliseum,* and theatres and opera-houses so named tend to be spelt that way too (only one *o*, and only one *s*).

commemoration first a double *m*, then a single *m*: *com-* + *memory*.

committee double *m*, double *t*, double *e*.

common sense, commonsense the noun, meaning 'native good judgment', is always written as two words; on the other hand, the adjective, as in *a commonsense approach*, is best written as one word, though it can be hyphenated: *common-sense*.

comparatively *-parat-*; not *-paret-* or *-parit-*, as might be suggested by *compare* or *comparison*.

complacent, complaisant see separate entry.

compliment, complement see separate entry.

confidant, confident a *confidant* (*confidante* is the feminine) is a person you confide in. The form *confident* is sometimes used in this way too, but is best reserved for the adjectival senses.

conjurer/conjuror both are fully acceptable.

connoisseur double *n* (like *connote*) and double *s* (like *masseur*), and a double vowel *-oi-* between them.

consensus the only *c* is the first letter — *s*'s thereafter: *-sensus*, unlike *census*.

cooperate, coopt, coordinate these are now usually fused into single words, but spelling any of them with a hyphen is also accepted: *co-operate, co-opt, co-ordinate*. The use of a dieresis, as in *coöperate*, is still allowed in American spelling.

correlative two *r*'s as in *correspond*; one *l*, like *relative*.

coruscating only one *r*, unlike *corrugation* or *correspondence*.

curb, kerb see separate entry.

current, currant see separate entry.

curriculum double *r*, as in *current*; single *c*, in the middle, as in *matriculate*.

cygnet, signet the young swan is a *cygnet* — not to be confused with the word meaning a seal, as in *signet ring*.

dais not × *dias*, on the mistaken model of *bias*.

dare say the British expression *I dare say* is often, needlessly and dubiously, written or printed as *? I daresay*.

decrepit *t* on the end, unlike *intrepid*.

defence, defensive *c* in the noun, *s* in the adjective; but in American English, an *s* can be used in both.

delicatessen begins with *delicate*: only a single *l*; and the informal contraction is *deli*, unlike *telly*.

delineate a single *n*, as in *line*; ends *-neate*, not *-niate* as in *calumniate*.

deliquescent not *dele-* as in *deleterious* or *deletion*.

deliverance retains the second *e* of *deliver*, even though it is often omitted in pronunciation; contrast *remembrance*.

demagogue, demagogic the nouns *demagogue* and *pedagogue* have a *ue* after the second *g* (though in American English the *-ue* can be omitted); but the adjectives *demagogic* and *pedagogic* lose the *u*, to look (and sound) like *logic*; the abstract nouns *demagogy* and *pedagogy* similarly have a soft second *g* by preference, since they too drop the *u*, though *demagoguery* has both *g*'s hard, of course.

demesne different in spelling and meaning from *demean*, though sometimes pronounced the same.

demur ends *-ur*; not like *purr* or *defer*.

denouement do not forget the middle *e*; the accent over the first *e* — *dé-* — is optional.

dependent, dependant the adjective, meaning 'contingent or reliant', is spelt *-ent*; the noun, meaning 'one who depends', is spelt *-ant*; in North American writing, the noun is often spelt *-ent*, and the adjective occasionally *-ant*.

depredation *-pre-* as in *predatory*, not *-pri-* as in *deprivation*, and not *-pra-* as in *depravity*.

desert, dessert The double *-s* spelling is used only of the last course of a meal: think of having a second helping of *dessert*, and you will remember the second *s*. In all other senses, *desert* is the correct spelling: *your just deserts* (related to the verb *deserve*), *to desert your post, a deserted village, the Sahara desert,* and so on.

desiccated a single *s*, a double *c*: *de-* + *sicca* (Latin for 'dry').

desperate *-per-*, not *-par-* as in *separate*.

dexterous/dextrous both spellings are quite acceptable, the first being slightly more common perhaps; yet *ambidextrous* cannot take the extra *e*.

diagram never *-gramme* as in *programme*.

diarrhoea *-rrh-*, as in *haemorrhage*; and remember the *o*, though North American English often does without it.

dichotomy *-ch-*; not like *narcotic*.

dilapidated *di-*; not *de-* as you might expect.

dilettante only one *l*, unlike *dilly-dally*; then a double *t* in the middle, unlike *debutante*.

diphtheria not *dipth-*, though often pronounced as if it were.

diphthong *diphth-*, again with two *h*'s.

disc, disk see separate entry.

discomfit, discomfort see separate entry.

dispatch/despatch both spellings are acceptable, the first being the more usual now.

dissect double *s* — like *dissent*, unlike *bisect*.

disseminate *dis-* (not *de-*) + *seminate*; double *s*, one *m*, like *dissemble*; *-min-* as in *seminal*, not *-men-* as in *semen*.

dissension double *s* as in *dissent*, rather than *-sc-* as in *condescension* (compare *assent* and *ascent*); and ending *-sion* as in *dimension* rather than *-tion* as in *detention*.

dissertation note the double *s*, unlike *desertion* or *disorientation*; and do not forget the *r*.

dissipate double *s*, like *dissident*; one *p*, like *anticipate*.

dissociate *dis-* + (*as*)*sociate* — hence double *s*.

distil one *l*, unlike *distillery* or *fill*, but in American English, it has a double *l*.

diverse, divers see separate entry.

doomsday/domesday *doomsday* is the more common form, as in *wait until doomsday*, but the *Domesday Book* is the usual form for the written survey of English property ordered by William the Conqueror.

dote/doat both are acceptable: *dote* is slightly more usual, and more in keeping with the related nouns *dotage* and *dotard*.

douse, dowse see separate entry.

draft, draught see separate entry.

Duffel *-el*, unlike *muffle*; hence *duffelcoat*.

dyke/dike the usual British spelling for all senses is with a *y*, though the spelling with an *i* is a possible variant. The standard American spelling is always with an *i*.

dysentery very different from *disinter* and *dissent*. For the prefix *dys-*, compare *dysfunction*, *dyslexia*, and *dyspepsia*.

eczema *-cz-*, not *-cs-*; and do not forget the *e* in the middle.

eighth two *h*'s; do not drop the original *h* of *eight* when adding the new *h* at the end.

elegiac *-iac* as in *maniac*; not *-aic* as in *prosaic*.

enforceable the second *e* of *enforce* is retained; without it, the *c* would become hard as in *forecast* or *implacable*.

enquiry, inquiry see separate entry.

enrol spelt with one *l* in British English, two *l*'s in American English.

ensconced do not omit the first *n*, on the mistaken model of *escape* or *escort*.

enthral single *l* unlike *thrall*, but American English does have the double *l*.

ephemeral *-ph-*; not *-ff-* as in *effervescent*; one *m* as in *emerald*.

epitome despite the pronunciation, the ending is *-ome* (compare *hyperbole*) not *-omy* as in *tonsillectomy*.

erogenous a single *r*, unlike *erroneous*; and *-gen-*, not *-gyn-* as in *misogynist*.

ersatz the *s* comes before the *z*, though the pronunciation would suggest the reverse.

exaggerate a single *x*, a double *g*.

exalt, exult see separate entry.

excel a single *l* (even in American English), but *excellent* has a double *l*; do not forget the *c*.

exhilarating note the *h*, as in *hilarity*.

exhort do not leave out the *h* on the mistaken model of *exorcise*.

exorbitant no *h* here, unlike *exhilarating*, *exhort*, or *abhorrent*.

expatriate this is the correct spelling for the noun as well as the verb; ✗ *expatriot*, on the model of *compatriot*, is a very common spelling error; the form *ex-patriot* is a possible word, referring to a person who is no longer a patriot.

extirpate *-tir-* as in *stir*; not *-ter-* as in *exterminate* or *-tur-* as in *turpentine*.

Fahrenheit this was the name of the German physicist who developed the mercury thermometer and the Fahrenheit temperature scale. The word has no connection with the *height* of the mercury column, an association that often causes misspelling.

fait accompli not *fête*; and no *-e* on the end of *accompli*.

fallopian double *l*, as in *fallow*; single *p*, as in *utopian*.

falter no *u* as in *fault*.

faun, fawn the goat-like deity of mythology is a *faun*; *fawn* refers to a young deer or a brownish colour; there is another word *fawn*, the verb meaning 'to show affection, or flatter'.

faux pas not *faut pas*, which would mean 'must not'; *faux pas* means 'a false step'; the plural is spelt the same way.

fay, fey see separate entry.

feasible *-ible*, not *-able* the way *reasonable* is.

fiery note the reversal of the last two letters of *fire*.

fledgling/fledgeling both spellings are acceptable, the former slightly preferable.

flotation this form is now preferable to *floatation*, especially in financial contexts.

flu fully established in its own right now, no longer just a contraction of *influenza*; it does not require an apostrophe in front of it, let alone one behind it; and do not confuse with *flue*, 'the inside of a chimney or other duct'.

flunky/flunkey the former is preferable, the latter permissible — but not × *flunkie*.

(pâté de) foie gras not *foi*, which means 'faith', or *fois*, 'a time or times', but *foie*, 'liver'.

fuchsia first the *ch*, then the *s*: named after a German botanist called *Fuchs*.

funicular no double letters; note that the first vowel is a *u*, and the last an *a*.

gaberdine, gabardine the form *gaberdine* refers to a worsted cloth, to a raincoat made from it, or to a rough cloak worn in the Middle Ages. The form *gabardine* refers only to the cloth.

gamble, gambol see separate entry.

Gandhi the *h* follows the *d*, not the *g* as it does in *Ghana*, *Ghent*, *Afghan*, and so on.

garrotte/garotte/garrote double *r* and double *t* in the usual spelling, but the two variants are possible; remember that there is always an *e* on the end.

gauge *-au-* not × *guage* as in *language*; in nautical contexts and in North American English, the variant *gage* is sometimes used.

genealogy *-al-* as in *mineralogy*, not *-ol-* as in *geology*.

gherkin note the *h* after the *g*.

gibe, jibe, gybe see separate entry.

goodbye preferably one word, though the hyphenated form is also acceptable. In North American English, the *-e* tends to be omitted.

graffiti two *f*'s like *giraffe*; not *-ph-* as in *graphic*; one *t* unlike *tutti frutti*.

granddad three *d*'s altogether — this is far preferable to *?* *grandad*.

grey so spelt in British English; Americans use *gray*, though still preferring *greyhound*. Note: Lady Jane *Grey*, Charles *Grey* (the second Earl Grey) the British Prime Minister, Zane *Grey* the novelist, but Thomas *Gray* the poet, and *Gray*'s Inn in London.

grisly, grizzly, gristly *a grisly sight, a grizzly bear, a gristly steak.*

guerrilla/guerilla the double *r* is slightly preferable to the single *r*; the Spanish original has the double *r*, being the diminutive of *guerra*, 'war'.

Gurkha the *h* usually goes after the *k*; very occasionally it is found after the *G* instead.

guttural note that this has two *u*'s, not an *e* as in *gutter*.

gymkhana *gym-* as in *gymnasium* + *-khana* with an *h,* like *khaki*.

Gypsy/Gipsy sometimes small *g*; both spellings are possible, but since the word derives from

Egyptian, perhaps the spelling with the *y* is preferable.

haemorrhage, haemorrhoid the only double letter is the *r* — the combination *rrh* occurs also in *catarrh, cirrhosis, diarrhoea, gonorrhoea, amenorrhoea*; note the first vowel/s: *ae* in British English, but generally a simple *e* in American English.

hangar *-ar* as the garage for aircraft; *hanger*, as in *coat hanger*, is a quite different word.

harass one *r*, double *s*, like *morass*.

harridan double *r*, one *d*, like *horrid*; *-an* as in *Sheridan*, not *-en* as in *hidden*.

Hawaii note the double *i* at the end; in *Hawaiian*, there are four vowels in a row.

hazel, hazelnut *-el*; not *-le* the way *dazzle* is.

hello/hallo/hullo all acceptable; as listed, they are probably in order of current frequency.

hoard, horde see separate entry.

honorary see separate entry.

hors d'oeuvre(s) *oeuvre* like *manoeuvre*; can be pluralised in English either by adding an *s* at the end of the whole phrase, or simply by leaving the spelling unaltered as in French.

humerus the bone in the arm (the 'funny bone'); do not confuse the second and third vowels with those of *humorous* ('funny').

hygiene *hy-*, not *hi-*.

idiosyncrasy ends *-asy* like *ecstasy*, not *-acy* the way *democracy* does; note too the vowels: there are two *i*'s and two *y*'s.

impostor ends *-or* in British English, not *-er* as in *poster*, though North American spelling allows *-er* as a variant.

impresario only one *s*, unlike *impress*.

indict, indite see separate entry.

indigenous not × *indiginous*: the stem *-gen-* is common to *genetics, genus, progenitor*, and so on.

indispensable *-able*, not *-ible* the way *inexhaustible* is.

innocuous double *n* and single *c*, like *innocent*.

inoculation single *n*'s, unlike *innocuous*; single *c* too.

integrate not *inter-* or *inti-*.

inventor *-tor*, not usually *-ter*.

invertebrate not *-terb-*.

iridescent a single *r*, like its source *iris*; do not be distracted by the model of *irritate* or *irradiate*; note the *-sc-*.

jeopardise *-eo-* like *leopard*.

jewellery more acceptable spelt thus in British English; *jewelry* is the American spelling.

judgment/judgement both forms are quite acceptable: *judgment* is now slightly favoured, though some British publishers still insist on *judgement* for the legal sense.

labyrinth the *y* comes before the *i* — unlike *bicycle*.

lacquer *c* before the *qu*; ends -*er*, not -*eur* the way *liqueur* does.

laryngitis the *y* comes before the *i*'s; *laryn*- from *larynx*, not -*in*- as in *meningitis*.

lead, led see separate entry.

leprosy -*osy*; not -*ocy* as in *idiocy*, or -*ousy* as in *jealousy*. The adjective, however, is *leprous*.

leukaemia three double-vowels, though the American spelling drops the *a* in the middle.

lich gate/lych gate either spelling is acceptable; Middle English *lycheyate* was spelt with a *y*, but the word comes from Old English *lic*, 'a body or corpse' + *gate*, *yate*, 'a gate'.

lightning see separate entry.

liquefy this is the preferred spelling, as is *liquefaction* — with an *e* after the *qu* rather than an *i* as in *liquid*; *liquify* is, however, now widespread enough to have found its way into the dictionaries as a secondary variant.

liqueur -*ueur*, as in *longueur*, for the after-dinner sweet alcoholic drink.

liquor -*uor* as in *languor*, for any kind of alcoholic drink; no *c* before the *q*, the way *lacquer* has. Compare *liquorice* (also spelt *licorice*, especially in American English).

loath/loth both forms are quite acceptable for the old-fashioned adjective meaning 'unwilling, reluctant'. The verb meaning 'to detest' is spelt *loathe*.

lodestone, lodestar The *lode*-element is far preferable to *load*-.

longueur from the French — -*ueur* at the end usually, though *longeur* is sometimes considered an acceptable variant spelling.

loofah not -*er* but -*ah* (rarely *a*) at the end, like *pariah*; in American English, however *loofa* and *luffa* are often used.

maisonette this is the usual form, though a double *n* is also acceptable.

Manila the Philippine capital has one *l* like *Attila*, not two like *vanilla*; but the hemp fibre, cigar, paper, or colour (usually taking a small *m*) can have either a single or a double *l*.

manoeuvre a triple vowel in the middle, -*oeu*-. The American spelling is *maneuver*. Formerly the *o* and *e* were fused into a digraph, -*œ*-, but this is now unnecessary and very rarely seen.

mantle, mantelpiece see separate entry.

marquess, marquis strictly speaking, the British nobleman ranking between duke and earl is a *marquess*. The variant *marquis* is probably more common now, and refers too to noblemen from other European countries.

Matisse one *t*, double *s* (like *tissue*) for the painter Henri Matisse or any of his paintings.

mattress double *t*; not like *mat*, but like *buttress*.

medieval/mediaeval these are both standard in British English: *medieval* is now more usual, overwhelmingly so in American English.

mediocre no *h* the way *ochre* has.

Mediterranean *medi*, 'middle' + *terra*, 'earth'; one *d*, one *t*, two *r*'s.

membrane do not misspell the second syllable on the mistaken model of *brain*.

memento *mem*- as in *memory*; do not use the model of *moment*.

metallurgy an extra *l* after *metal*; ends -*urgy*, not -*ergy* as in *energy*.

meter, metre see separate entry.

métier should have an acute accent on the first *e*.

millenarian double *l* as in *million*; ends -*enarian* like *octogenarian*; no double *n* the way *millennium* has.

millennium double *l* like *million*; double *n* like *annual*.

mineralogy retains the -*al* of *mineral*; not -*ol* as in *geology*.

miniature -*iat*- not × *minituare* or × *miniture*.

minuscule *minus*- not *mini*-; do not confuse with the *mini* of *minimum*; compare *majuscule*.

mischievous no more *i*'s than necessary — not × *mischievious*.

misogynist not -*gen*- or -*gin*- but -*gyn*-, from the same source as *gynaecology*, from the Greek word for 'woman'.

misspell often *misspelt* through leaving out one of the *s*'s; no hyphen is needed to break the double *s*.

molten no *u*, the way *moult* has.

monstrous the *e* of *monster* is dropped; contrast *murderous*, in which the *e* is retained.

mortgage do not forget the silent *t* in the middle.

mote, moat see separate entry.

mountebank do not omit the *e* in the middle, and do not substitute an *i* for it.

murmur the second syllable is identical to the first, not *mer* as in *mermaid*; unlike *occur* or *concur*, the *r* does not double in other forms of the verb — *murmured*, *murmuring*.

naive, naivety these can now be regarded as the standard spellings in British English. The French forms *naïve/naïf* for the adjective, and *naïveté* for the noun, are still standard in American English, but elsewhere seem old-fashioned or affected. But in the rare sense of 'a person who is naive', the spellings *naïf* (male) and *naïve* (female) are perhaps still standard everywhere. And the adjective or noun *faux-naïf* seems to be spelt in this way only.

597

naught, nought see separate entry.

necessary one *c*, double *s*.

nickel ends *-el*, not *-le* the way *pickle* does.

none the less see separate entry.

obbligato/obligato this musical term can be spelt with a single *b* as in *oblige*, but the preferred spelling has a double *b*, as it has in Italian.

oculist a single *c*, unlike *occult*.

occurred double *r*, unlike *occur* or *occurs*.

offender not × *offendor* on the mistaken model of *vendor*.

omelette the usual British English spelling is *-ette*; the spelling *omelet* is chiefly North American. Do not forget the first *e*.

opprobrium not *appro-* as in *approval*; *-brium* like *equilibrium* — do not omit the second *r* on the mistaken model of *odium*.

ordinance, ordnance see separate entry.

ostentatious *-atious*, not *-acious* as in *spacious* or *pertinacious*.

paean this is the standard spelling for the word meaning 'a song of praise'; an occasional U.S. variant is *pean*. A *paeon* is a metrical unit in Greek verse, and a *peon* is a farmworker in Latin America or a poor person.

palette this is the usual spelling for the artist's mixing board (which can also be spelt *pallet*). *Palette* can also refer to the plate that protects the armpit on a suit of armour, though a preferable spelling here is *pallette*. *Pallet* usually refers to a tool used by a potter or bookbinder, or a portable platform on which goods are stored or transported, typically by a fork-lift truck. Another word *pallet* refers to a straw mattress or hard bed.

palisade single *l*, single *s* — unlike *palladium* or *glissade*.

pallor *-or* at the end, in British spelling as well as American.

pander *-er* not *-ar*, although the original *pander* of legend or literature was called *Pandaros* or *Pandare*, and so on.

parallel single *r*, double *l*, then single *l*.

pariah not *-aiah* as in *Isaiah*; and not *per-* as in *peroxide*.

parley, parlay see separate entry.

passed, past see separate entry.

pavilion a single *l*, unlike *million* or *villain*.

pedagogue, pedagogic see the item on *demagogue, demagogic* above.

pejorative not *per-* the way *perjury* is.

Peloponnese the only double letter is the *n*.

penicillin the only double letter is the *l*: think of *pencilling*.

perennial double *n* like *annual*; compare *millennial*.

perseverance *-ance*, even though the verb *persevere* ends with an *e*; contrast *coherence*.

personify single *n* like *conifer*.

personnel *-nnel* on the end, like *tunnel*; note the difference from *personal*.

pertinacious *-acious* like *tenacious*, not *-atious* as in *ostentatious*.

pharaoh *-aoh*, not *-oah* or *-oh*; *-ara-* in the middle, like the *scarab* beetle that the pharaohs believed to be sacred.

Philippines single *l*, double *p*.

philistine single *l*, as in *philanderer*.

phone although this was originally a contraction of *telephone*, it is now fully established — so writing *'phone* with an apostrophe is unnecessary.

phoney this is the favoured British spelling; North Americans prefer *phony* slightly.

plain, plane see separate entry.

plenitude single *n*, as in *plenty*.

pleurisy *-isy* as in *hypocrisy*; not *-acy* as in *lunacy*.

pliers the second vowel is an *e*, not an *a* as it is in *liars* or *pliable*.

poltergeist *polt-*; no *u* as in *poultice* or *poultry*.

pore, pour see separate entry.

Portuguese do not forget the *u* after (as well as before) the *g*, needed to keep the *g* hard.

practice, practise see separate entry.

practitioner *-tioner* not *-cioner* or *-sioner* despite *practice* and *practise*; do not model it on *suspicion* or *pensioner*.

preceding no double *e* as there is in *proceeding*.

premise as both noun and verb, this is the standard spelling, but in the sense of 'a proposition in logic', *premiss* is also possible.

prerogative not *perog-*.

prescience *-sc-*: *pre* + *science*.

pretentious *-tious* like *sententious*, despite the nouns *pretence* and *pretension*; do not model it on *conscious* or *suspicious*.

primeval this is now the usual British spelling, as well as North American, though British English still allows *primaeval*.

principal, principle see separate entry.

privilege no *d* as in *ledge*.

professor one *f*, double *s*, like *confessor*: *profess* + *-or*.

proffer two *f*'s like *offer*; not like *prefer*.

profuse single *f*.

programme, program see separate entry.

promontory the first three vowels are *o*'s.

propeller in British English, *-er*; not *-or* the way *chancellor* is; North American English allows *-or* as well.

prophecy, prophesy see separate entry.

proselytise from *proselyte*, therefore spelt *-lyt-*.

psychedelic *psyche-*, not *psycho-* as in *psychology*; one *l* like *indelible*.

pusillanimous only the *l* is doubled; compare *miscellaneous*.

putrefy *-efy* like *liquefy*, even though the adjective is *putrid*. Similarly, *putrefaction*.

pygmy, pigmy either spelling is possible; capital *p* when referring specifically to peoples of Africa or Asia, or the midgets of Greek legend; the Middle English form was *pigmie*, but the word goes back via Latin *pygmaeus*, 'dwarfish', to the Greek *pugme*, 'a fist, or the length from the elbow to the knuckles'; so *y* is perhaps preferable to *i*.

Pyrrhic *-yrrh-*, like *myrrh*.

questionnaire double *n* unlike *commissionaire* and *millionaire*.

rancour *-our* like *succour*, *colour* (*-or* only in American English), but *rancorous* drops that *u* — do not model it on *cantankerous*.

rarefied, rarefy preferably *-efied* not *-ified* as in *terrified*; *rare* keeps its *e*, though some dictionaries, both British and American, now admit *-ified* as a variant.

raspberry *-p-* in the middle, though it is not pronounced.

receipt, recipe the guide to cooking a dish is commonly a *recipe* today — /**ress**i-pi/. Formerly, *receipt* was possible, and is still used in this way in regional English, but it should then be pronounced /ri-**seet**/.

recommend one *c*, two *m*'s — contrast the double *c* of *accommodate*; *re-* + *commend*.

reconnaissance three *n*'s altogether; one more than *Renaissance*.

reconnoitre only one *c*, unlike its informal British derivative *recce*.

recount, re-count see separate entry.

remembrance note that the last *e* of *remember* is dropped here.

repertory, repertoire do not omit the middle *r* on the mistaken model of *repetition*.

rescind do not omit the silent *c*.

restaurateur it is nonstandard to insert an *n* on the model of *restaurant*.

resurrect note the double *r*, and the *u*; doubly different from *erect*.

reverent, reverend see separate entry.

review, revue see separate entry.

rhododendron *rho-* as in *Rhodes*, and *-dod-* in the middle, like *dodo*; *-on* on the end, not *-um*.

rhythm do not forget the first *h*.

rigour in the sense of 'harshness', *-our* in the British spelling (*-or* in American), but *rigorous* drops that *o*. But in medical senses, the Latin

spelling *rigor* is retained, as in *rigor mortis*.

Romania this is now the official spelling; *Rumania* is still extremely common, however; *Roumania* less so.

rococo single consonants throughout, not like *sirocco* or *Morocco*.

saccharin/e *-cch-* in the middle like *Bacchus*; *saccharin*, the noun, refers to the sweetener; *saccharine* with an *e* is the adjective, as in *a saccharine smile*.

sacrilegious note that the first *i* comes before the *e* — the reverse of *religious*.

sapphire note that this has two *p*'s.

schizophrenic no *t* before the *z*, despite the pronunciation.

separate *-par-*, not *-per-* as in *desperate*.

sciatica the first *c* is silent, and is all too easily forgotten in the spelling.

sheriff the word referring to the legal officer has one *r* and two *f*'s like *tariff*; but there is a different word, *sherif*, referring to a Muslim ruler.

sibyl *i* then *y*; the word goes back to Greek *sibulla* via Middle English, Old French, and Latin *sibylla*. The woman's name, however, is usually spelt *Sybil* (as in Dame Sybil Thorndike), especially since Disraeli (mis)spelt the title of a novel thus; note that *sibylline* has two *l*'s, *sibylic* only one.

Siena the Italian town has one *n*.

sienna the colour — burnt, raw, or otherwise — has a double *n*.

silicosis one *l* as in *silicon*

silvan/sylvan The Latin source is *silva*, 'a forest', so *silvan* is the preferred spelling; *sylvan* is now more commonly used, however.

siphon/syphon *si-* is more usual and traditional, going back to the same word in Greek meaning 'a pipe or tube'; *sy-* is now an acceptable variant.

skiing two *i*'s, no hyphen; the past form is *skied* — identical to the past form of the verb *to sky*.

sleight of hand note the *ei*; do not confuse with *slight*.

snorkel *-el* not *-le*; so write *snorkelling* not × *snorkling*; but *snorkeling* in North American spelling.

sober *-er*, unlike *sombre*.

sola topi not *solar*, despite being a protection against the sun; the hat is made from the pith of the *sola*, a swamp plant in Asia.

solace *-ace* as in *grimace*; not *-ice* as in *solstice*.

soporific *-por-* as in *torpor*, not *-per-*; one *r* unlike *horrific*.

sorrel double *r*, one *l*.

spirt, spurt see separate entry.

squalor in British as well as American spelling,

599

-or like *pallor*, not *-our* as in *colour*.

staccato double *c*, single *t*'s; plural *staccatos* or *staccati*.

stanch, staunch see separate entry.

stationary, stationery see separate entry.

stiletto single *l*, double *t*; plural *-tos* is preferable to *-toes*, though both are acceptable.

straitened as in *straitened circumstances*; do not 'correct' this to *straightened*, which has a different meaning.

strychnine the first syllable has a *y*, the second an *i*.

stupefy *-efy* not *-ify,* despite *stupid*; compare *putrefy*, *liquefy*, *rarefied*.

stupor in British as well as American spelling, *-or* as in *torpor*, not *-our*.

sty/e the eye-infection can be spelt *sty* or *stye*, the pigpen only *sty*.

subtilise do not omit the first *i*.

suffrage no *e* before the *r*, as there is in *suffering* and *sufferance*. (See separate entry.)

summertime, summer time usually one word for the summer season; two for the daylight saving time as in *British Summer Time*.

supersede *-sede,* not *-cede* as in *precede* or *intercede*.

surveillance note the *ei* in the middle.

swap, swop see separate entry.

swat, swot see separate entry.

syllabub/sillabub either *y* or *i* is acceptable, as in *syllable* or *silliness*; *sillabub* used to be standard, but *syllabub* is increasingly common; double *l* unlike *silicon*; *-abub*, not *-ebub* as in *Beelzebub* or *-ubub/-ubbub* as in *hubbub*.

taboo/tabu *taboo* is standard, but in specialised contexts, as in social anthropology, the old-fashioned spelling *tabu* is sometimes still preferred.

Tangier preferable to *Tangiers* (which is modelled on *Algiers*); the official name in roman script is now *Tanger*.

tariff one *r* two *f*'s, like *sheriff*.

tassel *-el*, not like *hassle*; hence *tasselled*, *tasselling* (U.S. *tasseled*, *tasseling*).

teenage/teenaged either form is acceptable as the adjective: *a teenage/d boy*.

Teheran this is the commoner spelling of the capital of Iran, but *Tehran* is also acceptable.

tenet one *n* like *tenure*, not two like *rennet* or *tennis*.

Tennessee double *n*, double *s*, double *e*.

threshold single *h* at the syllable break, unlike *withhold*.

today one word, as are *tonight* and *tomorrow*; the hyphenated forms are no longer current.

torpor *-or* like *stupor*; not *-our*.

tremor *-or*, not *-our* as in *humour*.

trooper, trouper a soldier is a *trooper*; an actor is a *trouper*, belonging to a *troupe* of actors. A person of experience, or a good sport or colleague, is by extension an *old trouper*, not × *old trooper*.

tsar, czar see separate entry.

tuber *-er* like *sober*, not *-re* as in *sabre*.

tutelage, tutelary do not model them on *tutor* or *pupillage*.

tyre, tire see separate entry.

tyro/tiro *tyro* is usual, *tiro* a possible variant.

vaccinate double *c* like *success*, *eccentric*.

vacillate one *c*, two *l*'s; like *bacillus*, not like *vaccinate*.

variegated note the first *e* between the *i* and the *g*.

veld/veldt either with or without a final *t* is acceptable, though in South Africa itself *veld* is now always used.

veranda/verandah both are fully acceptable.

vermilion/vermillion both forms are acceptable — the single *l* is perhaps slightly preferable.

veterinary do not omit the *-er-*, and note the *-in-* that follows, unlike *veteran*.

vibrancy this is the noun from *vibrant*; the form × *vibrance* is not standard.

vilify only a single *l*, as in its synonym *revile*; do not use the mistaken model of *villain*.

violoncello *-on*, not like *violin*.

virulent one *r* and a *u*, like *virus*.

wander, wonder see separate entry.

whetstone note the *h*: a *whetstone* is for whetting (sharpening) knives on. Whether you *wet* it or not beforehand is incidental.

whisky, whiskey see separate entry.

whither, wither see separate entry.

withhold two *h*'s, unlike *threshold*; *with* + *hold*.

wondrous note that the *e* of *wonder* is dropped; compare *monstrous*, but contrast *thunderous* and *slanderous* in which the *e* is retained.

wych elm/wich elm the first word comes from Old English *wice,* 'drooping', and has nothing to do with witches, even though it is sometimes spelt × *witch elm*; *wych elm* is preferred, though *wich elm* is acceptable too; a hyphen is sometimes inserted, but is not recommended.

yolk, yoke see separate entry.

spill The past tense and past participle form of the verb *to spill* is *spilt* in British English, with *spilled* a perfectly acceptable though less common alternative. In American English, *spilled* is the preferred form.

In both varieties, however, *spilled* tends to be

favoured when the verb is intransitive (that is, without a direct object) and means 'overflowed': *The water spilled onto the floor.* And in both varieties, *spilt* is favoured as the adjectival form when used directly in front of the noun: *Don't cry over spilt milk.*

See also -ED, -T.

spirt, spurt   *Spurt* is the usual spelling of this word, though *spirt* is possible in some of the senses. When the meaning is 'a sudden or forcible gush or outburst' (as of water or emotion), the word can acceptably be spelt *spirt,* as it can in its related verb senses, 'to flow suddenly, gush' and 'to force out in a burst, squirt'.

However, the *spurt* of energy an athlete makes, or the verb *to spurt* meaning 'to make a short burst of effort', can be spelt only with a *u.*

The reasons for this division are not clear. Both forms seem to come from the earlier *spirt, sprit,* 'to sprout', from Middle English *sprutten,* from Old English *spryttan.* Perhaps *spirt* was thought to be related to *squirt,* and so was never used in the looser, more figurative sense.

An easy way to remember the acceptable forms is this: a liquid (containing both a *u* and *i*'s) can either *spurt* or *spirt*; a runner (containing only a *u*) can only *spurt*.

In American English, *spirt* is used much less often than *spurt*.

split infinitive   One of the best-known schoolroom 'rules' of grammar — and one of the most irrational — is 'Don't split infinitives'. Phrases such as   *? to boldly go where no man has gone before* and   *? began to silently hope* are guaranteed to set the pedant's teeth on edge — despite the greater metrical regularity of *to boldly go* and *to silently hope* than *to go boldly* or *to hope silently.* Many split infinitives, on the other hand, do sound distinctly jarring, and should be avoided for that reason if no other:

> *? Although it has been suggested the forgery was an attempt to in some way rehabilitate Hitler, all those concerned now pin it firmly on Kujau, with the clear assumption he had only one motive — money.*
> – Tony Catterall, *The Observer*

This would sound more natural if worded *an attempt to rehabilitate Hitler in some way.*

The infinitive form of a verb is commonly (though not always) preceded by the particle *to*; this *to* is apparently regarded by many people as an actual part of the verb, as though attached to it by an invisible hyphen, and therefore not to be

separated from it by any intrusive adverb.

The origin of the 'rule' (laid down in the 17th century, and elaborated in the 18th) probably lies in Latin grammar, which used to be thought of as the model of English grammar. In Latin, the infinitive form of a verb has no preceding particle: it is fully expressed by a single word, such as *ire,* 'to go', or *sperare,* 'to hope'. It is impossible to 'split an infinitive' in Latin. So, it was argued, nobody should split infinitives in English. But Latin grammar is not really the basis of English grammar (as the lack of an infinitive particle equivalent to *to* precisely makes clear).

Moreover, the objection seems to apply only to infinitives of the *to go* type: *? to boldly go* is frowned on, but there is apparently nothing wrong with saying *Let us boldly go, can boldly go, make us boldly go,* any more than *by boldly going, to have boldly gone, is boldly going, to be silently hoped, began silently hoping.* There is no awkwardness in any of these constructions, no ambiguity, no loss of sharpness, no blurring of distinctions ... nor is there any in such constructions as   *? to boldly go* either.

And yet the 'rule' persists, and most careful users continue to observe it. Sometimes it is clearly preferable to abide by the rule: *He wants to see you immediately* is obviously more natural than *?? He wants to immediately see you.* And all the more, *He wants to see you immediately and urgently* is better than *?? He wants to immediately and urgently see you.* But even where it feels more natural to split the infinitive, purists will still avoid doing so, and instead abide consistently by the 'rule'. They do this partly out of respect for tradition (no matter that the tradition in this case has no sensible foundation to speak of), and partly out of fear of being regarded as philistines.

Perhaps in reaction to the tyranny of this illogical taboo, many of the best writers and speakers frequently defy it. Raymond Chandler, for example, wrote to a magazine editor:

> Would you convey my compliments to the purist who reads your proofs and tell him or her ... that when I split an infinitive, God damn it, I split it so it will stay split.
> – Raymond Chandler (U.S.),
> quoted in F. MacShane (U.S.),
> *The Life of Raymond Chandler*

The famous lexicographer Eric Partridge also seemed to enjoy outraging the purists by glaringly splitting his infinitives:

> Naturally I checked with Dr Onions himself,

for I certainly did not intend to even try to compete with a work written by him. He was very good about the matter.

– Eric Partridge,
The Gentle Art of Lexicography

Elsewhere Partridge wrote, in his witty way:

Usage has decided to approve of final prepositions and split infinitives. Usage has been right to so decide.

– Eric Partridge, *A Charm of Words*

Usage may well have decided to approve of split infinitives, but the rule persists nevertheless, even if supported by nothing more than tradition.

Of course, mere tradition is not a good basis for a rule, but equally, mere defiance is not a good reason for breaking it. It is worth at least being aware that you are breaking a rule, and pondering your reasons for doing so.

There may well be good reasons.

● It is sometimes impossible to keep the infinitive unsplit:

... a new method of carrying out carbon-14 dating of archaeological and palaeontological specimens that promises to more than double the time span from which ancient organic objects can be dated.

– Boyce Rensenberger (U.S.),
The New York Times

It is as if the verb in question here is not *double* so much as *more-than-double,* and the infinitive is thus not being split at all.

● It may be that the split infinitive alone gives the precise emphasis and sense you want to convey, and that shifting the adverb changes the meaning slightly:

Remember to partly boil the potatoes before putting them in the oven (compare the verb *to parboil*).
It is best to so structure your sentences that no ambiguous reading is even possible.
You have to really feel Hamlet's tormenting dilemma before you can play the part convincingly.
Read my comments carefully, mark them, learn them, and try to inwardly digest them.
It is difficult not to at least suspect a mistake.

Splitting the infinitive has the further advantage of making clear exactly which verb the adverb refers to. If you shift the adverb, then a possible ambiguity or even absurdity sets in: *? In a menacing tone she asked me kindly to keep my com-*

ments to myself. And note the likely change in meaning when the word *further* is shifted in the following sentence: *You ought to further check loose connections / You ought further to check loose connections / You ought to check further loose connections.* Or consider, finally, the following passage:

? They are planning quietly to scrap the regulations which require the manufacturers of white bread to replace the nutrients that the process of refining takes out.

– Katharine Whitehorn, *The Observer*

Is it the *planning* or the *scrapping* that is being done *quietly* here? Probably *scrapping,* since if *quietly* referred to *planning* it would more naturally be placed in front of it. But equally, it sounds more 'natural' to place *quietly* directly in front of *scrap* if that is what it refers to.

And in the following example, the adverb *fully* probably relates to *appreciate,* but in its 'safe' position before rather than after the *to,* it could be understood to relate to *have read* instead:

? It is not necessary to have read Rosamond Lehmann's novel *The Weather in the Streets* fully to appreciate the quiet power that is generated in Julian Mitchell's television adaptation.

– Peter Davalle, *The Times*

● This leads on to the third advantage of a split infinitive: it often follows the natural rhythm of an English sentence, whereas an unsplit infinitive — as in the previous quotation — tends to jar and break the flow. The following passage has a fine rhythm to it that it would be unfair and unnatural to disrupt:

? Bill's wife had worshipped him from afar long before they ever met: in fact, she used to secretly admire the famous young actor as he ate sundaes in Schwob's drugstore.

– Vladimir Nabokov, *Lolita*

Such justifications of the split infinitive do not apply in all cases, of course. In the following extract, for instance, nothing would be lost by moving the adverb *systematically* to a position immediately after the verb *confront*:

? It is, incidentally, the first book to systematically confront the illegal exchange of pilfered goods.

– Jason Dutton, *The Times Higher
Education Supplement*

Such needless split infinitives often succeed, rightly or wrongly, in outraging the reader or listener. Even if they do no more than distract him momentarily, you have still defeated your object, which is, after all, to communicate ideas to him. It is always worth being mindful of his holy cows, and keeping a safe distance from them. Simply reword your sentence.

Of course, some rewordings are better than others. The simplest form of rewording is to shift the offending adverb either towards the beginning of the sentence or, preferably, to the end. If you wish to avoid saying *? They wanted him to deliberately flout the law,* it is better to say *They wanted him to flout the law deliberately* than to say *They wanted him deliberately to flout the law.* The phrase *deliberately to flout* suggests a 'deliberate' effort to avoid splitting the infinitive; *to flout ... deliberately* has an ease and naturalness about it which suggests that it was your first thought rather than your second. Here are two quotations that would have read more elegantly if the adverb had come at the end of the sentence rather than before the *to*:

> Cushman not only narrates the show, he sings, revealing a gritty and Lehrer-like relish for the grotesque. 'Fingers' finished last night, alas, but goes to Edinburgh in August, when it is destined greatly to cheer up the Fringe.
> – Michael Ratcliffe, *The Observer*

> Labour seemed to be making a bit of progress on the future of the welfare state, but not enough significantly to affect the result.
> – Alan Watkins, *The Observer*

The difference in 'feel' between *deliberately to flout the law* and *to flout the law deliberately* may have to do with an underlying objection to the split infinitive itself. In English the normal position for an adverb of manner is after the verb, and often at the end of the sentence: *to flout the law deliberately*; *to speak clearly.* Putting the adverb elsewhere creates an effect of special emphasis or contrast. So *He defiantly splits infinitives* is more 'marked' than *He splits infinitives defiantly.* It is bad style to overuse emphatic or contrastive forms, and it is possible that the objection to the split infinitive is really that it is marked in this way. Thus there is a sense in which *to deliberately flout* and *deliberately to flout* are both marked, whereas *to flout ... deliberately* is normal. To summarise:

1. *to flout the law deliberately* — normal and acceptable.

2. *deliberately to flout the law* — marked but acceptable.

3. *to deliberately flout the law* — marked and unacceptable to purists.

The further argument against placing the adverb earlier in the sentence is that it might then seem to apply to a preceding verb instead. The sentence *They urged him deliberately to flout the law* would be not just 'marked', but ambiguous as well, whereas *They urged him to flout the law deliberately* is both unambiguous and more natural — and hence clearly preferable.

One interesting side-effect of the split-infinitive rule is that overcareful writers take great pains to shift the adverb from its natural position even when its natural position is a fully legitimate one:

> Owing to the comparative remoteness of the cottage no neighbours were sufficiently near easily to be drawn in.
> – Anthony Powell,
> *O, How the Wheel Becomes It!*

> The humiliation and embarrassment of being defeated systematically not only by Russians, but by the East Germans, a nation of just 17 million, propelled the United States government to heed the words of former football-playing President Gerald Ford.
> – Alan Hubbard, *The Observer*

There was no need at all for the artificial re-positioning of the adverbs here. The natural wording — *sufficiently near to be easily drawn in* and *embarrassment of being systematically defeated* — would not in fact have involved a split infinitive, and should not have been tampered with.

● *Recommendation* In reply to the injunction *Don't split infinitives,* it is very easy and appropriate to say *Don't split hairs.* And yet that is not the end of the matter. The force of tradition, no matter how irrational, commands a certain respect, and although appeal to tradition is not in itself a full justification of a rule, appeal to current usage is not a conclusive argument against the rule either.

Bear in mind that purists do still object to the split infinitive. If you refuse to pander to this irrational objection of theirs, and if you are unconcerned that people might think you know no better, then by all means split your infinitives. But remember the possible consequences: your reader or listener may give less credit to your arguments (because he thinks of you as a careless speaker or writer), or he may simply lose the thread of your argument entirely (because he has been distracted by your grammatical 'error').

At the same time, it is also inadvisable to wrench

a sentence into ambiguity or ugliness simply in order to avoid splitting an infinitive. Doing this can cause equal distraction in your reader or listener, or it might once again reduce his regard for your views — as being those of a pedant this time, rather than of an ignoramus. The best course may be to skirt such a predicament altogether, and simply recast your sentence, wording it in an entirely different way.

spoil   *Spoilt* is used as the past tense and past participle of the verb *to spoil* in British English, with *spoiled* a less common though perfectly acceptable alternative. In American English, however, *spoiled* is the preferred form. *Spoilt* is the correct adjectival form to use in British English, as in *a spoilt child*; *She's thoroughly spoilt*. Americans too sometimes favour *spoilt* here, especially before the noun.

See also DESPOIL.

spurious   See SPECIOUS.

spurt   See SPIRT.

square brackets   **1.** Square brackets, [ ], also called *brackets* in America, are rather technical marks of punctuation. Many typewriter keyboards do not have them; an attempt at square brackets can be made by combining the solidus or slash (/) with hyphens typed at the top and bottom (this is done by giving the roller a half-twist up and down). Many people simply put in square brackets by hand if required.

2. a. Square brackets are used to enclose editorial corrections, comments, or explanations in material written by someone else:

'Shakespeare died in 1615 [1616], well before the time of the Civil War.'
There is a line from a 15th-century morality play, 'Thi olde mercy, let me remene [remember]', that may perhaps have some bearing here.
'The author of *Orlando Furioso* [Ariosto] influenced many later poets, both Italian and non-Italian.'

b. A typical comment of this kind is the [*sic*] that informs readers that the preceding text is to be taken literally, however odd or incorrect it may appear:

There is a British book called *Analyzing* [sic] *English* that I recommend highly.

Here the [*sic*] is used because the word before it would normally be spelt *Analysing* in Britain.

The word *sic* is often enclosed in round brackets instead, however. (See SIC.)

c. Square brackets also identify changes in the text that have been introduced by the person commenting:

I enjoyed the ambiguity: 'Lydgate's manuscripts merit ... study ..., *not because he is a great poet* [my italics], but because of his great popularity and influence.'
                        – Basil Cottle,
          The Times Literary Supplement

d. Sometimes the source of the material in square brackets is identified, as being by —*ed.* (= the editor):

'Shakespeare died in 1615 [1616—*ed.*], well before the time of the Civil War.'

However, this explicit identification is not usually necessary.

e. Square brackets also enclose words (or even letters) inserted into a text instead of or in addition to the words originally there. Such inserted words are not comments or corrections, but are intended to be read as part of the text, which should as a result be clearer or easier to follow:

If the main participants are to be believed — risky, this, since according to their amanuensis, Piers Paul Read, 'thieves [are] facile liars' — the robbery and its aftermath also involved widespread corruption by many police officers and prison warders.
          – Clancy Segal (U.S.), *The Listener*

Thirdly, Foster J. employed his own acquaintance with the practice of leasehold conveyancing ...: '[To this clause], I think, should be added the words "such consent not to be unreasonably withheld." [If this were done] I think that such covenant would be a usual one and ought to be inserted.'
                  – Gordon Woodman,
            The Law Quarterly Review

How scrupulous a writer should be in quoting a text is a matter of some debate. Some purists insist on complete fidelity to the original, resulting in such passages as this:

As Marlowe argues, '[t]hat is special pleading ... [and] begging the question at one and the same time ...'

Some writers allow much more elasticity:

As Marlowe argues, 'that is special pleading [and] begging the question at one and the same time.'

See PUNCTUATION for a fuller discussion of these different approaches.

f. The use of square brackets is particularly important in preventing confusion about the source of one sort of 'comment': the question mark inserted into a text to indicate doubt. Compare the following two sentences:

Shakespeare died in 1615 (?).
'Shakespeare died in 1615 [?].'

In the first example, the doubt is in the mind of the author of the original sentence, of which (?) is a part. In the second example, the doubt is in the mind of the editor or reviewer, who has inserted [?] into a sentence that did not at first contain it. This difference is conveyed entirely by the choice of round brackets or square ones.

3. Square brackets are sometimes used to enclose a parenthesis within a parenthesis:

My uncle (I never knew his Christian name [he was much older than I]) died ten years ago.

This practice may lead to confusion about whether the material in square brackets is part of the original text or an editorial interpolation. So it is perhaps better to use either round brackets within brackets or, preferably, some other punctuation:

? My uncle (I never knew his Christian name (he was much older than I)) died ten years ago.
My uncle (I never knew his Christian name — he was much older than I) died ten years ago.

4. In books about language, square brackets have another, specialised use. They enclose symbols that show how the distinctive sounds of a language are pronounced in particular environments, whereas symbols for the distinctive sounds themselves are enclosed in slashmarks:

The symbol [t^h] represents the English sound /t/ as pronounced with an accompanying puff of breath, as in the word *tip*.

And in dictionaries square brackets are often used to enclose the etymology of a headword. See also BRACKETS.

stalactite, stalagmite *Stalactites* grow downwards, *stalagmites* grow upwards. The names are easily confused, but if you visit a limestone cavern you can distinguish at once these two varieties of calcium-carbonate pillar. The

dripping of mineral-rich water produces *stalactites* resembling icicles, and *stalagmites* resembling half-burnt candles.

The history of the two words does little to make this distinction memorable. *Stalactite* comes from the Greek *stalaktos* meaning 'dripping, dropping'; *stalagmite* comes from the Greek *stalagma* meaning 'a drip, a drop'.

A good way to fix the difference in your memory is: *c* from the ceiling, *g* from the ground. Alternatively, remember this formula: 'Stalactites hang on tight to the ceiling; stalagmites might one day reach the ceiling.'

The British pronunciations are /stal-əg-mīt/ and /stal-ək-tīt/, but in North America the words are usually pronounced with the stress on the second syllable: /stə-**lag**-mīt/ and /stə-**lak**-tīt/.

stanch, staunch The verb meaning 'to stop from flowing' can be spelt either *stanch* or *staunch*. The form *stanch* is, surprisingly perhaps, pronounced /staanch/; the form *staunch*, /staanch/ or /stawnch/. Both can be used in all the following ways: *to stanch the wound, to stanch the blood from the wound*, and *to stanch the flow of blood from the wound*.

The adjective meaning 'steadfast, firm', 'strongly constructed', or 'watertight' is almost always *staunch* (the variant *stanch* has now fallen into disuse). It is usually pronounced /stawnch/, though /staanch/ is possible. It is often used of people, to convey their strength of character and loyalty: *a staunch ally*; *a staunch campaigner*.

The verb and the adjective come, via slightly different Middle English routes, from the same source in Old French and Vulgar Latin.

standard English, correct English, appropriate English Who decides what is acceptable English and what is not?

In the long run, a word or sense or grammatical construction lives or dies by a process akin to natural selection: what is useful comes to be accepted, what is not useful goes under.

But at any given moment, there are many disputed items whose fate has not yet been sealed, and whose current usefulness is precisely what is at issue, with much lively discussion going on for and against.

The discussion is not limited to 'experts', and is not moderated by any Academy. (Even if there were one, as there is in France, would its decisions about the language really be binding?) The discussion is open to all those who care enough about English to pick their words deliberately and to reflect on the merits of one choice of words over another. It is these people who, in effect, decide in the short term what is acceptable English and what is not. The standards, you might say, are set by those who are interested in setting standards. Not that standards are rules: they are just the consensus of this community of concerned language-users. Such a consensus can be rejected, of course, and should certainly be examined critically, but it should at least be taken seriously.

This book lists the disputed items, and tries to establish, explain, and analyse the consensus about them, and to equip you with the knowledge or confidence needed to join the debate.

Bear in mind that only a dead language stands still. English, with its vibrancy and its remarkable capacity to absorb from other tongues, has traditionally been open to change. Words and ways of using them that are perfectly natural in one generation or decade may not be appropriate for another. Phrases or formations shunned in one era might be used freely and unobjectionably in the next.

This is not an argument against the existence of standards — just an admission that standards themselves change. This makes it all the more necessary to be aware of them, in order to respond sensitively to the idiom of the day. In this book, some words and usages are accepted or recommended, while others are criticised as unacceptable — whether 'nonstandard', 'incorrect', or 'inappropriate'. What do these judgments mean?

Standard English For speech or writing to be regarded as standard English, four conditions should, ideally, be satisfied.

1. *standard English is the English that is used now.* Much as we may admire the language of Chaucer, Shakespeare, and Jane Austen, the model for standard English is the language of educated adults in this generation who use it as their mother tongue. Milton may have used *prevent* to mean 'to arrive before', but today it means 'to stop, or keep from happening'. In the 18th century, the word *mob* was reviled as slang, and purists used *to surprise* to mean 'to catch unawares', rejecting the 'modern' sense of 'to astonish'. No longer. This is all part of the language's history.

But when such changes take place before our eyes, there is often a natural resistance to them. A new sense or usage has to fight for acceptance. At present, many younger people consider it quite natural to say *Hopefully we'll succeed*, even though this seems objectionable to many whose views on language were formed before the 1970s.

There seems little doubt that this use of *hopefully* to mean 'I hope' will become standard English in a few years' time. But it is probably not standard quite yet. The resistance to it seems to be too strong still. The word *prestigious*, on the other hand — 'having prestige' — is equally deplored by some purists, but their battle is in effect lost: the resistance has fallen below the necessary threshold, and *prestigious* seems to have gained access to standard English. If the language is to stay vigorous, words and senses will come and go, and usages will change.

2. *standard English is the English that is used most widely.* *Anyroad* and *outwith* are as good as *anyway* and *without*. But the first two words are restricted in their use to a few regions, whereas the last two words are used wherever English is spoken. It is in that sense that *anyroad* and *outwith* are not standard. Standard English does not include expressions found only in regional dialects.

English is used so widely that it has developed not only regional dialects, but several regional and national standards as well. The most striking case is that of American English, which has gone so far as to use conventions of spelling that differ (sometimes deliberately) from those of British English. It cannot be said that *color* is a nonstandard spelling of *colour*, however, or that *elevator* is a nonstandard word for *lift*, or that *robot* (as used in South African English) is a nonstandard word for *traffic light*. Instead, people say that *color* is the American English spelling of *colour*, that *elevator* is the American English word for *lift*, and that *robot* is a South African English word for *traffic light*. But there is a difference: *traffic light* is used very widely, and so is classed as World English; *elevator* too is perhaps widespread enough to qualify as World English, but *lift*, in this sense, has to be classified as British English.

When an expression from one variety enters another, some people will accept it readily and use it naturally while others continue to regard it as somewhat alien. An expression such as *? Do you have the time?* is perfectly natural and standard for some speakers of British English; for others it is an Americanism; and for others it is nonstandard (and should instead read *Have you (got) the time?*). It is, of course, standard American English. But note that the expression × *We'd like for them to visit us*, though American, is *not* standard American English.

3. *standard English is free of 'performance errors'.* Some errors occur so frequently as to become familiar intruders into what is otherwise well-considered speech and writing. But their regular occurrence is no justification for them: they remain errors, and cannot be accepted as standard English. It is understandable that, under pressure, people might say ✗ *as well or better than* instead of *as well as or better than*. Hesitation between *by far the best* and *far and away the best* produces the blend ✗ *by far and away the best*. Such expressions are no longer isolated mistakes. But they remain mistakes. They have become institutionalised and so are no longer merely overlooked: they are identified, analysed, and labelled 'nonstandard'.

4. *standard English is English that is accepted as standard by people who use it habitually.* This definition chases its own tail, yet it encapsulates an interesting fact about usage. Some expressions can be current, widespread, and even error-free, and yet still raise doubts in most people who stop to think about them. There is general agreement, for instance, that *ain't* is nonstandard.

Correct English The notion that language should be governed by a fairly rigid set of rules came to prominence in the 18th and 19th centuries — and the timing is significant. This was a period when science and industrialisation were advancing rapidly, and when education, at least in the 'Three R's', became available for everybody. The emergent physical sciences seemed to offer clear and rigorous laws, and it was believed that logical and rigorous rules could be found for language too.

Such rules could be learnt and followed by any educated person who wished to move upwards in society, whereas the traditional elite were content to speak as their ancestors had spoken. Ill-founded though many of the early rules were, the people who proposed them were promoting social mobility and advocating rational debate rather than unquestioning adherence to tradition. They were acting in the spirit of the Enlightenment, and their rule-discovering (really rule-inventing) was soon followed by the modern scientific study of languages — a description (rather than prescription) of their structures, and an account of their history, development, and relations to one another.

Nevertheless, the shadow of 'prescriptivism' persisted. Small wonder that generations of schoolchildren grew up with a prejudice against starting a sentence with *But* or ending one with a preposition.

There is a more relaxed attitude towards such rules today; but if you intend to break a rule it is always better to act in the full knowledge of what you are doing, and of the effect it may have.

What, then, are the general rules that 'incorrect' expressions are believed to violate?

1. *correct English is unambiguous.* In writing, the phrase *three year old horses* is ambiguous: does it mean *three year-old horses* or *three-year-old horses*? Without punctuation to clarify the sense, the phrase is not 'correct' in its presentation.

Some ambiguities are not easily avoidable, however: *I must replace that record* can suggest that I must put it back where it belongs, or that I must buy a new one, or that I must exchange it for a copy that is not faulty. The ambiguity does not make the sentence 'incorrect', though it does reduce its usefulness. (See AMBIGUITY.)

In some controversial constructions, the ambiguity is more apparent than real. In *I only borrowed five pounds*, the *only* could in theory be taken to apply to *borrowed*, and the sentence could mean 'I didn't spend five pounds'. Some careful users would therefore prefer the wording *I borrowed only five pounds*. Yet the first version is not really 'incorrect': the context would usually make the meaning clear, and in speech the intonation would certainly make it clear. Besides, an English sentence is not simply arranged like beads on a string: *only* can modify a distant word or a whole phrase as well as a neighbouring word. (See ONLY.)

2. *correct English makes more rather than fewer distinctions.* *Disinterested* originally meant 'not interested', and is now often used in this way again. But careful speakers reserve that meaning for *uninterested* (which originally meant 'unbiased'), and use *disinterested* to mean 'unbiased'. To use (or misuse) *disinterested* in the sense of 'bored, not interested' is to blur a useful distinction.

This is a convincing argument. One of the ways in which language grows is the making of fine distinctions of meaning. Any usage that needlessly goes against this healthy tendency can be considered 'incorrect'.

3. *correct English is logical.* The phrase ✗ *between you and I* is incorrect. No fluent English speaker would say *between I and you*: the natural form is *between me and you*, and so, 'logically', the other correct form is *between you and me*.

A sentence such as ? *She ran faster than him* is also often considered incorrect: the full thought is expressed in the words *She ran faster than he did*, and so, 'logically', the shortened form should be *She ran faster than he*.

Logic and strict grammar are often at odds with idiom, however. There is no danger of misunderstanding *She ran faster than him* (in the way there is a theoretical danger of misunderstanding *She likes running more than him*), and many grammarians might accept the sentence as 'correct', since it feels natural, is unambiguous, and can even be justified 'logically' by changing the rules slightly (defining *than* as a preposition here, instead of a conjunction). (See AS; PRONOUNS; THAN 1.)

A more obvious conflict between idiom and logic or grammar occurs in the response to the question *Who's there?* According to traditional grammar, the answer is *It is I* — in keeping with the rule that *I* not *me* follows the verb *to be* in a simple sentence like this. Yet the idiomatic response is *It's me* — perfectly clear, and usually far more natural and socially appropriate than the stilted *It's I*. The answer *I am* gets round the problem — it is both correct and unstilted. (See IT'S ME.)

4. *correct English avoids redundancy and duplication of resources.* The objection to such phrases as *?? new innovation* and *?? to divide up the spoils* is that they contain unnecessary words: the noun *innovation* already implies something new, so the adjective *new* is superfluous; *to divide up the spoils* seems to add nothing to the more economical form *to divide the spoils*. (See TAUTOLOGY.)

Or consider the word *hopefully* again, as in *Hopefully we'll succeed.* One of the arguments against this modern use of it is that the word duplicates the expression *it is to be hoped*, which is already at our disposal.

5. *correct English sounds right.* In *Hamlet*, Shakespeare wrote *To be or not to be* because it sounded right: it would have shattered the rhythm had he written *To be or to not be.*

His preference was based on the simple matter of rhythm and elegance, not on any wish to avoid a 'split infinitive'. The rule about the 'split infinitive' developed a long time after Shakespeare's day: it is a good rule to the extent that it serves the cause of elegance. Yet not all split infinitives are inelegant: the words *to boldly go where none has gone before* could almost be a line of Shakespearean poetry: technically, they make a perfect iambic pentameter, with the same rhythm as that used in his sonnets and plays — as in this line, again from *Hamlet*: *'Tis now the very witching time of night.* (See SPLIT INFINITIVE.)

If you want to mark down a disputed word or construction as incorrect on the ground that it is ugly or inelegant, make sure that this is true of it in all cases. If it is not, you should reconsider

your objection to it.

6. *correct English is true to its history.* English spelling often reflects the origin of the word rather than the pronunciation of it — that is why English spelling often seems so difficult. So *night* is the correct form, rather than *nite*, for good historical reasons: the spelling contains a reminder of the way the word was once pronounced — with a guttural /kh/ sound in the middle, as in the German *Nacht* (to which *night* is historically related).

Yet spelling does change, as does pronunciation. So too does the grammatical status or function of words. *Agenda* is now a singular noun, whereas it used to be considered plural (the Latin plural of *agendum*). But *data* and *bacteria* remain plural nouns, even though they are often mistakenly used as singular nouns. (See DATA; MEDIA; PLURALS.)

The meaning of a word often changes too; to insist that it remain 'true to its history' is to commit the 'etymological fallacy': *to prevent*, as noted above, has changed its meaning over the centuries, and diverged from its origins, the Latin roots *prae-*, 'before' + *venire*, 'to come'. *To decimate* originally meant 'to kill one in ten'; today it is more often used to mean 'to kill an enormous number, to devastate'. (See DECIMATE.) Traditionalists protest, and still regard the new sense as 'incorrect'. But time is on its side. Sooner or later, words come to mean what most people take them to mean.

These six criteria of correct English are all important. But it is obvious that they cannot be used mechanically to evaluate an item of disputed usage. Apply them with subtlety and care.

Appropriate English Without realising it, people adjust their language to their audience or to the occasion. Only an extremely eccentric person would use the same level of language in all contexts, formal or informal, spoken or written. The English that is appropriate for addressing a meeting is not appropriate for use in a family discussion, or for talking to a friend — just as a dinner suit is not appropriate clothing to wear on a picnic. One reason that Queen Victoria disliked Mr Gladstone was, she said, his habit of speaking to her as if she were a public meeting.

In general, the greater the distance between the two participants — physical distance, social distance, the distance that comes from unfamiliarity — the more formal the language will be. That is why the language of this book, and in fact in most non-fiction, tends to be fairly formal: it is addressing readers who are physically distant, and whose personalities are quite unknown.

It may, however, be appropriate in some circumstances to insert nonstandard expressions deliberately into a stretch of standard English. Some examples of this practice have become widely accepted: the use of *ain't* in such expressions as *That just ain't so*; the use of *dun* for *did* in *a whodunit*.

Sometimes, as mentioned earlier, appropriate English may be at odds with correct English. Suppose somebody asks the question *Which one of you is Jack Jones?* It would be appropriate, though 'incorrect', for Jack Jones to answer, *That's me*. It would be 'correct', though usually not appropriate, for him to say *That's I*. If he answered *I am*, he would be using the language appropriately and correctly.

The accomplished user of English knows the rules, but he knows too that it is better to break a rule appropriately than to obey it inappropriately. The aim of this book is to provide enough information about the rules to enable the reader to select the right word at the right time — and that means the appropriate word or construction, and wherever possible the correct and standard one as well.

stationary, stationery A traditional spelling trap for the unwary here. *Stationary* is the adjective meaning 'standing still, motionless'; *stationery* is the noun referring to paper, pens, staples, and so on. It should be easy to remember the spelling: *stationery* is what is sold by a *stationer* — which, like *grocer* or *fishmonger,* is spelt with *-er* at the end.

Both words come from the same source, the Latin *statio* 'a standing still' (from *stare,* 'to stand'), and later 'a standstill' — hence *stationary* — and 'a fixed stall in a market', as distinct from an itinerant pedlar. *Statio* gave rise to the Medieval Latin *stationarius,* 'a shopkeeper', and Middle English adopted the word as *staciouner.* The word tended to refer not to any shopkeeper but to a bookseller specifically, and was later further specialised to refer, as today, to a seller of writing materials.

A survival of these earlier senses of *stationery* is to be found in HMSO, 'Her Majesty's Stationery Office', an organisation for the publication and sale of British government documents, reports, and the like.

staunch See STANCH.

stile See STYLE.

still more, still less See MUCH MORE.

stimulus, stimulant *Stimulus* comes straight from the Latin noun *stimulus*, meaning 'a goad'. The English word means broadly 'anything causing a response, or initiating physical or mental activity; an incentive or motivation': *Plants respond to the stimulus of light*; *He needed the stimulus of his teacher's approval to encourage him to study*.

Stimulant as a noun refers to something that causes a brief increase in bodily or mental energy, especially a drink or drug. It strongly suggests the temporary *heightening* of mental or physical activity; a *stimulus*, by contrast suggests rather the *initiation* of such activity. Obviously, there is an overlap of meaning between the two words. A story may be both a *stimulus* to the imagination, setting it in motion, and a *stimulant* to the imagination, increasing its activity temporarily.

Stimulant can also be an adjective meaning 'serving as a stimulant' — *a stimulant drug*. The word comes from the Latin *stimulans,* the present participle of *stimulare,* 'to stimulate'.

Note that the plural of *stimulus* is *stimuli,* pronounced /**stim**mew-lī/ or sometimes /**stim**mew-lee/.

storey, story The word *storey,* referring to a floor or level of a building, is the source of several difficulties. First of all, its spelling. In British English it is usual to spell the word *storey* (plural *storeys*), thus distinguishing it from *story,* 'a tale'.

In American English, the usual spelling is *story* (plural *stories*), though *storey* can also be found, as in the American title of Thomas Merton's autobiographical book *The Seven Storey Mountain* (in Britain also called *Elected Silence*).

Secondly — the adjective form: *three-storeyed* or *three-storey*? In fact, both are found and accepted. (In American spelling, *three-storied* and *three-story* are also possible.) The tendency is for *-storey* rather than *-storeyed* to be used of buildings (especially tall ones) other than private houses: *a 110-storey skyscraper*.

Finally, despite British-American differences in the numbering of *floors* (see FLOOR), there is no significant difference in the number of *storeys*: *a three-storey(ed) building* is likely to be the same size anywhere in the English-speaking world. It would consist of a set of rooms at street level, and two raised levels above it (and any number of basements or lower-ground levels: these are not taken into account). In countries using British English, therefore, an office block whose top floor is the fifth floor would in fact be a *six-storey(ed) building*.

Storey and *story* probably both derive from the

same source: Latin *historia,* 'a story'. A *storey* may owe its name to the row of painted windows or statues, telling a story, that marked off the layers of a building in bygone ages.

stratum   The noun *stratum* keeps the Latin plural form, *strata*: *All strata of society are affected.* *? Stratums* is rare and doubtful, and × *stratas* is incorrect. *Stratas* has given rise to a singular form, *strata*, as in × *This strata of society has been most affected.* Although it is becoming increasingly common, this singular use of × *strata* is widely criticised and should be avoided.

× Alan Bennett's script for *A Private Function* ... examined a narrow strata of society in an ironic, almost fastidious way.
– Richard Rayner, *The Fiction Magazine*

Compare CRITERION; DATA; ERRATA; MEDIA; PHENOMENON.

street   *Streets* are usually in towns, and *roads* in the country. But in British English in particular, there are many exceptions, and it is not possible to state simple rules explaining why *road*, *avenue*, *way*, and the like are used. American English often omits the term in speech: *I live at 360 Parker* (that is, Parker Street). And in British English people say *I live in Parker Street* whereas Americans say *I live on Parker Street.*

Writing of the 'beat' scene in America, a British author says:

Kerouac duly rang, and the consequent date at Howard Johnson's diner in Eighth Street went on — and off — for the next two years.
– Michael Horovitz, *The Spectator*

The phrase *in Eighth Street* sounds extremely odd to Americans: they would say *on Eighth Street.* Conversely, an American version of the British children's song about the Muffin Man has him living *on Drury Lane*; this sounds extremely odd in Britain, where he lives *in Drury Lane.*

stricture   The noun *stricture* has little relation to *strictness,* though it does have the same Latin source — *strictus,* 'tight, narrow', from *stringere,* 'to tighten'. *Stricture* is today used most commonly as a formal word for 'a criticism or censure or adverse remark':

The reviewers were quite severe in their strictures, yet the play had a successful run.

As a technical term in medicine, *stricture* refers to an abnormal narrowing of a duct or passage: *a congenital stricture of the lower bowel.*

stringed, strung   *Stringed* is an adjective meaning 'having strings'. It comes from the noun *string* + the *-ed* that you find in *black-hatted* or *white-shirted. Strung* is the past tense or past participle of the verb *to string,* meaning 'to fit with strings'.

Stringed tends to be used in front of the noun it refers to, not after it. Although it is just possible to speak of *the zither, a board-like instrument, which is stringed and which rests on the knee while being played,* it would be much more usual to speak of *the zither, a board-like instrument which has strings* ... , and best of all to speak of *the zither, a board-like stringed instrument.* The commonest combination, in fact, is simply *a stringed instrument*; also commonly heard is *a stringed racket* (though this seems tautologous). But: *Her tennis racket was strung with nylon; His violin has to be restrung by an expert.*

Another difference between *stringed* and *strung* follows directly from their origins in the noun *string* and the verb *to string* respectively. The verbal origins of *strung* mean that it can have adverbs before it: *a badly strung guitar, a tightly strung racket.* But adverbs are not used before *stringed,* so you cannot say × *a badly stringed guitar.* On the other hand, adjectives and numerals can precede *stringed* — *a twelve-stringed guitar* — but not *strung*: × *a twelve-strung guitar.*

Since the *stringed instruments* (the violin, viola, cello, and double bass) are also known as the *strings* or the *string section* of an orchestra, the phrase *string instruments* has developed, and is now widely accepted as a variant of *stringed instruments.*

Note the forms *unstrung* and *stringless. Stringless* means 'without strings': *The stringless, dusty violin lying in the attic turned out to be a Stradivarius; tender, stringless French beans. Unstrung* is the past tense or past participle of the verb *to unstring,* 'to loosen or remove the strings of': *He unstrung the broken bow, and fitted the string to his new one; An unstrung violin is less likely to warp. Unstrung* can also be used to mean 'emotionally upset, unnerved': *Sylvia was feeling quite unstrung after being blamed by the boss.*

stroke   See SOLIDUS.

strong verbs   See VERBS 1.

style, stile   There are two words spelt *stile,* and it is only through an etymological accident that the word *style* is not spelt *stile* as well.

The first *stile* — 'a set of steps for getting over

a fence or wall'; also 'a turnstile' — comes from the Old English *stigel.*

The second *stile* — 'an upright support in a panel or frame' — is probably from the Dutch *stijl,* 'a doorpost', probably in turn derived from the Latin *stilus,* 'a pole or post'.

A more common sense of this Latin word *stilus* was 'pen', and it was this sense (extended to 'manner of writing') that probably gave rise to the present senses of *style*: 'the way in which something is written or done', and so on. The Latin *stilus* became *style* as well as *stile* in Old French, probably because it was wrongly associated with the Greek word *stulos,* 'a column' (the Greek vowel *upsilon* tended to be rendered as a *y* in French and English derivatives). Hence the spelling *style* rather than *stile* in English today.

subjective See OBJECTIVE.

subjunctive   The usual 'mood' of a verb (that is, its 'mode', the indication of the speaker's attitude to the sentence or to the addressee) is known as the *indicative mood*: *He is 16*; *He's not yet 16*; *Is he really 16?* Here, the indicative form *is* is used to express, deny, or question a fact. The *imperative mood* is used for instructions or commands: *Act your age! Be quiet! First catch your hare.* The *subjunctive mood* expresses what could or should happen, rather than what actually does or did; it is used for desires, doubts, necessities, hypotheses, proposals, and certain conditions, particularly those that are contrary to fact.

Today, the subjunctive is probably most common in certain fixed phrases: *Far be it from me*; *Heaven forbid!*; *Suffice it to say*; *If need be*; *As it were*; *Be that as it may*; *God bless you*; *God save the Queen*; *Long live the King*; *Grammar be damned!*

In form, the subjunctive of an ordinary verb, whether present or past, is its basic form, without the *-s.* This means that in the present tense the difference between subjunctive and indicative appears only in the third person singular: *heaven forbid* replaces *heaven forbids*, but *they forbid* is the same in both moods. The verb *to be*, unlike other verbs, has the separate past tense subjunctive *were.*

Apart from the idiomatic phrases quoted above, the subjunctive is used in two sets of circumstances: to express some unreal conditions, and in certain clauses introduced by *that.*

Conditions that can take the subjunctive are typically introduced by *if, though, as if, as though, supposing,* or the rather old-fashioned *lest.* In the following examples, *were* is

subjunctive:

> I wouldn't try it if I were you.
> If she were a man, I'd punch her nose for her.
> She acts as if she were the boss around here.
> As though I were in any state to help!
> If it were to snow, we could not come.
> If it weren't for Mary, we'd be in trouble.
> Oh, that my love were in my arms!

And in the following examples — all rather old-fashioned — *be* is the subjunctive:

> If anyone be found guilty, he shall have the right to appeal against the verdict.
> Whatever be the reason, we will not allow it.
> Though he be the chairman himself, he must obey the rules.

This *be*-subjunctive in *if*-clauses, being so old-fashioned, is little used now. Even less common is the subjunctive of other verbs in such constructions:

> If he find us guilty, we shall have the right to appeal.

Today, the indicative *finds* would almost always be used here. Just how old-fashioned the subjunctive here really is can be seen by reference to a book by Archbishop Trench, written in the last century:

> One who now says, 'If he *call*, tell him I am out' — many do say it still, but they grow fewer every day — is seeking to detain a mood, or rather the sign of a mood, which the language is determined to get rid of.
> — Richard Chenevix Trench,
> *English Past and Present*

The subjunctive *be*, then, is seldom used after *if* today. There are restrictions too on the use of the subjunctive *were* after *if*. It cannot be used, for instance, in sentences where *if* could be replaced by *whether*:

> He looked to see if/whether she was angry (not *were angry*).
> We must find out if/whether it was true.
> There's some doubt if/whether she was married.
> She asked if/whether I was ready.

Nor should the subjunctive *were* follow *if* in conditions that are not purely hypothetical:

> If he was in the street at the time, he must have seen the accident.

The *if . . . were* construction sounds a good deal

more formal to British ears than to American ones. In everyday usage, particularly in speech, British speakers often prefer to say *as if she was the boss* and *if it wasn't for Mary*.

The other major setting for subjunctives is in clauses introduced by *that* — typically clauses expressing a proposal, wish, desire, or necessity:

They insist that she leave at once.
They insisted that she leave at once.
It is vital that this letter reach him within a week.
His demand that the president intervene is as firm as ever.

This kind of subjunctive too is more popular and natural in American than in British English, though it is coming increasingly into modern British use under American influence. The older British alternative would have been to use *should*: *insist that she should leave*; *vital that the letter should reach him*; *demand that the president should intervene*. British writers also sometimes use the indicative in such circumstances: *vital that the letter reaches him*.

Both of these British alternatives can produce ambiguity. Consider the sentences *They insist that she should leave at once* and *They insisted that she left at once*: the first might be taken to mean that they think she ought to leave; the second might be taken to suggest that they are anxious to convince us that she did in fact leave. No such misunderstanding is possible when using the subjunctive forms: *They insist/insisted that she leave at once*.

Take care not to mix subjunctive and indicative in the same construction: × *If he be found guilty and receives a prison sentence* . . .

In most contexts, of course, the subjunctive form of the verb is actually indistinguishable from the indicative. If one of the earlier examples had read *His demand that the politicians intervene is as firm as ever*, it would be impossible to know which mood was intended.

All these considerations apply also to negative *that*-clauses:

He is eager that they (should) not withdraw.
They recommend that we (should) not pay.

There is an interesting difference in the way that the subjunctive *be* is negated in *that*-clauses and in *if*-clauses. Here is a positive sentence illustrating the two kinds of *be* (the one in the *if*-clause is more old-fashioned):

If he be guilty, I demand that he be punished.

If both clauses are negated, the *not* is positioned differently in the two clauses:

If he be not guilty, I demand that he not be punished.

Remember that if the subjunctive feels awkward, whether in positive or negative sentences, it can often be avoided by rephrasing. The earlier example *They recommend that we not pay*, for instance, can be reworded as *They advised us not to pay*.

See also IF; WHETHER.

subsequent See CONSEQUENT.

substantial, substantive Both of these adjectives are related to the noun *substance*, and there is considerable overlap in their meaning. Both, for instance, can mean 'real, genuine, not imaginary': *There was no substantial/substantive reason to disbelieve him*.

In many contexts, however, one form or the other is favoured. *Substantial* tends to refer to *substance* in its more physical sense: 'matter', 'size', and so on. So: *a substantial meal*, won by *a substantial distance*, and informally, *a woman of substantial proportions*.

> The present policies of Western governments and the international agencies are predicated on the belief that substantial servicing by these debtors in real terms is manageable in the years ahead.
> — Lord Lever, *Time and Tide*

Substantial has sometimes been criticised as a fancy substitute for *big* or *large*: *a substantial house* is suitable if the house is strong or particularly solid, but if it refers simply to 'a large house', then say *a large house* instead.

Substantial also means 'virtual, in the main' — *in substantial agreement* — and 'prosperous and influential': *substantial citizens*.

Substantive suggests substance in its more abstract senses of 'essence', 'important characteristics', and so on. Whereas *substantial talks* would suggest large-scale and lengthy talks, *substantive talks* suggest talks dealing with important or essential concerns.

> As at Lancaster House, there will be many crises during the negotiations. This became apparent on Friday when the meeting ran into a protocol wrangle and almost broke down before any substantive discussions began.
> — Allister Sparks, *The Observer*

Some of the corrections are substantive, and

at least one is of such importance that it will have considerable effect upon the interpretation of the whole book.

> – Professor Richard Ellman (U.S.), quoted in the *Daily Telegraph*

Substantive also has technical senses in grammar, law, and the armed services. Note that it is usually stressed on the first syllable, whereas *substantial* is stressed on the second.

substitute, replace 1. Take care not to confuse these two verbs. The typical patterns are: *to substitute A for B*; and *to replace B by A*, or *A replaces B*. It is now very common, but still incorrect, to use *to substitute* in the place of *to replace*, and *substitution* in the place of *replacement*. So:

× Hedley is substituting McAlister as opening bowler.
× Natural cotton has been substituted by synthetic fibres in most of our fabrics.
× The substitution of fuel-efficient cars by 'gas-guzzlers' was the most notable change in the market during the 1970s.

× At a recent international energy seminar Academician Styrikovich, a senior Soviet energy specialist, confirmed that his country was planning to substitute 200 million tonnes of domestic oil consumption by natural gas supplies by the end of the 1980s.
> – Steve Vines, *The Observer*

Remember: *to substitute* means 'to put in the place of'; *to replace* means 'to take the place of'; *to substitute* tends to take the preposition *for*, and *to replace* tends to take *by* or *with*.

2. *To replace* is in danger of being used ambiguously. The sentence *I must replace this record* can, without a clarifying context, mean three different things: 'I must put this record back in its rack'; 'I must buy you another record, having accidentally broken this one'; or 'I must return this record to the people at the record-shop, and get them to give me an undamaged copy'. Make sure that you convey the intended sense. If the context does not make your meaning clear beyond the possibility of misunderstanding, choose another verb instead: *exchange*, *return*, *put back*, or the like.

such 1. There is a traditional objection to the use of *such* in place of *so* as an intensive: *? such naughty children*; *? such a trivial complaint*. The objection is twofold. First, since the intensive applies to the adjective, not the noun, the adverb

so is apparently required: since we say *the complaint is so trivial*, we should speak of *so trivial a complaint*, not *? such a trivial complaint*. Secondly, *such* can cause ambiguity: *I refuse to put up with such naughty children* can be understood to mean either 'I refuse to put up with naughty children, such as these are' or 'I can put up with reasonably naughty children, but I refuse to put up with children as naughty as these'.

Certainly, we can rephrase *? such a trivial complaint* as *so trivial a complaint* quite easily. But how do we rephrase *? such naughty children*? The only way is to twist the phrase around: *children so naughty*. And this wrench might do considerable damage to the natural feel and rhythm of our sentence. To change *Such naughty children ought to be taught a lesson* to *Children so naughty ought to be taught a lesson* is hardly to make it more elegant.

It is time that this common use of *such* before an adjective was fully accepted (particularly before plural nouns, or mass nouns where there is no article present) as an unobjectionable and unavoidable English idiom.

2. The traditional rule is that pronouns following the phrase *such as* should take the subject form: *I have never before seen a bald woman such as she*. That is, *such as* should apparently be regarded as a conjunction not a preposition, and the sentence should be understood as *I have never before seen a bald women such as she is* or *of the kind that she is*.

Such usage sounds extremely formal today, however, and in most contexts *such as* can be treated as a preposition, and the pronouns following can take the object form: *I have never before seen a bald woman such as her*; *You've always been jealous of people such as me*. Of course, informal English would probably have *like* instead of *such as* in both these sentences. (See AS; LIKE.)

3. The relative pronoun that forms a correlative pair with *such* is *as*: *We are such stuff as dreams are made on*. There is a common tendency, however, especially in long sentences, to use *that*, *which*, *who*, or *where*, instead of *as*:

× The concession applies not to all workers, but only to such members of the permanent staff who registered before the specified deadline.
× He handled the machine in such a way that made it impossible for me to use afterwards.

The mistake here seems to be based on a confused blend of two different constructions: *to such members as registered/to those members who registered*; *in such a way as made it impossible/in a way that made it impossible.*

Of course, the combination *such . . . that,* in its proper place, is a common and helpful and perfectly acceptable usage:

> The machine was subjected to such rough handling that it was impossible for me to use it afterwards.

This too might explain the common temptation to use *such . . . that* in the place of *such . . . as.*

4. A similar confusion of constructions occurs in such awkward sentences as:

> The condition can be treated in various ways, such as by taking a cure at a spa or simply by massaging the affected areas with wintergreen.

The two appropriate constructions are *such as taking a cure* and the rather old-fashioned *as by taking a cure.* But the prepositional phrase *such as* should not be followed by another preposition: it has to be followed by a noun or by the *-ing* form of a verb.

5. Note that the negative form of *such an X* is *no such X*; it is incorrect to say ✗ *no such an X*:

> By isolating such an element as oxygen, Priestley effectively proved that there was no such substance as phlogiston

— not ✗ *no such a substance.*

6. Avoid the pompous and awkward substitution of *such* for the pronouns *this, it, them, those,* and so on:

> ? Anyone noticing diseased elms is urged to report such to the local conservation officer.

This should read *to report them/these.* In the following quotation, *such* is deliberately chosen as a playfully pompous substitute for *this*:

> ? It is not given to everyone to lunch with a man wearing top of the range Coxmoore's in a subtle burgundy and cream diamond intarsia knit with inset ventilation panels, but such was my good fortune last Wednesday when I attended a conference called 'The Shape Of Feet To Come' run by the Foot Care Council.
> — Sue Arnold, *The Observer*

Similarly, avoid using the official-sounding *such* in place of *the, this, that, these,* and *those,* when repeating a noun:

> ? If a company purchases a property outright, only to find that such property was falsely

represented at the time of purchase, it always has recourse to the courts.

It was well-advised here to repeat the word *property* (since a simple *it* would have been ambiguous, and capable of referring either to *company* or to *property*); but why say *such property* when it would be less pompous and more elegant to say *the property*?

See also AS SUCH; LIKE; SUCHLIKE.

suchlike Whether as pronoun or adjective, *suchlike* is today considered too casual a word for formal usage: *? pens, pencils, and suchlike* (also *? pens, pencils, and such*); *? lions, wolves, and suchlike carnivores.*

It sounds less colloquial, and less lazy, to say *pens, pencils, and other items of stationery,* for instance, or even *pens, pencils, and the like*; similarly, *lions, wolves, and other (such) carnivores* is preferable. And *like items/carnivores* is also correct, though rather formal.

See also ET CETERA.

sufferance, suffrage Although *sufferance* once meant 'suffering or patient endurance', this sense is now old-fashioned and very rare, and should not be taken as the usual meaning of the word. A more acceptable sense of *sufferance,* though also seldom encountered nowadays, is 'the ability to tolerate pain or distress' — not suffering itself but the capacity for suffering: *Her sufferance of extreme hardship was remarkable.* The common meaning of *sufferance* today is 'consent, acceptance, toleration': *Your continuous sufferance of John's bad habits is going to spoil the boy.* It usually refers to passive acceptance rather than active permission. The word occurs most frequently in the phrase *on sufferance,* meaning 'tolerated reluctantly; accepted but not really wanted':

> The vote of no-confidence was overwhelming, but he remains president on sufferance until a replacement is agreed upon.

Note that *sufferance* is always spelt with the *e* in the middle, although it is often pronounced /ˈsuffrənss/. The alternative pronunciation is /ˈsuffərənss/; both are acceptable. The word goes back, as *suffer* does, to the Latin verb *suffere,* 'to sustain'.

Suffrage is not related to *sufferance* or *suffering. Suffrage* means 'the right or privilege of voting, or the exercise of such right, or a vote itself'. It derives, via Old French and Medieval Latin, from the Latin *suffragium,* 'the ballot or the right of voting'.

Suffrage is spelt without an *e* in the middle, and pronounced /**suff**rij/.

Universal suffrage is the phrase used to refer to the right of every adult citizen to vote, especially (when this was an issue) including women. *Universal* is not strictly accurate in Britain, even now that there is *universal suffrage*. In Britain, the exceptions to this universality, apart from minors, are foreigners, committed criminals, certified lunatics ... and peers — who cannot, as members of the House of Lords, elect MPs to the House of Commons, and can vote only in local elections.

A *suffragan* (/**suff**rəgən/) or *suffragan bishop* is an assistant or subordinate bishop. *Suffragan* derives ultimately from the Latin *suffragium* as well, which in Medieval Latin acquired the extended sense of 'support or assistance'.

The *suffragettes* were female supporters of female suffrage in various countries, notably members of the Women's Social and Political Union (founded by Emmeline Pankhurst), who early this century campaigned for the vote for women in Britain. The term *suffragette,* which was coined by the press, is somewhat condescending: the *-ette* ending is, strictly speaking, diminutive and not simply feminine (it indicates the sense 'little' as well as 'female'). The neutral term for a campaigner (male or female) for women's suffrage is a *suffragist*, and this is now again in favour with feminist writers, but *suffragette* caught on and remains the standard term for women suffragists. The wide use of the term has probably encouraged the misconception that *-ette* is simply a feminine suffix: hence the formation *usherette*, and such informal coinages as *undergraduette*.

Note that *suffragette* can be stressed on either the first or (more usually) the third syllable, but *suffragist* can be stressed only on the first syllable.

suffixes See PREFIXES AND SUFFIXES.

superlative See ADJECTIVES 2.

supine See PRONE.

supplement See COMPLEMENT.

suppose, supposing Both *suppose* and *supposing* can be used to express a theoretical or possible event: *Suppose/Supposing he doesn't turn up? Suppose/Supposing somebody finds out!* They can also be used to make a suggestion: *Suppose/Supposing we offer him a better price?*

Some people consider *supposing* a little more casual than *suppose* in such sentences, and so avoid it in formal speech or writing. However, *supposing* is the correct, and only possible, form to use when the meaning is *assuming* rather than *what if?*: *Even supposing he were invited, he might decide not to turn up*; *We'll talk to her at the meeting tomorrow, always supposing she turns up.*

susceptible *Susceptible* is followed by *to* when it means 'easily affected by, having little resistance to': *very susceptible to flattery*; *susceptible to rheumatism*. It is followed by *of*, or very occasionally by *to*, in its more formal meaning of 'capable of undergoing': *a theory susceptible of several interpretations*. The use of *susceptible to* to mean 'frequently displaying', as in *?? She is susceptible to fits of pique*, has attracted criticism, and should be avoided in careful usage. *Liable* or *prone* would be possible here, or simply say *She tends to have fits of pique*. See also ADMIT; LIKELY, APT, LIABLE, PRONE.

suspect, suspicious Both these adjectives can mean 'giving rise to suspicion': *suspicious/suspect behaviour*; *a shifty, suspect/suspicious little man*. *Suspicious*, but not *suspect*, can also mean 'feeling suspicion, distrustful':

> I admit to being instinctively suspicious of stories remembered from schooldays, and my suspiciousness increased as I read each preposterous episode in Raven's saga.
> – Rupert Morris, *The Times*

When there is a danger that *suspicious* might be ambiguous, use *suspect* if possible in the sense of 'giving rise to suspicion'. If a detective, for instance, is under suspicion of being corrupt, it would be better to refer to him as *the suspect detective*, since the phrase *the suspicious detective* would usually be taken to refer to a conscientious detective who is not inclined to take people or things at face value.

The adverb, however, is almost always *suspiciously*, in both senses: *The detective looked suspiciously around the room* (= distrustfully); *The detective had been behaving suspiciously for some time* (= questionably).

Suspect has a shade of meaning that *suspicious* lacks — 'of doubtful quality or appropriateness': *a suspect bridge* is one that might just possibly collapse; *suspect meat* is possibly a hazard to health. You would be unlikely to speak of *?? suspicious meat*, though you might say *This meat smells suspicious* (or *suspect*). In the following extract *suspect* means 'not altogether suitable' rather than 'under suspicion':

> The suspect but able Leningrad chieftain who lived it up a little too obviously ...
> – Edward Crankshaw, *The Observer*

Note that *suspect* as adjective, and as noun, is stressed on the first syllable, unlike the verb, which is stressed on the second.

swap, swop   *Swap* is the standard spelling of this informal word meaning 'to exchange' or 'an exchange'. But *swop* is now a common enough variation to have found its way into dictionaries.

swat, swot   *To swat*, meaning 'to hit or slap with a sharp blow', is a variant of the word *squat*, in its earlier sense of 'to hit sharply, or lay flat with a blow'. It is often spelt *swot*, though some writers still regard this form as unacceptable.
To swot has the further sense in British English of 'to study hard'. The word is a dialect variant of *sweat*.
Both *swat* and *swot* can also be used as nouns. A *swat* is a slap. A *swot* is a period of hard study, or a subject that needs hard study, or a person who studies hard. In this last sense, it often has a disapproving tone that is absent from the verb.
Both words remain slightly informal in tone, except in the phrase *to swat flies*, which is fully standard.

swell   The usual past participle form of the verb *to swell* is *swollen*: *The river/Her neck was swollen*. But *swelled* is often used when an increase in size or amount is being expressed: *The crowd was swelled by a large number of young people*. A contrast in meaning is sometimes possible, with *swollen* implying a harmful or unwanted increase in size: compare *Their numbers have swelled to nearly a thousand* (statement of fact) and *Their numbers have swollen to nearly a thousand* (an undesirable development). The form used adjectivally before a noun is *swollen*, as in *swollen ankles*; *swelled* can occur in the idiomatic phrase *swelled head*, though this is chiefly an American usage, British English still favouring *swollen head* (and *swollen-headed*).
Compare LIGHT; MELT; SHRINK; SINK.

syllepsis   See ZEUGMA.

symbiosis   See SYNTHESIS.

sympathy, empathy   *Empathy* is increasingly being used as an impressive-sounding synonym of *sympathy,* but strictly speaking it should not be used in this way. *Empathy* was coined early this century, as a translation of the German word *Einfühlung,* but using ancient Greek roots meaning 'feeling into'. *Empathy* and the verb *to empathise* refer to a person's ability to project himself 'into' the mind of another person, or the feelings of an animal, or the spirit of a book, or the like, to the point where he can virtually share those other emotions or participate imaginatively in another life. A common synonym of *to empathise with* is *to identify with* (see IDENTIFY). Identical twins are often thought to display great empathy with each other.

> The skill of Meryl's film performance is that she is able to make the transition, to coarsen her behaviour, even her looks, to such an extent that there is only a passing physical resemblance between her real self and her portrayal of Karen Silkwood. She did feel a great empathy with Karen. 'I've done more literary types in the past, but Karen Silkwood is closer to what I'm really like than, say, The French Lieutenant's Woman. ....'
> – Joyce Eggington, *The Observer*

> The days passed and Alexis decided they were waiting for something. ... He had an uncommonly good eye for seeing such things far ahead of his colleagues. When it came to empathising with Jews, he believed that he lived in a kind of vacuum of excellence.
> – John le Carré,
> *The Little Drummer Girl*

This is a fairly specialised and restricted sense, and so it should be. For the wider, more general sense of 'pity, emotional understanding, compassion', there is no reason to use *empathy* when the common and long-established word *sympathy* is available. *Sympathy* goes back through Latin to ancient Greek roots meaning either 'feeling together with' or 'having similar feelings'. *Sympathy* has many other related meanings of course: 'an expression of pity or commiseration': *My sympathies to you on your defeat*; 'mutual understanding and affection': *little sympathy between the chairman and the shareholders*; 'agreement, harmony, or accord': *His views are in sympathy with my own*; and so on.
Empathy has a second sense: the word is used when a person suggests that an object (such as a painting or a tree) experiences thoughts and emotions rather than simply producing them in him. When a poet speaks of 'brooding clouds' or 'a sculpture full of love', he is using or dis-

playing empathy. A more familiar term with much the same meaning is *pathetic fallacy*.

The related adjectives are *sympathetic*, sometimes *sympathetical*, and *empathetic*, sometimes *empathic*.

Note finally, that *sympathy* tends to take the preposition *for* when used in the sense of 'pity, compassion' — *sympathy for the underdog* — but *with* (or *to* or *between*) in most other cases.

syndrome The word *syndrome*, pronounced /**sin**-drōm, -drəm/, is a technical medical term, referring to a group of signs or symptoms that occur together and are characteristic of a particular mental or physical disorder. By extension, *syndrome* can refer to the disorder or abnormality itself. The condition formerly known as *mongolism*, for instance, is referred to technically as *Down's syndrome*: it is a genetic disorder that is accompanied by a set of physical symptoms, such as slanting eyes and a broad short skull, that indicate the condition. Another *syndrome* much in the news lately is AIDS: *acquired immuno-deficiency syndrome*.

Syndrome has gradually transferred itself from medical usage to general English usage. It has become a vogue word, referring to a set of reactions, actions, and so on that usually occur together in a particular situation to form a more or less predictable pattern. For example, *He is suffering from the mid-life syndrome* — this means that he is showing all the signs usually associated with the beginning of middle-age, such as doubts about his job, his virility, his marriage, and what he should be doing next.

This use is perhaps just acceptable, but if there is no real pattern of indications, then the word should be avoided: *? She is beginning to show a career-woman syndrome*. And if the intended sense is no more than 'a symptom' or 'an obsession' or 'a pattern', then use the appropriate one of these terms rather than forcing *syndrome* into a role it does not fit: × *He's got a physical fitness syndrome*; × *What are the syndromes of a nervous breakdown?*

The word comes through New Latin and Greek from the Greek roots *sun-*, 'together' + *dromos*, 'a race or racecourse': the idea being of symptoms running or occurring together.

synecdoche See METAPHOR.

synthesis, symbiosis Formerly restricted chiefly to specialist scientific and philosophical contexts, *synthesis* has now become a vogue word in general use — any combination, fusion, union, or the like is now a *synthesis*: *? This revolutionary new product is a synthesis of shampoo, conditioner, and setting lotion*; *? His style is a synthesis of Kafka and Mel Brooks*. The Greek roots of the word mean 'a putting together'.

A more recent vogue word is *symbiosis*, from Greek roots meaning 'living together'. Technically the word refers to plants or animals living in close association, each benefiting from, or even depending on, the welfare of the other. By metaphorical extension, the word is now used in political and social contexts too: *? the symbiosis of the miners' union and the Labour Party*, and so on. It is difficult to regard the word as anything other than pretentious.

systematic, systemic The usual adjective from *system* is *systematic*: *a systematic philosophy*. In a slightly extended use, *systematic* can also mean 'methodical, step-by-step, well-planned', and so on: *a systematic search, a systematic housekeeper*.

This extended sense is now the dominant one: to study something *systematically* would tend to mean to study it methodically, item by item. If you wanted to refer to an approach that considers the parts of something in relation to one another and to the whole, you could speak about studying it *systemically*. This would be a very useful distinction, but *systemic* is still too rare a word to allow the distinction wide currency, and many people consider it little more than a rather pretentious variant of *systematic*.

Systemic and *systematic* each have a specialised meaning that is not covered by the other term. *Systemic* is used in a specialised medical sense: 'of or affecting the whole body'. So *a systemic disease* is one that affects the entire system. Occasionally *systemic* is used as a noun, meaning 'a systemic poison or medicine'. The word can be pronounced either /si-**stem**mik/ or /si-**stee**mik/.

The specialised sense of *systematic*, or *systematical*, occurs in biology and zoology — 'relating to the classification of living organisms': *a radical rearrangement of the established systematic classification of large worms and caterpillars*.

T

-t See -ED, -T.

target **1.** During the Second World War, the noun *target* came to be widely used in its metaphorical sense of 'a desired end or quota, an objective': *a target of 200 shell casings per worker per day.* The word became so much a part of everyday speech that it soon seemed to lose its metaphorical feel altogether: instead of simply *aiming at a target* or *hitting the target* or *just missing the target* or *falling short of the target* — all these phrases keep in the spirit of the original metaphor — people now speak of *?? exceeding the target, ? being on course for the target, ?? chasing the target, ?? circling the target,* and *?? increasing the target* (which should, if you think of it, make the task easier rather than more difficult).

True enough, this is the way that language develops: metaphorical extensions become literal meanings in their own right. When we speak of *the hands of a clock*, for instance, we are not expected to conjure up an image of two human hands. An extended meaning becomes in due course quite independent of the original meaning; concrete and abstract senses can seem quite unrelated — the two commonest senses of *goal*, for instance, are quite distinct: 'a scoring move or the scoring area in a sport' and 'the purpose or objective towards which an action is directed'. Similarly the two chief senses of *to aim*: 'to direct (a weapon)' and 'to strive or intend'. Perhaps it is through the association with these two related words that *target* is now used as though its two chief senses were also quite distinct.

The trouble is that things have moved too fast. Language needs time before such changes can be fully accepted. Older speakers can still remember all too clearly when the word *target* was used chiefly of archery or rifle practice. Until the metaphorical origins of the new sense are obscured by time, it is best still treated as a residual metaphor, and paired with appropriate counterparts such as *hit, miss,* or *fall short of.*

2. The verb *to target* is now widely accepted in the sense of 'to have as a target, or to make a target of' — more or less in the original sense of the noun *target.* So:

It was eventually decided to target Dresden for the bombing raid.

Last month Cardinal Glemp was handed a list of more than 60 priests who have been targeted as troublemakers by the Government.

– Sunday Telegraph

But in its more extended sense, 'to strive for, to intend, to work towards', *to target* is something of a vogue word, much favoured in the jargon of economists and politicians: *? A five-per-cent inflation rate before January has been targeted by the Exchequer.*

taste See -LY.

tautology The English language has huge resources; much exuberant writing, from Chaucer or Shakespeare to Dylan Thomas or the Monty Python scripts, spends these resources with abandon. But most writing and speaking is dedicated to more straightforward communication, and is most efficient when most economical with language. Unless some special emphasis is required, or some stylistic effect such as pathos or comedy, the language's resources should be drawn on with restraint.

The appeal of two words where one will do is something that most speakers and writers yield to from time to time. They say *at the present time* rather than *now, owing to the fact that* instead of *because, weather conditions* instead of *the weather.* Verbosity of this kind might impress listeners or readers briefly, but it soon grows tiresome and suspect.

One common form of verbosity is 'redundancy' — in effect, saying the same thing twice, the needless repetition of a single item of information (as in this sentence). It is like killing a fly twice over.

Two technical terms referring to redundancy in language are *tautology* and *pleonasm. Tautology* goes back to the Greek roots *tautos*, 'identical' (from *to*, 'the' + *autos*, 'the same') + *logos*, 'saying, or a word'. In logic, a *tautology* is a statement that is true no matter what happens: *Either it will rain tomorrow or it will not rain tomor-*

row. In language, *tautology* is the repetition of an idea in different words: × *Pair off in twos*; × *7.30 p.m. in the evening.*

Pleonasm is rather broader. It does not necessarily entail the repetition of an idea. It is the overelaboration of the idea through using more words than are necessary. To speak of *? meeting up with a friend* is pleonastic, since *meeting a friend* conveys the meaning quite adequately. The word *pleonasm* goes back through Late Latin to the Greek *pleonasmos*, 'a superabundance', from *pleonazein,* 'to be more than enough', from *pleon,* 'more'.

Many tautologies or pleonasms are built into the natural idiom of English, and it is quite pointless trying to drive them out of the language as obstructions to streamlined communication. There is no getting rid of such phrases as *silly fool, young lad, old crone,* and *over and done with,* for instance. Even some individual words have a built-in element of redundancy: *reiterate,* for instance, is made up of elements that mean 'again' and 'to do again', yet this does not make it an invalid word (though to speak of *?? reiterating again* or *?? repeating again* would usually be ill-advised). Legal jargon and religious language are full of redundancies: *lift up, rise up, join together, null and void, last will and testament,* and so on.

Many other common redundant phrases are not so deep a part of the language as to claim immunity as idioms. Here is a list of widely used tautologies, of different kinds and different degrees of unacceptability:

past history
future prospects
grateful thanks
usual habits
free gifts
new innovations
an indirect allusion
an essential prerequisite
no other alternative
the general consensus
the consensus of opinion
to mix things together
to circle round something
to divide it up
to rest up
more preferable
unjustly persecuted
the reason is because
a new addition to the family
when it was first founded
to set a new world record

Entrance is restricted to ticketholders only.
Two further points must be added.
There were other consequences apart from bankruptcy and distress.
Zappo kills flies dead.
There is no need for undue alarm.
From time immemorial it has always been the custom.
For the 20th time the OAU convenes again.

Here now is a selection of quotations displaying redundancy. A short comment follows each example to explain what is wrong:

> *?* One other factor does not really help: at 11 pm Radio 4 divides up, and the remainder of *The World Tonight* is consigned to the long and medium waves, and falls victim to a very horrid loss of sound quality.
> – David Wade, *The Times*

The *up* of *divides up* is superfluous.

> *??* But that course of action was rejected by News Editor Allan M. Siegal last week. Said he: 'Everybody feels, I think unanimously, that that wouldn't sound like the New York *Times.*'
> – *Time* (U.S.)

If *everybody* feels the same way, then the feeling is unanimous, and the word *unanimous* can be left unstated.

> × Both 'November 1918', and 'Snow' which gives its title to the book, are in complete contrast to the delicate sketches of the Italian countryside. Both could have been developed into novels and both of them leave us wanting to know more about the chief protagonists.
> – Joan Haslip, *The Literary Review*

A *protagonist* is the *chief* character as it is. (See PROTAGONIST for further details.)

> *?* A more prolific exponent of the present cat cult is the artist Martin Leman, who paints nothing but cats. A genuine primitive, he asks us to contemplate the cat as icon. He reduces them down to being mounds of fur brooding on a brick wall or by the seashore, or arising from a bed of formalised flowers.
> – Sir Roy Strong, *The Times*

The word *down* is, strictly speaking, superfluous after *reduce.*

> × That idea has also interested me for a long time, and the two ideas happened to merge together. What then emerged was a story of

strong family tensions and conflicts, as you say.

> – Emma Tennant,
> interviewed in *The Literary Review*

To *merge together* is pleonastic. Omit *together*.

?? The actual facts are that I began this book impulsively and wrote it continuously.

> – Joseph Conrad,
> Author's Note to *The Secret Agent*

Can *facts* be anything other than *actual*?

?? Alas, these agreeable qualities were balanced by weaknesses ... He had a mercurial, change-able temperament which disinclined him to stick to any course of life for long.

> – Lord David Cecil,
> *A Portrait of Jane Austen*

A *mercurial* temperament is much the same thing as a *changeable* temperament, and so is a temperament that disinclines one to stick to any course of life for long.

tea cake See MUFFIN.

temerity *Temerity* is sometimes confused with *timidity* or *timorousness*. In fact, it means almost the opposite — 'foolish or reckless disregard of danger; impetuous boldness; rashness': *He had the temerity to answer back*. It goes back to the Latin adverb *temere*, 'blindly, rashly'.

The stress is on the second syllable: /tə-**merr**ə-ti/.

There is a related adjective *temerarious*, pronounced /**temm**ə-**rair**-i-əss/ and meaning 'reck-lessly daring', but it is a far more formal and far rarer word than *temerity*.

tend Be careful when using *to tend* and *to attend* in formal English. Both *tend* and *attend* (more formal) can be used as transitive verbs with the meaning 'to take care of, nurse': *She tended/ attended the sick and wounded*. This is not to be confused with *to attend to*, which is used in the closely related sense of 'to see to': *Please attend to this customer*. Here *to tend* is not permissible. To *attend to* also means 'to give one's attention to', as in *Attend to your work!* For some American speakers *tend to* can also be used col-loquially in this sense, but that would not be acceptable in British English.

tense 1. The *tense* of a verb is any of a set of par-ticular forms that show the time, nature, or degree

of completeness of the event under discussion. (The use of verbs to indicate the nature or degree of completeness is also known as 'aspect'.)

English verbs have really only two tenses: the present tense, as in *Today is Thursday*, and the past tense, as in *Yesterday was Wednesday*. There is no obvious future tense corresponding to these. Instead, the future is formed with *will, shall,* or *be going to*, or the like — *It will be Friday tomorrow; It is going to rain* — or is simply represented by the present tense: *She is flying to New York next week.* (See section 3 below.) In an English verb, everything else about the time when an action takes place is described by com-bining *be* or *have* with one of the two 'participles' of the verb in question.

The English tense system distinguishes three types of event. First, there are events that simply happen or happened. Here, the simple present and past forms of the verb are used: *She talks a lot; I shall read your story; We worked late.*

Secondly, there are events that are happening or were happening at a particular moment. Here an *-ing* form of the verb is used — the present participle — preceded by the verb *to be*: *She is talking; I was reading; We'll be working then.*

Thirdly, there are events that happen in a period of time stretching up to a particular point. Here the *-ed* form of the verb is used — the past par-ticiple — preceded by the verb *to have*: *She has spoken for an hour; I shall have read the story by then; We had worked from midnight to dawn.*

The second and third patterns can be combined: *She had been talking; I have been reading; We shall have been working.*

If the past participle is used after the verb *to be*, the 'passive' of the verb is formed: *We shall be drowned; They were rejected.* The passive indicates that the subject of the sentence under-goes the action rather than performs it.

See also ACTIVE AND PASSIVE; PARTICIPLES; SUBJUNCTIVE.

2. When two or more verbs are used in the same sentence, the time relation, or *sequence of tenses*, is important and sometimes troublesome. The verb in the subordinate clause might well follow the lead of the verb in the main clause:

> I remember that I owe him a favour.
> I remembered that I owed him a favour.

But if the two clauses refer to different times, the two verbs might be in different tenses:

> I remember that I once owed him a favour.
> I then remembered that I still owe him a favour.

I owed him a favour because he had helped me to find a place to stay.

In the third example here, the subordinate clause refers to a preceding event, and therefore has a verb in the past perfect tense.

A peculiarity of the English tense system is that when the main clause is in the future tense, the subordinate clause tends to have its verb in the present tense:

I shall repay the debt when I next see him.

When the subordinate clause expresses a permanent or universal truth, its verb is usually in the present tense even when the main verb is in the past tense:

Even then they knew that tides are caused by the moon.
As a child she was taught that honesty is the best policy.

According to the rules of sequence of tenses, *shall* becomes *should*; *will, would*; *can, could*; *may, might*: *They think they will win* becomes *They thought they would win*.

The *must* indicating necessity or obligation becomes *had to* or remains unchanged: *They think they must leave* becomes *They thought they had to/must leave*. The *must* of assumption or possibility is unchanged: *They think he must be guilty* becomes *They thought he must be guilty*.

Ought to and *used to* remain unchanged: *They think he ought to do it* becomes *They thought he ought to do it*.

Dare and *need*, if not followed by *to*, remain unchanged: *They think they needn't do it* becomes *They thought they needn't do it*. But when followed by *to*, *dare* and *need* change tense just like ordinary verbs: *They think they need to do it* becomes *They thought they needed to do it*.

When *should, would, could*, and *might* do not refer to past time, the sequence of tenses is optional. Idiom might favour a past or a present verb for the subordinate clause according to the construction: *I should imagine that she is here* (though *was* is possible); *I could swear she was here* (more likely than *is*); *Would you say that she is/was here?* (equally likely).

3. The present tense is often used to refer to future time, as in two of the examples already discussed: *She is flying to New York next week* and *I shall repay the debt when I next see him*. Radio and television announcers have been criticised for using the simple present tense when giving details of future programmes: *At 9.30 tonight, Robert Knight interviews the Home Secretary*. Purists apparently prefer *will interview* or *will be interviewing* here. But the simple present is a well-established way of referring to some definite future event — *She flies to New York next week* may in some contexts be just as appropriate as *She is flying* or *She will fly* or *She will be flying*. And in some cases the simple present seems clearly preferable to the alternatives:

In tonight's birthday tribute to Graham Greene on Radio 3, the late James Mason talks about the filming of 'Dr Fischer of Geneva'.

Surely this is less awkward than *? the late James Mason will be talking . . .* would be.

The present tense is also used to refer to past time: *Dickens is* ('was') *the greatest of the Victorian novelists*; *The weather report says* ('said' or 'has said') *that floods are expected*. Once again, radio and television have been criticised for taking liberties with this usage. Adopting the style of newspaper headlines, news readers now sometimes begin a news broadcast with 'headlines' of their own — couched for dramatic effect in the present tense:

The space shuttle returns safely . . . Australia win the toss and score 300 by tea . . . The Prime Minister hints at a new 'tax on wealth' . . .

So long as such constructions remain confined to headlines, it again seems unfair to object to them.

terminal, terminus Both *terminal* and *terminus* mean 'a station at the end (and beginning) of a route'. *Terminal* is usually used of airline buildings — those at airports that deal with arrivals and departures, and those within cities that provide services for passengers.

In British English, *terminus* is usually used of bus and rail stations. A rail *terminus* is a main-line station where trains terminate — in London, for example, this would refer to Victoria rather than Clapham Junction. A bus *terminus* is also the end (or beginning) of the line, but above all for *local* buses. A station where inter-city buses ('coaches') end or begin their runs may also be a *terminus*, but there is now a chance that it will be called, more glamorously, a *terminal*. So: in front of Victoria Station in London there is a *terminus* for local London buses; near Victoria Station is Victoria Coach Station, which is perhaps more likely to be called a *terminal* than a *terminus*.

In American English *terminus* is rare; if used at all it tends to refer to the towns, rather than the stations, at the end of transport routes. Major air, rail, and long-distance bus stations can all be called *terminals*.

Terminal has several other senses, of course — in the context of electrical circuits or of computer systems, for instance. It also functions as an adjective meaning 'at the end or boundary of anything, final'; and 'fatal': *a terminal illness*. And in informal or humorous usage it can mean 'utter or hopeless', as in *terminal laziness*.

The plural of *terminus* is much argued about; both the Latin plural *termini* (pronounced /-ī/) and the anglicised *terminuses* are acceptable.

terrible, terrific Many adjectives with unfavourable suggestions have come to be used as general terms of disapproval: *horrible*, *dreadful*, *frightful*, and so on. *Terrible* follows suit: *The film was terrible*. Uncharacteristically, however, *terrific* has come to be used as an adjective of approval: *The film was terrific*.

The words do have a meaning in common, however — 'very great', as in *a terrible lot to do*, *a terrific amount of work*. And the adverb forms, curiously, come together again, and can be used as intensifiers in both favourable and unfavourable contexts: *That was a terribly/terrifically boring film*; *That was a terrifically/terribly interesting film*. The nuances are slightly different in each case.

What is notably missing in these examples is anything of the original idea of *terror* — the Latin source, *terrere*, 'to frighten', seems to have lost all bearing on the meaning. In theory, it is true, *terrific* can still mean 'causing terror': *the terrific voice of his master*. But this use is now extremely rare. And if *terrible* were used in its place in such a context — *the terrible voice of his master* — it would almost certainly be understood in the sense of 'extremely ugly or unpleasant'. The old sense of 'causing terror' is now conveyed almost exclusively by *terrifying*.

Do keep your use of *terrible* and *terrific* within limits. Restrict the words to informal speech, and use them sparingly even then. There is something irritatingly childish about the words, especially when they are used to exaggerate the value of what is at best perhaps agreeable or disagreeable.

than 1. When *than* appears in a sentence, it is usually followed by a verb or at least an implied verb: *Joan works faster than Mike (does)*.

Than is a conjunction here. But it can sometimes be a preposition — that is, there is no verb or implied verb following: *It cost more than £100*;

The mystery guest was none other than Mick Jagger.

A common problem with *than* is whether the following pronoun is in the subject or object form. Should it be *than he* or *than him*? The traditional rule is quite simple: if there is no implied verb, *than* is a preposition, and takes the object form: *The mystery guest was none other than him*. If there is an implied verb, then *than* is a conjunction: add the implied verb mentally to the sentence, and that will decide the form of the pronoun. So:

> She treats you worse than I (= worse than I do).
> She treats you worse than me (= worse than she treats me).

The sentences have quite different meanings, and the difference would be blurred if the pronouns were misused. But in informal speech and writing, the form *?? She treats you worse than me* is used for the first as well as the second sense. And the form *?? Joan works faster than him* is widely used instead of the grammatically correct form *Joan works faster than he* (= than he works).

Unfortunately, the *than I* and *than he* forms here, which are correct, sound rather stilted, whereas the *than me* and *than him* forms, though sounding quite natural, are not strictly in keeping with good grammar (or at least, with an 18th-century 'rule' of grammar). To be both correct and natural, add the missing verb explicitly whenever you can:

> She treats you worse than I do.
> Joan works faster than he does.

The danger of ambiguity is more serious where the final pronoun is *you* (which remains unchanged in form whether subject or object) or where *than* is followed by a noun. The following examples are hopelessly ambiguous:

> *?* She treats me worse than you.
> *?* She treats me worse than Mary.

> *?* In a letter to the SDP leader, Dr David Owen, Mr Noel-Baker said that he agreed generally with the Government on domestic policy. He concluded: 'I find the Tories more credible than you.'
>
> – *The Observer*

Here again, it would be clearer to add the missing verbs (and other missing words):

> She treats me worse than you do/than she treats you.
> She treats me worse than Mary does/than she

treats Mary.

I find the Tories more credible than I find you/than you find them.

2. Strict grammar favours *Joan works faster than he* over **??** *Joan works faster than him*, but in one construction grammar always yields to idiom — *than whom*: *She is a writer than whom no one works faster*. This construction is so old-fashioned that it is now used only for humorous or other stylistic effects, but it is interesting to note that it often, as here, goes against the strict requirements of grammar. (Not that *than who* is any better: it would be quite unidiomatic.)

3. a. Take care not to lose the thread of an *as*-construction and use *than* mistakenly in place of *as* (or vice versa). The writer of the following example has made the wrong choice:

✗ The standards, which are accepted in Britain, allow for nearly twice the pressure in the gun barrel than do the equivalent British rules.
— *New Scientist*

What has happened here is that two possible patterns have been confused: *twice + as*, and *more + than*. The form *allow for more pressure in the gun barrel than. . .* or alternatively *allow for twice as much pressure in the gun barrel as do. . .* would have been perfectly correct.

b. *Than* is also often mistakenly used in place of *when*. This occurs in constructions after *hardly, barely*, and *scarcely*:

✗ Scarcely had he entered the room than the telephone rang.

Use *when* here, not *than*.

c. And *than* is sometimes mistakenly used in place of *to* after *superior, inferior, senior*, and *junior*:

✗ The modern piano is much superior in tone than the 18th-century instrument.

Use *to* here, not *than*.

4. Another fairly common error (in British though not in American English) is to introduce an unnecessary *what* after *than*:

✗ He looks much happier than what he did yesterday.

This combination should be avoided except in very informal English. There is no *what* in the correct form: *He looks much happier than he did yesterday*.

See also DIFFERENT; OTHER THAN; RATHER.

thankfully See HOPEFULLY.

that **1.** *that* vs *which*. Consider these two sentences:

The family that/which prays together stays together.
The family, which is the basic unit of human society, is losing its appeal.

In the first sentence, either *that* or *which* is suitable. The relative clause is here a restrictive clause — that is, it defines the noun *family*, specifying the kind of family in question. (See RESTRICTIVE AND NONRESTRICTIVE CLAUSES.) The clause usually has no commas before or after.

In the second of the specimen sentences, only *which* is suitable. The relative clause is here a nonrestrictive clause — that is, it simply gives some incidental information about the noun *family*. It is usually cordoned off by commas, to show that it is not really an essential part of the sentence. In the following quotation, *which* rather than *that* should have been used to introduce the nonrestrictive clause:

?? It was 'Roy Hobbs Day', that had been in the making since two weeks ago, when Max Mercy printed in his column: 'Roy Hobbs, El Swatto, has been ixnayed on a pay raise.'
— Bernard Malamud (U.S.),
The Natural

In restrictive clauses, the choice between *that* and *which* is not a completely random one. There is occasionally a preference for one or the other according to the construction, though the 'rules' here are far too complicated to be worth repeating fully. *Which* is probably more widely used nowadays (though some old-fashioned usage experts urge *that* wherever possible, in order to keep a neat distinction between restrictive and nonrestrictive clauses).

If there is already a *which* in the sentence, then *that* tends to be preferred: *Which is the horse that won last time?* And vice versa: *Is that the horse which won last time? We ate that which was put before us.*

So I will continue for the time being to temper my indulgence in the best things of life with a modicum of that kind of activity which provides stimulation as well as interest.
— Sir Anthony Parsons, *The Times*

These books remind one of the blood that is shared, as well as that which was spilled in an unnecessary war.
— Nicholas Rankin,
The Literary Review

And there does seem to be a slight preference for *that* in three important constructions:
● in clauses relating to the pronouns *anything*, *everything*, *nothing*, and *something*: *Can you think of anything that has to be finished before the weekend?*
● in clauses following a superlative: *the most versatile computer that has ever been produced in a British factory.*
● in relative clauses following *it is* constructions: *It was the dog that died, not the man.*

2. *that* vs *who*. It is quite acceptable, in certain restrictive clauses, to use *that* in reference to human beings, particularly where it replaces *whom*: *The brother that/whom you're referring to lives in Perth.* It is slightly less natural, though still acceptable, to use *that* in place of *who*: *The brother that/who lives in Perth is a dentist.*

Some people still object to the use of *that* in reference to a specific person, on the ground that it sounds disrespectful. There is something in this objection, but it surely does not apply when the preceding noun refers to people in general or a type of person or a vague group of people, rather than to individually specified people. It can sound much more natural, in fact, to use *that* than to use *who* or *whom*.

3. *omitting or retaining that.* The relative pronoun *that* (or *whom*) can sometimes be omitted — specifically, when *that* serves as the object rather than subject of the relative clause: *The car (that) I saw has been towed away.*

As a conjunction, *that* can be omitted more easily still, after various simple verbs such as *say*, *think*, *tell*, *feel*, *know*, *suppose*, *admit*, *realise*, and *believe*: *I thought (that) the car had been towed away, but now I'm told (that) it was in fact stolen.* In the following quotation, *that* is omitted three times:

> At first I thought he referred to some sort of medical treatment, harking back to the conversation of the chaplains the night before, then realised the question had something to do with reading. I had to admit I did not take any digests. Bithel seemed disappointed at this answer.
> – Anthony Powell,
> *The Valley of Bones*

Of course, this omission of *that* is not appropriate in all constructions, or after all verbs: We can say *He suggested a vote be taken* but probably not *? He urged a vote be taken* or *? The silence of the committee members suggested little opposition would be raised to his other proposals.* And in extremely formal usage, even the fully

idiomatic examples quoted above might be frowned on, though they are elsewhere regarded as quite acceptable by all but the most pedantic.

In four special cases, however, it is unwise to omit the *that* even when natural idiom allows it.

First, when the clause is remote from the verb, *that* is best retained (or repeated or reinstated) in order to pick up the syntax properly again:

> Do you know for certain that she was out last night?

> I thought, in my usual unsuspecting way, that I could trust you.

> But Robert ... said he could not bear to part with the boy, and that the pair of them would lodge with Monsieur and Madame Fiat.
> – Daphne du Maurier,
> *The Glass Blowers*

This last example is open to the objection that it violates the parallelism of the sentence as a whole. The author would have done better to write *But Robert ... said that he could not ..., and that the pair ...*

Take care, however, not to insert a second *that* when only one relative clause is involved. Such overconscientiousness is a common error: × *I thought that, since we've been friends for so long, that I could trust you.*

Secondly, the omission of *that* might momentarily give the reader or listener the impression that a different construction is being used. For example, *? I propose a toast be drunk* might initially be understood as *I propose a toast,* where the object of *propose* is a simple noun rather than a clause.

Or consider this example:

> *?* I do not for a moment believe all those elaborate they-do-this-so-we-do-that scenarios the double-dome strategists expect these military men to put into effect could happen: a nuclear war wouldn't be so considerately tidy and tame.
> – Meg Greenfield (U.S.), *Newsweek*

The omission of the conjunction *that* after *believe* leads the reader into thinking that the construction is *I do not believe all those scenarios* whereas the construction intended is in fact *I do not believe that all those scenarios could happen.* (The further omission of the relative pronoun *that* after *scenarios* in the quotation only succeeds in making the sentence even more difficult to understand.) If there is any danger of leading your reader astray in this way, then the conjunction *that* should be retained.

The extreme case is the rather old-fashioned type of sentence that begins with a *that*-clause: *That he is tall is true.* Here the word *that* must be retained, if only to show that the sentence continues after the word *tall*. If the sentence is reformulated, the *that* can be omitted but is typically retained: *It is true (that) she is tall.*

Thirdly, if there is any danger of ambiguity caused by leaving out *that*, then again it should be retained. For example, the sentences ✗ *She said several times she had lost hope* and ✗ *I felt sure last Friday the sale was going through* are needlessly ambiguous. The meaning can be made clear by inserting a *that* either before or after the phrases *several times* and *last Friday.*

Fourthly, you cannot usually omit the conjunction *that* in so-called appositional clauses. For example, in the sentence *The fact that we discussed it yesterday is irrelevant*, the conjunction *that* cannot be left out; when *that* is a relative pronoun, however, as in *The fact that we discussed yesterday is irrelevant*, it can be left out — in this example at any rate. In the first example, *that we discussed it yesterday* is the fact itself; in the second example, *that we discussed yesterday* merely identifies the fact.

● *Recommendation* In all but the most formal contexts, it is quite acceptable to omit the conjunction *that* where you can, as a way of streamlining your sentences. However, if there is any danger of losing the thread of your grammatical construction or of lapsing into ambiguity, or if it helps the rhythm of the sentence, then the *that* should be retained.

4. *that as adverb — using it or avoiding it.* The use of *that* as an adverb in the sense of 'so, to the extent' is often heard in dialect, but is unacceptable in standard English: ✗ *He's that sure of himself that he never listens to criticism.* As an adverb in the sense of 'as that, to that degree or amount', it sometimes attracts criticism too: ? *A car that old is a bad risk*; ? *If it costs that much, you should think again.* The more formal way of wording such sentences would be with *so*, or in this pattern: *A car as old as that is a bad risk*; *If it costs as much as that, you should think again.* But the shorter version is so widespread today, and so harmless, that it is fast becoming fully acceptable. It is difficult to think of a more convenient wording for sentences such as *If you fall behind, you will just have to work that much harder to catch up* or *It was about that wide and that long.*

Rather stronger exception can be taken to the negative forms *not that* and *not all that*: ? *I'm really not that interested in your problems*;

? *She's not all that fond of me, is she*? The *not that* and *not all that* are simply colloquial substitutes for *not very* or *not especially*, and are unsuitable for formal usage. However, the constructions are more acceptable where they are used for strong emphasis: *He's well off, but he's not **that** rich!*

5. *at that.* This idiom, originally American, is very useful but is still considered somewhat loose in British English. It can mean 'furthermore' or 'into the bargain': ? *The opera was given in a warehouse — and a dirty warehouse at that.* Do not use the phrase in formal speech and writing. Another of the meanings of *at that* is something like 'all things considered' or 'after all':

? I sometimes think how poor I am. Then I look at my yacht and swimming pool, and reflect that maybe I'm not so poor at that.

Again, this use should be limited to informal contexts.

See also AND ALL; AND WHICH; BUT **6**; THIS **3**; WHATEVER; WHICH; WHO.

---

the **1.** The pronunciation of *the* presents a few difficulties. Broadly, the rule is this: if the following word begins with a vowel-sound (regardless of its spelling), *the* is pronounced /thee/; before consonants and the 'glides' or 'weak' consonants — /h, w, y/ — *the* is pronounced /thə/.

The traditional warning was always against the use of the weak /thə/ before vowels. Today, perhaps in reaction to this old schoolroom warning, the opposite tendency has developed: the unvarying use of /thee/. It has attracted considerable criticism recently — it tends to sound stiff and overmethodical, or else crass and pretentious, if used in such an indiscriminate way.

However, /thee/ is permissible before consonants in certain cases. Before a weakly pronounced *h* (usually when the *h*-syllable is unstressed), the strong /thee/ is probably acceptable, though not really advisable; so /thee/ *hotel* and /thee/ *habitual liar,* but not ✗ /thee/ *hostel* or ✗ /thee/ *horrible liar.* And when some special emphasis is wanted, as in a contrast, *the* is given the strong /thee/ pronunciation, whether before a vowel or a consonant:

You're not *the* Robert Wilson?
I said *a* supreme achievement, not *the* supreme achievement.

See A, AN **1** and **2** for a more detailed discussion of this subject.

2. A single *the* can be used to refer to several elements listed together:

The cat, dog, and parrot seem to get along very well with one another.

Further *the*'s before *dog* and *parrot* are optional here — though you cannot insert one without the other.

When the elements are clearly part of a single concept, then no subsequent *the*'s can be inserted:

The proud soldier waved the red, white, and blue flag above his head.
The Oxford and Cambridge boat race will take place on the 23rd this year.

Conversely, when the elements have to be considered singly, it is advisable to insert *the* each time:

The red, the white, and the blue cloths and napkins are kept in separate cupboards.
The Oxford and the Cambridge trials will take place on the 22nd and the 23rd.

This repetition of *the* may sound rather stiff, but it does help to avoid ambiguity.

3. There is no consensus on the use of *the* in the names of newspapers, ships, and so on. Some publishers prefer to consider the *the* an intrinsic part of the title — whether their convention is to use italics or quotation marks for the title — and some relegate the *the* to a subordinate position:

I first read about it in 'The Sunday Times' (or: the 'Sunday Times').
I first read about it in *The Sunday Times* (or: the *Sunday Times*).

Note, however, that some official titles do not include *the*. The British periodical formerly called *The New Scientist* is now called simply *New Scientist,* and if the word *the* is used, it should usually take a small *t* and should not be in italics. Similarly, Handel called his oratorio *Messiah*, not ✗ *The Messiah*; and the ship *R.M.S. Titanic* should be referred to as the *Titanic* rather than as ✗ *The Titanic*.

Even where the *the* is part of the official title, it again has to be subordinated if the title serves an adjectival role, prefacing some other noun: the *the* now refers primarily to the other noun, and so should not be in italics or within the quotation marks:

If you ask me, the *Sunday Times* crossword is compiled by a sadist.

4. As with *A,* when *The* is the first word of a literary, musical, or other artistic work, it is often omitted if its presence would interfere with the flow of the sentence.

My favourite novel is Henry James's *Portrait of a Lady.*
Did you borrow my *Shorter Oxford English Dictionary?*

This is now a widely accepted convention in publishing, though some purists still frown on it, and would reinstate the *The* as the first word of the title in both of the examples above. There are a few other contexts where *the* is sometimes omitted:

● before established pairs or lists of nouns:

(The) President and (the) Congress are once again at odds.
You must allow lawyer and client to discuss their case in private.

● when the noun is in apposition to a person's name — that is, when placed directly after the name to explain it:

Jane Grigson, (the) author of several outstanding cookery books, has agreed to join the panel of judges.

However, when the elements are reversed, as in ? *Author Jane Grigson has agreed*, the *the* should be reinstated in formal writing.

● with nouns naming 'unique' offices after such verbs as *become, elect, appoint*, or after *as* and *of*: So:

in her role as/of captain of this team (the team has only one captain)
He became (the) Prime Minister at the age of 46 (there is only one PM).
She became MP for Bermondsey at the age of 40 (there is only one such MP at any one time).

But not:

✗ She became MP at the age of 40 (there are hundreds of MPs).

● before *Synod*, *Conference*, and similar nouns referring to major meetings, organisations, or the like:

? That is a matter for Conference to decide.
? Synod will debate the divorce-question tomorrow.

This last usage sometimes attracts criticism. It suggests perhaps an unwarranted sense of the organisation's unique importance, and it rather smugly represents an insider's view, as though excluding the world at large.

See also YE.

then Careful speakers of English sometimes object to the use of *then* as an adjective, as in *the then Prime Minister*, preferring such phrases as *the Prime Minister at that time*. However, its succinctness is a virtue that perhaps outweighs its awkwardness and grammatical impropriety; the construction is now firmly established, particularly in political journalism, and it can safely be used even in quite formal contexts.

thence, thither *Thither* is archaic, except in the phrase *hither and thither,* and should not be used except in official or jocular contexts. A simple *there* is usually enough; if ambiguity threatens — *? The drive there is tree-lined all the way* — then replace *there* with *to it* rather than *thither.*

Thence, though now very formal, survives in its three distinct senses:
— 'from that place':

I drove to the Ritz to fetch Phoebe, and thence to the banquet in Whitehall.

— 'from that time':

She lived the life of a princess in Moscow until 1917; thence the life of an impoverished emigrée in Zurich. (*Thenceforth* or *thenceforward/s* is perhaps preferable here; *thereafter* is clearly preferable.)

— 'from that source; as a result':

Churchill observed the Soviets' westward advance; thence his view that the seeds of future conflict were being sown.

See also ARCHAISMS; HENCE; WHENCE.

there is 1. The phrase *there is/are* (or *there was/ were* or *there seems/seem*) is a useful way of indicating the existence or location of something or introducing a topic for discussion. But it should be used sparingly. George Orwell, for example, disliked its timid tone and its impersonality, and preferred a stronger construction with an active verb. Instead of *There's apple pie for dessert,* you can often express the same idea more vividly by saying *We're having apple pie for dessert* or *I've baked an apple pie for dessert.*

2. It ought to be clear when to say *there is/was* and when to say *there are/were*: when the noun following is in the singular, *there is* is used; when the noun following is plural, *there are* is used.

However, it is not always this way in practice. First, if the plural noun is thought of as a single unit, usage favours *there is* over *there are*: *There is £4 in my account.* Then, in ordinary conversation, it is very common to hear such sentences

as *?? There's apples for dessert* or *?? There's four of us at home.*

?? I haven't said a word to you about a psychiatrist. In fact, I haven't got a great deal of time for them, myself. They all hold different theories. There's hardly two who would treat a patient in the same way.
— Dr Jarvis, in Muriel Spark's *The Mandelbaum Gate*

The reason for this common error is probably that it is so much quicker and easier to say *there's* than *there are* or *there're*. In formal speech, and in writing of course, such faulty constructions should be avoided. So too with *here's* and *where's*: *?? Here's the apples you ordered*; *?? Where's the flowers I sent you?*

But what about a construction such as *? There is an apple and a pear for dessert*? It probably reflects the tendency for the verb to agree with what is nearest it. The plural would be used in *There are apples and a pear for dessert,* and the singular would tend to return in *There is an apple and pears for dessert.* Similarly:

We went to parties with other English children, and for picnics to beautiful formal Mogul gardens, with sheets of water reflecting domes and minarets. Here there was no dust, no dancing horses, no hyenas running near the camp in the early morning.
— Lord Butler, *The Art of the Possible*

The interior had been furnished by Lingard when he had built the house for his adopted daughter and her husband, and it had been furnished with reckless prodigality. There was an office desk, a revolving chair, bookshelves, a safe: all to humour the weakness of Almayer.

— Joseph Conrad, *An Outcast of the Islands*

Some language experts now regard *there is* as a fixed, unvarying idiom that can precede a (plural) list of nouns so long as the first noun is in the singular: *In any church there is typically a nave, aisles, pews, and an apse.*

Still, the constructions with a singular verb might attract criticism from old-fashioned purists. If you are still hesitant, you can often avoid the difficulty altogether by using a more active construction in preference: *We've got an apple and some pears for dessert.*

3. *There,* as used in impersonal constructions, is not restricted to such phrases as *there is, there seem to be, there happen to be,* and so on. More

active verbs can be used: *There came a great spider*; *Beyond the hill, there lies some fresh, green land,* and so on. But such constructions tend to sound old-fashioned today, and should be kept for contexts that are either very formal or else deliberately jocular. A sentence such as *There comes a time in a man's life when he has to take a stand* requires a solemn occasion — or a mock-solemn occasion — to sound appropriate.

An interesting characteristic of such constructions, pointed out by the American linguist Dwight Bolinger, is that they are used to 'present' to the hearer what is already 'on stage' or is coming 'on stage' rather than what is going 'off stage'. People will say *At nine o'clock there remained/arrived 15 guests* more readily than *? At nine o'clock there left 15 guests.*

they, them, their 1. English is unfortunate in lacking a third-person singular personal pronoun that can refer to a human being regardless of sex: *he, him*, and *his* usually refer exclusively to a man or a boy (or a male animal); *she, her* and *hers* to a woman or girl (or a female animal, or sometimes a ship, car, or the like). When you want to refer to one human being, whether male or female, there are various strategies available to you:

a. If the winner is under 18, he or she will not receive the money directly, but a trust will be opened in his or her name.

b. If the winner is under 18, he will not receive the money directly, but a trust will be opened in his name.

c. If you win but are under 18, you will not receive the money directly, but a trust will be opened in your name.

d. If the winner is under 18, the money will be held in trust rather than awarded directly.

e. ? If the winner is under 18, they will not receive the money directly, but a trust will be opened in their name.

All of these can be criticised in one way or another.

a. he or she/his or hers — these are awkward to say, sound pedantic, and take up considerable space. (See HE OR SHE.)

b. he/his — this is often considered unfair to women nowadays, even though no one is really likely to misunderstand it. (See HE, HIM, HIS.) Some feminists would use *she* and *her* instead of *he* and *his* here. This may 'redress the balance', but it creates a new problem.

c. you — a temporary solution at best. Although the second-person pronoun is becoming increasingly popular in documents and textbooks (see YOU, YOUR, YOURS), it is of limited use. For one thing, its tone is sometimes inappropriately intimate or hectoring. For another, as soon as one starts referring to past times or distant places or anything in fact that does not involve one's listeners or readers directly, then it becomes very awkward, if not impossible, to substitute the second-person for the third: *? In the 18th century, of course, you would have no anaesthetic before you underwent your operation.*

d. avoiding pronouns altogether — well and good, but if you keep avoiding tricky pronouns in this way, your language is in danger of sounding very stiff or artificial.

e. they/their — but, the standard objection goes, *they/their* are plural pronouns, and the preceding noun in this case, *winner*, is in the singular.

(It is a pity that one other common strategy is not available here, that of making all the relevant nouns and pronouns plural. The most acceptable construction of all would be: *If the winners are under 18, they will not receive the money directly, but trusts will be opened in their names*. But in our specimen sentence, unfortunately, there is only one winner.)

The objection to *e.* is a very strong one. The principle of agreement is one of the basic principles of English: a singular noun should take a singular verb and singular pronouns and singular possessive adjectives. None the less, throughout the history of English, *they* and associated forms have been used as though singular, standing in place of *anybody, everybody, each, someone,* and so on — and even in place of phrases containing a noun, such as *that person* or *any teacher*:

Each of them should ... make themself ready.
— William Caxton,
Sonnes of Aymon (1489)

Now this king did keepe a great house, that everie body might come and take their meat freely.
— Philip Sidney, *Arcadia* (1580)

Now leaden slumber with life's strength doth fight,
And every one to rest themselves betake ...
— Shakespeare,
The Rape of Lucrece (1594)

Every body fell a laughing, as how could they help it.
— Henry Fielding, *Tom Jones* (1749)

A person can't help their birth.
— William Makepeace Thackeray,
Vanity Fair (1847)

Now, nobody does anything well that they cannot help doing.
— John Ruskin,
The Crown of Wild Olive (1866)

If that person gets sick ... they are in the hospital for more than two weeks.
— John F. Kennedy (U.S.),
The New Republic

It is therefore the first duty of any teacher of literature to give their pupils a chance of enjoying it.
— Lord David Cecil, letter to *The Times*

The assumption now is that no one will read it, and wouldn't understand or enjoy it if they did.
— Philip Larkin, *Required Writing*

The poem exists if everyone who finds it finds themselves in it and becomes absorbed in it.
— Professor John Bayley, *The Listener*

It is a tendency very difficult to resist, though most careful users of English do still try to resist it. But they too sometimes drop their guard, especially when the subject is *everybody, nobody*, or *none*, and above all, when more than one clause is involved: *Everybody came to the party last night, didn't they? Everybody came to the party last night, and they enjoyed themselves.*

It is worth remembering that the second-person *you*, today the standard form for both singular and plural, was formerly used only as the plural, with *thou* for the singular. Words do change their meaning or range over time — even words as simple and fundamental as pronouns. It may well be that in a hundred years' time, *they/them/theirs* will be fully and unthinkingly accepted as singular common-gender pronouns, not just as plurals. But they are not accepted in that way yet.

See also AGREEMENT; ME; EVERYBODY; PLURALS Part II.

2. Idiom tends to favour such constructions as *?That's them at last, ? Are these them?*, and so on. Given strict grammar, *they* is meant to be used rather than *them*, though the first example can hardly be reformulated as *?? That's they at last* or *?? These are they at last.* For a fuller discussion, see IT'S ME; ME; PRONOUNS.

3. In dialects, especially in America, *them* is used instead of the adjective *those*: *?? Hand me some more of them beans.* It is sometimes used

in this way too, for jocular effect, by speakers of standard English, but the usage is of course nonstandard. This nonstandard *them* is often reinforced by *there* — *?? There's gold in them there hills* — perhaps because *them* by itself lacks the meaning of 'distance' that *there* has. Constructions like *?? them beans there* are also used.

See also THIS HERE.

they say   Such sentences as *They say it's going to be a wet summer* sometimes attract criticism from pedantic users of English. 'And who exactly might *they* be?' is the complaint.

But how else can we express unattributed rumours or theories that lack a specified source? To write *It is said that it's going to be a wet summer* is to be laughably formal or old-fashioned (and might, after all, invite the question: 'Said by whom?'). And you cannot really write *One says it's going to be a wet summer* (on the model of the French *On dit ...*), because English *one*, unlike French *on*, generally implies that the speaker is included in the subject of the sentence.

In other words, *they* has come unavoidably to serve as an indefinite pronoun (excluding both speaker and hearer), and its usefulness now far outweighs any doubts about its acceptability.

this   **1.** The use of *this* as an adverb in the sense of 'to this extent, so, as this' is discouraged by purists. It tends to occur most often in negative or interrogative constructions, though it does sometimes occur in positive statements:

? I was told you were tall, but not this tall!
? Is it always this crowded on market-day?
? A play this silly is sure to be a hit.

Rather less exception is taken when the adjective following *this* is *much* or *many* —

? He never dreamt he'd get this much support

— but such constructions are again best avoided in formal contexts. The formally correct alternative to *? this much support* is *so much support* or, even better, *as much support as this.*

Compare THAT 4.

2. *This* (or *that*) has also been criticised when introducing a subordinate phrase or clause:

? VAT is up, personal allowances are down — · this in spite of the government's pledge to increase the worker's spending-power.
? Speak of the crusades, and you are speaking of pillage, massacre, spoliation — and this in the name of the gentle Saviour.

The *this* or *and this* in each case is virtually redundant, it is argued, and tends to sound arch or affected. Yet it can serve a useful purpose, gathering up or summarising a preceding list of items before discussing them jointly. Before using it, however, remember the traditional criticism, and pause to consider whether the *this* really is necessary.

3. Elsewhere *this* (or *these*) as a pronoun is often used when *she, him, it,* and so on (or *they* or *them*) would be preferable:

> ? Her own favourite among her many novels is *Hart at Bay,* for this is the one most closely modelled on her own life.

Good usage would prefer *it* or *this book* to *this.* But *this* (or *that*) is easier to stress than *it,* and so *this* or *that* may be retained if special emphasis is desired. The following example, however, cannot really be defended in this way:

> ? Queen Anne was succeeded by her second cousin, George I; this was an ill-equipped monarch, barely able to speak English, and little interested in his subjects.

Preferable to *this* would be *this king* or simply *he.*

4. The use of *this* (or *that*) as a pronoun referring to a previous sentence or clause is also sometimes discouraged:

> It emerged yesterday that prices rose a full one per cent last month — this has given the opposition further ammunition for the economic debate next week.

Those objecting to this usage would prefer *this news* or *this price-rise* to the pronoun *this.* The objection seems needlessly restrictive, and would do away with a convenient shorthand means of summarising foregoing ideas. As a relative pronoun, *which* serves much the same purpose: *He's just got remarried, which is very nice*; the objection would presumably apply here too, again depriving English of a very useful resource. Whatever merit the objection may have is more than outweighed by the value of these broader functions of *this* (or *that*) and *which.* The objection should be disregarded.

Remember too that *this* can refer to a following clause, not simply to a preceding one:

> Then conquer we must, for our cause it is just —
> And this be our motto, 'In God is our trust!'
> – Francis Scott Key (U.S.),
> 'The Star-Spangled Banner' (1814)

5. *This* (and sometimes *these*) is used very freely in spoken, and sometimes written, English without any previous mention of what *this* might refer to: ? *I met this man, didn't I, and we went to this restaurant* ... Using *this* in that way is not recommended.

> Roy turned into a winding dirt road and before long they came to this deserted beach, enclosed in a broken arc of white birches.
> – Bernard Malamud (U.S.),
> *The Natural*

6. It is possible to use either *this* or *that* in responses:

> 'Our side is good.' 'This/That is true.' 'But their side is better.' 'This/That is the problem.'

While nobody objects to *that* here, some people object — often with surprising strength of feeling — to *this.*

7. The phrase *this is it* has recently come into extremely widespread use, typically as a way of agreeing with or summing up a statement — often a depressing statement:

> 'We're a good team, but we keep missing our chances.' 'This is it.'

The phrase is in fact a useful and unpretentious alternative to *I quite agree* or *Exactly*, but it is used with such irritating frequency now, especially by less well-educated speakers, that it has attracted the attention both of language critics and of comedians. Use it sparingly, if at all. The phrase *That's it* or *That's just it* is better.

See also SORT OF 2.

this here, that there   *This here* and *that there* have long been used in regional varieties of English, British as well as American, as demonstrative phrases: ?? *This here coffee's cold*; ?? *That there dog is looking for trouble.* These constructions may well be usefully emphatic (they parallel the French pronouns *celui-ci, ceci* and *celui-la, cela*), but remain unacceptable in standard English. You can of course say *this coffee here* and *that dog there* instead.

Note that the plurals of these nonstandard constructions are not parallel. The plural of *this here* is *these here*, but the plural of *that there* is usually not × *those there* but *them there:* ?? *There's gold in them there hills!* That is because the nonstandard plural of *that* is *them.*

those   This is often used redundantly as a demonstrative adjective:

? Will those councillors in favour of the proposal please vote now.

This construction seems to be a fusion of two simpler forms; one using *those* as a pronoun — *Will those in favour* . . . — and the other using *the* (or nothing) before the noun: *Will (the) councillors in favour* . . . Perhaps *those* came to be favoured because it can be stressed more easily than *the*. At all events, the construction *Will (all) those councillors in favour* is so widespread now that it passes unnoticed by all but the purists. For their sake, it is still worth avoiding the controversial form in formal contexts.

Of course *those councillors* is a perfectly permissible combination in other contexts: *Those councillors are in favour, and these are against.*

though See ALTHOUGH.

through 1. The spellings *thro'* or *thru'* (often without the apostrophe) should not be used today except in very informal writing.

In American English, however, one of the words for *motorway* is *thruway*; this is its official spelling, adopted to save space on signs.

2. The Americans have an extremely useful function for the preposition *through*: *The project lasts from March through September.* The cumbersome equivalent in British English is *The project lasts from March up to and including September* or *The project lasts from March until the end of September* or *The project lasts from March to September inclusive.* The use of *to* (or *through to*) without elaboration is ambiguous in such contexts, failing to make clear whether September is included or not.

Unfortunately, the economical use of *through* is still regarded outside North America as an Americanism.

3. Various modern uses of *through* — again originating in America — are still not considered standard in British English. First, in the literal sense of 'finished': *Are you through with the phone yet?* Secondly, 'finished' in an extended and colloquial sense — 'ruined, having no more chance of success': *She's through financially.* Finally, 'finished' in a more extended sense still — 'having no further dealings': *I'm through with that woman! She and I are through!*

thus 1. Care is needed in the placing of *thus* in a sentence. It tends to sound rather inelegant at the beginning of a sentence, and many purists reject it in favour of *therefore, accordingly, and so,* or *consequently.* There can be no blanket prohibi-

tion, however; in fact, the harsh monosyllable and the unrhythmical pause that follows it are often dramatically effective in capturing the attention before stating an important conclusion:

Let us . . . tear our pleasures with rough strife
Thorough the iron gates of life:
Thus, though we cannot make our sun
Stand still, yet we will make him run.
— Andrew Marvell,
'To His Coy Mistress' (c. 1652)

2. *Thus* is occasionally followed by inverted word-order, as in *Thus did we triumph.*

Thus do newcomers to *The Times,* for example, learn that in Printing House Square the spelling of *recognise* is *recognize.*
— Keith Waterhouse, *Daily Mirror Style*

Such inversion is clearly old-fashioned, though it can — as here — be used to good effect.

3. *Thus* is an adverb. The formation ?? *thusly,* now quite common in jocular American usage, is therefore a totally unnecessary elaboration:

?? Kris Kristofferson describes her thusly:
'She's still sexy in a strange way . . .'
— *Boston Herald American* (U.S.)

It should of course be avoided in formal usage, unless some particular arch effect is intended.

titillate, titivate To *titillate* comes from the Latin *titillare,* 'to tickle'. Like *tickle,* it means 'to produce a tingling or itching sensation, by touching or stroking lightly'. Nowadays it is most often used figuratively, in connection with exciting the mind or 'tickling the fancy', and means 'to stimulate pleasantly': *The child's clowning titillated my sense of humour; Her vanity was titillated by his effusive flattery.*

Contemporary Americans are less stifled. Their affluent economy, selling them things they don't need but can't do without, can survive only by titillating fantasy and achieving, once money has changed hands, its instantaneous realisation — the willing of fantasy into reality.
— Peter Conrad, *The Observer*

In some contexts the word is used intransitively to mean 'to excite mild sexual pleasure'; the related noun is *titillation:*

This may be true, but 'Portnoy' remains the only novel in which Roth's contorted genius managed to shed its inhibitions. With the case of Nathan Zuckerman, the self-revelation exhausts its power to titillate or scandalise, and the reader starts looking for the artistic content of the work, not the symbols, the decor, so much as the phrasing, the responsiveness.

– Martin Amis, *The Observer*

So long as Vanessa put up with his caprices, showed him affection, copied his ideas, and took his advice seriously, he could indulge himself in the titillations of her seductiveness.
– Professor Irvin Ehrenpreis (U.S.),
Swift: The Man, His Works, and The Age

On the whole the word and its derivatives now have negative connotations. *Titillation* suggests flightiness, superficiality, and self-indulgence. It often suggests immediate enjoyment with the sacrifice of good sense or morality: *Some people are titillated by reading about rape.*

To titivate is sometimes confused with *to titillate*. The word was once *tidivate* and seems to be a blend of *tidy* and *cultivate*. It means 'to tidy, pretty up, smarten up, preen', and is usually used in the pattern *to titivate oneself*: *We'll be late for the party — she's still in her room titivating herself.* However, such a sentence is almost certain to be used in a self-conscious way.

Titivate is sometimes spelt *tittivate*, but this change is not recommended.

to   The tiny word *to* has so many functions in English that it can easily clutter a text if left unchecked:

?? With regard to your apparent need to understand every single computer-term that happens to come to your attention, you really ought to try to learn to refer to a dictionary rather than always coming over to my desk and expecting me to explain the meaning to you.

This plague of *to*'s can be kept under control by careful rewording: a *have to* can become a *must*, a *happen to* can simply be omitted, and so on. But take care not to go to the other extreme and leave out an essential *to* for fear of overcrowding the sentence:

× Please put your mind to what the author could be referring here.
× We're quite baffled as to whom it is addressed.

These should read: *be referring to here* and *is addressed to*. The presence of an earlier *to* in each

sentence is no reason for omitting the later one: the earlier *to* cannot serve the two distinct purposes in each case.

See also DIFFERENT; SPLIT INFINITIVE; TRY AND; WHAT **5**.

till   See UNTIL.

tolerance, toleration   In most contexts, there is little danger of confusing these two words. *Tolerance* principally means 'the capacity to tolerate', and *toleration* 'the action of tolerating'. So: *His tolerance was amply proved by his toleration of John's bad temper.*

However, there is sometimes a grey area, in which either word sounds and is acceptable: *In not leaving the room at once he showed a certain tolerance/toleration.* The distinction here is very fine: perhaps between a general or permanent disposition (*tolerance*) and a specific willingness on this one occasion (*toleration*).

Tolerance has a number of specialised meanings, not covered by *toleration*. It can mean 'the acceptable leeway or deviation from a standard or specified value': *This gauge is engineered to a tolerance of less than one hundredth of a centimetre*. It can mean 'the capacity to endure': *He took painkillers only when he reached the limit of his tolerance*. And it can mean 'the capacity to resist potentially harmful substances': *His tolerance for alcohol is not what it was.*

Toleration, too, has a specialised meaning — 'the official recognition of the right to hold dissenting opinions, especially on religion': *The national constitution lays down the principle of religious toleration.*

Interestingly enough, the form *intolerance* seems to serve as the opposite of both *tolerance* and *toleration*.

too   **1.** As an adverb placed directly in front of the adjective or adverb it governs, *too* is the commonest way of conveying the idea of excess: *These shoes are too big for me*; *You're driving too slowly.*

In usages that depart from such straightforward examples, *too* can present a number of problems.

a. *Too* sometimes replaces *so* or *very* in affected colloquial usage: *? Oh, your poodle is too charming!* This should be avoided in formal speech and writing.

b. *Too* should not be used to govern absolute adjectives and adverbs, such as *perfectly*, *exhausted* and *unique*. You cannot really say *?? His story is too unique to be believed* any more than you can say *?? His story is more unique than* *yours.* See ADJECTIVES 3; PERFECT; UNIQUE.

c. Similarly, *too* cannot be used appropriately with certain past participles; namely, those that cannot take *very* as an intensifier. Just as you cannot easily say *?? very maligned* and *?? very disliked* (use *much maligned* and *greatly disliked* instead), so you cannot easily say *?? too maligned* and *?? too disliked.* See VERY.

d. When *too* modifies an adjective, that adjective should be placed after the noun it qualifies: *The luxury edition is too expensive for me; The luxury edition, too expensive for regular customers, was finally bought by a wealthy American collector.*

When the adjective is used attributively — that is, when it comes before the noun it modifies — *too* is best avoided. Four hundred years ago, Shakespeare made Hamlet say: *Oh that this too too solid flesh would melt . . . .* Today we would be more likely to speak of *this excessively solid flesh* or perhaps *over-solid flesh.*

The best solution is often to rearrange the sentence altogether. *? The accident was caused by a too-sharp application of the brakes* is very ungainly: *by an excessively sharp application* is preferable, and *by too sharp an application* is also possible. But better still would be a sentence reconstructed along these lines: *The accident occurred because the brakes were applied too sharply.*

2. Considerable care must be taken when using *too* in negative constructions.

a. Statements or commands containing *too* are often little more than tautologies. If someone says *? Don't take it too much to heart,* or *? Not too many potatoes for me, please,* you might be tempted to reply *Well obviously not!* Such constructions probably developed through a blend of two related statements such as *I don't want many potatoes* and *You are giving me too many potatoes.* Although well-established idioms now, sentences of this kind will be avoided by careful speakers.

b. The phrase *not too* is being used increasingly in place of *not very* or *not entirely: ? Her performance during rehearsals was not too convincing, but she brought it off perfectly on the opening night.*

> *?* Over the last fortnight, people have done just that. Business, throughout the vast LA basin, has been terrible. And last week's burst of advertising was not too successful.
> – William Scobie *The Observer*

Formal usage still requires something like *was not very convincing/successful* or *was not entirely*

convincing/successful here.

c. A further argument against the use of *not too* in the sense of 'not very' is the danger of ambiguity: *? There was not too much interest in his proposals* Is *too* here to be understood as 'very' or as 'excessively, unduly, disproportionately'? But since *not too* is, rightly or wrongly, used to mean 'not very', take care even when using it in its old correct sense of 'not excessively' to avoid laying yourself open to misinterpretation.

d. The phrase *not too* is also widely used in understatements: *She was not too pleased when her husband crashed the car she had just bought herself.* In formal usage, *none too pleased* and (in British English) *not best pleased* are perhaps slightly preferable; and also *not very pleased,* though some of the irony would then be lost. Another possible phrase, *not exactly pleased,* also has an informal ring to it.

3. The adverb *too* is also commonly used to mean 'also' or 'in addition'. Unlike these words, however, it should not be used as the first word of a sentence, although it is increasingly being used in this way in American English, especially in journalism:

> × A large and growing concentration of lower-income citizens . . . are increasing the cost of city services. . . . Too, there is a growing 'skills mismatch'.
> – Wayne King (U.S.),
> *The New York Times*

Such awkward constructions can be avoided by moving *too* to the middle or end of the sentence, or by using *furthermore, moreover,* or *in addition* in its place, or by using *Then* in front of *too,* producing the acceptable phrase *Then too . . . .*

tornado See CYCLONE.

tortuous, torturous These two adjectives are often confused. *Tortuous* means 'twisting, winding', and figuratively means 'complex' or 'overelaborate', as in *a tortuous argument.*

> The short cut in question got worse and worse, bumpier and bumpier, muddier and muddier, and when I attempted to turn back after some ten miles of purblind, tortuous and tortoise-slow progress, my old and weak Melmoth got stuck in deep clay. All was dark and muggy, and hopeless. My headlights hung over a broad ditch full of water.
> – Vladimir Nabokov, *Lolita*

The tortuous road which has led from Montgomery to Oslo is a road over which millions of Negroes are travelling to find a new sense of dignity.

> – Martin Luther King, Jr. (U.S.),
> Nobel Prize acceptance speech

Dynasty. The tortuous plots thicken and reach a fiery climax in the last episode of the present series. Is Adam's deranged past repeating itself? Has Fallon stumbled on the truth about Jeff's 'illness'?

> – Peter Davalle, *The Times*

It is a considerable defeat for the Government. The Lords spoke passionately against the regulations. Lord Denning described their 'tortuosity and obscurity'. They are indeed obscure and tortuous.

> – *The Times*

Tortuous goes back ultimately to the Latin verb *torquere,* 'to twist'. So too does *torturous,* the adjective from *torture,* though here a quite different kind of twisting is suggested. *Torturous* means 'like or causing torture, agonising, extremely painful':

> It was Duncan who spent the most time with John Wolf during Wolf's torturous dying of lung cancer. Wolf lay in a private hospital in New York sometimes smoking a cigarette through a plastic tube inserted in his throat.
> – John Irving (U.S.),
> *The World According to Garp*

The difference between *torturous* and *tortuous* can be seen in such a phrase as *a torturous assault course through a tortuous ravine.*

There are several reasons for the frequent confusion between these two words. First, their similarity of sound, of course. Then, the verb *to torture* can, in one of its senses, mean 'to distort' or 'to twist out of shape', as in *the tortured branches of the blasted oak.* And, conversely, a complex or *tortuous* line of thought is difficult to follow, and involves an agonising or *torturous* mental activity for those concerned: *The brilliant but self-tormenting novelist engaged in torturous/tortuous arguments with himself.* In the following examples, *tortuous* could be replaced by *torturous:*

> Negotiating the purchase of the jumbo might have proved easier if Virgin had been a public company. Tortuous discussions included a marathon 48-hour session between Boeing, Barclays Mercantile, Chemical Bank and Virgin's financial advisers, County Bank.
> – Victor Smart, *The Observer*

The resistance claimed that ten thousand murders on a given day were within the capacity of Auschwitz Two ... Throughout Europe that summer some millions of people, Oskar among them, and the ghetto dwellers of Cracow, too, tortuously adjusted the economies of their souls to the idea of Belzec-like enclosures in the Polish forests.

> – Thomas Keneally, *Schindler's Ark*

If you want to avoid a possible charge of confusion in contexts such as this, you can always choose another appropriate word — *convoluted* for *tortuous,* and *agonising* for *torturous,* for instance.

In the following two quotations, *tortuous* and *tortuously* are dubious words in context: in all probability, the intended words are *torturous* and *torturously.*

?? But, as Shepard's story unfolds, it is clear that Eddie and May are bound in blood and tears to part and reunite violently, tortuously and endlessly. They share the same father, an intolerable fact that they discovered too late.

> – Ros Asquith, *The Observer*

?? While his wife and Bulu led him up the stairs, hauling him up and propping him upright by their shoulders as though he were some lifeless bag containing something fragile and valuable, he tried to think when he had last attempted or achieved what now seemed a tortuous struggle up the steep concrete steps to the warped green door at the top.

> – Anita Desai, *Games At Twilight*

total 1. Some purists have criticised the modern tendency to overwork *total* and *totally.* The words should be used, they argue, only when there is a sense of various parts being added together to produce a whole: *The total cost for the various items was six dollars exactly*; *The jigsaw puzzle is still not totally finished.*

If there is no such idea of component parts, then *total* and *totally* are best avoided: ? *The attempt was a total disaster*; ? *He was totally unmoved by my threat*; ? *The wall is totally purple.* Use *utter, quite, absolutely, completely,* or the like in preference.

? I predict they will live as classics of radio — grave, passionate, moving, shot through with an ironic humour, and taking a unique flavour from Elkins's totally unmistakable delivery.

> – John Wain, *The Listener*

2. *Total* or *totally* is often used redundantly. In *the sum total*, *totally demolished*, and so on, the word can be omitted: it adds some small emphasis perhaps, but it adds nothing to the meaning, and for the sake of efficient and economical speech should be omitted as superfluous.

The overuse and often needless use of *total* and *totally* are well illustrated in the following extracts, all from a single short newspaper article. (Note too the writer's controversial use of *hopefully* and the split infinitive.)

?? The first Golf was a total Guigiaro design. There are those who say that he is a one man-one car designer. ...

The ventilation system should, on paper, be better: the car I have been driving for the past month never fails to condense on all window areas when parked overnight. It can take an hour to totally clear. The basic fascia layout is better but the heated rear window tell-tale (which you might often need) is totally obscured whereas the hazard warning light (which you would hopefully not want) is obvious. ...

And the wipers themselves are totally inexcusable. ...

The ... Jetta ... has a totally different feel from the Golf.

   – Roy Harry, *The Guardian*

3. The American slang sense of the verb *to total*, 'to damage (a vehicle) beyond repair in a road accident', is now increasingly heard in British English. It is not appropriate for formal contexts, of course.

trade union   *Trade union* is the standard form, with its plural *trade unions,* though *trades union* is fairly common in British English: the TUC in Britain is in fact the *Trades Union Congress*.

I also asked about his membership of the SDP's trade union council. He told me, and his recording machine, that he was resigning from the body 'which I only joined to help set it up'.

   – Peter Hillmore, *The Observer*

The blueprint tries to enshrine Solidarity ideals of social justice ... the continuing struggle of Solidarity for independent trades unions; a more active participation in workers' councils at the factory level ...

   – Roger Boyes, *The Times*

In American English there seems less objection to the form *trades union* than there is in British English. But that is probably because both *trade union* and *trades union* are less common in American English than the Americanism *labor union*.

transcendent, transcendental   Both these adjectives have technical uses in philosophy and mathematics. In general use, *transcendent* chiefly means 'surpassing, pre-eminent': *a matter of transcendent importance*; *the transcendent excellence of his verse*. *Transcendental* is rarely used in general contexts; when it is, it would then tend to mean 'mystical, abstruse, or exalted': *He uses transcendental terminology that I cannot translate and can barely understand*.

Theologians use *transcendent* with reference to God, in affirming that He exists above and more or less independently of the universe. (Compare IMMANENT.)

Transcendental meditation is a simple form of meditation and mental relaxation derived from Hinduism but practised mainly in the West.

transient, transitory   These words mean 'lasting only a short time', and are more or less synonyms. They share the Latin roots *trans-,* 'across' + *ire*, 'to go', suggesting the idea of disappearance.

Transient sometimes suggests that the short duration is caused by rapid movement, as in *transient hotel guests*. *Transitory* may suggest that desirable things disappear too swiftly: *the transitory nature of fame*. Since *transitoriness* is a rather awkward word, most writers seem to prefer *transience* for the noun:

But it is not only a sense of transience that inscriptions on tombs evoke. They remind us, too, of the intimacies of ordinary life, its sweetness and precariousness.

   – Peterborough, *Daily Telegraph*

Note that in both words, pronunciation with a *z*-sound is slightly preferred, unlike in *transform*, for instance. So: /tranzi-ənt/ and /tranzi-tri/. Several variants are possible, however.

transitive and intransitive   *Transitive* verbs are verbs that need a direct object to complete their meaning; or they can be thought of as verbs that can be used in the passive. The verb *to vanquish*, the phrasal verb *to give away*, and the reflexive verb *to pride* (*oneself*) are all transitive (though reflexive verbs cannot be used in the passive), since they cannot be used alone: one vanquishes or gives away *someone* or *something*, and one prides *oneself* on something.

The verb *to vanish* and the phrasal verb *to hang back* are intransitive, since they do not take a direct object: *The tickets vanished*; *The shy child hung back*. Intransitive verbs cannot be used in the passive.

To know, to want, and *to put* are all transitive: *I know that he is here*; *We want you to go*; *Put it on the shelf.* (Note that the direct object is sometimes a clause: *that he is here*.)

A verb may be transitive in some constructions and intransitive in others: *to fly* is intransitive in *These planes fly*, transitive in *I fly these planes*; *to grow* is intransitive in *The puppy is growing*, transitive in *We grow tomatoes*; *to smell* is intransitive in *It smells delicious*, transitive in *I can smell onions*.

To smell in the sentence *This smells delicious* is an example of an intransitive verb that tends to be followed by something, but not by a direct object. This necessary 'something' is often called the *complement*. It may be a noun, an adjective, or a nounlike or adjectivelike expression, and it refers directly back to the subject of the sentence. The verb *to be* takes a complement in *This is my father* or *She was thirsty*. Other intransitive verbs that take a complement are *to become*, *to remain*, *to seem*, and *to appear*: *She became a vet*; *He remained calm*; *It seems a pity*; *The story appears true*. So too with *to cost, to weigh, to measure*: *It cost £10*; *The baby weighs 8lbs*; *The room measures 12 feet by 11*.

Such verbs, since they may be followed by a noun, may appear to be transitive, but are really intransitive: the noun following is simply the complement (that is, it *completes* the construction), but it really relates to the subject of the sentence and is not the object of the verb.

Other intransitive verbs worth noting are those that are followed by a specified distance or extent (and so might again appear to be transitive): *to run a mile, to swim a long way*; and also those, such as *to smell* again, that refer to our senses and sensations: *You look tired*; *It tasted bitter*; *The music sounded extremely strange*; *I felt such a fool*.

Many verbs that would normally be transitive are sometimes used intransitively to express the idea that something undergoes the process implied by the verb. This is true of *to publish* in *The newspaper did not publish during the strike*, of *to read* in *This book reads well*, and of *to sell* in *The house sold for £70,000*.

Some transitive verbs may have an indirect object before their direct object — *I gave them a book* — or a complement after their direct object: *They considered him foolish/a fool*.

transitory See TRANSIENT.

transpire Purists object to the most recent sense of this verb — 'to happen' (even though it dates back to the 18th century). It certainly can sound affected:

? Tell me what transpired when you finally met her.
? They never spoke to each other again, as it transpired.
? It transpired that the weather was unsuitable.

? The nation ... sold its products to the entire world, but otherwise it largely ignored what transpired beyond its borders.
— J. Paul Getty (U.S.), *As I See It*

An earlier sense of the word (which gave rise to the questionable later meaning) — 'to become known, come to light, emerge slowly' — is fully acceptable:

The pact was a secret one, and when news of it transpired at last, the government was deeply embarrassed.
It later transpired that he had not been ill at all at the time, but was playing truant.

Neutral Switzerland is at the heart of a storm over the alleged supply of warplanes to Iran ... It transpires that of some 380 PC-7s turned out over the past seven years from the Pilatus works at Stans, near Lucerne, all but four orders have been from developing countries' military establishments.
— *The Observer*

A skilful opening montage cuts between a group of people preparing for a funeral and the corpse, its white slashed wrists neatly sewn up, being dressed for a late autumn burial. The seven principal mourners, it transpires, were close friends at the University of Michigan in the mid-1960s and marched with Mailer's army of the night.
— Philip French, *The Observer*

The word comes from Latin roots, *trans*, 'out, through' + *spirare,* 'to breathe'. The old sense of the word, 'to perspire', is used mainly of plants nowadays. Formerly, it was in more general use:

And while thy willing soul transpires
At every pore with instant fires,
Now let us sport us while we may.
— Andrew Marvell,
'To His Coy Mistress' (*c.*1652)

Compare MATERIALISE.

transport, transportation In British English, *transport* is the usual word both for the system of conveying — *public transport*, *the means of transport*, *Ministry of Transport* — and for the vehicle used for conveyance: *a troop transport*. American English often uses *transportation* for the first of these:

> Some of the wedding guests brought elephants to the party. They weren't really conscious of showing off, they were just using the elephants for transportation.
> — John Irving (U.S.),
> *The World According to Garp*

This usage is filtering into British English, though it is still widely regarded as an Americanism.

The British and Americans alike speak of *transports of joy*, and of the *transportation* of convicts to a penal colony.

trauma The word *trauma*, originally pronounced /trowmə/, now more usually pronounced /trawmə/ in British English, has its origins in the medical world. It comes from the Greek word for 'a wound'. It is still used as a technical term in medicine to refer to a physical injury: the plural in technical use sometimes still has the Greek form *traumata*, /trawmətə/, though *traumas* is now more common. In some hospitals you will find, as part of the casualty department, a *trauma clinic* dealing with broken arms, legs, and so on.

The term is also used in psychological medicine and psychiatry to indicate the cause of mental or emotional stress, or the stress itself, such as the shock following the death of a relative or involvement in a car accident. In psychoanalysis, *trauma* often refers to some distressing experience in childhood that affects the child's psychological development and can lead to neurosis later on.

Like so many other technical words, *trauma* has become something of a vogue word, used too often and too loosely. Overuse diminishes the force of words — and *trauma* is a very forceful word — until they become almost meaningless. So we find people referring to the trauma of having to stay late at work, the trauma of missing the last bus home, or the trauma of finding the bank closed. Such events are annoying and perhaps troublesome, but they do not constitute real *traumas*.

The adjectival form *traumatic* and the verb *to traumatise* are also used far too widely and loosely, being fine examples of 'psychobabble':
?? *I had a traumatic meeting with the boss today*;
?? *I was really traumatised by seeing my mother drinking last night.*

Not that all such extended uses are unacceptable. The words are often very effective in slightly metaphorical uses: *the lingering trauma of the Vietnam war.*

> While the U.S. remains traumatised by the Three Mile Island incident, other industrialised nations are moving rapidly in the field of nuclear power.
> — *Time* (U.S.)

triumphal This adjective cannot usually exchange roles with *triumphant*. *Triumphant* is now commonly used in the sense 'exulting in success or victory' — *a triumphant return home* — though it can also mean simply 'successful, victorious': *The triumphant team congratulated their defeated opponents.*

Triumphal is used in a more restricted way, referring to the formal celebration or commemoration of a victory: *a triumphal arch*. A *triumphal procession* might in fact be very subdued, anything but triumphant. In the following quotation, *triumphant* would have been more in keeping with current usage than *triumphal* is:

> ? It may look as if Judi Dench's theatrical career has been one long triumphal progress; but this doesn't quite correspond to the facts and her feelings.
> — Richard Findlater, *The Observer*

trouble In informal English, the noun *trouble*, in the construction *to have trouble,* is often followed directly by the *-ing* form of a verb:

> ? I had a lot of trouble finding the right book for you.

Formal usage requires the insertion of the preposition *in*:

> I had a great deal of trouble in finding the right book for you.

Two other common constructions with *trouble* — *to take the/some trouble* and *to go to the/some trouble* — should both really be followed by *to* + the infinitive rather than by the *-ing* form of the verb:

> I took the trouble to find the right book for you.
> I went to a great deal of trouble to find the right book for you.

truism Strictly speaking, a *truism* is a tautology — a statement about the subject of a sentence that repeats part of the definition of that subject, as in *Criminals break the law.* But the word now usually refers to any statement of a truth so obvious as to be not worth mentioning, such as *One feels colder in the winter.* A truism is not simply anything that happens to be true; the word cannot be used as a smart synonym for *fact* or *truth,* as in ✕ *the truism that 99 books are written for every one that gets published.*

try and   *Try and* is a more casual way of saying *try to,* and is very common in informal usage today. But it is far less flexible than *try to.* It cannot easily be used in the negative, for instance. Compare these two sentences:

He didn't try to stop smoking after all.

?? He didn't try and stop smoking after all.

And although you can use the forms *try to, tries to, tried to,* and *trying to,* the only possible informal form is *try and.*

The two forms differ not just in level of formality and degree of flexibility, but in meaning as well: *try to do it* gives more importance to 'try' than *try and do it* does. So if failure is anticipated, *try to* may be more appropriate:

Just try to open that door, and you'll realise it's locked.

For the second day, police used horses to try to control the women, who were blockading the road to prevent traffic entering and leaving the base.
– Pat Healy, *The Times*

Try and is thought to have a slightly greater sense of urgency or determination or encouragement. (Note that these distinctions are very slight, however, and can be reversed by the context or — in speech — by the amount of stress on the word *try.*)

Try and seems to be particularly common in three contexts.

● After *to,* because *to try and* sounds better than *to try to* (but see the previous quotation):

To try and cheer her up, the King now put in hand a scheme ... for a little country house in the gardens of Trianon.
– Nancy Mitford, *Madame de Pompadour*

The slow, forceful trundle of the bike gave an impression of certainty, almost of remorselessness, of aims it was useless for anyone to try and frustrate.
– Peter Dickinson, *The Last House-Party*

● In expressions of defiance: *I won't do it! Just you try and make me!*

● In informal speech, or in writing that quotes or implies informal speech:

Well, without going into a lot of sordid details, which are neither here nor there, I was compelled to try and raise money. I cast about in all sorts of likely and unlikely directions.
– Arthur Norris, in Christopher Isherwood's *Mr Norris Changes Trains*

I went back to Dr Maxwell, the GP Graham had sent me to, and he told me I should try and rest as much as possible. I explained the situation to him and he said well, he couldn't help that, morning sickness was morning sickness.
– Lynne Reid Banks, *The L-Shaped Room*

tsar, czar   These are variant spellings of the word referring to any of the former Russian emperors. (Another variant, quite rare now, is *tzar.*) *Tsar* is the more accurate rendering of the Russian word, as written in the Cyrillic script and pronounced with a distinct *ts*-sound, /tsar/; it is the preferred spelling in British English, even though the word is commonly pronounced /zar/ in English.

The form *czar* dates from a 16th-century German text: this spelling reflects the interesting origin of the word — from the Gothic *kaisar,* 'an emperor' (compare the modern German form *Kaiser*), going back ultimately to the Latin *Caesar.*

Czar has extended senses in American English: it can refer more generally to an authoritarian or autocratic person, a petty tyrant, or to any important or leading figure in a specified field, especially one with official supervisory powers — *the czar of major-league baseball.* In this last sense it is roughly equivalent to the British English term *supremo.*

In derivatives, the *ts*-form is very much preferred in British English, and the *cz*-form in American English: *tsarevitch,* 'the eldest son of a tsar'; *tsarevna,* 'the daughter of a tsar or the wife of a tsarevitch', and *tsaritsa,* 'a Russian empress, or the wife of a tsar' (spelt *czaritsa* in American English). A common English variant of *tsaritsa* is *tsarina,* which is borrowed from German and influenced by Romance words such as *signorina.*

turbulent, turbid, turgid, tumid *Turgid* and *tumid* mean much the same; *turbid* has a quite different sense, though in figurative use it does approach the other two quite closely.

Turgid (pronounced /**tur**jid/) means literally 'swollen, bloated': *The camel's stomach was tight and turgid after it had drunk its fill.* The adjective *tumid* (pronounced /**tew**mid/) would have been equally appropriate here, though rather less common.

Turgid can be used in a more metaphorical way too: 'overtight, rigid':

> But Oxford University Convocation, in theory the MAs' parliament, is far too turgid a body to produce such a solution at anything less than the point of a gun.
> – John Ezard, *The Guardian*

Turgid comes from the Latin *turgere*, 'to swell or be swollen'; *tumid* from the Latin *tumere*, 'to swell' (from which *tumour* also derives).

Both *turgid* and *tumid* can be used in another metaphorical sense of 'inflated', applying to speech or writing: *turgid language* or *tumid rhetoric* suggests high-flown, ornate, pompous use of words — more style than content.

> For example, writing on Francis Thompson, Larkin follows a turgid quotation beginning 'At the last trump thou wilt arise Betimes!' with the tart comment: 'It was Thompson's attempt to get himself out of bed. It did not work.'
> – Martin Walker,
> *The Literary Review*

> *Dolores,* published in the same year as Lawrence's *The White Peacock* ... had been a thoroughly misconceived homage to George Eliot .... Its very turgidity shows how fiercely Ivy had struggled, like the great moderns, with a dead form.
> – Hilary Spurling, *The Times*

It is here that the adjective *turbid* becomes a possible source of confusion. The commonest literal sense of *turbid* is 'muddy, unclear, cloudy', as in *turbid water.* In metaphorical use, this too could apply to speech or writing: *a turbid argument* is a confused, unclear argument. (One wonders whether in the last quotation above the writer perhaps intended *turbidity* rather than *turgidity*.) So we could talk about *a speech that was turbid because it was so turgid.* *Turbid* has two other literal senses: 'thick or dense', as in *turbid smog*, and 'muddled, in turmoil', as in *the turbid streetlife of Bangkok*.

Another danger of confusion arises with the adjective *turbulent*, in the sense of 'agitated or disturbed': *a turbulent river.* This is not quite the same thing as *a turbid river. Turbulent* also has the more metaphorical senses of 'restless, chaotic' — *a turbulent period of history* — and 'unruly, disorderly': *a turbulent group of protesters* or even *a turbulent priest* (as Henry II referred to Thomas à Becket).

> The Zuckerman novels look like life looks, before art has properly finished with it. And Roth's corpus still gives the impression of a turbulent talent searching for a decorous way to explode.
> – Martin Amis, *The Observer*

Both *turbid* and *turbulent* go back to the same Latin source word *turba*, 'confusion or uproar' (from which *disturb* also derives).

Tumid, turbid, and *turgid* can all form nouns by adding either *-ity* or *-ness* at the end (if *-ity*, the stress moves from the first to the second syllable in each case). The noun from *turbulent* is *turbulence.*

type of See SORT OF.

typhoon See CYCLONE.

tyre, tire Although *tyre* (= the covering of a wheel) is now the standard British spelling, and *tire* is restricted to American English, *tire* is in fact as old as *tyre* in British English. The word seems to be a contracted form of *attire*: tyres 'attired' or 'dressed' the wheels of a cart or carriage. (Originally, a tyre was a metal rim; wood and cork tyres were also possible — rubber tyres were introduced in 1868.) During the 16th and 17th centuries both *tire* and *tyre* were used, but it seems that by 1700 *tyre* had died out and *tire* had become the accepted form. The re-emergence of *tyre* as the popular spelling in British English is fairly recent, and for some time it encountered resistance from traditionalists — *The Times,* for instance, long held to the spelling *tire* before conceding and admitting *tyre* in its place.

The verb *to tyre,* in British English, is used only in the sense 'to fit with a tyre or tyres'. The verb meaning 'to weary' or 'to become fatigued' is spelt *tire.*

U

U and non-U These terms were devised in the mid-1950s by Professor Alan Ross, a British linguist and sociologist, as abbreviations of *Upper Class* and *non-Upper Class*. Professor Ross's thesis was this: 'It is solely by its language that the (English) upper class is clearly marked off from the others.' No longer by its education, its cleanliness, its wealth, its influence in government — simply its use of English (and a few social likes and dislikes).

Professor Ross's researches, undertaken initially with a serious scholarly purpose, provoked a lively controversy — dinner-party arguments, heated letters to *The Times*, and so on. Several noted writers of the time were drawn into the fray — Nancy Mitford, Evelyn Waugh, Christopher Sykes. And John Betjeman wrote a satirical poem on the subject.

Here are a few details that emerged in the course of the debate. (Remember, this was in the mid-1950s.) U people, though still subtly different in their social habits — confidently using the correct mode of address, shunning doilies and cruets, preferring the milk to be poured after the tea, refusing to carry an umbrella in the countryside, and so on — were distinguishable chiefly by their linguistic habits. And this distinctive use of language was discernible almost exclusively in pronunciation and vocabulary, not in grammar.

In pronunciation, for example, *formidable* and *temporarily* are both stressed on the first syllable by U-speakers. Non-U-speakers stress *formidable* on the second syllable, and like Americans add a strong third-syllable stress to *temporarily*. Here are some more examples:

	U	non-U
either	/ī-thər/	/**ee**-thər/
fault	/fawlt/	/folt/
forehead	/**forr**id/	/**fawr**-hed/
medicine	/**med**-s'n/ (two syllables)	/**medd**i-sin/ (three syllables)
Ralph	/rāf/	/ralf/
really	/**ree**-ə-li/ (three syllables)	/**rair**-li, **reel**i/ (two syllables)
salt	/sawlt/	/solt/

U-speakers sometimes pronounced *girl* as /gal/ or /gel/, *golf* as /gof/ or /gōf/ or /gawf/; *gone*

as /gawn/, *just* as /jest/, and Edwardian (like Americans) as /Ed-**waar**di-ən/.

And non-U-speakers sometimes, attempting to be genteel, pronounced *ride* as /rayd/, *garage* (like Americans) as /gar**raazh**/, *plastic, piano*, and *substantial* as /**plaa**stik/, /**pyaa**nō/, and /səb-**staan**shəl/, *scone* as /skōn/ (though this is the usual unaffected pronunciation in some parts of Britain), and *involved* as /in-**vōlvd**/.

And here are some of the vocabulary differences noted between U-speakers and non-U-speakers:

U	non-U
false teeth	dentures
to have my bath	to take a bath
knave (in card-games)	jack
lavatory	toilet
my wife	the wife
napkin, table-napkin	serviette
pudding	sweet
rich	wealthy
scent	perfume
(silence)	Miss (addressing a telephone operator or barmaid)
(silence)	Cheers! God bless! (an informal toast when drinking)
drawing room	lounge
telegram	wire

Dinner is U for the evening meal, non-U for the midday meal. *Boring* is a general adjective of disapproval among U-speakers. Some typical non-U expressions are *Eat your greens*; *I don't mind if I do*; *If you don't mind my mentioning it*; *Pardon?*; *Pardon me!*; *Pleased to meet you*; *How rude!*; *Bye-bye*; *Ta ever so*; *a nice lie-down*; *one for the road*.

A few comments: Professor Ross did not intend U-speech to be taken as 'better' than non-U speech (except perhaps when non-U speech is the result of a fumbling imitation of U-speech: see below). The public, however, took over the terms *U* and *non-U* and gave them distinctly approving and disapproving overtones: *Ascot is becoming so non-U these days*.

British English is not unique in having these linguistic distinctions, but they are perhaps more undoubtedly

striking in British English than they are in other European languages — just as class-consciousness still seems more intense in Britain, or at least in England, than elsewhere in Europe.

The distinctions between U and non-U speech are really distinctions between upper-class and middle-class speech. In fact, they are of far less importance than the differences between middle-class and working-class speech, and those between dialects and standard speech.

U-speech changes from generation to generation: even in the 1950s, the old U-habit of pronouncing the *-ing* suffix as /-in/ — *huntin'*, *shootin'*, *fishin'* — was considered all but dead. And it is surely no longer non-U to say *mirror* instead of *looking glass*. Terms once considered deplorably non-U — such as *weekend* — have graduated to full acceptance.

The distinction between *U* and *non-U* English, however dubious it was even in the 1950s and however tenuous it may be today, does serve to focus attention on two linguistic matters that are still important — first, that the way people talk (or write) says a tremendous amount about them: their upbringing, present social status, and aspirations; their intelligence, sensitivity, and general personality, and so on.

Secondly, the *U/non-U* distinction has a timeless lesson for all speakers — that the *appropriate* style or 'register' is the right one. To strive to be purer than the pure is to risk a great fall; to affect a refined, or 'refained', accent is likely to distract and irritate your listeners rather than impress them. Dickens and dozens of other satirists have had a field-day with snobs or pretentious *nouveaux riches* who put on linguistic airs — mouthing long fashionable terms in la-di-da accents but occasionally dropping an *h* or using a vogue word in the wrong sense. The judgments of 'vulgar' or 'genteel' are passed not on honest plain speakers but on speakers aping a 'grander' style that is not natural to them — pronouncing *spite* as if it were *spate*, for example, or using the words *assist, desire,* and *sufficient* instead of the simple *help, want,* and *enough.*

Now that the adjective *non-U* has become a negative rather than a neutral term (being applied more often to social habits and domestic objects than to language use), it can legitimately be directed against 'fancy' words and pretentious pronunciations — but not simply to the plain, forthright speech of people (the vast majority) who happen not to belong to the upper class.

unaware, unawares *Unaware* is usually an adjective, meaning 'not aware', often used with *of* or *that*: *He was unaware of any change; He was unaware that anything had changed.*

The hurt silence with which her refusal had been accepted had implied the importance of these 'social duties' of which Bina remained so stubbornly unaware.
– Anita Desai, *Games at Twilight*

It can also be an adverb, meaning 'by surprise, unexpectedly, without forethought' (though in the second of the examples below, *unaware* may also be regarded as an adjective):

A spring of love gushed from my heart,
And I blessed them unaware.
– S.T. Coleridge,
'The Ancient Mariner' (1798)

Office workers and shoppers caught unaware by the sudden announcement of the 24-hour curfew raced for their cars, only to get caught up in one of the worst traffic jams the city has ever seen.
– *The Observer*

Adverbial use is traditionally, however, the province of *unawares*, which remains the more common form: *He came upon them unawares. Unawares* cannot be used with *of* or *that*, or as an adjective. Here are two examples, separated in time by over 350 years:

Be not forgetful to entertain strangers: for thereby some have entertained angels unawares.
– Hebrews 13:2
(King James Bible, 1611)

Churches hold nothing of the numinous for him. But he is taken unawares in a cathedral by an image of Christ and he collapses.
– Anthony Burgess, *The Observer*

unceremonious See CEREMONIAL.

under way, underway See WAY 2.

undiscriminating See DISCRIMINATING.

undoubtedly, doubtless, no doubt, without a doubt Two of these terms can be understood literally: *undoubtedly* and *without a doubt* express a strong sense of certainty. (Various other related terms express equal certainty: *indubitably, without the shadow of a doubt, beyond a doubt, there is no doubt whatsoever that,* and so on.)

She's undoubtedly the best candidate for the

post, but can we afford to pay her the salary she expects?

That man is guilty without a doubt.

The other two terms, *doubtless* and *no doubt,* are very much weaker than this, and often seem to convey a distinct sense of doubt despite their structure:

> Gilbert Sorrentino is one of America's most celebrated practitioners of the sort of playful novel Donleavy no doubt had in mind as competition.
> – Valentine Cunningham,
> *The Observer*

Ask any university administrator what his chief teaching anxiety is and he is likely to reply that he has lost the wrong people, and has a lopsided age profile among teaching staff. Sir Keith doubtless now leans towards a little mild coercion, in order to lose the *right* people.
> – leading article, *Daily Telegraph*

Truman's success in the election, as you no doubt know, went against all the polls and predictions.

You doubtless have your usual good excuse for being late.

Three points to note: first, *doubtless* is rather old-fashioned nowadays, and is far less common than *no doubt*. Secondly, *doubtless* is the correct form of the adverb — x *doubtlessly* is unnecessary and nonstandard. Thirdly, the mild sarcasm often invested in *doubtless* and *no doubt* is not an essential part of their sense: they can in fact be used to convey a sense of politeness or delicacy, by toning down a criticism or indicating an assumption or concession:

> You're no doubt under a lot of strain at the moment, so I'll make allowances.

> He's doubtless been caught in the traffic. No doubt you're right.

> How angry she felt that poor little children and old people were being made to suffer like this, no doubt through someone's inefficiency.
> – D.M. Thomas, *The White Hotel*

unearthly See EARTHY.

uneatable See EATABLE.

unexceptional See EXCEPTIONAL.

unimaginable See UNTHINKABLE.

uninterested See DISINTERESTED.

unique The adjective *unique* means primarily 'being the only one of its kind'. This is an 'absolute' sense; something is either *unique* or *not unique*; there are no degrees in between. It cannot be *more unique* or *less unique* therefore, or *very unique* or *rather unique* or *so unique*.

And yet such usages do occur quite often, particularly in American speech and writing:

> *?* When you are visiting the beauty spots of this country, don't overlook Frank Phillip's ranch and game preserve at Bartlesville, Okla. It's the most unique place in this country. Got everything but reindeer.
> – Will Rogers (U.S.), *Autobiography*

> *?* The customs and traditions that make Thai culture so unique date back over two thousand years. At Thai International we're pleased to say that nothing has changed.
> – advertisement, *The Observer*

There appear, then, to be a number of secondary senses of *unique* in widespread use today — 'non-absolute' senses, which do allow for degrees of comparison. These senses range from 'unequalled' or 'unrivalled', through 'outstanding', 'unusual', and 'rare', to merely 'impressive' or 'of high quality'. Sometimes the word is used so loosely that it loses all sense of meaning except for a vague sense of enthusiastic approval: *?? London's most unique vegetarian restaurant is now even more unique.*

This development marks a sad weakening of the unique and powerful quality of *unique*. To apply it too freely is to make it lose its basic and absolute flavour, so such an application should be resisted in all but the most casual speech and writing.

If *? more unique, ? very unique,* and so on are not really permissible, are there no words then that can be used to modify *unique*? It is true that there are no degrees of uniqueness, but there are degrees of *nearness* to being unique. And so it is quite acceptable to say *almost unique* or *nearly unique,* just as it is to say *far from unique*. And since *nearly unique* is permissible, so too are *more nearly unique* and *most nearly unique*.

What about *utterly unique* or *absolutely unique*? These forms are very common, and serve the purpose, in informal usage, of intensifying the adjective — in the same way as you might say *I'm absolutely certain*. (The same is true of *quite unique,* provided that *quite* is used to mean 'absolutely' and not 'somewhat'.) But logically, an intensifier such as *absolutely* is pointless, since *unique* is already absolute and cannot be improved upon. In formal speech and writing, intensifiers are therefore best omitted.

Finally, the adjectival phrase *unique to*: although some purists used to disapprove of its use, it is a perfectly acceptable synonym of 'peculiar to', in the sense of 'restricted to':

> While the production of Beaujolais is widespread throughout the region, there are dozens of individual varieties, each unique to its particular vineyard.

● *Recommendation Unique,* like any other word, is freely available to all for use as a sharp or blunt instrument. The meaning of *unique* has an absolute force, so if you want to keep the instrument sharp, do not say *more unique* or *less unique* (or *very unique* and so on). If you want to discuss degrees of rarity or impressiveness, then say *more nearly unique* or *less nearly unique* (or simply *nearly unique*). Or avoid the word *unique* altogether, and find an alternative: *the most unusual, more remarkable, rarer,* and so on. In informal writing and casual speech, there is nothing objectionable in using *utterly unique* or a similar emphatic form, but avoid it in very formal usage. The word *unique* is quite strong enough to stand by itself, without help from such intensifiers.

See also ADJECTIVES 3; PERFECT; VERY.

United Kingdom See BRITAIN.

United States The abbreviations *U.S.* and *U.S.A.* (now often written without full stops) are in widespread use in informal English, and in newspaper headlines. (In postal addresses *U.S.A.* is preferable.) In formal speaking and writing, the appropriate form is *the United States*: the abbreviated forms can sound rather offhand and chatty:

> ? As President Reagan, who will open the Games at the LA Memorial Coliseum on 27 July, recently discovered for himself, a sharp sense of commerce is something the US and the Chinese have in common.
> – Alan Hubbard, *The Observer*

Only in official or extremely formal contexts is it necessary to use the full name *the United States of America.* The name *America* by itself can refer to several different areas, and should therefore be used with great caution. (See AMERICA.)

As an adjective, *U.S.* is more acceptable than it is as a noun, and is often more acceptable even than *United States*: *a U.S. president. U.S.A.* cannot be used as an adjective. *American* is often used, but should be avoided if there is any danger of ambiguity.

In the early days of the nation, it was still unclear just how united the 13 former colonies — now 13 united states — really were. The name *the United States* was often regarded as a straightforward plural form requiring a plural verb:

> The United States were settled by emigrants from different parts of Europe.
> – Noah Webster (U.S.), *Dissertation on the English Language* (1789)

Nowadays, however, the name is always treated as singular: *The United States is sending a fact-finding mission to Cyprus.*

In certain patriotic and rhetorical contexts, the phrase *these United States* is still used, often to stress the unity-in-diversity of the country, and here a plural verb would be the appropriate one to choose.

See also BRITAIN.

unlawful See ILLEGAL.

unreal See REAL.

unrealistic See REALISM.

unsatisfied See DISSATISFIED.

unthinkable Most things can be thought about: whether or not we are able to *visualise* God, or a square circle, we can surely *think* about them. They are not really *unthinkable.* Nor are they *unimaginable*: if we cannot *imagine* them in the sense of conjuring up an image of them in our minds, we can at least *imagine* them in the sense of contemplating the ideas, of considering what they might be like.

It is perhaps reasonable to use *unthinkable* (or *unimaginable* or *inconceivable*) in a slightly extended way, as referring to things that are very painful to think about (but *outrageous* or *intolerable* or *appalling* can serve this purpose) or that are very difficult to believe (but *incredible* and *impossible* are available here):

> It would be unthinkable for the government to turn a blind eye to the mass-starvation ravaging parts of Africa.

The search was called off after two days: it was inconceivable that any human could survive so long in such icy waters.

Nuclear war raises the unimaginable horror of the extinction of all human life.

The late Herman Kahn's book about nuclear war, *Thinking About the Unthinkable in the 1980's,* has an admittedly effective title: it neatly combines the ideas of 'too difficult to imagine' and 'too horrible to contemplate'.

But *unthinkable,* together with *unimaginable* and *inconceivable,* has overstepped these bounds, and become a vogue word, used — unthinkingly — of anything from another Falklands war to a salary-increase to an economic policy that is not only conceivable but is actually in operation:

?? The Chancellor's inconceivably stupid project has already cost the industry well over 3000 jobs.

?? The seven-per-cent pay-rise demanded by the union is unthinkable at the moment.

In general, *unthinkable, inconceivable,* and *unimaginable* are in danger of being reduced to mere synonyms of *impracticable, undesirable, unacceptable,* or *unlikely.* The appeal of the words came no doubt from their extreme and emphatic tone, much like *terribly, fantastic,* and so on; and as with these words, overuse of *unthinkable, inconceivable,* and *unimaginable* has served only to drain them of their power. It was once advisable to shun them as unduly vigorous and emphatic — as overstatements; it is now advisable to shun them as stale, hollow, and ineffective — as impotent grumbling.

until, till 1. *Until* is slightly more formal than *till,* both as preposition and as conjunction. This is not to say that *till* is informal or in the least slangy. *Till* is not an abbreviation of *until* (as the common misspelling × *'til* would seem to suggest): it is, in fact, the older form in Old English, with *until* developing in Middle English as an expansion of *till.*

Observer management hung on until the early hours of yesterday before abandoning attempts to print the intended run of 875,000 copies. The loss is estimated at £400,000.
— John Ardill, *The Guardian*

Thereafter, munitions production more than doubled, till by mid-1944 Germany at its peak had more munitions than at any time in the war.
— Andrew Wilson, *The Observer*

× Up 'til Sunday last, it had only two substantiated claims to fame. Mr Meany, a local publican, holds the world record for being buried underground, and that irreverent balladeer Percy French mentioned it in song:

But Donegan's daughter from over the water
'Twas little they taught her in Ballyporeen.
— Jeananne Crowley, *The Listener*

The two forms are virtually always interchangeable, though certain contexts may favour one or the other. For a start, *till* is much more common in spoken English, and *until* can sound slightly stiff in speech. Again, *until* is preferable in very formal contexts, the great exceptions being the archaic phrases *till death us do part* and *true till death.* Then, the rhythm of a sentence might urge one word in preference to the other: *stayed until dawn; till a' the seas gang dry.* In particular, when used as the first word of a sentence, *until* occurs far more often than *till: Until I hear otherwise I shall continue taking the tonic.*

Negative sentences can create ambiguities with *till* and *until.* What, for example, is the meaning of *Don't work until you're 35?* It could mean either 'Don't start working before you're 35' or 'Stop working before you're 35'.

Such ambiguities should be avoided by rephrasing the sentence, but fortunately they are rarer in practice than in theory. A sentence such as *Don't work until you're ready* will surely be interpreted to mean 'Don't start working before you're ready'; whereas a sentence such as *Don't work until you're tired* will surely be interpreted to mean 'Stop working before you're tired'.

Till and *until* can refer to space as well as time: *Carry straight on till/until the bus stop* (though it would be more usual to say *till/until you reach the bus stop*). They can also refer to cause and effect, in the sense 'to the point or extent that': *He just nagged and nagged until I finally lost patience and walked out on him.* In such cases as this last one, *until* is definitely preferable to *till.*

2. *up till* or *up until.* This is an increasingly common variant of *till* or *until* as preposition: ? *Summer uniform is worn up till 21 September.* Such constructions attract considerable criticism: they are regarded either as redundant, or as uneducated transformations of *up to. Up until,* even more than *up till,* seems thoughtless or clumsy. It might be said in their favour that they do emphasise the sense of a continuous period ending at a specified time:

? Up until 1929 only women aged thirty and over were allowed to vote. Suddenly, in the middle of a debate about something quite different, Jix was alleged to have said that at the next election the Conservatives would give the vote to women of twenty-one.

  – Ronald Blythe, *The Age of Illusion*

But if *till* or *until* is thought to be too weak on its own, the resourceful writer has any number of ways — unobjectionable ways — of accentuating and refining his meaning.

 3. *until such time as.* This is another increasingly common phrase, and the charge of redundancy is clearly a just one this time. To say ? *You will all stay behind until such time as one of you owns up* is to say nothing more than *You will all stay behind until one of you owns up.*

 4. *unless and until.* A favourite formula in legal and very formal language: ? *This agreement will remain in force unless and until either of the signatories informs the other of his decision to withdraw.* To omit the words 'unless and' would not damage the sentence at all: *until* is a tentative word after all, and already carries within it the suggestion of *unless.* So avoid the elegant but empty phrase ? *unless and until* unless you are quite sure it deserves to be used.

unwonted This adjective means 'unusual, out of the ordinary, contrary to habit', as in *an unwonted display of temper from such a placid child.*

  The plot turns on a group of respectable Parisians who collide in a fleabag hotel on a night of unwonted adventure.

   – Victoria Radin, *The Observer*

Such adventure or such a display of temper may well be *unwanted* too, but that is not what is meant in the phrases above. The confusion arises not just because both *unwonted* and *unwanted* often fit the same slot in a construction, but also because *unwonted* is so often incorrectly pronounced to sound the same as *unwanted.* In fact, the correct pronunciation of *unwonted* is /un-**wōn**tid/, with the *o* as in *won't.*

 The adverb *unwontedly* is also still used, to mean 'unusually, or contrary to habit':

  Yes. I remember Adlestrop —
  The name, because one afternoon
  Of heat the express train drew up there
  Unwontedly. It was late June.
   – Edward Thomas, 'Adlestrop'

Argerich's subsequent proclamation that Pogorelich was a genius lit the fuse under a vast publicity machine; he was swiftly signed by a record company, proved unwontedly photogenic and hasn't looked back.

  – Andrew Clements, *The Observer*

The positive form *wonted*, meaning 'usual, accustomed', is now archaic or extremely formal. It is placed in front of the noun it refers to, never after it. The following example is now 50 years old, and probably sounded slightly old-fashioned even in 1935:

  I had rehearsed a partial reconciliation, on magnanimous terms. But Arthur, of course, was to make the advances. Instead of which, here he was, opening his wine cupboard with his wonted hospitable air.

   – Christopher Isherwood,
   Mr Norris Changes Trains

Wonted is, however, still encountered in the phrase *at the wonted hour*, usually used nowadays only for deliberate jocular effect.

 The word *wont*, as both noun and adjective, is more common, though still rather old-fashioned. (As a verb, however, 'to accustom or be accustomed', it is now archaic, as is the related verb *to won*, 'to dwell or inhabit'.) As an adjective, *wont* means 'accustomed'; it usually follows the verb *to be* and is followed by an infinitive: *He is wont to take a small sherry before dinner.*

  I was very happy; and if sometimes the familiarities in our relationship were of an irritating nature (like the way he teased me, as he had always teased me, about my sticking-out ears, for instance) I pushed them aside and refused to acknowledge them — even when they were quite important, the sort of things on which the nagging small voice was once wont to pounce as reasons against any positive commitment.

   – Lynne Reid Banks,
   The L-Shaped Room

As a noun, *wont* means 'a custom', and is usually used in the pattern *as is one's wont: She rose before sunrise, as was her wont, and stole from the cottage.*

  Though I often went over to Gin Sau's to talk to her, her husband, or her mother-in-law, I never found her sitting idle drinking a cup of tea as was her husband's habit in the evening, or taking a mid-afternoon nap as was her mother-in-law's wont.

  – Steven W. Mosher (U.S.), *Broken Earth*

The correct pronunciation of *wont* is identical to that of *won't* — /wōnt/.

up See DOWN.

upstairs, upstair *Upstair* is a rare form of the adjective. *Upstairs* is now used for both adjective and adverb: *an upstairs* (or *upstair*) *room*; *to go upstairs*.

us See ME; WE.

U.S., U.S.A. See UNITED STATES.

use 1. The noun *use* (/yōoss/) is now fully accepted as a synonym of *good* or *point* in certain idioms:

What's the use of worrying?
There's no use in worrying.
What use is there in worrying?

Other constructions now generally accepted as standard are:

This tyre is no use to me.
Is it any use to you?
What use is it?

Purists would still prefer an *of* in each of these examples: *of no use to me*; *Is it of any use? Of what use is it?* But the idioms are now well established.

In the absence of *no*, *any*, *what*, *how much*, or the like before *use*, however, the *of* is definitely preferable —

? It's little use to her.
? It's some use to him.

(And of course it is impossible to omit the *of* in *It's of use to me*.)

Other constructions in which a preposition should be reinstated are:

? There's no use worrying (similarly, *no point/ trouble/difficulty worrying*).
? What use is there worrying?

— the *in*, as shown earlier, should be inserted before *worrying*. It is probably acceptable, however, to say:

What use is it worrying?
It's no use worrying

and also:

Worrying is no use

though, as suggested, purists would tend to place an *of* before *no use*.

2. The verb *to use* (/yōoz/) has a modern sense that still attracts criticism — 'to exploit for one's own purposes; take advantage of':

? He used the voters' legitimate fears in order to advance his own career.

The word *exploited* would be preferable to *used* here.

The particular objection is to giving the verb *to use* a human object without a qualifying adverb:

? She said she loved me, but she was just using me.

(The construction *She used me unkindly*, on the other hand, is if anything rather old-fashioned.) Though well on their way to acceptability, such sentences are still best restricted to informal usage.

See also UTILISE.

used to 1. As an adjectival expression, in the sense of 'accustomed to', *used to* is suited to such constructions as:

He is used to this kind of word-processor (or *He is not used to . . .* or *He is very used to . . .*)
He has become very used to typing on this kind of word-processor.

But not:

× He has become very used to type on this kind of word-processor.

This incorrect use of the infinitive after the *to* is probably due to confusion with *used to* as an auxiliary verbal expression.

2. As an auxiliary verbal expression, *used to* survives only in the past tense. It means 'did continuously or habitually':

He used to live in Boston.
He used to type on this word-processor.

The negative, emphatic, and interrogative forms of such constructions are problematic; if you say:

He used not to type on this word-processor (*usedn't to* is still current in Australian and New Zealand English)

or:

He never *used* to type on this word-processor,

the suggestion is that he formerly did not but that he now does. If, however, you merely intend to deny his past association with the machine, disregarding the present, then the wording might be:

He never used to type on this word-processor

(leaving the *used* unstressed)

or:

? He didn't use to type on this word-processor.

This last example, though once quite standard, came to be regarded as unacceptable in formal British English, and is still frowned on by purists. (In American English, it is seldom objected to.) Similarly:

? He did (not) use to type on this word-processor.

? Did he (not) use to type on this word-processor? (or: *? Didn't he use to ...*)

? 'And what did they use to give you on Sundays?' he was asking as I came in. 'We got pea-soup with a sausage in it. Not so bad.'
    – Christopher Isherwood,
    Mr Norris Changes Trains

There seems to be no alternative to the emphatic forms, but the interrogative forms should, strictly speaking, be worded as:

? Used he (not) to type on this word-processor? (or: *? Usedn't he ...*)

But these constructions now sound laughably old-fashioned or overformal. (Note the preferred spellings — *Did he use to ...* not *✗ used*; and *Usedn't he to ...* not *✗ usen't*.)

On balance, the slightly informal *? Did he use to ...* is preferable to the excessively formal *? Used he to ...* But, as with all such impasses, you can always avoid having to make the choice — just restructure the sentence. Either:

Is this the word-processor that he used to type on?

or simply:

Would/Did he type on this word-processor?

Note that the *used* of *used to* (in both the senses discussed) is pronounced /yo͞oss(t)/. Elsewhere, *used* is pronounced /yo͞ozd/, even when preceding *to*: *A screwdriver was used to prise off the hinges* — /yo͞ozd/.

See also USE.

utilise In business and official jargon, *to utilise* has become a favourite variant of the simple *to use*. It sounds grander, no doubt, but careful readers and listeners will suspect the intentions of someone who chooses a fancy — and dubious — variant over the simple, unpretentious, established term.

?? In view of your anomalous status, it has been agreed that you may utilise all the recreation facilities normally reserved for our membership.

In this welter of officialese, the word *utilise* holds its own as a piece of ugly jargon.

Careful usage favours retaining (or reinstating) a distinction between *to use* and *to utilise*. In the general sense of 'to put into service', *to use* is correct: *The machinery should be used as little as possible. To utilise* should be reserved for the narrower sense of 'to make productive use of, to exploit profitably': *We can utilise the spare parts to save on running costs; We must utilise all available resources to the full.*

vagary The noun *vagary* does not mean 'vagueness', though the two words do both go back to the Latin adjective *vagus*, 'wandering, undecided'. A related Latin verb *vagari*, 'to wander', produced the English *vagary*, which originally meant 'a roaming tour, a ramble'. It has since departed from this literal meaning: *vagaries* — the word is commonly used in the plural — are fluctuations or flights of fancy, whimsical ideas or eccentric actions: *the vagaries of the stock market.*

> Pakamac, a name synonymous for the past quarter-century with the vagaries of the British weather, has fallen into the hands of the receiver.
> By a cruel irony, the very unpredictability of British rain on which the company built its folding plastic raincoat fortune was in the end its downfall; this year's long dry summer dealt sales a mortal blow.
> – Alan Hamilton, *The Times*

> But the greatest landmark in the development of lexicography was Dr. Sam. Johnson's *Dictionary of the English Language,* completed in 1755. For this employed much more *fully* and effectively the method of illustrating by quotations which Bailey had only occasionally used. Moreover, its definitions, despite some humorous or individual vagaries, were the first to be really clear, scholarly and effective.
> – Professor C.L. Wrenn, *The English Language*

> The Comte de Charolais was a ripsnorting oddity; he dressed like a gamekeeper and ordered his coachman to run over any monks he might see on the road, but he could afford such vagaries as he was a cousin of the King's.
> – Nancy Mitford, *Madame de Pompadour*

The word was formerly pronounced /vǝ-**gair**-i/, with the stress on the second syllable, but today it is almost always pronounced with the stress on the first syllable, as /**vayg**ǝri/.

venal, venial These words are unrelated and should not be confused with each other. *Venal* basically means 'for sale': it comes from the Latin *venum*, meaning 'that which is for sale, goods on sale'. Applied to people, it means 'open to bribery, corrupt', or 'greedy for money': *a venal customs official.*

> ... a charming boy with a great love of beauty and of luxury, a little venal perhaps (but which of us is not if we get the opportunity to be?).
> – Nancy Mitford, *Love in a Cold Climate*

Similarly, one speaks of *venal conduct*. And applied to a political or judicial system, *venal* means 'corrupt, operating by bribery':

> Life was grindingly poor, as they say, with a fair amount of priestly sanction over everyday existence. A series of governments, venal or brutal or simply negligent, occupied the unimaginably distant capital of Athens.
> – Christopher Hitchens, *The Literary Review*

Venial comes from the Latin *venia*, 'pardon', and means 'forgivable'. It refers to sins or offences, and in Roman Catholic theology describes a sin that is not punishable by eternal damnation. (Its opposite is a *mortal* sin.) In common use it means 'not grave' (of crimes):

> She was a flop at cooking and sewing, detested cleaning and spent money carelessly. In the circumstances the sins were venial. They could afford cooks, maids and extravagance.
> – Arthur M. Schlesinger, Jr (U.S.), *Robert Kennedy and His Times*

> Letters from vigilant readers flood in to point out in triumph, rage or *Schadenfreude* the tiniest literal or the most venial solecism in their daily newspaper.
> – Philip Howard, *New Words for Old*

The related nouns are *veniality* (or *venialness*) and *venality*:

Nowadays money is the *only* thing that doesn't stink. In modern Chicago there is nothing infra dig, socially, about venality and graft. The money is its own just cause: it speaks for itself. The rest is flim-flam.

– Martin Amis, *The Observer*

vengeance See REVENGE.

verbal See AURAL.

verbal nouns See -ING FORMS OF VERBS.

verbs 1. A verb refers to an action, or tells us that something exists or occurs. These are all verbs: *agree, sing, cut, be, vanquish, vanish, win*. Most verbs are regular in form; that is, if you know the basic spelling you can predict what the other forms will be: *I agree, we agreed, they have agreed*. Such verbs are called *regular verbs*. But some verbs are *irregular verbs*, such as *sing, sang, sung*, or *cut, cut, cut*, or *go, went, gone*. English verbs like *sing*, which show the differences in tense by an internal vowel change, are sometimes also called *strong verbs*.

One of the forms that a verb can take is its *infinitive*, the basic form, which is used with or without *to* in various grammatical patterns. *Agree* is used in the infinitive in *They might agree; They're unlikely to agree; To agree would be unwise*. (See HAVE; INFINITIVE.) The other possible forms of a verb are its *-s* form, used in the present tense with a singular subject, as in *Mary agrees*; its *past-tense* form, as in *George sang* or *The tickets vanished*; and its two participles: the *present participle*, formed with *-ing*, as in *He's singing*; and the *past participle*, as in *We've won, They were vanquished, a vanished race*. (See PARTICIPLES; TENSE.)

2. Besides having various possible forms, verbs differ in their function. A *transitive* verb needs a direct object to complete its meaning (or else it can be in the passive). The verb *to vanquish* is transitive, since it cannot be used alone: you *vanquish* somebody or something. The verb *to vanish* is *intransitive*, since it does not take a direct object (and cannot be in the passive): *The tickets have vanished*. Some verbs, such as *to win*, can be either transitive or intransitive. You can say either *George won* or *George won the tournament*. (See TRANSITIVE AND INTRANSITIVE.)

3. An *auxiliary* verb, or 'helping' verb, is used with another verb to form a unit expressing tense or suggesting possibility, necessity, or obligation. The commonest auxiliaries are *to be, to have*, and *to do*, as in *I am working; He has arrived; They didn't come*. One function of *to be* is to form the *passive*,

as in *They were rejected*. (See ACTIVE AND PASSIVE.)

Some other auxiliary verbs are *can, could, shall, should, will, would, may, might, need, ought*, and *dare*: *He can't swim; It may rain; You needn't eat it*. (See also SUBJUNCTIVE.)

4. *Reflexive* verbs are transitive verbs whose object and subject are the same thing or person. Some verbs are always reflexive: we may *pride ourselves on* something, but we cannot *pride* anything else. Other verbs may or may not be used reflexively: we can *enjoy ourselves* or *enjoy the concert*. There is often a choice between using a reflexive verb and expressing the same idea with an intransitive verb: *She dressed herself* or simply *She dressed*. There is in fact a modern tendency to reduce certain reflexives and other transitive verbs to an intransitive form, as when saying to someone ?? *Enjoy!* or ?? *Let's discuss*.

Reflexive verbs are used with reflexive pronouns, such as *myself* or *themselves*. (See MYSELF; SELF.)

5. a. A *phrasal verb* is a combination of a verb with an adverb, such as *give up* in *give up smoking*; or of a verb with a preposition, such as *take to* in *take to the woods*; or both, such as *put up with* in *to put up with it*. Phrasal verbs are a vivid and productive part of the language, and are very welcome so long as they really mean more than the sum of their parts: to *give up* something is to renounce it. There is a tendency today, however, to create phrasal verbs that mean no more than the simple verb standing alone. *He consulted with her* means merely *He consulted her*, and *We met up with some friends* usually means no more than *We met some friends*. The same may be said of *to drown out* for *to drown; to miss out on* for *to miss; to rest up* for *to rest*, and *to win out* for *to win*.

In the following quotations, *check out* and *end up* could have been written as *check* and *end* alone:

? The guidance given here on such matters is patchy. I checked out 30 popular catachreses, usages that are actually destroying useful words by making them ambiguous.

– Kingsley Amis, *The Observer*

? I came up against this shortage of female language most acutely when writing my novel *The Waterfall*, which is the most female of all my books, beginning with childbirth, travelling through sex, and ending up with a thrombic clot resulting from contraceptive pill-taking.

– Margaret Drabble,
'Words', BBC Radio 3

Always pause to consider whether the adverb or

preposition really does change the sense of the verb, and thereby earn its keep. If it does not, leave it out.

b. Note, however, that there are some cases where a preposition is preferred to no preposition in standard British English. *To approximate the truth*, *to protest the war*, and *to provide him an excuse* are possible (though not always preferred) in North American English, but *to approximate to the truth*, *to protest against the war*, and *to provide him with an excuse* are preferred in British English. Conversely, *to agree a plan* is frequent in British English for *to agree on a plan* or *to agree to a plan*, but the last two constructions are alone acceptable in North American English and are preferred by purists in Britain. (See AGREE.)

6. a. One very common way of forming new verbs is by the process called 'conversion' — the use of a word belonging to another part of speech, usually a noun, to make a verb. This process has been going on in English for a long time. We made the verb *to question* from the noun *question* in the 15th century, and the verb *to knife* from the noun *knife* in the 19th. The verb *to lunch*, meaning 'to eat lunch', was derived from the noun *lunch* in the 19th century, and has since developed a transitive sense meaning 'to buy lunch for (someone)': *He lunched us sumptuously*. This is an unobjectionable way of extending the vocabulary where something new needs to be said. The verb *to service*, meaning 'to perform routine maintenance on', is very useful now that machines play such an important part in most of our lives. The process of conversion seems to get somewhat out of hand, however, when people take to using *? to author* instead of *to write*.

b. One kind of conversion is that by which *compound verbs* are formed, such as *to air-condition*, *blue-pencil*, *downgrade*, *single-space*, *soft-pedal*, and *signpost*. Again, there seems to be no objection to such expressions in principle, though the isolated modern case might attract criticism: *to round-table*, for instance, or *to compulsory-purchase*. One problem they do raise is whether to hyphenate them or spell them as one word. Consult a dictionary if in doubt, but bear in mind that the dictionaries themselves often disagree with one another over such spellings. (See NOUNS 2.)

7. Another way of forming verbs is by *back-formation*. This is the process of making a new verb from an existing noun or adjective that might itself appear to be derived from the verb: *to laze* (1592), for instance, comes from *lazy*, rather than the other way round. And *to edit* (1791) comes from *editor* (1649), even though *publisher* (15th century) comes from *to publish* (14th century).

Many such words certainly earn their place in the language. We need the verbs *to edit*, *to extradite*,

to legislate, to manipulate, to televise, to automate, and *to diagnose*; and the verbs *to laze*, *to scavenge*, and *to burgle* are at least convenient ways of expressing those ideas; but many careful speakers disapprove of such coinages as *to liaise* (from *liaison*), *to self-destruct* (from *self-destruction*), and *to enthuse* (from *enthusiasm*). *Enthuse* at least should be avoided in formal speech and writing.

8. Yet another kind of verb is formed by adding *-ise* or *-ize* to an existing word: *legalise* from *legal*, *magnetise* from *magnet*. Again, some careful users feel that altogether too many new verbs are being constructed on this pattern, and dislike such formations as *finalise*, *hospitalise*, *privatise*, and × *politicise*. (See -ISE.)

vertex, vortex   The Latin verb *vertere*, 'to turn', gave rise to a Latin noun with two forms, *vertex* or *vortex*. It meant either 'a highest point' or 'a whirl'. *Vertex* has now taken on the first of these meanings, *vortex* the second.

The *vertex* is the highest point of a hill or structure, or the apex of a cone or upright triangle standing on its base. It also has various specialised senses. In anatomy and zoology it is the crown of the head. In astronomy it is the zenith — or the highest point reached in the apparent motion of a celestial body, especially the sun. In geometry it can mean the point at which two or more lines or edges intersect.

A *vortex* is a flow round an axis, or a whirl — of air, water, or flame. It is often used to refer to a cyclone or whirlpool, and sometimes specifically to the core or centre of such a whirl. Used figuratively, it refers to any activity or situation that is characterised as a whirl, or that draws into its centre and engulfs what surrounds it: *She lived in a vortex of parties and socialising*; *They were swept up in the vortex of political activism*.

The plurals of *vertex* and *vortex* are technically *vertices* and *vortices*, pronounced /**ver**ti-seez/ and /**vor**ti-seez/. *Vertexes* and *vortexes* are often encountered, however, and are considered acceptable in general usage.

very, much   The familiar adverb *very* serves to intensify an adjective or adverb when placed directly in front of it. It is the commonest way of expressing the idea of 'extremely' or 'to a great degree': *She was very lucky*; *They worked very diligently*.

Common though it is, *very* cannot be applied to every adjective and adverb.

1. Some adjectives and adverbs have an absolute sense: *certain, essential, worthless, perfectly,* *unique,* and so on. (See ADJECTIVES 3; PERFECT; UNIQUE.) Strictly speaking, something is either certain or it is not; there are no *degrees* of certainty. So you cannot really say *? more certain* or *? less certain* (though you can say *more nearly certain*). And in the same way, you should not really say ✗ *very certain* or ✗ *very perfectly* (though you can, except in very formal contexts, say *utterly certain* or *absolutely perfectly,* to reinforce the sense of totality).

One apparent exception:

? When the gang had finished with the informer, he was very dead indeed.

The odd or comic effect of *very dead* derives precisely from the unacceptability of this combination in ordinary straightforward usage.

2. A further problem with *very* arises with adjectives or apparent adjectives that consist of past participles. There is no difficulty in saying *very tired* or *very pleased*. But can we say *? very displeased*? Perhaps, but it doesn't feel quite so natural any longer. And it feels quite wrong to say ✗ *very criticised*. The intensifying adverb needed here is *much* (or *greatly*): *much criticised*; *greatly criticised*.

The difference seems to be this: *pleased* has been accepted in English as a full adjective in its own right, even though it still has the form of the past participle of the verb 'to please'. Hence: *very pleased*. (Similarly, we would say spontaneously *very interested, very annoyed, very experienced, very assured, very embarrassed, very worried*.)

At the other end of the scale, *criticised* has kept an extremely strong connection with the verb 'to criticise', and lacks the status of an independent adjective. Hence: *much criticised*. (Similarly we would write *much discussed, much improved, much used, much maligned, much admired*.)

The word *displeased* lies somewhere in the middle — together with *vexed, inconvenienced, obsessed, engrossed, preoccupied,* and so on. Any of the intensifiers is acceptable here:

Simon is very preoccupied with his exam preparations just now.
Simon is much preoccupied with his exam preparations just now.
Simon is greatly preoccupied with his exam preparations just now.

There is another slight difference between the use of *very* and the use of *much* as intensifier. The use of *much* often produces a greater sense of formality, even archaic stiltedness:

Webster was much possessed by death

And saw the skull beneath the skin.
— T.S. Eliot,
'Whispers of Immortality'

He is feeling much maligned sounds more formal than *He is feeling very insulted*. The reason for this difference in formality may be simply that words requiring *much* tend to be more difficult and unusual words than those requiring *very*. At all events, there is one way of toning down the formality of *much,* and that is by adding the word *very* as well. *He is feeling very much maligned* sounds less stiff than *He is feeling much maligned*.

3. There are certain past participles which, although once again functioning as adjectives, are not usually intensified by adding either *very* or *much*. It sounds awkward to say either *much injured* or *very injured* — it would be far more natural to say *badly injured* or *seriously injured*.

When intensifying such past participles, in other words, refer them to a standard of quality (*good/bad, severe/mild,* and so on) rather than quantity (*much/little*): *badly botched, well written, severely burnt, slightly disfigured*.

The word *affected,* it is interesting to note, can take *very* or *much* or *seriously* as its intensifier, according to the sense in which it is used:

She's a very affected young woman, I must say (= conceited and insincere).
The widow was much affected by all the messages of good will (= emotionally moved, touched).
His performance in the 200 metres was seriously affected by a pulled tendon in his left leg (= adversely influenced, damaged).

via This preposition means 'by way of; in transit through': *travelling from Trieste to Athens, via Belgrade*. It should not be used as an affected synonym of 'by' or 'by means of': ✗ *sent a message via your brother*; ✗ *was sent via parcel post*; ✗ *We're going there via motorbike*; ✗ *forced a confession via unfair interrogation methods*.

Compare PER.

viable This adjective seems to have become a fashionable catch-all term, standing in for the plain old-fashioned *possible, real, workable, effective, important, believable, practicable, lasting, profitable, valid, feasible,* and so on. Such phrases as *? a viable solution, ? a viable alternative,* and *? economically viable* have become clichés, mouthed parrot-fashion by politicians and public spokesmen. *Viable* may sound impressively earnest, but it usually does not add anything to the meaning of a sentence that the other, unpretentious, adjectives could not provide just as well:

? His fate hangs on the result of a snap election he himself called, arguing that his one-seat majority in the 91-seat parliament was no longer viable. The situation, he said, had arisen because he could no longer rely on the support of a woman MP.
     – David Garvey, *The Observer*

? A salesman to his fingertips, he naturally assumes — no doubt with justice — that those in his employ would welcome the options of high earnings from a modern industry and generous redundancy for those from pits without a viable future.
     – leading article, *Daily Telegraph*

? Miss Le Moignan had defeated Miss Devoy in the final of the French Open at the end of last month, and her performance yesterday suggested once again that her flamboyant style poses the most viable threat to the New Zealander's continuing reign.
     – David Hunn, *The Observer*

Although these modern senses are clearly here to stay, purists reserve *viable* for its older sense: 'capable of living'. The word goes back through French and Old French to *vie*, and the Latin *vita*, meaning 'life'. *A viable foetus* is a foetus that has reached a stage of development that will allow it to survive and develop. *A viable seed* or *spore* is one that is capable of germinating under favourable conditions. *A viable settlement* is one capable of becoming a permanent town or community.

By extension, *a viable scheme* is a scheme that could really be put into practice, that is capable of being realised — as opposed to a 'pie-in-the-sky' scheme, a 'purely theoretical' scheme, a 'pipe dream', a 'stillborn' scheme, an 'impracticable' scheme — or a 'nonviable' scheme. The noun *viability* is used in a corresponding way:

Concentrating on London and the West Country Sarah spent three months testing the viability of such a company and is now engaged on the much bigger task of putting together a report for the Arts Council giving definitive figures and projected results.
     – Elizabeth Bunster,
     The Fiction Magazine

The Government is already known to be seriously concerned about the viability of Mercury, which has so far proved unable to build its customer base.
     – Colin Clifford, *The Observer*

This seems a reasonably fair development of the earlier sense, but it has unfortunately led to the excessively general and unacceptably frequent use of the words. Use *viable* and *viability* with great caution when applying it to anything other than embryonic or very young living organisms.

virtuosity   This refers to the great technical skill of a *virtuoso*. It has nothing to do with *virtue*:

'Un Re in ascolto' is undoubtedly a score of consummate virtuosity.
     – Peter Heyworth, *The Observer*

But certainly there would be no excitement if you carried on repeating metaphors. Virtuosity for itself would go dead.
     – Emma Tennant, interviewed
     in *The Literary Review*

The Latin noun *virtus* (derived from *vir*, 'a man') meant 'manliness, strength, or ability' rather than 'goodness'. In English and French, it has long had this sense of power or ability too: 'efficacy, potency, skill', and so on. We can still speak of *the virtue of herbal remedies*. But the adjective *virtuous* has now lost this association, and is used only in reference to moral good and bad, not practical good and bad.

The noun *virtuoso*, borrowed from Italian, refers typically to a musician of great brilliance. What *a virtuoso* displays is *virtuosity*, 'great technical skill'. Its meaning is not too far from that one special sense of *virtue*, but is very far from the meaning of *virtuousness*.

virus   See GERM.

visitation   *Visitation* is often used, without much thought, as a supposedly elegant synonym of *visit*. But it should be used in this way only when a jocular effect is intended, in particular when referring to a tedious and unwelcome visit.

Used properly, *visitation* refers to various special kinds of visit: a formal or official visit, as by an inspector, or by a bishop to his diocese, or above all a visit by a ghost. There are further religious and supernatural senses of the word, as the following phrases indicate: *the visitation of the sick* (from the Book of Common Prayer); *the visitation of plagues on the peoples of Egypt*; *a visitation by the angels*. With a capital *V, the Visitation* refers to the visit of the Virgin Mary to her cousin Elizabeth, and to the minor church festival held on 2 July in commemoration of this visit. In the following example, *visitation* is used to suggest something almost supernatural:

> His wife had accepted his dictum, when he arrived that night in a white man's bakkie with a visitation of five white faces floating in the dark.
> — Nadine Gordimer, *July's People*

In American English, *visitation* refers to the right of access that a divorced or separated parent has to his or her children.

viz When read from the printed page, this abbreviation is usually rendered as *namely*; in informal conversation, however, /viz/ is often heard. It is an abbreviation of *videlicet,* Latin for 'it is permitted to see'. It is pronounced /vi-**deeli**-set, vī-, -**day**li-ket/, though there is seldom any need to say it at all.

The word *viz* is used when listing items just mentioned or hinted at:

> The three candidates — viz, Brown, Green, and Mrs White — are now in the waiting-room.

It is similar to *i.e.*, but the slight distinction is worth retaining: *i.e.* tends to explain rather than simply to list:

> The three candidates for the job — i.e., the editorial vacancy, not the typist's job — are now in the waiting-room.

The form *viz* is often followed by a full stop, but there is really no need for one: the *z* in fact represents the closing *-et* of *videlicet* (see ABBREVIATIONS).

Further in keeping with modern streamlining, *viz* tends no longer to be italicised in print; moreover it often does without a comma directly after it:

> Britain's legacy to the sub-continent is complex and multi-faceted. But many features of it are clearly identifiable, viz the widespread use of the English language, some domestic and public architecture, basic communications infrastructure, the style and tradition of the armed forces and police, the parliamentary system of government in India, to name a few of the more obvious manifestations of the impact of one culture on another.
> — Sir Anthony Parsons, *The Times*

Note: it could be argued that *e.g.* would be more suitable than *viz* here, since the list of examples is not exhaustive.

See also E.G., I.E.

vogue words Fashion is a fickle mistress, bestowing her favours — apparently arbitrarily, and usually very briefly — on a particular hairstyle or pop group, a ski resort ... or a word or phrase: *parameter, quantum leap, aware* (in the sense of 'tuned in' — another vogue term), the notorious *ongoing*, and so on.

Vogue words are those words and phrases that suddenly and perhaps needlessly come into vogue, to be heard in so many fashionable conversations and read in so many pretentious pieces of journalism. Vogue words are adapted either consciously as impressive-sounding and 'trendy' (to use a vogue word) or unconsciously as a lazy and often imprecise way of conveying an idea.

The first of these promptings is clearly at work in the following quotation:

> The handsome 34-year-old world No 6 has emerged from a lazy coaching summer to be savaged in the Premier League by hungry young Englishmen ... David Lloyd, of Edgbaston Priory, Gawain Briars, of Nottingham, and, this week, Geoff Williams, of Manchester Northern. As if to illustrate that the syndrome is one of age differential, rather than national complex, he also fell in the World Masters championship to the new 20-year-old world No 2, Chris Dittmar of Australia.
> — Colin McQuillan, *The Times*

There are three indisputable vogue words here — *syndrome, differential*, and *complex* — and a further three contenders: *savaged, hungry,* and *fell*. So far from sounding impressive, such journalism comes across as strained and sometimes merely silly.

Here is another quotation heavily weighed down with vogue words: *escalation* is again an 'impressive' vogue word; *realistically, genuine,* and perhaps *scale* are 'imprecise' vogue words:

> To date Alfonsin has shown no sign of coping realistically with the very genuine possibility of an escalation into hyper-inflation on a Weimar scale, and if this happened, as it very well might, Argentina might become another Lebanon.
> — Peregrine Worsthorne, *Sunday Telegraph*

The term *vogue word* was coined about 60 years ago by the usage expert H.W. Fowler. The older term *catchword* was rather limiting, retaining its association with political slogans and rallying-cries. (And *catch phrase* tends to be associated nowadays with individual comedians or broadcasters.) The more recent terms *buzz word, fad word,* and *weasel word* are also rather narrower in range, perhaps, and are used chiefly in American English. The *buzz* of *buzz word* suggests not just the frequency but also the meaninglessness of the word in question. *Weasel words* are usually attributed to politicians and officials, and are designed to obscure or even skirt the truth, or to evade a direct commitment; overuse and misuse unobtrusively sucks the meaning out of a *weasel word* in the way that a weasel supposedly sucks out the contents of an egg without doing any obvious damage to the shell.

The term *vogue word* is a better 'catch-all' (another vogue word?). It refers to several different categories of overused words which are listed below.

Vogue words are not, as a rule, newly coined words. They are established words that, suddenly and mysteriously, seem to be on everyone's lips, either in their original sense or with some slightly changed meaning. They are usually 'instant clichés' — careful speakers and writers will avoid them if possible. Many vogue words fade after a single season, but some are surprisingly resilient.

Consider the case of the verb *to relate.* For hundreds of years it had been quietly and unremarkably doing its work conveying such senses as 'to establish a connection between', 'to tell, or give an account of', and so on.

In the 20th century, the word acquired an extended sense in the specialised vocabularies of psychologists and sociologists — 'to have a specified relationship with or response to': *He relates well to babies and animals; suffering from a depression and generally relating poorly to her environment.*

In the 1960s, this psychological-sociological use of the verb was taken up by laymen, and became one of the hallmarks of the decade, especially in the United States: *I really relate to your ideas; How do you relate to macrobiotic foods?* You were no longer *interested* in things or *attracted* to other people — you *related* to them. (And unless otherwise specified, *relating* had by now come to mean *relating well.*)

In due course, the word became so automatic, unthinking, and often empty of meaning, that it dropped out of fashion — lost its 'credibility' perhaps. At all events, people stopped relating to it in a positive way, and only very un-hip or nostalgic people would allow themselves to use such a *passé* term. (Not surprisingly, however, it is revived from time to time, as in the television advertising campaign for a California wine that you could *really relate to.*)

One important qualification: not every widely used new term or sense should be branded a vogue word and shunned as mindlessly conformist. A new term or sense is often introduced to fill a gap in the English vocabulary. The term *supply-side economics* is fashionable because the *concept* of supply-side economics is fashionable, and some phrase is needed to represent it. (The convenience and conciseness of this carry a corresponding danger, however — that the *naming* of the concept encourages an easy *acceptance* of it, since it comes to be regarded as a simple, unanalysable whole.)

Two other terms that have been unfairly castigated as vogue words are *low profile* and *scenario* — *low profile* in the sense of 'an unobtrusive pattern of behaviour; a restrained public stance; especially, an avoidance of militancy, publicity, or intervention' (the phrase was originally a military term, referring to the tendency of tanks and other likely targets to stay on low ground or in hiding in order to reduce the chances of being hit by enemy gunfire); and *scenario* in the sense of 'an outline of a hypothetical chain of events; a possible state of affairs or course of action'. It is difficult to think how these complicated ideas could be economically expressed if the terms *low profile* and *scenario* were excluded (though *profile* itself clearly is a vogue word in various senses).

It may be a reflection of the complex world we live in, rather than of the impoverished state of the English language, that such terms are so frequently used. Similarly, perhaps, with *anti-social, bottleneck* (but to say *big bottleneck* is to ruin the metaphor), *cold war, community* (as in *the homosexual community*), *copy-cat crime, counterproductive, heritage, ivory tower, lookalike, pattern, permissive, status symbol, upmarket, yardstick*, and so on. Used sparingly, these are all very helpful terms in their proper place.

In short, not all words enjoying a vogue are real vogue words of little value.

That said, here is a brief classification and list of vogue words, with several clear-cut examples.

● words that have broken out of some specific sphere of discourse — legal, political, scientific, psychological, or the like — into general use (often distorting the original meaning, not just extending it):

acid test
adrenalin
allergic
ambivalent
blueprint
catalyst
chain reaction
charisma
clone
crescendo
cross-section
decimate
dichotomy
differential
double bind
ecology
end product
equate
evaluate
extrapolate
fascist
feedback
fellow traveller
fixation
flashpoint
format
genocide
geometrical progression
interface
internecine
leading question
logistics
masochism
metaphysical
orchestrate
overkill
parameter
paranoid
personal equation
predicate
prelude
propaganda
psychological moment
rat-race
repression
special pleading
state-of-the-art
strategy
symbiosis
syndrome
task force
track record
transplant
trauma
viable
winds of change
workshop
zero in on

Note the following quotation for an example of the vogue use of *quantum leap*, borrowed from the domain of nuclear physics:

> While the image of St Helena as a quaint English toy town is compelling it falls short of the truth. For the aftermath of the Falklands war has provided the Saints — as they are known — with a quantum leap in knowledge of their parlous condition as a dependency of Britain.
>
> — Ray Coonan, *The Times*

For *born-again*:

> If the Government needs to cater for the legitimate interests of the farming community, it should see the contradiction in both subsidising increased agricultural production and then expecting farmers to be born-again conservationists.
>
> — leading article, *Daily Telegraph*

For *spin-off*:

> In considering any proposal for disposal, whether to a United Kingdom or a foreign bidder, the Government will bear very much in mind the technology spin-off effects for the United Kingdom.
>
> — Norman Tebbit, quoted in the *Daily Telegraph*

● words that have a wide range of senses and can be used again and again, like a versatile overcoat, in quite different contexts. The user is spared having to tailor his vocabulary to any particular occasion. Why struggle to find a sharp specialised word to dress your idea in, when a lazy vogue word is available that more or less passes as suitable? (This is not to say that these words should never be used — only that they should not be used where a sharper, more precise word is available.)

amenities
authentic
background
backlash
basic
colourful
constructive
contemporary
credible
dynamic
engaged
environment
establishment
facility
factor
feature
function
glamorous
in-depth
involve
issue
level
major
marginal
massive
meaningful
mechanism
model
operative
overall
phenomenal
pivotal
plausible
process
profile
realistic
redundant
relevant
rewarding
scale
significant
situation
system
total

For *dimension* and *perspective*:

> And that was how I felt having the baby. It called for the same complete concentration — dedication, almost. I felt as if I were projecting myself into a new dimension, and it was so important that everything else acquired a new and relatively tiny perspective.
>
> — Lynne Reid Banks, *The L-Shaped Room*

For *constructive*:

> Mr Kinnock opened the duel by accusing the Prime Minister of complete humbug in earlier comments about the need for moderate, responsible, reasonable and constructive trade unionism.
>
> — Julia Langdon, *The Guardian*

vogue words

For *profile*:

> Ask any university administrator what his chief teaching anxiety is and he is likely to reply that he has lost the wrong people, and has a lopsided age profile among teaching staff.
>
> — leading article, *Daily Telegraph*

These 'vague words' are sometimes used not as an easy substitute for a sharper word, but as a needless piece of verbal padding. Such lean, efficient wording as *experts in nuclear physics*, might be fattened up into *experts in the field of nuclear physics*. Plain old *wet weather* supposedly sounds more impressive as *wet weather conditions*. A simple *from me* is inflated to *from these quarters* or *from this direction*.

● highfalutin or up-to-date equivalents, adapted in order to sound impressive or expert:

academic = theoretical, impractical
aggressive = active, energetic
ambience = surroundings
archetypal = typical
challenging = interesting
compassionate = understanding
concept = a rough plan
conceptualise = to imagine
confrontation = a disagreement
dedicated = hard-working
deploy = to use or place
dialogue = discussions
embattled = worried, hard-pressed
ersatz = artificial
escalate = to rise or increase
euphoria = happiness
eventuate = to happen
fiefdom = power base, territory controlled
finalise = to finish
global = worldwide
image = reputation
implement = to carry out or achieve
literature = printed information
manipulate = to control or sway
meaningful = important
mentality = mind, attitude
meticulous = careful
minimal = small
motivation = encouragement
objective = unbiased or fair
ongoing = current, continuing
optimal = ideal, best
optimistic = hopeful
palpable = obvious
paradigm = an example or model
pedigree = record, experience

perception = an opinion or view
personnel = staff, or worker
pragmatic = practical
proportion = part
rationale = reasons
reaction = an opinion or answer
recrudescence = renewal or repetition
repercussions = results
sabotage = to spoil or wreck
subjective = personal or biased
supportive = encouraging, kind, sympathetic
synthesise = to combine or combine into
tendentious = biased
utilise = to use
venue = a place or setting

For *dialogue*:

> Mr Oswald Clark, chairman of the synod's House of Laity, who led the opposition in 1978, said arguments supporting women's ordination were neither cohesive nor complete: 'The dialogue is unfinished.'
>
> — Martyn Halsall, *The Guardian*

For *stance* and *escalation*:

> He warded off brickbats aimed at himself and his executive and also a series of moves by militants to guide the union into an extreme stance in an escalation of industrial trouble.
>
> — *Daily Telegraph*

For *philosophy*:

> His rugby philosophy is to move the ball. 'You might make a lot of mistakes but you have got to try for that is the only way to make opportunities.'
>
> — Clem Thomas, *The Observer*

For *ongoing*:

> Since he had stopped writing, the only ongoing friction in Garp's life concerned his relationship with his best friend, Roberta Muldoon.
>
> — John Irving (U.S.), *The World According to Garp*

Here are a few quotations in which vogue words are used deliberately and self-consciously:

> When I saw him again in 1955, and thereafter quite often, he seemed fairly unchanged — as comical and fascinating as ever. Had he 'matured', to use a current vogue word for grown up?
>
> — Jessica Mitford, *The Observer*

Then for someone who is not speaking, you are giving away volumes of information. . . .
I mean that if I were younger and more trendy I should probably say that I could deconstruct the signifiers of your discourse.
– Philip Neville, in Anita Brookner's
Hotel du Lac

Mr Hart's performance invites the opposite criticism. He did well to win four primaries. But in the language of 'momentum', Mr Hart seems to have 'peaked' some time last week and since then suffered some 'slippage'.
– leading article, *Daily Telegraph*

● slangy synonyms, typically from journalism or the various sub-cultures of modern urban society. These vogue words are adapted in order to sound either tough or 'with it':

bid = an attempt
enjoy! = enjoy it, or enjoy yourself
flak = criticism
hype = publicity
in = fashionable
laid back = easygoing
must = a necessity
nous = common sense, intelligence
probe = an investigation
relax! = calm down!
sensation = a surprise, or a great success
smear = an insulting or libellous allegation
sort out = to solve, untangle, mollify, silence, fight, and so on

For *flak*:

When the London Economic Summit ended nine days ago President Reagan must have drawn a deep sigh of relief. Although he took a fair amount of flak over the impact of United States fiscal policy on international interest rates, his fellow summiteers were keen not to embarrass him in an election year.
– *Daily Telegraph*

For *number*:

Mr Sellers said that a Toronto manufacturer had just brought out the first computer-designed sock, an ergonomically constructed non-slip number which worked on the principle that when the foot went down, the sock went up.
– Sue Arnold, *The Observer*

For *supremo*:

Mr Brittan, Home Secretary, has appointed a supremo to direct the Government fight against the increasing abuse of drugs and to help stem the flow of hard drugs into the country.
– John Weeks, *Daily Telegraph*

For *ego trip* and *overkill*:

Mr Alan Greengross, Conservative group leader on the council, described the decision as a multi-million-pound ego trip to promote Mr Kenneth Livingstone at the ratepayers' expense.
He added: 'Far from saving the GLC, this is massive overkill. We are almost certain to destroy the GLC's case and to alienate public opinion from it.'
– Valerie Elliot, *Daily Telegraph*

For *deliver*:

Britain cannot obtain political consensus inside Northern Ireland, and still less can Britain deliver a United Ireland.
– Conor Cruise O'Brien,
The Observer

For *hit list*:

One of the central arguments in the miners' strike has been the existence of a Coal Board hit list of collieries marked for closure.
– Graham Jones, *Daily Telegraph*

● silly overstatements, no longer the monopoly of teenagers:

amazing	magic
awfully	mega
bloodbath	obscene (*an obscene*
cataclysm	*new tax*)
cosmic	revolution (*a revolution*
crisis	*in men's headwear*)
dire	sensational
epoch-making	super
fabulous	tragic
fantastic	ultimate
great	unique
grotesque	unbelievable
inconceivable	unreal
infinitely	unthinkable

● pretentious or threadbare metaphors:

bombshell = a surprise
breakthrough = an advance or success
facelift = an improvement
front-runner = a favourite, leading contender
knee-jerk = unthinking and automatic, predictable

marathon = going on for a long time
massage = to falsify or distort slightly
orchestrate = to organise deliberately
overtones = hints
strongman = a political despot, a dictator
summit = an important conference
target = to strive for, intend
thaw = an improvement in relations
traumatised = distressed
violence = almost any action that you happen
  to disapprove of
within the framework of = in, at

For *flavour of the month*:

Six Northern spy networks were closed down
in the South. Mr Kim is not exactly the
flavour of the month in Pyongyang
espionage circles and, to ensure that their
prize exhibit stays alive, the South Koreans
have allocated him a personal bodyguard
skilled in the martial arts and the use of small
arms.
— Alexander Frater, *The Observer*

For *mileage*:

It is also a malign paradox that many big
British companies see no mileage either in
doing more to help blacks or drawing attention to their virtue in this respect.
— David Watt, *The Times*

For *cliffhanger*:

Birmingham East is the most marginal constituency in Europe, needing a swing of only
0.2 per cent for Labour to take control from
the Conservatives, yet it is unlikely that a
third of the half-million will bother to take
part in this cliffhanger.
— James Allan, *Daily Telegraph*

For *grass roots*:

We went quite near the table placed by the
office where father sat to receive petitions
and give judgements and settle quarrels.
Thus we witnessed the grass roots of
government.
— Lord Butler, *The Art of the Possible*

See also CLICHÉS; JARGON; NEWSPAPER
ENGLISH; SLANG.

voice See ACTIVE AND PASSIVE.

vortex See VERTEX.

wait, await *To wait* takes a direct object in the phrases *to wait one's turn, to wait one's chances,* and informally in such expressions as *Let's wait dinner till she gets home* or the Americanism *to wait table in a restaurant.* It is also sometimes used transitively (that is, with a direct object, or in the passive) in the general sense of 'to remain in expectation of' — *? I waited the results anxiously*; *? She waits our decision*; *? He waits his fate* — but it is far preferable here to use *await* or *wait for* instead: *I waited anxiously for the results*; *She awaits our decision*; *He awaits his fate.*

To await, conversely, is now no longer used intransitively. It has to take a direct object, or be used in the passive. But it is by no means always appropriate when used in this way: it usually sounds extremely formal when referring to people or physical objects: *? I shall await her* (or *her arrival*) *until midnight*; *? We are awaiting the train.* It would be normal to use *wait for* in such sentences instead. And in the following construction, *to await* cannot be used at all in place of *to wait for* : *We are waiting for the train to arrive.*

The one case where *await* can take a human object without sounding overformal is when the sense wanted is 'to be in store for': *A surprise awaits her when she gets home*; *A prize of £5000 awaits the first person to find the solution.*

With direct objects that are intangible things or abstract notions, *to await* is usually acceptable, though still more formal than *to wait for*: *We are still awaiting the announcement*; *We await the outcome with trepidation.* Note that *await* is often used in the simple present tense, whereas *wait* often favours the continuous *-ing* form: *We are waiting for the outcome with trepidation.*

To wait on means, strictly, 'to serve': *You always expect me to wait on you.* It is sometimes used, especially in American English, as a variant of *to wait for* — *? I'll wait on the bus* — but this usage, although long-established, is still usually considered informal or dubious.

waive, wave, waiver, waver The verb *to waive* means 'to give up or defer (a right or claim) voluntarily': *to waive your diplomatic immunity*;

The defence counsel waived his right of reply.

A French marriage contract is a cold-blooded document listing everything of the bridegroom's that the bride may or may not share. Jagger wanted Bianca to agree to waive any right to his possessions in the event of a divorce. Bianca was upset by the calculation of it, and pleaded with Mick to call the wedding off.

– Philip Norman, *The Stones*

Albert was as good as his word and stayed 11 weeks. After that, of course, few people wanted to see a less-known actor reading a phone-book. I was required to waive my royalty, and after a four months' run the play closed.

– Peter Nichols, *The Observer*

Wave has numerous well-known meanings, both as noun and verb, and is not usually confused with *to waive.* But there is often a confusion over the phrase *to wave aside,* meaning 'to dismiss from consideration, as by a flick of the hand': *He waved aside my warnings and persisted in his disastrous policy.* Do not write it as × *to waive aside.*

× He was full of good humour and waived aside my apology for imposing on him when ill.

– Louis Nizer (U.S.),
My Life at Court

Waiver is the noun from *waive* and means 'the relinquishment of a right' and sometimes 'the legal document that contains this relinquishment'. *Waver* of course means 'one who waves'. But there is also a verb *to waver,* meaning 'to hesitate or falter, fail in courage or decisiveness': *His confidence wavered at the sight of the audience.*

This misuse of the word 'freedom' is intended to prevent thought rather than provoke it, and it has proved extremely effective. People are usually stupid rather than evil, and many staunch Tory supporters would waver if you challenged such catchphrases.

– Eva Figes, *The Literary Review*

These words have different histories. *To waver* comes from Old Norse via Middle English, both *waive* and *waiver* from Norman French via Middle English, and *wave* from Old English.

wake, awake, awaken, waken All four of these verbs can be used in both transitive and intransitive senses (roughly, with or without a direct object), though some forms and senses are far more idiomatic than others.

The commonest of these verbs is *to wake*, both transitive and intransitive: *Please wake me at 7*; *I woke (up) just in time*; *The baby was woken by the storm*.

Note the verb forms: *wake, woke, woken*; the past and past participle *waked* is also possible, though rather old-fashioned in British English; it is still current in American English:

> Wrestling together, they knocked over the tables and chairs, when the lights went on and waked him. Roy grabbed under the pillow for a gun he thought was there.
> – Bernard Malamud (U.S.), *The Natural*

To wake also used to mean 'to be awake, to remain awake', though it retains this sense today only in the idioms *waking or sleeping* and *waking hours*. For the standard verb uses today, use *be awake* or *stay awake* (or simply *stay up*) instead: *We stayed awake until she came home*. It would be archaic to use *waked* here; even more so to use *watched,* which formerly had the same meaning too.

In the literal sense of 'to wake up' (both transitive and intransitive), both *to awake* and *to awaken* are now rather formal or old-fashioned. When a metaphorical sense is intended, *to awaken* is the usual transitive verb, and *to awake* is the usual intransitive verb: *Don't awaken their suspicions*; *Our fears were awakened once again*; *Our fears awoke once again*; *When they awake to the realisation that they're trapped — it will be a rude awakening for them*. The form *awoken* used to be considered nonstandard — *woken* or *awaked* being preferred — but there seems no basis for the objection, and it is freely used, and widely accepted, today.

> Shortly before noon yesterday, the Conservative Party conference in Brighton was awakened from its slumbers by the sound of a man shouting at it. Speakers are not supposed to shout at Tory conferences because it wakes the representatives up.
> – Michael White, *The Guardian*

Waken is usually used as a transitive verb, more commonly occurring in the passive, and used in both literal and metaphorical contexts. It is now rather old-fashioned: *I was wakened by a strange noise*; *The OPEC countries were wakened from their complacency by the U.N. report*.

In the following quotation, *waken* is used in the active, and seems rather stiff, following as it does a use of the more idiomatic *wake*:

> I was much too disturbed to go to bed myself. I decided to wake Roy Calvert; it was a strange reversal of rôles, when I recalled the nights of melancholy in which he had woken me. ...
> He was peacefully asleep. He had not known insomnia since the summer, and always when he slept it was as quietly as a child. It took some time to waken him.
> – C.P. Snow, *The Masters*

See also RISE.

wander, wonder These two words are not likely to have their meanings confused, but do present a traditional problem in spelling and pronunciation. Remember that *wander*, 'to roam or digress', has an *a* as in *meander*; *wonder*, 'to marvel or doubt', has an *o* as in *ponder*.

The similar characteristics of the two words are exploited to good effect in the popular American religious song beginning *I wonder as I wander out under the sky*.

Both *wonder* and *wander* occur as nouns as well as verbs, of course (*wonder* more often than *wander*). Both derive from Old English roots.

Both words are pronounced differently from the way you would expect: *wander* (but not *wonder*) rhymes with *yonder*; *wonder* rhymes with *thunder*.

want 1. The primary meaning of *to want* in modern usage is of course 'to desire' or 'to wish for': *What do you want for Christmas? Do you want the parcel wrapped?*

To *want* may also be used, especially in British English, to mean 'to lack' — *The chair wants a leg* — or 'to need': *That child wants a good talking-to*; *That fence wants mending*.

To be wanting as an intransitive verb (taking no object) means: 'to be lacking': *A roof is wanting, but otherwise the house is finished*.

Sometimes the senses of 'desire', 'lack', and 'need' seem to overlap, as in: *The nation wants a democratically elected government*. A good writer will be aware of possible ambiguity.

2. In two of the sample sentences above, the

verb forms are sometimes reversed in regional British English: *Do you want the parcel wrapping?* and *? That fence wants mended.* The second of these is doubtful, possibly nonstandard, even in regional usage. The first is a colourful and widespread regional variant, but is best avoided in formal speech and writing. It does have a great deal to be said in its favour, however: it can be justified on grammatical grounds, and sometimes saves a sentence from ambiguity, as these two letters to the editor of the *Daily Telegraph* make clear:

> Either participle is really an abbreviated passive infinitive: 'Do you want it (to be) wrapped?' or 'Do you want it (to undergo) wrapping?' The former draws attention to the finished state, the latter to the action to be performed.
>
> In many contexts the difference of meaning will be slight. However: 'Do you want your turkey plucking?' is a clear offer to pluck a bird which still has its feathers. 'Do you want your turkey plucked' is ambiguous: it could simply mean that the shop stocks both plucked and unplucked birds.
>   – Paul Jackson

> 'I want the car parking' as opposed to 'I want the car parked' in fact conveys almost exactly similar information, *i.e.* 'Take the car and park it', but if you expand both slightly and say 'I want the car parking in the far corner' the information remains precise, whereas 'I want the car parked in the far corner' does not — you may mean 'Take this car and park it in the far corner' or you may mean 'Fetch me the car that is parked in the far corner'.
>   – H. Patrick Holden

None the less, a distinct regional flavour clings to such constructions as *Do you want your turkey plucking?* and *I want the car parking in the far corner*, no matter how effective they are in preventing ambiguity. Certainly it is important to avoid ambiguity, but there are better ways of doing that. The simplest is to reinstate the omitted words *to be* into the standard construction: *Do you want your turkey to be plucked?* and *I want the car to be parked in the far corner.* There is no ambiguity in these senses, and no distracting or controversial regional flavour either.

3. An expression such as × *She wanted we should travel by train* is nonstandard American English. Formal usage requires *She wanted us to travel by train.*

4. *want for.* The phrasal verb *to want for*, in its old-fashioned sense of 'to lack', survives chiefly in such idioms as *He wanted for nothing* and *She didn't want for anything.*

In the sense of 'to wish' it is often encountered in nonstandard American English: *She wanted for us to travel by train.* In standard usage, the *for* would be omitted.

The objections are less clear, however, when *to want* and *for* are separated. An expression such as *He wanted very much for me to go* sounds quite natural, though in formal usage it is still better to rephrase it as *He very much wanted me to go.* And an expression such as *What he wanted was for me to go* is probably acceptable as standard English everywhere.

5. *want in/out.* The expressions *to want in* and *to want out*, in their literal meaning of 'to want to enter' and 'to want to leave', are chiefly Scottish English or informal American English.

In the figurative sense of 'to want to participate or be included' and 'to want to withdraw or be released', the phrases are now fairly widespread in informal English, no longer just in American English but in British English too:

> My sources tell me an emotional Yablans said at one point that he 'wants out' of his contract.
>   – Dan Dorfman (U.S.), *New York*

> Details are shrouded in secrecy, but it appears that Boeing will take back the plane for more than $25 million at the end of 12 months if Virgin wants out. If there is any increase in the jumbo's value, Virgin will be able to sell it on the open market.
>   – Victor Smart, *The Observer*

> Children often relish being alone, because alone is where they know themselves and where they dream. But thanks to the war, these Belfast children are alone in a different way. Elizabeth is not dreaming of what she will be. She looks about her and knows quite well what she will be, what her life and that of her children will be in that dread city. She wants out.
>   – Roger Rosenblatt,
>   *The Children of War*

Several similar phrases are also sometimes used in both literal and figurative senses: *I want into the deal; She wanted off the show.*

-ward, -wards In British English, *-ward* is usually the adjective suffix, and *-wards* the adverb suffix: *a northward view, without a backward* glance, *an upward movement; looking north-wards, never glancing backwards, moving upwards.*

In American English, the *-ward* ending is commonly used for the adverb as well as the adjective, though *-wards* is usually also acceptable.

Some exceptions: in British English, *forward* can be used as the adverb in almost all cases, and in some constructions it is the only acceptable form: *Keep moving forward/forwards* (indicating direction); *Will Sgt Jones please step forward*; *Many witnesses came forward*; *I look forward to it*; *Forward march!*; *to bring the meeting forward* (indicating time). *Forwards* is distinctly preferable only when used in conjunction with *backwards*: *running forwards and backwards like scared chickens*; *the name reads the same backwards as forwards.* Even here, however, *forward* is possible.

Next, *onward*: this is just as acceptable an adverb as *onwards* in British English (and far preferable in American): *Onward, Christian soldiers; trudging onward through the icy wastes.* The one construction in which *onwards* is definitely preferred is that in which it follows a date directly: *from the sixth century onwards.* (In American English, *onward* and *onwards* would be equally acceptable here.) *Onward* is the only acceptable adjectival form.

Finally, *toward/s* and *afterward/s*: these have no current adjectival senses, though *untoward* is still a useful adjective; *towards* (preferably *toward* in American English) serves only as a preposition; *afterwards* (*afterward* is equally acceptable in American and probably in British English) only as an adverb.

wastage, waste *Waste* as a noun has many senses: 'rubbish or refuse', 'useless excess material', as in *chemical waste*, and above all, 'squandering; careless spending, consumption, or use': *a waste of time*; *It's a waste to throw that fruit out.*

Wastage is loss by decay, leakage, drying up, and so on, but not by human 'wastefulness'. There is *wastage* from an open reservoir because of evaporation. People speak of a reduction in staff by *natural wastage*, which refers to retirement, resignation, or death rather than dismissal or redundancy. Do not use *wastage* as just a grander-sounding variant of *waste*.

Waste, in its sense of 'squandering', implies moral censure; *wastage* seldom carries moral overtones.

wave, waver See WAIVE.

way 1. *Way* is frequently used as an adverb meaning 'to a great degree' in such phrases as *way over budget*, *way above my head*, *way back in 1916*, and *way ahead of the field*. It is in fact a shortened form of *away* here, and though well on its way to full acceptability, is still regarded as slightly informal.

2. *under way*. A ship (or voyage, or any project) is *under way*, never ✕ *under weigh*. This common error is of long standing:

✕ Bildad had told them that no profane songs would be allowed on board the Pequod, particularly in getting under weigh.
 – Herman Melville (U.S.),
 Moby Dick (1851)

The mistake is probably due to a confusion with the expressions *to weigh anchor* (= to raise the anchor) and *Anchors aweigh!* (never ✕ *Anchors away!*).

Note that *under way* is usually two words. Strictly speaking, the one-word form should be used only when it comes directly in front of the noun it qualifies: *underway refuelling*. However, the one-word form is being used increasingly in all contexts, and is approaching acceptability:

? The second movement was well underway when the first violinist suddenly collapsed.

3. *in the way of*. This is a strangely attractive piece of verbal padding — *There's not much in the way of food, I'm afraid.* Perhaps it serves to soften the forthrightness of *There's not much food, I'm afraid.* That apart, there is no reason for using the phrase. If you do use it, use it sparingly.

4. *by way of being*. This is another piece of verbal padding — *I am by way of being a liberal with a small l.* Avoid the phrase if possible; if not, use it very sparingly.

The phrase *by way of*, however, in the sense of 'as a means of; to serve as', is unobjectionable: *By way of apology, he bowed his head.*

-ways See -WISE.

we, us, our 1. *We* can mean 'you and I', or 'you and I and the others': *Shall we dance, Joan? Let's hire a coach, shall we?* It can mean 'the others and I but not you': *May we go now, miss?* Or it can mean just 'you', as used rather patronisingly to children and the sick: *How are we feeling today?*

A certain amount of ambiguity results when the range of *we, us,* and *our* is not made quite clear. *Shouldn't we get started?* might include or exclude the person addressed, thus producing two quite different possible answers: *But I'm not ready yet* or *Yes, you should have left an hour ago.* In discursive writing, the phrase *as we have noticed* presumably includes the reader, whereas *we believe...* presumably does not. But what about *and so we find...?* Take care to make clear your intended range when you use *we, us, our,* or *ours* in speech and writing.

2. The 'royal' or 'editorial' *we* is no longer very much in fashion: Queen Victoria apparently said *We are not amused,* but Queen Elizabeth II speaks plainly of *my Government* and *my husband and I.* Some newspaper editorials still use *we, us,* and *our* to preserve a collective anonymity, though increasingly some rephrasing is attempted to avoid personal pronouns altogether. Occasionally scientists write *We then heated the liquid* as a change from the tedious passive of *The liquid was then heated.* But *I* is preferable if the scientist was conducting the experiment on his own.

Note that the curious form *ourself* has been used as the 'reflexive pronoun' corresponding to the royal *we: We shall now take ourself to bed for a rest.* The normal reflexive form is of course *ourselves.*

3. Although clearly an object form, *us* sometimes appears in speech and writing as the subject of a sentence when joined to a plural noun: ✗ *Only us poor kids ever got to see the sun rise over Botany Bridge.* This use may be fairly common among children and in varieties of regional English, but it is not standard English, and should be avoided except in very informal usage, or in parody, or when presenting yourself as down-to-earth and unpretentious.

Unfortunately, in being careful to avoid this mistake, people sometimes go to the opposite extreme, and use *we* in contexts where *us* is in fact the correct form: ✗ *It's not fair to expect we people in public relations to know all the answers.*

In the following quotation, *us* is used correctly. It would be quite wrong to substitute *we* as supposedly more proper:

> Jargons are the private languages of those who need to say something new that cannot be said in the existing language. They are not strictly the concern of us outsiders.
> Philip Howard, *Weasel Words*

4. Note the spelling of *ours*: no apostrophe. And take care not to confuse *our* and *ours.* The correct forms are *our house and theirs*; *their house and ours*; but not ✗ *ours and their houses.*

5. For the problem of whether to say *They're*

in favour of us going or *They're in favour of our going,* see -ING FORMS OF VERBS. For the choice between *us* and *we* in *as fast as us/we,* and *faster than us/we,* see AS; THAN.

See also ME; MYSELF; PRONOUNS; SELF.

weasel words See VOGUE WORDS.

week See YEAR.

well See GOOD.

Welsh English In 1536, the Act of Union of England and Wales decreed that, henceforth, all courts would be held and all oaths sworn in the English language, in Wales and England alike; no Welsh-speaking person was to hold public office unless he had a command of English as well. At first, the spread of English was confined to the local aristocracy, with their connections with the Tudor court (which was itself of Welsh extraction). Later, as the Industrial Revolution expanded in southeast Wales, it brought with it a predominantly English-speaking class of managers. But even at the end of the 19th century, more than 60 per cent of the population of the industrial area was Welsh-speaking, many of them speaking no English; so too with the vast majority of the population in the rural north and west. During the 20th century, however, the language shift has gathered pace. After all, English was, until the middle of the century, the mandatory language of instruction and administration in all schools. Today there is scarcely anyone, in any part of Wales, who does not have a command of English.

As Welsh English has become established as the majority language, and the major language of commerce and public institutions, so it has come increasingly under the influence of standard English. But in earlier times, much of Welsh English resembled the dialects of the English counties bordering Wales; it was from these counties that English first spread westwards into Wales. A different influence was the Welsh language itself: as Welsh speakers learned English, they transferred features of their native language into the English they were acquiring. Today then, there are two distinguishable basic varieties of Welsh English, one characterised by its 'Welshness' and the other by its affinities with neighbouring dialects in England. Though the two varieties have many features in common, they are distinguished in their pronunciation, their grammar and — to a lesser extent — their vocabulary.

Pronunciation The dialects of the West and

North are distinguished by being 'rhotic' — that is, they pronounce all written *r*'s, after vowels and not just before them: the *r* in *car* or *cart*, for instance, is clearly sounded. This is a feature taken over directly from Welsh, which always pronounces the written *r*. (The standard English of southeastern Wales, however, like that of southeastern England — RP or 'received pronunciation' — is generally non-rhotic.)

The western and northern Welsh dialects show further traces of Welsh influence in also having a breathy *h*-sound — not just in words like *he* and *hat*, but also in *which* and *what*, and *Rhine* and *rhythm*. (Again, the dialect of the southeast does not have this feature — neither does RP. But /hw/ for *wh*- is found in other varieties of English, including Scottish, Irish, and much of American English.) The North is distinguished from both the southern and western varieties in having no *z*- or *j*-sound, again a feature carried over from Welsh: *buzz* is pronounced just like *bus*, and *zeal* like *seal*; and *gin* sounds like *chin*, and *ridge* like *rich*.

In the southern and western dialects, *y* and *w* are often not pronounced if followed by a vowel which has the same tongue position. Thus, *yeast* is pronounced just like *east*, and in the southeast, both *wood* and *hood* are pronounced /ōod/.

In pronouncing proper names, most dialects of Welsh English retain the native Welsh sounds expressed in writing by -*ch*- and -*ll*- — something like /kh/ (as in *loch*) and a breathy /hl/ sound (as in *Llewellyn*): so *Rhosllannerchrugog* is pronounced more or less /**hross-hlan**nerkh-**reeg**og/.

The *a* of *bath, last, chance*, and so on is short rather than long; *bath* is pronounced /bath/, not /baath/ as in RP.

The neutral vowel /ə/ has a markedly different distribution in Welsh pronunciation from that of RP. On the one hand, Welsh English tends to avoid it, preferring to give the written vowels *a* and *o* their proper value in unstressed as well as stressed syllables: the *a* in *atomic* and *cobra*, for example, and the *o* in *Olympic* or *convince*, are sounded as full /a/ and /o/ by Welsh people, rather than reduced to a slurred or neutral /ə/ as in RP. On the other hand, Welsh English uses /ə/ instead of /u/ even in stressed syllables: *butter* is pronounced /bətər/.

Some diphthongs are simplified in Welsh English: *game* and *tone* sound more like /ge-em/ and /to-on/ than /gaym/ and /tōn/. This tendency is particularly strong in northern Welsh dialects.

Grammar The most distinctive feature of Welsh English grammar is the verb-form expressing habitual activity in both present and past tenses. In both varieties, it differs from the simple present or simple past of standard English (*He goes/went to school every day*). In the southeast, the auxiliary verb *to do* is used with an uninflected verb:

He do go to school every day/He did go to school every day.

This pattern is borrowed from the dialects of neighbouring counties in England. In other parts of Wales, the pattern used derives from a Welsh model, with the auxiliary verb *to be* followed by the present participle of the verb:

He is going to school every day/He was going to school every day.

Another common pattern that translates a Welsh equivalent concerns possession:

There's no luck with the rich (= The rich have no luck).

This use of *there is* occurs also — again on the model of Welsh — in exclamations:

There's tall you are! (= How tall you are!)

And the Welsh language is again the source of the practice of bringing a word to the beginning of a sentence to emphasise it:

Coal they're getting out mostly.

Welsh English has some features in common with the vernacular English of other parts of Britain and other parts of the world too:
● double negatives are common — *I haven't been nowhere*.
● numerals can occur with singular nouns — *two pound*; *three mile*.
● the relative pronoun *who* is sometimes replaced by *as, which*, or *what* — *the boy as/what/which works in the shop*.
● the -*s* form of the verb is found in first-, second-, and third-person constructions, singular and plural, in the present tense — so, not just *he goes*, but also *I goes, you goes, we goes*, and *they goes*.
● an adverb or adjective is sometimes repeated for emphasis: *They are trying hard, hard*.
● the tag *isn't it?* can be attached to any statement, regardless of tense, person, or the like: *They did try hard, isn't it?*

Vocabulary A few Welsh words have found their way into Welsh dialects of English — the most common are the terms of endearment *del* ('pretty one') and *bach* ('little one'), and *tollut* ('a hayloft' — a regional term found elsewhere too: from Welsh *tawlod*). Standard English has benefited too, occasionally — the annual competitive arts festival, the *eisteddfod*, is now a common event, and word, throughout the English-speaking world; and the word *flummery*, referring to a sweet oatmeal dish or to various other bland desserts, and by extension meaning 'meaningless flattery, nonsense, humbug', comes from the Welsh *llymru*.

There are some words shared with neighbouring dialects in England — *askel* ('a newt'), *lumper* ('a youngster'), *dap* ('a bounce'), *pine-end* ('a gable-end'), *tundish* ('a funnel'), and *clem* ('to starve'). These words are heard mainly in southeastern Wales: in western dialects, where the Welsh language has been more resistant, the words imported have been of standard rather than dialectal English.

Some words have a distinctive meaning in Welsh English: *delight* ('interest'): *He has a delight in fishing*; *tidy* ('considerable; fairly large'): *a tidy way to go*; and *rise* ('to raise'): *He tried to rise money from the bank.*

The future of Welsh English Despite the differences — sometimes weighty differences — between Welsh English and standard English, the two forms are mutually quite intelligible, and the gap between them seems likely to narrow rather than widen. The 'Welshness' of Welsh English will increasingly be a matter of pronunciation rather than of grammar or vocabulary. A few distinctive words and grammatical constructions will no doubt remain, but Welsh English will probably come to be regarded as principally an *accent* rather than a *dialect* of English.

The reason for this likely convergence is that the language model with most status for English-speakers in Wales (as for those in dialect regions in England too) is that of the broadcasting media: a near-RP accent, and standard English grammar and vocabulary.

were   The combinations *I was, I am, Tom is, she was*, and so on are the usual forms (for first- and third-person singular), but sometimes the subjunctive form *were* can be used instead here — notably, after *if*, *as if*, and *as though* when these conjunctions introduce suggestions that are clearly imaginary or untrue:

> If only I were rich.
> If I were you . . .
> If I were in his place, I'd resign.
> He looked at me as if I were insane.
> She acts as though she were to blame, rather than you.

But if the supposition is a factual or possible or realistic one, then the indicative forms *is, am,* or *was* might be used instead:

> If she is here now, you can meet her.
> If she was here last night, you must have met her.

Compare the 'counterfactual' condition:

> If she were here now, you could meet here.

Was and *were* are sometimes equally appropriate, especially when the supposition just might be possible or factual, or where it is a cause of anxiety:

> If he were/was ever to find out, we would be in trouble.
> But just suppose she were/was telling the truth?
> She spoke as though everything were/was settled.
> If it were/was simply my own choice, I'd resign.

Here the use of *were* perhaps suggests greater doubt than the use of *was* does. And *were* is also likelier to be favoured in formal contexts, especially in American English.

When the *if* is followed by *not*, moreover, *were* is far preferable to *was*:

> If it were not for my family, I'd resign.

And in formal style, only *were*, not *was*, is posible nowadays as the first word in conditional sentences:

> Were it simply my own choice, I'd resign.

Note finally that only *was*, not *were*, can be used when the *if* can be replaced by *whether*.

> I asked her if/whether she was leaving.

See SUBJUNCTIVE.

West Indian English, Creole, and Black British English

Slaves were transported to the Caribbean (as to America) from all over West Africa. They spoke a wide range of languages: in order to communicate with one another, and to understand overseers, they would have had to acquire a pidgin language very quickly (pidgin English, for our purposes, though French and Dutch pidgins were in use too: see PIDGINS AND CREOLES).

Many of the slaves must have learnt pidgins either while being held at slaving-posts on the West African coast, or during the voyage across the Atlantic. Those who did not would have developed a rudimentary competence in pidgin within days of going to work on a plantation. Within a generation at most, the pidgin would have evolved into a creole — a full language in its own right, and a mother tongue, having a fuller vocabulary and more flexible grammar.

The West Indies consists of an archipelago extending across some 3500 kilometres (about 2000 miles) or more. (According to a broader definition, it includes parts of the South American mainland too, notably Guyana.) Naturally, the West Indian Creole of one island or region has a slightly different form from that of another. The standard English sentence *We plant yams where there is a lot of water*, for example, might be expressed in Jamaica as *Wi plaan yam we nof waata de*, and in Guyana as *We doz plaan yam we plenti waata de*. But — as this pair of examples makes clear — the similarities are very striking, in vocabulary, idiom, and grammar.

The description that follows is based chiefly on Jamaican Creole, the best-documented and most widely studied.

Vocabulary English is obviously the greatest influence on Creole vocabulary, and any word current in standard English is actually or potentially a Creole word too. But standard English has not been the only influence. French and Spanish words occur too, especially in islands, such as St Lucia and Trinidad, that have been under French or Spanish occupation: *crapaud* (for 'a frog or toad') and *pannier* (for 'a basket'), both French words in origin, are preferred in many parts of the West Indies to their standard English-based equivalents.

The indigenous Carib languages of the region contributed such words as:

jiga, jigger   an insect
kayman   a crocodile
macca   a thorn, something that can prick

And West African languages have provided:

akara   a beancake (from Hausa or Yoruba)
bosi   proud, show-off (from Yoruba)
fufu   pounded food (from Twi)
pinder   a peanut (from Kongo)
omi   water (from Yoruba)
unu   you — plural (from Igbo)

Other African borrowings include *bukra* ('a white man or woman'), *duppy* and *jumby* (both meaning 'a ghost'), *nyam* or *ninyam* ('food' or 'to eat'), and *tuku-tuku* ('short or squat').

West Africa has also been behind the numerous 'calques', or 'loan translations' — literal English translations of African idioms:

ai bebi   (eye baby) the pupil of the eye
big yai   (big eye) gluttony
de klin   (day + clean) dawn
haad ia   (hard ear/s) stubborn
kin teet   (skin + teeth) to grin or laugh
swiit maut/tok   (sweet mouth/talk) flattery

(The cultural affinities of the West Indies with West Africa go much deeper than this, of course. West Indian folktales retain their African roots, for instance, both in narrative techniques and in the plots and characters, notably the trickster hero Anancy or Nancy, a spider — from the Twi word for 'a spider'. And many West Indian proverbs are translations of African proverbs, stressing the need for vigilance or co-operation, for instance: *Monkey papa jump, monkey mama jump, monkey pickney mus jump*.)

Not all of the English contribution to Creole vocabulary has involved straightforward adoptions of standard English words. Creole sometimes retains archaic or obsolescent English terms — *box* in the general sense of 'to hit', for instance, or *beforetime, beknown, glean, glebe land*, and *proven*.

Sometimes the borrowings have been from British dialects:

bubby   a breast
buss   a kiss
fig   a segment of an orange
labrish   (noun) gossip (from the dialectal *lab*, 'to blab, reveal secrets')
tinnen   made of tin

Some borrowings have been from the United States:

blues   a type of soul music
bluetail   a type of lizard
bread   money

Often the form of the Creole word is a distortion of the standard English form, sometimes involving a slight change of meaning as well:

bleaky   bleak, overcast
cunny   cunning (noun or adjective); a trick
tief   to steal
ugly   sin, wickedness
was-was   a wasp; wasps

Even when the form stays much the same, the meaning of a word in Creole is often slightly different from that in standard English: *bat* means 'a large moth', for example; the flying rodent is known instead as a *rat-bat*. *Breakfast*, at least amongst older people, refers to the midday meal, and *evening* to the afternoon. *Foot, hand,* and *skin* can refer to the whole leg, arm, and body respectively. *Ignorant* can mean 'angry or quick-tempered'; *quality* can mean 'extremely'. The word *Babylon* is used by Rastafarians to refer to England and to everything in Western society that is viewed negatively, including the police.

The influence of Rastafarianism is evident too in some of the newly coined or remodelled terms in Creole: *I and I* (roughly 'we', but stressing 'insider'- or group-awareness), *overstand* ('to understand'), and *dreadlocks* ('tightly plaited locks of hair').

Dreadlocks, of course, has now emerged from Creole into World English. Other West Indian words now within the mainstream of general English usage include *calypso, obeah, reggae*, and *ska*.

Pronunciation Pronunciation changes considerably from one island or region to another: it is illustrated here chiefly by reference to Jamaica. Many of the vowel-sounds of Creole differ from those of RP — the 'received pronunciation' of educated people in southeast England. The neutral vowel /ə/, for example, so common in RP in unstressed syllables, is used far less often in West Indian speech: a Jamaican is likely to refer to his country as /ju-**mee**ku/ rather than as /jə-**may**kə/.

There is no consistent correspondence, however, in the different pronunciation of vowel-sounds in RP and Creole. The *a*-sounds in *man* and *bat*, for example, are virtually identical in RP; in Creole, they are not only different from RP, but they are different from each other as well — /maan/ and something between /bat/ and /but/.

The words *bay, bear*, and *beer* — requiring three different diphthongs in RP — are all realised in Creole as /bee-e/. Both *bud* and *bird* might be pronounced something like /bod/ by a Jamaican; both *boat* and *four* have /ōō-o/ for their vowel: /bōō-ot, fōō-o/; *broad* and *fall* both have the same /aa/ vowel as *bard* does; *toy* sounds like *tie*: /tī/.

The consonant system in West Indian English is, in contrast, very similar to that of RP — both varieties tend not to sound the written *r* except before a vowel. The main difference is in the 'dental' consonants: Creole uses /t/ and /d/ in the place of /th/ and /th/ — *the thin man* might sound something like /du tin maan/. One other interesting difference is the distribution of the sound /ng/: Creole usually reduces it to /in/ in the *-ing* form of verbs — *doing* is /dōō-in/. On the other hand, Creole sometimes uses /ng/ where RP does not: the RP-sound /-own/ tends to become /-ung/ or /-ong/ in Creole, so *town* and

ground might be pronounced /tong/ and /grungd/.

Some clusters of consonants are avoided in West Indian speech, especially at the end of words: *crisp* is pronounced /kris/, *fifths* /fif/, and *task* /taas/. And at the beginning of words the *s*-sound is occasionally dropped if it precedes a *p-, t-* or *k*-sound: *split, stiff*, and *squeeze* might be pronounced /plit/, /tif/, and /kweez/.

One result of this lesser flexibility in Creole is that some pairs of words are homophones in Creole — that is, are pronounced identically — whereas they are distinguished in RP.

English Words	Creole Pronunciation
rat, rot	/rat/
rye, Roy	/rī/
tear (when crying), tear (to rip)	/tee-e/
tin, thin	/tin/
den, then	/den/
thong, town	/tong/
mine, mind	/mīn/
coal, cold, colt	/kōl/
walk, walked	/waak/
laugh, laughed	/laaf/
mass, mast, mask	/mus/

Very little confusion results from this reduction of contrasts, however: for a start, context forestalls most potential ambiguities — as it does in RP, after all, with homophones such as *sun* and *son* or homonyms such as *leaves* (departs) and *leaves* (foliage).

Moreover, Creole sometimes introduces contrasts rather than reduces them, and thereby avoids ambiguity. So, even though *rat* and *rot* might sound alike, *cat* and *cot* do not, since Creole inserts a *y*-sound between /k/ or /g/ and the /a/: *cat* is pronounced more or less /kyat/, whereas *cot* lacks the *y*-sound, and sounds like /kat/. Similarly *garden* is pronounced /**gyaa**d'n/, whereas *Gordon* is pronounced /**gaa**d'n/. Sometimes a *w*-sound is inserted in a similar way: *boil* and *bile* have the same vowel sound, but remain distinct in Creole pronunciation as /bwīl/ and /bīl/ respectively.

Finally, ambiguity is averted by means of tone. Most West African languages are tone-languages — that is, they can distinguish two words not just by their vowel and consonant values, but also by the rise and fall of the voice in speaking them. The sound /lav/ in Lamnso (a Cameroon language), for example, can mean 'a thread', 'a house', 'to tie', or 'to build', according to the tone used.

West Indian English has to a small degree retained this West African feature: Jamaicans say /kyaan/ for both 'can' and 'cannot', but the tones are different, and misunderstanding is therefore most unlikely to happen. Similarly, the phrase *Mary is white*, in which the *is* is typically omitted in Jamaican speech, would not be confused with the name *Mary White*, since the tones would distinguish them clearly.

Creole Grammar There is a core of grammatical features common to all the English-speaking islands and regions of the West Indies. One of the most striking is the lack of inflection — *three dog, John walk, Winston hat, Mary go home.* (It would be easy, but shortsighted, to regard this tendency to use 'root' forms as a sign of linguistic immaturity. In most cases inflectional endings are redundant, and meaning is made clear from the context.) Whenever it is important to resolve ambiguity, creole languages use other devices, quite distinct from anything found in English, and based on structures found in West African languages. The suffix *-dem*, for instance, is sometimes used to mark a plural:

Give me di ticket-dem.
Beverley-dem (= Beverley and her friends) put it back.

And various auxiliaries (differing in form from island to island) are often placed in front of the verb to indicate both tense and aspect. Here are some examples from Jamaica, using the auxiliaries *a*, *did*, *bin*, and *go*:

Mi a tell you no (= I'm telling you no).
If me did have it, mi would look after it (= If I had it, I would look after it).
She bin come home yesterday (= She came home yesterday).
Dem go come home (= They will come home).

Then, possessives can be expressed with *fi*:

fi John hat (= John's hat)
fi Mary book (= Mary's book)
A fi mi book dis (= This is my book).

The Jamaican Creole pronoun system is similarly 'simplified'. Unlike standard English, it does not mark case and gender. Thus:

me = I, me, my
you = you, your (singular)
him/im = he, him, his, she, her
it = it, its
we = we, us, our
unu = you, your (plural)

dem = they, them, their.

So we find examples like:

Im give im moda di food (= He/she gave his/her mother the food).

Note, however, the distinction between *you* and *unu* — the singular and plural forms of *you* or *your*. This is a distinction, based on West African languages, that standard English long ago lost.

West Indian Creoles have a wide range of other features (which should be regarded as signs of flexibility rather than as limitations) not found in standard English. For instance, adjectives tend not to take the verb 'to be', or rather, adjectives themselves can function as verbs:

Mi ready (= I'm ready).
Mi a ready (= I'm getting ready).
Mi did ready (= I was getting ready).

Instead of the verb *to be*, Jamaican Creole has two verbs: *a*, the 'equating' verb, and *deh*, the 'locating' verb:

Im a di captain (= He is the captain).
Di book deh pan di table (= The book is on the table).

Other common Creole features are:

● the use of *se* (from Twi) to introduce a clause:

Im taak se di book a fi mi (= He said that the book is mine).

● the tendency to use verbs where standard English uses adverbs (again the result of African influence):

Tek dis book go (= Take this book away).
Tek di book gi me (= Take the book give me = Take the book for me).

● bringing the verb to the front of the sentence, and repeating it, as a way of emphasising it:

Iz ron im ron (= He really ran).
No gaan im gaan (= He's not gone for good).

● reduplication of words generally:

naka-naka (to pull to pieces)
wan-wan (one at a time)
se-se (to mention)

● the active voice to express the passive:

It kyaan eat (It can't be eaten).
Di gras kot (The grass has been cut).

● and, even in West Indian speech that is closer to standard English than to Creole, the use of regular rather than inverted word order in questions:

What day it is?
Who that is?
Why he is going?

The Creole continuum West Indians are continuously being exposed to and influenced by standard English, and the more educated they are, the nearer to standard pronunciation, grammar, and vocabulary their speech will be.

Social setting affects the form of speech considerably: regardless of a speaker's level of education, an informal conversation with family and friends will contain a higher proportion of Creole features than a formal exchange with employers or teachers. These sensitive fluctuations between one form of speech and another present a problem to linguists when it comes to describing 'West Indian English'. The commonest solution, though one involving a slight simplification, is to speak of a 'continuum' between broad Creole and standard English: within this continuum, any one speaker typically occupies a span rather than a single point.

Linguistic adaptation in Britain Black people have lived in England for hundreds of years. Their presence was a talking-point even in the days of Elizabeth I. It was not until the 1950s, however, and the post-war industrial boom, that substantial numbers of British citizens from the West Indies began to arrive in England in response to the urgent demand for labour.

The speech of these West Indians, and of the subsequent generations of immigrants, has often been dismissed as 'broken' English. But as has been shown, West Indian English in its various forms, though clearly different from standard British English, is in no way deficient.

Although West Indians newly arrived in Britain would have used their most 'English' speech, they none the less retained many Creole grammatical and pronunciation features, and often had trouble, initially at least, in making themselves understood to British-born listeners. By contrast, virtually all black children in British schools today were born in Britain, and their speech is often outwardly indistinguishable from that of their white fellow-schoolchildren. But it would be quite wrong to assume that Creole has therefore ceased to play an important role in the life of the black British community.

For a start, a number of young black people (and even some of their white friends) take pride in 'talking black', even in conversation with white people. This is largely a manifestation of a strong black identity, forged from experience of extensive discrimination and a consequent rejection of the values of mainstream British society.

Even among those British blacks who choose not to assert their blackness openly in this way, and who would always use standard English in conversation with white people, Creole remains available for exchanges among themselves. It is widely used in the black Pentecostal churches, for instance, and in predominantly black youth clubs. (It is here, above all, that some white teenagers, attracted by reggae and other aspects of black culture, have apparently learnt to use Creole.) Creole — or Patois, as it is more commonly called in the West Indian community — often alternates rapidly with English. The switch from one variety to the other can take place even within a single sentence:

Mi see di bwoy a ron dong di street, but I never managed to catch him (= I saw the boy running down the street, but I never managed to catch him).

Rapid switching of this kind does not indicate an inability to keep the two systems separate: it is rather a normal stylistic device in bilingual communities — one that has been recorded in communities as far apart as Wales and Texas. Speakers' real competence in Creole, and the extent to which they use it, are related to their social networks — the more integrated they are into the black community, the more competent their Creole. If racial discrimination persists or intensifies, black people in Britain will look inwards to their own community all the more, and Creole will remain a major linguistic force.

wet, wetted In British English, the verb to wet has two forms for the past tense or past participle: *wet* and *wetted*. (In American English, the form *wet* usually covers all functions.) The distinction seems to be this: if the verb involves deliberate action, its past form is *wetted*; if the action is involuntary or without deliberation, the past form is *wet*. So: *It was only a light drizzle, but it wet us through*, and *The baby wet the bed* (not deliberate); but *They wetted the wallpaper with stripper before scraping it off* (deliberate).

Note also that for clarity's sake it is better to use *wetted* than *wet* in a passive sentence. In this way you will avoid any chance of confusion between *wet* the verb and *wet* the adjective:

verbal use: The wallpaper was wetted with stripper (by the decorators).

adjectival use: The wallpaper was wet with stripper (when I came home).

wet, whet The old-fashioned word *whet* is sometimes misspelt as the more common word *wet*. *Whet* is usually used as a verb, meaning 'to sharpen or hone (a knife or tool)' — hence *whetstone*, a stone on which knives are sharpened. Figuratively, *to whet* means 'to stimulate or heighten': *The pictures whetted his curiosity about the place*. *Whet* is also a rare noun, meaning 'something that sharpens or stimulates'.

The phrase in which misspelling is most likely to occur is *to whet the appetite*; some people seem to assume that the word here is *wet* — perhaps understanding the phrase as meaning something like 'oiling the appetite in readiness', or associating the stimulated appetite with salivation.

Wet, as verb, noun, or adjective, goes back to Old English *wæt* or *wet*; *whet* goes back to Old English *hwettan*.

See also WET, WETTED.

what 1. *What* is a peculiar relative pronoun, and gives rise to several common grammatical errors. It is peculiar in that it refers both forward and back — both to the noun preceding it (whether stated or just implied) and to the clause that follows it. So it is really the equivalent of two or more words: *that which* or *those which*, or *the thing that* or *the things that*, or *anything that* or *everything that*, and so on:

We should stop for food, since what we have is quite insufficient (= We should stop for food, since that which we have is quite insufficient).
What I like about him is ... (= The thing that I like about him is ...).
They did what they could to save him (= They did everything that they could to save him).
For what proved to be very good reasons ... (= For reasons that proved to be very good reasons ...).

What cannot be used as the equivalent of a simple *that* or *who* or *which*, as it often is in dialect or by children or in nonstandard usage:

× The dog what bit me was just trying to be friendly.
× It's the rich what gets the pleasure, it's the poor what gets the blame.

In general, *what* cannot directly follow (or 'postmodify') a noun or pronoun.

There are further grammatical restrictions on the use of *what* that can be summed up in a second useful rule: if *what* can be omitted altogether, then it should be omitted (and often must be omitted). This is especially true after *as* and *than*, which seem so often to tempt users of British English (far more than users of American English) into adding an unacceptable *what* immediately afterwards:

× There is no need to do it the same way as what she does.
× She sings too loudly, the same as what her teacher does.
× I heard it as clearly as what I hear you now.
× She's younger that what he is.
?? That dog looks even fiercer today than what it did last time.
?? The damage was slighter than what I'd expected.
? Is that bicycle the same as what you used to use a couple of years ago?

The last of these sentences is perhaps just the right side of the borderline, though it would be better to replace *what* by *the one that* — *the same as the one that you used to use* — or else, as with the others, to leave out *what* altogether.

The last sentence but one — ?? *The damage was slighter than what I'd expected* — perhaps sounds reasonably acceptable too, but this is probably because of its similarity to perfectly correct forms such as *The damage was different from what I'd expected*. The two sentences are not really parallel, however: *from* is a preposition, and must be followed by a noun phrase or noun clause, but *as* and *than* can be conjunctions as well as prepositions, and do not need *what* to introduce a following clause.

2. If there is more than one relative clause requiring *what*, certain precautions are necessary. The correct form is:

I hold you responsible for what is probably a fatal blunder, and what is certainly an expensive one.

It is quite acceptable here to omit the second *what*:

I hold you responsible for what is probably a fatal blunder, and is certainly an expensive one.

But if the gap between the two *what*'s were any larger, it would be advisable to retain the second *what*, in order to pick up the thread of the syntax again (see THAT 3).

What is unacceptable, however, though very

common, is to change the second *what* into a *which:*

× I hold you responsible for what is probably a fatal blunder, and which is certainly an expensive one.

3. *What* sometimes seems to have a plural force but nevertheless requires a singular verb. Clearly we would say *What is needed here is a spotlight*, but what if *spotlights* — the plural form — is used instead. The options then are these:

What is needed here is spotlights.
? What are needed here are spotlights.
× What is needed here are spotlights.

The first construction, with both verbs in the singular, is the best by far. *What* could here be replaced by *That which* — which has to take a singular verb, as in the first construction; it could not really be replaced by *Those which* — which would take a plural verb as in the second construction. The third construction is unacceptable, since it has one singular verb and one plural verb relating to a single subject.

Similarly:

What worries him is the rumours (= That which worries him is the rumours).
? What worry him are the rumours.
× What worries him are the rumours.

In the following quotation, the singular verb is, correctly, used each time:

What has been consistently underplayed and is tragic is the real fears and emotions of many of the students most closely involved in this incident.

— *The Guardian*

In other contexts, however, it may be quite appropriate to use a plural verb after *what*:

He should stop for sandwiches, since what he has are too few for the journey (= ... since *those that* he has are too few ...).
For what were of course very good reasons ... (= ... For *reasons that* were of course very good reasons ...).
She always backs what seem to me to be the least promising horses (= She always backs *the horses that* seem to me ...).

4. Note the ambiguity in the sentence *The examiners asked me what I knew*. It can mean 'They asked me something that I knew; they asked me questions to which I knew the answers' or it can mean 'They asked me "What do you know?" ' Unless the context makes it clear which

of these meanings you intend, it is best to avoid such constructions.

5. A problem always arises with constructions containing *what* and the verb *to do*. The acceptable forms are these:

What he did was take his shoes off.
What he did was to take his shoes off.
What he did was this: he took his shoes off.

But it is not strictly acceptable to fuse these forms into:

?? What he did was he took his shoes off.
See also AND WHICH; BUT 7; WHICH 4.

what for As a synonym for *why*, the phrase *what ... for* sometimes attracts criticism as being unacceptably casual: ? *What did she punish you for?* Certainly it would be out of place in very formal contexts, but in ordinary speech and writing it seems appropriate enough. If the objection to it is simply that it encourages the use of a preposition at the end of a sentence, then that objection has very little to be said for it (see PREPOSITIONS ENDING A SENTENCE).

One danger that you should be alert to is the danger of ambiguity: the words *what* and *for* can, after all, be used in a more literal way. So the sentence ? *What did he sell his car for?* is ambiguous enough, for example, to prompt two quite different replies. If the *what ... for* is understood to mean 'why', then the reply might be *Because he needed the money to pay his speeding fine*. But *what...for* might be understood to mean 'for what price, for how much', in which case the reply to the question might be *For less than he could have got*.

what is more This clause has become an idiom, synonymous with *moreover* or *in addition,* and seems to function almost as though it were a single word, regardless of the grammar of the sentence in which it occurs:

He didn't even apologise when he backed into my bicycle — and what's more, he expected me to pay for his broken tail-light!

There is little point in objecting to a usage that is so long established that scarcely anyone notices anything awkward about it. None the less, it is worth noting that the grammar of such a sentence is, strictly speaking, incorrect: just try replacing *what* by *that which*. The 'correct' clause is *which is more*, not *what is more — which is more* being short for *which fact is more*.

The correct form occurs in the last (and much

misquoted) of these famous lines:

> If you can fill the unforgiving minute
> With sixty seconds' worth of distance run,
> Yours is the Earth and everything that's in it,
> And — which is more — you'll be a Man,
> my son!
>
> – Rudyard Kipling, 'If'

Though you have to bow to usage in the case of *what is more*, you can at least continue a rearguard action against the expanded forms of this clause, such as ? *what is more important*, ? *what is more relevant*, and so on. The relative pronoun here should be *which*, not *what*:

> He cashed the forged cheques, and — which is more reprehensible — falsely accused his brother of having done so.

whatever, what ever   Take care not to spell *what ever* (an interrogative pronoun) as one word, or *whatever* (a relative pronoun) as two words.

In the phrase *what ever*, the *ever* serves simply to make the *what* more emphatic. The phrase usually appears at the start of a direct question — *What ever is Father up to now?*

In *whatever*, as one word, the *-ever* element serves to make the *what* general, to make it embrace everything: among its many uses, *whatever* can function as the equivalent of the phrase *all things that* or *anything that* — *I'll go along with whatever you suggest*; it can also function as a pronoun or adjective in clauses of concession as the equivalent of *granting anything that* or *granting everything that* — *Whatever you do, don't tell them I helped you.*

In view of the two different functions of *whatever,* there is a slight danger of ambiguity when using the word. A sentence such as ? *Whatever he said he now withdraws* could possibly be understood in two different ways: as the equivalent of either *He withdraws everything that he said* or *He may have said he would not withdraw, but in fact he is withdrawing*. If the second sense had been intended, however, there would probably have been a comma halfway through the original sentence: *Whatever he said, he now withdraws*. (Better still, *Whatever he said, he is now withdrawing*.)

Take care, finally, not to insert a needless *that* after *whatever*. As the earlier definitions suggest, the relative pronoun *that* or *which* is already, as it were, contained in *whatever*, and should therefore remain unstated. It is incorrect, for example, to say × *Keep calm in whatever difficulties that you may encounter*. The *that* is here

not just unnecessary, but positively intrusive, and should be omitted.

With slight adjustments, the various factors considered here apply also to *whenever/when ever*, *whoever/who ever*, *wherever/where ever* (note that *wherever* has only three *e*'s, not four), and *however/how ever*.

See also EVER 1.

whence, whither   These two words are now archaic or at best extremely formal, and are likely to be used only self-consciously today, in official, religious, literary, or jocular contexts:

> The image of Russia as a river or a slow-moving ship is one that occurs again and again in her music, literature and painting. 'The Song of the Volga Boatmen' inspired perhaps the most politically effective picture of the 19th century — Ilya Repin's 'Barge Haulers on the Volga' — which shows a gang of peasants heaving a ship against the current. The laden ship is returning from a mysterious eastern land, whence will come a saviour to redeem a suffering people.
>
> – Bruce Chatwin, in
> *Great Rivers of the World*

> ? His visit is being treated as very important by the Socialist Government in Madrid, and thousands of posters in shop windows salute 'Dr Alfonsin, President of Argentina and grandson of Spain'. He is to visit the ancestral home in Galicia whence his grandfather emigrated.
>
> – *Daily Telegraph*

In the first of these examples, *whence* is deliberately literary and allusive — and quite effective. In the second of the examples, *whence* sounds affected or unduly old-fashioned.

Whither is usually understood as a synonym of *to where*, and *whence* of *from where*. These longer forms, however, are not very idiomatic. The modern substitute for *whence* would tend to be *from which* or *where . . . from*:

> The plane developed mechanical trouble, and we had to return to Gatwick, from which we had set out only 15 minutes earlier.
> Where does that coat of yours come from?

And *whither* would today be represented by *to which* or simply by *where*:

> Where are you going? (a *to* at the end is superfluous).
> The resort, to which we had driven overnight, turned out to be very different from

the way we'd imagined it (*to which* could be replaced by *where*).

The form *from whence* is frequently criticised as redundant. The best-known example of it is in Psalm 121:

I will lift up mine eyes unto the hills, from whence cometh my help.

(*From whence* is not the only redundant phrase here: the *up* in *lift up* is excessive too, though perfectly idiomatic.) But since *whence* is itself archaic and hence alien to modern standard usage, there is little point in preferring it to *from whence*. In a jocular setting, for example, *from whence* is probably more effective than *whence* precisely because of its even greater ungainliness:

The gatecrashers were met at the door by a 300-pound bouncer, who quickly persuaded them to return to that part of town from whence they had come.

See also ARCHAISMS; HENCE; THENCE.

whenever, when ever See EVER 1; WHATEVER.

wherever, where ever See EVER 1; WHATEVER.

whet See WET, WHET.

whether, if 1. Both *if* and *whether* can be used to introduce an indirect question. *Whether* sounds slightly more formal:

The leader of the opposition asked whether/ if the Prime Minister intended to respond to the transatlantic provocation.

Whether is preferable to *if* whenever two or more conditions are being fully expressed and linked by *or*:

He asked whether Nick would arrive in time or whether he would be late.

Only *whether* is possible when a preposition precedes:

It depends on whether he has recovered in time.

And *whether* alone should be used where *if* would result in ambiguity. Consider this sentence:

? Tell me if you want an answer.

It could mean either 'Tell me whether you want an answer' or 'If you expect an answer, there is something you should tell me'.

2. In constructions such as *He asked whether she intended to respond,* there may be a temptation to add the phrase *or not* at the end, or else to add an explicit alternative option, such as *or to submit tamely.*

We then got into a series of tangles, never fully unravelled, about the way cinema managers let under-age lads into X-certificate films and whether it was or was not OK to show adult viewing late at night.
  – Katharine Whitehorn, *The Observer*

But it is quite acceptable, perhaps even preferable today, to leave such alternatives unstated (unless they are considered equally important):

They will be judged on whether they have delivered an economic turnaround.
  – Dr David Owen, *The Guardian*

Pup, by his transaction in wintertime up on the old railway line, gains the whole world, including good looks, business success and a beautiful wife. Whether he loses his soul in the process and how much his sister's witchcraft has to do with it is for the reader to decide.
  – Ruth Rendell, *Bookcase*

3. In the sense of 'regardless of the circumstances that', however, *whether* must be followed explicitly by both (or all) the options:

I'm going to leave now, whether you like it or not.
Whether he wins, draws, or loses, I shall love him just the same.

Note that there is no objection to having three or more options following *whether* here, in the way that there is considered to be in the case of *either*. (See EITHER 5.)

Note too that the subjunctive form of the verb is often used here in preference:

Whether he win, draw, or lose, I shall love him just the same.

It can sound a bit stilted today, but is quite acceptable in formal writing. (See SUBJUNCTIVE.)

Note finally that the phrase *whether or no,* once more commonly used than *whether or not,* now sounds very old-fashioned, and is used extremely seldom.

4. When the option is explicitly stated after *whether,* make sure that it is stated only once, not twice.

× Whether or not a play is a success or not depends very little on the critics' reviews.

× Whether or not Lendl wins or loses the final, he gets my vote as player of the year.

In the first example, omit either one *or not* or the other. In the second example, omit either *or not* or *or loses*.

See also AS TO; DOUBT.

which **1.** Compare these two sentences:

This horse, which won last time, is now up for sale.
The horse that won last time is now up for sale.

In the first example, *which* cannot be replaced by *that* — the clause it introduces is a 'nonrestrictive' clause. In the second example, however, *which* could replace *that* — the clause here is a 'restrictive' clause. (See RESTRICTIVE AND NONRESTRICTIVE CLAUSES.) Some old-fashioned usage books urge *that* rather than *which* in restrictive clauses, in order to keep a clear distinction. In fact, *which* is probably more common than *that* in such clauses now, and is usually just as acceptable. (For the handful of constructions in which *that* is perhaps preferable, see THAT **1**.)

Make sure not to forget the comma before *which* in nonrestrictive clauses. In the following extract, the author — or the typesetter — has mistakenly omitted it:

× Home was an odd word to use for the Pera Palace which had the appearance of an eastern pavilion built for a world fair.
– Graham Greene, *Travels With My Aunt*

Which is usually preferable to *that* when another *that* appears in the sentence (and vice versa): *Is that the horse which won last time?*

And *which* is often preferred to *that* in a relative clause involving a preposition. A correctly worded sentence such as *The boat that you usually sail in is undergoing repairs today* is often dropped in favour of *The boat in which you usually sail is undergoing repairs today*. This preference for *in which* is probably based on the traditional fear of ending a sentence or clause with a preposition (see PREPOSITIONS ENDING A SENTENCE). Even Winston Churchill, who apparently scorned the contrived avoidance of final prepositions, often used *which* (preceded by the preposition) instead:

Headmasters have powers at their disposal with which Prime Ministers have never yet been invested.
– Winston Churchill, *My Early Life*

He could have said simply: ... *powers at their*

disposal that Prime Ministers have never yet been invested with* (though the sentence might then have lost something in balance and impact).

In certain complicated restrictive clauses, *that* simply cannot be used; *of which,* or preferably *whose,* has to stand in: *The suitcase in whose lining drugs were hidden is being examined by the police* (or *The suitcase in the lining of which drugs were hidden ...*).

2. This leads to the question of how acceptable *whose* is as a substitute for the phrase *of which.* Certainly it is widely used in this way today (see WHO **1**), and although pedants may object that *whose* cannot really be used of nonhuman subjects, this development clearly offers a welcome way of streamlining relative clauses. Compare, for lightness of touch, the following three sentences:

? That old desk of yours, the drawers of which are stuck and the legs and struts of which are coming off, is beyond repair and should be replaced.

? That old desk of yours, of which the drawers are stuck and the legs and struts coming off, is beyond repair and should be replaced.

That old desk of yours, whose drawers are stuck and whose legs and struts are coming off, is beyond repair and should be replaced.

Whose can itself be used in prepositional phrases such as *in whose, to whose,* and so on, as in the example quoted earlier: *The suitcase in whose lining drugs were hidden is being examined by the police.* Such wording is surely preferable to *The suitcase in the lining of which drugs were hidden ...* If you feel uncomfortable about using *whose* to refer to a suitcase, you can always rephrase the entire sentence: *The suitcase which/that had drugs hidden in its lining is being examined by the police.*

3. One interesting type of clause is worth noting — the clause that refers not to the preceding noun, but to the entire preceding clause: *Errol has a young daughter, which is very nice.* The clause *which is very nice* is known as a 'sentential relative clause'; what it refers to here is the entire previous statement: what is *nice* is the *fact* that Errol has a young daughter. The only relative pronoun that can be used in such a construction is *which.* It is equivalent to the phrase *and this.* Contrast the sentence: *Errol has a young daughter, who is very nice.* Here the relative clause refers only to the preceding noun, *daughter.*

Make sure, when using this *which*-construction, that you are not creating an ambiguity. The sentence *? He has a young poodle, which is very nice,* for example, can be understood in two different ways and should therefore be avoided. Instead of using the 'sentential relative clause', rephrase the sentence as *He has a young poodle — this* (or *that*) *is very nice.*

> *?* His views, he admits, are guided by Freudian psychology and guesswork, which may be two ways of saying the same thing.
> – Michael Foot, *The Observer*

4. *which* vs *what*. Both words can often be used in identical settings: *Which/What did you decide on? Which/What flight is she taking?*

The difference is this: *which* presupposes a limited or specified range of candidates; *what* is a more general query, and assumes no prior knowledge of the possible answers. So if you say *Which flight is she taking?*, you might in effect be asking *Is she taking the morning flight or the afternoon flight or the evening flight?* But if you say *What flight is she taking?*, you are probably ignorant of the various options.

5. Traditionally, *which* occurs as the first word of a sentence only in questions. There is a modern tendency, however, to use it at the start of statements too — that is, as a relative pronoun rather than an interrogative pronoun. Which is not quite in keeping with standard grammar, but which can produce a striking effect.

> No one else has quite her ability to lead us along paths where the abominable and the outrageous have a cool, quiet aspect and where men adapt their lives to the sick urges of the mind and to blind relentless motivations. Which is perhaps what crime fiction ought to be about.
> – Ruth Rendell, *Bookcase*

Traditionalists would urge the replacement of *Which* by *This* or *That*, or the replacement of the first full stop by a dash. Either course would certainly yield the same meaning, but each would lose something in effectiveness. There is a certain emphatic tone of confidence and certainty about the *Which* at the start of the sentence. Which is particularly effective as a summing-up or final assertion at the end of an article or report.

See also AND WHICH; WHAT IS MORE; WHO.

while, whilst **1.** The primary meaning of *while* as a conjunction is 'during the time that' or 'as long as': *It was fun while it lasted.* Two further meanings are still criticised by pedants, but are otherwise usually considered fully acceptable today:

● 'although': *While I respect your opinion, I cannot agree with you.* (Note that *while* is more positive, and hence slightly more polite perhaps, than *although*.)

● 'whereas': *John takes things very easy, while the rest of us are always rushing about and panicking.*

Two points to note: first, when *while* is used in the sense of 'although', its clause always comes before the main clause; when *while* is used in the sense of 'whereas' its clause can come before or after the main clause.

Secondly, ambiguity can occur, sometimes with comic results:

> My wife likes to have a bath, while I use the shower.
> The overture was played very solemnly, while the finale was performed with great exuberance.

(The comma in these examples perhaps just saves them from ambiguity; but if the *while*-clause were placed at the start of the sentence — that is, before the main clause rather than after it — the ambiguity would be undeniable.) The word *whereas* should, for safety's sake, have been used in these sentences.

2. *While* is used in still more extended senses — 'but', 'and', 'what is more' — and these are not considered fully acceptable:

● 'but' —

> *?* Your dental appointment is at 12 o'clock, while you're meant to be meeting the manager for lunch at 12.15.

● 'what is more' or 'and similarly' —

> *?* Postal charges are due to rise by 10 per cent, while telephone charges may increase even more.

● 'and' —

> *?* There used to be an old rule of thumb that the Conservative Party's scandals are usually about sex, while Labour's are about money.
> – David Watt, BBC Radio 3

In all these examples, *while* is little more than an affected substitute for *and* or *but*. And ambiguity frequently occurs. It is best to use *and* or *but* instead, which are unambiguous and unpretentious.

● *Recommendation* The basic sense of *while* has priority — 'during the time that'. Provided that no ambiguity with this sense is possible, then *while* can also be used with the meanings 'although' and 'whereas'. But if *while* can be replaced by *and* or *but,* then use these simple conjunctions instead.

3. In view of the possible ambiguity, some purists prefer the form *whilst* to *while* when the intended sense is 'whereas' or 'although':

> Having left Dillons Margaret spent a few months in America and returned to London without any definite plans for her career. She did a stint at the Royal Academy Bookshop during the Chinese Exhibition and whilst she quite enjoyed the job the work itself was very limited. Customers were only there because of the exhibition and only wanted a certain kind of book.
> – Elizabeth Bunster,
> *The Fiction Magazine*

> Whilst a large proportion of his method depends on the careful testing of hypotheses and the construction of syllogisms, he is forced to acknowledge the necessarily random nature of much detection.
> – Philip Lloyd-Bostock,
> *The Literary Review*

But strictly speaking, *whilst* can be used in all senses of *while,* though it does sound old-fashioned and is little used nowadays. And Americans regard *whilst* as chiefly British.

4. *While* as a verb, used usually with *away* ('to pass the time idly'), can also be spelt *wile: She whiled/wiled away the long afternoon by making daisy chains.* Take care, however, not to spell the noun *while* ('a period of time') as *wile* ('trickery, or a deception'): *Won't you stay for a while? He fell for the salesman's wiles, and bought the new vacuum cleaner.*

5. The adverb *awhile,* meaning 'for a short time', is usually used in the expression *to stay awhile* (or *to linger awhile*). Equally acceptable are *to stay a while* or *to stay for a while,* but not ✗ *to stay for awhile.*

whirlwind See CYCLONE.

whisky The spirit produced in Scotland (or Canada) is called *whisky*: this is also the usual British spelling. The spirit distilled in the United States or Ireland is correctly described as *whiskey*, and this is the main American English spelling, used frequently for all spirits of this type.

whither, wither If you are uncertain which word has the extra *h* in it, then bear this in mind: the old-fashioned word *whither* — meaning 'where

to' (as in *Whither are you going?*) or 'to where' (as in *the distant land whither he went*) — begins, like so many related words, with *wh*-. Compare, for instance, *who, where, why, when, whence. Whither* is the modern form of the Old English *hwider.*

The verb *to wither,* meaning 'to dry up or shrivel', has only the one *h.* It comes from the Middle English *widderen,* perhaps a variant of *wederen,* 'to weather'.

Finally, a horse's *withers* — the point between its shoulder blades: this word too has only one *h.* It probably goes back to the Old English *wither,* 'against', as this part of a horse's back 'opposes' a load.

See also WHENCE.

who, whom, whose 1. *who* vs *which* and *that.* The general rule is: *who* is used of people; *which* (like *what*) is used of things; *that* is used of both people and things.

There are certain exceptions to this rule: *who* can sometimes be used of nonhuman things, provided that they are being personified or in some way regarded as having human qualities. The following sentences are quite acceptable usage:

> It was quite by chance that we acquired Muffy, who had evidently run away from his previous owner, and retained a deep suspicion of all humans.
> Australia, who are still batting, have already made 115 runs.

Of course, considered purely as a national or geographical unit, *Australia* should not take *who* as its relative pronoun:

> ✗ Australia, who has an extremely large immigrant population, has a correspondingly rich and varied cultural life.

Just as *who* can sometimes be used of something not human (but thought of as almost human), so conversely *which* is sometimes used of small children (much as the pronoun *it* is used in *Is it a boy or a girl?*).

> Babies, which are particularly vulnerable to this virus, should be kept well clear of anyone affected.
> Babies which need special care are kept in a separate ward.

Note also the following examples:

> The committee, who are always fighting among themselves, have yet to reach a decision.

The committee, which consists of 15 members, has yet to reach a decision.

When a group noun such as *committee* takes a plural verb (*have,* in the first example), *who* can refer to its members. But with a singular verb (*has,* in the second example), *who* would probably not be used.

Note too that although you might often refer to ships, cars, and the like as *she,* you would not go on to use *who:*

She's a fine ship, in which I've often sailed and which I always find very comfortable.

The rule, as formulated above, makes it clear that *that,* not just *who* and *whom,* can be used in reference to people. So long as it does not sound disrespectful or unnatural, *that* can replace *who* and especially *whom* in restrictive clauses. (See THAT **2**.)

By far the commonest exception to the general rule (*who* for people, *which* for things) involves the possessive form *whose.* There is much greater freedom here in applying *whose* as a relative pronoun to nonhuman things:

The company, whose antiquated managing director and timorous financial advisers lack the necessary dynamism and imagination, is heading inexorably towards bankruptcy.

It would be very old-fashioned to insist that nonhuman things should be prohibited from taking *whose* as their relative pronoun, and should take *of which* instead. How clumsy the previous example would then sound:

? The company, of which the antiquated managing director and timorous financial advisers lack the necessary dynamism . . .

or even worse:

? The company, the antiquated managing director and timorous financial advisers of which lack the necessary dynamism . . .

And how clumsy the following quotations would sound if *whose very acronym* or *whose solvency* were changed to *the very acronym of which* or *the solvency of which:*

With a Greek flag in hand, and with a strange vocabulary, they announced that the war of liberation had begun. Here was ELAS, the Greek Popular Liberation Army, whose very acronym seemed the essence of the patriotic.
— Christopher Hitchens,
The Literary Review

The world will not prosper with a banking system whose solvency is chronically dependent on unsupported optimism about future debt payments and with South American, Asian and African economies struggling with grim economic and political difficulties.
— Lord Lever, *Time and Tide*

Whose is all the more convenient when further prepositions, in addition to *of,* are involved — *to whose, in whose,* and so on:

The old chestnut tree, in whose embrace of branches I nestled so often as a child, was uprooted in last night's storm.

This reads so much more smoothly than *in the embrace of the branches of which*, and only an extreme purist would object to its use. Similarly:

I'm afraid that Mr Rushdie is at present in the grip of a rather serious ailment with whose depredations I am familiar, both in my own country, Ireland, and in various parts of Africa and Asia.
— Conor Cruise O'Brien, *The Observer*

Beyond the huts there is a stagnant water-tank on whose farther bank are laid out to dry the long coloured sarees and murky rags belonging to the black-skinned, braceleted, bare-legged women who stand thigh-high in the water, washing themselves and their clothes.
— Paul Scott, *The Jewel in the Crown*

Nevertheless, there are several restrictions on the use of *whose* as a substitute for *of which*. First of all, when *whose* is used in a question or indirect question, it can refer only to persons: *Whose is this necklace?* or *Whose necklace is this?* For animals or things, a different construction is needed. You cannot say × *Whose is this leash?* or × *Whose leash is this?* when referring to a group of dogs. The question would have to take a different form, such as *Which of the dogs does this leash belong to?*

Secondly, *whose* is never, strictly speaking, a substitute for *of which*; it is really a substitute for *of which the* or *the . . . of which*; thus, *an old tree whose branches are broken = an old tree of which **the** branches are broken.* So *whose* has the same sense of definiteness as the definite article *the* has: *whose,* by itself, implies *all* not *some* or *several* or *three* or the like. So:

The gang, the leaders of which were arrested last night, is a spent force. = The gang,

whose leaders were . . .
The gang, the three leaders of which were . . .
= The gang, whose three leaders were . . .

But note that this last sentence differs from:

The gang, three leaders of which were . . .

Here, the subordinate clause lacks the definite article *the,* so a simple *whose* cannot be substituted: the phrase *of whose* has to be used instead (or *some of whose, several of whose, three of whose,* and so on). In the last example above, the correct variation is *The gang, three of whose leaders* . . . not ✗ *The gang, whose three leaders* . . .

The rule is, rather oddly, that *whose = of which the,* whereas *of whose = of which.*

The third restriction on converting *of which* into *whose* occurs when the phrase *of which* does not indicate possession at all. Consider the sentence: *The plot, of which I was quite ignorant, involved serious currency frauds*; this cannot be simply converted into a sentence using *whose.* (The best that one can do is to add an extra word such as *existence* or *details*: *The plot, of whose details I was quite ignorant* . . .)

2. *who* vs *whom. Who* and *whom* serve as both relative and interrogative pronouns:

The woman who is carrying the bouquet . . . (relative)
Who is that woman carrying the bouquet? (interrogative)
The baker whom the bank manager decided to sue . . . (relative)
Whom did he sue? (interrogative)

In traditional usage, *who* is always the subject form, and usually takes a singular verb even when the answer is plural:

'Who does the cooking here?' 'John and Mary both do.'

Whom is the form for the object of a verb or a preposition:

Whom are you going to visit today?
For whom are you going to vote?

(One helpful guideline: if the response to a question can be *him* or *her* — rather than *he* or *she* — then the correct form in the question is *whom,* rather than *who.*)

The Emergency Powers Act gave the Home Secretary under Regulation 18B authority to arrest and detain anyone whom he regarded with suspicion.
– A.J.P. Taylor, *The Observer*

They do not make literary fame on the Kipling scale any more — not in Britain, anyway. But then, strictly speaking, his was hardly a literary fame at all. The greater part of those who most admired Kipling, and whom he most admired, had barely a literary bone in their bodies.
– Nigel Andrew, *The Listener*

Increasingly, however, the use of *whom* is declining in everyday English, whether spoken or written, especially when asking a question. The questions *Whom are you going to visit today?* and *For whom are you going to vote?* are correct, but are beginning to sound rather formal, even artificial and stilted. They are far more likely today to be worded as:

? Who are you going to visit today?
? Who are you going to vote for?

As a relative pronoun, however, *who* should not usually be allowed to oust *whom* in careful writing:

?? The baker who the bank manager decided to sue has now gone out of business.

However, when *whom* has a related preposition following it, it can sound rather stilted today:

Bob made a point of taking a benevolent interest in Morris over the next few days, to balance out Dyson's hostility. He got him an office towel for the washroom. He told him to whom to apply for union membership.
– Michael Frayn,
Towards the End of the Morning

A more natural, though less grammatically correct, way of saying this would be:

? He told him who to apply to for union membership.

Similarly:

? In the lane, the children tried to make the chauffeur tell them who he worked for.
– John le Carré,
Tinker, Tailor, Soldier, Spy

On the other hand, when the governing preposition comes directly in front of *whom,* you cannot use *who* instead:

✗ For who are you going to vote?
✗ The candidate for who you voted . . .

(Note, however, that *who* can sometimes follow a preposition directly. See the examples below at the end of section 3.)

Note that, as a relative pronoun, *whom* is often omitted — especially before another pronoun (such as *he* or *you*):

The baker he sued has now gone out of business.
The candidate you voted for duly topped the poll.

Who as a relative pronoun cannot usually be omitted in this way, although it often is omitted in regional forms of English: *? There's no lad in the world works as hard as my Ben.* In standard English such constructions are unacceptable, though in American English and increasingly in British English too, the omission of *who* is approaching acceptability in clauses that already contain another *who* or a *whoever*:

? Who was it discovered oxygen, did you say?
? Primo Carnera, or whoever it was beat Jack Johnson in that heavyweight title fight, also destroyed a myth in doing so.

Note that there are restrictions on the use of *whom* as the indirect object of such verbs as *give, send,* or *make.* Usually, *whom* has to be accompanied by a preposition in such cases, whereas *him* can stand alone or take a preposition. So we can say, for example:

You sent a postcard to him / You sent him a postcard.
They made a kite for me / They made me a kite.

But:

You sent a postcard to whom? / ? You sent whom a postcard?
They made a kite for whom? / ? They made whom a kite?
To whom did you send a postcard? / × Whom did you send a postcard?
For whom did they make a kite? / × Whom did they make a kite?
She asked me to whom you sent a postcard / × She asked me whom you sent a postcard.
There goes Max, for whom they made a kite / × There goes Max, whom they made a kite.

● *Recommendation* It is acceptable, in all but the most formal English, to say or write *who* as the object form when asking a question. As a relative pronoun, *whom* or *that* (or nothing at all) should be used as the object form, though not if it sounds too stilted. If preceded by a governing preposition, then *whom* must always be used.

3. *hypercorrection.* Aware of the tendency to use *who* where *whom* is more correct, some writers and speakers go too far at times and use *whom* where it is in fact inappropriate.

This usually occurs when the relative clause seems to be the object of a verb, especially a verb like *say, hear,* or *report.* The correct forms are these:

We met the president, who the newspapers had reported was gravely ill.
We met the president, whom the newspapers had reported to be gravely ill.

In the first example, the clause *the newspapers had reported* functions more or less independently (it could even be put in brackets), and the verb *reported* does not determine the form of the relative pronoun *who.* In the second example, *reported* has the pronoun as its direct object. The pronoun therefore has to take the object form *whom.* A frequent error is to confuse these two constructions:

× We met the president, whom the newspapers had reported was gravely ill.

An easy test is to rewrite the secondary clauses in the form of full sentences:

The newspapers had reported (that) *he* was gravely ill.
The newspapers had reported *him* to be gravely ill.

The corresponding relative pronouns are *who* and *whom* respectively — subject and object.

In the following quotation, *who* should be *whom*:

× The project was brought to us by Michael Sissons, who I consider to be one of the most reputable agents on either side of the Atlantic. He has never sold us anything spurious.

— Lord Weidenfeld, quoted in *The Observer*

Another way of looking at it is this: what determines the forms *who* or *whom* is always the pronoun's role *within the clause it introduces.* So long as the pronoun serves as the subject of its own clause (as in the first quotation below), or as the complement of the verb *to be* or *become* or the like (as in the second quotation below) it remains *who* not *whom,* no matter what comes before it (*who* is more like an interrogative pronoun than a relative pronoun in such cases). Even when immediately preceded by a preposition, the pronoun remains *who* not *whom*:

I predict establishment canvassing and ambitious rivalry about who goes in there [into the museum, as historical exhibits] as intense as the rivalry about who gets his Field colours.

– Philip Howard, *The Times*

To write about the English language is to discover something about who we are and who we are not, and this is true not only in what we say but also in how we say it.

– Professor Leonard Michaels (U.S.), in *The State of the Language*

In both examples, the objects of the preposition *about* are the whole clauses *who goes in there* and *who gets his Field colours*; *who we are* and *who we are not*.

A famous problem involving the choice of *who* or *whom* with the verb *to be* is presented in the Bible (Matthew 16:13 and 16:15). In the Authorised (King James) version of 1611, Jesus puts these two questions to the disciples:

Whom do men say that I the Son of man am?
But whom say ye that I am?

In the Revised Standard version of 1952, the two questions are now phrased as follows:

Who do men say that the Son of man is?
But who do you say that I am?

By our rules, *who* is the correct form here: *I am he*; *I am who?*; *Who am I?*; *Who do you say that I am?*

On the same basis, *whom* is incorrect in the following quotation:

✕ Very few leading persons of the day would have been generally known on sight. It is worth remembering that when Wellington met Nelson at the Colonial office in September 1805, the latter had to enquire from an official whom the then Sir Arthur Wellesley was.

– R.E. Foster, *History Today*

Finally, there are such phrases as *Heaven knows who* or *you know who*. Here, *who* is always correct, even in such a sentence as *We were criticised by Heaven knows who*: this sentence means something like 'We were criticised by Heaven knows who it was'.

● *Recommendation* It may be a very common mistake (although considered less and less serious today) to write *who* instead of *whom*. But it is just as much a mistake to go to the other extreme and write *whom* instead of *who*.

4. *commas.* Compare these two sentences:

My brother who lives in Perth is a dentist.
My brother, who lives in Perth, is a dentist.

In the first of these, *who* introduces a 'restrictive' clause — defining or specifying the noun *brother*. In the second, *who* introduces a 'nonrestrictive' clause, merely describing the noun *brother*. (See RESTRICTIVE AND NONRESTRICTIVE CLAUSES for fuller details.)

The first example suggests that I have more brothers than one, and that I am identifying a particular brother as the one who lives in Perth: the clause introduced by *who* here is clearly essential to the meaning of the sentence, and the lack of commas around it is evidence of its integration and inherent importance in the sentence.

The second of the specimen sentences suggests that I have only one brother. The clause introduced by *who* adds some incidental information about him. This is cordoned off by commas, showing that the clause is not crucial in the sentence, and could even be dropped without drastically affecting the sense.

Clauses introduced by *whom, whose, of whose,* and so on can also take commas or do without them according to the sense:

The pilot, whose plane was shot down in that raid, was awarded the DSO.
The pilot whose plane was shot down in that raid was awarded the DSO.

5. *and who, but who.* Consider these sentences:

The man who loved me and (who) said he would marry me has now disappeared.
? The man I loved and who said he would marry me has now disappeared.
✕ Soldiers whose leave is cancelled at short notice and are therefore seriously inconvenienced are in theory entitled to double compensation.
✕ Soldiers whose children have an itinerant home life and who grow up in a variety of countries are naturally interested in the army's education policy.

In the first example, the *who* after *and* is optional (see AND WHICH) — it can be left out, since it can be 'understood' from the earlier *who* in the sentence.

In the second example, the *who* after *and* is compulsory: it cannot be omitted as though 'understood', since *who* does not appear earlier in the sentence. If any relative pronoun had appeared earlier, it would not have been *who* but *whom* or *that*: *The man whom/that I love . . .*

For the sake of a proper balance in the sentence, this *whom* or *that* should really have been inserted explicitly.

In the third example, a *who* should be inserted after the *and*: *who* cannot simply be 'understood' here since there is again no earlier use of *who* in the sentence. (See PARALLEL CONSTRUCTIONS.)

In the fourth example, the *who* after *and* is wrong: *who* refers grammatically to *soldiers*, whereas the clause about growing up in a variety of countries refers to the *children*. Omit the *who*, and the meaning is conveyed correctly.

6. *whose, who's.* Do not confuse these forms. *Whose* is the possessive form in both questions and statements:

Whose handbag is that?
Lord Danbury, whose father had been a lowly bookseller, was justly proud of his elevation.

By contrast, *who's* is the contraction of *who is* or *who has:*

It must be Jack who's knocking at the door.
Who's gone and left the fridge open again?

7. The verb following *who* is formed according to the noun or pronoun before *who*: So:

I, who am no one, adore you.
It is you who are to blame.
I gave the book to him, who is so scatter-brained that he's now lost it.
She presumed to instruct me, who have spent half my life studying the subject.

In the last example, *have* is the correct verb form because the implied subject — which *who* is replacing — is *I*.

8. *whoever, whomever.* Use *whoever* (or *whosoever*) when referring to the subject of a sentence; *whomever* (or *whomsoever*) when referring to the object. Much the same guidelines apply to them as to *who* and *whom*:

Whoever wants to attend the meeting is welcome.
You can discuss it with whomever you care to.

Note the rare possessive forms *whosever* and *whosesoever*.
Do not confuse *whoever* with *who ever*:

Who ever did something for nothing?
Who ever worked without expecting some return?
Whoever has worked voluntarily for charity knows that virtue is its own reward.

(For further details, see EVER 1; WHATEVER.)
See also AGREEMENT; ONE; THAT; WHICH.

whoever See EVER; WHATEVER.

will See SHALL.

-wise, -ways 1. These forms are added to nouns to produce adverbs or adjectives. In many cases, both forms are appropriate: *lengthwise, lengthways.* The *-wise* ending is slightly more popular in American English, the *-ways* form in British English.

In some cases, only one form can be used: *always, sideways, clockwise, otherwise.*

New formations, coined for the occasion, tend to take *-wise* only: *We crawled leopardwise through the long grass.*

2. New formations of this kind are perhaps due to the American habit of inventing one-word sentence modifiers by adding *-wise* to the end of a noun:

? Road-safetywise, the pedestrian crossing has almost as good a record as the traffic light.
? Strategywise, the bombarding of Port Stanley airstrip was an obvious priority.
? January is the resort's worst month weatherwise.

Such new forms are widely criticised: the gain in economy is accompanied by an increase in ugliness that more than offsets it. Avoid such excessive streamlining and say: *As far as road safety is concerned, . . .* or *As to strategy, . . .* (or *Strategically, . . .*) or *The resort's worst weather occurs in January.* All the examples given below could be improved by rephrasing, though there would be a small loss too — the cheeky, 'wisecracking' flavour of the *-wise* formations would be forfeited:

? And she discovers pretty spooky powers of her own, too, in the way of automatic writing — which may be stretching the terms of the genre a bit but proves very helpful sleuth-wise in this witty and relaxed tour of the best-seller undergrowth.
— Christopher Wordsworth,
The Observer

? Luckily, no one has ever got going on the concept of an Anglo-Scottish Ascendancy . . . In any case, any sort of ascendancy, talentwise, is probably held by the Scots in the South at the expense of the English.
— Lady Antonia Fraser,
The Listener

? Competition-wise Mr Lawson attempted several jokes of the laboured variety in which the party specialises.
– Michael White, *The Guardian*

? John Wolf finally sent the book, complete book jacket and all ... Garp managed a restrained letter to his editor; he expressed his sense of personal hurt, his understanding that this had been done with the best intentions, businesswise.
– John Irving (U.S.),
The World According to Garp

It should be pointed out that *-wise* in its other sense of 'having wisdom' can also be used in combinations (to form adjectives, not adverbs) and that such combinations are usually quite unobjectionable. The adjective *weather-wise*, for instance, as in *a weather-wise farmer* (usually with a hyphen) is perfectly acceptable, whereas the adverbial *weatherwise* (usually one word) in the earlier example is to be discouraged. A new adjectival formation of this sort, current since about 1965, is *streetwise*, 'experienced in the ways of rough urban areas'.

with 1. When *with* links a singular subject to a following noun or noun equivalent, the verb should remain in the singular: *The king, with his two sons, has arrived*, not × *The king, with his two sons, have arrived*. In casual speech, the plural meaning of the whole sometimes causes speakers to make the verb plural, but this is better avoided. The same rules apply to the expressions *together with*, *as with*, *along with*, and also *as well as*, *in addition to*, and *like*.

2. It is best not to use *with* to link parts of a sentence unless the relationship between these parts is really clarified by the presence of *with*: ? *The favourite could manage only third place, with victory going to a rank outsider*. It is better to say *The favourite could manage only third place*; *victory went to a rank outsider*. But it is all right to say: *With victory slipping away, we were forced to struggle harder*.

wither See WHITHER.

without 1. *Without* is nowadays very seldom used in the sense of 'outside' — it sounds far too formal or old-fashioned: ? *warm within but cold without*. It has the distinct tone of hymns or Shakespearean plays:

There is a green hill far away,
Without a city wall,

Where the dear Lord was crucified,
Who died to save us all.
– Cecil Frances Alexander,
'There is a Green Hill Far Away' (1848)

Macbeth: ... Sirrah, a word with you. Attend those men our pleasure?
Attendant: They are, my Lord, without the palace gate.
– Shakespeare, *Macbeth* III i

Added to this archaic ring is a slight danger of ambiguity: ? *the horses without the stable*.

2. *Without* is no longer used in the sense of 'unless' — in standard English, at any rate. It survives perhaps in various regional forms of English, including Scottish English: ? *I can't accept your offer without I first consult my husband*. The standard form, of course, is ... *without first consulting my husband or ... unless I first consult my husband*.

3. The combination *without hardly* has a strange attraction for speakers and writers: ? *Without hardly a grimace, he twisted the poker into the shape of a horseshoe*. This should read *With hardly a grimace ... or Almost without a grimace ....* (See DOUBLE NEGATIVE.)

woman, lady, girl, female Each of these words is commonly used to refer to a female adult human being, but their associations and their respective ranges of application and acceptability are changing constantly. A rough guideline is the best that one can hope for.

Lady is still a title of nobility, and retains some of its aristocratic glow accordingly. It tends therefore to be used in official, formal, or polite settings, the way *gentleman* would be used in referring to a man: *Show the lady to her seat; Has one of you ladies dropped a glove?* To use *woman* here, in dealing with strangers, would be blunt and familiar to the point of rudeness. There is a complication: the word *lady* (unlike *gentleman*) has a quite different association too, especially in the United States, deriving perhaps from the Blues era. It developed a much more informal tone then, having something of the easy familiarity of the word *dame*, though rather more affectionate and less disrespectful. Various modern expressions in American English probably derive from this change of tone. There is the use of *lady* in direct address, for example: *Hey lady, you dropped your purse*. And there is the use of *lady* in a clearly complimentary sense: *She's a really together lady*. Such usages are still informal.

Perhaps in reaction against the allegedly

overgenteel associations of the word *lady*, many modern women today object to the term, preferring the forthright term *woman*, with its apparent lack of nuances. Yet in former times, *woman* had many overtones, almost all of them negative. The term carried suggestions of low class or bad character, and of foolishness, fickleness, and feebleness:

> Teach her to subdue the woman in her nature.
> — Sir Henry Taylor,
> *Philip van Artevelde* (1834)

Historically, the word *woman* was almost always defined in terms of the word *man* (and found wanting). According to feminists, the word has now been reclaimed by modern women, and is defined independently. If only it were that easy!

Some men, confused by the changing fashion, have taken recourse in the blanket term *female*. This is often a good compromise when used as an adjective, but its increasing use as a noun is an inelegant and unnecessary development. Not surprisingly, *female* as a noun has already started to generate disrespectful overtones of its own, and it is unlikely to gain widespread acceptance: *? All we need now to complete the party is a female or two.*

Ultimately, there are no rules for deciding between *woman* and *lady*: so much depends on the social setting. But the current tendency in the average polite context can perhaps be summed up in this way: the term *woman* is used when referring to someone who is out of hearing; when referring to someone present, people still use the term *lady* in preference.

However, in one context at least, *woman* is definitely the preferred neutral form — that is, the context of professions. Used adjectivally, *woman* is the appropriate form in such terms as *a woman magistrate*, *women teachers*, *a woman police officer*. The use of *lady* here would sound arch or even satirical. Only in humbler jobs, paradoxically, is the term *lady*, used now as a noun, the appropriate form: *tea lady*, *cleaning lady*. (Even these expressions are being replaced by grander-sounding alternatives, such as *home help*.)

In many settings there is little to choose between *woman* and *lady*. It seems perfectly natural to say either *ladies' final* (and *Ladies' Day at Wimbledon*) or *women's final* (and *Women's Professional Tennis Association*), though the analogy of *men's final* may favour the latter phrase. And *young lady* and *young woman* are equally acceptable in most contexts: *young lady*

may be preferable when extreme courtesy or formality is needed, but it has the adverse danger once again of sounding satirical.

The word *girl*, finally, is falling out of favour as a term applying to adults. It has traditionally been used in several specific contexts: in offices, especially in the United States, a secretary or receptionist might be referred to as *the girl*. A female domestic servant, no matter how old she might be, would be called *the girl*, and in some parts of the English-speaking world is still referred to quite unselfconsciously in this way — even by people who would now think twice about calling an adult male servant *the boy*. At parties or outings, men might refer to their wives jointly as *the girls*. And women would often refer to themselves collectively as *girls*. Under the pressure of modern feminist disapproval, all these usages have now developed a disrespectful tone (except perhaps the last, which has a deliberate cheeky defiance about it) and should be used with great caution.

See also CHAIRMAN; -ESS; MISS; PARALLEL STYLE; SEXISM IN THE ENGLISH LANGUAGE.

wonder See WANDER.

wont See UNWONTED.

woods Referring to a dense growth of trees, whether wild or planted, the form *woods* is more common today than *wood* — *If you go down to the woods today, you're sure of very good hunting*. And it is always used when making general statements: *Many people love walking in the woods.* Note that *woods* always takes the definite article *the*; *wood* tends to take the indefinite article *a*:

> Two roads diverged in a wood, and I —
> I took the one less travelled by,
> And that has made all the difference.
> — Robert Frost (U.S.),
> 'The Road Not Taken'

Whether the singular used is *wood* or *woods,* the plural is always *woods*. When *woods* is used as a plural, it takes a plural verb of course: *The woods of England were devastated by Dutch elm disease.* But what about when *woods* is used as a singular? It is sometimes written with a singular verb, especially when the woods is named: *Broughton Woods lies just two miles north of the castle.* But it is far more common today to use a plural verb, even when referring to a single wood. Here is part of another poem by Robert Frost:

The woods are lovely, dark and deep,
But I have promises to keep,
And miles to go before I sleep,
And miles to go before I sleep.
      – Robert Frost (U.S.), 'Stopping
      by Woods on a Snowy Evening'

word order See INVERTED WORD ORDER.

word origins See SOURCES OF THE ENGLISH
VOCABULARY.

worthwhile, worth while **1.** The old rule was
that *worth while* — two words — was used after
the noun and verb, and *worthwhile* — one word
(previously hyphenated) — was used before the
noun: *The trip was worth while*; *It was surely a
worthwhile trip.*

> Now, 45 years later, I have achieved my
> ambition. It has been a long haul, but the
> first six months have confirmed that it has
> been worth while. I have always found it dif-
> ficult to understand those of my colleagues
> ... who have openly dreaded the moment
> of release, wondering what on earth they
> would find to do after breakfast on their first
> day with no office to go to.
>   – Sir Anthony Parsons, *The Times*

Increasingly, however, the two-word phrase tends
to be fused, and the form *worthwhile* is perhaps
becoming acceptable in all positions. Purists still
observe the old rule, and it is risky to provoke
them. The two-word form should at least be
retained when the adverb *well* is placed before it
for emphasis: *The trip was well worth while*. If
very replaced *well* in this example, then the one-
word form *worthwhile* might be acceptable.
    2. Avoid using *worthwhile* as a simple catch-all
adjective of approval: *? a worthwhile concert*;
? as any worthwhile teacher will know. In such
examples, *worthwhile* is not only a cliché but
imprecise as well: was the concert well-performed,
interestingly varied, or what? A more carefully
chosen adjective would make the meaning clearer.
    3. Do not use *worth while* if an *-ing* form
follows: *? What she said is worth while repeating.*
The *worth* is quite enough by itself: *What she said
is worth repeating.*

would See SHOULD.

wrath, wroth *Wrath* is an old-fashioned noun
meaning 'anger' and pronounced /rawth/ or
/roth/ (and in American English, /rath/): *The
king's wrath was terrifying*. There are two adjectives related to *wrath* and meaning 'angry' —
wrathful and *wroth*, pronounced /rōth/,
sometimes /roth/ (and in American English,
/rawth/). Traditionally, *wrathful* occurs only
before a noun — *a wrathful mood*; *a wrathful
king* — and *wroth* occurs only after a verb, at
the end of a clause or sentence: *The king was
wroth*; *Now she waxed most wroth*.
    As the words become increasingly archaic, the
traditional distinctions are fading too: writers who
do still use the words tend to use both *wrath* and
wroth as a noun (though strictly speaking *wrath*
is the noun and *wroth* the adjective), and *wrathful*
as an adjective in any position.

write The verb *to write* can take both a direct
and an indirect object: *I shall write him a letter
at once*. In American English, though not in
British English, it is possible to use the indirect
object without the direct object: *? I shall write
him at once*. In British English, the preposition
to would have to be added here: *I shall write to
him at once*.
    In the passive, however, the *to* must be used,
in both British and American English: *He was
written to last week*.

wrong *Wrong,* like *right,* can be used as an
adverb as well as an adjective. It is still correct
to say *He guessed wrong* or *She spelt it wrong,*
and *wrongly* may even seem affected in such short
phrases. (The most obvious example — *to go
wrong* — is not in fact the best example: it could
be argued that *wrong* remains an adjective here
and is not an adverb at all.)
    In more uncommon combinations, however, the
form *wrongly* is clearly preferable: *He failed his
driving-test because he indicated directions
wrongly*. And if the adverb comes before a participle or adjective, even in the common combinations, then *wrongly* is the only correct form: *a
wrongly spelt word*.

X, Y, Z

Xmas This abbreviation for *Christmas* is one of the oldest informal usages in our language — in its Old English form it occurs in the *Anglo-Saxon Chronicle* (roughly 870–1154). The *X* stands for the Greek letter *chi* (which is shaped like the *X* of our alphabet), the first letter of the Greek name for Christ (*Khristos* = Christ, 'the Anointed').

Xmas is informal: it is often used in personal letters, for example. It is also sometimes used in Christmas cards and where there is a need to save space, as in newspaper headlines. Some use it to play down the religious force of the word *Christmas*. However, many people object to this abbreviation, regarding it as commercial or even offensive to Christians. And there is a particularly strong objection to the pronunciation /**ekss**-məss/.

● *Recommendation* The form *Xmas* is best avoided in formal writing. And in speaking or reading out loud, pronounce *Xmas* as if it were written *Christmas,* unless you particularly want to make it clear that the abbreviation has been used.

ye The use of *ye* as a supposedly archaic form of *the* occurs in both British and American English, chiefly in house-names and shop-signs: *Ye Olde Coffee Shoppe*. Whether you find it quaint or irritating is a matter of taste, but it is worth remembering that the pronunciation /yee/ is a gross misrepresentation of the real early forms of *the*. The *y* in *ye* is really a distortion of the obsolete runic letter þ in Old and Middle English, now replaced by *th*. (It was called a *thorn,* and still survives in Icelandic.) It was always pronounced as *th* is today, both /th/ and /th̲/.

year, month, week, day 1. Any of these nouns, when placed in front of another noun to indicate the length of time, can be used in the singular form if combined by a hyphen with a number: *a two-year expedition round the world, a three-month stay in France, a one-day test match.*

A more formal way of expressing some of these ideas is by using the possessive form, but the hyphen is then omitted: *a three months' stay in France*. If no number is present, then the possessive form must be used: *a day's grace, a*

month's stay in France. Alternatively, rephrase things slightly: *a month-long stay in France.*

2. After an adjective or adverb in the superlative degree, the phrase *for months, for weeks*, or the like is often used to round out the comparison. It is used in simpler constructions too:

I haven't laughed so much for months — it's Woody Allen's funniest film for years.

In American English, both *in* and *for* are used in such expressions: the construction with *in* has now become widespread in British English too — *in months/weeks/years* — and although still frowned on by some purists as an Americanism, is really fully established and acceptable.

See also PREPOSITIONS OMITTED 3.

yes See NO 2.

yet 1. It used to be acceptable usage to place the verb rather than the subject immediately after the conjunction *yet:*

? Doctor Johnson received little encouragement — yet did he persevere and bring the dictionary to a conclusion.

Such inversion of the normal word-order is archaic today, and would sound unacceptably pretentious if attempted.

2. The use of the adverb *yet* in the sense of 'as before' is also archaic, though it persists in certain regional varieties of English: ? *He is yet at school*. In Scotland, that sentence might be widely accepted, and the following question would be ambiguous: ? *Is it snowing yet?* ('Has it begun to snow?' vs 'Is it still snowing?') But in the standard English of most English-speaking countries, *yet* and *still* are no longer interchangeable here.

They are more or less interchangeable when the sense is 'in the future; in the time remaining' (*A solution has yet/still to be found*); or 'up to a particular time' (*She has not decided yet* and *She has still not decided* — notice the change in position); or 'even' (*a yet/still less impressive debut; a yet/still sadder story*).

In the first and third of these senses, however, *yet* is slightly stilted, *still* being more in keeping with modern idiom.

3. Note that *yet* in the sense of 'up to a particular time' is used with the present perfect or past perfect tense: *They had not yet reached the Pacific*; *Has she decided yet?* The simple past tense is often used instead, especially in informal American English: *? Did she decide yet?* This is not acceptable in standard English. (See JUST 1.)

4. *Yet,* like *but,* is sometimes used unnecessarily or incorrectly (see BUT 3). It is redundant if used in conjunction with a synonym such as *but, however, nevertheless,* or *still*:

× Yet he nevertheless managed to alert his officer.

And it is incorrect to use *yet* to link two clauses (or sentences or phrases) that are in harmony rather than in opposition:

× The government repudiated the inquiry's conclusions that official incompetence was the cause of the bank's collapse. Yet the Prime Minister yesterday called the inquiry's report biased and politically motivated, and repeated his view that the world recession was to blame.

The *yet* should be omitted. The second sentence is not in opposition to the first, but simply an expansion of it. If the first sentence had begun *The inquiry concluded that . . .,* then the second sentence could legitimately retain the *yet.*

5. Whereas *however* (in the sense of 'but') is usually followed by a comma, *yet* (like *but*) usually has no comma afterwards. When special emphasis is needed, or a dramatic pause is intended, then a comma can be used, though a dash would be preferable:

It looked quite safe now. Yet — the dangers were far from over.

The punctuation that comes immediately before *yet* is more complicated. When *yet* simply links two words or phrases, it takes no punctuation either side: *an invention of limited yet undoubted usefulness*; *a thoughtful yet ultimately unhelpful adviser.* When two clauses are linked, the *yet* tends to take a comma before it if the subject is omitted after it: *He lived to be over 90, yet remained alert and witty to the end.*

If the subject after *yet* is retained, then a comma is again appropriate, though in more complex constructions, a semi-colon might help to keep the syntax clear and emphasise the contrast:

He led a demanding life and survived to well over 90; yet he was in full possession of his faculties until the day he died.

Dr Johnson received little encouragement during the years he was compiling his dictionary; yet he persevered and brought the project to a triumphant conclusion.

In more complex constructions still, it is best to keep the two linked elements as separate sentences. No one seems to object to using *yet* (in the way that some people, needlessly, object to using *but*) as the first word of a sentence.

6. In informal American English, *yet* can be used in a very distinctive way. It is placed at the end of an exclamation, directly after the word or phrase it relates to. It serves to emphasise that word or phrase, and perhaps to indicate surprise. Its meaning is roughly 'moreover' or perhaps 'really; even': *Not just a coat — a fur coat yet! Aha, breathless yet — you must be in a hurry!* The usage is usually self-conscious and jocular. It probably developed through the influence of Yiddish or German. It is far from being accepted as standard English. Compare the slang use of *already* (see ALREADY 3).

See also AS YET.

yolk, yoke   A *yolk* is the yellow part of an egg. A *yoke* is the connecting crossbar, as for a pair of oxen, or the tight part at the neck or hips of a woman's garment, or a bond, as in *the yoke of marriage*, and so on.

Both words come from Old English, the Old English word for 'yolk', *geolca* or *geoloca*, deriving from *geolu*, 'yellow'. To remember the spelling then, bear in mind that *yolk*, with an *l*, is related to *yellow*.

you, your, yours   1. These words are rather more widely used today than they used to be.

a. *You* is readily used in place of *one*:

You cannot lock a man up in jail with a lot of hardened criminals, and expect him to come out reformed.

Such constructions are now regarded as fully acceptable even in fairly formal contexts, whereas formerly *one* (or *one's*) would have been preferred to *you* (or *your* or *yours*) — and still is in very formal or upper-class speech (see ONE).

The impersonal *you* used to be considered less formal in tone, or reserved for homilies such as *You can take a horse to water but you can't make it drink.*

If you do use *you* in place of *one,* use it consistently. A mix of the two is unacceptable:

× If one wants affection, it is best if you offer some affection in the first place.

b. *You* is widely used in place of *I* (or *one*) where the writer (or speaker) is trying to draw the reader (or listener) into personal involvement in his own experiences:

> At Auteuil it was beautiful to watch each day. They raced when you could be there and see the honest races with the great horses, and you got to know the course as well as any place you had ever known. You knew many people finally.
> — Ernest Hemingway (U.S.),
> *A Moveable Feast*

It is worth noting that in British English, *I* is often conversely used in place of *you* when giving advice: *I should dress warmly (. . .if I were you)* means 'You should dress warmly'.

c. *You* is used increasingly in official documents such as contracts and application forms, where previously the third person was always used. Instead of reading *The lessee* (or *signatory* or *party of the first part) shall make his own tax arrangements, the lessor disclaiming responsibility therefor,* we often nowadays find something such as *You will have to make your own tax arrangements — we are not responsible for them.*

In many parts of the United States, manufacturers and leasing agents are now required by law to couch their contracts in 'plain language' — typically using second-person pronouns. This is a very welcome development. Any slight loss of legal precision is more than offset by the huge gain in comprehensibility. (See JARGON.)

A recent British *Tax Return Guide* takes a similar approach. It says:

> If you are a woman and the Return is addressed to you, you should enter your income. outgoings, chargeable gains and chargeable assets acquired in the column headed 'self'.

> If you are a married man, and your wife is living with you, you must show all her income, chargeable gains and chargeable assets acquired on your Return. If you married after 6 April 1982, however, both you and your wife continue to be taxed separately for 1982-83.

Imagine if such instructions and explanations were still couched in the third person!

One added advantage of using the second instead of the third person is that *you, yours,* and *your* are of indefinite gender and indefinite number. An old-style contract might have read:

> The purchaser or purchasers shall lose his or

their right to a refund if he or they fail to report the defect within one month of purchase.

There is no such awkwardness when you switch to *you* and *your.*

In particular, one very common grammatical error can be avoided by using *you* rather than the third person. Speakers and writers nowadays tend to be worried about using *he, his,* and *him* when the (singular) person referred to may be of either sex, and in their anxiety resort to *they, them, their,* and *theirs,* even though the sentence is strictly in the singular:

> ?? If the winner is under 18, they will not receive the money directly but a trust will be opened in their name.

(See THEY, THEM, THEIR.)

And the more accurate *he or she* or *his or her* has the disadvantage of awkwardness (see HE, HIM, HIS; HE OR SHE). Increasingly, therefore, writers and speakers are switching to the second person, which produces sentences that are at once grammatically correct, stylistically elegant, and non-sexist:

> If you win but are under 18, you will not receive the money directly, but a trust will be opened in your name.

2. Note the spelling of *yours*: no apostrophe.

3. Do not confuse *your* and *you're,* which many speakers pronounce identically. *You're* to ensure that *your* spelling of them is correct.

4. *You* is either singular or plural, and so are all its associated forms except *yourself* (singular) and *yourselves* (plural). In some varieties of English an effort is made to indicate plurality when plurality is meant: *? youse, ? you all,* and so on. Most of these constructions are regional or nonstandard. But two are now widely used in informal English. One is *you lot,* which is British, and the other is *you guys,* which is American. Both can be used of groups of either sex, or mixed groups, even though *guy* (singular) is masculine only. Note, however, that *you lot* may well have negative or ironic overtones that are not present in *you guys.*

you and I See BETWEEN YOU AND I.

you know The repeated use of these words in conversation is widely criticised, and with good reason. The phrase certainly is overused — indicative of mental laziness or lack of confidence. And its meaning, if it has one, is often virtually the opposite of 'as you know': the frequent retort 'I *don't* know' reflects the understandable irritation that many people feel at the overuse of the phrase — much as they do at the overuse of *of course* (see OF COURSE).

Nevertheless, a simple blanket disapproval of *you know* is too extreme. The phrase is a kind of spoken punctuation mark — just as *like*, *I mean*, *sort of*, *basically*, and *actually* are. It can serve many useful purposes. The pause it makes in the flow of ideas allows the speaker to gather his thoughts for a moment (though a moment's silence would allow him to do that just as well). Or the phrase might lend a certain emphasis or a note of caution or an ironic tone to what is being said: *He wasn't driving inattentively exactly, but he was — you know — enjoying the conversation.* Or the phrase might help to maintain contact with the listener, and monitor his concentration and his comprehension.

These are small rewards, however, for the sacrifice of fluency and euphony that a machine-gun volley of *you-know's* involves: *?? The road gets really winding there, you know, and it takes a lot of — you know — concentration, and all the time he was, you know, turning round to talk to me or Jim ....* Like a twitch, the recurrent phrase comes to dominate the attention of the listener, and instead of ensuring that he follows your ideas, it succeeds only in distracting him from them. The cure is to order your thoughts before expressing them in the first place, and to relax while conveying them to your listener.

It is only fair to add that the acceptability of *you know* probably varies with its position in the sentence. It seems to be fairly acceptable at the beginning or end of a clause, less acceptable in the middle of a clause, and least acceptable in the middle of a phrase. So in our last example, the three *you know*'s could be ranked from best to worst as follows:

? The road gets really winding there, you know ...

?? ... and all the time he was, you know, turning round to talk to us.

× ... and it takes a lot of — you know — concentration ...

And remember that *you know* is not always a 'comment clause' of this kind. It can also be the main clause of a sentence, of course; often it is only a comma, or intonation, that distinguishes these two uses of *you know* in initial position:

You know, I find her rather attractive. (comment clause)

You know I find her rather attractive. (main clause)

Only the second sentence can have *that* in it, and only in the first sentence can *you know* be moved to the end.

yourself *Yourself* is not acceptable as a substitute for *you* in formal style, though it is commonly so used in everyday speech: *? She wants to see Joan and yourself*; *? Yourself and the others will be expected later*; *? How's yourself?* It is particularly common in Irish English.

Standard English now uses *yourself* and *yourselves* to distinguish singular from plural in the second person: *You can do it yourself*; *You can do it yourselves.*

Compare MYSELF; SELF.

zeugma, syllepsis These two figures of speech, remnants of classical rhetoric, are closely related. In both, a single word is used to apply to two or more other words. In *zeugma*, the single word (usually a verb or adjective) is appropriate to only one of the two words (nouns) that it applies to. An example of *zeugma* is *He held his tongue and his promise.* In hurried speech, this might pass unnoticed, but on analysis it turns out to be poorly constructed: *× He held ... his promise.* The full sentence should read *He held his tongue and kept his promise.*

Zeugma is loosely used, however, to refer to what is strictly speaking a *syllepsis* — that is, a construction in which one word applies to two others, but in a different way each time. Examples of syllepsis are *She lost her coat and her temper* and *She left in a hurry and a taxi.* Here the word *lost* is appropriate both for *coat* and for *temper*, but it means something different in each case. Similarly, the *in* in the phrase *in a hurry* means something different from the *in* in the phrase *in a taxi.* Syllepses are usually contrived deliberately for a humorous effect. Zeugmas, on the other hand, are usually accidental, and tend to be regarded as errors.

Note the plural *syllepses*. The pronunciation of *syllepsis* is /si-**leep**-siss/ or /si-**lep**-sis/ (only the latter in American English); and of *zeugma*, /**zewg**-mə/. *Syllepsis* goes back to Greek roots meaning 'taking together'; *zeugma* in Greek means 'a joining, unity, or yoking'.